Lecture Notes in Computer Science   12433

More information about this series at http://www.springer.com/series/7407

Eduardo Lalla-Ruiz · Martijn Mes ·
Stefan Voß (Eds.)

Computational Logistics

11th International Conference, ICCL 2020
Enschede, The Netherlands, September 28–30, 2020
Proceedings

 Springer

Editors
Eduardo Lalla-Ruiz (iD)
University of Twente
Enschede, The Netherlands

Martijn Mes (iD)
University of Twente
Enschede, The Netherlands

Stefan Voß (iD)
University of Hamburg
Hamburg, Germany

ISSN 0302-9743   ISSN 1611-3349   (electronic)
Lecture Notes in Computer Science
ISBN 978-3-030-59746-7   ISBN 978-3-030-59747-4   (eBook)
https://doi.org/10.1007/978-3-030-59747-4

LNCS Sublibrary: SL1 – Theoretical Computer Science and General Issues

This Springer imprint is published by the registered company Springer Nature Switzerland AG
The registered company address is: Gewerbestrasse 11, 6330 Cham, Switzerland

Preface

The increasing complexity of present-day logistics operations as well as the increasing availability of information, makes it imperative to jointly use optimization and artificial intelligence for devising computational data-driven intelligent decision support. Recently, important efforts and initiatives from all sides of optimization and artificial intelligence have been undertaken to improve logistics operations with sophisticated algorithms and information systems. This resulted in advances in both theoretical and practical aspects as well as technical innovations in several logistics sectors, such as maritime shipping, freight transportation, urban distribution, multi-modal transportation, warehousing, and inventory management. This way, the trend towards computational logistics, as the glue between decision making and operations, has become a key component for economic and industrial growth. On the other hand, in the middle of the COVID-19 world crisis, advances in this area are more necessary than ever to support speedy operations, to flexibly adapt supply chains to distribution disruptions, and to avoid potential shortages.

Computational Logistics covers the management of logistics' activities and tasks through the joint use of computational technologies and advanced decision support and optimization techniques. It is applied in several areas, e.g., the flow and storage of goods and services as well as the flow of related information. In this context, modeling and algorithmic approaches are developed, verified, and applied for planning and executing complex logistics tasks, e.g., for finding the most efficient routing plan and schedule to transport passengers or distribute goods. The models and algorithms are integrated with computing technologies, not only for getting satisfactory results in reasonable times, but also exploiting interactivity with the decision maker through visual interfaces, and for extracting knowledge from data to improve future decision making. This promotes the joint effort of practitioners and scholars for better understanding and solving the logistics problems at hand.

The International Conference on Computational Logistics (ICCL) is a forum where recent advances in the computational logistics research area are presented and discussed. This volume offers a selection of 49 peer-reviewed papers out of 93 contributions submitted to the 11th ICCL edition, virtually held at the University of Twente, The Netherlands, during September 28–30, 2020. The papers show various directions of importance in computational logistics, classified into five topic areas reflecting the interest of researchers and practitioners in this field. The papers in this volume are grouped according to the following parts:

1. **Maritime and Port Logistics**
   Maritime logistics is the backbone of global supply chains and international trade. The performance and functioning of its related activities are remarkably influenced by the quality of its planning and management. In ICCL 2020, the contributions that fall into this area relate to, among others, port development, waterway transport, stowage planning, container management, and various real-world applications.

2. **Vehicle Routing and Scheduling**
   This well-known family of optimization problems constitutes an important part of real-world transport and logistics activities. Due to the many specific real-world features, there is a strong necessity of modeling and developing efficient solution approaches as well as formalizing cases that permit advancements in this area. The papers in this category address, among others, dynamic vehicle routing, collaborative logistics, inventory routing, cross-docking, green and electric vehicle routing, pickup and delivery, customer prioritization, and drivers' considerations.
3. **Freight Distribution and City Logistics**
   The progress in transportation and economic trade as well as the development of cities and regions require the adaptation and update of current systems to cope with changes that also involve sustainability and environmental impact. The works in this part relate to a diverse range of topics, such as vehicle repositioning, carsharing, travel time predictions, smart cities, waste collection, and truck platooning.
4. **Network Design and Scheduling**
   Designing and scheduling logistics networks is among the most important tactical and strategic decisions in supply chain management. This area pursues the efficient organization, modeling, and management of the diverse resources and operations involved in such a way that the flow of products, services, or persons is as good as possible. Contributions considering supply chain networks, logistic flow problems, shortest path algorithms, and matching problems fall into this category.
5. **Selected Topics in Logistics**
   The papers that appear in this area relate to a range of topics concerning various computational logistics topics such as cash distribution, logistics-related serious games, e-commerce, game theory applications, pricing, order picking and loading problems, and quality investments.

The ICCL 2020 was the 11th edition of this conference series, following the earlier ones held in Shanghai, China (2010, 2012), Hamburg, Germany (2011), Copenhagen, Denmark (2013), Valparaiso, Chile (2014), Delft, The Netherlands (2015), Lisbon, Portugal (2016), Southampton, UK (2017), Salerno, Italy (2018), and Barranquilla, Colombia (2019). The editors thank all the authors for their contributions as well as the program committee and reviewers for their invaluable support and feedback. Finally, we would like to express our gratitude to Julia Bachale for her helpful support and assistance during the preparation of the conference. We trust that the present volume supports the continued advances within computational logistics and inspires all participants and readers to its fullest extent.

September 2020

Eduardo Lalla-Ruiz
Martijn Mes
Stefan Voß

Organization

Program Committee

Panagiotis Angeloudis	Imperial College London, UK
Tolga Bektas	The University of Liverpool, UK
Francesco Carrabs	University of Salerno, Italy
Carlos Castro	Universidad Federico de Santa María, Chile
Raffaele Cerulli	University of Salerno, Italy
Joachim Daduna	Berlin School of Economics and Law, Germany
Adriana Daza	Universidad del Norte, Colombia
René De Koster	Erasmus University Rotterdam, The Netherlands
Yingjie Fan	Erasmus University Rotterdam, The Netherlands
Elena Fernández	Universidad de Cádiz, Spain
Monica Gentili	University of Louisville, USA
Rosa González Ramírez	Universidad de Los Andes, Colombia
Hans-Dietrich Haasis	University of Bremen, Germany
Richard Hartl	University of Vienna, Austria
Geir Hasle	SINTEF Digital, Norway
Wouter van Heeswijk	University of Twente, The Netherlands
Leonard Heilig	University of Hamburg, Germany
Alessandro Hill	California Polytechnic State University, USA
Jan Hoffmann	UNCTAD, Switzerland
Manuel Iori	University of Modena and Reggio Emilia, Italy
Jiangang Jin	Shanghai Jiao Tong University, China
Raka Jovanovic	QEERI, Qatar
Herbert Kopfer	University of Bremen, Germany
Eduardo Lalla-Ruiz	University of Twente, The Netherlands
Jasmine Siu Lee Lam	Nanyang Technological University, Singapore
Gilbert Laporte	HEC Montréal, Canada
Janny Leung	University of Macau, Macau, China
Dirk Mattfeld	TU Braunschweig, Germany
Frank Meisel	University of Kiel, Germany
Gonzalo Mejía	Universidad de La Sabana, Colombia
Belen Melián-Batista	Universidad de La Laguna, Spain
Martijn Mes	University of Twente, The Netherlands
José Marcos Moreno-Vega	Universidad de La Laguna, Spain
Ioannis Lagoudis	University of Piraeus, Greece
Rudy Negenborn	Delft University of Technology, The Netherlands
Dario Pacino	Technical University of Denmark, Denmark
Julia Pahl	University of Southern Denmark, Denmark
Carlos Paternina-Arboleda	Universidad del Norte, Colombia

Mario Ruthmair	University of Vienna, Austria
Juan José Salazar González	Universidad de La Laguna, Spain
Frederik Schulte	Delft University of Technology, The Netherlands
Marco Schutten	University of Twente, The Netherlands
Xiaoning Shi	University of Hamburg, Germany
Douglas Smith	University of Missouri-St. Louis, USA
Grazia Speranza	University of Brescia, Italy
Shunji Tanaka	Kyoto University, Japan
Kevin Tierney	Bielefeld University, Germany
Thierry Vanelslander	University of Antwerp, Belgium
Stefan Voß	University of Hamburg, Germany

Additional Reviewers

Adina Aldea	Alberto Locatelli
André Amaral	Johan Los
Breno Beirigo	Javier Maturana-Ross
Rob Bemthuis	Pedro Nunes
Melissa Buballa	Makbule Ozler
Giovanni Campuzano	Nadia Pourmohammadzia
Kaimin Chen	Michael Roemer
Jésica De Armas	Alex Sangers
Alan Dávila	Dingena Schott
Roberto Díaz	Jakov Schulte
Yun Fan	Peter Schuur
Alejandro Fernández	Silvia Schwarze
Berry Gerrits	Dimitris Souravlias
Stefan Guericke	Uilke Stelwagen
Nicolás Gálvez	Robert van Steenbergen
Mariam Gómez	Pieter Vansteenwegen
Hipolito Hernandez Pérez	Daniel Wetzel
Martijn Koot	Giorgio Zucchi

Contents

Maritime and Port Logistics

Evaluating Port Development Strategies for a Modal Shift:
A Norwegian Case Study. 3
  Andreas Breivik Ormevik, Stein Ove Erikstad, and Kjetil Fagerholt

Pickup and Delivery Problem with Transshipment for Inland Waterway
Transport. 18
  *Yimeng Zhang, Bilge Atasoy, Dimitris Souravlias,
  and Rudy R. Negenborn*

Ferry Service Network Design for Kiel fjord 36
  *Ingvild Eide Aslaksen, Elisabeth Svanberg, Kjetil Fagerholt,
  Lennart Christian Johnsen, and Frank Meisel*

Smart Containers with Bidding Capacity: A Policy Gradient Algorithm
for Semi-cooperative Learning 52
  Wouter van Heeswijk

Analyzing the Impact of the Northern Sea Route on Tramp Ship Routing
with Uncertain Cargo Availability. 68
  Mingyu Li, Kjetil Fagerholt, and Peter Schütz

Stowage Planning with Optimal Ballast Water 84
  *Beizhen Jia, Kjetil Fagerholt, Line Blander Reinhardt,
  and Niels Gorm Malý Rytter*

Waterborne Hinterland Transports for Floating Port Terminals 101
  *Gerrit Assbrock, Jens Ley, Ioannis Dafnomilis, Mark B. Duinkerken,
  and Dingena L. Schott*

An Optimization Model for Defining Storage Strategies for Export Yards
in Container Terminals: A Case Study. 119
  Daniela Ambrosino and Haoqi Xie

Vehicle Routing and Scheduling

Dynamic Assignment Vehicle Routing Problem with Time Windows 135
  *Kim J. Los, Frank Phillipson, Elisah A. van Kempen, Hans J. Quak,
  and Uilke Stelwagen*

Time-Dependent Travel-Time Constrained Inventory Routing Problem   151
  Faycal A. Touzout, Anne-Laure Ladier, and Khaled Hadj-Hamou

Vehicle Routing Problem with Reverse Cross-Docking: An Adaptive Large
Neighborhood Search Algorithm.   167
  *Aldy Gunawan, Audrey Tedja Widjaja, Pieter Vansteenwegen,
  and Vincent F. Yu*

Solving a Bi-Objective Rich Vehicle Routing Problem with Customer
Prioritization.   183
  Tim van Benthem, Mark Bergman, and Martijn Mes

A Genetic Algorithm to Minimise the Number of Vehicles in the Electric
Vehicle Routing Problem.   200
  Bertran Queck and Hoong Chuin Lau

Decentralized Combinatorial Auctions for Dynamic and Large-Scale
Collaborative Vehicle Routing   215
  *Johan Los, Frederik Schulte, Margaretha Gansterer, Richard F. Hartl,
  Matthijs T. J. Spaan, and Rudy R. Negenborn*

Metaheuristic Approaches for the Fleet Size and Mix Vehicle Routing
Problem with Time Windows and Step Cost Functions   231
  João L. V. Manguino and Débora P. Ronconi

Cyclical Inventory Routing with Unsplittable Pick-Up and Deliveries   246
  Jakob Schulte, Michael Römer, and Kevin Tierney

The Multistage Stochastic Vehicle Routing Problem with Dynamic
Occasional Drivers   261
  *Jørgen Skålnes, Lars Dahle, Henrik Andersson, Marielle Christiansen,
  and Lars Magnus Hvattum*

Cumulative VRP with Time Windows: A Trade-Off Analysis.   277
  *Alejandro Fernández Gil, Mariam Gómez Sánchez, Eduardo Lalla-Ruiz,
  and Carlos Castro*

Freight Distribution and City Logistics

Formulations of a Carsharing Pricing and Relocation Problem   295
  Giovanni Pantuso

Evolutionary Approach for the Multi-objective Bike Routing Problem.   311
  Pedro Nunes, Ana Moura, and José Santos

Quantifying the Effect of Flexibility and Information Sharing
in Transportation Planning   326
  Ebba Celius, Madeleine Reehorst, Heidi Dreyer, and Peter Schütz

A Bin Packing Problem with Mixing Constraints for Containerizing Items
for Logistics Service Providers 342
    Sajini Anand and Stefan Guericke

Distance Approximation for Dynamic Waste Collection Planning 356
    Fabian Akkerman, Martijn Mes, and Wouter Heijnen

Daily Distribution of Duties for Crew Scheduling with Attendance Rates:
A Case Study 371
    Martin Scheffler and Janis Sebastian Neufeld

A Heuristic Algorithm for Finding Attractive Fixed-Length Circuits
in Street Maps 384
    Rhyd Lewis

Minimizing Movements in Location Problems with Mobile
Recycling Units 396
    Eduardo Alarcon-Gerbier and Udo Buscher

Travel Time Prediction Using Tree-Based Ensembles 412
    He Huang, Martin Pouls, Anne Meyer, and Markus Pauly

Platooning of Automated Ground Vehicles to Connect Port and Hinterland:
A Multi-objective Optimization Approach 428
    Nadia Pourmohammad-Zia, Frederik Schulte, Dimitris Souravlias,
    and Rudy R. Negenborn

Dynamic Pricing for User-Based Rebalancing in Free-Floating Vehicle
Sharing: A Real-World Case 443
    Nout Neijmeijer, Frederik Schulte, Kevin Tierney, Henk Polinder,
    and Rudy R. Negenborn

Automated and Autonomous Driving in Freight Transport - Opportunities
and Limitations. 457
    Joachim R. Daduna

Learning-Based Co-planning for Improved Container, Barge
and Truck Routing 476
    Rie B. Larsen, Bilge Atasoy, and Rudy R. Negenborn

Overcoming Mobility Poverty with Shared Autonomous Vehicles:
A Learning-Based Optimization Approach for Rotterdam Zuid 492
    Breno Beirigo, Frederik Schulte, and Rudy R. Negenborn

Idle Vehicle Repositioning for Dynamic Ride-Sharing 507
    Martin Pouls, Anne Meyer, and Nitin Ahuja

Smart City: A Perspective of Emergency and Resilience at a Community
Level in Shanghai.   522
  Xiaoning Shi, Wenchen Sun, Stefan Voß, and Jiangang Jin

Network Design and Scheduling

A Shortest Path Algorithm for Graphs Featuring Transfer Costs
at Their Vertices.   539
  Rhyd Lewis

A Global Intermodal Shipment Matching Problem Under Travel
Time Uncertainty   553
  *Wenjing Guo, Bilge Atasoy, Wouter Beelaerts van Blokland,
  and Rudy R. Negenborn*

Cutting Planes for Solving Logistic Flow Problems.   569
  Kishan Kalicharan, Frank Phillipson, and Alex Sangers

Deep Reinforcement Learning and Optimization Approach
for Multi-echelon Supply Chain with Uncertain Demands   584
  Júlio César Alves and Geraldo Robson Mateus

The Multi-period Petrol Station Replenishment Problem:
Formulation and Solution Methods   600
  Luke Boers, Bilge Atasoy, Gonçalo Correia, and Rudy R. Negenborn

Simulation Approach for Container Assignment Under Uncertainty.   616
  Wouter J. de Koning, Frank Phillipson, and Irina Chiscop

A Mathematical Model to Route Technicians for Inland
Waterway Shipping.   631
  Melissa Buballa, Daniel Wetzel, Kay Lenkenhoff, and Kevin Tierney

Selected Topics in Logistics

Reactive GRASP-Based Algorithm for Pallet Building Problem
with Visibility and Contiguity Constraints   651
  *Manuel Iori, Marco Locatelli, Mayron C. O. Moreira,
  and Tiago Silveira*

Game Theoretic Analysis of State Interventions to Reduce Customer
Returns in E-Commerce.   666
  Maria Beranek

Fair User Equilibrium in a Transportation Space-Time Network   682
  Lianne A. M. Bruijns, Frank Phillipson, and Alex Sangers

Comparison of Manual and Automated Decision-Making with a Logistics
Serious Game.   698
   Martijn Mes and Wouter van Heeswijk

Pricing and Quality Investments in a Mixed Brown-Green Product Market. . .   715
   Arka Mukherjee and Margarida Carvalho

Increasing the Practical Applicability of Order Picking Operations
by Integrating Classification, Labelling and Packaging Regulations   733
   Sarah Vanheusden, Teun van Gils, Katrien Ramaekers, and An Caris

A Solution Approach to The Problem of Nesting Rectangles with Arbitrary
Rotations into Containers of Irregular Convex and Non-Convex Shapes.   747
   Alexandre Romanelli and André R. S. Amaral

Cash Distribution Model with Safety Constraints   763
   William J. Guerrero, Angélica Sarmiento-Lepesqueur,
   and Cristian Martínez-Agaton

Correction to: Stowage Planning with Optimal Ballast Water C1
   Beizhen Jia, Kjetil Fagerholt, Line Blander Reinhardt,
   and Niels Gorm Malý Rytter

Author Index   779

Maritime and Port Logistics

Evaluating Port Development Strategies for a Modal Shift: A Norwegian Case Study

Andreas Breivik Ormevik[1], Stein Ove Erikstad[1], and Kjetil Fagerholt[2(✉)]

[1] Department of Marine Technology, Norwegian University of Science
and Technology, 7491 Trondheim, Norway
{andreas.ormevik,stein.ove.erikstad}@ntnu.no
[2] Department of Industrial Economics and Technology Management,
Norwegian University of Science and Technology, 7491 Trondheim, Norway
kjetil.fagerholt@ntnu.no

Abstract. We study the design of a multi-modal distribution network for the transportation of incoming containers from a container terminal to nearby customer regions. The motivation for the study has been the relocation of the existing cargo terminal in the Port of Bergen, which is expected to increase the road transportation need in the region. To mitigate the consequences of increased driving distances, maritime solutions have been suggested as replacements for truck transportation, but as no such concepts currently exists, more knowledge and insight is needed. Therefore, in this paper we propose a Mixed Integer Programming (MIP) model for optimizing and evaluating strategies for a modal shift in the final stage of the supply chain, i.e. the short distance final distribution from the main terminal to the customer regions. We use it on the case study for the Port of Bergen to analyze whether it is possible to come up with solutions where a significant share of the distribution is done by small electric (and possibly autonomous) container ships instead of trucks. The analyses indicate that a multi-modal distribution network can be a cost-effective option for this particular case..

Keywords: Maritime transportation · Modal shift · Mixed Integer Programming

1 Introduction

More than 90% of the global trade is performed by ships (IMO 2019). Container shipping, which has more than doubled in the last 15 years, is a substantial part of this. Among the busiest routes for containerized cargo is the route from East Asia to Northern Europe, with the ports in Rotterdam, Antwerp and Hamburg being the three largest. From these ports, several optional transportation modes for further distributions exist, including truck or rail transportation, as well as further distribution by smaller ships to different end customer regions all across Europe.

© Springer Nature Switzerland AG 2020
E. Lalla-Ruiz et al. (Eds.): ICCL 2020, LNCS 12433, pp. 3–17, 2020.
https://doi.org/10.1007/978-3-030-59747-4_1

In Norway, the total volume of distributed cargo is expected to increase by approximately 70% towards 2050, where truck transportation is expected to have the largest share (The Ministry of Transport 2017). Trucks are often the preferred transportation mode due to lower costs and a higher flexibility through more frequent deliveries than ship transportation can offer. Despite being a flexible and cost-efficient way of distributing cargo, an increase in road-based transportation using current technologies might contribute to amplify some of the challenges that hinders a sustainable development. This is seen in several Norwegian (and European) cities, where road transport is a significant source to air pollution and noise. Some ports, such as the Port of Bergen on the west coast of Norway, shown in Fig. 1, is today located near the city center, which generates large amounts of traffic through urban areas. The port also restricts the access to the sea and occupies large land areas suited for urban development (Gulbrandsen et al. 2018). To overcome these challenges, it has been decided to move the cargo terminal of the Port of Bergen from the city center to one of the surrounding regions in 2025 (Bergen Havn 2018). However, this will induce a larger transportation need as the distance to the main customer regions increases. One of the suggested solutions to mitigate the increase in road traffic, has been to strengthen the maritime transportation in the region, also for shorter distances from the main terminal to surrounding end customer regions (Berg and Haram 2018). This will be consistent with both national and international goals and visions for future transportation systems.

The European Union has set a goal of shifting 30% of the road transportation to other transportation modes such as rail or maritime transport by year 2030, and a similar benchmark of at least 50% by year 2050 (European Commission 2011). The largest container port in Europe, the port of Rotterdam, has formulated an even more ambitious vision for inland transportation of cargo handled in the port - at most 35% of the further distribution should take place by trucks, 45% transported on inland waterways (barges) and the remaining 20% should be distributed by rail transport (OECD 2010). Also in Norway there is a national interest beyond the port of Bergen of working towards a modal shift in the domestic cargo transportation, with a goal of shifting 30% of the current road transportation to alternative transportation modes within 2030 (The Ministry of Transport 2017).

It should be noted that the above mentioned visions mostly apply for larger transportation distances, defined as more than 300 km. Less attention has been given to the final stages of the supply chain over shorter distances, where requirements to delivery frequencies can, in many cases, still be satisfied by ships. However, as the sailing distances get shorter, port fees, cargo handling activities and manning costs contribute to a larger portion of the total ship transportation cost. It has traditionally been hard to reduce the impact of these cost drivers, which will be a necessity to increase the share of maritime transportation. The introduction of new ship concepts, such as autonomous (and unmanned) ships, may facilitate such a change.

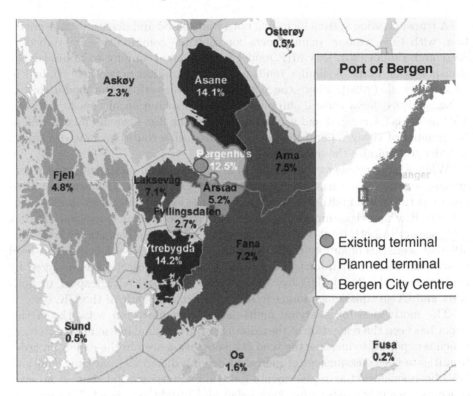

Fig. 1. Geographical distribution of cargo to different geographic locations in the Bergen region (Sundfjord 2015).

In the Norwegian shipping segment, several new concepts have been developed in recent years aiming to replace significant amounts of the current road-based transportation. In collaboration with the Kongsberg group, the Norwegian fertilizer company Yara has developed the world's first fully electric and autonomous container ship, Yara Birkeland. The vessel will have a capacity of 120 TEUs (Twenty-foot Equivalent Units), and is estimated to reduce the annual emissions of NO_x and CO_2 corresponding to 40 000 journeys by trucks between the facilities at Herøya, Brevik and Larvik (Kongsberg 2017). The Norwegian grocery wholesaler ASKO has also developed a similar concept for reducing the need for truck transportation, by using an electric and autonomous ro-ro vessel with a capacity of 16 trucks. The concept will replace two million ton-kilometers per year, and cut the CO_2 emissions by 5000 tons (ASKO 2019). The logistics company North Sea Container Line developed a concept for transshipment of containers at sea, using smaller feeder vessels to serve ports along the Norwegian coast and synchronize the routes with the route of the main vessel distributing cargo from the European ports. This concept has been further studied with respect to optimizing its performance (Holm et al. 2019).

A transportation system including both road-based and maritime transportation, with time window requirements for multiple commodities, is studied in Ayar and Yaman (2012). A MIP model is formulated, aiming to minimize the transportation costs. A similar multi-modal distribution network is studied in Chandra et al. (2020), where the potential for a growth in the modal shift is being analyzed for a coastal shipping case for distribution of cars in India. A MIP model is formulated and used to determine the fleet size and mix as well as the number of voyages performed on a set of feasible routes generated a priori, in order to minimize the overall costs.

While a large number of the reviewed articles focus on minimizing cost, there are also some studies considering mitigation of CO_2-emissions. Zhou et al. (2018) point out the lack of multi-objective studies in the existing literature, and present network flow models aiming to optimize a multi-modal transportation network with respect to both total costs and emissions of CO_2 equivalents (CO_2e). Five different scenarios of supply chain design in the UK, each with a different level of investments in port infrastructures and expansion projects, are analyzed by Rodrigues et al. (2015). The five scenarios are analysed with respect to both costs and CO_2e emissions, aiming to motivate a modal shift in the UK.

The motivation for studying multi-modal transportation networks in this paper has been the relocation of the existing cargo terminal in the Port of Bergen, which is expected to increase the road transportation need in the region. In order to mitigate the consequences of increased driving distances, maritime solutions have been suggested as replacements for truck transportation, but as no such concepts currently exists, more knowledge and insight is needed. Therefore, in this paper we propose a Mixed Integer Programming (MIP) model for optimizing and evaluating strategies for a modal shift in the final stage of the supply chain, i.e. the short distance final distribution from the main terminal to the customers. Furthermore, we use it on the case study for the Port of Bergen to see whether it is possible to come up with solutions where a significant share of the distribution is done by small electric (and possibly autonomous) container ships instead of trucks. In this MIP model, we take as input an estimated cargo demand from the Port of Bergen to the different customer regions surrounding Bergen, as well as cost data for a few alternative small-sized container ships that can potentially be used in this distribution. The model will then, for a given number of different input scenarios, determine the share of truck vs. ship transportation for the final distribution and the optimal fleet of small-sized container ships, and as such provide valuable decision support for analyzing the effects from a modal shift after the relocation of the Port of Bergen. Bergen and its surroundings consists of numerous fjords and islands, which makes the topography especially interesting for this, see Fig. 1.

Section 2 provides a problem definition and presents a MIP model for analyzing it. Section 3 presents the computational results from the case study for the Port of Bergen, while concluding remarks are provided in Sect. 4.

2 Problem Definition and Mathematical Formulation

In the following we provide a problem definition in Sect. 2.1 together with the mathematical notation, while the MIP model is presented in Sect. 2.2.

2.1 Problem Definition and Notation

The planning problem deals with designing a distribution network for the transportation of containers from a main terminal to a given set of customer regions (as illustrated in Fig. 1). There are two possible alternatives for transportation available: 1) Direct truck transportation from the main terminal to the customer regions, and 2) Multi-modal transportation with ships to unloading port(s) in or close to the customer regions, and then truck transportation from the unloading port(s) to the customers. The problem can be defined as to determine:

- which ships to use, i.e. the optimal fleet size and mix,
- the deployment of the ships, i.e. the ship routes,
- which unloading ports to use, and
- the cargo flow through the network, including mode of transportation.

To define this problem mathematically, we need the following notation. There is a set of customer regions, $\mathcal{K}$, where region k has a given monthly demand from the main terminal given by D_k. We assume there is a set of available ship types, $\mathcal{V}$, to choose from, each with a given capacity, $\overline{Q}_v$. There is also a set of candidate unloading ports, $\mathcal{P}$, that can be used in the distribution of containers from the main terminal to the customer regions. Furthermore, we define $\mathcal{R}_v$ as the set of candidate routes that can be used by ships of type v, while $\mathcal{P}_r$ is the set of unloading ports along route r. The parameter T_{vr} is the time it takes for a vessel of type v to perform route r (including the loading and unloading time, assuming that the ship is fully loaded).

We need to define the following cost parameters: C_v^F represents the fixed costs per vessel of type v, i.e. it represents the time charter rate that is also supposed to cover the building costs. C_{vr}^{VS} is the variable sailing cost for a vessel of type v to operate route r. C^{VM} is the unit cost (per container) for loading the vessels in the main terminal, while C_i^{VH} is the unit handling cost at unloading port i. C_k^{DT} and C_{ik}^{FT} represent the unit cost for direct truck distribution from the main terminal and the final truck distribution from unloading port i to customer region k, respectively. In this particular case study, the candidate unloading ports either do not exist or need to be upgraded. It will therefore be a decision regarding which unloading ports to open (i.e. build or upgrade), and we assume that the fixed cost for opening port i is given by C_i^F. The fixed costs for investing in ships, C_v^F, and ports, C_i^F, have been translated into equivalent periodic costs for the planning horizon, $\overline{T}$ (set to 30 days), based on an expected lifetime (chosen as 20 years for the ships and 40 years for the ports) and a given discount rate (set to 5%).

The decision variables are as follows: The integer variable u_v represents the number of ships of type v to be used, while y_{vr} is the total number of voyages on route r performed by vessels of type v over the planning horizon. q_{vr}^L represent the total quantity transported along route r by all vessels of type v, while q_{ivr}^U is the total quantity unloaded in port i by vessels of type v sailing route r. The total quantity transported directly by truck from the main terminal to customer k is given by l_k^{DT}, while the total quantity transported by trucks as final distribution from port i to customer region k is given by l_{ik}^{FT}. Finally, we let the binary variable δ_i be equal to 1 if unloading port i is opened, and 0 otherwise.

2.2 Model

By using the notation introduced in the previous section, we can formulate our planning problem with the following MIP model.

$$
\begin{aligned}
\text{minimize} \quad z = &\sum_{k\in\mathcal{K}} C_k^{DT} l_k^{DT} + \sum_{v\in\mathcal{V}} C_v^F u_v + \sum_{i\in\mathcal{P}} C_i^F \delta_i \\
&+ \sum_{v\in\mathcal{V}}\sum_{r\in\mathcal{R}_v} C^{VM} q_{vr}^L + \sum_{v\in\mathcal{V}}\sum_{r\in\mathcal{R}_v} C_{vr}^{VS} y_{vr} \\
&+ \sum_{v\in\mathcal{V}}\sum_{r\in\mathcal{R}_v}\sum_{i\in\mathcal{P}_r} C_i^{VH} q_{ivr}^U + \sum_{k\in\mathcal{K}}\sum_{i\in\mathcal{P}} C_{ik}^{FT} l_{ik}^{FT}
\end{aligned}
\tag{1}
$$

subject to

$$
q_{vr}^L - \sum_{i\in\mathcal{P}_r} q_{ivr}^U = 0, \quad v\in\mathcal{V}, r\in\mathcal{R}_v
\tag{2}
$$

$$
\sum_{v\in\mathcal{V}}\sum_{r\in\mathcal{R}_v} q_{ivr}^U - \sum_{k\in\mathcal{K}} l_{ik}^{FT} = 0, \quad i\in\mathcal{P}
\tag{3}
$$

$$
l_k^{DT} + \sum_{i\in\mathcal{P}} l_{ik}^{FT} \geq D_k, \quad k\in\mathcal{K}
\tag{4}
$$

$$
q_{vr}^L - \overline{Q}_v y_{vr} \leq 0, \quad v\in\mathcal{V}, r\in\mathcal{R}_v
\tag{5}
$$

$$
u_v \geq \frac{1}{T} \sum_{r\in\mathcal{R}_v} T_{vr} y_{vr}, \quad v\in\mathcal{V}
\tag{6}
$$

$$
\sum_{v\in\mathcal{V}}\sum_{r\in\mathcal{R}_v} q_{ivr}^U \leq \sum_{k\in\mathcal{K}} D_k \delta_i, \quad i\in\mathcal{P}
\tag{7}
$$

Non-negativity requirements are imposed for the load variables, i.e. all variables q_{ivr}^U, q_{vr}^L, l_k^{DT}, and l_{ik}^{FT}, while we make sure that the fleet selection and deployment variables, u_v and y_{vr} take non-negative integer values. Finally, we impose binary requirements on the port selection variables, δ_i.

The objective function (1) minimizes the total cost over the planning horizon, which consists of the following cost components: a) costs for the direct truck distribution from the terminal to the customer regions, b) fixed cost for the selected ships, c) fixed costs for the selected unloading ports, d) variable loading costs at the main terminal, e) variable sailing costs, f) variable handling costs at the unloading ports, and g) the costs for the final truck distribution from the unloading ports to the customer regions.

Constraints (2) ensure that the load balance for all vessel types is maintained, i.e. the total cargo quantity loaded on board the vessels of each type that sail a given route must equal the sum of the cargo quantity unloaded to all ports along the given route. Constraints (3) express the cargo flow balance between unloaded and further distributed cargo in each port, i.e. the total quantity unloaded in a given port i must equal the cargo quantity distributed by final truck transportation to all customer regions from that port. Constraints (4) ensure that the demand in each customer region is satisfied, while constraints (5) make sure that the ship capacity is respected for each ship type and route. Constraints (6) are time constraints that make sure that the number of vessels is sufficiently large to perform the selected routes for each ship type. Finally, constraints (7) ensure that cargo can be unloaded at a given port only if the port is in use.

The MIP model presented above requires a set of candidate routes for each vessel type as input. Each route will start at the main terminal and visit at least one unloading port before returning to the main terminal. Since the number of ports for this case study is rather small, it is easy to generate all feasible route combinations. For routes only visiting one or two unloading ports, the sequence of the port calls does not affect the total sailing distance of the route. However, for the routes including three or more unloading ports, the visiting sequence affects the sailing distance. We therefore solve a Traveling Salesman Problem for each subset of ports with three or more unloading ports, so as to only include the non-dominated routes for each subset.

3   Computational Study

In the following, Sect. 3.1 provides the input data for our case study, while computational results are presented and discussed in Sect. 3.2.

3.1   Input Data for the Case Study

The estimated distribution of the cargo flow to the different regions in and around the city of Bergen is shown in Fig. 1 presented in Sect. 1. Based on this, we exclude the regions with very small demands from our analyses. We also remove the region Fjell, as this coincides with the location of the new container terminal, meaning that all cargo from the container terminal to this region will most likely in any case go by truck. We are then left with the following nine demand or customer regions: 1) Askøy, 2) Ytrebygda, 3) Laksevåg, 4) Bergenhus, 5) Åsane, 6) Fyllingsdalen, 7) Årstad, 8) Arna, and 9) Fana. Based on interviews with representatives of the Port of Bergen, the total monthly demand to these nine regions is approximately 2000 TEUs, which we distribute among the nine regions according to the distribution in Sundfjord (2015), and as shown in Fig. 1.

Based on this cargo flow distribution, as well as what are suitable locations based on existing infrastructure, we have selected five candidate port locations.

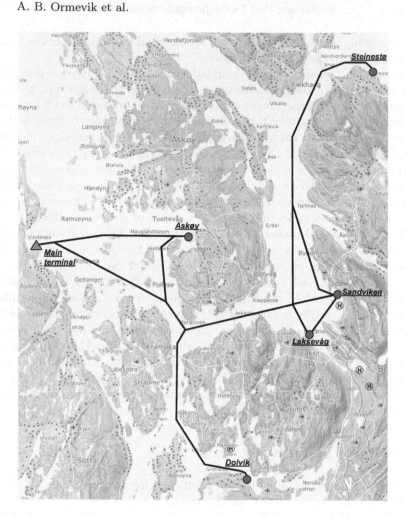

Fig. 2. Proposed port network with feasible sailing routes between the selected ports. Background map is retrieved from The Norwegian Mapping Authority (2019).

Figure 2 shows the port locations and the sailing paths between them, which are used to calculate the sailing distances. From each of these six port locations, including the new main terminal, we have calculated the driving distances on road to the geographical centre of each of the nine demand regions. However, some restrictions are imposed on the final distribution from an unloading port to a customer region:

- Region 1, which covers the island of Askøy, can only be served from the unloading port that is located on the island or by direct distribution from the main terminal.

– To avoid unnecessary transport through the city centre, no cargo distribution
  is allowed from the unloading ports north of the city center (i.e. Sandviken
  and Steinestø) to customer regions south of the city center, and vice versa.

According to Berg and Haram (2018), the costs for truck transportation in
the Bergen region, in Norwegian Kroner (NOK), can be found as $1500 + 31d$,
where d is the driving distance (in km).

Few existing container vessels exist with a loading capacity in the range of 10–
30 TEUs, which is the capacity considered to be most relevant for this case study.
Inspired by the existing projects of Yara Birkeland and the maritime supply
chain project at ASKO briefly discussed in Sect. 1, a set of vessel characteristics
as presented in Table 1 has been obtained. The vessels involved in the projects
mentioned above are fully electric, and we assume that the infrastructure in the
relocated port of Bergen will be able to accommodate electric vessels as well. As
the vessels are assumed to be electric, the maximum sailing range will strongly
depend on the battery capacity and energy consumption during a voyage, as
shown in Table 1. A consumption equal to 15% of the vessel's installed power is
assumed to be used during cargo handling activities in port.

Table 1. Vessel characteristics used to calculate both investment costs and feasible
routes for each vessel type.

Vessel type		1	2	3
Loading capacity	TEUs	10	20	30
Engine power	kW	150	250	300
Sailing speed	kts	12	10	10
Battery capacity	kWh	1200	1500	1800
Energy consumption	kWh/km	6.7	13.5	16.2
Building costs	MNOK	20	25	35
Annual maintenance costs	MNOK	0.3	0.6	1.0

With an energy consumption as shown in Table 1, and by assuming a cost of
energy of 2 NOK/kWh, the cost for operating the vessels can be found. Whether
the vessels are manned or autonomous is not explicitly considered in this study.
However, an additional unit cost of 50 NOK per km sailed is included to capture
additional variable costs that is not related to the usage of energy.

There are three cost components associated with the activities in the selected
ports: 1) Investment cost for upgrading an existing port to become an operative
unloading port in the distribution network, 2) unit costs (per container) for
loading of the vessels in the main terminal, and 3) unit costs (per container)
for unloading the containers in the unloading ports, from the vessel to a truck
ready for final distribution to the end customer. We have used cost figures for
the ports which are based on existing port charges (Dale et al. 2018) and similar
port infrastructure upgrades (Amundsen 2019).

3.2 Computational Results

When minimizing costs, as in objective function (1), the optimal distribution network design has a total cost of 5.22 MNOK. In this solution, 940 TEUs are distributed at sea by one vessel of type 2 before being further distributed by trucks to its final destination. The remaining 1,060 TEUs (of the total monthly demand of 2,000 TEUs), which are destined to customer regions 1, 2, 3, 6, 7 and 9, are transported by trucks directly from the main terminal. The total truck transportation for this solution, including the final distribution from the unloading ports, is approximately 79,010 km (km).

By fixing the ship variable u_v to zero, we obtain a solution where only direct truck transportation takes place. This solution has a cost of 5.24 MNOK, which is only slightly higher than the cost-minimizing solution. However, the total road transportation increases to 131,950 km.

Since one aims at reducing the road traffic, as discussed in Sect. 1, another interesting objective would be to minimize the total truck transportation. This solution gives a total cost of 5.74 MNOK and there is no direct truck distribution to any customer region. In this solution, all available unloading ports are used, except for Sandviken (see Fig. 2). The final distribution from the unloading ports requires 26,780 km of truck transportation, which is a significant reduction compared to both the cost-minimizing solution with 79,010 km, and even more so compared with the pure truck solution with 131,950 km. Two vessels of type 2 are used in this solution.

Table 2. Costs and truck driving distance for three solutions based on minimizing total costs, minimizing total truck transportation, and pure trucks, respectively.

	Cost-minimizing	Truck-minimizing	Pure truck
Total cost [MNOK]	5.22	5.74	5.24
Total truck transportation [km]	79,010	26,780	131,950

Table 2 summarizes the total cost and the total truck transportation for the solutions based on minimizing costs, minimizing total truck transportation and pure truck distribution, respectively.

To examine more closely the trade-off between costs and the amount of truck transportation, we can solve the problem as a bi-objective optimization problem by the epsilon-constrained method. We keep the cost in the objective function, and add a constraint to restrict the amount of truck transportation. By solving the model for different values of the maximum amount of truck transportation, we obtain the Pareto frontier between costs and truck transportation as shown in Fig. 3.

As seen from Fig. 3, the maximum reduction of road transport will equal more than 50,000 km per month. However, this will increase the total operational costs by nearly 10%. If the goal is to obtain a modal shift of at least 30% of the total

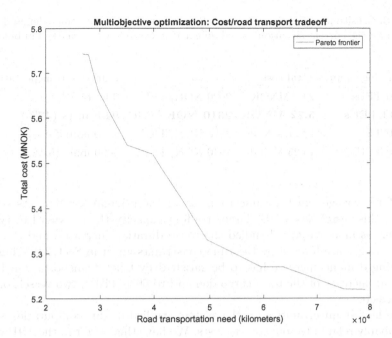

Fig. 3. Illustration of the trade-off between minimizing the truck transportation and minimizing the total cost for the distribution network. The solutions along the Pareto frontier can be seen as "equally good".

truck transportation to a maritime alternative, in accordance with the goals set by EU and the Norwegian government, this can be done at a rather moderate cost increase.

Several input parameters used in this computational study are uncertain. In order to evaluate the robustness of the solutions, a sensitivity analysis is performed, where we run the model with different values for certain input parameters. The sensitivity analysis is performed with respect to two groups of uncertain data, demand and costs, which will be evaluated further in the following.

The customer demands were established based on port statistics and existing studies of the cargo flows from the port of Bergen. From Berg and Haram (2018), the incoming cargo through the port of Bergen represents approximately 20% of the total market share of goods to the region. In other words, the total demand for cargo in the region equals 10,000 TEUs per month. Table 3 shows the optimal solutions with respect to costs, as well as other key performance parameters, for different shares of cargo through the port of Bergen, while assuming the same distribution among the customer regions.

As seen in Table 3, for small cargo flows through the port, a unimodal distribution network including only truck transportation is found to be the most cost-efficient. As the total cargo flow increases, the unit cost decreases. It should be noted that for the case of 4,000 TEUs, a decrease in the share of maritime transportation is observed. In this particular solution, a vessel of type 3 is selected

Table 3. Sensitivity analysis with respect to uncertainty in customer demands. The solution for the current situation, based on existing cargo flows, is marked in bold text.

Incoming supply	Total cost	Unit cost	Maritime transportation
1000 TEUs	2.62 MNOK	2620 NOK/TEU	0 units (0%)
2000 TEUs	**5.22 MNOK**	**2610 NOK/TEU**	**940 units (47%)**
4000 TEUs	10.21 MNOK	2550 NOK/TEU	1530 units (38%)
6000 TEUs	15.25 MNOK	2540 NOK/TEU	3090 units (52%)

to perform voyages on the same route as in the original solution. As seen in Table 1, this vessel has a 50% larger loading capacity than a vessel of type 2. However, as more cargo is handled the route duration increases, and the number of voyages are limited by the time constraints given in Sect. 2.2. Thus, the remaining demand increase has to be satisfied by truck transportation. In the case of an increase of the total cargo demand to 6000 TEUs, two vessels of type 3 are selected.

The largest uncertainties for the system studied in this computation study, are probably related to some of the costs. We have therefore run the MIP model for the following five different scenarios, varying one cost component at the time.

- Scenario 1: Increased acquisition costs for all vessel types, C_v^F, tested for an increase of both 10% (1a) and 20% (1b)
- Scenario 2: Increased port investment costs. Tested for an increase of both 20% (2a) and 40% (2b).
- Scenario 3: A 20% increase of the maintenance costs, for both the vessels of all types and the suggested unloading ports.
- Scenario 4: Increased (a) and reduced (b) variable sailing costs, C_{vr}^{VS}, of 20%, where the reduced sailing costs can be relevant in the autonomous (unmanned) case.
- Scenario 5: A 20% increase of the truck transportation costs, which could for example represent toll charges, which have not been included originally.

The optimal solutions for each of these scenarios are presented in Table 4. It can be noted that all scenarios from 1a to 4a equal either the cost-minimizing solution or the only truck-solution (see Table 2). Further, this sensitivity analysis shows that an increase in the port investment costs only leads to minor increases in the total operating monthly costs. The main reason for this is that in all solutions, only one unloading port is chosen (Sandviken, ref. Fig. 2). Lastly, the results illustrate an "instability" in the solutions. By introducing vessels for maritime transportation, several additional investments such as vessel acquisition, port investments and annual maintenance costs need to be taken into account, each with an uncertainty in the specified input value. Due to the relatively low cost reduction this will induce, too large changes in one of the cost parameters will cancel out the cost reduction obtained by taking the vessels in use. Instead, a solution where only trucks perform cargo distribution is selected.

Table 4. Sensitivity analysis with respect to uncertainty in cost components. The initial cost-minimizing solution is defined as scenario 0.

Scenario	Total cost	Vessel distribution	Road transportation
0	5.219 MNOK	940 TEUs	79,010 km
1a	5.236 MNOK	940 TEUs	79,010 km
1b	5.241 MNOK	0 TEUs	131,950 km
2a	5.239 MNOK	940 TEUs	79,010 km
2b	5.241 MNOK	0 TEUs	131,950 km
3	5.236 MNOK	940 TEUs	79,010 km
4a	5.241 MNOK	0 TEUs	131,950 km
4b	5.188 MNOK	1100 TEUs	72,190 km
5	6.052 MNOK	1100 TEUs	72,204 km

On the other hand, the results presented show that if the truck costs increase as in scenario 5, this will strengthen the competitiveness of maritime transportation and lead to a further increase in the share of cargo distributed by vessels.

Despite the dramatic changes in the structure of the obtained solutions in Table 4 due to modest changes in cost parameters, the total costs seem to be relatively stable or robust with respect to these cost changes. Thus, the obtained results indicate a relatively "flat" objective function, where a large number of different solutions yield relatively similar costs. This finding is also illustrated through the solutions along the Pareto frontier in Fig. 3, and can actually be seen as beneficial in the case of redeveloping the Port of Bergen. The political goals of moving significant amount of cargo from road to sea can be achieved at relatively small cost increases and through several combinations of strategic investment decisions.

4 Concluding Remarks

The performed analyses indicate that a multi-modal distribution network can be a viable option for the case of Bergen after relocating the main cargo terminal. For a given set of parameters and assumptions used as model input, the most cost-efficient solution proved to contribute to satisfy nearly 50% of the total cargo demand by multi-modal transportation. This share can be further increased at a relatively low increase of the overall costs. If the social costs of road congestion, air pollution and accidents induced by road transport are included, this finding will strengthen the competitiveness of a multi-modal distribution network.

With the significant uncertainties related to cost components and customer demands, together with the assumptions made throughout the study, the exact values obtained from the results are not of great importance in this project. Instead, the results indicate that given the topography of Bergen and its surrounding, with many fjords and islands, establishing a multi-modal network may provide cost-savings and a significant reduction of the increased road transportation need initiated by the relocation of the port.

Despite being a study of the specific case for the Port of Bergen, the proposed model and findings can be applicable to other ports and cargo distribution networks. There are several other cities in Norway, as well as in other countries, experiencing similar challenges regarding road congestion and where the topography creates maritime "shortcuts" which currently are utilized to a low extent. However, it is reasonable to expect that major changes of the distribution network design will be easier to implement through a port redevelopment process, for instance through the relocation of a port terminal, such as in Bergen.

In this study we have only considered the distribution from the main terminal to the different customer regions. However, in reality there is also a flow of containers in the opposite direction. It would therefore be of interest to extend our model to include this flow, which is likely to make the multi-modal distribution even more competitive compared to only using trucks.

References

Amundsen, B.O.: Implenia skal bygge fergekaier på Nordmøre for 74 millioner kroner (2019) (in Norwegian). https://www.veier24.no/artikler/implenia-skal-bygge-fergekaier-pa-nordmore-for-74-millioner-kroner/465876. Accessed 03 Mar 2020

ASKO: ASKO planlegger en hel-elektrisk transportkjede på vei og sjø (2019). https://asko.no/nyhetsarkiv/asko-med-droneprosjekt. Accessed 03 Mar 2020

Ayar, B., Yaman, H.: An intermodal multicommodity routing problem with scheduled services. Comput. Optim. Appl. **53**(1), 131–153 (2012). https://doi.org/10.1007/s10589-011-9409-z

Berg, G., Haram, H.K.: Flytting av godshavna i Bergen til Ågotnes - konsekvensanalyse (2018) (in Norwegian). https://fido.nrk.no/cef4c2d4d96346d5511114237d6072a6a7601eb97fc526f5ceb11102c261b082/Konsekvensanalyse%20flytting%20Bergen%20godshavn%20-%20Flowchange%20as.pdf. Accessed 03 Mar 2020

Bergen Havn: Endeleg ja til ny godshamn på Ågotnes (2019) (in Norwegian). https://bergenhavn.no/endeleg-ja-til-ny-godshamn-pa-agotnes/. Accessed 03 Mar 2020

Chandra, S., Christiansen, M., Fagerholt, K.: Analysing the modal shift from road-based to coastal shipping-based distribution - a case study of outbound automotive logistics in India. Marit. Policy Manage. **47**, 273–286 (2020)

Dale, E., et al.: Kostnadskomponenter og - størrelser ved skipsanløp Report No.: 10083133–4, Rev. 1. DNV GL AS Maritime, p. 12 (2018) (in Norwegian). https://www.kystverket.no/globalassets/rapporter-og-brosjyrer/dnv-gl-2018_kostnadskomponenter-og-storrelser-ved-skipsanlop.pdf. Accessed 03 Mar 2020

European Commision: WHITE PAPER - Roadmap to a Single European Transport Area - Towards a competitive and resource efficient transport system. European Commision, p. 9 (2011). https://eur-lex.europa.eu/LexUriServ/LexUriServ.do?uri=COM:2011:0144:FIN:en:PDF. Accessed 03 Mar 2020

Gulbrandsen, M.U., et al.: Samfunnsøkonomisk analyse av å årelokalisere godshavnen i Bergen til Ågotnes Report no. 96/2018. Menon Economics, pp. 8–11 (2018) (in Norwegian). https://www.menon.no/wp-content/uploads/2018-96-S%C3%98A-av-%C3%A5-relokalisere-godshavnen-i-Bergen-til-%C3%85gotnes.pdf. Accessed 03 Mar 2020

Holm, M.B., Medbøen, C.A.B., Fagerholt, K., Schütz, P.: Shortsea liner network design with transhipments at sea: a case study from Western Norway. Flex. Serv. Manuf. J. **31**(3), 598–619 (2018). https://doi.org/10.1007/s10696-018-9317-y

IMO: IMO profile - overview (2019). https://business.un.org/en/entities/13. Accessed 03 Mar 2020

Kongsberg: Autonomous ship project, key facts about Yara Birkeland (2017). https://www.kongsberg.com/maritime/support/themes/autonomous-ship-project-key-facts-about-yara-birkeland/. Accessed 03 Mar 2020

OECD: Transcontinental Infrastructure Needs to 2030/2050. North-West Europe Gateway Area - Port of Rotterdam Case Study. The Organisation for Economic Co-operation and Development (OECD), p. 25 (2010). https://www.oecd.org/futures/infrastructureto2030/48321781.pdf. Accessed 03 Mar 2020

Rodrigues, V.S., et al.: UK supply chain carbon mitigation strategies using alternative ports and multimodal freight transport operations. Transp. Res. Part E Logistics Transp. Rev. **78**, 40–56 (2015)

Sundfjord, Ø.: Konseptvalgutredning logistikknutepunkt i Bergensregio- nen - Behovsanalyse Document No.: POU-00-A-00095, Rev. 2. Jernbaneverket, p. 23 (2015) (in Norwegian). https://www.jernbanedirektoratet.no/contentassets/052c20a27b1049b88beba9eb0370a772/kvu-behovsanalyse-rapport.pdf. Accessed 03 Mar 2020

The Ministry of Transport: Meld. St. 33 - Nasjonal Transport-plan 2018–2029, pp. 33–34, 190 (2017) (in Norwegian). https://www.regjeringen.no/contentassets/7c52fd2938ca42209e4286fe86bb28bd/no/pdfs/stm201620170033000dddpdfs.pdf. Accessed 03 Mar 2020

The Norwegian Mapping Authority: Kart - Turkart, eiendomskart, stedsnavn, kart for utskrift (2019). https://norgeskart.no/. Accessed 03 Mar 2020

Zhou, M., et al.: Capacitated multi-modal network ow models for minimizing total operational cost and CO2e emission. Comput. Ind. Eng. **126**, 361–377 (2018)

Pickup and Delivery Problem with Transshipment for Inland Waterway Transport

Yimeng Zhang$^{(\boxtimes)}$, Bilge Atasoy, Dimitris Souravlias, and Rudy R. Negenborn

Department of Maritime and Transport Technology, Delft University of Technology,
2628 CD Delft, The Netherlands
{Yimeng.Zhang,B.Atasoy,D.Souravlias,R.R.Negenborn}@tudelft.nl

Abstract. Inland waterway transport is becoming attractive due to its minimum environmental impact in comparison with other transportation modes. Fixed timetables and routes are adopted by most barge operators, avoiding the full utilization of the available resources. Therefore a flexible model is adopted to reduce the transportation cost and environmental impacts. This paper regards the route optimization of barges as a pickup and delivery problem (PDP). A Mixed Integer Programming (MIP) model is proposed to formulate the PDP with transshipment of barges, and an Adaptive Large Neighborhood Search (ALNS) is developed to solve the problem efficiently. The approach is evaluated based on a case study in the Rhine Alpine corridor and it is shown that ALNS is able to find good solutions in reasonable computation times. The results show that the cost is lower when there is more flexibility. Moreover, the cost comparison shows that transshipment terminals can reduce the cost for barge companies.

Keywords: Inland waterway transport · Pickup and delivery problem · Transshipment · Adaptive large neighborhood search

1 Introduction

Transportation of goods and people via different inland waterways such as rivers, lakes and canals, is commonly referred as Inland Waterway Transport (IWT). Compared to road and railway transportation, IWT offers competitive advantages including lower transportation costs, reduced greenhouse gas emissions as well as noise pollution [1]. For this reason, more and more transportation stakeholders want to increase the share of water transportation in their operations. According to the Port of Rotterdam, a total of 100,000 inland barges arrived in 2019 [2]. To handle the subsequent container flows in the future, the Port of Rotterdam aims to raise the utilization of waterborne transport to have the largest modal share over the next 20 years [3]. The EU Transport White Paper (European Commission, 2011) targeted for freight transport to shift from road to rail and IWT by more than 50% by 2050 [4].

© Springer Nature Switzerland AG 2020
E. Lalla-Ruiz et al. (Eds.): ICCL 2020, LNCS 12433, pp. 18–35, 2020.
https://doi.org/10.1007/978-3-030-59747-4_2

Barge operators are the key carriers when it comes to IWT and they usually work with fixed timetables [5]. However, it might be beneficial to adapt the routes during operations, e.g., serve a new transportation request halfway, in order to reduce costs and/or serve additional requests. In this situation, the optimization problem for the barge carrier/operator can be regarded as a pickup and delivery problem (PDP) [6], especially for big transportation companies, that operate over multiple terminals in a river. A representative example of such a company is Contargo [7], which operates barges in the Rhine-Alpine corridor.

In transport operations, it is shown that the shipment of goods to an intermediate destination before they reach their intended destination (i.e., transshipment) can reduce costs and emissions [8,9]. In case of IWT, one barge drives the request to a predetermined terminal, called transshipment terminal. The second barge picks up the request at the transshipment terminal and transports it to the delivery terminal. In this way, several requests can share a barge as long as capacity is not exceeded, the number of used barges can be minimized and the capacity of barges is utilized better. A real-world example is shown in Sect. 3. To the best of our knowledge, no study focused on the PDP with transshipment for intermodal freight transportation involving IWT. Moreover, most barge operators adopt the fixed timetable and routes for barges, which may lead to loss of flexibility. In this paper, the flexible barges, i.e., barges without predefined timetable and routes, are considered.

In this paper, we study the PDP with transshipment over an intermodal transportation network including inland waterways. To formulate this optimization problem, we propose a Mixed Integer Programming (MIP) model. The objective is to determine the routes of barges that minimize the overall cost, under several practical constraints that realize the transshipment between barges. Given that for real size networks, the studied problem cannot be solved to optimality in reasonable times, we additionally propose an adaptive large neighborhood search algorithm. Based on real-world data including barge timetables and technical specifications (speed profiles, capacities), a series of instances with different sizes and diverse characteristics are generated. An extensive experimental evaluation is conducted that demonstrates the efficiency of the proposed approach under various configurations and across different problem instances.

The remainder of this paper is structured as follows: Sect. 2 presents a brief literature review. The proposed MIP model is described in Sect. 3, while the solution methodology is given in Sect. 4. The experimental settings and results are reported in Sect. 5. The paper concludes and provides directions for future research in Sect. 6.

2   Literature Review

In this section, we briefly review the literature related to the role of transshipment in transportation. Also, we outline several research studies that investigate the use of inland barges in waterway transport operations, including transport routes optimization and service network optimization.

2.1 Transshipment in Transportation Domain

Transshipment is a common practice in various transportation operations and considered in various modeling approaches, including vehicle routing problem with trailers and transshipment (VRPTT), vehicle routing problem with cross-docking (VRPCD), and pickup and delivery problem with transshipment (PDPT).

The VRPTT considers a set of non-autonomous vehicles (trailers), which can only move when pulled by a lorry [10]. In the VRPTT, the trailers can be parked at transshipment locations, where the load is transferred from lorries to trailers. The VRPCD is concerned with defining a set of routes that satisfy transportation requests among different pickup and delivery points. In the VRPCD, the vehicles bring goods from pickup locations to a cross-docking platform, where the items may be consolidated for efficient delivery [11]. The PDPT is a variant of the PDP, where requests can change vehicle at transshipment points during their trip [12]. In the PDP, the pickup and delivery points of a request should be serviced by the same vehicle. By relaxing related constraints, a request can be transported by more than one vehicle. There is a common characteristic in the above problems due to transshipment: synchronization among different vehicles. These problems are Vehicle Routing Problems (VRPs) which exhibit additional synchronization requirements with regard to spatial, temporal, and load aspects [9]. The model proposed in this paper belongs to PDPT.

Some studies proposed heuristics to reduce computation time. To determine the benefits of transshipment in a daily route planning problem at a regional air carrier, a greedy randomized adaptive search procedure (GRASP) was developed to find optimal routes efficiently [14]. A branch-and-price algorithm was proposed for the VRPTT, using problem specific enhancements in the pricing scheme and alternative lower bound computations [15]. In this study, an adaptive large neighborhood search (ALNS) algorithm was additionally used to obtain good initial columns. To solve PDPT efficiently, a heuristic capable of efficiently inserting requests through transfer points was proposed and it was embedded into an ALNS algorithm [12].

Besides freight transportation, some scholars solve similar problems in passenger transportation. For example, a pickup and delivery problem with transfers is formulated and the proposed model is applied to passenger transport [13]. There are three differences between the approach in [13] and this research: a) From the mathematical model perspective, the transfer node in [13] is regarded as two separate nodes (start node and finish node) to model the transshipment. In this research, vehicle flow and request flow are modeled to achieve container transshipment between barges. b) From the solution methodology perspective, a branch-and-cut solution method is used in [13] and there are up to 6 requests, 2 vehicles, and 2 transshipment terminals. In this research, ALNS is used to improve the scalability so that large instances can be handled. c) From the application perspective, the model in [13] and the model proposed in this research are applied to passenger transport and IWT separately, and different transport characteristics are considered. For example, this research takes upstream/downstream speed into account.

2.2   Optimization Challenges for Inland Barges

Barge route optimization is mainly studied by focusing on the waterway transport itself. The optimal values of parameters, which influence the efficient utilization of barges, were investigated in [16]. Several years later, the barge routing problem was studied with the objective of maximizing the profit for a shipping company [17]. In the same study, the upstream and downstream calling sequence as well as the number of loaded and empty containers were also determined. To generate rotation plans for inland barges, an approach was developed on the integration of mixed-integer programming (MIP) and constraint programming (CP) [18]. To address long waiting times and congestion of inland barges in the port, a two-phase approach for planning inter-terminal transport of inland barges was proposed in the presence of several practical constraints [3].

The service network design for barges can be related to intermodal transport. The relations between barge network design, transport market, and the performance of intermodal barge transport is typically the central issue [19]. A general framework that describes design variables of barge networks and identifies their connection to the performance indicators of intermodal barge transport is presented in [20]. There are additional studies on the service network of barges that consider regional characteristics. A hub-and-spoke network was designed for a shipping company that is consistent with the characteristics of the Yangtze River [21]. The subset of ports needs to be called and the amount of containers need to be shipped are determined in [22]. In order to save possible leasing or storage costs of empty containers at the respective ports, the repositioning of empty containers is explored in [22].

Although the VRP with transshipment and waterway transport optimization are well studied, only a few research studies have been devoted to the VRP with barges, and the benefits of transshipment have been rarely exploited. Table 1 provides a detailed comparison among different studies of the relevant literature considering several aspects.

Table 1. Comparison on models in literature.

Literature	Method	Objective	Transshipment	Time & capacity constraints	Upstream/ downstream	Waiting time	Heuristic
[19]	QA	–	✗	–	✗	✗	–
[16]	NF	profit	✗	✓	✓	✗	✗
[17]	NF	profit	✗	✓	✓	✗	✓
[20]	NF	profit	✗	✓	✗	✗	✗
[21]	NF	cost	✓	✓	✓	✗	✗
[18]	NF	time	✗	✓	✗	✓	✓
[3]	NF	time	✗	✓	✗	✓	✓
[22]	NF	profit	✗	✓	✓	✓	✗
Our paper	PDPT	cost	✓	✓	✓	✓	✓

QA: Quantitative Analysis; NF: Network Flow Model.
– means the relevant item is not applicable to the paper.

3 Optimization Model for Inland Barges

We formulate the optimization problem for the barge carrier as a PDPT. Compared with traditional modelling approaches for barges, such as network flow optimization, the proposed model can reduce the cost due to its flexibility and transshipment benefits, as in Fig. 1. In Fig. 1a, a barge named Nova picks up two requests (0 and 1) at Antwerp, then delivers request 1 and picks up request 2 at Rotterdam, finally deliveries requests 0 and 2 at Neuss terminal. If the barge Nova has a fixed shuttle from Antwerp to Neuss, requests 1 and 2 can only be served by other barges, a choice that induces unnecessary costs. In Fig. 1b, request 0 needs to be transported from Frankfurt-Ost terminal to Rotterdam, and request 1 needs to be transported from Mannheim terminal to Rotterdam. As they share the same route segment, request 1 is transferred from barge Michigan to barge So Long at transshipment terminal Koblenz, which avoids extra travel for Michigan and makes full use of So Long's capacity.

The proposed model allows containers to be transferred from one barge to another at transshipment terminals, as shown in Fig. 2. Therefore, different from traditional PDP, the routes of requests and routes of barges need to be considered separately.

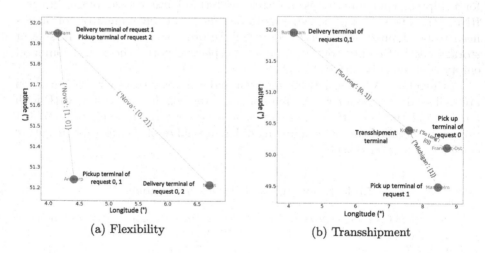

(a) Flexibility   (b) Transshipment

Fig. 1. Illustration of the flexibility and transshipment of the model.

The loading/unloading time is called service time for pickup/delivery, and it is called transshipment time in case of transshipment. Figure 2 also shows how the time is added in the model. The time from the arrival time till the service start time is the waiting time, and departure happens after service time or transshipment time is completed. There are three situations that lead to waiting time. The first one is when the barge arrives before the pickup/delivery time window, and so needs to wait for containers. The other two situations take place in the transshipment terminal. Assuming barge l will pickup containers and barge k will deliver containers at transshipment terminal. The second situation is that barge l arrives at the transshipment terminal before barge k completes the unloading, and l needs to wait for k. The last situation is that barge k arrives before barge l, and k needs to wait for l. For the first and second situations, the waiting time is necessary. For the last situation, as the reviewer suggested, barge k can unload container directly and doesn't need to wait for barge l. However, this paper doesn't consider the storage in the terminals, and the waiting time is used. Figure 2 shows the first and second situations.

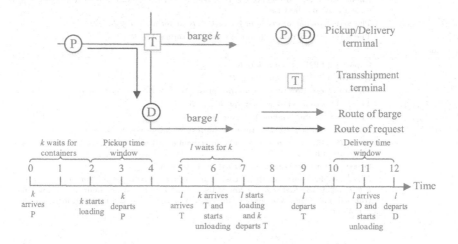

Fig. 2. Transshipment and time in the model.

The notation used in the mathematical model is provided in Table 2. A request consists of pickup and delivery time windows, and number of containers (TEU). The barge set includes barges' name, capacity, and speed. Terminals and arcs form the transport network of the carrier or barge operator. In the terminal set, there are some special terminals, including transshipment terminals, initial/final depots of barges and pickup/delivery terminals of requests. Each barge may start from different depot.

Table 2. Notation used in the model.

Sets	
R	Set of requests
K	Set of barges
N	Set of terminals
A	Set of arcs. For $i, j \in N$, the arc from i to j is denoted by $(i, j) \in A$
$T \subseteq N$	Set of transshipment terminals
$o(k)/o'(k) \subseteq N$	Initial/final depot of barge $k \in K$
$p(r)/d(r) \subseteq N$	Pickup/delivery terminal of request $r \in R$

Variables	
x_{ij}^k	Binary variable; 1 if barge $k \in K$ uses the arc $(i, j) \in A$, 0 otherwise
y_{ij}^{kr}	Binary variable; 1 if request $r \in R$ transported by barge k uses arc $(i, j) \in A$, 0 otherwise
z_{ij}^k	Binary variable; 1 if terminal $i \in N$ precedes (not necessarily immediately) terminal $j \in N$ in the route of the barge $k \in K$, 0 otherwise
s_{ir}^{kl}	Binary variable; 1 if request $r \in R$ is transferred from barge $k \in K$ to barge $l \neq k$ at node $i \in N$, 0 otherwise
$t_i^k/\bar{t}_i^k$	The arrival/departure time of barge $k \in K$ at terminal $i \in N$
$t'^{\,k}_i$	The service start time of barge $k \in K$ at terminal $i \in N$

Parameters	
u_k	Capacity (TEU) of barge $k \in K$
q_r	Quantity (TEU) of request $r \in R$
τ_{ij}^k	The transportation time (in hours) on arc $(i, j) \in A$ for barge $k \in K$
$[a_{p(r)}, b_{p(r)}]$	The pickup time window for request $r \in R$
$[a_{d(r)}, b_{d(r)}]$	The delivery time window for request $r \in R$
$t''^{\,k}_i/t'''^{\,k}_i$	The transshipment/service time (in hours) for barge $k \in K$ at terminal $i \in N$
v_k	Speed (km/h) of barge $k \in K$. The upstream speed and downstream speed for a same barge are different
d_{ij}	Distance (km) between terminal $i \in N$ and $j \in N$
c_k^{1-5}	c_k^1/c_k^2 are unit (one container) cost (euro) of transportation per km/hour using barge $k \in K$. c_k^3 is the fuel cost per km of barges. c_k^4 is the cost per hour of waiting time, transshipment time and service time at a terminal. c_k^5 is the transshipment cost per container

The objective of the model is to minimize cost, which consists of transportation cost of containers, fuel cost, transshipment cost, and cost associated with waiting, service, and transshipment time, defined as follows:

$$
\begin{aligned}
Minimize\ F = &\sum_{k \in K} \sum_{(i,j) \in A} \sum_{r \in R} (c_k^1 d_{ij} + c_k^2 \tau_{ij}) y_{ij}^{kr} q_r \\
&+ \sum_{k \in K} \sum_{(i,j) \in A} (c_k^3 d_{ij} x_{ij}^k + c_k^4 (\bar{t}_i^k - t_i^k)) + \sum_{k,l \in K, k \neq l} \sum_{r \in R} \sum_{i \in T} c_k^5 q_r s_{ir}^{kl}
\end{aligned}
\tag{1}
$$

Subject to:

$$\sum_{j \in N} x_{ij}^k \leqslant 1 \quad \forall k \in K, \ \forall i = o(k) \tag{2}$$

$$\sum_{j \in N} x_{ij}^k = \sum_{j \in N} x_{jl}^k \quad \forall k \in K, \ \forall i = o(k), \ \forall l = o'(k) \tag{3}$$

$$\sum_{k \in K} \sum_{j \in N} y_{ij}^{kr} = 1 \quad \forall r \in R, \ \forall i = p(r) \tag{4}$$

$$\sum_{k \in K} \sum_{j \in N} y_{ji}^{kr} = 1 \quad \forall r \in R, \ \forall i = d(r) \tag{5}$$

$$\sum_{j \in N} x_{ij}^k - \sum_{j \in N} x_{ji}^k = 0 \quad \forall k \in K, \ \forall i \in N \setminus o(k), o'(k) \tag{6}$$

$$\sum_{k \in K} \sum_{j \in N} y_{ij}^{kr} - \sum_{k \in K} \sum_{j \in N} y_{ji}^{kr} = 0 \quad \forall r \in R, \ \forall i \in T \setminus p(r), d(r) \tag{7}$$

$$\sum_{j \in N} y_{ij}^{kr} - \sum_{j \in N} y_{ji}^{kr} = 0 \quad \forall k \in K, \ \forall r \in R, \ \forall i \in N \setminus T, p(r), d(r) \tag{8}$$

$$y_{ij}^{kr} \leqslant x_{ij}^k \quad \forall (i,j) \in A, \ \forall k \in K, \ \forall r \in R \tag{9}$$

$$\sum_{j \in N} y_{ji}^{kr} + \sum_{j \in N} y_{ij}^{lr} \leqslant s_{ir}^{kl} + 1 \quad \forall r \in R, \ \forall i \in T, \ \forall k,l \in K, \ k \neq l \tag{10}$$

$$s_{ir}^{kl} \leqslant \sum_{j \in N} y_{ji}^{kr} \quad \forall r \in R, \ \forall i \in T, \ \forall k,l \in K, \ k \neq l \tag{11}$$

$$s_{ir}^{kl} \leqslant \sum_{j \in N} y_{ij}^{lr} \quad \forall r \in R, \ \forall i \in T, \ \forall k,l \in K, \ k \neq l \tag{12}$$

$$t_i^k \leqslant t'^k_i \quad \forall i \in N, \ \forall k \in K \tag{13}$$

$$t'^k_i \leqslant \overline{t}_i^k \quad \forall i \in N, \ \forall k \in K \tag{14}$$

$$\overline{t}_i^k + \tau_{ij}^k - t_j^k \leqslant M(1 - x_{ij}^k) \quad \forall (i,j) \in A, \ \forall k \in K \tag{15}$$

$$a_{p(r)} \leqslant t'^k_{p(r)}, \ \overline{t}_{p(r)}^k \leqslant b_{p(r)} \quad \forall r \in R, \ \forall k \in K \tag{16}$$

$$a_{d(r)} \leqslant t'^k_{d(r)}, \ \overline{t}_{d(r)}^k \leqslant b_{d(r)} \quad \forall r \in R, \ \forall k \in K \tag{17}$$

$$t'^k_{p(r)/d(r)} + t'''^k_{p(r)/d(r)} = \overline{t}_{p(r)/d(r)}^k \quad \forall r \in R, \ \forall k \in K \tag{18}$$

$$\overline{t}_i^k - t'^l_i \leqslant M(1 - s_{ir}^{kl}) \quad \forall r \in R, \ \forall i \in T, \ \forall k,l \in K, \ k \neq l \tag{19}$$

$$\overline{t}_i^k - t''^k_i = t''^k_i s_{ir}^{kl} \quad \forall r \in R, \ \forall i \in T, \ \forall k,l \in K, \ k \neq l \tag{20}$$

$$\overline{t}_i^l - t'^l_i = t''^k_i s_{ir}^{kl} \quad \forall r \in R, \ \forall i \in T, \ \forall k,l \in K, \ k \neq l \tag{21}$$

$$x_{ij}^k \leqslant z_{ij}^k \quad \forall i,j \in N, \ \forall k \in K \tag{22}$$

$$z_{ij}^k + z_{ji}^k = 1 \quad \forall i,j \in N, \ \forall k \in K \tag{23}$$

$$z_{ij}^k + z_{jl}^k + z_{li}^k \leqslant 2 \quad \forall i,j,l \in N, \ \forall k \in K \tag{24}$$

$$\sum_{r \in R} q_r y_{ij}^{kr} \leqslant u_k x_{ij}^k \quad \forall (i,j) \in A, \ \forall k \in K \tag{25}$$

$$x_{ij}^k \in \{0,1\} \quad \forall (i,j) \in A, \ \forall k \in K \tag{26}$$

$$y_{ij}^{kr} \in \{0,1\} \quad \forall (i,j) \in A, \ \forall k \in K, \ \forall r \in R \tag{27}$$

Constraints (2) and (3) ensure that a barge begins and ends at its begin and end depot, respectively. Constraints (4) and (5) ensure that containers for each request must be picked and delivered at its pick up and delivery terminal, respectively. Constraints (6) represent flow conservation for vehicle flow and (7)–(8) represent flow conservation for request flow. Constraints (7) are for transshipment terminals, and constraints (8) are for normal terminals. Constraints (9) link y and x variables in order to guarantee that for a request to be transported by a barge, that barge needs to be traversing the associated arc. Constraints (10)–(12) facilitate transshipment. (10) ensures that the transshipment occurs only once in the transshipment terminal. Furthermore, (11) and (12) let the transshipment only when the request is transported by both barges k and l. Constraints (13)–(15) are the time related constraints. Constraints (13) guarantee that the arrival time of barge is earlier than service start time. Constraints (14) maintain that the departure happens only after the service is completed. Constraints (15) ensure that the time on route is consistent with the distance travelled and speed, and M is a large enough positive number. Constraints (16) and (17) take care of the time windows. These constraints give possibility of waiting at terminals when barge arrives earlier. Constraints (18) add service time of pickup and delivery. Constraints (19)–(21) include time constraints for transshipment. If there is a transshipment from barge k to barge l, but barge l arrives before barge k departs, (19) allows barge l to wait until barge k completes its unloading. Constraints (20) and (21) add transshipment time at the transshipment terminal. Constraints (22)–(24) are the subtour elimination constraints, which provide tight bounds among several polynomial-size versions of subtour elimination constraints [23]. Constraints (25) are the capacity constraints. Constraints (26) and (27) set variables x and y as binary variables.

A MIP model for the PDPT in IWT is thus given by the objective function (1) and constraints (2)–(27) described above.

4   Solution Methodology

For the studied PDPT problem, we consider two main solution methodologies: (i) an exact solution by a solver, Gurobi [24], to the MIP, (ii) an ALNS. Section 5 presents comparative results for both approaches.

The ALNS was proposed in 2006 based on an extension of the large neighborhood search (LNS) heuristic [25], and ALNS adopted an adaptive mechanism to make it robust in different scenarios. ALNS has already been used for VRP problems successfully and it performs well on large-scale instances. There are other different approaches. But this adaptive nature of ALNS, i.e., choosing operators according to their past performances, is a significant advantage over other approaches which do not use it. The pseudocode of the ALNS in the paper is shown in Algorithm 1. X means the solution. For instance, $X_{initial}$ means initial solution, which is generated by Greedy Insertion proposed in Sect. 4.1. R_{pool} is a set of active requests, and it includes requests need to be inserted to routes.

The ALNS is composed of a number of competing sub-heuristics, i.e., insertion and removal operators. An insertion operator is concerned with inserting requests to the routes of barges. In contrast, a removal operator is used for

---

Algorithm 1: ALNS algorithm

Input: K, R; **Output:** X_{best};

set $X_{initial}$ as empty routes of K; $R_{pool} = R$;

$[X_{initial}, R_{pool}] = GreedyInsertion(X_{initial}, R_{pool})$;

while R_{pool} *is not empty* **do**

    | $[X_{initial}, R_{pool}] = RandomRemoval(X_{initial})$;

    | $[X_{initial}, R_{pool}] = GreedyInsertion(X_{initial}, R_{pool})$;

end

$X_{last} \leftarrow X_{initial}$; $X_{best} \leftarrow X_{last}$;

repeat

    refresh weights and choose operators at the beginning of each segment;

    $X_{current} \leftarrow X_{last}$;

    while R_{pool} *is not empty* **do**

        | $[X_{current}, R_{pool}] = RemovalOperator(X_{current})$;

        | $[X_{current}, R_{pool}] = InsertionOperator(X_{current}, R_{pool})$;

    end

    if $F(X_{current}) < F(X_{last})$ **then**

    | $X_{last} \leftarrow X_{current}$;

    else

    | $X_{last} \leftarrow X_{current}$ with probability p;

    end

    if $F(X_{last}) < F(X_{best})$ **then**

    | $X_{best} \leftarrow X_{last}$;

    end

until *stop-criterion met*;

---

removing requests from a route. The combination of insertion and removal operators is called *operations*. The process of using an operation until all requests are served is called an iteration. After each iteration, the algorithm will assign to the used insertion operator and removal operator the same score based on the operation's performance. The score criteria are reported in [25].

The entire search is divided into disjoint parts, henceforth called *segments*. A segment assumes a fixed number of iterations, and the number of iterations is denoted as s. The weights of the insertion operator and removal operator are updated after every s iterations, i.e., in every segment, according to their past performance, as follows:

$$w_{i,j+1} = w_{i,j}(1 - \mu) + \mu \frac{\pi_i}{\theta_i}, \tag{28}$$

where $w_{i,j}$ is the weight of operator i used in segment j, π_i denotes the score of operator i obtained during the last segment, and θ_i stands for the number of times operator i is used during the last segment. The reaction factor μ controls how quickly the weight reacts to changes in the performance of the operators.

A roulette wheel selection mechanism is employed to specify which operator will be applied next. This mechanism assumes a probability to select operator j, defined as follows:

$$\frac{w_j}{\sum_{i=1}^{n} w_i},\qquad(29)$$

where w_j is the weight of operator j, and n is the number of operators.

By using an operation, a feasible solution is detected at the end of an iteration. If the current solution is worse than the last solution, it will be accepted with a probability p in order to avoid local optima easier. Simulated annealing idea is used and probability p gradually declines in order to avoid local optima [25], as the following equation shows:

$$p = e^{\frac{-(F(X_{current}) - F(X_{last}))}{T}}\qquad(30)$$

where $T > 0$ is the temperature which starts from an initial temperature and gradually decreases in every iteration using the expression $T = T \cdot c$. c is the cooling rate and $0 < c < 1$.

After a number of iterations, the search tends to converge and finally a (sub)optimal solution is found.

4.1 Insertion Operators

Three insertion operators are used, namely greedy insertion, random insertion, and transshipment insertion.

Greedy Insertion: This insertion finds the best position in all routes for a request. The algorithm of greedy insertion without transshipment has been widely discussed in literature [14]. In algorithm with transshipment, the requests are segmented by transshipment terminals firstly, then every request is divided into two sub-requests for one transshipment terminal. For each sub-request, the algorithm without transshipment is used to find its best position. If both sub-requests satisfy constraints, they will be added to the candidate list and then the best will be chosen. In greedy insertion, the operator without transshipment is tried first. If it doesn't work, the transshipment will be considered.

The advantage of this operator is that it can find the best position for one request. However, it needs a longer time than other insertion operators as it may get stuck in a local optimum when the best position for one request is not the best position for the overall objective.

Random Insertion: To make up for the disadvantage of greedy insertion, the random insertion is designed such that the insertion position is chosen randomly, rather than trying all positions for both with and without transshipment case. Random insertion can expand the search space and avoid local optimum, and therefore needs less time.

Transshipment Insertion: The greedy insertion evaluates the insertion of each request sequentially and may miss good opportunities to use transshipment terminals. Some requests may benefit from the transshipment, as illustrated in [12], hence applying insertion with transshipment may detect the optimal solution quicker. Different from greedy insertion, this operator only uses the algorithm with transshipment.

4.2 Removal Operators

Five removal operators are considered to remove requests from routes and transfer them to the request pool: worst removal, random removal, delete node, clear route, and remove all.

Worst Removal: This operator removes the requests with the highest cost in each route. The cost of the request is calculated as follows:

$$cost_r = F(X) - F(X_{-r}), \tag{31}$$

where X_{-r} is the solution without request r. A request, that is served by more than one barge, will be removed completely from all routes.

Random Removal: Similar to the idea of random insertion, the random removal operator removes requests randomly, offering more unexplored spaces for insertion operators.

Delete Node: In most times, a barge carries multiple requests, therefore removing part of the requests may not change the routes of barges. However, most of the cost-savings are obtained from minimizing distance, i.e., changing routes of barges. To get better solutions quicker, Delete Node operator is designed, which deletes visited terminals in the routes. If one pickup terminal is deleted, the delivery terminal and relevant requests will be deleted too.

Clear Route: Insertion operators may not be able to find feasible solutions based on a small number of removals in a short time. In this case, the route needs to be cleared, which means all requests in a route are removed to the request pool. Another idea behind this operator is to guide the search to the direction of minimizing the number of used barges and making full use of capacity.

Remove All: This operator deletes all requests in routes and fills the request pool. This operator may change the search direction from the beginning and thus provide a larger neighborhood for insertion operators.

The synchronization for relevant barges is considered. Due to the transshipment, other barges may be influenced when one request is inserted to/removed from the route of a barge. These affected barges can cooperate with changes by extending or shortening the waiting time.

4.3 Performance Improvement

The application of an insertion operator typically involves the evaluation of the same move repeatedly, thereby resulting in a high number of duplicate computations during the optimization. Avoiding these repetitive computations can significantly reduce computation time, especially for large instances. Inspired by the idea proposed in [14], a cache structure that uses a hash table is implemented. Specifically, the hash table holds the best insertion positions and infeasible insertion positions for a given request and route. In total, eight hash tables are established. From these, four hash tables are devoted to best insertion while the rest four hash tables are built for failed insertion. There are two hash tables for insertion without transshipment, which include all possible positions and the best position during the search separately. The other two hash tables are for insertion with transshipment. Similarly, the other four hash tables for failed insertion include the same keys but they don't have values because the solution is infeasible.

Moreover, the complexity of transshipment is reduced by limiting the solution space. According to specific requests and barges, the transshipment terminals that are far away from them are not considered.

5   Case Study

In order to evaluate the proposed methodology, we carry out a set of experiments. All experiments are implemented in Python and run on a laptop with 8 GB of memory and an Intel Core i7 CPU with two 1.90 GHz and 2.11 GHz cores. First, we validate the ALNS algorithm with respect to the exact solution of the MILP for relatively small instances as a benchmark comparison. Then we perform numerical experiments on larger instances to show the performance of the ALNS algorithm for realistic size problems. For the experiments, we chose a case in the Rhine-Alpine water corridor that covers a wide area in Europe from Rotterdam/Antwerp to Basel. Improving transport across this corridor can benefit the transport operators in the Rhine river as well as transport stakeholders in the Trans-European Transport Network (TEN-T) [26].

5.1   Data

The Contargo company is one of the largest intermodal transportation providers in the Rhine-Alpine corridor, which is used as our case. In Rhine river, Contargo transports containers among 21 terminals, including deep-sea terminals in Rotterdam and Antwerp ports and inland terminals along the Rhine. According to figures [27] and timetables [28] in Contargo's website, it has nine services, which all have both import and export. The cost data used in the paper are reported in [29]. The speed data is obtained from an online ship monitoring system [30]. Affected by water flow, the upstream speed is lower than downstream speed.

5.2   Benchmark Comparison

Table 3 compares the results of exact approach by Gurobi and the best solution by ALNS in terms of average cost and computation time for small instances (1–8 requests, 2 barges and 1 transshipment terminal). For each instance, 20 independent experiments are conducted to get the average value. When Gurobi finds the optimal solution in the limited time (12 h), ALNS is able to provide the same solution in significantly less computational time. For the instance with 7 requests, Gurobi cannot reach optimality within the time limit and ALNS outperforms within a significantly lower computational time. As of 8 requests, Gurobi cannot provide a feasible solution within the time limit.

Table 3. The comparison between benchmark and ALNS.

Number of requests	Cost (euro)		Avg. running time (s)		Cost gap (%)
	Gurobi	ALNS	Gurobi	ALNS	
1	18048.3	18048.3	2.0	0.05	0
2	30033.1	30033.1	37.3	0.1	0
3	43660.7	43660.7	192.0	0.7	0
4	58431.2	58431.2	269.0	1.0	0
5	58518.4	58518.4	2482.6	2.6	0
6	58757.5	58757.5	10780.3	103.5	0
7	64160.5	59089.4	43200.0[a]	141.7	−7.9
8	–	59250.4	43200.0[a]	334.7	–

[a]Time limit reached (12 h).
–Gurobi can't find a feasible solution within the limited time.

5.3 Experiments with Large Instances

The possibility of transshipment in our model is one of the key complexities towards computational burden. Nevertheless, transshipment plays a vital role in supply chain today, allowing cargo to reach different parts of the world. It offers logistics players a high level of flexibility that can bring significant cost benefits. To obtain the saving cost of transshipment, the following experiments with large instances will compare the results of ALNS with/without transshipment.

Before proceeding with the results, we discuss the parameters of ALNS that affect the performance. Among those we analyzed the size of segments, s, and reaction factor μ based on an instance with 10 requests, 4 barges, and 1 transshipment terminal. These requests use Rhine-Main and Rhine-Upper services of Contargo company. To make sure the tuned parameters perform well under PDPT, these requests are designed to benefit from transshipment. There are 200 iterations in each experiment, and all experiments are repeated 5 times to get the average result. We concluded that the size of the segment needs to be sufficiently large compared to the number of operators in order to be able to update the weights accordingly in the early iterations. Otherwise it might lead to misleading weights. For example, for the case of 10 requests we need at least 8 iterations in a segment. When it comes to the reaction factor, our experiments showed that one should not ignore the history completely, i.e., μ should be smaller than 1. We chose 0.8 for the reactive factor μ. Note that, these parameters need to be carefully analyzed for ensuring the performance of ALNS for different problems.

Based on the above-mentioned tuning of parameters, we run larger instances as the results are shown in Table 4. Three large instances are designed with a naming convention such that "20r4k1T" means 20 requests, 4 barges and 1 transshipment terminal. The first instance contains 20 requests using same services with the small instance used in parameter tuning. Other two large instances include 30 requests, which cover all services of Contargo company. The only difference between these two instances is the loads of requests that are randomly drawn. The cost of the instances with 30 requests is lower than the instance with 20 requests because loads of requests and capacity of barges are different. Generally, the running time with large instances is less than 10 min.

Table 4. Results for large instances.

Instances	# Flexible barges	Transshipment		No transshipment		Cost gap (%)
		Cost	Running time	Cost	Running time	
20r4k1T	0	59438.0	220.6	59438.0	313.3	0
	1	59438.0	246.0	59438.0	175.4	0
	2	55423.8	17.7	59441.5	148.4	7.3
	3	54964.8	233.7	59439.3	229.7	8.1
	4	54986.3	397.2	58954.2	120.1	7.2
30r5k2T-I	0	31620.8	1.4	31620.8	1.6	0
	1	29070.7	219.0	29070.7	105.4	0
	2	26460.6	946.7	26584.1	489.1	0.4
	3	26575.0	233.3	28363.4	309.0	6.7
	4	21355.8	257.6	21355.8	100.5	0
	5	19861.2	658.7	19861.2	314.3	0
30r5k2T-II	0	25502.2	578.0	29284.8	2.2	14.9
	1	23714.4	332.6	23714.4	2.2	4.1
	2	23714.4	243.3	23714.4	231.3	0
	3	23277.5	250.0	23277.5	233.4	0
	4	18424.9	88.4	18424.9	16.0	0
	5	16930.2	7.1	16930.2	7.0	0

In Table 4, "# Flexible Barges" column represents the number of barges without fixed timetables. Except for flexible barges, other barges use real fixed timetable. When the number of flexible barges increases, the cost is reduced due to the flexibility of the proposed PDPT model.

The results show that the savings from transshipment vary a lot from one instance to another. The three factors that are playing an important role in an interdependent way are: (1) the cost of transshipment (based on the load) (2) the number of flexible barges (3) the capacity of the barges with respect to the loads. When the load is higher the transshipment costs are higher and it may not be preferable to use the transshipment option. When the number of flexible barges increases, more benefits from transshipment can be exploited, as shown in results of instances 20r4k1T (number of flexible barges from 0 to 2) and 30r5k1T-I (number of flexible barges from 0 to 3). Meanwhile, when there are enough flexible barges, the attractiveness of transshipment may decrease as the same phenomenon can be represented by the flexibility in routes, as shown in results of instances 30r5k1T-I (number of flexible barges from 3 to 5) and 30r5k1T-II (number of flexible barges from 0 to 5).

From the results, we can conclude that the following cases could benefit from transshipment: a) Requests that on the overlap (or similar) route of barge A and B can be transferred from one barge to another, and the cost-savings result from avoiding an unnecessary barge trip. b) Barge A's transport cost is lower than barge B, then part of requests of barge B can be transferred to barge A to make full use of its capacity.

6   Conclusions and Future Work

Inland waterway transport has been widely recognized as reliable, cost-efficient, and sustainable. To make full use of resources in waterway transport, a MIP model for Pick and Delivery Problem with Transshipment of inland barges is proposed. Because the solution of the studied problem is computationally expensive, an ALNS heuristic is proposed by developing operators specific to this problem. The results show that the ALNS approach reduces computation time significantly, and the best solution of large instances (up to 30 requests) can be obtained within 10 min. Due to the flexibility of PDPT, the cost decreases gradually when the number of barges without fixed timetable increases in the transport network. Additionally, the introduction of transshipment terminals brings reduction on costs (up to 14%), but it differs greatly from one instance to another. Future research will focus on the following aspects:

1. Multiple barge operators may want to cooperate to optimize their transport networks. Moreover, barge operators need to communicate with terminal operators about the arrival time and berth allocation. Therefore collaborative planning among different players will be studied.
2. New requests from a spot market may be released and new barges may be added into the transport network, which will lead to dynamic optimization. If the new request (new barge) is more suitable for a barge (a request), the original plan can be replaced with a penalty.
3. Boundaries of the work can be extended with the expansion of the network to include other modalities and the optimization for barges within the intermodal transport will be studied.
4. The storage in the terminal will be considered in the future, and the storage cost and terminal capacity will be added in the model.

Acknowledgments. This research is financially supported by the China Scholarship Council under Grant 201906950085 and the project "Complexity Methods for Predictive Synchromodality" (project 439.16.120) of the Netherlands Organisation for Scientific Research (NWO). In the meantime, we would like to express our sincere thanks to the reviewers for the constructive and positive comments.

References

1. Caris, A., Limbourg, S., Macharis, C., van Lier, T., Cools, M.: Integration of inland waterway transport in the intermodal supply chain: a taxonomy of research challenges. J. Transp. Geogr. **41**, 126–136 (2014)
2. Port of Rotterdam: Facts and figures about the port. https://www.portofrotterdam.com/en/our-port/facts-figures-about-the-port. Accessed 2 Apr 2020
3. Li, S., Negenborn, R.R., Lodewijks, G.: Planning inland vessel operations in large seaports using a two-phase approach. Comput. Ind. Eng. **106**, 41–57 (2017)
4. Ambra, T., Caris, A., Macharis, C.: Towards freight transport system unification: reviewing and combining the advancements in the physical internet and synchromodal transport research. Int. J. Prod. Res. **57**(6), 1606–1623 (2019)
5. Li, L., Negenborn, R.R., De Schutter, B.: Distributed model predictive control for cooperative synchromodal freight transport. Transp. Res. Part E Logist. Transp. Rev. **105**, 240–260 (2017)
6. Savelsbergh, M.W., Sol, M.: The general pickup and delivery problem. Transp. Sci. **29**(1), 17–29 (1995)
7. Contargo. https://www.contargo.net/. Accessed 2 Apr 2020
8. Rais, A., Alvelos, F., Carvalho, M.S.: New mixed integer-programming model for the pickup-and-delivery problem with transshipment. Eur. J. Oper. Res. **235**(3), 530–539 (2014)
9. Drexl, M.: Applications of the vehicle routing problem with trailers and transshipments. Eur. J. Oper. Res. **227**(2), 275–283 (2013)
10. Drexl, M.: Branch-and-cut algorithms for the vehicle routing problem with trailers and transshipments. Networks **63**(1), 119–133 (2014)
11. Grangier, P., Gendreau, M., Lehuédé, F., Rousseau, L.: A matheuristic based on large neighborhood search for the vehicle routing problem with cross-docking. Comput. Oper. Res. **84**, 116–126 (2017)
12. Masson, R., Lehuédé, F., Péton, O.: An adaptive large neighborhood search for the pickup and delivery problem with transfers. Transp. Sci. **83**(3), 344–355 (2013)
13. Cortés, C.E., Matamala, M., Contardo, C.: The pickup and delivery problem with transfers: Formulation and a branch-and-cut solution method. Eur. J. Oper. Res. **200**(3), 711–724 (2010)
14. Qu, Y., Bard, J.F.: A GRASP with adaptive large neighborhood search for pickup and delivery problems with transshipment. Comput. Oper. Res. **39**(10), 2439–2456 (2012)
15. Parragh, S.N., Cordeau, J.: Branch-and-price and adaptive large neighborhood search for the truck and trailer routing problem with time windows. Comput. Oper. Res. **83**, 28–44 (2017)
16. Maraš, V.: Determining optimal transport routes of inland waterway container ships. Transp. Res. Rec. **2062**(1), 50–58 (2008)
17. Maraš, V., Lazić, J., Davidović, T., Mladenović, N.: Routing of barge container ships by mixed-integer programming heuristics. Appl. Soft Comput. **13**(8), 3515–3528 (2013)
18. Li, S., Negenborn, R.R., Lodewijks, G.: Approach integrating mixed-integer programming and constraint programming for planning rotations of inland vessels in a large seaport. Transp. Res. Rec. **2549**(1), 1–8 (2016)
19. Konings, R.: Network design for intermodal barge transport. Transp. Res. Rec. **1820**(1), 17–25 (2003)

20. Braekers, K., Caris, A., Janssens, G.K.: Optimal shipping routes and vessel size for intermodal barge transport with empty container repositioning. Comput. Ind. **64**(2), 155–164 (2013)
21. Zheng, J., Yang, D.: Hub-and-spoke network design for container shipping along the Yangtze River. J. Transp. Geogr. **55**, 51–57 (2016)
22. Alfandari, L., Davidović, T., Furini, F., Ljubić, I., Maraš, V., Martin, S.: Tighter MIP models for barge container ship routing. Omega **82**, 38–54 (2019)
23. Öncan, T., Altınel, İ.K., Laporte, G.: A comparative analysis of several asymmetric traveling salesman problem formulations. Comput. Oper. Res. **36**(3), 637–654 (2009)
24. Gurobi. https://www.gurobi.com/. Accessed 2 Apr 2020
25. Stefan, R., David, P.: An adaptive large neighborhood search heuristic for the pickup and delivery problem with time windows. Transp. Sci. **40**(4), 455–472 (2006)
26. Trans-European Transport Network (TEN-T). https://ec.europa.eu/transport/infr-astructure/tentec/tentec-portal/site/index_en.htm. Accessed 2 Apr 2020
27. Contargo: Facts and figures. https://www.contargo.net/en/transport/inlandbarge/facts. Accessed 2 Apr 2020
28. Contargo: Timetables. https://www.contargo.net/en/transport/schedules/. Accessed 2 Apr 2020
29. Van Riessen, B., Negenborn, R.R., Lodewijks, G., Dekker, R.: Impact and relevance of transit disturbances on planning in intermodal container networks using disturbance cost analysis. Marit. Econ. Logist. **17**(4), 440–463 (2015). https://doi.org/10.1057/mel.2014.27
30. Marine Traffic. https://www.marinetraffic.com/. Accessed 2 Apr 2020

Ferry Service Network Design for Kiel fjord

Ingvild Eide Aslaksen[1], Elisabeth Svanberg[1], Kjetil Fagerholt[1],
Lennart Christian Johnsen[2]([✉]) [iD], and Frank Meisel[2] [iD]

[1] Department of Industrial Economics and Technology, Norwegian University
of Science and Technology, Trondheim, Norway
kjetil.fagerholt@ntnu.no
[2] Faculty of Business, Economics and Social Science, Christian-Albrechts-University
Kiel, Kiel, Germany
{lennart.johnsen,meisel}@bwl.uni-kiel.de

Abstract. This paper considers a ferry service network design problem
using autonomous ferries for the practical case of the Kiel fjord. Among
others, the city of Kiel, Germany, currently runs a number of initiatives
for developing an autonomous ferry system to open up new mobility
opportunities. The city is divided by the Kiel fjord into an eastern and
a western part and the current infrastructure is mainly built to accommodate car transportation on roads around the fjord. We provide a new
optimization model for the generation of schedules for an autonomous
ferry service, including route design and determination of departure frequencies. The model captures practically relevant aspects of minimum
required departure frequencies between specific port pairs and understandable ferry schedules, whilst maximizing customer service quality
(i.e., excess transit times and departure frequencies). We provide a two-
step optimization approach where candidate combinations of routes and
departure frequencies are heuristically generated a priori and fed into
an integer programming model. Experiments on real world data provide
managerial insights in regard to ferry fleet size, port network design and
ferry schedules.

Keywords: Network design problem · Autonomous ships · Kiel fjord

1 Introduction

Many countries currently develop autonomous ferry systems to open up new
mobility opportunities in coastal areas. A central idea is to replace the existing
conventional ferries (which are often large units to achieve economies of size)
by smaller autonomous units that can be deployed more flexibly. Among others,
the city of Kiel, Germany, currently runs a number of initiatives for developing

L.C. Johnsen—Supported by DFG - Deutsche Forschungsgemeinschaft through project
GZ: ME 3586/2-1.

such an autonomous ferry system. The city is divided by the Kiel fjord into an eastern and a western part. Up to now, two scheduled ferry lines bring people from east to west and vice versa, see Fig. 1. Each line is operated by one to three large ships with a capacity of 200 passengers each. The service frequency at the mooring spots is relatively low (one ship every 15 to 120 min) which is little attractive for customers.

Autonomy means that operations happen automatically, controlled by machines, and not humans [5]. Hence, a fully autonomous ferry could be operating on water without any captain or other crew stationed at the ferry. This facilitates new cost structures, and can enable the use of several smaller ferries, thus providing a more flexible and rapid ferry service offering. The technology, documentation and regulations needed for autonomous transportation are yet to some extent undeveloped [6]. However, the interest for the technology is high, and in 2018, Rolls-Royce and Finferries conducted a demonstration of the world's first fully autonomous ferry with 80 passengers on board. Mikael Makinen, Rolls-Royce President Commercial Marine, claims that "the demonstration proves that the autonomous ship is not just a concept, but something that will transform shipping as we know it" [13].

This paper presents and discusses solution methods regarding the design of routes for an autonomous ferry service, including the selection of departure frequencies, for a practical case at the Kiel fjord. This problem is henceforth

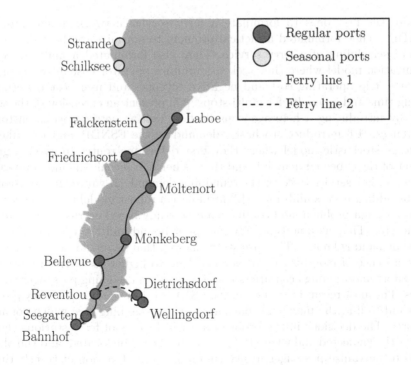

Fig. 1. Current ferry service at the Kiel fjord

referred to as the Ferry Service Network Design Problem (FSNDP). The paper contributes to a larger project at Kiel University, named *CAPTin Kiel*, "Clean Autonomous Public Transport in Kiel". The aim is to provide decision support to the implementation of a ferry service network for passenger transportation in the Kiel fjord using autonomous passenger ferries.

This paper makes the following contributions. We propose a new integer programming (IP) model, which can provide decision support for the FSNDP. The problem is solved in a two-step optimization approach where candidate combinations of routes and departure frequencies are generated a priori and fed as input to the IP model. To solve realistic problem instances, we provide a heuristic procedures to effectively generate candidate combinations of routes and departure frequencies. A computational study is provided using practical test instances based on the Kiel fjord in order to evaluate the optimization approach and to provide managerial implications.

The outline of this paper is as follows. Section 2 presents a review of relevant literature. A formal description of the FSNDP is presented in Sect. 3 including the IP model. Section 4 describes how the combinations of routes and departure frequencies are generated. A computational study is presented in Sect. 5. Lastly, Sect. 6 summarizes the managerial insights and concludes the paper.

2   Related Literature

[9] were the first ones to formulate a ferry service network design problem (FSNDP). They formulated a tactical problem to optimize the fleet size, routing and scheduling of a ferry service. They also formulated a multi-objective optimization model where they seek to minimize operator cost in terms of the fleet size, trip operating cost and negative revenue, and user cost in terms of waiting time and a penalty for multi-stops. [15] present an extension of the work of [9] by introducing a heterogeneous fleet as well as heterogeneous customer preferences. [10] introduce stochastic demand to the FSNDP, and formulate a two-stage stochastic model where they first determine routes to cover a given percent of the expected demand, and then, when the actual demand is revealed, offer an ad-hoc service to cover the remaining demand. [1] wrote an extension on this, by adding user equilibrium. [12] formulate a robust modelling of the service network design problem, and conducts a case study based on cases presented in [9] and [15]. They assume that only an upper bound and the mean of the passenger demand is known. The case study showed that using "loose information" in the absence of more exact values could lead to higher cost, which motivates more effort in obtaining accurate demand data when designing passenger transit routes. The most recent literature on the FSNDP is provided by [3]. They present a method to find the maximum passenger utility spanning tree which connects all ports. The decisions in the problem are which pairs of ferry stations should be directly connected and where the ferry hubs should be located, and the objective is to maximize passenger utility (minimize some function of transit time). They use the entropy maximization (EM) method to create a logit choice model

which in turn generates a random utility interpretation, and can then optimize an expected passenger utility. The problem is a strategic network design, hence disregarding frequencies and ferry capacity. They present two greedy heuristic approaches to solve the problem with up to 36 ports.

Network design problems are in general NP-hard [2]. Heuristics seem to be the general trending solution method. [11] propose three MIP-based heuristics: local branching, variable neighborhood branching, and variable neighborhood decomposition search. They find that variable neighborhood branching outperforms the other two heuristics as well as the commercial Cplex MIP solver. [8] propose a variable neighborhood search heuristic for the ship routing and scheduling problem with split loads. The heuristic provides good solutions and solves real-life instances within reasonable time. In our paper, we aim to find the sweet spot between tactical and strategic planning; taking it a step further than [3] by identifying specific routes and frequencies, but still disregard ferry capacity and not model exact load, thus keeping the model simple enough to be solved exact. The FSNDP is solved in a two-stage optimization procedure in the manner that a set of candidate routes are first generated, and then an optimal subset of these routes are chosen simultaneously with their respective frequencies. Therefore, lastly, we briefly discuss some literature on route generation. [7] present a heuristic which merges the two steps, thus the output being a final set of routes with associated frequencies. They start with an initial set of routes and generate several routes that can replace routes in the initial set if they meet some criteria and yield better solutions. For each pair of origin and destination, they generate two candidate routes; the shortest path (note that not all nodes are directly connected) and the shortest path which is sufficiently different from the first one. This ensures that the nodes with most demand get the most direct routes, whilst keeping the routes in the network sufficiently different, thus ensuring more connectivity in the network and good connections also between nodes with less demand. To the best of our knowledge within ferry service literature, no one has created a route generation algorithm with a rule-based heuristic which aims to reflect the geography of the case study. Moreover, we provide a new simple model formulation that represents the level of customer service through the trade-off between departure frequencies and excess transit time, while ensuring a satisfactory amount of departures between important ports.

3   Modelling of the FSNDP

Based on the categorization of algorithms for solving network design problems introduced by [4], the proposed model is a type of "selection of routes". Feasible routes are generated a priori, and the FSNDP seeks to find the best combination of routes and frequencies to transport the passengers through the network. The FSNDP considers a homogeneous fleet of autonomous ferries, where the size of the fleet is the only attribute of interest. Ferries repeat an assigned route, which is a cyclic sequence of port visits, i.e., they start and end in the same port. These routes are continuously repeated, and the ferries always travel their assigned route. Passenger demand exists between each pair of ports in the network, and the FSNDP aims to offer a service without the use of transfers. Assuming passengers can board only a single ferry, excludes the possibility of a hub structure. To avoid excessively long detours, a maximum transit time is imposed on the definition of *serving* a port pair, and it compares the actual transit time with the shortest possible transit times, i.e. the direct connection.

The FSNDP has a multi-objective approach which represents the trade-off between rapid departure frequencies and short transit times. It seeks to maximize perceived customer service, and in particular *departure frequency*, i.e., how often the ferries depart, and *transit times*, i.e., the time it takes for a passenger to travel in the ferry network. Customer service is represented by some artificial *user utility* for each combination of a route (r) and a frequency (f), which we will denote an *rf*-combination. In addition, each pair of origin and destination ports (OD-pair) is associated with a *minimum required frequency* ensuring certain service levels in the network. These minimum frequencies guarantee that a ferry travels between these ports at least a certain number of times per hour, regardless of which route it is assigned to. Moreover, to secure that the ferry schedule is understandable for the passengers, a maximum allowed number of unique routes included in the ferry schedule is imposed.

The route network is designed holistically, hence without modeling ferry specific passenger flow. The triangle inequality is satisfied for all transit times. This implies that an indirect route always yields higher transit times than a direct between the same pair of ports. Every route has a round-trip time, i.e., the time required for the ferry to traverse the route once. In order to satisfy the chosen departure frequency, a route may incur a waiting time after finishing the route. The model generates a network design for only one hour. However, the results can be used for the entire time horizon by repeating the solution. Therefore, we also assume that the input parameters are deterministic and constant within the considered time horizon. Moreover, we assume constant transit times, i.e the transit times are not influenced by e.g. weather conditions. The mathematical model with its notation summarized in Table 1 is as follows.

Objective

$$\max z = \sum_{r \in \mathcal{R}} \sum_{f \in \mathcal{F}_r} \sum_{i \in \mathcal{P}_r} \sum_{j \in \mathcal{P}_r} A_{rfij} (U_f^F + U_{rfij}^T) D_{ij} \, x_{rf} \qquad (1)$$

Table 1. Summary of notation

Indices:	
r	Route
i, j	Port
f	Departure frequency, per hour
Sets:	
$\mathcal{P}$	Set of ports
$\mathcal{P}_r$	Set of ports in route r
$\mathcal{R}$	Set of routes
$\mathcal{F}_r$	Set of available departure frequencies for route r
Parameters:	
V	Number of ferries available
A_{rfij}	Number of times route r with frequency f serves the port pair (i, j)
F_{ij}	Minimum frequency of departures from port i to j, per hour
D_{ij}	Demand from port i to port j per hour
R^{Max}	Maximum number of unique routes allowed
T_r	Total transit time of completing a round trip of route r
T_{rf}^{Wait}	Waiting time for a ferry on route r with departure frequency f
U_f^F	Utility associated with departure frequency f
U_{rfij}^T	Utility associated with excess transit time for port pair (i,j) in route r with frequency f
Decision variables:	
x_{rf}	1 if route r is served with frequency f, 0 otherwise

Constraints

$$\sum_{r\in\mathcal{R}}\sum_{f\in\mathcal{F}_r} A_{rfij}\, f\, x_{rf} \geq F_{ij}, \qquad (i,j)\in\mathcal{P},\, i\neq j \qquad (2)$$

$$\sum_{f\in\mathcal{F}_r} x_{rf} \leq 1, \qquad r\in\mathcal{R} \qquad (3)$$

$$\sum_{r\in\mathcal{R}}\sum_{f\in\mathcal{F}_r} (T_r + T_{rf}^{Wait})f\, x_{rf} \leq V \qquad (4)$$

$$\sum_{r\in\mathcal{R}}\sum_{f\in\mathcal{F}_r} x_{rf} \leq R^{Max} \qquad (5)$$

$$x_{rf} \in \{0,1\} \qquad r\in\mathcal{R}, f\in\mathcal{F}_r \qquad (6)$$

The objective function (1) selects the combination of routes and frequencies that maximizes user utility in the ferry network. Thus total user utility is modelled as a weighted sum of utility with respect to departure frequency, U_f^F, and to excess transit time, U_{rfij}^T. Let D_{ij} be an expected demand between port i and j and A_{rfij} be a parameter that states the number of times route r with frequency f serves port pair (i, j). The combination of D_{ij} and A_{rfij} is used to weigh U_f^F and U_{rfij}^T such that sought-after (i, j)-connections have more impact in the objective. Constraints (2) ensure every port-pair (i,j) is visited at least as often as the minimum required frequency F_{ij}. Constraints (3) ensure only one departure frequency is chosen per route r. Moreover, Constraint (4) ensures that the total number of required ferries does not exceed the number of ferries available. The transit time T_r of the route r is calculated by summing up the direct transit times and the berth times along the route r. The waiting time is calculated by $T_{rf}^{Wait} = \frac{\lceil f\,T_r \rceil - f\,T_r}{f}$. As an example, consider a transit time of 20 min $(1/3\,\mathrm{h})$ and a frequency of 4, the waiting time is $\frac{\lceil 4 \cdot \frac{1}{3} \rceil - 4 \cdot \frac{1}{3}}{4} = \frac{\frac{2}{3}}{4} = \frac{1}{6} \implies 10\,\mathrm{min}$. Then, with transit and waiting times given in hours and frequency f given in hours^{-1}, the product of times and frequency yields the number of ships to deploy on a route. Constraint (5) limits the number of unique routes in the network. Lastly, Constraints (6) define the feasible area for the decision variables.

4   Generation of Route and Frequency Combinations

In this chapter, we first propose rules for which to generate the routes and, afterwards, we present an algorithm to generate candidate combinations of routes and departure frequencies, denoted *rf*-combinations.

Our route generation procedure deploys a *chain* structure, which implies that each port can be visited at most twice in a route [14]. One way to generate the candidate routes is to combine the ports in all possible sequences for all route lengths, but the generation would experience a combinatorial explosion. We seek to generate as few routes as possible, while ensuring good candidate routes remain included. Therefore, we develop a route generation heuristic which aims to identify candidate routes that are deemed reasonable with respect to passenger transportation. The heuristic evaluates each route independently, and it is constructed such that generated candidate routes satisfy the following rules:

Rule 1 Do not generate identical route cycles.
Rule 2 Include only one directional direct link per port pair in the route.
Rule 3 Routes must contain at least one "large" port.
Rule 4 "Adjoining pairs" must be visited consecutively.
Rule 5 Disallow north/south "zigzagging" in the routes.

The first rule implies that a route with the same ports and visiting sequence, but with a different starting port, will not be included. As an example, consider the three routes $[A, B, C, A]$, $[B, C, A, B]$ and $[C, A, B, C]$. These routes are similar except for that they have different starting ports. The starting port is here defined as the port along the route where all the waiting time is allocated to. So by determining which port to have as starting port, so as to maximize the utility of the route, we can also determine which of these three routes to include as a candidate route. If for example port A is chosen as the starting port, only route $[A, B, C, A]$ will be included.

The second rule restricts the number of direct connections between a port pair in a route, thus disallowing e.g. $[A, B, C, A, B]$ since passengers going between ports A and B may as well enter the ferry on the first direct link.

The third rule aims to eliminate routes with low demand. We denote ports located in busy areas as *large ports*, i.e., ports with high demand, and rule three states that all routes must contain at least one of those large ports.

The fourth rule aims to avoid detours for ports located close to each other, i.e., *adjoining port pairs*. The algorithm rejects a route if it contains both of the ports in the *adjoining port pair* but these are not visited right after each other.

Lastly, the fifth rule disallows "zigzagging" in the north/south direction of the fjord. Since the routes are cyclic and not necessarily start in the most northern or southern ports, we allow them to turn two times, e.g. the route first goes south, then north and then south again. If the route turns more than two times, it is discarded. The rule is based on the ports having an attribute related to level in the north/south direction, similar to latitude. Note that, the concept of zigzagging is allowed in the east/west direction, because the benefits of utilising a ferry instead of alternative land transportation is larger when traveling across the fjord rather than along it.

The candidate combinations of routes and departure frequencies are generated in a two-step procedure: In the first step, candidate routes are generated with feasibility checks according to rules 1 to 5. In the second step, combinations of those candidate routes with departure frequencies are proposed with feasibility checks according to waiting times. Algorithm 1 presents the pseudocode of the candidate route generation procedure. The procedure constructs routes attractively by extending the length of the route by one port per iteration, checking the feasibility of the extended route according to rules 1 to 5, and if it is feasible, the extended route is added to the set of candidate routes. In particular, the first iteration generates routes with two ports. Then, a third port is added to each of these routes, checked for feasibility according to the rules mentioned above, and if the new route is deemed feasible, it is saved as a candidate route. By only extending routes which are in themselves feasible, we avoid enumerating all permutations of the routes, thereby decreasing computational time required to generate the routes. One exception to the feasibility requirement concerns routes with equal last and second last visit, e.g. $[A, B, A, A]$. These have to be temporarily feasible to construct other routes, e.g. $[A, B, A, C, A]$, but they will be discarded after they have been extended, such that they are not considered candidate routes.

We recall that the different combinations of routes and frequencies yield different waiting times, as described in Section 3. Some of these combinations may be undesirable due to excessively long waiting times in the port between scheduled departures. Therefore, we only generate the combinations with waiting

---

Algorithm 1: Candidate routes generation.

Initialize set of construction ports as all ports in the port case;
for *all ports in the port case* **do**
  if *the port is large* **then**
    create initial set of candidate routes by combining this port with each of
    the ports in the set of construction ports, except itself;
    for *routes in the set of candidate routes* **do**
      extend the route with each port in the construction port set;
      if *the extended route is feasible by all rules* **then**
        | save the route in the set of candidate routes;
      else
        | go to next route;
      end
    end
    remove this port from the set of ports to construct routes from;
  end
end

---

times less than a threshold, defined by W^{Max}, thus reducing the number of
variables in the problem.

5   Computational Study

Our test instances are based on a practical case of the Kiel fjord. Kiel is a
northern German city and houses nearly 250,000 people. Kiel is a seaport city,
where the western and eastern part of the city are divided by the fjord. A map
of the Kiel fjord with the ports is shown in Fig. 2b).

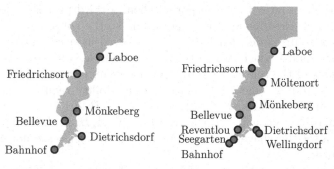

(**a**) Ports included in the *re-*   (**b**) Ports included in the *full*
duced port case.   port case.

Fig. 2. Illustration of the two port cases.

Table 2 lists all ports and their relevant attributes. Each port is defined as either "small" (S), "medium" (M), or "large" (L), and some ports are classified as "well connected" (*Well con.*), which are port pairs with excellent alternative on land connections, e.g., ports in walking distance. Both attributes will be reflected in demand generation. Adjoining ports (*Adj.*) are located directly next to each other. Further, ports have a defined location in the north/south (*N/S*) direction, which is related to their position on the map.

Table 2. Description of ports.

No.	Port name	Size	Well con.	Adj.	N/S
0	Laboe	L	-	-	3
1	Möltenort	M	-	-	5
2	Mönkeberg	M	-	-	6
3	Dietrichsdorf	L	4	4	8
4	Wellingdorf	L	3	3	8
5	Bahnhof	L	6, 7	6	10
6	Seegarten	S	5, 7, 8	5	9
7	Reventlou	L	5, 6, 8	8	8
8	Bellevue	S	6, 7	7	7
9	Friedrichsort	M	-	-	4

5.1 Instances

We present two different port cases, *reduced* and *full*. The *full* port case comprises all the ports used in today's ferry system, yielding a case with ten ports. The *reduced* case aims to create an alternative that covers the whole fjord, but with fewer ports, and thus it comprises six of the ten ports spread evenly across the fjord. The two port scenarios are visualized in Fig. 2a) and 2b). For each of these port cases, we define a set of test instances differing in the minimum required departure frequencies, the fleet size, and the maximum number of unique routes. Table 3 provides a summary of the test instances.

We construct three different settings for the minimum required frequencies per OD-pair. The minimum required frequency per OD-pair depends on the port size attribute. However, we choose to let the frequencies only depend on the size of the destination port. The minimum frequencies in the *moderate* setting are 1, 2, and 3 for *small/medium/large* ports, respectively. For the *relaxed* and *strict* settings we choose 0/1/2, and 2/3/4. For all *well connected* port pairs, the required frequency is set to zero, meaning we do not impose any requirement of visits between ports that are located close to each other. However, note that there may still exist demand between well connected ports, so the solution may

Table 3. Overview test instances.

Instance	Port case	Minimum frequency	Fleet size	Unique routes
Full port case				
Full-Mod-30-6	Full	Moderate	30	6
Full-Mod-20-6	Full	Moderate	20	6
Full-Mod-40-6	Full	Moderate	40	6
Full-Mod-30-3	Full	Moderate	30	3
Full-Mod-30-9	Full	Moderate	30	9
Full-Rel-30-6	Full	Relaxed	30	6
Full-Str-30-6	Full	Strict	30	6
Reduced port case				
Red-Mod-20-6	Reduced	Moderate	20	6
Red-Mod-30-6	Reduced	Moderate	30	6
Red-Mod-10-6	Reduced	Moderate	10	6
Red-Mod-20-3	Reduced	Moderate	20	3
Red-Mod-20-9	Reduced	Moderate	20	9
Red-Rel-20-6	Reduced	Relaxed	20	6
Red-Str-20-6	Reduced	Strict	20	6

offer a departure between the ports. Today, the ferries offer a departure frequency of less than once an hour for all OD-pairs, which relates to the challenges of the current ferry service. Therefore, all of our cases, except small ports in the *relaxed* case, are at least as good as the current offering, which is valuable when aiming to design a better ferry service.

Further, we solve the problem for a various number of available ferries, i.e., different values of V. We consider four settings with 10, 20, 30, and 40 ferries. Lastly, we solve the model for different values of maximum allowed number of unique routes in the solution, i.e., R^{Max}. We define settings with three, six and nine unique routes. For the instances of *reduced* port case, we run five samples of demand, whilst for *full* port instances three samples of demand are considered.

5.2   Parameters

To calculate direct transit times T_{ij}^{Direct} between all port pairs (i, j), *Google Maps* was used to find the distances between ports. The distances were not always a straight line, but the shortest distance that yielded a reasonable path given the restrictions of the fjord. We assume a sailing speed of 17 km/h for all instances, which is derived from the time table of the current ferry service. The transit times are then calculated by dividing the distances by speed. Based on empirical measurements conducted during a field trip, the berth time at each port is set to three minutes.

We assume that a passenger will not accept excess transit times of more than 100% of the direct travel time. This requirement must be fulfilled for a combination of route and frequency to satisfy demand between two ports, as given by the parameter A_{rfij}. The departure frequencies deemed feasible are restricted, because the ferry service aims to provide understandable schedules. For example, a frequency of seven times per hour would yield a route that departs every 8.57 min, which is not very intuitive. However, a frequency of six times per hour, would depart every tenth minute. Thus, the available departure frequencies (*departures/hour*) for the routes are 1, 2, 3, 4, 5, 6, and 8 implying that a ferry visits the ports every 60, 30, 20, 15, 12, 10 and 7.5 min.

Moreover, demand between each OD-pair is randomly drawn from uniform distribution in the interval [50, 100]. The demands are adjusted to account for differences in port size. Each sampled OD-pair demand is multiplied with the product of two factors. The first factor relates to the origin port, and it is set to 0.75, 1.00, and 1.25 for small, medium and large ports, respectively. The second factor depends on the destination port, and is set to 0.5, 1.0, and 1.5 for small, medium, and large ports, respectively. Furthermore, independent of port size, the demand between *well connected* ports is decreased by 90% to account for the low demand between ports located close to each other.

The users' utility, defined by U_f^F and U_{rfij}^T, is calculated as follows. The aim of our approach is to represent the trade-off between decreased transit time and increased departure frequency, weighted by demand on the different connections. The utility functions are based on s-curve shapes where the turning point can be interpreted as users' reference points.

For departure frequency utility U_f^F, we assume a turning point at a value of four. This implies that the marginal utility from higher departure frequencies diminishes after four departures per hour. Furthermore, the s-shape implies that two different routes with frequency of four times per hour, provide more utility than a single route with a frequency of eight times per hour. Thus, it aims to construct a network with more diverse connections between ports. We formalized the frequency utility as

$$
U_f^F = \begin{cases} f \cdot (0.05\,f + 0.8), & \text{if } 0 \le f \le 4 \\ f \cdot (-0.05\,f + 1.2), & \text{if } 4 < f \le 8 \\ 0, & \text{otherwise} \end{cases} \tag{7}
$$

where parameter values of the quadratic equations are defined such that the curves cross at the turning point, while ensuring that the slope of the curve is lower for departure frequency below four than above four.

U_{rfij}^T is the utility of excess transit time from port i to port j in route r with frequency f. It rewards decreases in transit time, i.e. more direct routes. We assume that passengers have a reference point for excess transit time at 40%. This preferences is justified as passengers know they make use of a public offering, implying that they to some extent are willing to accept a detour on their journey. The s-curve shape implies that decreasing user's excess ride time from 50% to 40% produces more utility gains than reducing it from 20% to 10%.

This is formalized in Eqs. (8), (9), and (10). U^T_{rfij} is a mean of U^T_{rfimjn}, where m and n are indices for *port calls* in the route for port i and port j respectively. For example, if port i is visited two times in route r, $m = 2$ indicates the second visit in port i in route r. M_i is the number of port calls, i.e. the number of visits of port i in route r, and N_j is the number of port calls in port j. T_{rfimjn} is the transit time when traveling from port i at visit m to port j at visit n in route r with frequency f. T^{RE}_{rfimjn} is the percentage of excess transit time, and it is computed in Eq. (10).

$$U^T_{rfij} = \frac{\sum_{m=1}^{M_i} \sum_{n=1}^{N_j} U^T_{rfimjn}}{M_i N_j} \tag{8}$$

$$U^T_{rfimjn} = \frac{1}{e^{\cdot T^{RE}_{rfimjn} - 0.4} + 1} \tag{9}$$

$$T^{RE}_{rfimjn} = \frac{T_{rfimjn} - T^{Direct}_{ij}}{T^{Direct}_{ij}} \tag{10}$$

5.3   Computational Results

In this section, we present and analyze the computational results. We use Gurobi Optimizer version 9.0.1 to solve the IP model. The procedure for the generation of route and frequency combinations has been implemented in Python 3.7. We performed all computations on a computer with a 2.7 GHz Intel Core i5 processor and 8 GB RAM which runs the Mac OS X El Capitan (version 10.11.6) operating system.

Table 4 displays the computational results of all test instances. All values reported are averages of the replications with different demand samples. The first column describes the test instances. The next column displays the objective value, z, while the two next show the run time of pre-processing, *Pre-proc*, and the run time for solving of the optimization problem with Gurobi, *cpu*, in minutes, respectively. Columns 5 to 8 present attributes of the solutions. Column 5, *Frequency*, shows the average departure frequency per hour across all port pairs in the network. Column 6, *Excess t.t.*, shows the average excess transit time for the *best* possible connection between the port pairs weighted by the demand between the port pairs. Column 7, *Unique routes*, gives the number of unique routes in the solution and the last column, *Call per port*, displays the average number of visits per port per hour.

Both when running the test instances for the *reduced* and the *full* port case, all instances were solved to optimality. The number of candidate routes for the *reduced* port case is 473, and the number of feasible *rf*-combinations is 2,177. For the *full* port scenario, the number of routes is 257,400 and the number of feasible *rf*-combinations is 1,155,059. We see from the table that the computational times are very small for the *reduced* port case. For the *full* port instances, the total run times are close to three hours. Moreover, within both port cases, the objective

Table 4. Results of all test instances.

Instance	z	Pre-proc, min	cpu, min	Frequency	Excess t.t, min	Unique routes	Calls per port
Full port cases							
Full-Mod-30-6	72,522	150.3	13.1	7.4	7.6	6	17.3
Full-Mod-20-6	47,651	150.3	26.6	4.7	7.6	6	11.6
Full-Mod-40-6	95,835	150.3	24.6	10.1	7.7	6	22.6
Full-Mod-30-3	67,289	150.3	9.5	7.3	7.8	3	16.8
Full-Mod-30-9	74,339	150.3	10.6	7.2	6.5	9	16.8
Full-Rel-30-6	73,422	150.3	14.1	7.6	7.6	6	17
Full-Str-30-6	71,014	150.3	14.9	7.3	7.7	6	16.8
Reduced port cases							
Red-Mod-20-6	31,261	0.09	0.004	7.9	3.6	5	13
Red-Mod-10-6	15,396	0.09	0.006	4	5.9	3	6.8
Red-Mod-30-6	45,346	0.09	0.003	11.9	4.3	6	20
Red-Mod-20-3	30,048	0.09	0.005	7.9	5.3	3	13.2
Red-Mod-20-9	32,122	0.09	0.005	7.3	2.8	8.2	12.5
Red-Rel-20-6	31,261	0.09	0.003	7.9	3.6	5	13
Red-Str-20-6	31,137	0.09	0.006	7.8	3.8	5	13

value seems to be mostly affected by the number of ferries available. This is natural as both short transit times and frequent departures are dependent of the number of ferries.

We next investigate managerial implications. The average departure frequency between every port pair (weighted by demand) seems to be mostly affected by the number of ferries available. With 20 ferries (Full-Mod-20-6) it lies at 4.7 times per hour for the *full* port case. Increasing the number of ferries to 30 increases the departure frequency to about 7.4 and with even 10 more ferries, we get around 11.9. The results for the *reduced* port case resemble these effects. Interestingly, we see that the departure frequency is also strongly affected by the number of ports as we observe that the departure frequency increases from 4.7 to 7.9 when moving from instance Full-Mod-20-6 to Red-Mod-20-6. It seems that in the *full* port cases about 10 ferries more are required to reach about the same departure frequencies as in the *reduced* port cases.

Moreover, the excess transit times in the *full* port case instances are especially good for the case when we allow a large number of unique routes (Full-Mod-30-9). This implies that allowing many different routes in the schedule offers at least one direct connection for more port pairs. Comparing the port cases (Full-Mod-20-6 with Red-Mod-20-6 and Full-Mod-30-6 with Red-Mod-30-6), we see that the average excess transit times are somewhat higher in the *full* port cases. This makes sense as there are more ports that have to be visited in the routes in order to cover the minimum required frequencies. This indicates that there are fewer direct connections in the *full* port cases than in the *reduced* cases. However, from comparing Full-Mod-30-6 with Full-Mod-30-9, we observe that also in the *full* port cases many unique routes seem to have a positive effect.

6 Conclusion

Our computational study provides several managerial insights for increasing the perceived customer service (i.e., excess transit times and departure frequencies) in an autonomous ferry system. First, we observe that with fewer, more relevant and less allied ports, the great demand from these ports will be served more efficiently. While fewer ports means longer distances from passengers' origins and destinations to the ports, this gap can be easily closed by the diverse transportation modes available on land, e.g., *dial and ride-service, bike-sharing, E-scooter*. Second, we observe that the number of ferries has a strong effect on both excess transit times and departure frequencies. For a high customer service with a departure frequency at the ports of on average every 5 min, a fleet with 20 ferries is required at Kiel fjord. Although the initial acquisition costs for autonomous ferries will be high, operating on water without captain or crew stationed at the ferry likely facilitates the use of more ferries in the long term. Moreover, our experiments show that the same level of service quality can be achieved with 10 fewer ferries if the number of ports in the network is reduced to the most relevant. Third, we observe that more complex time tables with more distinct routes decrease excess transit times by allowing more direct connections in the network. This demonstrates the importance of new technologies providing digital travel planners, allowing passengers to find their journey in an app without the need to study timetables.

Future research should develop a stochastic optimization model for finding the most reliable service network for a fleet of autonomous ferries that may be suspect to bad weather conditions. Another venue is to include the demand pattern into the candidate route generations. With this, one may reduce the number of candidate routes while ensuring that promising routes with direct connections between high demand ports are included. Lastly, one may investigate a combined transportation system, where the fixed schedule service is supplemented by a dial-a-ride service, in which ferries operate on-demand. The dial-a-ride ferries could then be used to serve those ports with less dense demand.

References

1. An, K., Lo, H.K.: Ferry service network design with stochastic demand under user equilibrium flows. Transportation Research Part B: Methodological **66**, 70–89 (2014)
2. Baaj, M.H., Mahmassani, H.S.: An AI-based approach for transit route system planning and design. J. Adv. Transp. **25**(2), 187–209 (1991)

3. Bell, M.G., Pan, J.J., Teye, C., Cheung, K.F., Perera, S.: An entropy maximizing approach to the ferry network design problem. Transp. Res. Part B: Methodol. **132**, 15–28 (2020)
4. Brouer, B.D., Karsten, C.V., Pisinger, D.: Optimization in liner shipping. Ann. Oper. Res. **271**(1), 205–236 (2018). https://doi.org/10.1007/s10479-018-3023-8
5. Cross, J., Meadow, G.: Autonomous ships 101. J. Ocean Technol. **12**, 23–27 (2017)
6. Gu, Y., Góez, J., Guajardo, M., Wallace, S.W.: Autonomous vessels: state of the art and potential opportunities in logistics. NHH Department of Business and Management Science Discussion Paper (2019/6) (2019)
7. Kiliç, F., Gök, M.: A public transit network route generation algorithm. IFAC Proc. Vol. **46**(25), 162–166 (2013)
8. Korsvik, J.E., Fagerholt, K., Laporte, G.: A large neighbourhood search heuristic for ship routing and scheduling with split loads. Comput. Oper. Res. **38**(2), 474–483 (2011)
9. Lai, M., Lo, H.K.: Ferry service network design: optimal fleet size, routing, and scheduling. Transp. Res. Part A: Policy Pract. **38**(4), 305–328 (2004)
10. Lo, H.K., An, K., Lin, W.H., uncertainty: Ferry service network design under demand uncertainty. Transp. Res. Part E: Logist. Transp. Rev. **59**, 48–70 (2013)
11. Maraš, V., Lazić, J., Davidović, T., Mladenović, N.: Routing of barge container ships by mixed-integer programming heuristics. Appl. Soft Comput. **13**(8), 3515–3528 (2013)
12. Ng, M., Lo, H.K.: Robust models for transportation service network design. Transp. Res. Part B: Methodol. **94**, 378–386 (2016)
13. Rolls-Royce: Rolls-Royce and Finferries demonstrate world's first fully autonomous ferry (2018). https://www.rolls-royce.com/media/press-releases/2018/03-12-2018-rr-and-finferries-demonstrate-worlds-first-fully-autonomous-ferry.aspx . Accessed 10 July 2020
14. Thun, K., Andersson, H., Christiansen, M.: Analyzing complex service structures in liner shipping network design. Flexible Serv. Manuf. J. **29**(3–4), 535–552 (2017)
15. Wang, D.Z., Lo, H.K.: Multi-fleet ferry service network design with passenger preferences for differential services. Transp. Res. Part B: Methodol. **42**(9), 798–822 (2008)

Smart Containers with Bidding Capacity: A Policy Gradient Algorithm for Semi-cooperative Learning

Wouter van Heeswijk[✉]

Department of Industrial Engineering and Business Information Systems,
University of Twente, P.O. Box 217, 7500 Enschede, AE, The Netherlands
w.j.a.vanheeswijk@utwente.nl

Abstract. Smart modular freight containers – as propagated in the Physical Internet paradigm – are equipped with sensors, data storage capability and intelligence that enable them to route themselves from origin to destination without manual intervention or central governance. In this self-organizing setting, containers may autonomously place bids on transport services in a spot market setting. However, for individual containers it might be difficult to learn good bidding policies due to their short lifespan. By sharing information and costs between one another, smart containers can jointly learn bidding policies, even though simultaneously competing for the same transport capacity. We replicate this behavior by learning stochastic bidding policies in a semi-cooperative multi-agent setting. To this end, we develop a reinforcement learning algorithm based on the policy gradient framework. Numerical experiments show that sharing solely bids and acceptance decisions leads to stable bidding policies. Real-time system information only marginally improves performance; individual job properties suffice to place appropriate bids. Furthermore, we find that carriers may have incentives not to share information with the smart containers. The experiments give rise to several directions for follow-up research, particularly addressing the interaction between smart containers and transport services in self-organizing logistics.

Keywords: Self-organizing logistics · Smart containers · Multi-agent reinforcement learning · Bidding · Policy gradient

1 Introduction

The logistics domain is increasingly moving towards self-organization, meaning that freight transport is planned without direct human intervention. The Physical Internet is often considered as the ultimate form of self-organizing logistics, having smart modular containers equipped with sensors and intelligence interacting with their surroundings and routing themselves [13]. Due to the standardized shapes of the containers, they can be easily combined into full truckloads and

© Springer Nature Switzerland AG 2020
E. Lalla-Ruiz et al. (Eds.): ICCL 2020, LNCS 12433, pp. 52–67, 2020.
https://doi.org/10.1007/978-3-030-59747-4_4

decomposed with equal ease. The self-organizing paradigm also suggests that the system should be able to function without a high degree of central governance, rather converging to an organically functioning system by itself. Moreover, it can be more efficient than traditional logistics systems, being able to dynamically respond to disruptions and opportunities in the logistics system utilizing intelligent decision-making policies. It is this notion of autonomy and self-organization that inspired the present study.

We model smart containers as independent job agents that – on behalf of their shippers – are able to place bids on the transport service that they wish to use. In a dynamic setting, the bid price should depend on the state of the system. Rather than having the fixed contract prices that preside in contemporary transport markets, dynamic bidding mimics financial spot markets that constantly balance demand and supply. For instance, if a warehouse holds relatively few containers waiting for transport, a low bid may suffice to get accepted for the transport service, whereas higher bids might be required during busy times. Additionally, there is also an anticipatory element involved in the bidding decision. Assuming each container has a given due date, the bidding strategy should also take into account the probability of future bids getting accepted.

The optimal bidding strategy may be influenced by many factors. We want to have a policy that provides us with the bid that minimizes expected transport costs given the current state of the system. Such an optimal policy is very difficult to derive analytically, but may be approximated by means of reinforcement learning. However, as each job terminates upon delivery of the smart container, lifespans of individual jobs are very limited. As the quality of a learned bidding policy to a large extent depends upon the number of observations made, it is therefore challenging to learn policies individually. Semi-cooperative learning [2] might alleviate this problem; even though each container aims to minimize its own costs rather than striving towards a common goal, smart containers can share observations to jointly learn better bidding policies that benefit the individual agents. On the other hand, if competing containers are aware of the exact bidding strategies of other containers, they may easily be countered. A fully deterministic policy might therefore not be realistic, we explore whether a stochastic policy yields sensible bidding decisions. Another question that we seek to answer is whether sharing additional information (other than bid prices and acceptance) helps in improving bidding policies. System information (e.g., total container volume in the warehouse) may allow for better bids, but the competing containers also utilize this information for the same purpose.

The contribution of this paper is as follows. First, we explore a setting in which smart containers may place bids on transport capacity; to the best of our knowledge this topic has not been studied before from an operations research perspective. In particular, we aim to provide insights into the drivers that determine the bid price and the effects of information sharing on policy quality. Second, we present a policy gradient reinforcement learning algorithm to learn stochastic bidding policies, aiming to mimic a reality in which competing smart containers may deviate from jointly learned policies. Due to the explorative nature of the paper, we present a simplified problem setting involving a single transport service with fixed capacity that operates on the real line. Our focus is on evaluating bidding dynamics in a world absent regulation and centralized control.

2   Related Work

This literature overview is structured as follows. First, we discuss the role of smart containers in the Physical Internet. Second, we highlight several studies on reinforcement learning in the Delivery Dispatching Problem, which links to our problem, yet from a carrier's perspective. Third, we discuss studies that address the topic of bidding in freight transport.

The inspiration from this paper stems from the Physical Internet paradigm. We refer to the seminal works of Montreuil [7,8] for a conceptual outline of the Physical Internet, thoroughly addressing its foundations. The Physical Internet envisions an open market at which logistics services are offered, with automated interactions between smart containers and other constituents of the Physical Internet determining routes and schedules. Sallez et al. [10] emphasize the active role that smart containers have, being able to communicate, memorize, negotiate, and learn both individually and collectively. Ambra et al. [1] present a recent literature review of work performed in the domain of the Physical Internet. Interestingly, their overview does not mention any paper that defines the smart container itself as a key actor. Instead, existing works seem to focus on traditional actors such as carriers, shippers and logistics service providers, even though smart containers supposedly route themselves in the Physical Internet.

The problem studied in this paper is related to the Delivery Dispatching Problem [6], which entails dispatching decisions from a carrier's perspective. In this problem setting, transport jobs arrive at a hub according to some external stochastic process. The carrier subsequently decides which subset of jobs to accept, also considering future jobs that arrive according to the stochastic process. The most basic instances may be solved with queuing models, but more complicated variants quickly become computationally intractable, such that researchers often resort to reinforcement learning to learn high-quality policies. We highlight some recent works in this domain. Klapp et al. [4] develop an algorithm that solves the dispatching problem for a transport service operating on the real line. Van Heeswijk and La Poutré [12] compare centralized and decentralized transport for networks with fixed line transport services, concluding that decentralized planning yields considerable computational benefits. Van Heeswijk et al. [14] study a variant that includes a routing component, using value function approximation to find policies. Voccia et al. [15] solve a variant that includes both pickups and deliveries. In contrast to our current paper, the aforementioned works use the mileage and utilization of the carrier to optimize dispatch decisions.

Finally, we highlight some works on optimal bidding in freight transport; most of these studies seem to adopt a viewpoint in which competing carriers bid on transport jobs. For instance, Yan et al. [18] propose a particle swarm optimization algorithm used by carriers to place bids on jobs. Miller and Nie [5] present a solution that emphasizes the importance of integrating carrier competition, routing and bidding. Wang *et al.* [16] design a reinforcement learning algorithm based on knowledge gradients to solve for a bidding structure with a broker intermediating between carriers and shippers. The broker aims to propose a price that satisfies both carrier and shipper, taking a percentage of accepted bids as its reward. In a Physical Internet context, Qiao *et al.* [9] model hubs as spot freight markets where carriers can place bids on transport bids. To this end, they propose a dynamic pricing model based on an auction mechanism. Most papers assume that shippers have limited to no influence in the bidding process; we aim to add a fresh perspective with this work.

3   Problem Definition

This section formally defines our problem in the form of a Markov Decision Process model. The model is designed from the perspective of a modular container – denoted as a job j – that aims to minimize its expected shipping costs over a finite discretized time horizon $\mathcal{T}_j$, with each decision epoch $t \in \mathcal{T}_j$ representing a day on which a bid for a capacitated transport service (the carrier) may be placed. In addition to this job-dependent time horizon (time till due date), we define a system horizon $\{0, \ldots, T\}$ with corresponding decision epochs denoted by t'. Thus, we use t when referring to the individual job level and t' for the system level.

The cost function and job selection decision of the transport service will be defined as well, yet the transport service agent has no learning capacity. As past bids and transport movements do not affect current decisions, the Markovian property is satisfied for this problem. Figure 1 illustrates the bidding problem.

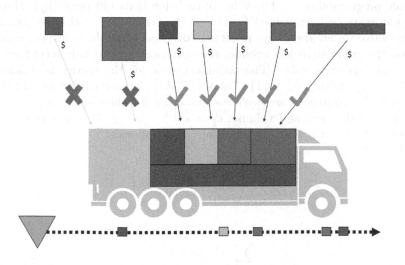

Fig. 1. Visual representation of the bidding problem. Modular smart containers (jobs with various sizes and destinations) simultaneously place bids on a transport service with finite capacity; bids are accepted or rejected based on their marginal contributions.

Modular containers with varying sizes and destinations (located on the real line, which implicitly may represent travel distances in more realistic networks) pose a bid for the transport service; the service selects the combination of jobs that maximizes its profit.

We now define the jobs, with each job representing a modular container that needs to be transported. A job is represented by the following attribute vector:

$$\boldsymbol{j} = \begin{pmatrix} j_\tau = & \text{time till due date} \\ j_d = & \text{distance to destination} \\ j_v = & \text{container volume} \end{pmatrix}$$

The integer attribute $j_\tau \in [0, \tau^{max}]$ indicates how many decision epochs remain until the latest possible shipment date. Containers are presumed to be indifferent to delivery time, as long as the due date is not exceeded. When a new job enters the system, we set $\mathcal{T}_j = \{j_\tau, j_\tau - 1, \ldots, 0\}$; note that this horizon may differ among jobs and decreases over time; the attribute j_τ is decremented with each time step. When $j_\tau = 0$ and the job has not been shipped, it is considered to be a failed job, incurs a penalty, and is removed from the system (implicitly assuming some more expensive backup transport and a fine for lateness). The attribute $j_d \in (0, d^{max}]$ indicates the position of the destination on the real line; the further away the higher the transport costs. The job volume $j_v \in [1, \zeta^{max}]$ – defined as an integer in this paper – indicates how much transport capacity the job requires. Let $\boldsymbol{J}_{t'}$ be the problem state, defined as a set containing the jobs present in the system at time t'. Furthermore, let $\mathcal{J}_{t'}$ be the set of feasible states at time t'.

At each decision epoch t', a transport service with fixed capacity C departs along the real line. For the transport service to decide which jobs to take, the selection procedure is modeled as a 0–1 knapsack problem that is solved using dynamic programming [3]. The value of each job is its bid price (x_j) minus its transport costs (c_j), explained further in the remainder of this section. Jobs with negative values are always rejected. Note that when the transport capacity exceeds the cumulative job volume, the transport service will accept all bids that yield a positive value. The decision vector for the carrier is denoted as $\boldsymbol{\gamma} = [\gamma_j]_{\forall j \in \boldsymbol{J}_{t'}}$, with $\gamma_j \in \{0, 1\}$. The set $\Gamma(\boldsymbol{J}_{t'})$ denotes the set of all feasible selections. The transport service's cost function for shipping a single job $\boldsymbol{j}$ is a function of distance and volume: $c_j = c^{mile} \cdot j_v \cdot j_d$. The transport service maximizes its direct rewards by selecting $\boldsymbol{\gamma}_{t'}$ as follows:

$$\underset{\gamma \in \Gamma(\boldsymbol{J}_{t'})}{\text{argmax}} \left(\sum_{j \in \boldsymbol{J}_{t'}} \gamma_j (x_j - c_j) \right) , \tag{1}$$

s.t.

$$\sum_{j \in \boldsymbol{J}_{t'}} \gamma_j \cdot j_v \leq C .$$

From the perspective of jobs, actions (i.e., bids) are defined on the level of individual containers. All bids $x_j \in \mathcal{X}_j \equiv \mathbb{R}$ are placed in parallel and independent of one another, yielding a vector $\boldsymbol{x} = [x_j]_{\forall j \in J_{t'}}$. Unshipped jobs with $j_\tau > 0$ incur holding costs and unshipped jobs with $j_\tau = 0$ incur a failed job penalty, both are proportional to the job volume. At any given decision epoch, the direct reward function for individual jobs is defined as follows:

$$r_j(\gamma_j, x_j) = \begin{cases} -x_j & \text{if} & \gamma_j = 1 \\ -c^{hold} \cdot j_v & \text{if} & j_\tau > 0 \wedge \gamma_j = 0 \\ -c^{pen} \cdot j_v & \text{if} & j_\tau = 0 \wedge \gamma_j = 0 \end{cases}.$$

To obtain x_j at the current decision epoch (which may be denoted by $x_j \equiv x_{t',j}$ when we need to explicitly include the decision epoch), we try to solve $\text{argmax}_{x_{t',j} \in \mathcal{X}_j} \mathbb{E}\left(\sum_{t''=t'}^{t'+|T_j|} r_j(\gamma_{t'',j}, x_{t'',j})\right)$, i.e., the goal is to maximize the expected reward (minimize expected costs) over the horizon of the job. Note that – as a container cannot observe the bids of other jobs, nor the cost function of the transport service, nor future states – we can only make decisions based on *expected* rewards depending on the stochastic environment. The solution method presented in Sect. 4 further addresses this problem.

Finally, we define the transition function for the system state that occurs in the time step from decision epoch t' to $t' + 1$. During this step two changes occur; we (i) decrease the due dates of jobs that are not shipped or otherwise removed from the system and (ii) add newly arrived jobs to the state. The set of new jobs arriving for $t' + 1$ is defined by $\tilde{\boldsymbol{J}}_{t'+1} \in \tilde{\mathcal{J}}_{t'+1}$. The transition function $S^M : (\boldsymbol{J}_{t'}, \tilde{\boldsymbol{J}}_{t'+1}, \boldsymbol{\gamma}) \mapsto \boldsymbol{J}_{t'+1}$ is defined by the sequential procedure outlined in Algorithm 1.

Algorithm 1. *Transition function* $S^M(\boldsymbol{J}_{t'}, \tilde{\boldsymbol{J}}_{t'+1}, \boldsymbol{\gamma}_{t'})$

0: Input: $\boldsymbol{J}_{t'}, \tilde{\boldsymbol{J}}_{t'+1}, \boldsymbol{\gamma}_{t'}$	▶ Current state, job arrivals, shipping selection
1: $\boldsymbol{J}_{t'+1} \hookleftarrow \emptyset$	▶ Initialize next state
2: $\boldsymbol{J}_{t'}^x \hookleftarrow \boldsymbol{J}_{t'}$	▶ Copy state (post-decision state)
3: $\forall j \in \boldsymbol{J}_{t'}$	▶ Loop over all jobs
4: $\quad \boldsymbol{J}_{t'}^x \hookleftarrow \boldsymbol{J}_{t'}^x \setminus j \mid \gamma_{t',j} = 1$	▶ Remove shipped job
5: $\quad \boldsymbol{J}_{t'}^x \hookleftarrow \boldsymbol{J}_{t'}^x \setminus j \mid j_\tau = 0 \wedge \gamma_{t',j} = 0$	▶ Remove unshipped job with due date 0
6: $\quad j_\tau \hookleftarrow j_\tau - 1 \mid j_\tau > 0$	▶ Decrement time till due date
7: $\boldsymbol{J}_{t'+1} \hookleftarrow \boldsymbol{J}_{t'}^x \cup \tilde{\boldsymbol{J}}_{t'+1}$	▶ Merge existing and new job sets
8: Output: $\boldsymbol{J}_{t'+1}$	▶ New state

---

4 Solution Method

To learn the bidding strategy of the containers, we draw from the widely used policy gradient framework. For a detailed description and theoretical background, we refer to the REINFORCE algorithm by Williams [17]. As noted earlier, the policy gradient algorithm returns a stochastic bidding policy, reflecting the deviations in bid prices adopted by individual containers. As bids can take any real value, we must adopt a policy suitable for continuous action spaces. In this paper we opt for a Gaussian policy, drawing bids from a normal distribution. The mean and standard deviation of this distribution are updated based on observations.

In policy-based reinforcement learning, we perform an action directly on the state and observe the corresponding rewards. Each simulated episode $n \in \{0, 1, \ldots, N\}$ yields a batch of selected actions and related rewards according to the stochastic policy $\pi_\theta^n(x_j \mid j, J_{t'}) = \mathbb{P}^\theta(x_j \mid j, J_{t'})$, where θ is the parametrization of the policy. Under our Gaussian policy, bids are drawn independently from other containers, i.e., $x_j \sim \mathcal{N}(\mu_\theta(j, J_{t'}), \sigma_\theta), \forall j \in J_{t'}$. We deliberately do not truncate the distribution, in order to observe the learning process in unrestricted form. The randomness in action selection allows the policy to keep exploring the action space and to escape from local optima. From the observed actions and rewards during each episode n, we deduce which actions result in above-average rewards and compute gradients ensuring that the policy is updated in that direction, yielding updated policies π_θ^{n+1} until we reach π_θ^N. For consistent policy updates, we only use observations for jobs that are either shipped or removed, for which we need some additional notation. Let $K^n = [K_0^n, \ldots, K_{\tau^{max}}^n]$ be a vector containing the number of bid observations for such completed jobs. For example, if a job had an original due date of 4 and is shipped at $j_\tau = 2$, we would increment K_4^n, K_3^n and K_2^n by 1, using an update function $k(j)$. Finally, we store all completed jobs (i.e., either shipped or failed) in a set $\hat{J}^n$. For each episode, the cumulative rewards per job are defined as follows:

$$\hat{v}_{t,j}^n(\gamma_j, x_j) = \begin{cases} r_j(\gamma_j, x_j) & \text{if} \quad t = 0 \\ r_j(\gamma_j, x_j) + \hat{v}_{t-1,j}^n & \text{if} \quad t > 0 \end{cases}, \forall t \in \mathcal{T}_j .$$

Let $\hat{v}_{t'}^n = [[\hat{v}_{t,j}^n]_{t \in \mathcal{T}_j}]_{\forall j \in J_t}$ be the vector containing all observed cumulative rewards at time t' in episode n. At the end of each episode, we can define the information vector

$$I^n = \left[[J_{t'}^n, x_{t'}^n, \hat{v}_{t'}^n, \gamma_{t'}^n]_{\forall t' \in \{0, \ldots, T\}}, K^n, \hat{J}^n \right] .$$

The information vector contains the states, actions and rewards necessary for the policy updates (i.e., a history similar to the well-known SARSA trajectory). The decision-making policy is updated according to the policy gradient theorem [11], which may be formalized as follows:

$$\nabla_\theta v_{j_\tau, j}^{\pi_\theta} \propto \sum_{t'=1}^{T} \left(\int_{J_{t'} \in \mathcal{J}_{t'}} \mathbb{P}^{\pi_\theta}(J_{t'} \mid J_{t'-1}) \int_{x_j \in \mathcal{X}_j} \nabla_\theta \pi_\theta(x_j \mid j, J_{t'}) v_{j_\tau, j}^{\pi_\theta}(\gamma_j, x_j) \right) .$$

Essentially, the theorem states that the gradient of the objective function is proportional to the value functions $v_{j_\tau, j}^{\pi_\theta}$ multiplied by the policy gradients for all actions in each state, given the probability measure $\mathbb{P}^{\pi_\theta}$ implied by the prevailing decision-making policy π_θ. Perhaps more intuitive: we derive a state distribution and corresponding values given the current policy and use this information to update our policy.

We proceed to formalize the policy gradient theorem for our problem setting. Let θ be a vector of weight parameters that defines the decision-making policy $\pi_\theta : (j, J_{t'}) \mapsto x_j$. Furthermore, let $\phi(j, J_{t'})$ be a feature vector that distills the most salient attributes from the problem state, e.g., the number of jobs waiting to be transported or the average time till due date. The inner product of the feature vector ϕ and weight vector θ yields the average bid price. We will discuss the features used for our study in Sect. 5. For the Gaussian case, we formalize the policy as follows:

$$\pi_\theta = \frac{1}{\sqrt{2\pi}\sigma_\theta} e^{-\frac{\left(x_j - \mu_\theta(j, J_{t'})\right)^2}{2\sigma_\theta^2}} ,$$

with x_j being the bid price, $\mu_\theta(j, J_{t'}) = \phi(j, J_{t'})^\top \theta$ the Gaussian mean and σ_θ the parametrized standard deviation. The action x_j may be obtained from the inverse normal distribution. The corresponding gradients are defined by

$$\nabla_{\mu_\theta}(j, I^n) = \nabla_\theta(j, I^n) = \frac{(x_j - \mu_\theta(j, J_{t'}))\phi(j, J_{t'})}{\sigma_\theta^2} ,$$

$$\nabla_{\sigma_\theta}(j, I^n) = \frac{(x_j - \mu_\theta(j, J_{t'}))^2 - \sigma_\theta^2}{\sigma_\theta^3} .$$

The gradients are used to update the policy parameters into the direction of the (local) optimum. Due to the randomly drawn actions, we observe whether deviating from the current policy is beneficial, e.g., whether the average bid price could be reduced. As the observations may exhibit large variance, we add a non-biased baseline value (i.e., not directly depending on the policy), namely the average observed value during the episode [11]. For the prevailing episode n, we define the baseline as

$$\bar{v}_t^n = \frac{1}{K_t^n} \sum_{j \in J^n} \hat{v}_{t,j}^n, \forall t \in \{0, \ldots, \tau^{max}\} .$$

For the Gaussian policy, the weight update rule for μ_θ – updating θ^{n-1} to θ^n and using learning rate $\alpha_\mu \in (0,1)$ – is:

$$\Delta_{\mu_\theta}(j, I^n) = \Delta_\theta(j, I^n) = \alpha_\mu \frac{1}{K_{j_\tau}^n}(\hat{v}_{j_\tau} - \bar{v}_{j_\tau})\frac{(x_j - \mu_\theta(j, J_{t'}))\phi(j, J_{t'})}{\sigma_\theta^2} . \quad (2)$$

The standard deviation σ_θ is updated – using learning rate $\alpha_\sigma \in (0,1)$ – as follows:

$$\Delta_{\sigma_\theta}(j, I^n) = \alpha_\sigma \frac{1}{K_{j_\tau}^n}(\hat{v}_{j_\tau} - \bar{v}_{j_\tau})\frac{(x_j - \mu_\theta(j, J_{t'}))^2 - \sigma_\theta^2}{\sigma_\theta^3} . \quad (3)$$

Note that the update functions consist of (i) the learning rate, (ii) the difference between observation and baseline and (iii) the gradient. Intuitively, this means that after each episode we update the feature weights – which in turn provide the state-dependent mean bidding price – and the standard deviation of the bids, proportional to the difference between observation and mean. The mean bidding price – taking into account both individual job properties and the state of the system – represents the bid that is expected to minimize overall costs. If effective bids are very close to the mean, the standard deviation will decrease and the bidding policy will converge to an almost deterministic policy. However, if there is an expected benefit in varying bids, the standard deviation may grow larger. The algorithmic outline to update the parametrized policy is outlined in Algorithm 2.

Algorithm 2. *Outline of the policy gradient bidding algorithm (based on [17])*

0: Input: π_θ^0	▶ Differentiable parametrized policy
1: $\alpha_\mu \leftharpoonup (0,1) \cap \mathbb{R}, \alpha_\sigma \leftharpoonup (0,1) \cap \mathbb{R}$	▶ Set step sizes
2: $\sigma^0 \leftharpoonup \mathbb{R}^+$	▶ Initialize standard deviation
3: $\theta \leftharpoonup \mathbb{R}^{|\theta|}$	▶ Initialize policy parameters
4: $\forall n \in \{0, \dots, N\}$	▶ Loop over episodes
5: $\hat{\boldsymbol{J}}^n \leftharpoonup \emptyset$	▶ Initialize completed job set
6: $\boldsymbol{J}_0 \leftharpoonup \mathcal{J}_0$	▶ Generate initial state
7: $\forall t' \in \{0, \dots, T\}$	▶ Loop over finite time horizon
8: $x_j^n \leftharpoonup \pi_\theta^n(j, \boldsymbol{J}_{t'}), \forall j \in \boldsymbol{J}_{t'}$	▶ Bid placement jobs
9: $\gamma^n \leftharpoonup \arg\max_{\gamma^n \in \Gamma(\boldsymbol{J}_{t'})}$	▶ Job selection carrier, Eq. (1)
$\left(\sum_{j \in \boldsymbol{J}_{t'}} \gamma_j^n (x_j - c_j) \right)$	
10: $\hat{v}_{j_\tau, j}^n \leftharpoonup r_j(\gamma_j^n, x_j^n), \forall j \in \boldsymbol{J}_{t'}$	▶ Compute cumulative rewards
11: $\forall j \in \boldsymbol{J}_{t'} \mid j_\tau = 0 \vee \gamma_j^n = 1$	▶ Loop over completed jobs
12: $\hat{\boldsymbol{J}}^n \leftharpoonup \hat{\boldsymbol{J}}^n \cup \{j\}$	▶ Update set of completed jobs
13: $\boldsymbol{K}^n \leftharpoonup k(j)$	▶ Update number of completed jobs
14: $\tilde{\boldsymbol{J}}_{t'} \leftharpoonup \tilde{\mathcal{J}}_{t'}$	▶ Generate job arrivals
15: $\boldsymbol{J}_{t'+1} \leftharpoonup S^M(\boldsymbol{J}_{t'}, \tilde{\boldsymbol{J}}_{t'+1}, \gamma_{t'}^n)$	▶ Transition function, Algorithm 1
16: $\boldsymbol{I}^n \leftharpoonup \left[[\boldsymbol{J}_{t'}^n, \boldsymbol{x}_{t'}^n, \hat{\boldsymbol{v}}_{t'}^n, \gamma_{t'}^n]_{\forall t' \in \{0, \dots, T\}}, \boldsymbol{K}^n, \hat{\boldsymbol{J}}^n \right]$	▶ Store information
17: $\forall t \in \{0, \dots, \tau^{max}\}$	▶ Loop till maximum due date
18: $\forall j \in \hat{\boldsymbol{J}}^n$	▶ Loop over completed jobs
19: $\mu_\theta^{n+1} \leftharpoonup \mu_\theta^n + \Delta_{\mu_\theta}(j, \boldsymbol{I}^n)$	▶ Update Gaussian mean, Eq. (2)
20: $\sigma_\theta^{n+1} \leftharpoonup \sigma_\theta^n + \Delta_{\sigma_\theta}(j, \boldsymbol{I}^n)$	▶ Update standard deviation, Eq. (3)
21: Output: π_θ^N	▶ Return tuned policy

5   Numerical Experiments

This section describes the numerical experiments and the results. Section 5.1 explores the parameter space and tunes the hyperparameters. After determining the policy, Sect. 5.2 addresses its performance and behavior. The algorithm is written in Python 3.7 and available online.[1]

---

[1] https://github.com/woutervanheeswijk/policygradientsmartcontainers.

5.1   Exploration of Parameter Space

The purpose of this section is twofold: we explore the effects of various parameter settings on the performance of the algorithm and select a suitable set of parameters for the remainder of the experiments in Sect. 5.2. We make use of the instance settings summarized in Table 1. Note that the penalty for failed jobs is the main driver in determining bid prices; together with holding costs, it intuitively represents the maximum price the smart container is willing to bid to be transported.

Table 1. Instance settings

Number of job arrivals	[0–10]
Due date	[1–5]
Job transport distance	[10–100]
Job volume	[1–10]
Holding cost (per volume unit)	1
Penalty failed job (per volume unit)	10
Transport costs per mile (per volume unit)	0.1
Transport capacity	80

To parametrize the policy we use several features, denoted by vector ϕ. First, we use a constant term that represents the average bid price. Second, we use the individual job properties of the job placing the bid, i.e., the time till due date, the job's transport distance and the container volume. Third – in case the job shares its own properties with the system – it also uses the generic system features: the total number of jobs, average due date, average distance, and total volume. These system features only include the data of other smart containers that share their information. All weight parameters in θ are initialized at 0, yielding initial bid prices of 0. The initial standard deviation is set at 1, i.e., we set out with a standard normal distribution.

We perform a sequential search to set the simulation parameters. First, we tune α_{μ} (learning rate for mean) and α_{σ} (learning rate for standard deviation). We test learning rates $\{0.0001, 0.001, 0.01, 0.1\}$ for both parameters and find that $\alpha_{\mu} = 0.1$ and $\alpha_{\mu} = 0.01$ are stable (i.e., no exploding gradients) and converge reasonably fast. Taking smaller learning rates yields no eminent advantages in terms of stability or eventual policy quality. Figure 2 shows two examples of parameter convergence under distinct learning rate settings.

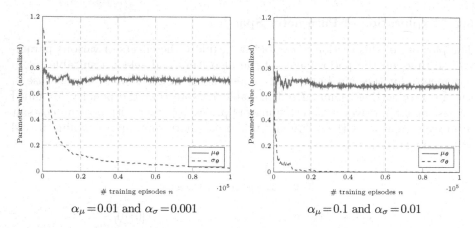

Fig. 2. Convergence of μ_θ and σ_θ (normalized) for various learning rates. Higher learning rates achieve both faster convergence and lower average bid prices.

Next, we tune the initial bias weight θ_0^0 (using values $\{-50, -40, \ldots, 40, 50\}$) and the initial standard deviation σ^0 (using values $\{0.01, 0.1, 1, 10, 25\}$). Anticipating non-zero bids, we test several initializations with nonzero bias weights. Large standard deviations allow for much exploration early on, but may also result in unstable policies or slow convergence. From the experiments, we observe that the bias weight converges to a small or negative weight and that there is no benefit in different initializations. For the standard deviation, we find that $\sigma^0 = 10$ yields the best results; the exploration triggered by setting large initial standard deviations helps avoiding local optima early on. In terms of performance, the average transport costs are 7.3% lower than under the standard normal initialization. Standard deviations ultimately converge to similarly small values regardless the initialization.

Finally, we determine the number of episodes N and the length of each horizon T. Longer horizons lead to larger- and therefore more reliable batches of completed jobs per episode, but naturally require more computational effort. Thus, we compare settings for which the total number of time steps $N \cdot T$ is equivalent. Each alternative simulates 1,000,000 time steps, using $T = \{10, 25, 50, 100, 250, 500, 1000\}$ with corresponding values N. To test convergence, after each 10% of completed training episodes we perform 10 validation episodes – always with $T = 1000$ for fair comparisons – to evaluate policy qualities. We find that having large batches provides notable advantages. Furthermore, in all cases 400,000 time steps appear sufficient to converge to stable policies. To illustrate the findings, Fig. 3a shows the average transport costs measured after each 100,000 time steps (using the then-prevailing policy); Fig. 3b shows the quality of the eventual policies for each time horizon.

The final parameters to be used for the remainder of the numerical experiments are summarized as follows: $N = 4,000$, $T = 100$, $\sigma^0 = 10$, $\alpha_\mu = 0.1$ and $\alpha_\sigma = 0.01$.

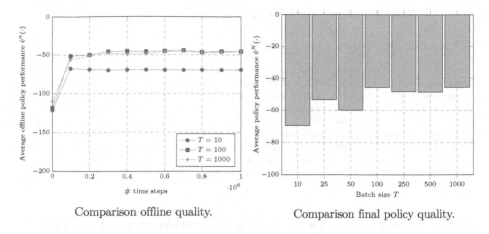

Comparison offline quality.   Comparison final policy quality.

Fig. 3. Policy performance for various time horizons. The horizon $T = 100$ yields the best overall performance; batches too small diminish performance.

5.2   Analysis of Policy Performance

Having determined the parameter settings, we proceed to analyze the performance of the jointly learned policies. This section addresses the effects of information sharing, the relevance of the used features in determining the bid, and the behavior of the bidding policy and its impact on carrier profits. All results in this section correspond to the performance of policies after training is completed. To obtain additional insights we sometimes define alternative instances; for conciseness we do not explicitly define the settings of these alternatives.

We first evaluate the effects of information sharing. According to preset ratios, we randomly determine whether or not a generated container shares its information with the system. Only containers that share information are able to see aggregate system information. Clearly, the more containers participate, the more accurate the system information will be. We test sharing rates ranging from 0% to 100% with increments of 10%; Table 2 shows the results. We observe that performance under full information sharing and no information sharing is almost equivalent, with partial information sharing always performing worse. The latter observation may be explained by the distorted view presented by only measuring part of the system state. In the policy parametrization all features are scaled to the $[0, 1]$ domain, such that the magnitudes of weights are comparable among each other. We see that the generic features have relatively little impact on the overall bid price. This underlines the limited difference observed between full information sharing and no information sharing. Job volume and job distance are by far the most significant drivers of a job's bid prices. This is in line with expectations: as the costs incurred by the carrier depend on these two factors, they require higher compensations for longer distances and larger volumes. Furthermore, holding- and penalty costs are proportional to the job volume. The relationship with the time till due date is negative; if more time remains, it

Table 2. Feature weights for various information sharing rates.

Feature	Rate										
	0%	10%	20%	30%	40%	50%	60%	70%	80%	90%	100%
Constant	−10.10	−10.28	−8.03	−11.83	−10.98	−4.81	−7.17	−10.46	−8.71	−9.46	−12.12
Average due date	–	−2.37	−2.73	−3.28	−2.57	−2.73	−2.69	−2.49	−1.79	−2.02	−1.56
Average distance	–	1.83	3.07	2.59	2.36	3.18	3.58	3.16	3.44	2.26	2.92
Total job volume	–	0.06	0.06	−0.12	0.44	0.03	0.29	0.42	1.18	0.64	0.63
# jobs	–	−0.03	−0.31	−0.69	−0.21	−0.86	−0.77	−1.39	−0.02	−1.25	−1.70
Job due date	−22.45	−23.25	−24.02	−21.16	−21.95	−23.89	−25.96	−22.89	−22.26	−22.82	−21.27
Job distance	49.49	48.37	45.88	49.38	48.81	45.98	45.27	46.85	48.00	49.15	49.54
Job volume	59.20	57.14	56.83	58.46	58.70	55.27	56.13	56.55	56.69	57.97	60.10
Average reward	**−46.87**	**−51.78**	**−55.96**	**−49.12**	**−49.54**	**−57.75**	**−56.75**	**−55.71**	**−53.12**	**−49.43**	**−46.32**

might be prudent to place lower bids without an imminent risk of penalties. On average, each job places 1.36 bids and 99.14% of jobs is ultimately shipped; the capacity of the transport service is rarely restrictive. Figure 4 illustrates bidding behavior with respect to transport distance and time till due date, respectively.

Next, we discuss some behavior of the bidding policy and its effect on carrier profits. As our carrier is a passive agent we omit overly quantitative assessments here. We simulate various toy-sized instances, adopting simplified deterministic settings with a single container type (time till due date is zero, identical volume and distance). If transport capacity is guaranteed to suffice, the learned bid prices converge to almost zero. If two jobs always compete for a single transport service slot and the other incurs a penalty, the bids will be slightly below the penalty costs. Several other experiments with scarce capacity also show bid prices slightly below the expected penalty costs that would otherwise be incurred. For our base scenario, the profit margin for the carrier is 20.2%. This positive margin

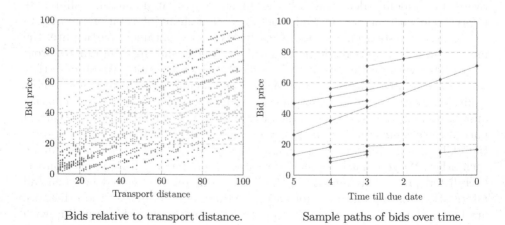

Bids relative to transport distance.   Sample paths of bids over time.

Fig. 4. Visualizations of bidding policies with respect to volume and due date. Bids tend to increase when (a) transport distance is larger and (b) the job is closer to its due date.

indicates that the features do not encapsulate all information required to learn the minimum bidding price. For comparison, we run another scenario in which the carrier's transport costs – which are unknown to the smart containers in our default setting – are the sole feature; in that case all jobs trivially learn the minimum bidding price. This result implies that carrier may have financial incentives not to divulge too much information to the smart containers.

For the carrier, the bidding policies deployed by the smart container greatly influence its profit. Scarcity of transport capacity drives up bid prices, yet also increases the likelihood of missed revenue. To gain more insight into this trade-off, we simulate various levels of transport capacity, from scarce to abundant. These experiments indeed confirm that a (non-trivial) capacity level exists that maximizes profit. In addition, a carrier needs not to accept all jobs whose bid exceed their marginal transport costs, as we presume in this paper. Having a carrier represented by an active agent stretches beyond the scope of this paper, but would certainly yield new insights.

We summarize the main findings, reiterating that the setting of this paper is a highly stylized environment. The key insights are as follows:

- Utilizing global system information only marginally reduces job's transport costs compared to sharing no system information;
- Jointly learned policies converge to stable bidding policies with small standard deviations;
- Jobs with more time remaining till their due date are prone to place lower bids;
- Carriers have an incentive not to disclose true cost information when transport capacity is abundant.

6   Conclusions

Traditional transport markets rely on (long-term) contracts between shippers and carriers in which price agreements are made. In contrast, self-organizing systems (e.g., the Physical Internet) are expected to evolve into some form of spot market where demand and supply are dynamically matched based on the current state of the system. This paper explores the concept of smart containers placing bids on restricted transport capacity. We design a policy gradient algorithm to mimic joint learning of a bidding policy, with autonomous smart modular containers sharing their observations. The job volume, transport distance and time till due date are used to parametrize the bidding policy. Our stochastic (Gaussian) policy reflects deviations made by individual containers, given that deterministic policies are easy to counter in a competitive environment. This stochastic approach appears effective. Standard deviations converge to small values, implying stable bidding policies.

Numerical experiments show that sharing system information only marginally reduces bidding costs; individual job properties are the main driver in setting bids. The limited difference in policy quality with and without sharing system information is a potentially relevant observation. This result implies that smart containers would only need to (anonymously and after the job has been completed) submit their key properties, bid price history and incurred costs. There is no apparent need to share real-time information on a system-wide level, which would greatly ease the system design. Further research on transport networks with intelligent carriers is needed to verify whether this result holds in more realistic settings.

The profitability of the transport service – which is modeled as a passive agent in this paper – strongly depends on the bidding policy of the smart containers. Experiments with varying transport capacities show that in turn, the carrier may also influence bidding policies by optimizing the transport capacity that is offered. Without central governance, unbalances between smart containers and transport services may result in unstable transport networks. Based on the findings presented in this paper, one can imagine that the dynamic interplay between carriers and smart containers is a very interesting one that begs closer attention.

We re-iterate that this study is of an explorative nature; there are many avenues for follow-up research. In terms of algorithmic improvements, actor-critic methods (learning functions for expected downstream values rather than merely observing them) would be a logical continuation. Furthermore, the linear expression to compute the bidding price could be replaced by neural networks that capture potential non-linear structures. In addition, the basic problem presented in this paper lends itself for various extensions. So far the carrier has been assumed to be a passive agent, offering fixed transport capacity and services regardless of (anticipated) income. In reality the carrier will also make intelligent decisions based on the bidding policies of smart containers. A brokerage structure might be helpful to match carriers and containers. Finally, we consider only a single transport service operating on the real line. Using the same algorithmic setup, this setting could be extended to more realistic networks with multiple carriers, routes and destination nodes.

References

1. Ambra, T., Caris, A., Macharis, C.: Towards freight transport system unification: reviewing and combining the advancements in the physical internet and synchromodal transport research. Int. J. Prod. Res. **57**(6), 1606–1623 (2019)
2. Boukhtouta, A., Berger, J., Powell, W.B., George, A.: An adaptive-learning framework for semi-cooperative multi-agent coordination. In: 2011 IEEE Symposium on Adaptive Dynamic Programming and Reinforcement Learning, pp. 324–331. Institute of Electrical and Electronics Engineers Inc, Piscataway, New Jersey (2011)
3. Kellerer, H., Pferschy, U., Pisinger, D.: Multidimensional knapsack problems. In: Floudas, C., Pardalos, P. (eds.) Knapsack problems, pp. 235–283. Springer, Boston (2004). https://doi.org/10.1007/978-0-387-74759-0_412
4. Klapp, M.A., Erera, A.L., Toriello, A.: The one-dimensional dynamic dispatch waves problem. Transp. Sci. **52**(2), 402–415 (2018)
5. Miller, J., Nie, Y.M.: Dynamic trucking equilibrium through a freight exchange. Transp. Res. Part C: Emer. Technol. **113**, 193–212 (2019)

6. Minkoff, A.S.: A Markov decision model and decomposition heuristic for dynamic vehicle dispatching. Oper. Res. **41**(1), 77–90 (1993)
7. Montreuil, B.: Toward a Physical Internet: meeting the global logistics sustainability grand challenge. Logist. Res. 71–87 (2011). https://doi.org/10.1007/s12159-011-0045-x
8. Montreuil, B., Meller, R.D., Ballot, E.: Physical internet foundations. In: Borangiu, T., Thomas, A., Trentesaux, D. (eds.) Service Orientation in Holonic and Multi Agent Manufacturing and Robotics, pp. 151–166. Springer, Heidelberg (2013). https://doi.org/10.1007/978-3-642-35852-4_10
9. Qiao, B., Pan, S., Ballot, E.: Dynamic pricing model for less-than-truckload carriers in the Physical Internet. J. Intell. Manuf. **30**(7), 2631–2643 (2016). https://doi.org/10.1007/s10845-016-1289-8
10. Sallez, Y., Pan, S., Montreuil, B., Berger, T., Ballot, E.: On the activeness of intelligent Physical Internet containers. Comput. Ind. **81**, 96–104 (2016)
11. Sutton, R.S., Barto, A.G.: Reinforcement Learning: An Introduction, 2nd edn. The MIT Press, Cambridge (2018)
12. Van Heeswijk, W.J.A., La Poutré, H.: Scalability and performance of decentralized planning in flexible transport networks. In: 2018 IEEE International Conference on Systems. Man, and Cybernetics, pp. 292–297. Institute of Electrical and Electronics Engineers Inc, Piscataway (2018)
13. van Heeswijk, W., Mes, M., Schutten, M.: Transportation management. In: Zijm, H., Klumpp, M., Regattieri, A., Heragu, S. (eds.) Operations, Logistics and Supply Chain Management. LNL, pp. 469–491. Springer, Cham (2019). https://doi.org/10.1007/978-3-319-92447-2_21
14. Van Heeswijk, W.J.A., Mes, M.R.K., Schutten, J.M.J.: The delivery dispatching problem with time windows for urban consolidation centers. Transp. Sci. **53**(1), 203–221 (2019)
15. Voccia, S.A., Campbell, A.M., Thomas, B.W.: The same-day delivery problem for online purchases. Transp. Sci. **53**(1), 167–184 (2019)
16. Wang, Y., Nascimento, J.M.D., Powell, W.B.: Reinforcement learning for dynamic bidding in truckload markets: an application to large-scale fleet management with advance commitments. arXiv preprint arXiv:1802.08976 (2018)
17. Williams, R.J.: Simple statistical gradient-following algorithms for connectionist reinforcement learning. Mach. Learn. **8**(3–4), 229–256 (1992)
18. Yan, F., Ma, Y., Xu, M., Ge, X.: Transportation service procurement bid construction problem from less than truckload perspective. Math. Probl. Eng. (2018)

Analyzing the Impact of the Northern Sea Route on Tramp Ship Routing with Uncertain Cargo Availability

Mingyu Li$^{(\boxtimes)}$, Kjetil Fagerholt, and Peter Schütz

Norwegian University of Science and Technology, Trondheim, Norway
{mingyu.li,kjetil.fagerholt,peter.schuetz}@ntnu.no

Abstract. The opening of the Northern Sea Route (NSR) provides an alternative in connecting Asia and Europe. We evaluate the impact of the NSR on tramp shipping through a two-stage stochastic programming model featuring tramp ship routing and scheduling with uncertain cargo availability. Decisions regarding deterministic cargoes with known availability are made in the first stage and decisions regarding spot cargoes and detailed routing and scheduling plans are made in the second stage when the available spot cargoes are revealed. We solve the problem by Sample Average Approximation. The case study shows that the introduction of the NSR leads to an increase in gross margin. It allows picking up more cargoes or picking up cargoes with higher revenues. The advantages of the NSR are more obvious when the bunker price increases. The effect of the NSR on tramp ship routing decisions depends on the region. The effect is most significant for transportation between Northern Asia and Northern Europe, while less interesting to Southern Asia. In general, the NSR is more favored than the Suez Canal Route for both transporting cargoes and repositioning vessels.

Keywords: Tramp ship routing and scheduling problem · Northern Sea Route · Uncertain cargo availability

1 Introduction

Tramp shipping is the backbone of maritime transportation. It is the major transportation mode for bulk cargo as well as oil and gas, which accounted for 47.54% and 29.04% of international maritime trade in cargo volume respectively in 2018 [16]. Traditionally, maritime transportation between Asia and Europe is realized through the Suez Canal Route (SCR). The opening of the Northern Sea Route (NSR) provides an alternative to the SCR. On one hand, using the NSR may reduce the sailing time by 43.75%, and thus the fuel costs [11]. On the other hand, additional costs should be considered to operate along the NSR, for example ice-breaking support fees, which complicates the evaluation of the impact of introducing the NSR into maritime transportation. The attractiveness of the NSR has received extensive research attention, and we refer the interested readers to [8,9] and [15] for the most up-to-date and complete review. The majority of the literature focus on establishing cost-effectiveness comparisons between NSR and other traditional routes, the SCR in most cases. The evaluation for NSR in tramp shipping is commonly based on the cost of a single voyage, for instance [11]. In terms of evaluation based on regular services, the existing literature focus on liner shipping. To the best of our knowledge, an evaluation of the NSR's impact on tramp shipping has not been conducted. The potential benefits of using NSR in tramp shipping are twofold. First, shorter distances may lead to shorter sailing times and consequently lower fuel costs. In addition, the saved time may allow vessels to transport more cargoes which would not be feasible when using the traditional route. The latter has not been included in the evaluation of the impact of the NSR.

The operation mode of tramp shipping is comparable to a taxicab [2]. Similar to a taxi serving passengers, a vessel may either sail transporting cargoes, or in ballast to reposition for next cargoes. The operator decides on which cargoes to accept, which vessels to transport the cargoes, the order of transporting the cargoes and the pickup time for each cargo, with an objective to maximize the profit per time unit [3].

The tramp operators also resemble taxi drivers in that they do not know all the transportation demands in advance. However, they may know some demands in advance and can enter into long term agreements referred to as Contracts of Affreightment (CoAs). A CoA usually specifies shipping rates, cargo quantities, pickup and delivery ports as well as associated time windows [2,17]. On the tactical level, the tramp operator decides which cargoes to sign a CoA for and commits to the corresponding schedule. These chosen contract cargoes must be transported. Given the contract cargoes, the operational level problem is to fill in the time slots that have not been committed to contract cargoes with available spot cargoes. This variant of the Tramp Ship Routing and Scheduling Problems (TSRSPs) includes deciding the contract cargoes, assigning the cargo to a vessel with a pickup time, then deciding spot cargoes and the detailed routes and schedules for the fleet, aiming to maximize the expected gross margin.

The TSRSP is categorized as a tactical planning problem in maritime transportation [2]. The planning horizon ranges from one to two months (e.g. [18]) and up to a year (e.g. [19]). There has been an increasing research interest in TSRSPs, see [10] and [1] for more general reviews on TSRSPs. Still, little attention has been paid to uncertain spot cargo availability. In [19], the authors consider the total number of spot cargoes is known, which may appear any time of the year. They solve the problem dynamically by first deciding routes and schedules based on the CoAs and revealed spot cargoes. Then based on updated spot cargo information, they allow giving up contract cargoes to pick up spot cargoes for more revenues and they compare the impact on the decisions under different penalties for giving up contract cargoes. They also design a Genetic Algorithm-based heuristic to solve the problem. None of the research has explicitly treated uncertain cargo availability in TSRSP. In addition, the direct route between two ports is always fixed in the literature. However, the flexibility in routing decisions such as using the NSR as an alternative to the SCR has not been addressed in research for TSRSPs.

To address the main objective of this paper, we formulate our research question as whether the routing decisions in tramp shipping change provided with the NSR as an alternative and if they change, to what degree. We analyze this problem based on the results from a two-stage stochastic programming model we propose for the TSRSP with uncertain cargo availability. In reality, available spot cargoes are gradually revealed and decisions are made sequentially. Hence, a multi-stage model would describe the real-world decision making process better. However, multi-stage stochastic programming models quickly become computationally intractable. We therefore approximate the real-world problem using a two-stage approach: In the first stage, tactical decisions on choosing contract cargoes to accept and the schedules for vessels to pick them up are made. In the second stage, the available spot cargoes are known and operational decisions, including the selection of spot cargoes as well as detailed routing and scheduling of the vessels, are made. The model will select the contract cargoes such that the expected gross margin from transporting contract cargoes and uncertain spot cargoes is maximized.

We contribute to the literature in that (1) we present a new variant of TSRSP with uncertain cargo availability, which we formulate into a two-stage stochastic programming model, (2) we introduce routing flexibility into TSRSP and (3) we evaluate the impact of routing flexibility of introducing NSR on tramp ship routing.

The reminder of this paper is organized as follows. Section 2 presents the problem. In Sect. 3 we first introduce our modeling approach then present the model formulation. Input data and the generation of scenario tree are described in Sect. 4. Results of a case study are discussed in Sect. 5 and Sect. 6 concludes the paper.

2   Problem Description

We present a TSRSP with uncertain cargo availability and routing flexibility. A tramp operator plans which cargoes to enter into contract together with routes and schedules for the fleet in two stages. At the first stage, with only knowing the information of deterministic cargoes which will be available and spot cargoes which may become available, the operator decides which deterministic cargoes to accept, the corresponding vessel to use for transporting the cargo and the cargo's pickup time. At the second stage, the uncertain spot cargoes are revealed. Given the first stage decisions, the operator then decides which spot cargoes to accept and the detailed routes and schedules for the fleet.

The company operates a heterogeneous fleet to transport cargoes between ports in Asia and Europe. A cargo is specified by pickup port, delivery port and revenue. The cargo has to be picked up within a given time window and delivered as early as possible. Depending on the locations of pickup and delivery ports, cargoes are divided into local cargoes, with both pickup and delivery ports in Asia or Europe, and inter-continental cargoes. Inter-continental cargoes can be transported either via the SCR or the NSR, introducing routing flexibility.

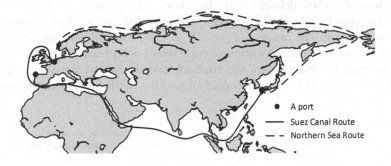

Fig. 1. Illustration of routes

The heterogeneous fleet varies in vessel performance, e.g. fuel consumption rate and speed. The vessel performances also vary on different routes. Figure 1 illustrates the routes. At the beginning of planning horizon, the vessels are located at different ports. A vessel has to deliver a cargo before picking up the next. Then we refer to the voyages loaded with cargo as *delivery voyages*, and voyages in ballast between transporting two consecutive cargoes as *repositioning voyages*. Similarly, routing flexibility also applies to inter-continental repositioning voyages.

We consider the voyage costs for delivery and repositioning voyages, which we refer to as delivery costs and repositioning costs respectively, and idle costs which incur when a vessel is neither delivering or repositioning. The voyage costs consist of fuel costs and port dues. For inter-continental voyages, the voyage costs also include canal fee for the SCR and ice-breaking support fees for the NSR. Note that to pick up a cargo, vessels are allowed to arrive early and wait til the pickup time window opens, but they are considered to be idle while waiting.

The operator decides in the first stage on which deterministic cargoes to accept as well as vessels and pickup times for the chosen deterministic cargoes. In the second stage, when the uncertain cargoes are revealed, the operator must decide which of those to choose, the sequence of transporting cargoes and the corresponding pickup times as well as routes for inter-continental voyages. The objective is then to maximize the expected gross margin from transporting cargoes.

3   Model Formulation

We formulate the problem as a two-stage stochastic programming model. Before presenting the mathematical formulation, we first introduce our approach to model voyages and routing flexibility, followed by the notation used in the model and preprocessing procedures.

3.1   Modeling Approach

As in our problem vessels either sail in ballast or loaded with one cargo, a voyage can be denoted by the sequence of cargoes, see Fig. 2. The vessel first picks up cargo i from P_i, then delivers it to D_i. After repositioning to P_j to pick up cargo j, the vessel visits D_j for delivery. Transporting cargo i and j sequentially implies a voyage in the order of $P_i \rightarrow D_i \rightarrow P_j \rightarrow D_j$. With this cargo-based voyage notation, the initial location of each vessel is represented by the delivery port of an artificial origin cargo, and similarly the location at the end of planning horizon is represented by a pickup port of another artificial destination cargo.

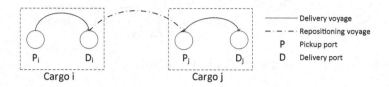

Fig. 2. Illustration of a voyage

We model the routing flexibility for delivery voyages through cargo duplication. For a given scenario s, we have a total of N cargoes, N^I inter-continental and N^L local cargoes. For an inter-continental cargo i, we use cargo i to refer to the cargo transported via SCR, and we duplicate it into a corresponding cargo $i + N$ to represent transporting the cargo via NSR. These two cargoes share the same pickup time window and revenue but differ in sailing times and costs. In addition to the duplicated NSR cargoes, we also add the artificial origin and destination cargoes for the fleet into the cargo set to form an extended cargo set $\mathcal{G}_s^E$.

3.2   Notation

Let us introduce the following notation:

Sets

$\mathcal{G}_s^E$	Extended set of cargoes, including the duplicated inter-continental cargoes, the artificial origin and destination cargoes in scenario s
$\mathcal{G}^D$	Set of deterministic cargoes
$\mathcal{G}_s^I$	Set of inter-continental cargoes in scenario s
$\mathcal{G}_s^L$	Set of local cargoes in scenario s
$\mathcal{G}^U$	Set of uncertain spot cargoes
$\mathcal{R}$	Set of routes
$\mathcal{S}$	Set of scenarios
$\mathcal{V}$	Set of vessels

Indices

i, j	Cargo index
r	Route index
s	Scenario index
v	Vessel index

Parameters

A_{is}	Earliest pickup time for cargo i in scenario s
B_{is}	Latest pickup time for cargo i in scenario s
C_v^F	Daily idle cost for vessel v
C_{vijrs}^R	Repositioning cost for vessel v between transporting cargo i and j via route r in scenario s
C_{vis}	Delivery cost for transporting cargo i with vessel v in scenario s
D_{is}	The availability of spot cargo i in scenario s, either 1 or 0
E_v	An artificial destination cargo for vessel v
H	Length of planning horizon
N	Number of cargoes
O_v	An artificial origin cargo for vessel v
P_s	Probability of scenario s
R_{is}	Revenue of transporting cargo i in scenario s
T_{vijrs}^R	Sailing time for a reposition voyage for vessel v between transporting cargo i and j via route r in scenario s
T_{vis}	Sailing time for transporting cargo i with vessel v in scenario s

Decision Variables

n_{vi}	1 if vessel v is assigned to transport deterministic cargo i, 0 otherwise
t_{vi}	The planned pickup time of a deterministic cargo i by vessel v
τ_{vis}	The planned pickup time of a cargo i by vessel v in scenario s
x_{vijrs}	1 if vessel v delivers cargo i, repositions via route r then directly picks up cargo j in scenario s, 0 otherwise

3.3   Preprocessing Procedures

We implement two preprocessing procedures in variable generation to reduce the problem size and solution time.

Time Window Limits. Here we eliminate the variables that connect incompatible pickup time windows. In a given scenario s, the earliest arrival time at the pickup port of cargo j for vessel v from the delivery port of cargo i can be estimated by adding the sailing time T_{vis} and the minimum repositioning time T_{vijrs}^R to the earliest pickup time for i. If the result is later than the latest pickup time for cargo j, the voyage is infeasible and thus eliminated beforehand.

Dominance Criteria. We apply a dominance criteria with regard to index r when creating variable x_{vijrs}. We fix the rest indices and compare the sailing times and repositioning costs for using r_1 and r_2. If both the sailing time and costs of r_1 are less than these of r_2, route r_2 is dominated by r_1 and we only create the variable with r_1, and vice visa. Otherwise, variables with both routes are created.

3.4 Model

With the notation introduced above we present the formulation of the two-stage stochastic TSRSP with uncertain cargo availability and routing flexibility.

$$\max \sum_{s \in \mathcal{S}} P_s \left\{ \sum_{v \in \mathcal{V}} \sum_{i \in \mathcal{G}_s^E} \sum_{j \in \mathcal{G}_s^E} \sum_{r \in \mathcal{R}} (R_{is} - C_{vis} - C_{vijrs}^R) x_{vijrs} \right.$$

$$\left. - \sum_{v \in \mathcal{V}} C_v^F (H - \sum_{i \in \mathcal{G}_s^E} \sum_{j \in \mathcal{G}_s^E} \sum_{r \in \mathcal{R}} (T_{vis} + T_{vijrs}^R) x_{vijrs}) \right\} \quad (1)$$

subject to

$$\sum_{v \in \mathcal{V}} n_{vi} \leq 1 \qquad\qquad i \in \mathcal{G}^D, \quad (2)$$

$$\sum_{j \in \mathcal{G}_s^E} \sum_{r \in \mathcal{R}} (x_{vijrs} + x_{v,i+N,jrs}) = n_{vi} \quad v \in \mathcal{V}, i \in \mathcal{G}^D \cap \mathcal{G}_s^I, s \in \mathcal{S}, \quad (3)$$

$$\sum_{j \in \mathcal{G}_s^E} \sum_{r \in \mathcal{R}} x_{vijrs} = n_{vi} \qquad v \in \mathcal{V}, i \in \mathcal{G}^D \cap \mathcal{G}_s^L, s \in \mathcal{S}, \quad (4)$$

$$\sum_{v \in \mathcal{V}} \sum_{j \in \mathcal{G}_s^E} \sum_{r \in \mathcal{R}} (x_{vijrs} + x_{v,i+N,jrs}) \leq D_{is} \qquad i \in \mathcal{G}^U \cap \mathcal{G}_s^I, s \in \mathcal{S}, \quad (5)$$

$$\sum_{v \in \mathcal{V}} \sum_{j \in \mathcal{G}_s^E} \sum_{r \in \mathcal{R}} x_{vijrs} \leq D_{is} \qquad i \in \mathcal{G}^U \cap \mathcal{G}_s^L, s \in \mathcal{S}, \quad (6)$$

$$\sum_{j \in \mathcal{G}_s^E} \sum_{r \in \mathcal{R}} x_{v,O_v,jrs} = 1 \qquad\qquad v \in \mathcal{V}, s \in \mathcal{S}, \quad (7)$$

$$\sum_{i \in \mathcal{G}_s^E} \sum_{r \in \mathcal{R}} x_{vi,E_v,rs} = 1 \qquad\qquad v \in \mathcal{V}, s \in \mathcal{S}, \quad (8)$$

$$\sum_{i \in \mathcal{G}_s^E} \sum_{r \in \mathcal{R}} x_{vijrs} - \sum_{i \in \mathcal{G}_s^E} \sum_{r \in \mathcal{R}} x_{vjirs} = 0$$

$$v \in \mathcal{V}, j \in \mathcal{G}_s^E \setminus \{O_v, E_v | v \in \mathcal{V}\}, s \in \mathcal{S}, \quad (9)$$

$$A_{is} \leq \tau_{vis} \leq B_{is} \qquad\qquad v \in \mathcal{V}, i \in \mathcal{G}_s^E, s \in \mathcal{S}, \quad (10)$$

$$\tau_{vis} + \sum_{r \in \mathcal{R}} (T_{vis} + T_{vijrs}^R) x_{vijrs} \leq$$

$$\tau_{vjs} + B_{is}(1 - \sum_{r \in \mathcal{R}} x_{vijrs}) \qquad v \in \mathcal{V}, i, j \in \mathcal{G}_s^E, s \in \mathcal{S}, \qquad (11)$$

$$\tau_{v,i+N,s} = t_{vi} \qquad v \in \mathcal{V}, i \in \mathcal{G}^D \cap \mathcal{G}_s^I, s \in \mathcal{S}, \qquad (12)$$

$$\tau_{vis} = t_{vi} \qquad v \in \mathcal{V}, i \in \mathcal{G}^D, s \in \mathcal{S}, \qquad (13)$$

$$\tau, t \geq 0 \qquad (14)$$

$$x, n \in \{0, 1\} \qquad (15)$$

The objective (1) is to maximize the expected value of gross margin. The first term is the revenues minus the delivery costs and repositioning costs for all cargoes. The second term calculates the idle cost, which is the product of the daily idle cost and the time when a vessel is neither transporting a cargo nor repositioning.

Constraints (2) ensure that at most one vessel is assigned to transport deterministic cargo i. Constraints (3) to (6) are the cargo selection constraints. The left-hand-side of (3) to (6) are the flows from the local or SCR cargo plus the flows from the corresponding duplicated NSR cargo if inter-continent in a scenario for deterministic cargoes and spot cargoes respectively. The right-hand-side (RHS) of Constraints (3) and (4) denote whether a deterministic cargo is chosen in the first stage. Constraints (3) and (4) stipulate that if a deterministic cargo is selected in the first stage, then in all the scenarios it has to be transported, either via the SCR or NSR. The RHS of Constraints (5) and (6) describe if a spot cargo i becomes available in scenarios s. Constraints (5) and (6) ensure whether to accept a spot cargo is optional. Constraints (7) to (9) are the flow conservation constraints. With Constraints (7), all vessels have to leave the original location. Similarly, Constraints (8) ensure all vessels end in the destinations. Constraints (9) require if a cargo is picked up then it has to be delivered. Constraints (10) force the planned pickup time for cargo i to be within the pickup time window. Constraints (11) make sure the difference between two consecutive cargoes i and j transported by the same vessel v is long enough for the vessel to transport cargo i and to reposition the vessel. Constraints (12) and (13) are the non-anticipativity constraints for the planned pickup times for deterministic cargoes. They together make sure, the pickup time for a deterministic cargo, regardless of transported via the NSR or SCR in the second stage, has to be equal to the time planned in the first stage. Constraints (14) and (15) are the nonnegativity constraints for the continuous variables and the binary requirements for the binary variables, respectively. Note that indices have been omitted.

4   Data and Scenario Generation

In this section we first introduce the input data for the case study with a 90-day planning horizon, then describe the scenario generation procedure.

4.1   Input Data

Port Information. Eight ports among the busiest ports in Asia and Europe are chosen for the case study, including Yokohama, Busan, Singapore, Vladivostok, Hong Kong, Rotterdam, Antwerp and Bilbao. In terms of the distances for local voyages and SCR voyages we refer directly to [12]. Note that the distances through NSR are calculated as follows. We use the distance between Port of Nome and Murmansk as the length of NSR. Then we add the distances from ports to Nome or Murmansk to the NSR length to acquire distances of NSR voyages. The distances are listed in Table 1.

Table 1. Distances between ports. Distances of local and SCR voyages are at the higher triangle while distances for NSR voyages are in bold at the lower triangle.

Distances (nm)	Yokohama	Busan	Singapore	Vladivostok	Hong Kong	Rotterdam	Antwerp	Bilbao
Yokohama	0	657	2892	937	1584	11,180	11,185	10,680
Busan	-	0	2503	509	1140	10,791	10,796	10,291
Singapore	-	-	0	3007	1460	8288	8293	7788
Vladivostok	-	-	-	0	1639	11,295	11,300	10,795
Hong Kong	-	-	-	-	0	9748	9753	9248
Rotterdam	**6885**	**7232**	**9697**	**6763**	**8334**	0	149	771
Antwep	**6980**	**7327**	**9792**	**6858**	**8429**	-	0	776
Bilbao	**7557**	**7904**	**10,369**	**7435**	**9006**	-	-	0

Vessel Information. The fleet consists of two types of vessels differing in fuel consumption rate, sailing speed and ice-class, three vessels for each type. We adopt the fuel consumption rate in [20] with 75 t/day for vessels with lower ice-class and 78.76 t/day for the other type. We refer to the design speed of 14.5 knots in [7] as the speed for vessels with lower ice-class for local and SCR voyages, and we estimate the average speed through the NSR to be 11 knots. Based on [4], we estimate the average speed of higher ice-class vessels during SCR and local voyages to be 14 knots and 13 knots for NSR voyages.

Costs and Revenues. We consider the fuel costs, port dues and transit fees for each voyage. The bunker price is set to be 175.5 USD/mt, average of Europe, the Middle East and Africa (EMEA) and Asia-Pacific bunker prices as of April 2020. The port dues are estimated to be 23,200 USD per voyage according to [20]. The transit fees for SCR are calculated based on [13]. For NSR, the transit fees are estimated through [14], which include the ice-breaking support costs for both vessel types.

We consider the fuel costs of being idle at a 50% fuel consumption rate.

According to [6], the tramp companies earn profit margin ranging from 4.1% to 14.2%. We estimate the cargo profit rate to be ranging between 4% and 15% based on the costs to transport a cargo with a lower ice-class vessel via local or SCR voyages.

4.2   Scenario Generation

The scenario tree contains cargo information with 20 scenarios. For a given problem, all scenarios share the same 30 deterministic cargoes, and at most 70 scenario-dependent spot cargoes will be available in each scenario. We describe the scenario generation in the following three steps:

Step 1: Cargo Pool Generation. We first generate 1000 cargoes as cargo pool for the scenario tree. The generation of cargoes involves generating the pickup and delivery ports, pickup time windows. Then cargo properties such as the delivery costs and revenues are calculated based on the input data presented above. We set the ratio of inter-continental cargoes to be 70%, and the remaining 300 cargoes are equally distributed as European and Asian local cargoes. As for the pickup time window, the earliest pickup time for each cargo is randomly generated in the whole planning horizon with equal probability. The length of the pickup windows are set to be three and seven days for local and inter-continental cargoes, respectively.

Step 2: Generating Deterministic Cargoes. The probability of a cargo being chosen as a deterministic one is assigned based on the earliest pickup time. Cargoes with earlier pickup time have higher probabilities to be chosen as deterministic cargoes, in an attempt to reflect that typically more information is available for the near future. We use a sample procedure to decide the deterministic cargoes. We first sample a cargo, then sample whether the cargo is deterministic or not. We stop once we have 30 deterministic cargoes.

Step 3: Generating Spot Cargoes and Uncertain Availability. The 70 spot cargoes are chosen with equal probability from the remaining 970 cargoes for each scenario and the probability for a cargo to be available is generated randomly with a probability of 50%.

5   Case Study

We solve the problem using Sample Average Approximation [5]. We generate 20 independent samples of 20 scenarios and use a reference sample of 1000 scenarios to find a best solution.

We create three cases, each of which consists of an instance where both the SCR and NSR are available (SCR + NSR) and a reference instance where only the SCR is allowed (SCR only). In the basic case, we include 700 inter-continental cargoes and 150 local cargoes for Europe and Asia each in the cargo pool, with the bunker price at 175.5 USD/mt from April 2020. We then raise the bunker price to 460.75 USD/mt to establish a higher bunker price case. Note that the higher fuel price case uses the exact same scenario tree with the basic case, meaning the deterministic cargoes, the spot cargoes and the realization of cargo availability are identical, with only difference in fuel price. In the last case we change the cargo distribution in the basic cargo pool to 300 inter-continental cargoes, 350 European cargoes and 350 Asian Cargoes. The results and discussions are presented below. Note that all the numbers are the average results over 1000 scenarios.

Basic Case. The costs and revenues of the best solutions from the basic case are summarized in Table 2.

Table 2. Costs and revenues in million USD in the best solutions from the basic case

	Cargo Revenues	Delivery costs	Repositioning costs	Idle costs	Objective function value
SCR only	11.29	7.16	0.49	1.02	2.62
SCR + NSR	13.66	7.32	0.91	0.83	4.61

We observe that, compared with only using the SCR, using both the SCR and NSR leads to a better gross margin. The revenues from transporting cargoes increase and the idle costs are reduced. We further examine the number of voyages in Table 3.

Table 3. Average number of voyages in the best solutions from the basic case

	Delivery voyages				Repositioning voyages				
	SCR	NSR	European	Asian	SCR	NSR	European	Asian	None
SCR only	10.92	0	3.87	2.43	0.12	0	3.31	3.19	10.60
SCR + NSR	4.87	8.43	3.20	2.66	0.10	0.58	4.04	4.85	9.59

For delivery voyages, compared to using SCR only, using both SCR and NSR allows picking up about 1.9 cargoes in addition, which contributes to the great increase in gross margin. For inter-continental cargoes, about 63.4% are transported via the NSR.

In terms of repositioning voyages, the largest share goes without repositioning, which means that after delivering a cargo, the vessel picks up a new cargo at the same port. The number of local repositioning voyages is greater than the number of inter-continental repositioning voyages. It is reasonable that inter-continental repositioning is unfavorable. An inter-continental voyage may take at least 20 days, which is quite long in a planning horizon of 90 days. During 20 days, several local delivery voyages can be made with revenues, while no revenues are gained during the long inter-continental repositioning voyage. But when inter-continental repositioning is needed, the NSR is much favored than the SCR, used about 5 times more often. With NSR preferred for both delivery and repositioning voyages, we find the total number of NSR voyages outweighs SCR.

Higher Bunker Price Case. In this case we raise the bunker price to see how this changes the usage of two routing options. The costs and revenues of the best solutions are listed in Table 4.

Table 4. Costs and revenues in million USD in the best solutions from the higher bunker price case

	Cargo Revenues	Delivery costs	Repositioning costs	Idle costs	Objective function value
SCR only	19.73	15.16	0.96	2.70	0.91
SCR + NSR	24.05	15.01	1.96	2.49	4.59

While the gross margin in the SCR+NSR instance is hardly affected, that of the SCR only case shrinks drastically. However, we observe the similar pattern that the SCR + NSR instance gives more revenues and has lower idle costs. We present the voyage information in Table 5 to see how the routing choices change.

Table 5. Average number of voyages in the best solutions from the higher bunker price case

	Delivery voyages				Repositioning voyages				
	SCR	NSR	European	Asian	SCR	NSR	European	Asian	None
SCR only	10.91	0	3.89	2.39	0.11	0	3.29	3.13	10.66
SCR + NSR	1.86	11.46	3.20	2.74	0.09	0.60	4.27	5.98	8.31

The total number of delivery voyages in this case is very close to the basic case. The most notable change here is that the percentage of NSR delivery voyages in inter-continental cargoes increases from 63.4% to as much as 86.1%. As for the repositioning voyages, there is a slight decrease in none repositioning and an increase in Asian repositioning, but none repositioning still outweighs the local repositioning, while the inter-continental repositioning remains the least favored. Despite the dominating position of NSR voyages in delivery voyages, it is worth mentioning that the NSR and SCR repositioning voyages are almost not affected at all.

To understand how the inter-continental delivery voyages change, we examine the voyages from NSR + SCR instances in both the basic and higher bunker price cases in detail. We divide the ports into groups by region. Yokohama, Busan and

Vladivostok are in Northern Asia (NA), while Singapore and Hong Kong are in Southern Asia (SA). Rotterdam and Antwerp are relatively north in Europe (NE) and we consider Bilbao to be in Southern Europe (SE). Delivery voyages by region are presented in Fig. 3 and 4, note that voyages in both directions are included.

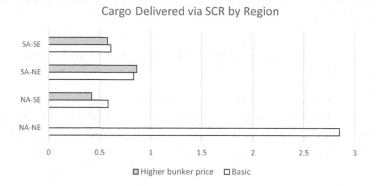

Fig. 3. Cargoes delivered via SCR by region

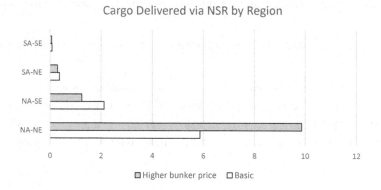

Fig. 4. Cargoes delivered via NSR by region

The impact of using NSR depends on the region and it is most significant between Northern Europe and Northern Asia. With a higher bunker price, in general almost all inter-continental deliveries reduce slightly but there is a major increase in usage of the NSR between NA and NE. In fact, these voyages use exclusively the NSR while the SCR is never used. Tracing back to the input data also supports that, using the NSR between these regions brings the most savings in both sailing times and delivery costs. In contrast, the NSR is always less interesting to SA ports. Note that NSR is used less often in both cases when Hong Kong and Singapore are involved.

Different Cargo Distribution Case. In previous cases, we observe that most inter-continental voyages are with cargoes. However, inter-continental cargoes are abundant in the previous scenario tree. We reduce the ratio of inter-continental cargoes in this case to see if there will be an increase in inter-continental repositioning. The costs and revenues are listed in Table 6 and the average numbers of voyages are summarized in Table 7.

Table 6. Costs and revenues in million USD in the best solutions from the different cargo distribution case

	Cargo Revenues	Delivery costs	Repositioning costs	Idle costs	Objective function value
SCR only	10.03	6.41	0.98	1.13	1.51
SCR + NSR	11.34	6.21	1.00	1.21	2.92

Table 7. Average number of voyages in the best solutions from the different cargo distribution case

	Delivery voyages				Repositioning voyages				
	SCR	NSR	European	Asian	SCR	NSR	European	Asian	None
SCR only	8.16	0	12.73	7.73	0.64	0	3.41	5.80	18.77
SCR + NSR	3.56	5.82	13.30	8.13	0.21	0.54	3.49	6.30	20.27

Compared to the basic case, the gross margin decreases due to lack of inter-continental cargoes. In this case, the average number of cargoes transported with only SCR is 30.8 and when allowing the NSR the number is 28.6 but the number of inter-continental cargoes delivered when allowing the NSR is actually one more. Consequently, the total gross margin when allowing the NSR is higher. So using NSR may allow picking up cargoes with higher profits. When it comes to the repositioning voyages, it is still true that the model tries to align delivery port of last cargo with pickup port of next cargo and inter-continental repositioning is the least popular.

6   Conclusion

We present a new variant of TSRSP with uncertain cargo availability and routing flexibility. In our problem, not all available cargoes are known in the first stage and for inter-continental voyages, two routes can be chosen from. We formulate the problem into a two-stage stochastic programming model and employ the model to evaluate the impact of introducing the NSR on tramp ship routing decisions.

The case study shows that using the NSR will allow picking up more cargoes or picking up cargoes with higher profits. The NSR is used more often than the SCR for both delivery and repositioning voyages. We also show that with higher bunker price, the advantages of NSR are more obvious. The advantages of the NSR are most significant in connecting the Northern Europe and Northern Asia, while it is less interesting to Southern Asia.

References

1. Christiansen, M., Fagerholt, K.: Ship routing and scheduling in industrial and tramp shipping. In: Toth, P., Vigo, D. (eds.) Vehicle Routing: Problems, Methods, and Applications, 2nd edn., pp. 381–408. SIAM–Society for Industrial and Applied Mathematics, Philadelphia (2014). https://doi.org/10.1137/1.9781611973594
2. Christiansen, M., Fagerholt, K., Nygreen, B., Ronen, D.: Maritime transportation. Handbooks Oper. Res. Manag. Sci. **14**, 189–284 (2007)
3. Fagerholt, K., Lindstad, H.: Turborouter: an interactive optimisation-based decision support system for ship routing and scheduling. Maritime Econ. Logist. **9**(3), 214–233 (2007)
4. Furuichi, M., Otsuka, N.: Proposing a common platform of shipping cost analysis of the northern sea route and the Suez canal route. Maritime Econ. Logist. **17**(1), 9–31 (2015)
5. Kleywegt, A.J., Shapiro, A., Homem-de Mello, T.: The sample average approximation method for stochastic discrete optimization. SIAM J. Optim. **12**(2), 479–502 (2002)
6. Macrotrends. https://www.macrotrends.net/. Accessed 13 Feb 2019
7. Propulsion trends in bulk carriers. https://marine.man-es.com/docs/libraries provider6/test/propulsion-trends-in-bulk-carriers.pdf?sfvrsn=7ff3dda2_8. Accessed 22 Apr 2020
8. Meng, Q., Zhang, Y., Xu, M.: Viability of transarctic shipping routes: a literature review from the navigational and commercial perspectives. Marit. Policy Manag. **44**(1), 16–41 (2017)
9. Milaković, A.S., et al.: Current status and future operational models for transit shipping along the northern sea route. Marine Policy **94**, 53–60 (2018)
10. Pache, H., Kastner, M., Jahn, C.: Current state and trends in tramp ship routing and scheduling. In: Digital Transformation in Maritime and City Logistics: Smart Solutions for Logistics. Proceedings of the Hamburg International Conference of Logistics (HICL), Vol. 28. pp. 369–394. epubli GmbH, Berlin (2019)
11. Schøyen, H., Bråthen, S.: The northern sea route versus the Suez canal: cases from bulk shipping. J. Transp. Geogr. **19**(4), 977–983 (2011)
12. Sea distances. https://sea-distances.org/. Accessed 2 Apr 2019
13. Tolls calculator. https://www.suezcanal.gov.eg/English/Tolls/Pages/TollsCal culator.aspx. Accessed 2 Apr 2019
14. Icebreaker assistance value calculating. http://www.nsra.ru/en/ledokolnaya_ i_ledovaya_lotsmanskaya_provodka/raschet_stoimosti_ledokolnoy_provodki_v_ akvatorii_smp.html. Accessed 2 Apr 2019
15. Theocharis, D., Pettit, S., Rodrigues, V.S., Haider, J.: Arctic shipping: a systematic literature review of comparative studies. J. Transp. Geogr. **69**, 112–128 (2018)
16. United Nations Conference on Trade and Development: Review of Maritime Transport 2019. UN Publications (2019)

17. Vilhelmsen, C., Larsen, J., Lusby, R.M.: Tramp ship routing and scheduling-models, methods and opportunities. DTU Management Engineering (2015)
18. Vilhelmsen, C., Lusby, R., Larsen, J.: Tramp ship routing and scheduling with integrated bunker optimization. EURO J. Transp. Logist. 3(2), 143–175 (2014). https://doi.org/10.1007/s13676-013-0039-8
19. Yu, B., Wang, K., Wang, C., Yao, B.: Ship scheduling problems in tramp shipping considering static and spot cargoes. Int. J. Shipp. Transp. Logist. 9(4), 391–416 (2017)
20. Zhu, S., Fu, X., Ng, A.K., Luo, M., Ge, Y.E.: The environmental costs and economic implications of container shipping on the northern sea route. Marit. Policy Manag. 45(4), 456–477 (2018)

Stowage Planning with Optimal Ballast Water

Beizhen Jia[1](✉), Kjetil Fagerholt[2], Line Blander Reinhardt[3],
and Niels Gorm Malý Rytter[4]

[1] Aalborg University, A. C. Meyers Vænge 15, 2450 Copenhagen, SV, Denmark
bj@m-tech.aau.dk
[2] Norwegian University of Science and Technology, Trondheim, Norway
[3] Roskilde University, Universitetsvej 1, 4000 Roskilde, Denmark
[4] University of Southern Denmark, Campusvej 55, 5230 Odense, Denmark

Abstract. Stowage planning is at the essence of a maritime supply chain, especially for short sea Ro-Ro ships. This paper studies stowage optimisation of Ro-Ro ships with a focus on stability constraints and the applicability of models. The paper contributes to short sea Ro-Ro ship stowage in two ways. First, we propose an integrated approach of designing stowage models with the consideration of loading computers. Second, we present a mathematical formulation of the Ro-Ro Ship Stowage Problem with Ballast Water with a discretisation method, to generate an optimal stowage plan which meets stability requirements by means of the weight of cargoes instead of excess ballast water, i.e. excess fuel consumption. Computational tests based on empirical data indicate significant savings and potential of model application in the real world. Preliminary results show 57.69% ballast water reduction, equivalent to 6.7% fuel savings and CO_2 reduction. Additional tests on instances with various cargo weight distribution and discretisation levels are conducted, and finally, improvements are suggested for further research considerations.

Keywords: Stowage optimisation · Ballast water · Maritime transportation · Environmental impact

1 Introduction

Roll-on/Roll-off (Ro-Ro) short sea shipping (SSS) has become one of the most important means in Europe for transportation of passengers and cargoes. Ro-Ro ships carry vehicles and passengers travelling with own journey plans as well as cargo units being trailers, cars, heavy machinery, containers, or anything that goes onto a rolling equipment. Trailers and rolling cargoes are transported either accompanied or unaccompanied by a (truck) driver. Compared to other means of intra-European transport, like for example, container shipping, rail or pure road

Supported by ECOPRODIGI.

The original version of this chapter was revised: Figure 1 was corrected. The correction to this chapter is available at https://doi.org/10.1007/978-3-030-59747-4_50

transport, Ro-Ro SSS has the advantage of being well integrated into the entire cargo supply chains from door to door. Short sea container shipping requires several modal shifts (road, rail, ship etc.), has longer transit times and low flexibility due to less frequent departures, and implies more document handling in comparison with Ro-Ro SSS.

The European Ro-Ro SSS market is growing [3], but also becoming increasingly competitive with currently approximately 100 short sea operators in Europe [1]. Several Ro-Ro companies have recently expanded their fleet capacity via ordering new mega Ro-Ro ships. One example is DFDS which recently ordered 6 × 6700 lane metre Ro-Ro ships to be delivered to their routes in 2019–2020 [19]. The increase in Ro-Ro tonnage, combined with recent Brexit and Corona virus developments, is likely to impact ship utilisation and rate levels going forward. Also the industry must comply with environmental regulations and International Maritime Organization (IMO)'s 2030 and 2050 targets for greenhouse gas emissions [6]. New ship designs, propulsion technologies and fuel alternatives are in progress to meet long term requirements, but in parallel cost control and energy efficient ship operations will be a strategic priority for existing Ro-Ro operators. A key element will be reduction in fuel consumption and costs on the sea leg via adjusting speed, trim, reduced deadweight etc. To achieve this, it is critical for ships to be stowed optimally before departing from port, which implies maximising cargo load, reducing ballast water intake and thereby deadweight without compromising stability, strength or safety requirements. Ship stowage is a key part of Ro-Ro SSS operations, and it includes a whole set of maritime related sub-processes from when a cargo unit gates into the terminal until when it gets picked up at the destination terminal. It is critical that the entire process is understood well to be able to plan and execute optimal stowage for Ro-Ro ships. In addition to what was mentioned above, high quality stowage planning also ensures efficient load and discharge processes at the terminal, and shortening of the port stay which again enables the ship to slow down and save fuel on the sea leg.

Through interviews with selected terminal managers, stowage planners, ship officers and other relevant stakeholders from one of the largest Ro-Ro shipping companies in Europe, the end-to-end cargo stowage process is defined as a process of a series of cargo-related activities including booking, gate-in, yard positioning at loading port, stowage planning, loading, discharging, yard positioning at destination port and gate-out.

As illustrated in Fig. 1, stowage planning acts as the core activity in the process. It takes booking information and cargo arrival status as input to the planning. The booking information offers a list of cargo booked for the departure with detailed cargo information, such as cargo type, transportation unit type, dimensions and weight, well in advance. In addition, cargo arrival status confirms the presence of booked cargo in the terminal on the day, due to the fact that no-show is a common phenomenon in shipping industry. Therefore, before making a stowage plan, the planner needs to know how much of the booked cargo have actually shown up, so that he does not plan stowage for cargo that will never show up and makes timely decision to pull forward optional cargo if the ship's capacity is not fulfilled, thus maximising the space utilisation onboard.

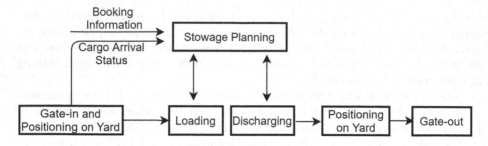

Fig. 1. The Ro-Ro shipping End2end stowage process.

Once the load list is updated, a stowage plan is made with consideration of ship stability and cargo characteristics. The stowage plan includes a plan for positions of all cargo to be loaded onboard the ship to ensure a good handling of cargo with regards to special requirements for dangerous goods, refrigerated goods, and goods with lashing needs. The loading operation is conducted according to the stowage plan, and it gets updated if there is any changes happening during the loading operation. Based on the updated stowage plan, the discharge operation is performed at the destination port, and customers can pick up cargo units according to the pick-up time and position in the yard. Finally, customers gate out with their cargo and usually continue road transportation to the next destination.

From above, it becomes visible that stowage planning interacts with all activities happening in the end-to-end cargo stowage process. Hence, it is essential to make a good stowage plan, as it impacts ship utilisation, fuel consumption, safety at sea and the ability to execute load and discharge operations efficiently. Moreover, it can also be used to derive accurate information of when cargo is available for pick-up by customers at the destination port [9].

2   Literature Review

Stowage planning of Ro-Ro ships has not attracted the same attention from researchers in operations research and optimisation as has container ships. Øvstebø et al. [13] were the first to introduce the Ro-Ro ship stowage problem (RSSP). For a set of mandatory and optional cargoes and a given route with multiple port calls, reflecting the situation of deep sea car carriers, the problem was to determine which additional cargoes to carry and how to stow all carried cargoes on board the ship in order to maximise the profit of the journey. Cargo consisted of a number of homogeneous vehicles. Decks were divided into several lanes which also explained why only rolling moment and vertical forces were constrained in the model for stability considerations. The paper proposed a mixed integer programming (MIP) approach as well as a heuristic algorithm to solve the RSSP. According to the authors, realistic size instances with 5–10 mandatory cargoes could be solved to optimality by MIP, while the heuristic worked better without stability constraints.

Hansen et al. [5] focused on the operational decisions related to the stowage of Ro-Ro ships visiting multiple ports. The paper restricted the stowage problem to a single deck and considered it as a special version of a 2-dimensional packing problem with some additional considerations. In addition, it also considered the shifting of cargoes to make an entry/exit path if needed during loading and unloading operations. Several versions of new MIP formulation for the problem were presented with the consideration of reducing the need of shifting. The goal was to stow all mandatory cargoes and as many optional cargoes as possible while trying to avoid shifting. Since it was focused on a single deck, stability constrains were therefore not included in the model. Furthermore, the model used a grid representation of the deck instead of dividing it into several lanes, which the authors thought may restrict finding of good solutions. The paper concluded that the model works well with small-size instances and suggested further research of a faster algorithm for realistic-size problem instances and eventually for not only one single deck but the whole ship.

Following their previous work [5], Hansen et al. [4] presented the stowage plan evaluation problem to determine which vehicles to shift at each port call, in order to minimise the extra time spent on shifting. For a given set of alternative stowage plans, the goal was to find the best plan of all with the minimal shifting time. A shortest path based heuristic was proposed for solving the problem and it showed that solution method was powerful for its fast computing time and high success rate in determining a better plan.

The above mentioned papers were focused on deep sea Ro-Ro ships, such as car carriers that operate globally with multiple port calls on the sailing route. The problems were usually considered with two types of cargoes, mandatory and optional. The objective was therefore focused on revenue related decisions, such as how many optional cargoes could be stowed, less shifting cost, and etc. Stability constraints were simplified and limited for the ease of modelling, and not included at all in the case [5] where only one deck is considered. Such handling of stability constraints might be due to the fact the RSSP with deep sea car carriers is more robust to changes in terms of cargo weight. There is limited variation for car weights. Thus it becomes more relevant for deep sea car carriers to focus on shifting costs along multiple ports on the route in their stowage planning. Nonetheless, when planning stowage for short sea Ro-Ro ships, stability is of utmost importance due to high variance of cargo weights. The difference of cargo weights can have a significant effect on ship's stability in many aspects.

Based on the state-of-art research on Ro-Ro stowage optimisation problem, Puisa [14] proposed three practical improvements, namely ship stability, fire safety and cargo handling efficiency. The author proposed a new grid method to discretise the stowage location onboard for accurate ship stability and strength calculation. Fire safety was ensured by adding additional constraints to high risk cargoes, average headroom and cargo spacing. With the argument that it was not a realistic solution to penalise cargo shifting with a cost as proposed by previous researches, elimination of such was proposed in the paper for a swift loading and unloading operation with multiple port calls. The study included different cargo types with the same weight within a type which might not be the case of containers and trailers for example. The test instance size was small with most cargoes being optional. So it is difficult to say the running performance when solving realistic sized problems. The study extended stability calculations with stricter and more constraints. However, without the inclusion of ballast tanks in the calculation, limits for stability constraints should be adjusted to the cases without ballast tanks.

Integration of various operations to improve terminal efficiency has been studied by some researchers in containers shipping, such as ship loading problems where stowage planning is taken into consideration as an input to the model [7,8,10], and stowage planning integrated with the quay crane scheduling [2].

Rethink of the stowage problem. No matter how fast the algorithm works or how much revenue the objective function can achieve, stability is always the prerequisite of a stowage plan. Without it, a ship can not sail. Therefore, it is mandatory to calculate stability for every ship departure to ensure its seaworthiness, which is enforced by IMO. Every ship has a loading computer onboard which connects to sensors that collect all information needed to calculate stability of the ship. Once all cargoes are loaded, ship officers will try to adjust the amount of ballast water in each tank to reach the desirable stability. This usually ends up with ships carrying around with excess ballast water, in other words, excess fuel consumption.

Therefore, the contribution of this paper is twofold - first, to introduce the integrated approach of stowage planning with considerations of loading computers, which has not been studied so far to the authors' knowledge, and second, to include ballast water optimisation in RSSP with the purpose of generating a stowage plan that reduces fuel consumption and at the same time provides a better stability condition that is closer to the loading computer requirements.

3   Integrated Stowage Planning

Stowage planing for Ro-Ro ships is typically done through a stowage module in combination with onboard loading computer software. A stowage module can be as advanced as stowage optimisation models or as simple as Excel sheets. Loading computers provide deck officers the ability to validate whether a given stowage plan complies with maritime authorities' stress and stability requirements. A ship is required to be seaworthy at any given moment in order for her to sail. At each ship departure, during and after finishing loading, the hull strength and stability of the ship are calculated and if necessary modified by adjusting the amount of water in ballast tanks to meet stability requirements. Currently in the market for Ro-Ro ships, there are several loading computer systems available, such as Kockumation's Loadmaster, NAPA's Loading Computer, Navis's MACS3 and Autoship's Autoload.

The common and traditional approach of designing stowage plans, as illustrated in Fig. 2, starts with a stowage module generating an initial stowage plan, optimises if possible and then sends it to the loading computer onboard to check the stability of the plan. If it passes the loading computer's stability requirement,

the plan can be executed in the loading process. Otherwise, the ship officer or
stowage planner manually adjusts the plan by adding ballast water and/or moving cargoes around to achieve desired stability. It is usually the case that the plan
does not fulfil the stability requirement from the loading computer, especially
when the stowage module provides an optimal plan with bad stability condition
to the loading computer. In the case of a stowage model with simplified stability
constraints, it may perform excellent in finding optimal solutions according to
the objective function. Nonetheless, it may result in undesirable overall performance due to the fact that manual adjustment can be expensive regarding the
excess amount of ballast water which is translated to excess fuel consumption.

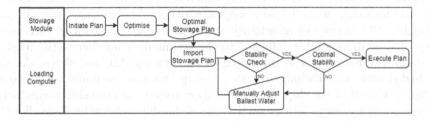

Fig. 2. Traditional stowage planning and interaction with loading computers.

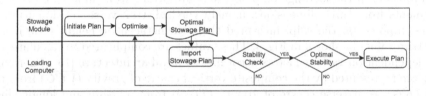

Fig. 3. Envisioned future approach for stowage planning with integration of loading
computers.

We propose an integrated approach of stowage planning as decision support,
illustrated in Fig. 3. Compared with the traditional approach, the difference is
that the loading computer is integrated into the planning phase, meaning that
when the optimal plan does not pass stability check, instead of manual adjustment, the information is sent back to the module with additional constraints
added to re-optimise and re-generate a new optimal solution. In this approach,
there is continuous communication and interaction between the stowage module and the loading computer to improve the plan for it to satisfy stability
requirements in the end. The envisioned future approach is automated to the
extent that the integration with the loading computer allows. Anyways, these
iterations can be expensive, and hence should ideally be eliminated or minimised. Therefore stability constraints should be set as close to reality as possible
for the stowage module to generate a good plan subject to a certain objective
function while keeping stability within required limits or even optimal stability.

In this paper, we focus on designing the stowage model with considerations of the integration with loading computers instead of the whole iterative process, which highly depends on the development of loading computers.

4   Ro-Ro Ship Stowage Problem with Ballast Water

Let us assume that a given Ro-Ro ship transporting two types of cargoes: general trailers (TRAs) and refrigerated trailers (TRARs). TRAs can be loaded anywhere, whereas TRARs can only be loaded at designated slots that have power connection through the ship. The ship has a fixed number of decks with various weight limits. In the case of short sea Ro-Ro ships, the majority of cargoes are standard trailers. For the sake of simplicity, we assume cargoes are homogeneous in dimensions with the same length, width, and height, however, different in weight. All cargoes are mandatory and available at the loading port, unaccompanied by drivers after delivered to the terminal. A number of tug masters are assigned for loading and unloading tasks between ship and shore. Cargoes are loaded onto and discharged from the ship through the main ramp usually located at the aft of the ship. Movement of cargoes within the ship is conducted through narrower ramps located on the side of the ship in between decks. For this characteristic of Ro-Ro ship, cargoes need to be loaded and discharged following precedence relations based on their positions on board.

In order to generate a stowage plan that is more likely to pass stability requirements in the loading computer, it is important to include stability measurements from three dimensions, namely vertical, transverse and longitudinal forces imposed on the ship, measured through metacentric height (GM), heel and trim values as shown in Fig. 4. These values are complicated to calculate and are dependent on various factors according to naval architecture [15]. Therefore, they are represented by the composite vertical centre of gravity ($\overline{VCG}$) from the keel (KG), transverse centre of gravity ($\overline{TCG}$) from midship and longitudinal centre of gravity ($\overline{LCG}$) from aft perpendicular to mimic the stability as close to reality as possible.

The vertical distance between composite $\overline{VCG}$ to the metacentre is GM, which is calculated by the equation $KG + GM = KM$, where KM is the height of metacentre from keel and can be found in the hydrostatic table from the ship builder. For the simplicity of the model, KM is treated as a constant. GM is one of the most important measurement when it comes to stability. GM is always positive to make sure that ships have the ability to bring themselves back to the upright position. Ship designers usually produce and define a set of values of minimum GM (GM_{min}) that meet all intact and damage stability criteria. If the actual GM value is higher than GM_{min}, then in most cases, other stability requirements will also be satisfied [18]. On the other hand, a very large GM meaning that the ship returns to the upright position too fast. At this stage, it has too much stability and becomes stiff, which can cause damage to cargoes and discomfort of crew. Therefore, a maximum GM (GM_{max}) value should be enforced as well. Hence, KG should satisfy $KM - GM_{max} \leq KG \leq KM - GM_{min}$.

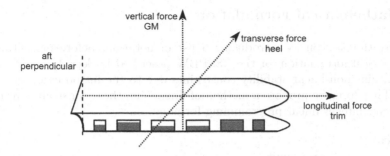

Fig. 4. Ship stability illustration.

Another two important parameters of stability are $\overline{TCG}$ and $\overline{LCG}$. $\overline{TCG}$ is an estimation of how much the ship heels, to ensure the ship does not roll too much to one side due to imbalanced heavy load. $\overline{LCG}$ is of similar concept to $\overline{TCG}$ but works in longitudinal direction, and serves as an estimation of trim to make sure the ship does not have a too heavy nose or bottom sitting in the water. Both $\overline{TCG}$ and $\overline{LCG}$ are constrained to a limit range to achieve close-to-zero heel and trim. Note that trim is a more complicated matter which has an impact on fuel consumption. However, it has a non-linear relation to displacement, draught and speed of the ship, hence, trim optimisation is left out in this article.

Ballast tanks are located at the bottom and along both sides of the ship, as illustrated in Fig. 4. There are two different types of ballast tanks on board - heeling tanks and regular tanks. Most of the ships have an anti-heeling system which is designed to balance the ship continuously and automatically with heeling tanks to minimise the angle of heel during loading and unloading operations. The total amount of water in all heeling tanks are required to be within a certain range in order to provide sufficient anti-heeling capability when the ship is heeled within a certain range of angles. However if it is beyond the ability of the anti-heeling system, then the amount of water in regular tanks needs to be adjusted to ensure stability. For carrying the same cargo load, the more ballast water a ship carries, the deeper it sits in the water due to the extra deadweight, the more fuel is consumed. In other words, fuel consumption has a positive correlation with the amount of extra ballast water a ship carries.

For a given Ro-Ro ship, transporting a set of cargoes from one loading port to one discharging port, we present an optimisation problem dealing with where to stow each cargo on board so that the ship can sail with a minimal amount of ballast water while still respecting the ship's stability requirements. We consider decisions such as the placement of individual cargo on board with regards to its weight and stowing restrictions, and the amount of ballast water in each tank. In order to integrate with loading computer, we introduce the inclusion of ballast tanks as well as more complete and accurate stability constraints introduced above, in order to achieve overall efficiency of stowage planning with a goal of reducing fuel consumption. We define this problem as Ro-Ro Ship Stowage Problem with Ballast Water (RSSPBW).

5   Mathematical Formulation

We start this section by introducing a list of notation, before presenting the mathematical formulation for the RSSPBW described in Sect. 4. This formulation contains non-linear stability constraints due to the introduction of ballast water. Therefore, we propose a method of linearising these constraints resulting in a binary integer linear programming formulation.

Indices

c	cargo unit
d	deck
s	slot
i	ballast tank

Sets

$\mathcal{C}$	set of cargo units
$\mathcal{C}^{\mathcal{R}}$	subset of refrigerated units
$\mathcal{D}$	set of decks
$\mathcal{S}$	set of slots
$\mathcal{S}_d$	subset of all slots on deck $d \in \mathcal{D}$
$\mathcal{S}_d^{\mathcal{R}}$	subset of all refrigerated slots on deck $d \in \mathcal{D}$
$\mathcal{T}$	set of ballast tanks
$\mathcal{T}^{\mathcal{H}}$	subset of regular ballast tanks
$\mathcal{T}^{\mathcal{B}}$	subset of heeling ballast tanks

Parameters

$H^{max/min}$	limiting water volume required in all heeling tanks
T_i^{max}	maximum volume capacity for ballast tank i
C_c^W	individual weight of cargo unit c
$D_d^{W,max}$	maximum allowable weight on deck d
$C_c^{\mathcal{R}}$	= 1 if cargo unit c is refrigerated, 0 otherwise
D_d^H	height of deck d
L^W	lightweight of the ship
L^{VCG}	VCG of lightship
T_i^{AoB}	Area of the base for ballast tank i
T_i^{TCG}	TCG of ballast tank i
T_i^{LCG}	LCG of ballast tank i
C_c^{VCG}	VCG of individual cargo unit
$S_s^{VCG/TCG/LCG}$	VCG/TCG/LCG of slot s
$KG^{max/min}$	maximum/minimum limiting KG value
$\overline{TCG}^{max/min}$	maximum/minimum limiting $\overline{TCG}$ value
$\overline{LCG}^{max/min}$	maximum/minimum limiting $\overline{LCG}$ value
ρ	sea water density, unit ton/m^3

Variables

x_{cds}	(binary) = 1 if cargo c is loaded on deck d at slot s
t_i	(continuous) the mass of water in ballast tank i
KG	composite VCG from keel
$\overline{TCG}$	composite TCG from midship
$\overline{LCG}$	composite LCG from aft perpendicular

5.1 Mathematical Formulation

$$\min \sum_{i \in T^B} t_i \tag{1}$$

$$\sum_{d \in \mathcal{D}} \sum_{s \in \mathcal{S}_d} x_{cds} = 1 \quad c \in \mathcal{C}, c \notin \mathcal{C}^R \tag{2}$$

$$\sum_{d \in \mathcal{D}} \sum_{s \in \mathcal{S}_d^R} C_c^R x_{cds} = 1, \quad c \in \mathcal{C}^R \tag{3}$$

$$\sum_{c \in \mathcal{C}} x_{cds} \leq 1, \quad d \in \mathcal{D}, s \in \mathcal{S}_d \tag{4}$$

$$\sum_{c \in \mathcal{C}} \sum_{s \in \mathcal{S}_d} C_c^W x_{cds} \leq D_d^{max}, \quad d \in \mathcal{D} \tag{5}$$

$$\rho H^{min} \leq \sum_{i \in T^H} t_i \leq \rho H^{max} \tag{6}$$

$$KG^{min} \leq KG \leq KG^{max} \tag{7}$$

$$\overline{TCG}^{min} \leq \overline{TCG} \leq \overline{TCG}^{max} \tag{8}$$

$$\overline{LCG}^{min} \leq \overline{LCG} \leq \overline{LCG}^{max} \tag{9}$$

$$x_{cds} \in \{0,1\}, c \in \mathcal{C}, d \in \mathcal{D}, s \in \mathcal{S} \tag{10}$$

$$0 \leq t_i \leq \rho T_i^{max}, i \in T \tag{11}$$

$$KG = \frac{\sum_{c \in \mathcal{C}} \sum_{d \in \mathcal{D}} \sum_{s \in \mathcal{S}_d} (S_s^{VCG} + C_c^{VCG}) C_c^W x_{cds} + L^W L^{VCG} + \sum_{i \in T} t_i \frac{t_i}{\rho T_i^{AoB}}}{\sum_{c \in \mathcal{C}} C_c^W + L^W + \sum_{i \in T} t_i} \tag{12}$$

$$\overline{TCG} = \frac{\sum_{i \in T} t_i T_i^{TCG} + \sum_{c \in \mathcal{C}} \sum_{d \in \mathcal{D}} \sum_{s \in \mathcal{S}_d} x_{cds} C_c^W S_s^{TCG} + L^W L^{TCG}}{\sum_{c \in \mathcal{C}} C_c^W + L^W + \sum_{i \in T} t_i} \tag{13}$$

$$\overline{LCG} = \frac{\sum_{i \in T} t_i T_i^{LCG} + \sum_{c \in \mathcal{C}} \sum_{d \in \mathcal{D}} \sum_{s \in \mathcal{S}_d} x_{cds} C_c^W S_s^{LCG} + L^W L^{LCG}}{\sum_{c \in \mathcal{C}} C_c^W + L^W + \sum_{i \in T} t_i} \tag{14}$$

The objective of the model (1) minimises the total amount of ballast water carried onboard a ship in order to reduce the fuel consumption caused by excess ballast water. Constraints (2) and (3) ensure that each cargo is loaded exactly once at a slot for general cargo and refrigerated cargo respectively. Whereas constraints (4) make sure that each slot will only have at most one cargo loaded. For ship safety and stability, constraints (5) make sure that the total weight of cargoes loaded on each deck does not exceed the maximum weight limit per deck. Constraint (6) keeps the total amount of water in heeling tanks within a safe margin so that the tanks have sufficient capability to heel the ship. Lastly, vertical, transverse and longitudinal stability calculations are presented in Eq. (12), (13) and (14), and are constrained through constraints (7), (8) and (9), respectively. Due to the inclusion of ballast tanks and the amount of water inside as decision variables, VCG of ballast tanks becomes a function of the decision variables as well. For a given ballast tank, its VCG depends on the volume of water inside, and its shape, or its area of base if the tank is shaped vertically straight. The model assumes the latter, as also shown in Eq. (12). Lastly, decision variables are bounded by (10) for binary indicator x_{cds}, and by (11) for both types of ballast tanks, whose upper limits are taken from ship builders.

5.2   Linearisation

As can be observed that constraints (7), (8) and (9) are non-linear when substituted with equation (12), (13) and (14), respectively, not only due to the division but also the quadratic function of decision variables t_i in equation (12).

   To eliminate the division existing in all three constraints, we simply multiply each constraint with its lower fraction, which is the sum of all weights including the ship itself. It is naturally positive, hence does not have any impact on the signs of the inequalities. It is however trickier when it comes to linearising the quadratic function in Eq. (12) - the product of the amount of water in the ballast tank and its vertical centre of gravity which is again determined by the amount of water whether the tank empty, full or in between. We propose a discretisation method using the following additional notations listed. In the discretisation method, we divide each tank i into several filling levels denoted by a set of discrete points $k \in \mathcal{K}_i$ and use binary variables y_{ik} to indicate whether the tank is filled to a certain level k. Each point or filling level corresponds to an amount of water T_{ik}^{VOL} and a VCG value T_{ik}^{VCG} when tank i is filled to the level k.

Indices	k	discretisation point, fill level of ballast tank
Sets	$\mathcal{K}_i$	set of discretisation point for ballast tank i
Parameters	T_{ik}^{VOL}	volume of ballast tank i if filled at level k
	T_{ik}^{VCG}	VCG of ballast tank b if filled at level k
Variables	y_{ik}	(binary) = 1 if ballast tank i is filled at level k

An example of the discretisation method is illustrated in Fig. 5. Let us look at one of the ballast tanks on board, tank i, which is located right above the keel. The maximum amount of water tank i can carry is $100\,\mathrm{m}^3$ and its maximum VCG value is 10 m. The tank is divided into three levels denoted by a set of points $\mathcal{K}_i = \{0, 1, 2\}$. At filling level $k = 0$, tank i is empty and therefore its corresponding VCG is 0 m. A half filled tank i corresponds to a filling level of $k = 1$, with a VCG of 5 m. Lastly a filling level of $k = 2$ meaning that the

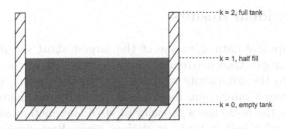

Fig. 5. Tank discretisation.

tank is full with $100\,\mathrm{m}^3$ of ballast water inside and a VCG of $10\,\mathrm{m}$. In the case illustrated here, the tank is filled to level $k = 1$, represented by binary variables $y_{i2} = 1$, and $y_{i0} = y_{i1} = 0$. As mentioned above, the discretised tank values corresponding to filling level $k = 2$ are $50\,\mathrm{m}^3$ of ballast water and a VCG of $5\,\mathrm{m}$. Therefore, the gravity moment of the tank i becomes the following linear calculation:

$$\sum_{k\in\mathcal{K}_i} \rho T_{ik}^{VOL} T_{ik}^{VCG} y_{ik} = \rho(0 \times 0 \times 0 + 50 \times 5 \times 1 + 100 \times 10 \times 0) = 250\rho \ (t\text{-}m)$$

The method represents the decision variables t_i, and their corresponding VCG in a discrete manner and replaces them in the original formulation in Sect. 5.1 so that the quadratic product can be linearised. The amount in ballast tank t_i, their corresponding VCG, and their gravity moment are now represented as

$$t_i = \sum_{k\in\mathcal{K}_i} \rho T_{ik}^{VOL} y_{ik} \qquad\qquad i \in \mathcal{T} \qquad\qquad (15)$$

$$T_i^{VCG} = \sum_{k\in\mathcal{K}_i} T_{ik}^{VCG} y_{ik} \qquad\qquad i \in \mathcal{T} \qquad\qquad (16)$$

$$t_i T^{VCG} = \sum_{i\in\mathcal{K}_i} \rho T_{ik}^{VOL} T_{ik}^{VCG} y_{ik} \qquad\qquad i \in \mathcal{T} \qquad\qquad (17)$$

Constraint (7) is then linearised and rewritten as the following:

$$KG^{min}(\sum_{c\in\mathcal{C}} C_c^W + L^W + \sum_{i\in\mathcal{T}}\sum_{i\in\mathcal{K}_i} \rho T_{ik}^{VOL} y_{ik}) \le$$

$$\sum_{c\in\mathcal{C}}\sum_{d\in\mathcal{D}}\sum_{s\in\mathcal{S}_d} (S_s^{VCG} + C_c^{VCG})C_c^W x_{cds} + L^W L^{VCG} + \sum_{i\in\mathcal{T}}\sum_{k\in\mathcal{K}_i} \rho T_{ik}^{VOL} T_{ik}^{VCG} y_{ik}$$

$$\le KG^{max}(\sum_{c\in\mathcal{C}} C_c^W + L^W + \sum_{i\in\mathcal{T}}\sum_{i\in\mathcal{K}_i} \rho T_{ik}^{VOL} y_{ik}) \qquad\qquad (18)$$

By substituting t_i with formula (15) in all other appearance in the original formulation and constraint (7) with (18), a new linearised formulation of RSSPBW is presented.

6   Computational Results

We collected empirical data from one of the largest short sea Ro-Ro shipping companies in Europe. One departure has been selected as the benchmark in this study due to the complexity of working with the loading computer. The departure was from Vlaardingen, the Netherlands to Immingham, the UK. The ship deployed for the route has a capacity of 4076 lane meters with two heeling tanks and 20 regular ballast tanks in various sizes. Empirical data regarding the departure consisted of a stowage plan carried out by the dispatcher and the crew, a list of cargo information, and a file from the loading computer on board containing the ship's condition upon departure. Limits for the stability constraints were roughly estimated based on zero trim condition with the help of an naval architect working with the loading computer. For this specific ship, the limits applied in the model are [11, 12.5], [87.83, 93.61] and [−0.5, 0.5] for KG, LCG and TCG respectively. The linearised RSSPBW was run in Julia with Gurobi optimiser on a window laptop with Intel(R) Core(TM) i7-7820HQ CPU @ 2.90 GHz and 16.0 GB RAM. The optimal solution was found in 65 s with an input size of 251 cargoes with a total weight of 6976 tons and 10 discretisation levels of ballast tanks.

Table 1. Ballast and fuel consumption saving results based on real stowage plan and sailing condition.

Parameters	unit	orig.	opt.	opt.s	opt.orig.s
Ballast water	amount (ton)	3448.5	911.4	1458.9	2115.5
	saving in (ton/%)	0.0/0.00	2537.1/73.57%	1989.6/57.69%	1333.0/38.65%
Stability	GM (metre)	1.51	1.43	1.23	1.28
from loading	Trim (metre)	0.00f	1.93a	0.91a	0.06a
computer	Heel (degree)	0.1s	1.8s	1.5s	0.4s
Fuel consumption	amount (ton)	10404.7	9520.3	9707.6	9946.9
*annual	saving (ton/%)	0.0/0.00	884.4/8.5%	697.1/6.7%	457.8/4.4%
	monetary saving	$0	$502339	$395953	$260030
CO_2 impact	emission (ton)	32412.0	29657.0	30240.4	30985.9
*annual	reduction (ton)	0	2755.0	2171.6	1426.1

Preliminary results on ballast water savings and stability conditions are shown in Table 1. The original stowage plan (orig.) collected from the empirical data carried 3448.5 tons of ballast water, whereas the optimal solution (opt.) from the linearised RSSPBW minimised the amount of ballast water down to 911.4 tons with a saving of 2537.1 tons, accounted for almost 75% of the original amount. However, the optimal solution provided a plan that is heavily trimmed by the aft with a risky GM and not approved by the loading computer due to the stability requirement. For the sake of the performance and comparison, we improve the optimal solution by manually adjusting the amount of ballast water on board to meet the loading computer's requirement (opt.s). The result when the ship is within stability is still astonishing - over half the original ballast intake was cut off. Moreover, we also improved the plan a step further by adjusting the ship to match the stability condition in the original stowage plan with a close-to-even trim and heel (opt.orig.s). Once again, we are still able to save 38.65%, which is equivalent to an amount of 1333 tons saving of the original amount of ballast water. Furthermore, to translate ballast savings into fuel consumption savings and CO_2 reductions, we roughly estimated the fuel consumption by using admiralty coefficient [12], average fuel consumption and CO_2 emission of a ro-ro ship close to the empirical ship [11], route distance [16] and an average bunker price of $568 per metric ton for MGO in Rotterdam in 2019 [17]. For one ship sailing on the selected route with a daily departure, the annual savings in fuel consumption are 697.1 and 457.8 tons for the cases where stability requirements are satisfied. Their respective monetary savings are $348,550 and $228,903. Moreover, a saving in fuel consumption has a positive impact on our environment. As presented in the table, CO_2 emission can be reduced significantly with an amount of 2171.6 tons. Note that the savings in "opt.s" and "opt.orig.s" are only minimal since they were based on manual improvement from a non-expert.

Table 2. Test instances and results.

Instance	% of cargo weigh between				$\|\mathcal{K}_i\| = 10$		$\|\mathcal{K}_i\| = 50$		$\|\mathcal{K}_i\| = 100$	
	5–15	15–25	25–35	35–45	t	t'	t	t'	t	t'
inst1	25	25	25	25	2.63	2.82	2.21	2.30	2.16	2.20
inst2	20	30	30	20	2.78	2.86	2.46	2.50	3.26	3.33
inst3	30	20	20	30	1.72	1.77	1.68	1.74	3.26	3.28
inst4	10	40	40	10	2.27	2.32	2.99	3.05	3.17	3.28
inst5	40	10	10	40	2.27	2.28	2.38	2.42	2.74	2.77
inst6	10	20	30	40	110.38	9.28	31.66	18.65	37.32	8.44
inst7	40	30	20	10	1.70	1.62	2.53	2.45	2.72	2.60
inst8	50	50	0	0	2.30	2.18	1.67	1.61	2.48	2.39
inst9	0	50	50	0	16.77	4.70	38.03	15.26	9.64	2.19
inst10	0	0	50	50	63.48	8.52	17.52	8.20	17.2	3.49

The preliminary results show that the RSSPBW has a significant benefit on ballast savings with stability constraints and integration with loading computer, even though it is based on only one departure. Setting the right limits for stability constraints in the linearised RSSPBW is a complicated matter involving one to master the knowledge of navel architecture. A better set of limits will definitely contribute to a ship condition closer to ideal stability. Furthermore, a larger set of discretisation points provides a higher level of granularity for the filling levels and in turn improves the flexibility of the model satisfying the stability constraints. However, it might be expensive. In order to evaluate the impact of different discretisation levels on the running time, we performed the following tests. Based on the above empirical load list, we generated 10 instances with different cargo weight distribution and run them against three discretisation levels $|\mathcal{K}_i| = \{10, 50, 100\}$ $\forall i$ to examine the performance variation, displayed in Table 2. In addition, we compare the running time when it solves to optimality (t) with the running time when it is terminated by 1% gap (t'), equivalent to less than 2 tons ballast water.

Most instances can be solved to optimality within 4 s regardless of the discretisation levels. For cases that are difficult for the model to find the optimal solution, such as inst6, inst9 and inst10, a larger discretisation level can significantly improve the running time as assumed above, but at the same time a too large discretisation level can be costly as indicated in the test results of inst6, where the running time was improved significantly from 110 s to 31 s from a discretisation level of 10 to 50, while with $|\mathcal{K}_i|$ increased from 50 to 100, the performance dropped. No obvious pattern has been found on the correlation between discretisation level and running time. There are several other deciding factors such as the strictness of stability constraints, the granularity of tanks and the cargo distribution as well. However, for cases where optimality is difficult to achieve, getting close to the lower bound with 1% gap can be done at a much lower computational cost. This indicates the ease of implementing the model in the real world, namely fast running time providing a close-to-optimum solution.

7   Conclusion and Discussion

This paper analyses the problem of stowage planning in short sea Ro-Ro shipping and proposes an integrated approach to model and solve stowage and stability problems. The new approach requires better formulation of stability constraints and the inclusion of ballast water compared to previous methods. The idea is to generate an optimal stowage plan which uses the weight of cargoes to satisfy stability requirements instead of using excess ballast water which is translated into excess fuel consumption. The paper defines a Ro-Ro ship stowage problem with ballast water and presents a quadratic mathematical formulation with the objective to optimise the amount of ballast water onboard. A discretisation method is applied to linearise the quadratic constraints due to the introduction of ballast tanks. The linearised model is then tested against empirical data collected from the collaborating company. Computational results on the selected departure indicate significant potential for ballast savings, showing the relevance of the model's application in the real world. Furthermore, additional tests on instances with various cargo weight distributions and discretisation levels are conducted, and results show no significant correlation among the factors.

Our preliminary study result from this research clearly indicates the industry potential of our integrated stowage approach and model which delivered between 4.4% and 6.7% of savings in fuel consumption and emissions. Due to the complexity of the problem, some details were simplified and compromised compared to reality, which can be further improved by a more complete and better formulated set of constraints. For example, additional deadweight elements, such as storage and fuel tanks can be included for a more accurate stability calculation; free surface movement can be implemented by penalising partially filled tanks; trim optimisation can be added since it has an obvious impact on fuel consumption etc. In addition, other discretisation methods such as piecewise linear functions might improve the solution without significantly increase computational costs. Another aspect which we suggest for future research is to analyse the robustness of the model, subject to changes of cargo amounts, mix and weight. As mentioned, the unpredictability of cargo amounts and composition, makes it difficult to apply our model in daily processes without making it more robust. Lastly, even though the majority of cargo is homogeneous in dimensions, cargo in reality differ in sizes compared to standard trailers. Future research and models for stowage planning can therefore also improve practical relevance by including this aspect.

References

1. European transport maps. https://www.europeantransportmaps.com/map/roro-ferry/operator
2. Azevedo, A.T., de Salles Neto, L.L., Chaves, A.A., Moretti, A.C.: Solving the 3D stowage planning problem integrated with the quay crane scheduling problem by representation by rules and genetic algorithm. Appl. Soft Comput. **65**, 495–516 (2018). https://doi.org/10.1016/j.asoc.2018.01.006
3. Eurostat: Maritime transport statistics - short sea shipping of goods. https://ec.europa.eu/eurostat/statistics-explained/index.php/Maritime_transport_statistics_-_short_sea_shipping_of_goods
4. Hansen, J.R., Fagerholt, K., Stålhane, M.: A shortest path heuristic for evaluating the quality of stowage plans in roll-on roll-off liner shipping. ICCL 2017. LNCS, vol. 10572, pp. 351–365. Springer, Cham (2017). https://doi.org/10.1007/978-3-319-68496-3_24
5. Hansen, J.R., Hukkelberg, I., Fagerholt, K., Stålhane, M., Rakke, J.G.: 2D-packing with an application to stowage in roll-on roll-off liner shipping. In: Paias, A., Ruthmair, M., Voß, S. (eds.) ICCL 2016. LNCS, vol. 9855, pp. 35–49. Springer, Cham (2016). https://doi.org/10.1007/978-3-319-44896-1_3
6. IMO: Greenhouse gas emissions. http://www.imo.org/en/OurWork/Environment/PollutionPrevention/AirPollution/Pages/GHG-Emissions.aspx
7. Iris, Ç., Christensen, J., Pacino, D., Ropke, S.: Flexible ship loading problem with transfer vehicle assignment and scheduling. Transp. Rese. Part B: Methodol. **111**, 113–134 (2018). https://doi.org/10.1016/j.trb.2018.03.009
8. Ji, M., Guo, W., Zhu, H., Yang, Y.: Optimization of loading sequence and rehandling strategy for multi-quay crane operations in container terminals. Transp. Res. Part E: Logist. Transp. Rev. **80**, 1–19 (2015). https://doi.org/10.1016/j.tre.2015.05.004
9. Jia, B., Rytter, N.G.M., Reinhardt, L.B., Haulot, G., Billesø, M.B.: Estimating discharge time of cargo units – a case of Ro-Ro shipping. In: Paternina-Arboleda, C., Voß, S. (eds.) ICCL 2019. LNCS, vol. 11756, pp. 122–135. Springer, Cham (2019). https://doi.org/10.1007/978-3-030-31140-7_8
10. Jovanovic, R., Tanaka, S., Nishi, T., Voß, S.: A GRASP approach for solving the Blocks Relocation Problem with Stowage Plan. Flex. Serv. Manuf. J. **31**(3), 702–729 (2018). https://doi.org/10.1007/s10696-018-9320-3

11. LIPASTO: Average emissions and energy use of a RORO and ROPAX ship in 2016. http://lipasto.vtt.fi/yksikkopaastot/tavaraliikennee/vesiliikennee/roroe.htm
12. Man Diesel & Turbo: Basic principles of ship propulsion. https://spain.mandieselturbo.com/docs/librariesprovider10/sistemas-propulsivos-marinos/basic-principles-of-ship-propulsion.pdf?sfvrsn=2
13. Øvstebø, B.O., Hvattum, L.M., Fagerholt, K.: Optimization of stowage plans for RORO ships. Comput. Oper. Res. **38**(10), 1425–1434 (2011)
14. Puisa, R.: Optimal stowage on Ro-Ro decks for efficiency and safety. J. Marine Eng. Technol. 1–17 (2018)
15. Rhodes, M.A.: Ship Stability for Mates. Seamanship International Ltd., Glasgow (2003)
16. Searoutes: Immingham - vlaardingen distance. https://www.searoutes.com/routing/4294967447/4294973215
17. Ship and Bunker: Rotterdam bunker prices. https://shipandbunker.com/prices/emea/nwe/nl-rtm-rotterdam#MGO
18. Wärtsilä: Wärtsilä encyclopedia of marine technology: Curve of minimum operational metacentric height gm. https://www.wartsila.com/encyclopedia/term/curve-of-minimum-operational-metacentric-height-gm
19. World Maritime News: Dfds names its largest roro ship - offshore energy (2019). https://www.offshore-energy.biz/dfds-names-its-largest-roro-ship/

Waterborne Hinterland Transports for Floating Port Terminals

Gerrit Assbrock[1](✉) (iD), Jens Ley[1], Ioannis Dafnomilis[2], Mark B. Duinkerken[2], and Dingena L. Schott[2]

[1] Development Centre for Ship Technology and Transport Systems,
Oststr. 77, 47057 Duisburg, Germany
assbrock@dst-org.de
[2] Department of Maritime and Transport Technology,
Mekelweg 2, 2628CD Delft, The Netherlands

Abstract. Port terminals on floating modular platforms are a conceivable solution for the problem of limited space and water depths restrictions of ports in estuary regions. A design of a dedicated Transport&Logistic hub has been developed in the scope of the Horizon 2020 project Space@Sea. This paper addresses dedicated options of waterborne hinterland transports and discusses opportunities for bypassing onshore terminals by means of river-sea or sea-going inland vessels. A tailored simulation method for ship operations utilises a specific cost model and is applied to derived demand scenarios. Cargo flow statistics of an onshore port have been projected onto the hub to identify relevant waterborne transports to the hinterland. Three different vessel types are implemented, whereas inland vessels are considered with two different sizes. A comparison of round trip durations and transport costs per transported container between a floating terminal and a relevant hinterland port pointed out, that a non-stop connection with sea-going inland vessels is the economically favourable solution. A feeder vessel is the faster solution in coastal waters but it can not compensate the time saved by omitted terminal visits on a direct hinterland connection.

Keywords: Port terminal at sea · Waterborne hinterland transport · Strategic simulation model

1 Introduction

Over the last decade global trade has increased noticeably in all dimensions like tonnage, number of containers, size and number of vessels and port size. However, the expansion of handling capacity is a major issue for many sea ports because of limited space and water depths restrictions in adjacent rivers or channels. Innovative solutions are required to overcome these problems. Kim and Morrison [1] as well as Baird and Rother [2] provide an overview of different floating concepts and their technical feasibility in a low-wave sheltered environment. A modular floating logistic hub, namely a Transport&Logistic (T&L) hub

© Springer Nature Switzerland AG 2020
E. Lalla-Ruiz et al. (Eds.): ICCL 2020, LNCS 12433, pp. 101–118, 2020.
https://doi.org/10.1007/978-3-030-59747-4_7

that has been developed in the Space@Sea project [3], constitutes one possible solution for this problem. It is assumed to be located in the North-Sea in front of the River Scheldt's estuary. Van den Berg and Langen [4] already discussed the added value in port development considering hinterland connections during expansion planning. A logistic concept including a terminal design [5] and hinterland connections bypassing ashore terminals was elaborated and optimised on a strategic level. Konings et al. [6] also proposed a container hub but along inland waterways to equalise the congestion in sea ports. Waiting times and congestion of inland vessels in sea ports is also discussed and modelled by Shobayo and van Hassel [7]. Most approaches focus on the assessment of waterborne inter terminal transport in sea ports as discussed by Li et al. [8]. Here, relevant connections to the hinterland are investigated including the combination of short-sea shipping and inland waterway shipping with two vessel types or a direct connection by river-sea shipping. Vantorre et al. [9] emphasised that inland vessels can establish a technically feasible hinterland connection as long as they are capable of navigating estuaries and coastal waters. These vessel types are considered in this publication.

Floating terminals near shore are meant to meet demands of vessels growing in size and capacity driven by an increasing cargo flow. Integrating those in an existing inter terminal transport is crucial for economic port expansion. It is expected that direct connections to the hinterland with vessels operating on coastal as well as on inland waterways can optimise the integration of a near shore terminal. Different types of vessel services are compared to identify the economically most favourable solution. The objective is to analyse the potential of direct hinterland connections from the offshore T&L hub with a strategic simulation method calculating round trip durations and transport costs.

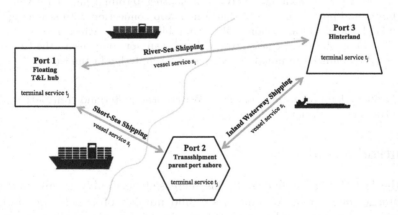

Fig. 1. Overview of modelled solutions. A combination of short-sea and inland waterway shipping or the utilisation of vessels being capable of river-sea shipping to serve a cargo request.

The strategic simulation bases on demand scenarios. This way, hinterland connections can be evaluated for their performance in a variety of boundary conditions and demands. The methodology applied considers four steps: It begins with an analysis of an origin-destination matrix to identify relevant cargo requests on hinterland connections for a proposed floating terminal location. The definition of a cost model that includes capital and operational costs for different types of vessels and transshipment at terminals follows. Including both a simulation method is developed. The assessment of transport paths by costs and number of vessels that service a given scenario of cargo requests concludes the analyses.

Relevant hinterland connections in the populated area of Central and North Europe are considered. Major container cargo flows are derived from statistics for the Port of Antwerp together with its cargo sources and drains in the hinterland, e. g. in the adjacent Benelux countries and federal states of Germany along the river Rhine. Under the premise of optimising the remote terminal integration traditional ways of shipping are combined to serve the hinterland connection. Figure 1 illustrates two different solutions connecting the hub to the hinterland. Focussing on inter terminal transport with an existing port ashore, one hinterland connection is realised with two types of vessels and an additional handling. The other proposed solution relies only on one vessel type being capable of navigating both waters, coastal and inland waterways.

2   Hinterland Transport Scenarios

Cargo throughputs are required as input for the strategic simulation. From trade statistics and prognoses for upcoming demands of transport throughput, scenarios and an origin-destination matrix are derived. The latter yields relevant connections between the T&L hub and the hinterland that are applied to the simulation method.

2.1   Assumptions

A scenario provides the required boundary conditions for the model. For the strategic simulation it sets the amount of TEU that are handled on T&L hub within a specific time scale, the cargo throughput respectively. Knowing the demand from the prognosis for a sea port in North-Central Europe in 2030, [10] the throughput at the T&L hub can be a portion of the total handled TEU at that port. It is assumed, that a T&L hub will relieve the Port of Antwerp by a throughput of 6 million TEU. Due to an additional demand for specific infrastructure for the storage and handling of reefer containers, a split of 6% is not handled at the hub. With a ratio of FEU and TEU of 1.5 (60% FEU and 40% TEU containers respectively) it leaves 3.525 million containers to be handled at the floating terminal each year. The simulation takes a daily throughput of 18193 TEU as input which is based on a one day dwell time and 310 days of operation.

2.2   Container Split on Hinterland Connections

A T&L hub is proposed to act as an additional terminal of a nearby onshore port on the one hand and as an independent hub on the other hand. As a hub other sea ports are served by short-sea connections and on direct hinterland transports. To identify and prioritise relevant hinterland destinations for the T&L hub, the major container cargo flows to and from Belgium were identified first. The Netherlands and Germany were found to be major trading partners for Belgium. Since Antwerp is Belgium's major container port, these cargo flows were expected to be representative of the considered use case. It was decided to focus on possible hinterland cargo drains and sources between Port of Antwerp and Germany and to project the results onto the T&L hub. The statistics from 2016 contain the distribution of containers for each federal state of Germany which is trading with the Port of Antwerp, being either the shipping or the receiving instance [11]. The three most important states are North Rhine Westphalia (NRW), Rhineland Palatinate (RP) and Baden-Wuerttemberg (BW). As expected, destinations far downstream the river Rhine (Rhine-kilometre > 500) take the greatest share of all containers. The cargo source or drain NRW is represented by the conglomeration of inland ports of Duisburg, Düsseldorf and Cologne. With 45%, it takes the largest split of the total container transport between Port of Antwerp and Germany. The total waterway distance between the T&L hub and the conglomeration of terminals in NRW is about 398 km and includes about 102 km to be covered by inter terminal transport between the T&L hub and the sea port onshore.

Based on the chosen scenario of cargo throughput at the T&L hub, see Sect. 2.1, this hinterland connection provides the portion of containers that has to be covered by a vessel service. The modal split at the Port of Antwerp for hinterland connections reveals 38% of waterborne container transport [12] in 2017, whereas 62%, represent the inter terminal transport. This split is also projected onto the T&L hub.

3   Simulation Model

General assumptions build the fundament of the strategic simulation method. With respect to time scales the operational downtime of a terminal influences the yearly throughput of cargo. The annual productivity of any service is subject to the assumption of 310 days of operation per year and 20 h of operation per day. Uneven distributions between shipping and receiving shares are averaged unweighted, since the import–export factor is assumed with 0.5.

3.1   Vessel Types

For the service of above discussed hinterland connections different types of vessels are considered. Two major characteristics are distinguished, since different operational areas need to be navigated. For the connection of the T&L hub to the hinterland, a short-sea segment and inland segments have to be completed. A vessel servicing the short-sea segment requires a classification of its structural strength to withstand wave loads and a dedicated crew for navigation in coastal waters. The critical parameters for transport on inland waterways are the maximum clearance under bridges and the draught to water depth ratio.

When the hub is operated as an additional terminal to an existing port ashore, a container feeder vessel is proposed to establish the waterborne inter terminal transport. This vessel type is denoted a feeder in the following. Direct hinterland connections can either be serviced with a transshipment in the parent onshore port or by a vessel type that can complete the river-sea connection non-stop. sea-going inland vessels can realise a direct connection and integrate the T&L hub in a network of hinterland terminals. To compare this solution to the established way with additional handling at an onshore port also inland vessels are introduced, which are less expensive than sea-going inland vessels. This type of vessel is entrenched with different sizes and corresponding container capacities, whereas two are considered for the analysis in combination with the feeder. The combination of vessel type and terminal has an influence on the processing time in port, since the number of cranes processing a vessel is limited by the vessel's length. The vessels given in Table 1 with examples for reference, are found to be suitable for the terminal integration.

The velocities over ground of each vessel are set constant for the conducted simulations and depend on the operational area. The approach of velocity estimation for the short-sea services is described in Sect. 3.2. Average velocities of the feeder and sea-going inland vessel in the operational area of coastal waters are linked to a sea state common for southern North Sea territories. The influence by current or by runoff in m^3/s, which is entrenched navigating on rivers, is only considered for services on inland waterways. Half the velocity over ground is assumed, when the vessel sails upstream. The velocity corresponds to a moderate usage of engine power and fuel consumption. Hence, higher velocities may be possible for round trips being time-sensitive. Although, it is recommended to assume moderate velocities, since the ratio of draught to water depth has a strong impact on maximum velocities over ground and is not considered throughout this analysis. For very deep hinterland penetrations, e.g. upstream the Rhine (Rhine-kilometre < 550), the river gets more shallow and an additional operational area allowing only smaller drafts and velocities needs to be modelled.

3.2 Ship Velocity at Sea

Round trip durations and transport costs depend on the achievable ship's speed. As connections between the T&L hub at sea and the hinterland are considered, the hydrodynamic behaviour of a ship is affected by two principle environments, namely by the sea and inland waterway. Wave loads are dominating the ship's speed at sea; currents and limited water depths significantly affect the achievable ship's speed on inland waterways. The applied approach of the velocity estimation for the waterborne transport service at sea is described next.

Table 1. Container capacity, main dimensions, ship speeds and assigned cranes per type or the Conférence Européenne des Ministres de Transport (CEMT) water way class

Vessel type	Feeder vessel	Sea-going inland vessel	inland class Va	"Jowi" class
Capacity [TEU]	734	380	240	510
Length L [m]	140.0	110.0	110.0	134.9
Breadth B [m]	21.5	17.0	11.45	16.9
Draught T [m]	7.0	4.0	3.0	3.0
Velocity short-sea segment [km/h]	22.0	8.0	-	-
Velocity up-/downstream [km/h]	-/-	8.0 / 16.0	8.0 / 16.0	8.0 / 16.0
No. of cranes at terminal to un-/load	3	2	2	3
TEU/FEU per move	4/2	4/2	2/1	2/1

It is obvious, that different vessel types come along with various seakeeping abilities leading to different ship speeds and operational days per year. For instance, small sea-going inland vessels are more sensitive to wave loads and equipped with less propulsion power than feeders. Thus, it is necessary to distinguish these ship types and to quantify their speed losses in waves.

For the ship speed estimation, wave loads are separated into two load components, namely first and second order loads. First order wave loads (wave amplitudes) rather cause ship motions and affect the seakeeping ability in terms of the required minimum bow height and freeboard. Second order wave loads increase the required propulsion power of the vessel or cause a speed loss for a given propulsion power. In case of head waves, the resulting forces are denoted as added resistance. The approach to estimate the speed loss in relevant sea state conditions is based on the following steps:

1. Ship type selection (hull dimensions and geometry)
2. Estimation of the calm water resistance R_T
3. Calculation of the Response-Amplitude Operators (RAO) for the second order wave forces for different wave frequencies.[1]
4. Calculation of the mean added resistance for irregular sea states by multiplying the RAOs with the spectral energy density function $S(\omega)$ for given sea states and integration over the relevant wave frequency range.
5. Calculation of the speed loss.

The fundamental assumption is that the effective propulsion and the provided power by the main engine stay unaffected during the operation at sea. For the moderate sea states considered, it is a reasonable assumption. For extreme and steep seas, the propulsion efficiency will change and more power is required. Hence, an additional speed loss induced by a lack of power may be the consequence.

---

[1] For the sake of simplification, head sea conditions are considered.

Calm water resistance prognoses for ships can be carried out on the basis of the empirical approach proposed in [17]. If required, even more sophisticated numerical methods based on the solution of Reynolds-Averaged Navier-Stokes Equations (RANSE) or model tests can be used as well as done in [18].

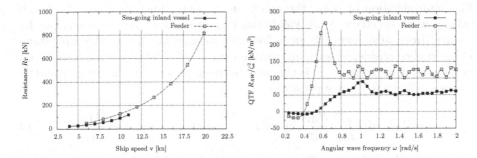

Fig. 2. Estimated calm water resistance R_T [kN] (left) and Response Amplitude Operators for the added resistance [kN/m²] of the Feeder at 12 knots and the sea-going inland vessel at 8 knots (right)

Exemplary results are shown here for the feeder and the sea-going inland vessel, see Fig. 2 (left). The resistance prognosis for the feeder bases on the approach by Holtrop&Mennen [17]; the prognosis for the sea-going inland vessel was based on model test results of a comparable vessel with similar ship dimensions. A Boundary Element Method (BEM) based on potential theory was applied to perform hydrodynamic diffraction calculations in waves. Potential theory is known to be suitable for proper prediction of ship motions in waves. In addition, the method can be used to estimate the second order drift forces. The vessel's responses were calculated in regular waves for a relevant range of wave frequencies and fixed speeds. Forces acting on the vessels in longitudinal direction were extracted from the diffraction calculation. The Quadratic Transfer Function (QTF) is plotted against the angular wave frequencies ω of the incident wave and presented for both vessel types in Fig. 2 (right). The maximum added resistance for the feeder is found at $\omega \approx 0.635$ rad/s; for the sea-going inland vessel at $\omega \approx 1.05$ rad/s. Irregular sea states are described by statistical properties such as the spectral energy density distribution S. In analogy to the added resistance, the exciting forces are expressed at different angular wave frequencies ω. A suitable semi-empirical expression for the North Sea was published in [19] and represents the well known JONSWAP spectrum. It reads

$$S(\omega) = \frac{\alpha g^2}{\omega^5} \cdot \exp\left[-\frac{5}{4} \cdot \left(\frac{\omega_p}{\omega}\right)^4 \right] \cdot \gamma^{\exp\left(-\frac{(\omega-\omega_p)^2}{2\sigma^2\omega_p^2}\right)} \text{ with } \sigma = \begin{cases} 0.07 : \omega \leq \omega_p \\ 0.09 : \omega > \omega_p \end{cases} \quad (1)$$

and covers the peak frequency ω_p, α controlling the overall energy of the spectrum, peak enhancement factor γ, and σ modifying shape and width of the spectrum. The significant wave weight H_S can be obtained by means of the zeroth order spectral moment m_0

$$H_S = 4\sqrt{m_0} \qquad \text{and} \qquad m_0 = \int_0^\infty \omega^0 S(\omega)d\omega \qquad (2)$$

The multiplication of both, the quadratic transfer function R_{AW}/ζ_a^2 and the exiting wave spectrum $S(\omega)$, yields the response acting on the vessel per frequency. Integrating over the given frequency range, the mean added resistance $\overline{R}_{AW}$ in the considered sea state can be estimated. The consecutive speed loss in percent, denoted by v_{loss}, is the ratio between mean added resistance and the corresponding calm water resistance.

$$\overline{R}_{AW} = 2\int_0^\infty \frac{R_{AW}}{\zeta_a^2} S(\omega)d\omega \qquad \text{and} \qquad v_{loss} = \frac{\overline{R}_{AW}}{R_T} \qquad (3)$$

As a result, the different sailing speeds can be derived for the relevant sea states at the T&L hub's site. Assuming a mean sea state with a significant wave height $H_S = 1.5$ m and peak period $T_p = 6.5$ s, the velocity of the feeder reduces about 18%, while the sea-going inland vessel looses speed by about 38%.

3.3   Cost Model

The concept in focus evaluates the beneficial effect of a direct hinterland connection with established vessels for river-sea shipping. The non-stop solution is compared with the connection including one transshipment at a parent onshore port. With the developed model also short-sea shipping can be addressed. A comparison of solutions for relevant connections is done calculating the duration of round trips between the hub and a hinterland destination. With a dedicated cost model that includes capital, maintenance, personnel and fuel costs for each vessel type the most efficient solution is calculated. The applied cost model makes use of the following assumption:

   The capital costs consist of a vessel's lightweight approximation that defines the costs for the hull and fixed rate for machinery and equipment, which is specific for the type of vessel and installed power. For the investment a fixed lending term of 20 years and a rate of interest of 1.5% are assumed. With 2 and 5% per year of the total investment, costs for maintenance and insurance are covered. The total capital costs per day for the considered vessels are summarised in Table 2.

   The personnel costs depend on the crew size and assumed salaries for personnel being skilled for either navigation on inland waterways or seaways. Since the operational hours throughout the analyses of terminal design and hinterland logistics are set to 20 h, the personnel works in two shifts. An associated employer outlay is already included in the personnel cost in Table 2. Capital costs and personnel costs are calculated for every operational hour. On a round trip, two different operational modes are distinguished and costs scale only with the corresponding mode. One mode is the processing at a terminal, that includes hours of vessel coordination in the port, and the loading and unloading at the terminal. In the second mode the vessel is under way in operation on a short-sea segment or on an inland segment considering sailing up- or downstream.

Fuel costs are only applied for the operational mode under way. Depending on the vessel's heading on an inland waterway, the necessary shaft power is related to the assumed velocity it sails up- or downstream (see Table 1). A margin of 15% is assumed and applied on the total costs per vessel on a round trip. More sophisticated cost models including a case study and aspects of pollution are provided by Al Enezy et al. [13] or Wiegmans and Konings [14].

Table 2. Costs per time unit and vessel in EUR

Vessel type/waterway class	Feeder vessel	Sea-going	Va class	"Jowi" class
Capital costs - per day	10548	1964	1133	1699
Personnel costs - per day	2310	858	762	762
Fuel costs - per hour	500	93	47	86

The major contributions to transport costs are those for handling. Terminal brochures provide the handling costs to analyse the connections. The transshipment on the T&L hub is charged with 23.71 EUR/TEU [5]. A research on costs for handlings at existing terminals at sea and inland ports is documented below. For example, the handling of one container FEU or TEU between a vessel and the terminal is charged with approximately 75.00 EUR [15]. At a representative inland terminal in NRW the handling of one container is charged with 10.00 EUR on average [16]. In case the solution with stopover is calculated, costs for handling in the Port of Antwerp are charged for each move unloading from the feeder and loading on the inland vessel. Since vessel capacities for the short-sea segment and inland waterway segment do not match, it is assumed that also partially utilised vessels are available. For these vessels the full capital and personnel costs are applied, whereas fuel costs are only considered relatively. Since all analyses assume only a one-day dwell time, solutions with storage of containers at stopover ports are not considered. Hence, it is secured that the calculation of needed vessels per day is sufficient. The following paragraph sums up all assumptions and boundary condition assigned to the mode of operation.

- Duration for **Processing at Terminal** in port
    - at the floating T&L hub in coastal waters at least 1 h
    - at hinterland or sea port for transshipment at least 2 h

A minimum duration for processing at terminals is set, since delays in ports commonly occur due to vessel coordination and the general risk of congestion. Thus, it considers the time the port needs to assign a vessel to its terminal after the vessel arrived. For the T&L hub this duration is assumed to be half of the time needed in established ports, since modern vessel and crane scheduling techniques will be applied. The actual time for loading or unloading scales with the number of cranes, their productivity in moves per hour, the spreader size setting, the TEU per move and the utilisation of the vessel for the cargo request. An example of concatenated durations is shown in Fig. 3.

- Cranes operate with a productivity of 20 moves per hour regardless of the terminal or port. This is a reasonable assumption following Baird and Rother [2]. The spreader and number of cranes that can be used to process one vessel depend on the vessel type. The number of cranes depends on the vessel's length. In case a vessel is equipped with cell guides a double spreader can be used. It is assumed that only the feeder and the sea-going inland vessel can be processed with a double spreader.
- At this stage of model development, it is assumed that only one vessel can be processed per terminal. Although, round trip durations are given per vessel service.
- At the terminal of stopover no ship to ship handling is assumed, which results in slightly higher durations and costs for the transhipment to the connecting vessel. It is a reasonable assumption, since no time for storage and transfer within a terminal are considered. It is further assumed, that the calculated minimum processing duration of 2 h per vessel before unloading, compensates it.
- Costs are calculated per handled container, whereas prices for TEU or FEU depend on the terminal. Costs for the vessel are calculated on an hourly basis but only capital and personnel costs are considered.
- The **Vessel under way in Operation** sails at a dedicated velocity in coastal waters assuming common moderate sea state conditions or rather up- or downstream on inland waterways.
- The necessary power is coupled to the sailing velocity and influences the fuel costs, whereas fuel costs depend on the vessel's utilisation.

3.4 Mathematical Model Formulation

The formulated approach calculates the transport costs $Z_{r,p}$ on a feasible path p as a concatenation of shipping s and handling services t for a cargo requests r. An assumed scenario sets the boundary conditions for the relevant hinterland connections being analysed. The model is implemented in Visual Basic for Applications (VBA) and is structured by the following indices, variables and parameters. Considered types of services are distinguished by the following indices in given intervals. The index $i \in [1, ..., 4]$ distinguishes vessel services $s_i \in S^{Vessels}$, whereas $j \in [1, 2, 3]$ differentiates terminal services $t_j \in T^{Cranes}$. The integer $r \in \mathbb{N}$ enables contrasting costs of different cargo requests. To differentiate partial costs e.g. for fuel or crane moves, s and t are used as indexes for parameters discussed below. Scaling of the objective quantities round trip duration τ and costs Z needs the following dimensionless variables: $n_i \in \mathbb{N}$, the number of vessel services of type s_i, $u_i \in [0, 1]$, the utilisation of vessel service of type and $m_j \in \mathbb{N}$, the number of terminal services of type t_j. Parameters specify the cargo request and the considered types of services. Each cargo request r is the product of a given scenario with its container throughput CT and a suitable hinterland connection with its cargo portion. It is characterised by the origin and destination of a round trip and CT_r denoting the container throughput on request r [TEU].

Each vessel service $s_i \in S^{Vessels}$ is characterised by its operational area OA_S namely an inland waterway up-/ downstream or an estuary or coastal waters. Moreover, the service is defined by $d_S(OA_S)$ denoting the spatial distance the service can cover depending on the operational area given in [km], the nominal capacity UN_S in [TEU] and $v_S(OA_S)$ the average velocity as a function of the waterway, the operational area and the average conditions along each area e. g. v_{loss} Eq. (3). Furthermore, there are CF_S denoting the fuel costs in [EUR/hour], the personnel costs CP_S in [EUR/day], CC_S for the capital costs in [EUR/day], NC_S as the dimensionless nominal number of cranes to un-/load the vessel and NM_S the spreader type that is suitable for un-/loading in [TEU/move]. Each terminal service $t_j \in T^{Cranes}$ is characterised by its operational area OA_T namely a remote terminal, an onshore terminal or an inland terminal. Moreover, it needs PM_T describing the performance of cranes in [moves/hour], $CH_T(OA_T)$ denoting the handling costs in [EUR/TEU] and the minimum duration τ_0 for processing a vessel at the terminal due to expected congestion in [hours].

The objective function minimises the total costs per container [EUR/TEU] for a request r as a result of the concatenated path p of services s_i and t_j. Let $x_{r,p} \in \{0,1\}$ be a binary variable equal to 1 if shipping s_i and terminal services t_j are compatible with respect to operational areas $OA_{S \vee T}$ and concatenate to a feasible path p for request r, 0 otherwise. The transport costs $Z_{r,p}$ are obtained following Eq. (4).

$$Z_{r,p} = \sum_{i,j} n_i x_{r,p} \left(u_{S,i} \left(\tau_i \cdot CF_{S,i} + UN_{S,i} \cdot CH_{T,j} \right) + \tau \cdot \left(CP_{S,i} + CC_{S,i} \right) \right) \quad (4)$$

A path $p = [s_i, ..., t_j, ...]$ is feasible to service a request r, if it satisfies the compatibility of operational areas OA_S, e.g. a vessel service with the OA_S coastal and estuary waters is necessary to reach a service t_j with OA_T remote terminal.

Following Eq. (5), the total duration τ to service a request r on path p with service combinations s_i and t_j is the sum of time elapsed at terminals and under way, it reads

$$\tau_{r,p} = \sum_{i,j} \left(\tau_i + \tau_j \right). \quad (5)$$

Here τ_i is the time each service s_i needs to cover the spatial distance of a request r and the velocity $v_S(OA_S)$. The time sailing and the time a vessel needs to be processed at a terminal τ_j, read

$$\tau_i = v_{S,i}(OA_{S,i}) \cdot d_{S,i} \quad \text{and} \quad \tau_j = \tau_{0,j} + \frac{UN_{S,i} \cdot u_{S,i}}{NC_{S,i} \cdot PM_T \cdot NM_{S,i}} \quad (6)$$

and are subject to

$$CT_r = \sum_i \left(n_i \cdot UN_{S,i} \cdot u_{S,i} \right). \quad (7)$$

The constrain given by Eq. (7) ensures that the container throughput of request r for a given scenario on a given hinterland connection is met by the assigned services. The most economic path p of all feasible paths is found, when $Z_{r,p}$ and $\tau_{r,p}$ reach a minimum. Minima are approached varying the type and number n_i, m_j as well as the utilisation u_i of assigned services which build a feasible path.

Table 3. Round trip durations per vessel for the hinterland connection T&L hub to NRW with stopover at Port of Antwerp a) and with non stop solution b).

Segment	Vessel type	No. Vessels (avg. utilisation)	Under way [h]	Processing at terminal [h]	Days in total
a)					
short-sea	Feeder vessel	2 (97.5%)	9.17	15.23	1.22
inland	"Jowi" class	3 (93.5%)	55.56	21.00	3.83
	Days in total		3.24	1.81	**5.05**
b)					
short-sea	Sea-going inland	4 (94.2%)	25.47	5.75	1.56
inland			55.56	11.50	3.35
	Days in total		4.05	0.86	**4.91**

4   Simulation Results

A scenario demanding 18193 TEU per one day dwell time was analysed. For a comparison always two feasible paths are calculated, one with transhipment and a non-stop connection. The cargo request between a T&L hub in the estuary of the River Scheldt and NRW breaks down to 1002 containers (573 TEU and 429 FEU) per day. The duration for a round trip fulfilling the request is compared for services in the two operational areas by Table 3 a). The path combines feeder vessels and the largest inland vessels ("Jowi" class) available with a capacity of 510 TEU. The round trip of one feeder takes 1.22 days (102 km one way) and the inland vessel needs 3.83 days for 296 km each way including loading and unloading at the port of destination and stopover. These durations depend on the vessels velocity in the respective operational area and its capacity that defines the time needed for processing in the port (see Table 1).

In Table 3 b) the path with a sea-going inland vessel is summarised. This non-stop solution requires more time, since the sea-going inland vessel is assumed to sail only with approximately one third of the feeder's velocity, but compensates time at the terminals. Although the sea-going inland vessel's capacity is about half of the feeder's, only two more vessels per type are necessary to fulfil this cargo request with 1002 containers each day. In total it is one vessel less than for the solution with stopover at the T&L hub's parent port onshore.

A detailed split of durations is shown in Fig. 3. Here port 1 abbreviates the T&L hub, port 2 the parent port ashore of stopover and port 3 the conglomeration of terminals in the hinterland. An illustration of the hinterland connection is provided by Fig. 1. All durations related to port 2, where the handling from sea-going to inland vessel takes place, are obsolete in case of the non-stop solution. This time saving amounts to about 3% of the path with stopover. The favourable solution is found to be the fastest and most beneficial one. Raising only the fastest path as the promising one for an economical integration of the T&L hub takes into account that fewer vessels are needed, since round trip durations reach a minimum even if the capacity of the deployed vessel is smaller.

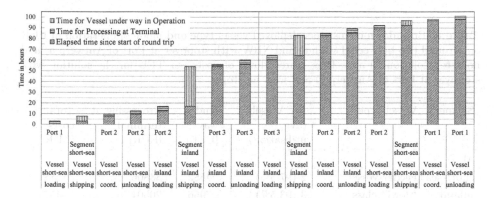

Fig. 3. Split of durations for individual operations (hatched horizontally in port and vertically under way) along a round trip between the T&L hub and NRW with a feeder and large inland vessel (Jowi). The cumulative sum shows the elapsed time (hatched diagonal) until the current operation (from left to right). Vessels are heading upstream/inbound first, left of the vertical line that indicates half way, and downstream on the way back.

As the non-stop solution reveals time savings, it is even worth to look at costs and their evolution. For the hinterland connection between the T&L hub and NRW a breakdown of costs per vessel service and by the two operational modes is given by Table 4 a) and b). These two tables deal with the costs per vessel, whereas Table 4 c) and d) present the costs per TEU. Comparing both paths by the total costs per TEU on a round trip the non-stop connection with the sea-going inland vessel is about 35% less expensive than the path including additional handlings at the parent onshore port between the large inland and the feeder vessel. As observed for the round trip durations, the sea-going inland vessel is slower and also more expensive. Costs per vessel are about 7% higher than for the combination of sea-going and inland vessel on the analysed hinterland connection. Looking at costs per TEU, the benefit is even more on the solution with two vessel types, since the capacity of the sea-going inland vessel is only 380 TEU. Thus, the sea-going inland vessel is 38% more expensive considering the costs during transit.

Another aspect can be observed at the partial costs in the two operational areas of short-sea and inland waterway shipping separately. Analysing costs per vessel service and operational area on the path with stopover, the feeder is much more expensive than the inland vessel, even though it completes only about a third of the distance on inland waterways. This is due to the high handling costs at the stopover. If the costs are normalised by the vessel capacity, the feeder vessel is slightly less expansive than the inland vessel on the inland waterway segment. Evaluating this split for the path with one vessel type, the short-sea segment is always less expensive, since the costs are almost equally distributed over both modes of operation (50.6% under way to 49.4% processing at the terminal).

Table 4. Breakdown of costs per deployed vessel type and mode of operation in EUR on a round trip between T&L hub and NRW with stopover at Port of Antwerp a) and non-stop solution b) as well as a breakdown of costs per TEU for the solution with stopover at Port of Antwerp c) and with no stopover d).

Segment	Vessel type	No. Vessels (avg. utilisation)	Under way [EUR]	Processing at terminal [EUR]	Total costs [EUR]
a)					
short-sea	Feeder vessel	2 (97.5%)	4582	33806	38388
inland	"Jowi" class	3 (93.5%)	7956	20501	28457
	Total costs in EUR		12538	54307	**66845**
b)					
short-sea	Sea-going inland	4 (94.2%)	4774	7118	11892
inland			8680	5990	14670
	Total costs in EUR		13453	13109	**26561**
c)					
short-sea	Feeder vessel	2 (97.5%)	6	46	52
inland	"Jowi" class	3 (93.5%)	16	40	56
	Total costs in	EUR/TEU	22	86	**108**
d)					
short-sea	Sea-going inland	4 (94.2%)	13	19	32
inland			23	16	39
	Total costs in	EUR/TEU	35	35	**70**

5   Conclusions

Regional cargo demands were analysed to assess the potential of different water-borne transport between hinterland ports and a floating T&L hub in coastal waters. A strategic simulation method was developed and applied to scenarios evaluating different paths of hinterland transport. Navigational and operational profiles for types of sea-going and inland vessels build the method's core in combination with a dedicated cost model. Round trip durations as well as transport costs for containers on relevant waterborne transports were calculated. Connections between the hub and the hinterland base on a cargo flow prognosis that focuses on established connections of the Port of Antwerp. If another waterborne transport is of interest, e. g. by short-sea shipping to other sea ports, a more extensive cargo flow analysis is required, which can be included in the developed model as a larger data base. The hinterland connection between the federal German state NRW and the T&L hub with a given cargo request was found to be representative for a relevant waterborne transport. Two feasible paths to fulfil the request with combinations of vessel services were compared, one with additional transhipment at the hubs parent port ashore and another one with a non-stop solution.

Servicing this cargo request on a path concatenated of two vessel services results in longer round trip durations and higher transport costs of about 35% per TEU than with the non-stop solution. The combination of short-sea and inland waterway shipping needs one more handling at a port ashore, here the Port of Antwerp. On the path with non additional stop, the transport costs of 70 EUR per TEU were estimated, while the path with an additional terminal service yielded about 108 EUR per TEU. The duration of a round trip along the non-stop path with the sea going inland vessel lasts up to 4.91 days which is about three hours faster than the path of two vessel services with stopover.

Moreover, it turned out that, as long as the demand scenario provides enough throughput of containers, the feeder vessel should be deployed in combination with the largest available inland vessel. Although, the sea going inland vessel is assumed sailing slower in coastal waterways, the non-stop solution is economically favourable as long as the depth of hinterland penetration permits it. Further research has to show if this may change when deep hinterland connections are serviced by inland waterway shipping, thus that an additional handling at the onshore port from the feeder to the inland vessel is negligible in terms of costs and time. An underestimated contribution to round trip durations is the vessel scheduling in ports, which can change the processing times at terminals significantly.

Acknowledgements. This project has received funding from the European Union's Horizon 2020 research and innovation programme under grant agreement No 774253. The opinions in this document reflect only the authors' view and in no way reflect the European Commission's opinions. The European Commission is not responsible for any use that may be made of the information it contains.

Nomenclature

Symbol	Description	Dimension
Latin Symbols		
B	Vessel Breadth	m
CC_S	Capital costs per hour	EUR/h
CF_S	Fuel costs per day	EUR/d
$CH_T(OH_T)$	Handling costs per TEU	EUR/TEU
CP_S	Personnel costs per day	EUR/d
CT_r	Container throughput on request r per day	TEU/d
$d_S(OA_S)$	Spatial distance covered by service s_i	km
g	Acceleration due to gravity	m/s^2
H_S	Significant wave height	m
L	Vessel length	m
m_j	Number of terminal services of type t_j	-
m_0	Zeroth spectral moment of $S(\omega)$	M^2
NC_S	Nominal number of cranes to un-/load the vessel	-
NM_S	Spreader capacity of service s_i per move	TEU
n_i	Number of vessel services of type s_i	-
OA	Operational area of service s_i or t_j	-
PM_T	Crane moves per hour	1/h
r	Cargo request per day	TEU/d
R_{AW}	Added resistance	N
R_T	Calm water resistance	N
s	Vessel service	-
$S(\omega)$	Energy density spectrum	m^2 s
t	Terminal service	-
T	Vessel draught	m
T_P	Peak period	s
u_i	Utilisation of vessel services of type s_i	-
UN_S	Nominal transport capacity of service s_i	TEU
v	Velocity	m/s or kn
v_{loss}	Velocity loss	-
$v_S(OA_S)$	Average velocity of vessel service s_i	m/s
$x_{r,p}$	Feasibility of path p with $x_{r,p} \in [0,1]$	-
$Z_{r,p}$	Transport costs on path p for cargo request r	EUR
Greek Symbols		
α	Constant scaling the spectrum $S(\omega)$	-
γ	Peak enhancement factor	-
σ	Factor modifying the shape of spectrum $S(\omega)$	-
$\tau_{r,p}$	Total duration to service request r on path p	h
τ_0	Minimum duration of processing a vessel in port	h
τ_i	Duration of service s_i under way in operation	h
τ_j	Duration of service t_j un-/loading a vessel	h
ω	Angular wave frequency	rad/s
ω_p	Angular peak frequency	rad/s
ζ_a	Wave amplitude	m
Indizes		
i	Type of vessel service s_i with $i \in [1,...,4]$	-
j	Type of terminal service t_j with $j \in [1,2,3]$	-

References

1. Kim, J., Morrison, J.R.: Erratum to: offshore port service concepts: classification and economic feasibility. Flex. Serv. Manuf. J. **24**, 246–247 (2012). https://doi.org/10.1007/s10696-011-9114-3

2. Baird, A.J., Rother, D.: Technical and economic evaluation of the floating container storage and transhipment terminal (FCSTT). Transp. Res. Part C Emer. Technol. **30**, 178–192 (2013). https://doi.org/10.1016/j.trc.2012.12.013
3. Totoloci, D.: Cargo and cargo streams - Deliverable 9.1. In: Horizon 2020 SpaceSea Project, Galati (2018)
4. Van den Berg, R., De Langen, P.W.: Hinterland strategies of port authorities: a case study of the port of Barcelona. Res. Transp. Econ. **33**(1), 6–14 (2011). https://doi.org/10.1016/j.retrec.2011.08.002
5. Dafnomilis, I., Duinkerken, M.B., Schott, D.L., Ley, J., Assbrock, G.: Optimization design of a floating modular port terminal. In: Kartnig, G., Zrnić, N., Bošnjak, S. (eds.) Proceedings of the XXIII International Conference on Material Handling, Constructions and Logistics 2019, MHCL, pp. 299–308. FME, Belgrade, September 2019
6. Konings, R., Kreutzberger, E., Maraš, V.: Major considerations in developing a hub-and-spoke network to improve the cost performance of container barge transport in the hinterland: the case of the port of Rotterdam. J. Transp. Geogr. **29**, 63–73 (2013). https://doi.org/10.1016/j.jtrangeo.2012.12.015
7. Shobayo, P., van Hassel, E.: Container barge congestion and handling in large seaports: a theoretical agent-based modeling approach. J. Shipp. Trade **4**(1), 1–26 (2019). https://doi.org/10.1186/s41072-019-0044-7
8. Li, S., Negenborn, R.R., Lodewijks, G.: Planning inland vessel operations in large seaports using a two-phase approach. Comput. Ind. Eng. **106**, 41–57 (2017). https://doi.org/10.1016/j.cie.2017.01.027
9. Vantorre, M., Eloot, K., Delefortrie, G.: Probabilistic regulation for Inland Vessels operating at sea as an alternative Hinterland connection for coastal harbours. Eur. Jo. Transp. Infrastruct. Res. **12**(1), 111–131 (2011)
10. Grossmann, H., Otto, A., Stiller, S., Wedemeier, J.: Strategy 2030 - Maritime Trade and Transport Logisitcs, Part A, p. 65 Fig. 39 Source Eurostat 2006 and Forecast HWWI, Hamburg (2006)
11. Statistisches Bundesamt (StBA, destatis.de) represented by Sarreither, D.: Güterverkehrsstatistik der Binnenschifffahrt 2016, Fachserie 8 Reihe 4, pp. 16–49, Wiesbaden (2017)
12. Nutsch, M.: Containerticker Modal Split Port of Antwerp. Journal Schiffahrt und Technik (SUT), p. 90. Schiffahrt und Technik Verlags GmbH, Sankt Augustin (August 2018)
13. Al Enezy, O., van Hassel, E., Sys, C., Vanelslander, T.: Developing a cost calculation model for inland navigation. Res. Transp. Bus. Manag. **23**, 64–74 (2017). https://doi.org/10.1016/j.rtbm.2017.02.006
14. Wiegmans, B., Konings, R.: Intermodal inland waterway transport: modelling conditions influencing its cost competitiveness. Asian J. Shipp. Logist. **31**(2), 273–294 (2015). https://doi.org/10.1016/j.ajsl.2015.06.006
15. PSA Antwerp Homepage: General rates for terminal operations and CFS activities 2018. https://www.psa-antwerp.be/sites/default/files/PSAAntwerpCFSandquay workrates20180101CFSAE.pdf. Accessed 4 Apr 2019
16. Duisburger Hafen AG (duisport) Homepage : Tarif über Hafen- und Ufergeld der Duisburger Hafen AG und Hafen Duisburg-Rheinhausen GmbH. https://www.duisport.de/wp-content/uploads/2018/07/Tarif-Hafen-und-Ufergeld-01-01-2017.pdf. Accessed 4 Apr 2019
17. Holtrop, J., Mennen, G.G.J.: An approximate power prediction method. Int. Shipbuild. Prog. **29**(335), 166–170 (1982)

18. Ley, J., Sigmund, S., el Moctar, B.: Added resistance of ships in waves. In: Proceedings of the 33th International Conference on Ocean, Offshore and Arctic Engineering, San Francisco, USA (2014)
19. Hasselmann, K., et al.: Measurements of Wind-wave Growth and Swell Decay During the Joint North Sea Wave Project (JONSWAP), Ergänzungsheft zur Deutschen Hydrographischen Zeitschrift Reihe 12 (1973). 95 pages

An Optimization Model for Defining Storage Strategies for Export Yards in Container Terminals: A Case Study

Daniela Ambrosino[✉] and Haoqi Xie

Department of Economic and Business Studies, Università di Genova,
Via Vivaldi, 5, 16126 Genova, Italy
ambrosin@economia.unige.it, valerioxhq163@gmail.com

Abstract. In maritime container terminals, yards have a primary role in permitting the efficient management of import and export flows. In this work, we focus on export containers and storage strategies to minimize the space used in the export yard. The main aim is to define the rules to use to allocate containers into the bay-locations of the yard for minimizing both the number of bay-locations used and the empty slots. The storage rules are related to the configuration of classes of weight in terms of the number of classes to use and the weight limitations of each class. The idea is to use a 0–1 linear programming model to periodically modify the storage rules for defining the groups of containers that can be stored together. This model uses updated input data derived by periodical data analysis. A real case study related to an Italian terminal is reported and preliminary results are given.

Keywords: Export containers · Storage policies · Optimization model · Yard space minimization

1 Introduction and Literature Review

Maritime container terminals are generally recognised as crucial intermodal change nodes in the logistic chains. In fact, about 80% of the world trade is realized via sea (UNCTAD, 2018) and the most part of general cargo is containerized. Maritime container terminals connect the seaside to the landside through storage yards [1]. Their relative services, reliabilities and infrastructures are pointed out by [2,3]. The import and export processes and the related problems in a container terminal have been analysed together with the useful optimization approaches in [4–6].

The storage yards have a primary role in permitting the efficient management of import and export flows [7]. The yard is an intermediate area between the frontier and the backward of a terminal used to store, control and handle the containers. This area occupies a considerable part in a terminal and can be divided into some segmentation for the inbound and outbound containers based

© Springer Nature Switzerland AG 2020
E. Lalla-Ruiz et al. (Eds.): ICCL 2020, LNCS 12433, pp. 119–132, 2020.
https://doi.org/10.1007/978-3-030-59747-4_8

on the process of import and export, respectively. Referring to the location of the input/output container points, two different configurations of layout are possible: Asian and European layout [8].

The container yard is basically divided into numerous *Blocks*, each one composed by a given number of *Bays*. Each bay is formed by several *Rows*; containers are thus stacked in *Tiers* [9]. In modern container terminals, the maximum tier to stock a container in a block is 4 and the utilization ratio ranges from 70% to 90% [10]. The exact position of each container is described by a code like the following: A01-07-03-1 that means that the container is stored in the Area/Block A01, bay 07, row 03, first tier.

An import container is unloaded from a vessel and transported to a pre-assigned block either in the import yard or in the rail yard, in accordance with the rail/road transport modality used to send it in the interland [11]. Dealing with export containers, the procedure is reversed. Containers approaching the terminal by trains or trucks and waiting to leave the terminal by ships are stored in the export yard. Dedicated areas for reefer, open top, tank, out of gauge, dangerous, transit and empty containers are usually present in container terminals.

Efficiency is always a major aim to be considered: efficiency in both picking containers from the yard, loading a ship/a train and reducing congestion inside the terminal when trucks are unloaded/loaded. The typical operations performed in the yard are the storage and the retrieval of containers, dispatching and routing of material handling equipment. All the related problems have been studied by many researchers. [7] presents a review and a classification scheme for the storage yard operations in container terminals.

In this paper, we consider an European layout where import and export yards are independent, and we deal with export standard containers. Each container is characterized by its type, size, weight and destination; these characteristics are important when defining the storage strategy. The ideal rule is to store together containers having both the same characteristics and the same loading vessel, in order to reduce the operation time and avoid bottleneck in the terminal when loading the ship [12,13]. This strategy is known as *consignment* strategy. Note that, this strategy requires large storage space (for example more than random policies [14]), but on the other hand permits to improve the storage yard operations during the vessel containers loading in terms of productivity of both pick up operations in the bays and movements of material handling equipment among bays. Note that when a random policy is used, generally in European layout terminals, another strategy follows to improve the efficiency in the loading process; this strategy can be either a pre-marshaling strategy that permits to reorganize the container stacking beforehand, in order to reduce reshuffles, or a re-marshaling strategy that permits to move containers from their current storage location to a location closer to their vessel.

The purpose of this work is to set the best rules for defining which containers to store together (i.e., in a bay), that is the characteristics of containers for applying the consignment strategy. In particular, the idea is to monitor the outbound flows in such a way to periodically update the characteristics to use in the consignment strategy as better explained in the next section.

A 0–1 linear programming model is proposed to define the characteristics to lead the storage strategy in such a way to both minimize the space used in the export yard and grant a certain level of efficiency in the terminal during the pick up of containers in the yard and during the containers loading on vessels.

This problem can be included in the class of storage space assignment to containers [7]. The storage space assignment deals with finding the best allocation of containers to storage spaces, in order to reduce the storage yard operations cycle time. The assignment can be related to either individual containers or groups of containers. Note that the present problem differs from the ones proposed in the existing literature for the specific decisions to take, the evaluation criteria, and also for the tactical contest, as explained in the next section.

Concerning the storage allocation for export containers, in [15] Light, Medium and Heavy weight classes, destination and size are used to decide an exact slot for an individual container. [16] tries to increase the loading operation efficiency by considering the travel distances of equipment. [17] includes new constraints related to the staking height and specific stack configurations. In [18] the optimal storage location is determined taking into consideration the container handling schedules.

[12] formulates the storage space allocation problem by using a rolling-horizon approach in a temporary working period; the aim is to disperse appropriate quantity of containers to each block and balance the workload of yard equipment. [19] uses a mixed-integer programming model to define the number of yard bays and a hybrid sequence algorithm to select the exact slots for storing containers. [20] focuses on the space allocation problem in the short-term. The authors introduce the new concept "segment" to define a block. Two boundaries are brought in as shifts and vessels constraints for each segment.

In [21] four rules to determine the number of blocks to allocate the groups of export containers are proposed. Rules are fixed and the main aim is to optimize the movements of yard equipment and the distance between the yard and the quay. Moreover, the authors evaluate the influence of the yard size on the efficiency of loading operations.

The reminder of this paper is organized as follows. The problem under investigation is described in Sect. 2; the 0–1 linear model is presented in Sect. 3. In Sect. 4, a case study related to an Italian maritime terminal is detailed. Finally, conclusions and future works are outlined in Sect. 5.

2   Problem Description

Let us consider an export yard splits into different zones according to the transport services offered by the terminal, and let us focus on the blocks dedicated to a particular service, that is dedicated to receive containers to be loaded on the vessels of the considered service. The problem consists in defining the best rules to use when storing containers in the bays of these blocks. Blocks are characterized by different capacities, depending on bays, rows and tiers. The capacity of each bay can be equal to 4, 8, 12 and 16, either 20' or 40' containers, depending on the number of tiers and the number of rows that, in this case, range from 1 to 4, as sketched in Figure 1. For example, Block 03 in Fig.1 is composed of 16 bays, with 4 rows and 4 tiers each; thus, each bay has a capacity of 16 containers.

In this work, we will refer to the cells belonging to the same bay of a block as *bay-locations*; only 20' bay-locations with a capacity of 8, 12 and 16 containers are considered. A bay-locations with 8 containers capacity has 8 slots in which we can store containers; the general aim is to fulfill the bay-locations minimizing the empty slots. For the storage of 40' containers, two contiguous 20' bays are required.

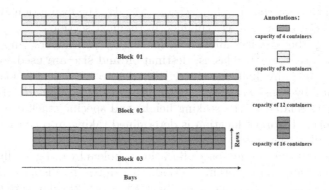

Fig. 1. Yard blocks with different capacities - view from above.

To define rules to store containers together means to list the characteristics that containers may have to be stored in the same bay-locations. These rules must grant an efficient pick-up and loading process. The efficiency is related to the handling equipment of the terminal. Following the instruction of ships and yards planners of the container terminal we are involved with, we prefer to store together containers having the same loading vessel, port of destination, size and "class of weight". These rules permit to have homogeneous containers in each bay-locations, i.e., to be able to pick them up in sequence for their loading on board, and to optimize the work of the reach stackers during their pick-up in the yard.

The containers included in the analysis have the following characteristics:

Size: 20 ft (20') and 40 ft (40') containers. The 20' container is the standard size and referred as a TEU. A 40' container is equivalent to two 20' (2 TEU). For storing a 40' container, two contiguous 20' bay-locations are required, and for security reasons, a 40' container cannot be stored under two 20' containers. Generally, stacks of one size (i.e., either 20' or 40') are preferred, both in the yard and on board.

Type: standard containers, 20' and 40' box and 40' HC containers are analysed. Box and HC containers are often mixed in the yard bay-locations. The choice to have bay-locations devoted to HC depends on both the pick-up and the loading strategy used during the loading process. The terminal we are involved with prefers to complete the pick- up process in a bay-locations and empty it before moving the reach stacker to another bay-locations. This means that, in case of a bay-locations devoted to HC, they transfer from the yard to the vessel a sequence of HC containers. If, due to the loading policy, they are stored on board in the same stack, this can create an inefficient usage of the vertical space in the hold of the ship.

Destination: containers are grouped in accordance with their destination, i.e. the port of call of the vessel of the considered service. In fact, containers, on board, are generally grouped for homogeneous destination, i.e., either a bay of the vessel, or a part of it, is dedicated to store containers of the same destination.

Weight: usually, empty 20', 40' and 40' HC containers weight, respectively, 2.3, 3.9, 4.1 tons. The full container weight can vary from 5 to more than 33 tons depending on cargo and loading degree. This standardization prioritizes to store containers in the same bay with similar weights also respecting the requirement of safety, generally saying that the weight of the container stored in a given tier has to be no greater than the weight of the container stored in tier below it, within a given tolerance. Many terminals group containers according to the weight classes, i.e., containers belonging to the same weight class can be stored together; the most common configuration used is based on three classes: Light (from 5 tons to 15 tons); Medium (from 15 tons to 25 tons); Heavy (over 25 tons).

The weight limitations of each class and the number of classes used for defining the storage rules have a significant impact on the space used in the yard, varying the number of containers of each group, and the number of groups to manage. The number of groups to manage corresponds to the required *patterns* of bay-locations.

Let us suppose to have to create 3 different patterns of bay-locations for each destination, for respecting the type and size rules (see Fig. 2). If we use 3 weight classes, each one of these bay-locations will generate 3 other patterns one for each weight class, thus having 9 patterns of bay-locations to manage. Moreover, the number of the required bay-locations of each pattern depends on the number of the containers of each group, and it is strongly related to the different weight limitations imposed for each weight class.

We consider the possibility of having to choose among 2, 3 and 4 classes. We will refer to the chosen class of weight as *Class configuration*. Each Class configuration can be characterized by many weight limitations, here *Weight configurations*.

Let us give an example: consider a class configuration with 2 classes: Light and Heavy. For this configuration 3 alternative weight configurations are considered, i.e. 1–23/23–33, 1–18/18–33 and 1–14/14–33. In the first example, 1–23/23–33, Light containers weight ranges from 1 ton to 23 tons, while Heavy containers weight ranges from 23 to 33 tons.

As already said, the basic rule is to store together containers with the same characteristics; these containers are considered of the same group. Note that, the

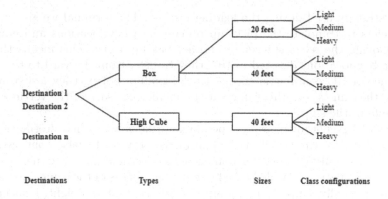

Fig. 2. Decision tree for defining patterns of bay-locations.

classes of weight, in terms of the number of classes to use and the weight limitations of each class, are key elements among the characteristics of containers (destinations, types, sizes and weights) when implementing the storage strategy. Thus, given a set C of containers characterized by their size, type, weight, destination, being representative of the average transport demand of a given service, the problem consists in deciding how to group them in order to minimize the space used in the export yard. We have to define the set of characteristics of the different patterns of bay-locations and the capacity of each bay-locations used to store containers. The objective is to use the minimum number of bay-locations and to minimize the total empty slots in the bay-locations. Also, the storage of box and HC in the same bay-locations is penalized. The 0–1 linear programming model used for that purpose is presented in the next section.

Note that this problem emerges at the tactical level for defining rules to use in the operative contests. These rules are not fixed once and ever adopt; the idea is to modify them following the trend of the export flow demand. Consider, for example, a service offered by the terminal, and suppose that the number of containers for a destination of this service increases; we are interested to observe which groups of containers increase. Only in this way, we are able to decide if the existing rules are adequate or not, and in this latter case, how to modify them.

3 The 0–1 Linear Programming Formulation

In this section, a basic 0–1 linear programming model to solve the problem described in Sect. 2 is presented. Table 1 gives the useful notation. The resulting model is the following:

$$Min \sum_{d \in D} \sum_{j \in B} y d_{dj} + \sum_{j \in B} z_j + \alpha \sum_{j \in B} m_j \qquad (1)$$

Subject to:

$$\sum_{j \in B} x_{ij} = 1 \quad \forall i \in C \tag{2}$$

$$\sum_{i \in C: d_i = d} x_{ij} \leq M y d_{dj} \quad \forall d \in D, \forall j \in B \tag{3}$$

$$\sum_{d \in D} y d_{dj} \leq 1 \quad \forall j \in B \tag{4}$$

$$\sum_{i \in C: s_i = s} x_{ij} \leq M y s_{sj} \quad \forall s \in S, \forall j \in B \tag{5}$$

$$\sum_{s \in S} y s_{sj} \leq 1 \quad \forall j \in B \tag{6}$$

$$\sum_{i \in C} x_{ij} \leq q y q_{qj} \quad \forall q \in Q, \forall j \in B \tag{7}$$

$$\sum_{q \in Q} y q_{qj} \leq 1 \quad \forall j \in B \tag{8}$$

$$\sum_{i \in C: h_i = h} x_{ij} \leq M y h_{hj} \quad \forall h \in H, \forall j \in B \tag{9}$$

$$\sum_{h \in H} y h_{hj} \leq 1 + m_j \quad \forall j \in B \tag{10}$$

$$y q_{qj} + y s_{sj} - 1 \leq t_{jqs} \quad \forall j \in B, \forall q \in Q, \forall s \in S \tag{11}$$

$$\sum_{j \in B} (t_{jq20} + 2 t_{jq40}) \leq n_q \quad \forall q \in Q \tag{12}$$

$$w_i x_{ij} \leq \sum_{f \in F} \sum_{w \in W_f} u_{wf} y w_{wfj} \quad \forall i \in C, \forall j \in B \tag{13}$$

$$w_i x_{ij} \geq \sum_{f \in F} \sum_{w \in W_f} l_{wf} y w_{wfj} \quad \forall i \in C, \forall j \in B \tag{14}$$

$$\sum_{w \in W_f} y w_{wfj} \leq 1 v_f \quad \forall j \in B, \forall f \in F \tag{15}$$

$$\sum_{f \in F} v_f = 1 \tag{16}$$

$$\sum_{q \in Q} q y q_{qj} - \sum_{i \in C} x_{ij} \leq z_j \quad \forall j \in B \tag{17}$$

Table 1. Useful notation for model (1)–(17)

Sets	Definitions
B	Set of bay-locations
C	Set of containers
D	Set of ports of destination
H	Set of heights (Box, High Cube)
S	Set of sizes (20, 40 ft)
Q	Set of bay-locations capacities (8, 12)
F	Set of configurations
W_f	Set of classes for configuration f, $\forall f \in F$

Data	Definitions
d_i	Destination of container i, $\forall i \in C$
s_i	Size of container i, $\forall i \in C$
h_i	Height of container i, $\forall i \in C$
w_i	Weight of container i, $\forall i \in C$
u_{wf}	Weight upper bound of class w in configuration f, $\forall w \in W_f$, $\forall f \in F$
l_{wf}	Weight lower bound of class w in configuration f, $\forall w \in W_f$, $\forall f \in F$
n_q	Max number of 20 bay-locations of capacity q, $\forall q \in Q$
M	Big M, parameter used to fix to one some binary variables
α	Parameter used to penalise the storage of box and HC in the same bay-locations

Variables	
$x_{ij} \in \{0,1\}$	$\forall i \in C, \forall j \in B, x_{ij} = 1$ if container i is stored in bay-locations j
$yd_{dj} \in \{0,1\}$	$\forall d \in D, \forall j \in B, yd_{dj} = 1$ if in bay-locations j are stored containers with destination d
$yh_{hj} \in \{0,1\}$	$\forall h \in H$, $\forall j \in B$, $yh_{hj} = 1$ if in bay-locations j are stored containers with height h
$ys_{sj} \in \{0,1\}$	$\forall s \in S$, $\forall j \in B$, $ys_{sj} = 1$ if in bay-locations j are stored containers having size s
$yq_{qj} \in \{0,1\}$	$\forall q \in Q$, $\forall j \in B$, $yq_{qj} = 1$ if bay-locations j has capacity q
$m_j \in \{0,1\}$	$\forall j \in B$, $m_j = 1$ if in bay-locations j are stored both Box and HC containers
$t_{jqs} \in \{0,1\}$	$\forall j \in B$, $\forall q \in Q, \forall s \in S$, $t_{jqs} = 1$ if bay-locations j with capacity q are stored containers of size s
$v_f \in \{0,1\}$	$\forall f \in F$, $v_f = 1$ if configuration f is chosen
$yw_{wfj} \in \{0,1\}$	$\forall f \in F$, $\forall w \in W_f, \forall j \in B$, $yw_{wfj} = 1$ if weight class w of configuration f is assigned to bay-locations j
$z_j \geq 0$	$\forall j \in B$, number of empty slots in bay-locations j

Equation (1) is the objective function that minimizes the number of bay-locations used, the empty slots in the bay-locations, and penalizes the storage of box and HC in the same bay-locations.

Thanks to constraints (2) each container must be stored in one bay-locations. Constraints (3)–(8) assign only one destination, one size and one capacity to each bay-locations. Note that M can be fixed equal to 16 (that is the maximum number of containers to store in a bay-locations) in constraints (3), (5) and (9).

Constraints (9) and (10) assign the height to each bay-locations; (10) fixed to one variables m_j when in bay-locations j both box and HC are stored. Equations (11) define variables t_{jqs} that indicate if bay-locations j has capacity q and size s, information necessary to compute the number of bay-locations of a given capacity, used for 20' and 40', with respect to the number of bay-locations of the corresponding capacity available in the yard (12).

Thanks to constraints (13) and (14) a container can be assigned to a bay-locations only if its weight is within the maximum and minimum weight limitations imposed to the bay-locations by the weight configuration assigned to it (15). Note that the weight configuration assigned to the bay-locations depends on the chosen class configuration (16). Thanks to constraint (16) only one configuration can be chosen. In (17) the number of empty slots in each bay-locations is computed.

4   Case Study

In this section, the case study of an Italian maritime terminal is introduced. Thanks to historical data analysis, together with a scenario analysis on different strategies to store export containers in the yard, we noted that it is possible to save space acting on the weight class configurations. Higher savings can be obtained if the storage strategies are periodically modified to take into account the real containers flows and their trend.

The rules for grouping containers and the bay-locations patterns resulting by solving the model, represent the parameters that are inserted in the TOS (Terminal Operating System) used by the terminal to manage containers when approaching the terminal by trucks or by trains. The idea is to modify these parameters when there is a change in the transport demand. How to modify them is determined by the mathematical model (1)–(17) that is solved using average updated input data information reflecting the trend of the transport demand.

In the following we report the analysis related to one of the transport services of the terminal under investigation. This service has a ship once a week; the ship loads containers for 9 destinations. The historical data analysis for computing the input for the model (1)–(17) is based on 2 months, i.e., 9 trips.

In the following figures, some results of this analysis are shown. Figure 3 shows the number of containers loaded in the last 9 trips. Containers are split in accordance with their destination; the line chart represents the average data of total trips for each destination.

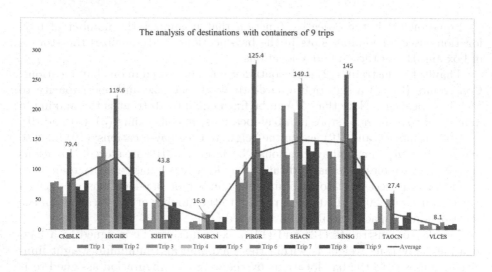

Fig. 3. Containers loaded split for their destination.

Distinguishing containers according to their size and their height (20' box, 40' box and HC), we obtained the graph reported in Fig. 4. The average number of loaded containers is 717.4, 33.74% are 20' box containers, while the 40' box and HC are, respectively, 12.94% and 53.3%.

The last analysed characteristic is the weight: the heaviest containers weigh 32.5 tons while the lightest ones 2.5 tons. The average weight of the containers is 18.7 tons. The class configuration used in this period is based on three classes:

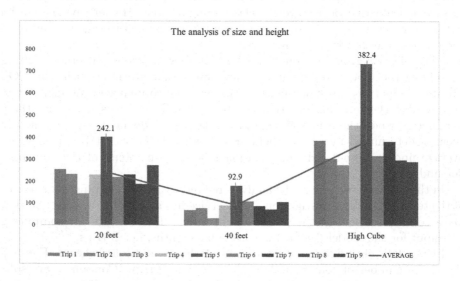

Fig. 4. Containers loaded split for their size and height

containers that weigh from 1 ton to 10.8 tons are pertained to *Light* class, while from 10.8 tons to 21.6 tons are in *Medium* and from 21.6 tons to 32.5 tons are in the *Heavy*. Figure 5 reveals the percentage of each class of weight loaded in each trip. The line chart in the Fig. 5 represents the average percentage of each class of weight in the 9 trips: Light containers represent 25.31% while 28.69% are Medium and 46.01% are Heavy.

Here below, we report the results obtained by applying model (1)–(17). It has been encoded in Mathematical Programming Language (MPL) and solved by the commercial solver GUROBI on a computer Intel Core i7.

Note that model (1)–(17) has been solved for one destination a time with a time limit of one hour. Some instances have been solved in less than one second (i.e., 3–4–8–9). The CPU time grows when the number of containers increases and larger instances require 30 min. The decomposition of the problem is possible since containers are always grouped according to their destination; moreover, we relaxed the capacity constraints on the number of bay-locations (the only shared resource) for checking it when the problem is solved for all the destinations. Note that this decomposition permits to choose the most appropriate weight class configuration for each destination (instead of only one for the whole vessel/trip).

In Table 2, the first column shows the 9 destinations and the number of containers to load for each of them. The second column shows the number of bay-locations used for storing the containers, while the third column reveals the number of empty slots in the bay-locations used to store containers. The following column indicates the number of bay-locations that combine Box and High Cube. In the last column, the weight configuration of each destination is shown. Note that, we solved the model by choosing among 3 different configurations (2, 3, and 4 classes) and for each class among 4–6 weight configurations (4 when two classes are considered and 6 in the other cases).

Analyzing the obtained solutions, we have computed the fulfill rate that is the occupancy of bay-locations computed as the ratio between the number of

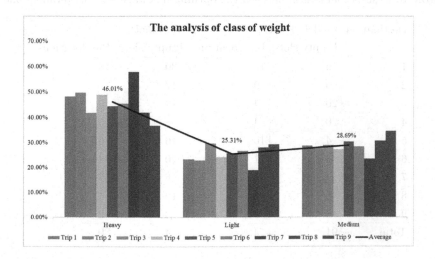

Fig. 5. The percentage of class of weight of containers loaded on the 9 trips.

Table 2. The obtained results

Destination-containers	Bay-locations used	Empty slots	Bay-locations combining Box/HC	Weight configuration
1–86	10	6	1	Light/Heavy
2–83	9	9	0	Light/Medium/Heavy
3–16	4	20	1	Light/Heavy
4–16	4	20	2	Light/Medium/Heavy
5–152	15	4	0	Light/Heavy
6–108	11	4	2	Light/Medium/Heavy
7–152	15	4	2	Light/Heavy
8–20	3	8	2	Light/Medium/Heavy
9–13	3	15	2	Light/Medium/Heavy
Tot	75	91	12	–

Note:
In Light/Heavy configuration the weight limits are following:
Light: from 1 ton to 23 tons; Heavy: from 23 tons to 33 tons;
In Light/Medium/Heavy configuration the weight limits are following:
Light: from 1 ton to 18 tons; Medium: 18 tons to 27 tons; Heavy: from 27 tons to 33 tons.

stored containers and the capacity of the bay-locations. This rate ranges from 44.44% to 97.43%, and it is on average 87.78%. This rate results higher than that obtained by the terminal 82.82%.

Table 3 shows a comparison between the results obtained by using the proposed approach and the real storage plan of the terminal. We can note that the proposed approach permits to obtain better results both in terms of empty slots

Table 3. Results comparison between the optimized storage and the terminal one.

Destination	Model (1)–(17)		Terminal	
	Empty slots	Bay-locations	Empty slots	Bay-locations
1	6	10	30	15
2	9	9	17	12
3	20	4	12	5
4	20	4	8	5
5	4	16	16	16
6	4	11	20	14
7	4	15	16	17
8	8	3	12	4
9	15	3	3	2
Total	91	74	134	89

and bay-locations. The savings are on average 32.83% and 13.79% in terms of empty slots and bay-locations, respectively.

5 Conclusion

This work focuses on the possibility of optimizing the storage space in an export container yard. Considering the contradiction between the huge quantity of containers and the yard's limitation, the main aim is to save spaces as more as possible while facilitating the container loading operations on vessels. A model for this purpose has been introduced. The idea is to plan the yard and to adequate it in accordance with the changes in the transport demand. The output of the model is the input parameters of the TOS of the terminal.

The preliminary results related to the case study seem to be promising. An extensive experimental campaign will be performed in the future. moreover, we will evaluate the possibility of mixing containers in a bay-locations in order to save space. Finally, more restrictions and more types of containers such as reefer will be taken into consideration.

References

1. Gouvernal, E., Lavaud-Letilleul, V., Slack, B.: Transport and logistics hubs: separating fact from fiction. In: Integrating Seaports and Trade Corridors, pp. 83–98 (2016)
2. Chen, S.L., Jeevan, J., Cahoon, S.: Malaysian container seaport-hinterland connectivity: Status, challenges and strategies. Asian J. Ship. Logist. **32**(3), 127–138 (2016)
3. Acciaro, A., Mckinnon, A.: Efficient hinterland transport infrastructure and services for large container ports, international transport forum (2013). https://tinyurl.com/y5m9fzvt
4. Steenken, D., Voß, S., Stahlbock, R.: Container terminal operation and operations research-a classification and literature review. OR Spect. **26**(1), 3–49 (2004)
5. Günther, H.O., Kim, K.H.: Container terminals and terminal operations (2006)
6. Stahlbock, R., Voß, S.: Operations research at container terminals: a literature update. OR Spect **30**(1), 1–52 (2008)
7. Carlo, H.J., Vis, I.F., Roodbergen, K.J.: Storage yard operations in container terminals: literature overview, trends, and research directions. Eur. J. Oper. Res. **235**(2), 412–430 (2014)
8. Wiese, J., Suhl, L., Kliewer, N.: Mathematical models and solution methods for optimal container terminal yard layouts. OR Spect. **32**(3), 427–452 (2010)
9. Legato, P., Canonaco, P., Mazza, R.M.: Yard crane management by simulation and optimisation. Marit. Econ. Logist. **11**(1), 36–57 (2009)
10. Sha, M., Zhou, X., Qin, T.B., Yu, D.Y., Qiu, H.L.: Study on layout optimization and simulation of container yard. Ind. Eng. Manag. 2 (2013)
11. Xie, Y., Song, D.P.: Optimal planning for container prestaging, discharging, and loading processes at seaport rail terminals with uncertainty. Transp. Res. Part E: Logist. Transp. Rev. **119**, 88–109 (2018)

12. Zhang, C., Liu, J., Wan, Y.W., Murty, K., Linn, R.: Storage space allocation in container terminals. Transp. Res. Part B Methodol. **37**, 883–903 (2003)
13. Saanen, Y., Dekker, R.: Intelligent stacking as way out of congested yards part 1. Port Technol. Int. **31**, 87–92 (2007)
14. Koster, R.D., Le-Duc, T., Roodbergen, K.J.: Design and control of warehouse order picking: A literature review. Eur. J. Oper. Res. **182**(2), 481–501 (2007)
15. Kim, K.H., Park, Y.M., Ryu, K.R.: Deriving decision rules to locate export containers in container yards. Eur. J. Oper. Res. **124**(1), 89–101 (2000)
16. Kim, K.H., Park, K.T.: A note on a dynamic space-allocation method for outbound containers. Eur. J. Oper. Res. **148**(1), 92–101 (2003)
17. Zhang, C., Wu, T., Kim, K.H., Miao, L.: Conservative allocation models for outbound containers in container terminals. Eur. J. Oper. Res. **238**(1), 155–165 (2014)
18. Kozan, E., Preston, P.: Mathematical modelling of container transfers and storage locations at seaport terminals. In: Kim, K.H., Günther, H.-O. (eds.) Container Terminals and Cargo Systems, pp. 87–105. Springer, Heidelberg (2007). https://doi.org/10.1007/978-3-540-49550-5_5
19. Chen, L., Lu, Z.: The storage location assignment problem for outbound containers in a maritime terminal. Int. J. Prod. Econ. **135**(1), 73–80 (2012). Advances in Optimization and Design of Supply Chains
20. Zhou, C., Wang, W., Li, H.: Container reshuffling considered space allocation problem in container terminals. Transp. Res. Part E: Logist. Transp. Rev. **136**, 101869 (2020)
21. Woo, Y.J., Kim, K.H.: Estimating the space requirement for outbound container inventories in port container terminals. Int. J. Prod. Econ. **133**(1), 293–301 (2011)

Vehicle Routing and Scheduling

Dynamic Assignment Vehicle Routing Problem with Time Windows

Kim J. Los[1,2], Frank Phillipson[1(✉)] (ID), Elisah A. van Kempen[1],
Hans J. Quak[1,3], and Uilke Stelwagen[1]

[1] TNO, PO Box 96800, 2509 JE The Hague, The Netherlands
frank.phillipson@tno.nl
[2] Erasmus University, Rotterdam, The Netherlands
[3] Breda University of Applied Sciences, Breda, The Netherlands

Abstract. Offering time windows to receivers of last-mile delivery is becoming a distinguishing factor. However, we see that in practice carriers have to create routes for their vehicles based on destination information, that is just being revealed when a parcel arrives in the depot. The parcel has to be assigned directly to a vehicle, making this a Dynamic Assignment Vehicle Routing Problem. Incorporating time windows is hard in this case. In this paper an approach is presented to solve this problem including Time Windows. A comparison is made with a real observation and with a solution method for the base problem.

Keywords: Home delivery · Dynamic Vehicle Routing · Time Windows

1 Introduction

Last-mile delivery has become increasingly important with the rise of e-commerce [1]. This is often complicated by the continuous stream of new demand. Ideally, routing decisions are made while having complete information regarding the daily demand. Unfortunately, such a static setting is often unrealistic and more often one has to work in a dynamic environment. Last-mile delivery falls in the area of Vehicle Routing Problems (VRP) [2]. To avoid ambiguities, we use the terms carrier, shipper and receiver. In last-mile delivery, the carrier transports the goods sent by the shipper to the receiver. In [3] and [4], the Dynamic Assignment Vehicle Routing Problem (DA-VRP) is introduced. Here, the planning is done dynamically, meaning that the planning is built up in time, where information is added during the planning process. In contrast to the common dynamic VRP [5], planning is done in advance, where the route is not being executed yet. This gives the possibility to change the order per vehicle, but not to interchange between the vehicles. In this work we extend the DA-VRP, by introducing time-windows to the problem, making it the Dynamic Assignment Vehicle Routing Problem with Time Windows (DA-VRPTW). We will first give a rationale for this.

© Springer Nature Switzerland AG 2020
E. Lalla-Ruiz et al. (Eds.): ICCL 2020, LNCS 12433, pp. 135–150, 2020.
https://doi.org/10.1007/978-3-030-59747-4_9

An important factor for the perceived quality of the delivery service is the variety of delivery options a receiver can choose from [6,7]. Examples of delivery options are next-day delivery, same-day delivery, alternative address delivery or predefined time window delivery. Here, time windows offer the benefit of potentially serving as a communication tool towards the receiver, allowing companies to increase the success rate of their deliveries. Naturally, a decrease in the number of delivery failures will increase the receiver's satisfaction level. Nonetheless, as the implementation of time windows reduces the efficiency of the routing, a trade-off has to be made between receiver's satisfaction and delivery costs. The possibilities to improve the efficiency of home delivery are investigated by [8]. They conclude that contact with the receiver can significantly increase the efficiency. In addition, a process called address intelligence seems to hold great potential by using historical data as a way of predicting future deliveries. Other promising options that apply to home delivery are the possibility to use sliding time windows [9] or to deliver at a different location, within a predefined time window or change the delivery time. Agatz [10] tackles the problem of selecting time windows to offer in different regions. In other words, receivers in certain regions are provided with specific choices to accommodate the ability to construct cost efficient routes. The results emphasise the trade-off between delivery efficiency and receiver's satisfaction since offering narrow time windows is convenient for the receiver but greatly reduces the efficiency of the routes.

To be able to offer time windows in the dynamic setting, we need to solve the DA-VRPTW. Note that already the VRPTW is as variant of the VRP a NP-hard problem [11], meaning that the DA-VRPTW is even more challenging. Every time a new request is received the DA-VRPTW can be seen as a static VRPTW. Pillat et al. [2] provide a review of the dynamic VRP, including a general description of the problem, an explanation of the degree of dynamism, possible applications and solution methods. A multi-objective Dynamic Vehicle Routing Problem with Fuzzy Time Windows (DVRPFTW) is presented and solved by [12] using a Genetic Algorithm. In this problem, part of the receiver's demand is known beforehand and the other part is revealed during the execution of the routes. To tackle the dynamic aspect of this problem a real-time optimisation method is proposed and a sequence of multi-objective static VRPFTW models is solved. After receiving a new request the VRPFTW will re-optimise the routing plan and information about route changes is communicated to the drivers of the vehicles. A comparable approach is chosen by [13], who proposes a meta heuristic based on an Adaptive Large Neighbourhood Search algorithm. Another Neighbourhood Search approach, benchmarked against the best known algorithms can be found in [14]. An Ant Colony Optimisation method is developed by [15] to solve a broad range of DVRPTW. Their approach seems to be very flexible and capable of attaining a good feasible solution within a limited amount of time. Additional research into the assignment of time windows to receivers is performed by [16] followed by an improved algorithm in terms of computation time and size of the instances by [17]. Both develop a branch-and-cut algorithm to solve a two-stage optimisation problem. In the first-stage, before the demand is known, time windows are assigned to the receivers and in the second stage, after the demand is revealed, vehicle routes are constructed satisfying the assigned time windows.

To summarise, the literature contains an extensive body of research concerning the static and dynamic version of the VRPTW. It turns out that heuristic approaches can often be improved by the use of local search methods or meta heuristics. A frequently used approach is to solve the DVRPTW as a sequence of static VRPTW. After a new request is received, the solution is re-optimised allowing the algorithm to reassign receivers which are not serviced yet by the vehicles, which is not allowed in the DA-VRPTW case.

In this work we propose a method to solve the DA-VRPTW and gain insight in the trade-off between delivery efficiency and receiver's satisfaction in this case. This problem was not studied earlier in literature. The remainder of this paper is as follows. In Sect. 2 a problem description is provided. In Sect. 3 the proposed algorithm is presented. Next, in Sect. 4 results of this approach for a case study are presented and benchmarked, for the case without time windows, against the realisation in practice of the case study and to the results of the approach of [3]. In Sect. 5, conclusions are drawn.

2   Problem Description

In this paper, the DA-VRPTW is considered, based on the definition in [3] and [4]. The problem considers a single depot, where parcels arrive both directly from receivers and from other (international) depots. The aim is to assign the incoming parcels to one of the vehicles, such that the routes along the receivers can be carried out at the lowest cost without violating the time windows and vehicle capacity constraints. Factors influencing the cost are the total travelling distance and the total driving hours of the vehicles. In achieving an efficient solution one should therefore attempt to minimise these factors.

Throughout the evening and night trucks arrive at the depot, where the parcels are unloaded. In the depot, the parcels are scanned and information about the location and preferred time window becomes known. We assume that this information, which parcels are arriving and what their destination is, is not available to the depot prior to this scan. Where this looks like a deficiency in the information management, this is not uncommon, even at larger carriers. After scanning, the parcels should be sent directly to one of the vehicles since it is not possible to store the parcels. Hence, even though the delivery vehicles may not leave until the early morning, this makes it impossible to first collect all the demand data and then solve a VRPTW. The route the vehicle will drive, depends on the parcels assigned to the vehicle and is calculated just before departure from the depot. Information about the parcels is revealed during the assignment process of the parcels to the vehicles (during the construction of the routes). This emphasises the dynamic component of the problem.

Introducing time windows makes it even more complicated. The method presented in [3] for the general DA-VRP case is not suitable to be extended for handling time windows, due to the optimisation step in the end. Therefore we present a different approach based on a dummy start solution based on historical data and smart insertion. This approach can be used for the general DA-VRP case and allows for handling time windows. In the next sections we present this approach, benchmark it against real observations and to the approach of [3], and, lastly, show the results for the situation with time windows. All time windows are assumed to be hard time windows.

3   Solution Approach

In this section we describe the method we propose to solve the dynamic VRP problem. For this, the problem is divided in two sub-problems, namely the Generalised Assignment Problem (GAP) and multiple Travelling Salesman Problem with Time Windows (TSPTW). We propose an interactive approach between the two.

3.1   Overview of the Approach

Solving multiple TSPTWs every time a parcel should be assigned is very time consuming, it is unclear how many vehicles we should consider in the first place and it does not take into account receivers that may follow. For this, it helps to have some preliminary notion of the complete problem such that we can make a more informed decision regarding how we should assign the parcels as they come in dynamically. This initial notion comes from historical data or from a dummy data set for which a good solution can be determined. For this historical or dummy data a solution can be created. We now have some general pattern that serves as starting point Each incoming parcel will replace a dummy parcel, based on some cost metric, building gradually the solution for the new day. We propose a three step approach:

1. Create initial solution based on dummy sample,
2. Create improved solution based on dummy sample,
3. Create a dynamic solution, substituting each dummy parcel with a real dynamic incoming parcel.

In step one and two we consider two methods. The difference in these methods is related to the information we have available: Method 1 uses randomly generated data and Method 2 uses historical data to create the dummy sample. We see in practice that there seems to be a great level of repetitiveness in the weekly data [18]. Hence we could exploit this information to attain a sample that should closely mimic the batch of future parcels that will arrive. Here we use data of the corresponding day during the last week to build our dummy sample. We present both approaches for the general case where this repetitiveness is not occurring and to show the benefit of this information.

3.2   Step 1: Create Initial Dummy Solution

In this step, we have two methods. Method 1 starts with the creation of the random sample. For this, we simply gather all zip codes that are assigned to the depot and randomly sample receivers from this set until we reach the desired sample size, based on the expected number of receivers to visit on the current day. Next, we employ K-means clustering [19] to cluster the receivers based on their geographical proximity. Next, the route corresponding to cluster k is initialised with the receiver closest to the depot. The route is built further using on a nearest neighbour approach. Method 2 uses historical data. Since we now have actual useful information regarding the density of demand in certain regions, we can solve a VRPTW to obtain a solution for the problem. Given the size of the problem, we use a sequential route building heuristic to solve it. By using a sequential route building heuristic we do not have to define the number of vehicles (K in the previous section) as we can leave the decision of the number of vehicles to the algorithm. The used sequential heuristic is based on the insertion heuristic introduced by [20].

3.3   Step 2: Create Improved Dummy Solution

In Step 2 the initial solution is improved by using interroute and intraroute local search methods. Here, an interroute method interchanges receivers between two different vehicles and an intraroute method re-positions a receiver within the route of a vehicle.

For interroute, the Relocate Operator [21] is used to improve the solution of a Vehicle Routing Problem by exchanging receivers between two different routes. Since the Relocate Operator searches between routes we should limit the searching space as to restrict the searching time. We can do this by looking at neighbouring routes only. To prevent searching in vehicles which are located too far from the receiver, we only allow to search in the X nearest neighbour vehicles. The number of neighbour vehicles is defined as a parameter which should be a positive integer value smaller than the total number of vehicles. In the analysis we used $X = 5$.

As the initial solution consists of K different routes. Each route can be solved using a Travelling Salesman Problems (TSP) formulation. We can improve every solution using the Or-Opt Operator [21]. This operator works intraroute which means that changes take place within a route of a vehicle, or in other words within a 'Travelling Salesman' tour. This implies that a receiver of the tour may be reallocated to another position in the tour. This is achieved by changing three edges of the tour, namely edges $(i-1,i)$, $(i,i+1)$ and $(j,j+1)$ which are then replaced by the edges $(i-1,i+1)$, (j,i) and $(i,j+1)$. As a result receiver i is relocated to another position in the tour. The Or-Opt Exchange Operator continues making exchanges until no further improvements can be made.

The searching time of the Or-Opt operator to find a feasible insertion place can be accelerated by omitting certain part(s) of the route. We can limit the search space by disregarding insertions between receivers that have to be visited in a time span that lies outside of the time span of the receiver that we are considering.

3.4 Step 3: Dynamic Solution

Up until this point we had the freedom to switch receivers between vehicles, as we were just trying to build a good preliminary prediction for the real data. The insertions that are made past this point have to be fixed, to comply with the assignment process within the depot. Furthermore it is important to note that before we start making our substitutions, we delete the time window requirements for our dummy set, such that they do not interfere with feasibility checks.

The main idea is that dummy receivers are slowly replaced by dynamic receivers. Any residual dummy receivers that remain once all dynamic receivers are assigned will be omitted.

For each incoming dynamic receiver u, we evaluate the tours, and substitute a dummy receiver for a dynamic receiver, such that this substitution provides the largest cost decrease, or smallest cost increase. Here, the cost (C) or benefit (B) is expressed in terms of travelling distance (d). The evaluation is done by taking a vehicle and consider for all receivers k in that tour:

- Type 1 insertion: if receiver k, with neighbours i and j, is a dummy receiver:
  - Gives replacing this receiver k a feasible solution, given the time restrictions?
  - Calculate the costs for this insertion, given by

$$C(i, u, j) = (d_{iu} + d_{uj}) - (d_{ik} + d_{kj}). \tag{1}$$

- Type 2 insertion: if receiver k, with neighbours i and j, is an already placed dynamic receiver:
  - Can we insert receiver u between receivers i and k, given the time restrictions? Calculate the costs for this insertion, given by

$$C(i, u, k) = (d_{iu} + d_{uk}) - d_{ik}. \tag{2}$$

  - Can we insert receiver u between receivers k and j, given the time restrictions? Calculate the costs for this insertion, given by

$$C(k, u, j) = (d_{ku} + d_{uj}) - d_{kj}. \tag{3}$$

  - Determine which dummy receiver m, with (different) neighbours i and j, can be deleted with the highest benefit, given by

$$B(i, m, j) = (d_{im} + d_{mj}) - d_{ij}. \tag{4}$$

Now for all possible insertion, replacing and or deleting possibilities, the cheapest, feasible solution is chosen.

The two insertions are explained in more detail. Figure 1 illustrates a tour containing only dummy parcels, in which we want to insert the dynamic receiver defined as 'dyn1'. Here we simply substitute dummy receivers one by one to figure out which substitution is the most favourable. Each step in Fig. 1 illustrates what happens when a certain receiver of the tour is excluded and the dynamic receiver is included in that position of the tour. We calculate the insertion cost of all possible substitutions, after which the insertion with the largest cost decrease, or smallest cost increase is chosen, which is the case for receiver 3.

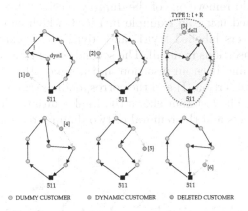

Fig. 1. Example of a type 1 insertion.

Next, we consider the insertion of the second dynamic receiver. The second tour of Fig. 3 shows the substitution of the first dynamic receiver, and this is our starting point for determining the most profitable insertion of the second dynamic receiver labelled 'dyn2'. An example is displayed in Fig. 2.

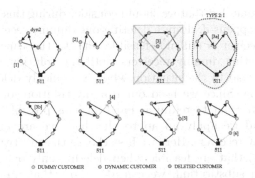

Fig. 2. Example of a type 2 insertion.

In Fig. 2 we consider the insertion of dynamic receiver 'dyn2'. To do this, we again consider the possible substitutions of the dummy receivers in the tour. For the first two customers in the tour the same technique is applied as for a type 1 substitution. The third receiver, however, cannot be substituted, because this receiver is already a dynamic receiver. Instead, we consider the two corresponding insertions as shown with receivers 3a and 3b. Here, we simply insert the dynamic receiver between a dummy receiver and a dynamic receiver. This results in another type of insertion and thus a different insertion cost. In the example shown in Fig. 2 receiver 3a seems the most profitable insertion. However, this type of insertion does not include a direct removal of one of the dummy receivers. Therefore, we should remove one of the dummy receivers from this vehicle. The heuristic is explained using an example in Fig. 3, which shows the insertion of two dynamic receivers labelled 'dyn1' and 'dyn2'. This example explains two different types of insertions in detail. The second tour in Fig. 3 illustrates a type 1 insertion, containing both an insertion and a removal (I+R). The third tour illustrates a type 2 insertion (I) and the corresponding removal (R) is illustrated in the fourth tour. The last tour shows the final solution, after the insertion of two dynamic receivers and the removal of two dummy receivers.

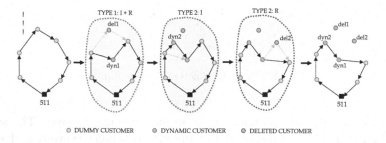

Fig. 3. An overview of the two different types of insertions/removals.

There are two issues left that we should consider during this process. The first question is, what happens if, despite deleting one dummy receiver, the insertion of the dynamic receiver is still not feasible, due to the time constraints. We could continue deleting dummy receivers until the solution becomes feasible, however, this may lead to the situation where we quickly delete large parts of our dummy solution. Since we need our dummy solution for assigning future points and therefore want to retain as much of it as possible, we should avoid this. Hence, instead we apply an approach where we are more 'cautious' in deleting our dummy receivers. Here we first choose the substitutions (among all considered vehicles) that are feasible when deleting only one dummy receiver. If there is no such substitution, we consider those that are feasible through deleting multiple dummy receivers, starting with all possible combinations of 2 receivers. In each of these cases we still choose the substitution according to the lowest costs, calculated through Eq. 1 or 2. If we are still unable to create a feasible substitution, even without deleting all the left over dummy receivers, a new vehicle is introduced. The second issue we have to consider is for which vehicles we should apply the above framework. Here we apply the same approach

Table 1. Number of parcels per day.

Day	Number	Day	Number	Day	Number	Day	Number
11.01	18,847	11.05	14,275	11.08	17,530	11.12	14,341
11.02	14,570	11.06	20,743	11.09	18,011	11.13	20,618
11.03	2,819	11.07	19,107	11.10	2,579	11.14	18,847

as in Sect. 3.3, and consider the X 'closest' vehicles. In addition, every time a dynamic receiver is assigned to one of the vehicles, the Local Search Or-Opt operator tries to improve the tour of the vehicle. The idea behind this Or-Opt operator is explained in Sect. 3.3. Now all dynamic receivers have been assigned and all residual dummy receivers are removed, as indicated in the main idea of Step 3.

4   Results

In this section, we report the results for the procedure as described in Sect. 3. We test the performance by using real data for a two week period (2018.11.01– 2018.11.14) for one depot in The Netherlands. The number of parcels per day is shown in Table 1. Note that 11.03 and 11.10 are both a Saturday. We look at two cases, first we look at the problem without time windows, which will be used as benchmark. Next we give the look at the problem with time windows to study the effect of time windows. The number of parcels per day in this period are depicted in Table 1. The results are generated using an i7-4700MQ CPU, 2.40 GHz and 8 GB RAM computer. The implementation is done in Matlab. We show the performance first in the more general case, without time windows, compared to other approaches, which are not suitable to be extended to the case with time windows. Then we show results for the case with time windows.

4.1   Discarding Time Windows

Here, we discuss the results obtained by applying both Method 1, based on random data, and Method 2, based on historical data, to the case without time windows. This means that every receiver can be visited during the entire time horizon. Mathematically this can be represented as follows: $[a_i, b_i] = [-\infty, \infty]$ for all receivers i.

Benchmarking Method. We use the approach of [3] for solving the general DA-VRP problem that is used as benchmark. The method is based on four steps, in which the work of [3] propose alternative approaches for each step. Note that here first tours are determined and later these tours are combined to routes and assigned to vehicles. We will indicate which method we use in every step:

Table 2. Comparison of Results: Travel Distances (km) of the methods and their relative difference from the observed results.

Day	Observed	Method 1 'random'	%	Method 2 'historical'	%	Method 3 'combining'	%	Method 4 'integrating'	%
11.01	16,612	15,061	−9.3	14,004	−15.7	15,293	−7.9	12,705	−23.5
11.02	16,998	15,260	−10.2	13,842	−18.6	12,705	−25.3	11,045	−35.0
11.03	6,048	7,216	+19.3	4,517	−25.3	4,641	−23.3	2,610	−56.8
11.05	15,260	15,179	−0.5	12,675	−16.9	13,180	−13.6	9,302	−39.0
11.06	22,803	23,026	+1.0	16,489	−27.7	17,540	−23.1	14,356	−37.0
11.07	17,851	18,853	+5.6	15,418	−13.6	16,278	−8.8	12,883	−27.8
11.08	18,152	17,709	−2.4	14,170	−21.9	15,075	−17.0	12,827	−29.3
11.09	17,665	19,352	+9.6	16,054	−9.1	15,445	−12.6	13,000	−26.4
11.10	5,697	5,668	−0.5	4,484	−21.3	4,104	−28.0	3,102	−45.6
11.12	15,946	14,899	−6.6	12,097	−24.1	12,919	−19.0	9,703	−39.2
11.13	19,124	23,452	+22.6	16,666	−12.9	17,466	−8.7	14,333	−25.1
11.14	17,606	20,689	+17.5	15,150	−14.0	16,053	−8.8	13,421	−23.8
Total	**189,763**	**196,364**	**+3.5**	**155,566**	**−18.0**	**160,699**	**−15.3**	**129,287**	**−31.9**

1. Initial assignment of direction to routes; we use the method based on separation by dummy location: performing a K-means clustering over all potential receivers and assign a dummy parcel, having as location one of the cluster means, to each route.
2. Dynamic decision of the daily fleet size; we use 'Tour capacity based': Start with 75% of the expected number of tours. When the tour load of a *specific tour* is higher than 99% when trying to assign a parcel to it, we add an extra tour and assign this parcel to it.
3. Dynamic assignment of arriving parcels; we use 'Based on minimal insertion costs': for all tours we calculate the minimal cost of inserting the arriving parcel's destination to the tour. The insertion that is cheapest is selected.
4. Post-processing: we use both 'Integrating', optimise further by integrating combined tours, such that they do not have to go to the depot in between and 'Combining', try to minimise the number of vehicles, given the tours. We do so in a greedy way, start with the longest tour and try to add the longest tour as possible that fits the requirements.

In the benchmark this approach, using all steps with 'Combining' in step 4, will be called Method 3. The approach with 'Integrating' in step 4 will be called Method 4. For more details on this approach the reader is referred to [3]. In general, Method 4 results in better results in distance. However, this method is harder to implement, where it requires more flexibility in the depot.

Comparison of Results. Table 2 compares the proposed Methods (1 and 2) to the benchmark methods (3 and 4) and to a realisation in practice, in terms of

Table 3. Comparison of Results: Number of vehicles

Day	REAL	Method 1	Method 2	Method 3/4 Initial	Method 3	Method 4
11.01	141	141	134	148	118	126
11.02	140	140	133	120	89	95
11.03	43	53	30	37	24	25
11.05	125	135	118	123	89	90
11.06	155	218	160	170	127	135
11.07	147	175	149	158	118	127
11.08	147	169	121	141	113	114
11.09	147	185	149	149	111	129
11.10	40	40	32	36	23	30
11.12	130	133	111	123	90	93
11.13	152	228	160	181	126	145
11.14	145	190	146	156	115	126
Total	**1,512**	**1,807**	**1,443**	**1,542**	**1,143**	**1,235**

the travel distance (displayed in kilometres). The comparison to the real routes is not completely fair since the restrictions in our solution approach may be different from the assumptions in reality. We limit our solution to tours of 9 h, while in reality some routes are longer. Also, in our solution approach we do not allow for reallocation after the assignment. However, in the real solution reallocation happens on each day by the drivers.

From Table 2 it follows that Method 1 performs better on 6 out of 12 days compared to the realisation. However, on some days the deviation is very large and the cumulative difference in the total travel distance favours the realised solution since this number lies 3.5% below that of Method 1. It follows that setting K equal to the number of vehicles used in reality in combination with a random estimation of the solution space does not provide impressive results.

Conversely, Method 2, based on the historical data, outperforms the real solution for each day. Cumulatively, this means that we are able to decrease the total travel distance with 18%. During this two week period this percentage decrease varies between 9% and 28%. In addition, we do not allow for the reallocation of parcels after the assignment has taken place, which is an additional benefit on top of the travel distance improvement. Our method has a reallocation percentage of 0% while this average daily proportion of reallocated parcels in practice is equal to 11%.

Method 2 is slightly better than Method 3 in distance. This is no surprise, as it uses more historical information to create the routes. Method 4, however, performs, in resulting distance, much better than all the other methods. However, as already mentioned, the optimisation step 'Integration' complicates the execution in practice, it needs a huge number of storage points in the depot and the integration of the routes afterwards makes the extension to time windows impossible.

Table 3 compares the number of vehicles used in the realisation to that of the four methods. As the number of vehicles in Method 1 is based on the number of vehicles in the realised solution, the final solution will always have a larger or equal number of vehicles. We see that on only three days of the sample period, the number of vehicles is not increased. On the other days there is a significant increase in the number of vehicles. Method 2 actually outperforms the realised solutions when looking at the (cumulative) number of used vehicles. Method 2 is able to decrease the number of vehicles by 69.

Running Times. Table 4 below displays the running times, using the specific computer as defined before, in seconds for every method for each day, where we display the running times for one week. As is obvious from Table 4, the benefit

Table 4. Running Times (s) for the four methods.

Day	Initial solution		Dummy solution		Dynamic solution		Benchmark
	Method 1	Method 2	Method 1	Method 2	Method 1	Method 2	Method 3/4
11.01	17	3,382	3,742	2,920	4,142	3,570	192
11.02	17	4,108	2,913	3,365	3,915	2,781	120
11.03	24	237	1,258	244	889	258	3
11.05	31	3,348	4,169	4,005	4,061	2,485	87
11.06	29	3,573	3,455	4,092	4,892	3,049	283
11.07	30	3,721	3,843	3,754	4,965	3,683	132

Table 5. The nine different time windows.

Length (h)	Overlapping	Examples
0.5	Non-overlapping	08:00–08:30 08:30–9:00 etc.
1	Overlapping	08:00–09:00 08:30–9:30 etc.
1	Non-overlapping	08:00–09:00 09:00–10:00 etc.
2	Overlapping	08:00–10:00 09:00–11:00 etc.
2	Non-overlapping	08:00–10:00 10:00–12:00 etc.
4	Non-overlapping	08:00–12:00 12:00–16:00 16:00–20:00
5	Overlapping	08:00–13:00 11:00–17:00 15:00–20:00
6	Non-overlapping	08:00–14:00 14:00–20:00
7	Overlapping	08:00–15:00 13:00–20:00

of Method 1 is that the solution is obtained quickly. A large drawback of this method however is that the number of vehicles (K in this case) should be determined beforehand. The performance of Method 1 is therefore strongly dependent on the correctness of the number of vehicles. When looking at the running times of Method 1 and Method 2 in the last phase, n1amely the creation of the dynamic solution, Method 1 has a higher running time. This can be explained by the fact that the initial solution in Method 1 is built while using a higher number of receivers. As a result more dummy receivers have to be considered/deleted when building the dynamic solution, which is more time consuming.

4.2   Incorporating Time Windows

In this section, the problem is extended by the introduction of time windows. As the observed solution nor the benchmark method use predefined time windows in their solution we cannot make the comparison here. Therefore, we choose to compare the results with predefined time windows with the results that we generated without time windows. From the previous section it followed that the performance of Method 2 was significantly better than Method 1. We expect this also for the case with time windows, therefore, we only look at Method 2 in this section.

Time windows are randomly distributed among the receivers. The number of receivers with a time window is defined beforehand. We consider cases in which 25%, 50%, 75% and 100% of the receivers have a predefined time window. In addition, we consider different types of time window combinations, varying in the number of time windows a receiver can choose from and whether the time windows are overlapping or non-overlapping. Table 5 shows the nine different time windows which will be analysed.

Figure 4 displays the relation between the total travel distance and the percentage of allocated time windows (allocation percentage) for the nine time window combinations for a specific day. These figures allows us to make three observations. The first and most obvious observation is the increase in the travel distance as the allocation percentage increases. This makes sense as a higher percentage adds more constraints/complexity to the problem, as more time windows have to be met. Second, it appears that allowing for time windows causes a increment in travel distance, however, the incremental costs for higher percentages decrease (decreasing additional costs). Third we can look at the effect of overlapping time windows. Allowing for overlapping time windows produces a lower travelling distance. One can simply interpret the overlap as a relaxation of constraints, therefore providing an intuitive explanation for the decrease. The running times for the case with time windows (based on the same configuration as earlier) are between 5 and 7 h, as shown in detail in [18]. Using a more advanced machine and parallelisation can reduce the running time to 1–2 h easily.

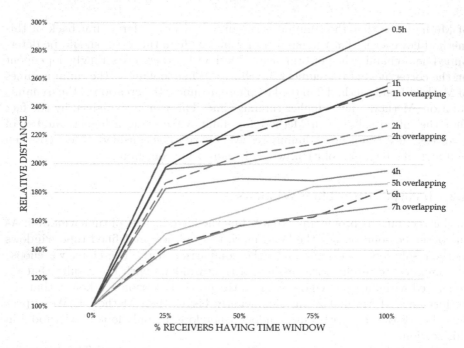

Fig. 4. The relation between the percentage of allocated time windows and the total travel distance for all time window lengths.

5   Summary and Conclusions

The goal of this paper was to propose a method that can handle time windows in a Dynamic Assignment Vehicle Routing Problem. Here, routing decisions have to be made instantly once parcels come in. This means that we cannot use static methods that need information on the full set of receivers to construct a route. Instead we have to incorporate methods to deal with the dynamic nature of the continuous stream of parcels that have to be assigned without knowing what the demand for the remainder of the day looks like. To do this we proposed a method based on the principle of creating a dummy solution first. This dummy solution can then be used as a guideline when adding the real parcels, as we now have a preliminary notion of what the final routes should approximately look like and we can use this to make a more 'informed' decision as to where to place these real incoming parcels. In creating the dummy solutions we make use of a random sample that requires no historic information (Method 1), and a historic sample consisting of the demand for the corresponding day exactly one week ago (Method 2). Once the dummy solution is attained we substitute parcels in the dummy solution for dynamic parcels that come in.

The performance of the methods was compared to the benchmark method from [3] and to travelling distances as attained by the original routing process in reality. These benchmark results are for deliveries without time windows, hence for the time window case we can only evaluate the relative differences that occur once we introduce time windows for more receivers. The method that employs the random sample in creating the dummy solution provides mixed results. However, when we use historic data in the creation of the dummy sample, the performance is much better than the observed realisation. This method performs less good that of [3], but the latter one is not expandable to be used with time windows.

When adding time windows to the problem, the proposed solution is able to solve this. The results show that when more receivers make use of time windows, the travelling distance increases due to the higher complexity and additional constrains of the problem. For our approach the time windows double the travelling distance. Overlapping time windows may provide better outcomes due to more flexibility in the constraints.

We can conclude that the inclusion of historical data can provide notable efficiency gains, when trying to use time windows in the dynamic case. Future research or adjustments to this approach could focus on the creation of the dummy sample/solution in more detail. For one, it would be useful to improve the dummy solution based on a random sample. Yet in an age of increasing data collection one could make an argument for actually focusing on a good implementation of the historical data. A 'middle road' between the two methods that we used in this research could be to use the parcels that were delayed (parcels that arrived at the depot the day before and were not loaded on a vehicle, or were not delivered and hence returned to the depot) to aid in constructing a dummy sample. If these parcels are somewhat similar to the overall demand one could potentially use this information to create a dummy solution, without having to rely on historical records.

Acknowledgements. The authors like to thank the Dutch Topsector Logistics (TKI Dinalog and NWO) for the support to Project SOLiD (NWO project number 439.17.551). The aims of the SOLiD project [22] is to bridge the gap between the long(er) term vision and the short term daily logistics operations in self-organising parcel distribution.

References

1. Joerss, M., Neuhaus, F., Schröder, J.: How customer demands are reshaping last-mile delivery. Travel Transp. Logist. **1**, 4 (2016)
2. Pillac, V., Gendreau, M., Guéret, C., Medaglia, A.L.: A review of dynamic vehicle routing problems. Eur. J. Oper. Res. **225**(1), 1–11 (2013)
3. Phillipson, F., De Koff, S., van Ommeren, C., Quak, H.: Dynamic assignment vehicle routing problem with generalised capacity and unknown workload. In: Proceedings of 9th International Conference on Operations Research and Enterprise Systems (ICORES) (2020)
4. Phillipson, F., de Koff, S.: Immediate parcel to vehicle assignment for cross docking in city logistics. In: Proceedings of 9th International Conference on Operations Research and Enterprise Systems (ICORES) (2020)
5. Baldacci, R., Toth, P., Vigo, D.: Recent advances in vehicle routing exact algorithms. 4OR **5**(4), 269–298 (2007)

6. Rincon-Garcia, N., Waterson, B., Cherrett, T.J., Salazar-Arrieta, F.: A meta-heuristic for the time-dependent vehicle routing problem considering driving hours regulations-an application in city logistics. Transp. Res. Part A Policy Pract. **137**, 429–446 (2018)
7. Yao, Y., et al.: ADMM-based problem decomposition scheme for vehicle routing problem with time windows. Transp. Res. Part B Methodol. **129**, 156–174 (2019)
8. Van Duin, J., De Goffau, W., Wiegmans, B., Tavasszy, L., Saes, M.: Improving home delivery efficiency by using principles of address intelligence for B2C deliveries. Transp. Res. Procedia **12**, 14–25 (2016)
9. Shao, S., Xu, G., Li, M., Huang, G.Q.: Synchronizing e-commerce city logistics with sliding time windows. Transp. Res. Part E Logist. Transp. Rev. **123**, 17–28 (2019)
10. Agatz, N., Campbell, A., Fleischmann, M., Savelsbergh, M.: Time slot management in attended home delivery. Transp. Sci. **45**(3), 435–449 (2011)
11. Solomon, M.M., Desrosiers, J.: Survey paper–time window constrained routing and scheduling problems. Transp. Sci. **22**(1), 1–13 (1988)
12. Ghannadpour, S.F., Noori, S., Tavakkoli-Moghaddam, R., Ghoseiri, K.: A multi-objective dynamic vehicle routing problem with fuzzy time windows: model, solution and application. Appl. Soft Comput. **14**, 504–527 (2014)
13. Chen, S., Chen, R., Wang, G.G., Gao, J., Sangaiah, A.K.: An adaptive large neighborhood search heuristic for dynamic vehicle routing problems. Comput. Electr. Eng. **67**, 596–607 (2018)
14. de Armas, J., Melián-Batista, B.: Variable neighborhood search for a dynamic rich vehicle routing problem with time windows. Comput. Indust. Eng. **85**, 120–131 (2015)
15. Schyns, M.: An ant colony system for responsive dynamic vehicle routing. Eur. J. Oper. Res. **245**(3), 704–718 (2015)
16. Spliet, R., Desaulniers, G.: The discrete time window assignment vehicle routing problem. Eur. J. Oper. Res. **244**(2), 379–391 (2015)
17. Dalmeijer, K., Spliet, R.: A branch-and-cut algorithm for the time window assignment vehicle routing problem. Comput. Oper. Res. **89**, 140–152 (2018)
18. Los, K.: Improving delivery efficiency using a dynamic assignment method. Master's thesis, Erasmus University (2019)
19. James, G., Witten, D., Hastie, T., Tibshirani, R.: An Introduction to Statistical Learning. STS, vol. 103. Springer, New York (2013). https://doi.org/10.1007/978-1-4614-7138-7
20. Solomon, M.M.: Algorithms for the vehicle routing and scheduling problems with time window constraints. Oper. Res. **35**(2), 254–265 (1987)
21. Bräysy, O., Gendreau, M.: Vehicle routing problem with time windows, Part I: route construction and local search algorithms. Transp. Sci. **39**(1), 104–118 (2005)
22. Quak, H., van Kempen, E., van Dijk, B., Phillipson, F.: Self-organization in parcel distribution-SOLiD's first results. In: IPIC 2019 6th International Physical Internet Conference London (2019)

Time-Dependent Travel-Time Constrained Inventory Routing Problem

Faycal A. Touzout$^{(\boxtimes)}$, Anne-Laure Ladier, and Khaled Hadj-Hamou

Univ Lyon, INSA Lyon, DISP, EA 4570, 69100 Villeurbanne, France
{faycal.touzout,anne-laure.ladier,khaled.hadj-hamou}@insa-lyon.fr

Abstract. The Inventory Routing Problem (IRP) is an integration of two operational problems: inventory management and routing. The Time-Dependent Travel-Time Constrained (TD-TC-IRP) is a new proposed variant of the IRP where the travelling time between two locations depend on the time of departure throughout the day and the length of a trip is time-constrained. The real-world discontinuous time-dependent data that we use will be modelled by a piece-wise linear continuous function. A mathematical formulation for the TD-TC-IRP is proposed, to emulate such transformation. Numerical experiments are conducted, to validate the mathematical formulation, on a new benchmark combining benchmarks from the IRP and time-dependent routing problems literature.

Keywords: Inventory routing problem · Time-dependent routing · Travel-time constrained routing · Piece-wise travelling time function

1 Introduction

Vendor Managed Inventory (VMI) is a logistic system where the inventories of the clients are controlled by the supplier. The supplier is thus able to globally optimise the replenishment plan while the client does not need to dedicate specific resources for inventory management [1]. In this context, the Inventory Routing Problem (IRP) emerges. It integrates inventory management and routing problems in order to decide, over a time horizon, when, how much and following which route the clients are replenished.

The IRP has attracted a lot of scholars' interests during the last decades. In order for the IRP to be representative of real-life situations, new variants are proposed in the literature, such as the IRP with time-windows, transshipment, travel-time constrained or the parameters are considered as uncertain, such as the clients' demand or the travelling time. Other scholars focused on proposing new efficient solving approaches due to the NP-hardness of the problem [2]. A common point of all these works is that the travelling time between locations is always considered constant. However, in urban logistics and last mile distribution, the time it takes to travel from one location to another can vary a lot

© Springer Nature Switzerland AG 2020
E. Lalla-Ruiz et al. (Eds.): ICCL 2020, LNCS 12433, pp. 151–166, 2020.
https://doi.org/10.1007/978-3-030-59747-4_10

during the day due to traffic congestion. Thus, we identify the need of considering time-dependent data for the routing component.

Time-dependent routing problems consider that the travelling time from one location does not depend only on the destination but on the time of departure as well. The literature of time-dependent routing problems, such as Travelling Salesman Problem (TSP), Vehicle Routing Problem (VRP) or Arc Routing Problem (ARP), is quite rich [3]. However, from the literature and to the best of our knowledge, it has never been considered for the IRP although the inventory aspect can have an important impact on the structure of time-dependent IRP solutions.

In this article, we present a new variant of the IRP, the Time-Dependent Travel-Time Constrained IRP (TD-TC-IRP), where the travelling times are time-dependent and the total duration of the trips are constrained. The real-world discontinuous time-dependent data that we use will be modelled by a piece-wise linear continuous function. The mathematical formulation for the TD-TC-IRP that is proposed emulates this transformation. The numerical experiments are conducted on a new benchmark that combines two benchmarks of the IRP and TD-TSP literature, to investigate the advantages of considering time-dependent travelling time functions over basic ones.

The article is organised as follows: Sect. 2 presents a brief literature review of the IRP and time-dependent routing problems. Section 3 presents mathematical formulations of the IRP and TD-TC-IRP and discusses the differences between them; a discussion is proposed on the piece-wise continuity of the time-dependent function. Section 4 shows and discusses the results of the numerical experiments while Sect. 5 concludes and gives perspectives for future research.

2   Literature Review

The IRP is set in a network where a supplier delivers goods to its clients, over a time horizon. The objective of the IRP is to decide for each period, whether a client is served, with which quantity, and a route for the vehicles, while minimising the total cost (transportation and inventory costs). However, since the actors and parameters of the IRP are multiple, this definition is hardly representative of all real-life situations. Therefore, many variants of the IRP exist: most consider one vehicle only. Furthermore, the IRP is known to be an NP-hard problem [2]. Consequently, scholars dedicated their work to find the most suitable solution approaches for these variants. In the following, a collection of the most common variants of the IRP are presented. For a more detailed literature review, interested readers can refer to [4–7]

IRP with time-windows: Due to constraints related to urban deliveries such as rush hours or availability of parking slots, and to scheduling problems such as workers availability, the clients may require to be visited in a certain time interval. The IRP with time-windows is proposed in this context. A review of the IRP with time-windows literature is presented in [8].

IRP with transshipment: In order to design a network that is efficient in an economical sense, but also ecological, reducing the number of vehicles used to replenish the clients as well as reducing the total travelled distance is necessary. [9] introduced the IRP with transshipment in this context, where the replenishment is not only done from the supplier to a client but can also be done from a client to another client.

Cyclic IRP: The irregularities brought by scheduling on a large time horizon inspired the cyclic IRP. The scheduling is done in a smaller time interval and is reproduced over and over. A work in this context is presented in [10].

Multi-echelon IRP: For a globally optimised network, the IRP can be studied in a multi-echelon environment where multiple layers of the supply chain are included: a supplier, retailers and clients. [11] tackled this problem recently.

Travel-Time Constrained IRP Due to legal limitations of the work hours per day, or the perishability of the products, the travel-time constrained IRP emerges. [12] are the last to tackle this problem.

All the variants presented above consider that the travelling time from one location to another is constant throughout the day. Since traffic volatility can be a concern in real-life instances, a time-dependent variant is needed to account for it. Given the fact that time-dependent IRP literature is nonexistent, we turn to pure routing problems to better understand how this parameter is included.

The objective of time-dependent routing problems is to design the best routes in a graph where the duration or cost of travelling an arc can vary according to the time it is travelled. Interest over this area has spiked during the last decades. In [3], the authors propose an extensive review of time-dependent routing problems in the literature. They show that the time-dependent aspect is only considered for pure transportation problems such as: Time-Dependent TSP (TD-TSP), Time-Dependent VRP (TD-VRP) and Time-Dependent ARP (TD-ARP). They also show that the time-dependent problems are hard to solve in comparison to their basic counterpart, thus the need for new efficient approaches to solve them. The study concludes by stating that although the literature for time-dependent routing problem is consequent, it is relatively recent and there is still room for improvements. Perspectives for future research are given. In the following, we cite a collection of works published after this review by [3].

In [13], the authors model the TD-TSP as a constraint programming (CP) problem and propose a new global constraint called the "Time-Dependent no-Overlap" that extends the no-Overlap constraint. The results show that including this new constraint outperforms the CP models of the literature. In [14], the TSP with time-dependent service times is presented. In this version, the service time depends on the time a node is visited. The authors of [15] tackle the problem of minimising the expected emissions of CO_2 for a time-dependent vehicle routing problem. The emission function depends in this case not only on the travelling time between two nodes but on the load of the vehicle as well. The results show that the improvement on emissions are proportionally larger than the deterioration of the tour length. In [16], a new ILP formulation for the TD-TSP is presented. Two tailored branch-and-cut algorithms are proposed with pre-processing rules, initial heuristics and valid inequalities. The proposed approaches are able to prove the optimality of more than 300 new instances of the literature and improve the number of nodes explored and the computational times. The authors of [17] propose a partially time-expanded network formulation that, instead of generating a time-expanded network in a static, a priori, fashion, does so in a dynamic and iterative manner. They propose an algorithm based on the dynamic discretisation discovery framework. The results show that the algorithm outperforms those of the literature and that it is robust with respect to all instance parameters, particularly the degree of travel time variability. In [18], the authors manage real-time perturbations on time-dependent functions in the context of a vehicle routing problem with time-windows. When perturbations occur and the delivery route is no longer feasible, due to time-windows violations or the violation of the horizon length, the time-dependent functions are updated and a re-optimisation with new-objectives is conducted. Most recently, [19] propose a new real-life benchmark for routing problems based on the traffic conditions of the city of Lyon, using a dynamic microscopic simulator of traffic flow. The purpose of their study is to show the impact of space granularity, i.e. the number of sensors deployed to monitor the traffic flow, and time granularity, i.e. the number and length of time steps, on the quality of the solutions for pick-up and delivery optimal tours. They conclude that when there is a full space coverage, exploiting time-dependent travelling time functions leads to better tours and that the smaller the time step, the better the tour gets.

The literature of the time-dependent routing problems provides benchmarks and ideas on how to model and solve efficiently time-dependent problems that are exploited throughout this paper.

3   IRP vs. Time-Dependent IRP (TD-IRP)

In this section, we discuss the difference between the IRP and the TD-IRP. A mathematical formulation for the IRP is presented, a time-dependent travelling time function and its properties presented and discussed and a mathematical formulation for the TD-IRP proposed.

3.1   Mathematical Formulation of the IRP

Let $\mathcal{G} = (\mathcal{V}, \mathcal{A})$ be a graph where vertex $0 \in \mathcal{V}$ represents the supplier, $\mathcal{V}' = \mathcal{V} \backslash \{0\}$ the set of clients and $\mathcal{A}$ a set of arcs. $\mathcal{H} = \{1, 2, ..., |\mathcal{H}|\}$ is the scheduling time horizon and $\mathcal{H}' = \{0\} \cup \mathcal{H}$ the horizon including the period 0 which represents the initial state. $p \in \mathcal{H}'$ represents the index of the period. Each client $i \in \mathcal{V}'$ has a demand D_i^p for period $p \in \mathcal{H}$, an initial inventory I_i^0 and a maximum inventory level $I_i^{\max}$. The supplier has an unlimited inventory capacity, an initial inventory I_0^0, R^p products available at each period $p \in \mathcal{H}$ and a vehicle with a maximal capacity C. Keeping one item in inventory for a period incurs a holding cost h_i for each actor $i \in \mathcal{V}$. Finally τ_{ij} represents the duration of travel through arc $(i, j) \in \mathcal{A}$ and c is the cost of one unit of time travelled.

Variables: let x_{ij}^p be a binary variable that equals to 1 if arc $(i,j) \in \mathcal{A}$ is travelled in period p, 0 otherwise. y_i^p a binary variable that is equal to 1 if client $i \in \mathcal{V}'$ is visited in period p, 0 otherwise. $I_i^p \in \mathbb{R}$ represents the inventory level of actor $i \in \mathcal{V}$ at the end of period $p \in \mathcal{H}'$ and $q_i^p \in \mathbb{R}$ the quantity sent from the supplier to client $i \in \mathcal{V}'$.

IRP

$$\min \, obj^{\mathrm{IRP}} = c \times \sum_{(i,j)\in\mathcal{A}} \sum_{p\in\mathcal{H}} \tau_{ij} \times x_{ij}^p + \sum_{i\in\mathcal{V}} \sum_{p\in\mathcal{H}'} h_i \times I_i^p$$

$$
\begin{aligned}
\text{s.t} \quad I_0^p &= I_0^{p-1} - \sum_{i\in\mathcal{V}'} q_i^p + R^p & \forall p \in \mathcal{H} && (1)\\
I_i^p &= I_i^{p-1} + q_i^p - D_i^p & \forall i \in \mathcal{V}' , \forall p \in \mathcal{H} && (2)\\
I_i^p &\leq I_i^{\max} & \forall i \in \mathcal{V}' , \forall p \in \mathcal{H} && (3)\\
q_i^p + I_i^{p-1} &\leq I_i^{\max} & \forall i \in \mathcal{V}' , \forall p \in \mathcal{H} && (4)\\
q_i^p &\leq y_i^p \times I_i^{\max} & \forall i \in \mathcal{V}' , \forall p \in \mathcal{H} && (5)\\
q_0^p &\leq C \times y_0^p & \forall p \in \mathcal{H} && (6)\\
\sum_{j\in\mathcal{V}'} x_{i,j}^p &= y_i^p & \forall i \in \mathcal{V} , \forall p \in \mathcal{H} && (7)\\
\sum_{j\in\mathcal{V}'} x_{ji}^p &= y_i^p & \forall i \in \mathcal{V} , \forall p \in \mathcal{H} && (8)\\
\sum_{(i,j)\in\mathcal{S}} x_{ij}^p &\leq |\mathcal{S}| - 1 & \forall \mathcal{S} \subseteq \mathcal{A} , t \in \mathcal{H} && (9)\\
x_{ij}^p &\in \{0,1\} & \forall (i,j) \in \mathcal{A} , \forall p \in \mathcal{H} && (10)\\
y_i^p &\in \{0,1\} & \forall i \in \mathcal{V} , \forall p \in \mathcal{H} && (11)\\
q_i^p &\geq 0 & \forall i \in \mathcal{V}' , \forall p \in \mathcal{H} && (12)\\
I_i^p &\geq 0 & \forall i \in \mathcal{V} , \forall p \in \mathcal{H} && (13)
\end{aligned}
$$

The objective computes the total holding cost for each client $i \in \mathcal{V}$ and time period $p \in \mathcal{H}'$ and the total travelling cost for $p \in \mathcal{H}$. Constraints (1) are flow conservation constraints that compute the inventory level of the supplier at each period $p \in \mathcal{H}$ from its previous inventory level, the quantity produced at p and the quantities sent to the clients at p. Similarly, constraints (2) state the flow conservation constraints regarding the clients. They compute the inventory level of each client $i \in \mathcal{V}'$ for each period $p \in \mathcal{H}$ from its previous inventory level, the quantity received from the supplier and its demand for period p. The inventory capacity is enforced through several constraints: Constraints (3) state that the inventory level of client $i \in \mathcal{V}'$ at any period $p \in \mathcal{H}$ must be lower than $I_i^{\max}$, and constraints (4) state that a replenishment of this client at period $p \in \mathcal{H}$ cannot exceed its maximal inventory level. Constraints (5) link variables y_i^p with q_i^p, stating that a client $i \in \mathcal{V}'$ which receives a quantity at period $p \in \mathcal{H}$, is necessarily visited at p. $I^{\max}$ is used here as an upper bound for q_i^p. Constraints (6) works similarly for the supplier, stating that the quantity leaving supplier 0 at period $p \in \mathcal{H}$ is limited by the vehicle capacity C. Constraints (7) and constraints (8) are flow conservation constraints for the routing component for each $i \in \mathcal{V}'$ and respectively state that if a client is visited, one arc arrives to it and another leaves from it. Constraints (9) eliminates sub-tours, where $\mathcal{S}$

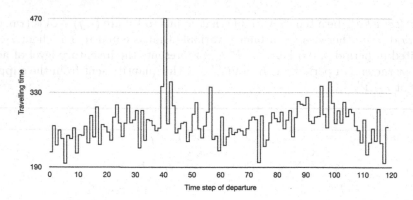

Fig. 1. A travelling time function between two locations where $\mathcal{M} = 120$

is a set of sub-tours. Finally, constraints (10) to (13) enforce integrality and non-negativity conditions on the variables.

3.2 Time-Dependent Travelling Time Function

The main difference between the IRP and the TD-IRP resides in its routing component. Let $\mathcal{T}$ be the length of a period $p \in \mathcal{H}$. $t \in \mathcal{T}$ represent the granularity in time for a period $p \in \mathcal{H}$. For example, $\mathcal{H}$ can represent the days and $\mathcal{T}$ the hours of the day. In IRP, for all $t \in \mathcal{T}$, the travelling time between a location i and j is constant and is equal to τ_{ij}. However, for the TD-IRP, the travelling time τ_{ij}^t is no longer constant but depends on the time t when the vehicle leaves from i.

Producing time-dependent functions for routing problems is a field that many scholars took interest in. A variety of functions exist in the literature for the Time-Dependent Travelling Salesman Problem (TD-TSP): some are artificial while others are based on real traffic data. Rather than reviewing the time-dependent functions in the literature, we refer to [19] who propose a compact review of the functions available in the literature and their limitations and present a new one based on the traffic conditions of the city of Lyon, using a dynamic microscopic simulator of traffic flow. It consists of constant piece-wise travelling time functions τ for each couple of locations with a number of time steps $|\mathcal{M}| = \{1, 12, 30, 60, 120\}$ and lengths (respectively) $L = \{720, 60, 24, 12, 6\}$ minutes, where $|\mathcal{T}| = |\mathcal{M}| \times L$. An example of a constant piece-wise travelling time function between two locations with $|\mathcal{M}| = 120$ time-steps and $L = 6$ minutes is presented in Fig. 1. In this case, the travelling time between any two locations and for each time-step is computed as the shortest path and is given in seconds. These travelling time functions will be used as the travelling time functions of the TD-IRP in the remaining of the paper.

A problem is faced when handling constant piece-wise travelling time functions is that the First In First Out (FIFO) property is not always satisfied.

3.3   First in First Out (FIFO) Property

A travelling time function τ that enforces the FIFO property is such that:

$$t' + \tau_{ij}^{t'} \geq t + \tau_{ij}^{t} \qquad \forall (i,j) \in \mathcal{A}, \forall t, t' \in \mathcal{T} \text{ where } t' \geq t$$

In other words, a travelling time function that enforces the FIFO property ensures that if leaving i to j at t, it is impossible to arrive later than when leaving i to j at t' when t' is later than t. The advantage of a travelling time function that enforces the FIFO property is that it is more realistic than one that does not. However, for constant piece-wise functions, the FIFO property is not satisfied for all $t \in \mathcal{T}$.

In the case of a piece-wise function, the length of a period $\mathcal{T}$ is split into $|\mathcal{M}|$ discrete time steps of duration L ($|\mathcal{T}| = |\mathcal{M}| \times L$). Let $m \in \mathcal{M}$ be the index of a time-step. Each time step $m \in \mathcal{M}$ is identified in a time interval denoted by t_m. Let $t_m = [t_m^{\min}; t_{m+1}^{\min}[$ where $t_m^{\min}$ represents the beginning of interval t_m. Finally, let τ_{ij}^{m} be the travelling time of traversing arc $(i,j) \in \mathcal{A}$ when $t \in t_m$. It is worth noting that in a constant piece-wise function, for all $t \in t_m$: $\tau_{ij}^{t} = \tau_{ij}^{m}$.

When there is an increasing discontinuity between time-step m and its successor $m+1$, i.e. $\tau_{ij}^{m} < \tau_{ij}^{m+1}$, the FIFO property is always satisfied in a piece-wise function since for all $t' \in t_{m+1}$ and $t \in t_m$: $t' > t$ and $\tau_{ij}^{m+1} > \tau_{ij}^{m}$. Therefore $t' + \tau_{ij}^{t'} > t + \tau_{ij}^{t}$. However, when a decreasing discontinuity occurs, an interval exists in t_m for which the FIFO property is not satisfied. This non-FIFO interval is denoted by $t_m^{\overline{FIFO}}$ where $t_m^{\overline{FIFO}} \subseteq t_m$. We will demonstrate this through an example of a constant piece-wise travelling time function, where $\mathcal{M} = 3$ and $L = 5$, presented in Fig. 2. We also show how to define the interval $t_m^{\overline{FIFO}}$ and transform the travelling time function τ, into one that enforces the FIFO property.

Following the non-FIFO travelling time function τ presented in Fig. 2, if we leave i for j at $t_{\text{departure}} = 0$, we arrive to j at $t_{\text{arrival}} = t_{\text{departure}} + \tau_{ij}^{m=1} = 0 + 2 = 2$, whereas when we leave i at $t'_{\text{departure}} = 4$, we arrive to j at $t'_{\text{arrival}} = t'_{\text{departure}} + \tau_{ij}^{m=2} = 4 + 7 = 11$. The FIFO property is satisfied in this case for all $t \in t_{m=1}$ and $t' \in t_{m=2}$ since it is an increasing discontinuity. Now, if we leave i at $t_{\text{departure}} = 4$, we arrive to j at $t_{\text{arrival}} = t_{\text{departure}} + \tau_{ij}^{m=2} = 4 + 7 = 11$. Whereas if we leave i at $t'_{\text{departure}} = 8$, we arrive to j at $t'_{\text{arrival}} = t'_{\text{departure}} + \tau_{ij}^{m=3} = 8 + 4 = 12$. The FIFO property is also satisfied. On the other hand, if we leave i at $t_{\text{departure}} = 6$, we arrive to j at $t_{\text{arrival}} = t_{\text{departure}} + \tau_{ij}^{m=2} = 6 + 7 = 13$ whereas if we leave i at $t'_{\text{departure}} = 8$, we arrive to j at $t'_{\text{arrival}} = t'_{\text{departure}} + \tau_{ij}^{m=3} = 8 + 4 = 12$. In this case, the FIFO property is no longer satisfied since we arrive earlier by departing later. The interval $t_m^{\overline{FIFO}}$ for which the function no longer satisfies the FIFO property is defined as $t_m^{\overline{FIFO}} =]\max\{t_m^{\min}, t_{m+1}^{\min} - (\tau_{ij}^{m} - \tau_{ij}^{m+1})\}; t_{m+1}^{\min}[$. In the case of the example, $t_2^{\overline{FIFO}} =]\max\{4, 8 - (7 - 4)\}; 8[=]5; 8[$.

Now that the interval $t_m^{\overline{FIFO}}$ is identified, we need to transform this function into one that satisfies the FIFO property. Several ways to transform a non-FIFO function into a FIFO one exist; we use the one by [20] that simulates waiting

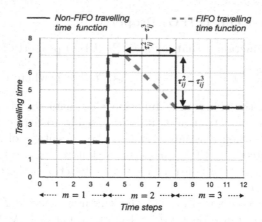

Fig. 2. FIFO travelling function transformation procedure

times. Indeed, if for all $t \in t_m^{\overline{FIFO}}$, instead of leaving right away we wait for the moment t_{m+1}^{min}, the FIFO property is always satisfied. In order to do this, the constant piece-wise function τ is transformed into a linear piece-wise function such as

$$\tau_{ij}^t = \min \left\{ \tau_{ij}^{m=\lfloor \frac{t}{L} \rfloor}, \min_{f \in \mathcal{F}} f(t) \right\} \qquad \forall t \in \mathcal{T}, \forall(i,j) \in \mathcal{A}$$

$\mathcal{F}$ is a set of linear functions f that are added for every decreasing discontinuity. The full procedure for the FIFO transformation is described in Algorithm 1.

3.4 Limits of the FIFO Travelling Time Function

Let x_{ijm}^p be a binary variable that is equal to 1 if the vehicle leaves $i \in \mathcal{V}$ to $j \in \mathcal{V}$ at time step $m \in \mathcal{M}$ and 0 otherwise, when the travelling time function is constant piece-wise (non-FIFO). For an instance where $|\mathcal{V}| = 5$, $|\mathcal{H}| = 3$, $|\mathcal{M}| = 120$ and $L = 360$, the number of variables x_{ijm}^p denoted by $\#x_{ijm}^p$ is equal to $\#x_{ijm}^p = (|\mathcal{V}| - 1)^2 \times |\mathcal{H}| \times |\mathcal{M}| = 4^2 \times 3 \times 120 = 5,760$ variables.

Algorithm 1: FIFO transformation

1: **input**: a constant piece-wise travelling time function τ, an arc $(i,j) \in \mathcal{A}$ and an empty set of linear functions $\mathcal{F}$
2: **for** $m \in \mathcal{M} = \{1, 2, ..., |M| - 1\}$ **do**
3:     **if** $\tau_{ij}^m > \tau_{ij}^{m+1}$ **then**
4:         create a linear function f such that $f(t) = \begin{cases} -t + \tau_{ij}^{t_{m+1}^{min}} + t_{m+1}^{min} & \forall t < t_{m+1}^{min} \\ +\infty & \forall t \geq t_{m+1}^{min} \end{cases}$
5:         add f to $\mathcal{F}$
6:     **end if**
7: **end for**
8: **return** τ and $\mathcal{F}$

Since the FIFO function is a linear step-wise function, knowing the time step in which location i is left is no longer sufficient. It is necessary to know the exact moment, in seconds. Therefore, discretising the length of the period into seconds is needed. Let x_{ijt}^p be a binary variable that is equal to 1 if the vehicle leaves $i \in \mathcal{V}$ to $j \in \mathcal{V}$ at second $t \in \mathcal{T}$ and 0 otherwise, when the travelling time function is linear piece-wise (FIFO). The problem faced in this case is the number of the binary variables. Indeed, for the same instance, the number of variables x_{ijt}^p denoted by $\#x_{ijt}^p$ is equal to $(|\mathcal{V}| - 1)^2 \times |\mathcal{H}| \times |\mathcal{M}| \times L = 4^2 \times 3 \times 120 \times 360 = 2,073,600$ variables. Optimising with such a number of variables, even though they can be reduced by cleaning the graph, is a tedious task. However, since the objective of our IRP is to minimise the cost of travelling but not the arrival time, and since the FIFO function simulates waiting at nodes, it is possible to produce solutions that satisfy the FIFO property with a non-FIFO function by allowing waiting at nodes. This prevents using a huge number of variables.

Let us consider an example presented in Fig. 3 where $|\mathcal{V}| = 3$, $|\mathcal{M}| = 3$ and $L = 5$ and for each arc (ij), a travelling time function is presented. Let us assume that an optimal solution is to visit locations $1, 2, 3$ in the order $1 \rightarrow 2 \rightarrow 3 \rightarrow 1$ and that the vehicle must leave location 1 at the beginning of the period, i.e. at $t = 0$. Therefore, we need to determine at what time the vehicle leaves 2 for 3 and at what time it leaves 3 for 1. Three cases are displayed: (i) non-FIFO travelling time function with no waiting allowed, (ii) FIFO travelling time function with no waiting allowed and (iii) non-FIFO travelling time function with waiting allowed. For (i) and (iii), the solution with minimum cost is to depart from 1 at $m = 1$, from 2 at $m = 1$ and from 3 at $m = 2$. For (ii) more than one optimal solution exist: leaving 1 at $t = 0$, leaving 2 at $t \in \{0, 1, 2, 3, 4\}$ and leaving 3 at $t \in \{5, 6, 7, 8, 9\}$. For (i) and (ii), these solutions are infeasible since no waiting at nodes is allowed. The optimal feasible solution is to leave 1 at $m = 1$, 2 at $m = 1$ and 3 at $m = 2$ for (i) and leave 1 at $t = 0$, 2 at $t = 1$ and 3 at $t = 2$ for (ii). The problem in this case is that although the vehicle leaves 3 at the same moment, it arrives later in the solution of (i) than in the solution of (ii). Therefore, the FIFO property is not satisfied. However, leaving 1 at $m = 1$, 2 at $m = 1$ and 3 at $m = 2$ is feasible for (iii). In this case, the arrival time in (ii) is equal to the arrival time in (iii), which means that the FIFO property is satisfied. We can conclude from this example that we are able to produce solutions that enforce the FIFO property while using a non-FIFO travelling time function by allowing waiting at nodes.

3.5   Mathematical Formulation of the TD-IRP

Let us start by defining a time-dependent path, using the definition by [21].

Definition 1. *Let $P = < v_1, ..., v_{k-1}, v_k, v_{k+1}, ..., v_n >$ where $v_k \in \mathcal{V}'$ and $v_1 = v_n = 0$ the supplier. Let $T = < m_1, ..., m_{k-1}, m_k, m_{k+1}, ..., v_{n-1} >$ be a set of departure times. A time-dependent path $[P, T]$ is a combination of P and T where T represents the departure times of $v_k \in P \backslash \{v_n\}$.*

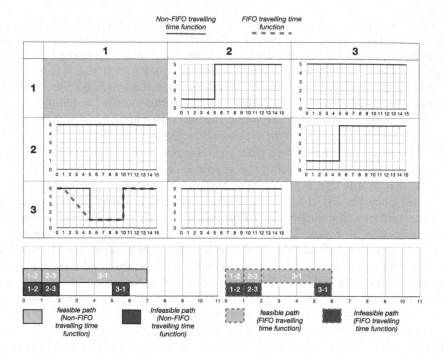

Fig. 3. Example 1: non-FIFO waiting not allowed vs. FIFO waiting not allowed vs. FIFO waiting allowed

Let t_{v_k} and s_{v_k} be, respectively, the earliest departure time and the service time of location $v_k \in P$ where:

$$- \ t_{v_k} = \begin{cases} 0 + s_{v_k} & v_k = 0 \\ \max\{t_{v_{k-1}} + \tau_{v_{k-1},v_k}^{\lfloor \frac{t_{v_{k-1}}}{L} \rfloor} + s_{v_k}, \ t_{m_k}^{\min}\} & \forall k \in P \backslash \{v_n, v_1\} \end{cases}$$

$- \ [P, T]$ is infeasible $\iff \exists v_k \in P : t_{v_k} \notin [t_{m_k}^{\min}; t_{m_k+1}^{\min}[$

Using this definition, infeasible paths can be detected and eliminated following the mathematical formulation presented below.

TD-IRP

$$\min obj^{\text{TD-IRP}} = c \times \sum_{(i,j)\in\mathcal{A}} \sum_{p\in\mathcal{H}} \sum_{m\in\mathcal{M}} \tau_{ij}^m \times x_{ijm}^p + \sum_{i\in\mathcal{V}} \sum_{p\in\mathcal{H}'} h_i \times I_i^p$$

s.t. (1) to (13)

$$\sum_{m\in\mathcal{M}} x_{ijm}^p = x_{ij}^p \qquad \forall (i,j)\in\mathcal{A}, \forall p\in\mathcal{H} \qquad (14)$$

$$\sum_{j\in\mathcal{V}'} x_{0j0}^p = y_0^p \qquad \forall p\in\mathcal{H} \qquad (15)$$

$$\sum_{v_k\in P\backslash\{v_n\}} \sum_{m_k\in T} x_{v_k,v_{k+1},m_k}^p \leq |P| - 2 \qquad \forall P, T\in\overline{[P,T]}, p\in\mathcal{H} \qquad (16)$$

$$x_{ijm}^p \in \{0,1\} \qquad \forall (i,j)\in\mathcal{A}, m\in\mathcal{M}, \forall p\in\mathcal{H} \quad (17)$$

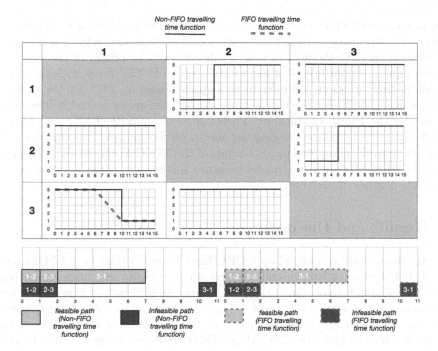

Fig. 4. Example 2: non-FIFO waiting not allowed vs. FIFO waiting not allowed vs. FIFO waiting allowed

The objective of the TD-IRP extends the objective of the IRP by incorporating the time dimension in the travelling cost. The model is extended with constraints (14) to (17). Constraints (14) link the variables x_{ijm}^p to variables x_{ij}^p stating that if an arc $(i.j) \in \mathcal{A}$, it is travelled in one time step only. Constraints (14) state that if a tour is scheduled, it starts from the supplier at the beginning of the period. Constraints (16) eliminate the infeasible time-dependent paths $\overline{[P,T]}$. Finally, constraints (17) enforce the integrality of variables x_{ijm}^p.

3.6   Time-Travel Constrained TD-IRP

Let us take a look at another example presented in Fig. 4, which is an alternative version of the example in Fig. 3. We reconsider the same three cases: (i) non-FIFO travelling time function with no waiting allowed, (ii) FIFO travelling time function with no waiting allowed and (iii) non-FIFO travelling time function with waiting allowed.

For (i) and (ii) the optimal feasible solutions are the same: departing from 1 at $t = 0$, from 2 at $t = 1$ and from 3 at $t = 2$. For (iii), an optimal solution is to depart from 1 at $t = 0$, from 2 at $t = 1$ and from 3 at $t = 10$. All these solutions enforce the FIFO property. However, the solution of (iii) does not only use waiting times to mimic the FIFO algorithm but uses it to improve the cost of solution by waiting even more. The problem with this kind of solutions is that they are not satisfactory in real life. Therefore, in order to avoid such solutions, it is necessary to constrain the total duration of travelling, hence the TD-TC-IRP.

Since in an IRP, the longest tour would visit all the clients of the network, we compute an upper bound of the solution of a TD-TSP for $\mathcal{V}$ with the FIFO travelling time function. We refer to this upper bound as $\mathcal{T}^{\text{new}}$ for the value in seconds and $|\mathcal{M}^{\text{new}}|$ for the one in time steps. This upper bound will serve as a limit for the length of the tour. Therefore, $\mathcal{T} = \max\{\mathcal{T}, \mathcal{T}^{\text{new}}\}$ and $|\mathcal{M}| = \max\{|\mathcal{M}|, |\mathcal{M}^{\text{new}}|\}$. Since the original length of the period $\mathcal{T}$ is very large in comparison to the computed upper bounds of the TD-TSP, the TD-IRP becomes a TD-TC-IRP. Moreover, the model becomes smaller and easier to solve due to a smaller number of variables.

4   Results and Discussion

All experiments are conducted on a CPU Intel Xeon E5-1620 v3 @3.5 Ghz with 64 GB RAM using a branch-and-cut procedure with an execution time limit of 3600 s. The sub-tour elimination constraints as well as the time-dependent infeasible paths constraints are added dynamically using Gurobi 9.0.2 as a solver with the lazyConstraints parameter and the default number threads. As stated before, in order to make the TD-IRP a TD-TC-IRP, we compute upper bounds for the TD-TSP. To that purpose, a simple Iterated Local Search (ILS) algorithm is used. All algorithms are implemented with Java.

The benchmark used for these experiments is the result of a combination between the most commonly used benchmark of the IRP presented in [2] and the benchmark of the TD-TSP presented in [19] and discussed in Subsect. 3.2. The combination is made by replacing the euclidean coordinates in [2] with constant travel time functions between each 2 locations from [19]. We tested instances with a number of clients $|\mathcal{V}| \in \{5, 10, 15, 20, 25, 30\}$ and a number of periods $|\mathcal{H}| = 3$. For each value of $|\mathcal{V}|$, 10 different instances are available. Each instance is combined with 6 different travelling time functions depending on the number of time steps $|\mathcal{M}| = \{1, 12, 30, 60, 120\}$. The case $|\mathcal{M}| = 1$ is the basic IRP.

In order to see the impact of optimising with time-dependent travelling time functions, we solve the basic problem and the time-dependent problems. Moreover, we also solve the time-dependent problem using the partial solution given by the solution of the basic IRP. The partial solution here means that all the values of variables x_{ij}^p, q_i^p, y_i^p and I_i^p are fixed to the one found when solving the basic IRP, leaving variables x_{ijm}^p to be determined.

Table 1 presents the results of these experiments. Columns z, g and $CPU(s)$ present, respectively, the objective value, the gap and the execution time, in average, of the basic IRP. Columns $z_\mathcal{M}$, $g_\mathcal{M}$ and $CPU_\mathcal{M}(s)$ represent, respectively, the objective value, the gap and the execution time, in average, of the TD-IRP. Finally, column $\bar{g}$ represents the gap between the solutions found using the basic solutions with time-dependent functions z to the time-dependent solutions $z_\mathcal{M}$ where $\bar{g} = \frac{z_\mathcal{M} - z}{z_\mathcal{M}}$.

Table 1. Results

$|\mathcal{V}|$	$|\mathcal{M}|$	z	$g\%$	$CPU(s)$	$z_\mathcal{M}$	$g_\mathcal{M}\%$	$CPU_\mathcal{M}(s)$	$\overline{g}\%$
5	1	2182.21	0.00	0.01				
	12	1964.21	0.00	0.00	1959.81	0.00	0.01	0.22
	30	1832.41	0.00	0.00	1832.21	0.00	0.01	0.01
	60	1734.61	0.00	0.00	1729.21	0.00	0.04	0.31
	120	1594.21	0.00	0.00	1575.16	0.00	0.09	1.21
10	1	3628.56	0.00	0.04				
	12	3373.66	0.00	0.00	3344.28	0.00	0.04	0.88
	30	3234.86	0.00	0.01	3189.87	0.00	0.47	1.41
	60	3059.26	0.00	0.02	3024.49	0.00	0.70	1.15
	120	2844.16	0.00	0.05	2790.79	0.00	2.15	1.15
15	1	4592.76	0.00	0.26				
	12	4292.66	0.00	0.01	4278.56	0.00	0.55	0.33
	30	4152.46	0.00	0.04	4132.36	0.00	3.61	0.49
	60	3943.76	0.00	0.20	3898.75	0.00	12.88	1.15
	120	3666.96	0.00	0.58	3598.49	0.00	58.09	1.90
20	1	5943.82	0.00	0.22				
	12	5561.62	0.00	0.02	5540.02	0.00	1.33	0.39
	30	5384.82	0.00	0.15	5314.13	0.00	24.70	1.33
	60	5147.72	0.00	0.78	5058.48	0.00	132.04	1.76
	120	4863.22	0.00	11.64	4778.23	0.94	997.54	1.78
25	1	6838.12	0.00	0.27				
	12	6506.12	0.00	0.05	6477.61	0.00	10.54	0.44
	30	6293.72	0.00	0.45	6256.21	0.00	591.80	0.60
	60	6063.92	0.00	2.67	6018.49	1.67	1689.16	0.75
	120	5769.52	0.06	747.36	5760.07	5.73	3600.06	0.76
30	1	8428.37	0.00	0.52				
	12	8061.97	0.00	0.19	8020.23	0.82	1247.00	0.52
	30	7806.37	0.00	4.53	7773.43	0.87	2183.56	0.42
	60	7543.67	0.00	434.07	7522.99	3.69	3135.61	0.27
	120	7184.87	0.57	1964.32	6839.65	10.08	3600.08	5.05

We can see from Table 1 that the gaps $\overline{g}$ between the basic solution when applied to a time-dependent travelling time-function and the time-dependent solution are fairly small, as the largest gap is 5% for $|\mathcal{V}| = 30$ and $|\mathcal{M}| = 120$. The reasons can be summarised in three points:

Departure Time From the Supplier: In this paper, we consider that the departure time from the supplier is always the beginning of the period, i.e. $t = 0$.

Although for the constant case this parameter does not have an impact, since the travelling times are constant over the entire length of the period, it can have a big importance for the time-dependent case. The cost of the tour can heavily decrease if leaving later avoids travelling during time intervals where the traffic is congested.

Number of Clients: For $|\mathcal{V}| = \{5, 10, 15, 20\}$ the number of clients does not seem influential as the gaps $\bar{g}$ are quite similar. This is due to the speed with which we can visit all the clients and get back to the supplier. As seen from Fig. 1, the travelling time function is not volatile in the first time-steps, and since it does not take a long time to visit up to 20 clients, all of the clients can be visited while avoiding congestion periods. However, for $|\mathcal{V}| = \{25, 30\}$ although the gaps does not show a big difference since the instances are not solved to optimality due to their hardness, we expect that the gaps will be bigger when optimality is achieved (Instances where $|\mathcal{V}| = 30$ and $|\mathcal{M}| = 120$ give a glimpse of this intuition). Indeed, when the number of clients is bigger, visiting all the clients requires more time and therefore it is not possible to entirely avoid congestion periods. This is where optimising with time-dependent travelling time functions becomes useful.

Structure of Time-Dependent Solutions: We observed that optimal time-dependent solutions are not very different from basic solutions, as the difference only resides in the values of variables x_{ij}^p and x_{ijm}^p. This means that the same clients are visited for each period with the same quantities. The only difference is in the sequence in which the clients are visited. Therefore, since the gap in the cost is only seen in the transportation cost, its impact is not of a big importance as the inventory cost remains the same.

Note that the results presented in Table 1 can be heavily impacted by the upper-bounds of the TD-TSP. If the TD-TSP is solved to optimality, then the waiting times will be used only to mimic the FIFO transformation algorithm. However, since in our case the TD-TSP upper bounds are generated using an ILS algorithms, the performance of the algorithm has an impact on the TD-TC-IRP solutions. Indeed, the better the ILS performs, the shorter $|\mathcal{T}|$ is, and vice-versa.

5   Conclusions and Perspectives

In this paper, we propose a new variant of the IRP, the TD-TC-IRP. In this variant, the travelling time between two locations is not constant throughout the day but depends on the time the arc is travelled and the length of a trip is constrained. A constant piece-wise time-dependent travelling time function of the TD-TSP literature is presented. We show that such functions do not necessarily satisfy the FIFO property and present a way on how to transform it to a linear piece-wise function that does. The limits of using a linear piece-wise function for optimisation purposes are discussed. To cater for this, a mathematical formulation for the TD-TC-IRP using a constant piece-wise function by allowing waiting at nodes, in order to always satisfy the FIFO property, is proposed. Numerical experiments are conducted on a new proposed benchmark where benchmarks from the literature of the IRP and the TD-TSP are combined using a branch-and-cut procedure. The results show that solving the TD-TC-IRP is harder than its basic counterpart. Moreover, it also shows that the solutions of the basic IRP performs almost as well as time-dependent solutions in a time-dependent environment. However, this last point can be the result of parameters such as the departure time from the supplier and the number of clients visited.

A future work would be to enhance the solving method by proposing new valid inequalities or new reformulations for the TD-IRP. Faster algorithms will help with two points: solving larger instances and considering the departure time from the supplier as a decision variable and no longer the beginning of the period. Another perspective is to consider a dynamic service time which will not be constant anymore but depends on the replenishment quantity.

Acknowledgments. The authors thank H. Cambazard and N. Catusse for their valuable contribution to this work.

References

1. Campbell, A.M.: The Inventory Routing Problem. Springer, Boston (1998)
2. Archetti, C., Bertazzi, L., Laporte, G., Speranza, M.G.: A branch-and-cut algorithm for a vendor-managed inventory-routing problem. Transp. Sci. **41**(3), 382–391 (2007)
3. Gendreau, M., Ghiani, G., Guerriero, E.: Time-dependent routing problems: a review. Comput. Oper. Res. **64**, 189–197 (2015)
4. Moin, N.H., Salhi, S.: Inventory routing problems: a logistical overview. J. Oper. Res. Soc. **58**(9), 1185–1194 (2007)
5. Andersson, H., Hoff, A., Christiansen, M., Hasle, G., Løkketangen, A.: Industrial aspects and literature survey: combined inventory management and routing. Comput. Oper. Res. **37**(9), 1515–1536 (2010)
6. Bertazzi, L., Speranza, M.G.: Inventory routing problems: an introduction. Eur. J. Transp. Logist. **1**(4), 307–326 (2012)
7. Coelho, L.C., Cordeau, J.F., Laporte, G.: Thirty years of inventory routing. Transp. Sci. **48**(1), 1–19 (2014)
8. Delgado, K.V., Alves, P.Y.A.L., Freire, V.: Inventory routing problem with time windows: a systematic review of the literature. In: Proceedings of the XIV Brazilian Symposium on Information Systems. pp. 215–222 (2018)
9. Coelho, L.C., Cordeau, J.F., Laporte, G.: The inventory-routing problem with transshipment. Comput. Oper. Res. **39**(11), 2537–2548 (2012)
10. Bertazzi, L., Laganà, D., Ohlmann, J.W., Paradiso, R.: An exact approach for cyclic inbound inventory routing in a level production system. Eur. J. Oper. Res. **283**(3), 915–928 (2020)
11. Farias, K., Hadj-Hamou, K., Yugma, C.: Model and exact solution for a two-echelon inventory routing problem. Int. J. Prod. Res. **0**(0), 1–24 (2020)
12. Lefever, W., Touzout, F.A., Hadj-Hamou, K., Aghezzaf, E.H.: Benders' decomposition for robust travel time-constrained inventory routing problem. International J. Prod. Re. **0**(0), 1–25 (2019)

13. Melgarejo, P.A., Laborie, P., Solnon, C.: A time-dependent no-overlap constraint: Application to urban delivery problems. In: CPAIOR, pp. 1–17 (2015)
14. Taş, D., Gendreau, M., Jabali, O., Laporte, G.: The traveling salesman problem with time-dependent service times. Eur. J. Oper. Res. **248**(2), 372–383 (2016)
15. Ehmke, J.F., Campbell, A.M., Thomas, B.W.: Vehicle routing to minimize time-dependent emissions in urban areas. Eur. J. Oper. Res. **251**(2), 478–494 (2016)
16. Montero, A., Méndez-Díaz, I., Miranda-Bront, J.J.: An integer programming approach for the time-dependent traveling salesman problem with time windows. Comput. Oper. Res. **88**, 280–289 (2017)
17. Minh Vu, D., Hewitt, M., Boland, N., Savelsbergh, M.: Solving time dependent traveling salesman problems with time windows. Optimization Online **6640** (2018)
18. Gmira, M., Gendreau, M., Lodi, A., Potvin, J.Y.: Managing in real-time a vehicle routing plan with time-dependent travel times on a road network. Working paper. Cirrelt-2019-45 (October) (2019)
19. Rifki, O., Chiabaut, N., Solnon, C.: On the impact of spatio-temporal granularity of traffic conditions on the quality of pickup and delivery optimal tours. Working paper. Univ Lyon (2020)
20. Ichoua, S., Gendreau, M., Potvin, J.Y.: Vehicle dispatching with time-dependent travel times. Eur. J. Oper. Res. **144**(2), 379–396 (2003)
21. Miranda-Bront, J.J., Méndez-Díaz, I., Zabala, P.: An integer programming approach for the time-dependent TSP. Electr. Notes Discr. Math. **36**(C), 351–358 (2010)

Vehicle Routing Problem with Reverse Cross-Docking: An Adaptive Large Neighborhood Search Algorithm

Aldy Gunawan[1(✉)], Audrey Tedja Widjaja[1], Pieter Vansteenwegen[2], and Vincent F. Yu[3]

[1] Singapore Management University,
80 Stamford Road, Singapore 178902, Singapore
{aldygunawan,audreyw}@smu.edu.sg
[2] KU Leuven Mobility Research Center - CIB, KU Leuven,
Celestijnenlaan 300, Box 2422, Leuven, Belgium
pieter.vansteenwegen@kuleuven.be
[3] Department of Industrial Management,
National Taiwan University of Science and Technology,
43, Section 4, Keelung Road, Taipei 106, Taiwan
vincent@mail.ntust.edu.tw

Abstract. Cross-docking is a logistics strategy that aims at less transportation costs and fast customer deliveries. Incorporating an efficient vehicle routing could increase the benefits of the cross-docking. In this paper, the vehicle routing problem with reverse cross-docking (VRP-RCD) is studied. Reverse logistics has attracted more attention due to its ability to gain more profit and maintain the competitiveness of a company. VRP-RCD includes a four-level supply chain network: suppliers, cross-dock, customers, and outlets, with the objective of minimizing vehicle operational and transportation costs. A two-phase heuristic that employs an adaptive large neighborhood search (ALNS) with various DESTROY and REPAIR operators is proposed to solve benchmark instances. The simulated annealing framework is embedded to discover a vast search space during the search process. Experimental results show that our proposed ALNS obtains optimal solutions for 24 out of 30 problems of the first set of benchmark instances while getting better results for all instances in the second set of benchmark instances compared to optimization software.

Keywords: Vehicle routing problem · Cross-docking · Reverse logistics · Adaptive large neighborhood search

1 Introduction

In a supply chain network, suppliers deliver their products to customers in two different ways, either through a direct shipment or a transhipment process.

E. Lalla-Ruiz et al. (Eds.): ICCL 2020, LNCS 12433, pp. 167–182, 2020.
https://doi.org/10.1007/978-3-030-59747-4_11

This supply chain is a vital function since customers want to receive products in quick and easy ways. In a direct shipment, each supplier may dispatch one or more vehicles in order to fulfil all customer demands, resulting in long origin-to-destination paths and a large number of vehicles dispatched [15]. On the other hand, adopting an intermediate facility for a transshipment process can improve supply chain performance as a whole and provide better delivery performance to customers. Products from suppliers are first sent to a cross-dock, sorted and consolidated according to customer demands, and then delivered to customers afterwards. It can provide enhanced customer service and it can speed up customer deliveries. Advantages of cross-docking will be enhanced by an efficient vehicle routing [6]. It is important for a distribution network because it reduces or eliminates the storage activities that belong to the warehousing system. Products are not allowed to be stored inside the cross-dock. [14] compared the performance between adopting the cross-docking strategy and direct shipments. The experiments conclude that cross-docking is capable to achieve cost savings compared to the direct-shipping under certain conditions.

The VRP plays an essential role in the field of supply chain management and logistics. It is associated with important role in distribution management and logistics, as well as the costs associated with operating vehicles with the objective of finding optimal delivery from a warehouse to a set of customers with respect to limited constraints. Customers are served by some identical vehicles with a limited capacity from suppliers. This combined VRP and cross-docking model is addressed as a vehicle routing problem with cross-docking (VRPCD) that has been widely studied [4,11,19]. Many industries or companies have started to pay more attention in reverse logistics as this concept has been recognized as a source of profitability and competitiveness for their businesses [1,8,10]. Apple, H&M, and Dasani are some examples of companies that implement reverse logistics. In reverse logistics, the returned products from customers are collected and sent back to the suppliers [9] for further processes such as break down or re-manufacture process. Due to the advantages of adopting cross-docking in the forward flow, [20] studied the VRPCD in reverse logistics flow, the so-called VRP with reverse cross-docking (VRP-RCD). We then re-visit this VRP-RCD which is suitable for companies with seasonal demand patterns, such as fashion, books, and electronics, and which commercialize the returned (unsold) products through secondary channels (e.g. outlet stores). The practice of introducing cross-docking as a viable strategy for handling returned products in the European apparel industry is highlighted by [22]. The main difference with the problem discussed in [9] is that VRP-RCD [20] happens in a four-level supply chain network consisting of suppliers, customers, outlets, and a cross-dock, while [9] only considers a three-level supply chain network: suppliers, customers, and a cross-dock. Furthermore, VRP-RCD [20] considers a multiple product scenario and a situation where some of the supplied products can be defective.

In this paper, we introduce a two-phase heuristic that employs an adaptive large neighborhood search (ALNS) to solve the VRP-RCD [20]. ALNS was firstly introduced by [16] as the extension of LNS [18]. It has been widely adopted to solve many variants of VRP such as the pollution-routing problem (PRP) [2], the two echelon VRP (2E-VRP) [7], the VRP with drones [17] and the VRPCD [4]. ALNS has also been implemented to perform the column generation process in a matheuristic approach to solve the VRPCD with time windows [3] and the VRPCD [5]. Due to the superiority of ALNS to solve various combinatorial optimization problems, we adopted the ALNS used in [4] to solve the VRP-RCD. However it should be noted that the algorithm needs several modifications due to different assumptions in both problems, such as: 1) VRPCD assumes all nodes are visited, while in VRP-RCD some nodes might not be visited, 2) VRPCD only involves customer and supplier nodes, while VRP-RCD involves customer, supplier, and outlet nodes, and 3) VRPCD considers an individual pickup (delivery) process in supplier (customer) nodes, while VRP-RCD also considers the simultaneous pickup and delivery processes in outlet nodes. In general, ALNS employs DESTROY and REPAIR operators to repetitively remove some nodes from a solution and to re-insert these back to a more profitable position. We also employ simulated annealing (SA) acceptance criteria that gives us a chance to accept a worse solution rather than always reject it, so as in order not to get stuck in local optima. The proposed ALNS performs well in solving the available benchmark VRP-RCD instances. For the first set of instances, it is able to obtain optimal solutions for 24 out of 30 instances. For the second set of instances which is a larger set, it outperforms optimization software, CPLEX, by obtaining 38.81% better results on average, with significantly faster computational times.

The rest of the paper is organized as follows. In the next section, we provide the problem description of the VRP-RCD. Section 3 presents the proposed ALNS algorithm. The computational results are presented in Sect. 4. Finally, Sect. 5 concludes the paper with our findings and directions of future research.

2 Problem Description

The VRP-RCD network (as shown in Fig. 1) involves $|C|$ customers, $|O|$ outlets, $|S|$ suppliers, and a cross-dock facility to handle the reverse logistics process. In this problem, customers can be shops or wholesalers that are trying to sell products, but may not be able to sell all. Since those products may almost reach their end of life (EOL) period to be sold on the customers site, they are then passed to the outlets for the second round of selling process with lower prices. However, those products may not be sold in outlets and have to be replaced with newer products, therefore they will be returned to the supplier who supplied those products, for further processing (e.g. re-manufacture or break down).

Each connected arc between customer and cross-dock nodes has a travel distance of e'_{ij} and a travel time of t'_{ij}. For outlet and cross-dock nodes, each connected arc has a travel distance of e''_{ij} and a travel time of t''_{ij}. Finally, between supplier and cross-dock nodes, we represent a travel distance of e'''_{ij} and a travel time of t'''_{ij} for each connected arc. Let c represent the transportation cost per unit distance.

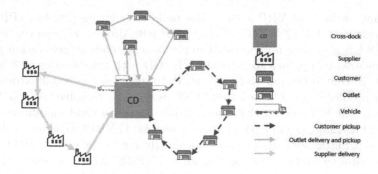

Fig. 1. VRP-RCD network

A set of homogeneous vehicles $V = 1, 2, \ldots, |V|$ with the same vehicle capacity q and operational cost H is available at the cross-dock to perform any one of three processes involved in VRP-RCD: 1) customer pickup process, 2) outlet delivery and pickup process, and 3) supplier delivery process. Let r'_{ik} be defined as the amount of returned products k from customer i and r''_{ik} as the amount of returned products k from outlet i.

In the first process, a vehicle starts from the cross-dock, visits one or more customers to pick up any returned products r'_{ik}, and back to the cross-dock at the end of its trip. Among the returned products type k, p_k percent is considered as defective products, which hence, only $(100 - p_k)$ percent of the returned products type k can be distributed to any outlet nodes for the reselling process. Therefore, outlet i with demand of product type k as much as d''_{ik} may not be able to receive all of its demand. If the non-defective unsold products k from all customers are able to fulfil all outlets demand of product k, then, all outlets with demands of product k will be visited. Otherwise, only several outlets will be visited, which depends on the number of non-defective unsold products k. The second process is thus implemented to cover this delivery process to outlet nodes, as well as to pick up their returned products r''_{ik}. Finally, all returned and defective products are sent back to each supplier that supplied that product in the third process. It is assumed that one supplier supplies one type of product. The VRP-RCD then aims to decide the number of vehicles used as well as to construct the route sequence of the used vehicles such that all processes are done within the T_{max} time horizon, while minimizing the total costs in the process (vehicle transportation and fixed operational costs). The VRP-RCD assumes a synchronous arrival scenario where the second process can only be performed after the first process is finished, and subsequently the third process can only be performed after the second process is done. This assumption is adopted from the original VRPCD [11,12,21].

The VRP-RCD addressed here is slightly different compared to the one of [20] in terms of defining the amount of returned products from customers and outlets. The VRP-RCD [20] considers the amount of customer returned products as a fraction of their demand in the previous cycle, while the amount of outlet returned products was defined as a fraction of the amount of products they received during the delivery process in the previous cycle. However, it might be hard to find the relationship between those two values in practice. Therefore, the VRP-RCD in this paper models the amount of returned products as known parameters r'_{ik} and r''_{ik} when the routing is planned, as how it is addressed in the literature [9].

3 Proposed Algorithm

Our proposed algorithm is divided into two phases. The first phase aims to decide the selected nodes and the second phase aims to construct the routing sequence given the selected nodes from the first phase, such that the total transportation and operational costs is minimized. The selected nodes from the first phase will be treated as the input and will not be modified during the second phase. Therefore, we carefully derive some rules to determine which nodes to be visited in Sect. 3.1. The second phase, described in Sect. 3.2, employs an adaptive large neighborhood search (ALNS) to find a set of routes sequence given the selected nodes from the first phase.

3.1 Phase 1: Node Selection

Since not all nodes are mandatory to be visited in this problem, we need to select which nodes to be visited. We define m'_i equals to 1 if node i must be visited during the customer pickup process; 0 otherwise ($i \in C$), m''_i equals to 1 if node i must be visited during the outlet delivery and pickup process; 0 otherwise ($i \in O$), and m'''_i equals to 1 if node i must be visited during the supplier delivery process; 0 otherwise ($i \in S$). The decision of m'_i is done in a very straightforward rule, where customer i is visited ($m'_i = 1$) if there is any returned products from customer i, and $m'_i = 0$ otherwise.

For deciding the value of m''_i, we need to calculate the amount of delivered product k to node i in advance, denoted as ϑ''_{ik}. If the amount of non-defective returned product k from all customers are more than outlets demand of product k, we set $\vartheta''_{ik} = d''_{ik}$ $\forall i \in O, \forall k \in S$. Otherwise, we apply a sorting criteria on the outlets and then iteratively assign ϑ''_{ik} according to this sorting until the amount of available units is reached. One of the following sorting criteria is randomly selected to decide the amount of ϑ''_{ik}:

- outlet with the highest demand of product k
- outlets that have demand of product k by splitting the same amount of non-defective returned product k from all customers to those outlets.
- outlet with demand of product k that is located nearest to the cross-dock and any other outlets
- outlet with the highest product types demand
- outlet with the highest cumulative demand of all product types
- outlet with the lowest unique returned product types
- outlet with the lowest cumulative returned products of all product types

Hence, outlet i will only be visited ($m_i'' = 1$) if there is any delivered and/or returned products from outlet i, and $m_i'' = 0$ otherwise. Finally, supplier k is visited ($m_k''' = 1$) if there is any returned products to supplier k, as formulated in Eq. (1).

$$m_k''' = \begin{cases} 1, & \text{if } \sum_{i \in C} r_{ik}' - \sum_{i \in O} \vartheta_{ik}'' + \sum_{i \in O} r_{ik}'' > 0 \\ 0, & \text{if } \sum_{i \in C} r_{ik}' - \sum_{i \in O} \vartheta_{ik}'' + \sum_{i \in O} r_{ik}'' = 0 \end{cases} \quad \forall k \in S \quad (1)$$

3.2 Phase 2: Adaptive Large Neighborhood Search (ALNS)

A two-dimensional solution representation with each row v representing the route sequence performed by a particular vehicle, $v \in |V|$ is designed. Hence, a solution has a fixed number of $|V|$ rows and a different number of columns in each row v, which depends on the number of visited nodes by vehicle v. This solution representation is illustrated in Fig. 2. For example, starting from the cross-dock (node 0), vehicle 1 visits suppliers 3, 2, 1, and 4 respectively, and returns back to node 0. The amount of non-defective returned products from customers can only fulfil demands of outlets 2 and 4, therefore only outlets 2 and 4 are visited by vehicle 2. Due to the vehicle capacity and time horizon constraints, one vehicle alone is unable to visit all customers. Vehicle 3 visits customers 3, 1, and 4, while vehicle 4 visits customers 2, 6, and 5. In this example, in total four vehicles are required to complete the entire process.

Vehicle 1	0	S3	S2	S1	S4	0
Vehicle 2	0	O2	O4	0		
Vehicle 3	0	C3	C1	C4	0	
Vehicle 4	0	C2	C6	C5	0	
Vehicle 5	0					

Fig. 2. Example of solution representation with $|S| = 4, |O| = 5, |C| = 6, |V| = 5$

3.2.1 Initial Solution

Based on the selected nodes from the first phase (Sect. 3.1), we perform the following five steps to construct an initial solution:

STEP 1: Node allocation. We allocate nodes to vehicles by solving the following mathematical model.

- $a_i'^v$ is a binary decision variable with value 1 indicating node i is visited by vehicle v in the customer pickup process; 0 otherwise ($i \in C, v \in V$)
- $a_i''^v$ is a binary decision variable with value 1 indicating node i is visited by vehicle v in the outlet delivery and pickup process; 0 otherwise ($i \in O, v \in V$)

- $a_i'''^v$ is a binary decision variable with value 1 indicating node i is visited by vehicle v in the supplier delivery process; 0 otherwise $(i \in S, v \in V)$
- x'^v is a binary decision variable with value 1 indicating vehicle v in used in customer pickup process; 0 otherwise $(v \in V)$
- x''^v is a binary decision variable with value 1 indicating vehicle v in used in outlet delivery and pickup process; 0 otherwise $(v \in V)$
- x'''^v is a binary decision variable with value 1 indicating vehicle v in used in supplier delivery process; 0 otherwise $(v \in V)$

The objective function (2) minimizes the number of vehicles used.

$$Min \sum_{v \in V} x'^v + x''^v + x'''^v \tag{2}$$

All mandatory visited nodes are visited by exactly one vehicle, as addressed in constraints (3) to (5).

$$\sum_{v \in V} a_i'^v = m_i' \ \forall i \in C \tag{3}$$

$$\sum_{v \in V} a_i''^v = m_i'' \ \forall i \in O \tag{4}$$

$$\sum_{v \in V} a_i'''^v = m_i''' \ \forall i \in S \tag{5}$$

The vehicle capacity constraints are presented by constraints (6) to (8). Constraint (6) ensures that the amount of picked-up products from any customers assigned to vehicle v does not exceed the vehicle capacity. Constraint (7) ensures that the amount of max(picked-up, delivered) products from/to any outlets assigned to vehicle v does not exceed the vehicle capacity. Constraint (8) ensures that the amount of delivered products to any suppliers assigned to vehicle v does not exceed the vehicle capacity. The amount of delivered products equals the sum of (the difference between customers returned products and amount of products delivered to outlets) and (outlets returned products).

$$\sum_{i \in C} \sum_{k \in S} a_i'^v r_{ik}' \le q \ \forall v \in V \tag{6}$$

$$\sum_{i \in O} a_i''^v \times \max \left(\sum_{k \in S} \vartheta_{ik}'', \sum_{k \in S} r_{ik}'' \right) \le q \ \forall v \in V \tag{7}$$

$$\sum_{k \in S} a_k'''^v \left(\sum_{i \in C} r_{ik}' - \sum_{i \in O} \vartheta_{ik}'' + \sum_{i \in O} r_{ik}'' \right) \le q \ \forall v \in V \tag{8}$$

Constraints (9) to (11) keep track of the used vehicle in each process and constraint (12) ensures that each vehicle is being used in at most one of the three processes.

$$|C| x'^v \ge \sum_{i \in C} a_i'^v \ \forall v \in V \tag{9}$$

$$|O|x''^{v} \geq \sum_{i \in O} a''_{i}{}^{v} \quad \forall v \in V \tag{10}$$

$$|S|x'''^{v} \geq \sum_{i \in S} a'''_{i}{}^{v} \quad \forall v \in V \tag{11}$$

$$x'^{v} + x''^{v} + x'''^{v} \leq 1 \quad \forall v \in V \tag{12}$$

STEP 2: Route sequence construction. We implemented a nearest neighbor heuristic to construct a route sequence in each vehicle.

STEP 3: Time feasibility checking. It is done by recording the maximum transportation time in each process, denoted as Tcp_{max}, $Todp_{max}$, and Tsd_{max}. If the total of Tcp_{max}, $Todp_{max}$, and Tsd_{max} does not exceed time horizon, we continue to STEP 5. Otherwise, go to STEP 4.

STEP 4: Repair time infeasibility. We remove a node from a vehicle that has the highest total transportation time, and relocate this node to another vehicle as long as it does not violate the vehicle capacity and time horizon constraints. Otherwise, this node will be relocated to a new vehicle. This step is repeated until time horizon constraint is satisfied.

STEP 5: Objective function value calculation. The objective function is calculated by adding up the total of transportation and operational costs.

3.2.2 Algorithm

ALNS employs DESTROY and REPAIR operators that aims to remove π nodes from a solution and then to reinsert them back in a more profitable position, such that a new solution is observed. The performance of each operator is then evaluated and is given a higher score if it generates a better solution. This score later becomes the base for calculating its weight, which adjusts its probability to be selected in the following iterations. When a combination of DESTROY-REPAIR operators is able to generate a better solution, its score is increased and also its weight and probability. Additionally, in order to escape from local optima, we incorporate simulated annealing (SA) acceptance criteria by giving chance to accept worse solution during the search process.

Let us define $R = \{R_r | r = 1, 2, \ldots, |R|\}$ and $I = \{I_i | i = 1, 2, \ldots, |I|\}$ as the set of DESTROY and REPAIR operators respectively (see Sect. 3.2.3). Every time DESTROY and REPAIR operators generate a new solution, we adjust its score using Eq. (13), where $\delta_1 > \delta_2 > \delta_3$ [13]. In our implementation, we use $\delta_1 = 0.5, \delta_2 = 0.33, \delta_3 = 0.17$.

$$s_j = \begin{cases} s_j + \delta_1, & \text{if } j \text{ is selected and the new solution is} \\ & \text{the best found solution so far} \\ s_j + \delta_2, & \text{if } j \text{ is selected and the new solution} \\ & \text{improves the current solution} \qquad \forall j \in R \cup I \\ s_j + \delta_3, & \text{if } j \text{ is selected and the new solution} \\ & \text{does not improve the current solution,} \\ & \text{but it is accepted} \end{cases} \tag{13}$$

After η_{ALNS} iterations, we calculate each operators weight by following Eq. (14). Subsequently, operators probability are adjusted by following Eq. (15).

$$w_j = \begin{cases} (1-\gamma)w_j + \gamma\frac{s_j}{\chi_j}, & \text{if } \chi_j > 0 \\ (1-\gamma)w_j, & \text{if } \chi_j = 0 \end{cases} \quad \forall j \in R \cup I \tag{14}$$

$$p_j = \begin{cases} \frac{w_j}{\sum_{k \in R} w_k} & \forall j \in R \\ \frac{w_j}{\sum_{k \in I} w_k} & \forall j \in I \end{cases} \tag{15}$$

The pseudocode is presented in Algorithm 1. ALNS starts by setting the current solution (Sol_0), the best solution so far (Sol^*), and the starting solution in each iteration (Sol') equals to INITIALSOLUTION, which is constructed based on Sect. 3.2.1 (line 1). The current temperature $Temp$ is set as initial temperature (T_0) (line 2) which will be reduced by α after η_{SA} (line 32). FOUNDBESTSOL is set as False in the beginning (line 4) and every η_{SA} iterations (line 31). Its value will only be True if a new better than Sol^* solution is found (lines 17–19). Subsequently, when it is True, then NOIMPR is reset as 0 (lines 28–30), otherwise it is increased by one (lines 25–27). At the beginning, all operators are initialized by the same score, weight, and probability (line 5).

In every iteration, π nodes are removed from Sol_0 (lines 8–11) by a DESTROY operator. Those π nodes are then reinserted to Sol_0 by a REPAIR operator (lines 12–15). A new solution is directly accepted if improves Sol^* or Sol'. Otherwise, it will only be accepted by a $e^{\frac{-(TC(Sol_0) - TC(Sol'))}{Temp}}$ chance (line 16), where $TC(x)$ represents the total cost of solution x. Subsequently, we update operators score, weight, and probability. The ALNS terminates when there is no solution improvements after θ successive temperature reductions.

3.2.3 Operators
We list down the operators used in the proposed algorithm:

Random removal (R_1): randomly remove a node from Sol_0.
Worst removal (R_2): remove a node that has the xth highest removal gain (i.e. the difference in objective function values between including and excluding this node). x is decided by following Eq. (16), where $y_1 \sim U(0,1)$, $p = 3$, and ξ is the number of candidate nodes which is formally formulated in Eq. (17), case 1.

$$x = \lceil y_1^p \times \xi \rceil \tag{16}$$

$$\xi = \begin{cases} |C| + |S| - \text{REMOVEDNODES}, & \text{for } R_2 \\ |C| + |S| - \text{REMOVEDNODES} - 2, & \text{for } R_4, R_5 \\ \text{REMOVEDNODES}, & \text{for } I_9 \end{cases} \tag{17}$$

Route removal (R_3): randomly select a vehicle and remove z visited nodes. $z = \min(\pi, \beta)$, where β is the number of nodes visited by that vehicle.

Algorithm 1: ALNS pseudocode

```
 1  Sol₀, Sol*, Sol' ← INITIALSOLUTION
 2  Temp ← T₀
 3  NOIMPR, ITER ← 0
 4  FOUNDBESTSOL ← False
 5  Set sⱼ and wⱼ such that pⱼ is equally likely
 6  while NOIMPR < θ do
 7  │   REMOVEDNODES ← 0
 8  │   while REMOVEDNODES < π do
 9  │   │   Sol₀ ← Destroy (Rᵣ)
10  │   │   UpdateRemovedNodes(REMOVEDNODES, Rᵣ)
11  │   end
12  │   while REMOVEDNODES > 0 do
13  │   │   Sol₀ ← Repair (Iᵢ)
14  │   │   UpdateRemovedNodes(REMOVEDNODES, Iᵢ)
15  │   end
16  │   AcceptanceCriteria(Sol₀, Sol*, Sol', Temp)
17  │   if Sol₀ is better than Sol* then
18  │   │   FOUNDBESTSOL ← True
19  │   end
20  │   Update sⱼ
21  │   if ITER mod η_ALNS = 0 then
22  │   │   Update wⱼ and pⱼ
23  │   end
24  │   if ITER mod η_SA = 0 then
25  │   │   if FOUNDBESTSOL = False then
26  │   │   │   NOIMPR ← NOIMPR + 1
27  │   │   end
28  │   │   else
29  │   │   │   NOIMPR ← 0
30  │   │   end
31  │   │   FOUNDBESTSOL ← False
32  │   │   Temp ← Temp × α
33  │   end
34  │   ITER ← ITER + 1
35  end
36  Return Sol*
```

Node pair removal (R_4): remove a pair of nodes that has the xth highest transportation cost. x is determined by Eq. (16) while ξ follows Eq. (17) case 2. The idea is to remove two adjacent nodes with a high transportation cost from the Sol_0, such that when REPAIR reinserts them back to Sol_0, they can be located in better, probably separated, positions.

Worst pair removal (R_5): similar to R_2, but R_5 chooses a pair of nodes instead of only one node. The underlying difference between R_4 and R_5 is that R_4 only focuses in the transportation cost between two nodes, while R_5 considers the overall costs. x is determined by Eq. (16) while ξ is determined by Eq. (17) case 2.

Shaw removal (R_6): remove a node that is highly related with other removed nodes in a predefined way, so as it is easier to replace the positions of one another during the repair process. Let us define node i as the last removed node and node j as the next candidate to be removed. The relatedness value of node j (φ_j) to node i is calculated by Eq. (18), where ϕ_1 to ϕ_3 are weights given to each of the related components in terms of travel distance, travel time, and node position

($l_{ij} = -1$ if nodes i and j are in the same vehicle; 1 otherwise). This means that the lower the φ_j is, the more related node j to i is. Therefore, node j with lowest φ_j is then selected and removed from Sol_0. We implement $\phi_1 = \phi_2 = \phi_3 = \frac{1}{3}$.

$$\varphi_j = \begin{cases} \phi_1 e'_{ij} + \phi_2 t'_{ij} + \phi_3 l_{ij}, & \text{if } i \in C \\ \phi_1 e''_{ij} + \phi_2 t''_{ij} + \phi_3 l_{ij}, & \text{if } i \in O \\ \phi_1 e'''_{ij} + \phi_2 t'''_{ij} + \phi_3 l_{ij}, & \text{if } i \in S \end{cases} \qquad (18)$$

Greedy insertion (I_1): insert a node to a position with the lowest insertion cost (i.e. the difference in objective function values between after and before inserting a node to a particular position).

k-regret insertion (I_2, I_3, I_4): a regret value is defined as the difference in objective function values when node j is inserted in the best position (denoted as $TC_1(j)$) and in the k-best position (denoted as $TC_k(j)$). A node with the largest regret value (see Eq. (19)) is then inserted in its best position.

$$\underset{j \in \text{RemovedNodes}}{\text{argmax}} \left\{ \sum_{i=2}^{k} (TC_i(j) - TC_1(j)) \right\} \qquad (19)$$

Greedy insertion with noise function (I_5): an extension of I_1 by introducing a noise function to the objective function value (20) when selecting the best position of a node, where $\bar{e}$ is the maximum transportation cost between nodes (problem-dependent), μ is a noise parameter (set to 0.1 in our case), and $y_2 \sim U(-1, 1)$.

$$TC_{new} = TC + \bar{e} \times \mu \times y_2 \qquad (20)$$

k-regret insertion with noise function (I_6, I_7, I_8): an extension of I_2, I_3, and I_4 by applying a noise function to the objective function value (20) when calculating the regret value.

GRASP insertion (I_9): similar to I_1, but instead of choosing a node with the lowest insertion cost, I_9 chooses a node that has the xth lowest insertion cost. x is determined by Eq. (16) while ξ is determined by Eq. (17) case 3.

4   Computational Results

Our proposed ALNS is tested on the available benchmark VRP-RCD instances introduced in [20]. The instances are available in https://www.mech.kuleuven. be/en/cib/op/opmainpage#section-50. The benchmark VRP-RCD instances consists of two sets, the first set of instances with 15 nodes and the second set of instances with 40 nodes, each having 30 problems. Parameter values of these instances are summarized in Table 1. OFAT (One-factor-at-a-time) method is used to tune parameters by solving randomly selected instances. The best values for parameters are summarized in Table 2. The following experiments are then conducted based on this setting.

Table 1. VRP-RCD parameter values

	Set 1	Set 2
$|S|$	4	7
$|C|$	6	23
$|O|$	5	10
$|V|$	10	20
q	70	150
c	1	1
H	1000	1000
T_{max}	16 h	16 h
$e_{ij}', e_{ij}'', e_{ij}'''$	U~(48,560)	U~(48,480)
$t_{ij}', t_{ij}'', t_{ij}'''$	U~(20,200)	U~(20,100)
$\sum_{k \in S} d_{ik}''$	U~(5,50)	U~(5,20)
$\sum_{k \in S} r_{ik}, \sum_{k \in S} r_{ik}''$	U~(5,50)	U~(5,20)
p_k	U~(0,0.05)	U~(0,0.05)

Table 2. ALNS parameter values

Parameter	Value
T_0	5, 10, **20**
α	0.85, 0.9, **0.95**
θ	10, **50**, 100
γ	0.7, 0.8, **0.9**
η_{ALNS}	100, 200, **300**
η_{SA}	$(|S| + |C| + |O|) \times 1, (\mathbf{|S|} + \mathbf{|C|} + \mathbf{|O|}) \times \mathbf{2}, (|S| + |C| + |O|) \times 3$

The proposed ALNS is coded in C++ and run on a computer with Intel Core i7-8700 CPU @ 3.20 GHz processor, 32.0 GB RAM. We perform 5 replications for each instance and the best total cost (TC) obtained is recorded. Subsequently, the average and total computational time of 5 replications are also presented. Tables 3 and 4 summarize results on Sets 1 and 2 instances, respectively. Since no state-of-the-art algorithms have been introduced to solve this problem, we compare our TC results against those obtained by CPLEX by calculating Gap (%) using the following Eq. (21). We also remark the lowest TC in each problem instance by **bold**.

$$Gap~(\%) = \frac{(TC_{ALNS} - TC_{CPLEX})}{TC_{CPLEX}} \times 100 \qquad (21)$$

Table 3. Results on Set 1 instances

Instance	CPLEX		ALNS			
	TC	Time (s)	TC	Avg. time (s)	Total time (s)	Gap (%)
1	**10982**	81.98	**10982**	0.17	0.87	0.00
2	**8304**	21.18	**8304**	0.12	0.62	0.00
3	**10076**	50.54	10304	0.11	0.55	2.26
4	**10753**	38.52	**10753**	0.13	0.66	0.00
5	**8584**	20.97	**8584**	0.11	0.54	0.00
6	**10965**	45.93	**10965**	0.11	0.54	0.00
7	**9703**	45.68	9855	0.12	0.60	1.57
8	**7630**	5.04	8226	0.11	0.53	7.81
9	**9519**	13.63	**9519**	0.11	0.53	0.00
10	**9486**	24.41	**9486**	0.11	0.56	0.00
11	**10581**	74.32	**10581**	0.11	0.56	0.00
12	**11381**	24.01	**11381**	0.12	0.60	0.00
13	**9432**	7.69	**9432**	0.13	0.63	0.00
14	**9428**	23.28	9705	0.10	0.49	2.94
15	**8993**	17.43	**8993**	0.09	0.47	0.00
16	**9591**	33.46	**9591**	0.11	0.53	0.00
17	**10049**	5874.90	**10049**	0.09	0.43	0.00
18	**9375**	9372.26	**9375**	0.09	0.47	0.00
19	**8012**	23.42	**8012**	0.09	0.47	0.00
20	**10881**	18.83	**10881**	0.10	0.49	0.00
21	**8235**	22.67	**8235**	0.14	0.68	0.00
22	**8875**	13.25	**8875**	0.10	0.52	0.00
23	**8728**	866.68	9145	0.09	0.46	4.78
24	**11719**	28.07	**11719**	0.10	0.49	0.00
25	**10686**	21.81	**10686**	0.09	0.44	0.00
26	**9042**	60.50	**9042**	0.11	0.53	0.00
27	**10545**	23.81	**10545**	0.10	0.50	0.00
28	**10636**	38.19	**10636**	0.10	0.49	0.00
29	**9130**	64.07	**9130**	0.13	0.65	0.00
30	**9700**	30.11	10111	0.09	0.46	4.24
Avg.		566.22		0.11	0.55	0.79

Results on the first set of instances show that our proposed ALNS is able to get the optimal solutions for 24 out of 30 problems with significantly shorter computational times compared to CPLEX (around 0.1% of CPLEX computational time). For the second set of instances, ALNS provides better solutions than

Table 4. Results on Set 2 instances

Instance	CPLEX		ALNS			
	TC	Time (s)	TC	Avg. time (s)	Total time (s)	Gap (%)
1	30988	7200	**12239**	1.69	8.44	−60.50
2	19270	7200	**12522**	1.38	6.88	−35.02
3	14062	7200	**11366**	1.27	6.37	−19.17
4	28668	7200	**11841**	1.43	7.16	−58.70
5	13945	7200	**12011**	1.40	6.99	−13.87
6	11837	7200	**10439**	1.24	6.20	−11.81
7	27184	7200	**12415**	1.35	6.76	−54.33
8	16111	7200	**12430**	1.30	6.49	−22.85
9	31137	7200	**13020**	2.28	11.41	−58.18
10	16107	7200	**12168**	1.00	5.02	−24.46
11	17817	7200	**11935**	1.17	5.83	−33.01
12	23026	7200	**12251**	1.31	6.54	−46.79
13	24684	7200	**12114**	1.36	6.82	−50.92
14	20889	7200	**12073**	2.16	10.79	−42.20
15	16497	7200	**12246**	1.76	8.79	−25.77
16	22017	7200	**11706**	1.00	4.98	−46.83
17	16256	7200	**13108**	1.10	5.49	−19.37
18	29582	7200	**12465**	1.48	7.38	−57.86
19	17653	7200	**12008**	1.16	5.80	−31.98
20	27966	7200	**12624**	0.97	4.83	−54.86
21	25482	7200	**12334**	0.90	4.52	−51.60
22	15263	7200	**12510**	1.08	5.40	−18.04
23	22747	7200	**11753**	1.36	6.80	−48.33
24	14834	7200	**11942**	2.52	12.62	−19.50
25	26117	7200	**12762**	1.00	5.00	−51.14
26	28020	7200	**12974**	1.23	6.17	−53.70
27	26497	7200	**12786**	1.16	5.80	−51.75
28	29305	7200	**13228**	1.36	6.79	−54.86
29	21786	7200	**12281**	1.26	6.30	−43.63
30	17600	7200	**12332**	1.04	5.19	−29.93
Avg.		7200		1.36	6.78	−38.81

CPLEX for all instances, with an average gap of 38.81% within again, only 0.1% of CPLEX's computational times. From the practical perspective, ALNS outperforms CPLEX since it only needs a few seconds. For larger instances, ALNS is expected to solve them within reasonable computational times. However, it may be possible that ALNS could not solve all larger instances to optimality.

5   Conclusion

This paper studies the reverse flow of the vehicle routing problem and cross-docking, namely vehicle routing problem with reverse cross-docking (VRP-RCD). The VRP-RCD considers a four level supply chain network involving suppliers, cross-dock, customers, and outlets. There are three processes that must be conveyed in the VRP-RCD, which are the customer pickup process, outlet delivery and pickup process, and supplier delivery process. We designed a two-phase heuristic that employs an adaptive large neighborhood search (ALNS) to solve the VRP-RCD. ALNS uses various DESTROY and REPAIR operators to generate neighborhood solutions. Furthermore, a simulated annealing (SA) framework is embedded to discover a vast search space during the search process.

We tested our proposed ALNS by solving the available benchmark VRP-RCD instances. Experimental results on the first set of instances show that our proposed ALNS is able to obtain optimal solutions for 24 out of 30 problem instances with significantly shorter computational time. When solving the second set of instances, ALNS is able to obtain better solution for all problem instances with an average improvement of 38.81% and only need 0.1% of CPLEX's computational times. Generating and solving larger instances, e.g. with 100 or 200 nodes, would be interesting for future research. It is noted that selecting which outlets to visit is fixed and it is not a part of the routing problem in our problem. However, this could be integrated in the future, but then the problem becomes much more complicated if selecting the outlets is considered as part of the routing problem. Other possible extensions, such as introducing exact algorithms, imposing penalties for unvisited nodes and partial deliveries, considering a mixture of direct-shipping and cross-docking, asynchronous arrival scenario, multi-period settings, can be further studied. Introducing new and larger instances can be explored as well in order to represent real-sized problems faced by industries.

Acknowledgment. This research is supported by the Singapore Ministry of Education (MOE) Academic Research Fund (AcRF) Tier 1 grant.

References

1. de Brito, M.P., Dekker, R.: A framework for reverse logistics. In: Dekker, R., Fleischmann, M., Inderfurth, K., Van Wassenhove, L.N. (eds.) Reverse Logistics, pp. 3–27. Springer, Heidelberg (2004). https://doi.org/10.1007/978-3-540-24803-3_1
2. Demir, E., Bektaş, T., Laporte, G.: An adaptive large neighborhood search heuristic for the pollution-routing problem. Eur. J. Oper. Res. **223**(2), 346–359 (2012)
3. Grangier, P., Gendreau, M., Lehuédé, F., Rousseau, L.M.: A matheuristic based on large neighborhood search for the vehicle routing problem with cross-docking. Comput. Oper. Res. **84**, 116–126 (2017)
4. Gunawan, A., Widjaja, A.T., Vansteenwegen, P., Yu, V.F.: Adaptive large neighborhood search for vehicle routing problem with cross-docking. In: Proceedings of the IEEE World Congress on Computational Intelligence (WCCI) (2020, accepted for publication)

5. Gunawan, A., Widjaja, A.T., Vansteenwegen, P., Yu, V.F.: A matheuristic algorithm for solving the vehicle routing problem with cross-docking. In: Kotsireas, I.S., Pardalos, P.M. (eds.) LION 2020. LNCS, vol. 12096, pp. 9–15. Springer, Cham (2020). https://doi.org/10.1007/978-3-030-53552-0_2

6. Hasani-Goodarzi, A., Tavakkoli-Moghaddam, R.: Capacitated vehicle routing problem for multi-product cross-docking with split deliveries and pickups. Proc. - Soc. Behav. Sci. **62**, 1360–1365 (2011)

7. Hemmelmayr, V.C., Cordeau, J.F., Crainic, T.G.: An adaptive large neighborhood search heuristic for two-echelon vehicle routing problems arising in city logistics. Comput. Oper. Res. **39**(12), 3215–3228 (2012)

8. Jayaraman, V., Luo, Y.: Creating competitive advantages through new value creation: a reverse logistics perspective. Acad. Manag. Perspect. **21**(2), 56–73 (2007)

9. Kaboudani, Y., Ghodsypour, S.H., Kia, H., Shahmardan, A.: Vehicle routing and scheduling in cross docks with forward and reverse logistics. Oper. Res. Int. J **20**, 1589–1622 (2018). https://doi.org/10.1007/s12351-018-0396-z

10. Lambert, S., Riopel, D., Abdul-Kader, W.: A reverse logistics decisions conceptual framework. Comput. Ind. Eng. **61**(3), 561–581 (2011)

11. Lee, Y.H., Jung, J.W., Lee, K.M.: Vehicle routing scheduling for cross-docking in the supply chain. Comput. Ind. Eng. **51**(2), 247–256 (2006)

12. Liao, C.J., Lin, Y., Shih, S.C.: Vehicle routing with cross-docking in the supply chain. Expert Syst. Appl. **37**(10), 6868–6873 (2010)

13. Lutz, R.: Adaptive large neighborhood search. Bachelor thesis, Universität Ulm (2015)

14. Nikolopoulou, A.I., Repoussis, P.P., Tarantilis, C.D., Zachariadis, E.E.: Moving products between location pairs: cross-docking versus direct-shipping. Eur. J. Oper. Res. **256**(3), 803–819 (2017)

15. Rezaei, S., Kheirkhah, A.: Applying forward and reverse cross-docking in a multi-product integrated supply chain network. Prod. Eng. **11**(4–5), 495–509 (2017). https://doi.org/10.1007/s11740-017-0743-6

16. Ropke, S., Pisinger, D.: An adaptive large neighborhood search heuristic for the pickup and delivery problem with time windows. Transp. Sci. **40**(4), 455–472 (2006)

17. Sacramento, D., Pisinger, D., Ropke, S.: An adaptive large neighborhood search metaheuristic for the vehicle routing problem with drones. Transp. Res. Part C: Emerg. Technol. **102**, 289–315 (2019)

18. Shaw, P.: Using constraint programming and local search methods to solve vehicle routing problems. In: Maher, M., Puget, J.-F. (eds.) CP 1998. LNCS, vol. 1520, pp. 417–431. Springer, Heidelberg (1998). https://doi.org/10.1007/3-540-49481-2_30

19. Wen, M., Larsen, J., Clausen, J., Cordeau, J.F., Laporte, G.: Vehicle routing with cross-docking. J. Oper. Res. Soc. **60**(12), 1708–1718 (2009). https://doi.org/10.1057/jors.2008.108

20. Widjaja, A.T., Gunawan, A., Jodiawan, P., Yu, V.F.: Incorporating a reverse logistics scheme in a vehicle routing problem with cross-docking network: a modelling approach. In: 2020 7th International Conference on Industrial Engineering and Applications, pp. 854–858. IEEE (2020)

21. Yu, V.F., Jewpanya, P., Redi, A.P.: Open vehicle routing problem with cross-docking. Comput. Ind. Eng. **94**, 6–17 (2016)

22. Zuluaga, J.P.S., Thiell, M., Perales, R.C.: Reverse cross-docking. Omega **66**, 48–57 (2017)

Solving a Bi-Objective Rich Vehicle Routing Problem with Customer Prioritization

Tim van Benthem, Mark Bergman, and Martijn Mes[✉]

Department of Industrial Engineering and Business Information Systems,
University of Twente, Enschede, The Netherlands
m.r.k.mes@utwente.nl

Abstract. This paper considers a rich vehicle routing problem in which a combination of transportation costs and customer perceived waiting times should be minimized and a differentiation is made between priority and non-priority customers. We illustrate the problem using a case study of a wholesaler with its own last-mile delivery network where customers can have pickup and delivery demand and are served by a heterogeneous fleet of vehicles. We propose a bi-objective mathematical problem formulation, minimizing the combination of transportation costs and customer dissatisfaction. We model customer dissatisfaction using a non-linear function that approximates the perceived waiting time of the customers. To be able to solve realistically sized problems in reasonable time, we propose a Simulated Annealing heuristic, Variable Neighborhood Search, and a combination of these. We perform various experiments considering different customer preferences (visit as soon as possible or at a specific time) and problem settings. For the combined objective, we see an average costs reduction for the dissatisfaction function approach compared to the standard time window approach of 48% over all experiments. Furthermore, we observe an average reduction in perceived waiting time of 48% and 20% for priority and non-priority customers, respectively.

Keywords: Vehicle Routing Problem · Customer satisfaction · Simulated Annealing · Variable Neighborhood Search · Time windows

1 Introduction

In this study, we consider a Vehicle Routing Problem (VRP) in which a combination of transportation costs and customer perceived waiting times should be minimized. Two types of customers have to be served: priority and non-priority customers. Customers are served from a depot with a heterogeneous fleet of vehicles having varying driving time limits. Also, customers have two types of demand: pickup demand from the customers to the depot and delivery demand from the depot to the customers. For this problem, we propose a bi-objective mathematical programming formulation, minimizing a combination

© Springer Nature Switzerland AG 2020
E. Lalla-Ruiz et al. (Eds.): ICCL 2020, LNCS 12433, pp. 183–199, 2020.
https://doi.org/10.1007/978-3-030-59747-4_12

of transportation costs and customer dissatisfaction. We model customer dissatisfaction with a non-linear function that approximates the perceived waiting time of customers, as opposed to modeling standard time windows. We aim to find solution generation methods that can find good solutions within reasonable computational time.

To illustrate the problem and to test our proposed solution methods, we use a case study of a wholesaler with its own last-mile delivery network. Using heterogeneous vehicles, this company aims to serve its customers within 1.5 h after order acceptance. Therefore, the time required for creating the transportation schedules should be limited. The company has 12 warehouses with more than 3000 customers, of which on average 1200 order products on a daily basis. To test our proposed solution methods, we use several real-life instances from this company with varying problem sizes and customer characteristics. These problem instances contain both priority and non-priority customers. Compared to non-priority customers, priority customers have smaller time windows in which they prefer to be served, and the penalty costs for serving customers outside these time windows increase faster as time elapses.

The contribution of this work is threefold. First, we provide a new formulation for this problem, extending existing formulations by including heterogeneous vehicles, customer prioritization, and various customer dissatisfaction functions. Second, to solve realistically sized problem instances, we propose a Simulated Annealing heuristic, Variable Neighborhood Search, and a combination of these. Third, we illustrate our approach using multiple instances from our real-life case study, providing insights into the benefits of our solution methods for various problem settings.

The remainder of this paper is structured as follows. Section 2 presents a literature review about exact mathematical problem formulations and heuristics that can find good solutions to this problem. Section 3 presents the mathematical problem formulation. Section 4 presents the heuristics used to solve the problem. Section 5 presents experiments that were conducted on several problem instances and Sect. 6 concludes on these experiments and provides directions for further research.

2 Literature Review

The core of the studied VRP is best described by a Pickup and Delivery VRP (PDVRP). In this variant, customers require simultaneous pickup and delivery, all transported to and from a single depot [3]. During the route, the vehicle's load is a mix of pickup and delivery loads, constrained by the vehicle's capacity. Cao and Lai [3] provide a mathematical model for the PDVRP; an improved version of this model includes time windows in which customers are to be served [11]. Zhang, et al. [22] also provide a model for the PDVRP; however, service times at customers are not considered. Finally, Zhang, et al. [23] model the PDVRP with service times at customers and time windows for customers. Compared to the standard PDVRP, our problem also includes prioritization amongst customers and customer satisfaction should be taken into account. In practice, firms often create tiered service levels and assign customers to these tiers based on, e.g., their sales (potential) [21]. Firms often benefit from implementing a prioritization strategy [6, p. 126]. To facilitate a prioritization strategy, one should first identify what influences customer satisfaction (i.e., service levels) [6, p. 126]. In literature, customer satisfaction related to the delivery service of logistics companies can be described by short waiting times, as customers often prefer to receive their orders as soon as possible [20]. However, customer satisfaction is typically modeled using a standard time window, see, e.g., Zhang, et al. [23], resulting in either maximum satisfaction when the order arrives within the time window, or minimum satisfaction when the order arrives outside the time window. Customer satisfaction can also be modeled by fuzzy time windows [1]. In fuzzy time windows, customer satisfaction is a function with values ranging between a minimum and maximum customer satisfaction. Fuzzy time windows are suitable to express the subjective function of satisfaction as they typically lead to maximum customer satisfaction [1, p. 532]. Ghannadpour, et al. [5] show that the width of the fuzzy time window can be adjusted to customer importance, where a smaller interval indicates a more important customer.

As our problem originates from the real-world and consists of a combination of known variants of the traditional VRP, it can be described as a Rich VRP (RVRP) [2]. These problems are NP-hard [10] and typically heuristics are being used to find good solutions in reasonable computational time [17]. Popular meta-heuristics that are used to solve RVRPs are, amongst others, Local Search and Variable Neighborhood Search (VNS) [2, p. 17]. Local Search methods, such as Simulated Annealing (SA) and Tabu Search (TS), are shown to provide good solutions for the VRP [13]. Tavakkoli-Moghaddam, et al. [18] show that SA provides good solutions for the VRP in reasonable computational time. Robusté, et al. [15] show that SA is an effective heuristic to solve VRPs, particularly when the problem is too large or too complex to be solved with traditional combinatorial optimization techniques. Kuo and Wang [8] use VNS in combination with SA, and show it is efficient and effective in solving VRPs. Stenger, et al. [16] show that VNS provides high-quality solutions to the VRP within short computational time. These improvement heuristics improve a given solution by making local changes. The starting solution is created by a so-called construction heuristic. Suitable construction heuristics for VRPs are the Clark and Wright savings, Cluster First Route Second, Route First Cluster Second, Nearest Neighbor, Nearest Insertion, and Farthest Insertion.

The mathematical model proposed by Cao and Lai [3] is used as the base model for the studied problem. To tailor this model to the studied problem, homogeneous vehicles are replaced by heterogeneous vehicles. To model customer satisfaction and prioritization among customers, we extend the base model. We combine the idea of fuzzy time windows as suggested by Afshar-Bakeshloo, et al. [1] with the ability to change the width of the interval to prioritize customers, as introduced by Ghannadpour, et al. [5]. To model the customer prioritization related to the shortest waiting time, we let customer satisfaction of priority customers decrease faster over time compared to non-priority customers, such that the priority customers are likely being served earlier, as done by Wang, et al. [19]. As the transportation costs should be minimized and customer satisfaction should be maximized, we minimize a combination of transportation costs and customer dissatisfaction. We model customer dissatisfaction with a non-linear function approximating the perceived waiting time of the customers.

To be able to solve realistic problem instances and to find good solutions in a short amount of time, we propose to use the metaheuristics SA, VNS, and a combination of SA and VNS. Furthermore, we propose a modified version of SA. The starting solution will be generated by a modified version of the Nearest Neighbor Heuristic, in which we not only take into account distances between customers, but also the perceived waiting times of customers.

3   Problem Formulation

Our proposed mathematical model minimizes a weighted average of the transportation costs and the perceived waiting times of customers while satisfying the following four conditions for each delivery moment: (i) each customer is visited exactly once, (ii) each vehicle can only be used once, (iii) the total driving time of a vehicle and its total service time at its customers should not exceed its driving time limit, and (iv) the vehicle's load capacity cannot be exceeded.

The following assumptions are used for the mathematical model: (i) the depot is always operational, has infinite capacity, and does not suffer from stockouts, (ii) freights cannot be divided and each customer is visited once, (iii) vehicles cannot go back to the depot for a refill, (iv) the service time at the customer and the travel time between two nodes are independent of the vehicle and the driver, (v) all vehicles are always operational, (vi) the transportation costs are fixed meaning that fuel consumption is equal for every driven kilometer, (vii) pickup and delivery demand is fixed implying that these demands cannot be canceled, (viii) travel times, distances, and service times are deterministic, meaning that no online changes occur, and (iv) customers are always ready to hand over pickup demand and to receive delivery demand.

To model the perceived waiting times, we propose a customer dissatisfaction function $\hat{f}_{i,t}$, which denotes the perceived waiting time of customer $i \in \mathcal{N}$ at time $t \in \mathcal{T}$, where $\mathcal{N}$ represents the set of customers and $\mathcal{T}$ represents the set of discrete time units. This dissatisfaction function is input for the mathematical model. The mathematical model determines the arrival time $A_{i,k}$ at customer i by vehicle $k \in \mathcal{K}$, where $\mathcal{K}$ represents the set of vehicles. Furthermore, we use the binary variable $\lambda_{i,t}$, which indicates whether a vehicle arrives at customer i at time t. The perceived waiting time of customer i can then be calculated as follows: $\sum_{t \in T} \lambda_{i,t} \hat{f}_{i,t}$. We propose the following constraints to ensure that $\lambda_{i,t}$ is set to 1 when $A_{i,k} = t$ (with $A_{i,k} = 0$ when vehicle k is not serving costumer i):

$$\sum_{t \in \mathcal{T}} t\lambda_{i,t} = A_{i,k} \qquad \forall i \in \mathcal{N}, \ \forall k \in \mathcal{K}$$

$$\sum_{t \in \mathcal{T}} \lambda_{i,t} = 1 \qquad \forall i \in \mathcal{N}$$

$$\lambda_{i,t} \in \{0,1\} \qquad \forall i \in \mathcal{N}, \ \forall t \in \mathcal{T}$$

We propose two types of dissatisfaction functions as shown in Table 1: a quadratic function and a step function, where the latter corresponds with the typical approach considered in the VRP literature. Furthermore, we evaluate our dissatisfaction functions under two different situations for customer preferences: (i) customers prefer to be served as soon as possible (ASAP) and (ii) customers prefer to be served at a specific time (AST). We use several parameters in these dissatisfaction functions.

For the step function, we consider a fixed penalty v_i for visiting customer i outside its time window. In case of AST, this time window is given by $[lb_i, \ ub_i]$, where the middle point of this time window is m_i and the width of the time window is w_i. In case of ASAP, this window is given by $[e_i, \ e_i + w_i]$, where e_i represents the earliest possible visiting moment of customer i, which depends on the driving time from the depot to this customer. For the quadratic function, we penalize the time after earliest visit time e_i or the deviation from a preferred visit time m_i in case of ASAP and AST, respectively. To distinguish between different priority customers, these time deviations are penalized by a factor a_i. The equations for the two dissatisfaction functions for both situations are given in Table 1 and an illustration is given in Fig. 1.

Table 1. Proposed dissatisfaction functions for two situations of customer preferences.

Situation	Quadratic function	Step function
ASAP	$\hat{f}_{i,t} = a_i(t - e_i)^2, \ t > e_i$	$\hat{f}_{i,t} = v_i, \ t > e_i + w_i$
	$\hat{f}_{i,t} = 0$, otherwise	$\hat{f}_{i,t} = 0$, otherwise
AST	$\hat{f}_{i,t} = a_i(m_i - t)^2, \ t < m_i$	$\hat{f}_{i,t} = v_i, \ t < lb_i$
	$\hat{f}_{i,t} = a_i(t - m_i)^2, \ t > m_i$	$\hat{f}_{i,t} = v_i, \ t > ub_i$
	$\hat{f}_{i,t} = 0$, otherwise	$\hat{f}_{i,t} = 0$, otherwise

When using the quadratic dissatisfaction function in the ASAP situation, customer dissatisfaction increases rapidly with increasing waiting times. This is also experienced in practice, as the customer dissatisfaction exponentially increases when the perceived waiting time increases [4]. When using step functions, penalties remain constant when being outside the time window. The standard modelling approach in case of AST is to use a time window around the preferred visit time, and the assumption is that customer dissatisfaction is the same over the whole interval, while this is not experienced in practice [4]. The quadratic

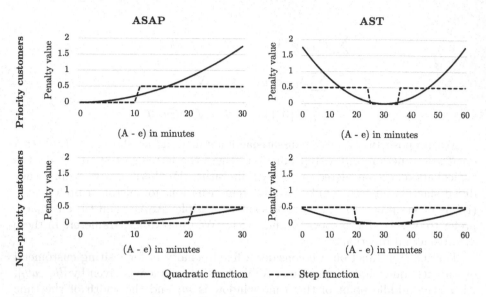

Fig. 1. Quadratic and step penalty functions for two situations of customer preferences.

function uses increasing penalties with increasing deviations from the preferred visit time m_i, thereby pushing the model to schedule the visit closer to the preferred time. The dissatisfaction functions ensure the distinction between priority and non-priority customers by letting the penalty value for priority customers increase faster than for non-priority customers. This distinction can be achieved by setting the parameter a_i higher for priority customers than for non-priority customers. When using the standard time window modeling approach, the width of the time window, denoted by w_i, is smaller for priority than for non-priority customers.

In the following, we introduce the notation for the mathematical problem formulation for the RVRP with customer prioritization. Besides the sets $\mathcal{N}$, $\mathcal{K}$, and $\mathcal{T}$ as introduced before, we also use $\mathcal{N}_0$ to denote the set of customers including the depot, i.e., $\mathcal{N}_0 = \mathcal{N} \cup \{0\}$. For the parameters solely related to customers, we define for each customer i pickup demand p_i, delivery demand d_i, and service time s_i. For the parameters related to the arcs between two nodes i and j, we define $t_{i,j}$ as the travel time and $c_{i,j}$ as the distance. For the parameters related to vehicles, we define for each vehicle k, its capacity q_k, driving time limit l_k, time-related costs tc_k, distance-related costs dc_k, and startup costs sc_k for using this vehicle. Furthermore, we have a parameter $\alpha \in [0, 1]$ to set the weight of the two objectives in the bi-objective goal function and a conversion factor β to convert the perceived waiting time penalty into the costs equivalent. Next, we introduce the variables in the mathematical model. The variable $X_{i,j,k}$ indicates whether arc (i, j) is traversed by vehicle k, $A_{i,k}$ is the arrival time of vehicle k at customer i, $Y_{i,j,k}$ is the demand picked up by vehicle k from customers up to node i and transported on arc (i, j), and $Z_{i,j,k}$ is the demand to be delivered by vehicle k to customers routed after node i and transported on arc (i, j). As mentioned before, $\lambda_{i,t}$ indicates whether the arrival time at customer i is at time t.

We define the proposed mathematical problem formulation as follows:

$$\min \left(\alpha \left(\sum_{(i,j) \in \mathcal{N}_0, k \in \mathcal{K}} \left(c_{i,j} dc_k + (t_{i,j} + s_j) tc_k \right) X_{i,j,k} + \sum_{j \in \mathcal{N}, k \in \mathcal{K}} sc_k X_{0,j,k} \right) \right.$$

$$\left. + (1 - \alpha) \left(\beta \sum_{i \in \mathcal{N}, t \in \mathcal{T}} \hat{f}_{i,t} \lambda_{i,t} \right) \right) \quad (1)$$

s.t.

$$\sum_{i \in \mathcal{N}_0, k \in \mathcal{K}} X_{i,j,k} = 1 \quad \forall j \in \mathcal{N} \quad (2)$$

$$\sum_{i \in \mathcal{N}_0} X_{i,j,k} - \sum_{i \in \mathcal{N}_0} X_{j,i,k} = 0 \quad \forall j \in \mathcal{N}_0, \ \forall k \in \mathcal{K} \quad (3)$$

$$\sum_{j \in \mathcal{N}} X_{0,j,k} \leq 1 \quad \forall k \in \mathcal{K} \quad (4)$$

$$A_{i,k} + s_i + t_{i,j} X_{i,j,k} - A_{j,k} \leq l_k (1 - X_{i,j,k}) \quad \forall i \in \mathcal{N}, \ \forall j \in \mathcal{N}_0, \ \forall k \in \mathcal{K} \quad (5)$$

$$A_{j,k} \geq t_{0,j} X_{0,j,k} \quad \forall j \in \mathcal{N}, \ \forall k \in \mathcal{K} \quad (6)$$

$$A_{0,k} \leq l_k \quad \forall k \in \mathcal{K} \quad (7)$$

$$\sum_{i \in \mathcal{N}_0, k \in \mathcal{K}} Y_{j,i,k} - \sum_{i \in \mathcal{N}_0, k \in \mathcal{K}} Y_{i,j,k} = p_j \quad \forall j \in \mathcal{N} \quad (8)$$

$$\sum_{i \in \mathcal{N}_0, k \in \mathcal{K}} Z_{i,j,k} - \sum_{i \in \mathcal{N}_0, k \in \mathcal{K}} Z_{j,i,k} = d_j \quad \forall j \in \mathcal{N} \quad (9)$$

$$Y_{i,j,k} + Z_{i,j,k} \leq q_k X_{i,j,k} \quad \forall (i,j) \in \mathcal{N}_0, \ \forall k \in \mathcal{K} \quad (10)$$

$$\sum_{t \in \mathcal{T}} t \lambda_{i,t} = A_{i,k} \quad \forall i \in \mathcal{N}, \ \forall k \in \mathcal{K} \quad (11)$$

$$\sum_{t \in \mathcal{T}} \lambda_{i,t} = 1 \quad \forall i \in \mathcal{N} \quad (12)$$

$$X_{i,j,k} \in \{0, 1\} \quad \forall (i,j) \in \mathcal{N}_0, \ \forall k \in \mathcal{K} \quad (13)$$

$$A_{j,k} \geq 0 \quad \forall j \in \mathcal{N}, \ \forall k \in \mathcal{K} \quad (14)$$

$$Y_{i,j,k}, \ Z_{i,j,k} \geq 0 \quad \forall (i,j) \in \mathcal{N}_0, \ \forall k \in \mathcal{K} \quad (15)$$

$$\lambda_{i,t} \in \{0, 1\} \quad \forall i \in \mathcal{N}, \ \forall t \in \mathcal{T} \quad (16)$$

The objective function (1) minimizes a weighted average of transportation costs and perceived waiting times of the customers, where the transportation costs consist of distance-related transportation costs, time-related transportation costs, and vehicle startup costs. Constraint (2) makes sure that each customer is visited exactly once and constraint (3) ensures that a vehicle always departs from the node at which the vehicle arrives. Constraint (4) indicates that a vehicle can be used only once, i.e., it can only leave the depot once. Sub-tours are eliminated by constraint (5) and constraint (6) ensures that the arrival time at a customer cannot be earlier than the driving time from the depot to that customer. Constraint (7) ensures that the total driving time and service time limit of each vehicle is not exceeded. The vehicle loads on each arc, for pickup demand and delivery demand, respectively, are calculated by constraints (8) and (9). Constraint (10) makes sure that the vehicle capacity is not exceeded. Constraints (11) and (12) ensure that the correct input is used for the dissatisfaction function. Finally, the domain restrictions for the variables are indicated by constraints (13)–(16).

4   Heuristics

As the studied problem is NP-hard [10], we use heuristics to find good solutions for large-size problem instances [17] in a short amount of time. To provide a starting solution for the improvement heuristics, we use the Nearest Neighbor Heuristic [14]. In the standard Nearest Neighbor Heuristic, a vehicle constructs its route by inserting the closest customer until its driving time limit or capacity limit is reached. So, the costs for adding customer j to the route of vehicle k is calculated as follows: $C(i, j, k) = c_{i,j}$, where the current location of vehicle k is denoted by i. So, only the travel distance is taken into account. In our problem, we also have to consider customer dissatisfaction and transportation costs; therefore, we modify the standard Nearest Neighbor Heuristic such that customer dissatisfaction and transportation costs are also taken into account. We propose to calculate the costs for making a route between nodes i and j with vehicle k with the following formula: $C(i, j, k) = \alpha(c_{i,j}dc_k + t_{i,j}tc_k) + (1 - \alpha)\beta \hat{f}_{j, A_{j,k}}$, where the current location of vehicle k is denoted by i. This construction heuristic is executed in a parallel manner. This means that we are gradually constructing the routes of all vehicles. In each iteration of the construction heuristic, we loop over all customers j and vehicles k to find the lowest value for $C(i, j, k)$ and then add customer j to the route of vehicle k. Then, we repeat this procedure until all customers are visited. If all customers are visited, all vehicles return to the depot.

After that, we improve the starting solution with improvement heuristics. In these improvement heuristics, we modify the current solution with neighborhood operators. We consider the following two neighborhood operators: (i) a move-operator, in which we insert a customer from a certain route into another route, and (ii) a swap-operator, in which we swap two customers on the same route or between different routes. When generating a neighbor solution, we select the move-operator and the swap-operator with equal probability. We use the following four improvement heuristics: (i) the standard version of Simulated Annealing [7], (ii) the standard version of Variable Neighborhood Search [12], (iii) the standard version of Simulated Annealing combined with the standard version of Variable Neighborhood Search [9], and (iv) a modified version of Simulated

Annealing. In the modified version of Simulated Annealing, we generate multiple neighbor solutions and evaluate the best solution among these neighbor solutions, as opposed to evaluating only one neighbor solution [7].

In Sect. 5, we benchmark (i) our proposed construction heuristic against the standard version of the Nearest Neighbor Heuristic and (ii) these improvement heuristics against the deterministic version of Simulated Annealing, which we refer to as 'Descent'. The Descent heuristic only accepts solutions that improve the best solution so far. We use the modified Nearest Neighbor Heuristic before using the improvement heuristics. We also apply a modeling trick to the construction and improvement heuristic. We relax constraint (7) by allowing vehicles to have overtime in which l_k is exceeded. Based on the overtime, we add overtime penalty costs to the objective function (1). This modeling trick helps to escape from local optima but can cause the heuristic to find infeasible solutions having vehicles with overtime. Therefore, it is possible that the construction heuristic finds an infeasible solution, which the improvement heuristic uses as starting solution. Moreover, it enables constructing good routes for large scenarios for which a feasible solution is hard to find or non-existent.

Finally, we apply post-processing to the solutions found by the construction heuristic and improvement heuristic. First, we improve the solution by swapping customers within every single route. Second, we improve the solution by swapping vehicles to find the best vehicle for each route, which might result in less overtime.

5   Experiments

In this section, we present the experiments and their corresponding results. In Sect. 5.1, we describe the data from the problem instances. In Sect. 5.2, we present the experiments with the mathematical model. In Sect. 5.3, we give an introduction to the experiments with the heuristics and present the parameter settings for the heuristics. In Sect. 5.4, we present the results of the experiments with the heuristics.

5.1   Description of Problem Instances

As mentioned in the introduction, we perform our experiments using real-life instances from our case study. The involved company has 12 warehouses, but for our experiments, we limit ourselves to one of these warehouses, which serves approximately 300 customers, of which on average 120 distinct customers place orders over six different delivery moments within day. The first vehicles leave the depot at 8:00 AM and the last vehicles leave the depot at 3:30 PM. Transportation costs include fuel costs, salaries, depreciation, vehicle packing costs, service costs, and cleaning costs; these data are extracted from a full year of company data. Real (asymmetric) travel distances and (asymmetric) travel times are extracted by using Google APIs. Besides that, a full year of GPS-data from the company is used to generate a customer service time distribution. We extracted

7 problem instances from company data, ranging from low demand (38 customers) to high demand (95 customers); scenario-specific information regarding the fraction of priority customers, volume of pickup demand p_i, volume of delivery demand d_i, travel distance $c_{i,j}$, travel time $t_{i,j}$, and preferred visit time m_i, are presented in Table 2. For these parameters, we provide the mean value and the standard deviation, of which the latter is presented between brackets. The scenario number corresponds with the number of customers that placed an order in this scenario.

Table 2. Scenario-specific information

Scenario	Priority (%)	Pickup demand	Delivery demand	Travel distance (m)	Travel time (s)	Preferred visit time (s)
38	13.16	4.4 (3.2)	14.1 (4.8)	23170 (13265)	1268 (595)	2683 (664)
45	13.33	5.4 (3.2)	12.3 (4.8)	22674 (12574)	1289 (573)	2648 (655)
54	5.56	4.7 (3.4)	12.8 (5.2)	27462 (14979)	1457 (655)	2767 (857)
67	8.96	4.8 (3.2)	12.0 (4.8)	25335 (14376)	1375 (636)	2648 (708)
75	12.00	5.0 (3.1)	11.2 (5.0)	25013 (13854)	1361 (603)	2811 (662)
86	8.14	4.8 (3.2)	12.8 (4.7)	25009 (14013)	1370 (629)	2831 (791)
95	9.47	5.3 (3.1)	12.5 (4.8)	25712 (14161)	1397 (624)	2753 (682)

Other data that are extracted from a full year of company data are the same for each scenario. These data include the (i) number of vehicles, which is 14, (ii) service time s_i, which has an empirical distribution with a mean of 138 s, a median of 107 s, and a standard deviation of 109 s, (iii) vehicle capacity $q_k = 500$, (iv) driving time limit of $l_k = 9000$ s for the first 4 vehicles and $l_k = 5400$ s for the other 10 vehicles, (v) distance costs $dc_k = €0.0001$ per meter, (vi) time costs $tc_k = €0.0028$ per second, and (vii) startup costs of a vehicle $sc_k = €1.68$ (equal to time costs for 10 min). Furthermore, as discussed in Sect. 3, α is the weight assigned to the transportation costs, and $1 - \alpha$ is the weight assigned to the penalty costs for the perceived waiting time of customers. Increasing α results in (i) a decrease in transportation costs and (ii) an increase in waiting times. The parameter β is a conversion factor to convert the perceived waiting time penalty into the cost equivalent. Increasing β results in (i) a decrease in waiting times and (ii) an increase in transportation costs.

To allow the involved company to make a trade-off between transportation costs and perceived waiting times, we performed a number of experiments with different values of α and β. From the results, the involved company decided that the values $\alpha = 0.5$ and $\beta = 100$ resulted in the best overall objective.

For both the ASAP and AST situation we use (i) $a_i = 5 \times 10^{-6.965}$ for priority customers and $a_i = 1 \times 10^{-6.85}$ for non-priority customers, and (ii) use a penalty $v_i = 0.5$. For the ASAP situation, we use $w_i = 600$ and $w_i = 1200$ for priority customers and non-priority customers, respectively. For the AST situation, we use the same w_i values to set the width of the windows $[lb_i, \ ub_i]$ around the preferred time m_i.

5.2   Experiments with the Mathematical Model

For each scenario, we try to solve the mathematical model for the two situations ASAP and AST. We try to solve both situations with the dissatisfaction function approach and the standard time window modeling approach. To achieve this, we implement the mathematical model in AIMMS using the general-purpose solver CPLEX version 12.8, on a machine equipped with an Intel Hexa-Core 4.1 GHz and 16 GB of RAM. We limit the computational time to 3600 s.

For none of the scenarios, the model is able to find an optimal solution; the gap, the fractional difference between the lower bound and the incumbent solution, is on average 89%. Therefore, we perform two modifications. First, we set the time units to minutes ($\mathcal{T} = \{1, \ldots, 150\}$) by modifying constraint (11) such that $\sum_{t \in \mathcal{T}} 60t\lambda_{i,t} \geq A_{i,k}$, resulting in a significant reduction in the number of decision variables $\lambda_{i,t}$. Second, we also consider smaller scenarios, with 15 and 24 customers. For the scenario with 24 customers, the model still does not find optimal solutions, and the gap is on average 63%. For the scenario with 15 customers, the model is able to find optimal solutions within 3600 s, taking 2735 s and 1895 s for the ASAP and AST situation, respectively. Note that changing the time units from seconds to minutes results in an over-approximation of the dissatisfaction penalty, causing an approximation error in the objective function. Therefore, there is no guarantee that the optimal solutions found are the true optima of the original problems.

5.3   Experimental Settings

As discussed in Sect. 5.2, it is hard to solve the instances to optimality by using the mathematical model. Furthermore, the corresponding computational time is not acceptable, as the company aims to serve customers within 1.5 h after order acceptance. Therefore, we only consider the heuristics in the remaining experiments. We refer to (i) the standard version of the Nearest Neighbor Heuristic as 'NN', (ii) the modified version of the Nearest Neighbor Heuristic as 'NN-IMPR', (iii) the standard version of Simulated Annealing as 'SA', (iv) the standard version of Variable Neighborhood Search as 'VNS', (v) the standard version of Simulated Annealing combined with the standard version of Variable Neighborhood Search as 'SA-VNS', and (vi) the modified version of Simulated Annealing as 'SA-STPD'. Furthermore, we use the Descent improvement heuristic for benchmarking purposes, which we refer to as 'Descent'.

To find suitable parameter settings for the heuristics, we have conducted experiments on all scenarios with a proper selection of parameter values. We chose the parameter values that found the best solutions over 25 replications (i.e., running every experiment 25 times with the same parameter settings to provide statistically significant results) with regard to the following KPIs: (i) the best objective value found, (ii) the average objective value found, (iii) the worst objective value found, and (iv) the fraction of the solutions containing overtime, i.e., where l_k is exceeded at least once. After having found these parameter values, we tried to minimize the computational time by varying the parameter values, taking into account that the performance on these KPIs should not diminish. The resulting parameter settings for the heuristics are presented in Table 3.

Table 3. Parameter settings for the heuristics

Parameter	Descent	SA	SA-STPD	SA-VN	VNS
Start temperature	–	50	50	50	–
Decrease factor	–	0.999	0.999	0.999	–
Length of the Markov Chain	–	100	10	100	–
Temperature of lower bound	–	0.5	0.5	0.5	–
Maximum neighborhood depth	–	–	–	3	5
Maximum number of moves	–	–	–	10^6	5×10^4
Number of neighbor solutions	–	–	15	–	–
Maximum number of iterations	5×10^5	–	–	–	5×10^8

We perform experiments with the quadratic dissatisfaction function (DF=Q) and the standard time window modeling approach (DF=S) for both the ASAP and AST situation. For each experiment, we perform 25 replications, i.e., we run every experiment 25 times with the same parameter settings, to provide statistically significant results. When no feasible solution can be found within one replication after running the combination of the construction heuristic and improvement heuristic 25 times, the scenario is classified as 'infeasible' for that heuristic. During the execution of the heuristics for a specific setting of the dissatisfaction function, the corresponding quadratic or step function is used during the optimization, and afterwards the objective value is calculated assuming a quadratic perceived waiting time function. We do not report the computation times as they are all negligible and do not deviate significantly among the different improvement heuristics.

5.4   Experimental Results

First, we show the results of the experiments for the ASAP situation. The results for the different heuristics can be found in Table 4. Here we show the best objective value found, with in between brackets the increase when considering the average objective value. With respect to the construction heuristics, we see that NN-IMPR always outperforms NN, and is able to find feasible solutions for more instances. All improvement heuristics can find feasible solutions. We see that the SA approaches (SA, SA-STPD, SA-VN) outperform both Descent and VNS. When comparing the dissatisfaction function approach and the standard approach, we find that the dissatisfaction function approach significantly outperforms the standard approach regarding the objective and the average perceived waiting times of customers.

Table 4. Comparison of heuristics using the ASAP situation

DF	Heuristic	38	45	54	67	75	86	95
Q	NN	2232 (88)	–	–	–	–	–	–
Q	NN-IMPR	144 (0)	223 (0)	–	514 (0)	–	–	–
Q	Descent	133 (1)	158 (6)	205 (15)	268 (32)	431 (41)	541 (65)	760 (73)
Q	SA	134 (2)	158 (3)	204 (4)	249 (12)	420 (14)	516 (24)	626 (47)
Q	SA-STPD	134 (1)	158 (2)	204 (6)	250 (11)	419 (14)	518 (20)	625 (18)
Q	SA-VN	133 (2)	158 (2)	204 (5)	256 (8)	424 (13)	521 (23)	632 (40)
Q	VNS	133 (1)	158 (7)	208 (13)	262 (33)	427 (40)	521 (86)	705 (150)
S	NN	2421 (241)	–	–	–	–	–	–
S	NN-IMPR	207 (0)	263 (0)	273 (3)	421 (5)	–	–	–
S	Descent	181 (26)	219 (13)	248 (10)	308 (33)	2108 (296)	941 (382)	2898 (529)
S	SA	175 (13)	200 (27)	241 (18)	288 (27)	453 (197)	761 (336)	1005 (574)
S	SA-STPD	175 (18)	213 (17)	242 (19)	299 (17)	474 (216)	681 (577)	1034 (551)
S	SA-VN	171 (17)	199 (24)	245 (15)	282 (34)	472 (190)	829 (404)	888 (482)
S	VNS	173 (31)	222 (12)	248 (12)	303 (64)	2102 (332)	859 (464)	2224 (1144)

Next, by using the SA heuristic, we compare the effect of the dissatisfaction function and the standard approach on the perceived waiting times of the priority and non-priority customers. The following results are shown in Table 5: (i) the average objective value, referred to as 'Obj', (ii) the average perceived waiting time, referred to as 'Avg', (iii) the standard deviation of the perceived waiting time, referred to as 'StDev', and (iv) the maximum perceived waiting time, referred to as 'Max'. The results related to perceived waiting time are presented for both priority and non-priority customers. When analyzing these results, we find that the perceived waiting times for both the priority and non-priority customers are significantly lower when using the dissatisfaction function approach. Furthermore, we find that the perceived waiting times of priority customers are significantly lower than for non-priority customers.

Table 5. Comparison of dissatisfaction functions using the ASAP situation

Scenario	Quadratic function							Step function						
	Priority				Non-priority			Priority				Non-priority		
	Obj	Avg	Std	Max	Avg	Std	Max	Obj	Avg	Std	Max	Avg	Std	Max
38	135	104	91	215	198	209	973	189	150	152	524	468	413	1197
45	161	88	143	437	274	256	1031	227	269	219	589	461	399	1195
54	208	131	112	344	321	303	1294	259	223	157	592	443	387	1197
67	261	149	155	638	394	342	1664	314	210	168	569	480	388	1198
75	434	190	206	750	584	473	1988	650	368	598	4527	658	609	5979
86	540	260	219	708	610	522	3206	1097	788	1047	6058	710	767	7137
95	673	181	193	847	708	558	3511	1579	476	785	4768	910	1069	7345
Average	345	158	160	563	441	380	1952	616	355	447	2518	590	576	3607

The comparison of heuristics under the AST situation are shown in Table 6. When comparing the two construction heuristics, we find that NN-IMPR outperforms NN when using the dissatisfaction function approach. When using the standard time window modeling approach, we find that NN-IMPR and NN can only find feasible solutions for a small number of scenarios; therefore, no conclusion can be drawn whether one construction heuristic outperforms the other construction heuristic. When comparing the improvement heuristics, we find that only SA and SA-VN can find solutions for all scenarios. Regarding the objective value, SA and SA-VN perform similarly and outperform the other improvement heuristics. Furthermore, SA and SA-VN have similar perceived waiting times for customers. SA-STPD outperformed VNS and Descent regarding the objective value and VNS outperformed Descent regarding the objective value. When comparing the dissatisfaction function approach and the standard time window modeling approach, we find that the dissatisfaction function approach significantly outperforms the standard time window modeling approach regarding the objective and the average perceived waiting times of customers.

Table 6. Comparison of heuristics using the AST situation

DF	Heuristic	38	45	54	67	75	86	95
Q	NN	1208 (20)	–	–	–	–	–	–
Q	NN-IMPR	308 (0)	246 (0)	–	–	–	–	–
Q	Descent	185 (16)	203 (12)	268 (13)	259 (25)	–	–	–
Q	SA	167 (8)	178 (13)	208 (13)	224 (17)	305 (20)	357 (23)	387 (43)
Q	SA-STPD	166 (9)	178 (14)	214 (14)	224 (27)	303 (22)	–	–
Q	SA-VN	168 (9)	182 (11)	205 (15)	232 (9)	302 (23)	353 (26)	406 (30)
Q	VNS	176 (23)	203 (11)	254 (27)	251 (27)	–	–	–
S	NN	1369 (291)	–	–	–	–	–	–
S	NN-IMPR	–	–	–	2820 (157)	–	–	–
S	Descent	514 (589)	361 (471)	436 (477)	–	–	–	–
S	SA	308 (93)	305 (74)	336 (62)	393 (66)	500 (153)	619 (184)	748 (210)
S	SA-STPD	318 (77)	312 (50)	339 (51)	380 (113)	–	–	–
S	SA-VN	272 (116)	298 (73)	334 (56)	386 (65)	529 (148)	630 (172)	717 (271)
S	VNS	333 (159)	324 (227)	408 (331)	–	–	–	–

Finally, we compare the effect of the dissatisfaction function and the standard time window modeling approach on the perceived waiting times of the priority and non-priority customers, by using the SA heuristic. The corresponding results are presented in Table 7. Similarly as in the ASAP situation, the dissatisfaction function approach will result in lower average perceived waiting times for both priority and non-priority customers. Furthermore, we find that the perceived waiting times of priority customers are significantly lower than for non-priority customers.

Table 7. Comparison of dissatisfaction functions using the AST situation

Scenario	Quadratic function							Step function						
	Priority				Non-priority			Priority				Non-priority		
	Obj	Avg	Std	Max	Avg	Std	Max	Obj	Avg	Std	Max	Avg	Std	Max
38	175	507	312	957	827	598	2347	401	896	639	1861	990	666	2389
45	191	529	261	987	918	578	2097	379	676	508	1874	1017	665	2632
54	220	319	165	647	831	568	2325	399	587	399	1658	966	668	2575
67	241	373	297	1029	808	570	2325	459	642	473	1861	965	649	3549
75	325	352	296	988	886	575	2277	653	723	674	2040	954	652	2400
86	380	397	273	1098	868	598	2535	802	766	804	3732	1041	781	5649
95	430	434	330	1111	1002	677	3548	958	596	655	4633	1204	919	6131
Average	280	416	276	974	877	595	2493	579	698	593	2523	1020	714	3618

6   Conclusion

We proposed a bi-objective mathematical programming formulation for rich vehicle routing problems, minimizing a combination of transportation costs and customer dissatisfaction, distinguishing between priority and non-priority customers. We modelled customer dissatisfaction with a non-linear function that approximates the perceived waiting time of customers. The proposed mathematical model could only solve instances up to 15 customers. To be able to solve realistically sized instances, we used heuristics. We first created an initial route with a construction heuristic and then improved this route with various improvement heuristics. For the construction heuristic, we found that it is beneficial to allow vehicles to violate restrictions, which later on would be repaired by the improvement heuristic. For the improvement heuristics, we considered Descent, Simulated Annealing, Modified Simulated Annealing, Variable Neighborhood Search, and a combination of the last two. We found that Simulated Annealing or the combination of Simulated Annealing with Variable Neighborhood Search always provided the best results. Furthermore, we found that the perceived waiting times for both the priority and non-priority customers are significantly lower when using the dissatisfaction function approach, as opposed to modeling standard time windows, with average savings of 48% and 20%, respectively. With respect to the combined objective of transportation costs and waiting time penalties, the dissatisfaction function approach resulted in average savings over all experiments of 48%.

With respect to further research, we propose (i) the development of a matheuristics that can help to find a good solution for the proposed mathematical problem in a shorter time and (ii) the use of Machine Learning techniques to decrease the solution space of the mathematical problem formulation.

References

1. Afshar-Bakeshloo, M., Mehrabi, A., Safari, H., Maleki, M., Jolai, F.: A green vehicle routing problem with customer satisfaction criteria. J. Ind. Eng. Int. **12**(4), 529–544 (2016). https://doi.org/10.1007/s40092-016-0163-9

2. Caceres Cruz, J., Arias, P., Guimarans, D., Riera, D., Juan, A.: Rich vehicle routing problem: survey. ACM Comput. Surv. **47**, 1–28 (2014)
3. Cao, E., Lai, M.: An improved differential evolution algorithm for the vehicle routing problem with simultaneous delivery and pick-up service. In: Third International Conference on Natural Computation, ICNC 2007, vol. 3, pp. 436–440, August 2007
4. Feng, S., Wu, H., Sun, X., Li, Z.: Factors of perceived waiting time and implications on passengers' satisfaction with waiting time. PROMET - Traffic Transp. **28**, 155–163 (2016)
5. Ghannadpour, S.F., Noori, S., Tavakkoli-Moghaddam, R.: A multi-objective vehicle routing and scheduling problem with uncertainty in customers' request and priority. J. Comb. Optimiz. **28**(2), 414–446 (2014)
6. Homburg, C., Droll, M., Totzek, D.: Customer prioritization: does it pay off, and how should it be implemented? J. Mark. **72**(5), 110–130 (2008)
7. Kirkpatrick, S., Gelatt, C.D., Vecchi, M.P.: Optimization by simulated annealing. Science **220**(4598), 671–680 (1983)
8. Kuo, Y., Wang, C.C.: A variable neighborhood search for the multi-depot vehicle routing problem with loading cost. Expert Syst. Appl. **39**(8), 6949–6954 (2012)
9. Lalla-Ruiz, E., Heilig, L., Voß, S.: Assessing simulated annealing with variable neighborhoods. In: Matsatsinis, N.F., Marinakis, Y., Pardalos, P. (eds.) LION 2019. LNCS, vol. 11968, pp. 298–303. Springer, Cham (2020). https://doi.org/10.1007/978-3-030-38629-0_24
10. Lenstra, J., Kan, A.: Complexity of vehicle routing and scheduling problems. Networks **11**, 221–227 (2006)
11. Mingyong, L., Erbao, C.: An improved differential evolution algorithm for vehicle routing problem with simultaneous pickups and deliveries and time windows. Eng. Appl. Artif. Intell. **23**(2), 188–195 (2010)
12. Mladenović, N., Hansen, P.: Variable neighborhood search. Comput. Oper. Res. **24**(11), 1097–1100 (1997)
13. Osman, I.H.: Metastrategy simulated annealing and tabu search algorithms for the vehicle routing problem. Ann. Oper. Res. **41**(4), 421–451 (1993). https://doi.org/10.1007/BF02023004
14. Reinelt, G.: The Traveling Salesman: Computational Solutions for TSP Applications. Springer, Heidelberg (1994). https://doi.org/10.1007/3-540-48661-5
15. Robuste, F., Daganzo, C.F., Souleyrette, R.R.: Implementing vehicle routing models. Transp. Res. Part B: Methodol. **24**(4), 263–286 (1990)
16. Stenger, A., Vigo, D., Enz, S., Schwind, M.: An adaptive variable neighborhood search algorithm for a vehicle routing problem arising in small package shipping. Transp. Sci. **47**, 64–80 (2013)
17. Talbi, E.G.: Metaheuristics: From Design to Implementation, vol. 74. Wiley, Hoboken (2009)
18. Tavakkoli-Moghaddam, R., Safaei, N., Gholipour, Y.: A hybrid simulated annealing for capacitated vehicle routing problems with the independent route length. Appl. Math. Comput. **176**(2), 445–454 (2006)
19. Wang, Y., Ma, X., Xu, M., Wang, Y., Liu, Y.: Vehicle routing problem based on a fuzzy customer clustering approach for logistics network optimization. J. Intell. Fuzzy Syst. **29**, 1427–1442 (2015)
20. Wong, R.T.: Vehicle routing for small package delivery and pickup services. In: Golden, B., Raghavan, S., Wasil, E. (eds.) The Vehicle Routing Problem: Latest Advances and New Challenges. ORCS, vol. 43, pp. 475–485. Springer, Boston (2008). https://doi.org/10.1007/978-0-387-77778-8_21

21. Zeithaml, V.A., Rust, R.T., Lemon, K.N.: The customer pyramid: creating and serving profitable customers. Calif. Manag. Rev. **43**(4), 118–142 (2001)
22. Zhang, T., Chaovalitwongse, W.A., Zhang, Y.: Scatter search for the stochastic travel-time vehicle routing problem with simultaneous pick-ups and deliveries. Comput. Oper. Res. **39**(10), 2277–2290 (2012)
23. Zhang, T., Chaovalitwongse, W.A., Zhang, Y.: Integrated ant colony and tabu search approach for time dependent vehicle routing problems with simultaneous pickup and delivery. J. Comb. Optimiz. **28**(1), 288–309 (2014). https://doi.org/10.1007/s10878-014-9741-1

A Genetic Algorithm to Minimise the Number of Vehicles in the Electric Vehicle Routing Problem

Bertran Queck and Hoong Chuin Lau[✉]

Fujitsu-SMU Urban Computing and Engineering Corporate Lab, School of Information Systems, Singapore Management University, Singapore, Singapore
klqueck.2015@sis.smu.edu.sg, hclau@smu.edu.sg

Abstract. Electric Vehicles (EVs) and charging infrastructure are starting to become commonplace in major cities around the world. For logistics providers to adopt an EV fleet, there are many factors up for consideration, such as route planning for EVs with limited travel range as well as long-term planning of fleet size. In this paper, we present a genetic algorithm to perform route planning that minimises the number of vehicles required. Specifically, we discuss the challenges on the violations of constraints in the EV routing problem (EVRP) arising from applying genetic algorithm operators. To overcome the challenges, techniques specific to addressing the infeasibility of solutions are discussed. We test our genetic algorithm against EVRP benchmarks and show that it outperforms them for most problem instances on both the number of vehicles as well as total time traveled.

Keywords: Electric Vehicle Routing Problem · Genetic algorithm

1 Introduction

With the rise of electric vehicles (EVs) and the charging stations' infrastructure, corporations may look to adopt an EV fleet as a green alternative. Traditional fuel-powered combustion engine vehicles are less energy-efficient than battery-powered EVs. However, one weakness of EVs is that they have a shorter driving range as compared to fuel-powered vehicles. This is largely related to the size of the battery in the EV. In [4], we see that in terms of cost-efficiency, EVs are only comparable to fuel-powered vehicles if they use a small battery.

Thus, it is important for EVs to incorporate charging station visits to recharge its battery in route planning. While charging stations are being built, they are not as ubiquitous as petrol stations. Charging of EVs is also unlike refueling traditional vehicles as it costs a considerable amount of time. Hence, there is a need to factor queuing time at charging stations as well [7]. Due to the higher upfront investment cost of acquiring an electric vehicle as compared to a fuel-powered vehicle, fleet sizing and management becomes even more important. In that regard, being able to know the minimum number of required EVs can help corporations plan their investment strategy.

E. Lalla-Ruiz et al. (Eds.): ICCL 2020, LNCS 12433, pp. 200–214, 2020.
https://doi.org/10.1007/978-3-030-59747-4_13

This paper provides a genetic algorithm (GA) approach to solve the Electric Vehicle Routing Problem (EVRP) that minimises the number of vehicles while accounting for charging and waiting times at charging stations. The classical Vehicle Routing Problem (VRP) is a well-researched topic, with many different variants like Vehicle Routing Problem with Time Windows, etc. However, as EV adoption and research are nascent, there are opportunities to adapt or explore new methods to solve the EVRP variants. The variant and constraints of EVRP we focus on is adopted from [7], and can be defined as follows (detailed mathematical notations can be found in [7]):

1. A single depot
2. Set of customer nodes with varying deterministic demands and service time; all customers have to be served
3. Set of identical charging stations, each of which can only be used sequentially, later arrivals are to wait in queue
4. Set of identical EVs V, each starting and ending at the depot, and each having a load capacity, an upper limit on battery capacity and a battery which cannot fall to 0, and an upper limit on the time taken for a route.

The objective is first to minimise the number of vehicles used, and secondarily to minimise total travel time. More precisely, our objective function is defined as follows:

$$\min (K \times M) + \sum_{k \in V} t^k. \tag{1}$$

where

K $(\leq V)$ is the number of vehicles used
M is a large constant representing the penalty coefficient
t^k is the total travel time of vehicle k

As seen in [7], with the same constraints, finding optimal solutions for a 10-customer problem takes longer than 3 h. Rather, our aim is to achieve good results by a genetic algorithm. In this paper, we will discuss the challenges that arise from applying genetic algorithm operators to obtain feasible solutions for EVRP. To overcome these challenges, we discuss modifications to the selection, crossover, and mutation operators of the GA, respectively. For each technique, we explain the challenge we address as well as the reasons why the proposed approach is suitable. In addition, were sent methods to enhance the diversity of search and improvement of runtime performance.

This paper proceeds as follows. Section 2 gives a brief literature review. In Sect. 3, we provide the limitations of the current GA approach. Sections 4–6 give our detailed solution approach in terms of the modified crossover, mutation, and enhancing diversity. We discuss our experimental analysis in Sect. 7, and conclude in Sect. 8.

2 Literature

Prior research in EVRP focused on minimising electric consumption using a hybrid-GA approach with Tabu Search (TS) [3]. The authors' approach was to use GA and

TS as a local search, and a Tabu List to avoid getting stuck in a local optimum. [7] proposes to solve EVRP by a GA with popular operators, such as tournament selection, partially matched crossover, and also local search. Some papers discuss how infeasibility is handled through the use of a penalty function to chromosomes that violate constraints, while other approaches include repairing the chromosome by fixing the infeasibility [6, 11, 13]. In [2], the authors discuss a crossover for CVRP to not even create infeasible solutions in the first place. Also, using a crossover that is designed for their constraint gave them superior results as compared to using the commonly good crossover operators. When it comes to mutation operators, commonly used mutation operators like swap and insertion are used [12]. These operators work is a way where nodes are randomly selected, and they have their positions changed, without regards to their context or feasibility. In [7], a local search technique that is similar to the insertion mutation operator is used, but it only accepts the new solution if there is an improvement. On population selection and diversity management, there are a few methods. One is the diversity-controlling adaptive genetic algorithm [15], which calculates the current population diversity, and increase and decrease the rate of crossovers and mutations to achieve a targeted diversity. Other methods include a Fitness Uniform Selection Scheme, and a Fitness Uniform Deletion Scheme where population selection is based on their fitness value [5, 8]. The claim is that by selecting chromosomes of differing fitness, they are able to maintain population diversity.

3   Limitations of the Base Genetic Algorithm

A GA consists of 3 key steps: selection, crossovers as well as mutation. A solution is encoded as a chromosome and multiple chromosomes are maintained in a population, and each has a fitness value. The steps to a basic genetic algorithm are as follows.

1. Initialise the population of chromosomes and compute their fitness values.
2. The crossover between 2 good chromosomes to create a new chromosome.
3. The mutation operation is applied randomly on any chromosome.
4. Recalculate fitness value of chromosomes.
5. The selection mechanism is used to determine who makes it to the next generation.
6. Repeat from step 2 until we complete the stipulated number of generations.

Our work extends the existing GA from [7]. Having a baseline algorithm to work with, we can observe the performance of the algorithm to identify potential gaps and address them accordingly. Specifically, the challenge is to find good feasible routes that satisfy the *vehicle load capacity*, *battery levels*, and *vehicle time taken limit*. We term the three crucial constraints as the *triple constraints*. Intuitively, for a route where any of these constraints is binding, we know that it is unable to include another customer node at any position without additional modifications (such as local search). Any algorithm not only has to account for travel time to the charging station but also the charging time and waiting time (if there are other vehicles in queue). A random mutation can easily cause the resulting solution to become infeasible. In the following, we will describe the challenges and proposed techniques to deal with the triple constraints.

4 Modified Crossover

The triple constraints tend to create an offspring solution that is infeasible. In this section, we present our modified crossover operator which improves the one proposed in [7].

Table 1 illustrates the used chromosome representation. Depot denotes the start and end of a single route, same as [7], Cust is a customer, and CStat is a charging station.

Table 1. Single-point crossover example

Parent1	Depot	Cust1	CStat1	Cust2	CStat2	Cust3	Depot	Cust4	Depot
Parent2	Depot	Cust1	Cust2	Depot	Cust3	CStat2	Cust4	Depot	
Offspring1	Depot	Cust1	CStat1	Cust2	Cust3	CStat2	Cust4	Depot	
Offspring2	Depot	Cust1	Cust2	Depot	CStat2	Cust3	Depot	Cust4	Depot

From the example, we observe that Offspring1 which previously had 2 routes, has become a single route. While this is an improvement to reduce the number of vehicles by 1, from the Cust2 to Cust3, it is essential to make a stop to CStat2, like in Parent1 to recharge the battery, otherwise, it will cause a battery level violation. This is just a simple case where constraints are violated. Others that make random crossovers challenging are, for example, crossovers or routes which have missing customer nodes, or repeated visits to the same customer. Additional steps are required to remedy the infeasibility and violations. Unfortunately, randomly occurring crossovers are ineffective as they frequently generate infeasible offspring.

Some interesting points to note are that while a solution has multiple routes, 2 constraints, i.e. vehicle load utilisation and battery levels, are route-specific and will not change if the route does not. While the constraint on used vehicle time is affected by changes in other routes, it is largely only affected by a change in charging station visits. Hence, the crossover operator would ideally be one that can pass on desirable routes from parents to offspring, with minimal or no changes to individual routes. Also, it should have minimal changes to charging station visits. It should also be quick to compute because it is a common operator that would be run multiple times throughout the course of the genetic algorithm.

A crossover operator that fulfils these requirements is the Best Route Better Adjustment Recombination (BRBAX) proposed in [2]. From two parents, the operator will pass on the top 50% of routes verbatim from one parent to the offspring, then insert the rest of the nodes not in the offspring from the second parent, preserving the same order. The top 50% of routes are determined by the vehicle load utilisation, and higher utilisation is preferred. With that, BRBAX works within the triple constraints in a fitting manner, with vehicle load utilisation and battery level remaining the same, or even reduced in the offspring. The only possibly affected constraint is the used vehicle time as there might be changes to charging station visit times.

5   Modified Mutation

Due to the triple constraints of our problem, random mutations tend to generate infeasible solutions. In this section, we propose modified mutation operators.

We observe that the mutation operation in [7] exploited some form of local search. Something noteworthy about the local search mutation operator used is the mitigation technique employed when the mutation causes routes within the solution to become infeasible. What was done previously to remedy the solution was that for routes that were infeasible, their customer nodes were removed until they became feasible, and the evicted nodes were placed into a newly created route. While this might work well for the objective in [7] to minimise total travel, it only serves to worsen the objective value of minimising the number of vehicles. Hence, the conventional mutation operators with the focus of primarily improving population diversity would not be effective. In the following, we propose a method that is more akin to the existing local search mutation where there is a higher chance of a good mutation that improves the solution.

5.1   Route Elimination Algorithm

A desirable mutation operator is one that can effectively work within the triple constraints, is quick to compute, and able to improve the objective value. The Route Elimination Algorithm in [9] proposed to immediately eliminate one route by putting all nodes into an ejection pool and then inserting them into existing routes. However, inserting nodes into existing routes proves to be challenging. To address this, the authors introduced Squeeze and Perturb operators which iteratively attempt to remove nodes from the ejection pool and insert them into routes. In essence, the concept is to insert the customer nodes which are *hard* to insert first, followed by the easier customers later. The difficulty to insert is represented by a heuristic penalty term, which is derived through multiple iterations. These operators are not suitable in the mutation operator because it is an iterative process, which is computationally expensive.

5.2   Node Insertion with Triple Constraints

Even though we are unable to utilise the Squeeze and Perturb operators directly, the route elimination algorithm can be adapted. The idea is to insert a customer into a relatively good route and position, without having to do so iteratively. A critical problem is to insert ejected customer nodes into existing routes that will satisfy the triple constraints. First, ensuring vehicle capacity constraints is easy, since cumulative loads can be computed in constant time. Second, the constraint on total vehicle time per route is the most challenging, because it cannot be computed on a route level due to possible queuing time caused by *other* vehicles waiting at charging stations. Furthermore, even if a route has not changed, it might become infeasible due to changes on a different route. Thirdly, we have a constraint on the battery level. Unlike the constraint on vehicle time per route, this constraint is self-contained. However, it is not as simple as the vehicle capacity constraint, because when a new node is inserted to the route, we must calculate whether it is feasible in terms of battery level.

In our problem, we always charge the battery to full in every charging station visit; therefore, we can calculate the battery levels starting from the depot or charging station prior to the insertion until the depot or charging station, whichever comes first. However, this means that the computation for battery level feasibility is always done retrospectively after a new customer node has been inserted. To reduce the number of failed insertions due to battery level constraints, we can precompute the minimum battery level requirement of each node, which is the lowest battery level a vehicle can be at when visiting that node in order to safely travel to a charging station to recharge.

5.3   Battery-Feasible Neighbours

To further improve the efficiency of deriving feasible nodes for insertion, we can make use of the minimum battery level to derive a set of battery-feasible neighbours for every node. A node's battery feasible neighbour is one that a vehicle can safely visit and be sure that the battery level constraint is not violated, i.e. we can subsequently make an insertion of a charging station to recharge the battery *prior to* arriving at the neighbour, if required. The algorithm to generate the set of battery-feasible neighbours should take into consideration that the vehicle may have had to travel from a previous node, and that there is a maximum battery level that a vehicle can have, once it is at that node. For example, assuming a full battery of 100, node i to node j takes 90 units battery cost, but node i is 20 units battery cost from its nearest charging station. Hence, the maximum battery level at node i is $100 - 20 = 80$, and a vehicle at node i will never make it to node j. The algorithm for computing battery level feasibility is given as follows:

Algorithm for Computing Maximum Battery Level for Node i

1. Iterate through all charging station nodes to find the *nearest* charging station to node i, denoted $cs1$
2. Calculate the battery cost for travelling from node i to $cs1$, $bc(i, cs1)$
3. Calculate the battery cost for travelling from node i to depot, $bc(i, depot)$
4. Calculate *minimumBatteryLevelRequirement* $= \min(bc(i, cs1), bc(i, depot))$
5. Calculate *maximumBatteryLevel* $=$ *fullBatteryLevel* $-$ *minimumBatteryLevelRequirement*

For a node j to be a battery-feasible neighbour of node i, we check if it is reachable with the maximum battery level of node i, and if it has sufficient battery to visit a charging station afterwards. For example, assuming a full battery of 100 units, node i to node j takes 90 units battery cost, but the nearest charging station is 20 units battery cost away. Once a vehicle travels from node i to node j, it will have a remaining battery level of $100 - 90 = 10$, which is insufficient for going to the nearest charging station. Hence, node j should not be included in node i's battery-feasible neighbour set.

Algorithm for Generating Battery-Feasible Neighbours for Node i
Iterate through every node $j \neq i$

a. Calculate battery cost from node i to node j, $bc(i,j)$

b. If *maximumBatteryLevel* > *minimumBatteryLevelRequirement* + bc(i,j) add node j
to the battery-feasible neighbour set of node i

5.4 Route Merge Local Search (RMLS) as Mutation Operator

We integrate the above two subsections to form our mutation operator. The first step of
the route elimination is to remove a route. Given a chromosome, we would compute
the total vehicle load utilisation of each route, and select the route with the lowest load
utilisation for elimination. All customer nodes of the eliminated route will be added to
an ejection pool, ignoring depot and charging stations.

For insertion, it is done one node at a time. First, a node to be inserted, node i,
is randomly selected from the ejection pool. Then, the route with the lowest vehicle
load utilisation with nodes in the node i's battery-feasible neighbour set is selected as
a candidate route for insertion. If battery level constraint causes infeasibility, there is a
remedy in the form of charging station reallocation, explained in the next section.ote
that we might still violate the used vehicle time constraint. Then, we proceed to find the
position to insert node i that adds the shortestdistance to the route.

The algorithm will repeat node insertion until the ejection pool is empty or it is
unable to insert any nodes due to violating the constraints. If it fails to insert, we would
consider it a failed mutation and skip it entirely. One possible downside to the route
merges local search is that it can be too aggressive in hill-climbing, as it is following a
simple greedy strategy. However, the mutation is only performed on a certain percentage
of the population in the genetic algorithm, and that it would be able to pass the good
sections of the solution to the next generation. Moreover, this is just one part in the
overall genetic algorithm, we look to employ other methods to prevent convergence into
a local optimum.

5.5 Charging Station Reallocation

After every node has been inserted, it is still possible that the battery level constraint is
violated. However, we can perform some reallocation of charging stations to ensure that
the constraint is satisfied. An example where battery level constraint is violated before
and after charging station reallocation is given in Table 2. Assume that it costs exactly
20 battery units to move from one customer node to another, and exactly 10 battery units
to move to a charging station.

Table 2. Reallocate charging stations

Before – Route	Cust1	Cust2	Cust3	
Before – Battery Level	30	10	−10	
After – Route	Cust1	Cust2	CStat1	Cust3
After – Battery Level	30	10	100	80

Algorithm for Charging Station Reallocation for a Route

1. Remove all charging stations in the route.
2. Iterate through the route to calculate the battery cost for every node the vehicle visits and find out at which node the battery is lower than 0, node i.
3. From node i, we will then iterate backwards until we identify a charging station or depot node, node j.
4. Insert a charging station where there is the smallest increase in route travel time.
5. Repeat from Step 2 until the solution is battery-feasible.

6 Diversity Induced Population Selection

The diversity-controlling adaptive genetic algorithm [15] is only useful if an increased rate of crossovers and mutations is able to introduce diverse offspring or solutions. Based on our prior experiments with BRBAX and Route Merge Local Search operators, the observed diversity is reduced as the GA continues into the later generations. In the following, we discuss our approach for ensuring population diversity.

6.1 Fitness Function vs Objective Function

For our work, there is a distinct difference between the objective function and fitness function. One such application of differing objective function and fitness function is fitness sharing [10], a popular method to increase diversity in a population. The idea is to penalise the fitness of chromosomes that are closely similar to other chromosomes in the population, hence "sharing" their fitness with look-alikes.

Note that our objective function is to minimise the number of vehicles used. To encourage diversity we derive the fitness value depending on how different a chromosome is from the rest of the population, by adding a multiplier to its objective value. In doing so, the chromosome with the best fitness might not be one with the best objective value.

Our proposed fitness function after accounting for diversity is as follows:

$$fCi = nCi \times \left(\frac{\text{average } similarityScore}{diversityMultiplier} \right) \tag{2}$$

where fCi is the fitness of Chromosome i and nCi is the number of vehicles in Chromosome i

The idea is to have higher diversity in the early generations and to add selection pressure in the later generations, a diversity multiplier is added. It is set at the start and reduced in every iteration. In our experiments, the range is from 1.0 to 5.0.

6.2 Similarity Score: Hamming Distance

To derive the similarity scores, we study different types of measures, such as genotypic and phenotypic. [14] proposed that the genotypic similarity between chromosomes can be measured by the Hamming distance, and phenotypic similarity can be measured with the difference of the objective value, e.g. A chromosome that uses 11 vehicles is more similar to a chromosome that has 10 vehicles than a chromosome with 13 vehicles.

For example in Table 3, suppose each chromosome has a single route and the distance is 1 for every non-match.

Table 3. Hamming distance between chromosomes

Chromsome1	Depot	Cust1	Cust2	Cust3	Cust4	Depot
Chromsome2	Depot	Cust4	Cust1	Cust2	Cust3	Depot
Distance	0	1	1	1	1	0

The Hamming distance between Chromosome1 and Chromosome2 will be 4, even though they serve the same nodes, and also share a common subsequence [1–3]. Clearly, there are some features of similarity that are not captured by Hamming distance. Hamming distance would be a good measure to use for when the sequence of visits matters. In addition, if we were to introduce more routes, there would also be the complexity of deciding which pairs of routes would be used to calculate the Hamming distance. Since our focus is on minimising the number of vehicles, the sequence of visits would be less important, because no matter which sequence of visits, it is still served by 1 vehicle. Using a phenotypic measure, such as the objective value is also not desirable, since 2 chromosomes with good, diverse solutions will be penalised purely for having the same objective result. What is preferred is a population comprising a diverse set of good chromosomes, instead of only 1 good chromosome with the other chromosomes having a poor performance just for the sake of diversity.

6.3 Jaccard Index for Chromosomes

The key feature to capture is which customers are visited by the same vehicle. Here, we can utilise the features of an unordered collection of unique elements. For a given chromosome, it contains a set of routes, and within each route, contains a set of nodes to visit. A simple measure for set similarity is the Jaccard Index:

$$J(A, B) = \frac{|A \cap B|}{|A \cup B|} \tag{3}$$

In Table 4, since the two chromosomes share 1 common route, Chromosome3 ∩ Chromosome4 = 1, and since the number of unique routes combined is 3, Chromosome3 ∪ Chromosome4 = 3. Hence, J(Chromosome3, Chromosome4) = 1/3.

Table 4. Chromosomes for Jaccard Index example

Chromosome3	Depot	Cust1	Cust2	Cust3	Depot	Cust4	Cust5	Cust6	Depot
Chromosome4	Depot	Cust3	Cust1	Cust2	Depot	Cust7	Cust8	Cust9	Depot

6.4 Double Jaccard Index

We now introduce the Double Jaccard Index as our similarity measure, as it can handle sets of routes that are highly similar even though they are not *exact* matches. The idea is that the Jaccard Index on chromosome-level is calculated with the Jaccard Index on route-level, with set membership determined by a pre-defined threshold (routeMatchThreshold).

As shown in Table 5, even though RouteA and RouteB are similar (out of 7 nodes, first 5 are the same), the routes are not an exact match and will not be considered as a match in the Jaccard Index calculation above.

Table 5. Routes for Double Jaccard Index example

RouteA	Dpot	Cust1	Cust2	Cust3	Cust4	Cust5	Cust6	Cust7	Dpot
RouteB	Dpot	Cust5	Cust1	Cust2	Cust3	Cust4	Cust8	Cust9	Dpot

To account for such cases, when determining if routes match, we would also use the route Jaccard Index, and consider it a match when the Jaccard index is greater than a predefined route matching threshold. For simplicity, we will only calculate the route Jaccard Index based on customer nodes only. In the above, Cust1 to Cust5 are common in both RouteA and RouteB, hence RouteA $\cap$ RouteB $= 5$. The number of unique routes in RouteA $\cup$ RouteB $= 9$. Hence, J(RouteA, RouteB) $= 5/9$.

Then, to calculate the Jaccard Index between Chromosomes i and j, we iterate every route in Chromosome i, and compare with every route in Chromosome j to calculate the Jaccard Index between each route pair given above. If this Jaccard Index exceeds the *routeMatchThreshold*, we increment the size of the intersection size (i.e. numerator) by 1. A similar calculation is performed on the denominator.

Finally, to calculate the similarity score of a chromosome with respect to the population, we apply the following algorithm:

Naïve Algorithm to Calculate Similarity Score for a Chromosome i:

1. Initialise *sumJaccardIndex* to 0
2. Iterate through all chromosomes in population except for chromosome i to compute Jaccard Index with these chromosomes and add the computed value to *sumJaccardIndex*
3. *similarityScore = sumJaccardIndex*/(population size $- 1$)

The Double Jaccard Index calculation, if performed naively, is computationally expensive. In essence, the above algorithm exhaustively iterates through all combinations. Let R denote the number of routes, and N denote the number of customer nodes. Since every pair of nodes of a given pair of routes must be considered, and every possible route pair is compared, the time complexity is $O(R^2 N^2)$ to calculate one Double Jaccard Index. Since the calculation of similarity score has to be done in every generation and for every chromosome, the resulting complexity is high. From our experiments, when we included the Double Jaccard Index calculation, the runtime of the GA increases tremendously. As such, this algorithm must be made more efficient.

One way to achieve that is to use a lookup table that maps which nodes are on which route. The algorithm is given as follows:

Efficient Double Jaccard Index Algorithm between Chromosomes(i, j)

1. Initialise *numUniqueRoutes* to be number of routes in Chromosome i
2. Initialise *numRoutesIntersectBothChromosome* $= 0$
3. Iterate through every customer node in Chromosome i, and create a lookup table of node to route mapping for Chromosome i, *nodeIdToRouteCiMapping*
4. Iterate through every route r in Chromosome j

   a. Initialise set of customer nodes from r, *c2RouteNodes*
   b. Initialise *minNumNodeMatchesForC2Route* = ⌈size of *c2RouteNodes* * *routeMatchThreshold*⌉
   c. Iterate through every customer node in route r, and get their corresponding route in Chromosome 1 by looking up *nodeIdToRouteCiMapping*, then keep a count of how many occurrences on each route into a separate table, *routeToCountTable*
   d. Using the largest count from the *routeToCountTable*, if it is smaller than *minNumNodeMatchesForC2Route*, increment *numUniqueRoutes*
   e. Otherwise, union route r and route with the largest count from Chromosome1, and get the size of the union set.
   f. If the size of the union set * *routeMatchThreshold* is greater than the largest count, increment *numUniqueRoutes*, else increment *numRoutesIntersectBothChromosome*

5. Set Jaccard Index $=$ *numRoutesIntersectBothChromosome/numUniqueRoutes*

With the above algorithm, we have reduced the complexity from the naïve algorithm of $O(R^2N^2)$ to $O(N)$, which greatly improves the run time complexity of GA.

7   Experimental Analysis

7.1   Experimental Setup

To evaluate the effectiveness of our algorithm, we performed experiments on the same problem instances as those provided in [7], which is a set of modified Solomon instances with charging stations as well as battery capacity. We will omit instance c101_21 as there is no feasible solution. The instances are divided into 3 categories: clustered (C) random (R) and randomly clustered (RC).

We first obtained a set of EVRP benchmark results by running the GA proposed in [7] with the *modified* objective function defined in Sect. 1 (to ensure fairness in comparison) with the value of M set as 100,000. We used a population size of 100, and 5000 generations. Crossover occurs once per generation, with parents selected using binary tournament selection. The mutation occurs twice per generation, one is for the chromosome with the best fitness, another is selected using uniform-random. All experiments were performed for 5 times, and the best results were presented. We then tested the effectiveness of our proposed crossover and mutation operators individually to evaluate their performance. Finally, we applied them together with the diversity population selection technique, with the route matching Jaccard index thresholds at 1.0 and 0.25. This way, we evaluated how well the operators work together, as well as the impact of different route matching thresholds.

Table 6 shows the benchmark instances and results obtained on all 100-customer modified Solomon instances presented in [7]. The numbers in brackets () represent the results published in [7] with their *original* objective function (that minimises total travel duration). It can be seen that the modified objective achieves a smaller number of vehicles in 20 out of 28 instances, equal numbers in 4 instances, and more vehicles in 4 instances.

Table 6. EVRP benchmarks

Instances	# of Vehicles	Instances	# of Vehicles
c102	11 (13)	r107	12 (14)
c103	13 (12)	r108	13 (14)
c104	12 (15)	r109	15 (15)
c105	12 (13)	r110	15 (14)
c106	14 (11)	r111	12 (14)
c107	14 (17)	r112	14 (12)
c108	11 (13)	rc101	13 (15)
c109	10 (19)	rc102	14 (17)
r101	14 (14)	rc103	15 (18)
r102	13 (16)	rc104	15 (15)
r103	13 (13)	rc105	14 (17)
r104	13 (14)	rc106	14 (18)
r105	14 (17)	rc107	15 (15)
r106	15 (12)	rc108	14 (15)

7.2 Minimum Number of Vehicles Comparison

Figure 1 shows the comparison of results of best solutions obtained by each combination of our proposed approaches against the EVRP benchmarks.

From Fig. 1, we observe improvement over the EVRP benchmarks (as shown in Table 6). Interestingly, our proposed approach could outperform both the old and new results given in Table 6, for both the old and new results. In fact, for the clustered instances, we managed to achieve the minimum number of vehicles possible. For these clustered instances the total demand of all customers is 1810, and the load capacity per vehicle is 200. Hence, the minimum number of vehicles required $= \lceil 1810/200 \rceil = 10$.

Another interesting point is that RMLS yields slightly better results compared with BRBAX+RMLS+Diversity(1.0). However, using BRBAX+RMLS+Diversity(0.25), we can obtain the same average performance as RMLS for the best result. We suspect that

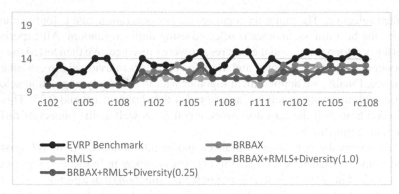

Fig. 1. Best minimum number of vehicles

a route matching threshold of 1.0 might be too conservative, leading to high population similarity. In other words, allowing partial matching between routes can potentially yield an improvement in results.

BRBAX+RMLS+Diversity(0.25) runtime performance across all instances averages to around 50 min per run.

7.3 Average Minimum Number of Vehicles Comparison

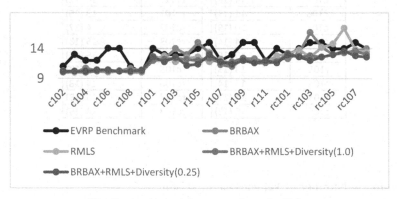

Fig. 2. Average minimum number of vehicles

Figure 2 shows the *average* (instead of best) performance over the 5 runs. Apart from 4 outlier instances, both BRBAX and RMLS showed improved performance against the benchmark.

We observe that regardless of route matching threshold value, BRBAX+RMLS+Diversity outperformed RMLS. We believe this phenomenon is observed because RMLS is highly exploitative and can easily be stuck in a local optimum.

In summary, BRBAX+RMLS+Diversity would be the preferred algorithm if consistent results are preferred. For best results, use a low route matching threshold like 0.25 as a threshold of 1.0 can be too conservative.

7.4 Total Travel Duration Comparison

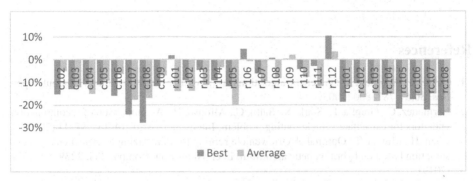

Fig. 3. Total route duration, BRBAX+RMLS+Diversity(0.25) vs [7]

Figure 3 compares BRBAX+RMLS+Diversity(0.25) against [7] on the total route duration measure based on percentage change. We observe that there is a significant reduction in the total route duration across all (C) and (RC) instances. However, for (R) instances, there is a small handful where our algorithm performs worse. This might be because there is a correlation between the number of used vehicles and the total route duration for each category of problem instances. The reason that our algorithm tends to perform better in clustered than uniform-random instances is that its focus is to reduce the number of used vehicles. With fewer vehicles, individual vehicles would have to serve more customers, and if customers are part of a cluster, travel time and battery usage will be reduced if the cluster is served by the same vehicle. On the contrary, random instances of customer nodes are unable to take advantage of cluster characteristics.

On average, we observe an 11% reduction in total route duration for both best and average measures. This further validates the efficacy of the algorithm; not only were we able to achieve reductions in the number of vehicles, but also in the total travel duration.

8 Conclusion and Future Works

In this paper, we proposed an efficient GA that solves EVRP which minimises the total number of vehicles. While the experimental results look very promising, we believe there are many opportunities to improve both solution efficiency and effectiveness. One possibility to explore is to find another heuristic to remove nodes for RMLS instead of the greedy heuristic on vehicle load utilization. Removal of nodes into the ejection pool does not need to be strictly from one route. GA will come to a point where it is challenging to reduce the number of routes, where it might be good to start improving on the secondary objective, to reduce the total of the needed time. GA seems to perform well for clustered instances; this would probably be because the BRBAX and RMLS were using vehicle load utilisation as a heuristic measure. One possibility to explore is using different heuristic measures to select good routes for BRBAX.

Acknowledgements. This research is supported by the National Research Foundation, Singapore under its Corp Lab @ University scheme and Fujitsu Limited as part of the A*STAR-Fujitsu-SMU Urban Computing and Engineering Centre of Excellence.

References

1. Baker, B., Ayechew, M.: A genetic algorithm for the vehicle routing problem. Comput. Oper. Res. **30**(5), 787–800 (2003)
2. Bermudez, C., Graglia, P., Stark, N., Salto, C., Alfonso, H.: A comparison of recombination operators for capacitate vehicle routing problem. Inteligencia Artif. **14**(46), 34–44 (2010)
3. Chen, H., Murata, T.: Optimal electric vehicle routing for minimizing electrical energy consumption based on hybrid genetic algorithm. Lect. Notes Eng. Comput. Sci. **2239**, 526–531 (2019)
4. Gustafsson, T., Johansson, A.: Comparison between battery electric vehicles and internal combustion engine vehicles fueled by electrofuels—from an energy efficiency and cost perspective (2015)
5. Hutter, M., Legg, S.: Fitness uniform optimization. IEEE Trans. Evol. Comput. **10**(5), 568–589 (2006)
6. Kumar, S., Panneerselvam, R.: A survey on the vehicle routing problem and its variants. Intell. Inf. Manag. **04**(03), 66–74 (2012)
7. Li, B., Jha, S.S., Lau, H.C.: Route planning for a fleet of electric vehicles with waiting times at charging stations. In: Liefooghe, A., Paquete, L. (eds.) EvoCOP 2019. LNCS, vol. 11452, pp. 66–82. Springer, Cham (2019). https://doi.org/10.1007/978-3-030-16711-0_5
8. Miller, B., Goldberg, D.: Genetic algorithms, selection schemes, and the varying effects of noise. Evol. Comput. **4**(2), 113–131 (1996)
9. Nagata, Y., Bräysy, O.: A powerful route minimization heuristic for the vehicle routing problem with time windows. Oper. Res. Lett. **37**(5), 333–338 (2009)
10. Oliveto, P., Sudholt, D., Zarges, C.: On the benefits and risks of using fitness sharing for multimodal optimization. Theoret. Comput. Sci. **773**, 53–70 (2019)
11. Ombuki, B., Ross, B., Hanshar, F.: Multi-objective genetic algorithms for vehicle routing problem with time windows. Appl. Intell. **24**(1), 17–30 (2006). https://doi.org/10.1007/s10 489-006-6926-z
12. Pereira, F.B., Tavares, J., Machado, P., Costa, E.: GVR: a new genetic representation for the vehicle routing problem. In: O'Neill, M., Sutcliffe, R.F.E., Ryan, C., Eaton, M., Griffith, N.J.L. (eds.) AICS 2002. LNCS (LNAI), vol. 2464, pp. 95–102. Springer, Heidelberg (2002). https://doi.org/10.1007/3-540-45750-X_12
13. Prins, C.: A simple and effective evolutionary algorithm for the vehicle routing problem. Comput. Oper. Res. **31**(12), 1985–2002 (2004)
14. Zhu, K.: Population Diversity in Genetic Algorithm for Vehicle Routing Problem with Time Windows (2004). http://www.cs.sjtu.edu.cn/~kzhu/papers/zhu-ecml04.pdf. Accessed 6 Apr 2020
15. Zhu, K.: A diversity-controlling adaptive genetic algorithm for the vehicle routing problem with time windows. In: Proceedings of the 15th IEEE International Conference on Tools with Artificial Intelligence (2003)

Decentralized Combinatorial Auctions for Dynamic and Large-Scale Collaborative Vehicle Routing

Johan Los[1](✉), Frederik Schulte[1], Margaretha Gansterer[2], Richard F. Hartl[3], Matthijs T. J. Spaan[4], and Rudy R. Negenborn[1]

[1] Department of Maritime and Transport Technology,
Delft University of Technology, Mekelweg 2, 2628 CD Delft, The Netherlands
{J.Los,F.Schulte,R.R.Negenborn}@tudelft.nl
[2] Department of Operations, Energy, and Environmental Management,
University of Klagenfurt, Universitätsstraße 65–67, 9020 Klagenfurt, Austria
Margaretha.Gansterer@aau.at
[3] Department of Business Decisions and Analytics, University of Vienna,
Oskar-Morgenstern-Platz 1, 1090 Vienna, Austria
Richard.Hartl@univie.ac.at
[4] Department of Software Technology, Delft University of Technology,
Van Mourik Broekmanweg 6, 2628 XE Delft, The Netherlands
M.T.J.Spaan@tudelft.nl

Abstract. While collaborative vehicle routing has a significant potential to reduce transportation costs and emissions, current approaches are limited in terms of applicability, unrealistic assumptions, and low scalability. Centralized planning generally assumes full information and full control, which is often unacceptable for individual carriers. Combinatorial auctions with one central auctioneer overcome this problem and provide good results, but are limited to small static problems. Multi-agent approaches have been proposed for large dynamic problems, but do not directly take the advantages of bundling into account. We propose an approach where participants can individually outsource orders, while a platform can suggest bundles of the offered requests to improve solutions. We consider bundles of size 2 and 3 and show that travel costs can be decreased with 1.7% compared to the scenario with only single order auctions. Moreover, experiments on data from a Dutch transportation platform company show that large-scale collaboration through a platform results in system-wide savings of up to 79% for 1000 carriers.

Keywords: Collaborative vehicle routing · Collaborative transportation · Platform-based transportation · Combinatorial auctions · Multi-Agent System · Bundling · Logistics · Dynamic Pickup and Delivery Problem

1 Introduction

Horizontal collaboration is an effective approach to increase transportation efficiency (Verdonck et al. 2013; Gansterer and Hartl 2018b; Pan et al. 2019). While

© Springer Nature Switzerland AG 2020
E. Lalla-Ruiz et al. (Eds.): ICCL 2020, LNCS 12433, pp. 215–230, 2020.
https://doi.org/10.1007/978-3-030-59747-4_14

traditional collaborative vehicle routing focuses on exchange of orders between limited numbers of carriers, the rise of transportation platform companies allows large-scale cooperations, where shippers could directly connect to the platform as well. This raises the need for systems that can assist in both allocating and reallocating orders to carriers in real time without having direct control over the cooperative (but nevertheless rational) participants.

Centralized collaboration approaches have been studied to assess the possible gains of collaboration (Fernández et al. 2018; Molenbruch et al. 2017; Schulte et al. 2017), but these generally make the assumption of complete control and full information availability—which cannot always be assumed in real-world applications. Decentralized approaches with a central auctioneer, and combinatorial auctions in particular (Berger and Bierwirth 2010; Gansterer and Hartl 2018a), overcome these problems, but available computational studies are limited to static problems with small numbers of carriers and orders. For order allocation in larger dynamic problems, Multi-Agent Systems (MASs) have been used, where shippers iteratively offer jobs in auctions, and carriers can bid on them (Máhr et al. 2010; Mes et al. 2013; Los et al. 2020). Although different improvements to the basic auction system have been proposed, interaction effects of orders have not been considered, to the best of our knowledge. Offering bundles of orders, however, is relevant if the individual orders could not be accepted when they are offered in sequence, but are profitable if they are combined. We expect that offering bundles within a MAS could improve results, while the extra effort for carriers to compute a bid on a bundle is limited.

Further, MASs are generally used for allocation, rather than reallocation of orders, although they are suitable for both. By focusing completely on reallocation of orders among carriers, we are able to investigate the possible gains of cooperation among a large number of carriers, while such gains have only been investigated for cooperation between a few carriers so far.

Hence, the contribution of this article is twofold. First, we explore whether and to which extent applying bundling principles to multi-agent approaches can improve results for large-scale dynamic settings. Second, we investigate the possible gains of cooperation among a large number of carriers using this approach.

2   Related Work

Two main collaborative vehicle routing research areas have been distinguished: centralized collaboration and decentralized collaboration (Gansterer and Hartl 2018b, 2020).

Centralized collaboration models mainly assume a set of orders for each carrier and compute what gains could theoretically be obtained if orders are shared. Approximation algorithms are used to compare the solution where each carrier performs only its own orders and the solution where (part of) the orders can be exchanged. It is assumed that all required information is known, which might be difficult in practice. Centralized collaboration models have been developed for different applications: Fernández et al. (2018) consider a problem where customers request service from different companies and will be attended by only a subset of these companies. Molenbruch et al. (2017) study cooperation of different dial-a-ride providers. Montoya-Torres et al. (2016) compare a non-cooperative and a cooperative scenario for a specific case of city logistics. The number of cooperating carriers in the computational studies, however, ranges from 2–4 (see Table 1). Schulte et al. (2017) use larger instances of up to 50 carriers to investigate emission reductions by carrier cooperation in port-related truck operations.

Table 1. Overview of collaborative transportation approaches.

Cat	Reference	R	A	T	P	L	#Ord	#Carr	#Veh	I	B
CC	Fernández et al. (2018)	✓			✓		18–30	2	∞		
	Molenbruch et al. (2017)	✓		✓	✓	✓	400	4	32		
	Montoya-Torres et al. (2016)	✓					61	3	3		
	Schulte et al. (2017)	✓			✓	✓	10–75	4–50	4–50		
DC	Berger and Bierwirth (2010)	✓			✓		<100	3	3		✓
	Dai et al. (2014)	✓		✓	✓	✓	15–24	3	3–30	✓	✓
	Gansterer and Hartl (2018a)	✓			✓	✓	30–210	3	3		✓
	Gansterer et al. (2020)	✓			✓	✓	30–90	3–6	9–18		✓
	Lai et al. (2017)	✓			✓		30–245	3–24	∞	✓	
	Li et al. (2015)	✓			✓	✓	9–15	3	6	✓	
	Lyu et al. (2019)	✓		✓	✓	✓	9–45	3	9	✓	✓
	Wang and Kopfer (2014)	✓		✓	✓	✓	104–266	2–5	19–61	✓	✓
	Wang and Kopfer (2015)	✓			✓	✓	~1767	NAv	NAv	✓	✓
DL	Dai and Chen (2011)	✓		✓	✓	✓	9	3	3–30	✓	
	Figliozzi et al. (2004)		✓	✓	✓		NAv	4	8		
	Figliozzi et al. (2005)		✓	✓	✓		NAv	NAv	4		
	Van Lon and Holvoet (2017)		✓	✓	✓		120–1200	NAp	10–100	✓	
	Los et al. (2020)		✓	✓	✓	✓	1000	150	150	✓	
	Máhr et al. (2010)		✓	✓	✓		65	NAp	40	✓	
	Mes et al. (2013)		✓	✓	✓		NAv	10	10	✓	
	This article	✓	✓	✓	✓	✓	1000–2000	1–1000	150–1000	✓	✓

CC: Centralized collaboration; **DC:** Decentralized collaboration with central auctions; **DL:** Decentralized collaboration with local auctions; **R:** Reallocation of orders; **A:** Allocation of unassigned orders; **T:** Time windows; **P:** Pickups and deliveries; **L:** Less than truckload; **#Ord:** Number of orders; **#Carr:** Number of carriers; **#Veh:** Number of vehicles; **I:** Iterative auctions; **B:** Bundling of orders.

Within the literature on decentralized collaboration, two approaches can be distinguished: decentralized collaboration with central auctions and decentralized collaboration with local auctions (see Table 1).

Decentralized collaboration with central auctions assumes that one central auctioneer interacts with all carriers but does not have complete information. An advantage is that the auctioneer can give some guarantees, e.g., it can ensure that all orders are assigned by solving the winner determination problem. The generally large complexity of such subproblems for the coordinator, however, restricts the size of instances that can be solved. In combinatorial auctions (Berger and Bierwirth 2010; Gansterer and Hartl 2018a; Gansterer et al. 2020), each carrier submits unprofitable orders to the auctioneer. To reduce complexity, the auctioneer proposes only a limited subset of attractive bundles of these orders, and all carriers bid on them. The auctioneer then computes the optimal assignment. Different iterative variants where bundles of orders are considered and the auctioneer finally determines a solution based on the information of different carriers have been studied by Dai et al. (2014), Lyu et al. (2019) and Wang and Kopfer (2014, 2015) (see Table 1). Other variants where bids are made only for single orders have been considered by Lai et al. (2017) and Li et al. (2015).

In decentralized collaboration with local auctions, no central auctioneer is considered. In contrast, any actor can act as auctioneer at any time by starting an auction on (part of) the order(s) that it is responsible for. Hence, local improvements can be made without guarantees on the feasibility of other orders and on global solution quality. Consequently, quick adjustments in dynamic large-scale problems are possible. Generally, this approach is used for allocation of orders to carriers (or even to separate vehicles of one carrier), but Dai and Chen (2011) apply it for reallocation as well (see Table 1). Máhr et al. (2010) and Van Lon and Holvoet (2017) consider MASs with local auctions to examine whether such a decentralized approach can outperform centralized approaches, without focusing on incentives for different carriers. Different carrier strategies and learning mechanisms are considered by Figliozzi et al. (2004, 2005). Mes et al. (2013) investigate the interaction of several look-ahead policies for shippers and carriers, namely delaying commitments, breaking commitments, and valuation of opportunities with respect to future orders. Los et al. (2020) examine the value of information sharing in a MAS.

While bundling of orders is often considered in decentralized collaboration approaches with central auctions, this is not the case for decentralized collaboration approaches with local auctions. Since interaction effects could be relevant in these approaches as well, the focus of this article is on including combinatorial aspects within local auctions. Furthermore, we approximate possible cooperation gains for up to 1000 carriers with our decentralized approach, while the current centralized collaboration literature considers significantly lower carrier numbers.

3   Problem Description

We consider a transportation platform that connects shippers and carriers, and improves routes by allowing carriers to outsource orders. We focus on a dynamic Pickup and Delivery Problem (PDP) where an order either is submitted to the platform by the shipper, or is directly assigned to a specific carrier. In the later case, the contracted carrier can be seen as the owner—the original shipper is then irrelevant. The platform organizes auctions to contract carriers for the unassigned orders. Furthermore, carriers cooperate in the sense that already contracted orders can be sold to other carriers that can deliver them cheaper.

A problem instance consists of a set of shippers S, a set of carriers C, a set of orders O_s for each shipper $s \in S$, a set of initially assigned orders O_c for each carrier $c \in C$ (with $O_S = \bigcup_{s \in S} O_s$ the total set of unassigned orders, $O_C = \bigcup_{c \in C} O_c$ the total set of assigned orders, and $O = O_S \cup O_C$ the total set of orders), and a set of capacitated vehicles V_c for each carrier $c \in C$ (with $V = \bigcup_{c \in C} V_c$ the total set of vehicles).

Each order $o \in O$ represents a load of a certain quantity that must be transported from a pickup location p_o to a delivery location d_o. The pickup or delivery, taking a certain service duration, must start in a time window $[e_i, l_i]$, for $i \in \{p_o, d_o\}$. The release time r_o denotes when the order becomes known to the system. For $o \in O_S$, a reservation price f_o is defined, i.e., a maximum value that the shipper is willing to pay for transportation.

Each vehicle $v \in V$ has an availability time window $[e_v, l_v]$; it becomes available at the initial location α_v at e_v and needs to be at the end location ω_v at l_v. All vehicles $v \in V_c$ become known to the system at the release time r_c of the carrier.

Travel time and travel costs from location i to location j are assumed to be identical for all vehicles, and are denoted by t_{ij} and z_{ij}, respectively. By τ, we denote the time horizon of the problem instance.

A (temporary) solution at time t for a problem instance is given by a set of routes $R^t = \{\langle \rho^{1t} \rangle, \cdots, \langle \rho^{|V|t} \rangle\}$, where each route (plan) $\langle \rho_i^{vt} \rangle_{i=1}^{m^{vt}}$ is a sequence of m^{vt} locations representing the (partially completed) path of vehicle v at time t, respecting time, capacity, and precedence constraints. A formal description can be found in Los et al. (2020).

Individual shippers have the goal of outsourcing their orders at a price as low as possible, but not exceeding their reservation prices. Carriers have the goal of maximizing profit, and do this by accepting and outsourcing orders such that the differences between the payment (made to them in case the order is accepted, or paid by them in case the order is outsourced) and the marginal travel costs for the orders are maximized. Together, they contribute to the global goal of obtaining a final solution R^τ with minimal total travel costs.

4 Auction Approach

We propose a multi-agent approach were orders are iteratively offered in reverse auctions. All available carriers (acting as sellers of service) can bid for them, and the carrier with lowest bid wins the auction: it pays the price of its bid, and becomes responsible for filling the order. In contrast to previous approaches (Máhr et al. 2010; Mes et al. 2013; Los et al. 2020), we do not restrict an auctioneer to be a shipper or carrier offering a separate order: we introduce bundle auctioneers as well, denoted by A_B, offering a group of orders $B \subseteq O$. The orders within a bundle are not necessarily owned by the same shipper or carrier, since bundle auctioneers can be generated by the platform.

4.1 Auction Procedure

When order $o \in O$ becomes available at r_o, auctioneer $A_{\{o\}}$ (acting on behalf of shipper s if $o \in O_s$ or acting on behalf of carrier c if $o \in O_c$, but operated by the platform) is initialized and becomes active. Furthermore, the platform immediately generates, if possible, bundle auctioneers A_B with $o \in B$ and $|B| > 1$ (based on similarity of o and previously released orders that are known to the platform, as we will define in Sect. 4.2) and activates them shortly after $A_{\{o\}}$ has been activated.

When active, auctioneer A_B iteratively organizes auctions. Given a maximum number of auctions a per auctioneer and its activation time r_{A_B}, the time between subsequent auctions is set to $(\min_{o \in B} l_{p_o} - r_{A_B})/a$. The auction at time t then is as follows:

- Each carrier $c \in C$ bids its marginal costs $MC_c^t(B)$ for bundle B at time t, i.e., the extra travel costs for inserting all orders in B into its routes, given the situation at time t. If one or more of the orders in B are already planned in the routes of the carrier, the marginal costs are computed as if these orders were not yet planned.
- A_B compares the bids; let b_0 be the lowest bid provided by carrier c_0.
- A_B examines the current costs $CC^t(B)$ for bundle B at time t, given by the sum of the marginal costs for assigned orders and the reservation prices for unassigned orders at time t:

$$CC^t(B) = \sum_{c \in C} MC_c^t(B \cap O_c^t) + \sum_{o \in B \cap O_S^t} f_o,$$

where $O_c^t = \{o \in O \mid \exists v \in V_c \; \exists i \in \{1, \cdots, m^{vt}\} \; \rho_i^{vt} = p_o\}$ is the total set of orders that carrier c has in its route plans at time t and $O_S^t = \{o \in O \mid \neg \exists v \in V \; \exists i \in \{1, \cdots, m^{vt}\} \; \rho_i^{vt} = p_o\}$ is the set of unassigned orders at time t.
- If $b_0 < CC^t(B)$, the bid is accepted. The platform informs all involved shippers and carriers, who update their contracts and routing plans. Furthermore, the platform receives in total $CC^t(B)$ from the outsourcing shippers and carriers and pays b_0 to the winning carrier c_0. The gain of $CC^t(B) - b_0$ is divided over the participants as incentive to cooperate, following some profit distribution function.
  To avoid unserved orders, the bid is accepted as well if $b_0 \geq CC^t(B)$ and one or more of the orders in B are (due to initial assignment) owned by a carrier who cannot serve them. In this case, they have to cover the difference between b_0 and $CC^t(B)$ with shares proportional to the reservation prices. In other cases when $b_0 \geq CC^t(B)$, no (re)allocations and no payments take place.

When transportation of one of the orders in B starts or the latest pickup time of one of the orders has passed without a contract for that order, A_B becomes inactive.

4.2   Bundle Generation

Selling bundles of orders within a MAS is relevant if for (some of the) individual orders, the best bid is higher than the current costs, while the best bid for the bundle is below the current costs for the bundle. This is likely to happen if orders are close to each other (both in space and time) since they might be combined within the same vehicle route with lower marginal costs.

Relatedness of orders has been defined by Ropke and Pisinger (2006) for PDPs in the context of Large Neighborhood Search (LNS). Since the goal there is to select orders from routes that can be reinserted at each other's places, both pickup locations and delivery locations need to be similar and actual visiting times are compared. For our application, it is already sufficient if one of the locations of one order is similar to one of the locations of the other order and the time windows are not too different. Gansterer and Hartl (2018a) have investigated bundle criteria based on isolation, density and tour length. Isolation, however, is not useful in our context (since we do not require partitions of the complete set of requests) and time windows are not considered in their approach. Hence, we propose a new relatedness measure and bundling procedure that can be applied in the MAS.

We define a relatedness measure $R(o, \hat{o})$ for two orders o and $\hat{o}$ as follows:

$$R(o, \hat{o}) = \min(\text{sim}(p_o, d_{\hat{o}}), \ \text{sim}(d_o, p_{\hat{o}}), \ 0.5(\text{sim}(p_o, p_{\hat{o}}) + \text{sim}(d_o, d_{\hat{o}}))), \quad (1)$$

where the similarity of two pickup or delivery locations i and j is defined based on both travel time and time windows:

$$\text{sim}(i, j) = \gamma t_{ij} + W(i, j). \quad (2)$$

Here, W represents the minimal waiting time (due to time window restrictions) at one of the locations if a vehicle serves both locations immediately after each other. Formally,

$$W(i, j) = \max(0, \ \min(W_D(i, j), W_D(j, i)), \quad (3)$$

where

$$W_D(i, j) = \begin{cases} \infty & \text{if } e_i + t_{ij} > l_j; \\ \max(e_i + t_{ij}, e_j) - \min(l_i + t_{ij}, l_j) & \text{otherwise.} \end{cases} \quad (4)$$

In Eq. 2, γ is a parameter (generally $\gamma > 1$) representing the cost of travel time relative to waiting time. In this article, we use $\gamma = 2$. In Eq. 1, the minimum over three terms is taken. If the pickup of one of the orders is similar to the delivery of the other order, the orders might form a good match, irrespective of the other pickup and delivery locations and times. If, however, both pickup locations are similar, it does matter whether the delivery locations are similar. If they are at opposite directions, combining the orders might appear less useful than if they are similar as well. Hence, the third term in Eq. 1 involves similarity of both pickup and delivery locations.

The platform dynamically generates bundles based on the relatedness measure R. Given a new order o at release time t and the pool of not yet being transported orders O^t, x bundles of size 2 and y bundles of size 3 are generated as follows:

– **Bundles of size 2.** The platform generates bundles $\{o, \hat{o}\}$ for $\hat{o} \in O^t$ and keeps the x bundles with minimal $R(o, \hat{o})$.

- **Bundles of size 3.** The platform generates bundles $\{o, \hat{o}, \check{o}\}$ for $\hat{o}, \check{o} \in O^t$ and keeps the y bundles for which $\min(R(o, \hat{o}) + R(\hat{o}, \check{o}), R(o, \check{o}) + R(\check{o}, \hat{o}),$ $R(o, \hat{o}) + R(o, \check{o}))$ is minimal. Not all three orders have to be highly related to each other to form an attractive bundle, but each order in the bundle needs to be highly related to at least another order in the bundle.

4.3 Theoretical Analysis

By applying bundling, the relatively easy subproblems of the carriers become more difficult. For a carrier $c \in C$ approximating its marginal costs for a bundle B, a basic insertion heuristic that iteratively inserts the order that can be inserted at least costs has a complexity of $\mathcal{O}(|B|^2 |V_c| (l + |B|)^3)$, with l the maximum length of a vehicle route.[1] For single orders, this reduces to $\mathcal{O}(|V_c| l^3)$. In practice, however, a lot of options might be quickly pruned due to time, precedence and capacity constraints.

To get insights into the possible impact of bundling within a MAS, we assume that (estimates of the) real marginal costs are always reported. Although strategic bidding might occur in practice, it is not straightforward (Gansterer and Hartl 2018a). For carriers or shippers mentioning the marginal costs or reservation prices for outsourcing orders, we make the following observations.

- They do not report a value above the true value, since they need to pay this.
- They might report a lower value, but this comes with the risk that the lowest bid b_0 is not lower than $CC^t(B)$, hindering the trade. Indeed, they might report lower values and slightly increase them in next auction rounds, but due to the dynamic environment, there is no guarantee on success.

For carriers placing a bid to acquire a bundle B, we can reason as follows, where $MC_c^t(B)$ denotes the carrier's marginal costs, b_0 denotes the carrier's bid, and g denotes the profit that a winning carrier makes, i.e., g is a fraction of $CC^t(B) - b_0$, dependent on the used profit distribution function.

- They will not bid a value $b_0 < MC_c^t(B)$ if g is expected to be relatively small, since the compensation $b_0 + g$ will not cover the extra costs $MC_c^t(B)$.
- They might place a bid $b_0 < MC_c^t(B)$ if g is expected to be relatively high. If $b_0 + g > MC_c^t(B)$, lowering the bid is a good strategy to outbid another carrier with a bid between b_0 and $MC_c^t(B)$.
- They might bid a value $b_0 > MC_c^t(B)$ to get a higher compensation, but this comes at the risk of not winning the auction anymore.

---

[1] Per main iteration ($|B|$ in total), the insertion costs for all resulting orders (at most $|B|$) at all routes ($|V_c|$ in total) need to be checked. Insertion of both the pickup and the delivery needs to be checked for each position in the route (which can be up to $l + 2|B| - 2$ positions when the last order of the bundle must be inserted), and a chain of time consistency checks might be necessary along the complete route in the worst case as well.

The approach guarantees that no carrier is worse off per auction. They might, however, be worse off on the long term if they get dynamically revealed yet assigned tasks that produce bad interactions with the tasks they acquired before. Nevertheless, individual rationality is guaranteed if all assigned tasks are known by the carriers beforehand.

5   Computational Study

Our experiments are based on a real-world data set consisting of well over 12000 orders that have been received by the Dutch transportation platform company Quicargo. To investigate the impact of bundling, we created 6 instances of 2000 orders where half of the orders are assigned to carriers (to generate initial routes), and the other half is unassigned and released during operations. All orders were available for (re)allocation. To examine the possible gains of cooperation among a large number of carriers, we created 6 instances of 1000 orders and varied the number of carriers that own them.

The MAS was implemented in Go and all experiments were performed on a single machine with Intel Core i5-750 CPU at 2.67 GHz and 6 GB of RAM. Within our experiments, we used the insertion heuristic described by Campbell and Savelsbergh (2004), adapted to pickup and delivery problems, for computation of marginal costs and construction of initial routes.

5.1   Impact of Bundling

We generated 6 instances of 2000 orders and 150 carriers. Each carrier has a single randomly chosen depot with 1 to 3 vehicles of capacity 13.6 (loading meters). Half of the orders were randomly assigned to one of the 10% closest carriers in terms of distance between pickup location and depot. About 66% of the carriers are always available, and the others have restricted availability times based on the assigned orders. Release times of assigned orders were always set equal to release times of the corresponding carriers, to make sure that routes can be constructed immediately. Pickup and delivery locations (in and close to the Netherlands) and estimated load quantities are as in the original data set. Pickup and delivery time windows have been kept, as well as release times for the unassigned orders, but random shifts of a whole number of days have been made such that all orders fell within a time horizon of 10 days. Travel speed was set to 0.015 km/s and reservation prices were set to 2.5 times the travel costs between pickup and delivery locations.

We ran experiments where only single orders were auctioned, and compared them with runs in which 3 bundles of size 2 and 1 of size 3 were introduced per order. First, we allowed a maximum of 10 auctions per auctioneer. The results in terms of travel costs, the number of rejected orders, and the increase in computation time are given in Table 2 (set 1). Addition of the bundles decreases the travel costs by about 4% on average, but increases the computation time by a factor 10.

Table 2. Results for single order auctions (S) and bundle auctions (B).

Instance			Settings		Results					
I	C	RP	A_S	A_B	TC_S	TC_B	D(%)	R_S	R_B	T
1	150	2.5	10	$10+4\times10$	9705.58	8955.25	7.73	1	2	6.43
2	150	2.5	10	$10+4\times10$	9440.72	8997.33	4.70	1	1	9.03
3	150	2.5	10	$10+4\times10$	9383.03	9151.61	2.47	0	1	10.34
4	150	2.5	10	$10+4\times10$	9405.44	8923.82	5.12	1	1	11.72
5	150	2.5	10	$10+4\times10$	8806.27	8716.37	1.02	0	1	11.72
6	150	2.5	10	$10+4\times10$	8945.61	8639.87	3.42	2	3	12.91
Average of set 1							4.08	0.83	1.5	10.36
1	150	2.5	50	$10+4\times10$	9253.74	8955.25	3.23	1	2	0.66
2	150	2.5	50	$10+4\times10$	9169.23	8997.33	1.87	0	1	0.99
3	150	2.5	50	$10+4\times10$	9149.17	9151.61	-0.03	0	1	1.15
4	150	2.5	50	$10+4\times10$	9179.95	8923.82	2.79	1	1	1.14
5	150	2.5	50	$10+4\times10$	8658.51	8716.37	-0.67	0	1	1.23
6	150	2.5	50	$10+4\times10$	8856.09	8639.87	2.44	1	3	1.35
Average of set 2							1.61	0.5	1.5	1.09
1*	500	2	30	$10+4\times5$	9185.33	8934.01	2.74	3	0	1.39
2*	500	2	30	$10+4\times5$	9014.15	9002.89	0.12	1	0	1.85
3*	500	2	30	$10+4\times5$	9231.21	9058.68	1.87	2	2	1.92
4*	500	2	30	$10+4\times5$	9273.16	9027.70	2.65	2	3	2.18
5*	500	2	30	$10+4\times5$	8864.34	8706.58	1.78	1	0	2.19
6*	500	2	30	$10+4\times5$	8917.12	8828.61	0.99	0	0	2.55
Average of set 3							1.69	1.5	0.83	2.01

I: Instance number (instances marked with a * differ only in number of carriers and reservation prices); **C:** Number of carriers; **RP:** Reservation price factor (relative to travel costs); $\mathbf{A}_{\{S,B\}}$: Maximum number of auctions per order in the experiments without (S) or with (B) bundling ($a+bc$ denotes a maximum of a auctions for the single order and b times a maximum of c auctions for bundles with the order); $\mathbf{TC}_{\{S,B\}}$: Total travel costs obtained without (S) or with (B) bundling; **D(%):** Decrease in travel costs for bundling compared to no bundling. $\mathbf{R}_{\{S,B\}}$: Number of rejected orders without (S) or with (B) bundling; **T:** Computation time increase factor for bundling compared to no bundling.

To check whether the improvements are caused by bundling or rather by the increased total number of auctions, we ran a second experiment where we allowed a maximum of 50 auctions per single order auctioneer, such that both the scenario without bundling and the scenario with bundling have the same maximum total number of auctions (see set 2 in Table 2). Although there is a small reduction in travel costs on average (1.6%) when bundles are used, two individual cases have slightly higher travel costs (instance 3 and 5). Furthermore, the number of rejected orders is generally larger with bundling than with single order auctions. Hence, no clear improvement due to bundling can be observed within this set.

One might conjecture, however, that the reservation prices are too high to take any advantage of bundling. If reservation prices are lower, it is more likely that serving some individual orders is too expensive, but combinations still could be advantageous. Hence, we ran a third set of experiments where we lowered the reservation price of the orders to 2 times the travel costs between pickup and delivery locations. At the same moment, we increased the number of carriers to 500 to avoid large numbers of rejected orders. The results (Table 2, set 3) show that travel costs can be reduced by about 1.7%, and the number of rejected orders generally does not increase if bundles are used. The computation time for the bundling scenario (about 4 h on average) is twice as high as that of the single order auction scenario (about 2 h).

5.2   Cooperation Gains

To assess the possible gains from cooperation, we created another series of instances were each order is initially assigned to a carrier. We created 6 different instance sets of 1000 orders, and used 4 carrier configurations (1000, 100, 10 carriers, or 1 carrier) and 2 assignment configurations (close or random) per set. Within each set, 50 depots with 20 vehicles each were defined, which were distributed equally among 1000, 100, 10 carriers, or 1 carrier, such that each carrier has 1, 10, 100, or 1000 vehicles, respectively. Each order is always associated with the same depot—the depot closest to the pickup location of the order in case of close assignment, and a random depot in case of random assignment. Then, the order was assigned to a random carrier having vehicles in that depot. All carriers are continuously available, but original order release times were kept. Other properties are the same as described in Sect. 5.1.

Because carriers do not optimize their individual routes (but only use the insertion heuristic), the MAS can serve as a system that reassigns orders to the same carrier if the selling carrier is the same as the lowest bidder, i.e., carriers can improve their own routes through the auction system. To avoid this behaviour in our cooperation gain assessment, we added an individual improvement phase consisting of 50 hill-climbing LNS iterations (see Pisinger and Ropke 2019) after each insertion of an order into a carrier's plan.

In Fig. 1a, we show the decrease in total travel costs if carriers collaborate compared to the scenario where each carrier only serves its own orders. Savings of up to 79% and 70% (for 1000 carriers, with random and close assignment, respectively) are observed. The savings with close assignments are lower than the savings with random assignments, as expected, but are still rather large.

Note that a 22% gain through self-reassignment can be obtained if only one carrier is present that does not apply individual improvement phases. With individual improvements, however, this is not possible, as expected. Furthermore, gains through self-reassignment are lower for larger numbers of carriers, since the number of orders per carrier is smaller. With only 1 order per carrier (which

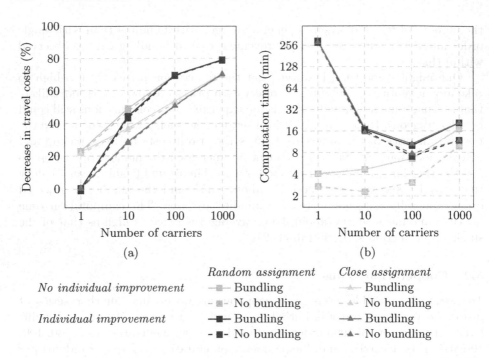

Fig. 1. Results for varying numbers of cooperating carriers: (a) decrease in total travel costs compared to a non-cooperative setting; (b) computation times.

is the average for the 1000 carrier instances) the insertion heuristic will already find the best individual solution. Indeed, the individual improvement phase does not significantly change the gains if 1000 carriers collaborate.

When LNS improvement is applied, the computation time (see Fig. 1b) slightly increases if carriers' subproblems are relatively small (for large numbers of carriers) but increases a lot if the subproblems are more complex (for lower numbers of carriers). In practice, a suitable individual optimization method should be selected, based on the individual carriers' available resources and time.

To give an indication of advantages for individual carriers, we show the distribution of the gains among the platform and the carriers in Fig. 2, and the minimum and maximum shares of the total gain that are obtained by individual carriers in Table 3. The used profit distribution function in each auction (see Sect. 4.1) is as follows: 30% of the gain was assigned to the winning carrier, 60% to the selling carriers and shippers (proportional to their current costs), and 10% was kept by the platform itself. In case of pure self-reassignment (which sometimes occured, despite the LNS improvement), no payments were made. The platform's share of total gains is larger when lower numbers of carriers participate (except for the trivial case of 1 carrier where no payments are made) and larger for close assignments than for random assignments. In extreme cases, a single carrier can obtain 3.9% (1000 carrier instances) to 60.9% (10 carrier instances) of the total profits made. Maximum losses (due to the fact that car-

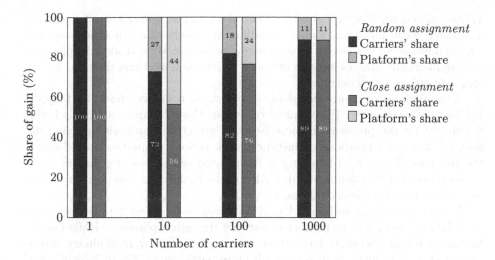

Fig. 2. Shares of the cooperation gains that are obtained by the carrier collective and by the platform.

riers acquire or outsource orders without knowing or even considering future orders that are assigned to them) are considerably lower when orders are randomly assigned (0.1% of the total gains for 1000 carriers up to 16.3% for 10 carriers) than when orders are assigned to the closest carrier (0.3% for 1000 carriers up to 59.1% for 10 carriers). This might be attributed to the high interaction effects of future orders for a carrier: outsourcing an early order might be relatively costly, given similar jobs that later on still appear to be executed.

Table 3. Minimum and maximum percentages of the total gains that are obtained by an individual carrier with single order auctions only (S) and with bundle auctions (B).

	Carriers	1		10		100		1000	
	Setting	S	B	S	B	S	B	S	B
Random	Minimum	100.0	100.0	−16.3	−12.0	−1.1	−1.0	−0.1	−0.1
	Maximum	100.0	100.0	52.1	43.6	10.5	14.6	3.5	3.3
Close	Minimum	100.0	100.0	−59.1	−50.7	−14.4	−14.0	−0.3	−0.3
	Maximum	100.0	100.0	54.1	60.9	23.9	22.9	3.9	3.7

6 Conclusions

We have investigated the potential savings by auctioning bundles of orders within a multi-agent approach for dynamic large-scale collaborative vehicle routing.

While combinatorial auctions with a central auctioneer provide good results on small-size static problems, similar bundling approaches have not been applied within multi-agent systems to solve dynamic problems. We considered a platform that dynamically creates bundles of 2 or 3 orders, and auctions them, as well as separate orders, to all carriers.

A computational study based on a real-world data set shows that applying bundling can save 1.7% of travel costs, but that the applicability is highly dependent on the problem characteristics. A structured analysis applying different bundle configurations on instances with various properties should clarify the full potential of local bundling in distributed vehicle routing. In this work, we used one policy to define bundles. Alternatively, different compositions, sizes, and numbers of bundles could also be used.

Moreover, the approach and data set allowed us to investigate the potential of collaboration of a large number of carriers through a platform, while current literature hardly considers more than 3 or 4 carriers. Our preliminary results show that cost reductions increase with more participants. Up to 79% of travel costs can be saved with 1000 cooperating carriers. However, besides the assumptions in problem properties, the quality of carriers' local route optimization could have an impact on the exact savings, especially if their subproblems become more complex. Future work should examine what quality of subproblem solutions is desirable and what resources and time to obtain them are acceptable.

In this article, we assumed true value reporting by carriers and shippers. Although false bidding is not trivial in the proposed setting, an experimental study on possible individual gains by reporting false values is planned as part of future work. Furthermore, second price auctions can be used to eliminate incentives of false bidding on the short term. An interesting question is whether the extra payments could be covered by bundling gains. Finally, we plan to investigate a scenario with mixed levels of autonomy, where shippers and carriers either can be in charge of auctioning orders themselves, or outsource this process to the platform.

Acknowledgements. This research is supported by the project "Dynamic Fleet Management (P14-18 – project 3)" (project 14894) of the Netherlands Organization for Scientific Research (NWO), domain Applied and Engineering Sciences (TTW).

References

Berger, S., Bierwirth, C.: Solutions to the request reassignment problem in collaborative carrier networks. Transp. Res. Part E **46**, 627–638 (2010)

Campbell, A.M., Savelsbergh, M.: Efficient insertion heuristics for vehicle routing and scheduling problems. Transp. Sci. **38**, 369–378 (2004)

Dai, B., Chen, H.: A multi-agent and auction-based framework and approach for carrier collaboration. Logist. Res. **3**, 101–120 (2011)

Dai, B., Chen, H., Yang, G.: Price-setting based combinatorial auction approach for carrier collaboration with pickup and delivery requests. Oper. Res. Int. J. **14**(3), 361–386 (2014). https://doi.org/10.1007/s12351-014-0141-1

Fernández, E., Roca-Riu, M., Speranza, M.G.: The shared customer collaboration vehicle routing problem. Eur. J. Oper. Res. **265**, 1078–1093 (2018)

Figliozzi, M.A., Mahmassani, H.S., Jaillet, P.: Competitive performance assessment of dynamic vehicle routing technologies using sequential auctions. Transp. Res. Rec. **1882**, 10–18 (2004)

Figliozzi, M.A., Mahmassani, H.S., Jaillet, P.: Impacts of auction settings on the performance of truckload transportation marketplaces. Transp. Res. Rec. **1906**, 89–96 (2005)

Gansterer, M., Hartl, R.F.: Centralized bundle generation in auction-based collaborative transportation. OR Spectr. **40**(3), 613–635 (2018a). https://doi.org/10.1007/s00291-018-0516-4

Gansterer, M., Hartl, R.F.: Collaborative vehicle routing: a survey. Eur. J. Oper. Res. **268**, 1–12 (2018b)

Gansterer, M., Hartl, R.F.: Shared resources in collaborative vehicle routing. TOP **28**(1), 1–20 (2020). https://doi.org/10.1007/s11750-020-00541-6

Gansterer, M., Hartl, R.F., Savelsbergh, M.: The value of information in auction-based carrier collaborations. Int. J. Prod. Econ. **221**, 107485 (2020)

Lai, M., Cai, X., Hu, Q.: An iterative auction for carrier collaboration in truckload pickup and delivery. Transp. Res. Part E **107**, 60–80 (2017)

Li, J., Rong, G., Feng, Y.: Request selection and exchange approach for carrier collaboration based on auction of a single request. Transp. Res. Part E **84**, 23–39 (2015)

Van Lon, R.R.S., Holvoet, T.: When do agents outperform centralized algorithms? A systematic empirical evaluation in logistics. Auton. Agent. Multi-Agent Syst. **31**, 1578–1609 (2017)

Los, J., Schulte, F., Spaan, M.T.J., Negenborn, R.R.: The value of information sharing for platform-based collaborative vehicle routing. Transp. Res. Part E **141**, 102011 (2020)

Lyu, X., Chen, H., Wang, N., Yang, Z.: A multi-round exchange mechanism for carrier collaboration in less than truckload transportation. Transp. Res. Part E **129**, 38–59 (2019)

Máhr, T., Srour, J., de Weerdt, M., Zuidwijk, R.: Can agents measure up? A comparative study of an agent-based and on-line optimization approach for a drayage problem with uncertainty. Transp. Res. Part C **18**, 99–119 (2010)

Mes, M., van der Heijden, M., Schuur, P.: Interaction between intelligent agent strategies for real-time transportation planning. CEJOR **21**, 337–358 (2013)

Molenbruch, Y., Braekers, K., Caris, A.: Benefits of horizontal cooperation in dial-a-ride services. Transp. Res. Part E **107**, 97–119 (2017)

Montoya-Torres, J.R., Muñoz-Villamizar, A., Vega-Mejía, C.A.: On the impact of collaborative strategies for goods delivery in city logistics. Prod. Plann. Control **27**, 443–455 (2016)

Pan, S., Trentesaux, D., Ballot, E., Huang, G.Q.: Horizontal collaborative transport: survey of solutions and practical implementation issues. Int. J. Prod. Res. **57**, 5340–5361 (2019)

Pisinger, D., Ropke, S.: Large neighborhood search. In: Gendreau, M., Potvin, J.-Y. (eds.) Handbook of Metaheuristics. ISORMS, vol. 272, pp. 99–127. Springer, Cham (2019). https://doi.org/10.1007/978-3-319-91086-4_4

Ropke, S., Pisinger, D.: An adaptive large neighborhood search heuristic for the pickup and delivery problem with time windows. Transp. Sci. **40**, 455–472 (2006)

Schulte, F., Lalla-Ruiz, E., González-Ramírez, R.G., Voß, S.: Reducing port-related empty truck emissions: a mathematical approach for truck appointments with collaboration. Transp. Res. Part E **105**, 195–212 (2017)

Verdonck, L., Caris, A., Ramaekers, K., Janssens, G.K.: Collaborative logistics from the perspective of road transportation companies. Transp. Rev. **33**, 700–719 (2013)

Wang, X., Kopfer, H.: Collaborative transportation planning of less-than-truckload freight. OR Spectr. **36**(2), 357–380 (2014). https://doi.org/10.1007/s00291-013-0331-x

Wang, X., Kopfer, H.: Rolling horizon planning for a dynamic collaborative routing problem with full-truckload pickup and delivery requests. Flex. Serv. Manuf. J. **27**(4), 509–533 (2015). https://doi.org/10.1007/s10696-015-9212-8

Metaheuristic Approaches for the Fleet Size and Mix Vehicle Routing Problem with Time Windows and Step Cost Functions

João L. V. Manguino[✉][ID] and Débora P. Ronconi[ID]

Department of Production Engineering, University of São Paulo,
Av. Luciano Gualberto, 1380, Cidade Universitária, São Paulo, SP 05508-010, Brazil
jmanguino@gmail.com

Abstract. The vehicle routing problem is a traditional combinatorial problem with practical relevance for a wide range of industries. In the literature, several attributes have been tackled by dedicated methods in order to better reflect real-life situations. This article addresses the fleet size and mix vehicle routing problem with time windows in which companies hire a third-party logistics company. The shipping charges considered in this work are calculated using step cost functions, in which values are determined according to the type of vehicle and the total distance traveled, with fixed values for predefined distance ranges. The problem is solved with three different metaheuristic methods: Variable Neighborhood Search (VNS), Greed Randomized Adaptive Search Procedure (GRASP) and a hybrid proposition that combines both. The methods are examined through a computational comparative analysis in 168 benchmark instances from the literature, small-sized instances with known optimal solution, and 3 instances based on a real problem from the civil construction industry. The numerical experiments show that the proposed methods are efficient and show strong performance in different scenarios.

Keywords: Vehicle Routing Problem · Step cost functions ·
Metaheuristics · Local search · Third party logistics

1 Introduction

The vehicle routing problem (VRP) has been extensively studied in the literature due to its relevance to industry and broad applications. In the last decades, several variants of the problem were proposed to explore the diversity of operating rules and constraints encountered in real-life applications. To address the actual

Supported by FAPESP (grants 2016/01860-1 and 2013/07375-0) and CNPq (grant 306083/2016-7).

E. Lalla-Ruiz et al. (Eds.): ICCL 2020, LNCS 12433, pp. 231–245, 2020.
https://doi.org/10.1007/978-3-030-59747-4_15

needs of carriers and industry, the problem has been enriched with additional restrictions, as well as clients' and fleet's characteristics [12,25].

This article addresses the situation in which companies hire a third-party logistics company (3PL), whose freight charges are calculated using discontinuous step cost functions, with fixed costs for each distance range according to the type of vehicle being used. The problem also takes in account a diverse fleet to choose from for the routing and time windows in every client and in the deposit. This problem is the Fleet Size and Mix Vehicle Routing Problem with Time Windows and Step Cost functions and it is referred with the acronym FSMVRPTWSC, according to the usual nomenclature.

In this problem, the company prepares its own routing, evaluating all the restrictions and costs, but it does not own the fleet of vehicles, it belongs to a 3PL. In general, such providers have a vast fleet with multiple vehicles of each kind to offer to the clients. The use of 3PL allows the company to focus on its core business and to avoid costs related to the acquisition and maintenance of a fleet, equipment depreciation, drivers and employees' payroll, among other costs. The shipping charges, considered in this problem, are calculated using step cost functions in which values are determined according to the type of vehicle and the distance traveled, with fixed values for predefined distance ranges. This form of freight table is common in certain segments of the industries, as clients and providers can calculate and verify the chargers quickly and conveniently, avoiding costs of personnel or software in the calculation of each invoice exchanged.

The first proposition of the VRP was made by [4] and ever since has been widely studied and more characteristics were considered. A fleet with multiple vehicle types was introduced to the problem by [8] to generate the FSMVRP (Fleet Size and Mix Vehicle Routing Problem). Time windows were introduced by [22], the first approach to the VRPTW, the same paper generated 56 instances of 100 clients that became an important benchmark for evaluating methods. The FSMVRPTW (Fleet Size and Mix Vehicle Routing Problem) was introduced by [14], who also added different vehicle costs and capacities to the problems generated by [22], combining to 168 reference problems.

The use of third party logistics providers (3PL) has already been studied in the literature in many occasions with different approaches. The first approach was made by [2], in which the decision is to choose, for each route, if the company uses its own fleet, or a 3PL's fleet. In a market research, [13] point out that, by 2013, the 3PL industry had evolved into an important outsourcing option for logistics managers around the globe, generating nearly $700 billions in annual operating revenues. An extensive review on the relationship between companies and 3PL partners is presented in [17]. Finally, the combination of FSMVRPTW with the step function freight costs, generating the FSMVRPTWSC, was proposed by [16].

Solution quality is lost when solving the FSMVRPTWSC by artificially creating a linear freight cost curve based on the freight table of the problem and applying a linear cost optimization method. As exemplified in [16], the decision to add more clients to a route may cause a zero cost addition as long as the distance after adding such client still fits in the same distance range and the updated demand can be carried by the same kind of vehicle as before. On the other hand, adding a client that increases the route distance just a small amount can cause a spike in transportation cost, as the small distance change might be just enough to change the distance range. That is why a method that addresses the step cost functions can provide better results.

The use of metaheuristic has been frequent in the multi attribute VRP problems. [12] points out multiple methods of this kind applied to the VRP problem during the 50 years since it started being studied. [24] provide a very extensive review of the evolution of metaheuristics and local search for MAVRP (Multi Attribute VRP). In a survey with the intent to classify and review the taxonomy of the multiple variations of the vehicle routing problems, [3] classify 277 articles of journals with strong impact factor from 2009 and 2015. Among these papers, over 70% of them apply metaheuristic methods.

In Manguino and Ronconi [16], a MILP formulation and two constructive heuristics with local search methods are proposed. This work will further explore the problem through the proposition of metaheuristics approaches that can generate solutions taking advantage of the problem's characteristics. The metaheuristics are GRASP, VNS and a hybrid method combining both. A computational study is carried out with 168 reference instances, three real case inspired instances and small sized instances for comparison with optimum results.

The next section (Sect. 2) describes details of the problem. Sect. 3 explains the proposed metaheuristics. The result of computational experiments are presented and analysed at Sect. 4, followed by the conclusion in Sect. 5.

2 Problem Description

In the problem, there are $n + 1$ points geographically scattered, $N = \{0, 1, 2, \ldots, n\}$. Each route begins and ends at the central depot ($i = 0$), respecting its working hours limited by $[e_0, \ell_0]$. Each client i ($i = 1, 2, \ldots, n$) has a predetermined demand q_i, a service time s_i, and the start time of the service should be within a specific time window, i.e. between time instants e_i and ℓ_i. The distance d_{ij} and travel time t_{ij} between every pair of points are known before the routing plan is defined. There are K different types of vehicles available. Each type of vehicle k ($k = 1, 2, \ldots, K$) has a load capacity a_k ($a_1 < a_2 < \cdots < a_K$).

The cost of each vehicle has a fixed value for each predefined distance range, i.e. each vehicle k has a cost C_{kf} whether its total traveled distance varies from W_f to W_{f+1} for $f = 0, 1, 2, \ldots, F - 1$, where $F - 1$ is the penultimate distance range. The last range, F, is an exception, since it has no upper bound and the cost grows linearly, starting from $C_{k,F-1}$, plus C_{kF} for each unit of distance added. Thus, given a traveled distance $d > 0$, the step cost function C_k for vehicle k can be defined as

$$C_k(d) = \begin{cases} C_{kf}, & \text{if } W_f < d \leq W_{f+1} \text{ for} f \in \{0, 1, \ldots, F - 1\}, \\ C_{k,F-1} + C_{kF}(d - W_F), & \text{if } W_F < d. \end{cases}$$

To illustrate the cost calculation, Fig. 1 presents an illustrative example.

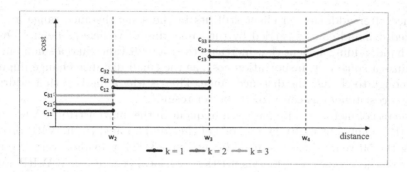

Fig. 1. A illustrative figure from [16] with the step cost function chart representation for case with 3 vehicle types ($k = 1$, 2 and 3) and 4 distance ranges ($f = 1$, 2, 3 and 4). Every distance range starts at w_f and each cost is fixed at c_{kf}. For the last distance range ($F = 4$), cost starts in c_{kF-1} and adds c_{kF} at each extra distance unit.

3   Proposed Metaheuristics

In this work, the FSMVRPTWSC is approached using metaheuristics. In [16] two constructive sequential insertion heuristics are proposed, as well as two local search procedures. This work utilizes the knowledge of the problem and the most successful constructive method (SCIH2), as well as the local search movements, and proposes additional local search movements and the development of metaheuristics.

The choice of the methods to approach was based on [1]. In this paper, it is discussed that there is not one definitive method that achieves best results, but rather methods that can explore and extract the best of each problem's characteristics. With such inspiration, GRASP and VNS were chosen. While the latter uses local searches alternated with increasing amounts of shakes to achieve best results, the first adds controlled variances to a constructive method in a multi-start procedure. Also, taking advantage of possible synergy among methods, a hybrid combination of both is explored.

The main components of the proposed methods were calibrated in 54 instances extracted from the complete set of instances described in Sect. 4.1. This set combines all considered characteristics, with three instances of each combination. More details can be found in [15].

3.1   Local Searches

As the local search is a crucial element for the proposed methods, this section describes their structures and applied movements. Two local searches are proposed by [16], Cross and Relocate. In this work the two methods are reviewed and the 2-opt* is explored.

Relocate consists of removing a client from a route and re-inserting it back to the solution in a different position, either in the same route or a different one. The procedure follows along the proposed by [11], but with one criteria for removing and inserting clients to routes. Figure 2 is an illustration to aid the understanding of the movement.

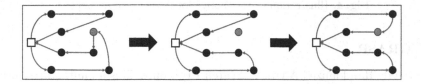

Fig. 2. Illustration of the Relocate local search movement.

The client whose removal generates the biggest cost reduction is chosen. To be re-inserted, the position that causes the minimal cost increase, as long as it is not the same position it was removed from, is chosen. In each iteration up to 60% of the clients with the greatest remove criteria values will be evaluated for the relocation to find the largest total cost reduction.

Cross is an exchange of sections between two different routes of the problem, as it is illustrated in Fig. 3. It was first proposed by [23]. The movement is performed by selecting two distinct routes and for each one a starting position and number of clients of the section is chosen. In this work, the neighborhood is composed by the exchanges of every pair of routes, with sections starting in every position of each route and with section sizes from 1 to 5 clients. The cross exchange that generates the biggest cost reduction is selected.

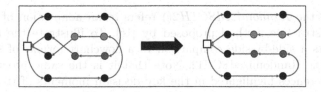

Fig. 3. Illustration of the Cross local search movement.

2-opt* exchanges final sections of routes, as it is illustrated in Figure 4. It was first proposed by [20]. The movement is performed by selecting two distinct routes and for each of them the position from which the section will be exchanged. In this work, the neighborhood is composed by the exchanges of every pair of routes, with sections starting in every position of each route. The 2-opt* exchange that generates the biggest cost reduction is selected.

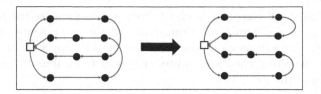

Fig. 4. Illustration of the 2-opt* local search movement.

3.2 GRASP

The Greedy Randomized Adaptive Search Procedure [5] is a multi start method with the execution of a randomized constructive method followed by a local search. The randomized decisions are made with the use of Restricted Candidate Lists (RCLs), that are very well discussed by [21], which are lists with the best candidates for the next decision. It is not a random move, it has criteria for selecting which candidates will be in the list and selecting a candidate from it.

Some further detail of the GRASP was provided by [6]. It lays out some concepts from which the Algorithm 1 was drawn.

Algorithm 1. GRASP

1: **Input:** $Instance_Data$, $MaxTime$
2: **Output:** $BestSol$
3: **for** $CPUTime < MaxTime$ **do**
4:     $SolTemp \leftarrow RandomizedSCIH2()$
5:     $SolTemp \leftarrow LocalSearch(SolTemp)$
6:     UpdateSol(SolTemp,BestSol)
7: **end for**
8: **return** $BestSol$

At line 4, the $RandomizedSCIH2()$ refers to an adaptation of the SCIH2 insertion constructive method proposed by [16]. To illustrate the adaptation, Fig. 5 presents a side-by-side comparison in a flowchart format of the original SCIH2 and the RandomizedSCIH2. Note that it is the same procedure, with the main differences highlighted in the key decision moments of the sequential insertion, when starting a new route, and when deciding which client to add to the route under construction.

SCIH2 is a sequential insertion constructive method, based on the procedure originally proposed for the VRPTW (Vehicle Routing Problem with Time Windows) by [22] and adapted for other multi attributes routing problems throughout the literature. It interactively creates new routes using the furthest unrouted client available and starts adding clients to this route. Clients that can be added to the route, if their demand is not greater than what would be the available capacity if the route was served by the biggest vehicle available are evaluated for insertion through criteria C1 and C2. C1 is the impact caused by the insertion of a client to the route by a cost increase, reducing the vehicle's capacity, using distance of the distance range and time available for the route. C1 is calculated for each position of the route and the minimum value is considered, always with care to never violate the time windows in every client of the route. C2 is the benefit of avoiding an exclusive route to the candidate client after considering C1. A positive C2 means that it is advantageous to insert the client to the route, a negative value means this insertion should be disregarded. The client with the greatest C2 should be inserted and a new list of candidates formed for another consideration of C1 and C2. If there is no client with positive C2, that route is done and a new one should be generated. This process is repeated until no clients are left unrouted.

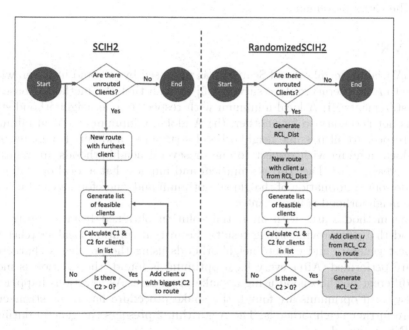

Fig. 5. Side-by-side comparison of the flowcharts for SCIH2 and RandomizedSCIH2 with highlights for the changes among each procedure.

For the RandomizedSCIH2 procedure, instead of starting new routes using the furthest client, a RCL of most distance is formed and the new route is started with a client chosen from this list. Also, instead of choosing the client with the greatest C2, a RCL of clients with positive C2 is generated, from which a client is chosen to be inserted.

The RCLs of the RandomizedSCIH2 are formed and clients are chosen with the following rules:

- *RCL_Dist*:
  - Fixed size list with up to 5 candidates;
  - The 5 furthest clients from the deposit are inserted;
  - Client is chosen randomly from the RCL.
- *RLC_C2*:
  - Clients are accepted based on their C2 value, there is no maximum number of clients to be accepted;
  - From the biggest positive C2 value, every client with C2 greater than 10% less is included;
  - Clients are chosen randomly, with bias to their C2 values.

After the generation of each new solution, it is enhanced using a local search with the Cross movement.

3.3 VNS

VNS (Variable Neighborhood Search) was proposed by [18] and has been widely utilized in the literature. In a survey, [10] explain that the method is based on facts statements: (i) A local minimum with respect to one neighborhood structure is not necessary so for another; (ii) A global minimum is a local minimum with respect to all possible neighborhood structures; and (iii) For many problems local minima with respect to one or several neighborhoods are relatively close to each other. Fact (iii) is empirical and implies that a local optimum can provide some information of the global optimum and, therefore, a careful search of the neighborhood is important.

The method starts with an initial solution obtained from a constructive method that can provide strong results. From that solution local searches that can best generate and explore neighborhoods using the problem's characteristics are performed. After every local optimum is found, the solution is moved to a different neighborhood using a shake procedure. As iterations happen and no new local optimums are found, the shake procedure has to be stronger, to explore further neighborhoods. The Algorithm 2 presents the general outline of the VNS proposed.

As explained in Sect. 3.1, three different local search procedures are used in this work. According to [9], the search in the different neighborhoods should start from the smallest to the largest. That is a form of intensifying the search near to the local minimum since, as the three stated facts suggest, local minimums tend to have similar characteristics.

In a neighborhood analysis, 2-opt* has the smallest neighborhood, as it combines two routes at a time and all positions in each of them. Cross is next, as it adds to the neighborhoods of 2-opt* up to 5 different section sizes. Relocate is the biggest as it combines up to 60% of the clients with every position available in the current solution. Therefore, the sequence of neighborhoods is: 2-opt*, Cross, and Relocate.

During the shake step, each local search performs a random move. For 2-opt*, two routes are selected randomly as well as the positions for exchange in each

Algorithm 2. VNS

1: **Input:** $Init_Sol, MaxNeighborhoods, MaxTime$
2: **Output:** $BestSol$
3: $BestSol \leftarrow Init_Sol$
4: **repeat**
5:     $TempSol \leftarrow BestSol$
6:     $Neighborhood \leftarrow 1$
7:     **while** $Neighborhood \leq MaxNeighborhoods$ **do**
8:         $SolTemp \leftarrow Shake(SolTemp)$
9:         $SolTemp \leftarrow LocalSearch(SolTemp, Neighborhood)$
10:         **if** $Cost(SolTemp) < Cost(BestSol)$ **then**
11:             $BestSol \leftarrow SolTemp$
12:         **else**
13:             $Neighborhood \leftarrow Neighborhood + 1$
14:         **end if**
15:     **end while**
16: **until** $CPUTime > MaxTime$
17: **return** $BestSol$

---

of them. For Cross, after the same selections as 2-opt*, also a random section size is selected. Finally for Relocate, a client is randomly chosen for removal and inserted in a route and position chosen randomly. Infeasible solutions are never accepted, so if the shake generates an one, it is discarded and the shake is repeated until a feasible solution is achieved.

If after going through all the local searches no improvement in the current solution is achieved, the shake is intensified. That is done only after 10 iterations without improvement. The shake starts with one random move for each local search and is added one extra movement at each intensification and can scale up to 50% of the solution routes for 2-opt*, 1% of the solution routes for Cross and 40% of the number of clients in the problem for Relocate.

The proposed VNS version will have the following sequence:

- constructive heuristic SCIH2 from [16] as seed;
- Local Searches:
    - 2-opt*;
    - Cross;
    - Relocate.
- For each Local Search a specific shake is performed;
- For each full cycle of performing all the local searches without any improvement, the shake is intensified, starting from a minimal shake;
- Repeat process for a predetermined CPU Time.

In each and every step of the process, if a new best solution is found, it is always accepted. Infeasible solutions are never considered.

3.4   Hybrid

As mentioned in the previous sections, both methods have the same background idea that local optimal solutions have similar characteristics and search could be performed nearby. On the other hand, each one uses different strategies in different steps of the solution, so a combination of both does not present conflict, but it is rather complimentary.

Hybrid metaheuristic methods are vastly used in the literature to take advantage of strong search procedures of different methods. [7] explore multiple forms of applying GRASP as the chosen strategy, but also combined in hybrid methods, including the VNS. [7] claim that GRASP can generate a proper seed to start the search procedure of the VNS, as the present paper attempts. The combination of GRASP as a seed generator for a VNS procedure is also experimented by [19] for the orienteering problem.

For the FSMVRPTWSC, a hybrid procedure based on the GRASP and VNS metaheuristic is proposed as described in Algorithm 3.

Algorithm 3. GRASP+VNS Hybrid Metaheuristic

1: **Input:** *InstanceData, MaxTime, GRASPTimeShare*
2: **Output:** *BestSol*
3: *BestSol* ← *SCIH2*
4: **while** *CPUTime* ≤ (*GRASPTimeShare* × *MaxTime*) **do**
5:     RandomizedSCIH2(*TempSol*);
6:     **if** *Cost(SolTemp)* < *Cost(BestSol)* **then**
7:         *BestSol* ← *SolTemp*
8:     **end if**
9: **end while**
10: **while** *CPUTime* ≤ *MaxTime* **do**
11:     *Neighborhood* ← 1
12:     **while** *Neighborhood* ≤ *MaxNeighborhoods* **do**
13:         *SolTemp* ← *Shake(SolTemp)*
14:         *SolTemp* ← *LocalSearch(SolTemp, Neighborhood)*
15:         **if** *Cost(SolTemp)* < *Cost(BestSol)* **then**
16:             *BestSol* ← *SolTemp*
17:         **else**
18:             *Neighborhood* ← *Neighborhood* + 1
19:         **end if**
20:     **end while**
21: **end while**
22: **return** *BestSol*;

The procedure starts in line 3, where the solution from the greedy original constructive heuristic is used as an initial solution. From that point on, a share of the solution time (*GRASPTimeShare*) is dedicated for executing the RandomizedSCIH2 procedure and capturing the best solution from this phase. After the time share, the remainder of the execution time is dedicated to the execution of the VNS search.

GRASPTimeShare was calibrated by running the calibration for 12 min with values ranging in: 1%, 3%, 5%, 10%, 15%, 20%, ... , 50%. After analysis and calibration, the time share for the GRASP procedure (*GRASPTimeShare*) was determined in 5%. Even though this apparently runs the VNS share for much longer than the GRASP part, the GRASP process is much faster to run, as it is a multi start of a constructive method that in average lasts less than 1×10^{-4} s, therefore a great number of solutions is generated in the same time as a local search can generate new solutions for a much longer time.

4 Numerical Experiments

Computational experiments were conducted to evaluate the proposed methods. The codes of the proposed procedures were written in C programming language and tests were conducted on a 2.1 GHz Intel Core i7-3612QM with 8 GB of RAM memory. Each instance was executed for 12 min.

The proposed methods were applied in the instances presented in [16], which include a set of 168 instances with 100 clients adapted from the literature, three instances inspired in a real case and 72 small sized instances.

4.1 Literature Adapted Instances

The 168 instances adapted from the literature were adapted from the 56 instances generated by [22] for the VRPTW that were further adapted by [14] for the FSMVRPTW. The instances are grouped with the following characteristics, picking one option for each aspect:

- **Physical distribution of clientes:**
  R: Randomly spread; *C*: Clustered; *RC*: Part randomly spread, part clustered
- **Time Windows Length:**
  1: Tight; *2*: Large
- **Vehicle Costs:**
  a: Most expensive; *b*: Medium; *c*: Least expensive.

Table 1 presents and compares the results obtained by the three proposed methods for the reference instances. For comparison, the original SCIH2 method followed by local search with the Cross movement was implemented (SCIH2+LS). Values are compared through the average objective function value for each group of instances as well as how many of the best known results are obtained.

It is noticeable that the three proposed methods outperform the SCIH2+LS in every group of instances. Among the proposed methods, VNS and GRASP have similar performances, with a smaller total average cost by VNS, but more best known results percentage by GRASP, with a very strong dominance in the RC2 instance group. There is a strong performance by the Hybrid method, with a smaller average total cost smaller then all the other methods. When the share of best known solutions is analysed, the dominance of the Hybrid method becomes clear, as it provides 55.4% of the best known results.

Aiming to determine if there is a relevant difference between the results obtained by the proposed methods, statistical tests were applied. First, the Kolmogorov-Smirnov test was applied to accept or reject the normality of the results distribution, which was rejected. Based on that, the Wilcoxon signed-rank test was applied for every pair of method's results. With a significance level of

Table 1. Average Cost and percentage of best known solutions for each group of the instances. Values in bold are the best known average for each group and biggest percentage of known best results. The percentage of the methods may sum to over 100%, as more than one method may obtain the same best known value.

Data set	#Inst	SCIH2+LS		GRASP		VNS		Hybrid	
		Cost	%Best	Cost	%Best	Cost	%Best	Cost	%Best
C1a	9	6,168.8	0.0	6,151.4	11.1	6,145.4	55.6	**6,140.9**	**66.7**
C1b	9	1,597.5	0.0	**1,571.3**	**100.0**	1,584.0	33.3	1,579.1	33.3
C1c	9	1,025.7	0.0	**995.6**	**77.8**	1,011.8	11.1	1,002.1	44.4
C1	27	2,930.7	0.0	**2,906.1**	63.0	2,913.7	33.3	2,907.4	48.1
C2a	8	5,292.0	0.0	5,277.8	0.0	5,243.3	50.0	**5,240.0**	**62.5**
C2b	8	1,292.0	0.0	1,287.6	0.0	1,240.1	62.5	1,242.9	**75.0**
C2c	8	802.6	0.0	775.9	25.0	743.3	**62.5**	746.4	50.0
C2	24	2,462.2	0.0	2,447.1	8.3	2,408.9	58.3	2,409.8	**62.5**
R1a	12	2,805.7	0.0	2,756.0	8.3	2,749.0	25.0	**2,738.5**	**66.7**
R1b	12	799.8	0.0	763.6	25.0	765.5	0.0	**755.2**	**75.0**
R1c	12	539.8	0.0	503.5	8.3	500.8	33.3	**495.8**	**58.3**
R1	36	1,381.7	0.0	1,341.0	13.9	1,338.5	19.4	**1,329.8**	**66.7**
R2a	11	2,709.8	9.1	2,689.4	0.0	2,640.2	**72.7**	2,654.5	36.4
R2b	11	887.9	9.1	862.5	18.2	**828.0**	**90.9**	834.5	72.7
R2c	11	648.5	0.0	**588.9**	**63.6**	624.6	9.1	591.5	36.4
R2	33	1,415.4	6.1	1,380.3	27.3	1,364.3	**57.6**	**1,360.2**	48.5
RC1a	8	3,313.8	0.0	**3,247.9**	**87.5**	3,290.9	0.0	3,254.3	25.0
RC1b	8	1,036.7	0.0	1,006.0	12.5	997.4	25.0	**994.7**	**62.5**
RC1c	8	683.5	0.0	650.7	0.0	635.4	**50.0**	633.3	**50.0**
RC1	24	1,678.0	0.0	1,634.9	33.3	1,641.2	25.0	**1,627.4**	45.8
RC2a	8	3,119.9	0.0	3,057.9	**62.5**	3,086.5	25.0	**3,055.3**	50.0
RC2b	8	871.5	0.0	828.5	**87.5**	864.5	0.0	**828.4**	50.0
RC2c	8	534.6	12.5	**514.0**	**100.0**	534.6	12.5	517.5	62.5
RC2	24	1,508.7	4.2	**1,466.8**	**83.3**	1,495.2	12.5	1,467.0	54.2
Total	168	1,852.1	1.8	1,818.2	36.3	1,815.3	34.5	**1,805.7**	**54.8**

1%: SCIH2+LS is different from all the other methods; VNS and GRASP cannot be differentiated and the Hybrid method is different.

4.2 Real Case Inspired Instances

The instances based on a real case presented in [16] reflect the operation of three days of a distribution center of a major construction material supplier in São Paulo, Brazil.

Table 2. Cost and quantity of routes generated by each metaheuristic versus the reported values. Best results are highlighted in bold.

Day	Reported		GRASP		VNS		Hybrid	
	Cost	#Routes	Cost	#Routes	Cost	#Routes	Cost	#Routes
1	27,676.6	58	26,425.2	64	**24,433.5**	**41**	24,683.9	44
2	35,151.3	65	28,650.0	61	**27,500.0**	**50**	27,800.0	53
3	32,379.9	59	27,781.2	64	25,604.5	43	**25,419.8**	**40**
Total	95,207.8	182	82,856.4	189	**77,538.0**	**134**	77,903.7	137

The results in Table 2 show that VNS presented the best results, with a very similar, but slightly lower cost when compared to the Hybrid method. GRASP, dominated by the other methods, has better results than the Reported values, despite generating more routes.

4.3 Small-Sized Instances

To enable the comparison of proposed methods to known optimal results, [16] generated 72 small-sizes instances based on the literature adapted instances. For each combination of characteristics there are four quantities of clients: 10, 15, 20 and 25, summing up to a total of 72 problems. These were solved in a commercial solver and 42 optimal solutions were achieved.

Table 3. Results obtained in the small-sized instances when comparing the results from the solver. "Optimal solutions" compare how many optimal solutions were found by each method; "Gap to optimal" evaluate the average percentage cost difference from the optimal and the method's objective function cost; "Gap to LB" compare the results found with the lower bound provided by the solver.

	Solver	GRASP	VNS	Hybrid
Optimal solutions	42	28	42	36
Gap to Optimal (%)	–	3.3	0.0	1.2
Gap to LB (%)	17.3	19.7	16.7	17.7

Table 3 presents a comparison of the results obtained by the three proposed methods and the solver. VNS found all of the known optimal results and, among the problems without a known optimal, it obtained a result better than the best feasible solution found by the solver. The Hybrid method failed to find 6 of the optimal values, but the gap to optimal is only 1.2% and a similar gap to the lower bound as the solver. GRASP, on the other hand, is less successful when solving these problems when compared to the other methods. Even so, it finds more than half of the optimal values, with a gap of 3.3% to the optimal values.

5   Conclusion and Further Research

This work presented new methods for the FSMVRPTWSC, a rich vehicle routing problem that consider fixed costs per distance ranges and vehicle type. The investigation of this problem, that reflects a form of freight charge often present in the industry, shows opportunities for savings by using the length of the distance ranges to include clients to routes without additional costs, as well as avoiding that small distance increase cause a jump in the route cost.

Three metaheuristics, GRASP, VNS and Hybrid, were proposed with the purpose of generating methods that can best explore the particularities of the problem, that has a novelty aspect with a very particular characteristic of having the objective function determined by fixed values for distance ranges for each vehicle type. The methods combine the experience accumulated in the literature about VNS and GRASP, with the knowledge of the opportunities of minimizing the costs by exploiting the specific characteristics of the problem.

Numerical experiments confirm that the chosen methods have strong performances, outperforming other methodologies. The Hybrid method has a strong performance in benchmark instances, as well as in other instances, with also good results by the VNS in other instances. Further researches can be conducted in multiple fronts. New metaheuristics of different strategies, such as genetic methods, can be evaluated. Exact methods can also be further explored and combined with metaheuristics as a seed.

References

1. Arnold, F., Sörensen, K.: What makes a VRP solution good? The generation of problem-specific knowledge for heuristics. Comput. Oper. Res. **106**, 280–288 (2019)
2. Ball, M.O., Golden, B., Assad, A., Bodin, L.: Planning for truck fleet size in the presence of a common-carrier option. Decis. Sci. **14**(1), 103–120 (1983)
3. Braekers, K., Ramaekers, K., Van Nieuwenhuyse, I.: The vehicle routing problem: state of the art classification and review. Comput. Ind. Eng. **99**, 300–313 (2016)
4. Dantzig, G.B., Ramser, J.H.: The truck dispatching problem. Manag. Sci. **6**(1), 80–91 (1959)
5. Feo, T.A., Resende, M.G.: A probabilistic heuristic for a computationally difficult set covering problem. Oper. Res. Lett. **8**(2), 67–71 (1989)
6. Feo, T.A., Resende, M.G.: Greedy randomized adaptive search procedures. J. Global Optimiz. **6**(2), 109–133 (1995)

7. Festa, P., Resende, M.G.C.: Hybrid GRASP heuristics. In: Abraham, A., Hassanien, A.E., Siarry, P., Engelbrecht, A. (eds.) Foundations of Computational Intelligence Volume 3. SCI, vol. 203, pp. 75–100. Springer, Heidelberg (2009). https://doi.org/10.1007/978-3-642-01085-9_4

8. Golden, B., Assad, A., Levy, L., Gheysens, F.: The fleet size and mix vehicle routing problem. Comput. Oper. Res. **11**(1), 49–66 (1984)

9. Hansen, P., Mladenovic, N.: A tutorial on variable neighborhood search. Groupe d'Études et de Recherche en Analyse des Décisions, HEC Montréal (2003)

10. Hansen, P., Mladenović, N., Pérez, J.A.M.: Variable neighbourhood search: methods and applications. Ann. Oper. Res. **175**(1), 367–407 (2010). https://doi.org/10.1007/s10479-009-0657-6

11. Koç, Ç., Bektaş, T., Jabali, O., Laporte, G.: A hybrid evolutionary algorithm for heterogeneous fleet vehicle routing problems with time windows. Comput. Oper. Res. **64**, 11–27 (2015)

12. Laporte, G.: Fifty years of vehicle routing. Transp. Sci. **43**(4), 408–416 (2009)

13. Lieb, R.C., Lieb, K.J.: The north American third-party logistics industry in 2013: the provider CEO perspective. Transp. J. **54**(1), 104–121 (2015)

14. Liu, F.H., Shen, S.Y.: The fleet size and mix vehicle routing problem with time windows. J. Oper. Res. Soc. **50**(7), 721–732 (1999)

15. Manguino, J.L.V.: Heuristic methods applied to the mixed fleet vehicle routing problem with time windows and step costs per distance range. Ph.D. Thesis, Escola Politécnica, Universidade de São Paulo, São Paulo (2020). www.teses.usp.br

16. Manguino, J.L.V., Ronconi, D.P.: Step cost functions in a fleet size and mix vehicle routing problem with time windows. Ann. Opera. Res. (2020, submitted)

17. Marasco, A.: Third-party logistics: a literature review. Int. J. Prod. Econ. **113**(1), 127–147 (2008)

18. Mladenović, N., Hansen, P.: Variable neighborhood search. Comput. Oper. Res. **24**(11), 1097–1100 (1997)

19. Palomo-Martínez, P.J., Salazar-Aguilar, M.A., Laporte, G., Langevin, A.: A hybrid variable neighborhood search for the orienteering problem with mandatory visits and exclusionary constraints. Comput. Oper. Res. **78**, 408–419 (2017)

20. Potvin, J.Y., Rousseau, J.M.: An exchange heuristic for routeing problems with time windows. J. Oper. Res. Soc. **46**(12), 1433–1446 (1995). https://doi.org/10.1057/jors.1995.204

21. Resende, M.G., Ribeiro, C.C.: Greedy randomized adaptive search procedures: advances, hybridizations, and applications. In: Gendreau, M., Potvin, J.Y. (eds.) Handbook of Metaheuristics. ISOR, vol. 146, pp. 283–319. Springer, Boston (2010). https://doi.org/10.1007/978-1-4419-1665-5_10

22. Solomon, M.M.: Algorithms for the vehicle routing and scheduling problems with time window constraints. Oper. Res. **35**(2), 254–265 (1987)

23. Taillard, É., Badeau, P., Gendreau, M., Guertin, F., Potvin, J.Y.: A tabu search heuristic for the vehicle routing problem with soft time windows. Transp. Sci. **31**(2), 170–186 (1997)

24. Vidal, T., Crainic, T.G., Gendreau, M., Prins, C.: Heuristics for multi-attribute vehicle routing problems: a survey and synthesis. Eur. J. Oper. Res. **231**(1), 1–21 (2013)

25. Vidal, T., Crainic, T.G., Gendreau, M., Prins, C.: A unified solution framework for multi-attribute vehicle routing problems. Eur. J. Oper. Res. **234**(3), 658–673 (2014)

Cyclical Inventory Routing with Unsplittable Pick-Up and Deliveries

Jakob Schulte[1], Michael Römer[1(✉)], and Kevin Tierney[2(✉)]

[1] Decision Analytics Group, Bielefeld University, 33615 Bielefeld, Germany
{jakob.schulte,michael.roemer}@uni-bielefeld.de
[2] Decision and Operation Technologies Group, Bielefeld University,
33615 Bielefeld, Germany
kevin.tierney@uni-bielefeld.de

Abstract. We address a milk run logistics problem in which goods must be transferred between facilities on a regular basis to support a company's production. The resulting optimization problem is a form of cyclical, multi-commodity inventory routing problem with pick-ups and deliveries. This problem becomes particularly challenging when either all available cargo of a particular commodity must be picked up or none of it, so as to simplify internal logistics procedures. We model the problem mathematically and introduce a two-phase heuristic to solve the problem. The first phase consists of an adaptive large neighborhood search (ALNS), and the second phase uses a relaxed version of the mathematical model to improve the routes for the vehicles. We present experimental results on a dataset based on real-world data from a company in Germany and show that our two-phase procedure can find high quality solutions even to real-world sized problems in reasonable amounts of computation time.

Keywords: Cyclical inventory routing · Unsplittable cargo · ALNS

1 Introduction

Modern supply chains can involve hundreds or even thousands of steps to build a product in multiple production facilities. Components of products are regularly transported between a single company's facilities to support production activities. These routing activities are time-critical, especially with regards to current inventory stocks as delays or incorrect transports could lead to production interruptions.

We investigate the case of a multinational company with a base of production in Germany involving several geographically separated facilities requiring milk runs between them to keep production lines supplied with components. To reduce the overall planning complexity, the company creates a single plan used for every day of the week for replenishing their inventories. However, the company wishes to plan different routes for each day. These plans are used for about

© Springer Nature Switzerland AG 2020
E. Lalla-Ruiz et al. (Eds.): ICCL 2020, LNCS 12433, pp. 246–260, 2020.
https://doi.org/10.1007/978-3-030-59747-4_16

three months before being replanned to better correspond to the current production of the company. The company produces many different products and has a heterogeneous fleet of vehicles, leading to a complicated routing and scheduling problem. Making the problem further complex is the way pick-ups and deliveries are handled. The flow of goods is unsplittable, meaning if goods are to be transferred from one facility to another on a particular day, the truck must take all of the goods or none of them. Since goods are constantly being produced, on the next day the amount of goods is higher, making the mathematical model particularly challenging to solve.

We call the resulting optimization problem the cyclical inventory routing problem with unsplittable pick-up and deliveries (CIRUPD). The CIRUPD is a type of milk run problem (see [7]) consisting of a scheduling and routing subproblem similar to [4]. First, a cyclical, weekly, unsplittable delivery scheduling problem (CWUDSP) spanning five days, and, second, an unsplittable pick up and delivery problem (UPD) with multiple, heterogeneous vehicles for each of the five days.

We consider palletized cargo in which a given amount of each product is produced each day. To simplify loading procedures, either all pallets of a particular cargo type must be carried or none of them. In contrast, most of the inventory routing and production routing literature lacks such constraints, although some versions of maritime inventory routing are notable for the fact that ships should start voyages completely filled for stability [10].

Inventory routing problems describe a broad class of vehicle routing problems that can include holding and production costs, and a variety of different production/consumption schedules, among other aspects [3]. Coordinated production and distribution has been considered in a number of forms in the literature, and a full review can be found in [2]. In these problems, determining inventory levels and in which periods to route cargo make up the main challenges, see, e.g., [1,6]. Compared to these problems, our problem stands apart by demanding a cyclical plan and by the all-or-nothing constraints on pallet transports.

Cyclic inventory routing is a common way of reducing the operational complexity of performing regular routing tasks. Many approaches in the literature model challenging routing problems. Raa and Aghezzaf (2009) [9] consider a single vehicle cyclical routing problem and solve it with a heuristic. Ekici et al. (2015) [5] determine routing schedules using a two-phase solution approach that first clusters customers, then makes a delivery schedule for each cluster. However, in our problem the routing is not the main difficulty: there are only a handful of routing nodes, and it is the scheduling and pickup/delivery constraints that make the problem challenging.

We provide a novel mixed-integer linear model of the problem along with a novel two-phase heuristic for finding high quality solutions to the CIRUPD in a reasonable amount of computational time. The first phase of the heuristic runs an adaptive large neighborhood search (ALNS) [11] approach with several problem-specific destroy and repair operators. The second phase of the heuristic takes the ALNS solution and fixes the scheduling components and resolves the free portions of the mathematical model, using a relaxed model for guidance on which parts of the solution to fix. We create a dataset of instances based on data from a real company and evaluate both our mathematical model and our ALNS approach, showing that the ALNS is able to scale to real-world sized instances and solve them within a reasonable timeframe for a tactical problem.

This paper is organized as follows. We provide a problem description in Sect. 2, followed by the formulation of our mathematical model in Sect. 3. We then discuss our two-phase approach in Sect. 4. We provide computational results in Sect. 5 and conclude in Sect. 6.

2   Problem Description

We now describe the CIRUPD and its decomposition into the CWUDSP and UPD subproblems, along with an example. The CWUDSP schedules the delivery of orders $o \in O$ from source nodes v_o^s to their target, or destination, node $v_o^t \neq v_o^s$ on one or more days of the week. Every node $v \in V$ can be both a source and target node of multiple orders. Every order is constantly produced at the source node with rate of p_o per day, where p_o is expressed in fractions of pallets, and is consumed at the same rate as the target node. The delivery scheduling must respect limited inventory space at both the source and the target node, and it needs to ensure that the target node does not run out of supply. For each order, multiple deliveries can be scheduled per week. An unusual characteristic of the CWUDSP is that if a delivery of an order o is scheduled on a certain day d, the full amount of inventory of o available at day d needs to be picked up.

The scheduled deliveries are coupled with unsplittable pick up and delivery problems (UPD), one for each of the five days in the cyclical horizon. Each day, multiple heterogeneous capacitated vehicles, each associated with a depot node and with its own fixed and variable costs, can be routed to transport the scheduled order deliveries from their source to their target nodes. Note that while fractional amounts of pallets can be produced each day, when being transported this quantity is rounded up to the nearest number of pallets. The unsplittable pickup property (when picking up an order, the full amount of inventory needs to be picked up) also holds for the routing problem. Nonetheless, if a node is a source or target for more than one order, it can be visited more than once during a single route. In addition to vehicle capacity, routes are time-constrained, that is, the total time spent on a route comprising both travel time and handling time at nodes is not allowed to exceed a given number of hours per day. For certain orders, the delivery can be outsourced to contractors for a fixed cost per order.

Example. Figure 1 shows an example CIRUPD problem (a), along with a solution in (b). There are three facilities producing goods (A, B, C) and a depot (D) where a single truck with a capacity of two pallets is located. Facility A produces a full pallet of goods every day that needs to be taken to facility B, facility B produces a half a pallet daily destined for A, and C produces 1.5 pallets per day for B. In this example, we ignore capacity constraints in the facilities themselves, but note that in real problems storage space may be limited.

Figure 1(b) shows a solution to the instance given along with the amount of goods ready for pick up. We assume that daily production is completely finished by the time goods are picked up. Fractional pallets are rounded up for transport. Note that we exclude the routing from this example, but of course for each day we need to route the truck from D to the pick-ups and deliveries, e.g., on Thursday the truck needs to drive to all facilities. Even though the truck only has a capacity of two pallets, this does not violate the capacity restriction of the vehicle since we can first bring two pallets from C to B, then pick up one pallet at B, bring it to A, pick up two pallets at A, bring them to B, and then drive back to the depot. Note also the cyclical nature of the problem; since the truck does not pick up any pallets at A on Friday, there are two pallets ready for pick up at A on Monday. We note that this example leaves out some complexities of the problem outside of routing, such as consumption amounts at each of the nodes.

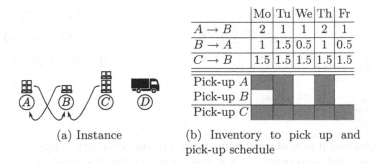

	Mo	Tu	We	Th	Fr
$A \to B$	2	1	1	2	1
$B \to A$	1	1.5	0.5	1	0.5
$C \to B$	1.5	1.5	1.5	1.5	1.5
Pick-up A					
Pick-up B					
Pick-up C					

(a) Instance   (b) Inventory to pick up and pick-up schedule

Fig. 1. An example problem instance and solution schedule (without routing).

3   Mathematical Model

In this section, we present a mixed-integer linear programming formulation for the CIRUPD. Following the structure of the problem description, we first describe the CWUDSP part of the model, followed by the UPD.

3.1   CWUDSP Submodel

The CWUDSP submodel is a feasibility problem. We assume that there are no inventory costs, and delivery costs are handled in the UPD part of the model. The main variables of the CWUDSP are the non-negative inventory variables $z_{t,o}^{\text{source}}$ and $z_{t,o}^{\text{target}}$ per order o, node v and day t at the order's source and target facility, the non-negative delivery variables $d_{t,o}$ and a binary variable $y_{t,o}^{\text{deliver}}$ per order and day indicating if the order is delivered at that day. All variables related to the order quantity (inventory and delivery) arise in two variants: a continuous variable representing the amount of each order in fractional pallets and their rounded-up, positive integral counterparts representing pallets taking up storage and vehicle space signified by an upper bar resulting in the variables $\bar{z}_{t,o,v}$ and $\bar{d}_{t,o}$.

Using these variables, the constraints of our model for the CWUDSP can be written as follows:

$$z_{t,o}^{\text{source}} = z_{prev(t),o}^{\text{source}} + p_o - d_{t,o} \qquad \forall t \in T, o \in O \qquad (1)$$

$$z_{t,o}^{\text{target}} = z_{prev(t),o}^{\text{target}} - p_o + d_{t,o} \qquad \forall t \in T, o \in O \qquad (2)$$

$$d_{t,o} \leq M_o y_{t,o}^{\text{deliver}} \qquad \forall t \in T, o \in O \qquad (3)$$

$$d_{t,o} \leq z_{t,o,v_o^t} \qquad \forall t \in T, o \in O \qquad (4)$$

$$d_{t,o} \geq z_{t,o,v_o^t} - M_o(1 - y_{t,o}^{\text{deliver}}) \qquad \forall t \in T, o \in O \qquad (5)$$

$$d_{t,o} \leq \bar{d}_{t,o} \qquad \forall t \in T, o \in O \qquad (6)$$

$$z_{t,o}^{\text{source}} \leq \bar{z}_{t,o}^{\text{source}} \quad , \quad z_{t,o}^{\text{target}} \leq \bar{z}_{t,o}^{\text{target}} \qquad \forall t \in T, o \in O \qquad (7)$$

$$\sum_{o \in O:s(o)=v} \bar{z}_{t,o}^{\text{source}} \leq b_v^{\text{out}} \qquad \forall t \in T, v \in \mathcal{V}^{\text{pickup}} \qquad (8)$$

$$\sum_{o \in O:t(o)=v} \bar{z}_{t,o}^{\text{target}} \leq b_v^{\text{in}} \qquad \forall t \in T, v \in \mathcal{V}^{\text{delivery}} \qquad (9)$$

The first two groups of constraints represent the inventory balance constraints for each day and each order both at the source and at the target location. The function $prev(t)$ returns the day before t in the cyclical time horizon, in particular, $prev(1)$ corresponds to $|T|$. Recall that the production rate p_o is not a decision variable, but a constant, and that the consumption rate at the destination equals the production rate. Constraints (3) link the delivery amount on each day for each order to the corresponding binary delivery variable. The value M_o is chosen as tightly as possible: it is set to the full production amount of order o in the cyclical planning horizon; we also introduce $\bar{M}_o := \lceil M_o \rceil$. Constraints (4) state that at most the inventory amount can be delivered. Constraints (5) ensure the unsplittability requirement: If an order is delivered, the full inventory must be delivered. Constraints (6) and (7) round the continuous delivery and inventory variables up to their integer counterparts. Finally, for each node v from the set $\mathcal{V}^{\text{pickup}}$ of pickup locations, constraints (8) ensure that the storage capacity for outgoing goods (those for which the source node $s(o)$ is v) b_v^{out} is respected. Analogously, constraints (9) consider the incoming storage capacity at each delivery node v for all orders o for which v is the target node $t(o)$.

3.2   UPD Submodel

The CWUDSP part of the model described so far deals with determining the delivery days and amounts per order. These decisions can be viewed as forming the input for the UPD submodels solving the unsplittable pickup and delivery routing of the orders for each day.

In the UPD submodel associated with a given day, the routes of the vehicles and flow of the orders are modeled as a multicommodity flow (vehicles and orders correspond to commodities) in a layered directed graph $G = (V, E)$. Each layer contains all order source and target locations from the "flat" graph $\mathcal{G} = (\mathcal{V}, \mathcal{E})$, in which factories are nodes and edges represent feasible connections between them, considered in the CWUDSP part of the model. Each layer in G is associated with the number of nodes visited so far, and thus, each trip between two nodes induces a transition between two consecutive layers. In our case study, the number of layers corresponds to 12, which is the maximum number of visits a vehicle can perform during a day given the time constraint described above. In addition to the pickup and delivery nodes on the layers, G contains each vehicle's source depot node, which is linked to each node of the first layer. A vehicle route then corresponds to a path (a unit flow) from the source depot node and to the target depot node of the vehicle. Furthermore, there is a directed arc from each node on each layer to a sink depot node for each vehicle. For each day t and each vehicle k, there is also a circulation arc $e_{k,t}^{\text{circ}}$ from its sink to its source node. A unit flow on a circulation arc means that the vehicle is used on the day under consideration. All nodes that vehicle k may visit on day t form the set $V_{k,t}^{\text{vehicle}}$; correspondingly, the set $E_{k,t}^{\text{vehicle}}$ consists of all arcs $(i, j) \in G$ for which both i and j are elements of vehicle$_{k,t}$.

For a given order o and day t, the non-depot nodes in the layered graph V can be partitioned into the node sets $V_{t,o}^{\text{pickup}}$ representing the pickup location of order o in all layers, $V_{t,o}^{\text{pickup}}$ representing the delivery location of order o in all layers, and $V_{t,o}^{\text{transship}}$, representing the remaining factory locations which, with respect to order o, serve as transshipment nodes. Given an order o and a day t, all edges (i, j) in E for which $i \in V_{t,o}^{\text{pickup}}$ constitute the set of pickup edges $E_{t,o}^{pickup}$ of o on day t. Analogously, the set $E_{t,o}^{pickup}$ is formed by all $(i, j) \in E$ for which $j \in V_{t,o}^{\text{pickup}}$.

The vehicle flow, modeled with a binary flow variable $x_{k,t,e}$ for vehicle k, day t and arc e, provides the transportation capacity for the order delivery flow represented by the integer variable $w_{k,t,o,e}$ of order o on the same arc. In addition to the order flow variable, there are binary variables $y_{k,t,o,e}^{\text{transport}}$ indicating if any amount of o is transported by k on day t using arc e. These variables are used for modeling the unsplittable requirement.

In addition, there are outsourcing variables: The binary variables $y_{t,o}^{\text{extern}}$ represent that the transportation of order o on day t is outsourced, and the integer variables $w_{t,o}^{\text{extern}}$ represents the outsourced flow of full pallets with order o on day t.

The portion of the objective function related to the UPD consists of fixed costs per vehicle and day that are associated with the vehicle circulation arcs, the variable costs (handling time, distance driven) associated with the arcs representing vehicle travel and the outsourcing costs c_o^{extern} per order o. Since all vehicle related costs can be represented using cost coefficients $c_{k,t,e}^{\text{vehicle}}$ of the vehicle flow variables $x_{k,t,e}^{\text{vehicle}}$ for each of the arcs $e \in E_{k,t}^{\text{vehicle}}$ that a vehicle k may use on day d, the objective function can compactly be written as:

$$\min \sum_{k \in K} \sum_{t \in T} \sum_{e \in E_{k,t}^{\text{vehicle}}} c_{k,t,e}^{\text{vehicle}} x_{k,t,e} + \sum_{t \in T} \sum_{o \in O} c_o^{\text{extern}} y_{t,o}^{\text{extern}} \quad (10)$$

The first three sets of constraints of the UPD submodel couple it to the CWUDSP submodel:

$$w_{t,o}^{\text{extern}} + \sum_{k \in K} \sum_{e \in E_{o,t}^{\text{pickup}}} w_{k,t,o,e} = \bar{d}_{t,o} \qquad \forall t \in T, o \in O \quad (11)$$

$$w_{t,o}^{\text{extern}} + \sum_{k \in K} \sum_{e \in E_{o,t}^{\text{delivery}}} w_{k,t,o,e} = \bar{d}_{t,o} \qquad \forall t \in T, o \in O \quad (12)$$

$$\sum_{k \in K} \sum_{e \in E_{t,o}^{\text{pickup}}} y_{k,t,o,e}^{\text{transport}} + y_{t,o}^{\text{extern}} = y_{t,o}^{\text{deliver}} \qquad \forall t \in T, o \in O \quad (13)$$

In particular, constraints (11) and (12) link the delivery quantities determined in the CWUDSP to the quantity picked up (the flow on arcs from the set $E_{t,o}^{\text{pickup}}$, representing a pickup of order o on day t) and delivered (the flow on arcs from the set $E_{t,o}^{\text{delivery}}$ representing a delivery of order o on day t) and the outsourced quantity. Constraints (13) couple the binary delivery variables from CWUDSP to the binary pickup and the outsourcing decisions in the UPD submodel. Note that these constraints not only couple the model parts, but also ensure that in case of a planned delivery on day t, the delivery is either outsourced or delivered by a single vehicle k. Furthermore, (13) ensures that in case of using a vehicle, each order is only picked up once per day which implies that a pickup is not split.

The remaining constraints of the UPD read as follows:

$$\sum_{e \in v^+} w_{k,t,o,e} = \sum_{e \in v^-} w_{k,t,o,e} \quad \forall k \in K, t \in T, o \in O, v \in V_{t,o}^{\text{transship}} \quad (14)$$

$$w_{k,t,o,e} \leq \bar{M}_o y_{k,t,o,e}^{\text{transport}} \qquad \forall k \in K, t \in T, o \in O \quad (15)$$

$$\sum_{e \in v^+} y_{k,t,o,e}^{\text{transport}} = \sum_{e \in v^-} y_{k,t,o,e}^{\text{transport}} \quad \forall k \in K, t \in T, o \in O, v \in V_{t,o}^{\text{transship}} \quad (16)$$

$$\sum_{o \in O} w_{k,t,o,e} \leq b_k^{\text{vehicle}} x_{k,t,e} \qquad \forall k \in K, t \in T, e \in E_{k,t}^{\text{transport}} \quad (17)$$

$$\sum_{e \in v^+} x_{k,t,e} = \sum_{e \in v^-} x_{k,t,e} \quad \forall k \in K, t \in T, o \in O, v \in V_{k,t}^{\text{vehicle}} \quad (18)$$

$$\sum_{e \in E_{k,t}^{\text{vehicle}}} a_{k,e}^{\text{time}} x_{k,t,e} \leq b_k^{\text{time}} \qquad \forall k \in K, t \in T \quad (19)$$

$$w_{t,o}^{\text{extern}} \leq \bar{M}_o y_{t,o}^{\text{extern}} \qquad \forall t \in T, o \in O \quad (20)$$

Constraints (14) form the flow balance constraints for transported pallets of order o on day t and on vehicle k. They are only defined for the transshipment nodes $V_{t,o}^{\mathrm{transship}}$ of an order o on day t. That is, they exclude vehicle depot nodes as well as exclude the pick up and delivery location of order o. Note that the flow out of the pickup and into the delivery nodes of the orders is implied by constraints (11) and (12) and by the fact that for each order and for each day, only a single arc out of a pickup node and a single in-arc of a delivery node can have a positive order flow.

Constraints (15) link the order transportation flow variables to the binary variables $y_{k,t,o,e}^{\mathrm{transport}}$ indicating if order o is transported using arc e on day t by vehicle k. As explained above, this variable is used to establish the unsplittability requirement. Constraints (16) form a kind of "flow balance" for these variables; they can be interpreted as propagating the unsplittable pickup enforced by constraint (13) to the transportation and delivery of the orders. Constraints (17) link the order transportation flow to the vehicle flow on arcs $E_{k,t}^{\mathrm{transport}}$, representing transportation activity of vehicle k on day t and ensure that the vehicle's capacity b_k^{vehicle} is not exceeded. Constraints (18) model the flow balance of the vehicles; recall that due to the introduction of the circulation arcs, the vehicle flow is circular. Constraints (19) model the time constraint for each day t and each vehicle k by limiting the time consumed on each route (modeled by the coefficient $a_{k,e}^{\mathrm{time}}$ representing both travel and handling time induced by a flow on a vehicle arc) to the maximum allowed time b_k^{time} per day. Finally, constraints (20) relate the outsourced delivery flow (in terms of pallets) modeled by variable $w_{t,o}^{\mathrm{extern}}$ to the binary variables $y_{t,o}^{\mathrm{extern}}$ indicating if the delivery of order o is outsourced on day t.

Note that the fact that the model formulation is based on a layered network, there is no need for subtour elimination constraints. In addition, a vehicle route may visit a node more than once, e.g. to pick up different orders.

4   Two-Phase Heuristic

The CIRUPD is a difficult, large-scale optimization problem that poses a challenge to exact solution approaches. Even though we are in a tactical setting, we would like to be able to find high-quality solutions in a relatively low amount of CPU time. We thus introduce a two-phase heuristic procedure in which we first run an ALNS [11], and then a variable fixing improvement procedure using guidance from a relaxed model. We first describe the ALNS and its destroy and repair operators, then the relaxation-based improvement procedure.

4.1   Phase 1: ALNS

ALNS has proven to be a highly effective metaheuristic technique for a wide range of vehicle routing and scheduling problems. For example, Adulyasak et al. (2014) [1] use an ALNS to solve a production routing problem. Our ALNS focuses mainly on finding good solutions to the CWUDSP and uses a greedy

Algorithm 1. Pseudocode for the ALNS, based on [8]. The algorithm is provided an initial starting solution s.

1: **function** ALNS-CIRUPD(s)
2:     $\rho^\lozenge \leftarrow (1, \ldots, 1) \ \forall \lozenge \in \{-, +\}$
3:     **repeat**
4:         Select $d \in \Omega^-$, $r \in \Omega^+$ using roulette wheel
5:         $s' \leftarrow r(d(s))$
6:         **if** s' infeasible **then**
7:             $\psi \leftarrow \omega^I$ ▷ Throw out current solution
8:         **else**
9:             $s'' \leftarrow$ GREEDY-ROUTING(s')
10:            **if** $f(s'') \leq f(s)$ **then**
11:                $\psi \leftarrow \omega^G$
12:                $s \leftarrow s''$ ▷ Update best solution
13:            **else**
14:                $\psi \leftarrow \omega^R$ ▷ Throw away non-improving solution
15:         Update ρ^- and ρ^+ using ψ and $f(s)$
16:     **until** Termination criteria satisfied
17:     **return** s

---

heuristic for solving the UPD for each day of the planning horizon. A solution is represented as an assignment of orders to days when they should be fulfilled. Note that orders can be (and are) mapped to more than one day.

We use a standard ALNS procedure in which all destroy and repair operators start with an equal probability of being selected in a given iteration. Adopting the notation from [8], we are given a set of destroy operators Ω^- and repair operators Ω^+. Each destroy (repair) operator j is assigned a probability ρ_j^- (ρ_j^+). Starting from an initial solution, in each iteration we apply a randomly selected destroy operator followed by a repair operator, and then the greedy route constructor (see Algorithm 1). We use a standard roulette wheel operator selection procedure in which the probability of selecting destroy or repair operator j is $\rho_j^\lozenge / (\sum_{k=1}^{|\Omega^\lozenge|} \rho_k^\lozenge)$, $\lozenge \in \{-, +\}$. At the end of the iteration, we update the probabilities of each operator with the update formula

$$\rho_j^\lozenge \leftarrow \lambda \rho_j^\lozenge + (1 - \lambda)\psi$$

where λ is called the *decay* parameter for adjusting how fast new information is integrated into the probability distributions and might be better termed a learning rate. We assign the parameter ψ either ω^I, ω^G or ω^R, according to whether the solution after destroying and repairing is infeasible, is better than the global best, or is feasible, but rejected, respectively. We note that our ALNS does not accept worsening solutions, rather it keeps trying to destroy and repair until it finds something better or eventually terminates if nothing better can be found.

Destroy Operators. We introduce three destroy operators. **DestroyRandom** simply unassigns $p\%$ of the orders from their assigned days uniformly at random. Although straightforward, such operators are important in ALNS procedures to ensure all parts of the solution have a chance at being destroyed in an iteration. The operators **DestroyFromNode** and **DestroyToNode** pick a node uniformly at random. A number is chosen uniformly at random between one and the number of orders with this node as their origin or destination, respectively. We chose a random subset of orders with this node as their origin or destination, respectively, and unassign them. The **DestroyFromNode** and **DestroyToNode** operators allow the ALNS to redistribute all tasks at a particular node at the same time, which can be especially helpful for the routing subproblem.

Repair Operators. We also introduce three repair operators. For each unassigned order, **RepairRandom** loops through the days of the week and flips a coin for each one to determine whether or not that day will be assigned as a pick up day. It does this while respecting capacity restrictions at the facilities for each day, meaning if the capacity would be exceeded by not picking up the order, then it is set to be picked up. Although it may seem counterproductive to have a random repair, recall that we still need to route the vehicles once the orders are assigned to days, and that the outcome of the routing problem is difficult to take into account in the repair procedure. Thus, performing a random repair (from time to time) ensures that the ALNS tries out a variety of options.

The repair operator **RepairIncreaseDeliveries** examines the unassigned orders in the solution and selects the pick-up plan from them with the most assigned days is selected as the new plan for all unassigned orders. If only a single order is unassigned, then the order is assigned to be picked up on every day of the week. This operator helps break up large orders across the week, ensuring that large, expensive trucks do not need to be used for transport.

Conversely, the operator **RepairDecreaseDeliveries** examines the unassigned orders for the pick-up plan with the fewest pick-up days and selects this as the plan for all unassigned plans. Note that as in the case of **RepairRandom**, extra pick-up days may need to be assigned to some orders to prevent facilities from having too much inventory. This is done by randomly selecting a day that the order is not assigned to and assigning it to the order. This process is repeated until the order can be carried. If only a single order is removed, then the order is assigned a pick-up plan in which as few as possible pick-up days are used, again depending on the size of the order and the capacity of the facilities.

Greedy Routing Procedure. Given a schedule for when to pick up each order, we now must solve a routing problem for each day. We use a greedy insertion heuristic. We note that more effective heuristics could be used, but since we have five routing problems to solve in each iteration of the ALNS, the procedure should be computationally inexpensive. The heuristic starts with a fleet of empty vehicles. We then loop over every vehicle and every order not yet assigned to a vehicle and compute the costs for inserting the pick up and delivery of that order into the route at the cheapest position possible. We only consider vehicles in which the order still fits.

Initial Solution Procedure. We introduce two initial solution procedures for the CIRUPD. Since they are not that computationally expensive to compute, we simply compute both and take the solution with the lower costs to start the ALNS. The first heuristic is a simple naive construction heuristic. We simply assign every order to be picked up every day. Of course on some instances this will result in high costs, however it might not be such a bad solution for instances with high amounts of daily production.

Our second initial solution heuristic works as follows. The idea is to try to better utilize the trucks transporting goods each day than the naive heuristic does. One option to complement the naive heuristic would be to compute the minimum number of days each order could be picked up. However, this is a computationally difficult problem, especially considering capacity interactions between orders. Thus, instead of looking at orders individually, we group all orders together and consider the minimum number of days on which the whole bundle can be picked up. Since we only consider a single week in the problem, we need only to look at all possible patterns of picking up deliveries, of which there are $2^5 = 32$. However, there are many symmetries due to the cyclical nature of the problem, as, for example, picking up everything on a Monday is equivalent to picking up everything on a Tuesday. Table 1 shows the non-symmetrical patterns for a single week. We examine each option, starting from the fewest number of pickup days, checking to see whether the capacity restrictions are satisfied and if there are enough trucks available to transport all orders.

Table 1. Non-symmetrical initial solution pick-up patterns.

	Mo	Tu	We	Th	Fr
Pattern 1	■	■	■	■	■
Pattern 2	■			■	
Pattern 3	■		■		
Pattern 4	■	■			
Pattern 5	■				

4.2 Phase 2: Variable Fixing Procedure

The second phase of the heuristic focuses on improving the routing. During the ALNS, we use a simple greedy heuristic, which has the advantage of being fast to compute, but is prone to getting stuck in a local optimum. We initially tried to just use an exact algorithm to compute the routing for each day, but we note that this is actually still a very hard problem, and takes much too long for integration into a heuristic. With this in mind, we develop a variable fixing approach.

For each day in the ALNS solution's plan, we perform two steps. First, we solve a relaxed version of the mathematical model in which all variables except for the binary flow variables $x_{k,t,e_{k,t}^{\text{circ}}}$ associated with the vehicle circulation arcs are relaxed to be continuous. Recall that these variables determine whether or not vehicle k is used on day t. Relaxing these variables leads to routing solutions that make little practical sense, as vehicles can be partially utilized. After solving the relaxed model, we now fix all $x_{k,t,e_{k,t}^{\text{circ}}}$ to 1 that are set to 1 in the relaxed model. We restore all variables to be binary and solve the resulting routing model to get a new routing solution. If at any time the lower bound of the model in the second step goes above the solution found using the greedy insertion heuristic we can stop the model and just use the greedy routing instead.

5 Computational Results

We evaluate our ALNS approach on a dataset of instances based on industrial scenarios. We evaluate the quality of the ALNS against solutions from Gurobi 9.0.

5.1 Dataset

We create an instance set of 15 instance split into four different categories. We base our instances on real data from a company. Since these instances are very large and difficult to solve, we create smaller instances with similar structures. We describe each instance according to the format {G, R}-⟨# orders⟩-⟨# nodes⟩-⟨# vehicles⟩-i, where G stands for a generated instance and R for a real instance, and i is a counter to provide a unique identifier to instances with similar sizes.

5.2 ALNS Performance

We test the performance of our approach on a 2.3 GHz dual-core Intel Core i5 7360U with 8 GB of RAM. Our ALNS is written in Python 3. We use Gurobi 9.0 to find optimal solutions to the CIRUPD on a separate machine consisting of Intel Xeon E5-2670 CPU at 2.60 GHz with 32 GB of RAM. We note that using exact algorithms proved rather fruitless; even with 48 h of runtime with 8 parallel cores, we only find optimal solutions on four out of the 15 instances with Gurobi 9.0. Thus, we believe a metaheuristic approach is necessary for providing decision support for the CIRUPD.

Table 2 shows the computational results of the ALNS. Our instance set consists of twelve generated instances of various sizes for three real instances from the industry. First, we note that the mathematical model struggles with even small instances of the CIRUPD; we find only four optimal solutions over all of our instances within a 48 h time limit. Even one of the instances with only four production locations is not solved to optimality. However, our ALNS approach is able to find solutions to all instances. On the four instances solved to optimality with Gurobi, the ALNS finds solutions with an average gap of only 4.2% to optimality. However, our gaps to the best known solutions tend to be somewhat higher than those to the optimal solutions, with several gaps over 20%. Our results on the real instances are especially encouraging, as the ALNS finds solutions on two of the instances that are better than those found by Gurobi, despite requiring significantly less wall clock time[1]. In addition, the best run of five returns solutions with gaps of below 10% on 12 out of 15 instances, indicating that the heuristic is able to effectively scale.

Table 2. ALNS experimental results over five executions per instance, showing the mean wall time; standard deviation of the CPU time; mean objective function value; standard deviation of the objective function value; average gap to the optimal solution, when one is available, or the best known solution from Gurobi (marked with a star); best objective function found; and the gap of the best objective function to the optimal solution or best found.

Instance	Time (s)		Obj.		Gap (%)	Best run	
	Avg.	Stdev.	Avg.	Stdev.		Obj.	Gap
G-4-3-3-0	6	5	4660.00	0.0	0.86	4660	0.86
G-4-3-3-1	2	1	4100.00	0.0	3.90	4100	3.90
G-4-3-3-2	52	14	5442.00	115.0	7.39	5240	3.82
G-7-4-3-0	152	42	5903.00	139.7	20.55*	5765	18.65*
G-9-5-3-0	47	7	1438.00	27.1	4.73	1395	1.79
G-9-5-3-1	95	41	3801.00	100.3	18.84*	3745	17.62*
G-9-5-3-2	127	45	4560.00	614.3	26.55*	3890	13.88*
G-9-5-3-3	202	42	5658.00	685.5	24.35*	4510	5.10*
G-9-6-4-0	539	81	5224.00	103.3	3.33*	5130	1.56*
G-15-6-4-0	372	78	2636.00	227.9	17.68*	2380	8.82*
G-15-6-4-1	534	156	1159.00	142.7	24.50*	915	4.37*
G-15-6-4-2	639	258	4022.00	237.8	13.97*	3630	4.68*
R-12-8-4-0	583	60	8213.20	95.4	−1.64*	8134	−2.59*
R-18-8-4-0	1760	254	9383.40	64.5	0.49*	9337	0.00*
R-24-8-4-0	6243	1870	1822.92	30.0	−1.25*	1793	−2.87*

The ALNS requires a significant amount of time to solve the real instances, with the largest needing around 1.75 h. About a third of this time is spent in the second stage of the heuristic, although this varies on an instance by instance basis, with some taking up to half the total time. We consider this an acceptable

---

[1] Although the models are run on different machines, the mathematical model was run on a faster machine than the ALNS.

amount of time since the problem is of a tactical nature and only solved about once a quarter.

6 Conclusion

We presented a mathematical model and two-phase solution heuristic for a real-world cyclical inventory routing problem with unsplittable pick-up and deliveries. The unsplittablity of the produced goods makes the problem especially challenging to model, although this aspect of the problem does not pose a big challenge to the heuristic. Our two-phase heuristic uses an ALNS and a variable fixing procedure to find high quality solutions, and is able to solve real-world instances to under a 1% gap to the best solution from Gurobi, with two solutions even being better than those found with Gurobi after two days of run time.

For future work, we intend to improve the performance of the ALNS with further operators and focus on improving the routing computation during each ALNS iteration. Furthermore, as a tactical problem, the CIRUPD is rife with uncertainty. Production amounts could vary throughout the week for a variety of reasons, and this ought to be taken into account when planning as a two-stage stochastic model.

Acknowledgments. We thank the Paderborn Center for Parallel Computation (PC^2) for the use of the *OCuLUS* cluster.

References

1. Adulyasak, Y., Cordeau, J.F., Jans, R.: Optimization-based adaptive large neighborhood search for the production routing problem. Transp. Sci. **48**(1), 20–45 (2014)
2. Adulyasak, Y., Cordeau, J.F., Jans, R.: The production routing problem: a review of formulations and solution algorithms. Comput. Oper. Res. **55**, 141–152 (2015)
3. Bertazzi, L., Savelsbergh, M., Speranza, M.G.: Inventory routing. In: Golden, B., Raghavan, S., Wasil, E. (eds.) The Vehicle Routing Problem: Latest Advances and New Challenges. ORCS, vol. 43, pp. 49–72. Springer, Boston (2008). https://doi.org/10.1007/978-0-387-77778-8_3
4. Chitsaz, M., Divsalar, A., Vansteenwegen, P.: A two-phase algorithm for the cyclic inventory routing problem. Eur. J. Oper. Res. **254**(2), 410–426 (2016)
5. Ekici, A., Özener, O.O., Kuyzu, G.: Cyclic delivery schedules for an inventory routing problem. Transp. Sci. **49**(4), 817–829 (2014)
6. Lei, L., Liu, S., Ruszczynski, A., Park, S.: On the integrated production, inventory, and distribution routing problem. IIE Trans. **38**(11), 955–970 (2006)
7. Meyer, A.: Milk Run Design: Definitions, Concepts and Solution Approaches. KIT Scientific Publishing, Karlsruhe (2017)
8. Pisinger, D., Ropke, S.: Large neighborhood search. In: Gendreau, M., Potvin, J.Y. (eds.) Handbook of Metaheuristics. ISOR, vol. 146, pp. 399–419. Springer, Boston (2010). https://doi.org/10.1007/978-1-4419-1665-5_13
9. Raa, B., Aghezzaf, E.H.: A practical solution approach for the cyclic inventory routing problem. Eur. J. Oper. Res. **192**(2), 429–441 (2009)

10. Rakke, J.G., Andersson, H., Christiansen, M., Desaulniers, G.: A new formulation based on customer delivery patterns for a maritime inventory routing problem. Transp. Sci. **49**(2), 384–401 (2015)
11. Ropke, S., Pisinger, D.: An adaptive large neighborhood search heuristic for the pickup and delivery problem with time windows. Transp. Sci. **40**(4), 455–472 (2006)

The Multistage Stochastic Vehicle Routing Problem with Dynamic Occasional Drivers

Jørgen Skålnes[1(✉)], Lars Dahle[1], Henrik Andersson[1], Marielle Christiansen[1], and Lars Magnus Hvattum[2]

[1] Department of Industrial Economics and Technology Management, Norwegian University of Science and Technology, Trondheim, Norway
jorgen.skalnes@ntnu.no
[2] Faculty of Logistics, Molde University College, Molde, Norway

Abstract. Widespread use of smart phones and cellular networks allow for new solutions to lower the costs of last mile delivery to customers. We consider a setting where a company not only uses its own fleet of vehicles to deliver products from their store, but can also make use of ordinary people who are already on the road. This may include people who visit the store and are willing to take a detour on their way home for a small compensation. The availability of these *occasional drivers* is naturally highly uncertain, and we assume that some stochastic information is known about them. This leads to a multistage stochastic vehicle routing problem, with dynamic appearance of vehicles. The contributions of this work is to present a formulation of the multistage stochastic programming problem, identifying what type of problem structures that makes this model superior to that of a two-stage formulation, and when a two-stage formulation can be an adequate simplification.

Keywords: Stochastic programming · Uncertainty · Crowdshipping · Mixed-integer programming

1 Introduction and Literature

Transportation services, and especially last-mile transportation and same-day deliveries, are costly operations. Advances in digital technology allow for ever more creative solutions for performing such operations. Both Amazon and Walmart consider using *crowdshipping*, which utilizes regular people already on the road to pick up packages from their stores and deliver to their customers [3,4], in addition to transporting their products with their own fleet of vehicles. This new mode of transportation can become profitable for both the company and ordinary people appearing as occasional drivers (ODs) by utilizing the vehicles better. There is also an increasing number of companies providing platforms to connect ODs with people or enterprises that need to transport goods to some

© Springer Nature Switzerland AG 2020
E. Lalla-Ruiz et al. (Eds.): ICCL 2020, LNCS 12433, pp. 261–276, 2020.
https://doi.org/10.1007/978-3-030-59747-4_17

end customer, such as Roadie, OrderUp, and PiggyBaggy [10]. Moreover, this new possibility has a potential for reducing climate gas emissions.

The problem considered here is similar to the problem considered in [5]. A company is responsible for delivering a set of small parcels from a warehouse to its customers. In addition to the company's own regular fleet of vehicles, it may use dynamically appearing ODs that are already on the road. We assume that the company has a sufficient amount of goods, and that each regular vehicle is filled up so that it can potentially serve all customers. There is no penalty for returning to the store with excess goods in the vehicle. The ODs, however, have to bring the right amount of goods from the store, because they should be empty when they have finished their deliveries and arrive at their destination. This rules out deliveries of unique packages, but does not imply a single product. A practical example can be deliveries of electronics, such as small home appliances, where the regular vehicles can easily carry additional units and the customers do not care whether the delivery is made by a regular vehicle or an occasional driver.

Crowdshipping is a general term describing that ordinary drivers perform a detour to pick up and deliver goods from a company in exchange for a small compensation. There is an increasing number of academic papers studying variants of vehicle routing problems where such behavior is allowed. A deterministic vehicle routing problem with ODs was introduced by [1]. This work was extended in [11] by considering time windows and allowing ODs to make multiple visits. Time windows in combination with a heterogeneous vehicle fleet were considered in [8], and a pick-up and delivery problem with ODs was considered in [6].

Green vehicle routing with ODs have been considered in other papers. First, [12] minimized the sum of routing costs of conventional and electric vehicles and the compensation to ODs and provided an integer linear programming formulation. This work was continued in [13] by introducing a cost related to emissions in the objective function.

In many cases, information about ODs is not available with certainty when planning the use of the company's own fleet. This was acknowledged by [2], where a deterministic pick-up and delivery problem was solved each time new information arrived. A stochastic and dynamic vehicle routing problem with crowdshipping was discussed in [17]. The objective was to minimize the average waiting time of customers. The authors used discrete event simulation to evaluate the benefit of ODs, and solved a mathematical programming model in each step to make routing decisions. Simulation was used in [16] to evaluate the effects on traffic and emissions from adopting crowdshipping by carriers delivering parcels in the city center of Rome, Italy. Both ODs and online orders arrive throughout the working day in the problem considered by [7].

When acknowledging that information about ODs is not available with certainty, the problem can be modelled while explicitly taking into account the uncertainty. In an early contribution, [5] considered a two-stage stochastic programming model where all information about the ODs is revealed at a single point in time. Next, [9] presented a bi-level stochastic model where there is a probability that a given OD will reject the assigned delivery. Later, [14] described a two-stage stochastic programming model incorporating uncertainty in OD availability. The first stage decisions include the location of mobile depot locations. A two-stage stochastic programming model where uncertainty about OD availability follows a binomial distribution was derived in [18]. The model was solved using branch-and-price.

However, there has been little to no focus on multistage stochastic models which are well suited to model the dynamic behaviour of ODs. In this work we propose a multistage stochastic model for the vehicle routing problem with dynamic ODs, and compare this to a two-stage stochastic model from [5]. The multistage stochastic model is taking into account the dynamic behaviour of ODs in terms of separate stages where the information regarding the availability of a given OD is revealed gradually. We show that more accurately modelling of this behaviour can give substantially different first stage routing decisions. In addition, we have a more accurate evaluation of the expected cost of the first stage decisions when the company has to accept or reject ODs in the order they arrive. The two-stage model ignores this fact and allows for a routing of the ODs in the second stage with a higher degree of information, which in practice may not be available to the decision maker. In addition, we provide a discussion on the value of information demonstrating the potential gain of utilizing services such as Roadie in order to reveal information about arriving ODs earlier.

In Sect. 2 we present the vehicle routing problem with dynamic ODs along with a multistage stochastic mathematical formulation. The instances and corresponding results are presented and discussed in Sect. 3, followed by concluding remarks in Sect. 4.

2 Mathematical Formulation

In this section the mathematical formulation of the implemented multistage model is presented. Sect. 2.1 defines the notation and presents a compact mathematical model. In Sect. 2.2 we describe how the non-linear constraints are linearised. Finally, Sect. 2.3 is devoted to valid inequalities and symmetry breaking constraints to improve solution time.

2.1 Notation and Compact Model

The multistage stochastic vehicle routing problem with dynamic ODs consists of a set of customer nodes $\mathcal{N} = \{1, \ldots, n\}$. A homogeneous fleet of regular vehicles $\mathcal{K}^R$, and a fleet of ODs $\mathcal{K}^O$, are available to service these nodes. Vehicle $k \in \mathcal{K} = \mathcal{K}^R \cup \mathcal{K}^O$ has an origin $o(k)$ and a destination $d(k)$. The origin is at the depot (or store) and is the same for all vehicles. The destination is at the depot for all regular vehicles, while for the ODs the destination is at a different location for each OD. Let $\mathcal{N}_k \subseteq \mathcal{N} \cup \{o(k), d(k)\}$ be the set of nodes vehicle k may visit, and $\mathcal{A}_k \subset \mathcal{N}_k \times \mathcal{N}_k$ be the set of possible arcs for vehicle k, and denote the arc from node i to node j as (i, j).

All vehicles have time windows for their origin node $[\underline{T}_{o(k)}, \overline{T}_{o(k)}]$ and destination node $[\underline{T}_{d(k)}, \overline{T}_{d(k)}]$. This typically spans the entire planning horizon for the regular vehicles, while the ODs are only available for a shorter period of time. The start and end of the planning horizon are denoted $[\underline{T}, \overline{T}]$. The deliveries can be done at any point during the day, but for modelling purposes a time window $[\underline{T}_i, \overline{T}_i]$ is defined for each customer i. There is a cost of C_{ijk} and travel time of T_{ijk} to travel from node i to node j with vehicle k. Let S_j be the time needed to serve node j.

Let $\mathcal{W}$ be the set of all scenarios. A scenario is denoted by $\omega \in \mathcal{W}$ and p^ω is the probability of scenario ω. For each scenario ω, the set of available vehicles is denoted as $\mathcal{K}^\omega \subseteq \mathcal{K}$. The binary variable x_{ijk}^ω indicates whether or not vehicle k uses arc (i, j) in scenario ω. The variable t_{ik}^ω denotes the time when vehicle k leaves node i in scenario ω. Let a stage s be initiated by the possible arrival of an OD, and denote the set of stages by $\mathcal{S}$. Let s^+ denote the stage number for the stage following stage s. Let T^s be the start time of stage s. For OD k arriving in stage s we have $T^s \leq \underline{T}_{o(k)}$. Note that for the multistage setting the information regarding when an OD k arrives is revealed at the arrival time, while for the two-stage setting all information is revealed at T^2. For the two-stage setting the vehicles will still arrive at the time T^s.

A scenario tree is defined, and an illustration of the scenario tree for instances with three ODs can be found in Fig. 1. The first stage of all scenarios is collected in the root node and the decisions made in this stage are required to be equal. Two successor nodes are created for the next stage, one where the first OD is available and one where it is not, dividing the scenarios in two sets. All decisions made in the second stage for these two sets of scenarios have to be equal within the sets. Each new OD further adds two successor nodes to each leaf node, giving a full scenario tree. Denote by $\mathcal{T}^I$ the set of internal nodes of the scenario tree, i.e. all nodes where more than one scenario share history. Furthermore, let $\mathcal{W}_v$ denote the set of scenarios that share history in the internal node v, e.g. $\mathcal{W}_v = \mathcal{W}$ for the root node.

Let T^{s+} be the end time of stage s, and also the start time of the next stage when applicable. In Fig. 1 we have that $T^{3+} = T^4$. To simplify, let $T_v = T^{s_v}$ be the start time of stage s_v for node v in the scenario tree. In addition, let $T_{v+} = T^{s_v+}$ be the end time of the stage for the node v in the scenario tree, and also start time for the stage of the successor nodes when applicable. In Fig. 1 we have that $T_{e+} = T_j$.

Let s_v be the stage number for node v in the scenario tree, e.g. $s_e = 3$ for node e in the scenario tree in Fig. 1. Furthermore, let s_{v+} be the stage number for the successor nodes of v in the scenario tree, e.g. $s_{e+} = 4$ in Fig. 1. A scenario tree node number corresponding to stage s and scenario ω is denoted $v(s, \omega)$. In Fig. 1 they are labeled alphabetically to avoid confusion between scenario tree nodes and scenarios. For instance, stage 3 with scenario 3 and 4 would both return node e, $v(3, 3) = e$ and $v(3, 4) = e$.

The ODs can be used to serve one or more of the customers. Customers can be assigned to OD k and a compensation $f_k(x^\omega)$ is given to this OD in

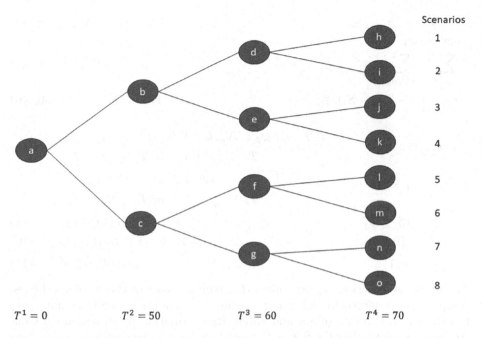

Fig. 1. Illustration of the scenario tree used for instances with three ODs. Consider the up-branches as an arriving OD and the down-branches as a non-arriving OD.

scenario ω, where x^ω denotes the arcs used in scenario ω. The compensation is set to make up for the detour of the OD, times a compensation parameter P, such that $f_k(x^\omega) = P(\sum_{(i,j)\in\mathcal{A}_k} C_{ijk}x_{ijk}^\omega - C_{o(k),d(k),k})$. The binary variable y_i^ω is 1 if customer i is not served in scenario ω, and 0 otherwise. If customer i is not served, a penalty γ_i is given. A feasible solution contains a set of routes, one for each vehicle in each scenario, that share history in certain parts of the scenario tree. The objective is to minimize the expected cost, consisting of the routing cost plus the compensation to the ODs and the penalties of not serving a customer.

A formulation of the problem becomes:

$$\min \sum_{\omega\in\mathcal{W}} p^\omega \left(\sum_{k\in\mathcal{K}^R} \sum_{(i,j)\in\mathcal{A}_k} C_{ijk}x_{ijk}^\omega + \sum_{k\in\mathcal{K}^\omega\backslash\mathcal{K}^R} f_k(x^\omega) + \sum_{i\in\mathcal{N}} \gamma_i y_i^\omega \right) \quad (1)$$

subject to

$$\sum_{j\in\mathcal{N}\cup\{d(k)\}} x_{o(k)jk}^\omega = 1 \qquad\qquad \omega\in\mathcal{W}, k\in\mathcal{K}^\omega \quad (2)$$

$$\sum_{i\in\mathcal{N}\cup\{o(k)\}} x_{ijk}^\omega - \sum_{i\in\mathcal{N}\cup\{d(k)\}} x_{jik}^\omega = 0 \qquad\qquad \omega\in\mathcal{W}, k\in\mathcal{K}^\omega, j\in\mathcal{N} \quad (3)$$

$$\sum_{i \in \mathcal{N} \cup \{o(k)\}} x^{\omega}_{id(k)k} = 1 \qquad\qquad \omega \in \mathcal{W}, k \in \mathcal{K}^{\omega} \quad (4)$$

$$\sum_{k \in \mathcal{K}^{\omega}} \sum_{j \in \mathcal{N} \cup \{d(k)\}} x^{\omega}_{ijk} + y^{\omega}_i = 1 \qquad\qquad \omega \in \mathcal{W}, i \in \mathcal{N} \quad (5)$$

$$(t^{\omega}_{jk} - t^{\omega}_{ik} - T_{ijk} - S_j)x^{\omega}_{ijk} \geq 0 \qquad\qquad \omega \in \mathcal{W}, k \in \mathcal{K}^{\omega}, (i,j) \in \mathcal{A}_k \quad (6)$$

$$x^{\omega_1}_{ijk} = x^{\omega_2}_{ijk} \qquad \begin{array}{c} v \in \mathcal{T}^I, \omega_1, \omega_2 \in \mathcal{W}_v, k \in \mathcal{K}^{\omega_1} \cup \mathcal{K}^{\omega_2}, (i,j) \in \mathcal{A}_k | \\ T_v \leq t^{\omega_1}_{ik} < T_{v^+} \text{ or } T_v \leq t^{\omega_2}_{ik} < T_{v^+} \end{array} \quad (7)$$

$$t^{\omega_1}_{ik} = t^{\omega_2}_{ik} \qquad \begin{array}{c} v \in \mathcal{T}^I, \omega_1, \omega_2 \in \mathcal{W}_v, k \in \mathcal{K}^{\omega_1} \cup \mathcal{K}^{\omega_2}, i \in \mathcal{N}_k | \\ T_v \leq t^{\omega_1}_{ik} < T_{v^+} \text{ or } T_v \leq t^{\omega_2}_{ik} < T_{v^+} \end{array} \quad (8)$$

$$\underline{T}^{\omega}_i \leq t^{\omega}_{ik} \leq \overline{T}^{\omega}_i \qquad\qquad \omega \in \mathcal{W}, k \in \mathcal{K}^{\omega}, i \in \{o(k), d(k)\} \quad (9)$$

$$x^{\omega}_{ijk} \in \{0,1\} \qquad\qquad \omega \in \mathcal{W}, k \in \mathcal{K}^{\omega}, (i,j) \in \mathcal{A}_k \quad (10)$$

$$y^{\omega}_i \in \{0,1\} \qquad\qquad \omega \in \mathcal{W}, i \in \mathcal{N} \quad (11)$$

The objective function (1) minimizes the expected cost of the regular vehicles, compensations offered to ODs and penalties. Constraints (2) and (4) make sure that a vehicle exits its origin and enters its destination in all scenarios. Constraints (3) ensure that the flow is balanced from origin to destination. Furthermore, constraints (5) force every delivery to be performed or a penalty is paid if the customer is not served. Constraints (6) are the scheduling constraints, and ensure that time passes when an arc is traversed, and waiting is allowed. Constraints (7) and (8) ensure that the same decisions are made in scenarios that share history. Note that if all other constraints are satisfied, then the t^{ω}_{ik} variables can be set a posteriori to satisfy constraints (8). Constraints (9) set time windows on origin and destination nodes. Due to the definition of t^{ω}_{ik} as departure time, these time windows are on the departure. Finally, the binary restrictions for the arc and node variables are given in (10) and (11), respectively.

No Rerouting of ODs

As there is no penalty for returning to the store with excess goods in the regular vehicles, this allows for rerouting of the regular vehicles during the day without having to revisit the depot. As described in the introduction, the ODs have to bring exactly the right amount of goods from the store. From a business perspective, it is reasonable that the company will not ask ODs to wait and that they propose a route or a set of customers to the OD, and no rerouting is expected of the OD after the OD accepts to participate. This means that for each internal node in the scenario tree, all decisions made thereafter for the corresponding OD have to be the same in all scenarios belonging to that node. For the branches where the OD did not arrive this is also true, but no constraints are needed as the vehicle is not used in any of them. The following constraints are added,

$$x^{\omega_1}_{ijk} = x^{\omega_2}_{ijk} \qquad k \in \mathcal{K}^O, v \in \mathcal{T}^I_k, \omega_1, \omega_2 \in \mathcal{W}_v, (i,j) \in \mathcal{A}_k, \quad (12)$$

where $\mathcal{T}_k^I$ gives the set of all internal nodes in the scenario tree where the arrival of OD k is revealed. For the second OD, this will in Fig. 1 be the nodes d, e, f and g. If two or more ODs potentially can arrive at the same time, then an epsilon difference in time is used to build the full scenario tree. Note that these constraints are not necessary for the last arriving OD, i.e. $\mathcal{W}_v$ only contains one scenario in the leaf nodes of the scenario tree.

2.2 Linearisation

The model (1)–(12) contains non-linearities in several of the constraints. We linearise the scheduling constraints (6) as follows:

$$t_{ik}^\omega + T_{ijk} + S_j - t_{jk}^\omega \le (1 - x_{ijk}^w)(\overline{T}_{d(k)} + T_{ijk} + S_j - \underline{T}_{o(k)}),$$
$$\omega \in \mathcal{W}, k \in \mathcal{K}^\omega, (i,j) \in \mathcal{A}_k \tag{13}$$

Next, we linearise the non-anticipativity constraints (7) by introducing a new binary variable $u_{ijk}^{s\omega}$, which is 1 if arc (i,j) is used by vehicle k in stage s and scenario ω. Then, the following constraints replace the non-anticipativity constraints (7):

$$\sum_{s \in \mathcal{S}} u_{ijk}^{s\omega} = x_{ijk}^\omega \qquad \omega \in \mathcal{W}, k \in \mathcal{K}^\omega, (i,j) \in \mathcal{A}_k \tag{14}$$

$$T^s \sum_{j \in \mathcal{N}_k} u_{ijk}^{s\omega} \le t_{ik}^\omega \qquad \omega \in \mathcal{W}, s \in \mathcal{S}, k \in \mathcal{K}^\omega, i \in \mathcal{N}_k \tag{15}$$

$$\overline{T} - (\overline{T} - T^{s^+}) \sum_{j \in \mathcal{N}_k} u_{ijk}^{s\omega} > t_{ik}^\omega \qquad \omega \in \mathcal{W}, s \in \mathcal{S}, k \in \mathcal{K}^\omega, i \in \mathcal{N}_k \tag{16}$$

$$u_{ijk}^{s_v\omega_1} = u_{ijk}^{s_v\omega_2} \qquad \begin{aligned} &v \in \mathcal{T}^I, \omega_1, \omega_2 \in \mathcal{W}_v, \\ &k \in \mathcal{K}^{\omega_1} \cup \mathcal{K}^{\omega_2}, (i,j) \in \mathcal{A}_k \end{aligned} \tag{17}$$

$$u_{ijk}^{s\omega} \in \{0,1\} \qquad \omega \in \mathcal{W}, s \in \mathcal{S}, k \in \mathcal{K}^\omega, (i,j) \in \mathcal{A}_k \tag{18}$$

Constraints (14) enforce that if an arc is used, then it is used in exactly one stage defined by $u_{ijk}^{s\omega}$. Constraints (15) and (16) use this to set time windows on the corresponding t_{ik}^ω variables. Note that strict inequalities are not supported in most commercial solvers, requiring rounding off travel times to some digit and adjusting constraints (16) accordingly. Constraints (17) are linear non-anticipativity constraints, and constraints (18) define the new variables. Constraints (17) make sure that an arc is assigned to the same stage for all scenarios that share history. The non-anticipativity constraints (8) can be fulfilled a posteriori as long as the linearisation (13)–(18) is fulfilled.

2.3 Valid Inequalities and Symmetry Breaking

As we use a mixed-integer programming solver to solve the proposed model, we explore some directions to derive a stronger formulation. Deriving a stronger formulation may lead to better bounds, which can be useful to reduce the number of nodes in a branch-and-bound scheme or to improve the gap between the best solution found and the upper bound if the best solution found is not proven optimal. Several families of valid inequalities have been derived for the model. In addition, we have developed symmetry breaking constraints that are added to the formulation. In this problem, the fleet of regular vehicles are homogeneous, with the same origins and destinations. This leads to mathematical symmetry where routes can be assigned to any permutation of the vehicles. These solutions are mathematically different but identical in practice and generally slow down the branch-and-bound.

First, we describe some arc consistency inequalities. For all scenarios, if there has been any arc into node j in stage s, then there has to be an arc out of j in s or later giving:

$$\sum_{z=s}^{|\mathcal{S}|} \sum_{k\in\mathcal{K}^w} \sum_{j\in\mathcal{N}\cup d(k)} u_{ijk}^{zw} \geq \sum_{k\in\mathcal{K}^w} \sum_{j\in\mathcal{N}\cup o(k)} u_{jik}^{sw} \qquad w\in\mathcal{W}, s\in\mathcal{S}, i\in\mathcal{N} \qquad (19)$$

Furthermore, if there is no arc into node i up to stage s, then there are no arc out of i up to stage s, giving:

$$\sum_{z=1}^{s} \sum_{k\in\mathcal{K}^w} \sum_{j\in\mathcal{N}\cup o(k)} u_{jik}^{zw} \geq \sum_{z=1}^{s} \sum_{k\in\mathcal{K}^w} \sum_{j\in\mathcal{N}\cup d(k)} u_{ijk}^{zw} \qquad w\in\mathcal{W}, s\in\mathcal{S}, i\in\mathcal{N} \qquad (20)$$

Subtour elimination constraints are added to improve the LP-relaxation, giving:

$$\sum_{s\in\mathcal{S}} \sum_{k\in\mathcal{K}^w} \sum_{i\in\mathcal{L}} \sum_{j\in\mathcal{L}, i\neq j} u_{ijk}^{sw} + \sum_{i\in\mathcal{M}} y_i^w \leq |\mathcal{L}| - 1 \qquad w\in\mathcal{W}, \mathcal{M}\subset\mathcal{L}\subseteq\mathcal{N}, \qquad (21)$$
$$|\mathcal{M}| = |\mathcal{L}| - 1$$

All node sets $\mathcal{L}$ of size 2 and 3 are added to the formulation a priori.

Another family of valid inequalities is related to the time to complete a route. A given route in any scenario ω has a maximum route length limited by the time windows at the origin and destination of vehicle k, giving:

$$\sum_{(i,j)\in\mathcal{A}_k} (T_{ijk} + S_j) x_{ijk}^\omega \leq \overline{T}_{d(k)}^\omega - \underline{T}_{o(k)}^\omega, \qquad w\in\mathcal{W}, k\in\mathcal{K}^\omega \qquad (22)$$

We have also derived valid inequalities related to customers that can be visited in the same route. The time windows of the nodes may be such that a vehicle cannot manage to serve selected customers on the same route. Therefore, if two customers i and j can be visited by vehicle k, but it is not possible to visit these two customers on the same route, we have the following valid inequalities:

$$\sum_{l\in\mathcal{N}} (x_{ilk}^w + x_{jlk}^w) \leq 1 \qquad w\in\mathcal{W}, k\in\mathcal{K}^\omega, i,j\in\mathcal{N} \qquad (23)$$

We also extend these valid inequalities to the three customer (i,j,h) case, giving

$$\sum_{l \in \mathcal{N}} (x_{ilk}^w + x_{jlk}^w + x_{hlk}^w) \leq 1 \qquad w \in \mathcal{W}, k \in \mathcal{K}^\omega, i, j, h \in \mathcal{N} \qquad (24)$$

Finally, we include the following symmetry breaking constraints which exploit that the fleet of regular vehicles is homogeneous:

$$\sum_{j \in \mathcal{N}} (x_{ijk}^1 + x_{jik}^1) = 0 \qquad k \in \mathcal{K}^R \setminus \{1\}, i \in \{1, ..., k-1\} \qquad (25)$$

Constraints (25) state that vehicle k cannot serve customers i with lower index number than k, i.e. $i < k$ in one of the scenarios, arbitrary chosen to be scenario 1 in this case. The final model consists of (1)–(5) and (9)–(25).

3   Computational Results

All instances of our mathematical programming models are solved using Mosel Xpress 8.4 on an 8 core 2×3.5 GHz Intel Xeon Gold 6144 processor with 384 GB RAM. The computational time limit was set to maximum 10 h for the instances presented in this paper. Sect. 3.1 explains how the instances and scenarios are generated, and in Sect. 3.2 we compare the presented multistage model with the two-stage model from [5], discussing the results gaining added managerial insights.

3.1   Instance Generation

The instances are adapted from [15] as in [5], where the n first delivery nodes in each instance are used. The instances have the following characteristics, where four instances with 15 delivery locations (customers) each are randomly generated on a square of 50×50, and named A, B, C and D. These are each divided into three sizes of the first 5, 10 and 15 (S, M, L) deliveries. A concatenation of these are used as reference, such that AL refers to the instance with the first 15 customers in A. The destination of the ODs are distributed at the border of the square, ordered with increasing arrival times clockwise along the border.

From preliminary tests we have chosen values for several parameters of the problem that seem to be suitable to demonstrate the effects of the uncertainty in the problem. The planning horizon starts at $\underline{T} = 0$ and ends at $\overline{T} = 100$, and ODs arrive throughout the planning horizon. The ODs are compensated $P = 1.3$ times the cost of their detour, and are available from the time they arrive to the end of the planning horizon. The penalty for not serving a customer is set to 50, and two regular vehicles are available in all instances. All possible realizations of ODs are used in the scenarios, giving $|\mathcal{W}| = 2^{|\mathcal{K}^O|}$ scenarios, with equal probability $p^\omega = \frac{1}{|\mathcal{W}|}$ for each scenario. We focus on instances with two or three ODs. We consider that ODs arrive at different points in time, as opposed to [5] who assumed that all ODs arrive at the same time. For the multistage model, the first OD may arrive at a fixed time T^2, the second OD may arrive at $T^3 = T^2 + 10$, and the third OD may arrive at $T^4 = T^3 + 10$. However, for the two-stage model, all ODs that arrive at the depot are known from time T^2, but arrive at the same points in time as the multistage model. It is only the revelation of information that is different.

3.2   Results and Discussion

In this section we compare the multistage model with the two-stage model from [5], showing that the structure of the solutions can change quite drastically when we no longer assume a two-stage revelation of the uncertain information. Experiments reported in [5] showed that the two-stage solution on average outperforms deterministic strategies. Therefore, we only focus on the multistage and two-stage solutions in this work. In addition, we provide an alternative interpretation of these results where they can be used to discuss the value of information giving added managerial insights.

Figure 2 shows an example of how different the first stage decisions of the two models might be. Here it is worth noting that both the selection of nodes visited in the first stage and the order of the visited nodes are different. We start by considering the two-stage solution shown in Fig. 2a. If one of the two first ODs arrive they are used to serve customer 2, and if not it is served by the company's own fleet. In the multistage solution shown in Fig. 2b this is not possible, because the company has to wait longer before they know whether the second OD arrives or not. Since rerouting is not allowed, the company does not have time to wait with its own vehicle at customer 4 until this information is revealed. Therefore, customer 2 will not be served by the company's own fleet in any of the scenarios and only visited if an OD arrives. Let us denote such a customer (customer 2) a *critical node*. Generally, a *critical node* in this context is a node in a route that cannot be visited by the company's own fleet if they have to wait until the very moment an OD arrives before deciding whether they serve this customer with a company owned vehicle or not. We see from this example that the subtle difference where the information is revealed at a later point in time results in a substantially different first stage solution due to the presence of a critical node.

Looking at the aggregated results for each instance in Table 1 we can identify a similar trend, where the multistage solution waits as long as possible before committing to a solution. Both tables in this paper have the same structure where the columns 'FSV' show the number of first stage visits, the columns 'SSV' show the average number of visits in the remaining stages and the columns 'SV' show the average number of customers not visited. The columns 'Z' show the objective value and the row 'Average ratio' shows the average across all instances when each cell is divided by their respective instance size. Note that the sum across the columns 'FSV', 'SSV', and 'SV' for each row add up to the instance size. Thus, the average ratio for the same columns add up to 1. We have defined the first stage visits to be the visits occurring before the first possible arrival of an OD.

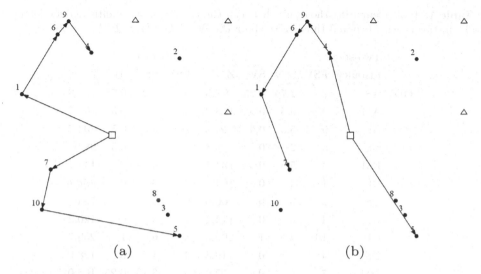

Fig. 2. The DM instance with three ODs and the first arriving at $T^{OD} = 50$. The depot is located at the square in the middle, the customers are located at the circular nodes, while the destination of the ODs are located at the triangle nodes. Figures (a) and (b) show the first stage solution for the two-stage and the multistage model, respectively.

From Table 1 we observe that the number of first stage visits (FSV) is slightly decreased from the two-stage model to the multistage model. Then, naturally the number of second-stage visits (SSV) are increased from the two-stage model to the multistage model. However, this trend does not always result in structurally different routes in the first stage as in Fig. 2, but rather that the decisions are delayed as long as possible in order to exploit the ODs in case they arrive.

For the instances where the first stage decisions are not structurally different and there is no presence of critical nodes we can still observe a different evaluation of the expected cost. This comes from the revelation of the information in several stages rather than one. When the company does not know if more ODs will arrive at a later point in time it is better to let the first OD drive a suboptimal route serving more customers compared to what would be optimal if we also knew the second OD would arrive.

Another interesting observation from Table 1 is that the option of skipping a visit (SV) is more frequent in the multistage model. This is due to the effect discussed regarding Fig. 2, where the only way to guarantee serving the last customer (in this example customer 2) is to start driving towards this customer with the company's own vehicle before they know whether the OD arrives or not, i.e. the presence of a critical node. The savings of utilizing the OD is so large that the expected cost becomes lower by only serving this customer if the OD arrives. Sometimes this leads to structurally different routes in the first stage as in Fig. 2, other times not.

Table 1. Table comparing the results between the two-stage and multistage model for the instances with two and three ODs where the first OD arrive at $T^{OD} = 50$.

	Instance	Two-stage				Multistage			
		FSV	SSV	SV	Z	FSV	SSV	SV	Z
3 ODs	AS	2	2.75	0.25	97.5	0	4.25	0.75	105.8
	AM	3	6.5	0.5	163.2	5	4.5	0.5	167.7
	AL	9	5.5	0.5	*199.7*	10	4.5	0.5	203.7
	BS	3	2	0	89.3	3	1.5	0.5	98.0
	BM	4	5.5	0.5	134.7	4	5	1	143.4
	BL	11	4	0	164.4	9	6	0	*166.6*
	CS	2	3	0	66.5	0	5	0	75.6
	CM	4	6	0	114.2	5	5	0	120.2
	CL	10	4	1	209.5	8	6	1	209.7
	DS	4	1	0	119.3	4	1	0	128.0
	DM	7	3	0	157.6	6	3.75	0.25	166.0
	DL	9	6	0	*161.1*	6	8.75	0.25	*173.0*
2 ODs	AS	3	1.75	0.25	105.6	3	1.75	0.25	105.6
	AM	7	3	0	168.2	7	3	0	168.2
	AL	9	5.25	0.75	206.1	6	8	1	213.0
	BS	3	2	0	93.3	3	2	0	95.3
	BM	5	4.75	0.25	142.0	5	4.75	0.25	143.3
	BL	4	10.5	0.5	168.7	4	10.5	0.5	169.3
	CS	2	3	0	68.9	2	3	0	76.1
	CM	5	5	0	116.5	5	5	0	120.1
	CL	8	6	1	211.5	10	4	1	211.7
	DS	4	1	0	118.2	4	1	0	122.7
	DM	7	3	0	156.5	7	3	0	161.1
	DL	9	6	0	160.1	10	5	0	162.6
Average ratio		0.56	0.42	0.02	15.24	0.52	0.45	0.03	15.88

Moreover, it is interesting to see how the two-stage solution behaves in a multistage setting. By fixing the first stage decisions from the two-stage solution evaluating it with the multistage model, we can get a measure of how much worse the expected cost becomes if we plan for a two-stage setting, when it in fact is a multistage setting. From Table 2 we can see this effect. Due to our definition of the first stage visits, the columns 'FSV' are not necessarily equal, as some visits might be shifted from the second stage to the first stage when re-evaluated in the multistage model. For the 'DM' instance, the two-stage solution has an expected cost of 167.4. This gives an increase of expected cost of about 0.84% compared to the multistage solution. Looking at the average expected cost across all instances

Table 2. Table comparing the results between the two-stage solution and the two-stage solution evaluated in the multistage model. The first OD arrive at $T^{OD} = 50$. The column 'Z*' shows the best integer solution found by the multistage model.

	Two-stage					Two-stage evaluation				
	Instance	FSV	SSV	SV	Z	FSV	SSV	SV	Z	Z*
3 ODs	AS	2	2.75	0.25	97.5	3	1.5	0.5	106.1	105.8
	AM	3	6.5	0.5	163.2	5	4.5	0.5	167.7	167.7
	AL	9	5.5	0.5	*199.7*	9	5	1	213.9	203.7
	BS	3	2	0	89.3	3	1.5	0.5	110.2	98.0
	BM	4	5.5	0.5	134.7	4	5	1	143.4	143.4
	BL	11	4	0	164.4	11	4	0	168.8	*166.6*
	CS	2	3	0	66.5	2	3	0	76.3	75.6
	CM	4	6	0	114.2	4	6	0	120.2	120.2
	CL	10	4	1	209.5	10	4	1	209.7	209.7
	DS	4	1	0	119.3	4	0.75	0.25	129.1	128.0
	DM	7	3	0	157.6	7	2.75	0.25	167.4	166.0
	DL	9	6	0	*161.1*	10	5	0	166.2	*173.0*
2 ODs	AS	3	1.75	0.25	105.6	4	1	0	110.2	105.6
	AM	7	3	0	168.2	7	3	0	168.2	168.2
	AL	9	5.25	0.75	206.1	9	5	1	216.9	213.0
	BS	3	2	0	93.3	4	1	0	96.5	95.3
	BM	5	4.75	0.25	142.0	5	4.75	0.25	143.9	143.3
	BL	4	10.5	0.5	168.7	4	10.5	0.5	169.3	169.3
	CS	2	3	0	68.9	2	3	0	77.0	76.1
	CM	5	5	0	116.5	5	5	0	120.1	120.1
	CL	8	6	1	211.5	8	6	1	211.7	211.7
	DS	4	1	0	118.2	4	0.75	0.25	124.9	122.7
	DM	7	3	0	156.5	7	2.75	0.25	163.3	161.1
	DL	9	6	0	160.1	9	6	0	165.1	162.6
Average ratio		0.56	0.42	0.02	15.24	0.59	0.37	0.03	16.12	15.88

there is an increase of expected cost of about 1.54%. Ignoring the instance 'DL' where the multistage model was not solved to optimality and it found a bad integer feasible solution the increase in expected cost is 1.70% instead.

However, further testing indicates that the routing decisions from the two-stage model are fairly good. When only fixing the arc-variables from the first stage, letting the scheduling of the visits to be freely set, the two-stage evaluation in the multistage model becomes much better, only 0.18% worse than the multistage model on average. This indicates that the biggest drawback with the two-stage model is to find the correct scheduling of the customer visits, but that the order of visits are quite good.

Moreover, the observation regarding critical nodes could be exploited in heuristics aiming at solving larger instances. After solving the two-stage model a post processing procedure could identify critical nodes and if any are found, make alterations in the first stage decisions. How to make these alterations and whether the exploitation of critical nodes are scalable require more research. However, our findings indicate that adjusting the scheduling of customer visits from the two-stage solution might give significant improvements of the solutions. The indication that parts of the two-stage solution is contained in the multistage solution is important for developing more advanced solution methods, because it already exists several good methods to solve two-stage stochastic programs, both heuristically and exact.

Another interesting observation from Table 2 is regarding the 'C'-instances. In these instances the majority of the customers are located relatively close to the depot. Here the evaluation of the two-stage solution is close or equal to the full multistage solution. The company has time to wait until the second or third OD arrives and thus visit the remaining customers with its own vehicles only if they do not arrive.

Alternatively, we can consider the two-stage model as a representation of a different business practice. Instead of having ODs arriving randomly in separate stages we can consider a case where the company has invested in a system where possible ODs have to register before noon the day they arrive. Using such a system, the problem has a two-stage structure, where at the beginning of the day they have to start serving their customers with their own fleet, and at some point during the day the information regarding the ODs are revealed. Comparing the two models from this perspective, we can interpret the difference in the objective value as the value of receiving the information of the arriving ODs at an earlier point in time. We see from Table 1 that the expected cost is improved on average by 4.2% by receiving the information earlier on the day. It is also worth noting that the difference between the expected cost of the two practices seems to increase with increasing number of ODs. For a real business the number of ODs are likely to be much higher, and these observations give reasons to investigate whether investing in a system to register ODs earlier is profitable in the specific business case.

4   Concluding Remarks

In this work we have shown that modelling the uncertain arrival of occasional drivers more realistically, i.e. with a multistage formulation, can give substantially different first stage decisions. We have also gained additional insight to the problem by identifying the typical structure explaining when and why the multistage solution differs from the two-stage solution, namely the presence of critical nodes. In addition, we have found indications that changing the scheduling of the customer visits from the two-stage solution can improve the solution in a multistage setting. These two observations can both be exploited in future research when developing more advanced solution methods. Finally, we give an alternative interpretation of the results pointing out the potential of investing in systems that can reveal uncertain information earlier.

To apply the multistage model in practice, alternative solution methods must be explored. A possible solution procedure could be to first solve the two-stage model with a more effective algorithm and then use the notion of critical nodes to give an indication of solution quality. The presence of critical nodes is likely to require alterations of the first stage decisions while the absence of such nodes is likely to indicate higher solution quality. How to make these alterations remain to be addressed in future research.

References

1. Archetti, C., Savelsbergh, M., Speranza, M.G.: The vehicle routing problem with occasional drivers. Eur. J. Oper. Res. **254**(2), 472–480 (2016)
2. Arslan, A.M., Agatz, N., Kroon, L., Zuidwijk, R.: Crowdsourced delivery - a dynamic pickup and delivery problem with ad hoc drivers. Transp. Sci. **53**(1), 222–235 (2018)
3. Barr, A., Wohl, J.: Wal-mart may get customers to deliver packages to online buyers. Reuters (2013). http://www.reuters.com/article/2013/03/28/us-retail-walmart-delivery-idUSBRE92R03820130328
4. Bensinger, G.: Amazon's next delivery drone: you. Wall Street J. (2015). https://www.wsj.com/articles/amazon-seeks-help-with-deliveries-1434466857
5. Dahle, L., Andersson, H., Christiansen, M.: The vehicle routing problem with dynamic occasional drivers. ICCL 2017. LNCS, vol. 10572, pp. 49–63. Springer, Cham (2017). https://doi.org/10.1007/978-3-319-68496-3_4
6. Dahle, L., Andersson, H., Christiansen, M., Speranza, G.: The pickup and delivery problem with time windows and occasional drivers. Comput. Oper. Res. **109**, 122–133 (2019)
7. Dayarian, I., Savelsbergh, M.: Crowdshipping and same-day delivery: employing in-store customers to deliver online orders (2017). Available at optimization-online.org
8. Feng, L., et al.: Solving generalized vehicle routing problem with occasional drivers via evolutionary multitasking. IEEE Trans. Cybern. 1–14 (2019)
9. Gdowska, K., Viana, A., Pedroso, J.: Stochastic last-mile delivery with crowdshipping. Transp. Res. Proc. **30**, 90–100 (2018)
10. Le, T.V., Ukkusuri, S.V.: Crowd-shipping services for last mile delivery: analysis from American survey data. Transp. Res. Interdiscip. Perspect. **1**, 100008 (2019)
11. Macrina, G., Di Puglia Pugliese, L., Guerriero, F., Laganà, D.: The vehicle routing problem with occasional drivers and time windows. In: Sforza, A., Sterle, C. (eds.) ODS 2017. SPMS, vol. 217, pp. 577–587. Springer, Cham (2017). https://doi.org/10.1007/978-3-319-67308-0_58
12. Macrina, G., Guerriero, F.: The green vehicle routing problem with occasional drivers. In: Daniele, P., Scrimali, L. (eds.) New Trends in Emerging Complex Real Life Problems. ASS, vol. 1, pp. 357–366. Springer, Cham (2018). https://doi.org/10.1007/978-3-030-00473-6_38
13. Macrina, G., Pugliese, L.D.P., Guerriero, F.: Crowd-shipping: a new efficient and eco-friendly delivery strategy. Proc. Manuf. **42**, 483–487 (2020)
14. Mousavi, K., Bodur, M., Roorda, M.: Stochastic last-mile delivery with crowd-shipping and mobile depots (2020). Available at optimization-online.org

15. Ropke, S., Cordeau, J.F.: Branch and cut and price for the pickup and delivery problem with time windows. Transp. Sci. **43**(3), 267–286 (2009)
16. Simoni, M.D., Marcucci, E., Gatta, V., Claudel, C.G.: Potential last-mile impacts of crowdshipping services: a simulation-based evaluation. Transportation **47**, 1933–1954 (2019). https://doi.org/10.1007/s11116-019-10028-4
17. Sun, L., Sun, Y., Zheng, W.: The stochastic and dynamic vehicle routing problem with crowdshipping. In: CICTP 2017, pp. 1500–1510. ASCE (2017)
18. Torres, F., Gendreau, M., Rei, W.: Vehicle routing with stochastic supply of crowd vehicles and time windows. Technical report, CIRRELT (2020)

Cumulative VRP with Time Windows:
A Trade-Off Analysis

Alejandro Fernández Gil[1]([⊠]), Mariam Gómez Sánchez[1], Eduardo Lalla-Ruiz[2],
and Carlos Castro[1]

[1] Departamento de Informática, Universidad Técnica Federico Santa María,
Valparaíso, Chile
{affernan,mggomez}@jp.inf.utfsm.cl, Carlos.Castro@inf.utfsm.cl
[2] Department of Business Information Systems and Industrial Engineering,
University of Twente, Enschede, The Netherlands
e.a.lalla@utwente.nl

Abstract. In this work, the Cumulative Vehicle Routing Problem
(CumVRP) is studied. It is a routing optimization problem, in which
the objective is to construct a set of vehicle routes with the minimum
cumulative cost in terms of distance and weight over a traveled arc. The
CumVRP can be defined with hard and soft time windows constraints
for incorporating customer service. To tackle this problem, a matheuristic approach based on combining mathematical programming and an
iterative metaheuristic algorithm Greedy Randomized Adaptive Search
Procedure (GRASP) is proposed. In each step of our approach, a feasible solution (set of routes) is built using GRASP, and, afterward, the
solution is optimized using a MILP optimizer. The main objective of
this research is to analyze the trade-off between the environmental cost
produced by the delivery of goods complying with the limits of time
windows and the customer's dissatisfaction when these limits are violated at a certain time limit previously defined. The results show that
the environmental cost is reduced if the violation of the upper limits
of the customers' time windows is allowed. These violations generate a
cost associated with penalties that are well balanced with respect to the
reduction of emissions.

Keywords: Cumulative Vehicle Routing Problem · Green VRP ·
Time windows · Matheuristic · GRASP · MILP

1 Introduction

Nowadays, there is increasing concern at enterprise and social levels concerning
greenhouse gas emissions. The transportation companies seek to offer a good
service to the customers while taking into account solutions that tackle climate
change. This circumstance has been widely studied in the area of Green Logistics (GL), which considers a set of activities that propose measuring the environmental impact of different product distribution strategies, minimizing the

© Springer Nature Switzerland AG 2020
E. Lalla-Ruiz et al. (Eds.): ICCL 2020, LNCS 12433, pp. 277–291, 2020.
https://doi.org/10.1007/978-3-030-59747-4_18

energy usage in logistics activities, reducing waste and managing its treatment [1]. Currently, burning fossil fuels causes 80% of environmental pollution in the world, and around 60% of this fuel is generated by the freight transport sector [2]. Optimizing fuel consumption helps reduce the rate of environmental pollution and health impacts. Moreover, fuel consumption by a vehicle is affected by several factors, e.g.., distance traveled, weight and speed of the vehicle and traffic, among others [3]. The inclusion of these factors in optimization models increases the realism of the solutions but, on the other hand, increases their complexity.

One of the main optimization problems in logistics to model freight distribution is the well-known Vehicle Routing Problem (VRP, [4]). It is commonly used for modeling transportation and logistics scenarios while optimizing a given objective function, e.g., distance, traveling time, etc. A recent VRP variation considering the reduction of the *cumulative cost*, calculated based on the distance traveled by a vehicle carrying a certain load, is the Cumulative VRP (CumVRP, [5,6]), which is an $\mathcal{NP}$-Hard problem. CumVRP belongs to the problems within Green VRP area as it considers the reduction of fuel consumption [3,7]. Another relevant aspect studied in the VRP related literature is the inclusion of time window constraints such as in the VRP with time windows (VRP-TW), where customers must be served within a predefined time interval [8,9]. When considering time windows, it can be distinguished between hard and soft time windows. In the hard time windows case, a vehicle must serve the customers right at a specified time interval, if the vehicle arrives earlier than the time window, it has to wait, late arrival is not allowed. The soft time window case permits the violation of the time window constraints subject to some penalty [10].

Considering previous discussion, in this work, we focus on analysing the inclusion of time windows on the CumVRP. Firstly, we consider the case where the freights distribution is constrained by hard time windows, and secondly, the case where the service time is constrained by soft time windows so that time window violations are permitted subject to penalization, i.e., the service is allowed to begin outside the time windows at the cost of a given penalty. Depending on the application, the use of soft time windows can reflect practical situations much better than hard time windows [11].

The goal of including time windows into the CumVRP aims at analyzing the trade-off between the environmental cost produced by the transportation of goods to customers, complying with the intervals of the time windows and infringement of quality service to the customers. Investigating on soft time windows permits analyzing the contribution of soft time windows penalty and environmental related costs. Furthermore, to provide feasible solutions for these problem variants, this work proposes a hybrid approach, specifically a matheuristic (named *MathGRASP*). *MathGRASP* is based on combining a mathematical programming approach (MILP optimizer) within the Greedy Randomized Adaptive Search Procedure (GRASP) metaheuristic.

The remainder of the paper is organized as follows. Section 2 reviews related work. Section 3 describes the mathematical formulation of the CumVRP and

CumVRP with hard and soft time windows. The solution approach based matheuristic algorithm is given in Sect. 4. Computational experiments and results are given in Sect. 5 and finally, we present the conclusions and future work in Sect. 6.

2   Related Works

In the freight transportation industry, the importance of achieving optimal vehicle routing considering sustainability factors is growing [12]. The area of Green Vehicle Routing Problems (Green VRPs) is characterized by incorporating environmental features (e.g., emissions per type of vehicle, energy minimization, etc.). Solution approaches in this area aim at proposing effective routes to satisfy the environmental concerns and commercial indicators of enterprises and societies. An extensive survey on this can be found in the work of Lin et al. [13].

In recent years, the Cumulative Vehicle Routing Problem (CumVRP) has received considerable attention from researchers. CumVRP has been introduced by Kara et al. [5] and referred to as a linear model of fuel consumption [7], and also as an energy minimization model [6]. The objective of the CumVRP is to find a set of routes that minimize the total cumulative cost, calculated based on the distance traveled by a vehicle transporting a specific weight load. In [3], it is stated that CumVRP is a type of problem that belongs to the area of Green VRPs, and in the study proposed in [7], some variations are suggested where the models consider factors aimed at reducing fuel consumption.

Several algorithms and approaches have been designed and developed for solving the CumVRP. Regarding exact algorithms, in [14] a mathematical model for CumVRP is presented as a Set Covering Problem and solved by a Column Generation Algorithm (CGA). However, the exact proposed algorithms demonstrate solving a considerable number of instances optimally, but always require a high amount of computational time and excessive memory consumption to solve more complex ones. For large instances, it is known that this type of approaches are not efficient enough to obtain the global optimum in reasonable times [15].

Heuristic and metaheuristic algorithms are able to find good quality solutions in relatively small times [16]. These types of algorithms have shown promise in solving VRPs: Clarke and Wright Savings algorithm (C&W) has been used in [17] to address CumVRP with Limited Duration; a Simulated Annealing (SA) is proposed in [18] for solving the previous problem considering the multi-trip factor and minimize fuel consumption; in [19], a memetic heuristic is reported that is aimed at solving CCVRP; an Iterated Greedy procedure is presented in [20] to achieve larger instances of CCVRP, and the proposed metaheuristic proves to be competitive.

3   Cumulative VRP

In this work, we address the Cumulative Vehicle Routing Problem (CumVRP) proposed in [5]. The goal of the CumVRP is to reduce *cumulative costs*, calculated based on the distance traveled by a vehicle carrying a certain load. The following parameters are defined in the problem:

- V, set of customer nodes.
- A, set of edges or arc $(i, j) \in A$ between each pairs of customers $i, j \in V$.
- d_{ij}, representing the travel distance between each arc $(i, j) \in A$.
- k, number of vehicles.
- $\mathcal{W}$, curb weight without associated weight load for each vehicle.
- Q, the maximum weight load for each vehicle.
- R, the flow capacity of the arcs of the network.

Let $G = (V, A)$ be a directed graph where each node $i \in V$ represents a customer and each arc $(i, j) \in A$ the distance between two customers $i, j \in V$. The node 0 represents the depot vertex from where a homogeneous fleet of k vehicles depart to satisfy the demand of the $|V| - 1$ customers. For each vehicle, its curb weight $\mathcal{W}$ is known and the maximum weight load that it can carry is Q. The flow capacity of each arc of the network R is known (maximal value of the flow in any arc of the network, for example, curb weight plus the capacity of the vehicles). For each customer $i > 0$, there is a demand $Q \geq Q_i > 0$. The cumulative cost of moving a vehicle from a customer i to a customer j is defined as $w_{ij} \cdot d_{ij}$. The decision variables are as follows:

- $x_{ij} \in \{0, 1\}$, $\forall i, j \in V$, set to 1 if the arc (i, j) is in the tour of a vehicle, and 0 otherwise.
- w_{ij}, $\forall i, j \in V$, the flow on the arc (i, j) if the vehicle goes from i to j, and 0 otherwise.
- c_{ij}, $\forall i, j \in V$, the cost of traversing an arc (i, j), is defined as $w_{ij} \cdot d_{ij}$.

The objective function of CumVRP (1) is to find a set of routes of minimum total cost where the cost is defined as the product of the distance of the arc (i, j) and flow on this arc.

$$Min \sum_{i=0}^{V} \sum_{j=0}^{V} d_{ij} w_{ij} \tag{1}$$

In the CumVRP the following constraints are considered:

(a) Each customer has to be served exactly by one vehicle.
(b) Each route starts and ends at the depot.
(c) For each tour, the flow on the arcs accumulate as much as preceding node's supply in the case of collection or diminish as much as preceding node's demand in the case of delivery.
(d) The flow on any arc of each tour does not exceed the flow capacity of the arcs.
(e) For each customer, the demand required must be satisfied.

In this research, we investigate the additions of time windows constraints in the CumVRP. The following two variants of CumVRP are evaluated: (i)

CumVRP-hTW, where the time windows cannot be violated, and (ii) CumVRP-sTW, where the upper bound of the time windows can be violated at a certain delay threshold.

The objective when solving CumVRP-hTW is based on obtaining a set of subtours, in such a way that the cumulative cost added to the number of vehicles used to supply the total demand is minimized. In the case of CumVRP-sTW, we will minimize the cumulative cost added to the penalties for service delay and use of vehicles. Both variants will be studied as delivery cases. Two variants are proposed in the following subsections.

3.1 CumVRP with Hard Time Windows

The addition of the hard time windows constraints to the CumVRP allows establishing strict frames of time to indicate when the customer has to be served. To properly include such features, the following parameters have to be incorporated:

Parameters:

- L_i, $\forall i \in V$, lower bound of the time window from which the customer i must be served.
- U_i, $\forall i \in V$, upper bound of the time window until which the customer i must be served.
- S_i, $\forall i \in V$, service time to serve customer i.
- M, big enough value.

Using the above parameters, the time interval $[L_i, U_i]$ represents the time windows during which the customer i must be served.

Decision variable:

t_i : time at which customer i starts to be serviced.

Objective function:

$$f_1 = \sum_{i=0}^{V} \sum_{j=0}^{V} d_{ij} w_{ij} \tag{2}$$

$$f_2 = Mk \tag{3}$$

$$Min \quad f_1 + f_2 \tag{4}$$

In the CumVRP-hTW, besides the constraints presented for CumVRP from (a) to (d), the following ones have to be considered for the correct consideration of the time windows:

(f) The starting time for servicing a customer $i \in V$ has to be equal to or greater than L_i time windows lower bound.
(g) The end service time of a customer i cannot exceed the U_i time window bound.

3.2   CumVRP with Soft Time Windows

Adding soft time windows constraints to the CumVRP allows establishing customers' time windows where its upper limit U_i does not have to be necessarily satisfied, in such a case a penalization is applied. Thus, it is necessary to add the parameters μ and P representing the allowed delay threshold and the penalty applied to each time unit of delay, respectively. In addition, it is necessary to include the following decision variables:

- $y_i \in \{0,1\}$, $\forall i \in V$, set to 1 if not complied with the upper limit for the time window in the customer i, and 0 otherwise.

The objective function, besides considering f_1 and f_2 as defined in the model for CumVRP-hTW, must incorporate the cost associated with penalties for violations (5), so it must be redefined as:

$$f_3 = \sum_{i=1}^{V}(P(t_i + S_i - U_i))y_i \qquad (5)$$

$$Min \quad \lambda_1 f_1 + f_2 + \lambda_3 f_3 \qquad (6)$$

The previous constraints from (a) to (f) remain in this formulation. The constraint (g) is redefined as:

(h) The end service time of a customer $i \in V$, U_i, cannot be exceeded by more than μ, i.e., $U_i + \mu$.

Finally, with regards to the depot, there is a time windows upper limit, U_0, associated with it, therefore, the following constraint has to be incorporated:

(i) The depot upper time windows U_i cannot be violated.

4   A *MathGRASP* Approach for the CumVRP

Matheuristics are algorithms that have been used successfully in routing problems [21]. These algorithms are based on combining heuristic or metaheuristic schemes and mathematical programming models to obtain high quality solutions. There are various applications of these techniques to solve variants of VRPs, such as time windows [22], multi-depot [23], electric vehicle [24], and cross-docking [25]. A matheuristic for the Pollution Routing Problem (PRP) is presented in [26], where a metaheuristic based on local search is combined with a MILP model. In [23] Multi-Depot CCVRP is solved using the POPMUSIC matheuristic algorithm (see [27]). This matheuristic consists in dividing a large problem into parts and then several of those parts are seen as subproblems to be solved through an exact approach.

For solving the CumVRP with time windows, we present a matheuristic based approach termed as *MathGRASP*. It is based on the hybridization of the Greedy Randomized Adaptive Search Procedure (GRASP) with an solving to optimality the optimization model. Our matheuristic is described in the context of a GRASP metaheuristic (see Algorithm 1). The GRASP algorithm [28] is an iterative method where each iteration has two phases: (i) construction and (ii) local search (lines 5–6).

Algorithm 1. *MathGRASP* Pseudocode

   Input: C vehicles, V customers, rcl, Max_Iter

 1: $T_F = \emptyset$;
 2: Preprocessing();
 3: **while** ($Max\_Iter > 0$) **do**
 4:     $T = \emptyset$;
 5:     $T = \text{Construction\_Algorithm}(rcl, V, C)$;
 6:     $T^* = \text{Local\_Search}(T)$;
 7:     **if** ($f(T^*) < f(T_F)$) **then**
 8:        $T_F = T^*$;
 9:     **end if**
10:     Max_Iter -=1;
11: **end while**
12: **return** T_F;

Initially a preprocessing of data (line 2) is performed. The constructive algorithm is provided with the set of vehicles and customers, in addition to the parameter rcl (size of restricted candidate list) and provides feasible solutions consisting of a set of subtours ($\tau_i \in T$) (line 5). After construction procedure, the best solution is selected and a local search procedure is applied to it (line 6). Finally, the algorithm updates the best tour found (lines 7-9) and returns the best solution obtained in all iterations T_F (line 12). In the following subsections we describe the components of the algorithm.

Solution Representation. The solution of the problem is stored in T_F, represented by a matrix, where each row represents a subtour τ_i, and in each subtour there is a sequence of ($Customers \in \tau_i$) to visit (see Fig. 1).

$$T_F = \begin{matrix} \tau_1 \\ \tau_2 \\ \vdots \\ \tau_n \end{matrix} \begin{bmatrix} Depot & Customer_9 & Customer_8 & \dots & Depot \\ Depot & Customer_3 & Customer_7 & \dots & Depot \\ \vdots & \vdots & \vdots & \ddots & \vdots \\ Depot & Customer_6 & Customer_5 & \dots & Depot \end{bmatrix}$$

Fig. 1. Solution structure composed of subtours.

Construction Algorithm. In each iteration of Algorithm 2, a feasible solution to the problem is constructed. It aims at making as few subtours as possible.

Each subtour considers the depot as the starting node. To create a subtour at each iteration, the array of customers is sorted in ascending order with respect to the distance between each customer and the last customer added to the subtour (initially the depot) (line 4). A restricted candidate list of customers RCL is constructed with rcl size, and on it the first RCL customer from V is added (line 5–6). After that, a customer is randomly selected from the restricted candidate list (line 7) and takes into account the available capacity of the vehicle, the candidate is added to the corresponding subtour (lines 8–12). Once the maximum capacity of the vehicle is completed, the variables are updated to form a new subtour (line 13). The procedure is performed while there are customers without visiting (line 3). Once the subtours have been established, the route to be carried out complying either with the hard or soft time windows is locally optimized (procedure described in the following subsection) and each subtour is updated (line 16). Finally, a feasible solution to the problem is returned (line 17).

Algorithm 2. Construction_Algorithm(rcl, V, C) Pseudocode
___
1: $\mathcal{T} = \emptyset$;
2: $c =$ Choose the initial Vehicle of C;
3: **while** (!V.empty()) **do**
4:     Sort array of Customer V;
5:     $Ub = min(rcl, |V|)$;
6:     $RCL = V[0 : Ub]$;
7:     $cand = RCL[random(1, |RCL|)]$;
8:     **if** ($c.Current\_Load + cand.Demand \le c.Maximum\_Payload$) **then**
9:         Add $cand$ to $\mathcal{T}$ at $c.index$;
10:         Update $Current\_Load$;
11:         Delete the $cand$ from V;
12:     **else**
13:         $c =$ Choose the next Vehicle of C;
14:     **end if**
15: **end while**
16: $\mathcal{T} = $ Solve_MILP$(\mathcal{T})$;   ▷ see Exact solution subsubsection
17: **return** $\mathcal{T}$;

– **Exact solution:** The model proposed in [5] incorporating the time windows constraints as discussed in Subsect. 3.1 are reformulated to optimize each subtour obtained by (Algorithm 2, lines 1–16). In both cases, to cover the total demand of each subtour, only one vehicle will be necessary, since the sum of the customers' demand considered each time is less than the maximum load supported by the vehicle. After completing the previous step in both formulations, the decision variable k is eliminated and the new assumption is added:

(j) For each subtour, only one loop can be performed.

In both cases, it is not necessary to assess the penalty for using vehicles in the objective function, therefore the Eqs. (4) and (6) are reformulated as the Eqs. (7) and (8) for CumVRP-hTW and CumVRP-sTW respectively.

$$Min \quad f_1 \tag{7}$$

$$Min \quad \lambda_1 f_1 + \lambda_3 f_3 \tag{8}$$

Local Search Algorithm. The Local Search (LS) algorithm is based on Hill-Climbing (HC) algorithm with the first improvement strategy. The pseudocode of the algorithm is shown in Algorithm 3. The used Hill-Climbing algorithm works with the best feasible solutions constructed by the Algorithm 2. The defined movement is inspired by [29] where two subtours are randomly selected (lines 3–4). After that, two customers are selected so that the distance between them is minimal (line 5) and a swap is performed (lines 6–7). Subsequently, the vehicle capacity constraints are checked in each subtour and if these were satisfied, the modified subtours are again optimized (line 9), and T is updated with the best solution found (lines 10–12). Finally, after LS_Iter iterations, the algorithm returns the best solution found so far.

Algorithm 3. Local_Search(T) Pseudocode

1: **while** ($LS\_Iter > 0$) **do**
2: $\quad T' = T$;
3: $\quad \tau_a = T'[random(0, |T'|)]$;
4: $\quad \tau_b = T'[random(0, |T'|)]$ with $\tau_b \neq \tau_a$;
5: $\quad C_a, C_b =$ Choose Two *Customer* of Minimum Distance from τ_a and τ_b;
6: $\quad$ Add c_a into τ_b, Delete c_a from τ_a;
7: $\quad$ Add c_b into τ_a, Delete c_b from τ_b;
8: $\quad$ **if** (Capacity Constraints for τ_a and τ_b) **then**
9: $\quad\quad T' =$ Solve_MILP(T');
10: $\quad\quad$ **if** ($f(T') < f(T)$) **then**
11: $\quad\quad\quad T = T'$;
12: $\quad\quad$ **end if**
13: $\quad$ **end if**
14: **end while**
15: **return** T;

---

5 Computational Study

In this section, we analyze the performance of *MathGRASP* for solving the previously discussed CumVRP variants. All implementations were done in C++11 using Visual Studio v15.9.2. The associated MILP formulations are solved using IBM ILOG CPLEX v12.9.0 API. The equipment used for the tests was a processor Intel(R) Xeon(R) Platinum 81171M CPU 2.60 GHz with 16 GB RAM memory on Windows 10 OS. The matheuristic was run in single thread mode.

5.1   Problem Instances

We perform tests on a selected set of 9 instances of PRPLIB proposed in [30], this dataset consists of 9 sets of 20 instances each one, where the customers or nodes quantities are in the range of 10 to 200 customer, and the values $\omega = 6350\,\mathrm{kg}$ and $Q = 3650\,\mathrm{kg}$. In Table 1 shows the features for the set of selected instances.

Table 1. Features of PRPLib instances.

Instance	Customers
UK10_01	10
UK15_01	15
UK20_20	20
UK25_01	25
UK50_01	50
UK75_01	75
UK100_05	100
UK150_12	150
UK200_01	200

5.2   Parameter Setting

A parameter tuning process was performed using ParamILS [31], an iterated local search algorithm that works searching for better-quality parameter settings in the neighborhoods of the current one. We provide to the tuner the following set of parameters: $rcl \in \{3, 5, 7\}$, $Max\_Iter \in \{25, 50\}$, and $LS\_Iter \in \{25, 50\}$. The results of this parameter setting indicate that values of $Max\_Iter{=}50$, $LS\_Iter{=}50$ and $rcl{=}5$ are the most suitable parameters.

5.3   Results

Our matheuristic approach executed on the selected instances shows that it keeps a stable performance mainly in small instances. This performance is due to the wide scalability of the problem that we solve and the construction of the initial subtours, trying to incorporate in each subtour the largest (see box-plots in Fig. 2).

Table 2 shows the results of the matheuristic approach proposed in this work (see Sect. 4) for CumVRP-hTW and CumVRP-sTW. In this table, column 1 reports the instance studied, columns 2 and 4 and columns 3 and 6 provide the cumulative cost values and the number of vehicles with which the tour can be traveled in CumVRP-hTW and CumVRP-sTW, respectively. Column 5 represents the cost of penalties due to delays of end of service, only valued for

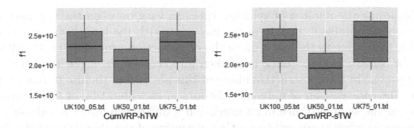

Fig. 2. Box-plot showing the f_1 values (*cumulative cost*) for CumVRP-hTW and CumVRP-sTW on PRPLib selected instances.

CumVRP-sTW. In the column (Gap (%)) the gap between both solutions (see column 2 and 4) is calculated according to: $100 \times (f_{1Col4} - f_{1Col2})/f_{1Col4}$, f_{1Col4} represents the best solution obtained in each instance. In this sense, it shows that the best results are obtained by solving CumVRP with soft time windows. A negative value in this column indicates that an improvement in terms of the objective function value is obtained.

Table 2. Computational results of the proposed matheuristic on PRPLib selected instances. We consider $\mu = 1800$ s and $P = 1$ cost/s.

Instance	MathGRASP					
	CumVRP-hTW		CumVRP-sTW			Gap (%)
	f_1	k	f_1	f_3	k	
UK10_01	3153462870	2	3153462870	0.000	2	0.000
UK15_01	6304836673	2	6189389516	0.000	2	−1.865
UK20_20	8625693080	3	8510155558	299.000	3	−2.507
UK25_01	6403951960	3	6401431234	0.000	3	−0.039
UK50_01	14863720450	7	14822031464	0.000	8	−0.281
UK75_01	19127115942	15	19001902452	846.002	14	−0.659
UK100_05	18568502490	23	18504497844	1269.003	21	−0.346
UK150_12	39788688093	21	39094971926	792.000	21	−1.774
UK200_01	36133585632	25	34569374470	144.030	25	−4.525

The results on the instances UK10_01, UK15_01, UK25_01, and UK50_01 does not show a reduction in the cumulative cost between CumVRP-hTW and CumVRP-sTW, because the time windows interval in these instances is very wide, and it is not necessary to violate the upper limit U_i. The results for UK20_20, UK75_01, UK100_05, UK150_12, and UK200_01 shows a minimization of cumulative cost incurring in several penalties values by allowing violations in the end times of services in some customers.

Regarding the number of vehicles, this can vary between the soft and hard variant of the problem, mainly in the instances with the largest number of customers, this is due to the fact that in the construction procedure in Algorithm 2 used for constructing subtours, it is taken into account the capacity of the vehicle. However, in the constructive phase of this algorithm, the use of randomness causes the construction of different subtours in each iteration of the algorithm. Thus, for the same instance in an execution a different number of subtours can be generated when compared to another execution of the algorithm, that implies the variation on the number of vehicles.

The results obtained show that when time window violations are permitted, the routes obtained have lower cumulative costs than problem with hard time windows is solved. Due to the fact that the emissions of greenhouse gases can be proportional to the cumulative cost, when this cost is reduced it also causes some dissatisfaction of the customers (in terms of satisfying the time window constraints), so it is possible to reduce the emissions.

The level of emissions reduction depends considerably on the attitude that a company shows in compromising its service process. In this sense, if the allowed delay time is very low or the penalties are very high, then it is not feasible to violate the time window. In addition, a company could estimate different penalties values P depending on how much each customer represents. Figure 3 shows the calculation of CO_2 emissions for each of the variants studied.

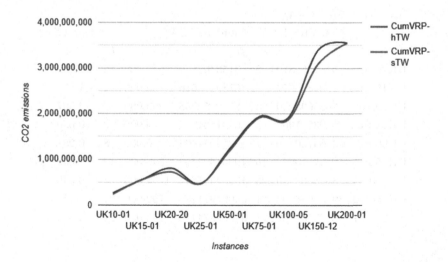

Fig. 3. Comparison of total CO_2 emissions values for CumVRP-hTW and CumVRP-hTW on the selected instances.

The calculation of emissions is done by using the following equation:

$$CO_2\, emissions\,(kg) = distance\, travelled(km)$$
$$\times payload(t) \qquad (9)$$
$$\times emission\, factor(kg\, CO_2e/t\, km)$$

where emission cost is obtained using the emission factor value of 0.41693 kg $CO_2e/t\, km$, averagely value for diesel-powered rigid vehicles weighted between 7.5 t and 17 t, suggested by DEFRA (2010) [32].

6 Conclusion and Future Research

In this work, we have investigated the Cumulative VRP with hard and soft time windows. For solving these problem variants, we have developed a matheuristic optimization approach that combines a Greedy Randomized Adaptive Search Procedure with the exact solution of the optimization model.

The results show that including soft time windows constraints, lead to significant reductions in environmental costs. In this sense, this consideration of the time windows might reflect better situations than hard time windows, especially considering dynamic changes in problem features. However, when considering the violation of a time window, a customer's dissatisfaction occurs, but despite this, there is a correct trade-off between time windows penalties and environmental related costs.

Our matheuristic approach shows that the quality of the solutions increase when each subtour is seen as a low complexity subproblem that can be solved by a mathematical programming approach.

Finally, as future work, we will propose a benchmark that encompasses novel features and new challenges for CumVRP with hard and soft time windows constraints. In addition, we propose to extend CumVRP with soft and hard constraints by considering fleets of heterogeneous vehicles.

Acknowledgments. This work has been partially supported by ANID-PFCHA/ Doctorado Nacional /2020-21200871 and CONICYT-PFCHA (Doctorado Nacional /2017-21171857), and in part by Proyectos de Línea de Investigación Regular (PI_LIR_2020_67, UTFSM) and Programa de Incentivo a la Iniciación Científica (PIIC, UTFSM). We are grateful to anonymous referees, whose valuable comments helped us to strongly improve the paper.

References

1. Sbihi, A., Eglese, R.W.: Combinatorial optimization and green logistics. Ann. Oper. Res. **175**(1), 159–175 (2010). https://doi.org/10.1007/s10479-009-0651-z
2. Sahin, B., Yilmaz, H., Ust, Y., Guneri, A.F., Gulsun, B.: An approach for analysing transportation costs and a case study. Eur. J. Oper. Res. **193**(1), 1–11 (2009)
3. Demir, E., Bektaş, T., Laporte, G.: A review of recent research on green road freight transportation. Eur. J. Oper. Res. **237**(3), 775–793 (2014)

4. Dantzig, G.B., Ramser, J.H.: The truck dispatching problem. Manag. Sci. **6**(1), 80–91 (1959)
5. Kara, İ., Kara, B.Y., Yetiş, M.K.: Cumulative vehicle routing problems. In: Vehicle Routing Problem, pp. 85–98. In-Teh (2008)
6. Kara, İ., Kara, B.Y., Yetis, M.K.: Energy minimizing vehicle routing problem. In: Dress, A., Xu, Y., Zhu, B. (eds.) COCOA 2007. LNCS, vol. 4616, pp. 62–71. Springer, Heidelberg (2007). https://doi.org/10.1007/978-3-540-73556-4_9
7. Singh, R.R., Gaur, D.R.: Cumulative VRP: a simplified model of green vehicle routing. In: Cinar, D., Gakis, K., Pardalos, P.M. (eds.) Sustainable Logistics and Transportation. SOIA, vol. 129, pp. 39–55. Springer, Cham (2017). https://doi.org/10.1007/978-3-319-69215-9_3
8. Solomon, M.M.: Algorithms for the vehicle routing and scheduling problems with time window constraints. Oper. Res. **35**(2), 254–265 (1987)
9. Desaulniers, G., Madsen, O.B.G., Ropke, S.: The vehicle routing problem with time windows (chap. 5). In: Vehicle Routing: Problems, Methods, and Applications, 2nd edn., pp. 119–159. SIAM (2014)
10. Kallehauge, B.: Formulations and exact algorithms for the vehicle routing problem with time windows. Comput. Oper. Res. **35**(7), 2307–2330 (2008). Part Special Issue: Includes selected papers presented at the ECCO 2004 European Conference on combinatorial Optimization
11. Fagerholt, K.: Ship scheduling with soft time windows: an optimisation based approach. Eur. J. Oper. Res. **131**(3), 559–571 (2001)
12. Bektaş, T., Ehmke, J.F., Psaraftis, H.N., Puchinger, J.: The role of operational research in green freight transportation. Eur. J. Oper. Res. **274**(3), 807–823 (2019)
13. Lin, C., Choy, K.L., Ho, G.T.S., Chung, S.H., Lam, H.Y.: Survey of green vehicle routing problem: past and future trends. Expert Syst. Appl. **41**(4, Part 1), 1118–1138 (2014)
14. Gaur, D.R., Singh, R.R.: Cumulative vehicle routing problem: a column generation approach. In: Ganguly, S., Krishnamurti, R. (eds.) CALDAM 2015. LNCS, vol. 8959, pp. 262–274. Springer, Cham (2015). https://doi.org/10.1007/978-3-319-14974-5_25
15. Laporte, G.: The vehicle routing problem: an overview of exact and approximate algorithms. Eur. J. Oper. Res. **59**(3), 345–358 (1992)
16. Gendreau, M., Potvin, J.-Y., et al.: Handbook of Metaheuristics, vol. 2. Springer, Cham (2010). https://doi.org/10.1007/978-3-319-91086-4
17. Cinar, D., Cayir Ervural, B., Gakis, K., Pardalos, P.M.: Constructive algorithms for the cumulative vehicle routing problem with limited duration. In: Cinar, D., Gakis, K., Pardalos, P.M. (eds.) Sustainable Logistics and Transportation. SOIA, vol. 129, pp. 57–86. Springer, Cham (2017). https://doi.org/10.1007/978-3-319-69215-9_4
18. Cinar, D., Gakis, K., Pardalos, P.M.: Reduction of co2 emissions in cumulative multi-trip vehicle routing problems with limited duration. Environ. Model. Assess. **20**(4), 273–284 (2015). https://doi.org/10.1007/s10666-014-9434-2
19. Ngueveu, S.U., Prins, C., Calvo, R.W.: An effective memetic algorithm for the cumulative capacitated vehicle routing problem. Comput. Oper. Res. **37**(11), 1877–1885 (2010). Metaheuristics for Logistics and Vehicle Routing
20. Nucamendi-Guillén, S., Angel-Bello, F., Martínez-Salazar, I., Cordero-Franco, A.E.: The cumulative capacitated vehicle routing problem: new formulations and iterated greedy algorithms. Expert Syst. Appl. **113**, 315–327 (2018)

21. Archetti, C., Speranza, M.G.: A survey on matheuristics for routing problems. EURO J. Comput. Optimiz. **2**(4), 223–246 (2014). https://doi.org/10.1007/s13675-014-0030-7
22. Sartori, C.S., Buriol, L.S.: A matheuristic approach to the pickup and delivery problem with time windows. In: Cerulli, R., Raiconi, A., Voß, S. (eds.) ICCL 2018. LNCS, vol. 11184, pp. 253–267. Springer, Cham (2018). https://doi.org/10.1007/978-3-030-00898-7_16
23. Lalla-Ruiz, E., Voß, S.: A POPMUSIC approach for the multi-depot cumulative capacitated vehicle routing problem. Optimiz. Lett. **14**, 671–691 (2019). https://doi.org/10.1007/s11590-018-1376-1
24. Keskin, M., Çatay, B.: A matheuristic method for the electric vehicle routing problem with time windows and fast chargers. Comput. Oper. Res. **100**, 172–188 (2018)
25. Grangier, P., Gendreau, M., Lehuédé, F., Rousseau, L.-M.: A matheuristic based on large neighborhood search for the vehicle routing problem with cross-docking. Comput. Oper. Res. **84**, 116–126 (2017)
26. Kramer, R., Subramanian, A., Vidal, T., Lucídio dos Anjos, F.C.: A matheuristic approach for the pollution-routing problem. Eur. J. Oper. Res. **243**(2), 523–539 (2015)
27. Lalla-Ruiz, E., Voß, S.: POPMUSIC as a matheuristic for the berth allocation problem. Ann. Math. Artif. Intell. **76**(1–2), 173–189 (2016). https://doi.org/10.1007/s10472-014-9444-4
28. Feo, T.A., Resende, M.G.C.: Greedy randomized adaptive search procedures. J. Global Optimiz. **6**(2), 109–133 (1995)
29. Sánchez, M.G., Gil, A.F., Castro, C.: Integrating a SMT solver based local search in ant colony optimization for solving RCMPSP. In: 2019 IEEE Latin American Conference on Computational Intelligence, LA-CCI, pp. 1–6 (2019)
30. Demir, E., Bektaş, T., Laporte, G.: An adaptive large neighborhood search heuristic for the pollution-routing problem. Eur. J. Oper. Res. **223**(2), 346–359 (2012)
31. Hutter, F., Hoos, H.H., Stützle, T.: Automatic algorithm configuration based on local search. In: Proceedings of the 22nd National Conference on Artificial Intelligence - Volume 2, AAAI 2007, pp. 1152–1157. AAAI Press (2007)
32. Food Statistics Pocketbook Defra and Ecosystems Evidence Plan. Department for environment. Food and Rural Affairs (2010)

Freight Distribution and City Logistics

Formulations of a Carsharing Pricing and Relocation Problem

Giovanni Pantuso[⊠] [ID]

Department of Mathematical Sciences, University of Copenhagen,
Universitetsparken 5, 2100 Copenhagen, Denmark
gp@math.ku.dk

Abstract. This article presents and compares two formulations for a pricing-based carsharing relocation problem. Given a target planning period, the problem consists of deciding simultaneously the price of carsharing rides between different zones of the city and the relocations of vehicles to perform to better serve demand. Customers response to pricing decisions are captured by utility functions. Results illustrate that the more compact of the two formulations is superior in terms of ease of solution and scalability.

Keywords: Carsharing · Relocation · Pricing

1 Introduction

The increase in car ownership and usage, coupled with high dependency on private vehicles and low occupancy rates, have determined serious traffic congestion problems in many cities of the world [10] resulting pollution and poor urban air quality. Improvements of public transport [25] and road pricing measures [9,13] have, to a large extent, failed to provide sustainable solutions [2,10,21]. In this context, carsharing has emerged as a viable alternative, linked to a decrease in congestion [12], pollution, land used [26] and transport costs [14,23].

Nevertheless, the attractiveness of carsharing, and its potential to replace car ownership, is heavily dependent on the actual availability and proximity of vehicles to users and its cost [6]. Ensuring the necessary levels of service in an economically viable manner poses novel complex planning problems to carsharing operators (CSOs). Failure to deal with this complexity results in early failure such as those reported in [1,11,27]. The focal problem in this article is that of pricing carsharing rides and ensuring a spatial distribution of the fleet that complies with demand.

A central challenge faced in such systems is that one-way rentals, coupled with demand tides and oscillations [30,31], create frequent imbalances in the distribution of vehicles. This results in an accumulation of vehicles in low-demand zones, and vehicle shortage in high-demand zones [4,6] with levels of service dropping accordingly. Failure to ensure a spatial distribution of vehicles consistent with demand determines unreliable levels of service.

© Springer Nature Switzerland AG 2020
E. Lalla-Ruiz et al. (Eds.): ICCL 2020, LNCS 12433, pp. 295–310, 2020.
https://doi.org/10.1007/978-3-030-59747-4_19

The research literature is slowly catching up and offering analytics methods for facing such challenges. Methods have been proposed for planning staff-based relocation activities [3,4,6–8,18–20,24,31], possibly combined with recharging [15] (see also the surveys [17,23]). These methods, typically based on optimization techniques, employ a mathematical problem (e.g., a MILP problem) to decide which vehicles should be relocated and where, and possibly which operators should perform the relocations. Methods have also been proposed for pricing carsharing services [16] and for inducing user-based relocations through pricing strategies [4,28,29].

This article addresses the problem of simultaneously setting pricing and deciding relocation activities. First, it expands a carsharing pricing formulation provided by [16] to account for relocation activites. Second, it proposes a pure IP reformulation. Finally, it compares the two formulations in terms of ease of solution. The use of the two formulations is envisaged in the context of scenario analysis or simulation.

In Sect. 2 we provide a brief description of the problem followed by modeling assumptions. In Sect. 3 we present an extensive formulation in a discursive manner in order to clarify all details of the problem. In Sect. 4 we present a compact formulation. In Sect. 5 we describe a computational study and its results. Finally, we draw conclusions in Sect. 6.

2   Problem Overview and Modeling Assumptions

Given a *target period* representing a portion of the day, e.g., a number of hours in the afternoon or morning, the distribution of vehicles at the time of planning, and the cumulative transport demand outlook for the target period, we address the problem of determining the prices to offer in the target period and the relocations to perform in preparation for the target period. Prices must be set taking into account customers preferences and the competition of alternative transport services (e.g., bus, metro, bicycle) and can vary with the origin and destination of the carsharing ride. The following assumptions are made.

A1 The price is made of a *drop-off fee*, which depends on the origin and destination of the rental, plus a per-minute fee which is identical to all zones. This is consistent with current pricing schemes in a number of carsharing services[1]. The drop-off fee may be negative to encourage desired movements of cars.

A2 The CSO can adjust the drop-off fee during the day, e.g., in response to demand waves.

A3 The CSO is able to inform customers about the current price from their location to every other zone, prior to rentals.

A4 Alternative transport services (e.g., public transport and personal bicycles) have unlimited capacity.

---

[1] See e.g., the pricing model recently adopted by Car2Go https://www.car2go.com/IT/en/milano/costs/.

A5 A customer chooses exactly one transport service among the available ones (i.e., the market is closed) and, particularly, the one that gives them the highest utility.

A6 An outlook of the cumulative demand of transport between different zones of the city is available (e.g., a forecast point or historical realization).

A7 Customers traveling with shared cars drive directly from their origin to their destination zone.

A8 Both the CSO and the customers are aware of all available transport services and of their characteristics (e.g., price, travel time and waiting time). Such characteristics are identical for all customers.

3 Extensive Formulation (F1)

Consider a urban area represented by a finite set $\mathcal{I}$ of zones and a CSO offering a finite set of shared vehicles $\mathcal{V}$. Before the beginning of the target period, the CSO is to decide the drop-off fee between each pair of zones and the relocations to perform to better serve demand in the target period.

At the time of planning, vehicles $v \in \mathcal{V}$ are geographically dispersed in the urban area as the result of previous rentals. Let parameter X_{vi} be equal to 1 if vehicle $v \in \mathcal{V}$ is initially in zone $i \in \mathcal{I}$, 0 otherwise, with $\sum_{i \in \mathcal{I}} X_{vi} = 1$ for all $v \in \mathcal{V}$. Let decision variable x_{vij} be equal to 1 if vehicle $v \in \mathcal{V}$ is relocated from zone $i \in \mathcal{I}$ to zone $j \in \mathcal{I}$, 0 otherwise. A vehicle can be relocated at most one time, that is

$$\sum_{j \in \mathcal{I}} x_{vij} \leq X_{vi} \qquad \forall v \in \mathcal{V}, i \in \mathcal{I} \tag{1a}$$

Let decision variable z_{vi} be equal to 1 if vehicle v is available for rental at zone i in the target period, 0 otherwise. It must hold that

$$z_{vi} = X_{vi} - \sum_{j \in \mathcal{I}} x_{vij} + \sum_{j \in \mathcal{I}} x_{vji} \qquad \forall v \in \mathcal{V}, i \in \mathcal{I} \tag{1b}$$

Let $\mathcal{L}$ be a finite set of drop-off fees the CSO is considering, and let decision variable λ_{ijl} be equal to 1 if fee l is applied between i and j, 0 otherwise. Only one drop-off fee can be selected between each pair of zones

$$\sum_{l \in \mathcal{L}} \lambda_{ijl} = 1 \qquad \forall i, j \in \mathcal{I} \tag{1c}$$

The city counts a set $\mathcal{A}$ of alternative transport services such as metro, bus and bicycle. Let decision variable p_{vij} be the price of service $v \in \mathcal{V} \cup \mathcal{A}$ between zones i and j. The price of a carsharing ride between i and j is

$$p_{vij} = P_v^V T_{vij}^{CS} + \sum_{l \in \mathcal{L}} L_l \lambda_{ijl} \qquad \forall v \in \mathcal{V}, i, j \in \mathcal{I} \tag{1d}$$

where parameter P_v^V is the per-minute fee of vehicle $v \in \mathcal{V}$, T_{vij}^{CS} the driving time between zones i and j and L_l the value of drop-off fee at level $l \in \mathcal{L}$. Instead, the price of alternative services is set as

$$p_{vij} = P_{vij} \qquad \forall v \in \mathcal{A}, i, j \in \mathcal{I} \tag{1e}$$

where parameter P_{vij} is the price of alternative service $v \in \mathcal{A}$ between i and $j \in \mathcal{I}$.

Let $\mathcal{K}$ be the set of customers, with $\mathcal{K}_i \subseteq \mathcal{K}$ being the set of customers traveling from zone $i \in \mathcal{I}$ and $\mathcal{K}_{ij} \subseteq \mathcal{K}_i$ the set of customers traveling from $i \in \mathcal{I}$ to $j \in \mathcal{I}$ in the target period. Each customer is uniquely characterized by a utility function $F_k(p_{vij}, \pi_{vij}^1, \ldots, \pi_{vij}^N)$ of the price p_{vij} and a number of characteristics $\pi_{vij}^1, \ldots, \pi_{vij}^N$ of transport service $v \in \mathcal{V} \cup \mathcal{A}$ between zones i and $j \in \mathcal{I}$ (e.g., travel and waiting time), and a random term $\tilde{\xi}_{kv}$ representing the portion of the preferences of customer k that the CSO is not able to describe by $F_k(\cdot)$. Any distribution for $\tilde{\xi}_{kv}$ is valid, leading in turn to different choice models such as the Logit model when $\tilde{\xi}_{kv}$ follows an extreme value distribution (see [5]). Let u_{ijkv} be a decision variable representing the utility obtained by customer $k \in \mathcal{K}$ when moving from i to $j \in \mathcal{I}$ using service $v \in \mathcal{V} \cup \mathcal{A}$. The utility is determined by

$$u_{ijkv} = F_k(p_{vij}, \pi_{vij}^1, \ldots, \pi_{vij}^N) + \xi_{kv} \qquad \forall i, j \in \mathcal{I}, k \in \mathcal{K}_{ij}, v \in \mathcal{V} \cup \mathcal{A} \tag{1f}$$

where ξ_{kv} is a realization of $\tilde{\xi}_{kv}$. Constraints (1f) are linear if $F_k(\cdot)$ is linear in p_{vij}.

Let binary variable y_{ikv} be equal to 1 if service $v \in \mathcal{V} \cup \mathcal{A}$ is offered to customer $k \in \mathcal{K}_i$, 0 otherwise. Alternative services $v \in \mathcal{A}$ are always offered to customers whenever they are available at all, that is

$$y_{ikv} = Y_{vi} \qquad \forall i \in \mathcal{I}, k \in \mathcal{K}_i, v \in \mathcal{A} \tag{1g}$$

where parameter Y_{vi} is equal to 1 if alternative service v is available in zone i, 0 otherwise. Conversely, a shared car $v \in \mathcal{V}$ can be offered to customers in zone i whenever it is physically available at i, that is

$$y_{ikv} \leq z_{iv} \qquad \forall i \in \mathcal{I}, k \in \mathcal{K}_i, v \in \mathcal{V} \tag{1h}$$

Let decision variable w_{ijkv} be equal to 1 if customer $k \in \mathcal{K}_{ij}$ chooses service $v \in \mathcal{V} \cup \mathcal{A}$, 0 otherwise. A customer will choose exactly one service

$$\sum_{v \in \mathcal{V} \cup \mathcal{A}} w_{ijkv} = 1 \qquad \forall i, j \in \mathcal{I}, k \in \mathcal{K}_{ij} \tag{1i}$$

And a service can be chosen only if it is offered to the customer

$$w_{ijkv} \leq y_{ikv} \qquad \forall i, j \in \mathcal{I}, k \in \mathcal{K}_{ij}, v \in \mathcal{V} \cup \mathcal{A} \tag{1j}$$

Among the available services, the customer will chose the one yielding the highest utility. Therefore, for a given zone $i \in \mathcal{I}$, let decision variable ν_{ivwk} be equal to 1 if both services v and w in $\mathcal{V} \cup \mathcal{A}$ are available to customer $k \in \mathcal{K}_i$, 0 otherwise, and decision variable μ_{ijvwk} be equal to one if service $v \in \mathcal{V} \cup \mathcal{A}$ yields a greater utility than service $w \in \mathcal{V} \cup \mathcal{A}$ to customer $k \in \mathcal{K}_{ij}$ moving from i to j, 0 otherwise. The following constraints state that ν_{ivwk} is equal to one when both services v and w are available

$$y_{ikv} + y_{ikw} \leq 1 + \nu_{ivwk} \qquad \forall i \in \mathcal{I}, k \in \mathcal{K}_i, v, w \in \mathcal{V} \cup \mathcal{A}, \tag{1k}$$

$$\nu_{ivwk} \leq y_{ikv} \qquad \forall i \in \mathcal{I}, k \in \mathcal{K}_i, v, w \in \mathcal{V} \cup \mathcal{A}, \tag{1l}$$

$$\nu_{ivwk} \leq y_{ikw} \qquad \forall i \in \mathcal{I}, k \in \mathcal{K}_i, v, w \in \mathcal{V} \cup \mathcal{A}. \tag{1m}$$

A service is chosen only if it yields the highest utility

$$w_{ijkv} \leq \mu_{ijvwk} \qquad \forall i, j \in \mathcal{I}, k \in \mathcal{K}_{ij}, v, w \in \mathcal{V} \cup \mathcal{A} \tag{1n}$$

that is, as soon as μ_{ijvwk} is set to 0 for some index w, w_{ijkv} is forced to 0 and service v is not chosen by customer k on i-j. The following constraints ensure that decision variable μ_{ijvwk} takes the correct value according to the utility

$$M_{ijk}\nu_{ivwk} - 2M_{ijk} \leq u_{ijkv} - u_{ijkw} - M_{ijk}\mu_{ijvwk}$$
$$\forall i, j \in \mathcal{I}, k \in \mathcal{K}_{ij}, v, w \in \mathcal{V} \cup \mathcal{A} \tag{1o}$$

and

$$u_{ijkv} - u_{ijkw} - M_{ijk}\mu_{ijvwk} \leq (1 - \nu_{ivwk})M_{ijk}$$
$$\forall i, j \in \mathcal{I}, k \in \mathcal{K}_{ij}, v, w \in \mathcal{V} \cup \mathcal{A} \tag{1p}$$

where constant M_{ijk} represents the greatest difference in utility between two services between i and $j \in \mathcal{I}$ for customer $k \in \mathcal{K}_{ij}$, that is $M_{ijk} \geq |u_{ijkv} - u_{ijkw}|, \forall v, w \in \mathcal{V} \cup \mathcal{A}$. Constraints (1o)–(1p) work as follows. When both services v and w are available ($\nu_{ivwk} = 1$) and $u_{ijkv} > u_{ijkw}$, (1p) forces μ_{ijvwk} to take value 1, while (1o) reduces to $0 \leq u_{ijkv} - u_{ijkw}$. When both service v and w are available and $u_{ijkv} < u_{ijkw}$, (1o) forces μ_{ijvwk} to take value 0, while (1p) reduces to $0 \geq u_{ijkv} - u_{ijkw}$. When one of the two services is not available ($\nu_{ivwk} = 0$), constraints (1o)–(1p) are satisfied irrespective of the value of μ_{ijvwk}. In case of ties ($u_{ijkv} = u_{ijkw}$) we impose

$$\mu_{ijvwk} + \mu_{ijvwk} \leq 1 \qquad \forall i, j \in \mathcal{I}, k \in \mathcal{K}_{ij}, v, w \in \mathcal{V} \cup \mathcal{A} \tag{1q}$$

A service can be preferred only if offered

$$\mu_{ijvwk} \leq y_{ikv} \qquad \forall i, j \in \mathcal{I}, k \in \mathcal{K}_{ij}, v, w \in \mathcal{V} \cup \mathcal{A} \tag{1r}$$

Let decision variable α_{ijkvl} be equal to 1 if fare l is applied between i and j and customer k chooses shared car $v \in \mathcal{V}$, 0 otherwise. The following constraints ensure the relationship between λ_{ijl} and w_{ijkv} and α_{ijkvl}

$$\lambda_{ijl} + w_{ijkv} \leq 1 + \alpha_{ijkvl} \qquad \forall v \in \mathcal{V}, i, j \in \mathcal{I}, k \in \mathcal{K}_{ij}, l \in \mathcal{L} \tag{1s}$$

$$\alpha_{ijkvl} \leq \lambda_{ijl} \qquad \forall v \in \mathcal{V}, i, j \in \mathcal{I}, k \in \mathcal{K}_{ij}, l \in \mathcal{L} \tag{1t}$$

$$\alpha_{ijkvl} \leq w_{ijkv} \qquad \forall v \in \mathcal{V}, i, j \in \mathcal{I}, k \in \mathcal{K}_{ij}, l \in \mathcal{L} \tag{1u}$$

Each car $v \in \mathcal{V}$ can accommodate only one customer. If more than one customers wish to use car v, the car is taken by the first customer arriving at the car. Assuming that customers are indexed according to their arrival time at the car, i.e., customer k arrives before $k+1$, we impose that a vehicle is offered to a customer only if it is offered also to the customer arriving before them (who perhaps did not take it), that is:

$$y_{ikv} \leq y_{i(k-1)v} \qquad \forall i \in \mathcal{I}, k \in \mathcal{K}_i, v \in \mathcal{V} \tag{1v}$$

A vehicle becomes unavailable for a customer if any customer has arrived before them and rented the car, that is:

$$z_{iv} - y_{ikv} = \sum_{j \in \mathcal{I}} \sum_{q \in \mathcal{K}_{ij}:q<k} w_{ijqv} \qquad \forall i \in \mathcal{I}, k \in \mathcal{K}_i, v \in \mathcal{V} \tag{1w}$$

that is, if car v is in zone i ($z_{iv} = 1$), but it is not offered to customer k ($y_{ikv} = 0$) we obtain

$$1 = \sum_{j \in \mathcal{I}} \sum_{q \in \mathcal{K}_{ij}:q<k} w_{ijqv}$$

meaning that one customer has arrived before k and rented the car. On the other hand, if the car is offered to customer k, ($y_{ikv} = 1$), then it must be in zone i ($z_{iv} = 1$ – see (1h)), and we obtain

$$0 = \sum_{j \in \mathcal{I}} \sum_{q \in \mathcal{K}_{ij}:q<k} w_{ijqv}$$

meaning that no customer arriving before k has taken the car. The same equality holds if the vehicle is not available at all ($z_{iv} = 0$ and $y_{ijkv} = 0$).

The CSO maximizes their profit by means of the following objective function

$$\max \sum_{v \in \mathcal{V}} \sum_{(i,j) \in \mathcal{I} \times \mathcal{I}} \left(P_v^V T_{vij}^{CS} - C_{vij}^U \right) \sum_{k \in \mathcal{K}_{ij}} w_{ijkv} \tag{1x}$$

$$+ \sum_{v \in \mathcal{V}} \sum_{(i,j) \in \mathcal{I} \times \mathcal{I}} \sum_{k \in \mathcal{K}_{ij}} \sum_{l \in \mathcal{L}} L_{ijl} \alpha_{ijkvl} \tag{1y}$$

$$- \sum_{v \in \mathcal{V}} \sum_{(i,j) \in \mathcal{I} \times \mathcal{I}} C_{vij}^R x_{vij} \tag{1z}$$

where C_{vij}^U is the cost born by the CSO when vehicle v is rented between i and j and (1x) represents the net revenue generated by the per-minute fee, (1y) represents the revenue generated by the drop-off fee, C_{vij}^R is the cost of relocating vehicle v from i to j and (1z) represents the total relocation cost.

Therefore, F1 consists of objective function (1x)–(1z) subject to (1a)–(1w). F1 is a MILP when a realization of $\tilde{\xi}$ is known and $F_k(\cdot)$ is linear in p_{vij}. However, it can be treated as a stochastic program if $\tilde{\xi}$ explicitly dealt with as a random variable.

4 Compact Formulation (F2)

Given a realization ξ_{kv} of $\tilde{\xi}_{kv}$, e.g., in a scenario analysis, a compact reformulation of the problem can be derived by preprocessing customers preferences. This formulation has a double advantage: its size is in general smaller than F1, and it does not require the utility function to be linear in the price.

Algorithm 1. Pseudo-code for the generation of requests.

$\mathcal{R} = \emptyset$

for $i, j \in \mathcal{I}$ and $k \in \mathcal{K}_{ij}$ **do**

  if $\exists l \in \mathcal{L} : u_{ijkv} > u_{ijka}$ for $v \in \mathcal{V}$ and $a \in \mathcal{A}$ **then**

    Create request r with $k(r) = k$, $i(r) = i$, $j(r) = j$

    Set $l(r) = \arg\max_{l \in \mathcal{L}} : u_{ijkv} > u_{ijka}$ for $v \in \mathcal{V}$ and $a \in \mathcal{A}$

    $\mathcal{R} \leftarrow \mathcal{R} \cup \{r\}$

  end if

end for

We introduce the concept of a request. A request represents a customer who wishes to use carsharing for moving from its origin to its destination. Let $\mathcal{R}$ be the set requests. The set $\mathcal{R}$ is generated as follows: for each customer $k \in \mathcal{K}$ for which there exists at least one drop-off level $l \in \mathcal{L}$ such that the customer would prefer carsharing to alternative transport services (that is, for which $u_{ijkv} > u_{ijkw}$ with $v \in \mathcal{V}$ and $w \in \mathcal{A}$) add a request r to $\mathcal{R}$. Set $i(r)$, $j(r)$ and $k(r)$ as the origin, destination and customer associated with request r, respectively, and $l(r)$ the highest drop-off fee at which customer $k(r)$ would prefer carsharing to other services. Note, that customer $k(r)$ would still prefer carsharing at any drop-off fee lower than $l(r)$ (under the reasonable assumption that the customer is sensitive to price). For each $r \in \mathcal{R}$ let $R_{vrl} = P_v^V T_{v,i(r),j(r)}^{CS} - C_{v,i(r),j(r)}^{U} + L_l$, for $l \leq l(r)$, be the profit generated if request r is satisfied by vehicle v with drop-off fee l. Let $C_{vi}^R = C_{vji}^R$ if v is initially in $j \neq i$, 0 otherwise, be the cost of making vehicle v available at i. Let $\mathcal{R}_r = \{\rho \in \mathcal{R} : i(\rho) = i(r), k(\rho) < k(r)\}$ be the set of requests which have a precedence over r. Let $\mathcal{R}_{ij} = \{r \in \mathcal{R} : i(r) = i, j(r) = j\}$. Let $\mathcal{L}_r = \{l \in \mathcal{L} : l \leq l(r)\}$. Finally, let decision variable y_{vrl} be equal to 1 if request r is satisfied by vehicle v at level l, 0 otherwise. Let z_{vi} if vehicle v is made available at zone i, 0 otherwise. Finally, let λ_{ijl} be equal to 1 if drop-off level l is applied between i and j, 0 otherwise. Formulation F2 is hence

$$\max \sum_{r \in \mathcal{R}} \sum_{v \in \mathcal{V}} \sum_{l \in \mathcal{L}_r} R_{vrl} y_{vrl} - \sum_{v \in \mathcal{V}} \sum_{i \in \mathcal{I}} C_{vi}^R z_{vi} \tag{2a}$$

$$\sum_{v \in \mathcal{V}} \sum_{l \in \mathcal{L}_r} y_{vrl} \leq 1 \qquad\qquad r \in \mathcal{R} \tag{2b}$$

$$\sum_{r \in \mathcal{R}} \sum_{l \in \mathcal{L}_r} y_{vrl} \leq 1 \qquad\qquad v \in \mathcal{V} \tag{2c}$$

$$\sum_{i \in \mathcal{I}} z_{vi} = 1 \qquad\qquad\qquad v \in \mathcal{V} \quad (2\text{d})$$

$$\sum_{l \in \mathcal{L}_{r_1}} y_{v,r_1,l} - z_{v,i(r_1)} + \sum_{r_2 \in \mathcal{R}_{r_1}} \sum_{l \in \mathcal{L}_{r_2}} y_{v,r_2,l} \le 0 \qquad r_1 \in \mathcal{R}, v \in \mathcal{V}$$

$$y_{v,r_1,l_1} \ge \lambda_{i(r_1),j(r_j),l_1} + z_{v,i(r_1)} \qquad\qquad (2\text{e})$$

$$- \sum_{r_2 \in \mathcal{R}_{r_1}} \sum_{l_2 \in \mathcal{L}_{r_2}} y_{v,r_2,l_2} - \sum_{v_1 \in \mathcal{V}: v_1 \neq v} y_{v_1,r_1,l_1} - 1 \quad r_1 \in \mathcal{R}, v \in \mathcal{V}, l_1 \in \mathcal{L}_{r_1} \quad (2\text{f})$$

$$\sum_{l \in \mathcal{L}} \lambda_{ijl} = 1 \qquad\qquad\qquad i \in \mathcal{I}, j \in \mathcal{J} \quad (2\text{g})$$

$$\sum_{v \in \mathcal{V}} y_{vrl} \le \lambda_{i(r),j(r),l} \qquad\qquad r \in \mathcal{R}, l \in \mathcal{L}_r \quad (2\text{h})$$

$$y_{vrl} \in \{0,1\} \qquad\qquad r \in \mathcal{R}, v \in \mathcal{V}, l \in \mathcal{L}_r \quad (2\text{i})$$

$$z_{vi} \in \{0,1\} \qquad\qquad\qquad i \in \mathcal{I}, v \in \mathcal{V} \quad (2\text{j})$$

$$\lambda_{ijl} \in \{0,1\} \qquad\qquad i \in \mathcal{I}, j \in \mathcal{I}, l \in \mathcal{L}. \quad (2\text{k})$$

The objective function (2a) represents the revenue obtained by car rentals minus the cost of relocating vehicles. Constraints (2b) ensure that each request is satisfied at most once and constraints (2c) that each vehicle satisfies at most one request. Constraints (2d) ensure that a vehicle is available in exactly one zone. Constraints (2e) state that a request r_1 can be satisfied by vehicle v only if the vehicle is in zone $i(r_1)$ and the vehicle has not been taken by a customer arriving at the vehicle before $k(r_1)$ (a lower index k). Constraints (2f) state that a request r_1 must be satisfied at level l_1 by vehicle v if the fare level l_1 has been selected and the vehicle is available at $i(r_1)$, unless the car has been used by a customer with a higher priority, or r_1 has been satisfied by another vehicle. Constraints (2g) state that for each i and j only one drop-off fee can be set. Finally, constraints (2h) states that a request can be satisfied at level l only if fare l is applied to all customers traveling between i and j.

5   Computational Study

Formulations F1 and F2 include a number of arbitrary elements subject to uncertainty, such as customers unknown preferences ξ_{kv}, their location and destination. As such, the envisaged usage of F1 and F2 is within a simulator, scenario analysis or as a component of a larger stochastic program, where different scenarios of the uncertain elements are assessed. Therefore, the scope of the computational study is to compare the two formulations on the case study illustrated in Sect. 5.1 in terms of solve time, percentage of problems solved, tightness of their LP relaxation and size. Results are presented in Sect. 5.2 and example solutions are presented in Sect. 5.3.

5.1   Case Study

To compare the two formulation we use a case study that replicates the carsharing system in the city of Milan. We assume the decision maker is a CSO with a homogeneous fleet $\mathcal{V} = \{1, \ldots, V\}$, servicing customers $\mathcal{K} = \{1, \ldots, K\}$. The alternative transport services are *public transport* (PT – bus and metro) and *bicycles* (B). Therefore we set $\mathcal{A} = \{PT, B\}$. A discretization of the business area of the city of Milan into ten zones is provided by [16], thus $\mathcal{I} = \{1, \ldots, 10\}$.

To each vehicle v we randomly assign an initial zone i (parameter X_{vi}). Similarly, we randomly partition customers into sets $\mathcal{K}_i$ and then further into sets $\mathcal{K}_{ij}$. Each customer k is characterized by a variant of the utility function provided by [16] and derived from [22]. The function is linear in the price thus F1, for a given ξ, is a MILP. For each customer $k \in \mathcal{K}$ traveling between i and j with transport service v, the utility can be stated as (3).

$$F_k(p_{vij}, T^{CS}_{vij}, T^{PT}_{vij}, T^{B}_{vij}, T^{Walk}_{vkij}, T^{Wait}_{vij}) = \beta^P_k p_{vij} + \beta^{CS}_k T^{CS}_{vij}$$

$$+\beta^{PT}_k T^{PT}_{vij} + \tau(T^B_{vij})\beta^B_k T^B_{vij} + \tau(T^{Walk}_{vij})\beta^{Walk}_k T^{Walk}_{vij} + \beta^{Wait}_k T^{Wait}_{vij} \quad (3)$$

where

- T^{CS}_{vij} is the time spent riding a shared car between i and j when using service v. This quantity is strictly positive only when v is a carsharing service, otherwise it is 0.
- T^{PT}_{vij} is the time spent in public transport between i and j when using service v. This quantity is strictly positive only when v is PT, otherwise it is 0.
- T^B_{vij} is the time spent riding a bicycle between i and j when using service v. This quantity is strictly positive only when v is B, otherwise it is 0.
- T^{Walk}_{vkij} is the walking time necessary for customer k to move with transport service v between i and j. This includes the walking time to the nearest service (e.g., shared car or bus stop), between connecting means (e.g., when switching between bus and metro to reach the final destination), and from to the final destination.
- T^{Wait}_{vij} is the total waiting time when using service v between i and j, and includes the waiting time for the service (e.g., bus or metro) as well as for connection.

The function $\tau(t) = \lceil \frac{t}{5} \rceil$ allows us to model the utility of cycling and walking as a piece-wise linear function: the utility of walking and cycling decreases faster as the walking and cycling time increases. Coefficients β^P_k, β^{CS}_k, β^{PT}_k, β^B_k, β^{Walk}_k and β^{Wait}_k represent the sensitivity of customer k to price, carsharing ride time, time spent in public transport service, cycling time, walking and waiting time, respectively.

For each (i, j) pair [16] provide a specification in minutes of the above mentioned T-parameters calculated on the actual services in Milan, as well as base values for the β coefficients. Particularly, they set $\beta^{CS} = -1$, $\beta^{PT} = -2$, $\beta^B = -2.5$, $\beta^{Walk} = -3$ and $\beta^{Wait} = -6$ and $\beta^P = -188.33$ if a customer belongs to the *lower-middle class* or $\beta^P = -70.63$ if a customer belongs to the *upper-middle class.* In order to create K unique customers, we characterize each customer by a perturbation of the β coefficients provided by [16]. Particularly, β_k^P will be uniformly drawn in $[-188.33, -70.63]$ in order to obtain customers between the upper- and lower-middle class and the remaining β coefficients will be uniformly drawn in $[0.8\beta, 1.2\beta]$, where β is the value provided by [16]. As an example, for each k we will draw β_k^{PT} in $[-1.6, -2.4]$.

The price of a bicycle ride is set to $P_{Bij} = 0$ for all (i, j) pairs. Based on current prices in Milan we set $P_{PT,ij} = 2$ (in Euro – €) for all (i, j) and $P_v^V = $ €0.265 corresponding to the average carsharing per-minute fee in Milan. The drop-off fees considered are €−2,−1,0,1, and 2 in order to include the possibility that the company provides a bonus for the desired movements of cars. The relocation cost C_{vij}^R represents the cost of the fuel necessary for a ride between i and j (we assume Fiat 500 cars with classical combustion engine and consumption of $0.043l/h$) and the per-minute salary of the driver multiplied by the driving time. The fuel cost is calculated assuming an average speed of 50km/h and a fuel price of 1.60 €/l. The per-minute salary of the driver is calculated as the average of the last four retribution levels in the Italian national collective contract for logistics services valid at October 1st 2019[2] and amounts to approximately €0.11 (assuming 26 working days per month and 8 working hours). This amount does not include elements such as seniority and night shifts thus most likely underestimates the real per-minute salary. The cost C_{vij}^U is set equal to the fuel necessary for a ride between i and j.

Finally, realizations of $\tilde{\xi}_{kv}$ are independently drawn from a Gumbel (Extreme Value type I) distribution with mean 0 and standard deviation σ calculated as the empirical standard deviation of $U_{ijkv} = F_k(p_{vij}, T_{vij}^{CS}, T_{vij}^{PT}, T_{vij}^B, T_{vij}^{Walk}, T_{vij}^{Wait})$ for all $i, j \in \mathcal{I}, v \in \mathcal{V} \cup \mathcal{A}, k \in \mathcal{K}_{ij}$.

We solve a set of small instances with $V \in \{20, 35, 50\}$ and $K \in \{50, 75, 100\}$ and a set of medium instances with $V \in \{50, 75, 100\}$ and $K \in \{200, 300\}$. For each combination of V and K we randomly generate five instances (each of the five instances will be different in terms of position and characteristics of the customers and distribution of vehicles).

5.2 Results

Problems are solved with Cplex 12.10 on a machine equipped with CPU 2×2.4 GHz AMD Opteron 2431 6 core and 24 GB RAM. A time limit of 360 s is set on all runs.

Table 1 reports the average solve time and percentage of problems solved for the small and medium instances. The time required to generate requests for F2 has not been included as it is in the order of fractions of a second and therefore negligible in our context. Already on the small instances it can be observed that F2 is superior to F1. F2 solves all problems to optimality (i.e., within the default Cplex 0.01% tolerance) in at most 2.635 s on average, while F1 solves only all the smallest instances and, also in that case, it spends a significantly

---

[2] https://www.lavoro-economia.it/ccnl/ccnl.aspx?c=328.

Table 1. Average solve time [sec] and percentage of problems solved for the small instances. The symbol "–" indicates that the solution process failed for excessive consumption of memory resources.

V	K	Time [sec]		Solved [%]	
		F1	F2	F1	F2
20	50	67.485	0.465	100	100
20	75	187.209	0.506	80	100
20	100	309.379	0.658	40	100
35	50	342.699	0.784	20	100
35	75	360.953	1.230	0	100
35	100	362.098	1.771	0	100
50	50	361.400	1.432	0	100
50	75	361.060	2.048	0	100
50	100	363.038	2.635	0	100
50	200	–	6.763	–	100
50	300	–	13.680	–	100
75	200	368.963	10.964	0	100
75	300	397.119	18.955	0	100
100	200	384.174	19.546	0	100
100	300	376.794	34.848	0	100

higher amount of time compared to F2. On the medium instances F1 does not solve any of the problems, and in a number of cases the solution process fails due to an excessive use of memory resources. On the same instances, F2 solves all problems to optimality with an average solution time much smaller than the allocated time limit.

The better performance of F2 is motivated by the tightness of its LP relaxation and its compact size. Regarding the quality of the LP relaxation, Table 2 reports the optimal objective value of the five randomly generated instances with $V = 20$ and $K = 50$ (the only instance size for which F1 solved all instances to optimality – see Table 1) together with the optimal objective value of the LP relaxations of F1 and F2. It can be noticed that F2 has a very strong LP relaxation as its optimal objective value corresponds to that of the IP formulation on all 5 instances in Table 2. At the same time, the LP relaxation of F1 provides a bound which is approximately from two to four times the optimal objective value. For the remaining instances not shown in Table 2, the LP gap for formulation F2 is zero on all the small instances, while on the medium instances it is zero for 24 of the 30 instances. For the remaining 6 instances the average LP gap is 0.018%, the maximum is 0.224% and the standard deviation is 0.052%. However, despite the relatively small LP gap, the solution to the LP relaxation is highly fractional, with limited chances obtaining the optimal solution by means of a simple rounding procedure.

The size of the two formulations also explains the different performances. The average size of the instances is reported in Table 3. The table illustrates how the size of F1 is orders of magnitude larger than the size of F2. Among the reasons for the significant different in size there is the fact that the number of requests is typically much smaller than the number of customers, and that most of the binary variables used to capture customer choices in F1 are replaced by a preprocessing phase in F2.

Table 2. Optimal objective value compared to the optimal objective value of the LP relaxations for the instances with $V = 20$ and $K = 50$.

Instance	V	K	Optimal objective value	LP objective value	
				F1	F2
1	20	50	53.58	124.22	53.58
2	20	50	40.64	128.12	40.64
3	20	50	25.94	117.19	25.94
4	20	50	25.94	119.35	25.94
5	20	50	38.44	124.75	38.44

Table 3. Average size of the instances in 10^4 variables/constraints.

V	K	# Variables		# Binary		# Constraints	
		F1	F2	F1	F2	F1	F2
20	50	5.24	0.17	5.14	0.17	19.48	0.16
20	75	7.87	0.21	7.72	0.21	29.67	0.22
20	100	10.41	0.25	10.21	0.25	39.63	0.27
35	50	14.10	0.26	13.94	0.26	53.74	0.26
35	75	21.22	0.34	20.97	0.34	81.61	0.37
35	100	28.13	0.41	27.79	0.41	108.72	0.46
50	50	27.25	0.35	27.01	0.35	104.92	0.36
50	75	41.04	0.46	40.68	0.46	159.12	0.51
50	100	54.41	0.56	53.94	0.56	211.70	0.65
50	200	109.05	1.01	108.10	1.01	432.08	1.26
50	300	164.23	1.46	162.79	1.46	660.95	1.87
75	200	235.16	1.49	233.75	1.49	931.39	1.88
75	300	354.17	2.16	352.05	2.16	1418.59	2.79
100	200	409.06	1.98	407.20	1.98	1619.71	2.49
100	300	616.12	2.87	613.31	2.87	2461.23	3.70

5.3 Solutions

The optimal solution to an example problem with four requests and three vehicles is reported in Fig. 1. Vehicles $V2$ and $V3$ are initially in zone 1 while $V1$ is in zone 4. Request $R1$, from zone 2 to 3 is valid only if the drop-off fee is $l(1) = €-2$ or lower. Similarly, $R2$ is valid up to $l(2) = €1$, $R3$ up to $l(3) = €1$ and $R4$ up to $l(4) = €-1$. The optimal drop-off fees are reported in the figure. The optimal solution sets a drop-off fee of $€-1 > l(1)$ from 2 to 3, thus request $R1$ is not valid anymore. Similarly, a drop-off fee of 0 between 7 and 6 vanishes $R4$. Requests $R2$ and $R3$ are satisfied by $V1$ and $V2$, respectively. $V2$ is relocated from zone 1 to 5 bearing a cost of $€3.68$. This cost is lower than the revenue of request $R3$.

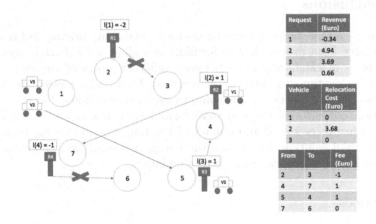

Fig. 1. Optimal solution for an example problem.

Table 4 reports a summary of the optimal solution for the smallest instances tested. In general, less than one third of the vehicles are relocated, and that more than 70% of the requests are satisfied. A negative drop-off fee is set on the large majority of the routes. Nevertheless, a positive profit is achieved on all instances. A further investigation of these results and managerial insights are left for future research.

Table 4. Drop-off fees, % of vehicles relocated and % of requests satisfied applied in the five instances with $V = 20$ and $K = 50$.

Instance	Drop-off fees applied [%]					Relocations [%]	Req. satisfied [%]
	€-2	€-1	€0	€1	€2		
1	76.60	5.55	4.44	6.66	6.66	30.00	73.91
2	85.55	3.33	1.11	5.55	4.44	10.00	76.92
3	88.88	3.33	2.22	1.11	4.44	25.00	73.33
4	86.66	7.77	0.00	3.33	2.22	30.00	76.47
5	84.44	6.66	1.11	3.33	4.44	25.00	70.00

6 Conclusions

An extensive and a compact formulation for a carsharing pricing and relocation problem have been proposed. The formulations allow a carsharing operator to set the price of carsharing rides between different zones of the city and the decide the relocations to better serve demand. Customers choices are modeled by means of utility functions. The computational study shows that the compact formulation outperforms the extensive formulation in terms of solution time, number of instances solved and quality of the linear programming bound. The relatively small solution time makes the compact formulation amenable to use in the context of a scenario analysis or simulation.

References

1. Straits Times (2008). Honda car-sharing scheme in singapore to end. https://wildsingaporenews.blogspot.com/2008/03/honda-car-sharing-scheme-in-singapore.html. Accessed 30 Sep 2010
2. Barnes, I., Frick, K., Deakin, E., Skabardonis, A.: Impact of peak and off-peak tolls on traffic in san francisco-oakland bay bridge corridor in california. Transport. Res. Record **2297**, 73–79 (2012)
3. Barth, M., Todd, M.: Simulation model performance analysis of a multiple station shared vehicle system. Transport. Res. Part C: Emerg. Technol. **7**, 237–259 (1999)
4. Barth, M., Todd, M., Xue, L.: User-based vehicle relocation techniques for multiple-station shared-use vehicle systems (2004)
5. Bierlaire, M., Sharif Azadeh, S.: Demand-based discrete optimization. Technical report (2016)
6. Boyacı, B., Zografos, K.G., Geroliminis, N.: An optimization framework for the development of efficient one-way car-sharing systems. Euro. J. Oper. Res. **240**(3), 718–733 (2015)
7. Boyacı, B., Zografos, K.G., Geroliminis, N.: An integrated optimization-simulation framework for vehicle and personnel relocations of electric carsharing systems with reservations. Transport. Res. Part B: Methodol. **95**(Supplement C), 214–237 (2017)
8. Bruglieri, M., Colorni, A., Luè, A.: The vehicle relocation problem for the one-way electric vehicle sharing: an application to the Milan case. Networks **64**, 292–305 (2014)

9. Carpintero, S., Gomez-Ibañez, J.A.: Mexico's private toll road program reconsidered. Transport Policy **18**(6), 848–855 (2011)
10. Choudhury, C.F., Yang, L., de Abreu e Silva, J., Ben-Akiva, M.: Modelling preferences for smart modes and services: a case study in lisbon. Transport. Res. Part A: Policy Pract. **115**, 15–31 (2018)
11. CPH Post: Car2go shutting down in Copenhagen. http://cphpost.dk/news/car2go-shutting-down-in-copenhagen.html (2016)
12. Crane, Keith, L.E.S.H., Nataraj, S.: Energy services analysis: An alternative approach for identifying opportunities to reduce emissions of greenhouse gases. Technical report, RAND Corporation, Santa Monica, California (2012). https://www.rand.org/pubs/technical_reports/TR1170.html
13. Dudley, G.: Why do ideas succeed and fail over time? the role of narratives in policy windows and the case of the london congestion charge. J. Euro. Public Policy **20**(8), 1139–1156 (2013)
14. Duncan, M.: The cost saving potential of carsharing in a us context. Transportation **38**, 363–382 (2011)
15. Folkestad, C.A., Hansen, N., Fagerholt, K., Andersson, H., Pantuso, G.: Optimal charging and repositioning of electric vehicles in a free-floating carsharing system. Comput. Oper. Res. **113**, 104771 (2020)
16. Hansen, R.G., Pantuso, G.: Pricing car-sharing services in multi-modal transportation systems: an analysis of the cases of copenhagen and milan. In: Cerulli, R., Raiconi, A., Voß, S. (eds.) ICCL 2018. LNCS, vol. 11184, pp. 344–359. Springer, Cham (2018). https://doi.org/10.1007/978-3-030-00898-7_23
17. Illgen, S., Höck, M.: Literature review of the vehicle relocation problem in one-way car sharing networks. Transport. Res. Part B: Methodol. **120**, 193–204 (2019)
18. Jorge, D., Correia, G.H.A., Barnhart, C.: Comparing optimal relocation operations with simulated relocation policies in one-way carsharing systems. IEEE Trans. Intell. Transport. Syst. **15**(4), 1667–1675 (2014)
19. Kek, A., Cheu, R., Chor, M.: Relocation simulation model for multiple-station shared-use vehicle systems. Transport. Res. Record: J. Transport. Res. Board **1986**, 81–88 (2006)
20. Kek, A.G., Cheu, R.L., Meng, Q., Fung, C.H.: A decision support system for vehicle relocation operations in carsharing systems. Transport. Res. Part E: Logistics Transport. Rev. **45**(1), 149–158 (2009)
21. May, A., Nash, C.: Urban congestion: a European perspective on theory and practice. Annual Rev. Energy Environment **21**(1), 239–260 (1996)
22. Modesti, P., Sciomachen, A.: A utility measure for finding multiobjective shortest paths in urban multimodal transportation networks. Euro. J. Oper. Res. **111**(3), 495–508 (1998)
23. Mourad, A., Puchinger, J., Chu, C.: A survey of models and algorithms for optimizing shared mobility. Transport. Res. Part B: Methodol. (2019)
24. Mukai, N., Watanabe, T.: Dynamic location management for on-demand car sharing system. In: Khosla, R., Howlett, R.J., Jain, L.C. (eds.) KES 2005. LNCS (LNAI), vol. 3681, pp. 768–774. Springer, Heidelberg (2005). https://doi.org/10.1007/11552413_109
25. Prud'homme, R., Koning, M., Lenormand, L., Fehr, A.: Public transport congestion costs: the case of the paris subway. Transport Policy **21**, 101–109 (2012)
26. Shaheen, S.A., Cohen, A.P.: Carsharing and personal vehicle services: worldwide market developments and emerging trends. Int. J. Sustainable Transport. **7**(1), 5–34 (2013)

27. The Local: Car2go drives out of Copenhagen after flop - The Local. https://www. thelocal.dk/20160120/car2go-on-copenhagen-road-to-nowhere (2016)
28. Wang, L., Ma, W.: Pricing approach to balance demands for one-way car-sharing systems. In: 2019 IEEE Intelligent Transportation Systems Conference (ITSC), pp. 1697–1702. IEEE (2019)
29. Waserhole, A., Jost, V.: Pricing in vehicle sharing systems: optimization in queuing networks with product forms. EURO J. Transport. Logistics **5**(3), 293–320 (2016)
30. Waserhole, A., Jost, V., Brauner, N.: Pricing techniques for self regulation in vehicle sharing systems. Electronic Notes Discrete Math. **41**, 149–156 (2013)
31. Weikl, S., Bogenberger, K.: A practice-ready relocation model for free-floating car-sharing systems with electric vehicles-mesoscopic approach and field trial results. Transport. Res. Part C: Emerg. Technol. **57**, 206–223 (2015)

Evolutionary Approach for the Multi-objective Bike Routing Problem

Pedro Nunes(✉) , Ana Moura , and José Santos

University of Aveiro, Aveiro, Portugal
pnunes@ua.pt

Abstract. In this paper, a multi-objective approach for the bike routing problem is presented. Bike routing represents specific challenges, since cyclists have different experiences, concerns, and route preferences. Our approach considers two criteria: the total traveled distance and the cyclists safety. Finding the optimal Pareto set is computationally unfeasible for these problems, therefore, the goal of this work is to create a non-exact method capable of producing a set of quality solutions in a timely manner. A heuristic that modifies the multi-label setting algorithm is used to create an initial population and a genetic elitist algorithm is used to find an approximated Pareto set of optimal routes. The proposed methodology is applied on a practical case study, in which real data from OpenStreetMaps (OSM) and Shuttle Radar Topography Mission (SRTM) was used to model the graph for the road network of the city of Aveiro, with 9506 nodes and 21208 edges. The results show that the approach is fast enough for interactive use in a planning tool and produces a set of quality solutions, regarding two criteria, the traveled distance and the safety of the path.

Keywords: Genetic algorithm · Bike routing · Multi-objective · Searching algorithm · Heuristic

1 Introduction

The bicycle use as a means of transport is becoming increasingly popular, especially for commuting trips, as it avoids car congestion in large urban centers [18]. For some journeys, it may be the fastest transport, because it avoids long stops due to car traffic, which gives the bicycle an enormous growth potential, when one acknowledges that almost half of all car trips in the cities are less than five kilometers [8]. In addition, it is cheap, promotes a reduction in pollutant emissions while contributes to improve user's health [16].

The bicycle manufacturing and related industries are expected to grow with an annual rate of 5.5% until 2022 [9]. However, there are some challenges associated with cycling, with safety being a major concern. According to the annual report of the ANSR (National Road Safety Authority), in 2018 there were 17 cyclists who were fatal victims on Portuguese roads, 114 seriously injured, and

E. Lalla-Ruiz et al. (Eds.): ICCL 2020, LNCS 12433, pp. 311–325, 2020.
https://doi.org/10.1007/978-3-030-59747-4_20

1984 being the total number of victims that year. There are several reasons for this worrying number, such as lack of appropriate cycling infrastructures or motor vehicle drivers misbehavior. In addition, cycling may be a challenge, specially for beginner cyclists with poor knowledge of the surrounding cycling network. For this reason, more people would consider using a bicycle if a bike route planner was available [1].

However, the choice of routes for cycling is much more complex than in the case of motor vehicles. In the latter case, the driver is mainly concerned with two aspects, the distance traveled and the time to reach the destination [26]. Thus, when making decisions, the great advantage lies on the shortest and fastest routes. However, a cyclist takes into account a much greater diversity of factors [3], such as the condition of existing bicycle paths [24], since cyclists prefer bike paths completely separated from motorized traffic [23]. Other factors such as obstacles in the road or the proximity to parked vehicles are not appealing, because cyclists visibility is reduced and they may be forced to make deviations from the parked vehicles or other obstacles. Tracks with hills or bridges are usually avoided by cyclists [29]. Junctions represent specific challenges for cyclists safety, since there are different types of intersections with different safety risks perceived by cyclists. The junctions controlled by traffic lights are perceived as the safer interceptions, but these tend to be avoided [21]. On the other hand, the junction type that gathers the biggest concern among cyclists is the roundabout [30]. This concern becomes more important, because since the beginning of the 1990s intersections have been converted into roundabouts [6]. There are some aspects and circumstances that influence the risk perception of a roundabout, such as the number of motorized vehicles, approaching, circulation and exiting speed and the existence of cycling facilities, especially those who have separation between bicycles and other vehicles [22].

In fact, any type of route that provides proximity between the cyclist and motorized vehicles is a discouraging factor for the use of this type of transport, especially in the case of main streets, where the maximum allowed speed is usually higher [4]. Generally, cyclists are willing to travel longer distances and spend more time on their route when traveling on ones they consider more comfortable, safer or calmer [31], and prefer avoiding large crowds of motorized traffic or other cyclists [32].

This work is divided in six sections. In Sect. 2, the main motivations and objectives of this work are addressed, while Sect. 3 presents some related work. In Sect. 4, the proposed methodology and algorithms are covered in detail. Section 5 presents the results. Finally conclusions and future work are highlighted in Sect. 6.

2   Motivation and Objectives

The motivation for this work comes from the increasing demand for soft mobility means of transport in urban environments. In this field, the bicycle has a determinant role nowadays, and for this reason, it is imperative that the technological development and investigation studies evolve towards ensuring better conditions for cyclists, especially for beginners or for those who have poor knowledge of cycling network.

Despite of several works developed for motorized vehicle routing, bike routing is much more complex, as mentioned. The main objective of this work is to provide a set of quality solutions (approximated Pareto set), regarding two criteria: safety and total travel distance. Regarding its quantification, the difference between these two criteria is that while the distance covered is an objective criterion, safety is not. Being the first criterion more complex and subjective, a set of relevant features classified as fundamentals in the literature for cyclists preferences was used, namely road slope, road type, type of intersection, existence of cycling infrastructures as separated cycle paths and existence of obstacles or road singularities as bumps or speed tables. The trade off between travel distance and safety depends on the cyclist's profile. One approach for the problem is to attribute weights to each criterion and create a cost function that combines both. This simplifies the problem to a shortest path problem. However, this approach may miss some interesting Pareto solutions that could be most suitable to the cyclist's preferences. For this reason, a multi-objective approach was used. The proposed approach is based on a genetic algorithm, which is a meta-heuristic inspired by the evolution of species in nature [33]. It begins with an initial population of individuals, who are evaluated, in order to choose the best ones to reproduce (crossover operator). Other operators such as mutation can be applied during the process. In this work, a lighter version of the multi-label setting algorithm is used to create an initial population which, may be improved though a genetic algorithm, since it is a commonly used approach in multi-objective problems [7], however, its use in bike routing problem is not widely explored.

3   Related Work

Some work directly or indirectly related to the bike routing problem has been published. The first approach to multi-objective routing problem was formalized by [20], who proposed multiple objective functions to describe the problem and created the multi-criteria label-setting algorithm to solve it. A multi-label correcting algorithm was used by [28] to select a set of Pareto routes, together with a route selection algorithm based on hierarchical clustering to reduce the set of Pareto routes. Despite the improvements to the existing label-setting algorithms, the computational time for this approach is prohibitive for interactive use.

Evolutionary approaches have been used in routing problems. For example, genetic algorithms have been used by [2], who implemented a parallel genetic algorithm (PGA) using High-performance Cluster (HPC) and by [17], in order to create a practical procedure to compute the cost function of each edge in a network for cyclists, incorporating distance and perceived risk. However, these works did not consider the multi-objective approach for bike routing.

Other authors use multiple criteria for bike routing and optimize each criterion separately. For example, [12], created a web-based bicycle trip planning using the ArcGIS Server framework together with some Google APIs. In [13] the A-Star algorithm is used together with a cost vector for each criterion (travel time, comfort, quietness, and flatness), a method based on artificial neural networks to find a heuristic function for the A-Star algorithm was used by [5], while [19] used contraction hierarchies together with OpenStreetMap data, in order to find the shortest path in a graph.

More recently some approaches to the multi-objective bike routing problem have been proposed and demonstrated to be feasible in real networks. The authors in [14], proposed speedups for bike routing algorithms and [15] proposed a heuristic-enabled Dijkstra algorithm with the multi-criteria approach for bike routing.

Despite the developments in the field of bike routing, there is a lack of multi-objective approaches that solve the problem in a reasonable computational time. This work proposes a new methodology based on a genetic algorithm to find an approximation of the optimal Pareto set, since genetic approaches have the potential to solve multi-objective problems and their use in this concrete problem is sparse.

4 Methodology

In this work, the bike routing problem is addressed. Let us represent the cycling network by a directed graph $G(V,E,\vec{c}\,)$, where V is the set of nodes, E is the set of edges and $\vec{c}$ is a cost vector associated to each edge. The nodes represent junctions or a places with any relevant feature, such as traffic lights, crosswalks, walkways, bumps, among others. Nodes are also used to define accurately the road geometry, for example, the curves need more nodes to be defined than a straight line road.

$E \subseteq \{(u,v)|(u,v \in V) \wedge u \neq v\}$ represents the edges, which are the segments that connect two adjacent nodes. If the route is one-way, there is only one edge connecting the two nodes, otherwise, there are two edges, one for each direction.

$\vec{C}$, $\vec{C} = (c_{distance}, c_{safety})$ is a vector of non-negative costs, that represents the cost of passing each edge (u, v), according to each criterion. It should be noted that each element of the cost vector can be a function of several parameters, such as distance, road slope, road and surface types, and existing features in each edge.

A path π is a sequence of nodes to visit $\pi = \{n_0, n_1, n_2..., n_n\}$ where n_0 represents source node, and n_n is the destination node. The cost of each path is a vector, and the goal of the proposed approach is to find a set with a reasonable diversity of non-dominated solutions, i.e., solutions for which improving any objective value means degrading other ones.

4.1 Definition of Cost Functions from Data

The data used to instantiate the problem is from two different data sources: OSM and SRTM. With these data, a directed graph for the road network and the cost functions, to weight the edges, are created. The first data source, OSM, is a collaborative and open source mapping project that aims to create a free and editable map of the world. We obtained the data for the bounding box that contains the city of Aveiro using the OSM turbo overpass API. The collected data is divided into two different types of elements: nodes and links. Each element may have additional information in a field designated by "tag", which gives additional important information about the element, such as existence of road singularities, intersections, road type, traffic signals, among others. The nodes also have the geographical coordinates, latitude and longitude, which allows the distance calculation, as will be further detailed.

The SRTM is a spatial mission that aims to obtain a digital model of the Earth. It consists of a specially modified radar system to acquire the altimetric data. This data has a resolution of 1 arc second, or 30 m and is available almost worldwide since 2014 [10]. To download and parse it, a library for Python was used.

Traveled Distance: This criterion is objective, since it only considers the total distance of a path. The cost function is given in meters and corresponds to the sum of lengths of each edge. None of the data sources used have the information about distances available. However, we extracted the nodes coordinates from OSM and used them to calculate the distance, through the haversine formula. This approach is possible, because there are enough nodes to define accurately the road geometry, for example in links with curves, the number of nodes is considerably greater compared to straight links. Considering two consecutive nodes from an edge $(u, v) \in E$, the length $\overline{uv}$ is calculated by Eq. 1.

$$\overline{uv} = 2R \times \sqrt{\alpha^2 + \cos(lat(u)) \times \cos(lat(v)) \times \theta^2} \qquad (1)$$

Where α and θ are given by Eqs. 2 and 3 respectively and R is the Earth's radius, 6371 Km, lon and lat are the respective longitude and latitude of each node. This approach has the advantage of being fast to compute, and the results are close to the distances created by Google Maps.

$$\alpha = \frac{\sin(lat(u)) - lat(v)}{2} \qquad (2)$$

$$\theta = \frac{\sin(lon(u)) - lon(v)}{2} \qquad (3)$$

Safety: The safety criterion is more subjective than the travel distance, because it includes several road features and the risk perception of each one may differ for each cyclist. This criterion aims to create routes that have cycle-ways or where traffic is not shared with motorized vehicles. For this reason, main roads have a higher cost than pedestrians paths separated from traffic. Intersections, roundabouts, and bridges also have a negative impact on the cyclist's safety [11].

The cost for this criterion is defined as an equivalent distance, i.e., the distance can be perceived as shorter by the rider, if he/she has bike paths or other infrastructures that can make his trip safer. Thus, the perceived distance is calculated by Eq. 4, in meters. $Node_{fs}$ and $Edge_{fs}$ are parameters that reflect the safety perception with regard to node and edge features, respectively.

$$Safety_{cost} = L \times Edge_{fs} \times slope_{coefficient} + Node_{fs} \qquad (4)$$

Where L designates the edge length and is calculated by the haversine formula. The parameter $slope_{coefficient}$ reflects the influence of slope in safety perception and is calculated according to Eq. 5.

$$slope_{coefficient} = 2 - \frac{V_{edge}(sl)}{V_{max}(sl)} \qquad (5)$$

Where sl designates the slope, $V_{edge}(sl)$ is an estimated speed of a cyclist, measured in m/s on a given edge, according to its slope percentage. It is a non linear function and is represented by Eq. 6, where $V_{max}(sl)$ is the maximum estimated speed (6.87 m/s), reached for a negative slope of 0.92% (according to [25]).

$$V_{edge}(sl) = \begin{cases} 7.582 \times e^{0.1072 \times sl}, if\ sl < -0.92 \\ 5.787 \times e^{-0.1880 \times sl}, if\ -0.92 < sl \le 6 \\ 0.833, if\ 6 < sl \le 10 \\ 0, if\ 10 < sl \end{cases} \qquad (6)$$

The above expression was obtained from [25], which studied the cyclists speed according to the road slope. It reveals that there is an exponential relationship between the speed and slope values, lower than 6%. The maximum speed occurs for a negative slope of 0.92%. If the slope becomes steeper, the maximum speed decreases because the riders tend to brake for safety reasons. For slope between −0.92% and 6%, the speed decreases due to the increasing effort. For bigger slopes, the speed is very low and almost constant. Note that 10% is the maximum positive slope admitted by the cyclists for riding the bike.

As the link length is not directly available from the data sources, the slope is calculated with the altitude values obtained from SRTM data, according to Eq. 7.

$$sl(u, v) = 100 \times \frac{\Delta h}{l} \qquad (7)$$

It is a trigonometric relation, where Δh is a difference between the altitude of each node, i.e., $\Delta h = h(u) - h(v)$ and l is the horizontal length. The slope value is in percentage (%) and the nodes order is important, since $sl(u, v) = -sl(v, u)$.

The parameters $Edge_{fs}$ and $Node_{fs}$ reflect the existence of features that influence the cyclists safety perception. These features are extracted from OSM data, namely from the information contained in the element's tags. The adopted values and considered features are expressed in Tables 1 and 2. These values result from an adaptation of the works [29–32].

Table 1. Edge features that influence safety perception

Element (OSM)	Key	Value	$Edge_{fs}$
way	highway	footway	0.81
		pedestrian	0.81
		cicleway	0.43
		steps	1.85
		track	0.81
		path	0.81
		primary	1.19
	bicycle	yes	1
		designated	0.43
	junction	roundabout	3
	bridge	yes	1.19
		movable	1.19
		suspension	1.19
	crossing	marked	1.30
		zebra	1.30
		island	1.40
		traffic_signals	1.50

Table 2. Node features that influence safety perception

Element (OSM)	Key	Value	$Node_{fs}$ (m)
way	highway	give_way	100
		crossing	120
		traffic_signals	70
		stop	70
	crossing	uncontrolled	120
	traffic_calming	bump	5
		table	5

4.2 Multi-objective Algorithm

The proposed methodology to solve the multi-objective problem includes a modified multi-label search algorithm, in order to create an initial population for a genetic algorithm. This algorithm is able to find the optimal Pareto set, however, at the costs of high computational time. For this reason, we modified the search algorithm to stop when it reaches the destination node and we used a new heuristic-based methodology to sort the labels. Figure 1 shows the pseudo code for the proposed approach. The algorithm starts by initiating two "bags", the *temporary_bag* and the *permanent_bag*. Each bag will be filled with labels, that are data structures of the type $label = (node, predecessor, c_{distance}, c_{safety}, c_{estimated})$, where *node* is the node associated to that label, *predecessor* is the previous node in the search process, $c_{distance}$ and c_{safety} are the distance and safety costs of going from the origin "O" to the labeled node, respectively. Finally, $c_{estimated}$ is an estimated distance. It is the summation of $c_{distance}$ and the cost given by a heuristic that estimates the distance between the current node and the destination "D". This heuristic computes the straight-line distance calculated by the haversine formula. This heuristic is used to speed up the searching process, since the function $find\_shortest(temporary\_bag)$ returns the label with the shortest $c_{estimated}$.

The labels for each node connected to the labeled node are determined and are added to the *temporary_bag* when they are non-dominated by any other existing label in that list. Since there may exist several non-dominated paths to reach one node, each of them may have multiple labels. One label $L_1 = (node_1, predecessor_1, c_1, c_2, c_3)$ dominates another one, $L_2 = (node_1, predecessor'_1, c'_1, c'_2, c'_3)$ when they are related to the same node and

$c_1 <= c_1' \wedge c_2 <= c_2'$. If a label is inserted into the *temporary_bag*, it is checked if it dominates any existing label. In these cases, the dominated labels are removed.

```
Input: Oriented Graph "G", Source point "O", Destination point "D"
Output: Approximated optimal Pareto set "S"
initialize permanent_bag = Ø
initialize temporaty_bag = Ø
initialize label = (O,"n",0,0,heuristic(O,D))
insert label into temporary_bag

while temporary_bag ≠ Ø:
    label = find_shortest(temporary_bag)
    node = node(label)
    remove label from temporary_bag
    add label to permanent_bag
    if node in label == D:
        initial_poulation = backtrack(permanent_bag,O,D)
        S = genetic (initial_population,G,O,D)
        break
    for ng ∈ G.neighbors(node):
        heuristic = haversine(neighbor, goal)
        new_label = (ng, node, c_distance, c_safety, c_distance+heuristic)
        if not check_dominated(temporary_bag, new_label):
            add new_label to temporary_bag
            for each label in temporary_list(neighbor):
                if check_dominance(temporary_bag,new_label):
                    remove label from temporary_bag
```

Fig. 1. Pseudo code of the modified multi-label search algorithm

When the the search reaches the destination node, a random backtrack algorithm is applied. As is shown in Fig. 2, each node may have several predecessors extracted from the *permanent_bag*. The backtracking algorithm consists in the construction of several solutions, starting by the destination node "D" and choosing a random predecessor, until the source point "O" is reached. This process is repeated until initial population size "N" (the number of individuals) is reached. In some cases, the safest path is much longer than the shortest one. In these cases, the safest path may not be reached. To ensure that it does not occur, we used the A-Star algorithm, to find the safest path and include it in the initial population. The A-Star algorithm was chosen, because it is widely used to solve shortest path problems, due to its computational performance [27].

Once the initial population is created, a genetic algorithm is executed, as illustrated in Fig. 3.

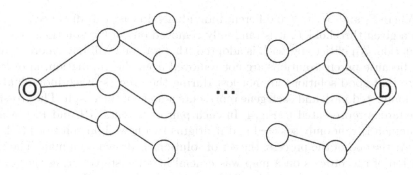

Fig. 2. Initial population with backtrack algorithm

```
Input: Initial population "IP", Oriented Graph "G", Source point "O",
Destination point "D"
Output: Approximated optimal Pareto set "S"
initialize Number_of_generations
initialize pop = IP
for a in range(Number_of_generations):
   fitness = fitness_population(pop,G)
   best_pop = sel_pop(pop,fitness)
   pop = crossover(best_pop)
draw_path(pop)
```

Fig. 3. Pseudo code of the genetic approach

In our pseudo code, fitness is a matrix, where the number of rows is equal to the number of individuals in the population, and the two columns contain the travel distance and the safety perceived distance for a given solution. The function $sel\_pop(pop, fitness)$ filters the non-dominated solutions of a given population. The parameter $Number\_of\_generations$ defines the number of times that the evolutionary process is repeated. It is important, since few generations may produce a poor set of solutions, but a large number of generations may make the algorithm slow, with limited increase in solutions quality. There is no population size control, since all the non-dominated solutions are accepted. In order to achieve more diversity of solutions, also the Euclidean distance between solutions is considered, as represented by Eq. 8.

$$Euclidean(S_1, S_2) = \sqrt{(c_{distance}(S1) - c_{distance}(S2))^2 + (c_{safety}(S1) - c_{safety}(S2))^2}$$

(8)

Where S_1 and S_2 are two different individuals. In case this distance is smaller than a given threshold T, it is randomly removed one of the solutions from the population. An elitist approach is adopted, this way one will have more individuals, because parent solutions are not removed from the population, in order to ensure that good solutions are not lost during the process. Each individual is a non-dominated path and each gene represents a node of the graph. The crossover procedure is represented in Fig. 4. In each pair of parents (P1 and P2), a node in common is randomly selected and it origins two new child solutions (C1 and C2). At the end of the process, the set of solutions is drawn on a map. The visualization of the process on a map was crucial in some steps during the process of construction of the genetic algorithm, namely in choosing the population size. We started with a population of 80 individuals and increased it in steps of 20 individuals, until we reached 500 individual, as the solution diversity does not increase any further. For this reason, the size adopted for the initial population was 500 individuals. Besides that, the number of new solutions generated by crossover is equal to the size of the non-dominated solutions, since each parent cross once with another randomly chosen parent, producing two new individuals. Note that each parent only cross once in the same iteration.

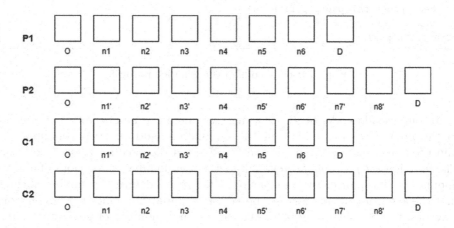

Fig. 4. Genetic algorithm crossover

5   Results and Discussion

The proposed approach was tested using a real graph of the city of Aveiro with 9506 nodes and 21208 edges. Figure 5 shows the initial population (500 individuals) generated by the backtracking algorithm after the searching algorithm was executed. The source point (A) is a street near the University of Aveiro and the destination point (B) is the city train station. These nodes were chosen because they have a great potential, since the number of people moving daily from these places is considerable. Sometimes, the optimal route for safety criterion is much longer than the other ones reached by the searching algorithm, for example, route C in Fig. 5 is the safest route between node point A and B, and is much longer than the other solutions. In these cases, the searching algorithm does not reach that solution, as mentioned in Sect. 4. To guarantee that it also makes part of the initial population, the A-Star algorithm is used to find the optimal route for safety criterion. This algorithm has a reduced computational time (only few milliseconds) [27], and will not degrade the overall performance.

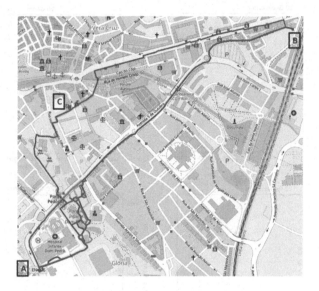

Fig. 5. Initial population

The number of generations is one of most important parameters for evolutionary algorithms. We tested different number of generations, from 2 to 24. Some of the obtained results can be seen in Fig. 6. The number of non-dominated solutions reached by the genetic algorithm increase with increasing number of generations, until 22 generations. Thereafter, the number of reached solutions

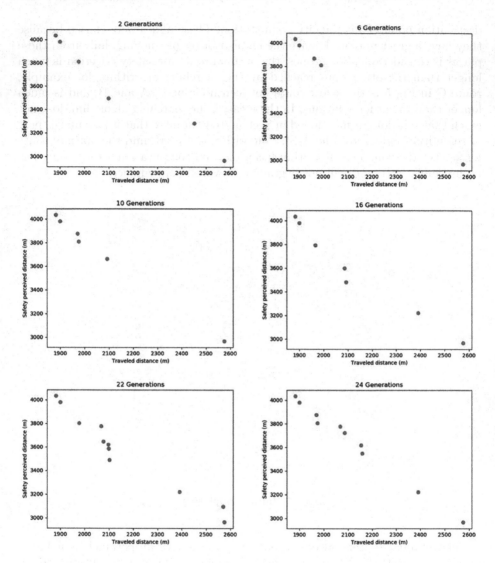

Fig. 6. Obtained solutions for different number of generations

tend to stabilize. For this reason, we set the number of generations as 22, because it is the best value to speed up the algorithm and reach a considerable number of non-dominated solutions. Figure 7 shows the obtained paths for 22 generations.

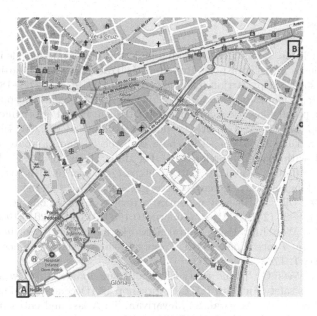

Fig. 7. Approximated Pareto set

6   Conclusions and Future Work

In this work, a new approach has been proposed to solve the multi-objective bike routing problem, based on a genetic elitist algorithm. It represents a simple and effective method to generate a set of diverse solutions, which can help the decision maker, since the trade-off between safety and distance is personal. The safety parameter was modeled as a perceived distance and is described by a set of features that influence cyclists safety perception, using open source data from OSM and SRTM.

As future work, we would like to test our approach with more than two criteria, including, for example a turn criterion, with the objective to minimize the number of turns during a trip. The implementation of a mutation operator could contribute to increase the number of non-dominated solutions achieved by the genetic algorithm, for this reason, it will be considered in future works.

Acknowledgments. The authors acknowledge the financial Support through project POCI-01-0247-FEDER-033769 - "Ghisallo - Investigação e Desenvolvimento de uma nova solução de comutação urbana, assente num novo conceito de veículo elétrico de próxima geração" which was funded by the Operational Program for Competiveness and Internationalization (COMPETE 2020) in its component FEDER and UID/EMS/00481 /2013-FCT CENTRO-01-0145 FEDER-022083 POCI-01-0247-FEDER-033769.

324   P. Nunes et al.

References

1. Akar, G., Clifton, K.: Influence of individual perceptions and bicycle infrastructure on decision to bike. Transport. Res. Rec. J. Transport. Res. Board 2140(2140), 165–172 (2009). http://trrjournalonline.trb.org/doi/10.3141/2140-18
2. Arunadevi, J., Johnsanjeevkumar, A., Sujatha, N.: Intelligent transport route planning using parallel genetic algorithms and MPI. In: High Performance Computing Cluster, pp. 578–583 (2008). https://doi.org/10.1109/adcom.2007.76
3. Broach, J., Dill, J., Gliebe, J.: Where do cyclists ride? a route choice model developed with revealed preference GPS data. Transport. Res. Part A: Policy Pract. 46(10), 1730–1740 (2012). https://doi.org/10.1016/j.tra.2012.07.005, https://linkinghub.elsevier.com/retrieve/pii/S0965856412001164
4. Buehler, R., Dill, J.: Bikeway networks: a review of effects on cycling. Transport Rev. 36(1), 9–27 (2016). https://doi.org/10.1080/01441647.2015.1069908
5. Chen, H.C., Wei, J.D.: Using neural networks for evaluation in heuristic search algorithm. In: Proceedings of the Twenty-Fifth AAAI Conference on Artificial Intelligence, 1, 1768–1769 (2011)
6. Daniels, S., Wets, G.: Traffic safety effects of roundabouts: a review with emphasis on bicyclist's safety. In: 18th ICTCT workshop 18 (December 2007), 1–12 (2005)
7. Deb, K., Pratap, A., Agarwal, S., Meyarivan, T.: A fast and elitist multiobjective genetic algorithm: NSGA-II. IEEE Trans. Evol. Comput. 6(2), 182–197 (2002). http://ieeexplore.ieee.org/document/996017/
8. EC: Mobility and transport (2019). https://www.ec.europa.eu/transport/themes/clean-transport-urban-transport/cycling_en. Accessed 10 Sep 2019
9. ECF: The benefits of cycling. Technical report, November 2018. https://ecf.com/sites/ecf.com/files/TheBenefitsOfCycling2018.pdf
10. Farr, T.G., et al.: The shuttle radar topography mission. Rev. Geophys. 45(2), RG2004 (2007). https://doi.org/10.1029/2005RG000183
11. Flower, J., Parkin, J.: Understanding attitudes to priorities at side road junctions. Transport. Res. Part F: Traffic Psychol. Behaviour 62, 246–257 (2019). https://doi.org/10.1016/J.TRF.2019.01.005, https://www.sciencedirect.com/science/article/pii/S136984781830809X
12. Hochmair, H.H., Fu, Z.: Web based bicycle trip planning for broward county, Florida. In: ESRI User Conference, pp. 1–12 (2009). http://digitalcommons.fiu.edu/gis/31digitalcommons.fiu.edu/cgi/viewcontent.cgi?article=1001&context=gis
13. Hrncir, J., Song, Q., Zilecky, P., Nemet, M., Jakob, M.: Bicycle route planning with route choice preferences. Front. Artif. Intell. Appl. 263(September), 1149–1154 (2014). https://doi.org/10.3233/978-1-61499-419-0-1149
14. Hrncir, J., Zilecky, P., Song, Q., Jakob, M.: Speedups for multi-criteria urban bicycle routing. OASIcs - OpenAccess Series in Informatics 48, 28 (2015). http://drops.dagstuhl.de/opus/volltexte/2015/5458/
15. Hrncir, J., Zilecky, P., Song, Q., Jakob, M.: Practical multicriteria urban bicycle routing. IEEE Trans. Intell. Transport. Syst. 18(3), 493–504 (2017). https://doi.org/10.1109/TITS.2016.2577047
16. Hsu, Y.T., Kang, L., Wu, Y.H.: User behavior of bikesharing systems under demand-supply imbalance. Transport. Res. Rec. J. Transport. Res. Board 2587(1), 117–124 (2016). http://journals.sagepub.com/doi/10.3141/2587-14
17. Kang, L., Fricker, J.D.: Bicycle-route choice model incorporating distance and perceived risk. J. Urban Plann. Dev. 144(4), 04018041 (2018). https://doi.org/10.1061/(asce)up.1943-5444.0000485

18. Lindsay, G., Macmillan, A., Woodward, A.: Moving urban trips from cars to bicycles: impact on health and emissions. Australian and New Zealand Journal of Public Health **35**(1), 54–60 (2011). https://onlinelibrary.wiley.com/doi/pdf/10.1111/j.1753-6405.2010.00621.x

19. Luxen, D., Gmbh, N., Vetter, C.: Real-time routing with OpenStreetMap data categories and subject descriptors. In: Proceedings of the 19th ACM SIGSPATIAL GIS Conference pp. 513–516 (2011)

20. Martins, E.Q.V.: On a multicriteria shortest path problem. Euro. J. Oper. Res. **16**(2), 236–245 (1984). https://doi.org/10.1016/0377-2217(84)90077-8

21. Menghini, G., Carrasco, N., Schüssler, N., Axhausen, K.W.: Route choice of cyclists in Zurich. Transport. Res. Part A: Policy and Practice **44**(9), 754–765 (2010). http://dx.doi.org/10.1016/j.tra.2010.07.008

22. Møller, M., Hels, T.: Cyclists' perception of risk in roundabouts. Accident Anal. Prevention **40**(3), 1055–1062 (2008). https://doi.org/10.1016/j.aap.2007.10.013, https://www.sciencedirect.com/science/article/pii/S0001457507002084

23. Piet, H., Bradley, M.A.: Route Choice Analyzed with Stated-Preference Approaches pp. 11–20 (1985)

24. Pucher, J., Buehler, R.: Making cycling irresistible: lessons from the netherlands. Denmark and Germany. Transport Rev. **28**(4), 495–528 (2008). https://doi.org/10.1080/01441640701806612

25. Romero, J.P., Moura, J.L., Ibeas, A., Alonso, B.: A simulation tool for bicycle sharing systems in multimodal networks. Transport. Plan. Techno. **38**(6), 646–663 (2015). http://dx.doi.org/10.1080/03081060.2015.1048946

26. Schmitt, J.P., Baldo, F.: A method to suggest alternative routes based on analysis of automobiles' trajectories. In: 2018 XLIV Latin American Computer Conference (CLEI), pp. 436–444. IEEE, October 2018. https://doi.org/10.1109/CLEI.2018.00059, https://ieeexplore.ieee.org/document/8786307/

27. Seo, W.J., Ok, S.H., Ahn, J.H., Kang, S., Moon, B.: An efficient hardware architecture of the a-star algorithm for the shortest path search engine. In: 2009 Fifth International Joint Conference on INC, IMS and IDC, pp. 1499–1502. IEEE (2009). https://doi.org/10.1109/NCM.2009.371, http://ieeexplore.ieee.org/document/5331336/

28. Song, Q., Zilecky, P., Jakob, M., Hrncir, J.: Exploring pareto routes in multi-criteria urban bicycle routing. In: 2014 17th IEEE International Conference on Intelligent Transportation Systems, ITSC 2014 (September), 1781–1787 (2014). https://doi.org/10.1109/ITSC.2014.6957951

29. Stinson, M.A., Bhat, C.R.: Analysis using a stated preference survey. Burns **03**, 107–115 (2003)

30. Summala, H.: Car drivers adjustments to cyclists at roundabouts **2014–2018**, 2018 (2000). https://doi.org/10.1207/STHF0201

31. Tilahun, N.Y., Levinson, D.M., Krizek, K.J.: Trails, lanes, or traffic: valuing bicycle facilities with an adaptive stated preference survey. Transport. Res. Part A: Pol. Pract. **41**(4), 287–301 (2007). https://doi.org/10.1016/j.tra.2006.09.007

32. Vedel, S.E., Jacobsen, J.B., Skov-Petersen, H.: Bicyclists' preferences for route characteristics and crowding in Copenhagen - a choice experiment study of commuters. Transport. Res. Part A: Pol. Pract. **100**, 53–64 (2017). https://doi.org/10.1016/j.tra.2017.04.006

33. Whitley, D.: A genetic algorithm tutorial. Stat. Comput. **4**(2), 65–85 (1994). https://doi.org/10.1007/BF00175354

Quantifying the Effect of Flexibility and Information Sharing in Transportation Planning

Ebba Celius, Madeleine Reehorst, Heidi Dreyer, and Peter Schütz(✉) ⓘ

Department of Industrial Economics and Technology Management, Norwegian University of Science and Technology, Trondheim, Norway
{ebbac,annamg}@stud.ntnu.no, {heidi.c.dreyer,peter.schuetz}@ntnu.no

Abstract. In this paper, we analyze the effect of information sharing between a wholesaler and a transport company in the Norwegian grocery supply chain. The planning process of each company is formulated as a set covering problem, where the input data of the transport company depends on the optimal solution of the wholesaler model. Information sharing is modeled through controlling which information from the wholesaler model is sent to the transport company model. We define three different cases of information sharing and introduce two types of flexibility, namely the abilities to deviate from the planned delivery date and selected routes. We use real-world data to calculate the effect of information sharing for the different cases. Our results indicate that the benefits from information sharing are limited if there is no flexibility in the system.

Keywords: Information sharing · Transportation planning · Flexibility · Set covering problem

1 Introduction

In the Norwegian grocery industry, transportation cost represent approximately 33% of the wholesalers' total operating cost [16]. Improving transport efficiency can therefore lead to improved profit margins. According to Norwegian transport companies and their partners, limited information sharing is the main obstacle to increased efficiency [1]. However, the literature has a nuanced view on the value of information sharing: one stream of literature considers (increased) sharing of information as generally positive for the supply chain, but acknowledges the trade-off between value of information sharing and costs due to added complexity, see e.g. [7,25]. Other authors state that the potential benefits are highly limited, mainly due to complexity, cost and risk [18]. Within transportation planning, sharing information horizontally, i.e. among transport companies, for the purpose of collaborative planning is examined. A recent example is [21], studying a collaborative vehicle routing problem where the transport companies

© Springer Nature Switzerland AG 2020
E. Lalla-Ruiz et al. (Eds.): ICCL 2020, LNCS 12433, pp. 326–341, 2020.
https://doi.org/10.1007/978-3-030-59747-4_21

have different attitudes towards information sharing. See also [12] for a review on collaborative vehicle routing. Despite the interest in information sharing, the utilization of shared information has not received much attention in the literature, notable exceptions are [17,20,22].

Daily demand in the grocery industry is uncertain [10], but exhibits a predictable, repetitive weekly pattern. This weekly pattern is characterized by daily variations in demand, with demand increasing towards the end of the week [6]. Promotions disturb the daily demand pattern and thus affect its predictability [11], but often lead to a predictable increase in demand for the promotional products. However, promotions are known well in advance of the promotion period [19]. Combining the knowledge of a planned promotion period with the weekly demand pattern allow the wholesaler to predict the cargo volumes that need to be transported during a given week.

Transport companies often receive information regarding the cargo volume that has to be transported less than 24 h before departure [14]. Earlier access to this information might improve transport planning and consequently reduce the cost of transportation. This paper analyses how the cost of transportation is affected by a Norwegian grocery wholesaler sharing cargo information with the transport company. To account for the different decision makers and to study the effect of information sharing, we model the decision processes of both the wholesaler and the transport company as independent optimization problems, where the outcome from the wholesaler's planning problem becomes input to the transport company's planning problem. We then investigate how a transport company can utilize the shared information under two types of flexibility: First, we consider delivery flexibility, i.e. the ability to change the delivery time of cargo. The second type of flexibility is route selection flexibility, where we allow the transport company to freely choose a route from a set preselected routes.

The remainder of this paper is organized as follows: in Sect. 2 we describe the planning process for the wholesaler and the transport company. We also introduce how information is shared between the two actors and how the types of flexibility can be exploited to reduce the cost of transportation. The mathematical model formulations are presented in Sect. 3. Case data and computational results are provided in Sect. 4. We conclude in Sect. 5.

2   Transportation Planning and Information Sharing

The grocery supply chain we consider in this paper belongs to one of the largest grocery companies in Norway, covering both wholesale and retail activities. The physical distribution of goods is organized according to a typical single-channel structure [24]: a third-party carrier transports the goods from the wholesaler to the retailer. The companies plan the distribution of goods from the wholesaler to the retail stores in two main stages: The first stage is carried out by the wholesaler, who is responsible for the general and mid-term planning in the form of a tactical route plan. The tactical route plan specifies the available routes that are supposed to be used for the distribution of goods. These tactical routes are determined using average demand data for given regions, taking into account frequency requirements as well as delivery time windows at retails stores. The objective is to minimize the delivery costs while ensuring a high truck utilization, see also [15]. Due to the short planning horizon, we assume the tactical route plan to be constant in the remainder of the paper.

The second planning stage is the operational distribution planning carried out by both the wholesaler and the transport company. The wholesaler determines the amount of cargo to be transported the following day and the set of tactical routes that the transport company can choose from. Due to requirements of the retail stores, e.g. delivery time windows, tactical routes are usually specific to the day of departure, i.e. a route planned for being used on Mondays can only be selected on Mondays. The transport company then allocates goods to trucks and trucks to routes. The transport company can also select to serve shorter subroutes of the tactical routes, e.g. if actual demand on a tactical route exceeds the capacity of a truck. Note that the objective for the two companies is different: The transport company wants to minimize the number of trucks used to transport the goods, whereas the wholesaler minimizes the cost of the transport volume plus a penalty for deviating from a given target volume. This penalty provides an incentive to the wholesaler to ship more or less the same volume each day, facilitating a more efficient resource utilization [7].

Formulating the wholesaler and transport company's decision problems as single, integrated optimization problem with multiple objectives might result in better distribution plans. This is due to the fact that the information of both companies would be captured in the same model. However, this approach implies a single decision maker as well as the availability of full information. Neither of these assumptions holds in case of the problem considered in this paper.

To study the value of information sharing between the wholesaler and the transport company, we focus on operational distribution planning. We distinguish between three different information sharing cases. The cases differ in how the wholesaler plans distribution and shares tactical routes and cargo volume with the transport company. The different cases are illustrated in Fig. 1. The planning horizon is considered to be one week. In the first information sharing case (DD), the wholesaler plans distribution on a daily basis. This information is shared with the transport company each day, which can only plan one day ahead. In the second case (WD), the wholesaler plans distribution for the entire week, but still shares routes and volumes on a daily basis only. The third case (WW) considers the situation where the wholesaler shares the distribution plan for the entire week with the transport company. This is also the only case where the transport company can plan for the entire week.

The daily distribution plan resulting from the operational distribution planning combines the chosen subset of tactical routes with the actual demand. However, actual demand may exceed the demand that was used to determine the tactical routes. In this case, the transport company may have to deploy more than one truck on the route, each serving a subset of the retail stores along the route. A possible consequence of this is a reduced utilization of the available trucks.

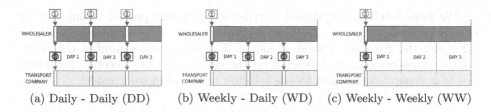

(a) Daily - Daily (DD)   (b) Weekly - Daily (WD)   (c) Weekly - Weekly (WW)

Fig. 1. Three different combinations of planning and information sharing

We introduce two types of flexibility and study their effect on the transportation cost: The first type of flexibility is delivery flexibility, i.e. here defined as the ability to deviate from the originally planned delivery date. Delivery flexibility can only exploited when planning for the entire week and only for goods that can be stored without deteriorating. We distinguish between three groups of goods, namely non-storable (NS), promotional storable (PS) and ordinary storable (OS) goods. Non-storable goods must be transported in accordance to planned delivery date. The wholesaler is allowed change the delivery date of PS goods to an early point in time for the WD and WW information sharing cases. The transport company can postpone the delivery of OS goods in the WW information sharing case. Changing the delivery date can only happen within the planning horizon of one week.

Route selection flexibility allows the transport company to choose different routes than the ones selected by the wholesaler. In the base case, the transport company can only use the wholesaler's selected routes for each given day. Under conditional route selection flexibility, the transport company can choose from the routes in the wholesalers has selected, irrespective of which day they were supposed to be driven. In the case of an unconditional route selection flexibility, the transport company may choose any route from the set of tactical routes, independently of choices made by the wholesaler.

3   Model Formulations and Solution Approach

For transportation planning, routing problems are the most common group of quantitative models. The Vehicle Routing Problem (VRP) is one of the most well-known and studied transportation routing problems, see [13, 26] for excellent overviews of the problem, extensions and solution methods.

A common way to model a VRP is using a set covering formulation, see e.g. [2,3,23]. The set covering formulation is very general and constructed to find the routes that will satisfy the delivery requirements at minimum cost. Two main approaches for generating the set of routes to choose from can be distinguished: The first approach entails the iterative generation of routes on-the-fly, e.g. through column generation [4,9]. See [8] for a thorough literature review of the advancement of column generation and the use of set covering formulations in VRPs. In the second approach, the set of routes is generated a priori, i.e. before solving the optimization model [5].

We formulate the operational distribution planning problem using two set covering models with a set of a priori generated routes. The model for the wholesaler uses the given set of tactical routes. The set of routes used in the model for the transport company depends on the degree of route selection flexibility, but is in general determined by the solution to the wholesaler model.

3.1 Notation

We first introduce the notation for the wholesaler and transport company models:

- Sets

$\mathcal{N}$	Set of retailers
$\mathcal{R}$	Set of available routes
$\mathcal{V}$	Set of trucks
$\mathcal{T}^W$	Set of days in the week
$\mathcal{T}^P$	Set of time periods in the week
$\mathcal{T}_d^D$	Set of time periods in day d, $\mathcal{T}_d^D \subseteq \mathcal{T}^P$
$\mathcal{P}$	Set of breakpoints

- Parameters

A_{ir}	1 if retailer i is on route r, 0 otherwise
B_{rt}	1 if route r can be chosen in time period t, 0 otherwise
C_r^P	Cost of transporting one pallet on route r
C_p^L	Penalty for deviating from daily target demand in breakpoint p
C_r^R	Cost of serving route r
C^{Own}	Cost of using an owned truck
C^{Rent}	Cost of using a rented truck
$\overline{D}$	Daily target demand
D_{it}^{NS}	Retailer i's demand of NS pallets scheduled for time period t
D_{it}^{PS}	Retailer i's demand of PS pallets scheduled for time period t
D_{it}^{OS}	Retailer i's demand of OS pallets scheduled for time period t
E	Number of time periods a SP pallet can be delivered earlier
I_i	Retailer i's inventory size
I_i^0	Retailer i's inventory in the beginning of the week
K_r	Number of consecutive time periods a truck is unavailable if assigned to route r
L	Number of time periods delivery a SO pallet can be postponed
m	Number of owned trucks
Q^V	Truck capacity
α	Share of pallets that can change delivery date
β_p	Allowed number of pallets for breakpoint p

– Variables

$w_{i\rho t}$ Number of pallets for retailer i scheduled for time period ρ with actual transport in time period t

x_{rtv} 1 if truck v leaves in time period t on route r, 0 otherwise

y_{irt}^{NS} NS pallets for retailer i on route r leaving in time period t

y_{irt}^{PS} PS pallets for retailer i on route r leaving in time period t

y_{irt}^{OS} OS pallets for retailer i on route r leaving in time period t

δ_v 1 if truck v is used during the week, 0 otherwise

γ_{it} Number of SP and SO pallets at retailer i's inventory in time period t

σ_{dp}^+ Pallets above target demand on day d for breakpoint p

σ_{dp}^- Pallets below target demand on day d for breakpoint p

Please note that transport requirements such as delivery time windows are already incorporated in the given routes. All retailer demand is specified in terms of number of pallets at the departure time.

3.2 Model Formulations

The wholesaler model and the transport company model have many similarities. We first present the objective function and unique constraints of each model separately before presenting the constraints the two models have in common.

The Wholesaler Model. The unique part of the wholesaler model is given as

$$\min \quad \sum_{d \in T^W} \sum_{p \in \mathcal{P}} C_p^L (\sigma_{dp}^+ + \sigma_{dp}^-) + \sum_{i \in \mathcal{N}} \sum_{r \in \mathcal{R}} \sum_{t \in T^P} C_r^P (y_{irt}^{NS} + y_{irt}^{OS} + y_{irt}^{PS}) \quad (1)$$

subject to

$$\sum_{r \in \mathcal{R} | A_{ir} = 1} (y_{irt}^{OS} + y_{irt}^{PS}) - \gamma_{it} + \gamma_{i(t-1)} = D_{it-1}^{OS} + D_{it-1}^{PS} \quad i \in \mathcal{N}, t \in T^P \quad (2)$$

$$\gamma_{it} \leq I_i \qquad\qquad\qquad i \in \mathcal{N}, t \in T^P \quad (3)$$

$$\gamma_{i0} = I_i^0 \qquad\qquad\qquad i \in \mathcal{N} \quad (4)$$

$$\sum_{i \in \mathcal{N}} \sum_{r \in \mathcal{R}} \sum_{t \in T_d^P} (y_{irt}^{NS} + y_{irt}^{OS} + y_{irt}^{PS}) + \sum_{p \in \mathcal{P}} (\sigma_{dp}^- - \sigma_{dp}^+) = \overline{D} \qquad d \in T^W \quad (5)$$

$$\sigma_{dp}^+ + \sigma_{dp}^- \leq \beta_p \qquad\qquad\qquad d \in T^W, p \in \mathcal{P} \quad (6)$$

$$\sigma_{dp}^+, \sigma_{dp}^- \geq 0 \qquad\qquad\qquad d \in T^W, p \in \mathcal{P} \quad (7)$$

$$\gamma_{it} \geq 0 \qquad\qquad\qquad i \in \mathcal{N}, t \in T^P \quad (8)$$

The objective function (1) reflects different the wholesaler's two cost incentives. The first term expresses is the penalty cost for deviating from the target transport volume. The unit penalty cost, C_p^L, increases piecewise linearly with breakpoint p. Both the unit penalty cost and the total deviation, given by σ_{dp}, increase with increased deviation from the target demand and contribute to the resulting total penalty cost. The second term represents the cost related to transporting a pallet on a given route. The unit cost of transporting a pallet on route r, C_r^P, is positively correlated with the length of the route.

Retailer inventory balance and restrictions are formulated in constraints (2)–(4). Pallets for non-storable goods (NS) are assumed to be placed in the store at once, therefore the retailer inventory only concerns storable pallets. Constraint (2) is the mass balance constraint for the inventory. Constraint (3) prevents each retailer's inventory size from being exceeded at any time. The retailer's initial inventory at the beginning of the week is defined in constraint (4). Constraints (5) and (6) calculate the deviation from the target transportation volume. The deviation is calculated in constraint (5), whereas constraint (6) limits the deviation variables according to the breakpoints of the penalty function. Constraint (7) and (8) are the non-negativity constraints for the decision variables.

The Transport Company Model. Note that the set of available routes $\mathcal{R}$ in the transport company model depends on the information sharing case and the solution from the wholesaler model. The objective function and the unique constraints for the transport company model are given as

$$\min \ \sum_{r \in \mathcal{R}} \sum_{t \in \mathcal{T}^P} \sum_{v \in \mathcal{V}} C_r^R x_{rtv} + \left(\sum_{v=1}^{m} C^{\text{Own}} \delta_v + \sum_{v=m+1}^{|\mathcal{V}|} C^{\text{Rent}} \delta_v \right) \tag{9}$$

subject to

$$Q^V \sum_{v \in \mathcal{V}} x_{rtv} - \sum_{i \in \mathcal{N} | A_{ir}=1} (y_{irt}^{NS} + y_{irt}^{OS} + y_{irt}^{PS}) \geq 0$$
$$r \in \mathcal{R}, t \in \mathcal{T}^P \tag{10}$$

$$\sum_{r \in \mathcal{R}} \sum_{t'=t}^{t+K_r} x_{rt'v} \leq 1 \qquad\qquad t \in \mathcal{T}^P, v \in \mathcal{V} \tag{11}$$

$$\sum_{r \in \mathcal{R}} \sum_{t'=t}^{t+K_r} \sum_{v \in \mathcal{V}} x_{rt'v} \leq |\mathcal{V}| \qquad t \in \mathcal{T}^P | (t + K_r) \leq |\mathcal{T}^P| \tag{12}$$

$$\sum_{v \in \mathcal{V}} x_{rtv} \leq |\mathcal{V}| B_{rt} \qquad\qquad r \in \mathcal{R}, t \in \mathcal{T}^P \tag{13}$$

$$M_1 \delta_v - \sum_{r \in \mathcal{R}} \sum_{t \in \mathcal{T}^P} x_{rtv} \geq 0 \qquad\qquad v \in \mathcal{V} \tag{14}$$

$$\delta_{v+1} - \delta_v \leq 0 \qquad\qquad v \in \mathcal{V} \tag{15}$$

$$x_{rtv} \in \{0,1\} \qquad\qquad r \in \mathcal{R}, t \in \mathcal{T}^P, v \in \mathcal{V} \tag{16}$$

$$\delta_v \in \{0,1\} \qquad\qquad v \in \mathcal{V} \tag{17}$$

The first term of objective function (9) is represents the operational costs of serving the selected routes. Here, route cost reflects the time it takes to complete the route. The second term is the cost of the used of trucks during the week.

Constraint (10) ensures that the capacity of all trucks assigned to a route is larger than the demand on the route. Further, constraint (11)–(13) makes sure that a truck v can only be in use once in each time period t. According to constraint (12), it is not possible to use more trucks than available in the fleet. Constraint (13) is a big M-formulation, which ensures that only feasible x_{rtv} are chosen. Constraints (14) and (15) keep track of which trucks are in use when. Constraint (14) connects δ_v and x_{rtv}, requiring δ_v to be equal to 1 if truck v is in use at least once during the week. Furthermore, constraint (15) is a symmetry breaking constraint, ensuring that the trucks with the lowest index are used first. Constraints (16) and (17) impose binary requirements on δ_v and x_{rtv}.

Common Constraints. The following constraints are structurally similar in both models and primarily consider demand. The constraints are here presented in terms of the wholesaler model. Note that the wholesaler can change the delivery date of the promotional storable (PS) goods, whereas the transport company can change the delivery date of the ordinary storable (OS) goods. Please see the text below the constraints for an explantion on how this affects the different constraints.

$$\sum_{r \in \mathcal{R} | A_{ir}=1} y_{irt}^{NS} = D_{it}^{NS} \qquad\qquad i \in \mathcal{N}, t \in \mathcal{T}^P \qquad (18)$$

$$\sum_{r \in \mathcal{R} | A_{ir}=1} y_{irt}^{OS} = D_{it}^{OS} \qquad\qquad i \in \mathcal{N}, t \in \mathcal{T}^P \qquad (19)$$

$$\sum_{t \in \mathcal{T}^P} (y_{irt}^{NS} + y_{irt}^{OS} + y_{irt}^{PS}) \leq M_1 A_{ir} \qquad\qquad i \in \mathcal{N}, r \in \mathcal{R} \qquad (20)$$

$$\sum_{i \in \mathcal{N}} (y_{irt}^{NS} + y_{irt}^{OS} + y_{irt}^{PS}) \leq M_2 B_{rt} \qquad\qquad r \in \mathcal{R}, t \in \mathcal{T}^P \qquad (21)$$

$$\sum_{t=\rho-E}^{\rho} w_{i\rho t} = D_{i\rho}^{PS} \qquad\qquad i \in \mathcal{N}, \rho \in \mathcal{T}^P | t > 0 \qquad (22)$$

$$\sum_{r \in \mathcal{R} | A_{ir}=1} y_{irt}^{PS} - \sum_{\rho=t}^{t+E} w_{i\rho t} = 0 \qquad\qquad i \in \mathcal{N}, t \in \mathcal{T}^P | \rho \leq |\mathcal{T}^P| \qquad (23)$$

$$w_{i\rho\rho} \geq (1-\alpha) D_{i\rho}^{PS} \qquad\qquad i \in \mathcal{N}, \rho \in \mathcal{T}^P \qquad (24)$$

$$w_{i\rho t} \geq 0 \ \ \& \ \text{integer} \qquad\qquad i \in \mathcal{N}, \rho \in \mathcal{T}^P, t \in \mathcal{T}^P \qquad (25)$$

$$y_{irt}^{NS}, y_{irt}^{OS}, y_{irt}^{PS} \geq 0 \ \ \& \ \text{integer} \qquad\qquad i \in \mathcal{N}, r \in \mathcal{R}, t \in \mathcal{T}^P \qquad (26)$$

Constraint (18) and (19) ensure that goods that cannot change delivery date are transported in according to schedule. Note that constraint (19) for the transport company is formulated for y_{irt}^{PS} and D_{it}^{PS}. Constraint (20) ensures y_{irt} is zero if a retailer i cannot be served on route r (i.e. $A_{ir} = 0$). Correspondingly, Constraint (21) ensures that y_{irt} only takes a positive value if route r can be used (leave/depart) in time period t (i.e. $B_{rt} = 1$). Changing the delivery date of goods is handled in constraint (22)–(24). In the wholesaler model, PS pallets can be delivered earlier than scheduled by introducing $w_{i\rho t}$. Constraint (22) makes sure that all deliveries happen within the allowed time window. Furthermore, Constraint (23) connects the two decision variables y_{irt}^{PS} and $w_{i\rho t}$. The transport company can postpone the delivery of OS pallets, constraints (22) and (23) are therefore replaced with

$$\sum_{t=\rho}^{\rho+L} w_{i\rho t} = D_{i\rho}^{OS} \qquad\qquad i \in \mathcal{N}, \rho \in \mathcal{T}^P | t \leq |\mathcal{T}^P| \quad (27)$$

$$\sum_{r \in \mathcal{R}|A_{ir}=1} y_{irt}^{OS} - \sum_{\rho=t-L}^{t} w_{i\rho t} = 0 \qquad\qquad i \in \mathcal{N}, t \in \mathcal{T}^P | \rho > 0 \quad (28)$$

Constraint (24) defines the upper limit of cargo that can change delivery date. Note that in the transport company model, this constraint is defined for $D_{i\rho}^{OS}$. Constraints (25) and (26) impose integer requirements and non-negativity.

4   Computational Study

The optimization models are implemented in Xpress Mosel version 3.8.0 and solved with FICOXpress Optimizer version 27.01.02. All calculations have been carried out on a computer with a 3.60 GHz Intel Core i7-4790S processor and 16.0 GB RAM running Microsoft Windows 7 Enterprise operating system.

4.1   Case Data

The case data is based on real world data from a Norwegian grocery wholesaler and transport company. The area of analysis is shown in Fig. 2. The transport area defines the geographical area where the retail stores are located. The wholesaler location is where all cargo is shipped from.

The analysis is carried out using daily demand data for one representative week. The main characteristics of the case are summarized in Table 1. Note that the operational routes include routes that only visit a subset of the retails stores on a tactical route.

4.2   Results

We combine the three information sharing cases (DD, WD, WW) with four different levels of flexibility: no flexibility (NF), delivery flexibility (D), route selection flexibility (R) and combined flexibility (C), i.e. both delivery and route selection flexibility. For the instance combing the weekly-weekly information sharing case with routing flexibility, we distinguish between two levels of routing flexibility,

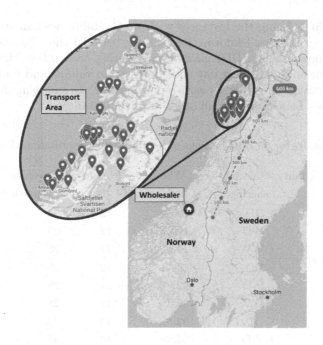

Fig. 2. Location of the wholesaler and the transport area

Table 1. Main characteristics of the case.

Description	Value
Number of retailers	39
Number of tactical routes	23
Number of daily routes/departures	[1,5]
Number of operational routes	222
Number of pallets of demand	1081
Number of PS pallets	128
Share of PS pallets that can be delivered early	0.9
Number of OS pallets	489
Share of OS pallets that can be delivered late	0.2

namely conditional, WW^{cond}, and unconditional, WW^{uncond}, routing flexibility that differ in the size of the set of available routes. For all instances, we report the relative distribution cost (in %) for the wholesaler as well as the required number of trucks and departures for the transport company. The results for the different combinations of available flexibility and information sharing cases are summarized in Table 2 and discussed in more detail below.

No Flexibility. Using the instances with no flexibility, we can study the isolated impact of increased information sharing between the wholesaler and the transport company. The (DD) information sharing case, where the wholesaler plans distribution for the next day and shares cargo volume and routes with the transport company on a daily basis, represents the current planning situation and serves as a benchmark for all other problem instances.

Table 2. Results for all combinations of flexibility and information sharing cases.

Flexibility	Information sharing	Wholesaler Rel. cost	Transport Company	
			Trucks	Departures
NF	DD	100%	12	28
	WD	100%	12	28
	WW	100%	12	28
D	DD	100%	12	28
	WD	92.3%	11	28
	WW	92.3%	11	28
R	DD	92.8%	14	35
	WD	92.8%	14	35
	WW^{cond}	92.8%	13	36
	WW^{uncond}	92.8%	9	24
C	DD	92.8%	14	35
	WD	79.1%	16	42
	WW^{cond}	79.1%	15	40
	WW^{uncond}	79.1%	10	30

We find that all the three information sharing cases give identical results. The models in each information sharing case choose the same routes, both tactical and operational, use the same number of trucks and have the same number of departures the same day of the week. This implies that there is no or little benefit of increased information sharing alone.

Delivery Flexibility. Introducing delivery flexibility allows changing the delivery date for some of the goods. PS goods can be delivered up to 7 days ahead of time in the wholesaler model, whereas OS goods can be postponed by up to 3 days in the transport company model. Exploiting delivery flexibility is only possible if the planning horizon is longer than one day. The DD instance is therefore identical to the benchmark case with no flexibility.

The wholesaler chooses the same tactical routes in all three information cases, but the cost for the wholesaler is reduced by 7.7% when the wholesaler plans increases the planning horizon for distribution planning from one day to one week. Note that the results for the wholesaler in the WD and WW information sharing cases are identical due to identical model input. The wholesaler's cost reduction is mainly due to a reduction in penalty cost for deviating from the transport volume target. Being able to change the delivery date for most of the PS pallets makes it easier for the wholesaler to achieve a constant transport volume. In fact, 52 PS pallets or approximately 75% of the goods that can be delivered earlier are scheduled for an earlier shipment.

The results from the transport company model change for each information sharing case with delivery flexibility. Most notably, the number of trucks needed to transport all cargo is reduced by one when the wholesaler extends its planning horizon to one week. In information sharing case WD, the transport company still receives transport information on a daily basis and can therefore not exploit delivery flexibility. The reduction in number of trucks can thus be attributed to the more evenly distributed transport volumes planned by the wholesaler. When delivery flexibility is enabled for the transport company in the WW information sharing case, the transport company chooses to postpone the delivery of 23 OS pallets or approximately 35% of the pallets that could have been postponed. The transport company exploits delivery flexibility less than the wholesaler, which might be due to the fact that the levelling of demand has already been done by the wholesaler. Exploiting delivery flexibility does not reduce the number of trucks or departures further. The main improvement for the transport company is due to the wholesaler exploiting delivery flexibility, rather than sharing information earlier.

Route Selection Flexibility. So far, the set of available routes has been limited to the routes specific for the day of departure. When introducing route selection flexibility, we relax this assumption and make all routes in the tactical route available on all days. Note that this relaxation may violate the agreements the wholesaler has with the retail stores. For the WW information sharing case, we distinguish between two levels of route selection flexibility for the transport company: in the case conditional route selection flexibility, the transport company can chose from all routes selected by the wholesaler, whereas in the case of unconditional route selection flexibility, the transport company can chose from all routes in the tactical route plan.

When introducing route selection flexibility, the wholesaler can reduce her cost by 7.2% compared to the instances without flexibility. This is slightly worse than the solution from the delivery flexibility instances. Note that the solutions from the wholesaler model are identical for all the three information sharing cases. Extending the planning horizon does not contribute to a reduction in cost. Information sharing does not cause any benefits for the wholesaler in this instance. As the cargo volumes cannot be changed, the cost reduction in this instance is due to changing different routes. The model tries to choose the shortest route for serving the different retailers each day. Therefore, the chosen routes consist of many short routes compared to fewer and longer routes that serve more retailers in the instances with no flexibility.

With the exception of WW^{uncond}, the transport company is generally worse off in terms of number of trucks and departures than compared to the instances without route selection flexibility. This is due to the high number of short routes selected by the wholesaler, which forces the transport company to deploy more trucks in order to serve all retail stores. Sharing of information enables the transport company to reduce the number of trucks by one at the expense of an additional departure as the set of chosen routes is now available for the entire week rather than a single day. Still, even with information sharing, the results for transport company in instance WW^{cond} are worse in than in the previous instances. These results clearly highlight that a reduction in transport cost for the wholesaler does not necessarily lead to cost savings for the transport company.

With unconditional route selection flexibility, the transport company can choose any route, independent of routes chosen by the wholesaler. This increase in flexibility allows the transport company to considerably reduce the number of trucks and departures. In fact, the results are even better than ones in the previous instances. Still these results also indicate the degree of routing flexibility is more important for the transport company than information sharing.

Combined Flexibility. In these instances we allow exploiting delivery flexibility and route selection flexibility at the same time. Note that delivery flexibility can only be exploiting when using a planning horizon of one week. Note that the solution for the DD information sharing case is identical to the DD solution from the route selection case, as change of delivery date is not possible. For the transport company we again distinguish between conditional and unconditional route selection flexibility in the WW information sharing case.

Compared to the instances without any flexibility, the wholesaler can reduce her transportation cost by 20.9% by extending the planning horizon to one week. Due to being able to exploit both delivery and route selection flexibility, the wholesaler is able to both even out the transported volumes per day and select the most efficient routes for serving the different retailers.

Without information sharing, the cost reduction for the wholesaler comes at the expense of the transport company, who has to deploy a total of 16 trucks in the WD information sharing case, the highest number in all of the instances. After introducing information sharing, the transport company is able to reduce the number of trucks and departures slightly under conditional route selection flexibility. Still, the numbers of trucks and departures remain higher than the instances without flexibility. Again we see that cost reductions for the wholesaler increase the costs for the transport company.

Under unconditional route flexibility, the transport company can reduce the number of trucks by 33% and the number of departures by 25% compared to the solution under conditional route flexibility. As we saw for the instances with only routing flexibility, the degree of flexibility has a larger impact on the costs of the transport company than mere information sharing.

5   Concluding Remarks

In this paper, we investigate the effect of information sharing and flexibility between a wholesaler and a transport company in the Norwegian grocery industry. The planning problems for each of the companies are formulated as individual optimization problems. The models are linked as the outcome from the wholersaler model serves as input to the transport company model. Information sharing is then modeled by controlling which information from the wholesaler model is available for the transport company model.

The different information sharing cases are combined with two different types of flexibility: delivery flexibility and route selection flexibility. Our results show clearly that information sharing alone has very limited benefits. Without flexibility to adjust decisions, the transport company cannot utilize the shared information. While delivery flexibility has a positive effect on the costs of both wholesaler and transport company, the results are less clear for route selection flexibility. The results indicate that there is a possible conflict of interest: under conditional route selection flexibility, the wholesaler's savings come at the expense of the transport company, who has to deploy more trucks. Introducing more flexibility in the planning process therefore has to consider the effect on all members of the value chain.

Different approaches for modeling the relationship between the wholesaler and the transport company, e.g. multiobjective optimization, bilevel programming or agent-based simulation, might provide additional insights, not only regarding the value of information sharing, but also for designing new, improved collaborative planning processes. The use of these approaches is subject of future research.

References

1. Bø, E., Grønland, S.E., Henning, L.: Bedre utnyttelse av lastebiler: integrering i forsyningskjeder gir økt transporteffektivitet (in Norwegian). VD Report, Vegdirektoratet, Oslo, Norway (2011)
2. Baldacci, R., Bartolini, E., Mingozzi, A., Valletta, A.: An exact algorithm for the period routing problem. Oper. Res. **59**(1), 228–241 (2011)
3. Balinski, M.L., Quandt, R.E.: On an integer program for a delivery problem. Oper. Res. **12**(2), 300–304 (1964)
4. Cacchiani, V., Hemmelmayr, V.C., Tricoire, F.: A set-covering based heuristic algorithm for the periodic vehicle routing problem. Discrete Appl. Math. **163**(1), 53–64 (2014)
5. Campbell, A.M., Thomas, B.W.: Challenges and advances in a priori routing. In: Golden, B., Raghavan, S., Wasil, E. (eds.) The Vehicle Routing Problem: Latest Advances and New Challenges, Operations Research/Computer Science Interfaces, vol. 43, pp. 123–142. Springer, Boston (2008). https://doi.org/10.1007/978-0-387-77778-8_6
6. Celius, E., Goldsack, M.: Quantifying the value of information sharing: a case study between a regional wholesaler and a transport company in the grocery supply chain. Project report, Department of Industrial Economics and Technology Management, Norwegian University of Science and Technology, Trondheim, Norway (2017)

340   E. Celius et al.

7. Chopra, S., Meindl, P.: Supply Chain Management: Strategy, Planning, and Operation, 6th edn. Pearson, Boston (2016)
8. Dayarian, I., Crainic, T.G., Gendreau, M., Rei, W.: A column generation approach for a multi-attribute vehicle routing problem. Euro. J. Oper. Res. **241**(3), 888–906 (2015)
9. Desrochers, M., Desrosiers, J., Solomon, M.: A new optimization algorithm for the vehicle routing problem with time windows. Oper. Res. **40**(2), 342–354 (1992)
10. Dreyer, H.C., Kiil, K., Dukovska-Popovska, I., Kaipia, R.: Proposals for enhancing tactical planning in grocery retailing with S&OP. Int. J. Phys. Distribut. Logistics Manage. **48**(2), 114–138 (2018)
11. Ettouzani, Y., Yates, N., Mena, C.: Examining retail on shelf availability: promotional impact and a call for research. Int. J. Phys. Distribut. Logistics Manage. **42**(3), 213–243 (2012)
12. Gansterer, M., Hartl, R.F.: Collaborative vehicle routing: a survey. Euro. J. Oper. Res. **268**(1), 1–12 (2018)
13. Golden, B., Raghavan, S., Wasil, E. (eds.): The vehicle routing problem: latest advances and new challenges. Operations Research/Computer Science Interfaces, vol. 43. Springer, New York (2008). https://doi.org/10.1007/978-0-387-77778-8
14. Hagen, A., Stefansson, G.: A framework for transport planning processes - a logistics service provider perspective. In: Arnäs, P.O., Arvidsson, N., Bergqvist, R., Johansson, M., Pahlén, P.O. (eds.) Proceedings of the 25th NOFOMA Conference. Gothenburg, Sweden (2013)
15. Hübner, A.H., Kuhn, H., Sternbeck, M.G.: Demand and supply chain planning in grocery retail: an operations planning framework. Int. J. Retail Distrib. Manage. **41**(7), 512–530 (2013)
16. Johannson, T.: Effektivitet og bærekraft i hele verdikjeden - sett fra ASKO's ståsted (in Norwegian). Transport & Logistikk 2015, Gardermoen, Norway. https://docplayer.me/6551195-Transport-logistikk-2015-19-20-10-2015.html, Accessed 24 April 2020
17. Jonsson, P., Myrelid, P.: Supply chain information utilisation: conceptualisation and antecedents. Int. J. Oper. Prod. Manage. **36**(12), 1769–1799 (2016)
18. Kembro, J., Näslund, D.: Information sharing in supply chains, myth or reality? a critical analysis of empirical literature. Int. J. Phys. Distrib. Logistics Manage. **44**(3), 179–200 (2014)
19. Kiil, K.: Aligning Supply and Demand in Grocery Retailing. Doctoral theses at NTNU, 2017:366, Department of Mechanical and Industrial Engineering, Norwegian University of Science and Technology, Trondheim, Norway (2017)
20. Kiil, K., Hvolby, H.H., Trienekens, J., Behdani, B., Strandhagen, J.O.: From information sharing to information utilization in food supply chains. Int. J. Inf. Syst. Supply Chain Manage. **12**(3), 85–109 (2019)
21. Los, J., Schulte, F., Spaan, M.T., Negenborg, R.R.: Collaborative vehicle routing when agents have mixed information sharing attitudes. Transport. Res. Procedia **44**, 94–101 (2020)
22. Myrelid, P.: Utilisation of shared demand-related information for operations planning and control. Licentiate thesis 2015:076, Department of Technology Management and Economics, Chalmers University of Technology, Gothenburg, Sweden (2015)
23. Rousseau, L.M., Gendreau, M., Pesant, G.: Solving VRPTWs with constraint programming based column generation. Ann. Oper. Res. **130**(1–4), 199–216 (2004)

24. Rushton, A., Croucher, P., Baker, P.: The Handbook of Logistics and Distribution Management: Understanding the Supply Chain, 6th edn. Kogan Page, London (2017)
25. Simchi-Levi, D., Kaminsky, P., Simchi-Levi, E.: Designing and Managing the Supply Chain: Concepts, Strategies and Case Studies, 3rd edn. McGraw-Hill, New York (2008)
26. Toth, P., Vigo, D.: Vehicle Routing: Problems, Methods, and Applications. Society for Industrial and Applied Mathematics, Philadelphia (2014)

A Bin Packing Problem with Mixing Constraints for Containerizing Items for Logistics Service Providers

Sajini Anand[1]([⊠])(iD) and Stefan Guericke[2](iD)

[1] A.P. Moller Maersk R&D, Bangalore, India
`sajini.anand@maersk.com`
[2] A.P. Moller Maersk R&D, Copenhagen, Denmark
`stefan.guericke@maersk.com`

Abstract. Large logistics service providers often need to containerize and route thousands or millions of items per year. In practice, companies specify business rules of how to pack and transport items from their origin to destination. Handling and respecting those business rules manually is a complex and time-consuming task. We propose a variant of the variable sized bin packing problem applicable to the containerization process occurring at logistics service providers. This novel model variant extends the bin packing problem with color constraints by adding multiple item mixing constraints. We present a binary integer program along with a first-fit decreasing heuristic and compare the performance on instances from a global logistics service provider. The numerical results indicate promising results to solve this computationally hard combinatorial optimization problem.

Keywords: Load planning problem · Variable sized bin packing with color constraints · Variable sized bin packing with multiple item mixing constraints

1 Introduction

Every year, millions of standardized containers are transported across the world [25,27]. [26] reports that the value transported through containers is more than 50% of the worldwide seaborne value. Containerized cargo varies from automobile spare parts to scrap metals and refrigerated cargo to consumer goods. In this paper, we focus on commodities that can be packed into rectangular stackable boxes with variable weights and volumes that are transported in dry containers, as it is the case for e.g. large retail enterprises.

Organizing and orchestrating the transport is either handled by large manufactures directly or outsourced to third parties, such as freight forwarders and third/ fourth party logistics providers. We keep referring to these third parties as logistics service providers (LSP) throughout this paper. LSPs enable the end-to-end transport of cargo from an origin location (either a manufacturer or a

© Springer Nature Switzerland AG 2020
E. Lalla-Ruiz et al. (Eds.): ICCL 2020, LNCS 12433, pp. 342–355, 2020.
https://doi.org/10.1007/978-3-030-59747-4_22

producer) to its final point of destination (warehouse, market or a customer) ensuring a worldwide distribution of products. LSPs usually containerize the cargo into full container loads (FCL) to reduce costs by using efficient container shipping lines. This containerization process considers items of different types and origins from one (or potentially multiple) customer(s). Items have properties associated, such as their origin plant, and we refer to these item properties as cargo attributes.

Today, the containerization process is a time-consuming manual task. Customers use complex business rules that define how items can be mixed in a single container. For example, a customer would like to avoid mixing items of more than 4 different production plants. The large volume of items that needs to be containerized combined with the rules make it challenging to identify good solutions on a day-to-day basis. Fast and efficient solution methods can help the planners in their decision process. The underlying optimization problem is a variant of the one-dimensional (e.g. volume, weight restrictions) Variable Sized Bin Packing Problem (VSBPP) that minimizes the total container costs while adhering to the business rules that constrain the mixing of items.

To the best of our knowledge, a generic approach for considering multiple mixing constraints for cargo consolidation has not been presented before. Therefore, this paper contributes to the state-of-the-art by:

- Introducing a novel variant of the one-dimensional variable sized bin packing problem with multiple item mixing constraints, applicable for instance to the containerization problem of logistics service providers,
- Proposing a binary integer problem that can solve small instances to optimality,
- Proposing a fast and efficient extension to the well-known first-fit decreasing heuristic to solve the problem for practical instances.

The remainder of this paper is organized as follows: Sect. 1.1 provides details of the underlying containerization and load planning problem, followed by a literature review in Sect. 1.2. Section 2 formalizes the problem, presents a binary integer program and a heuristic solution approach. Section 3 introduces test-instances and a numerical analysis of the solution methods. We conclude the work and reflect on future extensions in Sect. 4.

1.1   The Load Planning and Containerization Problem

A logistics service provider operates facilities, called container freight stations (CFS), to consolidate less than container load (LCL) cargo from different customers, factories and properties into standardized containers for container shipping. CFS can either be used for consolidation or de-consolidation, e.g. to cross-dock cargo at its destination. Full container loads are then transported in an intermodal network, often using container shipping lines for the long haul. The containerization and specification of a routing on a shipping line (a specific vessel departure) is referred to as the load planning process in practice. Once

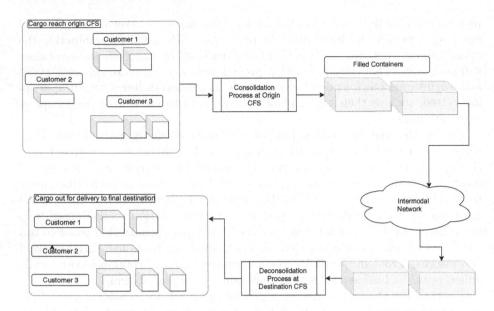

Fig. 1. Consolidation and deconsolidation of cargo at container freight stations.

containers reach their destination port, they are forwarded to the destination CFS, de-consolidated and transported to their final destination. See Fig. 1 for an overview of this process.

A LSP receives cargo bookings with a list of attributes that contain information about the cargo, such as date of arrival, factory, stock keeping unit (SKU), vendor or cargo type. We have observed on average 35 attributes that influence the load planning process. These can be distinguished between those 1) influencing the mix of cargo within a container (called cargo attributes) and those 2) determining the vessel departure (routing attributes). An example of a mixing constraint is 'cargo from two different vendors or containing more than four different SKUs cannot go in the same container'. The objective of business rules is to simplify the handling at the destination CFS, support the packing at the warehouses and ensure safety regulations. In practice, those rules usually differ by origin-destination pair and customer.

The objective of packing cargo into containers is to minimize the total container costs. Different types of standardized dry containers are used, for instance twenty-foot equivalent units (TEU) and forty-foot equivalent units (FFE), each with different volume and weight capacities. Each cargo needs to be assigned to a container while respecting capacity and cargo mixing constraints. In the remainder of this paper we will refer to items and bins instead of cargo and containers to be consistent with previous work in the bin-packing literature.

1.2   Literature Review

The classic Bin Packing Problem (BPP) of assigning items to a minimum number of identical bins without exceeding their capacity [15] is a well explored NP-hard optimization problem [20]. We refer to the work of [4–6,9,10] for extensive surveys throughout the last decades. In this paper we focus on one-dimensional bin packing problems and refer to [23] and [3] for recent advances in multi-dimensional bin packing algorithms. BPPs are solved to optimality using mathematical programming [9], metaheuristics [21] and well-known approximation algorithms such as First-Fit Decreasing (FFD) [16].

A relevant extension to the classic BPP are variable sized bins (VS-BPP) and variable costs [13]. This variant has been solved using various algorithms, such as Branch-and-Price or an extended FFD, and we refer to [1,14] and [17] for an overview.

Another extension related to the containerization problem presented above is the Bin Packing with Conflicts (BPPC) that assign items to a minimum number of bins while avoiding joint assignments of items that are in conflict [11]. A graph structure is used where nodes represent the items and edges represents the conflicts between a pair of items. [11] do not consider variable bin sizes, multiple capacity constraints and, most importantly, mixing constraints beyond pairwise conflicts. We refer to [24] and [2] for further solution methods on the BPPC.

A relatively recent work that is closely related to our problem is the variable sized bin packing problem with color constraints (VBPC) [8]. Items have an associated color and not more than two colors can be packed together in the same bin. [8] also introduce the generalized VBPC (GVBPC) problem where at most p colors can be packed into the same bin. They propose a first-fit variant to solve the GVBPC and derive bounds of their approach. [19] solve the bin packing problem with color constraints using a Branch-and-Price method. [18] apply a variable neighborhood search matheuristic to solve a variant of the VBPC where each item can have a set of colors. [7] study another variant where each color can only be associated with one item.

Summarizing, our work builds upon and extends work in the field of the generalized (one-dimensional) variable sized bin packing problems with color constraints (GVBPC). To the best of our knowledge, multiple attribute constraints have not been studied in literature before. We'll refer to the containerization problem as a generalized (one-dimensional) variable sized bin packing problems with multiple item mixing constraints (GVBPMC).

2   Solution Approach

In this section we present the formal definition of the problem, propose a binary integer program formulation and a first-fit decreasing based heuristic.

346 S. Anand and S. Guericke

2.1 Problem Formalization

Let J be the set of bins, where each bin $j \in J$ has cost Q_j and a maximum capacity of resource type R, $V_{r,j}$. In this work, we focus on the resource volume in cubic meters, but others, such as weight, could be considered as well. Let V_j be the vector of all resource capacities for container j. Let I be the set of items and $v_{r,i}$ the utilization of resource $r \in R$ by item $i \in I$. Let v_i be the vector of all resource utilizations of item i.

We now present the extensions for multiple item mixing constraints, i.e. limiting the number of different values of items attributes in a single bin. Let A be a set of relevant item attributes and C_a the set of unique values for attribute a. Partitions $P_c \subseteq I$ define all items sharing the same attribute value c. Note that $\{P_c\}_{c \in C_a}$ represents a partition of I into subsets such that each of the subset contains items belonging to the uniquely chosen attribute $a \in A$ such that $\cup_{c \in C_a} P_c = I$ and $\cap_{c \in C_a} P_c = \emptyset$. We denote $|P_c|$ as the number of items sharing the attribute value. Finally, parameter d_a defines how many different attributes values can occur in a single bin concurrently, similar to [8].

2.2 Mathematical Program

We propose a binary integer programming formulation for the generalized (one-dimensional) variable sized bin packing problems with multiple item mixing constraints (GVBPMC). It extends the classic variable sized bin packing problem and its variant with color constraints.

The objective of the optimization problem is to assign all items to bins while minimizing total bin costs so that no conflicts between items occur and no capacity constraints are violated. Binary variables $x_{i,j}$ are used to assign item $i \in I$ to bin $j \in J$ and y_j indicate whether bin j is used in the solution. Binary variables $w_{g,j}$ indicate whether any item of mixing constraint group g's attribute value is present in bin j.

$$\min \sum_{j \in J} Q_j y_j \tag{1}$$

$$s.t. \sum_{j \in J} x_{i,j} = 1 \qquad\qquad \forall i \in I \tag{2}$$

$$\sum_{i \in I} v_{r,i} x_{i,j} \leq V_{r,j} y_j \qquad\qquad \forall j \in J, r \in R \tag{3}$$

$$\sum_{i \in P_c} x_{i,j} \leq |P_c| w_{c,j} \qquad\qquad \forall a \in A, c \in C_a, j \in J \tag{4}$$

$$\sum_{c \in C_a} w_{c,j} \leq d_a \qquad\qquad \forall a \in A, j \in J \tag{5}$$

$$x_{i,j} \in \{0,1\}, \forall i \in I, j \in J \tag{6}$$

$$w_{c,j} \in \{0,1\}, \forall a \in A, c \in C_a, j \in J, \tag{7}$$

$$y_j \in \{0,1\}, \forall j \in J \tag{8}$$

The objective function (1) minimizes the total cost of used bins after assignment of all items. Constraints (2) ensure that each item is assigned to exactly one bin. Constraints (3) ensure that the capacity of bin j in respect to resource type r is respected by summing the total resource utilization of items assigned to the bin. Constraints (4) and (5) limit the mix of items in the same bin. Specifically, Constraints (4) set the indicator variable $w_{c,j}$ to 1 if any item with attribute value c is assigned to bin j. Constraints (5) set an upper bound on the number of different attribute values that are allowed to be together in a single bin. Finally, (6)–(8) define the variable domains.

2.3   First-Fit Decreasing Based Heuristic

Integer models for the bin packing problem are known to suffer from symmetry due to identical bins and thus long runtimes for practical instances [12]. An algorithm that has been extensively used in previous work is the first-fit decreasing heuristic [22], [6]. We extend this heuristic by multiple counters to respect the constraints placed on the attributes of items. We present the pseudo-code in Algorithm 1 and refer to it as FFD with Multiple Constraints (FFDMC).

Algorithm 1: FFDMC heuristic for the load planning problem.

---

1 $S = \{\}$;
2 $J' \leftarrow sort\_descending(J, V_{cbm,j})$;
3 $I' \leftarrow sort\_descending(I, v_{i,cbm})$;
4 **while** $|I'| > 0$ **do**
5 $\quad$ $j \leftarrow pop(J')$
6 $\quad$ $V^R \leftarrow V_j$
7 $\quad$ $I^* \leftarrow \{i \in I' : v_{r,i} \leq V_{r,j} \forall r \in R\}$
8 $\quad$ **if** $|I^*| > 0$ **then**
9 $\quad\quad$ **while** $|I^*| > 0$ **do**
10 $\quad\quad\quad$ $i \leftarrow pop(I^*)$
11 $\quad\quad\quad$ **if** $!constr\_violated(j, i, S, V^R)$ **then**
12 $\quad\quad\quad\quad$ $S \leftarrow S \cup (j, i)$
13 $\quad\quad\quad\quad$ $V^R \leftarrow V^R - v_i$
14 $\quad\quad\quad\quad$ $remove(I', i)$
15 $\quad\quad\quad$ **end**
16 $\quad\quad$ **end**
17 $\quad$ **else**
18 $\quad\quad$ | **Result:** *Infeasible*
18 $\quad$ **end**
19 **end**
$\quad$ **Result:** *reduce_bin_sizes(S)*
20

The assignment process works as follows: First, the set of bin-item tuples holding the solution S is initialized in line 1. In lines 2 and 3 the bins J and the item set I are sorted and indexed in descending order by capacity V and utilization v such that the lowest indexed items have the highest values. Note that we take the volume in cubic meters cbm as the resource of R for the sorting.

The while loop in line 4 continues while there are still items to be assigned to a bin. Starting with the largest bin, line 6 initializes the residual capacity to its total capacity and selected items I^* that fit into the bin. An empty set I^* in line 8 means that item still haven't been assigned ($|I'| > 0$), however, none is fitting into container j according to its capacities/ utilization. Thus, the algorithm returns an $Infeasible$ state (line 17) as the next container has less capacity according to the sorting. Next, the loop in line 9 tries to assign items while constraints maybe violated. The function $constr\_violated(j, i, S, V^R)$, returning $\{true, false\}$ for bin j, item i, solution S and residual capacity vector V^R, is defined in Eq. 9. It returns $true$, if item i fits into the residual capacity V_r^R for all of resource types r and if the mixing constraints are not violated. Therefore, I'' defines the set of items currently assigned to bin j. The second line in Eq. 9 checks that the upper bounds d_a for all attributes hold by summing the number of unique values C_a for attribute a. Attribute value $c \in C_a$ appears in bin j, if the intersection between items already associated to bins I'' and items with that property P_C is not empty.

$$constr\_violated(j, i, S, V^R) = \forall r \in R : V_r^R - v_{r,i} \geq 0$$
$$\wedge \forall a \in A : d_a \geq \sum_{c \in C_a} \begin{cases} 0, if\ I'' \cap P_c = \emptyset \\ 1, otherwise \end{cases} \quad (9)$$
$$\text{with } I'' = \{i' : (j, i') \in S\} \cup \{i\}$$

If no constraints are violated, line 12 adds the bin-item assignment to the solution, updates the residual capacity vector and removes i from the items to be processed. Note that we assume the pop operator to remove items from the lists. The process repeats until all items of I' are assigned to bins. The post-processing function $reduce\_bin\_sizes(S)$ in line 19 tries to improve the solution further by assessing if a next smaller bin can accommodate an already assigned item volume in a bin (provided smaller bins are still available). Otherwise, the FFDMC algorithm returns the current load plan.

3 Numerical Results

In this section we present our test instances, numerical results and compare solution approaches. We start with the single-constraint cases and continue with the more complex multi-constraint ones. The results are calculated on an Azure Virtual Machine ($standard\_a1\_v2$) with one CPU, 2 GB RAM and Gurobi 7.5.2 with default settings. For all results, a maximum runtime of 30 min has been set. Our FFDMC heuristic is implemented in Python 3.6.

3.1 Test Instances

Preliminary experiments indicate that the binary program is very sensitive to the input data, in particular to the item size distribution. Based on real sample sets provided by a global logistics service provider, we generate instances covering a variety of item sizes (in terms of cubic meters), different number of items and containers, and mixing constraints. Thereby, we can test the applicability of our solution methods to different input data and ensure that the algorithms are applicable to customers with different item-size patterns. To generate realistic item-sizes, we fitted a beta distribution to the volume attribute of four different real-world instances. Figure 2 visualizes density functions using the estimated parameters for the four instances in a scale of $[0, 80]$ cbm (which is the maximum for a 45 foot container).

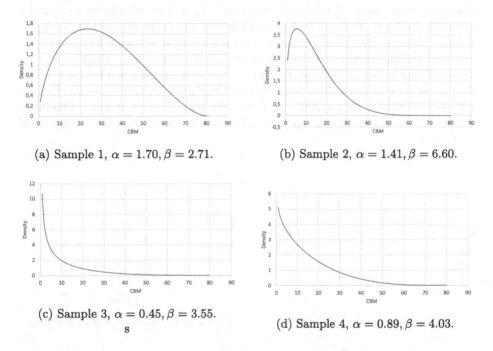

(a) Sample 1, $\alpha = 1.70, \beta = 2.71$.

(b) Sample 2, $\alpha = 1.41, \beta = 6.60$.

(c) Sample 3, $\alpha = 0.45, \beta = 3.55$.
s

(d) Sample 4, $\alpha = 0.89, \beta = 4.03$.

Fig. 2. Density functions of the beta-distribution for sample 1, 2, 3 and 4.

In total, we have generated 340 instances for two different analyses. The first set contains 275 and the second 65 instances. *Set 1* has a single item mixing constraint but different number of bins, parameters of the beta-distribution and number of items. For each of the four estimated beta-distributions, 50, 100, 150 and 200 items, for a uniqueness[1] of 5%, 10% and 25%, we created 25 samples. Additionally, we modified the number of bins to be 10, 20, 30, 40, 50, 75, 100 and 150 for a fixed number of items, uniqueness and distribution to evaluate the influence of that parameter on the runtime. *Set 2* evaluates 1,... 4 item mixing constraints and upper bounds while using a fixed amount of 100 items, 120 bins

---

[1] Uniqueness indicates how many items are sharing the same property value in percent, averaged over all rules of the instances.

and $\alpha = 1.41$ and $\beta = 6.6$, which is the most common pattern provided by the LSP.

3.2 Comparison of Mixed Integer Program and FFDMC Heuristic for a Single Item Mixing Constraint

In this section, MIP gaps[2] and runtimes between Gurobi and our suggested FFDMC heuristic are compared for a single item mixing constraint (similar to the GVBPC but with different costs).

As indicated in Fig. 3, all instances could be solved to an average gap of 1.1% (the maximum observed gap was less than 5%) within 30 min using Gurobi. Figure 3a shows that the average gap highly depends on the number of items in the instances. Practical instances typically contain between 100–150 items, showing the applicability of a binary integer formulation for a single item constraint. The number of bins (see Fig. 3b) have a clear impact on the runtime and the gap as they increase the complexity of the model. Figure 3c shows that the instances containing larger items (in terms of CBM) are clearly more difficult to solve which is challenging for the reliability of solution approaches for practical applications.

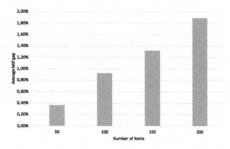

(a) Gaps by number of items.

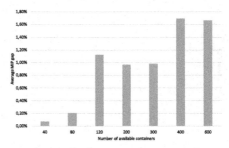

(b) Gaps by number of available bins.

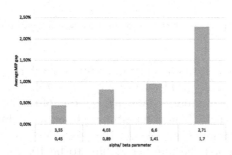

(c) Gaps by beta-distribution parameters.

Fig. 3. Gurobi MIP gaps in percent for different instance properties for test *Set 1*.

---

[2] We define MIP gap as $\frac{|best\_bound - incumbent|}{max(|best\_bound|, |incumbent|)}$.

In Table 1 the gap of Gurobi is compared to the FFDMC heuristic for different number of items. Timeout indicates the percent of instances for which Gurobi hit the timelimit of 30 min. We observe that the gap for Gurobi is consistently under 5% for all instances, also for larger instances. FFDMC performs reasonably well, with average gaps between 5.48–6.24%, depending on the number of items. Table 1 also indicates that for 30%–78% of the instances optimality could not be shown with Gurobi. As expected, this number increases with instances containing more items.

Table 1. Average MIP gaps for Gurobi and FFDMC for different number of items for test *Set 1*.

Items	Timeout [%]	Gap Gurobi [%]	Gap FFDMC[%]
50	30%	0.37%	5.48%
100	59%	0.93%	5.24%
150	78%	1.32%	5.54%
200	78%	1.67%	6.24%

Table 2 compares the runtime of Gurobi and the FFDMC heuristic. Gurobi's average runtime ranges from 554 s for small instances up to 1558 s for the largest ones. FFDMC in contrast never took more than 1/10th of a second. While measuring these low runtimes, we expect a large impact of side-processes running on the virtual machine and should thus been interpreted carefully.

Table 2. Average runtimes in seconds for Gurobi and FFDMC for different number of items for test *Set 1*.

Items	Runtime Gurobi [s]	Runtime FFDMC [s]
50	554	0.003
100	1195	0.010
150	1488	0.018
200	1558	0.030

Concluding the single item mixing constraint, our FFDMC heuristic provides solutions much faster than Gurobi but results in significantly larger gaps.

3.3 Comparison of Mixed Integer Program and FFDMC Heuristic for Multiple Item Mixing Constraints

In this section, we compare results of Gurobi with the FFDMC heuristic for instances with up to four item mixing constraints. We limit the number to four in the experimental study to still receive reasonable results for Gurobi.

Table 3. Average MIP gaps for Gurobi and FFDMC for instances with 1,...4 multiple item mixing constraints of test *Set 2*.

Mixing Constraints	Timeout [%]	Gap Gurobi [%]	Gap FFDMC [%]
1	96%	1.69%	5.74%
2	100%	18.94%	16.46%
3	100%	34.10%	15.62%
4	100%	48.35%	12.40%

Average gaps for Gurobi and FFDMC for different number of mixing constraints are presented in Table 3. As observed in the previous section, FFDMC's gap is worse than Gurobi's for a single mixing constraint. With increasing number of constraints, we observe a non-monotonic performance of FFDMC and believe that is connected to the randomness of the test instances. However, with an increasing number of constraints, FFDMC clearly outperforms Gurobi in terms of gap. Already for two constraints, FFDMC's gap is lower than Gurobi's. When considering four mixing constraints, FFDMC's gap is 75% lower than Gurobi's. Table 3 also highlights that in almost all cases Gurobi results in a timelimit of 30 min.

Table 4. Average runtime in seconds for Gurobi and FFDMC for instances with 1,...4 multiple item mixing constraints of test *Set 2*.

Mixing Constraints	Runtime Gurobi [s]	Runtime FFDMC [s]
1	1739	0.010
2	1800	0.014
3	1800	0.014
4	1800	0.013

The runtimes of Gurobi and FFDMC are presented in Table 4. Gurobi cannot prove optimality for almost all instances with more than one mixing constraint as it hits the maximum runtime. In contrast, FFDMC is still able to find solution in less of 1/10th of a second. The slight increase in runtime with more constraints can be explained by a more complex violation check function (see Eq. 9) that involves checking additional conditions.

Summarizing the findings for multiple item mixing constraints, we can state that FFDMC clearly outperforms our binary program solved with a state-of-the-art commercial solver, both in terms of runtime and MIP gaps. The very low runtimes suggest that it is very efficient for cases with many item mixing constraints. Thus, it can serve as an efficient construction heuristic or provide solution for warm starting the MIP solver. However, the results indicate that FFDMC still has relatively large remaining gaps and can be improved further.

4   Conclusion and Future Work

In this paper, we proposed a generalization of the classic bin packing problem with multiple item mixing constraints to solve the containerization problem arising at logistics service providers (such as third- or fourth-party logistics providers).

The problem is an extension to the BPP with color constraints. The problem addresses the packing issue where constraints can be placed on item attributes and thus limiting the mixing of items in each bin. Practical applications are, among others, creating load plans for multiple customers, reducing item type variations in containers and improving the item management.

We present a binary integer program to solve instances to optimality and a first-fit decreasing based heuristic to determine good solutions fast. To evaluate both methods, we generate a few hundred test-instances based on samples of a global LSP. Numerical results indicate that Gurobi performs reasonably well on instances with one mixing constraint, leading to an average gap of 1–2%. Instances with two item mixing constraints increase the average gap of 18.94%, and instance with four to more than 48%. Gurobi almost always reaches the timelimit of 30 min. Our FFDMC heuristic creates solutions for one mixing constraint with a gap of less than 6%, with a runtime of less than 1/10 of a second for all instances. For instances with four constraints, FFDMC provides a remaining MIP gap of less than 13% and clearly outperforms Gurobi for large, practical instances in both runtime and solution quality. We conclude that FFDMC is a reasonable starting point to solve the introduced problem for practical sized instances and can support future research as a benchmark algorithm.

Future work should be done in the area of solution algorithms. For instance, Branch-and-Price has been successfully applied to the bin packing problem with color constraints and is a promising approach. Besides, meta- or matheuristics such as [18] have also been used successfully. Finally, theoretical analyses of the approximation quality could provide new insights for solution algorithms.

References

1. Belov, G., Scheithauer, G.: A cutting plane algorithm for the one-dimensional cutting stock problem with multiple stock lengths. Euro. J. Oper. Res. **141**(2), 274–294 (2002)
2. Capua, R., Frota, Y., Ochi, L.S., Vidal, T.: A study on exponential-size neighborhoods for the bin packing problem with conflicts. J. Heuristics **24**(4), 667–695 (2018). https://doi.org/10.1007/s10732-018-9372-2
3. Christensen, H.I., Khan, A., Pokutta, S., Tetali, P.: Approximation and online algorithms for multidimensional bin packing: a survey. Comput. Sci. Rev. **24**, 63–79 (2017)

4. Coffman, E.G., Csirik, J., Galambos, G., Martello, S., Vigo, D.: Bin packing approximation algorithms: survey and classification. In: Pardalos, P.M., Du, D.-Z., Graham, R.L. (eds.) Handbook of Combinatorial Optimization, pp. 455–531. Springer, New York (2013). https://doi.org/10.1007/978-1-4419-7997-1_35
5. Coffman, E.G., Garey, M.R., Johnson, D.S.: Approximation algorithms for bin-packing — an updated survey. In: Ausiello, G., Lucertini, M., Serafini, P. (eds.) Algorithm Design for Computer System Design. ICMS, vol. 284, pp. 49–106. Springer, Vienna (1984). https://doi.org/10.1007/978-3-7091-4338-4_3
6. Coffman, E.G., Garey, M., Johnson, D.: Approximation algorithms for bin packing: a survey. Approximation algorithms for NP-hard problems, pp. 46–93 (1996)
7. Crévits, I., Hanafi, S., Mahjoub, A.R., Taktak, R., Wilbaut, C.: A special case of variable-sized bin packing problem with color constraints. In: 2019 6th International Conference on Control, Decision and Information Technologies (CoDIT), pp. 1150–1154. IEEE (2019)
8. Dawande, M., Kalagnanam, J., Sethuraman, J.: Variable sized bin packing with color constraints. Electron. Notes Discrete Math. **7**, 154–157 (2001)
9. Delorme, M., Iori, M., Martello, S.: Bin packing and cutting stock problems: mathematical models and exact algorithms. Euro. J. Oper. Res. **255**(1), 1–20 (2016)
10. Delorme, M., Iori, M., Martello, S.: Bpplib: a library for bin packing and cutting stock problems. Optimization Lett. **12**(2), 235–250 (2018)
11. Epstein, L., Levin, A.: On bin packing with conflicts. SIAM J. Optimization **19**(3), 1270–1298 (2008)
12. Fasano, G.: A mip approach for some practical packing problems: balancing constraints and tetris-like items. Q. J. Belgian, French and Italian Oper. Res. Soc. **2**(2), 161–174 (2004)
13. Friesen, D.K., Langston, M.A.: Variable sized bin packing. SIAM J. Comput. **15**(1), 222–230 (1986)
14. Haouari, M., Serairi, M.: Heuristics for the variable sized bin-packing problem. Comput. Oper. Res. **36**(10), 2877–2884 (2009)
15. Johnson, D.S.: Near-optimal bin packing algorithms. Ph.D. thesis, Massachusetts Institute of Technology (1973)
16. Johnson, D.S., Demers, A., Ullman, J.D., Garey, M.R., Graham, R.L.: Worst-case performance bounds for simple one-dimensional packing algorithms. SIAM J. Comput. **3**(4), 299–325 (1974)
17. Kang, J., Park, S.: Algorithms for the variable sized bin packing problem. Euro. J. Oper. Res. **147**(2), 365–372 (2003)
18. Kochetov, Y., Kondakov, A.: Vns matheuristic for a bin packing problem with a color constraint. Electron. Notes Discrete Math. **58**, 39–46 (2017)
19. Kondakov, A., Kochetov, Y.: A core heuristic and the branch-and-price method for a bin packing problem with a color constraint. In: Eremeev, A., Khachay, M., Kochetov, Y., Pardalos, P. (eds.) OPTA 2018. CCIS, vol. 871, pp. 309–320. Springer, Cham (2018). https://doi.org/10.1007/978-3-319-93800-4_25
20. Korte, B., Vygen, J.: Bin-Packing, pp. 407–422. Springer, Heidelberg (2000). https://doi.org/10.1007/978-3-540-76919-4_18
21. Levine, J., Ducatelle, F.: Ant colony optimization and local search for bin packing and cutting stock problems. J. Oper. Res. Soc. **55**(7), 705–716 (2004)
22. Martello, S., Toth, P.: Knapsack problems: algorithms and computer implementations. Wiley-Interscience series in discrete mathematics and optimization (1990)
23. Pisinger, D., Sigurd, M.: The two-dimensional bin packing problem with variable bin sizes and costs. Discrete Optimization **2**(2), 154–167 (2005)

24. Sadykov, R., Vanderbeck, F.: Bin packing with conflicts: a generic branch-and-price algorithm. INFORMS J. Comput. **25**(2), 244–255 (2013)
25. Statista Research Department: Estimated containerized cargo flows on major container trade routes in 2018, by trade route (in million teus). Accessed May 2020. https://www.statista.com/statistics/253988/estimated-containerized-cargo-flows-on-major-container-trade-routes/
26. UN Conference on Trade and Development: Review of maritime transport 2013. Technical report, United Nations (2013)
27. World Shipping Council: World shipping council trade statistics. Accessed May 2020.   http://www.worldshipping.org/about-the-industry/global-trade/trade-statistics

Distance Approximation for Dynamic Waste Collection Planning

Fabian Akkerman[✉], Martijn Mes[✉], and Wouter Heijnen

University of Twente, Department of Industrial Engineering and Business
Information Systems, Enschede, The Netherlands
f.r.akkerman@student.utwente.nl, m.r.k.mes@utwente.nl

Abstract. Approximating the solution value of transportation problems has become more relevant in recent years, as these approximations can help to decrease the computational effort required for solving those routing problems. In this paper, we apply several regression methods to predict the total distance of the traveling salesman problem (TSP) and vehicle routing problem (VRP). We show that distance can be estimated fairly accurate using simple regression models and only a limited number of features. We use features found in scientific literature and introduce a new class of spatial features. The model is validated on a dynamic waste collection case in the city of Amsterdam, the Netherlands. We introduce a cost function that combines the travel distance and service level, and show that our model can reduce distances up to 17%, while maintaining the same service level, compared to a well-known heuristic approximation. Furthermore, we show the benefits of using approximations for combining offline learning with online or frequent optimization.

Keywords: Distance approximation · Vehicle routing · Inventory routing problem · Waste collection

1 Introduction

There is an increasing need among logistics companies for faster solution methods to solve vehicle routing problems. In general, faster solving times are needed to cope with the addition of new problem attributes, fast-changing demands, disruptions, and increasing problem sizes. There are numerous applications for which these approximations can be helpful. What time-slots for delivery should we offer our customer, considering the current set of customers and the location of the new customer? How should customers be re-clustered when new customers are added, removed, or vehicles break down? Is it profitable to accept a far-away customer to include in the current vehicle routes, or should we reserve time for future customers? For these, and other situations, an approximation can be used to obtain an indication of the costs, without solving the actual problem.

In this paper, we develop an approximation method that utilizes regression models to approximate the costs within transportation problems related to distance and service level. We consider both the traveling salesman problem (TSP),

© Springer Nature Switzerland AG 2020
E. Lalla-Ruiz et al. (Eds.): ICCL 2020, LNCS 12433, pp. 356–370, 2020.
https://doi.org/10.1007/978-3-030-59747-4_23

creating the shortest route for a single vehicle visiting a given set of customers, and the vehicle routing problem (VRP), considering a fleet of vehicles with capacity restrictions. Both the TSP and the VRP are NP-hard combinatorial optimization problems, which means that realistic instances can typically only be solved heuristically [10]. We validate our model by applying it to a case study on dynamic waste collection in Amsterdam, the Netherlands. Fast approximation techniques can be advantageous in this case, as the problem size is huge, we have to consider a longer-term planning horizon, and demand is stochastic. The problem can be considered as an inventory routing problem, where we have to decide which containers to empty on which day, and how to route our vehicles to visit these containers. To reduce computational complexity, we split these decisions: first we select the waste containers to be emptied on the different days between the current day and the end of the horizon, and next decide on the routing of our vehicles for the current day. Even though we select the containers without solving vehicles routes, we use an approximation that predicts the costs and service levels for a selection of containers based on geographical information and fill levels of containers. To avoid excessive computation times in online or frequent decision making, we propose a combination of offline learning (training the approximation model) and operational decision making (VRP).

The remainder of this paper is structured as follows. In Sect. 2, we introduce the relevant scientific literature on combinations of online and offline methods, on waste collection problems, and describe our contribution. In Sect. 3, we describe the problem, introduce our approximation model and further discuss the combination of offline learning and online optimization. In Sect. 4, we validate and illustrate our model using the waste collection case. We close with conclusions and future research directions in Sect. 5.

2   Literature

In this section, we briefly review the literature on fast solution methods for the VRP. We first discuss the use of offline methods that support online or operational decision making, e.g., assigning customers to clusters and time slots before making a routing decision. Next, we treat the relevant literature about modelling the planning of waste collection related to our case study.

VRP research increasingly considers real-life, dynamic environments, which typically involve stochastic demands, stochastic travel times, and other disturbances [7]. This means that VRP models need to come up with robust plans that can handle changing environments. As opposed to exact solutions, approximation methods are generally better able to solve large problems and are typically more robust, hence they are often applied in real-life situations [8]. With increasing problem sizes or longer planning horizons, the need for faster solution methods increases. There are numerous options for limiting computational complexity, both for exact and approximate methods. The decision space can be reduced by, e.g., disregarding indisputably bad decisions, prioritizing customers, or restricting the decision space to the cheapest options [12]. Other methods focus on improving fast obtained heuristic solutions using metaheuristics, or split the heuristic solution in smaller sub-parts that can be solved to optimality using exact methods [14]. Approximating the unknown solution value, prior to solving, can help to reduce the decision space by excluding potentially weak solutions or unattractive problem instances. To keep computational effort low, a model can be split in an offline and online phase. Training the model on historic data can be done offline, while the application of the model is considered an online phase, since costs are incurred during the decision making process [20].

Several authors use offline methods to improve online decisions. In [24], approximate dynamic programming (ADP) is applied to the uncapacitated single-vehicle routing problem with stochastic service requests. Their approach has an offline value function approximation (VFA) component, which determines the value of a state using a heuristic and simulation, as further described in [25]. The state is defined by (i) the time of arrival to the current vehicle location, and (ii) the time budget, which is defined as the time left until the duration limit. The online routing decisions are then made using the already known VFA. They conclude that the geographical spread of customers is a good predictor for the success of an approximation. The approach in [19] is similar in the usage of ADP. They, however, define the state to be the current vehicle location, remaining vehicle capacity, and the demand yet to be delivered. Both approaches enable fast, online decision making by shifting computational effort to an offline stage.

Aside from ADP, research has been conducted on the use of machine learning methods to approximate the value of a VRP decision. In [2], the characteristics of a VRP solution are described by several features. Using classification algorithms (decision-trees, random forests, and support vector machines), they distinguish good and bad solutions. Their research shows that a good heuristic can be further improved by guiding the search process using classification data. The research in [18] is focused on the prediction of travel distance using linear regression, based on several customer-oriented features, like geographic information and demand. They show that the approximation of distance is accurate for the TSP and VRP, especially for Solomon instances [23] with clustered customers. For a comprehensive literature review on distance-approximation, we refer to [18].

The planning of waste collection is gaining a lot of attention in the scientific literature [5]. The main focus is on the collection of household waste. The collection from larger containers is typically modelled as an adapted VRP, also called the Waste Collection Vehicle Routing Problem (WCVRP) [5]. WCVRPs have as objective to find an optimal route for collecting waste from a set of containers. Collection vehicles leave the depot empty, collect waste and unload waste at a disposal facility when the route is completed or when the vehicle capacity has been reached. At the end of the day, the vehicles return to the depot [6]. The WCVRP requires the set of containers to be emptied to be known upfront. A distinctive feature of WCVRPs is the dynamicity, which entails the influence of today's decisions on the next-day decision space [3]. We distinguish the following options for including dynamicity: (i) run the model for a long planning horizon, (ii) solve a periodic VRP (PVRP), which concerns multi-period problems like in [1], and (iii) model the planning of waste collection as an inventory routing problem (IRP). The IRP combines the fields of inventory management (when to serve customers and how much to deliver to each customer) and routing (how to route the vehicles along the selected customers) [9]. The IRP is a medium-term problem, in contrast to the short-term character of the regular VRP or WCVRP [1]. The classification in [13] shows that most IRP literature uses a one-to-many topology, i.e., instances with a single depot serving many customers. Some authors extend the problem with satellite facilities, which function as additional depots, effectively increasing vehicle capacity [4]. Much waste collection research is done both for single-period models and multi-period models. However, since the long-term planning approach has positive effects on long-term outcomes [17], contemporary research tends to treat multi-period models [13]. An application of the IRP to a waste collection problem can be found in [15].

Our contribution to the scientific literature is threefold. First, we develop a solution methodology that reduces the problem size of multi-period, dynamic VRPs. Second, we introduce several new spatial features to better estimate the characteristics of VRP solutions. Third, we illustrate our solution methodology using a dynamic waste collection case.

3   Problem Description and Formulation

In this section, we subsequently introduce our case study and the approximation model. With respect to the model, we make a clear separation between case-specific elements and generic elements, enabling the model to be applied to a variety of problems. Furthermore, for the generic model, we distinguish between the TSP and VRP. Since VRPs include multiple vehicles, the basic TSP model needs to be expanded to consider vehicle capacity and expected demand. After the model description, we select features and evaluate the performance of both models on a test set. Next, we describe the adaptations of the generic model to apply it in our case study. We end this section with our framework for improving the approximation by combining online optimization and offline learning.

3.1   A Solution Structure for the Waste Collection Case

We consider the dynamic collection of waste from underground containers in Amsterdam, the Netherlands, as depicted in Fig. 1. Here we specifically focus on the collection of household waste from 7995 containers in Amsterdam. For illustrative reasons, we focus in our experiments on the Southeast district of Amsterdam. This district is a secluded part of the city that consists of 353 underground heterogeneous containers, one depot, and two satellite locations. The containers are scattered over an area of 21.7 km^2. The daily waste disposal at each container c is stochastic and modeled using a Gamma-distribution, given by $d_c \sim Gamma(k_c, \theta_c)$, as common for these type of problems [16]. We assume a homogeneous fleet of vehicles. Key performance indicators for comparing models are the service level and the distance traveled per ton of collected waste. The service level is dependent on the overflow of containers. An overflowed container has a fill level higher than the container capacity. We define the service level as the proportion of containers that are emptied on time, without overflow: $1 - $ (number of overflowed containers/number of emptied containers).

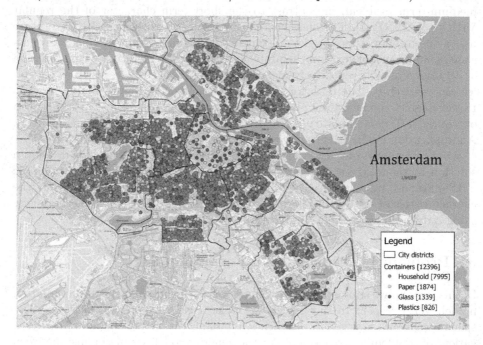

Fig. 1. Map of the waste collection containers in Amsterdam, The Netherlands (source: maps.amsterdam.nl)

We use a rolling horizon planning approach, where decisions are made on consecutive days t over a finite horizon $\mathcal{T} = \{1, ..., T\}$. Each day, we plan for T days ahead, but only the decisions of $t = 1$ are fixed. To be able to solve problem sizes of up to 7995 containers in reasonable time, we propose a solution methodology consisting of the following three phases: (i) container selection, (ii) day assignment, and (iii) route construction. The first phase concerns the selection of containers based on overflow probabilities of every container. When the overflow probability exceeds a certain threshold, the respective container is considered for the next phase. The second phase concerns the planning of collection days for the pre-selected containers. In this phase, both the service level and the travel costs are considered, i.e., both the time and space dimension. The third phase concerns the construction of routes for the first day ($t = 1$) of the planning horizon. We use a cluster-first-route-second approach, which constructs routes in four steps: (i) clustering containers using adapted k-means, (ii) feasible sequencing using nearest insertion, (iii) combining sequences into feasible routes and (iv) improving the feasible solution using a 2-opt metaheuristic. See [13] for more details on the route construction phase.

Our proposed method concerns the approximation to be used in the second phase: the allocation of containers to days. To benchmark our method, we consider a policy that sequentially builds a day assignment solution using the expected fill levels of containers for the time dimension, and the Daganzo-approximation for the space dimension, i.e., while iterating over all containers and days, it looks for the cheapest allocation of a container to a day, considering a combined term for service level and distance. The Daganzo-approximation is a fairly accurate approximation of a VRP distance [22] and is calculated as follows:

$$\text{VRP distance} \approx [0.9 + \frac{kN}{C^2}] * \sqrt{AN}, \tag{1}$$

where k is an area shape constant, N the number of customers, C the maximum number of customers a vehicle can serve, and A is the area size. The time dimension is covered using a penalty factor based on an acceptable overflow probability (AOP). The AOP is a tunable threshold, which allows for giving penalties when containers are emptied later than their desired emptying date (DED).

3.2   A Generic Model for Approximating Distance

We now introduce our approximation model, starting with a basic TSP model and later extending it to a VRP model. Various features are proposed and evaluated using (i) linear regression, (ii) random forests, and (iii) neural networks. We generate the training and testing data using our simulation of the waste collection case (see Sect. 4). Each day in the simulation, we use the three-phase planning approach to select the containers to empty and subsequently solve the VRP, treating the container as customers. Hence, this choice of generating the vehicle routes as training data does not affect the generic applicability. For the purpose of creating training data for the TSP, we randomly select the route of a single vehicle for each day. For both the TSP and VRP routes, we store the locations, the fill levels, as well as the location of the depot and possible planned visits of satellite locations. Note that for the purpose of generating the training and testing instances, we only focus on planned routes, and ignore possible disruptions during the day, which will be considered later on in Sect. 4.

Model for the Traveling Salesman Problem. For the approximation of a TSP route, we only consider spatial features. The features are summarized in Table 1 and, if deemed relevant, further explained below.

F5–F7 are based on the smallest rectangle that can be fitted around the locations. F8–F12 are distance related features for which we compute the average distances to the depot, cluster centroid, and cluster midpoint. The angle related features F13–F15 express the dispersion of the customers by taking the variance of several different bearings between customer and the depot, cluster centroid, and cluster midpoint. The bearing $\beta_{a,b}$ of two points (a, b) expressed in latitude and longitude, is the angle between the line connecting the two points and the north-south line of the earth, and can be calculated with (2), (3) and (4).

$$x = \cos(b_{lat}) * \sin(\Delta(a_{long}, b_{long})) \tag{2}$$

Table 1. Summary of features for the TSP

Feature ID	Feature or feature type	Source
F1	Number of customers	[2,18,21]
F2	Area	[21]
F3,F4	Convex Hull (area and perimeter)	[21]
F5–F7	Smallest cluster (width, height, perimeter)	[21]
F8–F12	Distance related (general)	[2,18,21]
F13–F15	Angle related	[2]
F16–F21	Geographical variance	[18]
F22–F24	Proximity related	-
F25–F32	Polygon related	-

$$y = \cos{(a_{lat})} * \sin{(b_{lat})} - \sin{(a_{lat})} * \cos{(b_{lat})} * \cos{(\Delta(a_{long}, b_{long}))} \quad (3)$$

$$\beta_{a,b} = \arctan{(x, y)} \quad (4)$$

F13–F15 are based on latitude and longitude but can be converted to a Cartesian system without loss of generality by substituting the north-south line by one of the Cartesian axes. F16–F21 express geographical variance and dispersion by means of variance in latitude and longitude, variance of latitude multiplied with longitude, and the variance of the distance from the depot, cluster centroid, or cluster midpoint, to all customers in a route. Finally, we introduce two new types of features. First, F22–F24 count the number of customers within a certain radius from the depot, cluster centroid or cluster midpoint. These features have similar descriptive power as other already described features but might be more convenient to calculate. Second, F25–F32 are polygon related features. We split the smallest possible rectangle that can be fitted around all points into several equally-sized smaller rectangles, called polygons. Several features can be extracted from the polygon structure, such as the distance between the depot and the centroid of the polygon with the most customers, and the average distance from the cluster centroid to all activated polygons, i.e., polygons that contain customers. These features can capture the extent of concentration of customers at geographical locations.

Model Extensions for the Vehicle Routing Problem. For the VRP, we consider geographical data as well as demand data. The addition of demand data is imperative since the VRP involves multiple vehicle routes and vehicle capacity. The extension on the current model is summarized in Table 2. Here, F32-F36 describe the VRP instance considering the demand and vehicle capacity. F36 is similar to F35, but rounds up to the nearest integer. F38 is a feature for which we count the polygons in which the demand is higher than the average polygon-demand.

Table 2. Summary of additional features for the VRP

Feature ID	Feature	Source
F32	Total demand per instance	[18]
F33	Avg demand per instance	[18]
F34	Variance of demand per instance	[18]
F35	$\frac{\text{Total demand per instance}}{\text{Vehicle capacity}}$	[18]
F36	Minimum required vehicles	[21]
F37	$\frac{\text{Maximum customer demand in an instance}}{\text{Vehicle capacity}}$	[21]
F38	Polygon demand weight	-

3.3 Model Evaluation

In this section, we evaluate our generic TSP and VRP model using linear regression, random forests, and neural networks. The data is split into a training set and test set. The hyperparameters are tuned using 5-fold cross-validation grid search, with the Scikit-Learn Python library, after which two different automatic feature selection methods are employed. Examples of these hyperparameters are the tree-depth and the minimum number of samples required to split a node (random forest), the activation function, L_2 penalty, hidden layer sizes, learning rate, and solver (neural network). Finally, the model is evaluated on the test set. In the next paragraph, the feature selection methods are briefly described. Next, the results of both the TSP and VRP model are presented.

Feature Selection. Feature selection is performed for several reasons. First, it indicates the individual importance of the features for the regression model. Second, features might be correlated, which potentially can distort some models. Also, a model can be overfitted because there are too many features relative to the available data. Finally, the computational costs need to be as low as possible for the approximation the be fast enough [21].

We employ two different methods for feature selection. The first method is called Elastic Net Regularization (ENR) [26]. ENR combines two linear regression methods: Lasso regression with L_1 penalization and Ridge regression with L_2 penalization. By combing the two methods, the advantages of both methods can be exploited, and the limitations reduced. Lasso regression shrinks large feature coefficients and can be an effective tool for automatic feature selection. However, the Lasso fails to select grouped features, i.e., features that suffer from multicollinearity [26]. Ridge regression, however, does recognize grouped features but does not do automatic feature selection. ENR successfully combines these two methods. Nevertheless, the assumptions for using linear regression need to be reviewed; we observe that the residuals are by estimation normally distributed and homoscedastic, i.e., we can safely assume linear regression is a valid method for our data. It should be noted that the features were standardized before fitting as this is necessary for coefficient shrinkage methods.

The second method employs recursive feature elimination, which can be used for random forests (RF-RFE). Random forests allow us to recursively remove features, based on feature importance. Since random forests is less affected by multicollinearity, we can assume that RF-RFE will render valuable results. For more details on both selection methods, we refer to [11] and [26]. Finally, all features are selected for the neural networks regressor, since neural networks are better able to learn complex relationships and weigh the importance of features.

Model Performance. We compare models using three different statistics: adjusted R^2, relative mean absolute error (rMAE) and relative root mean squared error (rRMSE). The adjusted R^2 indicates the proportion of variance in the dataset that can be explained by the regression model; it is adjusted for the number of features in the model. The measures rMAE and rRMSE provide an indication of the quality of the approximation. The regular MAE indicates the average magnitude of errors, without considering direction. The regular RMSE is useful for identifying large errors. Both MAE and RMSE are made relative, to the mean and standard deviation of the observed values, respectively.

$$\text{rMAE} = \frac{\frac{1}{N}\sum_{i=1}^{N}|Predicted_i - Actual_i|}{Actual} \tag{5}$$

$$\text{rRMSE} = \frac{\sqrt{\frac{\sum_{i=1}^{N}(Predicted_i - Actual_i)^2}{N}}}{\sigma_{Actual}} \tag{6}$$

Table 3 shows the performance of three models on the TSP dataset. We see that the adjusted R^2 is high for all models. The relative MAE is low, with ENR performing the worst with a rMAE of 7% of the average distance in the data. The relative RMSE is also low, so it does not indicate large errors. ENR performs notably well in comparison with RF and NN. ENR eliminated 8 features and RF-RFE eliminated 6 features. ENR removed 2 out of the 3 proximity features (F22–F24), only the feature representing the proximity to the depot is kept. Some seemingly good features were removed because of redundancy. All polygon features (F25–F32) are in the model. RF-RFE made a different selection: it removed 6 of the 7 polygon features, with the only one remaining being the average number of customers in an activated polygon.

Table 3. Model performance for the TSP (5-fold cross-validation)

Performance	ENR	RF-RFE	NN
Number of Features	24	26	32
Adjusted R^2	0.938	0.966	0.965
rMAE	0.070	0.049	0.051
rRMSE	0.248	0.185	0.188

Table 4 shows the performance of the three models on the VRP dataset. Compared to the TSP model, the adjusted R^2 data dropped significantly. Clearly, the distance becomes harder to predict when having multiple vehicles. Nevertheless, the performance is still acceptable, with a lower relative MAE but slightly larger errors compared to the TSP models. Again, linear regression performs relatively well compared to the more advanced methods. ENR removed several seemingly redundant features but kept all demand related features (F32–F38). RF-RFE now removed more features, which might be related to the noise in the data. For both the TSP and VRP model, we observe that the highest importance is given to the following features: number of customers (F1), convex hull area (F3), average distance between locations (F10), and the distance from the centroid of all activated polygons to the depot (F29).

Table 4. Model performance for the VRP (5-fold cross-validation)

Performance	ENR	RF-RFE	NN
Number of Features	27	23	38
Adjusted R^2	0.836	0.838	0.834
rMAE	0.048	0.047	0.047
rRMSE	0.404	0.402	0.406

3.4 Model Adaptations for the Waste Collection Planning

The waste collection problem and other IRPs differentiate from the standard VRP by being multi-objective: the distance needs to be minimized and the service level should be maximized (or attain a certain threshold). Practical problems will arise if there is too much overflow of containers. For our implemented benchmark method (Daganzo-approximation), we separately assess the service level requirements by adding an overflow penalty to the approximated distance. For our new approximation model, we can combine the performance indicators by both approximating the distance as the service level together.

We introduce two new features that are used to estimate the actual service level, namely the service level calculated using the expected fill levels (F39) and the average expected fill level of containers as a percentage of the container capacity (F40). For both features, we use the known container capacities to calculate the feature values. F39 can be calculated by considering for each container the days till last emptying, the average waste disposals per day for this container, and its capacity. We observe that F39 can estimate the service level reasonably well, when tested in a single-feature regression model aimed at predicting the service level we observe a mean absolute error of 9.3%. F40 is an error term that is added to take into account possible deviations from the expected fill levels: when the demand of a container is closer to the capacity, the chance is higher it has overflowed. So, in case of equal expected service level and distance, the container with a higher fill level is favored.

After scaling both target variables on the domain $[0, 1]$, we define a new cost function (7), that combines distance and service level terms in a sequential objective function. The regression model estimates the costs, i.e., it is trained to predict the value of $\zeta_{c,t}$.

$$\zeta_{c,t}(S_t, x_{c,t}) = w^d * d_{S_t, x_{c,t}} + w^\alpha * \alpha_{S_t, x_{c,t}}, \quad \forall c \in C : C \subseteq I, \forall t \in \mathcal{T} \quad (7)$$

with $\zeta_{c,t}$ being the combined cost for inserting container $c \in C$ on day $t \in \mathcal{T}$. C is the set of containers that are not yet inserted, I is the complete set of containers that has been pre-selected in phase 1 of the algorithm, so $C \subseteq I$. S_t is the current state from which we derive the feature values for the already selected set of containers for day t. $x_{c,t}$ is the decision to insert container c on day t. The costs are determined using the predicted distance d and service level α. The weights w strike a balance between the importance of the distance and the service level. In our experiments, we adjust both weights.

3.5 A Framework for Improving Approximations

The main advantage of learning models, as opposed to heuristic methods, is that they can be retrained and adapt to changing circumstances. The method of training a model (offline), using the approximation to optimize decisions (online), and retraining a model again is shown in Fig. 2. This framework can be applied to cases where the environment changes and the approximation model needs to be updated regularly, e.g., when the customer demand changes or the geographic area of operations changes. Alternatively, the framework can be used to improve the approximation of a stable environment by obtaining more data. In the next section, we will show how this framework can be applied to our case study.

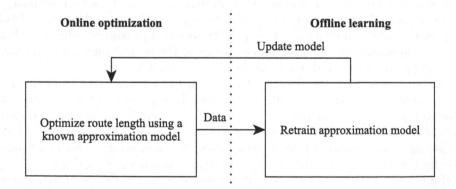

Fig. 2. Feedback loop with online optimization and offline learning

4 Computational Experiments and Results

To validate our proposed method, we created a discrete-event simulation model in Java, with two types of actors: the inhabitants who dispose waste in containers and the waste collectors who empty the containers. For simplicity we only focus on the planning phase and ignore possible disruptions during the execution of routes. At the beginning of each day, the three-phase planning procedure is executed to plan the waste collection routes for the corresponding day (see Sect. 3). We use a rolling horizon of three days, which is found to strike the best balance between performance and computational efficiency. For our simulation, we use 3 replications of 125 days each with a 25-day warmup period.

Three policies are compared: (i) the benchmark Daganzo-approximation with a service level penalty, (ii) our proposed machine learning model (ML), which combines distance and service level approximations, and (iii) a myopic policy that uses a horizon of $T = 1$ and always favors the containers with the highest expected fill levels. For both the benchmark policy and our ML-model, the respective overflow penalty and approximation weights can be tuned. The tuning of these parameters can shift the focus, either favoring service level or distance. Table 5 summarizes the relevant experimental parameters for each model. The acceptable overflow penalty (AOP) is only used for Daganzo-approximation since the myopic method only considers container fill levels and our ML-model has its own service level approximation.

Table 5. Experimental parameters

Policy	Planning horizon	AOP	(w^d, w^α)
Myopic	1	-	-
Daganzo	3	{0.1,0.2,0.3}	-
ML	3	-	{(1,1),(1,10),(10,1)}

To ease the presentation, we only show the results for the linear regression model, as its performance is close to those of the more advanced models, i.e., random forests or neural networks, see Sect. 3.3. The implemented model for the case contains 18 features and is trained using the VRP data obtained from the waste collection case.

Although the demand for the waste collection is stochastic, the system is stable, i.e., there are no external disruptions and the parameters for the demand, modeled with the Gamma-distribution, do not change. Nevertheless, it might still be the case that the approximation can be improved using the method described in Sect. 3.5. The data used to obtain the initial approximation is generated using Daganzo-approximation. With the new model, we can expect the planning to change, to which we can adapt by means of the feedback loop. Figure 3 shows the respective distance and service level for the three settings of ML during several iterations of the feedback loop. The performance of the best setting for the Daganzo-approximation is also shown.

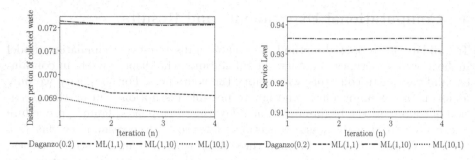

Fig. 3. Performance of approximation policies over several iterations, AOP = 0.2 (Daganzo) and $(w^d, w^\alpha) = \{(1,1),(1,10),(10,1)\}$ (ML), $N = 4$

First, we see that the weights in the cost function $\zeta_{c,t}$ have an effect on the performance of the model. When the weight for the distance (w^d) is relatively low, the model favors high service levels over distance reduction, and vice versa. The improvement over the iterations is limited, which indicates that for this case, the initial training on the training set as described at the beginning of this section, was sufficient.

A more detailed comparison of all experiments can be found in Table 6. First, the added value of a rolling planning horizon is confirmed by the bad performance of the myopic policy, in comparison with Daganzo and the regression model: the service level is relatively low, and the distance is over 15% more in comparison with the worst performing approximation method. Compared with the best performing approximation method, the myopic policy is more than 28% worse. Also, an additional vehicle is needed. Further, we observe that the regression model results in a better performance compared to using the Daganzo-approximation. There is an improvement in distance ranging from 0.13% to almost 17%, compared with similar or slightly worse service levels.

Table 6. Performance of approximation policies for all experiments, best ML-solution reported

Policy	Km/ton per vehicle	Service level	Nr. of vehicles
Myopic	0.0959	86.4%	5
Daganzo (0.1)	0.0830	96.5%	4
Daganzo (0.2)	0.0722	94.1%	4
Daganzo (0.3)	0.0827	90.5%	4
ML (1,1)	0.0691	93.2%	4
ML (1,10)	0.0721	93.5%	4
ML (10,1)	0.0684	91%	4

5   Conclusions

We developed an approximation method, encompassing a large range of temporal and spatial features, which can be used to predict distances and service levels within transportation problems, to reduce the computational complexity of finding suitable vehicle routes. We illustrated the approach considering a large dynamic waste collection problem. As a benchmark, we implemented the Daganzo-approximation with a service level penalty. The new distance and service level approximation model was introduced in such a way that it can be applied to a wide range of problems. We showed which features have the highest importance for TSP and VRP models, showed that we can predict distance fairly accurately without solving the TSP or VRP, and explained the automatic feature selection methods for linear regression and random forests. We described the approach of combining offline learning with online optimization, and how to iteratively update or improve the approximations. Finally, we validated our machine learning model on the waste collection case with stochastic demands. The case study showed that fast approximation methods are valuable because they enable fast decision making. Our proposed model performs reasonably better than the benchmark policy.

Further research can be done on features that describe the problem instances more specifically. We would like to stress that computational effort is an important factor in calculating features, especially when the approximation needs to be done often and relies on its speed compared with solving a TSP or VRP using heuristics. Another research direction we propose is to use approximate dynamic programming within the customer selection phase, to iteratively learn a value function approximation.

References

1. Archetti, C., Fernández, E., Huerta-Muñoz, D.L.: The flexible periodic vehicle routing problem. Comput. Oper. Res. **85**, 58–70 (2017)
2. Arnold, F., Sörensen, K.: What makes a VRP solution good? the generation of problem-specific knowledge for heuristics. Comput. Oper. Res. **106**, 280–288 (2019)
3. Baita, F., Ukovich, W., Pesenti, R., Favaretto, D.: Dynamic routing-and-inventory problems: a review. Transport. Res. Part A: Policy Practice **32**(8), 585–598 (1998)
4. Bard, J.F., Huang, L., Jaillet, P., Dror, M.: A decomposition approach to the inventory routing problem with satellite facilities. Transport. Sci. **32**(2), 189–203 (1998)
5. Beliën, J., De Boeck, L., Van Ackere, J.: Municipal solid waste collection and management problems: a literature review. Transport. Sci. **48**(1), 78–102 (2014)
6. Benjamin, A., Beasley, J.: Metaheuristics for the waste collection vehicle routing problem with time windows, driver rest period and multiple disposal facilities. Comput. Oper. Res. **37**(12), 2270–2280 (2010)
7. Braekers, K., Ramaekers, K., Van Nieuwenhuyse, I.: The vehicle routing problem: state of the art classification and review. Comput. Ind. Eng. **99**, 300–313 (2016)
8. Caceres-Cruz, J., Arias, P., Guimarans, D., Riera, D., Juan, A.A.: Rich vehicle routing problem, Survey. ACM Comput. Surv. **47**(2), 521 (2014)

9. Coelho, L.C., Cordeau, J.F., Laporte, G.: Thirty years of inventory routing. Transport. Sci. **48**(1), 1–19 (2014)
10. Dror, M., Laporte, G., Trudeau, P.: Vehicle routing with split deliveries. Discrete Appl. Math. **50**(3), 239–254 (1994)
11. Gregorutti, B., Michel, B., Saint-Pierre, P.: Correlation and variable importance in random forests. Stat. Comput. **27**, 13 (2013)
12. Gromicho, J., van Hoorn, J., Kok, A., Schutten, J.: Restricted dynamic programming: a flexible framework for solving realistic VRPS. Comput. Oper. Res. **39**(5), 902–909 (2012)
13. Heijnen, W.: Improving the waste collection planning of amsterdam, June 2019. http://essay.utwente.nl/78290/
14. Lalla-Ruiz, E., Voß, S.: A POPMUSIC approach for the multi-depot cumulative capacitated vehicle routing problem. Optimization Lett. **14**(3), 671–691 (2020)
15. Mes, M.: Using simulation to assess the opportunities of dynamic waste collection. In: Bangsow, S. (ed.) Use Cases of Discrete Event Simulation: Appliance and Research, chap. 13, pp. 277–307. Springer, Heidelberg (2012). https://doi.org/10.1007/978-3-642-28777-0_13
16. Mes, M., Schutten, M., Rivera, A.P.: Inventory routing for dynamic waste collection. Waste Manage. **34**(9), 1564–1576 (2014)
17. Moin, N.H., Salhi, S.: Inventory routing problems: a logistical overview. J. Oper. Res. Soc. **58**(9), 1185–1194 (2007)
18. Nicola, D., Vetschera, R., Dragomir, A.: Total distance approximations for routing solutions. Comput. Oper. Res. **102**, 67–74 (2019)
19. Novoa, C., Storer, R.: An approximate dynamic programming approach for the vehicle routing problem with stochastic demands. Euro. J. Oper. Res. **196**(2), 509–515 (2009)
20. Powell, W.B., Ryzhov, I.O.: Optimal Learning and Approximate Dynamic Programming, chap. 18, pp. 410–431. Wiley (2013)
21. Rasku, J., Kärkkäinen, T., Musliu, N.: Feature extractors for describing vehicle routing problem instances. In: Hardy, B., Qazi, A., Ravizza, S. (eds.) 5th Student Conference on Operational Research (SCOR 2016). OpenAccess Series in Informatics (OASIcs), vol. 50, pp. 7:1–7:13. Schloss Dagstuhl-Leibniz-Zentrum fuer Informatik, Dagstuhl, Germany (2016)
22. Robust, F., Daganzo, C.F., Souleyrette, R.R.: Implementing vehicle routing models. Transport. Res. Part B: Methodol. **24**(4), 263–286 (1990)
23. Solomon, M.M.: Algorithms for the vehicle routing and scheduling problems with time window constraints. Oper. Res. **35**, 254–265 (1987)
24. Ulmer, M.W., Goodson, J.C., Mattfeld, D.C., Hennig, M.: Offline-online approximate dynamic programming for dynamic vehicle routing with stochastic requests. Transport. Sci. **53**(1), 185–202 (2019)
25. Ulmer, M.W., Mattfeld, D.C., Köster, F.: Budgeting time for dynamic vehicle routing with stochastic customer requests. Transport. Sci. **52**(1), 20–37 (2018)
26. Zou, H., Hastie, T.: Regularization and variable selection via the elastic net. J. Royal Stat. Soc. Series B (Statistical Methodology) **67**(2), 301–320 (2005)

Daily Distribution of Duties for Crew Scheduling with Attendance Rates: A Case Study

Martin Scheffler[1]([⊠]) and Janis Sebastian Neufeld[1,2]

[1] Faculty of Business and Economics, TU Dresden, 01069 Dresden, Germany
{martin.scheffler,janis_sebastian.neufeld}@tu-dresden.de
[2] Chair of Management Science, Otto-von-Guericke-Universität Magdeburg,
39016 Magdeburg, Germany
http://www.industrielles-management.de, http://www.ms.ovgu.de

Abstract. The railway crew scheduling problem with attendance rates is particularly relevant for the planning of conductors in German regional passenger transport. Its aim is to find a cost-minimal set of duties. In contrast to other crew scheduling problems, only a given percentage of trains has to be covered by personnel. As a result, existing solution approaches for this complex planning task often generate schedules in which the number of duties per day varies significantly. However, schedules with an uneven distribution are often not applicable in practice, as an proper assignment of duties to conductors becomes impossible. Therefore, we discuss several ways how an even distribution can be considered in a column generation solution method, namely post-processing and integrated approaches. In addition, the daily distribution is also examined for each depot, where a given number of conductors may be assigned to. In a case study the presented approaches are examined and compared for three real-world transportation networks. It is shown that without much additional computational effort and only a minor increase of costs schedules with evenly distributed duties can be gained. Especially the depot-based integrated approaches show promising results. Hence, this study can contribute to an improved applicability in practice of automated railway crew scheduling.

Keywords: Railway crew scheduling · Column generation · Case study.

1 Introduction

Crew scheduling is a major planning step in the operation of a railway network. Its aim is to find a cost-minimal set of feasible duties for personnel. This schedule has to satisfy all legal regulations (e.g. working hours act) as well as operating conditions, and, at the same time, must enable the staff to fulfill all necessary

This research was supported by DB Regio AG.

© Springer Nature Switzerland AG 2020
E. Lalla-Ruiz et al. (Eds.): ICCL 2020, LNCS 12433, pp. 371–383, 2020.
https://doi.org/10.1007/978-3-030-59747-4_24

tasks. Especially for train drivers and conductors an efficient deployment of personnel is a crucial aspect for railway operators. On the one hand, many European railway companies face an increasing shortage of skilled workers. On the other hand, together with costs for the rolling stock personnel costs are one of the two major operational cost components [4,9].

Crew scheduling is based on the preceding timetabling and rolling stock rostering. Duties are usually generated as anonymous shifts, i.e. they still have to be assigned to specific employees in the following crew rostering step [7]. A challenge arising when implementing automated crew scheduling approaches in practice is that for the sake of simplification and efficiency usually some practical restrictions are not integrated into the underlying model. This, however, can lead to the problem that generated schedules are very cost-efficient but not applicable in reality.

One of these aspects, that came up during a long-term crew scheduling project at DB Regio AG in Germany [11], was an uneven daily distribution of duties for conductors. This is especially critical in regional passenger transport in Germany, where commonly attendance rates have to be taken into account. This means that only a given percentage of trips has to be attended by a conductor [5], which often results in a lower number of duties on certain days. This can lead to infeasibility of the whole schedule due to several reasons. For example, collective labor agreements may define a maximum percentage of duties on weekends, which may be conflicting with aim to find a cost-minimizing schedule. Furthermore, if the duties are concentrated on particular days of the week, the schedule complicates the downstream planning step of crew rostering. Possibly an assignment of conductors to duties is not possible legally. Despite these challenges, a consideration of an even distribution of duties is still missing in crew scheduling approaches.

Note, in general, the personnel capacity of a network or a depot, where a given number of conductors is located, is measured by a maximum number of duties per week. This measure can easily be integrated into crew scheduling models [6]. However, these constraints cannot be used for new networks, as no existing data is available for the number of conductors. Furthermore, this only sets an upper bound, but this does not prevent considerable fluctuations in the distribution.

The goal and major contribution of the study at hand are now twofold: First, we discuss several ways how an even distribution can be integrated in models for the crew scheduling problem with attendance rates (CSPAR) to generate applicable schedules for practice. Second, we present a case study for real-world railway networks to compare these different approaches regarding solution quality and to show the impact and relevance of an (un-)even distribution of duties in practice.

Therefore, the paper is structured as follows: In Sect. 2 the considered CSPAR is defined and a basic column generation approach from literature is presented. Furthermore, the relevance and challenges regarding an even distribution of duties per day are explained in more detail. Section 3 discusses different mea-

sures for evaluating the distribution of duties as well as ways of integrating it
to the column generation framework, namely an integrated planning and post-
processing. A case study with computational experiments on three real-world
networks serves as evaluation of the proposed methods and the impact of uneven
distributions of duties in Sect. 4. Finally, the results are summarized and future
research opportunities are pointed out in Sect. 5.

2   Distribution of Duties in Railway Crew Scheduling

2.1   The Railyway Crew Scheduling Problem with Attendance Rates

The CSPAR is defined as task to find a cost-minimizing schedule of duties for
conductors in railway passenger transport for a given planning horizon. Various algorithms have been presented to solve this complex planning problem and
nearly all of them have been developed for real-world railway networks in different countries (for a detailed overview see [4]). Among these two major modeling
approaches can be identified: network flow formulations (e.g. [12,13]) and set
covering or set partitioning models (e.g. [1,3,9]). Most studies have in common
that large-scale problems have to be solved, while many practical restrictions
are considered. However, so far the CSPAR has only been considered with the
second approach. Therefore, we present a simplified MIP formulation based on
[7], which models the CSPAR as set covering problem and makes use of a column generation approach. For an overview of column generation itself, we refer
to [10].

The planning horizon is given by a set of several days $k \in K$ (usually one or
two weeks). A trip $i \in M$ is the smallest planning entity, with M being a set of
all trips in the railway network. Each trip is defined by a departure and arrival
time as well as a departure and arrival station, and is a result of the preceding
timetabling. A duty $j \in N$, with N being a set of feasible duties, is defined by
a list of consecutive trips $i \in M$, added by required rest times, train-related
services or walks if trains are changed. Each duty represents a shift or working
day and has to meet all legal and technical restrictions (for a detailed description
of these see [6,8]).

Each trip $i \in M$ may exist on several days of the planning horizon, so that
M_k is defined as subset of M with all trips starting on day k. Likewise, N_k is a
subset of N, containing all duties starting on day k. The matrix $A \in \{0,1\}^{|M| \times |N|}$
contains all duties as columns, with $a_{ij} = 1$ if duty $j \in N$ covers trip $i \in M$ and
0 otherwise.

Each duty j leads to given costs c_j based on its paid working time. If the
binary decision variable $x_j = 1$, duty j is chosen in the solution schedule, 0
otherwise. The second binary decision variable y_{ik} is 1 if trip i is attended on
day k. Attendance rates are given by the transportation contract and defined
for each trip i. The given rate $g \in G$ of attended trips, with G representing a set
of all attendance rates and $g \in [0,1]$, is based on the total number of attended

kilometers. Therefore, the distance d_{ig} of trip $i \in M$ is used to calculate its fulfillment.

Based on this notation we use the restricted master problem (RMP):

$$[\text{RMP}]: \quad \min \sum_{j \in N} c_j x_j \tag{1}$$

$$\text{s.t.} \quad \sum_{k \in K} \sum_{i \in M_k} d_{ig} y_{ik} \geq g \sum_{k \in K} \sum_{i \in M_k} d_{ig} \qquad \forall\, g \in G \tag{2}$$

$$\sum_{j \in N_k} a_{ij} x_j \geq y_{ik} \qquad \forall\, k \in K, i \in M_k \tag{3}$$

$$x_j \in \{0, 1\} \qquad \forall\, j \in N \tag{4}$$

$$y_{ik} \in \{0, 1\} \qquad \forall\, k \in K, i \in M_k \tag{5}$$

The column generation approach is designed straightforward and based on [7]. Based on an initial solution the linear programming relaxation of RMP is solved in each iteration. Let p_{ik} be the dual value of Constraints (3), then the reduced costs are calculated by Eq. (6):

$$\bar{c}_j^{RMP} = c_j - \sum_{i \in M_k} a_{ij} \pi_{ik} \tag{6}$$

Subsequently, the pricing problem is solved to find new duties with negative reduced costs, which potentially further improve the objective value. As described by [1] it can be decomposed in K independent problems. In each iteration of column generation the pricing problem of a different day is solved by a genetic algorithm using the reduced costs as fitness. It searches for new duties with negative reduced costs. These are added to N and the algorithm moves on to the next iteration. The column generation terminates as soon as no new duties with negative reduced costs are found for the entire planning period or a given time limit is reached. The final schedule is obtained by solving RMP. For details we refer to [7].

2.2   Challenges Regarding the Distribution of Duties

Before automatically generated schedules can be implemented in practice, often minor manual adjustments are necessary, since it is neither advisable nor possible to integrate every practical detail in the mathematical model. But sometimes these necessary modifications can be very time-consuming or even be not manageable by a human planer, e.g. if a minor aspect leads to infeasibility of the whole schedule.

This can be the case for an uneven daily distribution of duties which is especially relevant for crew scheduling with attendance rate. Attendance rates are commonly found in German regional passenger transport [5] and are also the focus of this study. If all trips in a network have to be attended by personnel, the daily distribution of duties is mostly predefined by the trips of a network. In contrast, if only a certain percentage of trips needs to be covered, conventional algorithms regularly generate schedules with unevenly distributed duties. The example given in Fig. 1 illustrates this issue for a network with two stations A and B. Here, there is a trip from A to B and back only in the morning (upper row) and in the afternoon (lower row). We further assume that this network leads to a set of 14 feasible duties (7 in the morning, 7 in the afternoon) with identical costs. Each trip has an attendance rate of 50%. Since all trips have the same distance, exactly seven duties must be selected. For an even distribution over the week a worst case example is choosing duties of the first half of the week only (marked with gray color). In practice the distribution is random and causes considerable problems for the planners when assigning personnel to the duties.

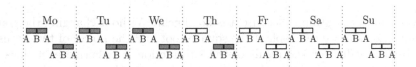

Fig. 1. Example for the daily distribution of duties

Use cases in practice have a much higher complexity than the chosen example, especially if duties contain trips with different attendance rates. Furthermore, the demanded distribution of duties might also follow different predefined patterns. Therefore, complex manual planning steps can be necessary regularly to generate or manipulate a feasible schedule. But due to the complexity of the crew scheduling problem with attendance rates (CSPAR) an automated decision support is necessary.

3   Solution Approaches

3.1   Measuring the Distribution of Duties

Measuring the distribution of duties can be done by using the standard deviation (STD) of the daily number of duties. For a simplified notation we introduce the following definitions. The number of all duties can be counted by X and is determined by Eq. (7). The number of all duties on day k can be counted by X_k and is determined by Eq. (8).

$$X = \sum_{j \in N} x_j \tag{7}$$

$$X_k = \sum_{j \in N_k} x_j = \sum_{j \in N} b_{jk} \cdot x_j \qquad \forall \quad k \in K \tag{8}$$

Note, parameter b_{jk} is introduced for an easy calculation of the reduced costs in Sect. 3.2. It becomes 1 if duty j takes place on day k.

For a practical application, minimizing STD is not always desirable. Often the timetable on weekends differs from the timetable on working days, so a different number of duties in both time periods is desired. Because of this, we aim for a given ratio p_k of duties per day $k \in K$, i.e. $\sum_{k \in K} p_k = 1$. In case of minimizing STD the parameter p_k equals $\frac{1}{|K|}$ for all $k \in K$. We will refer to this generalization as minimization the average deviation from the targeted distribution (AD). Based on this, STD and AD are given by statement (9).

$$\text{STD} = \sqrt{\sum_{k \in K} \frac{1}{|K|}\left(X_k - \frac{1}{|K|}X\right)^2} \to \text{AD} = \sqrt{\sum_{k \in K} \frac{1}{|K|}\left(X_k - p_k X\right)^2} \quad (9)$$

AD is hard to optimize because it is not linear. Without changing the goal of the optimization, we can replace the square root and the power of two by using the absolute value for the result of the subtraction. Furthermore, it does not matter whether we minimize the average or the sum. Hence, it is also possible to minimize the cumulated deviation of the targeted distribution (CD) without the constant $\frac{1}{|K|}$, leading to the Objective (10):

$$\min \text{AD} \to \min \text{CD} = \sum_{k \in K} |X_k - p_k X| \quad (10)$$

By using o_k as exceeding and u_k as deceeding of the targeted number of duties on day k, this can be linearized to:

$$\min \sum_{k \in K} u_k + o_k \quad (11)$$

$$\text{s.t.} \quad p_k X - X_k + o_k \geq 0 \qquad \forall \, k \in K, \quad (12)$$

$$X_k - p_k X + u_k \geq 0 \qquad \forall \, k \in K, \quad (13)$$

$$u_k, o_k \geq 0 \qquad \forall \, k \in K. \quad (14)$$

However, reaching a targeted distribution of duties over the week does not automatically lead to a corresponding distribution for each depot. This point is decisive for practical applications, as the conductors are assigned to depots. Therefore, the approach described above can be extended on the basis of the depots. Again, for a simplified notation we introduce some definitions. The number of all duties starting in depot e can be counted by X_e and is determined by Eq. (15). The number of all duties starting in depot e on day k can be counted by X_{ek} and is determined by Eq. (16).

$$X_e = \sum_{j \in N} b_{je} x_j \qquad\qquad \forall \ e \in E \quad (15)$$

$$X_{ek} = \sum_{j \in N_k} b_{je} x_j = \sum_{j \in N} b_{jk} b_{je} x_j = \sum_{j \in N} b_{jek} x_j \qquad \forall \ e \in E, k \in K \quad (16)$$

Again parameter b_{je} is introduced for an easy calculation of the reduced costs in Sect. 3.2. It becomes 1 if duty j starts on depot e. In the following we use b_{jek} as the product of b_{jk} and b_{ek}. Based on this we can minimize the depot based CD, referred to as dCD, by Objective (17):

$$\min \sum_{e \in E} \sum_{k \in K} u_{ek} + o_{ek} \qquad\qquad (17)$$

$$\text{s.t.} \quad p_{ek} X_e - X_{ek} + o_{ek} \geq 0 \qquad\qquad \forall \ k \in K, e \in E, \quad (18)$$

$$X_{ek} - p_{ek} X_e + u_{ek} \geq 0 \qquad\qquad \forall \ k \in K, e \in E, \quad (19)$$

$$u_{ek}, o_{ek} \geq 0 \qquad\qquad \forall \ k \in K, e \in E. \quad (20)$$

3.2 Integrated Planning

A first variant for gaining a targeted distribution of duties is an integrated approach. We are using the weighted sum in Objective (21) for minimizing the costs and CD during column generation. Parameter β can be interpreted as scale factor that transforms the value of CD into the same unit as the costs. We use the costs of the most expensive possible duty. This equals a duty with the legally maximum permitted length.

$$\min \left(\sum_{j \in N} c_j x_j \right) + \beta \left(\sum_{k \in K} (u_k + o_k) \right) \qquad\qquad (21)$$

The complete optimization problem RMP/CD is given by min (21), s.t. (12)–(14), (2)–(5). Let γ_k^o be the dual values of Constraints (12) and γ_k^u be the dual values of Constraints (13), than the reduced costs $\bar{c}_j$ are calculated by Eq. (22).

$$\bar{c}_j^{RMP/CD} = c_j - \sum_{i \in M_k} a_{ij} \pi_{ik}$$

$$- \sum_{k \in K} (-b_{jk} + p_k) \cdot \gamma_k^o \qquad\qquad (22)$$

$$- \sum_{k \in K} (+b_{jk} - p_k) \cdot \gamma_k^u$$

For minimizing the costs and dCD we use Objective (23).

$$\min \left(\sum_{j \in N} c_j x_j \right) + \beta \left(\sum_{e \in E} \sum_{k \in K} (u_{ek} + o_{ek}) \right) \qquad\qquad (23)$$

Again the complete optimization problem RMP/dCD is given by min (23), s.t. (18)–(20), (2)–(5). Let γ^o_{ek} be the dual values of Constraints (18) and γ^u_{ek} be the dual values of Constraints (19), than the reduced costs $\bar{c}_j$ are calculated by Eq. (24).

$$\bar{c}_j^{RMP/dCD} = c_j - \sum_{i \in M_{kj}} a_{ij}\pi_{ikj}$$
$$- \sum_{k \in K} (-b_{jek} + p_{ke}) \cdot \gamma^o_{ek} \qquad (24)$$
$$- \sum_{k \in K} (+b_{jek} - p_{ke}) \cdot \gamma^u_{ek}$$

Note that each variable x_j is only contained in Constraints (19)–(20) for a single depot. This means that the sum for all depots is eliminated for the calculation of the reduced costs.

3.3   Post-processing

A second variant for gaining a targeted distribution of duties is a post-processing (PP) step after solving the original RMP. This corresponds to the current practical procedure and is done by hand. However, the limits of what is humanly possible are quickly reached here, since the attendance rates make it highly complicated.

Set S contains all duties of the final min-cost schedule. This implies $x_j = 1 \ \forall j \in S$. In the following, we refer to all sets derived from S with an hat for a clear presentation. For each duty j of the min-cost schedule we can derive a set $\hat{S}_j$ containing j and all feasible duplicates of j on all other days. Again, we refer to the elements of the sets $\hat{S}_j$ with $\hat{j}$. For example, the solution schedule may contain a duty $j \in S$ on a Monday, that consist only of trips that are also valid on Tuesday. The same duty, but which is now considered on Tuesday, would be referred to as duty $\hat{j} \in \hat{S}_j$. In addition, we refer to the union of all $\hat{S}_j$ with $\hat{S}$. From this set, the duties should be selected aiming for the desired distribution. Therefore, we still need the daily subsets $\hat{S}_k$ of $\hat{S}$ for all days. Figure 2 gives an illustrative example of all mentioned sets.

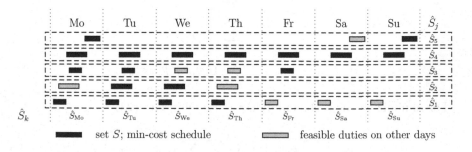

Fig. 2. Feasible duplicates of duties on other days

The goal of post-processing is to select a schedule from $\hat{S}$ in which the CD or dCD is minimized. For the first this can be done solving the original RMP with the following Objective (25):

$$\min \sum_{k \in K} \left| \sum_{\hat{j} \in \hat{S}_k} x_{\hat{j}} - p_k |S| \right|. \tag{25}$$

Again, we can extend this approach to a depot based variant. We use set S_e containing all duties of the final min-cost schedule starting at depot e. Additionally we define set $\hat{S}_{ek}$ following the same logic as used for $\hat{S}_k$ but with additional distinction of depots. Based on this we can minimize dCD as follows:

$$\min \sum_{e \in E} \sum_{k \in K} \left| \sum_{\hat{j} \in \hat{S}_{ek}} x_{\hat{j}} - p_k \cdot |S_e| \right|. \tag{26}$$

Note that both variants can be linearized in the same way as shown in Sect. 3.1. In addition to the targeted distribution, two crucial points have to be considered. On the one hand, the attendance rates must continue to be met. Because of this, it is not possible to simply shift any duty to other days. On the other hand, the objective value must not deteriorate significantly. The latter can be ensured by fixing the number of duties for each j:

$$\sum_{\hat{j} \in \hat{S}_j} x_{\hat{j}} = |S_j| \quad \forall \; j \in S \tag{27}$$

The complete optimization problem for PP is given by min (25) or min (26) s.t. (2)–(5), (27).

4 Computational Experiments and Discussion

We have tested the approaches presented in Sect. 3 in a case study with three different real-life instances. The generated schedules are directly transformable into action and can be used for realistic evaluation of the different approaches. The complete column generation algorithm was implemented in C#. The tests were run on Intel(R) Xenon(R) CPU E5-4627 with 3.3 GHz clock speed and 768 GB RAM. RMP and its relaxation were solved by Gurobi 7.5. The number of parallel threads for Gurobi was limited to 4. The genetic algorithm was run on a single core only. For each run we limited the computation time to 3 h for column generation and 1.5 h for solving the integer programming model. Since the GA is a probabilistic approach, each test was run five times. For an easy interpretation we set $p_k \forall k \in K$ and $p_{ek} \forall e \in E, k \in K$ to $\frac{1}{|K|}$. This means the results for minimizing CD equal minimizing STD and those for minimizing dCD equal the cumulated depot based STD (dSTD). We also show the resulting values for STD and dSTD explicitly.

Table 1 shows the results for the post processing (PP), the integrated approach (IA) and the depot based integrated approach (dIA). The costs are given
in millions, while the computing times for column generation, solving the RMP
and doing PP are given in seconds (CG, RMP, PP).

Table 1. Computational results for the considered real life instances

		Costs	CD	dCD	STD	dSTD	CG	RMP	PP	|S|
I	PP	2.365	3.4	19.8	1.0	3.6	10800	139	157	103
	IA	2.368	0.0	17.7	0.0	2.9	10800	173	-	105
	dIA	2.385	1.6	1.6	0.0	0.3	10800	22	-	107
II	PP	2.757	11.5	19.0	1.9	3.5	10800	21	78	109
	IA	2.759	1.6	20.9	0.3	4.2	10800	72	-	109
	dIA	2.783	0.3	0.3	0.1	0.1	10800	125	-	112
III	PP	4.888	15.8	27.3	3.0	4.9	10800	5400	252	209
	IA	4.879	0.0	24.0	0.0	4.2	10800	5400	-	218
	dIA	4.911	0.3	0.3	0.0	0.0	10800	5400	-	217

All three tested approaches do not differ in the computing times. The time
required for PP is negligible (maximum average value of 252 s for Instance III).
Note that the high computing times for solving the RMP for Instance III are
caused by the instance itself. For all three instances PP and IA gain almost
the same costs, but IA simultaneously eliminates the daily fluctuations almost
completely. The values of CD are much lower, which is equivalent to STD near
zero for all instances, whereas CD is up to 15.8 for the PP approach (Instance
III). A reason for this is the fact that PP cannot generate new duties when aiming
for an even distribution, but is limited to shifting duties of the final min cost
schedule to other days. This means the solution space for PP is very limited. In
general, the attendance rates account for a problem with many different solutions
with (almost) identical costs. The IA is able to consider these similar solutions
for minimizing CD, whereby the PP cannot do this.

Although IA achieves very good results for CD, there are still large daily
deviations for the individual depots (dCD). For example for Network II the
dCD is higher than 20.

To enable a better interpretation of the values, Fig. 3 shows randomly selected
solutions as examples for all three approaches on Instance II. Figure 3 (a) depicts
the solution for PP. It can be seen that the number of duties is significantly lower
on weekends (Sa and Su) and difference between the maximum and minimum
number of duties per day is up to three duties for Depots 3 and 4. Even though
the sum of duties per day shows a nearly even distribution if the integrated
approach is chosen, especially for Depot 1 and 3 the daily number of duties
still fluctuates significantly in Fig. 3 (b). The use of dIA, displayed in Fig. 3 (c),
achieves a much better distribution over the week than both other approaches.

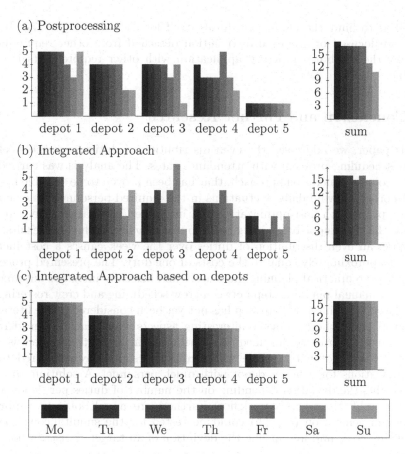

Fig. 3. Number of duties per day and depot for a real-life instance

Values close to zero for dSTD show that there are almost no daily fluctuations in the number of duties for each depot. This improvement in distribution causes only a minimal increase in costs of less than 1% for all instances compared to best solution gained by PP or IA (see Table 1). For all three instances, this increase of costs corresponds approximately to the cost of a single duty. It can also be noted that the integrated approaches require more duties in total. At the same time, the average paid time of a duty decreases minimally.

However, it is important to note that higher costs do not automatically lead to more needed conductors. For example, the minimum number of required conductors can be defined as the highest number of duties on one day of the week cumulated over all depots. For the given example in Fig. 3 this results in at least 19 conductors for PP and 22 for IA. But for dIA this results in only 16 conductors, which is a considerable advantage for the planner. Furthermore, in practice a schedule has to deal with many and sometimes also contradictory requirements. Hence, it is also common to keep the average paid time within predefined limits as well as to limit the number of duties itself for each depot (see [7]). In this study, we focused on the even distribution detached from other requirements, whereby the combined practical application with other requirements is easily possible.

5   Conclusion and Further Research

In this paper, we addressed the even distribution of duties over the week for a crew scheduling problem with attendance rates. The analysis was carried out using a column generation approach, that has been proven to be suitable in practice. In order to avoid daily fluctuations in the required personnel, we examined and compared both post-optimization and integrated approaches. We were able to show that the depot-based integrated approach achieves the best results. Furthermore, an even distribution of duties over the week causes a cost increase which is approximately equal to the costs of one duty. The presented procedure facilitates the practical planning immensely and basically increases automation, because a manual planning step between crew scheduling and crew rostering can be replaced. This intermediate step has not yet been considered in the literature.

Nevertheless, there are some interesting aspects which can be considered in future work. In practice, an unequal distribution in absolute numbers is more critical for a depot with relatively few conductors per day compared to the same deviations for a larger depot with much personnel. A solution approach that weights the deviation depending on the number of duties per depot would further simplify the practical work flow. Furthermore, a multi-objective approach for column generation (e.g. [2]) could be tested for the simultaneous goals of minimizing costs and minimizing the deviation of a targeted distribution.

References

1. Abbink, E.J.W., Wout, J.V., Huisman, D.: Solving large scale crew scheduling problems by using iterative partitioning. In: Liebchen, C., Ahuja, R.K., Mesa, J.A. (eds.) 7th Workshop on Algorithmic Approaches for Transportation Modeling, Optimization, and Systems (ATMOS 2007). OASICS, vol. 7. Internationales Begegnungs- und Forschungszentrum fuer Informatik (IBFI), Schloss Dagstuhl, Germany (2007)
2. Artigues, C., Jozefowiez, N., Sarpong, B.M.: Column generation algorithms for bi-objective combinatorial optimization problems with a min-max objective. EURO J. Computat. Optimizat. **6**(2), 117–142 (2018)
3. Chen, S., Shen, Y.: An improved column generation algorithm for crew scheduling problems. J. Inf. Computat. Sci. **10**, 175–183 (2013)
4. Heil, J., Hoffmann, K., Buscher, U.: Railway crew scheduling: models, methods and applications. Euro. J. Oper. Res. **283**(2), 405–425 (2020)
5. Hoffmann, K.: A hybrid solution approach for railway crew scheduling problems with attendance rates. In: Doerner, K.F., Ljubic, I., Pflug, G., Tragler, G. (eds.) Operations Research Proceedings 2015. ORP, pp. 243–250. Springer, Cham (2017). https://doi.org/10.1007/978-3-319-42902-1_33

6. Hoffmann, K., Buscher, U.: Valid inequalities for the arc flow formulation of the railway crew scheduling problem with attendance rates. Computers & Industrial Engineering (2018)
7. Hoffmann, K., Buscher, U., Neufeld, J.S., Tamke, F.: Solving practical railway crew scheduling problems with attendance rates. Bus. Inf. Syst. Eng. **59**(3), 147–159 (2017)
8. Jütte, S., Albers, M., Thonemann, U.W., Haase, K.: Optimizing railway crew scheduling at db schenker. Interfaces **41**(2), 109–122 (2011)
9. Jütte, S., Thonemann, U.W.: Divide-and-price: a decomposition algorithm for solving large railway crew scheduling problems. Euro. J. Oper. Res. **219**(2), 214–223 (2012)
10. Lübbecke, M.E., Desrosiers, J.: Selected topics in column generation. Oper. Res. **53**(6), 1007–1023 (2005)
11. Neufeld, J.S.: Efficient railway crew scheduling in german regional passenger transport. Impact **2019**(2), 7–10 (2019)
12. Şahin, G., Yüceoğlu, B.: Tactical crew planning in railways. Transport. Res. Part E: Logistics Transport. Rev. **47**(6), 1221–1243 (2011)
13. Vaidyanathan, B., Jha, K.C., Ahuja, R.K.: Multicommodity network flow approach to the railroad crew-scheduling problem. IBM J. Res. Dev. - Bus. optimizat. **51**(3), 325–344 (2007)

A Heuristic Algorithm for Finding Attractive Fixed-Length Circuits in Street Maps

Rhyd Lewis[✉]

School of Mathematics, Cardiff University, Cardiff CF24 4AG, Wales
LewisR9@cf.ac.uk

Abstract. In this paper we consider the problem of determining fixed-length routes on a street map that start and end at the same location. We propose a heuristic for this problem based on finding pairs of edge-disjoint shortest paths, which can then be combined into a circuit. Various heuristics and filtering techniques are also proposed for improving the algorithm's performance.

1 Introduction

The task of finding fixed-length routes on a map has various practical applications in everyday life. For example, we may want to go on a 10 km run, organise a cycling tour, or we may need to quickly determine a walk from our house in order to complete our daily number of steps as determined by our fitness tracker.

In practical circumstances, routes of a specific length are often quite easy to determine. As a trivial example, we may choose to travel back and forth on the same street repeatedly until the required distance has been covered. Similarly, we might also choose to perform "laps" of a city block. In this paper, we want to consider more attractive routes that avoid repetition. Specifically, we want to avoid routes that ask the user to travel along a street or footpath more than once. Two examples of such routes are shown in Fig. 1, using Times Square in New York City as a starting point.

To define this problem more formally, it is useful to first review some standard definitions from graph theory. Let $G = (V, E)$ be an undirected edge-weighted graph with n vertices and m edges, and let $w(u, v)$ denote the weight (or length) of an edge $\{u, v\} \in E$.

Definition 1. *A* walk *is a series of incident edges in a graph. A* trail *is a walk with no repeated edges. A* path *is a trail with no repeated edges or vertices.*

It is also usual to add the prefix u-v to the above terms to signify a walk/trail/path that starts at vertex u and finishes at vertex v. The following terms can then also be used in cases where $u = v$.

Definition 2. *A u-v-walk/trail/path is considered* closed *whenever $u = v$. Closed trails are usually known as* circuits; *closed paths are usually known as* cycles.

© Springer Nature Switzerland AG 2020
E. Lalla-Ruiz et al. (Eds.): ICCL 2020, LNCS 12433, pp. 384–395, 2020.
https://doi.org/10.1007/978-3-030-59747-4_25

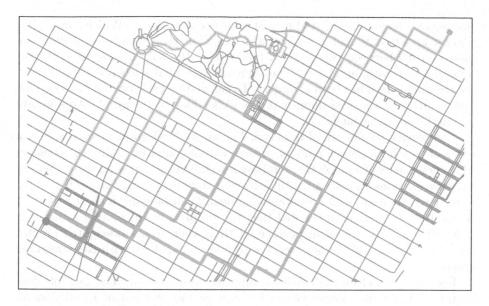

Fig. 1. Starting from Times Square (bottom-left) in New York City, the above map shows a 5 km (red) circuit and an 8 km (green) circuit. Central Park is at the top of the figure; the East river is at the bottom right. (Color figure online)

Similarly to the above, the term u-circuit (cycle) can be used to denote a circuit (cycle) that contains the vertex u. We can also extend this to multiple vertices: for example, a u-v-circuit is a circuit seen to contain vertices u and v.

The problem considered in this paper can now be stated as follows:

Definition 3. *Let $G = (V, E)$ be an undirected edge-weighted graph, $s \in V$ be a* source *vertex and k be a required length. The k circuit problem involves determining an s-circuit C in G such that the total length of its edges $L(C)$ does not exceed k, and $k - L(C)$ is minimal.*

In this paper, note that we focus on undirected graphs only. This is appropriate for practical applications that involve determining jogging and walking routes, though it is not sufficient in applications involving one-way streets. We also define our problem so that circuits with lengths exceeding k are disallowed. This again comes from practical considerations in that it is often easier to add a little extra distance to a route (e.g. by walking up and down a street), than it is to shorten it.

The examples in Fig. 1 show optimal solutions for $k = 5000$ m and 8000 m using Times Square as the source vertex. These particular cases are not cycles because certain vertices (intersections on the map) are visited more than once; however, they are both circuits, in that no edge (road section) is traversed more than once.

From a computational perspective very little work seems to have been conducted on the problem of finding fixed-length circuits and cycles in edge-weighted graphs. One recently suggested heuristic for cycles is due to Willems et al. [11] who use an adaptation of Yen's algorithm [12]. The basic idea is to calculate the shortest path between two vertices, followed by the second shortest path, the third shortest path, and so on. The algorithm then halts when a path close to the required length has been identified. To calculate a cycle containing a specific source vertex v, a special dummy vertex v' is added to the graph. Appropriate v-v'-paths are then sought.

Complexity results are also known. For unweighted graphs, the number of walks of length k between pairs of vertices can be found by taking the (binary) adjacency matrix of a graph G and raising it to the kth power. Currently, the best known algorithms for matrix multiplication operate in approximately $O(n^{2.3})$ [4], so for large values of k the resultant complexity can be quite high at $O(kn^{2.3})$. Basagni et al. [1] have also noted that the problem of calculating a u-v-walk of length k can be solved in polynomial time when using unweighted graphs, providing that $k = n^{O(1)}$; however, the problem is NP-hard with edge-weighted graphs.

For circuits and cycles, similar complexity results exist. The task of identifying a circuit in a graph G can be seen as the problem of identifying an Eulerian subgraph in G (recall that an Eulerian graph is a connected graph in which the degrees of all vertices are even). However, the problem of identifying the *longest* Eulerian subgraph in G is known to be NP-hard, both for weighted and unweighted graphs [8]. This tells us that our k circuit problem is also NP-hard, since it is equivalent to the longest Eulerian subgraph problem whenever $k \geq \sum_{\{u,v\} \in E} w(u,v)$. Similar reasoning can also be applied to the problem of finding cycles of length k in a graph, due to its relationship with the NP-hard Hamiltonian cycle problem.

In this paper we propose a heuristic for the k circuit problem with a particular focus on tackling graphs resembling maps of roads and footpaths. Our intention is for this heuristic to be fast while also producing accurate and visually pleasing solutions. In the next section we develop the overall framework of our algorithm. Section 3 then discusses methods for processing problem instances. In Sect. 4 we then analyse the performance of our methods, before showing how this performance can be further improved in Sect. 5.

2   Forming Circuits

In this paper our proposed strategy for the k circuit problem is to construct solutions by generating a pair of edge-disjoint paths between the source vertex s and a particular target vertex t. In an undirected graph, the union of these two s-t-paths forms an s-t-circuit. If these paths also happen to be vertex disjoint, then their union will also be an s-t-cycle. The problem now involves identifying the most appropriate target vertex—that is, the vertex $t \in V$ for which the sum of the lengths of the two s-t-paths is closest to, but not exceeding k.

A single path between a pair of vertices can be formed in various different ways. One strategy is to use depth first search, though this can often produce

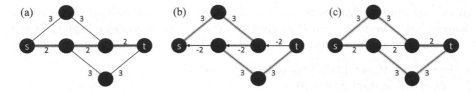

Fig. 2. (a) The shortest s-t-path in an example graph G; (b) a modified version of G and the corresponding shortest s-t-path (determined via MODIFIED-DIJKSTRA); (c) the resultant s-t-circuit (cycle) formed by "unweaving" the two paths.

long meandering paths that, for this application, may well be unattractive to the user. A better alternative is breadth first search, which generates paths between vertices containing the minimum numbers of edges. In our case, however, we choose to focus on using the *shortest* paths between vertices (in terms of the sum of the edge-weights within the path), as doing so seems to result in simpler-looking paths that involve less crisscrossing. The production of such paths can be achieved via various well-known polynomial time algorithms, such as those of Bellman-Ford [3] and Moore [6], which both feature a complexity of $O(nm)$. The approach we follow here, though, is the more efficient method of Dijkstra [5], which has a complexity of $O(m \lg n)$ when a binary heap is used for its priority queue [3].

An obvious way of determining two paths between s and t is to produce a single s-t-path, remove this path's edges from the graph, and then find a second s-t-path. However, this approach has faults. Figure 2(a), for example, shows a small edge-weighted graph and its corresponding shortest s-t-path. Removing the edges of this path then disconnects s and t, preventing a second s-t-path from being formed. However, it is obvious that two disjoint s-t-paths exist, as shown in Fig. 2(c). Better techniques are therefore needed.

Previously, Suurballe [9] and Bhandari [2] have proposed methods for finding the pair of edge-disjoint s-t paths whose edge-weight sums are minimal. An outline of Bhandari's method is given in Fig. 2. As shown, in the first step, the shortest s-t-path is found. In the second step, the graph is then modified by adding directions on this path so that its edges point towards s. The weights on these edges are then negated and the shortest s-t-path in this new graph is calculated. In the final step, the graph is reset, and the two paths are "unweaved" to form the final pair of paths, as demonstrated in Fig. 2(c). This unweaving process involves taking the symmetric difference of the two paths, resulting in a set of edges defining an Eulerian circuit.

Note that while Dijkstra's algorithm is sufficient for producing the first s-t-path in this method, it cannot be used for the second path because it is known to be incorrect for graphs featuring negatively weighted edges. Bhandari [2] proposes a modified version of Dijkstra's algorithm for this purpose. This MODIFIED-DIJKSTRA algorithm operates using the following steps.

In this description $L(v)$ is used the denote the length of the path between the source s and a vertex v, and $P(v)$ gives the vertex that precedes v in the shortest s-v-path. The method halts as soon as the shortest s-t-path has been established.

1. For all $v \in V$, set $L(v) = \infty$ and $P(v) = $ NULL.
2. Let $S = \emptyset$ and set $L(s) = 0$.
3. Let $u \in S$ such that $L(u)$ is minimal among all vertices currently in S. If $u = t$ then exit; otherwise, remove u from S and go to Step 4.
4. For all neighbouring vertices v of u, if $L(u) + w(u,v) < L(v)$ then: (a) set $L(v) = L(u) + w(u,v)$, (b) set $P(v) = u$, and (c) insert v into S. Now return to Step 3.

Note that MODIFIED-DIJKSTRA differs from Dijkstra's original algorithm in that vertices can be inserted and removed from the set S of visited vertices multiple times; however, Segewick and Wayne [7] note that this brings run times that are exponential in the worst case. As an alternative, Bhandari [2] also suggests a modified version of Moores algorithm that is able to halt as soon as the shortest s-t-path is identified. This features a more desirable complexity of $O(nm)$. Despite this, in our experimentation, we still found that MODIFIED-DIJKSTRA generally gave shorter run times, as shown in Sect. 4. It is therefore used in all test unless specified otherwise.

Having now reviewed methods for producing s-t-circuits, our overall algorithm framework GEN-k-CIRCUIT is described as follows.

1. Let $T = V - \{s\}$ be the set of target vertices to check and let $C^* = \emptyset$ be the best circuit observed during the run.
2. Use Dijkstra's algorithm to determine the shortest path tree rooted at s. This gives the shortest paths between s and all other vertices in the graph.
3. Randomly select and remove a target vertex t from T. Using the shortest s-t-path found in Step 2, employ the methods of Bhandari together with MODIFIED-DIJKSTRA to form an s-t-circuit C.
4. If $L(C) \leq k$ and $L(C) > L(C^*)$ then set $C^* = C$.
5. If $L(C^*) = k$ or $T = \emptyset$ then return C^* and end; else go to Step 3.

As shown, the basic idea in these steps is to take each vertex $t \in V - \{s\}$ in turn and generate the shortest s-t-circuit. The observed circuit C^* whose length is closest to but not exceeding k is then returned. In the worst case, this involves $n - 1$ separate iterations of the algorithm (i.e., applications of MODIFIED-DIJKSTRA). In the following sections, however we will discuss various ways in which this number can be reduced while not affecting the accuracy of the algorithm.

3 Problem Generation and Preprocessing

As mentioned, in this paper we want to focus on graphs resembling real-world networks of roads and footpaths. However, to help analyse behaviour, we also want to be able to alter their edge densities. We therefore started by looking

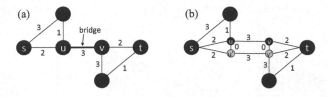

Fig. 3. (a) An example of a graph with an edge connectivity of one (due to the presence of the bridge $\{u,v\}$); (b) the modified graph, featuring an edge connectivity of two.

at the central districts of five large cities, namely Amsterdam, Kolkata, London, Melbourne and New York. These were found to have approximately 400 nodes (intersections) per square km. We then generated our own large problem instances that emulated these features.

To generate a single instance we started by taking a 10 km by 10 km square and placing 400,000 nodes within it at random coordinates. A Delaunay triangulation was then generated from these vertices, and a subset of this triangulation's edges was randomly selected to form a connected planar graph. Edge weights were then set to the Euclidean distances between end points, rounded up to the nearest metre. To allow circuits in any direction, the source vertex was also placed at the centre of the square at coordinate $(5000, 5000)$. For our experiments we considered three types of graphs: sparse, medium, and dense, featuring 500,000, 750,000 and 1000,000 edges respectively. Twenty such graphs were generated in each case.

Before producing circuits with these graphs, two preprocessing steps are required. Firstly, observe that any vertex v whose distance is more than $k/2$ units from the source can be removed from the graph since, in such cases, all s-v-circuits will be longer than k. For small values of k this can drastically reduce the number of edges and vertices, making computation much faster.

Our second preprocessing step is used to deal with any bridges in the graph (recall that a bridge is any edge whose removal increases the number of graph components). The presence of bridges in a graph can severely limit the number of circuits that are available and can therefore affect the quality of solution – in Fig. 3(a), for example, we see that only one s-circuit is possible. To avoid these issues, graphs containing bridges are extended so that their edge connectivity is raised to two, making circuits between all pairs of vertices possible. Our method of doing this is illustrated in Fig. 3(b). First, all bridges in the graph are identified[1], and the endpoints of these edges are inserted into a set A. For each vertex $v \in A$, a dummy vertex v' is then added to the graph and its neighbourhood is set to be equal to vertex v. The zero-weighted edge $\{v, v'\}$ is then also added.

Note that when executing our GEN-k-CIRCUIT algorithm, a dummy vertex v' of a vertex v does not need to be added to the set of target vertices T. This is

---

[1] This can be achieved in $O(m)$ time using the algorithm of Tarjan [10].

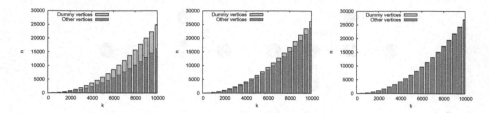

Fig. 4. Number of vertices in the graphs formed for differing values of k using sparse, medium, and dense problem instances respectively. All points are averaged across twenty problem instances.

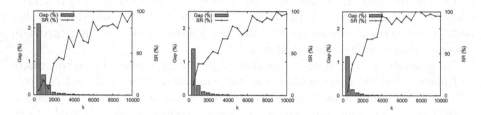

Fig. 5. Accuracy of our approach for differing values of k using sparse, medium, and dense problem instances respectively. All points are averaged across twenty problem instances.

because the generated s-v'-circuit will have the same length as the s-v-circuit. An instance containing n' dummy vertices therefore requires a maximum of $n - n' - 1$ iterations in total.

The effects of these preprocessing steps are illustrated in Fig. 4. In all cases, we see that the value for k has a large effect on the total number of vertices in the resultant graph. For the sparse graphs we also see that significant numbers of dummy vertices need to be added to eliminate the bridges that are present. Fewer additions are needed with denser graphs, however.

4   Basic Algorithm Performance

Our first set of results shows the accuracy of our approach for differing k values.[2] Here, accuracy is reported in two ways: (a) the percentage of instances for which $L(C^*) = k$ was achieved (the success rate), and (b) the percentage gap between $L(C^*)$ and k, calculated as $(1 - L(C^*)/k) \times 100$.

These results are summarised in Fig. 5. For the smallest values of k, the gap between k and $L(C^*)$ seems to be around one to two percent and success rates are low. These gaps exist because the graphs are small and, as a result, very few s-circuits are generated by the algorithm, giving us fewer options to choose between. For the same reason, larger values of k result in a much higher accuracy.

---

[2] All algorithms were written in C++ and executed on a 3.3 GHz CPU with 8 GB of RAM.

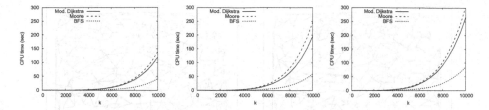

Fig. 6. Run times for different variants of GEN-k-CIRCUIT and differing values of k using sparse, medium, and dense problem instances respectively. All points are averaged across twenty problem instances.

Accuracy also improves slightly with denser instances because, as shown in Fig. 4, these tend to feature more vertices, but fewer dummy vertices. This also gives a greater number of s-circuits to choose from.

In Fig. 6 we show the run times of GEN-k-CIRCUIT with these instances. To reduce noise in these timings, we executed the algorithm for the maximum number of iterations – that is, we did not halt early if a circuit of length k was found. To contrast these results, we also include the times for two different variants. In the first of these, applications of MODIFIED-DIJKSTRA were replaced by Bhandari's modification of Moore's $O(nm)$ algorithm [2]. This variant therefore produces solutions of identical quality to the original. In the second variant, the shortest path algorithms used in Steps 2 and 3 of GEN-k-CIRCUIT were replaced by the $O(m)$ breadth first search (BFS) algorithm. This variant produces different solutions to the others because it determines s-t-circuits with the minimum number of edges as opposed to minimum lengths.

Figure 6 shows that the time requirements of these variants increase for denser graphs and larger graphs, with run times reaching up to 300 s in places. We see that using Moore's algorithm gives slightly higher run times compared to MODIFIED-DIJKSTRA, while the use of BFS shortens run times quite considerably. An issue with BFS, however, is that its preference for circuits with minimal numbers of edges can result in solutions that, subjectively, are sometimes less attractive to the user. An example of this is shown in Fig. 7.

5 Improving Algorithm Performance

In this section we show how the performance of GEN-k-CIRCUIT can be improved by (a) using information collected during a run to filter out members of T that cannot improve solution quality, and (b) strategically selecting members of T that are more likely result in high-quality solutions being found earlier in a run. For (a) we first give the following theorem.

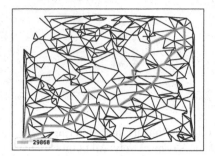 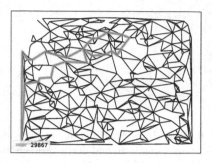

Fig. 7. Circuits produced by MODIFIED-DIJKSTRA (left) and BFS (right) using a planar graph with $n = 400$ and $m = 800$, and a desired length of $k = 30000$. The source appears at the bottom-left corner.

Theorem 1. *Let $G = (V, E)$ be an edge-weighted graph with no negative weights. In addition, let P_1 be the shortest s-v-path in G, and let C be the shortest s-v-circuit, determined using P_1 together with the methods of Bhandari (Sect. 2).*

(i) If $u \in C$, then the shortest s-u-circuit has a length of at most $L(C)$.
(ii) If u is a descendent of v in the shortest path tree rooted at s, then the lengths of all s-u-circuits in G equal or exceed $L(C)$.

Proof. Part (i) is trivial: if $u \in C$ then C also defines an s-u-circuit; hence an s-u-circuit of length $L(C)$ is known to exist.

To prove Part (ii), let P_2 be the shortest v-u-path in G. The shortest s-u-path therefore has length $L(P_1) + L(P_2)$, where $L(P_2)$ is nonnegative. In addition, using the methods of Bhandari let P_1' and P_2' be the second paths generated from s to v and s to u respectively. We now need to show that $L(C) = L(P_1) + L(P_1') \leq L(P_1) + L(P_2) + L(P_2')$ or, in other words, $L(P_1') \leq L(P_2) + L(P_2')$. To do this, assume the opposite, giving $L(P_1') > L(P_2) + L(P_2')$. This now implies that the shortest s-v-circuit has length $L(P_1) + L(P_2) + L(P_2')$, which is a contradiction. ∎

The findings of Theorem 1 allow us to filter out members of T through the application of the following two rules, which are applied between Steps 3 and 4 of GEN-k-CIRCUIT. Recall that at this point in the algorithm, C is the shortest s-t-circuit in G.

1. If $L(C) \leq k$, then remove all vertices $u \in C$ from T. (All s-u-circuits will be equal or inferior in quality compared to C.)
2. If $L(C) \geq k$, then remove from T any descendents u of t in the shortest path tree rooted at s. (The lengths of all s-u-circuits in G will equal or exceed $L(C)$.)

Instead of removing just one vertex from T in each iteration of the algorithm, these rules therefore allow the removal of multiple vertices, thereby speeding up the algorithm while not compromising the quality of solution produced. Note,

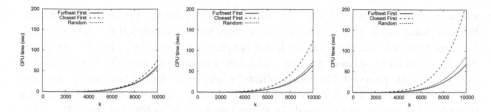

Fig. 8. Run times for GEN-k-CIRCUIT using filtering and heuristic selection. Results are summarised for differing values of k using sparse, medium, and dense problem instances respectively. All points are averaged across twenty problem instances.

however, that these rules rely on the use of shortest paths and circuits – they are therefore not suitable for the BFS variant of the algorithm.

Our second strategy for improving algorithm performance is to modify Step 3 of GEN-k-CIRCUIT so that t is chosen according to some heuristic. We suggest three strategies here: furthest-first, where the $t \in T$ furthest from the source s is selected; closest-first, where the $t \in T$ closest to s is selected; and the original random selection.

Figure 8 shows that these augmentations significantly reduce the run times of the algorithm. In general, the furthest-first rule seems to give the shortest run times because, in early stages of the run, it tends to produce overly long circuits with many vertices, allowing many elements to be removed from T according to the first rule above. Note that the second filtering rule is never actually applied using this heuristic because descendents of a vertex t will have already been considered and removed from T. Perhaps because of this, the random heuristic is often able to produce similar results in that it is able to remove elements from T according to both filtering rules.

As with our previous experiments, note that the run times shown in Fig. 8 were gained by executing GEN-k-CIRCUIT for the maximum number of iterations. That is, the algorithm did not halt early in cases where a circuit of length k was found. Doing so, however, can drastically cut run times. In Fig. 9 we show the times at which the best observed solution was found in each run with each

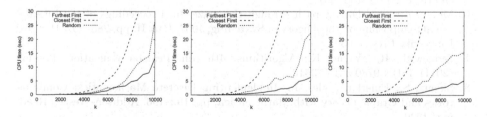

Fig. 9. Time at which the best solution was observed in runs of GEN-k-CIRCUIT using filtering and heuristic selection. Results are summarised for differing values of k using sparse, medium, and dense problem instances respectively. All points are averaged across twenty problem instances.

instance. The best performance again comes when using the furthest-first rule, because solutions with lengths close to k tend to be considered in early stages of the run. On occasion, the random heuristic produces better results, but we found its run times to be subject to a much higher variance, making its behaviour less predictable. In contrast the closest-first heuristic is clearly the worst because, early in the run, it tends to consider very short circuits whose lengths are far from k. This also seems to result in fewer vertices being filtered from T.

6   Conclusions

This paper has proposed a fast-acting heuristic algorithm for the NP-hard k circuit problem. Our method is based on finding pairs of edge-disjoint short-est paths between the source vertex s and a suitable target vertex t. The best observed performance comes when the targets that are furthest from s are con-sidered first, which seems to result in higher quality solutions being identified earlier in the run, while also allowing larger numbers of vertices to be filtered out of the set of potential targets T.

There are a number of extensions to this problem that might be considered in future work. These include identifying fixed-length circuits that remain within a given distance of the starting point (encouraging routes that "stay local"), or adding required destinations within a circuit, such as a local shop or a friend's house.

References

1. Basagni, S., Bruschi, D., Ravasio, S.: On the difficulty of finding walks of length k. Theoret. Inform. Appl. **31**(5), 429–435 (1997)
2. Bhandari, R.: Survivable Networks. Kluwer Academic Publishers, Dordrecht (1999)
3. Cormen, T., Leiserson, C., Rivest, R., Stein, C.: Introduction to Algorithms, 3rd edn. The MIT Press, Cambridge (2009)
4. Davie, A., Stothers, A.: Improved bound for complexity of matrix multiplication. Proc. Roy. Soc. Edinb. **143**(2), 351–369 (2013)
5. Dijkstra, E.: A note on two problems in connexion with graphs. Numerische Math-ematik **1**, 269–271 (1959)
6. Moore, E.: The shortest path through the maze. In: Proceedings of the Interna-tional Symposium on the Theory of Switching, 1957, Part II, pp. 285–292. Harvard University Press (1959)
7. Sedgewick, R., Wayne, K.: Algorithms, 4th edn. Pearson Education, London (2011). ISBN 9780 321 573513
8. Skiena, S.: Eulerian cycles. In: Implementing Discrete Mathematics: Combina-torics and Graph Theory with Mathematica, pp. 192–196. Addison-Wesley, Read-ing (1990)
9. Suurballe, J.: Disjoint paths in a network. Networks **4**, 125–145 (1974)
10. Tarjan, R.: A note on finding the bridges of a graph. Inf. Process. Lett. **2**(6), 160–161 (1974)

11. Willems, D., Zehner, O., Ruzika, S.: On a technique for finding running tracks of specific length in a road network. In: Kliewer, N., Ehmke, J.F., Borndörfer, R. (eds.) Operations Research Proceedings 2017. ORP, pp. 333–338. Springer, Cham (2018). https://doi.org/10.1007/978-3-319-89920-6_45
12. Yen, J.: Finding the K shortest loopless paths in a network. Manag. Sci. **17**(11), 661–786 (1971)

Minimizing Movements in Location Problems with Mobile Recycling Units

Eduardo Alarcon-Gerbier$^{(\boxtimes)}$ ⓘ and Udo Buscher

Chair of Business Management, especially Industrial Management,
Technische Universität Dresden, 01069 Dresden, Germany
eduardo.alarcon@tu-dresden.de
https://tu-dresden.de/bu/wirtschaft/lim

Abstract. This article addresses the twofold question of at which location and at what point in time waste is recycled. Immediate recycling is unnecessary since storage is available to a limited extent. One approach is to conduct large-scale recycling centrally at one location, but this would lead to high transport efforts for the waste. In this paper, a different, distributed approach is presented. Due to the miniaturization of production and recycling units and their being embedding in standard containers, it is possible to relocate them from site to site at short notice. We present a dynamic location problem for mobile recycling units (DLPMRU) to limit both the transport of waste and the movement of mobile recycling units. In addition to a mixed-integer programming (MIP) formulation, a bilevel decomposition algorithm is proposed, which, in an iterative process, determines the movement of recycling plants through several local search operations and a linear programming (LP) subproblem. Early computational tests show that our algorithm achieves competitive results, especially for large-sized problems.

Keywords: Mobile facility location problem · Distributed recycling · Inventory · Optimization · Waste management

1 Introduction

A significant problem in societies worldwide is the vast amount of garbage generated daily [24]. Fortunately, there are several methods of recycling much of this waste. For example, waste oil can be reprocessed in large refineries as refined oil that can be remarketed. Several types of plastic can be reused to manufacture new bottles, containers, and many other products [3]. Biomass is another example of waste that can be recycled and converted into biomaterials or bioenergy. Two crucial problems arise related to the recycling issue: reprocessing and transport. In many countries, due in part to lack of investment or infrastructure, waste is simply piled up at huge landfills, burned directly, or shipped to countries that purchase it [25]. These options have polluting effects on the environment due to the leakage of hazardous liquids, harmful gases released through burning, or long

© Springer Nature Switzerland AG 2020
E. Lalla-Ruiz et al. (Eds.): ICCL 2020, LNCS 12433, pp. 396–411, 2020.
https://doi.org/10.1007/978-3-030-59747-4_26

shipping distances. The second problem, which applies mainly to countries with the infrastructure to maintain a circular economy, is that of collection and transportation. Normally, recycling is conducted in large facilities, so all waste has to be transported long distances for further recycling. In the case of new products generated from recycled materials, these may require transportation and distribution on the market again. All this transportation generates unnecessary movement that could potentially be reduced with a network of geographically dispersed recycling plants.

For some time now, the concept of distributed manufacturing has gained increasing attention. The World Economic Forum (WEF) expects that this new production paradigm may even become the norm for future production systems [26]. Distributed manufacturing can be defined as a network of decentralized facilities that can be jointly coordinated, representing a paradigm shift away from the centralized-production approach. A major advantage is avoiding unnecessary transport by reducing transport distances, delivery times, and CO_2 emissions [23]. In the case of recycling, this new approach could be implemented using several of the new technologies available on the market. There are now companies that have developed small processing units that can even be relocated easily from one site to another because of their modular design. For example, modular and scalable equipment already exists for the recycling of waste oil [6], bulk waste [9], non-recyclable plastics [6], and woody biomass [19]. In addition, the European Union financed a project between 2015 and 2018 to develop and demonstrate mobile processes for the treatment of biomass [17].

One aim of this paper is to coordinate the operational recycling and transport of waste using a given number of mobile recycling units that can be relocated easily from one site to another. We have organized this article as follows. After this introduction, the second section classifies the problem in the related literature; in the third section, the problem is described in greater detail. The fourth section formulates the model mathematically, and the fifth section serves to introduce the developed bilevel approach. Early calculation results are presented in the sixth section, and in the seventh section, we conclude with a summary and an outlook on future research.

2   Literature Review

The problem considered in this paper is based on contributions that address the following problem areas: 1) multi-period (or dynamic) facility location problems with plant relocation, 2) mobile facility location problems, 3) mobile facility routing problems, and 4) problems that integrate location and inventory planning.

The dynamic facility location problem (DFLP) is a well-studied topic that aims to determine the spatial distribution of facilities at each period in order to, for example, minimize the total costs for fulfilling customer demands [7]. Nevertheless, the literature on relocating facilities is limited. Melo et al. [16] addressed the *dynamic location and relocation of facilities* and provided a comprehensive modeling framework. Jena et al. [13] presented a location problem that explicitly includes capacity expansion and relocation. Recently, Becker et al. [5] developed MIP models for the tactical planning of modular chemical-production plants. They presented three different levels of flexibility as follows: volume flexibility, process flexibility, and location flexibility. The last one makes it possible to relocate modules and, thereby, production capacity.

The second related topic is the *mobile facility location problem* (MFLP), which goes back to Demaine et al. [8], who perceived it as a certain class of movement problem. Here, customers and facilities are initially located at vertices, and the objective is to determine destination vertices with the aim of minimizing the total distances traveled by both clients and facilities and/or associated costs [10]. Demaine et al. [8] proposed a two-approximation algorithm for the minimum maximum movement MFLP. Friggstad and Salavatipour [10] demonstrated that it is NP-hard to achieve better than a two-approximation algorithm. Armon et al. [4] answered the question of approximating this problem in its unconfined form through LP-based methods. Several local-search-based algorithms were also developed by Ahmadian et al. [1] and Halper et al. [12]. More recently, Raghavan et al. [22] expanded the MFLP by adding capacity restrictions.

Halper and Raghavan [11] introduced the *mobile facility routing problem* (MFRP), whereby mobile facilities have to visit different locations in order to provide services, assuming a piecewise-constant function for the demand rate. Qi et al. [20] modified this problem by considering a demand rate that varies over the service time. In this case, the service time is associated with how long the mobile facility is installed at each site. Similarly, there is a problem known as location-routing problem [18]. Here, however, routing is for the distribution of goods and not for the movement of mobile facilities. A paper that addressed this integration was presented by Albareda et al. [2]. In their problem, decisions concerning routing were considered at each time period. By contrast, facility-location decisions are made only in specific periods of the planning horizon.

Only selected publications can be found that provide *integrated planning of location and inventory*. Melo et al. [16] introduced a mathematical modeling framework for the multi-period facility-location problem that integrates many aspects of strategic network design, such as the relocation of existing facilities between sites and, in particular, inventory decisions among others. Qiu and Sharkey [21] addressed the location and inventory problem for a single facility for the case of ships that serve as military bases at sea. More recently, Malladi et al. [15] presented a problem considering mobile modular production systems. They provided several MIP models in order to plan production and inventory by relocating transportable modular production capacity between different sites. They included in their problem the decision layer of production and inventory control for unmet demand. According to the authors, the time required to move the modules from one place to another is ignored since it would complicate their problem significantly.

The dynamic location problem for mobile recycling units (DLPMRU) presented in this article addresses partial aspects of the four problem areas presented. In contrast to what previous work has discussed, the time needed to move the mobile recycling units plays an important role because it reduces the recycling capacity at the target site. At the same time, the model formulation explicitly provides for limited storage of waste since the waste is generated in a distributed way and must be processed using these mobile recycling units. To the best of our knowledge, this problem has not been studied previously in the literature.

3 Problem Definition

Waste generation is a current and growing problem for all countries and regions of the globe. At the present time, garbage is continuously collected and transported to collection points for recycling. The problem considered in this paper results from a discussion with a young company interested in an effective and efficient use of the mobile recycling units they produce. The following list is intended to characterize the problem:

- In a multi-period approach, it is necessary to find a suitable location for a given number of mobile recycling units on a per-period basis. Due to the possibility of relocating the units at short notice, one period corresponds to one or more weeks.
- Suppliers are companies that collect waste or garbage from other companies. For example, the term *supplier* could refer to a waste-management company that collects waste oil from several customers. Such customers could include automotive repair shops and other companies whose production processes result in waste oil that must be disposed of according to national regulations.
- Where and when the waste is collected by the supplier is assumed to be known. Therefore, it is presumed that the amount to be collected can be fairly accurately predicted based on historical data.
- Trucks in unlimited numbers are available both for the transport of the mobile recycling units and for the transport of waste.
- Recycling is possible only at the location where a mobile recycling unit is available. It is possible to transport waste by truck from one place to another to have it recycled. In principle, the mobile recycling unit is installed at the supplier's site (or in his immediate vicinity) so that distance is irrelevant.
- Each supplier has a limited storage capacity; however, it is considerably larger than the transport capacity of a single truck. To ensure that the trucks are adequately utilized, only direct transports between suppliers take place.
- Since the aim is to minimize the total number of movements, a minimum utilization of mobile recycling units should be established in order to ensure a minimum amount of recycling in each period and maintain a profitable business. However, the saleable products resulting from the recycling process and its marketing and distribution are not explicitly considered.

Based on these characteristics, this problem can be represented graphically as shown in Fig. 1. In this example, a specific amount of waste is collected at each node. At the beginning of a period there is a certain stock level that is graphically represented by the different gray shades of the respective nodes. The transport of waste and machinery is necessary to meet the limited storage capacities. At the same time, however, it is important to keep the number of these transports as low as possible. Here, machine B is moved to the south (based on the standard cardinal points of a compass) at the beginning of the first period due to the large accumulation of waste in that area. Similarly, machine C is relocated at the beginning of period 2 to the northwest and installed at a node with a high inventory level. Without this relocation of the machines, a greater number of trucks would be required to transport the waste compared to the number of trucks needed to transport the mobile recycling units.

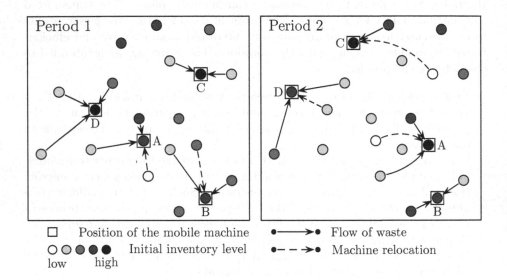

Fig. 1. Sample solution

4   Mathematical Formulation

The dynamic location problem for mobile recycling units (DLPMRU) will be formally described in the following. This problem is set on a graph $G(I, E)$ in which I denotes the set of nodes and E the set of edges. All edge values are positive and represent the distance between their end nodes. There are suppliers at each node $i \in I$ that collect a specific amount of waste in each period $p \in P$ and have a maximum inventory capacity. There are also N mobile recycling units initially positioned at a subset $K \subset I$. At the beginning of each period p, all the mobile recycling units and the collected waste can be relocated from node i to node j considering site-dependent transport distance $TD_{ij} \in E$. A feasible solution to this problem is to select a subset $C(p) \subset I$ for each period $p \in P$ in

which the mobile recycling units are installed and to ship waste to be recycled
between nodes in order to meet inventory and production constraints.

Within a total movement minimization set-up, this model aims to determine
the optimal relocation for each mobile recycling unit and to minimize transport
distances for the shipment of waste. Therefore, the waste is transported between
the nodes considering the current positions of the mobile recycling units, as well
as the amount of waste stored at each node. A detailed definition of indices,
parameters and decision variables can be found in Table 1.

Table 1. Indices, parameters and decision variables used in the model

Indices:	
I	Set of nodes
N	Set of mobile recycling units
P	Set of periods

Parameters:	
FM	Number of trucks required for moving a mobile recycling unit
II_i	Initial inventory at node $i \in I$
LC	Load capacity of a truck
M	Very large number
mPR	Minimum amount of production for each mobile recycling unit n
PR	Production rate for processing
SC_i	Inventory capacity at each node $i \in I$
TD_{ij}	Transport distance from node i to node j (measured in km)
RM_{ip}	Waste collected at node $i \in I$ in period $p \in P$
TT	Time capacity for each mobile recycling unit and period
V	Travel speed for relocating a mobile recycling unit
Y_{in}	Binary parameter taking the value 1 if the mobile recycling unit $n \in N$ has as its initial position the node $i \in I$

Decision variables		
il_{ip}	$\in \mathbb{R}^+$	Inventory level at node i at the end of period p
r_{ijp}	$\in \mathbb{R}^+$	Waste shipped from node i to node j in period p
s_{ijp}	$\in \mathbb{N}$	Number of trucks shipping raw material from node i to j in period p
x_{ip}	$\in \mathbb{R}^+$	Quantity of waste used for recycling at node i in period p
z_{ijnp}	$\in \{0,1\}$	Takes the value 1 if mobile recycling unit n is relocated from node i to node j in period p. The mobile recycling unit remains in the same place i if $z_{iinp} = 1$

In the following, the problem is modeled as MIP.

$$\min: \quad FM \cdot \sum_{i \in I} \sum_{j \in I} \sum_{n \in N} \sum_{p \in P} (TD_{ij} \cdot z_{ijnp}) + \sum_{i \in I} \sum_{j \in I} \sum_{p \in P} (TD_{ij} \cdot s_{ijp}) \quad (1)$$

subject to:

$$\sum_{j \in I} z_{ijn1} = Y_{in} \quad \forall\, i \in I, n \in N \tag{2}$$

$$\sum_{n \in N} z_{jinp} \leq 1 \quad \forall\, i,j \in I, p \in P \tag{3}$$

$$\sum_{i \in I} \sum_{j \in I} z_{ijnp} \leq 1 \quad \forall\, n \in N, p \in P \tag{4}$$

$$\sum_{i \in I} z_{ijnp} \leq \sum_{i \in I} z_{jin,p+1} \quad \forall\, j \in I, n \in N, p = 1, ..., P-1 \tag{5}$$

$$x_{ip} \leq M \cdot \sum_{j \in I} \sum_{n \in N} z_{jinp} \quad \forall\, i \in I, p \in P \tag{6}$$

$$\frac{x_{ip}}{PR} + \sum_{j \in I} \sum_{n \in N} \frac{TD_{ji}}{V} \cdot z_{jinp} \leq TT \quad \forall\, i \in I, p \in P \tag{7}$$

$$x_{ip} \geq mPR \cdot \sum_{j \in I} \sum_{n \in N} z_{jinp} \quad \forall\, i \in I, p \in P \tag{8}$$

$$s_{ijp} \geq \frac{r_{ijp}}{LC} \quad \forall\, i,j \in I, p \in P \tag{9}$$

$$il_{i0} = II_i \quad \forall\, i \in I \tag{10}$$

$$il_{ip} = il_{i,p-1} + RM_{ip} + \sum_{j \in I, i \neq j} (r_{jip} - r_{ijp}) - x_{ip} \quad \forall\, i \in I, p \in P \tag{11}$$

$$il_{ip} \leq SC_i \quad \forall\, i \in I, p \in P \tag{12}$$

In the above formulation, the objective function (1) aims to minimize the total number of movements caused by the relocation of the mobile recycling units and the transportation of waste. Equalities (2) include the initial position of each mobile recycling unit n in each tour. Constraints (3) specify that a node i can be visited, at most, by one mobile recycling unit n in each period p. With the introduction of (4), the mobile recycling unit n can be relocated, at most, once in each period p. Constraints (5) define the sequence for the relocation of each mobile unit n in each period p. Constraints (6) guarantee that production occurs at the node i only if a mobile recycling unit n is installed at that node. Inequalities (7) limit the quantity of waste used for recycling at node i by considering the production rate, relocation time (if a mobile recycling unit is relocated), and total time per period. Constraints (8) set a minimum quantity of production for each mobile recycling unit. Inequalities (9) define the number of trucks required for the shipment of waste. With the introduction of (10), the initial inventory level is considered at each node i. Constraints (11) calculate the inventory level of waste at node i as the sum of the inventory in the previous period $p-1$, the amount of new waste generated at node i, the amount shipped to this node, minus the amount used for recycling and the waste from node i to be relocated to another node j. Finally, (12) limits the amount of waste stored at each node i.

5   Bilevel Decomposition Algorithm for the DLPMRU

The production capacity at each node varies depending on whether there is a mobile recycling unit installed and on the time available for recycling. The latter depends directly on the time needed to relocate the mobile recycling unit from one node to another, thus creating a combinatorial problem for which it is difficult to identify an optimal solution. Therefore, we divided the problem into two parts and introduced a bilevel decomposition algorithm (BDA) that consists of sequentially solving both parts of the problem. The first part presents an LP model for the optimization of waste transport between nodes, which can be solved with the help of a global optimization solver. The second part solves the combinatorial aspect of the problem and determines the sequence for the movements of the mobile recycling units between nodes.

5.1   An LP Formulation for the Waste-Movement Problem

In order to determine the amount of waste to be transported from one site to another, it is necessary to define the position of each mobile recycling unit n in each period p as a parameter. With the position of these facilities declared as fixed, the relocation time can be pre-computed and also used as a parameter in the model. Therefore, and in addition to the parameters and variables defined in Table 1, the LP formulation requires the additional parameters listed in Table 2.

Table 2. New parameters for the LP formulation

Parameters:	
RT_{ip}	Time required for relocating a mobile recycling unit to node $i \in I$ in period $p \in P$
W_{ip}	Binary parameter taking the value 1 if a mobile recycling unit is installed at node $i \in I$ in period $p \in P$

The LP model (LP1) is then defined as:

$$\min : \sum_{i \in I} \sum_{j \in I} \sum_{p \in P} (TD_{ij} \cdot s_{ijp}) \qquad (13)$$

subject to:

$$x_{ip} \leq M \cdot W_{ip} \quad \forall\, i \in I, p \in P \tag{14}$$

$$\frac{x_{ip}}{PR} \leq TT - RT_{ip} \quad \forall\, i \in I, p \in P \tag{15}$$

$$x_{ip} \geq mPR \cdot W_{ip} \quad \forall\, i \in I, p \in P \tag{16}$$

We also need constraint sets (9)–(12). Constraints (14) guarantee that production occurs only in places where a mobile recycling unit is installed. Inequalities (15) calculate the time available for recycling as the difference between the total recycling capacity minus the time needed to relocate the mobile recycling unit. Finally, (16) sets a minimum quantity of production for each mobile recycling unit.

5.2   Start Solution: Greedy Algorithm

Our algorithm requires an initial solution that can be obtained using a greedy algorithm. Here, the main idea is to install the mobile recycling units in the nodes that are in areas with high inventory in order to reduce the total transport of the waste. This algorithm can be described as follows:

1. Calculate the weighted waste for each node $i \in I$. The main idea is to install the mobile recycling units at those nodes that have a greater amount of weighted waste, taking into consideration the material at each node $i \in I$ and its closest nodes. For this, as the distance between node i and another node, j, increases, the weighting of the waste of node j decreases, since the probability of waste being transported from this node to node i decreases as the distance increases (another mobile recycling unit is more likely to be closer). As shown in Fig. 2, we set up three zones with different weightings ($MaxDist$ = maximum distance between any node i and another node j).
2. Find node i with the maximum weighted inventory and relocate the nearest unassigned mobile recycling unit n to node i. Installing a mobile recycling unit at a node reduces the inventory for this node and has a direct effect on nearby nodes. For this, assign a dummy production value to this node equal to the maximum recycling quantity (Total time × Production rate).
3. Repeat the process until all mobile recycling units are assigned in all periods.

5.3   Solution Algorithm

As previously stated in this section, the BDA iteratively and discretely solves the problem of defining the sequence for the transfer of the mobile recycling units between each period and the problem of planning the transport and storage of waste at each node. However, as the size of the problem grows, the complexity increases considerably. Therefore, and in order to improve the performance of the BDA, the solution space that can be examined in each iteration must be reduced. To do so, two limitations related to the local search operations, which are shown graphically in Fig. 3, are added:

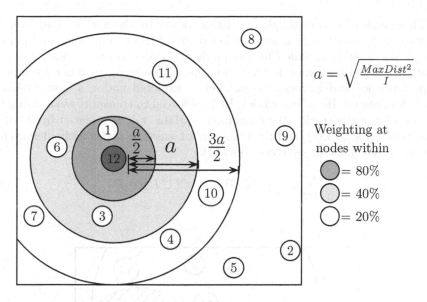

$$a = \sqrt{\frac{MaxDist^2}{I}}$$

Weighting at
nodes within

◯ = 80%

◯ = 40%

◯ = 20%

Fig. 2. Weighting of the waste at node 12. For example, nodes 3 and 6 are within the second region, so their inventories receive a 40% weighting.

1. The maximum transport distance should be limited when relocating a mobile recycling unit from one node i to another node j. This is explained by the fact that, since there are multiple mobile units installed in a distributed manner, a mobile recycling unit should not be moved between nodes that are far apart. Therefore, we add constraint (17), which limits the distance in relation to the square root of the estimated area for each mobile recycling unit and multiplies it by a growth factor $(\beta^N + 1)$.

$$TD_{ij} < \sqrt{\frac{MaxDist^2}{N}} \cdot (\beta^N + 1) \quad 0 < \beta < 1 \qquad (17)$$

2. The second limitation is that two mobile recycling units should not be installed too close to each other as this would represent a centralization of recycling, which would consequently tend to increase transport distances. This is formally represented by (18), which forces node j, chosen for installing a mobile unit, to be at a minimum distance from all the nodes $k \in C(p)$ at which a mobile unit has already been installed.

$$TD_{jk} > \frac{MaxDist}{(\alpha^N + 1) \cdot N} \quad \forall k \in C(p), 0 < \alpha < 1 \qquad (18)$$

These limitations are simple heuristics chosen by the authors based on the analysis of the problem (a more detailed study of these limitations and parameters is not directly included in this publication due to space constraints). In addition, a third limitation is added for the LP problem. In order to improve its performance and increase the number of explored nodes, a new version of LP1 is formulated. Here, this model (LP2) is forced to transport waste using the full capacity of the trucks (the continuous variable r_{ijp} is replaced by the integer expression $s_{ijp} \cdot LC$), and the transport of waste to nodes without recycling capacity is not allowed; see constraints (19).

$$\sum_{j \in I} r_{jip} \leq M \cdot W_{ip} \quad \forall\, i \in I, p \in P \tag{19}$$

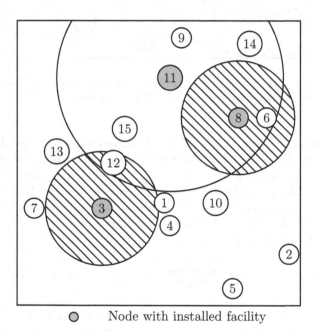

○   Node with installed facility

Fig. 3. Limited solution space: the mobile recycling unit at node 11 can be moved only to 9, 14, and 15 (H = {9,14,15}).

Thus, the BDA allows the reduction of movements of both the waste and the mobile recycling units, which can be seen in Algorithm 1.

Algorithm 1 Bilevel Decomposition Algorithm (BDA)

1: Set parameters (TimeLimit, MaxIteration, α, β)
2: Get an initial solution: Call procedure Greedy Algorithm
3: Solve model LP2 for the waste-transport problem
4: Save *BestSolution*
5: Set iteration $iter = 0$, var $time =$ Watch.StartNew
6: **while** $time.Elapsed \leq TimeLimit$ & $iter \leq MaxIteration$ **do**
7:     $iter \leftarrow iter + 1$
8:     Get a period $p \in P$ and a mobile recycling unit $n \in N$ randomly
9:     Find the position $i \in I$ of mobile unit n in period p
10:    Select a node $j \in H$ randomly. $H \subset I$ (see constraints (17), (18))
11:    Relocate mobile unit n from i to node j
12:    Solve model LP2 for the waste-transport problem
13:    Calculate $TotalMovement_{iter}$
14:    **if** $TotalMovement_{iter} < BestSolution$ **then**
15:        Update *BestSolution*
16:        Restart iteration $iter = 0$
17:    **else**
18:        Reject new solution
19:    **end if**
20: **end while**
21: Solve model LP1 for the waste-transport problem
22: **Return** *BestSolution*

6   Computational Results

Our first computational tests were performed on a computer running on a 3.3 GHz Intel Xeon CPU with 768 GB memory. The MIP model presented in Sect. 4 and the LP model in Subsect. 5.1 are solved using Gurobi version 9.0, and the heuristic is implemented in C# programming language with Microsoft Visual Studio 2017. For each problem size, we generated 10 different random instances, solving each one 10 times with the BDA in order to exclude random outliers and to show average results. Thus, a total of 800 runs were examined for the BDA. A summary of the parameters is provided in Table 3.

For the solution of the LP problem in BDA, we set the optimality tolerance to 1% and the maximum total CPU time for each iteration to 1 s. The heuristic stops after 400 iterations without improvement or once the maximum time of 1,000 s is reached. Regarding the global solver (MIP model), it is allowed a maximum CPU time of 3,600 s for the solution of each instance. With these restrictions and generating instances at random, the results shown in Table 4 were obtained. It can be seen that the solver is capable of finding the optimal solution for small problems. However, for larger problems, it can find only feasible solutions with a gap of up to 66.3%. In the table, we present the relative percentage difference (RPD) for the greedy algorithm and the BDA, which represents the percentage change of the solution found through the algorithms compared to the best solution obtained through the solver ($[sol.\ heuristic - sol.\ MIP]/sol.\ heuristic$).

Table 3. Parameter values

Parameter:	Value
α/β	0.8/0.25
Minimum recycling quantity per mobile recycling unit (50% TT)	7.5 tons
Number of mobile recycling units (N)	0.2 I
Number of trucks needed per relocation	2
Initial inventory	$U(5, 10)$ tons
Load capacity for a truck	3 tons
Production rate	$0.1 \frac{tons}{h}$
Inventory capacity	10 tons
Transport distance	677 km (avg.)
Travel speed	$80 \frac{km}{h}$
Waste generated in each period	$U(0.5, 4.5)$ tons
Time capacity	150 h

The greedy algorithm can achieve solutions that have an RPD of 30.9% on average. Regarding its computing time, we do not include the time needed to obtain the initial solution through this procedure because it is a matter of seconds and, thus, negligible. Based on these solutions, the BDA is able to considerably improve the start solutions and, for larger instances, find competitive results. In the case of small problems, the BDA is able to find good solutions in short amounts of computational time. However, because only better solutions are accepted in each iteration, it is likely that a local optimum will be reached, so the heuristic is not able to further improve the initial solution by possibly reaching even the optimum solution.

Table 4. Results of the computational study

Indices			Solver		Greedy	BDA				
P	I	N	T_{CPU}	Gap(%)	RPD(%)	T_{CPU}	RSD(%)	RPD(%)	# Iter	BS-iter
2	20	4	68	0	35.1	25.2	4.1	11.5	595.4	195.4
2	30	6	769	0	34.7	48.4	2.1	11.9	783.6	383.6
4	10	2	632	0	35.6	29.5	4.1	10.5	534.8	134.8
4	30	6	3,600	**32.5**	32.0	221.3	2.6	9.3	1,062.4	662.4
4	50	10	3,600	**46.8**	30.4	507.9	3.4	6.6	1,643.0	1,243.0
6	30	6	3,600	**55.3**	29.8	785.8	3.2	2.4	1,337.6	1,008.7
6	50	10	3,600	**62.9**	26.5	997.0	2.8	3.5	1,129.0	1,007.2
8	30	6	3,600	66.3	23.5	978.3	3.1	**-1.2**	1,177.7	1,029.8

*RSD: Relative standard deviation *RPD: Relative percentage difference
*T_{CPU}: CPU time in seconds *BS-iter: best solution found in iteration #

7   Conclusion

In this paper, the dynamic location problem for mobile recycling units was presented. It aims to minimize the number of waste transports in addition to the number of transports required for the relocation of mobile recycling units. As these units can be relocated at short notice, it is necessary to incorporate the specific relocation times in order to avoid overestimating the recycling capacity. In addition, the model explicitly takes into consideration limited waste-storage capacity at supplier locations. First, the problem was mathematically modeled using an MIP. In order to solve instances of larger problems, a bilevel decomposition algorithmic approach was presented; this determines optimal waste transport between the sites for a given allocation of mobile recycling units in the subproblem. The first computational tests showed that the BDA achieves competitive results for larger instances.

The approach presented can be expanded both methodologically and in terms of content. Methodologically, it can be stated that the BDA still requires a detailed parameter test to identify the best-possible parameter combination. It is also useful to identify such conditions that explicitly take into account the suitability of a relocation of units. Further considerations include allowing nonimproving solutions, altering the solution by moving multiple mobile recycling units in each iteration, and replacing the LP program with a heuristic solution. The advantages of these procedures would then have to be proven with a detailed computational study. Another direction of extension could be the implementation of a more sophisticated metaheuristic, such as GRASP or the Fixed Set Search [14].

From a content perspective, it might be interesting to identify solutions for different objective functions. For example, instead of minimizing transports, the associated emissions could be considered. A cost-oriented perspective could also be chosen, which, of course, requires knowledge of the corresponding cost parameters. A modification of the problem definition with considerable impacts on the solution approach would result if routing decisions were included. If, for example, the disposal companies described here as suppliers are small operators with comparatively low waste volumes and low storage capacities, planning collection routes could be advantageous.

Acknowledgements. The authors thank the Friedrich and Elisabeth Boysen-Foundation and Technische Universität Dresden for their financial support for this work during the third Boysen-TU Dresden-Research Training Group.

References

1. Ahmadian, S., Friggstad, Z., Swamy, C.: Local-search based approximation algorithms for mobile facility location problems: (extended abstract). In: Proceedings of the Twenty-Fourth Annual ACM-SIAM Symposium on Discrete Algorithms. Society for Industrial and Applied Mathematics (January 2013). https://doi.org/10.1137/1.9781611973105.115

2. Albareda-Sambola, M., Fernández, E., Nickel, S.: Multiperiod location-routing with decoupled time scales. Eur. J. Oper. Res. **217**(2), 248–258 (2012). https://doi.org/10.1016/j.ejor.2011.09.022
3. Allwood, J.M.: Squaring the circular economy. In: Handbook of Recycling, pp. 445–477. Elsevier (2014). https://doi.org/10.1016/b978-0-12-396459-5.00030-1
4. Armon, A., Gamzu, I., Segev, D.: Mobile facility location: combinatorial filtering via weighted occupancy. J. Comb. Optim. **28**(2), 358–375 (2012). https://doi.org/10.1007/s10878-012-9558-8
5. Becker, T., Lier, S., Werners, B.: Value of modular production concepts in future chemical industry production networks. Eur. J. Oper. Res. **276**(3), 957–970 (2019). https://doi.org/10.1016/j.ejor.2019.01.066
6. Biofabrik: https://biofabrik.com/. Accessed 3 Apr 2020
7. Correia, I., Melo, T.: A multi-period facility location problem with modular capacity adjustments and flexible demand fulfillment. Comput. Ind. Eng. **110**, 307–321 (2017). https://doi.org/10.1016/j.cie.2017.06.003
8. Demaine, E.D., Hajiaghayi, M., Mahini, H., Sayedi-Roshkhar, A.S., Oveisgharan, S., Zadimoghaddam, M.: Minimizing movement. ACM Trans. Algorithms **5**(3), 1–30 (2009). https://doi.org/10.1145/1541885.1541891
9. Dynamis-Energy. https://www.dynamisenergy.com/. Accessed 10 Apr 2020
10. Friggstad, Z., Salavatipour, M.R.: Minimizing movement in mobile facility location problems. ACM Trans. Algorithms **7**(3), 1–22 (2011). https://doi.org/10.1145/1978782.1978783
11. Halper, R., Raghavan, S.: The mobile facility routing problem. Transp. Sci. **45**(3), 413–434 (2011). https://doi.org/10.1287/trsc.1100.0335
12. Halper, R., Raghavan, S., Sahin, M.: Local search heuristics for the mobile facility location problem. Comput. Oper. Res. **62**, 210–223 (2015). https://doi.org/10.1016/j.cor.2014.09.004
13. Jena, S.D., Cordeau, J.-F., Gendron, B.: Modeling and solving a logging camp location problem. Ann. Oper. Res. **232**(1), 151–177 (2012). https://doi.org/10.1007/s10479-012-1278-z
14. Jovanovic, R., Tuba, M., Voß, S.: Fixed set search applied to the traveling salesman problem. In: Blesa Aguilera, M.J., Blum, C., Gambini Santos, H., Pinacho-Davidson, P., Godoy del Campo, J. (eds.) HM 2019. LNCS, vol. 11299, pp. 63–77. Springer, Cham (2019). https://doi.org/10.1007/978-3-030-05983-5_5
15. Malladi, S.S., Erera, A.L., White, C.C.: A dynamic mobile production capacity and inventory control problem. IISE Trans. **52**, 1–18 (2020). https://doi.org/10.1080/24725854.2019.1693709
16. Melo, M., Nickel, S., da Gama, F.S.: Dynamic multi-commodity capacitated facility location: a mathematical modeling framework for strategic supply chain planning. Comput. Oper. Res. **33**(1), 181–208 (2006). https://doi.org/10.1016/j.cor.2004.07.005
17. Mobile-Flip: The value of biomass (2018). http://www.mobileflip.eu/. Accessed 12 Apr 2020
18. Prodhon, C., Prins, C.: A survey of recent research on location-routing problems. Eur. J. Oper. Res. **238**(1), 1–17 (2014). https://doi.org/10.1016/j.ejor.2014.01.005
19. Pyrotech-Energy. https://pyrotechenergy.com/. Accessed 10 Apr 2020
20. Qi, M., Cheng, C., Wang, X., Rao, W.: Mobile facility routing problem with service-time-related demand. In: 2017 International Conference on Service Systems and Service Management. IEEE (June 2017). https://doi.org/10.1109/icsssm.2017.7996166

21. Qiu, J., Sharkey, T.C.: Integrated dynamic single-facility location and inventory planning problems. IIE Trans. **45**(8), 883–895 (2013). https://doi.org/10.1080/0740817x.2013.770184
22. Raghavan, S., Sahin, M., Salman, F.S.: The capacitated mobile facility location problem. Eur. J. Oper. Res. **277**(2), 507–520 (2019). https://doi.org/10.1016/j.ejor.2019.02.055
23. Rauch, E., Dallasega, P., Matt, D.: Distributed manufacturing network models of smart and agile mini-factories. Int. J. Agile Syst. Manag. **10**, 185–205 (2017)
24. Shulman, V.L.: Trends in waste management. In: Waste, pp. 3–10. Elsevier (2011). https://doi.org/10.1016/b978-0-12-381475-3.10001-4
25. Wang, C., Zhao, L., Lim, M.K., Chen, W.Q., Sutherland, J.W.: Structure of the global plastic waste trade network and the impact of China's import ban. Resour. Conserv. Recycl. **153**, 104591 (2020). https://doi.org/10.1016/j.resconrec.2019.104591
26. WEF: Technology and innovation for the future of production: accelerating value creation (2017)

Travel Time Prediction Using Tree-Based Ensembles

He Huang[1]([✉]), Martin Pouls[2][iD], Anne Meyer[3][iD], and Markus Pauly[1][iD]

[1] Department of Statistics, TU Dortmund University, 44221 Dortmund, Germany
he.huang@tu-dortmund.de
[2] Information Process Engineering, FZI Forschungszentrum Informatik,
76131 Karlsruhe, Germany
[3] Faculty of Mechanical Engineering, TU Dortmund University, 44221 Dortmund,
Germany

Abstract. In this paper, we consider the task of predicting travel times between two arbitrary points in an urban scenario. We view this problem from two temporal perspectives: long-term forecasting with a horizon of several days and short-term forecasting with a horizon of one hour. Both of these perspectives are relevant for planning tasks in the context of urban mobility and transportation services. We utilize tree-based ensemble methods that we train and evaluate on a data set of taxi trip records from New York City. Through extensive data analysis, we identify relevant temporal and spatial features. We also engineer additional features based on weather and routing data. The latter is obtained via a routing solver operating on the road network. The computational results show that the addition of this routing data can be beneficial to the model performance. Moreover, employing different models for short and long-term prediction is useful as short-term models are better suited to mirror current traffic conditions. In fact, we show that good short-term predictions may be obtained with only little training data.

Keywords: Travel time prediction · Tree-based ensembles · Taxi dispatching

1 Introduction

Predicting travel times of road trips is especially challenging in urban areas, as travel times considerably depend on the weekday, the time, and the current situation on the roads [18,19]. For both, the individual transport of people, and the transport of goods in urban areas, high quality predictions are necessary for planning reliable tours. For operators of classic taxi services as well as providers of shared economy services such as Uber or Lyft a good prediction of arrival times is crucial, not only for creating efficient tours but also for having satisfied customers who do not have to wait longer than expected. This is especially true if ride sharing services are offered, i.e., if different customers share one taxi in order to increase car utilization and decrease the price per person.

© Springer Nature Switzerland AG 2020
E. Lalla-Ruiz et al. (Eds.): ICCL 2020, LNCS 12433, pp. 412–427, 2020.
https://doi.org/10.1007/978-3-030-59747-4_27

Predictions for a time horizon of several days are necessary if guests book trips several days in advance and the taxi provider plans these tours ahead of time in order to guarantee a reliable service. Predictions of driving times for the next minutes or hour are necessary for dispatching, i.e., when assigning guests, who ask for an ad hoc service, to taxis on the short-term. Similar problems exist for other sectors such as same day deliveries of goods or food to consumers, but also deliveries to commercial customers such as restaurants, pharmacies, or shops which are often located in the city center. Hence, reliable travel time estimations in urban areas are necessary to (a) determine feasible plans, for example with respect to working time limits of drivers or opening hours of customers, and (b) to guarantee customer satisfaction. A good overview of applications for planning vehicle routes in an urban context is given in [20].

Historically, large traffic flow models (e.g., simulation, queuing theory) were built, calibrated with data from stationary devices such as induction loops or traffic cameras, to derive speed profiles for every section of the street network and to calculate the fastest route based on these profiles. Today, GPS tracks – referred to as floating car data – are available from cars, and navigation systems. This considerably improves the availability of data for a larges share of road sections, and in some cases additional information such as speed data are available. Routing services such as Google directions[1] or PTV Drive&Arrive[2] determine travel times based on these data for cars and trucks, respectively. Even if the travel time prediction of these services are of a high quality, the usage of a web API is often not possible: For dispatching decisions, the travel time for many relations is determined to assign a trip request to an adequate vehicle. If ride sharing services are offered, even more relations need to be considered. Since dispatching decisions are extremely time sensitive, web service calls are prohibitive. Also the pay per call plans are usually expensive. Finally, the predictions are provided for cars, pedestrians, or trucks but not for taxis, or small buses which are allowed to use special lanes in urban areas. In contrast to approaches based on complex traffic models estimating speed patterns on a link basis, we focus on simpler origin-destination based predictions: We only rely on information such as the location of the pickup and the deliveries and the corresponding time stamps. These data are, usually, available even if not all cars are equipped with tracking systems. If trajectories are available, selected nodes of the trajectory can be added as additional origin-destination data to the data base. Due to the various advantages of tree-based learning methods, we investigate their suitability for predicting the travel times in the described setup.

The remainder of this paper is organized as follows: In Section 2, we introduce the tree-based learning methods most appropriate to our problem at hand. Section 3 is dedicated to the computational study and evaluation of the methods for long-term prediction with a horizon of several days, and a short-term prediction for the next hours. We conclude the paper with a short discussion.

---

[1] https://developers.google.com/maps/documentation/directions/start (13.05.2020).
[2] https://www.ptvgroup.com/en/solutions/products/ptv-driveandarrive/ (13.05.2020).

2   Methodology: Tree-Based Learning

Travel time prediction can in principle be performed by any regression technique for metric outcomes. In particular, consider a theoretic model of the form

$$y = f(x_1, \ldots, x_p) + \epsilon = f(\mathbf{x}) + \epsilon,$$

where y denotes the travel time and $x_1, \ldots, x_p$ are corresponding features, also called explanatory variables, containing, e.g., information on historic travel times, destination or even weather data which are stacked in the vector $\mathbf{x} = (x_1, \ldots, x_p)$. Moreover, ϵ is an error term and f an unknown regression function that needs to be estimated to describe the relationship between y and $\mathbf{x}$. To this end, related applications on travel prediction have utilized approaches from time series analyses [7] or Artificial Intelligence and Machine Learning. Here, support vector machines [11], k-nearest neighbors [2] or neural networks and deep learning [5,10] have been proposed. We focus on methods that use trees as base learners. In particular, we study the performance of several tree-based methods such as CART and bagged or boosted ensembles. This includes *Random Forests* [1], *Extra (randomized) Trees* [6] as well as the recently proposed *XgBoost* and *LightGBM* algorithms [3,9]. These procedures are (i) known for being robust against feature co-linearity and high-dimensionality, (ii) usually more easy to train[3] and (iii) also need a lower computational burden than more enhanced deep learning algorithms, see also [4,12] for similar arguments. In fact, Random Forests or Stochastic Gradient Boosting models have already exhibit accurate predictions in the context of travel times [4,12,13]; though for other data sets and domains (e.g., travel time of buses or on free ways). In contrast to existing literature, we investigate whether more recent proposals (as XgBoost) are more appropriate than established methods (as Random Forest). Moreover, we compare all methods' accuracy for both, long and short term predictions for which we introduce additional features. A novel example for the latter is the travel time of the fastest route calculated with a routing engine assuming a street network without traffic.

For ease of presentation, we only summarize the basic ideas behind these methods and refer to the cited literature for the explicit definitions, see also the monograph [8] for further details. As all methods are based upon trees, let us first recall the idea behind a single tree.

2.1   Classification and Regression Trees

Let $\mathcal{D} = \{(y_1, \mathbf{x}_1), \ldots, (y_n, \mathbf{x}_n)\}$ denote the observed data with $\mathbf{x}_i = (x_{i1}, \ldots, x_{ip})$ representing the feature vector of the i-th observation. We focus on regression trees from the *CART* class. The key idea is to greedily split the feature space into disjoint regions, say $R_1, \ldots, R_m$, until a certain stop criterion

---

[3] At least compared to deep neural networks.

is fulfilled. At the end, for each of the resulting disjoint regions, also called terminal nodes, a separate prediction of the target variable (travel time) is performed by

$$\widehat{c}_j = \frac{1}{N_j} \sum_{\mathbf{x}_i \in R_j} y_i, \tag{1}$$

where $N_j = |\{\mathbf{x}_i : \mathbf{x}_i \in R_j\}|$. That is, the travel time of a new feature vector $\mathbf{x} \in \mathbf{R_j}$ is predicted by taking the mean over all y_i with feature vector $\mathbf{x}_i$ belonging to the region that contains $\mathbf{x}$. To obtain the mentioned partition, binary splits are performed recursively, starting with the complete feature set (root node) and continuing with the resulting nodes etc. as follows: For each node, the observed feature value that minimizes the total variance of the two nodes after splitting is selected. A toy example is given in Fig. 1 below, where we have chosen a tree depth of two. Here, the feature 'Weekday' with value 'Weekend' was chosen as first splitting point. Thus, two subsequent nodes partition the complete feature space into the observations belonging to Weekends (left node in the first row) and all other days (right node), respectively. Thereafter, the variable 'Time of day' with feature value '7 am' was chosen to split the data belonging to weekends. The two resulting sets are terminal nodes and the corresponding prediction values $\widehat{c}_1 = 25, 7$ min and $\widehat{c}_2 = 7, 8$ min were calculated according to (1). Similarly, for weekdays the feature 'Temperature' with the freezing point as splitting value was chosen and $\widehat{c}_3 = 17, 4$ min and $\widehat{c}_4 = 9, 2$ min were calculated.

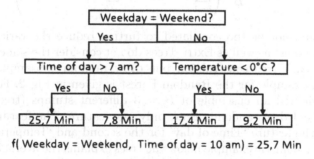

f(Weekday = Weekend, Time of day = 10 am) = 25,7 Min

Fig. 1. A simple regression tree with tree depth equal to 2.

One of the most important questions with CART is the choice of the tree size. A strategy is to grow a large tree B_0 first, than reduce the size of the tree by using a pruning technique. Here, several pruning techniques exist and we have chosen to use the *Cost of Complexity Pruning (CCP)* introduced by Breiman [14]. To describe this technique we define $B \subset B_0$ to be any sub-tree of B_0, which can be obtained by collapsing any number of its internal nodes. Let $Q_j(B) = \sum_{(\mathbf{x}_i, y_i) \in R_j} (y_i - \widehat{c}_p)^2 / N_j$ be the mean squared error in region R_p. Then the CCP is defined as $C_\alpha(B) = \sum_{j=1}^m N_j Q_j(B) + \alpha m$, where α is a tuning parameter for a trade-off between tree size and goodness of fit. The sub-tree with a minimal $C_\alpha(B)$ will be selected, so that large α values lead to smaller tree sizes. This is an important point as a major advantage of trees is their interpretability as illustrated in the example from Fig. 1. However, if the tree size is too large, interpretation can become cumbersome. Moreover, trees come with the cost of a rather simple prediction model which can usually be enhanced in terms of accuracy by turning to ensemble techniques.

2.2 Ensemble Techniques: Bagging and Boosting

Bagged ensembles as the Random Forest [1] or Extra Trees [6] usually improve the predictive accuracy of a single tree by following the wisdom of crowds principle: The basic idea is to randomly draw multiple subsamples, say B, from the (training) data and to grow a single tree for each of them and finally take the average tree prediction as random forest or Extra Tree prediction. To be a little bit more concrete, let $\mathcal{D}_b$ be a subsample (for the Random Forest this is usually of size $\lfloor .632n \rfloor$ and drawn with replacement from the training data $\mathcal{D}$) and $\mathbf{x} \mapsto \hat{f}_b(\mathbf{x})$ the corresponding single tree predictor based upon $\mathcal{D}_b$, $b = 1, \ldots, B$. Then a bagged ensemble regression predictor is given by $\mathbf{x} \mapsto \sum_{b=1}^{B} \hat{f}_b(\mathbf{x})/B = \hat{f}(\mathbf{x})$. The motivation behind this approach is that averaging reduces the variance. In fact, due to

$$Var(\hat{f}) = \frac{1}{B^2} \left(\sum_{b=1}^{B} Var(\hat{f}_b) + \sum_{b_1 \neq b_2} Cov(\hat{f}_{b_1}, \hat{f}_{b_2}) \right)$$

the trees should not be too correlated to further reduce the variance. That is why Random Forest as well as Extra Trees do not consider the same explanatory variables for each tree construction but draw random subsamples of feature variables. An example for the Random Forest is given in Fig. 2. For simplicity, we only considered an ensemble of $B = 3$ different stumps (trees). For each stump, we decided to randomly draw only one feature: The feature 'Weekday' for the first, the feature 'Time of day' for the second and 'Temperature' for the third tree. The numeric example below the trees explains the averaging principle. Random Forest and Extra Trees follow different approaches to generate (un-)correlated trees. The key difference is that in Random forest the single trees are

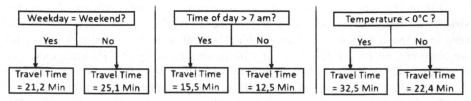

f (Weekday = Weekend, Time of day = 10 am, Temperature = -1 °C) = (21,2 + 15,5 + 32,5)/3 = 23,1 Min

Fig. 2. A simple Random Forest with $B = 3$ trees.

constructed as CARTs while the Extra Tree algorithm uses a different, even more random cut criterion to grow the trees. Roughly speaking, this should reduce the variance much faster (i.e. for smaller B) compared to Random Forests.

Different to these bagged ensembles, boosting is a more complex, iterative procedure. Therefore, we only explain some basic ideas and do not go too much into detail. One of its most common implementation is the gradient boosting algorithm [8] which can be interpreted as a gradient descent implementation for the optimization of a loss function. Roughly speaking, it computes a sequence of trees, where each new tree is fitted on a modified version of the data (so-called pseudo-residuals) in order to reduce the value of a pre-specified loss function. Due to the iterative nature, the final model prediction is the sum from all tree predictions at each step. There exist several different boosting implementations which are all equipped with certain techniques for regularization and stopping rules. For our purposes we have chosen two boosting methods: XgBoost [3] as it has recently been crowned the current *Queen of machine learning* [21] due to its dominating performance in many applied Machine Learning and Artificial Intelligence competitions, as e.g., on Kaggle. In addition, we considered Microsoft's LightGBM which is advertised as being highly efficient and accurate [9].

3   Travel Time Prediction

From common knowledge it may be apparent that travel time is affected by several variables such as the weekday, the time of the day, or the weather. In this section we start describing the used data sets, and show selected results from descriptive analyzes. For planning or dispatching transports, both, long-term predictions for travel times in several days, and short-term predictions for the next hour are necessary. Therefore, we consider different planning horizons and compare the resulting quality. For the short-term prediction, we also evaluate how much data for training (the last hour or the last couple of hours) is needed to reach good short-term predictions with acceptable run times.

3.1   Core Data Set and Data Enrichment

As data set for our computational study, we use the "TLC Trip Record Data" containing trip information of the yellow and green taxis in New York provided by the NYC Taxi and Limousine Commission for the last 10 years [22]. Since the information provided differs slightly between the years – for example, the records provided later than 2016 do no longer contain location data – we restrict our study to the period between January 2016 and June 2016. To avoid data sparsity, we furthermore filtered our data set to trips which started and ended in Manhattan, which corresponds to the vast majority of trips. In this period, the average number of trips per day is around 326 000, which results in an average number of trips per month of 9 949 000. Each trip is described by the date and the time, and the longitude and latitude value for its pickup and drop-off, respectively (in the following referred to as *pickup_datetime*, *dropoff_datetime*, *pickup_longitude*, *pickup_latitude, dropoff_ongitude, dropoff_latitude*). Longitude and latitude values are given on five decimal places, which corresponds to an accuracy of about one meter. Furthermore, the duration of the trips in seconds (*trip_duration*), the distance in miles (*trip_distance*), the number of passengers (*passenger_count*), and a code indicating the taxi provider (*vendor_id*) are provided.

Figure 3 shows the distribution of the trip duration, our target variable, for the area of Manhattan. The distribution seems to follow a log-normal distribution with a peak of trips lasting around 16 min (around 1 000 s). The trips with less than 10 s or with more than 100 000 s or more than 24 h do not appear plausible.

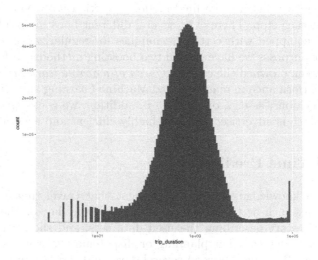

Fig. 3. Distribution of the trip duration in seconds (x-axis on logarithmic scale).

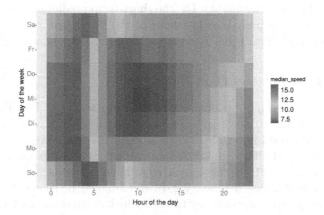

Fig. 4. Interaction between weekday and hours on travel speed. The medians of the speed for each combination of weekday and hour are scaled with color. The combination of these two features created a "low speed region" in the middle of the day and week. (Color figure online)

In this case we assume incorrect measurements. The explanatory variables can be divided into three categories, namely temporal variables, spatial variables, and others. The temporal variables are the *pickup_datetime* and *dropoff_datetime*. As expected, the day of the week, as well as the time of the day influence the travel time. To understand this interaction we plotted the travel speed for each combination of "weekdays" and "hours of the day" in Fig. 4 with a heat-map. It shows that the combination created a "low speed region" in the middle of the day and week. Such speed profiles over the course of the days are typical for urban areas, and they correlate negatively with the number of taxi trips. The speed goes down with an increase of road users during the day. During the night the speed, usually, corresponds to the so called free flow speed and is close to the legal speed limit for each road section. We also investigated the influence of weather on the speed using data provided by the National Weather Service[4]. The impact of heavy snowfalls in January on the travel speed was significant. Other weather phenomena, such as rainfall, do not have a similar impact on the travel speed. However, the reason can also be the shortcoming of our weather data set: It contains only average values per day, even though rainfall changes considerably over the course of the day. The spatial variables in our data set are the longitude and latitude values for the pick-up and the drop-off, and the distance of the trip. As shown in Fig. 5, the *trip_distance* has a strong positive correlation with our target variable *trip_duration*. The actual trip distance can only be measured ex-post, since the traffic situation influences the concrete route, and often taxi drivers use their geographical knowledge and use shortcuts. However, we can calculate the fastest route between the pick-up and the drop-off location with a routing algorithm assuming free flow speed on all road sections and use the resulting distance as an estimator for the trip distance which is available ex-ante. For our study, we applied the Open Source Routing Machine (OSRM)[5] on open street map data for New York. Besides the distance, referred to as *osrm_distance*, the response generated by the OSRM engine also contains the following information for the fastest (not necessarily shortest) route: the duration (*osrm_duration*), the total number of left-, right-, and u-turns (*total_turns*), the total number of left-turns (*total_left*), the total number of navigation instructions (*total_steps*), the name of the street with the longest duration (*main_street*), and the fraction of travel time on the main street (*main_street_ratio*).

Figure 5 shows that the *osrm_distance* and *osrm_duration* of the fastest route are highly correlated with the actual duration and distance. The *main_street_ratio* is weekly (negative) related to the actual trip duration. The *total_steps*, *total_left*, *total_turns* and *main_street_ratio* from OSRM are highly correlated with each other. Thus, it's not necessary to use all these features for prediction.

---

[4] The data can be downloaded from https://www.weather.gov.
[5] http://project-osrm.org/.

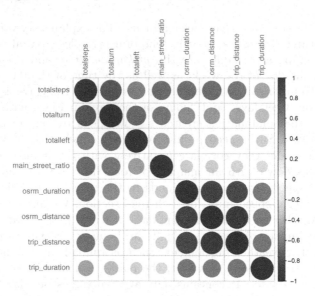

Fig. 5. Pairwise correlations of the features.

3.2 Long-Term Forecasting

Cleaning. Each model was trained on data from 1st June 2016 to 20th June 2016 (training data) and its prediction ability was evaluated in terms of RMSE on the data form 21st June 2016 to 30th June 2016 (test data). The training and test data contain 6,355,770 and 3,105,839 trips respectively, with 16 features for each trip. In Machine Learning, it is usually recommended to clean up the data before training. To this end, we first removed all trips with untrustworthy feature values, e.g., 10,000 trips with less than 10 s or more than three hours duration within Manhattan as well as 2,000 trips with an average speed of more than 60 mile per hour (noting that Manhattan's maximum speed limit is 50 mile per hour). In addition, we did a descriptive analysis of all feature variables to identify features without significant impact. Beyond summary statistics and graphical illustrations (not shown) we thereby also calculated the feature importance of all untuned models on the trip duration. Due to similarity we only show the resulting plots for the two boosting approaches in Fig. 6. Here, *vendor_id* and *passenger_count* had the least impact. As the exploratory analyses (bar- and boxplots) agree with this assessment, we excluded both from our further analyses. Moreover, *total_steps*, *total_left*, *total_turns* and *main_street_ratio* from OSRM express the next lowest feature importance. As Fig. 5 already revealed that these four features were highly correlated, we only keep the *main_street_ratio* and removed the other three.

Based on the remaining training data on these $p = 11$ features $\mathbf{x}$ and the target variable y, we performed an independent hyperparameter tuning for each of the five different modeling approaches. These were done on Python [16]. In particular, for CART and Extra Trees we used the library scikit-learn [15], for

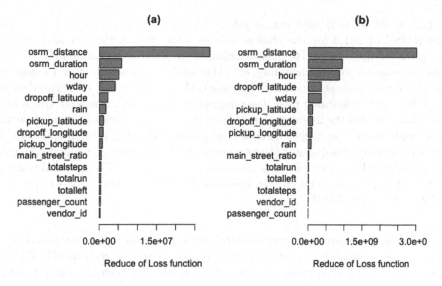

Fig. 6. Feature importance of (a) XgBoost and (b) lightGBM.

Random Forest and XgBoost the XgBoost-library from [3][6] was utilized and for lightGBM we turned to the Microsoft library[7]. As computational complexity can become an issue with boosting algorithms, we additionally compared the performance of the two boosting algorithms on both, CPUs and GPUs. For the latter, we turned to the plug-in GPU implementation of [17]. As this library only supports the faster histogram-based implementation of the XgBoost algorithm, we also restricted the CPU based XgBoost-implementation to this. This leaves us with seven different models to train.

Parameter Tuning. Starting with the single decision tree CART we tuned the size of the tree by max_depth and min_child_weight. To this end, we run a grid search for $max\_depth \in \{3, 8, 13, 18, 23, 38, 33\}$ and $min\_child\_weight \in \{10, 20, ..., 130\}$ resulting in the choices $max\_depth = 23$ and $min\_child\_weight = 100$. For Random Forest, the main parameters to be tuned are the subsampling rate on the training data ($subsample$), the subsampling rate on the features when building each tree ($colsample\_bytree$) and the total number of trees (n_trees). Apart from these bagging parameters, we also tuned the value max_depth for each single tree. We created a grid for these four parameters with $subsample$ and $colsample\_bytree$ in $\{0.6, 0.7, 0.8, 0.9, 1.0\}$, $n\_trees \in \{20, 40, 60, 80, 100\}$ and $max\_depth \in \{8, 13, 18, 23, 28\}$. The resulting best parameters with a minimal training RMSE of 254.21 were $max\_depth = 28$, $colsample\_bytree = 0.8$, $subsample = 0.9$ and $n\_trees = 80$. A similar grid search for the Extra Trees parameters (for which $subsample$ is redundant) with $colsample\_bytree \in \{0.6, 0.7, 0.8, 0.9, 1.0\}$, n_trees

---

[6] The source code of this library is available at https://github.com/dmlc/xgboost.
[7] The source code is available at https://github.com/microsoft/LightGBM.

$\in \{20, 40, 60, 80, 100\}$ and $max\_depth \in \{3, 8, 13, 18, 23, 28, 33\}$ led to a minimal RMSE of 261.3 for the choices $n\_trees = 60$, $max\_depth = 28$ and $colsample\_bytree = 0.6$. Compared to these bagging method, XgBoost and lightGBM need eight parameters to tune including, e.g., the minimum loss reduction to make an additional partition at each node ($gamma$), the coefficient of L2 regularization ($lambda$) and the learning rate ($learning\_rate$). As an 8-dimensional grid search would have needed the investigation of more than 72 Mio values (6 Mio for each of the 11 features and the target variable), we performed a step by step approach: at each step we only tuned some of the parameters with grid search while keeping the others fixed with the value we received from previous steps. The minimal training RMSE after this parameter tuning approach was 253.7 for the Xgboost approach and 256.46 for lightGBM.

Model Comparison. The performance of the resulting 'best' tree-based models were compared with respect to their predictive accuracy (measured in RMSE) on the test set and their computational effort needed for training. For a baseline comparison, a naive prediction was computed which uses the average trip duration for each combination of pickup and drop-off zipcode under the same hour of the same week day. The results are summarized in Table 1. Regarding computational time we considered two situations: The training time to obtain the corresponding 'best' model (second last column) and for illustration also the training time under the same tree and ensemble sizes (last column). These determine the complexity of the model and were set to $max\_depth = 16$ and $n\_trees = 60$. All computations were performed on an Intel Core i7-8700 3.20 GHz $\times$ 12 (CPUs) with GeForce GTX 1080/PCIe/SSE2 (GPUs) and 48 GB RAM.

It is apparent that the performance of all tree-based ensemble models were much better than the naive method and also better than the single CART tree. Among them, XgBoost on CPU was the model with the best RMSE (253.37) on test data directly followed by its GPU implementation (253.74). Moreover, Random Forest (254,21) and both lightGBM implementations ($\approx$256) only showed slightly worse accuracies while needing much less time for training. In fact, turning from XgBoost on its faster GPU implementation to the well-established Random Forest reduced the computational burden to train the best model by the factor 13.5. Turning to lightGBM (GPU implementation) even resulted in the factor 42.9. Finally, Extra Trees exhibits the worst RMSE among all ensembles while needing more time to train than lightGBM and the Random Forest.

To assess the effect of adding OSRM data for predictive modeling, we trained an XgBoost model without this auxiliary information resulting in a higher RMSE of 260.95 after parameter tuning. Thus, adding OSRM data can help to improve the accuracy in travel time prediction without incurring extra cost for buying map data or software.

Table 1. Comparison of the Tree-based Models. Some of the models, whose parameter haven't been tuned, have no data for the best models.

Model	RMSE	Training time [s] of best model	Training time [s] under same parameters
Naive	368.97	–	–
CART	271.23	72	–
Random Forest	254.21	442 (with 80 trees)	442
Extra Trees	261.3	825.6	493
XgBoost(GPU)	253.74	5916 (with 1685 trees)	72
XgBoost(CPU)	253.37	7240 (with 1662 trees)	196
LightGBM(GPU)	256.59	139 (with 597 trees)	9
LightGBM(CPU)	256.46	159 (with 524 trees)	11

We conclude that the tree based methods reach an improvement of around 30% compared to our naive estimator: The RMSE of the naive model of 368.97 s or 6.1 min is reduced to around 4.3 min in case of XgBoost and lightGBM. Considering an average trip duration of 10 to 15 min, this improvement is considerable. In combination with their low training times this justifies the application of XgBoost and lightGBM.

3.3   Short-Term Forecasting

Besides long-term predictions, short-term predictions for the next hours that react on recent conditions are needed. Here, an important question, especially with respect to storage and computation cost, is: how much information from the past is needed for training to obtain reasonable short predictions? To evaluate this, we trained several different XgBoost models, that only use the information from the last i hours. Moreover, we compare the obtained predictions with the one calculated by using the long-term forecasts. To this end, we randomly selected the week from 2016-06-23 to 2016-06-29 and separately considered the trips from every hour of this week as a single test data set. This resulted in 168 (7 d × 24 h/day) different test data sets. For each test data, we trained an XgBoost model on the trips in its past i hours, $i = 1, \ldots, 24$ as described in the last section excluding the temporal features *weekday* and all weather data. Thus, we trained 4,032 (168 × 24) XgBoost models in total. Their performance is shown in Fig. 7, in which each point represents a single model.

Here, several things stand out: First, for most hours of day and days of the week, the RMSE was almost constant over the different amounts of training data (1−24 h). This means that the trip duration of most hours and days have a rather short memory and mostly depend only on the trips from the last hour. An exception is given by the rush hours (5:00–8:00 on workdays), where the RMSE on test data was the lowest when using the past 24 h as training data. Beside that, all models exhibit the best performance on early morning hours (1:00–4:00)

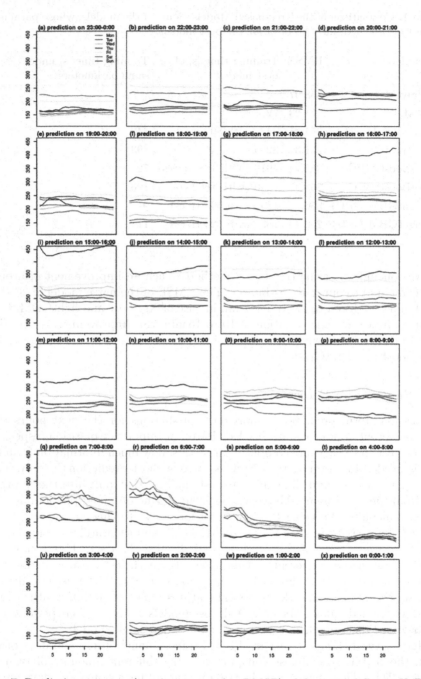

Fig. 7. Predictive accuracy (y-axis, measured in RMSE) of the 4,032 different XgBoost models corresponding to different days of the week (as indicated by different colors), hours of the day (header) and different amount of training data (x-axis, given in previous hours from 1–24). (Color figure online)

with RMSEs around 150 for all hour × day combinations. However, on Sundays between 10:00 to 18:00, the trip duration was relatively hard to predict resulting in RMSEs around 450 or even larger. The average training times for XgBoost (CPU) are very low: They range from below one second for the case, in which only trips of the last hour were considered, to around 9 s for the case in which data of the last 24 h were considered.

3.4 Short vs. Long-Term Prediction

The long-term prediction models can in principle also be used to predict the travel time for the trips in this randomly selected week. Choosing, the best CPU-based XgBoost long-term prediction model (Table 1), we also computed its RMSE for each of the 168 different test data sets (hours of this specific week). A comparison with the best short-term model is given in Fig. 8. It is surprising, that there is not much difference for most of the time. In fact, the short-term models are slightly better than the long-term model from Monday to Thursday and even much better on Sundays. An explanation may be that short-term models react more directly to the current traffic condition which is more hidden in the much larger training set of the long-term model. Thus, if the aim is short-term prediction, the consequences are very positive and save a lot of computation time: Simply use the short-term models.

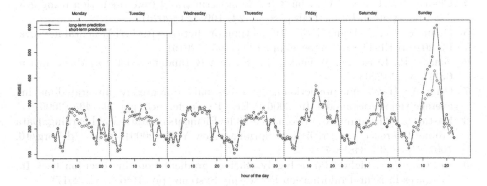

Fig. 8. Comparison of the RMSE of the best CPU-based XgBoost long-term prediction model and the best short-term model.

4 Discussion and Outlook

The results of our computational study show that ensemble tree methods deliver good travel time forecasts for both planning horizons, especially, if in addition to the core trip data, data related to the fastest route assuming a free flow speed, are considered. For short-term predictions, only data from the last few hours contain the information, which is necessary for a result outperforming models trained on a larger data set. Due to the relatively small training data sets, the resulting training times are very short, and allow for regular training runs on the most recent data. That means, at the same time, that for different planning horizons different models should be provided.

In future work we want to investigate how much data is needed for reliable forecasts for both time horizons, since there are significantly more trip data available for New York than for most other cities in the world. Especially in cases with less data records, different ways of integrating the short-term state of the traffic might be promising such as the global average speed of the last half an hour or the average speed of trips with similar origin destination locations. For many applications, it is also interesting to deliver arrival time (prediction) intervals or distributions expressing the uncertainty of the forecast.

References

1. Breiman, L.: Random forests. Mach. Learn. **45**(1), 5–32 (2001). https://doi.org/10.1023/A:1010933404324
2. Chang, H., Park, D., Lee, S., Lee, H., Baek, S.: Dynamic multi-interval bus travel time prediction using bus transit data. Transportmetrica **6**(1), 19–38 (2010)
3. Chen, T., Guestrin, C.: XgBoost: a scalable tree boosting system. In: Proceedings of the 22nd ACM SIGKDD Conference, pp. 785–794, August 2016
4. Chen, C.M., Liang, C.C., Chu, C.P.: Long-term travel time prediction using gradient boosting. J. Intell. Transp. Syst. **24**, 109–124 (2020)
5. Duan, Y., Lv, Y., Wang, F. Y.: Travel time prediction with LSTM neural network. In: 2016 IEEE ITS Conference, pp. 1053–1058 (2016)
6. Geurts, P., Ernst, D., Wehenkel, L.: Extremely randomized trees. Mach. Learn. **63**(1), 3–42 (2006)
7. Guin, A.: Travel time prediction using a seasonal autoregressive integrated moving average time series model. In: 2006 IEEE ITS Conference, pp. 493–498 (2006)
8. Hastie, T., Tibshirani, R., Friedman, J.: The Elements of Statistical Learning: Data Mining Inference and Prediction. Springer, New York (2009). https://doi.org/10.1007/978-0-387-84858-7
9. Ke, G., et al.: LightGBM: a highly efficient gradient boosting decision tree. In: Advances in Neural Information Processing Systems, pp. 3146–3154 (2017)
10. Van Lint, J.W.C., Hoogendoorn, S.P., van Zuylen, H.J.: Accurate freeway travel time prediction with state-space neural networks under missing data. Transp. Res. Part C **13**(5–6), 347–369 (2005)
11. Wu, C.H., Ho, J.M., Lee, D.T.: Travel-time prediction with support vector regression. IEEE Trans. ITS **5**(4), 276–281 (2004)
12. Yu, B., Wang, H., Shan, W., Yao, B.: Prediction of bus travel time using random forests based on near neighbors. Comput. Aided Civ. Infrastruct. Eng. **33**(4), 333–350 (2018)
13. Zhang, Y., Haghani, A.: A gradient boosting method to improve travel time prediction. Transp. Res. Part C **58**, 308–324 (2015)
14. Breiman, L., Friedman, J., Stone, C.J., Olshen, R.A.: Classification and Regression Trees. CRC Press, Boca Raton (1984)

15. Pedregosa, F., et al.: Scikit-learn: machine learning in Python. J. Mach. Learn. Res. **12**, 2825–2830 (2011)
16. P.C. Team: Python: a dynamic, open source programming language, Version 3.6. 8. Python Software Foundation, Wilmington, DE (2019)
17. Mitchell, R., Frank, E.: Accelerating the XgBoost algorithm using GPU computing. PeerJ Comput. Sci. **3**, e127 (2017)
18. TomTom: Traffic Index (2019). www.tomtom.com/en_gb/traffic-index/ranking/?country=CA,MX,US. Accessed 31 Mar 2020
19. NYC Department of Transportation: New York City Mobility Report (2016). http://www.nyc.gov/html/dot/downloads/pdf/mobility-report-2016-screen-optimized.pdf. Accessed 31 Mar 2020
20. Ulmer, M.: Approximate Dynamic Programming for Dynamic Vehicle Routing. Springer, Cham (2017). https://doi.org/10.1007/978-3-319-55511-9
21. Morde, V.: XgBoost Algorithm: Long May She Reign! (2019). https://towardsdatasc1ence.com/https-medium-com-vishalmorde-XgBoost-algorithmlong-shemay-rein-edd9f99be63d. Accessed 13 Apr 2020
22. NYC Taxi and Limousine Commission (TLC) Trip Record Data. https://www1.nyc.gov/site/tlc/about/tlc-trip-record-data.page. Accessed 7 May 2020

Platooning of Automated Ground Vehicles to Connect Port and Hinterland: A Multi-objective Optimization Approach

Nadia Pourmohammad-Zia(✉), Frederik Schulte, Dimitris Souravlias, and Rudy R. Negenborn

Department of Maritime and Transport Technology, Delft University of Technology, 2628 CD Delft, The Netherlands
{N.PourmohammadZia,F.Schulte,D.Souravlias,R.R.Negenborn}@tudelft.nl

Abstract. Automated ground vehicles (AGVs) are essential parts of container operations at many ports. Forming platoons—as conceptually established in trucking—may allow these vehicles to directly cater demand points such as dry ports in the hinterland. In this work, we aim to assess such AGV platoons in terms of operational efficiency and costs, considering the case of the Port of Rotterdam. We propose a multi-objective mixed-integer programming model that minimizes dwell and idle times, on the one hand, and the total cost of the system involving transportation, labor, and platoon formation costs, on the other hand. To achieve Pareto optimal solutions that capture the trade-offs between minimizing cost and time, we apply an augmented epsilon constraint method. The results indicate that all the containers are delivered by AGVs. This not only shortens the dwell time of the containers by decreasing loading/unloading processes and eliminating stacking but also leads to considerable cost savings.

Keywords: Platooning · Automated ground vehicles · Container terminals · Loading/unloading operations · Emission analysis

1 Introduction

Platooning of trucks has received significant attention in recent years because of its potential to reduce costs and emissions while preparing the ground for fully automated road transport. Automated Ground Vehicles (AGVs) have been used at many ports for several decades. While early generations were exclusively guided vehicles, newer generations of AGVs have been gradually adopting autonomous technologies. This growing trend has led researchers and practitioners to rethink the application of AGVs, especially considering their use in

This research is supported by the project "Dynamic Fleet Management (P14-18 – project 3)" (project 14894) of the Netherlands Organization for Scientific Research (NWO), domain Applied and Engineering Sciences (TTW).

an extended area of the port hinterland, possibly avoiding time-consuming and cost-intensive loading processes at container terminals. Smaller terminals and ports with adjacent dry ports, or generally, smaller subsets of containers handled at larger terminals could benefit from such ideas. Nonetheless, most roads are not yet ready and are not expected to be ready in the short or mid-term to safely be used by AGVs. In this expected transition period, vehicle platoons are considered a viable option for early adoption autonomous vehicle technology.

The concept platooning has been investigated by researchers as a way to benefit from automation in this transition phase [1]. For instance, Larrson et al. [12] have developed an approach to assess fuel savings achieved by truck platoons and more recently, Scherr et al. [17] have demonstrated how platoons can be used to bring AGVs from one autonomous zone to another. However, AGVs delivering containers from a ship to the hinterland directly, and thereby avoiding the traditional storage option (as illustrated in Fig. 1), still needs to be particularly investigated.

With the present work, we aim to make a first step towards evaluating the actual potential of applying AGV platoons in such settings. For this purpose, we develop a multi-objective mixed-integer programming model where AGV platoons are considered as transfer modes between ports and autonomous hinterland areas. We obtain Pareto optimal solutions using an augmented epsilon constraint method and obtain significant gains in terms of total costs, dwell times, and emissions, when AGV platoons are employed.

2 Related Work

Being integral parts of contemporary logistics systems, Automated Ground Vehicles (AGVs) are used to transport and handle various goods in diverse industrial environments over five decades. Especially in port terminals, AGVs are established transport modes typically transferring containers between ships and storage areas on land. The majority of research focuses on operation-level planning problems such as AGV scheduling [3,4,10], as well as routing [5]. For their solution, there exist a plethora of diverse studies that propose mathematical models, exact and heuristic approaches with the aim of minimizing mainly the container dwell times. Table 1 provides a comparison among relevant articles considering various aspects. For a comprehensive review on AGV scheduling and routing the reader is referred to Qiu et al. [15].

New technological advances have motivated recent research efforts to incorporate traffic control (e.g. collision avoidance mechanisms) into the planning process of AGVs in container terminals. Zhong et al. [21] study the integrated scheduling and path planning problem, while preventing potential conflicts among AGVs. To solve the problem, a mixed integer programming model along with two heuristic methods are introduced. Experiments with different numbers of containers and AGVs verify the potential of the proposed approach to minimize the delay of AVGs in large-scale problem settings.

Xin et al. [19] investigate the collision-free trajectory planning of free-ranging AGVs combined with the scheduling of different types of equipment for container

The Basic Problem with Conventional Trucks

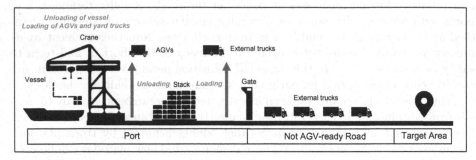

Platoons of Automated Ground Vehicles (AGVs)

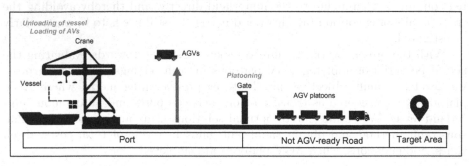

Fig. 1. The container drayage process with conventional trucks or AGV platoons

Table 1. Articles on automated ground vehicles and platooning

Reference	Objective		Problem		Method		Feature		Vehicle type	
	Time	Fuel	R	SC	EX	H	PL	TC	AGV	TR
Boysen et al. [2]		√		√	√		√			√
Briskorn et al. [3]	√			√	√	√			√	
Cheng et al. [4]	√			√	√			√	√	
Corréa et al. [5]	√		√	√			√		√	√
Kim et al. [10]	√			√			√		√	
Larson et al. [11]		√	√		√		√		√	
Larsson et al. [12]		√	√		√	√	√			√
Scherr et al. [17]	√			√			√	√	√	
Xin et al. [19]	√			√			√	√	√	
Zhang et al. [20]	√	√		√	√		√		√	
Zhong et al. [21]	√			√			√	√	√	
This paper	√	√		√	√		√		√	

Problems: R (Routing), SC (Scheduling)
Methods: EX (Exact), H (Heuristic)
Features: PL (Platooning), TC (Traffic control)
Vehicle types: AGV (Automated Ground Vehicle), TR (Truck)

transport. The proposed approach determines the sequence of jobs per piece of equipment by solving a hybrid flow shop scheduling problem. Based on the resulting sequences, conflict-free trajectories are identified by solving a series of mixed integer linear programming problems sequentially. The performance of the developed algorithm is evaluated by a simulation study, which shows that no collisions occur while the distance covered by the AGVs is significantly reduced.

Up-to-now, theoretical and practical studies have embraced AGVs for container transport only between ships and terminal storage areas. Hence, to the best of our knowledge, there is no approach that considers AGVs delivering containers from a ship to the hinterland directly, thereby avoiding the traditional storage option. Moreover, in these studies, AGVs are assumed to function in the restrained environment of a container terminal. Therefore, forming platoons of AGVs to render their operation feasible in non-controlled environments (e.g. public roads) is a new concept that has not been so far taken into consideration.

Platooning has emerged as a promising technology that not only offers significant fuel savings, but also prepares the ground of increased autonomy in freight transportation (Janssen et al. [9]). Research developments in the area, especially platooning problem classifications, operations research models and solution methods, are reviewed in Bhoopalam et al. [1]. A large part of the relevant literature has been devoted to technical and technological aspects of platooning including string sequence and stability, signal timing, longitudinal trajectory control, speed profile, connectivity issues, obstacle avoidance, vehicle-to-vehicle communications. However, none of these aspects is investigated in the current research. More information on these topics can be found in the works of Delimpaltadakis et al. [6], Liang et al. [13], and Zhong et al. [22].

Studies on the operational side of platooning, such as planning, routing, and scheduling, are still scarce in the logistics literature [7]. A first attempt to explore the benefits of platooning is presented in Larsson et al. [12]. The main objective is to maximize the fuel savings while considering the formation and routing of the platoon. In this study, several linear programming formulations for different problem variants are proposed with the aim of solving small instances. Experimental results show the gains of optimal platoon routing in fuel efficiency. For the same platooning problem, an improved model is developed in Larson et al. [11]. This approach results in a significant reduction of the problem size, thereby enabling to tackle realistic instances more efficiently.

Different aspects of the platoon formation problem are analyzed in Boysen et al. [2]. To this end, the authors formulate a basic platooning problem that addresses the truck-to-platoon assignment under the assumption that each truck considers an individual delivery window and the resulting platoons share the same path. Their computational analysis shows that the benefits of platooning on fuel consumption depend significantly on the number of platoon partners, restrictions on the platoon length as well as the size of the delivery windows. In the study of Zhang et al. [20], a platoon coordination and scheduling problem in the presence of travel time uncertainty is investigated. The problem is solved to optimality via an analytical model that considers different converging and diverging route networks. The authors conclude that differences in the scheduled arrival times of vehicles renders platooning an inefficient option.

A parcel delivery problem tackled via the use of heterogeneous autonomous fleets is introduced in Scherr et al. [17]. Autonomous vehicles travel only in specific zones while they are guided by manually operated vehicles forming platoons elsewhere. To the best of our knowledge, this is the only study in the literature where platooning plays a transfer mode role by connecting autonomous and ordinary driving zones. To model the problem, a linear programming formulation is proposed. Additionally, the problem complexity is reduced by utilizing a time-expanded model that discretizes the considered planning horizon.

In overall, despite the increasing interest on platooning, there is a limited number of research works in the freight transportation sector. This provides ample opportunities, especially for new decision making approaches that investigate its role in a wide spectrum of logistics applications. So far, platoon formation, scheduling and routing problems have claimed most of the research attention, while the role of platooning as a transfer mode still remains heavily unexplored. Moreover, up-to-now, fuel costs have been the main focus of platooning problems. Considering other types of cost will reveal the impact of platooning on additional aspects, thereby unlocking its full potential.

3   A Model for AGV Platooning

The proposed framework deals with container delivery from a port to its hinterland depot or adjacent dry port, henceforth referred as target zone. In the classic container terminal process, after unloading a vessel, its containers are moved to stack to wait for the rest of their delivery journey. Assume that a subset of these containers can be directly delivered to their target zone, without entering the stack, by application of external AGVs which belong to the carriers. For this subset of the containers, denoted as I in our model, we will investigate if direct delivery can bring savings in dwell time and costs. The transportation network is considered to be heterogeneous where the port and the target zone are appropriate for automated driving and the linking road segment which connects these two areas together is not suitable for AGVs. Therefore, the AGVs have to join a platoon with a human-driven leader to move in this linking road segment. Dwell time for either of the two delivery modes ($n = 1, 2$, 1 representing the classic delivery by trucks in presence of stacking and 2 by AGVs) is the accumulation

Table 2. Dwell time in two delivery modes

Dwell time	
Delivery by truck ($n = 1$)	Delivery by AGV ($n = 2$)
Loading containers on AGVs (t_1) Traveling to stack (t_2)	Loading containers on AGVs (t_1')
Unloading containers off AGVs (t_3) Stacking (t_4)	Traveling to gate (t_2')
Loading containers on trucks (t_5) Traveling to gate (t_6)	Joining platoons (t_3')

of the time components shown in Table 2. t_1, t_2, t_3, t_5, t_6, t'_1, t'_2, and t'_3 are fixed known parameters, whereas t_4 is a variable determined in the model.

The idea is to specify optimal transportation modes and schedules that minimize delivery time and costs of the considered containers. The notations used to formulate the model are listed as follows:

Sets

| I | Set of containers |
| P | Set of potential platoons |

Parameters

Cod_n	Transportation cost of mode n between the port and the target zone
Cl	Labor cost for external trucks
Cp	Platoon formation cost
AN_n	Number of available vehicles of mode n
To	Initial start time of the loading process at the quay side
Tod_n	Transportation time of mode n between the port and target zone
TA_i	Lower bound of admissible delivery time for container i
TB_i	Upper bound of admissible delivery time for container i
U_B	Minimum number of admissible AGVs in a platoon
L_B	Maximum number of admissible AGVs in a platoon
$m_1...m_4$	Lower bounds of the left-hand side of the respective constraints
$M_1...M_5$	Upper bounds of the left-hand side of the respective constraints

Variables

Z_{in}	1: if container i is delivered by mode n 0: otherwise
V_{ip}	1: if the AGV carrying container i joins platoon p 0: otherwise
σ_p	1: if platoon p is formed 0: otherwise
δ_i	1: if DF_i is positive 0: otherwise
ST_{in}	Delivery time of container i by mode n
RT_{in}	Arrival time of the vehicle of mode n carrying container i at its destination
IT_{in}	Idle time of vehicle carrying container i of mode n
DF_i	Auxiliary variable which is used to define stacking time of container i
t_{4i}	Stacking time of container i

Then, the proposed multi-objective optimization model is formulated as:

$$Min\, F_T = \sum_{i \in I} \left(w_1(t_1 + t_2 + t_3 + t_5 + t_6)Z_{i1} + w_1(t'_1 + t'_2 + t'_3)Z_{i2} + w_2 t_{4i} + w_3 \sum_{n=1,2} IT_{in} \right) \quad (1)$$

$$Min\, F_C = \sum_{i \in I} \sum_{n=1,2} Cod_n\, Z_{in} + \sum_{i \in I} Cl\, Z_{i1} + \sum_{p \in P} Cp\, \sigma_p \quad (2)$$

$$\sum_{i \in I} Z_{in} \leqslant AN_n \qquad \forall n = 1,2 \tag{3}$$

$$\sum_{n=1,2} Z_{in} = 1 \qquad \forall i \in I \tag{4}$$

$$Z_{i2} = \sum_{p \in P} V_{ip} \qquad \forall i \in I \tag{5}$$

$$\sum_{i \in I} V_{ip} \leq U_B \sigma_p \qquad \forall p \in P \tag{6}$$

$$\sum_{i \in I} V_{ip} \geq L_B \sigma_p \qquad \forall p \in P \tag{7}$$

$$ST_{in} \geq (To + DT_{in} + Tod_n)Z_{in} \qquad \forall i \in I, n = 1,2 \tag{8}$$

$$DT_{i1} = t_1 + t_2 + t_3 + t_{4_i} + t_5 + t_6 \qquad \forall i \in I \tag{9}$$

$$IT_{in} = ST_{in} - (To + DT_{in} + Tod_n)Z_{in} \qquad \forall i \in I, n = 1,2 \tag{10}$$

$$DF_i = TA_i Z_{i1} - (To + t_1 + t_2 + t_3 + t_5 + t_6 + Tod_1) \qquad \forall i \in I \tag{11}$$

$$DF_i \leq M_1 \delta_i \qquad \forall i \in I \tag{12}$$

$$DF_i \geq m_1(1 - \delta_i) \qquad \forall i \in I \tag{13}$$

$$t_{4_i} = DF_i \delta_i \qquad \forall i \in I \tag{14}$$

$$TA_i Z_{in} \leq ST_{in} \leq TB_i Z_{in} \qquad \forall i \in I, n = 1,2 \tag{15}$$

$$Z_{in}, V_{ip}, \sigma_p, \delta_i \in \{0,1\} \qquad \forall i \in I, p \in P, n = 1,2 \tag{16}$$

$$ST_{in}, IT_{in}, t_{4_i} \geq 0 \qquad \forall i \in I, n = 1,2 \tag{17}$$

The objective function (1) minimizes dwell time including loading/unloading, travel within zone and stacking time as well as idle time of the vehicles of two modes (w_1, w_2 and w_3 capture the relative importance of time components). In the objective function (2) the total cost of the system involving transportation, labor and platoon formation costs are minimized. Labor cost is the wage paid to the drivers of the external trucks and platoon formation cost expresses the cost of assigning a human-driven leading vehicle and its driver to each string.

Constraint (3) ensures that the limits on the available numbers of AGVs and external trucks are respected. Constraint (4) guarantees that each container is delivered by one of the transportation modes. Constraint (5) implies that an AGV can leave the port only if it joins a platoon. Constraints (6) and (7) confine the number of vehicles in a platoon. Consistency of service time is guaranteed by constraint (8). Dwell time of first transportation mode is obtained by constraint (9). Constraint (10) specifies the idle time of the vehicles of each transportation mode. The stacking time of each container is obtained through constraints (11) to (14). The constraints imply that each container of mode 1 is stacked only if it would arrive sooner than its admissible service time in case of no stacking. This is distinguished by variable δ_i. Time windows are represented by constraint (15). Finally, constraints (16) and (17) imply the type of variables.

Constraints (8), (10) and (14) are non-linear. These are linearized to transform the model into a mixed-integer linear programming (MIP) formulation as follows:

$$ST_{in} - To - DT_{in} - Tod_n \geq m_2(1 - Z_{in}) \qquad \forall i \in I, n = 1, 2 \qquad (18)$$

$$RT_{in} - To - DT_{in} - Tod_n \leq M_2(1 - Z_{in}) \qquad \forall i \in I, n = 1, 2 \qquad (19)$$

$$RT_{in} - To - DT_{in} - Tod_n \geq m_3(1 - Z_{in}) \qquad \forall i \in I, n = 1, 2 \qquad (20)$$

$$RT_{in} \leq M_3 Z_{in} \qquad \forall i \in I, n = 1, 2 \qquad (21)$$

$$IT_{in} = ST_{in} - RT_{in} \qquad \forall i \in I, n = 1, 2 \qquad (22)$$

$$t_{4_i} - DF_i \leq M_4(1 - \delta_i) \qquad \forall i \in I \qquad (23)$$

$$t_{4_i} - DF_i \geq m_4(1 - \delta_i) \qquad \forall i \in I \qquad (24)$$

$$t_{4_i} \leq M_5 \delta_i \qquad \forall i \in I \qquad (25)$$

Constraint (18) is a linearized version of constraint (8). Constraint (10) is linearized by constraints (19)–(22) and constraint (14) is linearized by constraints (23)–(25).

4   Solution Approach

In the proposed bi-objective model, it is impossible to obtain an individual solution that can simultaneously optimize both objective functions. For this reason, the augmented epsilon constraint method is used to achieve Pareto optimal solutions that capture the trade-offs between minimizing cost and time [14]. In this approach, we optimize one of the objective functions using the other as constraint accompanied by the original constraints of the problem. We take time (F_T) as the main objective function and calculate the range of F_C by creating the payoff table obtained by the lexicographic optimization of the objective functions. Then, the range of F_C is divided into k equal intervals resulting in $k + 1$ grid points for F_C. Subsequently, $k + 1$ optimization sub-problems are solved to obtain the Pareto front of the problem. The optimization sub-problem for the lth grid point is formulated as:

$$Min \ F_T - \varepsilon(\frac{S_l}{r}) \qquad (26)$$

s.t.

$$F_C + S_l = e_l \qquad (27)$$

Equations (3)–(7), (9), (11)–(13), (15)–(17), (18)–(25)

ε is a small number (10^{-6}–10^{-3}) and e_l is obtained as $e_l = ub - \frac{lr}{k}$ where ub and r are the upper bound and range of F_C, respectively.

In order to derive the best compromise solution from the obtained Pareto front, membership function in fuzzy sets is applied [18]. A linear membership function for each of the objective functions is introduced as:

$$\mu_m^l = \begin{cases} 0 & F_m^l \leq F_m^{\min} \\ \frac{F_m^{\max} - F_m^l}{F_m^{\max} - F_m^{\min}} & F_m^l \leq F_m^l \leq F_m^{\max} \\ 1 & F_m^l \geq F_m^{\max} \end{cases} \qquad (28)$$

Where $m = T, C$ and l indicate the two objective functions and grid points, respectively. Then, the overall membership function is normalized as:

$$\mu^l = \frac{\varpi_1 \mu_1^l + \varpi_2 \mu_2^l}{\sum_{g=1}^{k+1} \sum_{m=1,2} \varpi_m \mu_m^g} \qquad (29)$$

Where ϖ_m is the weight value of the mth objective function. Finally, the solution with the maximum membership function μ^l is selected as the best compromise solution.

5   Numerical Results

5.1   Experimental Settings

We consider container deliveries from the port of Rotterdam (western part of the seaport that is known as Maasvlakte area) to the logistic hub Venlo (Hutchison Ports Venlo) which is an important hinterland hub in Europe. This hub is located in the southeast of the Netherlands and within 200 km distance from the port of Rotterdam. The MIP model is coded in IBM ILOG CPLEX Optimization Studio 12.7 and due to its features, the model can be easily solved for large size instances in a reasonable time (namely 27.45 s for 1000 containers). Therefore, no heuristic solution approach was required. The experiments are carried out on a computer with Intel®Core i7-8650U CPU 1.9 GHz, 2.11 GHz, and 7.88 GB memory available.

To illustrate the features of the optimal solutions in details, it is considered that 50 containers can be directly delivered to their final destination. So, the remainder of the containers will follow the classic stacking procedure. As mentioned, scaling up does not impact the features of the problem and the model can be easily solved for larger sizes. We have taken 50 available AGVs as well as trucks to investigate optimal transportation modes for these containers. The planning horizon starts as the containers are unloaded off the ship. The destination time-windows for these containers can differ as their packed components may vary (Table 3):

Table 3. Destination time windows (in hours)

Containers	1–10	11–20	21–30	31–40	41–50
TA_i	3	3	4	4	4.5
TB_i	8	8	8	8	8

Distances are transformed into travel time by considering speeds of 75 km/h for trucks and 55 km/h for AGVs in the linking road of the origin to destination and 25 km/h for both modes within the container terminal of the port. Travel costs are proportional to distance and are higher for trucks due to higher fuel costs. Fuel cost reductions are observed when vehicles travel in a string which is due to lower air drag. The labor cost and platoon formation cost are 60 and 200 monetary units, respectively. The number of admissible AGVs in a platoon is confined to (2, 4).

5.2 Results

Optimizing the proposed model yields the following results (Table 4):

Table 4. Results

$F_1 = 22.316$	$Z_{1-50,1} = 0$	$IT_{1-40,2} = 0$	$\sigma_{1-13} = 1$
$F_2 = 11600$	$Z_{1-50,2} = 1$	$IT_{41-50,2} = 0.0767$	$\sigma_{14,15} = 0$

The results indicate that all the containers are delivered by AGVs. This not only shortens the dwell time of the containers by decreasing loading/unloading processes and eliminating stacking but also brings considerable cost savings.

The AGVs join 13 platoons to reach their destination and twelve of these platoons contain their maximum admissible AGVs in a string which is four in our problem. This is economically justifiable as it decreases the number of required platoons, hence platoon formation costs. Although using ordinary trucks for the remaining two containers is more economical than applying AGVs and forming a new platoon, these two containers are also delivered by AGVs joining the 13th platoon. That is because efficient time management is the top priority of the model which results in the application of AGVs.

In order to deep dive into the features of our proposed model, it is essential to analyze the impact of time-windows on the optimal solutions. Table 5 provides optimal solutions obtained by varying TA_i, $\forall i = 41-50$.

By increasing TA_{41-50} up to 6.5, the idle time of the AGVs rises. That is because the vehicles need to wait longer for delivery time window to be open. The optimal transportation mode is still the same, hence the dwell time and total cost of the system undergo no changes. As TA_{41-50} reaches 7, it is not optimal to use AGVs anymore and trucks are applied instead. Accordingly, the dwell time and total cost increase. The containers wait 3.28 h in stack before leaving the port. These convey an important insight: As the delivery time window shifts later, direct delivery by AGVs loses its efficiency due to longer idle times at the destination.

Table 5. The impact of time windows on the optimal solutions

Instance	TA_{41-50}	F_1	F_2	$Z_{41-50,n}$		$IT_{41-50,n}$		$t4_{41-50}$
				n = 1	n = 2	n = 1	n = 2	
#1	5	29.816	11600	0	1	0	0.577	0
#2	5.5	37.316	11600	0	1	0	1.077	0
#3	6	44.816	11600	0	1	0	1.577	0
#4	6.5	52.316	11600	0	1	0	2.077	0
#5	7	58.432	11800	1	0	0	0	3.28

The average dwell time of each container and total costs of the system for these five problem instances (as introduced in Table 5) in the classic and proposed approaches are illustrated in Fig. 2.

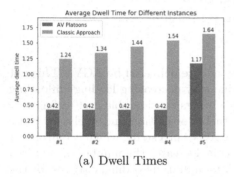

(a) Dwell Times

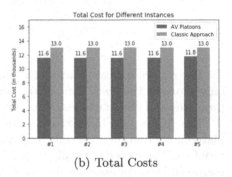

(b) Total Costs

Fig. 2. Comparison of dwell time and costs in two approaches

As shown, the average dwell time of the containers decreases by applying AGVs in all the problem instances. This is highly important since dwell time is a significant performance measure for ports. Moreover, the stacking is eliminated in this setting which is extremely desirable due to space limits and high container traffics in the yard of container terminals.

As platoon formation cost increases, forming a platoon becomes less economical. In order to investigate whether this increase affects the optimal solutions of the problem and specifically the transportation mode, a sensitivity analysis on C_p is carried out and the results are provided in Table 6.

With 25% increase in C_p, the optimal transportation mode is still selected as AGVs for all 50 containers. So, F_1 undergoes no changes and 25% boost in platoon formation costs raises F_2 to 12250. As C_p is increased by 50–75%, the optimal mode for two containers changes from AGVs to trucks preventing the

Table 6. The impact of platoon formation cost on the optimal solutions

Instance	C_p	F_1	F_2	Containers i	Z_{in} n = 1	n = 2	IT_{in} n = 1	n = 2	t_{4_i}
#6	250	22.316	12250	$\forall i = 1-50$	0	1	0	0.0767	0
#7	300	23.209	12740	$\forall i = 1-48$	0	1	0	0.0767	0
				$\forall i = 49, 50$	1	0	0	0	
#8	350	23.209	13340	$\forall i = 1-48$	0	1	0	0.0767	0
				$\forall i = 49, 50$	1	0	0	0	
#9	400	24.996	13820	$\forall i = 1-44$	0	1	0	0.0767	0
				$\forall i = 45-50$	1	0	0	0	

formation of 13th platoon. With further increase in C_p (100%), four more containers are delivered by trucks which decreases the number of required platoons to 11.

These results are compromised solutions in the Pareto front with the highest normalized membership value for the two objectives. Expressly, our approach takes into account possible solutions between optimizing either of the objective functions and selects the most promising one. As an instance, for $C_p = 400$, it is optimal to deliver all 50 containers by AGVs from the perspective of time (with $F_1 = 22.316$ and $F_2 = 14200$) and trucks are optimal for all 50 containers from cost view (with $F_1 = 56.9$ and $F_2 = 12500$). Then, with time as the first objective, the multi-objective approach suggests to use six trucks and 44 AGVs (with $F_1 = 24.97$ and $F_2 = 13820$).

Emission Analysis. Heavy duty vehicles are responsible for 27% of road transport CO_2 emission and European Commission is constantly proposing regulations on reducing CO_2 emissions from these vehicles. Accordingly, emissions should be captured in evaluation of any transportation setting. For heavy-duty vehicles, the UK Transport Research Laboratory has developed a function to estimate CO_2 emission of a travel [8]:

$$E = (\alpha_0 + \alpha_1 v + \alpha_2 v^2 + \alpha_3 v^3 + \frac{\alpha_4}{v} + \frac{\alpha_5}{v^2} + \frac{\alpha_6}{v^3})d \qquad (30)$$

where $\alpha_0, ..., \alpha_6$ are constant parameters for each vehicle type, v is the travel speed and d is the travel distance. For heavy-duty vehicles with gross weight 7.5–16 tones we have: $\alpha_0 = 871$, $\alpha_1 = -16$, $\alpha_2 = 0.143$, $\alpha_3 = \alpha_3 = \alpha_6 = 0$ and $\alpha_5 = 32031$. It should also be noted that platooning reduces fuel consumption due to reduction in air drag. This reduction is up to 9.7% for the following vehicles in the string that directly impacts emissions. Then, Eq. (30) should take into account this reduction for AGVs in a platoon. The total CO_2 emissions of the vehicles carrying 50 mentioned containers in the classic and proposed approach are obtained as 4810.69 and 3920.51 kg, respectively. This indicates that the proposed approach can bring 18% (890.17 kg) decrease in CO_2 emissions which is highly desirable. Then, the approach not only results in cost and time savings but also provides an environmentally friendlier setting.

6   Conclusions

Research on automated trucks and AVs has demonstrated the effectiveness of platooning to save fuel, costs, and emissions. Intelligent AGVs operated at ports may form platoons to establish an efficient and sustainable connection between port and hinterland, but models for these AGV platoons still need to be introduced and evaluated. In this work, we have proposed a multi-objective mixed-integer programming model for AGV platooning as a transfer mode between the port of Rotterdam and its hinterland. We have found that AGV platoons indeed offer a significant potential to reduce costs, dwell times, and emissions. In this way, our work transfers the platooning concept to port/hinterland operations and, by connecting two AGV-ready zones, it extends the work by Scherr et al. [16,17] who proposed platooning as a link between AV-ready areas in city logistics. In addition, the proposed multi-objective approach allows us to obtain Pareto optimal solutions, dealing with the trade-off between costs and time. Moreover, our emission analysis comparing conventional drayage trucks to port AGVs with air drag, provides detailed insight in the environmental impact of AGV platoons.

To the best of our knowledge, this is the first work to explore the potential of AGV platoons to connect ports with their hinterland, and our results provide first evidence for the advantages of this concept. In the long run, these findings may motivate further case studies and alternative concepts of AGV platoons in the port hinterland as well as gradual infrastructural investments that could allow us to scale up the approach. Nonetheless, while this study makes a first step, more research is needed to fully comprehend the potential of our approach and derive clear recommendations for policy makers to foster infrastructural adjustments. This research can be extended to a pickup-and-delivery structure where export containers may enter the port under a similar setting.

References

1. Bhoopalam, A.K., Agatz, N., Zuidwijk, R.: Planning of truck platoons: a literature review and directions for future research. Transp. Res. Part B: Methodol. **107**, 212–228 (2018)
2. Boysen, N., Briskorn, D., Schwerdfeger, S.: The identical-path truck platooning problem. Transp. Res. Part B: Methodol. **109**, 26–39 (2018)
3. Briskorn, D., Drexl, A., Hartmann, S.: Inventory-based dispatching of automated guided vehicles on container terminals. In: Kim, K.H., Günther, H.-O. (eds.) Container Terminals and Cargo Systems, pp. 195–214. Springer, Heidelberg (2007). https://doi.org/10.1007/978-3-540-49550-5_10

4. Cheng, Y.L., Sen, H.C., Natarajan, K., Teo, C.P., Tan, K.C.: Dispatching automated guided vehicles in a container terminal. In: Geunes, J., Pardalos, P.M. (eds) Supply Chain Optimization. Applied Optimization, vol. 98. Springer, Boston (2005). https://doi.org/10.1007/0-387-26281-4_11
5. Corréa, A.I., Langevin, A., Rousseau, L.M.: Scheduling and routing of automated guided vehicles: a hybrid approach. Comput. Oper. Res. **34**(6), 1688–1707 (2007)
6. Delimpaltadakis, I.M., Bechlioulis, C.P., Kyriakopoulos, K.J.: Decentralized platooning with obstacle avoidance for car-like vehicles with limited sensing. IEEE Robot. Autom. Lett. **3**(2), 835–840 (2018)
7. Gerrits, B., Mes, M., Schuur, P.: Simulation of real-time and opportunistic truck platooning at the port of Rotterdam. In: 2019 Proceedings of the Winter Simulation Conference (WSC), pp. 133–144. IEEE (2019)
8. Hickman, J., Hassel, D., Joumard, R., Samaras, Z., Sorenson, S.: Methodology for calculating transport emissions and energy consumption (1999)
9. Janssen, G.R., Zwijnenberg, J., Blankers, I., de Kruijff, J.: Truck platooning: driving the future of transportation - TNO whitepaper (2015)
10. Kim, K.H., Bae, J.W.: A look-ahead dispatching method for automated guided vehicles in automated port container terminals. Transp. Sci. **38**(2), 224–234 (2004)
11. Larson, J., Munson, T., Sokolov, V.: Coordinated platoon routing in a metropolitan network. In: 2016 Proceedings of the Seventh SIAM Workshop on Combinatorial Scientific Computing, pp. 73–82. SIAM (2016)
12. Larsson, E., Sennton, G., Larson, J.: The vehicle platooning problem: computational complexity and heuristics. Transp. Res. Part C: Emerg. Technol. **60**, 258–277 (2015)
13. Liang, X., Guler, S.I., Gayah, V.V.: Signal timing optimization with connected vehicle technology: platooning to improve computational efficiency. Transp. Res. Rec. **2672**(18), 81–92 (2018)
14. Mavrotas, G.: Effective implementation of the ε-constraint method in multi-objective mathematical programming problems. Appl. Math. Comput. **213**(2), 455–465 (2009)
15. Qiu, L., Hsu, W.J., Huang, S.Y., Wang, H.: Scheduling and routing algorithms for AGVs: a survey. Int. J. Prod. Res. **40**(3), 745–760 (2002)
16. Scherr, Y.O., Neumann-Saavedra, B.A., Hewitt, M., Mattfeld, D.C.: Service network design for same day delivery with mixed autonomous fleets. Transp. Res. Procedia **30**, 23–32 (2018)
17. Scherr, Y.O., Neumann-Saavedra, B.A., Hewitt, M., Mattfeld, D.C.: Service network design with mixed autonomous fleets. Transp. Res. Part E: Logist. Transp. Rev. **124**, 40–55 (2019)
18. Tavakkoli-Moghaddam, R., Sadri, S., Pourmohammad-Zia, N., Mohammadi, M.: A hybrid fuzzy approach for the closed-loop supply chain network design under uncertainty. J. Intell. Fuzzy Syst. **28**(6), 2811–2826 (2015)
19. Xin, J., Negenborn, R.R., Corman, F., Lodewijks, G.: Control of interacting machines in automated container terminals using a sequential planning approach for collision avoidance. Transp. Res. Part C: Emerg. Technol. **60**, 377–396 (2015)
20. Zhang, W., Jenelius, E., Ma, X.: Freight transport platoon coordination and departure time scheduling under travel time uncertainty. Transp. Res. Part E: Logist. Transp. Rev. **98**, 1–23 (2017)

21. Zhong, M., Yang, Y., Dessouky, Y., Postolache, O.: Multi-AGV scheduling for conflict-free path planning in automated container terminals. Comput. Ind. Eng. **142**, 106371 (2020)
22. Zhong, Z., Lee, J., Zhao, L.: Multiobjective optimization framework for cooperative adaptive cruise control vehicles in the automated vehicle platooning environment. Transp. Res. Rec. **2625**(1), 32–42 (2017)

Dynamic Pricing for User-Based Rebalancing in Free-Floating Vehicle Sharing: A Real-World Case

Nout Neijmeijer[1], Frederik Schulte[1(✉)], Kevin Tierney[2], Henk Polinder[1], and Rudy R. Negenborn[1]

[1] Department of Maritime and Transport Technology,
Delft University of Technology, Mekelweg 2, 2628 CD Delft, The Netherlands
N.Neijmeijer@felyx.nl,
{F.Schulte,H.Polinder,R.R.Negenborn}@tudelft.nl
[2] Faculty of Business Administration and Economics,
Bielefeld University, Universitätsstraße 25, 33615 Bielefeld, Germany
Kevin.Tierney@uni-bielefeld.de

Abstract. Dynamic pricing can be used for better fleet distribution in free-floating vehicle sharing (FFVS), and thus increase utilization and revenue for the provider by reducing supply-demand asymmetry. Supply-demand asymmetry refers to the existence of an undersupply of vehicles at some locations at the same time as underutilization of vehicles at other locations. We propose to use dynamic pricing as an instrument to incentivize users to rebalance these vehicles from low demand locations to high demand locations. Despite significant research in rebalancing vehicle sharing, the literature so far lacks experimental results on dynamic pricing in free-floating vehicle sharing. We propose to use an algorithm that minimizes the differences in the idle time of vehicles. The algorithm is tested in a real-life experiment that was conducted in cooperation with an FFVS provider. The results of the experiment are not statistically significant, but they clearly indicate that even slight differences in pricing and a simple algorithm can already influence user-behavior to counter supply-demand asymmetry. Improving the existing algorithm with more experimental research is advised to further uncover the potential of this strategy.

Keywords: Dynamic pricing · User-based rebalancing · Free-floating vehicle sharing · User-based operations · Living lab · Price sensitivity

1 Introduction

In recent years, one-way shared mobility has seen large growth. One-way shared mobility can be subdivided into station-based vehicle sharing (SBVS) and free-floating vehicle sharing (FFVS). The main difference between these two modes

This research is supported by Felyx E-Scooter Sharing.

E. Lalla-Ruiz et al. (Eds.): ICCL 2020, LNCS 12433, pp. 443–456, 2020.
https://doi.org/10.1007/978-3-030-59747-4_29

of vehicle sharing is that SBVS only allows pick-up and drop-off of vehicles at specific locations called stations. This mode of vehicle sharing is mostly present in bicycle sharing (BS) and the stations are often physical existing stations with a limited number of spots available for dropping off vehicles. FFVS allows the drop-off of vehicles at any locations inside a certain geofenced area. The result of this difference is that FFVS offers users more freedom and flexibility. However, balancing the fleet is easier to manage in SBVS. The large growth of one-way shared mobility in recent years is especially visible in FFVS according to a study by the Bundesverband Carsharing [1], a German carsharing organization.

Another recent trend is the usage of small vehicles, called micromobility. The term micromobility generally encompasses vehicles that weigh under 500 kg [9], including (e-)bikes, kick-scooters, and seated scooters (also known as mopeds). The potential market for micromobility has been estimated to make up for about 50% to 60% of all passenger miles traveled [11]. The same estimation concludes that these miles will translate into a potential market of between $330 billion to $500 billion worldwide, of which between $100 billion and $150 billion is in Europe alone, by the year 2030.

The successful adoption of FFVS as a part of an urban transport system requires reliability from the perspective of the user. Reliability can be achieved by ensuring the availability of a vehicle at nearly all times and places of demand. From the perspective of the FFVS operator, the availability of vehicles for customers can be increased by increasing the number of vehicles or restricting the service area. But rather than performing large investments by increasing the vehicle fleet or decreasing the number of potential customers by reducing the geofenced area, researchers have suggested a different approach to increase vehicle availability: rebalancing [7,13,16,17,19]. Rebalancing is the act of repositioning vehicles from low-demand to high-demand areas to overcome spatial asymmetry in supply and demand. This supply-demand asymmetry is a common difficulty in FFVS systems. Studies suggest that a successful rebalancing strategy can greatly increase the performance of a vehicle sharing system by increasing availability [17,19] or, in the case of ride-hailing, decreasing customer pick-up time [6,14].

Rebalancing of vehicles can be done by the operator (operator-based rebalancing) or by incentivizing users (user-based rebalancing). Dynamic pricing (DP) can be used to incentivize users to perform user-based rebalancing. Despite success with dynamic pricing to influence customer behavior in a variety of industries, it is still not common practice to apply DP to incentivize user-based rebalancing.

Responding to the current trends that were discussed in the first two paragraphs of this paper, we extend the academic research regarding user-based rebalancing. We investigate what dynamic pricing can do for user-based rebalancing in the upcoming free-floating vehicle sharing market. The rest of this paper will focus on answering the question:

How can dynamic pricing incentivize user-based rebalancing in free-floating vehicle sharing?

To answer this question we will first define what an optimal rebalancing strategy is in free-floating vehicle sharing. This strategy will be translated into a pricing strategy. We will make suggestions on how to evaluate such a pricing strategy, and finally, show how these results translate to other free-floating vehicle sharing platforms.

2   Literature Review

Multiple research articles have proposed relocation strategies for mobility on demand (MoD) systems that can decrease the average walking distance to one of the assets or decrease the average customer waiting time. Research on rebalancing for (autonomous) MoD has already extended to even incorporate different service levels [2] or a combination of parcel and person transport [3]. However, research in vehicle sharing is less advanced. Most of the research on vehicle sharing solves a static version of the rebalancing problem in BS [7,16]. Often this is done with the use of mixed-integer linear programming (MILP).

In the field of DP in mobility, Uber is probably one of the most experienced players. The DP system of Uber is called surge pricing and research into this system shows that it can increase total welfare according to the concept in transport economics [6,8,14]. Although it ought to be noted that maximizing revenue in these ride-hailing systems with dynamic pricing also has its downsides as it has a negative influence on congestion [15,18].

Congestion issues are less important for most forms of micromobility as they do not form traffic jams as easily. Also, the total number of miles driven in a ride-hailing system is higher than that of one-way vehicle sharing caused by vehicle miles traveled to the start point of the customer [12]. Another notable difference between DP in ride-hailing services and DP in one-way vehicle sharing is that DP in ride-hailing also affects the supply side of the demand-supply asymmetry, because the pricing affects the payments of the drivers [10]. Results of research into operator-based rebalancing of ride-hailing services points in different directions suggesting either large improvements even for small fleet sizes [20] or only marginal improvements [23].

A notable attempt on solving the rebalancing problem in one-way vehicle sharing that also considers user-based rebalancing is focused on SBVS [17]. This research finds that the ideal rebalancing strategy combines operator-based rebalancing with user-based rebalancing. A limitation of this research is that it does not consider latent demand, which is the demand that is not visible in the data because there were no vehicles available at a certain place and time, but rather assumes that historical data provides a full picture of demand for the service. Also, the results are only derived by simulation and not by a real-life experiment. This requires some assumptions about human behavior, like full rationality, which do not do justice to the complexity of the real-life problem.

The methods developed in [17] are applied in an experiment in BS [19]. This research extends on [17] with several insights. For example, it is shown that most of the rebalancing actions are done by only a small group of people. Survey-based research also finds that users are in general open to the idea of user-based rebalancing and are willing to comply with different methods of rebalancing [13].

Both [17] and [19] focus on increasing the *service level* although in the latter research it is renamed to *quality of service*. The definition of a *service level* is given as follows:

$$\text{Service level} = \frac{\text{Potential customers} - \text{No-service events}}{\text{Potential customers}}. \tag{1}$$

It is important to note is that latent demand is not taken into account. The no-service events in this metric are determined by assuming that the demand will stay the same independent of the rebalancing. The results of the experiment performed by [19] are also not used to evaluate the effect of rebalancing on the service-level of the SBVS system. To the best of our knowledge, this means that no research so far has provided any insights into the effect of user-based rebalancing in one-way vehicle sharing that are based on experimental results. This is also visible in Table 1, which contains the references used in this research. A general lack of experimental research, as well as a lack of research on user-based rebalancing in FFVS in general, can be concluded from this overview.

Table 1. Analysis of articles about rebalancing in Vehicle sharing showing the different research methods applied to different types of vehicle sharing and whether the research includes dynamic pricing (DP), operator-based rebalancing (OBR) and user-based rebalancing (UBR).

Reference	Type	DP	OBR	UBR	Method
Zhou [23]	Ride-hailing	✓	✓		Simulation
Qiu et al. [18]	Ride-hailing	✓	✓		Simulation
Kroll [15]	Ride-hailing	✓	✓		Simulation
Korolko et al. [14]	Ride-hailing	✓	✓		Simulation
Castillo et al. [6]	Ride-hailing	✓	✓		Simulation
Chemla et al. [7]	SBVS		✓		Simulation
Pal and Zhang [16]	SBVS		✓		Simulation
Spieser et al. [20]	AMoD		✓		Simulation
Wen et al. [22]	AMoD		✓		Simulation
Pfrommer et al. [17]	SBVS	✓	✓	✓	Simulation
Singla et al. [19]	SBVS	✓	✓	✓	Experiment
Herrmann et al. [13]	FFVS	✓		✓	Survey

3   Methodology

3.1   Optimal Rebalancing Method

The methodology of this research was outlined in the last paragraph of the introduction and starts with defining what the ultimate rebalancing strategy is for FFVS. The answer to this question is mainly based on the research done by [17]. The optimal strategy is the one that minimizes the deviation from the optimal distribution of vehicles. [17] use historical origin-destination pairs of rides to determine the departure and arrival rates of every station at different times and days. Based on this they build a simulation in which they attempt to positively affect the *service level* by applying a rebalancing strategy.

Following the lines of academic research so far, we construct a simulation based on historical origin-destination pairs from which we can draw demand patterns for different areas in the service area. We discretize the spatial data by clustering the rides to certain areas and model the system as an SBVS system. The data is divided into week/weekend days and one day is sliced into time frames of 1 h. The simulation draws random samples from the data based on the different data sets and simulates these rides. However, the simulation does not provide realistic results especially in areas in which the number of rides taken is relatively low. A reason is that origin-destination pairs ignore the latent demand of the system and, thus, areas that lack supply in particular do not give a good representation of the demand. For this reason, we refrain from using origin-destination pairs of rides to determine the demand. We propose to use a different metric instead as a basis for the rebalancing strategy: idle time.

Idle time is the amount of time between two consecutive rentals of one vehicle that is available for rent. Hours that are outside of the FFVS opening hours or the time during which a vehicle's battery has been empty are not part of the idle time of a vehicle. We assume that the preferred rebalancing strategy, from the customers' point of view, balances the vehicles such that the idle time of vehicles is equal across the whole service area. In this scenario the utilization of vehicles is equal across the service area, which is good for the service level. However, it does not take into account differences in ride length, and for that reason, might slightly differ from the most profitable scenario from the operators point of view. Rebalancing actions that have a positive utility are those for which the expected idle time of the vehicle is lower in the targeted area compared to the vehicles current area.

These definitions lead to a slightly altered version of the minimization problem that was set up in [17]. We use a as an index for a certain area that is part of the total service area A. The parameter v is an index of a certain vehicle. The idle time that a vehicle has spent in a certain area is $\theta_{a,v}$. The average idle time of an area is $I_a = \frac{1}{V}\sum_{v \in V}\theta_{a,v}$, where V is the complete set of idle times measured during a certain time interval. The expected idle time is derived from historical data and denoted with $\tilde{I}$, and the average idle time of the complete area $\bar{I}$. The average profit made per vehicle per unit time is denoted with R and the monetary incentive for a certain ride is p. In the experiment, the monetary incentive p is a reduction of the per minute price. Multiple different levels of reduction are tested in the experiment. The difference in idle time resulting from an applied incentive p is denoted by $\Delta I(p)$. We can define the following optimization problem:

$$\min_{p(v)} \quad \sum_{a \in A} \sum_{v \in V_a} (I_{a,v} - \overline{I})^2 + \alpha \sum_{a \in A} \sum_{v \in V_a} p_{a,v} \tag{2a}$$

$$\text{subject to } \Delta I_a(p)R - p > 0 \qquad\qquad \forall\ a \in A \tag{2b}$$

$$\Delta I_a(p) < \tilde{I}_a \qquad\qquad \forall\ a \in A \tag{2c}$$

The objective function (2a) minimizes the differences between the real scenario and the optimal scenario (in which idle time is equal across the whole service area) and the total sum of the costs of the incentives given. The factor α can be set in accordance with the importance of suppressing the costs of incentive payout. Constraints (2b) ensure that the result of a certain incentive payout has a positive influence on the operator's profit. Constraints (2c) take into account the upper limit of a decrease in idle time by an incentive p.

The minimization problem is used to determine the optimal pricing strategy. This pricing strategy is based on a set of two different predictions. Figure 1 shows how these two predictions influence the pricing strategy. Both of the predictions are drawn from historical data. The effect of pricing on the idle time can however

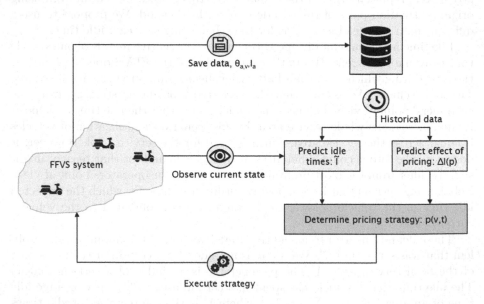

Fig. 1. The pricing strategy is determined based on historical data and the current state of the system as is shown in this block diagram. The current state consists of the amount of the current idle times of the vehicles in the system. The current fill levels should be taken into account when determining the expected idle times.

only be determined by experiment. This will be pointed out later in this paper as well.

The effect on the *service level* can be determined by looking at the average number rides in a certain time frame and the difference in idle time that was the result of applying certain incentives. If n_{rides} is the total number of rides during a certain time frame then the change in *service level* is given by the following:

$$\Delta \text{Service level}(p) = \sum_{a \in A} \Delta I_a(p) \frac{1}{\overline{I}_A \cdot n_{rides}}. \tag{3}$$

3.2   User-Based Rebalancing

When considering the payout of incentives for certain rebalancing actions it is important to keep in mind that it might be difficult to find users to perform these actions. A rebalancing action as described in the section above is called a *complete rebalancing* in this research. There are, however, also other possible ways to rebalance in FFVS. We distinguish between three different methods of rebalancing, as listed below. The difference between complete rebalancing and pushed rebalancing is made visible in Fig. 2.

1. **Complete rebalancing** incentivizes a complete rebalancing action. In this case, a customer is presented with an incentive to reposition a particular vehicle to a certain location. It is, in fact, similar to what an operator would do when rebalancing vehicles. It can be difficult, however, to find customers that are willing to reposition a vehicle when both the origin and destination of the trip are fixed. This requires the incentive to be high.
2. **Pulled rebalancing** incentivizes users to end a ride at a certain position. This is done by [19] and also considered by [17] when an extra reward is given for leaving a bike at a (nearly) empty bike station. Giving out these incentives requires the definition of high-demand areas and high-demand times. This information then needs to be communicated to the end-user such that they can be incentivized to leave behind a vehicle in such a position. Such incentives are determined and provided by [19] during the rental period of the client, taking into account also the current number of bikes at a certain bike-sharing station.
3. **Pushed rebalancing** incentivizes users to start a ride with a certain vehicle without specifying where the vehicle should travel to. This is also performed by other free-floating car-sharing and e-scooter-sharing companies. In this case, the operator incentivizes the use of certain vehicles. Often these vehicles are positioned in a low-demand area or have not been used for a certain amount of time. When this type of incentive reduces the idle time of the vehicle the vehicle can bring in extra revenue and create extra availability. This type of rebalancing assumes that on average many vehicles departing from low-demand areas will end up in areas in which the demand is higher.

Also important to note is that the values of $\Delta I(p)$ can only be determined by modeling user behavior or by experimental research. The lack of experimental research was already indicated in Sect. 2. Experimental research can uncover better insights into how effective a certain pricing strategy is. In the rest of this research, we set up a living lab that is based on *pushed rebalancing*.

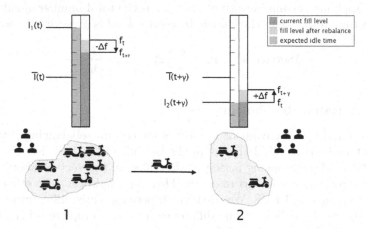

(a) In complete rebalancing, both the starting and ending position of a rebalancing move are known.

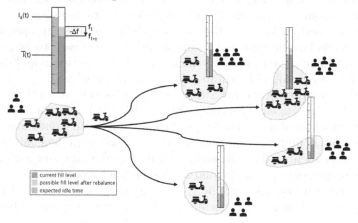

(b) Pushed rebalancing is performed from an area that is over-supplied. The vehicle will most likely end up in another area in which it is needed more.

Fig. 2. Schematic representation of different modes of rebalancing. Where f_t is the fill level of a certain are at time t, γ is the time required for a rebalancing move and Δf is the change in fill level resulting from the rebalancing.

4 Experiment in a Living Lab Setting

4.1 Setting up the Living Lab

The key principles of a living lab are *continuity, openness, realism, empowerment of users* and *spontaneity*, according to [21]. Examples of setting up a living lab are given by [4] and [5]. We take the most important lessons of these works into account to set up an effective living lab experiment for our use case. A notable difference between how the living lab has been set up in this research and that of [5] is that the concepts in our research are developed with very little co-creation (i.e., service design process with input from customers). The development of the concept, however, was the result of research into different possibilities that were all viewed from the customer's perspective. After this, the concepts are evaluated in a living lab setting. The main focus of this living lab experiment is to make the experiment very realistic and evaluate the concept in a user-centered way. The lessons learned from the experiment described below should take into account co-creation for the development of follow-up concepts. These co-creation characteristics of a living lab are not emphasized in this paper and should be set up as a continuation of this research.

To ensure *continuity* and *realism* we implement our pricing system in an existing FFVS system without making any changes to the service area, fleet size, or users. The pilot is communicated to the users only as it begins. Qualitative feedback is asked for directly, adhering to the *spontaneity* principle. The pricing system is visible and available to use for all users.

In the service area, we define a set of *low demand* areas L for which $L \subset A$ and $\bar{I}_{a,t} > \tilde{I}_t + \gamma$ where gamma is a factor that controls the size of the low demand area. In addition, we define a set of *control* areas C that have an idle time that is close to the average of the service area for which $C \cup L \subset A$ and $C \cap L = 0$. Both in L and C for a certain period, a set of vehicles is discounted. This reduction in price will be the same for different vehicles at the same moment in time, so there is only one level of discount tested at a certain moment in time. The experiment runs for a couple of weeks and tests multiple levels of discount.

As indicated in Fig. 3, the experiment bases its pricing strategy on a prediction of the idle time: $\tilde{I}$. The strategy that is executed only discounts a subset of the vehicles and does not discount the other vehicles. Both of the measurements I (of discounted and not discounted vehicles) are compared with the prediction made beforehand. Their relative differences can be calculated to show the effect of a price discount under the same external influences, $\frac{I - \tilde{I}}{\tilde{I}}$. The difference between discounted and not discounted vehicles will provide insight in the value $\Delta I(p)$.

A fixed incentive is applied to vehicles in these areas. After a certain time period the incentive is changed and the effects on the idle time of the vehicles for different incentives and different areas is compared. In total, two different incentives are applied: p_1, a 10% reduction in price and p_2, a 15% reduction in price. In both of the areas only 50% of the vehicles are discounted. The vehicles

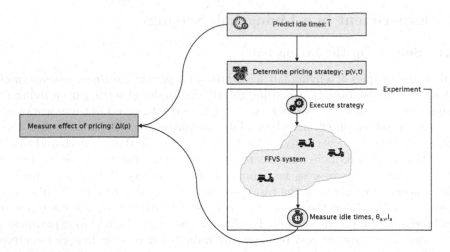

Fig. 3. The expected idle times are used to determine a pricing strategy. The execution of this strategy will then result in idle times which can be compared with the expected idle times. The comparison of the resulting values and expected values will show the effectiveness of a strategy.

Fig. 4. Screenshot of FFVS application, showing how discounted vehicles are made visible in the application.

that are discounted are made visible in the application with a different icon. This is shown in Fig. 4. The difference between the results of the discounted and not discounted vehicles are discussed in the next section.

Table 2. Averages of idle time of the living lab experiment. $\frac{I_a - \bar{I}_a}{\bar{I}_a}$ is the difference between the expected value of idle time and the average of the measured idle time samples as indicated in Fig. 3. The different values for discounted and not discounted vehicles lead to the measured impact of incentive $\Delta I(p)$.

		Not discounted		Discounted		Difference	
		$\frac{I_a - \bar{I}_a}{\bar{I}_a}$	n	$\frac{I_a - \bar{I}_a}{\bar{I}_a}$	n	$\Delta I(p)_a$	n
Low demand	p_1	+26%	658	+0%	676	26%	1,334
	p_2	+15%	542	−15%	634	30%	1,176
	Total	+21%	1,200	−6%	1,310	27%	2,510
Control	p_1	+15%	284	+12%	240	3%	524
	p_2	+6%	207	−12%	241	18%	448
	Total	+11%	491	+0%	481	11%	972

4.2 Results of the Living Lab

During the pilot period, we measured the idle times of different vehicles that were discounted and not discounted. The differences between these results and the value that was expected are noted in Table 2. This table measures the resulting idle times for two different incentives: p_1 and p_2 for which $p_2 > p_1$. The values in the table are the average idle time values of both the group of not discounted vehicles and discounted vehicles. From the results in Table 2, we draw several conclusions.

The first clear effect that is visible is the difference in the effect of different incentives: $\Delta I(p)$ is larger for p_2 than for p_1 in both the low demand areas and the control areas. This means that higher incentives have a larger effect. The second effect we note is that the values of $\Delta I(p)$ are higher in the low demand areas than they are in the control areas. This can easily be seen by comparing the total values for both of these areas. This means that the pricing has a larger effect in areas with higher idle times. A reason for this could be that users need a certain time before the discount is noticed, which will result in a relatively larger effect for longer idle times.

Another clear result in Table 2 is that the expected values of the idle times are relatively low. The measured values for idle times I are therefore relatively high in comparison. This leads to very positive values of $\frac{I_a - \bar{I}_a}{\bar{I}_a}$, whereas a negative value would have been expected. This is investigated closer later in this section. The expected value of the idle times is, however, not of importance when looking at the difference between the discounted and not discounted vehicles, so the above conclusions still hold.

Finally, the data of the living lab experiment shows that for different areas the effects vary heavily. For example, multiple areas marked as low demand areas show very different results on the effect of pricing $\Delta I(p)$. These differences could be dependent on characteristics of these areas such as the distance to the center of the service area or other characteristics. The total number of measurements n

in some of these areas is, however, relatively low. More measurements are needed in order to get a significant result to make comparisons between these areas as illustrated in Fig. 5. These differences are not visible in Table 2, because this table contains the average of all of the incentives. The average of discounted and not discounted vehicles in the same area does not significantly decline in comparison with the average idle times before the pilot. This is visible in Fig. 6. The average line shows no significant decline and is not stable during the period of the pilot due to significant influences of the weather. Some weeks show an overlap between two different incentives because the shift between these discount levels was made during the week. A reason for the average idle time not declining could be that the offered discounts are too low. The number of vehicles that are discounted is only about 5% of the number of rides. Moreover, the idle times fluctuate heavily with the influence of exogenous variables, which makes it very difficult

	W0 | No discount	W1 | No discount	W2 | No discount	W3 | No discount	W4 | No discount	W5 | No discount	W1 | p1	W2 | p1	W3 | p1	W3 | p2	W4 | p2	W5 | p2	W6 | p2
Low demand 1	1	2	1	19	6	-64	37	42	37	26	32	-6	-13
Low demand 2	-25	12	40	9	3	21	20	22	18	-9	36	27	5
Low demand 3	29	18	3	-67	-6	8	25	36	-28	53	-10	53	13
Low demand 4	7	-16	25	21	44	34	-22	13	34	46	36	48	21
Low demand 5	34	29	32	-35	-73	1	58	73	54	66	21	4	40
Control 1	-4	-2	-3	-19	26	21	12	-20	-10	22	10	15	35
Control 2	6	31	4	-27	2	-20	-28	29	23	-16	27	-9	3
Control 3	27	3	10	36	24	13	36	-16	-46	7	-5	30	-19

Fig. 5. The $\frac{I_a - \bar{I}_a}{\bar{I}_a}$ values for "low demand" and "control" areas applying the strategies, *nodiscount*, *p*1, and *p*2 in different weeks. Putting expected and measured idle times into relation, these values indicate how effective a pricing policy has been in a specific area and week.

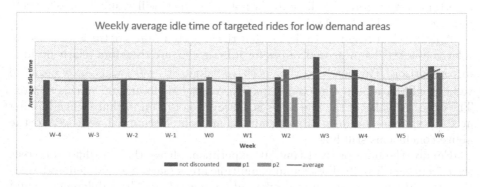

Fig. 6. The weekly averages of idle time for different vehicle groups.

to compare the results during the pilot with the historical data. This suggests that the incentives have probably triggered people to drive certain vehicles, but that these incentives might have been too low or not applied long enough to increase demand.

5 Conclusion

The success of dynamic pricing strategies for user-based operations in vehicle sharing highly depends on the users. Dynamic pricing algorithms, therefore, need to be implemented in real-world systems to fully evaluate their impact. To our knowledge, this is the first work that does this in the case of free-floating vehicle sharing. From the results, we conclude that even small price incentives and basic algorithms can be used to steer the behavior of the user. This means that dynamic pricing can be used as an instrument to incentivize user-based rebalancing in free-floating vehicle sharing. However, the effect on differences between idle times in different areas at the same time has not been significant. To reach more significant results in this regard, larger incentives might be needed or the pricing algorithm needs to be improved. Results for different living labs showed similar trends, but were still different. It could be interesting to investigate how well these results translate to other modalities of free-floating mobility, or how the effects of pricing can be different for different countries. It would also be useful to know what happens when all vehicles in a certain area are discounted. However, the resulting differences in idle time with idle times at other locations in the service area would have to be compared to times before and after applying the pricing algorithm. To make this comparison, more insight into the effect of exogenous variables on this difference would be needed. Lastly, this research does not investigate a price increase or negative incentives. Price increases are also part of dynamic pricing and can lead to an increase in revenue, but will probably not lead to an increase of *service level*.

References

1. Bundesverband carsharing e.v. (bcs) entwicklung der carsharing-varianten (2019). https://carsharing.de/presse/fotos/zahlen-daten/entwicklung-carsharing-varianten. Accessed 11 Nov 2019
2. Beirigo, B., Schulte, F., Negenborn, R.R.: A business class for autonomous mobility-on-demand: modeling service quality constraints in ridesharing systems (2019)
3. Beirigo, B.A., Schulte, F., Negenborn, R.R.: Integrating people and freight transportation using shared autonomous vehicles with compartments. IFAC-PapersOnLine 51(9), 392–397 (2018)
4. Bergvall-Kareborn, B., Hoist, M., Stahlbrost, A.: Concept design with a living lab approach. In: 2009 42nd Hawaii International Conference on System Sciences, pp. 1–10. IEEE (2009)
5. Bergvall-Kåreborn, B., Ståhlbröst, A.: Living lab: an open and citizen-centric approach for innovation. Int. J. Innov. Reg. Dev. 1(4), 356–370 (2009)

6. Castillo, J.C., Knoepfle, D., Weyl, G.: Surge pricing solves the wild goose chase. In: Proceedings of the 2017 ACM Conference on Economics and Computation, pp. 241–242. ACM (2017)
7. Chemla, D., Meunier, F., Calvo, R.W.: Bike sharing systems: solving the static rebalancing problem. Discret. Optim. **10**(2), 120–146 (2013)
8. Chen, M.K., Sheldon, M.: Dynamic pricing in a labor market: surge pricing and flexible work on the Uber platform. In: Ec, p. 455 (2016)
9. Dediu, H.: The micromobility definition (2019). Innovativemobility.org. Accessed 11 Nov 2019
10. Hall, J., Kendrick, C., Nosko, C.: The effects of Uber's surge pricing: a case study. The University of Chicago Booth School of Business (2015)
11. Heineke, K., Kloss, B., Scurtu, D., Weig, F.: Micromobility's 15,000-mile checkup (2019). https://www.mckinsey.com/industries/automotive-and-assembly/our-insights/micromobilitys-15000-mile-checkup. Accessed 11 Nov 2019
12. Henao, A., Marshall, W.E.: The impact of ride-hailing on vehicle miles traveled. Transportation **46**(6), 2173–2194 (2018). https://doi.org/10.1007/s11116-018-9923-2
13. Herrmann, S., Schulte, F., Voß, S.: Increasing acceptance of free-floating car sharing systems using smart relocation strategies: a survey based study of car2go Hamburg. In: González-Ramírez, R.G., Schulte, F., Voß, S., Ceroni Díaz, J.A. (eds.) ICCL 2014. LNCS, vol. 8760, pp. 151–162. Springer, Cham (2014). https://doi.org/10.1007/978-3-319-11421-7_10
14. Korolko, N., Woodard, D., Yan, C., Zhu, H.: Dynamic pricing and matching in ride-hailing platforms. SSRN (2018)
15. Kroll, J.: Dynamic pricing in shared mobility on demand service and its social impacts (2015)
16. Pal, A., Zhang, Y.: Free-floating bike sharing: solving real-life large-scale static rebalancing problems. Transp. Res. Part C: Emerg. Technol. **80**, 92–116 (2017)
17. Pfrommer, J., Warrington, J., Schildbach, G., Morari, M.: Dynamic vehicle redistribution and online price incentives in shared mobility systems. IEEE Trans. Intell. Transp. Syst. **15**(4), 1567–1578 (2014)
18. Qiu, H., Li, R., Zhao, J.: Dynamic pricing in shared mobility on demand service, pp. 1–9 (2018)
19. Singla, A., Santoni, M., Meenen, M., Krause, A.: Incentivizing users for balancing bike sharing systems, pp. 723–729 (2015)
20. Spieser, K., Samaranayake, S., Gruel, W., Frazzoli, E.: Shared-vehicle mobility-on-demand systems: a fleet operator's guide to rebalancing empty vehicles. In: Transportation Research Board 95th Annual Meeting, No. 16-5987. Transportation Research Board (2016)
21. Ståhlbröst, A.: Forming future IT: the living lab way of user involvement. Ph.D. thesis, Luleå tekniska universitet (2008)
22. Wen, J., Zhao, J., Jaillet, P.: Rebalancing shared mobility-on-demand systems: a reinforcement learning approach. In: 2017 IEEE 20th International Conference on Intelligent Transportation Systems (ITSC), pp. 220–225. IEEE (2017)
23. Zhou, S.: Dynamic incentive scheme for rental vehicle fleet management (2011)

Automated and Autonomous Driving in Freight Transport - Opportunities and Limitations

Joachim R. Daduna[✉]

Berlin School of Economics and Law, Badensche Str. 52, 10825 Berlin, Germany
daduna@hwr-berlin.de

Abstract. The development of mobility has always had a considerable influence on economic, social and political structures. Without efficient transport systems, the industrial revolutions of the last centuries would not have been possible or only to a much lesser extent. With the advancing digitalization and the development of automated and autonomous vehicles, new framework conditions are emerging, which are leading to far-reaching changes in the transport sector. In this contribution, the discussions regarding the existing automated and autonomous vehicles in the field of the main freight transport modes as well as possible developments will be presented and considered in the light of future demand structures.

Keywords: Freight transport · Transport modes · Automated and autonomous driving

1 Transport in the Context of Economic Developments

As history has shown, there is a direct connection between the development of economies and the mobility of people and goods available within them. Innovations in the transport sector in connection with a forced expansion of the corresponding transport infrastructure (see [55], pp. 186–188; [19]) were therefore very often associated with disruptive structural changes in the economy and society.

Of crucial importance in the last centuries was the *First Industrial Revolution* (see [31]) between the end of the 18th century and beyond the middle of the 19th century which essentially started from England. This led to far-reaching changes in the economic and settlement structures as well as in the markets due to the transition from a structure dominated by agriculture and handicraft business to an initial industrialization phase. This was based on improvements in the road network, especially through the expansion of turnpike roads in England (see [135], pp. 22–31; [17, 18]), as well as through a substantial expansion of the inland waterway network with the construction of canals (see [19]).

With the *Second Industrial Revolution* (see [32]) the expansion of mass production and an increasing division of labor began. At the same time decentralization and the development of medium-sized companies took place, which was made possible in particular by the establishment of a decentralized energy supply system based on electrical power networks (see [40]). During this period, inland waterway transport almost reached

E. Lalla-Ruiz et al. (Eds.): ICCL 2020, LNCS 12433, pp. 457–475, 2020.
https://doi.org/10.1007/978-3-030-59747-4_30

its greatest network expansion and thus the end phase of its life cycle, and lost its dominating position to freight transport by rail (see [135], pp. 74–86; [55], pp. 186–188; [12]). However, in the middle of the 20th century this transport mode also lost considerable importance and competitiveness, especially due to changing market requirements as well as the development of road transport infrastructure and road freight vehicle technology.

At the beginning of the *Third Industrial Revolution* (see [54]) at the end of the 1960s, the economy profoundly changed and transformed because the developments of electronic data processing. Road freight transport continued to dominate, due to the high density of road networks and the significant flexibility in the execution of transport operations. During this time, however, the first approaches towards an increased use of *Automated Guided Vehicles* (AGV) in the field of intralogistics were already being developed, but due to the lack in capable information technology, they were not or only partially suitable for practical use (see [136], pp. 8–9).

It was only with the far-reaching digitization of processes and data flows that the prerequisites for a *Fourth Industrial Revolution* (Industry 4.0) were available (see [136], pp. 10–11), which is most evident in the technical progress in manufacturing (see [15]) and intralogistics (see [136], pp. 10–11 and pp. 105–138). The developments in the field of automated and autonomous systems will be pushed further, but the question does not arise to what extent the structures of industry will have an influence on future forms of mobility. The question must be different, how and to what extent can possible advances in transport systems affect developments in Industry 4.0 and offer new technical design options.

The terms "automated" and "autonomous" are often not used in a sufficiently differentiated manner (see [119]). Automated driving refers to processes in which the movements of vehicles are remotely controlled from outside, for example by an external (central) control unit. There, all relevant data relating the traffic network and the vehicles moving in it are recorded and evaluated in order to manage all processes without conflicts. When driving autonomously, the control is carried out without external influence by the vehicle's internal system intelligence, which is decisive here. The basis for this is the evaluation of positioning and various environmental data, which are evaluated with the aid of appropriate software tools and then converted internally into control commands.

In the following sections, autonomous and automated driving in the classic freight transport modes are discussed in more detail: road and rail freight transport, transport on inland waterways, as well as sea and air freight transport. Not included are the developments in passenger transport.

2   Ground-Based Freight Transport

Ground-based freight transport has existed since the invention of the wheel, and for thousands of years it was also a major factor in the development of mobility. However, its performance was limited due to the technical conditions. It was only with the motorization of vehicles at the end of the 19th century that the decisive breakthrough came and with it the development into the dominant transport mode. With the unrestricted growth of automotive mobility, a dream of autonomous (or automated) driving was born, which, despite of some attempts in the 1950s, could not (yet) be realized comprehensively because of technical and traffic law reasons.

However, automated vehicle systems have been developed for use in closed environments, such as logistic facilities (see [136], pp. 37–103; [38, 97]), where operational practice had been proven. In recent years, the decisive development steps towards the introduction of autonomous vehicles in public road traffic have been taken (see [26, 121]) and also been implemented.

The main technical basis are the availability of evolved components from the field of *Advanced Driver Assistance Systems* (ADAS) (see [2, 5, 58]). This concerns capable radar and sensor systems for environment recognition and evaluation (see [28, 82, 85, 94, 143, 149]), which allow sufficiently exact satellite-based positioning on the basis of the *Global Navigation Satellite System* (GNSS) in conjunction with digital maps (see [69]) and the expansion of information and communication structures (for example relating to vehicle-to-vehicle (V2V) and vehicle-to-infrastructure (V2I) communication) (see [4, 95, 134, 143]). An essential step in this context is the platooning of trucks in the higher level road network (see [95, 105, 151]).

The possible uses of autonomous vehicles in transport logistics are strongly differentiated, whereby the capacitive vehicle design depends on the application, but in many cases the vehicle size is also influenced by the available road transport infrastructure. The focus is on delivery transport at the local (for instance in the field of city logistics [35, 115] and the regional level, which accounts for the largest share of road freight transport, but also on transport between logistics facilities. In addition, there are increasingly special applications in the off-road sector (see [94]) and in disaster logistics (see [7]).

The economic advantages are considerable, whereby the reduction of personnel costs is the main focus (see [22]) because road freight transport has the least favorable relation between transport costs and transported quantities compared with competing terrestrial transport modes. In addition, there is the elimination of strongly restrictive labor law conditions (limitation of working hours, prescribed breaks and rest periods, etc.), which have a negative influence on the planning and realization of service operations. Another important factor is the reduction of traffic accident-related costs by eliminating the dominant cause, the human error (see [2, 36, 56, 91]). In addition, there are very intensive political and regulatory discussions concerning the traffic law adjustments for of operating autonomous vehicles in public road traffic (see [2, 10]) as well as discussions relating the ethical problems of machine-made decisions in critical dilemma situations (see [56, 83]).

Another, but not uncontroversial, application for ground-based vehicles is the use for deliveries of parcel services with the help of automated or autonomous robots in the form of small vehicles (see [63, 68]). In this concept (see [20]), the robots are positioned by vans to the intended delivery area (if necessary also at different locations) and placed there. The route to the customer is automated or autonomous driven by the robots on the sidewalks, and the transfer point can be flexibly coordinated. The (operational and technical) tests carried out so far have shown the basic feasibility. However, the main problem is the legal framework (for example, with regard to the risk of accidents and liability issues). In addition, there is a lack of acceptance by the population due to safety concerns, also caused by the competing use of sidewalks.

Road freight transport has dominated in the *European Union* (EU) (and other economies) for many years with a share of 50.1% in 2017 (see [43], p. 36). If only terrestrial transport (excluding intra-European sea and air transport) is considered, the share is 73.2%. The main reasons for this large share are the demand structures, the (relatively) dense road network available in most countries and the flexibility of operating processes. With the availability of autonomous vehicles, these advantages will increase even further. If the politically forced decarbonization of road transport leads to a transition to electric drive (see [84, 106]) or fuel cell-based drive (see [96, 131]) in the future, the (ecologically based) comparative competitive advantage of the directly competing transport modes (rail and inland waterway) will be lost.

3 Rail Freight Transport

Rail freight transport was the backbone of industrialization worldwide in the 19th century. This leading role was lost with the developments in road transport vehicles at the beginning of the 20th century. At the same time there was an increase in rail passenger transport, which was given even greater priority over freight transport in terms of infrastructure use. Structural changes in industrial production led to a further decline in demand for rail transport, particularly in the European industrialized countries and this development will intensify in the future due to the accelerated use of renewable energies and the associated decline in bulk freight transport. The transition to automated driving (see [119]) is often associated with the hope of improving the competitive position in the transport market through higher service performance.

There are two main forms of this, which differ in the *Grade of Automation* (GoA) (defined by the *International Association of Public Transport* (UITP)). These are driverless train operations with the possibility of intervention by train conductors (GoA 3) and unattended train operations (GoA 4) (see [133]). The application of autonomous driving, however, is tightly restricted (see [80]).

Due to the restricted vehicle movements in the longitudinal direction caused by the track guidance, there is a significant technical advantage compared to other transport modes, which leads to a higher level of safety. The schedule-based track management excludes the possibility of competing use of the rail network. In addition, the *European Train Control System* (ETCS) provides efficient operational control and monitoring procedures which form the prerequisites for the transition to automated (and technically regulated) operation, as is currently shown by many implementations in the field of public rail passenger transport (see [119, 148]).

Achievable advantages for automated driving in rail freight traffic are (see [133, 139]) a better utilization of the available network capacity, an increase in the quality of service provision (timetable stability, punctuality, energy savings, noise reduction, wear reduction) as well as a significant cost reduction, especially in human resources (see [130]).

However, it must be taken into account that the current state of development of control and safety technology in the various network areas (regional, national, international) varies, also in Europe (see [119, 133]). The varied structure in freight transport, the lack of uniform vehicle standards at international level and the divergent national regulatory and legal framework conditions pose considerable problems with regard to the consistent use of ETCS.

However, in order to achieve a high market penetration of automated driving, the vehicles used must have suitable technical equipment (*Automatic Train Control - Onboard* (ATO-OB)) to be able to communicate with the track infrastructure systems (*Automatic Train Control - Trackside* (ATO-TS)) and the existing control centers (see [148]). The technical basis for communication at the various levels is (still) the *Global System for Mobile Communications-Rail* (GSM-R) based on G2 mobile radio technology. Within the (original) ETCS architecture, the recording of current train positions in the rail network is based on an odometrical procedure (see [13]). Further developments in the field of positioning include the integration of the *Global Navigation Satellite System* (GNSS) (see [13, 90]), including virtual balises to simplify the process and to reduce costs.

Because of the currently available vehicle systems and control technology, a next step with the transition to autonomous driving in the entire rail traffic will not be realizable within the next decade. The main restrictions are the limited range of the sensors for detecting the surroundings and (for non-straight routes) also for the radar systems, which are necessary to ensure sufficient braking distances, even at high speeds of passenger trains (see [120]). Restricting parts of the rail networks to freight trains with reduced safety requirements (see [114]) would require a segregation of the network, which is neither politically enforceable nor economically useful.

However, there are also specific applications in rail freight transport in which the transition to autonomous driving is possible and useful. For example, there are considerations to make this transport mode more flexible on the basis of the CargoMover, a freight wagon with its own drive that exists since 2002 (see [51, 119]). The aim was to make shunting operations in single wagonload transport more efficient and economical and also to operate the last leg of the trip from a marshalling yard to the customer's location in autonomous operation and back again (see [119]).

Another concept was a virtual coupling of autonomously driving units to quasi-trains in order to increase network utilization (see [44]) (analogous to the platooning in road freight transport, see Sect. 2). For example, in the Flex Cargo Rail project (see [119]), the aim was to serve customers via sidings without additional transshipment operations, whereby the individual units were to be discharged autonomously controlled and later reinserted into another quasi-train. However, for various reasons this concept has not yet been implemented. An essential weak point is that the drive and the load unit form a single vehicle, that means, it is a closed system in which wagons from conventional long-distance freight trains cannot be integrated or only with significant difficulties. The question therefore is whether a concept with smaller automated or semi-autonomous two-way locomotives maybe a more flexible and therefore better solution.

Another possibility is autonomous driving in defined networks, in which the transport operations cannot be planned or only to a limited extent. Examples of this are the autonomous control of locomotives within marshalling yards and harbor and industrial rail yards (see [53, 80, 119]). In the Bremerhaven harbor rail yard an implementation has been successful (see [80]). Other projects are currently being tested in Germany (see [119]).

The share of rail freight transport performance in the total freight transport (in t/km) within the EU (referring to 2017) is 11.3% (see [43], p. 36). A look at demand developments in recent years and current forecasts for the freight transport market shows that the politically wanted changes in the modal split in favor of rail freight transport are not very plausible. Extensive network expansions are not a solution for the next few years, as these require high investments and long time periods, due to long lasting planning and approval procedures as well as the construction work. At the same time, the continuity of industrial location structures has been significantly reduced in many regions in recent years, so that if the infrastructure is available, the expected customer demand may no longer exist.

Of essential importance will be the question, what modal shift potential exists, not only in terms of volume but also in terms of spatial distribution, and which share is suitable for rail freight transport. In local and regional transport, which, for example in German accounts to approximately 80% of road freight transport with domestic vehicles (see [23], 57), no relevant shift potential is identifiable due to the short distances and the strongly dislocated distribution. On the other hand, there are opportunities in long-distance transport, because this is where the system advantages of rail transport lie. However, since there are in most cases no direct origin-destination connections in rail networks available, pre-carriage and on-carriage must be included, which is usually done by road. Independent of the question of conventional or automated forms of operation, such bi-modal transport leads to overall cost increases (see [150]) due to the necessary transshipment processes and the higher costs in road freight transport, and thus in turn to advantages in (mono-modal) road freight transport.

4 Freight Transport on Inland Waterways

Inland waterway transport has been carried out on natural waterways for thousands of years and later also on artificial waterways (see [19]). Until the 19th century, the inland barge was also the most efficient terrestrial transport mode due to its capacity advantages over road transport. With the beginning of the railway age, however, its leading role was lost (see [55], pp. 186–188; [137]).

However, inland waterways are still important in the transport of bulk goods, because in terms of the quantities transported in relation to the emissions produced, the most favorable ratios are found when comparing terrestrial transport systems. The main problems of use, especially in Europe, result from the strongly differing capacities within the inland waterway networks (see [137]). This leads to controversial discussion of the adaptation of the waterways to the size of the ships, in order to enable cost-effective and efficient transport processes, or whether the ship sizes are determined by the waterways, with corresponding performance restrictions.

In inland navigation, four main fields of applications can be differentiated: transport on inland waterways (see [78]), also including *River-sea Shipping* (RSS) (see [34, 57]), use for ferry transport (see [50]), possible applications for internal transport within port areas (see [39, 128]) and, with the appropriate infrastructure, also in inner-city transport (see [70, 89, 138]).

Over the last years a development towards autonomous navigation has been observed (see [21]) as well towards automated (remotely controlled) navigation, which can serve as a fallback level if necessary. The basis for a classification in inland navigation are the *Autonomy Levels* (AL 0 to AL 6) defined by Lloyd's Register, where AL 6 describes fully autonomous navigation (see [21, 116]). In addition, there are more detailed classifications (see [116, 117]), however, which have no formally binding basis.

Autonomous (and also automated) navigation requires an appropriate infrastructure as well as vehicle design and equipment adapted to this (see [104, 116]). The technical basis in Europe (see Directive 2005/44/EC) is the system of *River Information Services* (RIS) (see [118]). The objective is to have a (continuously) online collected (and therefore actual) database of inland waterways and barge positions (see [86]) and to communicate this information accordingly (see [87]). This is an important basis for companies in the planning of transport operations and operational control as well as for the institutions responsible for the monitoring and control of traffic flows. System-technical support for navigation is provided by (national) *Digital Navigational Charts* (Inland ENC) and (national) *Electronic Card Display Information Systems* (Inland ECDIS) as well as associated information. An *Automatic Identification System* (AIS) is also included, which enables V2V and V2I communication.

In addition, further tools for information supply can be integrated into the RIS structures (see [59, 93]), such as (static) hydrographic information systems for decision support (see [92]) as well as (dynamic location-dependent) meteorological data for monitoring and control.

The framework conditions outlined above show that the necessary basis for the deployment of autonomous ships are in place. However, the technical and operation-al tests carried out so far under real conditions are not yet sufficient. In addition, there is a lack of uniform legal framework conditions, also within the EU (see [8, 42]), due to complex autonomy structures in the various sailing areas. A realization will most likely only be possible in restricted areas, such as within ports and urban areas as well as for ferry connections (see [132]). On the other hand, a use on inland waterways by autonomous barges may lead to discussions, as in many sections there is a competing use by recreational water sports. As these boats are usually not integrated into the RIS structures, safety problems may arise and possibly also the question of legal responsibility (see [142]).

When the safety issues and legal framework have been clarified, the use of autonomous (or automated) inland navigation barges could be a basis for improving the market position. Despite the ecological advantages of inland navigation, which can be further enhanced by appropriate drives, for example *Liquid Natural Gas* (LNG), its share in the modal split within the EU is comparatively small, only 3.9% in 2017 (see [43], p. 36). The reasons for this are, relating to situation within the EU, the sometimes very different geographical structures. In addition, as in rail freight transport, there will be strong structural changes in the demand for bulk transport, which will have a negative impact on inland waterway transport.

5 Sea Freight Transport

Since its early beginnings until the 20th century, sea freight transport was the only possibility to carry out intercontinental transport on a larger scale and thus the basis for the first steps to an economic globalization. This development was further intensified with the rise of steam navigation. At present (based on figures from 2015), ocean shipping has a share of about 70% in world trade (see [1]).

However, with the expected structural changes in world trade, a significant decline in sea transport (relative to 2050) is expected (see [49]). This will have a significant negative impact on the current main container traffic routes (USA/Europe and Europe/East-Asia) and the adjacent ports. In addition, bulk good transport will also be affected, because the demand will fall dramatically as a result of the decarbonization of the energy and transport sectors.

Based on various considerations, the development of technical concepts for autonomously operating vessels was started several years ago. The possible applications are broad, ranging from deep-sea cargo vessels (see [45, 65]), to ocean-going freighters in connection with feeder vessels (see [3, 64]), cargo vessels in *Short Sea Shipping* (SSS) (see [52, 99]), *roll-on/roll-off* (RoRo) vessels and sea-going ferries (see [29, 79]) up to smaller ships for various forms of use in coastal zones (see [41, 81]). In connection with these developments, a classification by Lloyd's Register with *Autonomy Levels* (AL 0 to AL 6) was established, whereby AL 6 represents the final stage of the developments (see [116]).

With the project *Maritime Unmanned Navigation through Intelligence in Networks* (MUNIN) (see [24] p. 14), essential basics for the development and deployment of autonomously operating ships were evaluated. Core topics were communication and information, ship operations and coastal services. Similar goals were pursued with the *ReVolt* project (see [111]) for applications in the SSS.

The main problem is the support of e-navigation with regard to stationary (see [41, 129]) and moving objects (see [107]). Only with sufficient performance of the technical systems with regard to accuracy and actuality of the collected data the necessary conditions for autonomous navigation can be ensured. In addition, the safety level can be increased by including *Shore Control Centers* (see [24, 110]). These can, for example, be used in critical coastal zones and port areas.

Efforts are focused on a significant reduction of human-caused errors (which have a share, based on different sources, between 60% and 94%) (see [21, 109, 146]) as well as of personnel costs in conventional operation (with a share between 30% and 44%) (see [146]). With regard to economic efficiency, however, the additional costs for the necessary technical equipment must also be taken into account. In this context, the question also arises which autonomy level should actually be realized (see [77, 99]), not only from a cost perspective but also with regard to operational requirements.

A fundamental problem will also arise in future in maritime transport, the simultaneous use of shipping areas by conventionally operating vessels and autonomously or automatically operated vessels (see [108]). The key point here are the *International Regulations for Preventing Collisions at Sea* (COLREGS) of the *International Maritime Organization* (IMO), which provide a global framework for maritime traffic rules (see

[110, 147]). Here, uniform and clearly defined guidelines are absolutely essential, also with regard to the question of legal responsibility (see [142]).

An interesting development is the integration of autonomously operated vessels into SSS concepts to increase the share of maritime transport and to enhance the efficiency. This is based on possible modal shift effects to the disadvantage of road freight transport (see [27, 113, 141]). A similar effect (see [3]) can be achieved if a number of ports in a region are to be served by a larger vessel, whereby the required running time increases with the number of port calls. The traditional approach in such cases is to serve only a few ports and to distribute the cargo by terrestrial transport modes in the hinterland. A reasonable alternative in this case could be the transshipment at sea with the use of autonomous or automated feeder vessels, whereby (also smaller) ports can be served directly.

6 Air Freight Transport

Commercial transport by aircraft is the youngest transport mode in the mobility market with a history of just over a hundred years. The actual beginning was a postal flight in India from Allahabad to Naini in 1911 (see [123], p. 14). Due to capacity restrictions, this market segment was of decisive importance for the development of air freight transport in the early years. Later also transport as belly freight in passenger aircrafts was added. With the development of larger and more powerful aircraft, the range of applications was increasingly expanded. However, the military requirements during the Second World War then played a major role in this development. During this phase, cargo gliders were also used (see [76]), but their civil application was no longer pursued in the post-war period due to the increasing performance of motorized aircraft. The real breakthrough of air freight transport came with the Berlin Airlift between June 1948 and September 1949, which quite clearly demonstrated the potential performance of this transport mode.

In the past decades, air freight transport has increased significantly due to growing globalization and also due to changing requirements for delivery processes. In relation to the total volume transported, however, air freight transport represents a residual volume. Within the EU the share is only about one percent (see [43], p. 36), but the value of goods transported by air freight is more than 10%. The technical and capacitive development of aircraft in the passenger and cargo sector occurred largely parallel, apart from special developments such as the Antonov AN 225 and AN 124 and the Airbus Beluga XL and Boeing 747-400 LCF Dreamlifter, which are specialized in (intra-company) volume transport between production sites. Another special area is the military cargo aircraft segment, as they have specific requirements for use.

The repeatedly discussed step towards *Unmanned Aircraft Systems* (UAS) is not yet far advanced. There are various applications, for example in marine sciences and nature conservation (see [30, 71]), in agriculture (see [62, 66]) and in atmospheric research (see [67]). Developments to date in the field of automated or autonomously operating *Unmanned Cargo Aircrafts* (UCA) are also very manageable (see [60]. Apart from the heavy drones existing in the military sector (see [61]), no marketable aircrafts are yet available, even if announcements are constantly being made (as in the case of the UCA FlyOx).

It is undisputed that a market emerge with corresponding offers, the question will be more the date and also the certification under aviation law. On the other hand, its use in passenger transport is quite unlikely in the foreseeable future, not so much because of technical reasons but due to psychological aversion of potential customers.

The development in the field of *Unmanned Aerial Vehicles* (UAV) looks completely different (see [61, 74, 102]). The currently known areas of application are very large, but transport logistics applications are not the main focus. Examples are remote sensing and geo data collection, also in connection with disaster situations (see [126]), in agriculture (see [72, 75]), forestry (see [100]) as well as in traffic monitoring (see [9]) and in object tracking (see [127]). The support of logistic measures in disaster situations by UAVs in the establishment of humanitarian supply chains (see [7]) is another field of application.

Discussions on logistics applications focus on the use of delivery drones in parcel logistics for "last mile" deliveries. This has been propagated for some years, and is often seen as a major step towards more environmentally friendly delivery processes (see [103, 112, 115]). Even if the technical framework conditions are in place, there is considerable debate as to whether broad market penetration can be achieved. Limitations arise in terms of performance parameters (for example due to a very limited capacity and operational range), cost structures, legal framework and security issues. If the performance of UAV increases, this can lead to changes relating to aviation laws and possibly to further restrictions on their use.

It is rather unlikely that a cost-covering price can be established for the use of UAV in parcel deliveries. Marketing considerations are likely to be at the forefront here. This does not mean, however, that in certain situations such transport will make no sense. In critical situations, applications to supply temporarily hard-to-reach islands in coastal regions (e.g. DHL Paketcopter 2) and within inaccessible mountain areas (e.g. DHL Paketcopter 3) can be important.

Another application can be (see [25]) the connection of truck transports on the last delivery step with drones if the road infrastructure does not allow direct access to the customer. Within the framework of autonomous flights to customer locations, however, the drones must have the technical capabilities for appropriate landing procedures (see [73, 98, 124]). A corresponding approach can also be implemented in connection with inland waterways.

The most important problems in the use of UCA and UAV are in the field of aviation law and public acceptance (see [6, 101, 112]). In some cases, there exist extended no-fly zones and overflight bans of facilities with public safety relevance, which considerably restrict the possibilities for UCA and UAV movements. The extent of the expected increase in drone movements also raises the question of ensuring adequate airspace control. Ultimately, there must be area-wide surveillance, also in airspace close to the ground to ensure the necessary safety there as well. In addition, potential threats from terrorist activities require further considerable regulations.

Possible applications in the field of UAV are very extensive as well as complex. This also applies to the field of logistic applications, even if the expectations discussed so far are overestimated, especially in parcel logistics. Ultimately, the question of long-term profitability will be decisive. Other areas are also not undisputed, such as the possibilities for military applications (see [14, 61, 122]), although some of these discussions are mostly on a rather abstract level.

7   Outlook and Further Developments

The use of automated and autonomously driven vehicles in transport logistics will increase with further technical developments. However, it will have to be considered in a differentiated way with regard to the various transport modes. A major reason for this is the changing structure of the worldwide mobility requirements in the coming years. Considerable effects will result from the unilateralist tendencies with a distinct orientation towards national interests that increasingly occur in economic policy. This is also associated with a de-globalization (see [145]), which is connected with the formation of regional economic blocks. Thus, the worldwide division of labor with its global supply chains as it was common practice up to now, is already showing clear changes. For example an increase of re-shoring (see [144]), which will lead to less (international) freight transport. The experience from the Covid-19 pandemic will intensify these developments, as securing supply of critical goods cannot be guaranteed within the framework of current logistics structures.

Added to this are the disruptive changes in industrial manufacturing and logistics caused by *Additive Manufacturing* (AM) (see [11, 47]). Key issues are decentralization in different manufacturing areas, on-demand and customer-oriented manufacturing with a decrease in transport and warehousing, and the first steps towards a re-industrialization of urban areas. This results in demands for goods transport, which are characterized by low order volumes, largely shorter distances, direct customer deliveries and high flexibility.

In this context, the dominance of road haulage will continue to increase by using (especially emission free) autonomous vehicles with very flexible operating options and favorable cost structures. The demand for (automated) rail freight transport and (autonomous or automated) freight transport on inland waterways will remain comparatively low, as there is a lack of sufficient demand potential, apart from non-time-critical long-distance transport (see [33]). Sea freight transport will decline overall (see [49]), but within the framework of the SSS there is potential demand for the use of autonomous or automated ships (see [3]). The extent to which UCA and UAV can establish themselves in the air freight sector cannot be estimated at present. Critical points are the load capacity and the cost structure as well as the necessary technical and legal integration into existing air traffic management, especially in the context of safety requirements.

In addition, two fundamental questions must be considered. One is the acceptance of *autonomous* vehicles with regard to their use (see [16, 46]), especially in road traffic where public space is shared with manually operated vehicles. *Automated* trains, such as those used in public transport (see [119, 148]) do not pose a problem in this respect, as they have an operations control center for monitoring and control, from which intervention can be made if necessary. However, driverless operations are also being discussed from a labor market perspective, since autonomous or automated operation imply considerable job losses (see [22, 48]). Furthermore, the question of cyber security arises in all transport modes (see [37, 88, 125, 140]). Security and safety are of vitally importance in respect of the technical side, in particular how to prevent unauthorized external attacks by third parties on the control systems, as well as how to solve the legal problems.

References

1. Acker, A., Kauppila, J.: How transport demand will change through 2050. In: OECD, International Transport Forum. ITF Transport Outlook 2019, pp. 21–46, OECD Publishing, Paris (2019)
2. Ainsalu, J., et al.: State of the art of automated buses. Sustainablity **10**(9), 3118 (2018)
3. Akbar, A., Aasen, A.K., Msakni, M.K., Fagerholt, K., Lindstad, E., Meisel, F.: An economic analysis of introducing autonomous ships in a short-sea liner shipping network. Int. Trans. Oper. Res. (2020, in Press)
4. Arena, F., Pau, G.: An overview of vehicular communications. Future Internet **11**, 27 (2019)
5. Arnold, E., Al-Jarrah, O.Y., Dianati, M., Fallah, S., Oxtoby, D., Mouzakitis, A.: A survey on 3D object detection methods for autonomous driving applications. IEEE Trans. Intell. Transp. Syst. **20**(10), 3782–3795 (2019)
6. Aurambout, J.-P., Gkoumas, K., Ciuffo, B.: Last mile delivery by drones - an estimation of viable market potential and access to citizens across European cities. Eur. Transp. Res. Rev. **11**(30), 1–21 (2019)
7. Azmat, M., Kummer, S.: Potential applications of unmanned ground and aerial vehicles to mitigate challenges of transport and logistics-related critical success factors in the humanitarian supply chain. Asian J. Sustain. Soc. Responsib. **5**(1), 1–22 (2020). https://doi.org/10.1186/s41180-020-0033-7
8. Bačkalov, I.: Safety of autonomous inland vessels: an analysis of regulatory barriers in the present technical standards in Europe. Saf. Sci. **128**, 104763 (2020)
9. Barmpounakis, E.N., Vlahogianni, E.I., Golias, J.C.: Unmanned aerial aircraft systems for transportation engineering - current practice and future challenges. Int. J. Transp. Sci. Technol. **5**(3), 111–122 (2016)
10. Bartolini, C., Tettamanti, T., Varga, I.: Critical features of autonomous road transport from the perspective of technological regulation and law. Transp. Res. Procedia **27**, 791–798 (2017)
11. Ben-Ner, A., Siemsen, E.: Decentralization and localization of production - the organizational and economic consequences of additive manufacturing (3d printing). Calif. Manag. Rev. **59**(2), 5–23 (2017)
12. Berger, T.: Railroads and rural industrialization - evidence from a historical policy experiment. Explor. Econ. Hist. **74**, 101277 (2019)
13. Beugin, J., Legrand, C., Marais, J., Berbineau, M., El-Koursi, E.M.: Safety appraisal of GNSS-based localization systems used in train spacing control. IEEE Access **6**, 9898–9916 (2018)
14. Bigman, Y.E., Waytz, A., Alterovitz, R., Gray, K.: Holding robots responsible - the elements of machine morality. Trends Cogn. Sci. **23**(5), 365–368 (2019)
15. Bildstein, A., Seidelmann, J.: Migration zur Industrie- 4.0-Fertigung. In: Vogel-Heuser, B., Bauernhansl, T., ten Hompel, M. (eds.) Handbuch Industrie 4.0 Bd.1. SRT, pp. 227–242. Springer, Heidelberg (2017). https://doi.org/10.1007/978-3-662-45279-0_44
16. Bissell, D., Birtchnell, T., Elliott, A., Hsu, E.L.: Autonomous automobilities - the social impacts of driverless vehicles. Curr. Sociol. **68**(1), 116–134 (2020)
17. Bogart, D.: Turnpike trusts, infrastructure investment, and the road transportation revolution in eighteenth-century England. J. Econ. Hist. **65**(2), 540–543 (2005)

18. Bogart, D.: Turnpike trusts and property income - new evidence on the effects of transport improvements and legislation in eighteenth-century England. Econ. Hist. Rev. **62**(1), 128–152 (2009)

19. Bogart, D.: Inter-modal network externalities and transport development - evidence from roads, canals, and ports during the English industrial revolution. Netw. Spat. Econ. **9**(3), 309–338 (2009)

20. Boysen, N., Schwerdfeger, S., Weidinger, F.: Scheduling last-mile deliveries with truck-based autonomous robots. Eur. J. Oper. Res. **8**(2), 253–265 (2018)

21. Bratić, K., Pavić, I., Vukša, S., Stazić, L.: A review of autonomous and remotely controlled ships in maritime sector. Trans. Marit. Sci. **8**(2), 253–265 (2019)

22. Bucsky, P.: Autonomous vehicles and freight traffic - towards better efficiency of road, rail or urban logistics? Urban Dev. Issues **58**, 41–51 (2018)

23. Bundesamt für Güterverkehr (BAG) (Hrsg.): Gleitende Mittelfristprognose für den Güter - und Personenverkehr - Mittelfristprognose Winter 2019/20. München/Köln (2020)

24. Burmeister, H.C., Bruhn, W., Rødseth, Ø.J., Porathe, T.: Autonomous unmanned merchant vessel and its contribution towards the e-navigation implementation - the MUNIN perspective. Int. J. e-Navig. Marit. Econ. **1**, 1–13 (2014)

25. Carlsson, J.G., Song, S.: Coordinated logistics with a truck and a drone. Manag. Sci. **64**(9), 4052–4069 (2017)

26. Chan, C.-Y.: Advancements, prospects, and impacts of automated driving systems. Int. J. Transp. Sci. Technol. **6**, 208–216 (2017)

27. Chandra, S., Christiansen, M., Fagerholt, K.: Analysing the modal shift from road-based to coastal shipping-based distribution - a case study of outbound automotive logistics in India. Marit. Policy Manag. **47**(2), 273–286 (2020)

28. Chindhe, G., Javali, A., Patil, P., Budhawant, P.: A survey on various location tracking systems. Int. Res. J. Eng. Technol. **5**(12), 671–675 (2018)

29. Christodoulou, A., Raza, Z., Woxenius, J.: The integration of RoRo shipping in sustainable intermodal transport chains - the case of a North European RoRo service. Sustainability **11**(8), 2422 (2019)

30. Colefax, A.P., Butcher, P.A., Kelaher, B.P.: The potential for unmanned aerial vehicles (UAVs) to conduct marine fauna surveys in place of manned aircraft. ICES J. Mar. Sci. **75**(1), 1–8 (2018)

31. Coluccia, D.: The first industrial revolution (c1760–c1870). In: Zanda, G. (ed.) Corporate Management in a Knowledge-Based Economy, pp. 41–51. Palgrave Macmillan, London (2012)

32. Coluccia, D.: The second industrial revolution (late 1800s and early 1900s). In: Zanda, G. (ed.) Corporate Management in a Knowledge-Based Economy, pp. 52–64. Palgrave Macmillan, London (2012)

33. Daduna, J.R.: Verkehrsträgerwettbewerb im Güterverkehr - Eine Scheindiskussion? In: Voss, S., Pahl, J., Schwarze, S. (eds.) Logistik Management, pp. 247–260. Physica, Heidelberg (2009)

34. Daduna, J.R.: Short sea shipping and river-sea shipping in the multi-modal transport of containers. Int. J. Ind. Eng. **20**(1/2), 225–240 (2013)

35. Daduna, J.R.: Developments in city logistics - the path between expectations and reality. In: Paternina-Arboleda, C., Voß, S. (eds.) ICCL 2019. LNCS, vol. 11756, pp. 3–21. Springer, Cham (2019). https://doi.org/10.1007/978-3-030-31140-7_1

36. Daduna, J.R.: Evolution of public transport in rural areas - new technologies and digitization. In: Marcus, A., Rosenzweig, E. (eds.) HCII 2020. LNCS, vol. 12202, pp. 82–99. Springer, Cham (2020). https://doi.org/10.1007/978-3-030-49757-6_6

37. de la Torre, G., Rad, P., Choo, K.K.R.: Driverless vehicle security - challenges and future research opportunities. Future Gener. Comput. Syst. **108**, 1092–1111 (2020)

38. De Ryck, M., Versteyhe, M., Debrouwere, F.: Automated guided vehicle systems, state-of-the-art control algorithms and techniques. J. Manuf. Syst. **54**, 152–173 (2020)
39. Devaraju, A., Chen, L., Negenborn, R.R.: Autonomous surface vessels in ports: applications, technologies and port infrastructures. In: Cerulli, R., Raiconi, A., Voß, S. (eds.) ICCL 2018. LNCS, vol. 11184, pp. 86–105. Springer, Cham (2018). https://doi.org/10.1007/978-3-030-00898-7_6
40. Devine, W.D.: From shafts to wires - historical perspective on electrification. J. Econ. Hist. **43**(2), 347–372 (1983)
41. Dohner, S.M., Pilegard, T.C., Trembanis, A.C.: Coupling traditional and emergent technologies for improved coastal zone mapping. Estuaries Coasts (2020, in Press)
42. Erceg, B.Č.: Inland waterways transport in the European union - flowing or still standing? In: Proceedings of the International Scientific Conference "Social Changes in the Global World", vol. 1, no. 6, pp. 123–137 (2019)
43. European Commission (EC): EU transport in figures. Publications Office of the EU, Luxembourgh (2019)
44. Fantechi, A.: Connected or autonomous trains? In: Collart-Dutilleul, S., Lecomte, T., Romanovsky, A. (eds.) RSSRail 2019. LNCS, vol. 11495, pp. 3–19. Springer, Cham (2019). https://doi.org/10.1007/978-3-030-18744-6_1
45. Felski, A., Zwolak, K.: The ocean-going autonomous ship - challenges and threats. J. Mar. Sci. Eng. **8**(1), 41 (2020)
46. Fraedrich, E., Lenz, B.: Societal and individual acceptance of autonomous driving. In: Maurer, M., Gerdes, J.C., Lenz, B., Winner, H. (eds.) Autonomous Driving, pp. 621–640. Springer, Heidelberg (2016). https://doi.org/10.1007/978-3-662-48847-8_29
47. Frandsen, C.S., Nielsen, M.M., Chaudhuri, A., Jayaram, J., Govindan, K.: In search for classification and selection of spare parts suitable for additive manufacturing - a literature review. Int. J. Prod. Res. **58**(4), 970–996 (2020)
48. Frey, C.B., Osborne, M.A.: The future of employment - how susceptible are jobs to computerisation? Technol. Forecast. Soc. Chang. **114**, 254–280 (2017)
49. Furtado, F., Martinez, L.: Disruptions in freight transport. In: OECD/International Transport Forum, ITF Transport Outlook 2019, pp. 153–216, OECD Publishing, Paris (2019)
50. Gagatsi, E., Estrup, T., Halatsis, A.: Exploring the potentials of electrical waterborne transport in Europe - the E-ferry concept. Transp. Res. Procedia **14**, 1571–1580 (2016)
51. Gattuso, D., Cassone, G.C., Lucisano, A., Lucisano, M., Lucisano, F.: Automated rail wagon for new freight transport opportunities. In: IEEE International Conference on Models and Technologies for Intelligent Transportation Systems (MT-ITS), pp. 57–62 (2017)
52. Ghaderi, H.: Autonomous technologies in short sea shipping - trends, feasibility and implications. Transp. Rev. **39**(1), 152–173 (2019)
53. Gleichauf, J., Vollet, J., Pfitzner, C., Koch, P., May, S.: Sensor fusion approach for an autonomous shunting locomotive. In: Gusikhin, O., Madani, K. (eds.) ICINCO 2017. LNEE, vol. 495, pp. 603–624. Springer, Cham (2020). https://doi.org/10.1007/978-3-030-11292-9_30
54. Greenwood, J.: The third industrial revolution - technology, productivity, and income equality. Econ. Rev. **35**(2), 2–12 (1999)
55. Grübler, A.: The Rise and Fall of Infrastructures. Physica, Heidelberg (1990)
56. Grunwald, A.: Autonomes Fahren – Technikfolgen, Ethik und Risiken. Straßenverkehrsrecht **19**(3), 81–86 (2019)
57. Guo, Z., Le, W., Wu, Y., Wang, W.: A multi-step approach framework for freight forecasting of river-sea direct transport without direct historical data. Sustainability **11**(15), 4252 (2019)
58. Haas, R.E., Bhattacharjee, S., Möller, D.P.F.: Advanced driver assistance systems. In: Akhilesh, K.B., Möller, D.P.F. (eds.) Smart Technologies, pp. 345–371. Springer, Singapore (2020). https://doi.org/10.1007/978-981-13-7139-4_27

59. Hammedi, W., Ramirez-Martinez, M., Brunet, P., Senouci, S.M., Messous, M.A.: Deep learning-based real-time object detection in inland navigation. In: IEEE Global Communications Conference (GLOBECOM), pp. 1–6 (2019)

60. Hardeman, A.B.: Sustainable alternative air transport technologies. In: Walker, T., Bergantino, A.S., Sprung-Much, N., Loiacono, L. (eds.) Sustainable Aviation, pp. 277–306, Springer, Cham (2020). https://doi.org/10.1007/978-3-030-28661-3_14

61. Hassanalian, M., Abdelkefi, A.: Classifications, applications, and design challenges of drones - a review. Prog. Aerosp. Sci. **91**, 99–131 (2017)

62. Hassler, S.C., Baysal-Gurel, F.: Unmanned aircraft system (UAS) technology and applications in agriculture. Agronomy **9**(10), 618 (2019)

63. Hoffmann, T., Prause, G.: On the regulatory framework for last-mile delivery robots. Machines **6**(3), 33 (2018)

64. Holm, M.B., Medbøen, C.A.B., Fagerholt, K., Schütz, P.: Shortsea liner network design with transhipments at sea - a case study from Western Norway. Flex. Serv. Manuf. J. **31**(3), 598–619 (2019)

65. Hoog, T., Ghosh, S.: Autonomous merchant vessels: examination of factors that impact the effective implementation of unmanned ships. Aust. J. Marit. Ocean Aff. **8**(3), 206–222 (2016)

66. Hunt Jr., E.R., Daughtry, C.S.T.: What good are unmanned aircraft systems for agricultural remote sensing and precision agriculture? Int. J. Remote Sens. **39**(15–16), 5345–5376 (2018)

67. Jacob, J.D., Chilson, P.B., Houston, A.L., Smith, S.W.: Considerations for atmospheric measurements with small unmanned aircraft systems. Atmosphere **9**(7), 252 (2018)

68. Jennings, D., Figliozzi, M.A.: A study of sidewalk autonomous delivery robots and their potential impacts on freight efficiency and travel. Transp. Res. Rec. **2673**(6), 317–326 (2019)

69. Jo, K., Kim, C., Sunwoo, M.: Simultaneous localization and map change update for the high definition map-based autonomous driving car. Sensors **18**(9), 3145 (2018)

70. Johnsen, L., Duarte, F., Ratti, C., Xiaojie, T., Tian, T.: ROBOAT - a fleet of autonomous boats for Amsterdam. Lands. Archit. Front. **7**(2), 100–110 (2019)

71. Johnston, D.W.: Unoccupied aircraft systems in marine science and conservation. Ann. Rev. Mar. Sci. **11**, 439–463 (2019)

72. Ju, C., Son, H.I.: Multiple UAV systems for agricultural applications - control, implementation, and evaluation. Electronics **7**(9), 162 (2018)

73. Kaljahi, M.A., et al.: An automatic zone detection system for safe landing of UAVs. Expert Syst. Appl. **122**, 319–333 (2019)

74. Kardasz, P., Doskocz, J., Hejduk, M., Wiejkut, P., Zarzycki, H.: Drones and possibilities of their using. J. Civ. Environ. Eng. **6**(3), 1–7 (2016)

75. Kim, J., Kim, S., Ju, C., Son, H.I.: Unmanned aerial vehicles in agriculture - a review of perspective of platform, control, and applications. IEEE Access **7**, 105100–105115 (2019)

76. Klemin, A.: Motorless flight. Sci. Am. **174**(1), 17–19 (1946)

77. Kobyliński, L.: Smart ships - autonomous or remote controlled. Sci. J. Marit. Univ. Szczecin **53**(125), 28–34 (2018)

78. Konings, R., Wiegmans, B.: Inland waterway transport - an overview. In: Wiegmans, B., Konings, R. (eds.) Inland Waterway Transport, pp. 1–17. Routledge, New York (2016)

79. Kotowska, I.: The role of ferry and ro-ro shipping in sustainable development of transport. Rev. Econ. Perspect. **15**(1), 35–48 (2015)

80. Krämer, I.: Shunt-E 4.0 - autonomous zero emission shunting processes in port and hinterland railway operations. J. Traffic Transp. Eng. **7**, 157–164 (2019)

81. Kum, B.C., et al.: Monitoring applications for multifunctional unmanned surface vehicles in marine coastal environments. J. Coast. Res. **85**(sp1), 1381–1385 (2018)

82. Kuutti, S., Fallah, S., Katsaros, K., Dianati, M., Mccullough, F., Mouzakitis, A.: A survey of the state-of-the-art localisation techniques and their potentials for autonomous vehicle applications. IEEE Internet Things J. **5**(2), 829–846 (2018)

83. Lenk, M.: Der programmierte Tod? Autonomes Fahren und die strafrechtliche Behandlung dilemmatischer Situationen. Straßenverkehrsrecht **19**(5), 166–171 (2019)

84. Liimatainen, H., van Vliet, O., Aplyn, D.: The potential of electric trucks - an international commodity-level analysis. Appl. Energy **236**, 804–814 (2019)

85. Lim, K.L., Bräunl, T.: A methodological review of visual road recognition procedures for autonomous driving applications. arXiv preprint:1905.01635 (2019)

86. Lisaj, A.: Implementation of e-navigation strategies for RIS centres supporting inland navigation. TransNav – Int. J. Mar. Navig. Saf. Sea Transp. **13**(1), 145–149 (2019)

87. Łubczonek, J.: Geoprocessing of high resolution imageries for shoreline extraction in the process of the production of inland electronic navigational charts. Photogram.-Fernerkundung-Geoinf. **2016**(4), 225–235 (2016)

88. Luo, Q., Cao, Y., Liu, J., Benslimane, A.: Localization and navigation in autonomous driving - threats and countermeasures. IEEE Wirel. Commun. **26**(4), 38–45 (2019)

89. Maes, J., Sys, C., Vanelslander, T.: City logistics by water: good practices and scope for expansion. In: Ocampo-Martinez, C., Negenborn, R.R. (eds.) Transport of Water versus Transport over Water. ORSIS, vol. 58, pp. 413–437. Springer, Cham (2015). https://doi.org/10.1007/978-3-319-16133-4_21

90. Marais, J., Beugin, J., Berbineau, M.: A survey of GNSS-based research and developments for the European railway signaling. IEEE Trans. Intell. Transp. Syst. **10**(18), 2602–2618 (2017)

91. Martínez-Díaz, M., Soriguera, F., Pérez, I.: Autonomous driving - a bird's eye view. IET Intell. Transp. Syst. **13**(4), 563–579 (2019)

92. Meißner, D., Klein, B., Ionita, M.: Development of a monthly to seasonal forecast framework tailored to inland waterway transport in central Europe. Hydrol. Earth Syst. Sci. **21**, 6401–6423 (2017)

93. Miciuła, I., Wojtaszek, H.: Automatic hazard identification information system (AHIIS) for decision support in inland waterway navigation. Procedia Comput. Sci. **159**, 2313–2323 (2019)

94. Milford, M., Anthony, S., Scheirer, W.: Self-driving vehicles - key technical challenges and progress off the road. IEEE Potentials **39**(1), 37–45 (2020)

95. Montanaro, U., et al.: Towards connected autonomous driving - review of use-cases. Veh. Syst. Dyn. **57**(6), 779–814 (2019)

96. Moriarty, P., Honnery, D.: Prospects for hydrogen as a transport fuel. Int. J. Hydrog. Energy **44**(31), 16029–16037 (2019)

97. Moshayedi, A.J., Jinsong, L., Liao, L.: AGV (automated guided vehicle) robot - mission and obstacles in design and performance. J. Simul. Anal. Nov. Technol. Mech. Eng. **12**(4), 5–18 (2019)

98. Mukadam, K., Sinh, A., Karani, R.: Detection of landing areas for unmanned aerial vehicles. In: IEEE International Conference on Computing Communication Control and automation (ICCUBEA), pp. 1–5 (2016)

99. Munim, Z.H.: Autonomous ships - a review, innovative applications and future maritime business models. Supply Chain Forum – Int. J. **20**(4), 266–279 (2019)

100. Näsi, R., et al.: Remote sensing of bark beetle damage in urban forests at individual tree level using a novel hyperspectral camera from UAV and aircraft. Urban For. Urban Green. **30**, 72–83 (2018)

101. Nentwich, M., Horváth, D.M.: The vision of delivery drones. Zeitschrift für Technikfolgenabschätzung Theorie Praxis **27**(2), 46–52 (2018)

102. Otto, A., Agatz, N., Campbell, J., Golden, B., Pesch, E.: Optimization approaches for civil applications of unmanned aerial vehicles (UAVs) or aerial drones - a survey. Networks **72**(4), 411–458 (2018)
103. Park, J., Kim, S., Suh, K.: A comparative analysis of the environmental benefits of drone-based delivery services in urban and rural areas. Sustainability **10**(3), 1–15 (2018)
104. Peeters, G., et al.: An unmanned inland cargo vessel - design, build, and experiments. Ocean Eng. **201**, 107056 (2020)
105. Piacentini, G., Goatin, P., Ferrara, A.: A macroscopic model for platooning in highway traffic. SIAM J. Appl. Math. **80**(1), 639–656 (2020)
106. Piatkowski, P., Puszkiewicz, W.: Electric vehicles - problems or solutions. J. Mech. Energy Eng. **2**(1), 59–66 (2018)
107. Polvara, R., Sharma, S., Wan, J., Manning, A., Sutton, R.: Obstacle avoidance approaches for autonomous navigation of unmanned surface vehicles. J. Navig. **71**(1), 241–256 (2018)
108. Porathe, T.: Maritime autonomous surface ships (MASS) and the COLREGS - do we need quantified rules or is "the ordinary practice of seamen" specific enough? TransNav – Int. J. Mar. Navig. Saf. Sea Transp. **13**(3), 511–517 (2019)
109. Porathe, T., Hoem, Å.S., Fjørtoft, K.E., Rødseth, Ø.J., Johnsen, S.O.: At least as safe as manned shipping? Autonomous shipping, safety and "human error". In: Haugen, S., Barros, A., van Gulijk, C., Kongsvik, T., Vinnem, J.E. (eds.) Safety and Reliability-Safe Societies in a Changing World, pp. 417–425. Taylor & Francis, London (2018)
110. Ramos, M.A., Utne, I.B., Mosleh, A.: Collision avoidance on maritime autonomous surface ships - operators' tasks and human failure events. Saf. Sci. **116**, 33–44 (2019)
111. Ramos, M., Utne, I.B., Vinnem, J.E., Mosleh, A.: Accounting for human failure in autonomous ships operations. In: Haugen, S., Barros, A., van Gulijk, C., Kongsvik, T., Vinnem, J.E. (eds.) Safety and Reliability-Safe Societies in a Changing World, pp. 355–363. Taylor & Francis, London (2018)
112. Rao, B., Gopi, A.G., Maione, R.: The societal impact of commercial drones. Technol. Soc. **45**, 83–90 (2016)
113. Raza, Z., Svanberg, M., Wiegmans, B.: Modal shift from road haulage to short sea shipping - a systematic literature review and research directions. Transp. Rev. **40**(3), 382–406 (2020)
114. Ristić-Durrant, D., Ćirić, I., Simonović, M., Nikolić, V., Leu, A., Brindić, B.: Towards autonomous obstacle detection in freight railway. In: XVII International Scientific-Expert Conference on Railways (2016)
115. Savelsbergh, M., van Woensel, T.: City logistics - challenges and opportunities. Transp. Sci. **50**(2), 99–110 (2016)
116. Schiaretti, M., Chen, L., Negenborn, R.R.: Survey on autonomous surface vessels: Part I - a new detailed definition of autonomy levels. ICCL 2017. LNCS, vol. 10572, pp. 219–233. Springer, Cham (2017). https://doi.org/10.1007/978-3-319-68496-3_15
117. Schiaretti, M., Chen, L., Negenborn, R.R.: Survey on autonomous surface vessels - Part II - categorization of 60 prototypes and future applications. In: Bektas, T., Coniglio, S., Martinez-Sykora, A., Voß, S. (eds.) Computational Logistics - ICCL 2017, pp. 234–252, Springer, Cham (2017). https://doi.org/10.1007/978-3-319-68496-3_16
118. Schilk, G., Seemann, L.: Use of ITS technologies for multimodal transport operations - River Information Services (RIS) transport logistics services. Procedia-Soc. Behav. Sci. **48**, 622–631 (2016)
119. Schindler, C.: Schienenverkehrstechnik 4.0. In: Frenz, W. (ed.) Handbuch Industrie 4.0: Recht, Technik, Gesellschaft, pp. 719–757. Springer, Heidelberg (2020). https://doi.org/10.1007/978-3-662-58474-3_38
120. Schindler, C., Nießen, N., Vallée, D.: Assistierter, automatischer oder autonomer Betrieb - Potentiale für den Schienenverkehr. Eisenbahntechnische Rundschau **66**(4), 32–37 (2017)

121. Schwarting, W., Alonso-Mora, J., Rus, D.: Planning and decision-making for autonomous vehicles. Ann. Rev. Control Robot. Auton. Syst. **1**, 187–210 (2018)
122. Sehrawat, V.: Legal status of drones under LOAC and international law. Penn State J. Law Int. Aff. **5**(1), 164–206 (2017)
123. Shamsudheen, P.V.: Growth and development of civil aviation in India. Thesis, Department of Business Administration Aligarh Muslim University, Aligarh (1982)
124. Silva, M.F., Cerqueira, A.S., Vidal, V.F., Honório, L.M., Santos, M.F., Oliveira, E.J.: Landing area recognition by image applied to an autonomous control landing of VTOL aircraft. In: IEEE International Carpathian Control Conference, pp. 240–245 (2017)
125. Silverajan, B., Ocak, M., Nagel, B.: Cybersecurity attacks and defences for unmanned smart ships. In: IEEE Smart Data, pp. 15–20 (2018)
126. Singh, K.K., Frazier, A.E.: A meta-analysis and review of unmanned aircraft system (UAS) imagery for terrestrial applications. Int. J. Remote Sens. **39**(15–16), 5078–5098 (2018)
127. Smyczyński, P., Starzec, Ł., Granosik, G.: Autonomous drone control system for object tracking - flexible system design with implementation example. In: IEEE International Conference on Methods and Models in Automation and Robotics, pp. 734–738 (2017)
128. Song, X., Jin, J.G., Hu, H.: Planning shuttle vessel operations in large container terminals based on waterside congestion cases. Marit. Policy Manag. (2020, in Press). https://doi.org/10.1080/03088839.2020.1719443
129. Stateczny, A., Kazimierski, W., Burdziakowski, P., Motyl, W., Wisniewska, M.: Shore construction detection by automotive radar for the needs of autonomous surface vehicle navigation. Int. J. Geo-Inf. **8**(2), 80 (2019)
130. Stene, T.M.: Automation of the rail - removing the human factor? In: Haugen, S., Barros, A., van Gulijk, C., Kongsvik, T., Vinnem, J.E. (eds.) Safety and Reliability-Safe Societies in a Changing World, pp. 1947–1955. Taylor & Francis, London (2018)
131. Tang, B., Arat, H.T., Baltacıoğlu, E., Aydin, K.: Overview of the next quarter century vision of hydrogen fuel cell electric vehicles. Int. J. Hydrog. Energy **44**(20), 10120–10128 (2019)
132. Tannum, M.S., Ulvensøen, J.H.: Urban mobility at sea and on waterways in Norway. J. Phys. – Conf. Ser. **1357**(1), 012018 (2019)
133. Tasler, G., Knollmann, V.: The introduction of highly automatic operation - towards fully automatic train operation. Signal. + Datacommun. **110**(6), 6–14 (2018)
134. Tiwari, A., Akhilesh, K.B.: Exploring connected cars. In: Akhilesh, K.B., Möller, D.P.F. (eds.) Smart Technologies, pp. 305–315. Springer, Singapore (2020). https://doi.org/10.1007/978-981-13-7139-4_23
135. Taylor, G.R.: The Transportation Revolution 1815–1860. Rinehart, New York (1951)
136. Ullrich, G. (ed.): Fahrerlose Transportsysteme. Springer, Wiesbaden (2014). https://doi.org/10.1007/978-3-658-27472-6_5
137. van Dorsser, C.: Existing waterway infrastructures and future need. In: Wiegmans, B., Konings, R. (eds.) Inland Waterway Transport, pp. 99–124. Routledge, New York (2016)
138. van Duin, J.H.R., Kortmann, L.J., van de Kamp, M.: Toward sustainable urban distribution using city canals - the case of Amsterdam. In: Taniguchi, E., Thompson, R.G. (eds.) City Logistics, vol. 1, pp. 65–84. Wiley, Hoboken (2018)
139. Venkateswaran, K.G., Nicholson, G.L., Roberts, C., Stone, R.: Impact of automation on the capacity of a mainline railway. In: IEEE International Conference on Intelligent Transportation Systems, pp. 2097–2102 (2015)
140. Vinnem, J.E., Utne, I.B.: Risk from cyberattacks on autonomous ships. In: Haugen, S., Barros, A., van Gulijk, C., Kongsvik, T., Vinnem, J.E. (eds.) Safety and Reliability-Safe Societies in a Changing World, pp. 1485–1492. Taylor & Francis, London (2018)
141. Vierth, I., Sowa, V., Cullinane, K.: Evaluating the external costs of trailer transport - a comparison of sea and road. Marit. Econ. Logist. **21**(1), 61–78 (2019)

142. Vojković, G., Milenković, M.: Autonomous ships and legal authorities of the ship master. Case Stud. Transp. Policy **8**(2), 333–340 (2020)
143. Wang, J., Liu, J., Kato, N.: Networking and communications in autonomous driving - a survey. IEEE Commun. Surv. Tutor. **21**(2), 1243–1274 (2018)
144. Wiesmann, B., Snoei, J.R., Hilletofth, P., Eriksson, D.: Drivers and barriers to reshoring - a literature review on offshoring in reverse. Eur. Bus. Rev. **29**(1), 15–42 (2017)
145. Witt, M.A.: De-globalization - theories, predictions, and opportunities for international business research. J. Int. Bus. Stud. **50**(7), 1053–1077 (2019)
146. Wright, R.G.: Intelligent autonomous ship navigation using multi-sensor modalities. TransNav – Int. J. Mar. Navig. Saf. Sea Transp. **13**(3), 503–510 (2019)
147. Xin, L., Ao, W.: Research on intelligent collision avoidance for unmanned surface vehicle with multi-ship obstacles based on COLREGS. Int. J. Mech. Eng. Robot. Res. **9**(2), 238–242 (2020)
148. Yin, J., Tang, T., Yang, L., Xun, J., Huang, Y., Gao, Z.: Research and development of automatic train operation for railway transportation systems - a survey. Transp. Res. Part C **85**, 548–572 (2017)
149. Zang, S., Ding, M., Smith, D., Tyler, P., Rakotoarivelo, T., Kaafar, M.A.: The impact of adverse weather conditions on autonomous vehicles - how rain, snow, fog, and hail affect the performance of a self-driving car. IEEE Veh. Technol. Mag. **14**(2), 103–111 (2019)
150. Zgonc, B., Tekavčič, M., Jakšič, M.: The impact of distance on mode choice in freight transport. Eur. Transp. Res. Rev. **11**(1), 1–18 (2019)
151. Zhang, L., Chen, F., Ma, X., Pan, X.: Fuel economy in truck platooning - a literature overview and directions for future research. J. Adv. Transp. (2020, in Press). https://doi.org/10.1155/2020/2604012

Learning-Based Co-planning for Improved Container, Barge and Truck Routing

Rie B. Larsen$^{(\boxtimes)}$, Bilge Atasoy , and Rudy R. Negenborn

Department of Maritime and Transport Technology,
Delft University of Technology, Delft, The Netherlands
{r.b.larsen,b.atasoy,r.r.negenborn}@tudelft.nl

Abstract. When barges are scheduled before the demand for container transport is known, the scheduled departures may match poorly with the realised demands' due dates and with the truck utilization. Synchromodal transport enables simultaneous planning of container, truck and barge routes at the operational level. Often these decisions are taken by multiple stakeholders who wants cooperation, but are reluctant to share information. We propose a novel co-planning framework, called departure learning, where a barge operator learns what departure times perform better based on indications from the other operator. The framework is suitable for real time implementation and thus handles uncertainties by replanning. Simulated experiment results show that co-planning has a big impact on vehicle utilization and that departure learning is a promising tool for co-planning.

Keywords: Cooperative planning · Synchromodal transport · Vehicle utilization

1 Introduction

Better co-planning between stakeholders in transport systems for planning barge schedules, truck and container routes in real time will help utilizing the transport capacity better. One of the main challenges of humanity at the moment is the climate changes. One way of alleviating our negative impact on the environment is to increase the efficiency of our activities. The transport sector is a large contributor of CO2 emissions and has a low efficiency, with e.g. trucks driving empty 26% of the kilometres they drive in the Netherlands [5]. CO2 emission is however not the only negative impact of freight transport. The report [4] estimates the external costs of transport, such as the cost of accidents, climate impact, and noise nuisance. Here it is concluded that maritime transport induces the lowest external cost, followed by rail, inland waterway and road transport

This research is supported by the project "Complexity Methods for Predictive Synchromodality" (project 439.16.120) of the Netherlands Organisation for Scientific Research (NWO).

in this order [4, Fig. 16]. It is therefore desirable not only to improve the vehicle utilization, and hence efficiency, of truck transport, but also the utilization across transport modes.

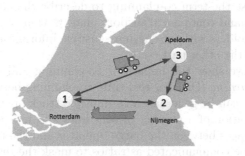

Fig. 1. Small Dutch transport network used as example in this paper.

Synchromodal transport uses a-modal bookings and change acceptance to enable transport providers to optimize plans in accordance with the realisation of uncertainties. In the traditional transport literature, decisions are divided into strategic, tactical and operational levels [15]. Strategic decisions have long lasting impact and usually high impact on revenue. Tactical decisions have impact over a tangible time horizons and are typically based on estimates of future events. Plans are often made on the tactical level and corrected at the operational level. Operational decisions regards what to do right now with the realised events. With synchromodal transport, decisions from the tactical and the operational levels are intertwined: uncertain long term plans for operational decisions can be formulated without commitment, and tactical decisions can be changed during operation. This intertwining requires additional research to utilize the potential of synchromodality. Model Predictive Control (MPC) provides a framework for combining predictions of future events with real time decision making. MPC has previously been used to route containers in several cases, e.g., [9,11] and [7].

Barge schedules are typically decided at the tactical level based on estimated demand [3]. When plans are made in advance, the realised demand is often different and external factors, like weather, cause unforeseen limitations. Some methods plan in accordance with these uncertainties [16], others adjust predefined departure times after the demand realization [1] or cancel unprofitable departures [18]. Truck routing is typically decided at the operational level based on pick up and delivery locations and times of the goods [12]. In [6] and [7] we demonstrated the negative impact of planning first container routes and then truck routes compared to planning them simultaneously in a synchromodal network. The results of [13] shows the same on a network with only one origin of the demand.

Barges and trucks are often operated by different stakeholders, so simultaneous planning requires co-planning. Co-planning can involve both information sharing and loss of autonomy. Many companies are interested in the benefits of cooperation [2], but participate reluctantly due to these implications. Co-planning schemes can be constructed such that missing information or sudden changes in the willingness to follow the scheme can damage the other partici-pating parties. Cooperation schemes vary from auctions [17] to distributed opti-mization [8]. We use the term co-planning to describe the act of cooperating to achieve the vehicle and container transport plans that are best for the group of cooperating stakeholders without sharing sensitive information or being vulner-able to defiance of the other parties.

In this paper, we show the impact of co-planning and develop a method, called *departure learning* (DL), for real time co-planning between a barge and a truck operator. DL can be generalized to multiple truck operators. The method requires communication of a number of schedules and indications of the corre-sponding performances between the barge operator and the truck operator. The performances can be communicated as ratios to mask the real numbers behind. It is assumed no party seeks to exploit the framework, but it does not severely damage cooperating parties if one party acts autonomously. The framework is based on Model Predictive Control (MPC) and uses ideas from Bayesian opti-mization to learn good departure times through continuous communication.

2   Real Time Co-planning in Synchromodal Networks

The synchromodal container transport networks we consider in this paper are described by graphs $\mathcal{G}(\mathcal{N}, \mathcal{A})$ where the nodes $\mathcal{N}$ are terminals and the arches $\mathcal{A}$ are connecting infrastructure. One arc corresponds to inland waterways and can thus only be used by barges and others are roads used by trucks. The set of road-arcs is denoted $\mathcal{R}$ and the two directions of the waterway comprise the set $\mathcal{W}$. Two nodes can be connected by both types of arcs. The operators' decisions can only be changed when the vehicles and containers are at the nodes. It is e.g. not possible to make the barge return to its departure terminal if a delay occurs. Furthermore, it is assumed only the truck operators have contact to clients and therefore the barge operator receives the demand only through truck operators. Figure 1 shows the transport network used as example in this paper.

It is assumed that barge and truck operators want to collaborate to decrease the total cost of transport and they have agreed how to share the profit. The truck operators are not willing to share information on release time, due date and quantity of their transport orders, but are willing to indicate how costly different barge schedules will be to them. The barge operator has the final authority to decide the schedule but adjusts it based on the feedback from the operators. The feedback from the operators are collectively considered by a weighted sum. For clarity, the DL is therefore presented for networks with one barge operator and one truck operator. It is furthermore assumed that both parties commit fully to the proposed framework. It is however worth noticing that agreement does not need to be reached since the barge operator has the final saying over the schedule and the truck company has authority to route the containers and is the only party who knows destinations and due dates.

Since the responsibilities of the barge and the truck operator are divided, the following description of the synchromodal transport network is also divided. Before this description, the real time aspect of the network and DL are discussed.

2.1   Real Time Aspect

Uncertainties are very common in the transport sector. To address them, DL is based on MPC, where time t is divided into timesteps k with Δt timeunits in between such that $t = k\Delta t$. The optimal decisions are found by optimizing the system performance over a prediction horizon T_p. Only the decisions regarding the current timestep k are implemented and at the next time $k + 1$ the process is repeated. MPC thus react to changes in the system or predictions every Δt time units and considers the period k to $k + T_p$ when it takes decisions. In the co-planning problem, a long prediction horizon is needed because of the long travel times of barges and the need to describe at least one departure from each terminal. Using MPC for problems that requires frequent updates, i.e. low Δt, and a long prediction horizon T_p requires fast optimization of the model. We therefore formulate the truck and container routing problem with continuous variables. Frequent updates can ensure sufficient precision when the continuous optimal decisions are rounded to integer variables [14]. The barge capacity is much larger than that of trucks and they are thus described by discrete variables.

2.2   Barge Operator

The barge operator is responsible for the barge schedule. It is assumed the synchromodal transport network only has two barge terminals: nodes 1 and 2. The travel time from node 1 to 2, τ_{12}^b, and the return, τ_{21}^b, include loading, travel time, mooring and unloading. Containers that arrive at the terminal after loading has started will not be accepted on the barge and containers can only be picked up after the barge has finished unloading all containers.

Two binary variables $y_1(k)$ and $y_2(k)$ are used to describe the departures of the barge at time step k from node 1 and 2 respectively. The dynamics of the barges can thus be described as

$$\bar{z}_i^b(k + 1) = \bar{z}_i^b(k) - \bar{y}_i(k) + \bar{y}_j(k - \tau_{ji}^b) \quad i,j \in \{1,2\}, i \neq j, \ \forall k \qquad (1)$$

where $\bar{z}_i^b(k) \in \{0,1\}$ is the number of barges at the quay of node i at time k. The superscript b is used to indicate the variable regards the barge and the bar on top, that it is the realized value. The barge operator knows the position of the barge at all time, since he has access to the barge state

$$\bar{x}^b(k) = \left[\bar{z}_1^b(k), \bar{y}_2(k - 1), \cdots, \bar{y}_2(k - \tau_{12}^b), \bar{z}_2^b(k), \bar{y}_1(k - 1), \cdots, \bar{y}_1(k - \tau_{21}^b)\right]^T.$$

The main cost for the barge operator is sailing the barge, since owning the equipment and hiring people are out of scope of this problem. There are additional costs involved with transporting containers on the barge, e.g., crane movements and increased weight of the barge. The total cost is thus $w_1^b \bar{y}_1(k) + w_2^b \bar{y}_2(k) + w_{12}^l \bar{u}_{12}^l(k) + w_{12}^l \bar{u}_{12}^b(k)$ $\forall k$, where w_i^b is the cost of sailing an empty barge from i to j, $\{i,j\} = \{1,2\}$, and $w_{ij}^l \in \mathbb{R}_{\geq 0}^{1 \times n_c}$ is the cost of transporting one additional container with the barge from i to j. $u_{ij}^b(k) \in \mathbb{R}_{\geq 0}^{1 \times n_c}$ is a vector with the number of containers of each commodity that is transported from i to j by barge departing at time k. n_c is the number of commodities. Since the barge and truck operators cooperate fully and share the profit after the transport has been performed, the cost per container is considered by the truck operator. The private cost for the bare operator is

$$J^b(k) = w_1^b \bar{y}_1(k) + w_2^b \bar{y}_2(k) \quad \forall k. \tag{2}$$

2.3   Truck Operator

The truck operator is responsible for choosing which modes and routes each container is transported by and for deciding the truck routes. The model used to describe this simultaneous planning problem is a simplification of on the method presented by us in [7]. The full model can be used with DL, but as it ads complexity to the description, the simplified model is used here. The key assumptions of the truck operator problem are:

– Any node in the network can be the origin and destination of transport demand, if it is defined as such, hence both import and export are considered.
– Demand is modelled as containers available to the network and needed from the network. Unsatisfied demand is penalized. The demand is fully known over the prediction horizon.
– Containers are modelled as continuous variable, commodity flows. This simplifies the model and captures the desired level of accuracy ([11] and [14]).
– Trucks are also modelled as continuous variable flows.
– The number of trucks is finite and each truck can transport one container.
– The barge has invariant, finite capacity. Other capacities and (un)loading rates are considered sufficient.
– Terminal operating hours, drivers resting hours, etc., are not considered.

All containers with the same destination are modelled as one commodity. Since the containers are described as flows, one container of a certain commodity can replace another. This assumption is also used in, e.g., [9]. More commodities can have the same destination, which allow us to distinguish e.g. different container sizes. In [11] a commodity is defined for each due date to ensure all containers arrive on time. We define virtual demand nodes adjacent to the nodes where containers can have origin or destination. The set of virtual nodes is denoted by $\mathcal{D}$. The dynamics of the virtual demand nodes are

$$\bar{z}_i^d(k+1) = \bar{z}_i^d(k) - \bar{u}_{di}(k) - \bar{u}_{id}(k) + \bar{d}_i(k) \quad \forall i \in \mathcal{D}, \; \forall k, \tag{3}$$

where $\bar{d}_i(k) \in \mathbb{R}_{\geq 0}^{n_c}$ is the realised new demand of each commodity at time k. Notice that all values are positive, so whether the demand indicates container releases or expected arrivals depends on the commodity, i.e. the element in the vector. The mappings $p_i^r \in \{0,1\}^{1 \times n_c}$ and $p_i^d \in \{0,1\}^{1 \times n_c}$ are defined such that $p_i^r \bar{d}_i(k)$ is the sum of containers that are released at node i at time k and $p_i^d \bar{d}_i(k)$ is the sum of containers that are due at node i at time k. The variable $\bar{z}_i^d(k) \in \mathbb{R}_{\geq 0}^{n_c}$ is the unsatisfied demand at node i at time k and $\bar{u}_{id}(k) \in \mathbb{R}_{\geq 0}^{n_c}$ is the containers of each commodity from terminal node i that are used to satisfy due dates at the virtual demand node at time k. $\bar{u}_{di}(k) \in \mathbb{R}_{\geq 0}^{n_c}$ is the opposite. To guide the direction of the demand satisfaction, the following must be true:

$$p_i^r \bar{u}_{id}(k) = 0 \quad \forall i \in \mathcal{D}, \, \forall k \tag{4}$$

$$p_i^d \bar{u}_{di}(k) = 0 \quad \forall i \in \mathcal{D}, \, \forall k \tag{5}$$

Each node in the network can be connected with three kinds of other nodes: $\mathcal{D}_i$, $\mathcal{W}_i$ and $\mathcal{R}_i$. $\mathcal{D}_i$ contains node i's adjacent virtual demand nodes and $\mathcal{W}_i$ the node to which i is connected by waterways. These sets are either empty or has one element. The set $\mathcal{R}_i$ contains all nodes that are connected to node i by road. Based on these sets, the dynamics of the stacks of containers are

$$\bar{z}_i^c(k+1) = \bar{z}_i^c(k) + \sum_{j \in \mathcal{D}_i} \left(\bar{u}_{di}(k) - \bar{u}_{id}(k) \right) + \sum_{j \in \mathcal{W}_i} \left(\bar{u}_{ji}^b(k - \tau_{ji}^b) - \bar{u}_{ij}^b(k) \right)$$

$$+ \sum_{j \in \mathcal{R}_i} \left(\bar{u}_{ji}(k - \tau_{ji}^r) - \bar{u}_{ij}(k) \right) \quad \forall i \in \mathcal{N}, \forall k. \tag{6}$$

The variable $\bar{z}_i^c(k) \in \mathbb{R}_{\geq 0}^{n_c}$ is a vector of how many containers of each commodity that are stacked at node i at time k. The superscript c indicates that the variable regards containers. $u_{ij}(k) \in \mathbb{R}_{\geq 0}^{n_c}$ has the same structure and is for the containers transported from i to j by road at time k. The travel takes τ_{ij} timesteps. The barge has a capacity of c^b and only carries containers that were ready for loading at the departure time. Hence

$$\mathbf{1}_{n_c} \bar{u}_{ij}^b(k) \leq c^b \bar{y}_i(k) \quad \forall <i,j> \in \mathcal{W}, \, \forall k, \tag{7}$$

where $\mathbf{1}_{n_c} \in \mathbb{R}^{1 \times n_c}$ is a vector of ones. The variable $\bar{z}_i^v(k) \in \mathbb{R}$ is the number of trucks parked at node i at time k, and has the dynamics

$$\bar{z}_i^v(k+1) = \bar{z}_i^v(k) + \sum_{j \in \mathcal{R}_)} \bar{v}_{ji}(k - \tau_{ji}^r) - \bar{v}_{ij}(k) \quad \forall i \in \mathcal{N}, \, \forall k, \tag{8}$$

where $\bar{v}_{ij}(k) \in \mathbb{R}$ is the number of trucks departing from i on the road to j at time k. To ensure containers only travel by roads if they are loaded on trucks, the sum of containers departing node i at time k on the road to node j must not exceed the number of trucks departing on the same road at the same time. Trucks are on the other hand allowed to drive empty. Both are modelled by

$$\mathbf{1}_{n_c} u_{ij}(k) \leq v_{ij}(k) \quad \forall j \in \mathcal{R}_i, \, \forall i \in \mathcal{N}, \, \forall k. \tag{9}$$

Since the truck and the barge operators cooperate fully and share the profit after the transport has been performed, the truck operator considers all costs that are directly related to his decisions, namely

$$J^t(k) = \sum_{<i,j>\in\mathcal{R}} w_{ij}^v \bar{v}_{ij}(k) + \sum_{<i,j>\in\mathcal{W}} w_{ij}^l \bar{u}_{ij}^b(k) + \sum_{i\in\mathcal{D}} w_d \bar{z}_i^d(k+1), \quad (10)$$

where $w_{ij}^v \in \mathcal{R}$ is the cost of driving a truck from i to j and w_d is the cost per timestep delay per container. The truck operator has always access to the state

$$\bar{x}^t(k) =$$

$$\begin{bmatrix} \left[\bar{z}_1^d(k) \cdots \bar{z}_{|\mathcal{D}|}^d(k) \right]^T \\ \left[\bar{u}_{j1}^b(k-\tau_{j1}^b), j \in \mathcal{W}_1, \cdots, \bar{u}_{j|\mathcal{N}|}^b(k-\tau_{j|\mathcal{N}|}^b), j \in \mathcal{W}_{|\mathcal{N}|} \right]^T \\ \left[\bar{z}_1^c(k), \bar{u}_{j1}(k-\tau_{j1}^r) \,\forall\, j \in \mathcal{R}_1, \cdots, \bar{z}_{|\mathcal{N}|}^c(k), \bar{u}_{j|\mathcal{N}|}(k-\tau_{j|\mathcal{N}|}^r) \,\forall\, j \in \mathcal{R}_{|\mathcal{N}|} \right]^T \\ \left[\bar{z}_1^v(k), \bar{v}_{j1}(k-\tau_{j1}^r) \,\forall\, j \in \mathcal{R}_1, \cdots, \bar{z}_{|\mathcal{N}|}^v(k), \bar{v}_{j|\mathcal{N}|}(k-\tau_{j|\mathcal{N}|}^r) \,\forall\, j \in \mathcal{R}_{|\mathcal{N}|} \right]^T \end{bmatrix}$$

3   Departure Learning

The cooperative planning between the barge and truck operator is based on exchange of information and commitment to find the solution that is cheapest for both parties. The truck operator is not willing to share information about specific containers and the barge operator wants autonomy over the schedule. We propose the novel method *departure dearning* (DL), where at each timestep, the barge operator sends a set $\mathcal{I}(k)$ of barge schedules to the truck operator. The truck operator hereafter computes the transport cost over the prediction horizon for each of the schedules. The costs are send to the barge operator, possibly after scaling to hide the exact information.

The actions corresponding to the current timestep in the schedule with the best performance are implemented by the barge operator and truck operator separately, and the process is repeated at the next timestep. To estimate which schedules will perform better, the barge operator uses the performances indicated by the truck operator at previous timesteps to estimate the performance at the current timestep. It is ensured that the set of potential schedules includes both schedules that will perform well and schedules that helps identifying good schedules in the future by using selection strategies that focus on both exploitation and exploration. The overview of the DL is shown in Fig. 2. In the following, it is described how the barge operator learns good schedules, and how the truck operator estimates the performance of a schedule.

Learning Good Departure Times. To estimate what the performance of all schedules are, all schedules must be identified. However, the first departure in a schedule must be from the terminal where the barge currently is, or to which it is travelling. It is thus possible to describe the performance of all feasible schedules if only half the schedules are identified as long as the location of the barge is known. This reduces the number of binary options per timestep to one (to depart or not). Such a reduced schedule is called an event e. Figure 3 shows

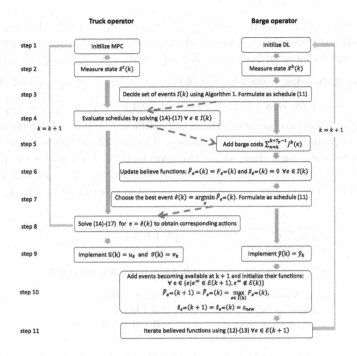

Fig. 2. Actions of DL. Blue, dashed arrows indicate communication. (Color figure online)

$$[y_1(k) \cdots y_1(k+T_p-1)] = [\,0\;0\;1\;0\;0\;0\,]$$
$$[y_2(k) \cdots y_2(k+T_p-1)] = [\,1\;0\;0\;0\;1\;0\,]$$
$$e \qquad\qquad\qquad\; = [\,1\;0\;1\;0\;1\;0\,]$$

Fig. 3. Schedule consists of two vectors of binary variables describing the departure times from the two end terminals. The corresponding event combines the two.

an example of a schedule and its corresponding event. Events can be decoded into schedules using the known location of the barge at time k and this relation:

$$y_i(k+\gamma) \leq z_i^b(k) + \sum_{\kappa=\tau_{ji}^b-\gamma}^{\tau_{ji}^b} y_j(k-\kappa) \quad \forall \gamma \leq \tau_{ji}, \forall < i,j > \in \mathcal{W}. \tag{11}$$

Each element of the event is a binary variable denoted by b_k. An event is thus $e = [b_k, ..., b_{k+T_p-1}]$ where each element is a specific realizations of $b_k \in \{0,1\}, ..., b_{k+T_p-1} \in \{0,1\}$. It takes time for the barge to travel between the terminals, and therefore not all events are feasible at all timesteps. The set of events that are feasible at time k is denoted by $\mathcal{E}(k)$. Events at two different timesteps may correspond to the same sequence of events when viewed over an infinite timespan, and are as such identical. e^∞ denotes an event over the infinite times-

pan and is defined as $e^\infty = \begin{bmatrix} \mathbf{0}_{1:k} & e & \mathbf{0}_{k+T_p:\infty} \end{bmatrix}$, where $\mathbf{0}_{a:b} = \{0\}^{b-a}$ is a zero-vector of suitable size. If two events are identical except for two subsequent elements, the events are said to be neighbours, i.e. for an event $e_1 = [b_k^1, ..., b_{k+T_p-2}^1] \in \mathcal{E}(k)$, the set of neighbouring events is $\mathcal{N}_{e_1^\infty}(k) = \left\{ e = [b_k^2, ..., b_{k+T_p-2}^2] \in \mathcal{E}(k) \,|\, b_i^2 = b_i^1 \,\forall i \setminus \{i = j+1\} \text{ for one } j \in \{1, ..., T_p - 2\} \text{ and } b_j^2 = b_{j+1}^1, b_{j+1}^2 = b_j^1 \right\} \setminus \{e_1\}$.
This corresponds to two barge schedules only differing in one departure time and for that departure only with one timestep. The set of neighbours are indexed with the event's e_∞ and time, since two events $e_1 \in \mathcal{E}(k)$ and $e_2 \in \mathcal{E}(k+1)$ with $e_1^\infty = e_2^\infty$ will have the same set of neighbours $\mathcal{N}_{e_\infty}$ for all k where $\mathcal{N}_{e_\infty} \in \mathcal{E}(k) \cap \mathcal{E}(k+1)$. Both e_∞ and $\mathcal{N}_{e_\infty}(k)$ are exemplified in Fig. 4.

$$
\begin{aligned}
e_{a1} \in \mathcal{E}(k) &= \quad [\,0\,1\,0\,0\,1\,0\,] \\
e_{a2} \in \mathcal{E}(k+1) &= \quad [\,1\,0\,0\,1\,0\,0\,] \\
e_{a1}^\infty = e_{a2}^\infty = e_a^\infty &= \quad 0\,0\,0\,0\,0\,1\,0\,0\,1\,0\,0\,0\,0\,0\,0\,0 \\
e_b \in \mathcal{N}_{e_a^\infty}(k) &= \quad [\,1\,0\,0\,0\,1\,0\,] \\
e_{c1} \in \mathcal{N}_{e_a^\infty}(k) &= \quad [\,0\,0\,1\,0\,1\,0\,] \\
e_{c2} \in \mathcal{N}_{e_a^\infty}(k+1) &= \quad [\,0\,1\,0\,1\,0\,0\,]
\end{aligned}
$$

Fig. 4. Illustration of e_∞ and $\mathcal{N}_{e_\infty}(k)$. Note that the set of neighbours varies over time.

It is expected that the performance indicator for events that share e^∞ evolve slowly over time, and that the performances of neighbouring events are related. The barge operator's estimate of the performance is called the event's expected fitness and is denoted by $\tilde{F}_{e_\infty}(k)$. To indicate how certain this estimate is, an uncertainty function $\tilde{s}_{e_\infty}(k)$ is used. $\tilde{s}_{e_\infty}(k)$ decreases when an event corresponding to e^∞ or its neighbours are evaluated and increases slowly over k. If the barge operator has received the performance indicator for an event e, we say event e has been evaluated. Like in Bayesian optimization, $\tilde{F}_{e_\infty}(k)$ and $\tilde{s}_{e_\infty}(k)$ are used to sample a number of candidate events that are expected to either correspond to good barge schedules or provide useful information for the future. Unlike most implementations of Bayesian optimization, the number of feasible events is finite in DL, and thus $\tilde{F}_{e_\infty}(k)$ and $\tilde{s}_{e_\infty}(k)$ can be computed for all events.

The set of candidate events $\mathcal{I}(k)$ is sampled using strategies based on ranking of $\tilde{F}_{e_\infty}(k)$, $\tilde{s}_{e_\infty}(k)$ and functions of the two, together with random selection as outlined in Algorithm 1 for balanced exploitation and exploration. The cardinality of $\mathcal{I}(k)$, denoted by n, is the number of schedules the truck operator must evaluate. Notice that the cost of each schedule is independent of the other schedules and the operator therefore can evaluate the schedules in parallel.

After the barge operator receives the performance indicators from the truck operator, the expected fitness of the evaluated events are updated and their uncertainty values are set to zero. Some events will be feasible at the next time $k+1$ which were not feasible at time k. These events are initialized with the

---

Algorithm 1. The strategy used to decide $\mathcal{I}(k)$

1: **input** $\tilde{F}_{e\infty}(k)$, $\tilde{s}_{e\infty}(k)$, $\mathcal{E}(k)$
2: **return** $\mathcal{I}(k)$ with n unique events
3: $\mathcal{I}(k) = \emptyset$
4: **for** $i \leftarrow 1$ to $floor(n/6)$ **do**
5:     $e_{new} = \arg\min_{e \in \mathcal{E}(k)\backslash\mathcal{I}(k)} \tilde{F}_{e\infty}(k) + \tilde{s}_{e\infty}(k)$
6:     $\mathcal{I}(k) = \mathcal{I}(k) \cup e_{new}$
7:     $e_{new} = \arg\min_{e \in \mathcal{E}(k)\backslash\mathcal{I}(k)} \tilde{F}_{e\infty}(k)$
8:     $\mathcal{I}(k) = \mathcal{I}(k) \cup e_{new}$
9:     $e_{new} = \arg\max_{e \in \mathcal{E}(k)\backslash\mathcal{I}(k)} \tilde{s}_{e\infty}(k)$
10:     $\mathcal{I}(k) = \mathcal{I}(k) \cup e_{new}$
11:     $e_{new} = \arg\min_{e \in \mathcal{E}(k)\backslash\mathcal{I}(k)} \tilde{F}_{e\infty}(k) - \tilde{s}_{e\infty}(k)$
12:     $\mathcal{I}(k) = \mathcal{I}(k) \cup e_{new}$
13:     **for** $j \leftarrow 1$ to 2 **do**
14:         $e_{new} = \text{rand}\,(e \in \mathcal{E}(k) \setminus \mathcal{I}(k))$
15:         $\mathcal{I}(k) = \mathcal{I}(k) \cup e_{new}$
16:     **end for**
17: **end for**
18: **for** $i \leftarrow floor(n/6)6$ to n **do**
19:     $e_{new} = \text{rand}\,(e \in \mathcal{E}(k) \setminus \mathcal{I}(k))$
20:     $\mathcal{I}(k) = \mathcal{I}(k) \cup e_{new}$
21: **end for**

---

maximum fitness evaluated at k and the uncertainty value s_{new}. Hereafter, all the fitness and uncertainty values of all events are updated as follows:

$$\tilde{F}_{e\infty}(k+1) = \alpha\tilde{F}_{e\infty}(k) + \frac{1-\alpha}{|\mathcal{N}_{e\infty}(k)|} \sum_{i \in \mathcal{N}_{e\infty}(k) \cup \mathcal{N}_{e\infty}(k+1)} \tilde{F}_i(k) \tag{12}$$

$$\tilde{S}_{e\infty}(k+1) = (\alpha+\beta)\tilde{S}_{e\infty}(k) + \frac{1-\alpha}{|\mathcal{N}_{e\infty}(k)|} \sum_{i \in \mathcal{N}_{e\infty}(k) \cup \mathcal{N}_{e\infty}(k+1)} \tilde{S}_i(k) \tag{13}$$

The learning parameter α balances the emphasis laid on each events' previous value and on neighbouring events' values and t he factor β controls the speed at which information from previous timesteps become uncertain. To initialize DL prior knowledge can be used, otherwise it is recommended that $\tilde{F}_{e\infty}(1) = \tilde{F}_{init} \forall e \in \mathcal{E}(1)$ where $\tilde{F}_{init}$ is higher than the expected maximum fitness and $\tilde{s}_{e\infty}(1) = s_{new} \forall e \in \mathcal{E}(1)$. s_{new} is the maximum uncertainty and is also used to update new feasible events at step 10 in Algorithm 1.

Evaluating the Performance. The truck operator evaluates the performance of the communicated schedules by planning container and truck routes simultaneously for each $e \in \mathcal{I}(k)$. To do so, he solves the optimization problem (14)–(17), initiated from the current state for the given schedule.

$$\tilde{F}_{e\infty}(k) = \min \sum_{\kappa=k}^{k+T_p-1} J^t(\kappa) \tag{14}$$

$$\text{s.t. } x^t(k) = \bar{x}^t(k) \tag{15}$$

$$\{< y_1(\kappa), y_2(\kappa) > |\kappa \in \{k, ..., k+T_p-1\}\} = e \tag{16}$$

$$(3) - (9) \quad \forall \kappa \in \{k, ..., k+T_p-1\} \tag{17}$$

$$\min \sum_{\kappa=k}^{k+T_p-1} J^t(\kappa) + J^b(\kappa) \tag{18}$$

$$\text{s.t. } x^t(k) = \bar{x}^t(k) \tag{19}$$

$$x^b(k) = \bar{x}^b(k) \tag{20}$$

$$(1), (3) - (9) \qquad \forall \kappa \in \{k, ..., k+T_p-1\} \tag{21}$$

$$y_1(\kappa) \in \{0,1\}, \ y_1(\kappa) \in \{0,1\} \quad \forall \kappa \in \{k, ..., k+T_p-1\} \tag{22}$$

4   Simulation Experiments

To illustrate the impact of co-planning of barges, trucks and containers, two sets of simulated experiments are carried out. The first small scale experiment provides a better understanding of the possibilities for better utilization of the barge and trucks. The second experiment shows both the impact of co-planning and of using DL in a realistic scenario for the network in Fig. 1. The experiments are performed in Matlab formulated with Yalmip [10] and solved by Gurobi.

DL is benchmarked against co-planning based on centralised optimization and planning based on fixed schedules. The former benchmark is the best possible solution, henceforth called optimal co-planning, while the latter represents common practice. Both methods use MPC. Optimal co-planning solves the optimization problem (18)–(22) at each time k and when the schedules are fixed, the truck problem (14)–(17) is solved for that predefined schedule.

4.1   Experimental Setup

Three scenarios, on the network in Fig. 1 are used in the experiments. It is assumed Rotterdam and Apeldorn are origin and destination for demand and that all containers are of the same size, leading to $n_c = 2$ different commodities.

Realistic Scenario. The simulated experiments take place over 5 days and new decisions are taken every $\Delta t = 15$ min. It is assumed trucks drive 90 km/h and (un)loading a truck in Rotterdam takes 20 min, while it is 10 min in Nijmegen and Apeldorn. With these assumptions, the 140 km distance between Rotterdam and Apeldorn corresponds to 123 min traveltime, and the 55 km distance between Nijmegen and Apeldorn takes 56 min. The barge between Dordrecht and Nijmegen is in [13] reported to take 5 h including loading, so we assume the total travel time between Rotterdam and Nijmegen is 6 h. The cost of using the barge is in the same paper stated to be €60 per barge and €4.29 + €23.89 = €28.18 per container. The hourly rate of trucking is stated at €30.98 with a starting fee of €15. Using these values, the costs and travel times shown in Table 1 are computed. To ensure the consequences of a barge return trip are considered, the prediction horizon is chosen to be $T_p = 70$. The barge capacity is $c^b = 100$ and 36 trucks start at node 1.

The demand to be released at each virtual demand node is drawn from a uniform distribution between 0 and 3 at each timestep. The containers have a minimum lead time of 70 timesteps. The number of containers due at a virtual demand node is drawn at each timestep from a uniform destitution between zero and the number of containers that can have due date at this destination at this time. A total of 949 containers are released from node 1 and 984 from node 3. The same demand profile was used for all experiments.

DL is initialized with $\tilde{F}_{init} = 10000$ and $s_{new} = 5000$. The learning parameters are $\alpha = 0.8$ and $\beta = 0.1$. $n = 28$ potential schedules is communicated between operators at each timestep.

The benchmark method that builds on a fixed schedule uses regular barge departures. This barge leaves node 2 at time $k = 1$ and departs hereafter every $\tau_{12}^b + 2 = 26$ timesteps.

Vehicle-Centered Cost Scenario. To analyse the effect of changing the cost from the containers to the barge, we lowered the cost of transporting a container by €15 to $w_{12}^l = w_{21}^l = €128.18$ per container. To make the total cost of sailing a full container the same, the cost of moving the barge was increased to $w_{12}^b = w_{21}^b = €210$. The other parameters are the same as in the realistic scenario.

Table 1. Scenario parameters

$c^b = 100$	$\tau_{12}^b = \tau_{21}^b = 24$	$w_{12}^b = w_{21}^b = 60$	$w_{12}^l = w_{21}^l = 28.181_{n_c}$
$\bar{z}_1^v(0) = 36$	$\tau_{13} = \tau_{31} = 9$	$w_{13}^v = w_{31}^v = 73.19$	$w_d = 1000$
$\bar{z}_2^v(0) = 0$	$\tau_{23} = \tau_{32} = 4$	$w_{23}^v = w_{32}^v = 33.93$	

Realistic scenario

$c^b = 10$	$\tau_{12}^b = \tau_{21}^b = 2$	$w_{12}^b = w_{21}^b = 10$	$w_{12}^l = w_{21}^l = 28.181_{n_c}$
$\bar{z}_1^v(0) = 4$	$\tau_{13} = \tau_{31} = 2$	$w_{13}^v = w_{31}^v = 73.19$	$w_d = 1000$
$\bar{z}_2^v(0) = 0$	$\tau_{23} = \tau_{32} = 1$	$w_{23}^v = w_{32}^v = 33.93$	

Tractable scenario

Tractable Scenario. This scenario is a simple case to better illustrate the potential improvements. The total simulation time is 10 timesteps and the prediction horizon is $T_p = 7$. Due to the short prediction horizon, the barge operator has less time to learn what a good departure is. On the other hand, less events are feasible. Therefore it is chosen to communicate $n = 12$ schedules every timesteps. The learning parameters remain $\alpha = 0.8$ and $\beta = 0.1$. The capacities, travel times, and costs have been adjusted to the size of the problem and are as shown in Table 1. A total of 7 containers are to be transported. Four containers are released at virtual demand node 3 at time $k = 1$ with destination in virtual demand node 1. Two of them are due at $k = 4$ and two at $k = 6$. Three containers are released at $k = 3$ in virtual demand node 1 with due date at $k = 9$ in virtual demand node 3. The schedule used by the fixed-schedule benchmark method has a departure from node 2 at time $k = 5$ and a departure from node 1 at $k = 8$.

4.2   Results

For the tractable scenario, the realised movements of barges and trucks are shown in Fig. 5 for each of the three control strategies together with the demand, stacked containers and parked trucks at each node. The results show that when the barge schedule is optimized together with the truck and container routes, a better utilization of the barge is achieved. Optimal co-planning departs the barge twice and transport two containers each time. When DL is used, the barge departs once with two containers. The fixed schedule is not aligned with the transport need, and the barge is thus empty on both departures. The truck utilization is the same for optimal co-planning and fixed schedule with 8 out of 22 timesteps driven by trucks being without containers. For DL the utilization is lower with 11 out of 23 timesteps driven empty.

For both realistic sized scenarios, Table 2 shows key results provided by DL and the benchmark methods. Optimal co-planning obtains as expected the lowest cost, followed by DL. This shows that planning barge schedules before the realization of the demand leads to less flexibility and thus higher costs. The total number of containers transported by barge and the average number of containers per barge are significantly lower in the fixed schedule case than for optimal co-planning, despite the fixed schedule having more departures. The barge schedules achieved by DL have fewer departures and lower occupancy than by optimal co-planning. The number of containers per barge seems however to be very cost dependent with a higher occupancy when the cost is vehicle-centered, where DL achieves better occupancy than the fixed schedule. The number of trucks used by all three methods are comparable for both scenarios. Generally few trucks drive empty. This is likely because truck and container routes are optimized simultaneously in all methods. When the costs from [13] are used, optimal co-planning postpones demand satisfaction, resulting in 766 unsatisfied container-timesteps, corresponding to 191 container-hours. When the cost is vehicle-centered, optimal co-planning satisfy all demand in time. DL satisfies more demand than the fixed schedule case.

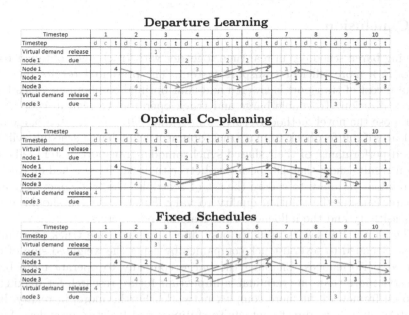

Fig. 5. Realised transport for the tractable scenario. Red numbers in column d are new demand and purple numbers in column c are containers stacked at the node. Black numbers in column t are vehicle parked at the node and green arrows indicate vehicle movements. Blue arrows are barge movements. (Color figure online)

Table 2. Results for the realistic scenario

Scenario	Costs from [13]			Vehicle-centered cost		
Planning method	DL	Optimal	Fixed	DL	Optimal	Fixed
Total cost (thousand €)	5982	5040	6148	5972	4928	6132
Unsatisfied demand	330.6	765.9	596.1	453.3	0	612.8
Barge departures	11	14	19	10	14	19
Containers transported by barge	207	501.4	385.1	278.1	551.7	396.0
Average barge occupancy (containers)	18.8	35.8	20.3	27.81	39.4	20.8
Truck departures	1746	1788.0	1745.8	1762	1813.8	1754
Empty truck departures	41.5	38.4	39	59.6	61.7	40

The results from both sets of experiments show that co-planning barge schedules with container and barge routes obtain better results in terms of cost. It furthermore increases the utilization rate of and number of containers transported by barge. Optimizing barge schedules together with container and truck routes achieves the best results. However, when one stakeholder does not have all information and authority over all decisions, DL provides a good alternative. The results show that DL is feasible in a realistic scenario and that it performs better than the fixed schedules case in terms of demand satisfaction and cost.

5   Conclusion

Planning barge schedules in real time together with truck and container routes results in a more efficient transport system. The presented results show that the total cost of transport is lowered and that optimal co-planning yields better barge utilization. To enable barge and truck operators to plan in cooperation, we propose the novel method *Departure Learning* (DL). With DL a barge operator learns from feedback from a truck operator what barge schedule will lead to good performance of their shared synchromodal transport system. The simulation results show that DL performs better than the fixed schedule case. DL uses random variables to choose the set of schedules the truck operator should evaluate, causing the solution quality to vary. Future research should analyse this sensitivity and the influence of the learning parameters.

The shown framework assumes only one barge and one truck company. It can be extended to several truck companies by using the weighted sum of their reported performances. Enabling the barge company to operate more barges and serve more than one terminal is important future research for making the proposed framework fit more complex networks. Furthermore, in reality, barge operators often have direct contacts to shippers and logistics providers. Future research could extend the framework to the case where the cooperation between the barge and truck operator only consider time-varying excess capacity. DL enables cooperative planning and relies on the honesty of the cooperating parties. Future research into sharing mechanisms and control schemes will make the framework more robust towards abuse.

References

1. Behdani, B., Fan, Y., Wiegmans, B., Zuidwijk, R.: Multimodal schedule design for synchromodal freight transport systems. Eur. J. Transp. Infrastruct. Res. **16**(3), 424–444 (2016)
2. Cruijssen, F., Dullaert, W., Fleuren, H.: Horizontal cooperation in transport and logistics: a literature review. Transp. J. **46**, 22–39 (2007)
3. Demir, E., Burgholzer, W., Hrušovskỳ, M., Arikan, E., Jammernegg, W., Van Woensel, T.: A green intermodal service network design problem with travel time uncertainty. Transp. Res. Part B: Methodol. **93**, 789–807 (2016)
4. van Essen, H., et al.: Handbook on the external costs of transport (2019). www.cedelft.eu
5. Eurostat: Database: annual road freight transport vehicle movements, loaded and empty, by reporting country
6. Larsen, R.B., Atasoy, B., Negenborn, R.R.: Simultaneous planning of container and vehicle-routes using model predictive control. In: Proceedings of European Control Conference, pp. 2177–2182 (2019)
7. Larsen, R.B., Atasoy, B., Negenborn, R.R.: Model predictive control for simultaneous planning of container and vehicle routes. Eur. J. Control (2020)
8. Li, L., Negenborn, R.R., De Schutter, B.: Distributed model predictive control for cooperative synchromodal freight transport. Transp. Res. Part E: Logist. Transp. Rev. **105**, 240–260 (2017)

9. Li, L., Negenborn, R.R., Schutter, B.D.: Intermodal freight transport planning - a receding horizon control approach. Transp. Res. Part C: Emerg. Technol. **60**, 77–95 (2015)
10. Löfberg, J.: YALMIP: a toolbox for modeling and optimization in Matlab. In: Proceedings of International Symposium on Computer Aided Control System Design (2004)
11. Nabais, J.L., Negenborn, R.R., Botto, M.A.: Model predictive control for a sustainable transport modal split at intermodal container hubs. In: Proceedings of the International Conference on Networking, Sensing and Control, pp. 591–596 (2013)
12. Psaraftis, H.N., Wen, M., Kontovas, C.A.: Dynamic vehicle routing problems: three decades and counting. Networks **67**(1), 3–31 (2016)
13. Qu, W., Rezaei, J., Maknoon, Y., Tavasszy, L.: Hinterland freight transportation replanning model under the framework of synchromodality. Transp. Res. Part E: Logist. Transp. Rev. **131**, 308–328 (2019)
14. Sager, S., Bock, H.G., Diehl, M.: The integer approximation error in mixed-integer optimal control. Math. Program. **133**(1), 1–23 (2012)
15. SteadieSeifi, M., Dellaert, N.P., Nuijten, W., Van Woensel, T., Raoufi, R.: Multimodal freight transportation planning: a literature review. Eur. J. Oper. Res. **233**(1), 1–15 (2014)
16. Van Riessen, B., Negenborn, R.R., Dekker, R., Lodewijks, G.: Service network design for an intermodal container network with flexible transit times and the possibility of using subcontracted transport. Int. J. Shipp. Transp. Logist. **7**(4), 457–478 (2015)
17. Xu, S.X., Huang, G.Q., Cheng, M.: Truthful, budget-balanced bundle double auctions for carrier collaboration. Transp. Sci. **51**(4), 1365–1386 (2017)
18. Xu, Y., Cao, C., Jia, B., Zang, G.: Model and algorithm for container allocation problem with random freight demands in synchromodal transportation. Math. Probl. Eng. **2015**, 1–13 (2015)

Overcoming Mobility Poverty with Shared Autonomous Vehicles: A Learning-Based Optimization Approach for Rotterdam Zuid

Breno Beirigo[✉], Frederik Schulte, and Rudy R. Negenborn

Delft University of Technology, Delft, The Netherlands
{b.alvesbeirigo,f.schulte,r.r.negenborn}@tudelft.nl

Abstract. Residents of cities' most disadvantaged areas face significant barriers to key life activities, such as employment, education, and healthcare, due to the lack of mobility options. Shared autonomous vehicles (SAVs) create an opportunity to overcome this problem. By learning user demand patterns, SAV providers can improve regional service levels by applying anticipatory relocation strategies that take into consideration when and where requests are more likely to appear. The nature of transportation demand, however, invariably creates learning biases towards servicing cities' most affluent and densely populated areas, where alternative mobility choices already abound. As a result, current disadvantaged regions may end up perpetually underserviced, therefore preventing all city residents from enjoying the benefits of autonomous mobility-on-demand (AMoD) systems equally. In this study, we propose an anticipatory rebalancing policy based on an approximate dynamic programming (ADP) formulation that processes historical demand data to estimate value functions of future system states iteratively. We investigate to which extent manipulating cost settings, in terms of subsidies and penalties, can adjust the demand patterns naturally incorporated into value functions to improve service levels of disadvantaged areas. We show for a case study in the city of Rotterdam, The Netherlands, that the proposed method can harness these cost schemes to better cater to users departing from these disadvantaged areas, substantially outperforming myopic and reactive benchmark policies.

Keywords: Mobility poverty · Shared autonomous vehicles · Approximate dynamic programming

1 Introduction

Service levels of residents from different areas of a city can vary significantly due to an uneven distribution of transport resources. Peripheral or low-income

This research is supported by the project "Dynamic Fleet Management (P14-18 – project 3)" (project 14894) of the Netherlands Organization for Scientific Research (NWO), domain Applied and Engineering Sciences (TTW).

© Springer Nature Switzerland AG 2020
E. Lalla-Ruiz et al. (Eds.): ICCL 2020, LNCS 12433, pp. 492–506, 2020.
https://doi.org/10.1007/978-3-030-59747-4_32

regions are typically more prone to suffer from accessibility poverty, that is, the difficulty of reaching certain key activities (e.g., employment, education, health-care) due to mobility poverty, which is concerned with the systemic lack of trans-portation and mobility options [10]. Since low-income and mobility poverty are strongly correlated, offering sufficient transportation choices to disadvantaged areas can ultimately improve social equity.

Shared autonomous vehicles (SAVs) and, more generally, autonomous mobility-on-demand (AMoD) systems, offer an opportunity to overcome mobil-ity poverty. Sharing services reduce the cost of personal mobility once all expenses of purchasing, maintaining, and insuring vehicles are distributed across a large user-base [15]. Recent research has demonstrated that efficient SAV fleet management can help AMoD providers fulfilling today's transportation demand using much fewer vehicles. However, typical performance measures fail to account for differences in demographics appropriately, lacking nuanced equity implications [5].

Due to natural demand patterns or deliberate profit-seeking policies, SAVs can end up re-enforcing existing inequalities by frequently moving to regions that are more prone to generate higher profits. Such a preference for affluent regions can already be identified in the current transportation landscape, where mobility options (e.g., ride-hailing, micro-mobility, ride-pooling, and transit) abound in cities' central areas.

In this study, we propose an approximate dynamic programming (ADP) algo-rithm to schedule and rebalance a fleet of AVs to improve the mobility of targeted disadvantaged areas. This algorithm uses demand data throughout an iterative process to derive value function approximations (VFAs) that convey the expected contribution of system states. These lookahead approximations are then consid-ered in the optimization process to assess the future outcome of current decisions. We illustrate our method using the case of Rotterdam, The Netherlands, where the northern region (Rotterdam Noord) encompasses the entire city center, out-performing the southern (Rotterdam Zuid) in a range of socio-geographical factors, such as income and transport connectivity. To improve the mobility of the residents in the Zuid region and ultimately their access to key activi-ties, we investigate to which extent ride subsidization and rejection penalties can contribute to overall fairness, adequately driving vehicles to underserviced areas.

We consider a first-mile case study in which users request vehicles from a pri-vate AMoD provider to access the closest train station (see Fig. 1). This setup is particularly relevant for the deployment of mobility-as-a-service (MaaS) solu-tions, which are based on the integration of different transport services. We show that a proper cost scheme setup can overcompensate the rebalancing bias towards densely populated and high-income areas improving mobility choices in underserviced areas. Ultimately, our results help city managers to understand the cost of laying out equitable transportation policies that balance providers' profitability and the service levels of underserviced users.

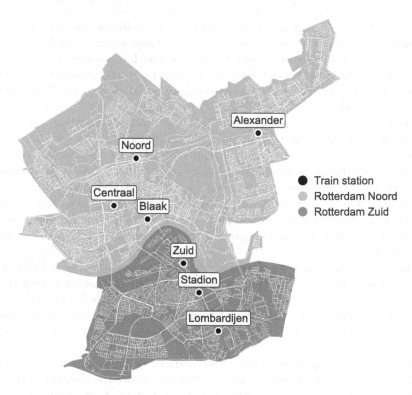

Fig. 1. Rotterdam regions (Noord and Zuid) and the seven train stations that are the destinations of all first-mile trips.

2 Related Work

AMoD systems rely on rebalancing strategies to find a reasonable compromise between asset utilization and user satisfaction. Supply and demand mismatches are typically addressed using ongoing imbalance cues (e.g., request rejections, idle vehicles) and predicted demand information (based on historical data). For example, Pavone et al. [12] propose an optimal transport problem in which locations with a surplus of idle vehicles continuously send empty vehicles to locations with a shortage of idle vehicles. Similarly, Alonso-Mora et al. [2] present a reactive rebalancing approach that sends idle vehicles to undersupplied areas, which are identified by the occurrence of unsatisfied requests. Through a linear program, vehicles are assigned to the departure locations of these requests, aiming to minimize the total sum of travel times. Later, Alonso-Mora et al. [3] use past historical data to compute a probability distribution over future demand and proposes an assignment algorithm to match vehicles to future requests. Fagnant et al. [6] relies on a rule to overcome supply-demand imbalances using a block-based division operational map. For each block, they compare the supply of idle stationary vehicles versus the share of currently waiting travelers plus soon expected travelers in the near future (according to the block historical trip rate).

Learning-based methods have also been successfully employed to enable anticipatory rebalancing. Through a reinforcement learning (RL) framework, Wen et al. [16] train a deep Q-network (DQN) using rewards based on waiting time savings of users picked up due to rebalancing movements. Conversely, penalties are applied when vehicles remain idle during the rebalancing period. Considering a grid map, they model states using grid-wise idle-vehicle distribution, in-service vehicles, and predicted demand (based on a Poisson process) in the surroundings. Guériau et al. [7] propose a decentralized RL approach based on Q-learning. They show that agents (i.e., vehicles) can contribute to global performance by learning how to optimize their own individual performance with local information only. Lin et al. [9] also takes advantage of the RL framework through a contextual multi-agent actor-critic (cA2C) algorithm. Their design stands out due to two main features, (i) the adoption of centralized value functions (shared by all agents), and (ii) context embedding that establishes explicit coordination among agents. Iglesias et al. [8] design a model predictive control (MPC) algorithm that leverages customer demand forecasts to rebalance vehicles. The forecasting model is based on a long short-term memory (LSTM) neural network. Al-Kanj et al. [1] use an ADP formulation that allows for anticipatory rebalancing and recharging of electric vehicles. Their approach maximizes vehicle contribution over time, using value function approximations to estimate the impact of each decision in the future.

Similarly to [1], we enable anticipatory rebalancing by using value functions to steer vehicles towards high-demand areas. In contrast with all proposed methods, however, we add nuance to service levels, acknowledging that users from different regions face distinct accessibility barriers to the transport system. Based on Lucas et al. [11], we consider transport accessibility primarily in terms of availability and affordability. Additionally, following Cohen et al. [5], our AMoD rebalancing policy aims to complement public transit and redistribute transport resources towards disadvantaged areas. Ultimately, from the user experience perspective, related literature focus on decreasing total delays (pickup and/or in-vehicle) whereas we focus on distributing service levels throughout regions.

3   Problem Formulation

We model the problem using the language of dynamic resource management (see [1,14]), where AVs (resources) service a sequence of trip request batches (tasks) dynamically revealed at discrete-time $t \in \{1, 2, \ldots, T\}$.

We assume all requests arrive in batch intervals of five minutes, occurring within the earliest time $t_e = 6:00$ and the latest time $t_l = 12:00$. To ensure the system has enough time to rebalance vehicles and deliver all users, we add thirty-minute offsets before t_e and after t_l, such that the total horizon $T = 84$ (i.e., 420/5).

The state of a single resource is defined by the attribute a representing the vehicle's location in the node-set N of $G = (N, E)$, a strongly connected graph drawn from a section of Rotterdam, The Netherlands. The city comprises six districts and 45 neighborhoods from which we select 40 to exclude the peripheries, such that node and edge sets have sizes $|N| = 10,364$ and $|E| = 23,048$, respectively (see Fig. 1).

By including the temporal dimension to location a, we have a_t, or the location of an SAV at time t. Let $\mathcal{A}$ be the set of all possible vehicle attributes. The state of all vehicles with the same state attribute is modeled using

$$R_{ta} = \text{Number of vehicles with attribute } a \text{ at time } t,$$
$$R_t = (R_{ta})_{a \in \mathcal{A}} = \text{The resource state vector at time } t.$$

Each request, in turn, is modeled using an attribute vector b comprised of origin and destination attributes $b_1, b_2 \in N$. Let $\mathcal{B}$ be the set of all possible request attribute vectors. The state of all rides with the same state vector occurring at time t is modeled using

$$D_{tb} = \text{The number of requests with attribute vector } b \text{ at time } t,$$
$$D_t = (D_{tb})_{b \in \mathcal{B}} = \text{The request state vector at time } t.$$

With the resource and request state vectors, we defined our system state vector as $S_t = (R_t, D_t)$. States S_t are measured before making decisions at each epoch $t \in \{1, 2, 3, \dots, T\}$. In this study, we consider each vehicle can realize three different types of decisions, namely, **service** a single user at a time, **stay parked** in its current location waiting to pick up users, and **rebalance** to a more promising location. Decisions are described using

$$d^{stay} = \text{Decision to stay parked in the current location,}$$
$$\mathcal{D}^R = \text{Set of all decisions } d \text{ to rebalance (i.e., move empty)}$$
$$\qquad \text{to a set of neighboring locations,}$$
$$\mathcal{D}^S = \text{Set of all decisions } d \text{ to service a user,}$$
$$b_d = \text{Trip } b \in \mathcal{B} \text{ covered by decision } d \in \mathcal{D}^S,$$
$$\mathcal{D} = \mathcal{D}^S \cup \mathcal{D}^R \cup d^{stay},$$
$$x_{tad} = \text{Number of times decision } d \text{ is applied to a vehicle with attribute } a \text{ at time } t,$$
$$x_t = (x_{tad})_{a \in \mathcal{A}, d \in \mathcal{D}}.$$

The decision variables x_{tad} must satisfy the following constraints:

$$\sum_{d \in \mathcal{D}} x_{tad} = R_{ta} \qquad\qquad \forall\, a \in \mathcal{A} \qquad\qquad (1)$$

$$\sum_{a \in \mathcal{A}} x_{tad} \leq D_{tb_d} \qquad\qquad \forall\, d \in \mathcal{D}^S \qquad\qquad (2)$$

$$y_{tb} = D_{tb} - \sum_{a \in \mathcal{A}} \sum_{\substack{d \in \mathcal{D}^S \\ b_d = b}} x_{tad} \qquad\qquad \forall b \in \mathcal{B} \qquad\qquad (3)$$

Constraints (1) and (2) guarantee flow conservation of vehicles and requests, respectively, and equalities (3) define the number y_{tb} of rejected trips b at time t. Once we aim to distinguish regions in N, we define $U(a) : N \rightarrow L$ as a function that maps each location $a \in N$ to a discrete geographical area in L, with $L = \{\text{Noord, Zuid}\}$. Applying a decision d to a resource with attribute a at time t generates a contribution c_{tad}, such that

$$c_{tad} = \begin{cases} p^a_{base} + p_{time}\delta\left(b_1, b_2\right) - c_{time}\left(\delta\left(a, b_1\right) + \delta\left(b_1, b_2\right)\right), & (service), \\ - c_{time}\delta\left(a, r\right), & (rebalance), \\ 0, & (stay). \end{cases}$$

Contributions c_{tad} of service, rebalance, and stay decisions are comprised of

$$p^a_{base} = \text{Base fare of trips departing from region } U(a) \in L,$$
$$p_{time} = \text{Time-dependent fare},$$
$$c_{time} = \text{Vehicle time-dependent costs (e.g., fuel)},$$
$$c^a_{penalty} = \text{Penalty for rejecting users from region } U(a) \in L,$$
$$\delta\left(a, b_1\right) = \text{Pickup duration},$$
$$\delta\left(b_1, b_2\right) = \text{Trip duration},$$
$$\delta\left(a, r\right) = \text{Rebalance duration (to neighboring location } r).$$

Assuming contributions are linear, the contribution function for period t discounted by rejection penalties is given by

$$C_t\left(S_t, x_t\right) = \sum_{a \in \mathcal{A}} \sum_{d \in \mathcal{D}} c_{tad} x_{tad} - \sum_{b \in B} c^{b_1}_{penalty} y_{tb}. \tag{4}$$

Let $X^\pi_t(S_t)$ be a decision function that represents a policy $\pi \in \Pi$, which maps a state S_t to a decision x_t at time t. We aim to determine the optimal policy π^* that, starting from an initial state S_0, maximizes the expected cumulative contribution, over all the time periods:

$$F^*_0\left(S_0\right) = \max_{\pi \in \Pi} \mathbb{E}\left\{\sum_{t=0}^{T} C_t\left(S_t, X^\pi_t(S_t)\right) | S_0\right\}. \tag{5}$$

4   Algorithmic Strategies

In principle, we can solve Eq. (5) by recursively computing (backward through time) Bellman's optimality equations, assigning to each state S_t at t, a value V_t, such that an optimal policy can chose decisions x_t that maximize expected contributions over time:

$$X^*_t(S_t) = \arg\max_{x_t \in \mathcal{X}_t}\left(C_t\left(S_t, x_t\right) + \mathbb{E}\left\{V_{t+1}\left(S_{t+1}\right) | S_t, x_t\right\}\right). \tag{6}$$

Solving Eq. (6), however, requires computing the expectation, which is computationally intractable for our problem setting. Doing so would incur in all the three "curses of dimensionality" (see [13]), since we would have to enumerate the state, outcome, and decision spaces.

4.1   An Approximate Dynamic Programming Algorithm

Once we cannot determine the true value V_t associated to each state S_t, we use an approximate dynamic programming algorithm (see [13] for a comprehensive treatment) to determine the value $\overline{V}_t^n$, which is an statistical estimate of V_t after n sample observations. First, at each time t in iteration n, applying the decision vector x_t to state S_t^n, before any new information has arrived, leads to a deterministic post-decision state

$$S_t^{x,n} = S^{M,x}(S_t^n, x_t^n),$$

where $S^{M,x}(.)$ is a transition function (or "system model") which describes how the system evolves from S_t^n to $S_t^{x,n}$. As exogenous information is unveiled, we can also use the post-decision state $S_t^{x,n}$ and the transition function to compute the subsequent pre-decision state

$$S_{t+1}^n = S^{M,W}(S_t^{x,n}, W_{t+1}(\omega^n)),$$

where $S^{M,W}(.)$ is a transition function from $S_t^{x,n}$ to S_{t+1}, and $W_{t+1}(\omega^n)$ is the exogenous information integrating a particular set of outcomes $W_1(\omega^n)$, ..., $W_T(\omega^n)$ of the resource and demand vectors measured over all periods in iteration n, following a sample path ω^n .

We solve (6) by replacing the expected value of being in S_{t+1} for $\overline{V}_t^{n-1}(S_t^{x,n})$, which corresponds to an approximation of the value of being in the post-decision state $S_t^{x,n}$ considering the first $n-1$ iterations. Then, we can make decisions at time t by solving the optimization problem

$$F_t(S_t^n) = \max_{x_t \in \mathcal{X}_t^n} (C_t(S_t^n, x_t) + \overline{V}_t^{n-1}(S_t^{x,n})), \qquad (7)$$

where we seek to determine the decision vector x_t in the feasible region $\mathcal{X}_t^n$ that maximizes the sum of the current contribution and the pre-calculated expected contribution $\overline{V}^{n-1}$ associated with post-decision state $S_t^{x,n}$.

4.2   Value Function Updates

We use the approximate value iteration algorithm from [13] to update value functions approximations using the solutions of (7) at each period t of iteration n. To streamline the process of stepping forward in time, we assume that the post-decision state is equivalent to the post-decision resource vector. Thus, after decision time, the post-decision demand vector $D_t^{x,n}$ is always empty, such that $\overline{V}_t^n(S_t^{x,n}) = \overline{V}_t^n(R_t^{x,n})$. In practice, this assumption entails that requests are not carried over periods. Consequently, users have to turn to alternative mobility options upon being rejected.

Assuming $\overline{V}_t^n(R_t^{x,n})$ is linear in R_{ta}, we have

$$\overline{V}_t^n(R_t^{x,n}) = \sum_{a' \in \mathcal{A}} \overline{v}_{t'a'}^n \sum_{a \in \mathcal{A}} \sum_{d \in \mathcal{D}} \delta_{a'}(a,d)\, x_{tad},$$

where $\overline{v}_{t'a'}^n$ is the marginal value of a vehicle with attribute a' at time t' at iteration n. The transition function $\delta_{a'}(a, d)$ is equal to 1 when $a^M(a, d) = a'$, and 0 otherwise, such that a' represents the post-decision location of a, and t' is the arrival time at a' of a vehicle departing from a at time t. When $d = d^{stay}$, $t' = t + 1$ and when $d \in \mathcal{D}^S \cup \mathcal{D}^R$, t' accounts for the travel time $\tau(t, a, d)$ to travel from a to a', such that $t' = t + \tau(t, a, d)$.

The marginal values $\overline{v}_{ta}^n$ approximate the overall contribution (i.e., until the end of the simulation horizon T) of assigning an incremental vehicle to a certain location at a certain time. Once costs depend on the region trips depart from (Noord or Zuid), these values will also reflect the benefits of working within these regions.

We update value functions $\overline{v}_{ta}^n$ using the samples $\hat{v}_{ta}^n$ drawn from attribute a at time t and iteration n. New samples are smoothed using stepsizes α_n which are updated every iteration according to the McClain's rule $\alpha_n = \frac{\alpha_{n-1}}{1 + \alpha_{n-1} - \overline{\alpha}}$, where $\overline{\alpha}$ is a constant that is approached as n advances. Initially, we set $\alpha_1 = 1$ such that value functions can start with the first sample value measured for each state. Algorithm 1 compiles all the steps of our ADP approach.

Algorithm 1. Approximate dynamic programming

1: **for** $n = 1, \ldots, N$ **do**
2:     Choose a sample path ω^n.
3:     **for** $t = 0, 1, \ldots, T$ **do**
4:         Let x_t^n be the solution of the optimization problem: $x_t^n = F_t(S_t^n)$.
5:         Let $\hat{v}_{ta}^n$ be the dual corresponding to the resource conservation.
6:         If $R_{ta} > 0$, update the value function using: $\overline{v}_{ta}^n = (1 - \alpha_n)\overline{v}_{ta}^{n-1} + \alpha_n \hat{v}_{ta}^n$
7:         Update the state: $S_t^{x,n} = S^{M,x}(S_t^n, x_t^n)$ and $S_{t+1}^n = S^{M,W}(S_t^{x,n}, W_{t+1}(\omega^n))$.
8:     **end for**
9: **end for**
10: Return the value functions, $\{\overline{v}_{ta}^n, t = 1, \ldots, T, \ a \in \mathcal{A}\}$.

4.3   Hierarchical Aggregation for Value Function Estimation

In order to estimate the value function of state attributes not yet observed, we use hierarchical aggregation coupled with the *weighting by inverse mean squared errors* (WIMSE) formula (see [14]). In this method, the state space is aggregated into a sequence of increasingly coarser state spaces, each of which associated with an aggregation level. By combining the values from superior levels through weights, we can estimate states' value functions without visiting them. We define three hierarchical levels experimentally, namely, 1, 2, and 3, that aggregate states both in space and time.

Spatially, the node set is aggregated in hexagon bins of $0.17\,\mathrm{km}^2$, $0.46\,\mathrm{km}^2$, and $5.16\,\mathrm{km}^2$, resulting in $1{,}016$, 198, and 38 bins, respectively (see Fig. 2). Valid bins cover at least one node of Rotterdam's street network and are identified by the closest node to their geographical center. As such, we assume that the travel time between two bins is based on the shortest path between their corresponding center nodes at 20 km/h speed. We aggregate temporally by increasing the length of the periods. We assume level 1 is the disaggregate five-minute period, whereas levels 2 and 3 correspond to ten- and fifteen-minute periods, therefore totaling 42, and 38 periods, respectively.

In practice, marginal values will aggregate up to the same value function, for example, at the third level, if they are within the same 5.16 km² hexagon and occur throughout the same fifteen-minute bin. Ultimately, the state-space size for each aggregation level declines from 85,344 to 8,316, and then to 1,444.

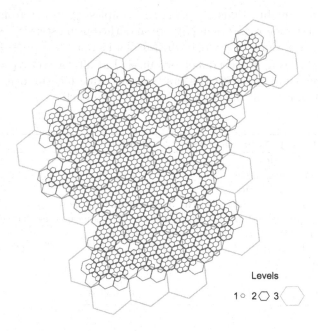

Fig. 2. The three spatial aggregation levels set up for the Rotterdam area encompassing the street network G. Starting from level 1, hexagon bins cover an increasingly higher number of locations of the node-set N.

4.4   Rebalancing Strategies

Slicing the area of network G using a hierarchy of geometric shapes allows us to infer a relation of proximity between nodes within the same region. We exploit this relation by assuming vehicles are allowed to rebalance to the center of the surrounding hexagon neighbors across all three hierarchical levels, totaling up to eighteen rebalancing options. This way, vehicles can explore increasingly farther neighborhoods, insofar as rebalancing targets become hexagon centers up in the spatial hierarchy. To prevent vehicles from flooding high demand locations, we bound the number of vehicles they can accommodate to v_{max}. Then, we consider that rebalancing trips can take place only when $v_{it} \leq v_{max}$, where v_{max} is the cumulative number of vehicles that are either inbound to or staying at each location $i \in N^{(g)}$ for $g = 1$ from current time period t onward. By doing so, we avoid both methodological and practical problems.

First, although we assume $\overline{V}_t^n (R_t^{x,n})$ is linear in R_{ta}, we acknowledge this assumption is prone to result in an oversupply of vehicles in regions associated with high marginal values. However, instead of dampening these values as the number of vehicles increases (using, for example, piecewise-linear approximations), we prefer to tune the value of constant v_{max}.

Second, from a practical perspective, a real-world application has to account for road capacity and curbside space before rebalancing vehicles. The maximum number of cars across regions can also depend on city regulations and vary according to local restrictions, for example, to avoid inconveniencing residents or businesses of a determined area.

5 Experimental Study

Spatial Demand Patters: To generate r request departure points, we use a weighted random process to select an origin neighborhood according to its relative population density using the Dutch census [4]. Next, we use a regular random process to select a street node within this origin neighborhood. We use this process to select 3,000 request origins, from which about one-third end up within the Zuid region. Figure 3 presents the probability distribution of selecting request origins across Rotterdam neighborhoods. Since we investigate first-mile trips, destination points correspond to the closest train stations of each origin point.

Temporal Demand Patters: Regarding the time the requests arrive at the system, we propose five scenarios in which we vary the demand patterns of residents departing from Noord and Zuid regions. We consider that the number of requests always peaks at 8:00 for the residents of Rotterdam Noord, whereas the number of requests originated in Rotterdam Zuid peak at 6:00, 7:00, 8:00, 9:00, and 10:00, leading to five request arrival scenarios labeled N8Z6, N8Z7, N8Z8, N8Z9, and N8Z10. By varying the demand peaks in Zuid, we can investigate how well the algorithm can distribute vehicles in the light of different levels of competition with the Noord demand. Moreover, the relative position between Noord and Zuid peaks allows us to assess the efficacy to which vehicles can move between regions in anticipation to demand. For instance, the earlier the demand peak in Zuid, the more time vehicles will have to move from Zuid to Noord. Conversely, the later the demand peak, the more time vehicles will have to move from Noord to Zuid. All these scenarios are modeled using a normal distribution truncated by t_e and t_l, with a standard deviation of one hour and means equal to the demand peaks entailed by each region.

Waiting Times: Upon receiving a five-minute request batch, the system sets up available trip decisions taking into account a pickup radius $w_{pk} = 10$ min.

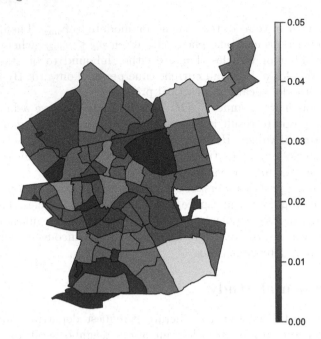

Fig. 3. Probabilities of choosing a departure location within each Rotterdam neighborhood based on the part-to-whole ratio of the number or residents.

If users cannot be accessed by any vehicle within w_{pk}, they are immediately rejected, having to resort to another transportation means. Since we assume the AMoD system integrates a broader MaaS ecosystem, a rejection means that the users will have to rely on alternative modes to fulfill their trips. Hence, in the worst-case scenario, serviced users wait at most fifteen minutes to be picked up.

Cost Schemes: We investigate the influence of six cost schemes on Zuid riders' service levels by manipulating both base fares and penalties. We refer to these schemes using the labels B1R0, B4R0, B8R0, B1R1, B1R4, B1R8, where B and R correspond to the p_{base} and $c_{penalty}$ constants, and the digits represent scaling factors. For instance, B1R0, B4R0, and B8R0 represent cost schemes in which the base fare p_{base} of Zuid users is one, four, and eight times higher. Regarding the values adopted, we consider $p_{base} = c_{penalty} = €2.5$, time-dependent fare $p_{time} = 1€/km$, and time-dependent operational costs $c_{time} = 0.1 €/km$. Finally, we assume B1R0 is our reference cost scheme and use it for all Noord users.

Fleet Configuration: We determine the fleet size following the model predictive control (MPC) algorithm proposed by [8]. Their approach assumes perfect information throughout the whole horizon and does not allow for delays, such that, at the end of each time step, there is a sufficient number of vehicles to pick up all requests at each location. To decrease computation times, we assume that all trip origins and destinations are associated with their respective third-level hexagon centers (38 in total). We have found that the average fleet sizes

achieved using the optimal MPC formulation across ten demand realizations
for each demand pattern scenario range from 382.8 (N8Z10) to 499.9 (N8Z8).
The results also indicated that the closer the demand peaks of Noord and Zuid
regions are, the higher is the fleet size required. To deliberately create a scarcity
scenario that splits the vehicle workforce between the two regions, we carry out
all experiments using a 300-SAV fleet. At the beginning of each ADP iteration,
we randomly distribute these vehicles throughout level-one hexagon locations.
Consequently, since Noord is broader and more populated than Zuid, a service
bias towards Noord will naturally emerge.

Benchmark: We benchmark our ADP π_{VFA} policy against two alternative
policies, namely, π_{myopic} and $\pi_{reactive}$, in which no information about the future
is available. Both policies aim to maximize the cost function in Eq. (4), but
while π_{myopic} seeks only to determine the optimal vehicle-request assignment
represented by Eqs. (1) and (2), the $\pi_{reactive}$ policy relies on an additional vehicle
rebalancing phase. The rebalancing is based on the state-of-the-art algorithm
proposed by Alonso-Mora et al. [2], which consists of a linear program where
idle vehicles are optimally rebalanced to under-supplied locations. Ultimately,
this program aims to minimize the total travel distance of reaching the pickup
locations of unassigned requests while guaranteeing that either all vehicles or all
requests are assigned.

6   Results

We implemented our approach using Python 3.6 and Gurobi 8.1. Test cases were
executed on a 2.60 GHz Intel Core i7 with 32 GB RAM. For all case studies,
we run our ADP algorithm throughout 1,000 iterations, considering stepsizes
$\overline{\alpha} = 0.1$, and maximum vehicle count $v_{max} = 5$, which have been found to show
good performance experimentally.

Since we aim to improve mobility for Zuid users, our analysis focuses mainly
on the service levels (i.e., the ratio of serviced requests) achieved for each region.
Still, provided that users can be picked up timely, delays are already bound to
w_{pk}. Table 1 presents the average service levels (across ten demand realizations)
for each policy π and cost scheme configuration. We separate the service levels
between users departing from each region to evaluate the effect of the proposed
cost schemes on driving vehicles towards Zuid. The results are subsumed under
three categories, namely, "Baseline", "Base fare," and "Rejection penalty." The
"Baseline" category comprises the averages achieved using the myopic and reactive policies, which we use to benchmark the performance of our learning-based
method. As hypothesized, when equity concerns are disregarded, service levels
differ markedly between regions, being consistently higher in Noord.

It can be seen from Table 1 that $\pi_{reactive}$ can already significantly improve the
service levels of Zuid users, servicing about 10% more requests than π_{myopic} in
all demand scenarios. Since the reactive rebalancing policy relies on trip rejection
stimuli to move vehicles to undersupplied areas, the fleet is disproportionately

Table 1. Average ratio of serviced users departing from Noord and Zuid regions for each policy, demand scenario, and cost scheme. Figures correspond to the mean average of ten demand distributions over 3,000 requests.

Policy(π)	Cost scheme	Origin in Noord					Origin in Zuid				
		N8Z6	N8Z7	N8Z8	N8Z9	N8Z10	N8Z6	N8Z7	N8Z8	N8Z9	N8Z10
					Baseline						
myopic	B1R0	.783	.788	.795	.790	.795	.637	.668	.688	.694	.682
reactive	B1R0	.807	.846	.850	.852	.853	.778	.775	.783	.790	.773
					Base fare						
VFA	B1R0	.926	.905	.908	.939	.963	.812	.876	.890	.904	.949
	B4R0	.892	.870	.871	.903	.933	.888	.923	.944	.956	.967
	B8R0	.883	.858	.828	.847	.925	.905	.946	.969	.976	.980
					Rejection penalty						
	B1R1	.903	.885	.886	.908	.949	.848	.919	.921	.935	.940
	B1R4	.903	.848	.863	.892	.919	.881	.957	.948	.966	.968
	B1R8	.874	.842	.812	.825	.899	.903	.961	.972	.956	.980

driven to Zuid. However, $\pi_{reactive}$ still leads to a moderate service bias towards the Noord region, regardless of the demand scenario.

We separate the results of our proposed π_{VFA} policy according to the main feature entailed by each cost scheme. Hence, the figures subsumed under the "Base fare" and "Rejection penalty" categories, highlight the effect of scaling up fares and penalties, respectively. It is worth noting that our π_{VFA} policy performs better than the baseline policies, even for cost scheme B1R0, in which no scaling is considered. The performance improvement is especially remarkable when demand peaks from Noord and Zuid are far apart, for example, in scenarios N8Z6 and N8Z10. These scenarios provide enough time for vehicles to rebalance in anticipation from one region to the other instead of reacting to imbalances in short notice. Moreover, during the thirty-minute rebalancing offset previous to the requests' arrival, vehicles also can harness the value functions to reach areas where users are more prone to appear. This explains how even the competitive scenario N8Z8 could benefit from using the π_{VFA} policy.

To investigate the trade-off between profits and Zuid service levels, we average the results of our VFA policy for each cost scheme over all the demand scenarios. Then, we compare the schemes' averages against the averages obtained for the reference cost scheme B1R0. Average profits are determined in terms of base fare accumulation, considering the number of requests departing from each region and the ratios of serviced users in Table 1. Cost schemes B4R0 and B8R0, lead to 104.8% and 249.6% higher profits to service about 4.9% and 6.9% more Zuid users over B1R0. In contrast, cost schemes B1R1, B1R4, and B1R8 incur 3.8%, 9.3%, and 16.7% losses compared to B1R0 average profit, to service about 2.6%, 5.8%, and 6.8% more Zuid users. For both cost scheme categories, the results indicate that further scaling up incentives or penalties is prone to diminishing returns, once less and less service level gains in the Zuid region can be seen.

Throughout all instances considered, scenario N8Z6 has consistently presented the lowest service levels. Since Noord starts with more vehicles than Zuid, and the demand peak in Zuid occurs earlier, this scenario necessarily demands that vehicles move from Noord to Zuid. With most requests happening at 6:00, most rebalancing operations have to be performed within the rebalancing offset. Considering that vehicles can start from remote parts of Noord, the results indicate that the thirty-minute offset is insufficient to rebalance all necessary vehicles to Zuid adequately. As the demand peak in Zuid is pushed forward (e.g., N8Z7), vehicles have more time to access Zuid user origins, and service levels increase.

7   Conclusion

In this study, we present a learning-based fleet rebalancing method that determines a compromise between company revenues and social equity between two distinct regions of Rotterdam, The Netherlands. Our anticipatory rebalancing strategy caters to the needs of targeted regions, compensates for biases towards more affluent and densely populated regions, and mitigates mobility poverty in disadvantaged areas. Based on a range of cost schemes, we show the tipping point at which cost manipulation can affect value function approximations enough to influence the rebalancing process. Ultimately, our approximate dynamic programming algorithm achieves superior service levels compared to myopic and reactive strategies, regardless of cost scheme and demand scenarios considered.

With respect to public polices, our results indicate that the public sector can work in tandem with private providers to guarantee that new mobility solutions consider the patterns of disadvantaged populations. In this way, as mobility technologies develop, private market innovation can be steered to achieve social equity goals, such as preventing mobility poverty. It is worth noting, however, that adequately fulfilling such goals depends on further policy-making. Since the private sector is at the forefront of new mobility systems, such as AMoDs, the public sector has to invest in incentives for the use of these systems in the broader scheme of city transportation. For instance, new services could integrate existing MaaS frameworks, complementing other transportation options (e.g., transit, walking, and cycling).

Future research will focus on designing equity-aware rebalancing strategies to increase user service levels based on alternative information (e.g., age, gender, income), rather than the departure location alone. Additionally, to improve the effectiveness of location-based equity policies, regional transport accessibility can be further investigated, for example, in terms of transit infrastructure, delays, and availability.

References

1. Al-Kanj, L., Nascimento, J., Powell, W.B.: Approximate dynamic programming for planning a ride-hailing system using autonomous fleets of electric vehicles. Eur. J. Oper. Res. **284**, 1–40 (2020). https://doi.org/10.1016/j.ejor.2020.01.033

2. Alonso-Mora, J., Samaranayake, S., Wallar, A., Frazzoli, E., Rus, D.: On-demand high-capacity ride-sharing via dynamic trip-vehicle assignment. Proc. Natl. Acad. Sci. **114**(3), 462–467 (2017). https://doi.org/10.1073/pnas.1611675114
3. Alonso-Mora, J., Wallar, A., Rus, D.: Predictive routing for autonomous mobility-on-demand systems with ride-sharing. In: 2017 IEEE/RSJ International Conference on Intelligent Robots and Systems (IROS), pp. 3583–3590 (2017). https://doi.org/10.1109/IROS.2017.8206203
4. Centraal Bureau voor de Statistiek (CBS): Wijk-en buurtkaart (2019). https://www.cbs.nl/nl-nl/dossier/nederland-regionaal/geografische-data/wijk-en-buurtkaart-2019
5. Cohen, S., Cabansagan, C.: TransForm: a framework for equity in new mobility (2017). https://trid.trb.org/view/1478022
6. Fagnant, D.J., Kockelman, K.M.: Dynamic ride-sharing and fleet sizing for a system of shared autonomous vehicles in Austin, Texas. Transportation **45**(1), 143–158 (2016). https://doi.org/10.1007/s11116-016-9729-z
7. Gueriau, M., Dusparic, I.: SAMoD: shared autonomous mobility-on-demand using decentralized reinforcement learning. IEEE Conference on Intelligent Transportation Systems, Proceedings, ITSC, pp. 1558–1563 (2018). https://doi.org/10.1109/ITSC.2018.8569608
8. Iglesias, R., Rossi, F., Wang, K., Hallac, D., Leskovec, J., Pavone, M.: Data-driven model predictive control of autonomous mobility-on-demand systems. In: 2018 IEEE International Conference on Robotics and Automation (ICRA), pp. 1–7 (2018). https://doi.org/10.1109/ICRA.2018.8460966
9. Lin, K., Zhao, R., Xu, Z., Zhou, J.: Efficient large-scale fleet management via multi-agent deep reinforcement learning. In: Proceedings of the 24th ACM SIGKDD International Conference on Knowledge Discovery & Data Mining, pp. 1774–1783 (2018). https://doi.org/10.1145/3219819.3219993
10. Lucas, K., Mattioli, G., Verlinghieri, E., Guzman, A.: Transport poverty and its adverse social consequences. Proc. Inst. Civ. Eng. - Transp. **169**(6), 353–365 (2016). https://doi.org/10.1680/jtran.15.00073
11. Lucas, K., van Wee, B., Maat, K.: A method to evaluate equitable accessibility: combining ethical theories and accessibility-based approaches. Transportation **43**(3), 473–490 (2015). https://doi.org/10.1007/s11116-015-9585-2
12. Pavone, M., Smith, S.L., Frazzoli, E., Rus, D.: Robotic load balancing for mobility-on-demand systems. Int. J. Robot. Res. **31**(7), 839–854 (2012). https://doi.org/10.1177/0278364912444766
13. Powell, W.B.: Approximate Dynamic Programming: Solving the Curses of Dimensionality, 2nd edn. Wiley, Hoboken (2011)
14. Simão, H.P., Day, J., George, A.P., Gifford, T., Nienow, J., Powell, W.B.: An approximate dynamic programming algorithm for large-scale fleet management: a case application. Transp. Sci. **43**(2), 178–197 (2009). https://doi.org/10.1287/trsc.1080.0238
15. Spieser, K., Treleaven, K., Zhang, R., Frazzoli, E., Morton, D., Pavone, M.: Toward a systematic approach to the design and evaluation of automated mobility-on-demand systems: a case study in Singapore. In: Meyer, G., Beiker, S. (eds.) Road Vehicle Automation. LNM, pp. 229–245. Springer, Cham (2014). https://doi.org/10.1007/978-3-319-05990-7_20
16. Wen, J., Zhao, J., Jaillet, P.: Rebalancing shared mobility-on-demand systems: a reinforcement learning approach. In: 2017 IEEE 20th International Conference on Intelligent Transportation Systems (ITSC), pp. 220–225 (2017). https://doi.org/10.1109/ITSC.2017.8317908

Idle Vehicle Repositioning for Dynamic Ride-Sharing

Martin Pouls[1]([✉]) [ID], Anne Meyer[2] [ID], and Nitin Ahuja[3]

[1] FZI Research Center for Information Technology, 76131 Karlsruhe, Germany
pouls@fzi.de
[2] TU Dortmund University, 44221 Dortmund, Germany
[3] PTV Group, 76131 Karlsruhe, Germany

Abstract. In dynamic ride-sharing systems, intelligent repositioning of idle vehicles enables service providers to maximize vehicle utilization and minimize request rejection rates as well as customer waiting times. In current practice, this task is often performed decentrally by individual drivers. We present a centralized approach to idle vehicle repositioning in the form of a forecast-driven repositioning algorithm. The core part of our approach is a novel mixed-integer programming model that aims to maximize coverage of forecasted demand while minimizing travel times for repositioning movements. This model is embedded into a planning service also encompassing other relevant tasks such as vehicle dispatching. We evaluate our approach through extensive simulation studies on real-world datasets from Hamburg, New York City, and Manhattan. We test our forecast-driven repositioning approach under a perfect demand forecast as well as a naive forecast and compare it to a reactive strategy. The results show that our algorithm is suitable for real-time usage even in large-scale scenarios. Compared to the reactive algorithm, rejection rates of trip requests are decreased by an average of 2.5% points and customer waiting times see an average reduction of 13.2%.

Keywords: Repositioning · Ride-sharing · Dial-a-ride-problem

1 Introduction

While the popularity of mobility-on-demand (MOD) services such as Uber and Lyft has increased significantly in recent years, this growth has also lead to increased traffic congestion [4]. Several cities have identified this issue and some have even taken countermeasures [8]. One way to tackle this problem is the increased usage of dynamic ride-sharing services such as UberPool or MOIA. In these services, multiple passengers with different destinations share a vehicle. This way, one maintains the flexibility of MOD services compared to traditional public transport, while at the same time improving vehicle utilization.

Planning problems regarding MOD services in general and dynamic ride-sharing, in particular, have generated significant research attention. Most works

© Springer Nature Switzerland AG 2020
E. Lalla-Ruiz et al. (Eds.): ICCL 2020, LNCS 12433, pp. 507–521, 2020.
https://doi.org/10.1007/978-3-030-59747-4_33

focus on the vehicle routing aspect, i.e. solving the dynamic dial-a-ride-problem arising in these applications [1,13]. In this work, we focus on the idle vehicle repositioning problem, i.e. the problem of sending idle vehicles to a suitable location in anticipation of future demand. In many practical applications with self-employed drivers, this problem is currently solved decentrally by incentivizing drivers to reposition towards areas with low vehicle supply. For instance, Uber employs so-called "surge pricing" which raises prices in areas with excess demand and thereby offers increased revenue opportunities to drivers [17]. We propose the usage of a central repositioning strategy that may improve system performance in use cases with a central fleet operator. In general, the overall performance of a ride-sharing system may be impacted significantly by suitable repositioning algorithms. Figure 1 illustrates this fact by comparing vehicle positions in scenarios without and with repositioning. Without repositioning vehicles become stuck in low-demand areas. In turn, requests in other areas are rejected due to a lack of nearby vehicles. This is due to the assumption of a maximum waiting time for customers in dial-a-ride problems. A vehicle must reach the customer within this time frame, otherwise the customer is rejected. Thus, vehicles in low-demand areas cannot reach many new trip requests in time and are consequently rarely assigned a new tour. This phenomenon may be avoided by using a suitable repositioning mechanism.

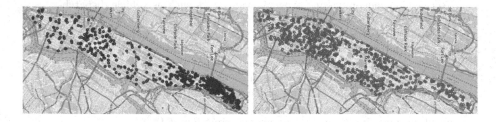

Fig. 1. Vehicle positions without (left) and with (right) repositioning.

The main contribution of this paper is the introduction of a novel forecast-driven repositioning algorithm. In particular, we propose a mixed-integer programming (MIP) model that maximizes the coverage of forecasted demand while minimizing driving times for repositioning movement. In contrast to prior works, our model utilizes a realistic demand forecast conforming to state-of-the-art forecasting models [11,19] and does not assume any further information regarding probability distributions of trip requests. The solution approach is embedded into a planning service for dynamic ride-sharing applications and evaluated on real-world taxi datasets from Hamburg, New York City and Manhattan through extensive simulation studies. The results show that our model can be used in real-time even on large-scale instances with up to 20,000 trip requests per hour. Compared to a reactive approach, our algorithm reduces rejection rates by an average of 2.5% points and customer waiting times by 13.2%.

The remainder of this work is organized as follows. Section 2 gives an overview of related work regarding idle vehicle repositioning. In Sect. 3 we briefly describe our planning service and the simulation that is used for evaluations. Our repositioning approach is detailed in Sect. 4. Finally, Sect. 5 presents our computational results and Sect. 6 summarizes our findings and gives some possible directions for future work.

2   Related Work

There has recently been an influx of papers dealing with repositioning in the context of MOD services. For bike- and car-sharing applications, several repositioning strategies have been proposed (e.g. [5,18]). However, all of these approaches differ from the problem at hand either due to their station-based nature or due to the missing consideration of ride-sharing. In the context of classical taxi services, some works consider repositioning and propose the usage of historical GPS data to identify potentially profitable regions [10,14]. In contrast to our work, these papers do not consider ride-sharing and have different objective functions as they view the problem decentrally from the perspective of individual drivers. Idle vehicle repositioning has also been modeled using queuing-based methods [3,16]. Although these works show that their approaches yield improvements compared to myopic strategies, they have not been evaluated on realistic large-scale scenarios. Moreover, they tend to be limited in the extent of the covered area and the spatial granularity of decisions.

To the best of our knowledge, there are only few papers considering idle vehicle repositioning in the context of large-scale dynamic ride-sharing applications. One approach is a reactive repositioning scheme with the idea of sending idle vehicles to the pickup locations of rejected trip requests [1]. Idle vehicles are matched to rejected requests while minimizing the travel time for repositioning movements. In a follow-up paper [2], the same authors present a more refined sampling-based approach. They include anticipated trip requests in their vehicle routes that are served with a low priority. The authors show that this approach leads to reduced waiting times and in-car travel delays compared to the reactive repositioning from [1]. However, no significant improvement in the number of served trip requests was made. Another paper presents two simple approaches in which vehicles reposition according to historical pickup probabilities [9]. Vehicles either move to a zone for roaming or to a depot. The probability of selecting a zone or depot is proportional to historical pickup probabilities. The authors compare these approaches to a setting without repositioning and evaluate them with a simulation scenario based on New York taxi data with approximately 145,000 trip requests over 8 h. Both repositioning algorithms improve the request acceptance rate at the cost of an increase in deadheading time. In contrast to our work, the authors do not consider detailed information about supply and demand. In particular, neither the current configuration of the vehicle fleet nor the total demand is considered during repositioning.

In this work, we view repositioning as an independent problem. As seen from [2], repositioning can also be treated as an integrated decision during vehicle routing. In that case, the problem may be viewed as a vehicle routing problem with stochastic customers. A variety of solution approaches have been presented for this problem, for a review see [15]. However, none of these approaches have been studied on large-scale scenarios and they often assume the presence of detailed information regarding trip request distributions that is not available in many practical settings.

3   System Overview

Our forecast-driven repositioning algorithm is embedded into a planning service for dynamic ride-sharing applications encompassing all components regarding dispatching, repositioning, demand forecasting, and routing. For evaluation, the planning service is coupled with a simulation that emulates relevant real-world events generated by customers and vehicles. The resulting overall system and the communication between components is depicted in Fig. 2.

By making a strict separation from the simulation, the planning service could theoretically be directly transferred to a real-world use case.

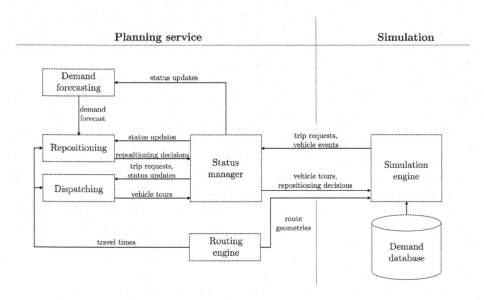

Fig. 2. Planning service, simulation and relevant communication.

3.1   Planning Service

All planning and forecasting functionality is consolidated in the planning service, which consists of separate decoupled modules. All external communication takes place via the central status manager that also maintains the current status of all vehicles and requests and provides this information to other modules.

The dispatching module contains functionalities for vehicle routing. Essentially, it solves a dynamic dial-a-ride-problem with the typical constraints: capacity, waiting time, and ride time [6]. We utilize a simple insertion heuristic inspired by [12] which tries to dynamically insert each incoming request into the current routing plan. If no feasible insertion is found, the request is rejected. The repositioning module implements our approach for idle vehicle repositioning which is detailed in Sect. 4.

Two further components are needed to provide the necessary input for planning. The routing engine operates on OpenStreetMap (OSM) data and provides travel times to the other modules. The demand forecasting module outputs the forecasted number of trip requests given a discrete set of areas (e.g. a grid-based partitioning of the map) and a forecast horizon (e.g. 30 min). This format conforms to state of the art demand forecasting methods [11,19] that could be integrated in this system. However, the forecasting methodology itself is not the focus of this work.

3.2 Simulation

The simulation operates on a database containing trip requests. Each trip request consists of the request time, origin and destination coordinates, and the number of passengers. The request may be obtained from actual taxi services or be derived from other sources such as public transport data or traffic simulations.

These trip requests are replayed by the simulation engine and sent to the planning service. If the trip request is accepted, it is assigned to a vehicle and the simulation receives an updated vehicle tour. It operates on this tour and simulates all relevant events such as arrival and departure at stops. Furthermore, the simulation emulates real-world GPS tracking by regularly sending position updates to the planning backend. The necessary information for these updates is obtained from a routing engine working on the road network.

4 Repositioning Approaches

In the following, we present our forecast-driven repositioning algorithm (FDR) as well as a simple reactive strategy (REACT) intended as a benchmark.

4.1 Forecast-Driven Repositioning

Our algorithm works with a demand forecast that provides the anticipated number of trip requests for a set of areas and a forecast horizon. The core part of FDR is a MIP model (FDR-M) in which we aim to maximize the coverage of forecasted demand by intelligently repositioning idle vehicles while minimizing the travel times for these movements. We assume that vehicles may cover trip requests near their current location as they can reach these requests within the maximum waiting time. Our model also takes the current state of vehicles into account and reflects the fact that vehicles may serve multiple requests at once. Model FDR-M takes decisions on an aggregated level. As an output, it determines the number of vehicles relocated between specific areas. The model is embedded into a planning process that provides the necessary inputs and translates the model output into actual repositioning assignments. In the following, we will first present this planning process and subsequently introduce the model itself with the necessary notation.

Planning Process. Model FDR-M is embedded into a rolling horizon planning process which is triggered at regular intervals f (e.g. every 3 min). The main steps of the planning process are as follows:

1. Obtain an up-to-date demand forecast.
2. Solve repositioning model FDR-M.
3. Determine actual repositioning assignments.

In the last step, we determine specific vehicles and targets for repositioning based on the aggregated output of FDR-M. Assume the model decides to reposition x_{ij} vehicles from area i to area j. Given that $j \in A$ represents an area, we have a set of feasible repositioning targets P_j in j. These are specific points to which we may send a vehicle. They are determined from prior trip requests, i.e. each past pickup location is a feasible repositioning target. We sample x_{ij} of these targets and subsequently greedily send the closest idle vehicle to each target.

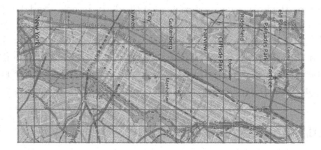

Fig. 3. Grid-based partitioning into areas (1×1 km).

Notation. Relevant notation for FDR is summarized in Table 1. K denotes the set of all vehicles. This set may be further subdivided into idle vehicles K^{id}, vehicles serving a tour K^t and vehicles on a repositioning trip K^r. In addition, we assume a set of areas A. For the remainder of this work, we utilize a partitioning of the region under study into grid cells (1×1 km) as seen in Fig. 3. For the purpose of travel time calculations, we assume that these areas are represented by their center and determine a travel time t_{ij} between the centers of i and j. We may now further divide the sets of vehicles by area as K_a^{id}, K_a^t, K_a^r. Note that the sets K_a^{id} and K_a^t contain those vehicles currently situated in area a. K_a^r on the other hand consists of vehicles currently repositioning towards a. Vehicles may only be repositioned to valid target areas $a \in A_r \subseteq A$. In practical applications A_r might be determined based on suitable waiting spots for vehicles. In this study, we limit A_r to areas with at least one prior pickup as we sample specific repositioning targets from past pickup locations. Our model works on a demand forecast denoted as $\hat{d}_a, a \in A$ over the forecast horizon h (e.g. 30 min). This forecast gives us the predicted number of trip requests originating in a within the horizon h. The areas that a vehicle may cover from its current area $a \in A$ are controlled by t^c which corresponds to the maximum waiting time of a customer. We refer to an area j as reachable from i ($r_{ij} = 1$), if $t_{ij} \leq t^c$. The assumption is that in this case a vehicle located at i may reach a request in j on time. Vehicles may serve multiple trip requests over the forecast horizon h. This aspect is included in the model by parameter p which corresponds to the assumed number of requests that an initially idle vehicle can serve. Vehicles currently serving a tour may also cover future demand. However, given the fact that they are already partially occupied with their current tour, their provided coverage is discounted by a factor $\alpha < 1$. Both α and p should be determined depending on the specific scenario under study. They may for instance be derived from historical data. A possible extension would be to determine these parameters adaptively and vehicle-specific.

Table 1. Notation for forecast-driven repositioning.

Sets	
K	Vehicles
$K^{id}\|K^t\|K^r$	Idle/touring/repositioning vehicles
A	Areas
A_r	Valid target areas for repositioning
$K_a^{id}\|K_a^t\|K_a^r$	Idle/touring/repositioning vehicles per area $a \in A$
P_a	Set of feasible repositioning targets in $a \in A$
Parameters	
t_{ij}	Travel time from $i \in A$ to $j \in A$
$\hat{d}_a$	Demand forecast for $a \in A$
h	Forecast horizon
p	Served requests over the given forecast horizon h
t^c	Coverage radius
r_{ij}	Reachability indication $\in \{0,1\}$; $r_{ij} = 1$, if $t_{ij} \leq t^c$
α	Discount factor for touring vehicles $k \in K^t$
β	Factor for travel times incurred by coverage

Mixed-Integer Formulation. Model FDR-M is given in Eqs. (1)–(8). Variables $c_{ij}|i,j \in A$ denote the coverage that is provided by vehicles in i for forecasted demand in j. This corresponds to the assumed amount of forecasted trip requests in j that would be served by vehicles from i. c_{ij} may take fractional values as forecasted demand $\hat{d}_j$ may be fractional and can be covered from multiple origin areas $i \in A$. Variables $x_{ij}|i,j \in A$ denote the number of vehicles repositioned from i to j. The hierarchical objective function (1) follows three goals which are reflected in the terms of the objective function:

1. Maximize the sum of covered demand, weighted by forecasted demand.
2. Minimize the number of repositioning movements.
3. Minimize weighted travel times.

Objective precedence is ensured by weights $W_1 >> W_2 >> 1$. The primary objective is to maximize the acceptance rate of future requests by covering predicted demand. Empirically, it has proven beneficial to prioritize coverage in high demand areas. Therefore, we add weights corresponding to the forecasted demand $\hat{d}_j$ in the covered area $j \in A$. The secondary objective stems from the operational concern that we want to move as few vehicles as possible. Particularly, we do not want to move any vehicles at all, if the current fleet configuration can cover all forecasted demand. The tertiary objective ensures that overall travel times are minimized and leads to suitable vehicles being selected for repositioning. Two travel time factors are considered. On the one hand, travel times are attached to x_{ij} variables as repositioning movements incur the movement of empty vehicles. Additionally, we consider anticipated travel times attached to c_{ij} variables. The assumption is that a vehicle located at $i \in A$ will have to move to $j \in A$ when a request arises. These anticipated travel times are penalized by a factor $\beta \geq 1$ which rewards moving vehicles closer to predicted demand. This tends to be beneficial as it reduces customer waiting times and improves vehicle utilization.

$$\text{(FDR-M)} \quad \sum_{i\in A}\sum_{j\in A} W_1 \cdot \hat{d}_j \cdot c_{ij} - \sum_{i\in A}\sum_{j\in A} W_2 \cdot x_{ij} \tag{1}$$

$$- \sum_{i\in A}\sum_{j\in A}(x_{ij} + \beta \cdot c_{ij})t_{ij} \to \max$$

$$\text{s.t.} \quad \sum_{j\in A} x_{ij} \leq |K_i^{id}| \qquad\qquad i \in A \tag{2}$$

$$\sum_{j\in A} c_{ji} \leq \hat{d}_i \qquad\qquad i \in A \tag{3}$$

$$\sum_{j\in A} c_{ij} \leq p \cdot \left(\sum_{j\in A} x_{ji} + |K_i^r| + \alpha \cdot |K_i^t|\right) \quad i \in A \tag{4}$$

$$c_{ij} = 0 \qquad\qquad i,j \in A, r_{ij}=0 \tag{5}$$

$$x_{ij} = 0 \qquad\qquad i \in A, j \notin A_r \tag{6}$$

$$x_{ij} \in \mathbb{N}_0^+ \qquad\qquad i,j \in A \qquad (7)$$
$$c_{ij} \in \mathbb{R}_0^+ \qquad\qquad i,j \in A \qquad (8)$$

Constraints (2) guarantee that the number of vehicles repositioned from $i \in A$ does not exceed the number of idle vehicles. Constraints (3) ensure that the maximum provided coverage for a given area is capped by the forecasted demand. Inversely, Constraints (4) limit the provided coverage from area i to the maximum available coverage. This maximum available coverage for area i is calculated based on the available vehicles and includes the assigned vehicles x_{ji}. In addition, provided coverage is based on vehicles repositioning to i or currently on a tour in i. The latter ones are discounted by factor $\alpha \leq 1$. The available coverage in trip requests is obtained by multiplying the available vehicles with the assumed number of served requests per period p. Reachability of covered areas is ensured by Constraints (5) while Constraints (6) limit repositioning movements to valid targets. Variable domains are given by Constraints (7) and (8).

4.2 Reactive Repositioning

As a benchmark, we implement a reactive approach (REACT). The algorithm is an adapted version of the reactive repositioning algorithm presented by the authors of [1]. We modify their approach to reflect the fact that we process trip requests individually whereas they work with batches. Therefore, after rejecting a request, we may also directly reposition an idle vehicle. Given a rejected request r an its pickup location p_r, we greedily reposition the nearest idle vehicle to p_r, i.e. the vehicle with the shortest travel time from its current position to p_r.

5 Computational Results

5.1 Data and Setup

We evaluate our repositioning algorithms on three real-world taxi datasets from Hamburg[1] (HH), New York[2] (NYC) and Manhattan (MANH). The latter is created from the NYC dataset by limiting it to trips within Manhattan. These datasets contain the pickup time, pickup location, dropoff location, and number of passengers for historical taxi trips. We filter the original data by eliminating obvious outliers and erroneous records. As a routing engine, we use RoutingKit [7] which operates on OpenStreetMap extracts covering the respective areas under study. Gurobi 8.1.0 serves as a MIP solver for model FDR-M. All experiments were run on the same machine with an Intel i7-6600U CPU and 20 GB of RAM.

---

[1] Provided by PTV Group, Haid-und-Neu-Str. 15, 76131 Karlsruhe.
[2] https://www1.nyc.gov/site/tlc/about/tlc-trip-record-data.page.

5.2   Scenarios and Parameter Settings

For each dataset, we run simulations covering two separate temporal scenarios: a Wednesday and a Sunday. This was done to evaluate the algorithm performance under different demand patterns as the spatial and temporal distribution of trip requests varies between weekdays and weekends. The precise dates and the number of trip requests are shown in Table 2.

Table 2. Temporal scenarios with dates and number of trip requests.

	HH		NYC		MANH	
	Date	Req.	Date	Req.	Date	Req.
Wed.	20.03.2019	13,556	16.03.2016	376,526	16.03.2016	297,457
Sun.	24.03.2019	10,669	20.03.2016	368,508	20.03.2016	269,346

We also vary the size of the vehicle fleet. We determined a base number of vehicles from preliminary testing (HH – 90, NYC – 1300, MANH – 900). With this base number, the fleet should be able to service around 95% of all trip requests. We then create scenarios with vehicle factors of 0.8, 0.9, 1.0, 1.1 and 1.2 where the actual number of vehicles per dataset is obtained by multiplying the base number with the vehicle factor. Combined with the temporal settings, we end up with 10 scenarios per dataset. Each of these scenarios is run with three different repositioning modes: no repositioning (NONE), reactive repositioning as described in Sect. 4.2 (REACT) and forecast-driven repositioning from Sect. 4.1 (FDR). The latter is run with two different demand forecasts: 1. a perfect demand forecast (FDR (P)) and 2. a naive demand forecast (FDR (N)). This naive demand forecast assumes that demand stays constant, i.e. the forecasted demand over the next horizon h is equal to the observed demand within the previous horizon h.

Parameters concerning FDR were determined based on preliminary results and historical data and are summarized in Table 3. Some parameters need to be determined dataset-specific, due to the significant differences in covered area and in demand density between the three datasets. For instance, in Manhattan a single vehicle may serve more requests in 30 min than in Hamburg due to much denser demand and a smaller covered area. The same factors also lead to the longer maximum waiting time for HH compared to MANH and NYC. All simulations are run with a warm-up time of 6 h, i.e. if we are evaluating the 20.03.2019, the simulation actually starts at 19.03.2019 18:00 and the first 6 h are not included in the gathered statistics.

5.3   Algorithm Performance with a Perfect Demand Forecast

In this section, we first evaluate the performance of FDR under a perfect demand forecast. Section 5.4 compares these results to a setting with a naive forecast.

Table 3. FDR parameter settings.

Description	All	HH	NYC	MANH
Forecast horizon (h)	30 min			
Repositioning frequency (f)	3 min			
Coverage travel time weight (β)	1.05			
Active vehicle factor (α)	0.7			
Grid cell size	1×1 km			
Objective weight for total coverage (W_1)	1000			
Objective weight for vehicle movements (W_2)	10			
Requests per forecast horizon (p)		5	8	9
Coverage limit (t^c)		8 min	4 min	4 min

Running Times. Our forecast-driven repositioning is real-time capable even on large problem instances. The average running times for one iteration of algorithm FDR was 475 ms (HH), 1938 ms (NYC) and 138 ms (MANH). Given that FDR is run once every 3 min, this running time is unproblematic. Including all other tasks such as dispatching and simulation, the average total running time for one scenario run was 8.7 min (HH), 315.9 min (NYC) and 138.4 min (MANH), a substantial speed-up over the simulated real-time equivalent of 1440 min.

Rejection Rates and Vehicle Travel Times. Figure 4 shows the request rejection rates, i.e. the fraction of requests that could not be served, depending on the dataset and fleet size factor. Across all scenarios, FDR yields the best results. The average improvement compared to REACT was 3.7, 2.2 and 1.5% points for HH, NYC, and MANH respectively. The improvement varies substantially between the datasets. We believe this is mainly due to the geographical distribution of requests and overall vehicle utilization. For instance, REACT works remarkably well on the Manhattan scenario where most trip requests occur in downtown Manhattan. In case of the other two datasets, the improvement in rejection rates is more significant. One trend across all datasets is that the difference between FDR and REACT grows as the number of vehicles is increased. FDR is better suited to exploit larger fleet sizes where almost all trip requests may be served, even ones in remote areas. In case of small vehicle fleets, the complete fleet may be occupied during peak hours, therefore leaving little room for improvement by smart repositioning.

Vehicle travel times and therefore operational costs are increased when using repositioning as seen in Fig. 5. On average, travel times with FDR are increased by 11.7% (HH), 1.7% (NYC) and 2.1% (MANH) compared to REACT. For the HH dataset this increase is larger than might be expected based on the improvement in served requests. One reason for this is that we now also serve those requests that are inefficient to serve, e.g. in remote areas. On the other two datasets the increase is roughly in line with the improvement in served requests.

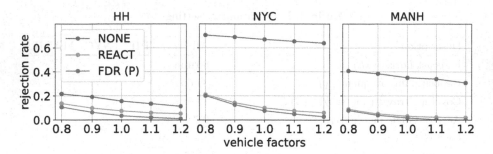

Fig. 4. Average request rejection rates.

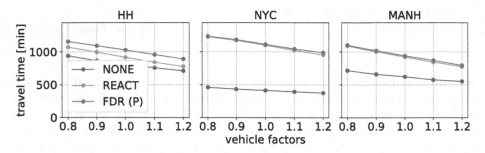

Fig. 5. Average vehicle travel times.

Customer Waiting Times. Besides reducing rejection rates, repositioning also decreases customer waiting times by moving idle vehicles closer to anticipated customer locations. Figure 6 compares the average customer waiting time, i.e. the time a customer has to wait before being picked up. With FDR the waiting time of a single customer is reduced by an average of 16.6% (66 s), 9.9% (23 s) and 13.2% (31 s) compared to REACT for HH, NYC, and MANH. Even in scenarios without a significant improvement regarding rejection rates, FDR manages to reduce waiting times. In practice, this reduction in waiting time will improve customer satisfaction and lead to improved vehicle utilization.

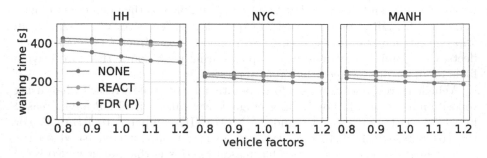

Fig. 6. Average customer waiting times.

Vehicle Utilization. Figure 7 shows the vehicle utilization compared between the different repositioning modes for one scenario. Several aspects of our algorithm FDR may be observed from this chart. During low-demand times (particularly at night between 02:00 and 04:00), most of the fleet is left idle and only minimal repositioning is performed. Before the morning peak, a significant portion of the fleet is repositioned. In comparison, REACT only starts to reposition notable numbers of vehicles after a small spike in rejected requests at around 07:00. Overall, when using FDR, the number of rejected requests is almost zero throughout most of the day. Only during the evening peak after approximately 18:00, when the complete fleet is occupied, requests are rejected.

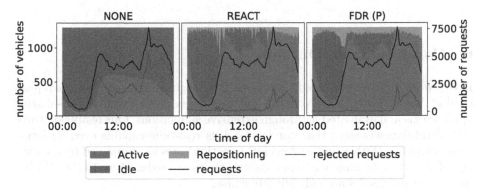

Fig. 7. Vehicle utilization throughout the day for one scenario (NYC, Wednesday, 1.0 vehicle factor) and three repositioning modes. Colored areas illustrate the number of vehicles in a specific state over time. Possible states are idle, active (i.e. serving a tour) and repositioning. Lines indicate the number of total and rejected requests over time (Color figure online)

5.4 Algorithm Performance with a Naive Demand Forecast

Figure 8 illustrates the average request rejection rates with FDR (N) compared to FDR (P) and REACT. In comparison with a perfect forecast, the results with a naive forecast are nearly identical with an average increase of 0.06% points. The picture regarding customer waiting times is similar with an average increase of 0.2%. These results illustrate that our algorithm is robust to minor forecast errors and may be used successfully with a simple forecasting model. However, it should be noted that for such short-term forecasts the utilized naive model performs remarkably well and would be difficult to outperform substantially even with complex forecasting models.

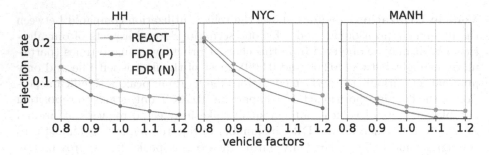

Fig. 8. Average rejection rates.

6 Conclusion and Outlook

In this work, we have presented a forecast-driven algorithm for idle vehicle repositioning. We embedded the algorithm a planning service for dynamic ride-sharing applications and evaluated it through extensive simulations. Our results on three real-world datasets show that our approach is real-time capable even on large-scale scenarios. With a perfect forecast, rejection rates are improved by an average of 2.5% points while customer waiting times are reduced by 13.2%. With a naive forecast, results are only slightly worse.

In the future, we aim to study how our algorithm reacts to forecasting errors and in which situations it might lead to undesirable repositioning movements. Additionally, we intend to improve our model in several ways. The provided coverage of currently traveling vehicles could be modeled in more detail by including spatial-temporal aspects such as current vehicle trajectories. Some model parameters such as the number of trip requests served over the forecast horizon could be determined adaptively and per individual vehicle, increasing the level of detail of the model and removing the need for preliminary parameter optimization.

References

1. Alonso-Mora, J., Samaranayake, S., Wallar, A., Frazzoli, E., Rus, D.: On-demand high-capacity ride-sharing via dynamic trip-vehicle assignment. Proc. Natl. Acad. Sci. **114**(3), 462–467 (2017). https://doi.org/10.1073/pnas.1611675114
2. Alonso-Mora, J., Wallar, A., Rus, D.: Predictive routing for autonomous mobility-on-demand systems with ride-sharing. In: 2017 IEEE/RSJ International Conference on Intelligent Robots and Systems (IROS), pp. 3583–3590. IEEE, Vancouver (September 2017). https://doi.org/10.1109/IROS.2017.8206203
3. Braverman, A., Dai, J.G., Liu, X., Ying, L.: Empty-car routing in ridesharing systems. Oper. Res. **67**(5), 1437–1452 (2019). https://doi.org/10.1287/opre.2018.1822
4. Castiglione, J., Cooper, D.: Tncs and congestion (2018). https://www.sfcta.org/projects/tncs-and-congestion. Accessed 11 Mar 2020

5. Chemla, D., Meunier, F., Wolfler Calvo, R.: Bike sharing systems: solving the static rebalancing problem. Discret. Optim. **10**(2), 120–146 (2013). https://doi.org/10. 1016/j.disopt.2012.11.005

6. Cordeau, J.F., Laporte, G.: The dial-a-ride problem: models and algorithms. Ann. Oper. Res. **153**(1), 29–46 (2007). https://doi.org/10.1007/s10479-007-0170-8

7. Dibbelt, J., Strasser, B., Wagner, D.: Customizable contraction hierarchies. J. Exp. Algorithmics **21**(1), 1–49 (2016). https://doi.org/10.1145/2886843

8. Doubek, J.: New York city temporarily halts more Uber and Lyft cars on the road (2018). https://www.npr.org/2018/08/09/637008474/new-york-city-temporarily-halts-more-uber-and-lyft-cars-on-the-road. Accessed 11 Mar 2020

9. Jung, J.Y., Chow, J.: Large-scale simulation-based evaluation of fleet repositioning strategies for dynamic rideshare in New York city, pp. 2019–01-0924 (April 2019). https://doi.org/10.4271/2019-01-0924

10. Li, B., et al.: Hunting or waiting? Discovering passenger-finding strategies from a large-scale real-world taxi dataset. In: 2011 IEEE International Conference on Pervasive Computing and Communications Workshops (PERCOM Workshops), pp. 63–68 (March 2011). https://doi.org/10.1109/PERCOMW.2011.5766967

11. Liao, S., Zhou, L., Di, X., Yuan, B., Xiong, J.: Large-scale short-term urban taxi demand forecasting using deep learning. In: 2018 23rd Asia and South Pacific Design Automation Conference (ASP-DAC), pp. 428–433 (January 2018). https:// doi.org/10.1109/ASPDAC.2018.8297361

12. Ma, S., Zheng, Y., Wolfson, O.: Real-time city-scale taxi ridesharing. IEEE Trans. Knowl. Data Eng. **27**(7), 1782–1795 (2015). https://doi.org/10.1109/TKDE.2014. 2334313

13. Ma, T.Y., Rasulkhani, S., Chow, J.Y., Klein, S.: A dynamic ridesharing dispatch and idle vehicle repositioning strategy with integrated transit transfers. Transp. Res. Part E: Logist. Transp. Rev. **128**, 417–442 (2019). https://doi.org/10.1016/ j.tre.2019.07.002

14. Powell, J.W., Huang, Y., Bastani, F., Ji, M.: Towards reducing taxicab cruising time using spatio-temporal profitability maps. In: Pfoser, D., et al. (eds.) SSTD 2011. LNCS, vol. 6849, pp. 242–260. Springer, Heidelberg (2011). https://doi.org/ 10.1007/978-3-642-22922-0_15

15. Ritzinger, U., Puchinger, J., Hartl, R.F.: A survey on dynamic and stochastic vehicle routing problems. Int. J. Prod. Res. **54**(1), 215–231 (2016). https://doi. org/10.1080/00207543.2015.1043403

16. Sayarshad, H.R., Chow, J.Y.: Non-myopic relocation of idle mobility-on-demand vehicles as a dynamic location-allocation-queueing problem. Transp. Res. Part E: Logist. Transp. Rev. **106**, 60–77 (2017). https://doi.org/10.1016/j.tre.2017.08.003

17. Uber: Surge pricing (2020). https://marketplace.uber.com/pricing/surge-pricing. Accessed 07 Apr 2020

18. Weikl, S., Bogenberger, K.: Relocation strategies and algorithms for free-floating car sharing systems. IEEE Intell. Transp. Syst. Mag. **5**(4), 100–111 (2013). https:// doi.org/10.1109/MITS.2013.2267810

19. Yao, H., et al.: Deep multi-view spatial-temporal network for taxi demand prediction. In: The Thirty-Second AAAI Conference on Artificial Intelligence (2018)

Smart City: A Perspective of Emergency and Resilience at a Community Level in Shanghai

Xiaoning Shi[1]([✉])[iD], Wenchen Sun[2][iD], Stefan Voß[1][iD], and Jiangang Jin[3][iD]

[1] University of Hamburg, Von-Melle-Park 5, Hamburg, Germany
{xiaoning.shi,stefan.voss}@uni-hamburg.de
[2] Shanghai Urban Construction and Communications Commission,
100 Dagu Road, Shanghai, China
swenchen@zjw.sh.gov.cn
[3] Shanghai Jiao Tong University, 800 Dongchuan Road, Shanghai, China
jiangang.jin@sjtu.edu.cn
http://www.bwl.uni-hamburg.de/iwi.html, http://jtys.naoce.sjtu.edu.cn/

Abstract. Natural disasters, contagious diseases and political conflicts might become emergencies which, to some extent, trigger abnormal form of traffic and logistics at the level of municipal cities as well as managerial control at the level of communities. In such context, level-of-service or cost-benefit-analysis are not considered as appropriate approaches for measuring governance performance of related cities and communities.

At the level of a municipal city, Shanghai (China) takes action considering the fact that it is a well-connected Chinese city comprising many transportation modes domestically and internationally. Stopping the further spread of the disease out of Wuhan City, by banning infected people from leaving Wuhan became a top priority on 23 January, 2020. Ever since then, Shanghai is taking actions step by step to avoid a secondary outbreak of COVID-19 in the city after the primary outbreak in Wuhan City. One of the actions is to control at the community level integrating manual measures together with advanced information technology applications.

At the community level, in this paper, some raw data of a residential community in a relatively suburban district in Shanghai is collected. As a goal of this paper, managerial measures are identified as effective. It does not necessarily mean that we hope these measures would have to be used elsewhere in the world. However, identifying and demonstrating the know-how on impact of public health interventions in specific cases has its merit, especially as the COVID-19 case turned out to be a global pandemic. After investigating the data, several insights regarding behaviors of human beings and patterns of demographics are provided.

Keywords: Smart city · Smart community · Resilience · Human mobility · Digitalization

Supported by National Natural Science Foundation of China with Grant No. 11602137, No. 71771149, and No. 71831008.

E. Lalla-Ruiz et al. (Eds.): ICCL 2020, LNCS 12433, pp. 522–536, 2020.
https://doi.org/10.1007/978-3-030-59747-4_34

1   Introduction

Disruptive events, depending on their scales and evolving speeds, might become emergencies which trigger abnormal patterns of traffic and logistics at the level of municipal cities as well as managerial control at the level of communities. In such context, either level-of-service or cost-benefit-analysis are not considered as appropriate approaches for measuring governance performance of related cities and communities. Hence, a holistic approach including classic and emerging elements within the field of urban planning, governance, emergencies and resilience should be considered and developed.

To narrow it down, in this paper, we address the residential community managerial measures in Shanghai at the beginning of 2020, after the contagious disease, in this case COVID-19, was spreading in Wuhan City in the end of the year 2019. As mentioned in a report released at the early stage of the Coronavirus disease outbreak in Wuhan City, there exists a mean 10-day delay between infection and detection; therefore, self-sustaining human-to-human transmission should not be ruled out [11]. China's health authorities and the government have been moving quickly [9]. Shanghai and Wuhan are well-connected in terms of many transportation modes. Therefore, the risk of a secondary outbreak in Shanghai is quite high. In such context, transport, traffic and urbanization shed lights on spontaneous residential demand including goods, medical services and supportive labors, respectively. After the lockdown of Wuhan City, there is a need to track information on transport and mobilities in order to facilitate control and restriction of epidemic processes in Shanghai.

The subsequent sections are structured as follows. After this introduction, a literature review is conducted in Sect. 2. By observing the data in Sect. 3, a few managerial measures are identified. After investigating the data, several insights regarding behaviors of human beings and patterns of demographics are provided in Sect. 4. Finally, conclusions and future research directions are listed and discussed in Sects. 5 and 6.

2   Literature Review

This section reviews existing literature in smart community, smart city, emergency governance and resilience performance, based on the terminologies defined by the urban planners, logistics researchers, geographers, social scientists and Information and Communication Technology (ICT) professionals.

2.1   Smart City and Smart Community

The concept of smart city has been leveraged since the early 2010s. It includes but is not limited to urbanization with digital innovations (e.g., mobile phone applications, APPs), city living labs, interactive human mobility and traffic flows, smart grids, smart hospital and health care services. In the context of the COVID-19 outbreak and pandemic, there have been many implementations of public health codes demonstrating estimated personal health status via APPs in quite a few municipal cities and provinces in China, e.g., Suishen Code in Shanghai, and Ankang Code in Anhui Province, etc. In the Chinese language, Suishen Code implies 'along with you in Shanghai', and Ankang Code has its meaning of 'staying safe and healthy in Anhui Province', respectively.

It should also be noted that when promoting the concept of smart city, leading cities and follower cities (or fellow cities) are often used to better describe the phenomena that some cities develop faster and share experiences, and some other cities catch up by implementing the shared experiences. In the context of resilience from the pandemic in early 2020, there are some leading cities, e.g., Shanghai, which start investigating the above-mentioned Code while lockdown and start using it at a very early stage of resilience, i.e. on 5th March. Some cities are followers and quick learners, e.g., Dalian, which started a similar implementation on 10th March, 2020.

Above-mentioned public health codes facilitate control measures on residents' mobilities by coloring their permits with red, yellow and green, just like what the traffic light does for monitoring vehicle transportation. Before obtaining the codes, one should submit accurate personal data including full name, identification card number, mobile number, etc., and a validation along with a mobility color would be issued after approval. Therefore, such APP installed on mobile phones might lead to serious debates and arguments on privacy protection concerns in normal contexts in China, or in other countries in the world. However, that is beyond the scope of this paper.

In the setting of smart cities and smart communities, ICT plays vital roles in various manner. Prior to the usage of emerging technological applications, mobile phone data is used to predict the spatial spread of another disease, i.e., Cholera [3]. In this research, movements of 2.9 million anonymous mobile phone SIM cards are used to create a national mobility network.

Regarding community transmission, restrictions on longer range population movement are shown to be a potentially useful additional control measure in some context [20]. The community level in Italian and Dutch societies has been studied in [17], together with three other levels, i.e., school level, household level and workplace level, in a multiplex network. In this research, level-specific (or layer-specific) patterns are observed.

Furthermore, there is evidence that a particular spatial setting is an important determinant of the overall magnitude of an epidemic. Shortening the onset-to-admission interval, as one of the measures, is suggested to be given high priority [8]. Contact-tracing studies are done to assess incubation periods and the nature of the contact resulted in transmission. However, the case-fatality rate is estimated based on cases in hospitals only. Therefore, this research also indicates that if additional infections in the community do not lead to admission to hospital or death, the case-fatality rate based on all infections would be lower. Therefore, community-based serological surveys to assess infection and recovery rates are a priority once a specific and sensitive serological test is available. Based on these discussions, we assume that data collection and analytics at the community level, especially with 'smart' technologies could be useful for deepening our understanding and sharpen the intervention measures.

Recently, the trend and experiments on smart city and smart community also raise the thinking on how urbanization would make sense when infection prevention of pandemics is needed on a short notice [12], and it indicates that urban planning should prepare density management in advance including thinking about decentralization of essential services. Smart community could play a role in this context. However, this research also raises the awareness that if urban planning concepts change to spread the city rather than densifying, that would have to go with much better connectivity of public transport. In other words, a city (not necessarily limited to be smart) has to balance its agility to emergency and redundancy in public health and public transport.

2.2   Geography, Demography and Complex Networks

There exists complexity in network-driven contagion phenomena, and research finds that the arrival times correlate weakly with geographic distance in the 2003 SARS epidemic [4]. The following idea is then deployed, i.e., replacing conventional geographic distance by a measure of effective distance derived from the underlying mobility network [4].

A Global Epidemic and Mobility (GLEaM) model is developed by integrating sociodemographic and population mobility data in a spatially structured stochastic disease approach to simulate the spread epidemics [2]. Such model could facilitate the analysis on different disease structures and local intervention policies.

Not only the geographical and the transport mobility structure have an impact on the transmission of infectious diseases, but also the total number or density of hosts that are candidates for infection play a role. A framework for discussing the population biology and demographical factors can be found in [1]. A contemporary research investigates the effect of travel restrictions on the spread of the COVID-19 outbreak [6], and individuals are assumed to occupy one of the following statuses: susceptible, latent, infectious and removed. Based on the aforementioned four status, the model generates an ensemble of possible epidemic scenarios described by the newly generated infections, time of disease arrival in each subpopulation, and the number of traveling infection carriers.

Besides, a familial cluster of pneumonia associated with COVID-19 is noted and reported [5], following discussion on several scenarios of possible transmission routes. Although the transmission routes are not certainly based on virus genome sequences test announced, the study showed that person-to-person transmission in family homes or hospitals, and intercity spread of the COVID-19 are possible. It is still crucial to isolate patients and trace and quarantine contacts as early as possible. This becomes our food for thought to analyze whether size of households in a residential community would matter for the control measures, especially at the early stage of the epidemic.

2.3 Humanities and Social Science

Similar historical cases can be found in Great Britain in the mid 18th century. Ever since (and even before), research on specific cases has its merit [7,20], especially in case of a global pandemic.

Super spreaders (or efficient spreaders) are key to be found out once an outbreak happens. The problem of finding efficient spreaders is not limited to disease epidemic models; it is possibly even more important for complex contagion phenomena (such as rumor spreading or the diffusion of innovations) [19], where humanities and social sciences get involved.

Moreover, some research assesses the likelihood of an outbreak when a case is introduced into a susceptible population, and draw preliminary conclusions about the impact of control measures [16]. The effectiveness of isolation, as one of the intervention measures, would be limited by the availability of isolation facilities, by the speed of the isolation process, and by failures of infection control for isolated patients. In other words, the population would need to understand via social media that the scale of interventions required to control an epidemic depends on the number of infectious cases present at the time the control measures are institutionalized and on logistical constraints. This perspective of conveying information and convincing related population needs knowledge and support from the field of humanities and social science.

2.4 ICT and Digitalization

Based on mobile operator data, two gravity models of population mobility are implemented for comparison [3], and it shows that mobile operator data is a highly promising data source for improving preparedness and response efforts during cholera outbreaks. The research also implies that ICT and digitalization applications may be particularly important for containment efforts of emerging infectious diseases, including high-mortality influenza.

The World Health Organization (WHO) has organized expert meetings to address response to epidemics, and following priorities for COVID-19 research have been set [21], which include infection prevention and control, and integration of social sciences into the outbreak response. Based on the above-mentioned priorities, this literature review is conducted. However, without loss of generality, we should be careful to balance the need to learn from previous research with the possibility that some virus has fundamentally changed [15] and is different from those that have been researched before.

In the specific case of COVID-19, the virus itself is different and quite unknown yet. Related disease containment measures and effects deserve research in-depth. There is a concern regarding whether China's COVID-19 strategies work elsewhere [14], when a rapid decline in cases is real. Therefore, in the following section, a sample residential community in Shanghai and its infection prevention and control measures are analyzed.

3 A Sample Community in Shanghai

The community discussed in this paper is located in one of the suburban districts, i.e., Minhang district, and one may find it in the south-west corner of Shanghai. The distance between this sample community and the classic city center of Shanghai, i.e., the Bund, would amount to approximately 20–22 km. The community has a total number of 25,373 households. Based on the estimated interval of household size, i.e., between 2.06 and 2.99 (calculation shown below), the overall residential population in this community would fall into the interval between 52,258 and 75,865.

Only number of households (instead of residential population) is available based on the preliminary data collection process involved in this research, and it might be due to the fact that the lockdown measure is conducted the first time ever and not every detailed data is considered at the early stage.

3.1 Timeline

The timeline of the data collection process lasts 20 days, ranging from February 1 to 20, 2020. It has to be admitted that the dataset is limited, and the data collection process ends when both of the two sources of cross-checking tracing data report 0.

February 1 – 7 days after the lockdown of Wuhan city and Hubei Province, Shanghai conducts control measures and data collection at the community level.

February 8 – the number of daily checks of this community reaches its highest value. This number includes compulsory checks based on information from the city level and information source from the community level. On February 14, 2020, the information source from the city level reports 0 the first time, which is depicted as a milestone in Fig. 1.

February 20 – the number of daily checks of the community reaches its lowest value, both sources of compulsory checks report 0. The timeline in Fig. 1 finishes.

3.2 Data

In this research, data regarding previous inbound trips is collected manually (see Figs. 2, 3 and 4). The reason is that this lockdown is performed in late January when there are neither experiences nor APPs available. Sources of data are two, i.e., city level and community level. Especially the data at the community level is collected mainly by newly established multi-functionality teams introduced in Sect. 4.3. The lockdown finished on 22nd February 2020. After 5th March 2020, an APP enabling health declaration code is deployed in Shanghai. However, the data collected manually in this research also play a vital role implementing the concept of smart city and smart community, because it reflects to which extent residents are sharing data and how long a lockdown takes until its effectiveness. Such data is not included in smart city discussions before, and it might be of interest to deepen the concept of smart city and smart community.

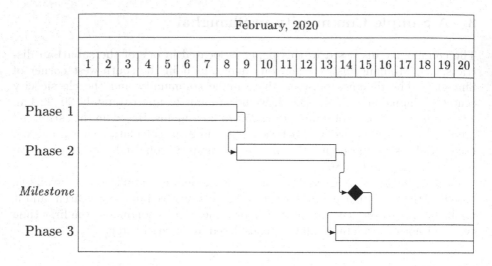

Fig. 1. Timeline of conducting control measures in the sample community

4   Effects and Sensitivity Analysis on Managerial Measures

4.1   Blocking Mobilities

The aim of locking-down a residential community or a city is to eliminate the risks of catching the virus and spreading it via mobilities, especially when there exists a delay between catchment and onset. Accordingly, an early signal that China has begun to turn the tide on the epidemic is that most newly reported cases begin to occur among known and quarantined contacts of confirmed cases [18], which implies the lockdown between late January and whole February, 2020 functions in terms of blocking interactions among health residents, confirmed positive cases, and quarantined contacts. Afterwards, three categories of uncertainties are also receiving special attention.

A) Low uncertainty: inbound and outbound of the residential community is blocked and only groceries logistics are performed and related data is verified. B) Medium uncertainty: other risky regions are already identified but lockdown of these regions are not performed. But data regarding trips from these regions is well documented. C) High uncertainty: other risky regions are not identified before the further outbreak and people are keeping traveling from these regions, therefore, data regarding trips is not expected to be well verified.

Sensitivity analysis based on three categories of uncertainties together with three-time phases is then conducted in Sect. 4.4.

4.2   Cross-Tracing Mechanism

There exists a gap between information from the city level and from the community level at the moment when the data of this paper are collected (see Fig. 5

Date	Leader team of the community (three members)		Number of residents under control measures														Total number of households 25,373
			Extra number of residents under control measures of the day			Number of residents free from control measures of the day			State-of-art number of residents under control measures								
	(Planned) Number of cross-checked residents of the day	Actual cumulated number of cross-checked residents	Info from city level	Info from community level	Total extra number of residents under control measures of the day	Info from city level	Info from community level	Total number of residents free from control measures of the day	Info from city level	Info from community level	Total under control measures	Origin Hubei Province	Origin non-Hubei Province	Number of households under control measures	Number of residents been to key regions	Number of close-contacts	Calculated household size
2020/2/1	21	239	3	26	29	9	16	-25	43	149	192	94	98	81	146	46	2.37
2020/2/2	19	258	3	16	19	0	4	-4	46	161	207	94	113	77	153	54	2.69
2020/2/3	13	272	0	11	11	3	3	-6	44	168	212	99	113	72	152	60	2.94
2020/2/4	6	277	3	3	6	2	13	-15	45	158	203	90	113	68	150	53	2.99
2020/2/5	27	309	0	16	16	8	14	-22	37	160	197	90	107	71	142	55	2.77
2020/2/6	24	333	5	17	22	7	34	-41	39	139	178	80	98	66	136	42	2.70
2020/2/7	23	356	4	7	11	4	21	-25	39	125	164	69	95	63	131	33	2.60
2020/2/8	30	386	7	29	36	7	32	-39	39	122	161	52	109	59	126	35	2.73
2020/2/9	15	401	1	19	20	12	33	-45	28	108	136	52	84	54	96	40	2.52
2020/2/10	17	411	3	6	9	6	30	-36	25	84	109	15	94	53	81	28	2.06
2020/2/11	26	437	5	16	21	3	7	-10	29	91	120	8	112	53	95	25	2.26
2020/2/12	15	450	2	16	18	2	2	-4	29	105	134	7	127	57	103	31	2.35
2020/2/13	16	470	4	6	10	4	12	-16	34	94	128	7	121	57	99	29	2.25
2020/2/14	15	485	0	19	19	1	9	-10	33	104	137	16	121	60	96	41	2.28
2020/2/15	6	491	0	3	3	2	9	-11	31	98	129	15	114	58	88	41	2.22
2020/2/16	7	498	3	4	7	1	11	-12	33	91	124	15	109	52	90	34	2.38
2020/2/17	11	509	4	7	11	4	17	-21	36	78	114	15	99	52	83	31	2.19
2020/2/18	7	516	1	8	9	2	1	-3	35	85	120	15	105	54	83	37	2.22
2020/2/19	2	518	0	1	1	5	9	-14	31	76	107	15	92	46	68	39	2.33
2020/2/20	0	518	0	0	0	2	14	-16	29	62	91	15	76	41	57	34	2.22

Fig. 2. Data collected from the sample community

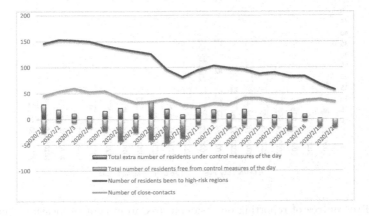

Fig. 3. Dynamics of the residents who are associated with control measures

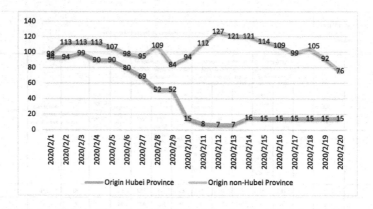

Fig. 4. Focusing on traffic and mobility from high-risk regions

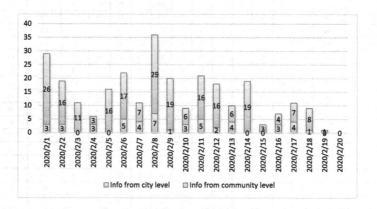

Fig. 5. Two sources of information tracing trips (number of residents)

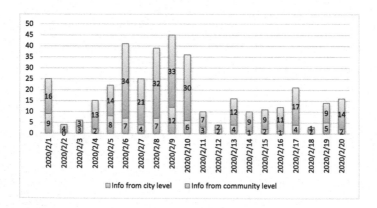

Fig. 6. Two sources of reporting on residents free from control measures (number of residents)

and 6). For instance, some inbound residents report to the city level about their previous trips to high-risk regions when entering Shanghai via highway, followed by a short stay somewhere else in Shanghai given the possibility that such residents might have more than one apartment in Shanghai. When such residents enter this sample residential community, the trip to high-risk regions finished days ago is a piece of missing information at the community level. To better synchronize information at both levels, a cross-tracing mechanism is performed.

4.3   Composing Multi-functionality Teams

To implement cross-tracing mechanism, some teams are built-up. Each team composes three team members, and each of them functions as community volunteer, medical support, and security guard, respectively. At the beginning, due to lack of experiences, some of the team members work overtime, e.g., 10–12 h per shift as per media reports.

4.4   Sensitivity Analysis

The sensitivity analysis is conducted based on an understanding of the current situation. In another research considering the UK and US context [10], it conducts scenarios on a combination of social distancing of the entire population, home isolation of cases and household quarantine of their family members. Justified by the periodic outcomes of temporal control measures, decision on further control is made. That is, it is a decision process based on rolling horizon planning.

The outcome of the lockdown of this sample residential community is regarded as effective. It needs to be noted that such lockdown functions well given the conditions that human mobility is suspended but logistics of medical protective equipments together with additional medical experts are never suspended. In addition, the logistics of daily groceries is still functioning, which means that the residents are not self-motivated to take risks and going out of the community and get groceries. Various implementation status of these two conditions, i.e., less mobility, and supportive logistics, would result in very different effectiveness of the lockdown. In case additional medical experts and protective equipments can not be 'imported' in a timely manner, human being's behaviors would be deviating due to the awareness of scarce medical resources. However, if the behaviors including accessing medical resources and daily consumption could be guided at a convincing rolling horizon, the limited amount of medical resources probably would avoid being burned out. The overall time horizon of dealing with the virus contagions and emergency need to be prolonged.

We conduct sensitivity analysis (see Fig. 7) based on the fact that the overall time horizon could be divided into three phases, as indicated in Fig. 1. Scenario 1 means for the whole three phases, the community and overall circumstance is locked down as A) mentioned in Sect. 4.1. Scenario 2 means for 8-day Phase 1 the community decreases the traffic and mobility as a strict lockdown, and its Phase 2 gets extended to 14 days followed by the Phase 3 extended to 46 days. A less restricted control measure is conducted in Phase 2 and 3, considering the category of medium uncertainty B) mentioned in Sect. 4.2. The information regarding degrees of risky regions is available then the residents do not need to abandon all trips. Scenario 3 means for 8-day Phase 1 the community is suggested to reduce mobility and activities as the residents are informed the category of high uncertainty C) mentioned in Sect. 4.2. Presumably the traffic and mobility get a 20 % decrease accordingly in Phase 1, and Phase 2 gets extended to 14 days followed by Phase 3 extended to 46 days.

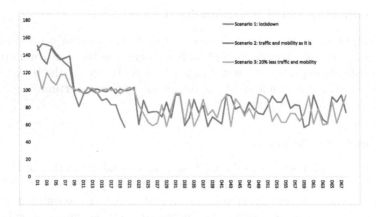

Fig. 7. Sensitivity analysis on traffic and mobility

5   Insights and Implications in Emergencies

5.1   Imbalanced Resources

The resources which are vital in the pandemic and its resilience phase include medical infrastructures, medical experts, etc. However, the working hours of medical experts in these phases might not be estimated to be extremely long, due to concerns on fragility of humans, the legal framework and labor unions, etc. Therefore, efficiently scheduling medical experts' capacities becomes a solution to obtain effectiveness of control measures. In the sample residential community, the team of check and validation comprises three members, including one medical expert, one community-service volunteer and one policeman.

The resources mentioned above are inevitably imbalanced for different regions across the country. The Gravity Model applied in the transport discipline indicates that imbalanced resources could motivate human mobility because people tend to move from a region containing fewer resources to another region containing richer resources. The bigger the diversity in terms of medical resources in different regions in a country, the higher possibility of motivating unusual travel behavior once contagious diseases spread.

In addition, especially when a pandemic occurs, absolute numbers of medical experts and medical infrastructures turn to be less important than comparable indicators of medical capacity, i.e., numbers of medical experts and medical infrastructures divided by number of residences of a region. That could twist the phenomenon of imbalance. Similarly, a recent discussion on the Gravity Model and its modification in specific resources condition can be found [13].

Other than that, once imbalanced medical resources are commonly recognized by associated residences, some unusual so-called Corona Parties are organized. Handwaving arguments also indicate that there is an irrational trend to intentionally get oneself infected at the early stage in order to access the imbalanced medical resources before an outbreak, when most medical resources may become scarce. Accessing medical resources is regarded as rational for individuals; however, in this case, cumulating individual rationalities does not necessarily lead to collective rationality which is a well-researched topic in the field of game theory. How to design in time a contemporary guidance to the associated residences becomes a vital concern of governance when confronted with a pandemic.

5.2 Imperfect Information

In this sample residential community, it is requested that the information on previous travel and stay in high-risk regions has to be reported to the community by the residents themselves. However, such reported information is neither complete nor perfect. As can be observed in Fig. 8, the blue dotted line and the yellow solid line are not always perfectly identical. In case these two lines are identical, the reported information regarding previous travel is complete.

Other than completeness of information, the perfection of information regarding previous trips is important, too. The perfection of information is an important notion in game theory when considering sequential and simultaneous games. It is a key concept when analysing the possibility of punishment strategies. In the context of pandemic prevention, filling out trip declaration forms and health declaration forms are ways to collect information as perfect as possible. If residents and governance capacities are all regarded as players in this information game, then perfect information refers to the fact that each player has the same information that would be available at the end of the game. In other words, each player knows or can see other player's actions. Each involved governance capacity knows or can see the resident's actions, i.e., proactive reporting.

Imperfect information appears when decisions have to made simultaneously and players need to balance all possible outcomes when making a decision. A resident, after some trips, would need to balance all possible outcomes when making a decision on reporting. It is observed that some residents consider quarantine as very inconvenient and based on that hide previous trips to high-risk regions at the first round of reporting, especially when APPs are not yet implemented and geographical location services are not yet available. In addition, imperfect information regarding previous trips could just happen due to the fact that the reporting resident's handwriting is not well recognized. It would need residential community's efforts to cross-check, figure out and take actions on control measures later. A latency then exists. Above mentioned phenomena on incomplete information and imperfect information result in the slight differences between the blue dotted line and the yellow solid line in Fig. 8.

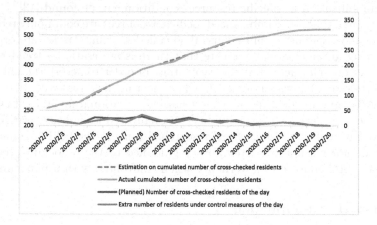

Fig. 8. Check and validation at the community level (Color figure online)

5.3   Average Household

Performance measurement of the spontaneous city logistics and load dependency phenomena may need to be categorized in detail.

The number of households and estimated population could be regarded as a meaningful configuration. In this context, we consider a community in metropolitan Shanghai. However, in other context similar numbers of population could compose a district in a city or even a city. Projecting the scale of this sample community might also makes sense for decision-makers of a city, given dedicated adjustment of the configuration and parameters analyzed above.

6   Discussion and Further Research

In this section, some further research perspectives are provided based on the above discussion.

6.1   Traffic Control at the City Level

This paper investigated at the community level. Within this sample residential community, there are no public transport services involved. Therefore, only in- and outbound moves of the residents are recorded. Mobility and interactions resulting from public transport are not discussed in this paper. However, at the city level, many control measures on public traffic and mobility, e.g., reducing numbers of departure per time unit during a lockdown and increasing numbers of departure per time unit in resilience, might need to be considered further.

6.2 Resilience at Multi-layer Networks

The performances of resilience during and after pandemic would need supports from different layers [17]. A multi-layer network could then be set-up including data and behaviors at the level of residential community, level of cargo transport network, and level of municipal city, respectively.

The contribution of this paper is unique, because it shares the data regarding lockdown at the community level. Due to the fact that there might not be physical barriers for residential communities in other countries during their control measures, such real-world record on mobility behaviors might not be available elsewhere. In addition, it also sheds light on how to proceed without physical barriers in residential communities to facilitate data collection and enhance effectiveness of control measures. One of the alternatives would be putting QR Codes on key locations, e.g., supermarkets and pharmacies, so that the close-contacts in the same time slot of visiting these specific locations can be easily tracked once a confirmed case occurs in the associated residential community. Another alternative would be providing preliminary medical test service in a decentralized pattern, i.e., within a stone-throw distance in the residential community. By so doing, psychological waiting time could be dramatically shortened and ease the panic, to some extent, in the pandemic. Hence, resilience at multi-layer networks is of interest and importance.

To summarize, this paper investigates and analyzes contagious diseases' impact at the level of residential community in a connected city from a perspective of emergency management and resilience measures. After the research at the level of community (as conducted in this paper), a research at the level of city could be further conducted (as indicated in Sect. 6.1), followed by another research at multi-level (or multi-layer) networks (as indicated in Sect. 6.2).

References

1. Anderson, R.M., Anderson, B., May, R.M.: Infectious Diseases of Humans: Dynamics and Control. Oxford University Press, Oxford (1991)
2. Balcan, D., Gonçalves, B., Hu, H., Ramasco, J.J., Colizza, V., Vespignani, A.: Modeling the spatial spread of infectious diseases: the global epidemic and mobility computational model. J. Comput. Sci. **1**(3), 132–145 (2010)
3. Bengtsson, L., Gaudart, J., Lu, X., et al.: Using mobile phone data to predict the spatial spread of Cholera. Scientific reports 5, article #8923 (2015)
4. Brockmann, D., Helbing, D.: The hidden geometry of complex, network-driven contagion phenomena. Science **342**(6164), 1337–1342 (2013)
5. Chan, J.F.W., Yuan, S., Kok, K.H., et al.: A familial cluster of pneumonia associated with the 2019 novel coronavirus indicating person-to-person transmission: a study of a family cluster. Lancet **395**(10223), 514–523 (2020)
6. Chinazzi, M., Davis, J.T., Ajelli, M., et al.: The effect of travel restrictions on the spread of the 2019 novel coronavirus (COVID-19) outbreak. Science **368**(6489), 395–400 (2020)
7. Cyranoski, D.: What China's coronavirus response can teach the rest of the world. Nature (2020). https://doi.org/10.1038/d41586-020-00741-x

8. Donnelly, C.A., Ghani, A.C., Leung, G.M., et al.: Epidemiological determinants of spread of causal agent of severe acute respiratory syndrome in Hong Kong. Lancet **361**(9371), 1761–1766 (2003)
9. Editorial: Stop the Wuhan coronavirus. Nature **577**, 450–450 (2020)
10. Ferguson, N.M., Laydon, D., Nedjati-Gilani, G., et al.: Impact of Non-Pharmaceutical Interventions (NPIs) to Reduce COVID-19 Mortality and Healthcare Demand. Imperial College London, London (2020). https://doi.org/10.25561/77482
11. Imai, N., Dorigatti, I., Cori, A., Riley, S., Ferguson, N.M.: Estimating the Potential Total Number of Novel Coronavirus Cases in Wuhan City, China. Imperial College London, London (2020)
12. Klaus, I.: Pandemics are also an urban planning problem (2020). https://www.citylab.com/design/2020/03/coronavirus-urban-planning-global-cities-infectious-disease/607603/. Accessed 6 Mar 2020
13. Kosowska-Stamirowska, Z.: Network effects govern the evolution of maritime trade. PNAS **117**(23), 12719–12728 (2020). https://doi.org/10.1073/pnas.1906670117
14. Kupferschmidt, K., Cohen, J.: Can China's COVID-19 strategy work elsewhere. Science **367**(6482), 1061–1062 (2020)
15. Lessler, J., Chaisson, L.H., Kucirka, L.M., et al.: Assessing the global threat from zika virus. Science **353**(6300), aaf8160 (2016)
16. Lipsitch, M., Cohen, T., Cooper, B., et al.: Transmission dynamics and control of severe acute respiratory syndrome. Science **300**(5627), 1966–1970 (2003)
17. Liu, Q.H., Ajelli, M., Aleta, A., Merler, S., Moreno, Y., Vespignani, A.: Measurability of the epidemic reproduction number in data-driven contact networks. Proc. Natl. Acad. Sci. **115**(50), 12680–12685 (2018)
18. Maxmen, A.: How much is coronavirus spreading under the radar. Nature (2020). https://doi.org/10.1038/d41586-020-00760-8
19. Pastor-Satorras, R., Castellano, C., Van Mieghem, P., Vespignani, A.: Epidemic processes in complex networks. Rev. Mod. Phys. **87**(3), 925 (2015)
20. Riley, S., Fraser, C., Donnelly, C.A., et al.: Transmission dynamics of the etiological agent of SARS in Hong Kong: impact of public health interventions. Science **300**(5627), 1961–1966 (2003)
21. WHO: World experts and funders set priorities for COVID-19 research (2020). https://www.who.int/news-room/detail/12-02-2020-world-experts-and-funders-set-priorities-for-covid-19-research. Accessed 12 Feb 2020

Network Design and Scheduling

A Shortest Path Algorithm for Graphs Featuring Transfer Costs at Their Vertices

Rhyd Lewis[✉]

School of Mathematics, Cardiff University, Cardiff CF24 4AG, Wales
LewisR9@cf.ac.uk

Abstract. This paper examines the problem of finding shortest paths in graphs that feature additional penalties – transfer costs – at their vertices. We propose a shortest path algorithm that can cope with these additional penalties without the need of first performing a graph expansion, which is the typical algorithmic strategy. While our method exhibits an inferior growth rate compared to existing approaches, we show that it is more efficient on sparse graphs.

1   Introduction

Consider the graph in Fig. 1. This might depict some small public transport system with edge colours representing transport lines and weights representing travel times. Now suppose that we want to find the shortest path from vertex v_1 to v_9. By inspection, this is (v_1, v_4, v_5, v_9) with a cost of $2 + 1 + 2 = 5$. However, this path involves changing lines at v_4 which, in reality, might also incur some time penalty. If this penalty is more than three units, then the shortest path from v_1 to v_9 now becomes $(v_1, v_4, v_7, v_8, v_9)$ with a cost of eight.

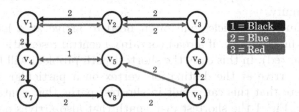

Fig. 1. A small network comprising $n = 9$ vertices, $m = 16$ edges and $k = 3$ colours. As per Definition 1 we have, for example, $E^-(v_1) = \{(v_2, v_1, 1), (v_2, v_1, 2)\}$, $E^+(v_1) = \{(v_1, v_2, 2), (v_1, v_4, 1)\}$, $C^-(v_1) = \{1, 2\}$ and $C^+(v_1) = \{1, 2\}$. (Color figure online)

In this paper we propose a flexible model in which colours of edges are used to help specify transfer costs at vertices. Let $G = (V, E)$ be an edge-weighted, loop-free, directed multigraph using k different edge colours. As usual, V is a set of n vertices $\{v_1, \ldots, v_n\}$ and E is a set of m coloured, directed edges taken

E. Lalla-Ruiz et al. (Eds.): ICCL 2020, LNCS 12433, pp. 539–552, 2020.
https://doi.org/10.1007/978-3-030-59747-4_35

from the set of all such edges $\{(u,v,i) : u,v \in V \wedge u \neq v \wedge i \in \{1,\ldots,k\}\}$. Hence $0 \leq m \leq kn(n-1)$. The weight of an edge of colour i travelling from vertex u to vertex v is denoted by $w(u,v,i)$.

In this paper we also use the following notation, exemplified in Fig. 1:

Definition 1. *Let* $E^-(v) = \{(u,v,i) : (u,v,i) \in E\}$ *be the set of edges whose endpoint is vertex* v, *and* $C^-(v) = \{i : \exists(u,v,i) \in E^-(v)\}$ *be the set of distinct colours that enter* v. *Similarly,* $E^+(v) = \{(v,u,i) : (v,u,i) \in E\}$ *is the set of edges whose starting point is* v *and* $C^+(v)$ *is the set of colours that leave* v.

Finally, we also need to define a set of *transfers* T. A transfer occurs when we arrive at a vertex v on an edge of colour i and leave v on an edge of colour j. Hence $T = \{(v,i,j) : v \in V \wedge i \in C^-(v) \wedge j \in C^+(v)\}$. The cost of a transfer is denoted by $t(v,i,j)$ and it is assumed that if $i = j$, then $t(v,i,j) = 0$.

Shortest path problems on graphs with transfer costs at the vertices have many practical uses. As noted, an obvious example is with public transport networks where additional costs (such as financial or time) can be incurred when switching between different lines. Another example is with the multi-modal shortest path problem where we are in interested in transporting goods efficiently between two locations using a combination of different travel modes (sea, train, road etc.), and where transfer costs represent the cost of moving the goods from one mode to another [5]. Constraints stemming from real-world road networks can also be defined using the above model by considering edges as roads and vertices as intersections. For example:

Intersection Delays. Often vehicles will need to wait at an intersection due to crossing traffic and pedestrians. Such delays can be modelled using an appropriate transfer cost at the vertex.

Illegal Routes and Turns. On occasion, large vehicles will not be permitted to drive on particular roads or make particular turns at an intersection. In these cases we can simply change the corresponding edge weights and transfer costs to infinity.

Kerbside Routing. Vehicles will often need to arrive at a location from a particular direction (e.g. if a road contains a central reservation and crossing is not permitted). In this case, the shortest path problem will be constrained so that we arrive at the destination vertex on a particular subset of edge colours. Note that this can result in shortest paths that contain cycles. For example, in Fig. 1 the shortest v_1-v_4-path that also arrives on a red edge is (v_1, v_4, v_5, v_4).

Initial Headway. Similarly to the previous point, vehicles may also need to leave a location in a particular direction (e.g. if they previously approached from a particular direction and turning is not possible). In this case, the shortest path should be specified as having to leave this vertex on a particular edge colour.

In this paper we propose a shortest path algorithm that accommodates transfer costs at the vertices and also allows us to evaluate paths in which the edge colours entering the source and target vertices are specified by the user. As we will see, previous methods for this problem rely on expanding graphs, resulting in many more edges and vertices. In contrast, our algorithm avoids this and, instead, operates on the original graphs without modification. The next section of this paper reviews the shortest path problem and surveys relevant expansion methods. Section 3 then presents our algorithm and proves its correctness, while Sects. 4 and 5 examine and compare asymptotic and empirical run times. Section 7 concludes the paper.

2   Identifying Shortest Paths

In general, three problems involving shortest paths on edge-weighted graphs can be distinguished: (a) the "single-source single-target" problem, which involves finding the shortest path between two vertices; (b) the "single source" problem, which involves determining the shortest path from a source vertex to all other vertices in the graph (thereby producing a shortest path tree); and (c) the "all pairs" problem, where shortest paths are identified between all pairs of vertices. A well-known algorithm for solving problems (a) and (b) is the Bellman-Ford algorithm, which operates in $\mathcal{O}(nm)$ time [4]. This is suitable for graphs featuring both positive and negative edge weights and can also be used for detecting negative cycles.

	DIJKSTRA $(s \in V)$
(1)	**for all** $v \in V$ **do**
(2)	$\qquad L(v) \leftarrow \infty, \ D(v) \leftarrow$ **false**, $P(v) \leftarrow$ NULL
(3)	$L(s) \leftarrow 0$
(4)	$Q \leftarrow \{(s, L(s))\}$
(5)	**while** $Q \neq \emptyset$ **do**
(6)	$\qquad$ Let $(u, L(u))$ be the element in Q with minimum value for $L(u)$
(7)	$\qquad Q \leftarrow Q - \{(u, L(u))\}$
(8)	$\qquad D(u) \leftarrow$ **true**
(9)	$\qquad$ **for all** $(u, v) \in E^+(u) : D(v) =$ **false do**
(10)	$\qquad\qquad$ **if** $L(u) + w(u, v) < L(v)$ **then**
(11)	$\qquad\qquad\qquad$ **if** $L(v) \neq \infty$ **then** $Q \leftarrow Q - \{(v, L(v))\}$
(12)	$\qquad\qquad\qquad L(v) \leftarrow L(u) + w(u, v)$
(13)	$\qquad\qquad\qquad Q \leftarrow Q \cup \{(v, L(v))\}$
(14)	$\qquad\qquad\qquad P(v) \leftarrow u$

Fig. 2. Dijkstra's algorithm for producing a shortest-path tree from a source vertex $s \in V$. To solve the single-source single-target problem, Line (5) should be replaced by the statement "while $D(t) \neq$ true do", where $t \in V$ is the target vertex.

If a graph contains only nonnegative edge weights, then a more efficient alternative is to use Dijkstra's algorithm [4]. The pseudocode of this method is given in Fig. 2. As shown, DIJKSTRA uses four data structures, D, L, P and Q. The first three of these contain n elements and will typically allow direct access (e.g.

by using arrays). Each entry $D(v)$ is used to mark whether a vertex v is classed as "distinguished" or not. Initially, only the source vertex s is distinguished. During the run, further vertices then become distinguished one by one, and this continues until all vertices are marked as such. Meanwhile, L is used to hold a "label" for each vertex. During execution, $L(v)$ stores the length of the shortest s-v-path that uses distinguished vertices only; hence at the end of the run, $L(v)$ will store the length of the shortest s-v-path in the graph. P then allows us to identify the shortest paths themselves by storing the predecessor of each vertex v in the shortest path tree.

The final structure used in DIJKSTRA is a priority queue Q. During execution this holds the label values of all vertices that have been considered by the algorithm but that have not yet been marked as distinguished. As shown on Line (6), in each iteration Q is used to identify the undistinguished vertex u with the minimal label value. In the remaining instructions, u is then removed from Q and marked as distinguished, and adjustments are made to the labels of undistinguished neighbours of u, if applicable.

The asymptotic running time of DIJKSTRA depends mainly on the data structure used to represent Q. A good option is to use a binary heap or self-balancing binary tree since this allows identification of the minimum label in constant time, with look-ups, deletions, and insertions then being performed in logarithmic time. This leads to an overall run time of $\mathcal{O}((n + m) \lg n)$, which simplifies to $\mathcal{O}(m \lg n)$ for connected graphs (where $m \geq n$). Asymptotically, a further improvement to $\mathcal{O}(m + n \lg n)$ can also be achieved using a Fibonacci heap for Q, though such structures are often viewed as slow in practice due to their large memory consumption and the high constant factors contained in their operations [2].

Solving the all pairs shortest path problem involves populating a matrix $\mathbf{D}_{n \times n}$, where each element D_{ij} holds the length of the shortest v_i-v_j-path. A well known approach for this problem is the Floyd-Warshall algorithm, which operates in $\mathcal{O}(n^3)$ time [4]. Another alternative – which usually gives better performance with sparse graphs – is to simply perform n applications of DIJKSTRA, with each application populating a single row of $\mathbf{D}$.

Although the Bellman-Ford, Floyd-Warshall, and Dijkstra algorithms all correctly calculate shortest paths in edge-weighted graphs, note that they cannot be directly applied to graphs featuring transfer penalties at the vertices. Instead, graphs are typically *expanded* to allow transfer penalties to be expressed via additional "transfer edges". This then allows shortest path methods to be applied as before. The most prominent expansion method is that of Kirby and Potts [10] who suggest using a cluster of dummy vertices for each vertex in the original graph. Specifically, using a graph $G = (V, E)$ as defined in Sect. 1, a new larger graph $G' = (V', E')$ is formed by creating two sets of dummy vertices for each vertex $v \in V$: one for each incoming colour in v and one for each outgoing colour in v. Transfer edges are then added between the dummy vertices in each set using edge weights equivalent to the corresponding transfer costs.

An example of the Kirby-Potts expansion method is shown in Fig. 3(a). As illustrated, the transfer edges within each cluster define a directed bipartite graph. This results in a new graph $G' = (V', E')$ comprising

$$n' = \sum_{i=1}^{n} |C^-(v_i)| + |C^+(v_i)| \tag{1}$$

$$m' = m + \sum_{i=1}^{n} |C^-(v_i)| \cdot |C^+(v_i)| \tag{2}$$

vertices and edges respectively. Note that a shortest path between two vertices in G' now also specifies the starting colour and arrival colour in the original graph's path. For example, the shortest path between the vertices marked by X and Y in Fig. 3(a) corresponds to the shortest v_1-v_5-path in Fig. 1 in which "arrival" at v_1 is assumed on a black edge and arrival at v_5 is on a red edge.

A similar but more restricted version of the Kirby-Potts expansion has also been used in various studies regarding small bus networks [1,3,7–9]. In this method each vertex v of the original graph is represented by a cluster of $|C^-(v) \cup C^+(v)|$ dummy vertices. Each vertex in this cluster then corresponds to a different colour, and edges are added between these vertices using weights equivalent to the corresponding transfer costs. However, although this restricted method can result in smaller graphs than those of Kirby-Potts, we have found that it can produce illogical results when the edge weights within a cluster do not obey the triangle inequality. Consider the Kirby-Potts expansion in Fig. 3(b) for example, where a cost of 3 is incurred at the vertex when transferring from blue to black. In the corresponding graph produced using the restricted expansion method (Fig. 3(c)) a smaller transfer cost of 2 will be identified by transferring from blue to red to black, which is clearly inappropriate when modelling things such as transfers on public transport. (This issue is not noted in any of the above works; however, it is actually avoided due to a constant value being used for all transfers, thereby satisfying the triangle inequality at each vertex.)

One further method of graph expansion is due to Winter [12] who suggests using the line graph of G (referred to as the "pseudo-dual" in the paper) for

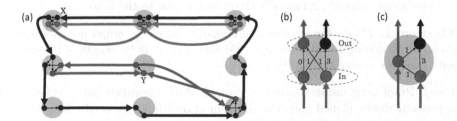

Fig. 3. (a) The graph $G' = (V', E')$ formed from Fig. 1 using the Kirby-Potts expansion method; (b) an example cluster of dummy vertices produced using the Kirby-Potts method; and (c) the corresponding cluster using the restricted expansion method. (Color figure online)

identifying shortest paths. However, this leads to a much larger graph comprising m vertices and $\sum_{v \in V} |E^-(v)| \cdot |E^+(v)|$ edges. A copy of the original graph G is also required with this method to facilitate the drawing of routes.

3   An Extension to Dijkstra's Algorithm

In this section we propose an extension to Dijkstra's algorithm that computes shortest paths in graphs featuring transfer costs at the vertices, but without the need for first performing an expansion.

The idea behind our proposed method can be explained by considering a cluster of dummy vertices in a Kirby-Potts expanded graph. As illustrated in Figs. 3(a) and (b), we see that vertices in each cluster can be partitioned into two sets: in-vertices and out-vertices. Moreover, a shortest path from an in-vertex must always next pass through an out-vertex from the same cluster before moving to a different cluster. As proven in Theorem 1 below, it is therefore sufficient to simply add the cost of the corresponding transfer (edge) to the path here, rather than consider the out-vertices as separate entities within the graph.

The idea in our approach is to therefore use a pair (u, i) for each vertex $u \in V$ and incoming colour $i \in C^-(u)$, giving $\sum_{u \in V} |C^-(u)|$ pairs in total. The source is also defined by such a pair (s, l), which is interpreted as meaning that the paths should start at $s \in V$, assuming initial entry to s on an edge of colour l. Similarly to DIJKSTRA, during execution this algorithm stores labels, predecessors and the distinguished status of each pair using the structures L, P and D respectively. At termination, all pairs reachable from the source are marked as distinguished, and a label $L(u, i)$ holds the length of the shortest path from the source to vertex u, assuming entry at u on an edge of colour i.

The pseudocode of our algorithm is shown in Fig. 4 and an example solution from this method is shown in Fig. 5. As shown, the main differences between this approach and DIJKSTRA are (a) the use of vertex-colour pairs, and (b) at Lines 11 and 13, where transfer costs $t(u, i, j)$ are added when comparing and recalculating label values. Note also that for $k = 1$ this algorithm becomes equivalent to DIJKSTRA, justifying our choice of the name EXTENDED-DIJKSTRA here.

The correctness of EXTENDED-DIJKSTRA is due to the following.

Theorem 1. *If all edge weights and transfer costs in a graph are nonnegative then, for all distinguished pairs (u, i), the label $L(u, i)$ is the length of the shortest path from the source (s, l) to (u, i).*

Proof. Proof is by induction on the number of distinguished pairs. When there is just one distinguished pair, the theorem clearly holds since the length of the shortest path from (s, l) to itself is $L(s, l) = 0$.

For the step case, let (v, j) be the next pair to be marked as distinguished by the algorithm (i.e., $L(v, j)$ is minimal among all undistinguished pairs) and let (u, i) be its predecessor. Hence the shortest (s, l)-(v, j)-path has length $L(u, i) + t(u, i, j) + w(u, v, j)$. Now consider any other path P from (s, l) to (v, j). We need to show that the length of P cannot be less than $L(u,i) + t(u,i,j) + w(u,v,j)$. Let (x,a) and (y,b) be pairs on P such that (x,a) is distinguished and (y,b) is not, meaning that P contains the edge (x,y,b). This implies that the length of P is greater than or equal to $L(x,a) + t(x,a,b) + w(x,y,b)$ (due to the induction hypothesis). Similarly, this figure must be greater than or equal to $L(u,i) + t(u,i,j) + w(u,v,j)$ because, as assumed, $L(v,j)$ is minimal among all undistinguished pairs.

4 Asymptotic Analysis

In this section we consider the asymptotic complexity of EXTENDED-DIJKSTRA and compare it to the process of using DIJKSTRA on graphs that have already been expanded using the Kirby-Potts method. As we might expect, the expense of both of these approaches increases for larger numbers of vertices and edges. In addition, they are also affected by the number of colours k used in the graph, though we avoid this variable in our analysis because it can lead to an overestimation of complexity due to a relationship with the graph colouring problem, as we now explain.

EXTENDED-DIJKSTRA $(s \in V, l \in C^-(s))$
(1)   **for all** $v \in V$ **do**
(2)   **for all** $i \in C^-(v)$ **do**
(3) $L(v,i) \leftarrow \infty$, $D(v,i) \leftarrow$ **false**, $P(v,i) \leftarrow$ NULL
(4) $L(s,l) \leftarrow 0$
(5) $Q \leftarrow \{(s,l,L(s,l))\}$
(6)   **while** $Q \neq \emptyset$ **do**
(7)   Let $(u,i,L(u,i))$ be the element in Q with minimum value for $L(u,i)$
(8) $Q \leftarrow Q - \{(u,i,L(u,i))\}$
(9) $D(u,i) \leftarrow$ **true**
(10)   **for all** $(u,v,j) \in E^+(u) : D(v,j) =$ **false**
(11)   **if** $L(u,i) + t(u,i,j) + w(u,v,j) < L(v,j)$ **then**
(12)   **if** $L(v,j) \neq \infty$ **then** $Q \leftarrow Q - \{(v,j,L(v,j))\}$
(13) $L(v,j) \leftarrow L(u,i) + t(u,i,j) + w(u,v,j)$
(14) $Q \leftarrow Q \cup \{(v,j,L(v,j))\}$
(15) $P(v,j) \leftarrow (u,i)$

Fig. 4. The Extended Dijkstra algorithm.

Let $G = (V,E)$ be a graph using k colours as defined in Sect. 1, and let $G^* = (V,E^*)$ be a copy of G with all edge directions removed. Finally let $G^*(i)$ denote the subgraph formed from G^* using edges of colour i only. Note that if two such subgraphs $G^*(i)$ and $G^*(j)$ have no common vertices, then no transfers are possible between colours i and j. In this case we have the opportunity to relabel all i-coloured edges with colour j (or vice versa), and potentially reduce the number of colours being used in the graph.

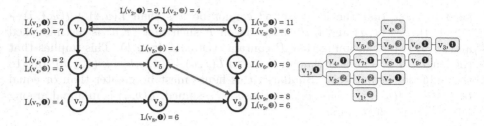

Fig. 5. Solution returned by EXTENDED-DIJKSTRA using the graph from Fig. 1 and source $(v_1, 1)$. All transfer costs are assumed to be 1. The shortest path tree defined by the contents of P is shown on the right.

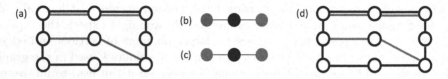

Fig. 6. (a) A graph G^* using $k = 3$ colours; (b) the underlying conflicts graph (and 3-colouring) prescribed by G^*; (c) a 2-colouring of this conflicts graph; and (d) the original graph G^* using $k = 2$ colours. (Color figure online)

In more detail, consider a conflicts graph created using an i-coloured vertex for each component of each subgraph $G^*(i)$ (for $i \in \{1, \ldots, k\}$), with edges corresponding to any vertex pair representing differently-coloured overlapping components in G^*. Note that the colours of the vertices in this conflicts graph define a proper k-colouring, in that pairs of adjacent vertices always have different colours; however, it may be possible to colour this conflicts graph using fewer colours. If this is so, then an equivalent graph to G with fewer colours can also be created. An example of this process is shown in Fig. 6. This illustrates that, while the number of edge colours k could have any value up to and including m, the minimum number of colours needed to express this graph might well be smaller. However, identifying this minimum can be difficult since it is equivalent to solving the $\mathcal{NP}$-hard chromatic number (graph colouring) problem [11].

Given these observations on k, a better alternative for analysing complexity is to consider the number of colours entering and exiting each vertex (given by $C^-(v)$ and $C^+(v)$) and, in particular, their maximum values $c_{\max}^- = \max\{|C^-(v)| : v \in V\}$ and $c_{\max}^+ = \max\{|C^+(v)| : v \in V\}$.

Now reconsider the pseudocode for EXTENDED-DIJKSTRA given in Fig. 4. As before, we assume the use of a binary heap for Q and direct access data structures for L, D and P. The initialisation of L, D, and P in Lines 1 to 5 has a worst-case complexity of $\mathcal{O}(nc_{\max}^-)$. For the main part of the algorithm, now note that each label in L is considered and marked as distinguished exactly once and, in the worst case, we will have $nc_{\max}^-$ such labels. Once a label (u, i) is marked as distinguished, all incident edges (u, v, j) are then considered in turn

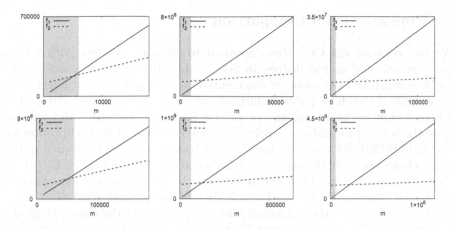

Fig. 7. Comparison of growth rates f_1 and f_2 with regards to the number of edges m. Rows show n-values of 1000 and 10000 respectively; columns consider values $c_{\max}^- = c_{\max}^+$ of 3, 10, and 20 respectively.

and are subject to a series of constant-time and log-time operations, as shown in Lines 12 to 15. This leads to a overall worst case complexity of $\mathcal{O}\left(nc_{\max}^-\right) + \mathcal{O}\left(\left(mc_{\max}^-\right)\lg\left(nc_{\max}^-\right)\right)$. Assuming graph connectivity, this simplifies to a growth rate for EXTENDED-DIJKSTRA of

$$f_1 = \mathcal{O}\left(\left(mc_{\max}^-\right)\lg\left(nc_{\max}^-\right)\right). \tag{3}$$

As noted, the complexity of DIJKSTRA using a binary heap is $\mathcal{O}(m\lg n)$. Using a Kirby-Potts expansion, in the worst case this leads to a graph G' with $n' = n(c_{\max}^- + c_{\max}^+)$ vertices and $m' = m + nc_{\max}^-c_{\max}^+$ edges, giving an overall complexity of $\mathcal{O}(m'\lg n')$, or

$$f_2 = \mathcal{O}\left(\left(m + nc_{\max}^-c_{\max}^+\right)\lg\left(n\left(c_{\max}^- + c_{\max}^+\right)\right)\right). \tag{4}$$

Figure 7 compares f_1 and f_2 for a range of different parameter values. Note that f_1 grows more quickly in all cases, demonstrating that EXTENDED-DIJKSTRA is less efficient with regards to increases in the number of edges m. The main reason for this is that, with EXTENDED-DIJKSTRA, each outgoing edge of a vertex v is considered for each incoming colour of v. This results in the term $(mc_{\max}^-)$ seen in Eq. (3). In contrast, although a Kirby-Potts expansion results in a graph G' with an increased number of edges and vertices, each edge in G' is considered only once using DIJKSTRA, which results in a slower growth rate overall. Note, however, that each chart in Fig. 7 features an intercept, suggesting that EXTENDED-DIJKSTRA is more efficient with very sparse graphs. For indicative purposes, the grey rectangles in the figure show the range of values for which planar digraphs exist (i.e., the right boundary of these rectangles occur at $m = 2(3n - 6)$, which is the maximum possible number of directed edges in a planar digraph). Planar graphs are considered further in the next section.

5   Computational Comparison

We now consider the CPU times required to calculate shortest path trees on the edge-coloured graphs defined in Sect. 1. In our case we will seek shortest paths in which transfer costs are not incurred at terminal vertices. This is useful in applications such as public transport, where a passenger will arrive at the source vertex by means outside of the network (e.g. by foot), and will then leave the network on arrival at their destination. To make this modification with EXTENDED-DIJKSTRA we can simply set all transfer costs at the source vertex s to zero before running the algorithm using an arbitrary in-colour $l \in C^-(s)$. The shortest s-v-path length in G is then indicated by the minimum value among the labels $L(v, i)$, where $i \in C^+(v)$. For a Kirby-Potts expanded graph G', a similar process is used: first, the weights of all transfer edges in the cluster defined by s are temporarily set to zero; next DIJKSTRA is executed from an arbitrary in-vertex within this cluster; finally, the minimum label value among all in-vertices in v's cluster is identified.

Two types of problem instances were considered in our tests. These were generated using a density parameter d that represents the average number of edges travelling from each vertex u to each vertex v. The first instance type, random graphs, were generated by randomly placing n vertices into the unit square. All potential edges (u, v, i) were then considered in turn and added to the graph with a fixed probability of d/k. During this process, care was also taken to ensure that the graph contained a random $(n - 1)$-cycle, making the graph strongly connected.

The second graph type, planar graphs, were considered to give an indication of algorithm performance on transport networks. Recall that planar graphs are those that can be drawn on a plane so that no edges cross. In that sense, like road networks, they are quite sparse, with vertex degrees being fairly low. Note that when things like roads physically intersect on land, there will often be an opportunity to transfer from one to the other; hence, the underlying graph will be planar. However, this is not always the case, such as when one road crosses another via a bridge, so the analogy is not exact. Planar graphs were formed by again randomly placing n vertices into the unit square. A Delaunay triangulation was then generated from these vertices, with the edges of this triangulation being used to form a pool of potential edges for the graph (that is, for each edge $\{u, v\}$ in the triangulation, all directed and coloured edges (u, v, i) and (v, u, i) (for $i \in \{1, \ldots, k\}$) were added to the pool). Edges were then selected randomly from this pool and added to the graph until the desired graph density was reached. Again, we also ensured that the resultant graph was strongly connected: in this case by including all edges from a bidirectional minimum spanning tree.

For both random and planar graphs, edge weights were calculated using the Euclidean distances between vertices plus or minus x percent where, for each edge, x was selected randomly in the range $(-10, 10)$. This prevents edges between the same pair of vertices from having the same weight. Transfer costs were set to the average edge weight across the graph plus or minus x percent.

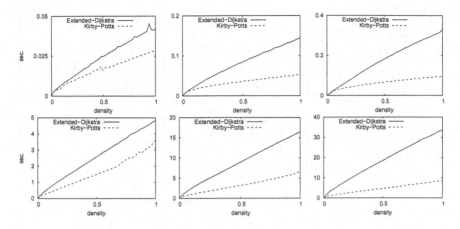

Fig. 8. CPU times required to produce a shortest path tree from a single source using random graphs of differing densities. Rows show n values of 1000 and 10000 respectively; columns consider k-values of 3, 10 and 20 respectively. The number of edges in a graph is determined by multiplying the density by $n(n-1)$.

All algorithms used in our tests were written in C++ and executed on 3.2 GHtz Windows 7 machines with 8 GB RAM. Our implementations used red-black trees for the priority queues Q and adjacency lists for storing edges, colours and weights.

Figure 8 shows the average CPU times required by EXTENDED-DIJKSTRA for random graphs with $n \in \{1000, 10000\}$ and $k \in \{3, 10, 20\}$. In all cases, five graphs were generated for each density $d \in \{0, 0.02, 0.04, \ldots, 1.0\}$. EXTENDED-DIJKSTRA was then run using each of the n vertices as a source in turn. Each point in the figure is therefore a mean of $5n$ different values. The figures also show the times required by DIJKSTRA on the corresponding Kirby-Potts expanded graphs. Note that the cost of performing the expansions is not included in these figures.

As expected, Fig. 8 shows that the run times of both algorithms grow for increases in n, k, and m. We also see that the Kirby-Potts method shows more favourable run times overall, particularly for large dense problem instances. Indeed, the most extreme difference occurs with graphs with $n = 10000$, $d = 1$, and $k = 20$, where an average difference of over twenty seconds per run is observed.

To contrast these results, Fig. 9 shows the average CPU times required for planar graphs. Here, for each n and k, graphs were generated for 25 different values for m, using an upper limit of $m = 2k(3n - 6)$ (this is the maximum number of edges in a planar, loop-free, multi-digraph using k edge colours). As before, the right boundaries of the grey rectangles in these charts indicate $m = 2(3n - 6)$ (the maximum number of edges in a planar digraph). All other details are the same as the previous experiments.

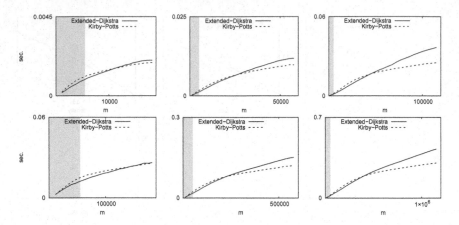

Fig. 9. CPU times required to produce a shortest path tree from a single source using planar graphs of differing densities. Rows show n values of 1000 and 10000 respectively; columns consider k-values of 3, 10 and 20 respectively.

Figure 9 reveals similar patterns to our analysis in Sect. 4. For sparse graphs, including all of those within the grey rectangles, EXTENDED-DIJKSTRA requires less run time. However, as previously seen in Fig. 7, these two lines eventually intersect, with EXTENDED-DIJKSTRA then requiring more run time for denser graphs.

6   Expansion Times

In the results of the previous section we have chosen not to include the time taken to perform Kirby-Watts expansions. This is because the decision on how a graph is represented and stored will often be made by the user beforehand and might therefore be considered a separate process. However, this will not always be the case. For example, Ahmed et al. [1] and Heyken Soares et al. [7] have proposed methods for optimising public transport systems that use heuristics to produce a whole series of graphs, each that is then expanded before evaluation. In these cases, it is therefore appropriate to consider the overheads consumed by these expansions.

In our case, an expansion takes a graph G and produces a corresponding adjacency list for the expanded graph G'. This involves stepping through each edge and each transfer cost in G and then adding an appropriate edge to G', leading to an overall complexity of $\mathcal{O}(m + nc_{\max}^- c_{\max}^+)$. Note that this has a slightly lower growth rate compared to executing DIJKSTRA on G', shown in Eq. (4).

Table 1 shows the conversion times for random and planar graphs of differing parameters. We see that these times increase for graphs featuring more edges, vertices, and colours, as we would expect. For graphs with $n = 1000$, conversion times are very small, coming in at less than 0.2 s in all cases; however, for larger

Table 1. Number of seconds to perform a Kirby-Potts expansion for random and planar graphs of differing parameters. Figures show the mean and standard deviation across twenty problem instances.

Random graphs			Planar graphs		
Parameters	Conversion time		Parameters	Conversion time	
	Mean	Std. dev.		Mean	Std. dev.
$n = 1000$:			$n = 1000$:		
$d = 0.05, k = 3$	0.006	<0.001	$m = 1998, k = 3$	<0.001	0.001
$d = 0.50, k = 3$	0.058	0.002	$m = 9661, k = 3$	0.003	0.001
$d = 0.95, k = 3$	0.113	0.001	$m = 17325, k = 3$	0.003	<0.001
$d = 0.05, k = 10$	0.017	<0.001	$m = 1998, k = 10$	0.001	<0.001
$d = 0.50, k = 10$	0.063	0.001	$m = 29781, k = 10$	0.016	0.002
$d = 0.95, k = 10$	0.113	0.001	$m = 57564, k = 10$	0.017	0.001
$d = 0.05, k = 20$	0.055	0.001	$m = 1998, k = 20$	0.001	0.001
$d = 0.50, k = 20$	0.108	0.002	$m = 58523, k = 20$	0.059	0.002
$d = 0.95, k = 20$	0.162	0.016	$m = 115049, k = 20$	0.068	0.004
$n = 10000$:			$n = 10000$:		
$d = 0.05, k = 3$	0.602	0.006	$m = 19998, k = 3$	0.008	<0.001
$d = 0.50, k = 3$	6.640	0.161	$m = 96781, k = 3$	0.028	0.001
$d = 0.95, k = 3$	38.369	6.452	$m = 173565, k = 3$	0.034	0.001
$d = 0.05, k = 10$	0.714	0.004	$m = 19998, k = 10$	0.009	0.001
$d = 0.50, k = 10$	6.550	0.229	$m = 298341, k = 10$	0.203	0.006
$d = 0.95, k = 10$	44.437	8.754	$m = 576684, k = 10$	0.232	0.008
$d = 0.05, k = 20$	1.193	0.014	$m = 19998, k = 20$	0.010	0.001
$d = 0.50, k = 20$	6.768	0.092	$m = 586283, k = 20$	0.689	0.002
$d = 0.95, k = 20$	53.360	7.904	$m = 1152569, k = 20$	0.770	0.016

graphs much longer times are sometimes required. Note that the largest Kirby-Watts graphs seen here (produced from random graphs with $n = 10000$, $d = 0.95$ and $k = 20$) required over 5 GB of RAM, so significant amounts of memory management (such as paging) may also be needed as part of this expansion process.

7 Conclusions

In this paper we proposed a new shortest path algorithm that copes with vertex transfer costs without having to first perform a graph expansion, a process that can sometimes be quite costly with large graphs. While our method exhibits an inferior growth rate compared to using Dijkstra's algorithm on Kirby-Potts expanded graphs, we have seen that it can exhibit shorter run times with sparse problem instances such as planar graphs.

In the future it would be useful to see if EXTENDED-DIJKSTRA might also be converted into a modified version of the A* algorithm, perhaps giving superior performance with the single-source single-target shortest path problem. This would involve modifying Line 7 of Fig. 4 so that a heuristic rule is used for selecting the pair (u, i). Properties of suitable heuristics are outlined in the work of Hart et al. [6].

References

1. Ahmed, L., Mumford, C., Kheiri, A.: Solving urban transit route design problems using selection hyper-heuristics. Eur. J. Oper. Res. **274**, 545–559 (2019)
2. Bauer, R., Delling, D., Sanders, P., Schieferdecker, D., Schultes, D., Wagner, D.: Combining hierarchical and goal-directed speed-up techniques for Dijkstra's algorithm. In: McGeoch, C.C. (ed.) WEA 2008. LNCS, vol. 5038, pp. 303–318. Springer, Heidelberg (2008). https://doi.org/10.1007/978-3-540-68552-4_23
3. Cooper, I., John, M., Lewis, R., Mumford, C., Olden, A.: Optimising large scale public transport network design problems using mixed-mode parallel multiobjective evolutionary algorithms. In: Proceedings of the 2014 IEEE Congress on Evolutionary Computation, pp. 2841–2848. IEEE (2014)
4. Cormen, T., Leiserson, C., Rivest, R., Stein, C.: Introduction to Algorithms. The MIT Press, Cambridge (2009)
5. Demir, E., Burgholzer, W., Hrusovsky, M., Arikan, E., Jammernegg, W., Van Woensel, T.: A green intermodal service network design problem with travel time uncertainty. Transp. Res. Part B **93**, 789–807 (2016)
6. Hart, P., Nilsson, N., Raphael, B.: A formal basis for the heuristic determination of minimum cost paths. IEEE Trans. Syst. Sci. Cybern. **4**(2), 100–107 (1968)
7. Soares, P.H., Mumford, C., Amponsah, K., Mao, Y.: An adaptive scaled network for public transport route optimisation. Public Transp. **11**, 379–412 (2019)
8. John, M.: Metaheuristics for designing efficient routes and schedules for urban transportation networks. Ph.D. thesis, School of Computer Science and Informatics, Cardiff University (2016)
9. John, M.P., Mumford, C.L., Lewis, R.: An improved multi-objective algorithm for the urban transit routing problem. In: Blum, C., Ochoa, G. (eds.) EvoCOP 2014. LNCS, vol. 8600, pp. 49–60. Springer, Heidelberg (2014). https://doi.org/10.1007/978-3-662-44320-0_5
10. Kirby, R., Potts, R.: The minimum route problem for networks with turn penalties and prohibitions. Transp. Res. **3**, 397–408 (1969)
11. Lewis, R.: A Guide to Graph Colouring: Algorithms and Applications. Springer, Cham (2016). https://doi.org/10.1007/978-3-319-25730-3
12. Winter, S.: Modeling costs of turns in route planning. GeoInformatica **6**(4), 345–361 (2002)

A Global Intermodal Shipment Matching Problem Under Travel Time Uncertainty

Wenjing Guo(✉), Bilge Atasoy, Wouter Beelaerts van Blokland,
and Rudy R. Negenborn

Department of Maritime and Transport Technology, Delft University of Technology,
Delft, The Netherlands
{W.Guo-2,B.Atasoy,W.W.A.BeelaertsvanBlokland,R.R.Negenborn}@tudelft.nl

Abstract. Global intermodal transportation involves the movement of
shipments between inland terminals located in different continents by
using ships, barges, trains, trucks, or any combination among them
through integrated planning at a network level. One of the challenges
faced by global operators is the matching of shipment requests with
transport services in an integrated global network. The characteristics
of the global intermodal shipment matching problem include acceptance
and matching decisions, soft time windows, capacitated services, and
transshipments between multimodal services. The objective of the problem is to maximize the total profits which consist of revenues, travel
costs, transfer costs, storage costs, delay costs, and carbon tax. Travel
time uncertainty has significant effects on the feasibility and profitability
of matching plans. However, travel time uncertainty has not been considered in global intermodal transport yet leading to significant delays
and infeasible transshipments. To fill in this gap, this paper proposes
a chance-constrained programming model in which travel times are
assumed stochastic. We conduct numerical experiments to validate the
performance of the stochastic model in comparison to a deterministic
model and a robust model. The experiment results show that the stochastic model outperforms the benchmarks in total profits.

Keywords: Global intermodal transportation · Shipment matching
problem · Travel time uncertainty · Chance-constrained programming

1 Introduction

With the increasing volumes of global trade and the trend towards time-sensitive
shipments, efficient global transportation becomes increasingly important in
global supply chains [18]. Intermodal transportation is the provision of efficient,
effective, and sustainable transport services thanks to the horizontal and vertical collaboration among players [15]. However, implementing intermodality in
global transport is still challenging from several aspects, including: the design of
collaboration contracts and pricing strategies that ensure fairness and attractiveness among players at the strategic level [8]; integrated service network design

© Springer Nature Switzerland AG 2020
E. Lalla-Ruiz et al. (Eds.): ICCL 2020, LNCS 12433, pp. 553–568, 2020.
https://doi.org/10.1007/978-3-030-59747-4_36

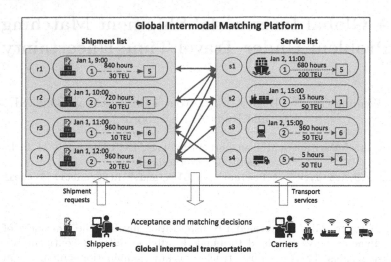

Fig. 1. A global intermodal matching platform.

that determines service frequencies and time schedules at the tactical level [12]; and integrated transport plan that assigns specific shipments with transport services under a dynamic or stochastic environment at the operational level [15]. This paper investigates a global intermodal shipment matching (GISM) problem under travel time uncertainty at the operational level.

With the development of digitization in the logistics industry, increasing matching/booking platforms have appeared in freight transportation [13], such as Uber Freight and Quicargo. We consider a platform owned by a global operator that receives shipment requests from shippers and receives transport services from carriers, as shown in Fig. 1. The global operator could be a logistics service provider or an alliance formed by multiple carriers, such as Maersk and COSCO Shipping lines. A shipment request is defined as a batch of containers that must be transported from its origin to its destination within a specific time window. For example, shipment r1 consists of 30 containers which require to be transported from origin terminal 1 to destination terminal 5 with a release time of Jan 1, 9:00, and a lead time of 840 h. A transport service is characterized by its mode, origin, destination, time schedule, and free capacity. For example, ship service s1 with capacity 200 TEU (twenty-foot equivalent unit) will depart from terminal 1 on Jan 2, 11:00, and arrive to terminal 5 with an estimated travel time of 680 h. The platform aims to provide optimal acceptance and matching decisions in a global intermodal network. A match between a shipment request and a transport service represents that the shipment will be transported by the service from the service's origin to the service's destination. The platform combines the matched services into itineraries to provide integrated transport for global shipments. For instance, shipment r2 will be transported by barge service s2 from origin terminal 2 to transshipment terminal 1 and by ship service s1 from transshipment terminal 1 to destination terminal 5. The objective of the platform is to maximize the total profits which consists of revenues and costs.

Due to travel time uncertainty and the utilization of multimodal services, the matches made for accepted requests might become suboptimal or even infeasible at transshipment terminals. Thanks to the development in data analytics, probability distributions of uncertainties are often available to transport systems [3]. However, while stochastic approaches that incorporate stochastic information of travel times in decision-making processes have been well investigated in vehicle routing problems [2,9] and inland intermodal transport planning [1,6], the stochastic approach for the GISM problem under travel time uncertainty is still missing. This paper contributes to the literature by developing a chance-constrained programming model to set confidence levels of chance constraints regarding infeasible transshipments in a global intermodal network.

In the literature, most similar to our work are the work of Demir et al. [1] and Guo et al. [4]. Demir et al. [1] investigated an inland intermodal service network design problem with travel time uncertainty. In comparison to [1], this paper considers fixed time schedules of multimodal services in a global network, and develops a model that integrates acceptance and matching decisions. Guo et al. [4] studied an inland intermodal shipment matching problem with request uncertainty. In comparison to [4], this paper considers travel time uncertainty in a global intermodal network.

The remainder of this paper is structured as follows. In Sect. 2, we provide a detailed problem description, followed by a mathematical formulation in Sect. 3. In Sect. 4, we develop the Chance-constrained programming model. In Sect. 5, we present the experimental results. Finally, in Sect. 6, we provide concluding remarks and directions for future research.

2   Problem Description

Let N be the set of terminals. Each terminal $i \in N$ is characterized by its loading/unloading cost lc_i^m, loading/unloading time lt_i^m with mode $m \in M = \{\text{ship, barge, train, truck}\}$, and storage cost per container per hour c_i^{storage}. We assume terminal operators provide unlimited loading/unloading and storage capacity to the global operator.

Let R be the set of shipment requests. Each request $r \in R$ is characterized by its container type CT_r (i.e., dry or reefer), origin terminal o_r, destination terminal d_r, container volume u_r, release time $\mathbb{T}_r^{\text{release}}$ (i.e., the time when the shipment is available for transport process), lead time LD_r, freight rate p_r, and delay cost c_r^{delay}. The due time of request r is $\mathbb{T}_r^{\text{due}} = \mathbb{T}_r^{\text{release}} + LD_r$.

Let S be the set of services. Each service $s \in S$ is characterized by its mode $MT_s \in M$, origin terminal o_s, destination terminal d_s, total free capacity U_s, free capacity U_s^k in terms of container type $k \in K = \{\text{dry, reefer}\}$, estimated travel time t_s, travel cost c_s, and generation of carbon emissions e_s^k for container type k. We consider ship, barge and train services as time scheduled services with scheduled departure time TD_s and scheduled arrival time TA_s for $s \in S^{\text{ship}} \cup S^{\text{barge}} \cup S^{\text{train}}$. Each truck service consists of a fleet of trucks that have flexible departure times. We define TD_{rs} as a variable that indicates the departure time of service $s \in S^{\text{truck}}$ with shipment $r \in R$. Moreover, different services with the same mode might be operated by the same vehicle. For two successive services operated by the same vehicle, transshipment is unnecessary at the intermediate terminal. Let l_{sq} be equal to 0 if services s and q are operated by the same vehicle, and service s is the preceding service of service q, 1 otherwise.

In practice, travel time uncertainties are quite common resulting from weather conditions and traffic congestion [1]. In this paper, we use common assumption that the travel times $[\tilde{t}_s]_{\forall s \in S}$ are continuous random variables following normal distributions, and are statistically independent [2]. Let $\tilde{t}_s \sim N(\mu_s, \sigma_s^2)$, in which μ_s is the mean travel time between terminal o_s and terminal d_s, and σ_s is the corresponding standard deviation. Due to the travel time uncertainties, the actual departure and arrival time of service $s \in S$ are also uncertain. The distribution of the departure time of service s is based on the distribution of the arrival time of its preceding service; the distribution of the arrival time of service s is based on the distributions of the departure and travel time of service s. For vehicle $v \in V$, we define the itinerary of vehicle v as the sequence of services that the vehicle operated, and define I_v^n as the nth service of vehicle v. Therefore, the departure time of service $s = I_v^n$ follows normal distribution given by:

$$\tilde{T}D_s \sim N(TD_{I_v^1} + \sum_{j \in \{1...n-1\}} \mu_{I_v^j} + \sum_{j \in \{1...n-1\}} 2lt_{d_{I_v^j}}^{MT_v}, \sum_{j \in \{1...n-1\}} \sigma_{I_v^j}^2),$$

where MT_v is the mode of vehicle v. We denote $\tilde{T}D_s \sim N(\mu_s^+, \sigma_s^{+2})$. Similarly, the arrival time of service $s = I_v^n$ follows the normal distribution given by:

$$\tilde{T}A_s \sim N(TD_{I_v^1} + \sum_{j \in \{1...n\}} \mu_{I_v^j} + \sum_{j \in \{1...n-1\}} 2lt_{d_{I_v^j}}^{MT_v}, \sum_{j \in \{1...n\}} \sigma_{I_v^j}^2).$$

We denote $\tilde{T}A_s \sim N(\mu_s^-, \sigma_s^{-2})$.

Travel time uncertainty of services in a global intermodal network may lead to infeasible transshipments in addition to the commonly studied outcome of late or early delivery at destinations [9,14]. An illustrative example is shown in Fig. 2. A shipment is planned to be transported by a train service from its origin terminal to port A, by a ship service from port A to port B, and by two barge services from port B to its destination terminal according to fixed time schedules. The outcomes of travel time uncertainty in global intermodal transportation include late delivery at destination terminal under realization 1 which causes delayed costs, early delivery at destination terminal under realization 2 which causes storage costs, and infeasible transshipment at port B under realization 3 which requires re-planning from port B to destination terminal.

The objective of the platform is to maximize the total profits by optimizing acceptance and matching decisions over a given planning horizon T. The total profits consist of revenues received from shippers, travel costs paid to carriers, transfer costs and storage costs paid to terminal operators, delay costs paid to shippers, and carbon tax charged by institutional authorities.

The notation used in this paper is shown in Table 1.

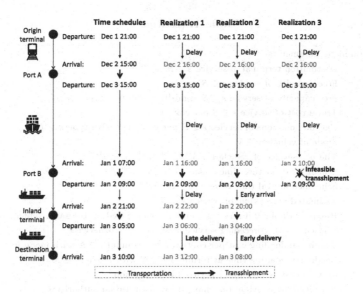

Fig. 2. Possible outcomes of travel time uncertainty in global transport.

Table 1. Notation.

Sets:	
N	Terminals N
K	Container types, $K = \{\text{dry, reefer}\}$
R	Shipment requests
R^k	Requests with container type $k \in K$
M	Modes, $M = \{\text{ship, barge, train, truck}\}$
V	Set of vehicles $V = V^{\text{ship}} \cup V^{\text{barge}} \cup V^{\text{train}} \cup V^{\text{truck}}$
S	Services, $S = S^{\text{ship}} \cup S^{\text{barge}} \cup S^{\text{train}} \cup S^{\text{truck}}$
S_i^+	Services departing at terminal i, $S_i^+ = S_i^{+\text{ship}} \cup S_i^{+\text{barge}} \cup S_i^{+\text{train}} \cup S_i^{+\text{truck}}$
S_i^-	Services arriving at terminal i, $S_i^- = S_i^{-\text{ship}} \cup S_i^{-\text{barge}} \cup S_i^{-\text{train}} \cup S_i^{-\text{truck}}$
Deterministic parameters	
T	Length of the planning horizon
α	Confidence level
CT_r	Container type of request $r \in R, CT_r \in K$
o_r	Origin terminal of request $r \in R, o_r \in N$
d_r	Destination terminal of request $r \in R, d_r \in N$
u_r	Container volume of request $r \in R$
$\mathbb{T}_r^{\text{release}}$	Release time of request $r \in R$
$\mathbb{T}_r^{\text{due}}$	Due time of request $r \in R$
p_r	Freight rate of request $r \in R$
LD_r	Lead time of request $r \in R$, $LD_r = \mathbb{T}_r^{\text{due}} - \mathbb{T}_r^{\text{release}}$
c_r^{delay}	Delay cost of request $r \in R$ per container per hour overdue
MT_s	Mode of service $s \in S, MT_s \in M$
o_s	Origin terminal of service $s \in S, o_s \in N$

(continued)

Table 1. (*continued*)

Deterministic parameters	
d_s	Destination terminal of service $s \in S, d_s \in N$
U_s	Free capacity of service $s \in S$
U_s^k	Free capacity of service $s \in S$ regarding container type $k \in K$
c_s	Travel cost of service $s \in S$ per container
e_s^k	Carbon emissions of service $s \in S$ per container with type $k \in K$
MT_v	Mode of vehicle $v \in V$
I_v^n	The nth service of vehicle $v \in V \backslash V^{\text{truck}}, I_v^n \in S \backslash S^{\text{truck}}$
TD_s	Scheduled departure time of service $s \in S \backslash S^{\text{truck}}$
TA_s	Scheduled arrival time of service $s \in S \backslash S^{\text{truck}}$
t_s	Estimated travel time of service $s \in S$
l_{sq}	Binary variable; 0 if services s and q are operated by the same vehicle, and Service s is the preceding service of service q, 1 otherwise
lc_i^m	Loading/unloading cost per container at terminal $i \in N$ with mode $m \in M$
lt_i^m	Loading/unloading time at terminal $i \in N$ with mode $m \in M$
c_i^{storage}	Storage cost at terminal i per container per hour
c^{emission}	Activity-based carbon tax charged by institutional authorities
M	A large number used for binary constraints
Random variables	
$\tilde{t}_s$	Travel time of service $s \in S, \tilde{t}_s \sim N(\mu_s, \sigma_s^2)$
$\tilde{T}D_s$	Departure time of service $s \in S \backslash S^{\text{truck}}, \tilde{T}D_s \sim N(\mu_s^+, \sigma_s^{+2})$
$\tilde{T}A_s$	Arrival time of service $s \in S \backslash S^{\text{truck}}, \tilde{T}A_s \sim N(\mu_s^-, \sigma_s^{-2})$
Variables	
y_r	Binary variable; 1 if request $r \in R$ is accepted
x_{rs}	Binary variable; 1 if request $r \in R$ is matched with service $s \in S$, 0 otherwise
z_{rsq}	Binary variable; 1 if request $r \in R$ is matched with service $s \in S$, $x_{rs} = 1$ And service $q \in S$, $x_{rq} = 1$, 0 otherwise
TD_{rs}	Departure time of truck service $s \in S^{\text{truck}}$ with request $r \in R$
f_{ri}	Transshipment cost of request $r \in R$ at terminal $i \in N$ per container
$\tilde{w}_{ri}$	Storage time of request $r \in R$ at terminal $i \in N$
$\tilde{\mathbb{T}}_r^{\text{delay}}$	Delay of request $r \in R$ at destination terminal $d_r \in N$

3   Mathematical Formulation

Let y_r be the binary variable which is 1 if request $r \in R$ is accepted, otherwise 0. We use the binary variable x_{rs} to represent the match between request $r \in R$ and service $s \in S$. A match between request r and service s means shipment r will be transported by service s from terminal o_s to terminal d_s. Due to the travel time uncertainty, the transport plan might become infeasible and requires re-planning. Therefore, the costs generated by accepted requests are uncertain and hard to estimate. We use $\tilde{C}_r(\mathbf{x})$ to denote the random cost generated for request $r \in R$ which consists of travel costs, transfer costs, storage costs, delay costs, and carbon tax. The mathematical formulation of the GISM problem is:

$$\mathbf{P0} \quad \max_{\mathbf{y},\mathbf{x}} \sum_{r \in R} p_r u_r y_r - \sum_{r \in R} \tilde{C}_r(\mathbf{x}) \tag{1}$$

subject to

$$y_r \leq \sum_{s \in S_{o_r}^+} x_{rs}, \quad \forall r \in R, \tag{2}$$

$$y_r \leq \sum_{s \in S_{d_r}^-} x_{rs}, \quad \forall r \in R, \tag{3}$$

$$\sum_{s \in S_i^+} x_{rs} \leq 1, \quad \forall r \in R, i \in N \backslash \{d_r\}, \tag{4}$$

$$\sum_{s \in S_i^-} x_{rs} \leq 1, \quad \forall r \in R, i \in N \backslash \{o_r\}, \tag{5}$$

$$\sum_{s \in S_{o_r}^-} x_{rs} \leq 0, \quad \forall r \in R, \tag{6}$$

$$\sum_{s \in S_{d_r}^+} x_{rs} \leq 0, \quad \forall r \in R, \tag{7}$$

$$\sum_{s \in S_i^+} x_{rs} = \sum_{s \in S_i^-} x_{rs}, \quad \forall r \in R, i \in N \backslash \{o_r, d_r\}, \tag{8}$$

$$\sum_{r \in R} x_{rs} u_r \leq U_s, \quad \forall s \in S, \tag{9}$$

$$\sum_{r \in R^k} x_{rs} u_r \leq U_s^k, \quad \forall s \in S, k = \text{reefer}, \tag{10}$$

$$\mathbb{T}_r^{\text{release}} + lt_{o_r}^{MT_s} \leq TD_{rs} + \mathbf{M}(1 - x_{rs}), \quad \forall r \in R, s \in S_{o_r}^{+\text{truck}}, \tag{11}$$

$$\mathbb{T}_r^{\text{release}} + lt_{o_r}^{MT_s} \leq \tilde{T}D_s + \mathbf{M}(1 - x_{rs}), \quad \forall r \in R, s \in S_{o_r}^+ \backslash S_{o_r}^{+\text{truck}}, \tag{12}$$

$$\tilde{T}A_s + lt_i^{MT_s} + lt_i^{MT_q} \leq \tilde{T}D_q + \mathbf{M}(1 - x_{rs}) + \mathbf{M}(1 - x_{rq}), \quad \forall r \in R, \\ i \in N \backslash \{o_r, d_r\}, s \in S_i^- \backslash S_i^{-\text{truck}}, q \in S_i^+ \backslash S_i^{+\text{truck}}, l_{sq} = 1, \tag{13}$$

$$TD_{rs} + \tilde{t}_s + lt_i^{MT_s} + lt_i^{MT_q} \leq \tilde{T}D_q + \mathbf{M}(1 - x_{rs}) + \mathbf{M}(1 - x_{rq}), \quad \forall r \in R, \\ i \in N \backslash \{o_r, d_r\}, s \in S_i^{-\text{truck}}, q \in S_i^+ \backslash S_i^{+\text{truck}}, \tag{14}$$

$$\tilde{T}A_s + lt_i^{MT_s} + lt_i^{MT_q} \leq TD_{rq} + \mathbf{M}(1 - x_{rs}) + \mathbf{M}(1 - x_{rq}), \quad \forall r \in R,$$
$$i \in N \backslash \{o_r, d_r\}, s \in S_i^- \backslash S_i^{-\text{truck}}, q \in S_i^{+\text{truck}}, \tag{15}$$

$$TD_{rs} + \tilde{t}_s + lt_i^{MT_s} + lt_i^{MT_q} \leq TD_{rq} + \mathbf{M}(1 - x_{rs}) + \mathbf{M}(1 - x_{rq}), \quad \forall r \in R,$$
$$i \in N \backslash \{o_r, d_r\}, s \in S_i^{-\text{truck}}, q \in S_i^{+\text{truck}}. \tag{16}$$

Constraints (2–3) ensure that request $r \in R$ will not be accepted by the platform if there is no matching possibilities. Constraints (4–5) ensure that at most one service transports request r departing from or arriving to a terminal. Constraints (6–7) are designed to eliminate subtours. Subtours might be formed since in one OD pair, there exist services in both directions. Constraints (8) ensure flow conservation. Constraints (9) ensure that the total container volumes of requests matched with service s do not exceed its total free capacity. Constraints (10) ensure that the total volumes of reefer containers matched with service s cannot exceed its free capacity on reefer slots. Constraints (11–12) ensure that the departure time of service s minus loading time must be earlier than the release time of request r, if request r will be transported by service s depart its origin terminal. Here, $\mathbf{M}$ is a large enough number which ensures the time compatibility between shipment r and service s when binary variable x_{rs} equals to 1, but leaves the constraints "open" if x_{rs} is 0. Constraints (13–16) ensure that the arrival time of service $s \in S_i^-$ plus loading and unloading time must be earlier than the departure time of service $q \in S_i^+$ if request r will be transported by service s entering terminal i and by service q leaving terminal i.

4   Chance-Constrained Programming Model

In the literature, different techniques have been developed to deal with travel time uncertainty: deterministic, stochastic, and robust programming [14]. While deterministic programming considers average travel times and robust programming considers minimum and maximum travel times, stochastic programming considers the probability distributions of travel times. Chance-constrained programming (CCP) is one of the major stochastic approaches to solve optimization problems under travel time uncertainty [9]. In this section, we develop a CCP model to approximate stochastic constraints (12–16) and random cost $\tilde{\mathbf{C}}_r(\mathbf{x})$ for request r in model **P0**. The CCP model does not take into account the correction costs caused by the re-planning of requests.

Under the CCP, each stochastic constraint will hold at least with probability α, where α is referred to as the confidence level provided by the platform. A high α means the matches have a low probability causing infeasible transshipments. When $\alpha = 0.5$, the CCP model becomes a deterministic model; when $\alpha = 1$, the CCP model becomes a robust model. The objective is to maximize expected total profits while ensuring that the probability of infeasible transshipments does not exceed α. The formulation of the CCP model is:

$$\mathbf{P1} \quad \max_{\mathbf{y,x}} \sum_{r \in R} p_r u_r y_r - \left(\sum_{r \in R} \sum_{s \in S} c_s x_{rs} u_r + \sum_{r \in R} \sum_{i \in N} f_{ri} u_r \right.$$

$$+ \sum_{r \in R} \sum_{i \in N} c_i^{\text{storage}} \mathbb{E}(\tilde{w}_{ri}) u_r + \sum_{r \in R} c_r^{\text{delay}} \mathbb{E}(\tilde{\mathbb{T}}_r^{\text{delay}}) u_r \tag{17}$$

$$\left. + \sum_{k \in K} \sum_{r \in R^k} \sum_{s \in S} c^{\text{emission}} e_s^k x_{rs} u_r \right)$$

subject to constraints (2–11),

$$P\{\mathbb{T}_r^{\text{release}} + lt_{o_r}^{MTs} \leq \tilde{T}D_s + \mathbf{M}(1 - x_{rs})\} \geq \alpha, \quad \forall r \in R, s \in S_{o_r}^+ \backslash S_{o_r}^{+\text{truck}}, \tag{18}$$

$$P\{\tilde{T}A_s + lt_i^{MTs} + lt_i^{MTq} \leq \tilde{T}D_q + \mathbf{M}(1 - x_{rs}) + \mathbf{M}(1 - x_{rq})\} \geq \alpha,$$
$$\forall r \in R, i \in N \backslash \{o_r, d_r\}, s \in S_i^- \backslash S_i^{-\text{truck}}, q \in S_i^+ \backslash S_i^{+\text{truck}}, l_{sq} = 1, \tag{19}$$

$$P\{TD_{rs} + \tilde{t}_s + lt_i^{MTs} + lt_i^{MTq} \leq \tilde{T}D_q + \mathbf{M}(1 - x_{rs}) + \mathbf{M}(1 - x_{rq})\} \geq \alpha,$$
$$\forall r \in R, i \in N \backslash \{o_r, d_r\}, s \in S_i^{-\text{truck}}, q \in S_i^+ \backslash S_i^{+\text{truck}}, \tag{20}$$

$$P\{\tilde{T}A_s + lt_i^{MTs} + lt_i^{MTq} \leq TD_{rq} + \mathbf{M}(1 - x_{rs}) + \mathbf{M}(1 - x_{rq})\} \geq \alpha,$$
$$\forall r \in R, i \in N \backslash \{o_r, d_r\}, s \in S_i^- \backslash S_i^{-\text{truck}}, q \in S_i^{+\text{truck}}, \tag{21}$$

$$P\{TD_{rs} + \tilde{t}_s + lt_i^{MTs} + lt_i^{MTq} \leq TD_{rq} + \mathbf{M}(1 - x_{rs}) + \mathbf{M}(1 - x_{rq})\} \geq \alpha,$$
$$\forall r \in R, i \in N \backslash \{o_r, d_r\}, s \in S_i^{-\text{truck}}, q \in S_i^{+\text{truck}}, \tag{22}$$

$$f_{ri} = \sum_{s \in S_i^+} x_{rs} lc_i^{MTs}, \quad \forall r \in R, i = o_r, \tag{23}$$

$$f_{ri} = \sum_{s \in S_i^-} x_{rs} lc_i^{MTs}, \quad \forall r \in R, i = d_r, \tag{24}$$

$$f_{ri} = \sum_{s \in S_i^+} \sum_{q \in S_i^-} \left(lc_i^{MTs} + lc_i^{MTq} \right) z_{rsq} l_{sq}, \quad \forall r \in R, i \in N \backslash \{o_r, d_r\}, \tag{25}$$

$$z_{rsq} \leq x_{rs}, \quad \forall r \in R, s \in S, q \in S, \tag{26}$$

$$z_{rsq} \leq x_{rq}, \quad \forall r \in R, s \in S, q \in S, \tag{27}$$

$$z_{rsq} \geq x_{rs} + x_{rq} - 1, \quad \forall r \in R, s \in S, q \in S, \tag{28}$$

$$\mathbb{E}(\tilde{w}_{ro_r}) \geq \mathbb{E}(\tilde{T}D_s) - lt_{o_r}^{MTs} - \mathbb{T}_r^{\text{release}} + \mathbf{M}(x_{rs} - 1), \forall r \in R, s \in S_{o_r}^+ \backslash S_{o_r}^{+\text{truck}}, \tag{29}$$

$$\mathbb{E}(\tilde{w}_{ro_r}) \geq TD_{rs} - lt_{o_r}^{MTs} - \mathbb{T}_r^{\text{release}} + \mathbf{M}(x_{rs} - 1), \forall r \in R, s \in S_{o_r}^{+\text{truck}}, \tag{30}$$

$$\mathbb{E}(\tilde{w}_{ri}) \geq \mathbb{E}(\tilde{T}D_q) - \mathbb{E}(\tilde{T}A_s) - lt_i^{MTs} - lt_i^{MTq} + \mathbf{M}(x_{rs} - 1) + \mathbf{M}(x_{rq} - 1), \tag{31}$$
$$\forall r \in R, i \in N \backslash \{o_r, d_r\}, s \in S_i^- \backslash S_i^{-\text{truck}}, q \in S_i^+ \backslash S_i^{+\text{truck}},$$

$$\mathbb{E}(\tilde{w}_{ri}) \geq \mathbb{E}(\tilde{T}D_q) - TD_{rs} - \mathbb{E}(\tilde{t}_s) - lt_i^{MTs} - lt_i^{MTq} + \mathbf{M}(x_{rs} - 1) + \mathbf{M}(x_{rq} - 1), \tag{32}$$
$$\forall r \in R, i \in N \backslash \{o_r, d_r\}, s \in S_i^{-\text{truck}}, q \in S_i^+ \backslash S_i^{+\text{truck}},$$

$$\mathbb{E}(\tilde{w}_{ri}) \geq TD_{rq} - \mathbb{E}(\tilde{T}A_s) - lt_i^{MTs} - lt_i^{MTq} + \mathbf{M}(x_{rs} - 1) + \mathbf{M}(x_{rq} - 1),$$
$$\forall r \in R, i \in N \backslash \{o_r, d_r\}, s \in S_i^- \backslash S_i^{-\text{truck}}, q \in S_i^{+\text{truck}}, \tag{33}$$

$$\mathbb{E}(\tilde{w}_{ri}) \geq TD_{rq} - TD_{rs} - \mathbb{E}(\tilde{t}_s) - lt_i^{MTs} - lt_i^{MTq} + M(x_{rs} - 1) + M(x_{rq} - 1),$$

$$\forall r \in R, i \in N\backslash\{o_r, d_r\}, s \in S_i^{-\text{truck}}, q \in S_i^{+\text{truck}}, \tag{34}$$

$$\mathbb{E}(\tilde{w}_{rd_r}) \geq \mathbb{T}_r^{\text{due}} - \mathbb{E}(\tilde{T}A_s) - lt_{d_r}^{MTs} + M(x_{rs} - 1), \quad \forall r \in R, s \in S_{d_r}^{-}\backslash S_{d_r}^{-\text{truck}}, \tag{35}$$

$$\mathbb{E}(\tilde{w}_{rd_r}) \geq \mathbb{T}_r^{\text{due}} - TD_{rs} - \mathbb{E}(\tilde{t}_s) - lt_{d_r}^{MTs} + M(x_{rs} - 1), \quad \forall r \in R, s \in S_{d_r}^{-\text{truck}}, \tag{36}$$

$$\mathbb{E}(\tilde{\mathbb{T}}_r^{\text{delay}}) \geq \mathbb{E}(\tilde{T}A_s) + lt_{d_r}^{MTs} - \mathbb{T}_r^{\text{due}} + M(x_{rs} - 1), \quad \forall r \in R, s \in S_{d_r}^{-}\backslash S_{d_r}^{-\text{truck}}, \tag{37}$$

$$\mathbb{E}(\tilde{\mathbb{T}}_r^{\text{delay}}) \geq TD_{rs} + \mathbb{E}(\tilde{t}_s) + lt_{d_r}^{MTs} - \mathbb{T}_r^{\text{due}} + M(x_{rs} - 1), \quad \forall r \in R, s \in S_{d_r}^{-\text{truck}}, \tag{38}$$

where f_{ri} is the planned loading and unloading cost of request r at terminal i; $\mathbb{E}(\tilde{w}_{ri})$ is the expected storage time of request r at terminal i; $\mathbb{E}(\tilde{\mathbb{T}}_r^{\text{delay}})$ is the expected delay in delivery of request r at destination terminal d_r; P is the probability measure; z_{rsq} is a binary variable which equals to 1 if request r has to transfer between service s and q, 0 otherwise; $\mathbb{E}(\tilde{T}D_s) = \mu_s^+$, $\mathbb{E}(\tilde{T}A_s) = \mu_s^-$, $\mathbb{E}(\tilde{t}_s) = \mu_s$.

The objective function **P1** is to maximize the expected total profits which consist of total revenues, travel costs, transfer costs, storage costs, delay costs and carbon tax. Constraints (18–22) ensure that the possibility of feasible transshipment at terminals will be higher than the confidence level α. Constraints (23–25) calculate the loading costs at origin terminals, the unloading costs at destination terminals, and the loading and unloading costs at transshipment terminals. Constraints (26–28) ensure that binary variable z_{rsq} equals to 1 if $x_{rs} = 1$ and $x_{rq} = 1$, 0 otherwise. Constraints (29–36) calculate the storage time at origin, transshipment, and destination terminals. Constraints (37–38) calculate delayed time at destination terminals.

To solve the CCP model, the traditional method is to convert the chance constraints into their corresponding deterministic equations. Based on the properties of normal distributions, chance constraints (18–22) can be linearized as:

$$\frac{\mathbb{T}_r^{\text{release}} + lt_{o_r}^{MTs} + M(x_{rs} - 1) - \mu_s^+}{\sigma_s^+} \leq \phi^{-1}(1 - \alpha), \forall r \in R, s \in S_{o_r}^{+}\backslash S_{o_r}^{+\text{truck}}, \tag{39}$$

$$\frac{lt_i^{MTs} + lt_i^{MTq} + M(x_{rs} - 1) + M(x_{rq} - 1) - (\mu_q^+ - \mu_s^-)}{\sqrt{(\sigma_q^+)^2 + (\sigma_s^-)^2}} \leq \phi^{-1}(1 - \alpha), \tag{40}$$

$$\forall r \in R, i \in N\backslash\{o_r, d_r\}, s \in S_i^{-}\backslash S_i^{-\text{truck}}, q \in S_i^{+}\backslash S_i^{+\text{truck}}, l_{sq} = 1,$$

$$\frac{TD_{rs} + lt_i^{MTs} + lt_i^{MTq} + M(x_{rs} - 1) + M(x_{rq} - 1) - (\mu_q^+ - \mu_s)}{\sqrt{(\sigma_q^+)^2 + (\sigma_s)^2}} \leq \phi^{-1}(1 - \alpha), \tag{41}$$

$$\forall r \in R, i \in N\backslash\{o_r, d_r\}, s \in S_i^{-\text{truck}}, q \in S_i^{+}\backslash S_i^{+\text{truck}},$$

$$\frac{TD_{rq} - lt_i^{MTs} - lt_i^{MTq} + M(1 - x_{rs}) + M(1 - x_{rq}) - \mu_s^-}{\sigma_s^-} \geq \phi^{-1}(\alpha), \tag{42}$$

$$\forall r \in R, i \in N\backslash\{o_r, d_r\}, s \in S_i^{-}\backslash S_i^{-\text{truck}}, q \in S_i^{+\text{truck}},$$

$$\frac{TD_{rq} - TD_{rs} - lt_i^{MTs} - lt_i^{MTq} + M(1 - x_{rs}) + M(1 - x_{rq}) - \mu_s}{\sigma_s} \geq \phi^{-1}(\alpha), \tag{43}$$

$$\forall r \in R, i \in N\backslash\{o_r, d_r\}, s \in S_i^{-\text{truck}}, q \in S_i^{+\text{truck}},$$

where ϕ^{-1} is the inverse function of standardized normal distribution.

5 Numerical Experiments

We evaluate the performance of the CCP on the GISM problem in comparison to a deterministic approach (DA) which uses average travel times (i.e., $\alpha = 0.5$) and a robust approach (RA) which considers the maximum and minimum travel times (i.e., $\alpha = 1$). Compared with the CCP, the DA is a risk neutral approach in which decision makers are indifferent to uncertainties, and the RA is a risk averse approach that seeks guarantee. The approaches are implemented in MATLAB, and all experiments are executed on 3.70 GHz Intel Xeon processors with 32 GB of RAM. The optimization problems are solved with CPLEX 12.6.3.

Unless otherwise stated, the benchmark values of coefficients are set as follows: loading cost (unit: €/TEU) $lc_i^{\text{ship}} = 18$, $lc_i^{\text{barge}} = 18$, $lc_i^{\text{train}} = 12$, $lc_i^{\text{truck}} = 12$ for $i \in N$; loading time (unit: hours) $lt_i^{\text{ship}} = 12$, $lt_i^{\text{barge}} = 4$, $lt_i^{\text{train}} = 2$, $lt_i^{\text{truck}} = 1$ for $i \in N$; storage cost (unit: €/TEU-h) $c_i^{\text{storage}} = 1$ for $i \in N$; carbon tax (unit: €/kg) $c^{\text{emission}} = 0.07$.

We consider a global intermodal network that consists of two terminals in Europe and three terminals in Asia that are connected by Suez Canal Route (SCR), Northern Sea Route (NSR), and Eurasia Land Bridge (ELB), as shown in Fig. 3. Compared with the SCR, the NSR has a shorter travel time but a higher travel cost caused by ice-breaking fees [11]. With the implementation of IMO 2020 regulations, shipping liner companies are required to use low-sulfur fuels on the sea, which in turn increases travel costs in the SCR and the NSR [10]. As an alternative, the ELB becomes more and more competitive thanks to its shortest travel time. However, without subsidies from governments, the ELB is still the most expensive route.

We consider 18 services operating on the network: 8 in Asia, 6 in Europe, and 4 connecting Asia and Europe as presented in Table 2. The hinterland-related data is adapted from the work of [5]; the intercontinental-related data is adapted from the works of [7,16,17]. We consider 6 shipment requests received by the platform at time 0. The detailed request data is shown in Table 3. Compared

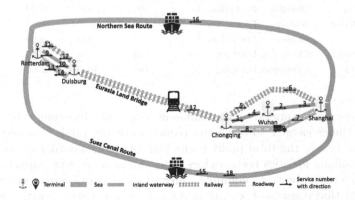

Fig. 3. The topology of a global intermodal network.

Table 2. Service data.

Service. ID	Mode	Origin	Destination	Total capacity (TEU)	Reefer slots (TEU)	Departure time	Arrival time	Travel time (h)	Travel cost (€)	Carbon emissions-dry (kg)	Carbon emissions-reefer (kg)	Preceding service	Succeeding service
1	barge	Chongqing	Wuhan	160	50	144	235	91	192	313	940		2
2	barge	Wuhan	Shanghai	160	50	243	328	85	178	291	874	1	
3	barge	Shanghai	Wuhan	160	50	144	229	85	178	291	874		4
4	barge	Wuhan	Chongqing	160	50	237	328	91	192	313	940	3	
5	train	Chongqing	Shanghai	90	30	144	181	37	269	526	1578		
6	train	Shanghai	Chongqing	90	30	144	181	37	269	526	1578		
7	truck	Shanghai	Chongqing	200	60			22	1823	1489	4466		
8	truck	Chongqing	Shanghai	200	60			22	1823	1489	4466		
9	barge	Rotterdam	Duisburg	160	30	1010	1027	17	35	57	170		
10	barge	Duisburg	Rotterdam	160	30	750	767	17	35	57	170		
11	train	Rotterdam	Duisburg	90	30	910	917	7	48	92	276		
12	train	Duisburg	Rotterdam	90	30	750	757	7	48	92	276		
13	truck	Rotterdam	Duisburg	200	60			3	334	219	658		
14	truck	Duisburg	Rotterdam	200	60			3	334	219	658		
15	ship	Shanghai	Rotterdam	200	50	350	988	638	1441	2161	6483		
16	ship	Shanghai	Rotterdam	200	50	350	900	550	2240	1631	4894		
17	train	Chongqing	Duisburg	90	30	350	723	373	2007	3517	10551		
18	ship	Shanghai	Rotterdam	200	50	518	1156	638	1441	2161	6483		

with reefer shipments (requests 1, 3, 5), dry shipments (requests 2, 4, 6) have longer lead times, lower freight rates, and lower delay costs.

5.1 Impact of Different Objective Functions

The effects of objective functions are tested under a deterministic environment without travel time uncertainties, i.e., mean of travel times $\mu_s = t_s$, standard deviation $\sigma_s = 0$, $\forall s \in S$. We set the confidence level $\alpha = 0.5$ for the CCP model, and therefore $\phi^{-1}(\alpha) = \phi^{-1}(1 - \alpha) = 0$.

Table 3. Request data.

Requests	Container type	Origin	Destination	Container volume (TEU)	Release time	Lead time (h)	Freight rate (€/TEU)	Delay cost (€/TEU-h)
1	Reefer	Shanghai	Rotterdam	5	100	720	4000	20
2	Dry	Shanghai	Rotterdam	5	100	840	3500	17.5
3	Reefer	Wuhan	Rotterdam	5	100	600	4500	22.5
4	Dry	Wuhan	Rotterdam	5	100	960	3000	15
5	Reefer	Chongqing	Duisburg	5	100	480	5000	25
6	Dry	Chongqing	Duisburg	5	100	1080	2500	12.5

The results generated under different objective functions are shown in Table 4. Under cases 1 to 6, all the requests are accepted. Comparing case 6 with cases 1 to 5, the total profit is the highest. It means that considering the trade-off among logistics costs, delays, and emissions is very important. While cases 1 to 6 are designed to minimize different costs, case 7 aims to maximize the total profit that consists of revenue and total costs. Compared with cases 1 to 6, the total profit is significantly higher under case 7. Comparing case 6 and case 7 shows that it may be necessary to reject the requests that are not profitable.

Table 4. Impact of different objective functions.

Cases	Objective function	Total profits	Revenue	Travel costs	Transfer costs	Storage costs	Delay costs	Carbon tax	Rejections	Delay (TEU-h)	Emission (kg)
1	Travel costs	−67978	112500	**48061**	2040	6914	113163	10300	0	4945	147146
2	Transfer costs	−34695	112500	50677	**1320**	8890	74925	11383	0	3416	162611
3	Storage costs	−47333	112500	59413	2400	**4814**	81063	12144	0	3482	173483
4	Delay costs	1590	112500	63648	1560	9317	**21439**	14947	0	**873**	213529
5	Carbon tax	−67375	112500	72030	2040	8367	89363	**8076**	0	3773	**115366**
6	Total costs	4946	112500	63282	2100	5983	21439	14750	0	873	210711
7	Total profits	**13107**	87500	53249	1980	4743	3364	11057	1	150	157957

5.2 Comparing Deterministic, Stochastic, and Robust Approaches

To investigate the differences between solutions generated by the CCP, DA, and RA under travel time uncertainty, we set the mean of travel times $\mu_s = t_s$ for $s \in S$, standard deviation of travel times $\sigma_s = 0.1t_s$ for $s \in S\backslash S^{\text{truck}}$, $\sigma_s = 0.5t_s$ for $s \in S^{\text{truck}}$. Besides, we let $0.9t_s$ be the fixed lower bound for travel times of service $s \in S$. Under the realization of travel times as shown in Table 5, barge service 2 is delayed, the transfers between barge service 2 and ship service 15 and 16 are therefore becoming infeasible. Regarding the CCP, we set the confidence level $\alpha = 0.7$, and therefore $\phi^{-1}(\alpha) = 0.524$, $\phi^{-1}(1 - \alpha) = -0.524$.

Table 5. The realization of travel times.

Service. ID	1	2	3	4	5	6	7	8	9	10	11	12	13	14	15	16	17	18
Actual travel time	98	99	89	101	40	36	23	21	18	15	7	7	3	4	631	537	384	657
Actual departure time	144	250	144	241	144	144			1010	750	910	750			350	350	350	518
Actual arrival time	242	349	233	342	184	180			1028	765	917	757			981	887	734	1175

Due to travel time uncertainty, the planned profits are different from the actual profits. Table 6 shows the results received before the realization of travel times. We note that the DA generates the highest planned profits with the lowest number of rejections and the highest delay in deliveries. In comparison, the CCP takes into account the trade-off between feasibility and profitability. It rejects requests 3 to 6 which might be non-profitable under travel time uncertainties and chooses rail service 6 instead of barge services 3 and 4 for request 2. The RA is the most conservative approach which has the lowest planned profits and the highest number of rejections. Regarding the results received after the realization of travel times, Table 7 shows that the DA generates the lowest actual profits due to infeasible transshipments at Shanghai Port for requests 4 and 6.

Table 6. Results received before the realization of travel times.

Approaches	Planned profits	Rejection	Delay (TEU-h)	Planned itinerary of requests					
				1	2	3	4	5	6
DA	13107	1	150	3,4,17,10	16	4,17,14	2,15		1,2,15,9
CCP	6553	4	0	6,17,10	16				
RA	4217	5	0		16				

Table 7. Results received after the realization of travel times.

Approaches	Actual Profits	Infeasible Transshipments	Rejection	Delay (TEU-h)	Actual itinerary of requests					
					1	2	3	4	5	6
DA	−438	2	1	911	3,4,17,10	16	4,17,14	2,18		1,2,18,13
CCP	6533	0	4	0	6,17,10	16				
RA	4151	0	5	0		16				

In comparison, the CCP has the highest actual profits thanks to the rejection of non-profitable requests 4 and 6. Compared with the DA and the CCP, the RA is the safest approach which avoids the possibility of infeasible transshipments but loses the opportunity to get higher profits.

The difference among the deterministic, stochastic, and robust solutions is graphically represented in Fig. 4. Under the DA, request 5 is rejected; requests 1 and 3 with reefer shipments are assigned to the ELB; requests 2, 4, 6 with dry shipments are assigned to the SCR and NSR. Due to travel time variations, requests 4 and 6 switch from service 15 to 18 at Shanghai Port. Under the CCP, request 1 arrives Chongqing terminal by using rail service 6 which is

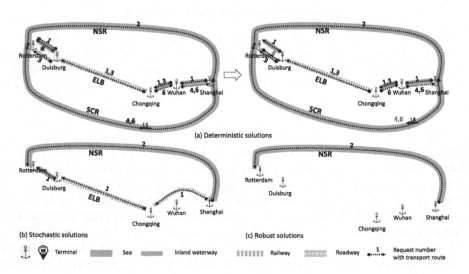

Fig. 4. Comparison of deterministic, stochastic and robust solutions.

faster than barges services 3 and 4. Under the RA, all the requests that require transshipments at terminals are rejected.

6   Conclusions and Future Research

In this paper, we investigated a stochastic shipment matching problem in global intermodal transport. The problem is stochastic since the uncertainties in travel times are incorporated. We developed a chance-constrained programming (CCP) model to address travel time uncertainties. We conducted experiments to validate the performance of the CCP in comparison to a deterministic approach (DA) in which decisions are made based on estimated travel times and a robust approach (RA) in which decisions are made based on maximum and minimum travel times. The experimental results indicate that the CCP increases total profits by 1591.55% in comparison to the DA and by 57.38% in comparison to the RA under the designed case.

This research can be extended in several promising directions. First, due to the computational complexity, we only conducted small experiments in this paper, future research can be extended to large-scale instances by designing efficient algorithms that benefit from parallelization and distributed structure. Second, this paper used fixed settings of parameters, conducting sensitivity analysis of parameters is a promising future research direction. Third, due to the fluctuation of freight rates in spot markets, future requests are quite uncertain. Combining travel time uncertainty with spot request uncertainty in global intermodal transport planning deserves further research.

Acknowledgments. This research is financially supported by the China Scholarship Council (Grant 201606950003) and "Complexity Methods for Predictive Synchromodality" (project 439.16.120) of the Netherlands Organisation for Scientific Research (NWO).

References

1. Demir, E., Burgholzer, W., Hrušovský, M., Arıkan, E., Jammernegg, W., van Woensel, T.: A green intermodal service network design problem with travel time uncertainty. Transp. Res. Part B: Methodol. **93**, 789–807 (2016)
2. Ehmke, J.F., Campbell, A.M., Urban, T.L.: Ensuring service levels in routing problems with time windows and stochastic travel times. Eur. J. Oper. Res. **240**(2), 539–550 (2015)
3. Gendreau, M., Jabali, O., Rei, W.: 50th anniversary invited article—future research directions in stochastic vehicle routing. Transp. Sci. **50**(4), 1163–1173 (2016)
4. Guo, W., Atasoy, B., van Blokland, W.B., Negenborn, R.R.: Dynamic and stochastic shipment matching problem in multimodal transportation. Transp. Res. Rec. J. Transp. Res. Board **2674**(2), 262–273 (2020)
5. Guo, W., Atasoy, B., van Blokland, W.B., Negenborn, R.R.: A dynamic shipment matching problem in hinterland synchromodal transportation. Decis. Support Syst **134**, 113289 (2020)

6. Hrušovský, M., Demir, E., Jammernegg, W., Van Woensel, T.: Hybrid simulation and optimization approach for green intermodal transportation problem with travel time uncertainty. Flex. Serv. Manuf. J. **30**(3), 486–516 (2016). https://doi.org/10.1007/s10696-016-9267-1

7. Jiang, Y., Sheu, J.B., Peng, Z., Yu, B.: Hinterland patterns of china railway (CR) express in china under the belt and road initiative: a preliminary analysis. Transp. Res. Part E: Logist. Transp. Rev. **119**, 189–201 (2018)

8. Lee, C.Y., Song, D.P.: Ocean container transport in global supply chains: overview and research opportunities. Transp. Res. Part B: Methodol. **95**, 442–474 (2017)

9. Li, X., Tian, P., Leung, S.C.: Vehicle routing problems with time windows and stochastic travel and service times: models and algorithm. Int. J. Prod. Econ. **125**(1), 137–145 (2010)

10. Lian, F., He, Y., Yang, Z.: Competitiveness of the China-Europe railway express and liner shipping under the enforced sulfur emission control convention. Transp. Res. Part E: Logist. Transp. Rev. **135**, 101861 (2020)

11. Lin, D.Y., Chang, Y.T.: Ship routing and freight assignment problem for liner shipping: application to the northern sea route planning problem. Transp. Res. Part E: Logist. Transp. Rev. **110**, 47–70 (2018)

12. Meng, Q., Wang, S., Andersson, H., Thun, K.: Containership routing and scheduling in liner shipping: overview and future research directions. Transp. Sci. **48**(2), 265–280 (2014)

13. Meng, Q., Zhao, H., Wang, Y.: Revenue management for container liner shipping services: critical review and future research directions. Transp. Res. Part E: Logist. Transp. Rev. **128**, 280–292 (2019)

14. Rodrigues, F., Agra, A., Christiansen, M., Hvattum, L.M., Requejo, C.: Comparing techniques for modelling uncertainty in a maritime inventory routing problem. Eur. J. Oper. Res. **277**(3), 831–845 (2019)

15. SteadieSeifi, M., Dellaert, N., Nuijten, W., van Woensel, T., Raoufi, R.: Multimodal freight transportation planning: a literature review. Eur. J. Oper. Res. **233**(1), 1–15 (2014)

16. Tran, N.K., Haasis, H.D., Buer, T.: Container shipping route design incorporating the costs of shipping, inland/feeder transport, inventory and CO_2 emission. Marit. Econ. Logist. **19**(4), 667–694 (2017)

17. Verny, J., Grigentin, C.: Container shipping on the northern sea route. Int. J. Prod. Econ. **122**(1), 107–117 (2009)

18. Yang, D., Pan, K., Wang, S.: On service network improvement for shipping lines under the one belt one road initiative of China. Transp. Res. Part E: Logist. Transp. Rev. **117**, 82–95 (2018)

Cutting Planes for Solving Logistic Flow Problems

Kishan Kalicharan[1,2], Frank Phillipson[2(✉)], and Alex Sangers[2]

[1] Delft University of Technology, Delft, The Netherlands
[2] TNO, PO Box 96800, 2509 JE The Hague, The Netherlands
frank.phillipson@tno.nl

Abstract. In logistic problems, an Integral Multi-Commodity Network Design Problem on a time-space network is often used to model the problem of routing transportation means and assigning freight units to those means. In Physical Internet and Synchromodal networks an interactive planning approach is preferable, meaning that calculation times of a single planning step should be short. In this paper we provide ways to reduce the size of the problem formulation based on cutting planes, that are effective in reducing the computation time for Integer Linear Programming problem-based solution methods.

Keywords: Logistic space time network · Logistic flow routing · Synchromodality · Cutting planes techniques

1 Introduction

In this paper we look at a transportation system where logistic units (e.g., containers) travel freely through this network. Decision makers here can be logistic service providers or clients controlling the stream of their containers, or intelligent containers or other smart logistic units themselves. This occurs in Physical Internet and in Synchromodal or Intermodal networks.

These types of transport networks allow for many different options of transportation. A unit can be trucked from its origin to its destination, but (part of) the route can also be done by barge, plane or train. In synchromodal and intermodal networks, a logistics service provider (LSP) is responsible for managing the flow of containers from their origins to their destinations. Especially in large logistics networks, LSPs may require assistance from algorithms to make good routing choices. These algorithms can be used to reach economic and emission-reduction targets by offering decision support for optimizing the (intermodal) transport chain [16]. In Physical Internet and Synchromodal networks, a more interactive planning scheme is preferable, following the dynamic and uncertain nature of the underlying networks. Here routing decisions can (or have to) be made, each time logistic units arrive at an intermediate node, incorporating the decisions of other agents and, possibly, the uncertainty of decisions or events in the future.

© Springer Nature Switzerland AG 2020
E. Lalla-Ruiz et al. (Eds.): ICCL 2020, LNCS 12433, pp. 569–583, 2020.
https://doi.org/10.1007/978-3-030-59747-4_37

In logistic (service) network planning problems Space-Time Networks (STN) are often used for the representation [9]. On this STN a non-negative integral minimum cost multi-commodity flow problem (MCMCF) is solved to get the overall optimal solution [6]. Here, all terminals are modelled as nodes. Services go from these terminals to other terminals in a certain amount of time. These services are modelled by arcs. To solve these problems, constraints can be relaxed to obtain a simpler problem. This yields lower bounds that together with heuristically found upper bounds can be combined in for instance a branch-and-bound algorithm, see, among others, the paper by Crainic et al. [7] and Holmberg and Yuan [12]. Holmberg and Hellstrand [11] propose an exact solution method for the uncapacitated problem based on a Lagrangian heuristic. A dual ascent procedure is treated by Balakrishnan et al. [3], which finds lower bounds within 1–4% of optimality. Heuristics and meta-heuristics (such as Tabu Search, Simulated Annealing and Genetic Algorithms) are also widely used. See for instance the paper by Crainic et al. [8], who look at a path-based formulation of the same problem and solve it with tabu search.

To allow for a more interactive use of this solution direction, short calculation times are crucial. In this paper we look at the problem of scheduling services and assigning transportation units to it. We start with modelling this problem as an Integral Multi-Commodity Network Design (MCND) problem. We will present tailored cutting planes to reduce the computation time when solving the problem. The MCND problem will be introduced in Sect. 2. In Sect. 3 the cutting planes are introduced. Next, in Sect. 4 computational results and conclusions will be presented.

2   Multi-Commodity Network Design Problem

The main goal of this paper is about efficiently and simultaneously routing transport means and scheduling transportation units. Without losing any generality, we will say container if we mean the transportation unit and use the terms barge and truck as example transport means. One of the models that could be used here is the Capacitated Fixed Charge Network Flow Problem from [10, 20]. We have a directed graph $G = (V, E)$ (or multigraph) that contains all the nodes and arcs in the network. We have a set of commodities K that represent the bookings/orders. Every commodity $k \in K$ has, without loss of generality, one source node s_k and one sink node t_k. The parameters c_e, for $e \in E$, are the capacities of the arcs. The parameters $f_{e,k}$, for $e \in E, k \in K$, determine the per unit cost of commodity k on arc e. The parameters $d_{v,k} = d_k$ if $v = s_k, d_{v,k} = -d_k$ if $v = t_k$ and $d_{v,k} = 0$ otherwise, where d_k is the demand/size of commodity k. The variables $x_{e,k}$ depict the magnitude of the flow of commodity k on arc e. Finally, we define the design variables $y_e, \forall e \in E$, that are one if the service at link e is active and zero otherwise. In intermodal transport these design variables are normally one if and only if the corresponding vehicle travels the corresponding link. Many possible arcs to travel are added for a vehicle and after the optimization process, it is decided which design variables are one; ergo, which routes the vehicles should travel. The graphs for these models are often time-space networks, but other graphs can also be used [24]. The optimization problem now looks like:

$$\min \sum_{k \in K} \sum_{e \in E} f_{e,k} x_{e,k} + \sum_{e \in E} g_e y_e \tag{1}$$

$$\text{s.t.} \sum_{e \in \delta^+(v)} x_{e,k} - \sum_{e \in \delta^-(v)} x_{e,k} = d_{v,k} \qquad \forall v \in V, \forall k \in K \tag{2}$$

$$\sum_{k \in K} x_{e,k} \leq c_e y_e \qquad \forall e \in E \tag{3}$$

$$x_{e,k} \geq 0, y_e \in \{0, 1\} \qquad \forall e \in E, \forall k \in K. \tag{4}$$

The first part of the objective function minimizes the cost using the $f_{e,k}$. The second part is a link cost, if a vehicle travels a certain link $e \in E$, then a certain fixed cost g_e is added. The flow conservation constraints (2) make sure that the total amount of a commodity that enters the node also leaves the node, except for the sources and sinks. The capacity constraints (3) say that if an arc in the network is not travelled by a vehicle, then no commodity flow may be on that arc. If a vehicle does travel an arc, then the container flow on that arc can be at most the capacity of the edge. This model is in some papers [4, 23, 25] extended to include what are called design-balanced constraints:

$$\sum_{e \in \delta^+(v)} y_e - \sum_{e \in \delta^-(v)} y_e = 0 \qquad \forall v \in V. \tag{5}$$

These constraints make sure that everywhere a vehicle arrives, it also leaves. This means that the routes for the vehicles are directed cycles. So the network we use, should contain directed cycles. When working over a time-space network, an additional arc should be added from the sink of vehicle type w of set W to the source of vehicle type w to make sure it is possible to have a directed cycle.

In [24] a similar continuous time ILP (Integer Linear Programming) problem is proposed. This model also has time variables and some more types of constraints. An extension of the design-balanced service network design problem is given in [19]. The model takes into account the usage of vehicles and the opening of corridors. In [2] another extension is derived and in [17] a model that shares some resemblances is applied to freight car distribution in scheduled railways. A completely different ILP problem that can handle the same sort of problem is given in [13].

The problem we will propose is similar, though contains a few key differences. First, we will consider two vehicle types: not flexible, high capacity, low cost vehicles that need to be scheduled in advance (barges, train etc.) and flexible, low capacity, high cost vehicles (trucks, transporters, etc.). From here we will refer to the first type as barge and to the second type as truck. Second, only the first part of the objective function of the service network design problem is used. Third, the flow conservation constraints for the vehicles are slightly different than the design-balanced constraints: in our model the number of non-truck vehicles is pre-specified and only for the non-truck vehicles, vehicle flow conservation constraints are added.

We call our problem the Integral Multi-Commodity Network Design (MCND) Problem. The model uses a time-space network, wherein the routes of the vehicles are not known in advance. The arcs in the time-space network are possible links that a vehicle can travel. For the trucks we add an arc for every time stamp from every terminal to every terminal. Naturally, the travel time is taken into account. We repeat this process for the first barge, second barge etc. Arcs corresponding to different vehicle (types) that run between the same time-space nodes are **not** merged.

This way it is assured that all the links of all the possible routes they can take are included in the time-space network. The **Integral MCND problem** then is:

$$\min \sum_k \sum_{e \in E} f_{e,k} x_{e,k} \tag{6}$$

$$\text{s.t.} \sum_{e \in \delta^+(v)} x_{e,k} - \sum_{e \in \delta^-(v)} x_{e,k} = d_{v,k} \qquad \forall v \in V, \forall k \in K \tag{7}$$

$$\sum_{e \in \delta^+(v) \cap E_w} y_e - \sum_{e \in \delta^-(v) \cap E_w} y_e = b_{v,w} \qquad \forall v \in V, \forall w \in W \setminus \{\text{truck}\} \tag{8}$$

$$\sum_k x_{e,k} \le c_e y_e \qquad \forall e \in E \setminus E_{\text{truck}} \tag{9}$$

$$\sum_k x_{e,k} \le c_e \qquad \forall e \in E_{\text{truck}} \tag{10}$$

$$x_{e,k} \ge 0, y_e \in \{0,1\}, x_{e,k} \in \mathbb{Z} \qquad \forall e \in E, \forall k \in K \tag{11}$$

For all non-truck arcs e in the network, we have created a discrete design variable $y_e \in \mathbb{Z}_{\ge 0}$, determining if the arc is used (11). The y_e are binary variables. The container flows are modelled with the variables $x_{e,k}$ and still have to be integral and non-negative (11). We assume that trucks do not necessarily need to be used the whole day, whereas barges do have to be used the whole day. For the paths of the barges to make sense we should add constraints that disallow the barge to teleport or travel multiple links at the same time. Flow conservation constraints for $w \in W \setminus \{\text{truck}\}$ (8) can do exactly this in the same flow conservation constraints (7) work for the commodities. In these constraints we have $b_{v,w}$ which describe the time-space nodes that are the sink and source for a $w \in W \setminus \{\text{truck}\}$. In more detail for such w we have that $b_{v,w}$ equals b_w if v is the source node of w, equals $-b_w$ if v is the sink node of w and 0 otherwise, where b_w is the number of vehicles of type $w \in W \setminus \{\text{truck}\}$. This is normally one, unless the vehicle reduction has been applied. The capacity of an arc is dependent on the number of vehicles that travel the arc (9). For the truck arcs we have different capacity constraints (10). Normally a vehicle has the same capacity the whole day. So we can then replace the c_e in the capacity constraints for the arcs, by capacity constants for the vehicle, c_w. For the trucks, however, c_e is the maximum number of trucks that can be deployed on link $e \in E_{\text{truck}}$. We assume a truck can carry exactly one container. Thus, the number of trucks that travel an arc $e \in E_{\text{truck}}$ is equal to the number of containers that are trucked on that arc $\sum_{k \in K} x_{e,k}$.

3   Cutting Planes

The feasible region of an Linear Programming (LP) problem may be unnecessary large, which may lead to a large computation time. For instance, there may be many equivalent solutions satisfying the constraints of the LP problem. Furthermore, for ILP problems in general the feasible region defined without the integrality conditions, contains many non-integral solutions. In practice constraints are often added or changed to refine the feasible region making it easier to solve the problem. These constraints are called cutting planes or cuts. In this section, we define cuts as constraints that are added before or during the optimization process, such that the optimal solution value of the problem does not change. An interesting heuristic for the integral MCND problem that uses cuts is discussed in [4].

3.1   General Cuts

For ILP problems different general cuts exist. The cuts only remove non-integral solutions from the feasible region defined by the constraints of the problem (without integrality constraints). These general cuts are automatically added by solvers like CPLEX [14]. A well-known cut is the Gomory mixed integer cut (GMIC) for ILP problems [1,18]:

$$\sum_{f_j \leq f} f_j x_j + \sum_{f_j > f} \frac{f(1 - f_j)}{1 - f} x_j \geq f, \quad f_j = a_j - \lfloor a_j \rfloor.$$

A GMIC is often based on an inequality/row of the simplex tableau, but can also be based on other valid inequalities. The cut is stronger than the fractional Gomory cut [1,18]

$$\sum_{j=1}^{n} (a_j - \lfloor a_j \rfloor) x_j \geq a_0 - \lfloor a_0 \rfloor.$$

A zero-half cut [15] is basically adding two inequalities dividing by two and taking the floor. Example: Suppose we have the inequalities $x_1 + 2x_2 \leq 3$ and $x_1 \leq 2$. Then we can combine them to $2x_1 + 2x_2 \leq 5$. We divide both sides by two $x_1 + x_2 \leq \frac{5}{2}$. Now we take the floor at both sides and get $x_1 + x_2 \leq 2$.

3.2   Symmetry Breaking Cut

If we have barge 0 and barge 1 in the model, then they correspond to different variables in the model. Suppose barge 0 and barge 1 are identical and they have the same start node and end node. In that case a solution with barge 0 taking path P_{j_1} and barge 1 taking path P_{j_2} is in practice equivalent with a solution in which barge 0 takes path P_{j_2} and barge 1 path P_{j_1} ceteris paribus. The symmetry leads to an unnecessary large feasible region and may result in a lengthy branch & bound process. There are ways to deal with the symmetry. An option is to reformulate the problem. Applying reduction C is such an approach. Another option is to add symmetry breaking constraints to the model in advance. Adding too many cuts might be detrimental to the computation time of the algorithms, motivating our choice of only adding $|W| - 2$ path-length cuts for the arc-based problems, where $W = \{\text{truck}, \text{barge0}, \text{barge1}, \text{barge2}, \dots \}$.

We use the fact that if we sum up all the y variables belonging to barge 0, we get the total path length of barge 0. The chosen numbering of the barges is then used to avoid some symmetry

$$\sum_{e \in E_{\text{barge0}}} y_e \le \sum_{e \in E_{\text{barge1}}} y_e$$

$$\sum_{e \in E_{\text{barge1}}} y_e \le \sum_{e \in E_{\text{barge2}}} y_e$$

$$\vdots$$

In these cuts only the length of the paths is calculated, do if in the last example P_{j_1} and P_{j_2} would be paths of the same length, then the cuts will not block this symmetry. If the paths have different lengths, then the cuts will help out. Although normally optimal solution will be removed from the feasible region by adding these cuts, at least one optimal solution will always remain.

For the path-based problems it is relatively easy to avoid symmetry. If $Q^{\text{barge0}} = Q^{\text{barge1}}$, then we number the paths of both barges the same way. Symmetric solutions can then be broken by adding constraints:

$$\sum_i i \zeta_i^{\text{barge0}} \le \sum_i i \zeta_i^{\text{barge1}}.$$

3.3   Arc Residual Capacity Cut

In [21, 22] two cuts for multi-commodity problems are described that can be used for our MCND problem. One of them is the *arc residual capacity cut*:

$$\sum_{k \in K'} x_{e,k} \le \sum_{k \in K'} d_k - r'(\mu' - y_e), \tag{12}$$

with $\mu' = \lceil \frac{\sum_{k \in K'} d_k}{c_e} \rceil$ and $r' = \sum_{k \in K'} d_k - (\mu' - 1)c_e$ for $K' \subseteq K$ for $e \in E \setminus E_{\text{truck}}$. In the MCND model constraints (9) hold, so for all $K' \subseteq K$ we have

$$\sum_{k \in K'} x_{e,k} \le c_e y_e \qquad \forall e \in E \setminus E_{\text{truck}}. \tag{13}$$

Note that a time-space graph has no cycles, together with constraints (7), (9) and (11), we know that

$$\sum_{k \in K'} x_{e,k} \le \sum_{k \in K'} d_k. \tag{14}$$

Theorem 1. *Let $e \in E \setminus E_{\text{truck}}$ and $K' \subseteq K$. Suppose y_e satisfies the integrality constraints (11) and constraints (13), (14) are satisfied for e and K' then (12) holds for e and K'.*

Proof. Let y_e be such that (11), (13) and (14) hold. If $y_e \geq \mu'$, then

$$\sum_{k \in K'} x_{e,k} \leq \sum_{k \in K'} d_k \leq \sum_{k \in K'} d_k - r'(\mu' - y_e).$$

So in this case if (14) holds, then (12) holds.

If $y_e < \mu'$, then by (11) we have $y_e = \mu' - s$ where $s \geq 1$. It then follows that

$$\sum_{k \in K'} x_{e,k} \leq c_e y_e = c_e \mu' - c_e s \leq \sum_{k \in K'} d_k - r's,$$

where the last inequality holds, because for $s = 1$ we have equality and

$$r' = \sum_{k \in K'} d_k - (\mu' - 1)c_e = \sum_{k \in K'} d_k - \left(\lceil \sum_{k \in K'} \frac{d_k}{c_e} \rceil - 1 \right) c_e$$

$$= \sum_{k \in K'} d_k - \lfloor \sum_{k \in K'} \frac{d_k}{c_e} \rfloor c_e = \sum_{k \in K'} \frac{d_k}{c_e} c_e - \lfloor \sum_{k \in K'} \frac{d_k}{c_e} \rfloor c_e$$

$$= \left(\sum_{k \in K'} \frac{d_k}{c_e} - \lfloor \sum_{k \in K'} \frac{d_k}{c_e} \rfloor \right) c_e < c_e.$$

Theorem 2. *We replace $\sum_{k \in K'} d_k$ by $\sum_{k \in K'} d_k + c_e$ in the arc residual capacity cut, then we get*

$$\sum_{k \in K'} x_{e,k} \leq \sum_{k \in K'} d_k + c_e - r''(\mu'' - y_e), \tag{15}$$

with $\mu'' = \lceil \frac{\sum_{k \in K'} d_k + c_e}{c_e} \rceil$ and $r'' = \sum_{k \in K'} d_k + c_e - (\mu'' - 1)c_e$ for $K' \subseteq K$. Then (15) is strictly dominated by (12) if $\frac{\sum_{k \in K'} d_k}{c_e} \notin \mathbb{Z}$. Furthermore (15) is equivalent to (12) if $\frac{\sum_{k \in K'} d_k}{c_e} \in \mathbb{Z}$.

Proof. We have

$$\mu'' = \lceil \frac{\sum_{k \in K'} d_k + c_e}{c_e} \rceil = \lceil \frac{\sum_{k \in K'} d_k}{c_e} \rceil + 1 = \mu' + 1$$

and

$$r'' = \sum_{k \in K'} d_k + c_e - (\mu'' - 1)c_e = \sum_{k \in K'} d_k - (\mu'' - 2)c_e = \sum_{k \in K'} d_k - (\mu' - 1)c_e = r'.$$

Then (15) is equivalent to

$$\sum_{k \in K'} x_{e,k} \leq \sum_{k \in K'} d_k + c_e - r'(\mu' + 1 - y_e) = \sum_{k \in K'} d_k - r'(\mu' - y_e) + c_e - r'.$$

In the case $\frac{\sum_{k \in K'} d_k}{c_e} \notin \mathbb{Z}$ we find

$$r' = \sum_{k \in K'} d_k - (\mu' - 1)c_e = \sum_{k \in K'} d_k - \left(\lceil \frac{\sum_{k \in K'} d_k}{c_e} \rceil - 1 \right) c_e$$

$$< \sum_{k \in K'} d_k - \left(\frac{\sum_{k \in K'} d_k}{c_e} - 1 \right) c_e = \sum_{k \in K'} d_k - \left(\frac{\sum_{k \in K'} d_k}{c_e} \right) c_e + c_e = c_e.$$

So with the above we conclude that the arc residual cut (12) strictly dominates (15):

$$\sum_{k \in K'} x_{e,k} \le \sum_{k \in K'} d_k - r'(\mu' - y_e) < \sum_{k \in K'} d_k - r'(\mu' - y_e) + c_e - r'.$$

If $\frac{\sum_{k \in K'} d_k}{c_e} \in \mathbb{Z}$, then we get

$$r' = \sum_{k \in K'} d_k - (\mu' - 1)c_e = \sum_{k \in K'} d_k - \left(\lceil \frac{\sum_{k \in K'} d_k}{c_e} \rceil - 1 \right) c_e$$

$$= \sum_{k \in K'} d_k - \left(\frac{\sum_{k \in K'} d_k}{c_e} - 1 \right) c_e = \sum_{k \in K'} d_k - \left(\frac{\sum_{k \in K'} d_k}{c_e} \right) c_e + c_e = c_e.$$

So in that case we conclude that the arc residual cut (12) is equivalent to (15):

$$\sum_{k \in K'} x_{e,k} \le \sum_{k \in K'} d_k - r'(\mu' - y_e) = \sum_{k \in K'} d_k - r'(\mu' - y_e) + c_e - r'.$$

Corollary 1. *The right-hand side of the arc residual capacity cut (12),*

$$\sum_{k \in K'} d_k - \left(\sum_{k \in K'} d_k - (\lceil \frac{\sum_{k \in K'} d_k}{c_e} \rceil - 1)c_e \right) (\lceil \frac{\sum_{k \in K'} d_k}{c_e} \rceil - y_e),$$

is not (monotonically) increasing in $\sum_{k \in K'} d_k$.

Proof. We first write the right-hand side as a function of $\sum_{k \in K'} d_k$

$$g : \mathbb{Z}_{\ge 0} \to \mathbb{R}$$

$$g(\sum_{k \in K'} d_k) = \sum_{k \in K'} d_k - \left(\sum_{k \in K'} d_k - (\lceil \frac{\sum_{k \in K'} d_k}{c_e} \rceil - 1)c_e \right) (\lceil \frac{\sum_{k \in K'} d_k}{c_e} \rceil - y_e).$$

Let $A \in \mathbb{Z}_{\ge 0}$ such that $\frac{A}{c_e} \in \mathbb{Z}$ and define $B := A - s$ for a $s \in \mathbb{Z} \cap [1, c_e - 1]$. We have $A - c_e < B < A < B + c_e < A + c_e$. Suppose g is monotonically increasing, then we would have

$$g(A - c_e) \ge g(B) \le g(A) \le g(B + c_e) \le g(A + c_e). \tag{16}$$

From Theorem 2 follows

$$g(A - c_e) = g(A) = g(A + c_e) \qquad (17)$$
$$g(B) < g(B + c_e). \qquad (18)$$

From (16) and (17) follows

$$g(A - c_e) = g(B) = g(A) = g(B + c_e) = g(A + c_e),$$

but this contradicts with (18). So we conclude the right-hand side of the arc residual capacity cut is not monotonically increasing in $\sum_{k \in K'} d_k$.

The structure of the time-space graph can be used to reduce the right-hand side of the arc residual capacity cut (12). Although this does not always help to find a stronger cut (Corollary 1), it still finds stronger cuts very often (Theorem 2). For an arc $e \in E$ no commodities should be included in the $K' \subseteq K$ for the arc residual capacity cut, that consist of bookings that cannot use that link. If we exclude these commodities, then the left-hand side does not change as $x_{e,k} = 0$ if commodity k cannot use arc e. The right-hand side is likely to decrease (Theorem 2), so if this is the case the cut will become stronger.

3.4 Cutset Cut

For every truck arc $e \in E_{\text{truck}}$ we add the variable $y_e \in \mathbb{Z}_{\geq 0}$ and the constraint

$$\sum_{k \in K} x_{e,k} = y_e \qquad \forall e \in E_{\text{truck}}. \qquad (19)$$

The second cut suitable for the MCND problem described in [21,22] is the cutset cut. Let $k \in K$ be a commodity that consists of one booking. Then it has a source node s_k. For the node we can add the cutset cut

$$\sum_{e \in \delta^+(s_k)} y_e \geq 1. \qquad (20)$$

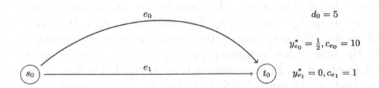

Fig. 1. Cutset cut example and LP problem relaxation solution y^*.

In Fig. 1 an example is visualized, where only half a barge is deployed to transport the container of a commodity at the start. In scenarios like that the cutset cut can be used to avoid the fractional solution that is found for the LP problem relaxation.

Constraints (9) imply

$$x_{e,k} \leq \sum_{k_1 \in K} x_{e,k_1} \leq y_e c_e \quad \Rightarrow \quad \sum_{e \in \delta^+(s_k)} y_e c_e \geq \sum_{e \in \delta^+(s_k)} x_{e,k} \quad \forall e \in E, \forall k \in K.$$

Constraints (7) and (11) imply

$$\sum_{e \in \delta^+(s_k)} x_{e,k} = d_k \quad \forall e \in E, \forall k \in K.$$

Substituting that and use the maximum arc capacity $c_{\max} := \max_{e \in E} c_e$ we get

$$c_{\max} \sum_{e \in \delta^+(s_k)} y_e \geq \sum_{e \in \delta^+(s_k)} y_e c_e \geq d_k \quad \Leftrightarrow \quad \sum_{e \in \delta^+(s_k)} y_e \geq \frac{d_k}{c_{\max}} \quad \forall k \in K.$$

Constraint (11) implies $y_e \in \mathbb{Z}_{\geq 0} \ \forall e \in E$. We can use this to get the enhanced cutset cut

$$\sum_{e \in \delta^+(s_k)} y_e \geq \lceil \frac{d_k}{c_{\max}} \rceil \quad \forall k \in K. \tag{21}$$

The demand d_k and the maximum capacity $c_{\max}$ are always integral so (21) is stronger than (20). This cut can be generalized.

Let $G = (V, E)$ be a directed graph. Suppose we have a subset of the nodes $S \subseteq V$. We denote the complement of S as $\overline{S} := V \setminus S$. The partition of the nodes $C := (S, \overline{S})$ is called a *cut*, to avoid ambiguity we will call this a *graph cut* in this thesis. Then $\delta(S, \overline{S}) = \{(i,j) \in E | i \in S, j \in \overline{S}\}$ is called the *cutset* of the graph cut $(S, \overline{S})$. The cuts in this section are named after it.

This allows us to define the general cutset cut

$$\sum_{e \in \delta(S, \overline{S})} y_e \geq \lceil \frac{\sum_{k | s_k \in S, t_k \notin S} d_k}{c_{\max}} \rceil \quad \forall S \subseteq V. \tag{22}$$

If we take $S = \{s_{k_1}\}$ for a $k_1 \in K$, then we get an enhanced cutset cut back (21) (if there is no $k_2 \in K$ with $k_2 \neq k_1$ and $s_{k_1} = s_{k_2}$). If there are multiple commodities with the same source, then sufficient capacity needs to be installed to handle the sum of their demands. So then (22) is stronger than (21). Suppose we have a graph cut $(S, \overline{S})$, then one could even say that sufficient capacity needs to be installed on the arcs of $\delta(S, \overline{S})$ to be able to transport at least the sum of the demands of the commodities that have their source in S and sink in $\overline{S}$. Every container of those commodities has to be transported from a node in S to a node in $\overline{S}$. Consequently, every such container is transported by at least one arc in $\delta(S, \overline{S})$. This reasoning gives some intuition why (21) can be generalized to (22). If the design variables y_e are binary variables, then we will use the flow cover cuts

$$\sum_{e \in Q} y_e \geq 1 \quad \forall Q \subseteq \delta(S, \overline{S}) \text{ with } \sum_{e \in Q} c_e < \sum_{k \mid s_k \in S, t_k \notin S} d_k, \forall S \subseteq V. \quad (23)$$

There are a huge number of node subsets $S \subseteq V$. So adding all cuts (22) is in general impractical. We can add some general cutset cuts during the branch & cut process. Finding violated cuts is called the *separation problem*. An $s_k - t_k$ cut for a $k \in K$ is a graph cut $C = (S, \overline{S})$ with $s_{k_1} \in S$ and $t_{k_1} \in \overline{S}$. Suppose we have a non-integral solution (x^*, y^*) found in one of the nodes of the branch & cut tree. To find violated cuts we take the following steps:

1. For all commodities $k_1 \in K$ repeat the following steps;
2. Set $S := \{s_{k_1}\}$ and $T := \{t_{k_1}\}$;
3. Put the values y_e^* as capacity on the arcs of the time-space graph;
4. Find a minimal $s_{k_1} - t_{k_1}$ cut by solving the max flow problem [5] on the time-space graph with s_{k_1} the source and t_{k_1} the sink (according to the max flow - min cut theorem [5]);
5. Check for the S constructed if the corresponding cut (22) is violated, if so add it to the ILP problem.

This way at a node in the branch & cut tree at most $|K|$ max flow problems need to be solved. The max flow problem is similar to the min cost flow problem.

Although the method can discover many violated cutset cuts, there are also some it cannot discover. The step-by-step plan above gives two minimum graph cuts in the graph of Fig. 2 with five truck arcs. The graph cut with $S = \{s_0\}$ and the graph cut with $S = \{s_1\}$. The corresponding general cutset cuts are not violated, because $y_{[s_1, v_0, \text{truck}]} \geq 1$ and $y_{[s_0, v_0, \text{truck}]} \geq 1$ hold (with equality). Although the general cutset cut with $S = \{s_0, s_1, v_0\}$, $y_{[v_0, v_1, \text{truck}]} \geq 2$, is violated.

Repeatedly solving max flow problems might take too much time in practice. So better options may be to add cuts (21) to the model. This can be done in advance or if they are violated during the branch & cut. Other useful cuts may be (22) for $S := \{s_k, (\tau(s_k) + 1, \chi(s_k)), \ldots, (\tau(s_k) + r, \chi(s_k))\}$ for all $k \in K$ for some small $r \in \mathbb{Z}_{\geq 0}$. If S and $\overline{S}$ are both large sets then the cut is normally not effective, because in that case there is a high chance that too many vehicles go from nodes in S to nodes in $\overline{S}$ rendering the corresponding cut (22) useless.

3.5 Strong Cut

Strong cuts from [4] are defined as:

$$x_{e,k} \leq d_k y_e \quad \forall e \in E, \forall k \in K. \quad (24)$$

These are only useful if all containers of a commodity are going through an arc $e \in E \setminus E_{\text{truck}}$. Then the corresponding strong cut ensures that at least one

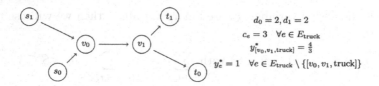

Fig. 2. Undiscovered violated cutset cut example.

vehicle should be used for that link. These cuts are less effective, when used in combination with vehicle and commodity reductions. With Reduction C the design variables are non binary making the cuts weaker. In case commodity reductions are used and/or commodities have high demands, then the chance is smaller that all containers of the commodity take the same arc. So then the cut is also less effective.

We have general integral design variables when vehicle reductions are used. In that case, we can make more effective cuts. If $x_{e,k} = d_k$, then we want to have that $y_e \geq \lceil \frac{d_k}{c_e} \rceil$. This means that we need to have $\lceil \frac{d_k}{c_e} \rceil d_k$ for the LHS (left-hand side). Furthermore, if $x_{e,k} = \lfloor \frac{d_k}{c_e} \rfloor c_e$, then we want to have $y_e \geq \lfloor \frac{d_k}{c_e} \rfloor$; so that means $\lfloor \frac{d_k}{c_e} \rfloor d_k$ for the LHS. Suppose $\frac{d_k}{c_e} \notin \mathbb{Z}$. Then we can define a linear function for the LHS that goes through the two points described:

$$ax_{e,k} + b \leq d_k y_e \qquad \forall e \in E, \forall k \in K, \tag{25}$$

with $a = \frac{\lceil \frac{d_k}{c_e} \rceil d_k - \lfloor \frac{d_k}{c_e} \rfloor d_k}{d_k - \lfloor \frac{d_k}{c_e} \rfloor c_e} = \frac{d_k}{d_k - \lfloor \frac{d_k}{c_e} \rfloor c_e}$ and $b = \lceil \frac{d_k}{c_e} \rceil d_k - a d_k$. We divide by d_k to get:

$$ax_{e,k} + b \leq y_e \qquad \forall e \in E, \forall k \in K, \tag{26}$$

with $a = \frac{1}{d_k - \lfloor \frac{d_k}{c_e} \rfloor c_e}$ and $b = \lceil \frac{d_k}{c_e} \rceil - a d_k$. For the substitution we use $\mu' = \lceil \frac{d_k}{c_e} \rceil$ and $r' = d_k - (\mu' - 1)c_e$ and we simplify to get:

$$x_{e,k} \leq d_k - r'(\mu' - y_e) \qquad \forall e \in E, \forall k \in K. \tag{27}$$

Theses are arc residual capacity cuts. This has a few implications. We do not have to show that this enhanced cut does not cut away integral solutions, because that is already shown for arc residual capacity cuts. It is not necessary to add strong cuts, because if they are effective, $x_{e,k} = d_k$, then the arc residual capacity cut forces the same bound for y_e and the arc residual capacity cut can be even stronger for integral design variables. These arc residual capacity cuts seems to be useful if $x_{e,k} \in \{d_k, \lfloor \frac{d_k}{c_e} \rfloor c_e\}$, but for most other values of $x_{e,k}$ it gives a non-integral lower bound for y_e. For the interested reader we refer to [4] for another cut; the flow pack cut.

4   Results and Conclusions

In this section we present the first results of the cutting planes in calculation time on a simple test instance. The instance has eight terminals locations and two groups of six barges. All barges that belong to the same group have the same capacities, travel times, and begin and end location. We assume an infinite number of trucks at every terminal, but restrictions may be added if that is desired. The travel times of the vehicles are based on data from practice and the truck travel times on data from Google Maps. Every truck can carry exactly one (40 ft) container. We choose to look at a time span of 36 h with time steps of one hour, where 50 bookings and 100 containers are scheduled. We let the cost on the non-horizontal truck arcs be equal to the travel time of the arc. This models a company that owns barges and has to pay additional cost when trucking containers. We make sure that it is possible to truck a booking to its destination, so its deadline should be (at least one time stamp) later than its release date. Besides the terminal locations, there are two customer locations in the model. The customer locations are not reachable by barge. So in the time-space network none of the barge arcs are incident to customer locations (that are not accessible by barge). Trains or other (types of) vehicles are initially not in the model, but could easily be added. We solved our ILP problems with IBM's CPLEX solver.

For the cutset cut, the counters determine the number of cutset cuts we take and which cutset cuts. If the counter is zero we only take the cutset based on the sink of the commodity. If the counter is one, we also take the cutset cut with the sink and the time-space node with the same location as the sink one time stamp earlier, etcetera.

Table 1. Numerical results of Cuts.

Cut	Active	Parameter	Comp. Time	Solution
Symmetry Breaking Cut	Yes	$|W| = 4$	292.32 s	3760 (optimal)
Symmetry Breaking Cut	No	$|W| = 4$	259.27 s	3760 (optimal)
Symmetry Breaking Cut	Yes	$|W| = 5$	641.11 s	3760 (optimal)
Symmetry Breaking Cut	No	$|W| = 5$	665.19 s	3760 (optimal)
Strong Cut	Yes		101.22 s	3760 (optimal)
Arc Residual Capacity Cut	Yes	All commodities	> 300 s	3850
Arc Residual Capacity Cut	Yes	Per commodity	54.58 s	3760 (optimal)
Cutset Cut	Yes	Counter = 0	61.16 s	3760 (optimal)
Cutset Cut	Yes	Counter = 1	58.42 s	3760 (optimal)
Cutset Cut	Yes	Counter = 2	47.83 s	3760 (optimal)
Cutset Cut	Yes	Counter = 3	100.97 s	3760 (optimal)

The symmetry breaking cut does not show its effectiveness in this example (Table 1). We expect that the instance is too small for this cut to be effective. The strong cut and the arc residual capacity cut are put together in one part of the table, because the arc residual capacity cut is a stronger version of the strong cut. Using the strong cut brings the calculation time back from more that 300 s to 101.22 s, still finding the optimal solution. Using the arc residual capacity cut per commodity is very effective. This may be because many commodities send all of their containers over one path. One could experiment with other sets of commodities to reach even better results. Using the cut for all commodities may lead to the case, with high probability, that this includes commodities that do not use the specific arc, making, probably, this cut weaker. Using this cut for more than two commodities is only recommended if you know that the arc is used by many commodities, and preferably which commodities. The cutset cut only helps a little it may be more effective more experiments with different types of cutsets and other instances should be done to see the full impact of this cut.

For further research we recommend to test the cuts on a variety of test instances to understand the best fit of the cuts on specific cases. This would also show whether the symmetry breaking cut does indeed perform on bigger instances. Also the effective use of (which) cutset cuts should follow from this analysis.

Acknowledgement. This work has been carried out within the project 'Complexity Methods for Predictive Synchromodality' (Comet-PS), supported by NWO (the Netherlands Organisation for Scientific Research), TKI-Dinalog (Top Consortium Knowledge and Innovation) and the Early Research Program 'Grip on Complexity' of TNO (The Netherlands Organisation for Applied Scientific Research).

References

1. Aardal, K., Weismantel, R., Wolsey, L.A.: Non-standard approaches to integer programming. Discrete Appl. Math. **123**(1–3), 5–74 (2002)
2. Andersen, J., Crainic, T.G., Christiansen, M.: Service network design with asset management: Formulations and comparative analyses. Transp. Res. Part C: Emerg. Technol. **17**(2), 197–207 (2009)
3. Balakrishnan, A., Magnanti, T., Wong, R.: A dual-ascent procedure for large-scale uncapacitated network design. Oper. Res. **37**(5), 716–740 (1989)
4. Chouman, M., Crainic, T.: MIP-based Matheuristic for Service Network Design with Design-balanced Requirements. CIRRELT (2012)
5. Cook, W.J., Cunningham, W.H., Pulleyblank, W.R., Schrijver, A.: Combinatorial Optimization. Wiley Interscience (1998)
6. Crainic, T.: Service network design in freight transportation. Eur. J. Oper. Res. **122**(2), 272–288 (2000)
7. Crainic, T., Frangioni, A., Gendron, B.: Bundle-based relaxation methods for multicommodity capacitated fixed charge network design. Discrete Appl. Math. **112**(1), 73–99 (2001)
8. Crainic, T., Gendreau, M., Farvolden, J.: A simplex-based tabu search method for capacitated network design. Inf. J. Comput. **12**(3), 223–236 (2000)
9. De Juncker, M.A.M., Huizing, D., del Vecchyo, M.R.O., Phillipson, F., Sangers, A.: Framework of synchromodal transportation problems. ICCL 2017. LNCS, vol. 10572, pp. 383–403. Springer, Cham (2017). https://doi.org/10.1007/978-3-319-68496-3_26
10. Ghamlouche, I., Crainic, T.G., Gendreau, M.: Path relinking, cycle-based neighbourhoods and capacitated multicommodity network design. Ann. Oper. Res. **131**(1–4), 109–133 (2004)

11. Holmberg, K., Hellstrand, J.: Solving the uncapacitated network design problem by a lagrangean heuristic and branch-and-bound. Oper. Res. **46**(2), 247–259 (1998)
12. Holmberg, K., Yuan, D.: A lagrangian heuristic based branch-and-bound approach for the capacitated network design problem. Oper. Res. **48**(3), 461–481 (2000)
13. Huizing, D.: General methods for synchromodal planning of freight containers and transports. Master's thesis, TU Delft (2017)
14. IBM: Cplex optimizer (2017). https://www.ibm.com/analytics/data-science/prescriptive-analytics/cplex-optimizer
15. IBM: Zero-half cuts (2017). https://www.ibm.com/support/knowledgecenter/SSSA5P_12.5.0/ilog.odms.cplex.help/CPLEX/UsrMan/topics/discr_optim/mip/cuts/38_zerohalf.html
16. Janic, M.: Modelling the full costs of an intermodal and road freight transport network. Transp. Res. Part D: Transp. Environ. **12**(1), 33–44 (2007)
17. Joborn, M., Crainic, T.G., Gendreau, M., Holmberg, K., Lundgren, J.T.: Economies of scale in empty freight car distribution in scheduled railways. Transp. Sci. **38**(2), 121–134 (2004)
18. Letchford, A.N., Lodi, A.: Strengthening Chvátal-Gomory cuts and Gomory fractional cuts. Oper. Res. Lett. **30**(2), 74–82 (2002)
19. Li, X., Wei, K., Aneja, Y., Tian, P.: Design-balanced capacitated multicommodity network design with heterogeneous assets. Omega **67**, 145–159 (2017)
20. Magnanti, T.L., Wong, R.T.: Network design and transportation planning: Models and algorithms. Transp. Sci. **18**(1), 1–55 (1984)
21. Magnanti, T.L., Mirchandani, P., Vachani, R.: Modeling and solving the two-facility capacitated network loading problem. Oper. Res. **43**(1), 142–157 (1995)
22. Marchand, H., Martin, A., Weismantel, R., Wolsey, L.: Cutting planes in integer and mixed integer programming. Discrete Appl. Math. **123**(1–3), 397–446 (2002)
23. Pedersen, M., Crainic, T., Madsen, O.: Models and tabu search metaheuristics for service network design with asset-balance requirements. Transp. Sci. **43**(2), 158–177 (2009)
24. Sharypova, K.: Optimization of Hinterland Intermodal Container Transportation. Ph.D. thesis, Eindhoven University of Technology (2014)
25. Vu, D.M., Crainic, T.G., Toulouse, M., Hewitt, M.: Service network design with resource constraints. Transp. Sci. **50**(4), 1380–1393 (2014)

Deep Reinforcement Learning and Optimization Approach for Multi-echelon Supply Chain with Uncertain Demands

Júlio César Alves[1,2]([⊠]) [iD] and Geraldo Robson Mateus[2] [iD]

[1] Universidade Federal de Lavras, Lavras, MG, Brazil
`juliocesar.alves@ufla.br`
[2] Universidade Federal de Minas Gerais, Belo Horizonte, MG, Brazil
`mateus@dcc.ufmg.br`
`http://www.ufla.br`
`http://www.ufmg.br`

Abstract. Deep Reinforcement Learning (RL) has been used recently in many areas achieving successful results. A multi-period supply chain operation can be viewed as a sequential decision-making problem for which Deep RL may be appropriate. Previous uses of such approach on related problems consider only serial or two-echelon supply chains with limited decision possibilities. In this research a four-echelon supply chain with two nodes per echelon and stochastic customer demands is considered. An MDP formulation and a Non-Linear Programming model of the problem are presented. Proximal Policy Optimization (PPO2) is used in order to find a good policy to operate the entire supply chain and minimize total operating costs. An agent based on a linearized model is used as a baseline. Experimental results indicate that PPO2 is a suitable and competitive approach for the proposed problem.

Keywords: Multi-echelon supply chain · Stochastic demands · Deep reinforcement learning · Proximal Policy Optimization

1 Introduction

Machine Learning has been used to solve problems in many fields, and the recent advances in the field, specially with the use of deep neural networks, have leveraged and extended their use. Reinforcement Learning (RL) is a sub-area of Machine Learning designed to solve sequential decision-making problems. The present work uses a Deep Reinforcement Learning approach to operate a multi-echelon supply chain with uncertain demands.

The supply chain considered is a four-echelon chain composed by suppliers, manufacturers (or factories), wholesalers and retailers, and it is operated by a central decision maker. Suppliers provide raw materials that are transformed into finished products by manufacturers. Products are distributed by manufacturers to wholesalers, and wholesalers, in turn, send products to retailers. Retailers

© Springer Nature Switzerland AG 2020
E. Lalla-Ruiz et al. (Eds.): ICCL 2020, LNCS 12433, pp. 584–599, 2020.
https://doi.org/10.1007/978-3-030-59747-4_38

are responsible for meeting uncertain (customer) external demands. Every node of the chain has a capacitated local stock and there is a constant delay (lead time) to produce raw material at suppliers and to send material from one node to another. There is also a capacity for suppliers in providing raw materials. The addressed scenario consists in two nodes per echelon, that is, there are two suppliers, two factories, and so on. The objective is to operate the entire chain, within a given horizon, to meet customer demands and minimize total operating costs. Costs are associated with the supply of raw materials by suppliers, in the processing of materials by manufacturers and in the stock and transport of materials and products. There is also a cost when customer demand is not met, representing the purchase price of a product on the market to complete its delivery. As the customer demand is uncertain, it is not trivial to define the best policy that can meet the customer demands and, at the same time, can minimize the total operating cost. Figure 1 illustrates the supply chain scenario addressed.

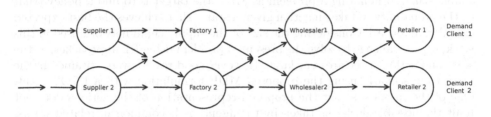

Fig. 1. Supply Chain example: there are four echelons (suppliers, factories, wholesalers and retailers) with local stocks; there is a lead time (in this case equal to 2 periods) to produce raw material at the suppliers and to send material from one node to another; there is an uncertain customer demand to be met by the retailers.

From the perspective of Operations Research, the problem addressed is a stochastic, non-linear, classic problem of production planning and product distribution. On the other hand, the problem can also be formulated as a Markov decision process (MDP). As the resulting model cannot be solved numerically due to the high dimension of the state space [8], Deep RL is an appropriate tool to deal with the problem. The basic RL mechanism [15] consists in an iterative process in which the agent observes the state of the environment and acts according to the state, then the environment changes to a new state due the action and gives a feedback (reward) to the agent. The purpose of the agent is to maximize the cumulative reward. In case of an episodic task, the idea is to maximize the total reward until the end of the horizon. Agent training consists of repeating this interaction over and over, starting with a trial and error approach and, throughout the process, learning to act for better cumulative rewards. In our case the environment is a simulation of the supply chain operation and the agent is the Proximal Policy Optimization (PPO2) [14] algorithm. Some works in the literature use Deep RL on related problems, but they deal with simpler supply chain networks (two-echelon or serial supply chains) [4,6,7,11,12]. In this research, PPO2 was chosen because it achieves high performance in many RL tasks with large spaces of states and actions [10].

In order to use the PPO2 agent it is necessary to formulate the problem as an MDP. The detailed formulation (that we consider a contribution of this research) is presented in Sect. 4.1, but can be summarized as follows. States are represented in a 27-dimensional continuous space, and they are composed of the customer's demands for the next period, the current amount of material (raw material or product) in each stock, the raw material supplied by suppliers and the material in transport throughout the chain. Actions are represented in a 14-dimensional continuous space, and they are composed of the amount of material that suppliers need to supply and the amount of material that each node needs to send to the next nodes in the tier (using this approach, inventory levels are indirectly defined). Retailers are not controlled as they need to meet demand whenever there is enough product in stock. Rewards are the negative of the total operating costs. The transition model is given by the simulation of the supply chain. When formulating a problem as MDP the target is to find a policy (that is, the probability to take an action given a state) that achieves the best expected cumulative reward. Considering the size of the supply chain network used in this work, it is a challenge to solve the presented problem using RL approaches, as the state and action space are very large. However good results were obtained in the case study scenario using the proposed MDP formulation with a PPO2 agent. One of the reasons is that the proposed representation of the actions does not limit the possible decisions taken by the agent, as is common in related works. Besides the PPO2 agent, a Non-Linear Programming (NLP) model is presented and a related LP model (considering deterministic expected mean demands) is solved. An LP-based agent built from the solution of the model is used as a baseline. In the experiments, after tuning the hyperparameters of PPO2, several training runs with different random seeds are executed. The results show that PPO2 can achieve good results on the proposed scenario.

The remainder of this article is structured as follows. Section 2 presents key aspects of Deep RL and the PPO algorithm. Related works are presented in Sect. 3. Section 4 presents the MDP formulation and NLP model. The case study, with experimental methodology and results, are presented and discussed in Sect. 5. A summary of the findings and proposed future research directions are finally given in Sect. 6.

2   Deep Reinforcement Learning

Problems formulated as MDP can be handled with RL algorithms. Many of the RL techniques are based on an iterative process that alternates between policy evaluation and policy improvement. The underlying theory of RL shows that considering infinity iterations the learned policy converges to an optimal policy. RL techniques can be either value-based, that is, they learn action (or state) values and then use such values to choose an action, or they can be policy-based, meaning they learn a parameterized policy that allows to choose actions without consulting value estimates [15].

The most simple RL algorithms are value-based methods (e.g., Q-Learning). The basic idea is to use a value function to represent the best action to be taken in each state and, during the learning process, to update these values in order to always improve the policy. But many problems have very large state and action spaces, and, in such cases, it is not possible to deal with a table for the value-function (state or action-values). The problem is not only with the time and storage constraints, but mainly because many states will probably never be visited during the learning process. Thus, it is necessary to use methods that can generalize from similar states. One recommended approach is to use the function approximation to represent the value function instead of tables. In this approach, when the weights of the function are updated for a state-action pair, the update also impact the values for other states-action pairs, enabling the desired generalization. Many of the approximated methods follow the same basic iterative mechanism, but using a function approximator, like a neural network for instance (e.g., DQN is an approximated approach based on Q-Learning).

Another approach to deal with large state and action spaces are policy-based algorithms (e.g., policy gradient methods [15]). These techniques try to find the best policy directly, instead of learning the value function to derive the best policy. Some of the policy gradient methods, called actor-critic methods, approximate not only the policy but also the value-function. The actor learns the policy, and the critic learns the value-function in order to evaluate the policy learned by the actor. This approach aims to accelerate the entire learning process, minimizing variance during the training process.

The most powerful actor-critic methods use deep neural networks for both, the actor and the critic, but it is not so easy to obtain good results with these methods. In general, they are very parameter sensible and sample inefficient. Proximal Policy Optimization (PPO) was proposed by Schulman et al. [14] in order to find a balance between implementation, parameterization and sample complexity (and PPO2 is the latest version, designed to run in parallel using GPU environments). The main idea of the method is to limit step size updates. The goal is to update the policy with a new one that it is not so different from the current one. This is important because big updates are responsible for a great variance in the learning process that leads to a poor performance. PPO pseudo-code is presented in Algorithm 1.

3   Related Works

There are several works that use RL for supply chain operation problems, but many of them are based on simpler RL techniques (e.g. Q-Learning) [2,3,9]. This section presents the most recent works that use Deep RL approaches to problems related to those explored here. Kemmer et al. [7] used Approximate SARSA and three versions of Vanilla Policy Gradient (REINFORCE) on a two-echelon supply chain. The scenario consists of a factory and one to three warehouses with increasing demands, and a horizon of 24 periods. The state is composed of the stock levels and the demands of the last two periods; the actions refers

---

Algorithm 1: PROXIMAL POLICY OPTIMIZATION (PPO)

---

1 Initialize Θ and Φ (policy and value-function parameters, respectively)
2 **for** $i=0,1,2,...$ **do**
3   **for** $actor=1,2,...,N$ **do**
4   Run policy $\pi(\Theta)$ for T steps and collect the trajectories.
5   Calculate advantage estimates $\hat{A}_1, ..., \hat{A}_T$ based on value-function V_ϕ.
6   Form a *batch*, of size NT, with collected trajectories and advantages.
7   **for** $epoch=1,2,...,K$ **do**
8   Shuffle *batch* and split into *minibatches*
9   **foreach** *minibatch* **do**
10   Update Θ wrt objective function via stochastic gradient.
11   Update Φ wrt mean-squared error of value-function V_ϕ.

---

to the factory production and product transportation (but the action space is reduced to only 3 production and transportation levels); and the rewards are the profit, considering operating costs and backlogs. $(r$-$Q)$-policy, a minimum stock approach, is used as baseline. All agents are better than baseline on the scenario with only one warehouse, and two versions of REINFORCE improve over the baseline in the scenario with 3 warehouses. The work is extended by Hutse [6], including non-zero lead times, two product types, continuous action spaces and four types of stochastic demand scenarios. The author uses a DQN (Deep Q-Network) for discrete actions and DDPG (Deep Deterministic Policy Gradient) for continuous actions. The state is composed of the stock, production, transport and the last x (a parameter) demands, for each node-product combination. The actions are, for each product, how much to produce and to send for each retailer (using aggregated levels in discrete case and limiting the maximum action values in the continuous case). The rewards are the profit, considering operating costs (including stock-outs). The baseline is the $(r$-$Q)$-policy and the agents are better than baseline in all scenarios (1 factory, 2 or 3 retailers and 1 or 2 products).

Gijsbrechts et al. [4] propose a proof of concept by using Deep-RL on three different problems: dual-sourcing or dual-mode, lost sales, and multi-echelon inventory models. In the multi-echelon setup the states are represented by the stock levels and orders of the warehouses and retailers, while the actions are the orders from each node (aggregated by state-dependent base-stock levels). They apply A3C (Asynchronous Advantage Actor-Critic) on two different scenarios with one warehouse and ten retailers, considering stochastic demands. The A3C agent performs better than a base-stock policy used as baseline. Oroojlooyjadid [11] uses a customized DQN to solve the MIT Beer Game, a four-echelon linear supply chain, considering deterministic and stochastic demands. They treat the problem as decentralized, with multi-cooperative agents. Each agent only knows the local information, and for avoid competition, there is an engineered mechanism to provide feedback to each agent at the end of an episode. In the experiments, only one agent uses DQN and the others follow a base-stock heuristic.

The state is composed of the stock levels, demands, arriving orders, and arriving products, from the past m (a parameter) periods. The actions refer to how much more or less to order than the received order, and the used intervals are $[-2, 2]$ and $[-8, 8]$. The rewards are the stock plus backlog costs. Experiments show that using DQN for one node achieves better results than using the base-stock policy for all nodes.

Peng et al. [12] use Vanilla Policy Gradient in a capacitated supply chain with one factory warehouse and three retailers (with balanced and unbalanced costs), and regular and seasonal stochastic demands. The state is composed of the stock levels and the last two demands; and the actions are how much to produce and to send to the each retailer. As the actions are state-dependent, they use two mechanisms to treat the inherent difficulty of using this approach with neural network outputs. The rewards are the profit, considering operating costs and penalization by not satisfying demand. The Deep RL agent achieves better results than baseline, $(r$-$Q)$-policy, in all experimented scenarios.

4 Problem Modeling

4.1 MDP Formulation

One of the most important activities (if not the most important) when using RL techniques to solve a problem is to model it as a Markov Decision Process (MDP), that is, define the states, actions, rewards and the transition model to be used to solve the problem. We believe that the problem formalization presented here is one of the main contributions of the present work.

State Space. Let S_{in} be the amount of material in stock in node n on period i, b_n^s the stock capacity of node n, T_{i*n} the amount of material that will arrive in node n on period i, l the supply and transport lead time, K the number of customers (one for each retailer), d_{ik} the demand of customer k on period i, d_{min} and d^{max} the minimum and maximum possible demand value, and H the size of the episode. The state on period i is composed of the demand values for the next period, $[d_{(i+1)1}, d_{(i+1)2}, \ldots, d_{(i+1)K}]$; for each node: current stock level, S_{in}, and material in transport to arrive on the next periods, $[T_{(i+1)*n}, T_{(i+2)*n}, \ldots, T_{(i+l)*n}]$; and, finally, the number of periods remaining until the end of the episode, $[H - i]$. We could define the state as a vector of such actual values, but given the good results of the used algorithm (PPO2) with continuous normalized values we have decided to normalize the values of state representation to the interval $[-1, 1]$ (in fact, this is advisable [5]). Demands are normalized by the minimum and maximum possible values ($\frac{d_{(i+1)k} - d_{min}}{d^{max} - d_{min}}$ for each customer k); stock and material in transport are normalized by node's stock capacity ($\frac{S_{in}}{b_n^s}$ and $\frac{T_{(i+j)*n}}{b_n^s}$, respectively); and the remaining time is normalized by the size of the episode ($\frac{H-i}{H}$). This representation leads to a continuous vector whose values lies in $[0, 1]$ interval and, therefore a transformation is done in order to use the target interval $[-1, 1]$. Considering a scenario as shown in Fig. 1 and supply and transport lead time $l = 2$, the state space would have 27 dimensions (2 for the demands, 3 for each node and 1 for the remaining time).

Action Space. Let a_n be the action value related to provide material at a first echelon node and b_{nm} the action value related to send material from the node n to the target node m (both real values in the $[0, 1]$ interval). Let S_n be the amount of material in stock in node n on the current period and b_n^p the supply capacity of the node n. Action value a_n determines the amount of material to be provided by node n, calculated by $a_n c_n$. The amount of material to be sent from node n to each possible node m is calculated by $S_n(b_{nm} - t(m))$, where $t(m) = \{0$ if $min_j b_{nj} = b_{nm}$; or $max_j \, b_{nj} \, | \, b_{nj} < b_{nm}$ otherwise $\}$. Such definition means that, for each node n, the action values are sorted and each of the values is viewed as a cut in the current amount of material kept in stock. For example, suppose there is a node n with current stock $S_n = 100$, and the action values to send material to its two possible target nodes are $b_{n1} = 0.8$ and $b_{n2} = 0.3$. First the values are sorted $(b_{n2}, b_{n1} = 0.3, 0.8)$ and then the first value indicates that the second target node will receive 30 units of material (because $t(2) = 0$; and $S_n(b_{nm} - t(m)) = 100(0.3 - 0) = 30$); the second value indicates that the first target node will receive 50 units of material (by doing $100(0.8 - 0.3) = 50$). The remaining material, 20 units, is kept in the stock. In this representation the actual action is a vector concatenating action values for suppliers (they have both a_n and b_{nm} actions) and action values for other nodes (they have only b_{nm} actions). Remembering that retailers don't have any actions as they will meet customer's demand whenever possible. In practice, as well as for the state space, it is advisable to use a normalized interval $[-1, 1]$ with PPO2, so the transformation is also considered for the action space. Regarding the same scenario (Figure 1), the action space has 14 dimensions (3 for each supplier plus 2 for each other node, except the retailers). The proposed action space representation is independent of the state and this facilitate the use of algorithms like PPO2 (see [12] for an example of state-dependent representation).

Transition Model. A simulation of the supply chain is used to give the transition model. Almost all supply chain operations are simulated in a deterministic way, that is, any amount of material defined by the action values (to be supplied or transported) is followed by the simulation, as the chosen action representation only generates viable quantities. The exceptions are: customer's demand, it is stochastic and sampled for the next period on each simulation step, and possible excess of material in stocks (each transport action is limited by sender's stock capacity, but the sum of materials arriving from different senders with current receiver's stock level can exceed receiver's stock capacity). Simulation considers that all arriving material need to pass by the stock, even if it is not kept for the next period. The excess of material is discarded and a related cost is considered.

Rewards. The design of the rewards is crucial for the success of an RL algorithm. For many problems is not clear the best approach to define how to give a feedback for the algorithm, specially because in many cases can be easy to define a feedback at the end of an episode (success or fail), but can be difficult to define a feedback on each simulation step. However, in the proposed supply chain problem, as it is a cost minimization problem, seems to make a lot of sense to use the negative of the total operating costs as the reward. Therefore the reward used is the negative of the sum of all incurred costs (production, transportation, manufacturing, stocks, material discarded due to exceed stock capacities and penalization by not meet customer demands) as stated by the objective of the NLP Model in Eq. 1.

4.2 Non-Linear Programming Model

In this section a Non-Linear Programming (NLP) model of the problem is presented. Let $n \in \{N\}$ be a node of the supply chain and $i \in \{I\}$ a period. The variables are: S_{in}, the stock level of node n on period i; T_{inm}, the amount of material sent from node n to node m and that will arrive on period i; P_{in}, the amount of raw material produced by node n (a supplier) and that will be available on period i; F_{in}, the amount of raw material processed by node n (a factory) on period i; D_{in}^s, the excess of material discarded due to exceed stock capacity of node n on period i; D_{in}^d, the amount of missing products to meet customer demand. The parameters of the model are presented on Table 1 (note that t_{nm} and f_n are binary, and all other parameters are integers). The objective is to minimize the total operating cost (Eq. 1).

Table 1. Parameters of the NLP Model.

Param.	Description
c_n^s	Cost of stocking one unit of material at node n
c_n^p	Cost of producing one unit of raw material at node n
c_n^f	Cost of processing one unit of raw material at node n
c^t	Cost of sending one unit of material
c^e	Cost of material discarded by exceed stock capacity
c^d	Cost incurred by unmet demand
b_n^s	Stock capacity of node n
b_n^p	Supply capacity of node n
b_n^t	Maximum amount of material that can be sent from node n
r_n	Processing ratio at node n
l	Transport and supply lead time
t_{nm}	Indicate if it is possible to send material from node n to node m
f_n	Indicate if it is possible to process raw material in the node n
s_n	Initial stock level on node n
p_{in}	Initial amount of material supplied from node n (defined for $i \leq l$)
t_{inm}	Initial amount of material sent by node n to node m (defined for $i \leq l$)
d_{in}	Stochastic customer demand to be met by node n on period i

$$min \quad \sum_{i \in I} \sum_{n \in N} \left(c_n^s S_{in} + c_n^f F_{in} + c^e D_{in}^e + c^d D_{in}^d \right) + \sum_{1 < i \le |I| + l} \sum_{n \in N} \left(c_n^p P_{in} + \sum_{m \in N} c^t T_{inm} \right) \quad (1)$$

The constraints are defined as follows. Constraints 2 and 3 control the stock, transport of material and demands. Capacities are handled by constraints 4, 5 and 6. Constraint 7 is used to calculate the amount of raw material processed at factories. And, finally, constraints 8 and 9 are used to take into account the initial supplied and transported materials.

$$S_{1n} = s_n + P_{1n} + \frac{\sum_{m \in N} t_{1mn}}{r_n} - D_{1n}^e - \sum_{m \in N} T_{(1+l)nm} - d_{1n} + D_{1n}^d \quad \forall \quad n \in N \quad (2)$$

$$S_{in} = S_{(i-1)n} + P_{in} + \frac{\sum_{m \in N} T_{imn}}{r_n} - D_{in}^e - \sum_{m \in N} T_{(i+l)nm} - d_{in} + D_{in}^d \quad \forall \quad i \in I \setminus 1, n \in N \quad (3)$$

$$0 \le P_{in} \le b_n^p \quad \forall \quad n \in N \tag{4}$$

$$0 \le S_{in} \le b_n^s \quad \forall \quad i \in I, n \in N \tag{5}$$

$$0 \le T_{inm} \le t_{nm} b_n^t \quad \forall \quad n \in N, m \in N \tag{6}$$

$$F_{in} = f_n \sum_{m \in N} T_{imn} \quad \forall \quad i \in I, n \in N \tag{7}$$

$$P_{in} = p_{in} \quad \forall \quad i \in \{1, ..., l\} \tag{8}$$

$$T_{inm} = t_{inm} \quad \forall \quad i \in \{1, ..., l\} \tag{9}$$

If we consider deterministic demands the presented model becomes a Linear Programming model. This related LP model is solved, considering expected mean demands, and an agent based on such solution is used as a baseline to evaluate the performance of the Deep RL algorithm.

5   Case Study

5.1   Methodology

The objective of the present work is to verify if a Deep RL approach can solve the supply chain operation problem with uncertain demands with good results. We have chosen PPO2 algorithm because it achieves high performance for many problems. In order to use the algorithm it is necessary to implement the simulation of the environment, the supply chain operation, following the formalization of the problem presented in Sect. 4.1.

After choosing the algorithm and implement the environment, the next step is to make the hyperparameters tuning of the algorithm. The proposed methodology uses 100 different combinations of randomly generated hyperparameters values. For each combination the agent is trained for one thousand episodes (with evaluations of the model on every 50 episodes). The values of the parameters used in the attempt with the best results are chosen for the experiments.

Experiment consists in using PPO2 to solve a scenario as that presented in Sect. 1, whose parameter values (following notation from Sect. 4.2), are presented in Table 2. All costs are applied by unit of raw material or product.[1]

Table 2. Parameters of the scenario used in the experiments.

Group	Param	Value	Details
Chain	N	1,...,8	2 suppliers, 2 factories, 2 wholesalers and 2 retailers (in this order)
Horizon	H	360	Episode length
Costs	c_n^s	1	For all nodes
	c_n^p	6,4	For each supplier, respectively
	c_n^f	12,10	For each factory, respectively
	c^t	2	On the whole chain
Pen. costs	c^e	10	Material discarded by exceed stock capacity
	c^d	216	Incurred by unmet demand
Capacities	b_n^s	200, 300	For each pair of nodes at the same echelon
	b_n^p	120, 150	For each supplier, respectively
	b_n^t	200, 300	For each pair of nodes at the same echelon
Prod. ratio/	r_n	3	For factories (1 for the other nodes)
Lead time	l	2	For the whole chain
Chain config.	t_{nm}	*	Modeling network as presented in Fig. 1
	f_n	1	For factories (0 for the others)
Initial values	s_n	0	For all nodes
	p_{in}	60	For each supplier
(defined for $i \leq l$)	t_{inm}	60	If m is a supplier or a factory
	t_{inm}	20	If m is a wholesaler or a retailer
Demands	d_{in}	[10,20]	Randomly sampled for each retailer

In order to verify the robustness of the results achieved by algorithms like PPO2 it is important to use different random seeds for the training process.

---

[1] Unmet demand cost c^d was considered as $3c^q$ where c^q is the total operating cost of delivering one unity of product. The value of c^q was calculated as 72 for the presented scenario (considering the highest supply and processing costs, total transportation costs and inventory costs over eight periods).

The proposed methodology is to train the algorithm 10 times. Each training consists in running the algorithm for 10 thousand episodes, evaluating the model on every 50 steps (considering 10 episodes on each evaluation step). The best model found on each training is used to evaluate the results. The evaluation of the results consists of simulating 100 episodes of the environment for each PPO2 model found in the training process. With this approach a total of one thousand episodes of evaluation is planned to be executed and the result metric is the average and standard deviation of all these episodes.

An agent based on the LP model (mentioned in Sect. 4.2) is used as a baseline to be compared to PPO2. To create this agent, the LP model is solved for a deterministic version of the problem considering the proposed scenario and constant demand values equal to the expected mean demand (15 in such scenario). The solution found by LP model is encoded as the actions of the agent, and therefore, the LP agent interact with the same scenario used for PPO2, with stochastic demands. With this approach the LP agent actions cause fluctuations at the stocks of the retailers, however as the demands are randomly sampled from the $[10, 20]$ interval, it is expected that the agent can obtain good results.

5.2   Experiments

Experimentation was conducted using Python 3.7.8 in a Dell Vostro notebook with a 2.4 GHz x 4 processor, 3.7 GB of RAM and Ubuntu Linux 20.04. The PPO2 version of the Stable Baselines 2.10 library [5] was used in the experiments; and RL Baselines Zoo library [13] was used for the hyperparameter tuning. The supply chain simulation was implemented following the OpenAI Gym standard [1]. The LP model was solved using CPLEX 12.10 via Python interface.

The proposed methodological steps for hyperparameter tuning was followed (Sect. 5.1). The values of the parameters were randomly sampled from the default intervals given by the RL Baselines Zoo library. Parameterization of the neural network architecture was included, considering three options with two internal layers containing 64, 128 or 256 nodes. During the process unpromising trials were early-stopped using median stopping rule, that is, an attempt was pruned if the intermediate results of the trial were worse than the median of the previous trials. The best values of parameters found are shown in Table 3.

The experiments were then conducted as presented in Sect. 5.1 using the tuned hyperparameter values for PPO2. Table 4 shows the comparison between PPO2 and LP agents. The first column shows the random seed used for the simulated environment, the second column presents a lower bound considering the demands generated with such random seed; the bound was obtained solving the LP model using the demands after they are all generated. The third and fourth columns presents the average and the standard deviation of the total operating cost obtained by LP agent, while the last two columns show the same data for PPO2. In case of LP agent the values refer to the average of 10 episodes, and for PPO2 the same 10 episodes are evaluated but for each training (therefore a total of 100 episodes). The results show that PPO2 is slightly better than LP agent with any of the used random seeds. The averaged gap above lower bound

Table 3. Best PPO2 parameter values found in hyperparameter tuning.

Parameter	Value	Description
N	4	Number of actors (fixed; serial environment)
T	128	Number of steps to collect trajectories
K	50	Number of epochs
α	1.48e-5	Learning rate
γ	0.95	Discount factor
λ	0.99	Trade-off of bias vs variance for GAE
nminibatches	1	Number of training minibatches per update
cliprange	0.2	Clipping parameter
ent_coef	0.03452	Entropy coefficient
net_arch	[256, 256]	Hidden layers of the neural networks

(i.e., optimal solution if demands were known in advance) is 6.2% for PPO2 and 7.6% for LP agent. It is interesting to note that PPO2 has low variance in all runs demonstrating the robustness of the results. Another comparison between the agents is presented in Table 5. The first column shows the type of cost, the second and third columns show the value for LP and PPO2 agent, respectively, and the fourth column shows the difference (PPO2 value minus LP value). The results show that the gain of PPO2 comes from lower amount of unmet demands (despite higher operation costs, the final result is worth it).

Table 4. Comparing LP and PPO2 agents in the proposed scenario. PPO2 achieves lower total operating costs in all evaluation runs.

Seed	Lower bound	LP agent		PPO2 agent	
		Avg	σ	Avg	σ
1	552,270	596,937	9,480	585,628	4,535
2	550,200	595,402	6,654	584,807	5,339
3	552,321	593,015	6,716	585,986	4,149
4	552,240	591,691	6,266	586,327	4,852
5	551,402	597,336	4,678	586,258	3,895
6	554,136	596,335	10,817	588,066	4,757
7	551,918	588,668	6,677	586,932	3,063
8	552,115	593,984	6,804	586,174	5,500
9	549,470	592,375	9,310	583,728	4,561
10	552,077	591,973	9,335	586,212	3,173
Average	**551,815**	**593,772**	**8,308**	**586,012**	**4,585**

To investigate in more detail the behaviour of the PPO2 agent in the proposed scenario we have summarized, by period, the unmet demands and the amount of material (raw material and product) in transport and in stock from all evaluation runs and the result is shown on Fig. 2. All the values are the average total sum for the whole chain. Top left graph shows the unmet demands by period and top right graph shows the cumulative unmet demands; both agents have very low values by period, but PPO2 agent is better and cumulative values emphasize the difference between the agents. Analysing the bottom left graph we can see that the LP agent keeps, as expected, a constant amount of material in transport (after releasing the initial products and before end-of-horizon), and PPO2 agent, in average, learns to keep the same level of transport. Finally, the bottom right graph shows that PPO2 agent tends to keep a constant stock level, while LP agent tends to increase the amount of product in stock (considering the average of all evaluation runs). It can be seen that the stock level of LP agent increases accordingly to the cumulative unmet demands.

Table 5. Comparing LP and PPO2 agents by cost types (on average). PPO2 gain comes from lower amount of unmet demands.

Cost type	LP agent	PPO2 agent	Diff.
Supply	125,760	129,264	3,504
Stock	22,056	21,475	−581
Processing	319,440	324,657	5,217
Transport	106,080	108,034	1,954
Unmet Demands	20,436	2,581	−17,855
Stock penalties	0	0	0
Total	**593,772**	**586,012**	**−7,760**

The learning curve of the PPO2 agent (average for the 10 training runs) is shown on Fig. 3. The graph shows the average of the total rewards by episode. It is noticed that the training is stable and converges after four thousand episodes. The average execution time of the training runs was around 3.5 h. It is important to note that parallelization was not used as the focus was on the behaviour of the algorithm. If wall clock time is a concern it would be easy to get better execution time results using parallelization in a GPU environment.

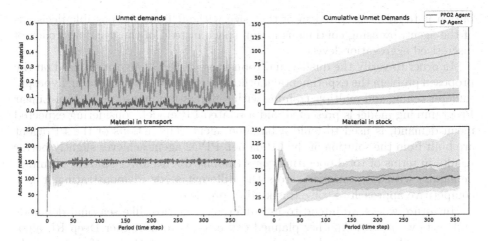

Fig. 2. Comparing LP and PPO2 agent performance by period (values refer to the whole chain and are averaged from all evaluation runs).

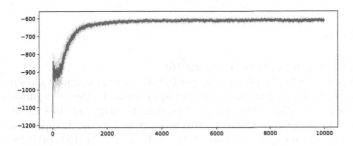

Fig. 3. PPO2 learning curve (on average) using the proposed scenario.

6 Conclusions

The present work uses a Deep Reinforcement Learning approach, namely the PPO2 algorithm, to operate a supply chain with stochastic demands. The experimental scenario consists of a network with four echelons and two nodes per echelon. On each period the RL agent needs to decide the amount of raw material that suppliers need to supply and the amount of material that each node needs to send to the next nodes in the tier (using this approach, inventory levels are indirectly defined). The goal is to meet uncertain customer demands attended by the retailers and minimize all involved costs (supply, stock, transport, processing and penalization if demand is not met). The formalization of the problem as MDP is a contribution of our work; the decisions taken by the RL agent are mapped in a continuous space instead of using aggregate levels, as is usual in the literature. To the best of our knowledge, this is the first work that uses a Deep RL technique for a multi-echelon supply chain with more than one node per echelon, and therefore to use such large state and action spaces. Another contribution is to solve the problem of that size without limit the possible decisions of the agent, by using continuous action space instead of the usual approach of discretized aggregation levels.

In order to verify the quality and robustness of PPO2 algorithm used on the proposed problem the experimental methodology was followed by doing hyperparameter tuning and multiple training with different random seeds. A Non-Linear Programming model is presented and a related LP model, considering expected mean demand, is used to build a baseline agent. The actions of the LP agent are built from the solution of the LP model. PPO2 agent achieves slightly better results in terms of total operating costs (mainly due to lower amount of unmet demands) with low variance across the different seeds, demonstrating it is a competitive approach to solve this kind of problem.

In future works we intend to use different scenarios, like seasonal demands and costs variations. Another planned extension is to use other Deep RL algorithms in order to verify which is the most appropriate technique for the supply chain problem. Other possible path is to use stochastic programming approach to solve the NLP model and use it as a baseline for the RL techniques.

References

1. Brockman, G., et al.: Openai gym (2016)
2. Chaharsooghi, S.K., Heydari, J., Zegordi, S.H.: A reinforcement learning model for supply chain ordering management: an application to the beer game. Dec. Supp. Syst. **45**(4), 949–959 (2008). https://doi.org/10.1016/j.dss.2008.03.007
3. Giannoccaro, I., Pontrandolfo, P.: Inventory management in supply chains: a reinforcement learning approach. Int. J. Prod. Econ. **78**(2), 153–161 (2002). https://doi.org/10.1016/S0925-5273(00)00156-0
4. Gijsbrechts, J., Boute, R.N., Van Mieghem, J.A., Zhang, D.: Can deep reinforcement learning improve inventory management? performance on dual sourcing, lost sales and multi-echelon problems (2019). https://doi.org/10.2139/ssrn.3302881
5. Hill, A., et al.: Stable baselines. https://github.com/hill-a/stable-baselines
6. Hutse, V.: Reinforcement Learning for Inventory Optimisation in multi-echelon supply chains. Master in business engineering, Ghent University (2019)
7. Kemmer, L., von Kleist, H., de Rochebouët, D., Tziortziotis, N., Read, J.: Reinforcement learning for supply chain optimization. In: European Workshop on Reinforcement Learning, vol. 14 (2018)
8. Laumanns, M., Woerner, S.: Multi-echelon supply chain optimization: methods and application examples. In: Póvoa, A.P.B., Corominas, A., de Miranda, J.L. (eds.) Optimization and Decision Support Systems for Supply Chains, pp. 131–138. Springer, Cham (2017). https://doi.org/10.1007/978-3-319-42421-7_9
9. Mortazavi, A., Arshadi Khamseh, A., Azimi, P.: Designing of an intelligent self-adaptive model for supply chain ordering management system. Eng. Appl. Artif. Intell **37**, 207–220 (2015)
10. OpenAI Baselines: Blog. https://openai.com/blog/openai-baselines-ppo/. Accessed 23 May 2020
11. Oroojlooyjadid, A.: Applications of Machine Learning in Supply Chains. Ph.D. thesis, Lehigh University (2019). https://preserve.lehigh.edu/etd/4364

12. Peng, Z., Zhang, Y., Feng, Y., Zhang, T., Wu, Z., Su, H.: Deep reinforcement learning approach for capacitated supply chain optimization under demand uncertainty. In: 2019 Chinese Automation Congress (CAC), pp. 3512–3517 (2019). https://doi.org/10.1109/CAC48633.2019.8997498
13. Raffin, A.: Rl baselines zoo (2018). https://github.com/araffin/rl-baselines-zoo
14. Schulman, J., Wolski, F., Dhariwal, P., Radford, A., Klimov, O.: Proximal policy optimization algorithms. arXiv preprint arXiv:1707.06347 (2017)
15. Sutton, R.S., Barto, A.G.: Reinforcement Learning: An Introduction. MIT Press, Cambridge (2018)

The Multi-period Petrol Station Replenishment Problem: Formulation and Solution Methods

Luke Boers[1], Bilge Atasoy[1(✉)], Gonçalo Correia[2], and Rudy R. Negenborn[1]

[1] Department of Maritime and Transport Technology,
Delft University of Technology, Delft, The Netherlands
lukeboers@gmail.com, {b.atasoy,r.r.negenborn}@tudelft.nl
[2] Department of Transport and Planning, Delft University of Technology,
Delft, The Netherlands
g.correia@tudelft.nl

Abstract. We present a "rich" Petrol Station Replenishment Problem (PSRP) with real-life characteristics that represents the complexities involved in actual operations. The planning is optimised over multiple days and therefore, the new variant can be classified as the Multi-Period Petrol Station Replenishment Problem (MP-PSRP). A Mixed Integer Linear Programming (MILP) formulation is developed and a decomposition heuristic is proposed as a solution algorithm, which is evaluated with a case study from a real-life petrol distributor in Denmark. To determine delivery quantities, the heuristic uses the newly introduced *simultaneous dry run* inventory policy. A procedure is applied to improve the initial solution. A commercial solver is able to find feasible solutions only for instances with up to 20 stations and 7 days for the MILP model where optimality is guaranteed for instances up to 10 stations and 5 days. The heuristic on the other hand provides feasible solutions for the full case study of 59 stations and 14 days, within a time limit of 2 h.

Keywords: Petrol Station Replenishment · Inventory routing · Simultaneous dry run inventory policy · Decomposition heuristic

1 Introduction

In this paper, we develop a variant of the Petrol Station Replenishment Problem (PSRP), that addresses the optimisation of the distribution of several petroleum products to a set of petrol stations over a given planning horizon. The products, stored in underground tanks, are delivered to petrol stations using a heterogeneous fleet of vehicles with multiple compartments. The vehicles are assumed to be equipped with flow meters, that allow to split the fuel in a compartment over multiple stations. Delivery amount is limited by the available capacity of a storage tank at a station and the capacity of vehicles. The aim is to determine the optimal route for the vehicles in order to minimize total travel distance. Figure 1 shows a schematic representation of the problem.

© Springer Nature Switzerland AG 2020
E. Lalla-Ruiz et al. (Eds.): ICCL 2020, LNCS 12433, pp. 600–615, 2020.
https://doi.org/10.1007/978-3-030-59747-4_39

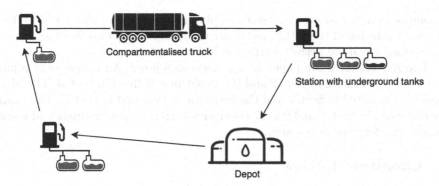

Fig. 1. A vehicle trip to multiple stations with different number of underground tanks

As the stations do not have to be replenished every day, the considered problem is solved over multiple days. The newly formulated problem can be classified as the Multi-Period Petrol Station Replenishment Problem (MP-PSRP). To decide when a station needs to be replenished the inventory levels at the stations are assumed to be known by the supplier. The supplier makes then, per time period, the following decisions:

- When stations are visited and which stations are combined into a trip (i.e., the routing decision for vehicles)
- Which vehicles are used to perform the trips
- The quantities per product that are transported to each station
- Which compartments are used to deliver the fuel
- For each trip the time a vehicle leaves and returns to the depot

These decisions comprise both inventory and routing decisions. Handling them simultaneously with Inventory Routing Problems (IRP) leads to more efficient operations since inventory and routing decisions are interrelated and these two factors are the main cost drivers of petroleum supply chain costs [9,23]. For a comprehensive review of IRP we refer to [7]. Moreover, the problem in this paper relates to vehicle routing problems with multiple compartments due to the nature of the problem and we refer to [13] for a review.

Delivery quantities are set sufficiently high to prevent stock out of a product at a station. The daily demand of a product at a station is given by a deterministic forecast. However, in the real-life situation, the fuel consumption is not known beforehand. In this research, a safety stock level set to at least the average daily demand is used to cope with this uncertainty. The daily planning is usually made over night, with the latest available inventory levels. The safety stock reduces the risk of running out of a product, regardless of the time of delivery.

In this paper, a Mixed Integer Linear Programming (MILP) model is proposed to formulate the problem. Due to the complexity of the problem, solutions for real-life size situations cannot be found by an exact approach. Therefore, a decomposition heuristic is proposed as a planning method for this problem. Both the exact solution of the MILP and heuristic approach are evaluated with a case study from a real-life petrol distributor in Denmark.

The remainder of the paper is organised as follows. An overview of related literature is presented in Sect. 2 and the problem is defined in Sect. 3. The MILP model is presented in Sect. 4 and the heuristic is provided in Sect. 5. The results are discussed in Sect. 6 and Sect. 7 concludes with the main findings and recommendations for further research.

2   Literature Review

The PSRP has received substantial attention in the literature over the last decades, after the problem was formulated for the first time by [5]. A comprehensive overview of the history of the PSRP is provided by [4,11]. The authors of [10] developed an exact algorithm for the single day PSRP, where the number of stops per trip was limited to two. The problem is extended to multiple days by [12], that presented a MILP model with the objective to minimise costs with a penalty for overtime use of vehicles. In [19], the authors defined a MILP model for the PSRP which minimises both inventory and routing costs over multiple days. The number of stations that can be visited in a trip is limited to three and a station cannot be visited by more than one vehicle during a time period. Traditionally, the PSRP has been solved over a single day time span mainly because of the complexity of the problem. Several researchers have, however, shown that solving the problem over multiple days leads to more efficient solutions [1].

In [20], a Variable Neighbourhood Search (VNS) heuristic is proposed with a shaking procedure based on shifting deliveries between days in the planning horizon with a homogeneous fleet of vehicles. [23] also used a homogeneous fleet of compartmentalised vehicles to distribute fuel and formulated the problem as a MILP with the objective to minimise both inventory and routing costs.

A variant of the PSRP with a homogeneous fleet is proposed in [16]. The stations are visited after a minimum delivery quantity can be delivered, which is set to improve vehicle utilisation. The problem is solved with a Tabu search algorithm that is proven to find near-optimal solutions. The lower bounds of a reasonable sized problem are determined with Lagrangian relaxation. A variant of the PSRP with multiple compartments and time windows is presented by [4]. The time windows represent the scheduling horizon for each vehicle and there are two types of vehicles with different compartment sizes. The problem is solved using commercial solvers for the MILP formulation and a heuristic.

A variant of the Vehicle Routing Problem with Time Windows (VRPTW) is the problem with multiple use of vehicles, where each vehicle can perform multiple trips per time period. This problem is studied in [3] with a homogeneous fleet of capacitated vehicles. The researchers presented a MILP model and solved the problem using a branch-and-price algorithm. Another MILP model for a single day VRPTW is presented by [17].

The contribution of this paper is twofold: (i) the design of a decomposition heuristic with a new inventory policy called *simultaneous dry run concept*, which aims to minimise the number of visits to a station considering the delivery quantities across all tanks at that station, and (ii) the consideration of a unique combination of real-life characteristics that makes the problem "rich" as later highlighted in Table 1. Therefore, in the remainder of this section, we present further literature related to decomposition heuristics and real-life characteristics in routing problems.

2.1 Decomposition Heuristics

The combination of characteristics makes the considered variant of the MP-PSRP NP-hard, since it is already shown to be an NP-hard problem even for simpler problems [1,12,16,23]. An effective method to solve such complex problems is decomposition heuristics that can be considered under the umbrella of matheuristics. Matheuristics is a category of heuristics that divides a problem into sub problems, of which at least one sub problem is a MILP. Another class of matheuristics are improvement heuristics, where MILP models are used to improve a solution [2]. The heuristic presented in this research is a decomposition heuristic, based on decomposing the decision process of the supplier.

In [22], a decomposition heuristic is proposed for the PSRP, in which inventory was not considered. The problem was decomposed into assignment, routing and improvement procedures. A local search technique based on switching any two stations between service days was used as the improvement procedure. The authors of [9] solved an IRP by decomposing the decision process of the vendor into a three-phase heuristic focusing on the decisions of replenishment plan, delivery sequence and which routes to drive, respectively. Inventory management has also been included by [10], who decomposed the problem in a Tank Truck Loading Problem (TTLP) and a routing problem. Similar models are used by [12], where the planning is constructed for each day of the planning horizon.

The distinction of our decomposition heuristic is the incorporated *simultaneous dry run* inventory policy to determine delivery quantities, which are set in a way that limits the number of visits to a station. Furthermore, petrol products are transported by compartmentalised vehicles. These vehicles are often assumed not to be equipped with flow meters [4,10,12,17,20,23]. The absence of flow meters limits the flexibility in utilisation of vehicles, since flow meters allow to split the load from one compartment over multiple stations [8]. The case studied in this research assumes the availability of flow meters, which allows splitting loads.

2.2 Real-Life Case Studies

Several researchers developed models to solve real-life cases. In [18], the distribution of petrol for a network in Hong Kong is improved by applying the Vendor-Managed Inventory (VMI) concept. The proposed approach helped the company to increase the delivery volume and decrease driver costs. The authors of [22] used real-life cases to evaluate the performance of the solution methods to solve the PSRP. Compared to a planning made by a human operator, a maximum saving of 17.7% was achieved. In [21], the PSRP is investigated for a distributor of petroleum products in Oman. A MILP model is presented that eventually can be used to prepare a bid for auctions of transportation procurement.

A large petroleum company in China is considered by [16]. The distribution of petroleum products in provinces was modelled as an IRP and a heuristic is developed that is shown to provide near-optimal solutions. In [15], the authors considered the petrol distribution in the United States. A MILP model was used to determine the optimal supply chain design, while considering multi-modal transportation methods when determining locations for the facilities. The case of distribution for an Algerian petroleum company has been evaluated by [4], with a model for the PSRP with compartmentalised vehicles and time windows. The method proposed by the authors outperformed the solution created by the company, in terms of number of vehicles and total travel distance.

The case studies mentioned underline the growing interest in "richer" models, what promises even more effective methods for the future. For the definition of "rich" routing problems we refer to the survey by [6] where they mention several characteristics of VRP variants that lead to this rich category. As we consider real-life constraints related to time and stations, dynamism, heterogeneous fleet, and have linkage between inventory and routing decisions our paper fits to this concept. An overview of the problem characteristics considered in this research in reference to the most relevant literature is shown by Table 1. With this positioning, it is clear that our paper addresses a problem with a unique combination of characteristics that is not done before to the best of authors' knowledge.

Table 1. Positioning of our work in the literature. TH: Time Horizon S: Single-period, M: Multi-period, ST: Single Trip, MT: Multiple Trip, MP: Multi-Product, VU: Vehicle Use, VF: Vehicle Fleet, Comp.: Compartments, SL: Split Loads, HO: Homogeneous, HE: Heterogeneous, SR: Station Restrictions, Time Con.: Time constraints

Paper	IRP	Stops/trip	TH	MP	VU	VF	Comp.	SL	Time Con.	SR
Al-Hinai and Triki [1]		Unlimited	M	✓	ST	HE	✓			
Azi et al. [3]		Unlimited	S		MT	HO		✓	✓	
Benantar et al. [4]		Unlimited	S	✓	ST	HE	✓		✓	✓
Coelho and Laporte [8]	✓	Unlimited	M	✓	ST	HE	✓	✓		
Cornillier et al. [12]	✓	Max. 2	M	✓	MT	HE	✓		✓	
Li et al. [16]	✓	Unlimited	S		SU	HO			✓	
Macedo et al. [17]		Unlimited	S		MT	HO		✓	✓	
Popović et al. [20]	✓	Max. 3	M	✓	ST	HO	✓			
Vidović [23]	✓	Max. 4	M	✓	ST	HO	✓			
This research	✓	Unlimited	M	✓	MT	HE	✓	✓	✓	✓

3   Problem Definition

Let $G = (V, A)$ be a complete directed graph, where $V = (0, 1, ..., n)$ is a set of nodes and $A = \{(i, j) : i, j \in V\}$ is the set of arcs. Each arc (i, j) is associated with a travel distance c_{ij} and a travel time t_{ij}. The stations are represented by nodes $N = (1, ..., n)$ and the depot is given as node 0 or $n + 1$, depending on whether it is the initial or final node in a trip. Each node has a fixed service time st_i. Set $T = (1, ..., n)$ defines the time periods (days) in the planning horizon.

Set R contains the trips that can be driven by vehicles, with $|R|$ chosen large enough to enable the maximum number of trips a vehicle can perform during a daily work schedule. The trip indices are used in increasing order, which means that $r' > r$ if a vehicle performs trip r' after trip r.

The stations are directly associated with nodes and have one or multiple underground tanks that store one type of product p. Set P contains all products, which are stored at the depot. Each underground tank has a maximum capacity C_i^p a safety stock IS_i^p and an initial inventory level at the start of the planning horizon I_{i0}^p. D_{it}^p gives the demand for each product at each station per day t.

Fuel is transported by a heterogeneous fleet of vehicles. Each vehicle $k \in K$ has multiple fuel compartments $f \in F_k$ with maximum capacity Q^{kf}. Station restrictions are included in the model by variable δ_i^k, which is 1 if station i can be visited by vehicle k. Operating hours of vehicles are represented by a time window $[a_t^k, b_t^k]$, where a_t^k is the start and b_t^k the end time for vehicle k during day t. M is an arbitrary large constant that is used to ensure a linear formulation.

Furthermore, the following assumptions are made:

- There is enough inventory at the depot to fulfil the replenishment plan.
- Inventory levels at stations are known by the supplier.
- Demand is considered as deterministic, based on a forecast. To deal with stochasticity and potential stock out, a safety stock level is determined for each tank at each station.
- A station can have only one underground tank per product.
- To transport the petrol products, a heterogeneous fleet of vehicles (equipped with flow meters) is used with compartments of known size.
- All vehicles are assumed to drive with the same speed, which means that they have the same travel time, given the same distance.
- Some vehicles cannot visit each station, due to spatial restrictions.
- Stations can be visited multiple times a day and 24/7, because it is assumed that a truck can always deliver the petrol products at the station.
- Vehicles run within the operating hours, i.e., work schedules of drivers.

4 Mathematical Formulation

The problem is formulated as an MILP. Let binary variable x_{ijrt}^k be 1 if and only if vehicle k drives arc (i, j) in trip r during day t. Binary variable y_{rt}^k is 1 if vehicle k drives trip r during day t. The same holds for binary variable z_{irt}^k, where i is added to define that station i is visited by vehicle k. If binary variable w_{rt}^{kfp} is 1, product p is loaded into compartment f of vehicle k during trip r on day t. If trip r' is driven after trip r by vehicle k during day t, binary variable $u_{rr't}^k$ is set to 1. Variable q_{irt}^{kfp} is used for the delivery quantity of product p, loaded in compartment f of vehicle k and delivered to location i during trip r

on day t. S_{irt}^k is the time vehicle k can start the service at station i during trip r on day t and I_{it}^p represents the inventory level of product p at station i at the end of day t. The problem can then be formulated as follows:

$$\min \sum_{t \in T} \sum_{r \in R} \sum_{k \in K} \sum_{(i,j) \in A} c_{ij}\, x_{ijrt}^k \tag{1}$$

Subject to

$$I_{it}^p \geq IS_i^p \qquad \forall p \in P, \forall n \in N, \forall t \in T \tag{2}$$

$$I_{i,t-1}^p + \sum_{r \in R} \sum_{k \in K} \sum_{f \in F_k} q_{irt}^{kfp} \leq C_i^p \qquad \forall p \in P, \forall i \in N, \forall t \in T \tag{3}$$

$$I_{it}^p = I_{i,t-1}^p + \sum_{r \in R} \sum_{k \in K} \sum_{f \in F_k} q_{irt}^{kfp} - D_{it}^p \qquad \forall p \in P, \forall i \in N, \forall t \in T \tag{4}$$

$$z_{irt}^k \leq \delta_i^k \qquad \forall k \in K, \forall i \in N, \forall r \in R, \forall t \in T \tag{5}$$

$$\sum_{j \in V} x_{0jrt}^k = 1 \qquad \forall k \in K, \forall r \in R, \forall t \in T \tag{6}$$

$$\sum_{i \in V} x_{ijrt}^k - \sum_{i \in V} x_{jirt}^k = 0 \qquad \forall k \in K, \forall j \in V, \forall r \in R, \forall t \in T \tag{7}$$

$$z_{irt}^k = \sum_{j \in V} x_{ijrt}^k \qquad \forall k \in K, \forall i \in N, \forall r \in R, \forall t \in T \tag{8}$$

$$q_{irt}^{kfp} \leq M\, z_{irt}^k \qquad \forall k \in K, \forall p \in P, \forall f \in F_k, \forall i \in N, \forall r \in R, \forall t \in T \tag{9}$$

$$\sum_{i \in N} q_{irt}^{kfp} \leq w_{rt}^{kfp} Q^{kf} \qquad \forall k \in K, \forall f \in F_k, \forall p \in P, \forall r \in R, \forall t \in T \tag{10}$$

$$\sum_{p \in P} w_{rt}^{kfp} \leq 1 \qquad \forall k \in K, \forall f \in F_k, \forall r \in R, \forall t \in T \tag{11}$$

$$S_{irt}^k \geq a_t^k \qquad \forall k \in K, \forall i \in V, \forall r \in R, \forall t \in T \tag{12}$$

$$S_{irt}^k \leq b_t^k \qquad \forall k \in K, \forall i \in V, \forall r \in R, \forall t \in T \tag{13}$$

$$S^k_{irt} + t_{ij} + st_i - M(1 - x^k_{ijrt}) \leq S^k_{jrt}$$
$$\forall k \in K, \forall (i,j) \in A, \forall r \in R, \forall t \in T \quad (14)$$

$$S^k_{0r't} + M(1 - u^k_{rr't}) \geq S^k_{n+1,rt} \qquad \forall r, r' \in R, r < r', \forall k \in K, \forall t \in T \quad (15)$$

$$\sum_{r \in R} \sum_{r' \in R | r' > r} u^k_{rr't} \geq \sum_{r \in R} y^k_{rt} - 1 \qquad \forall k \in K, \forall t \in T \quad (16)$$

$$z^k_{irt} \leq y^k_{rt} \qquad \forall k \in K, \forall i \in N, \forall r \in R, \forall t \in T \quad (17)$$

$$x^k_{ijrt} \in \{0,1\} \qquad \forall k \in K, \forall i,j \in V, \forall r \in R, \forall t \in T \quad (18)$$

$$y^k_{rt} \in \{0,1\} \qquad \forall k \in K, \forall r \in R, \forall t \in T \quad (19)$$

$$z^k_{irt} \in \{0,1\} \qquad \forall k \in K, \forall i \in N, \forall r \in R, \forall t \in T \quad (20)$$

$$w^{kfp}_{rt} \in \{0,1\} \qquad \forall k \in K, \forall f \in F_k, \forall p \in P, \forall r \in R, \forall t \in T \quad (21)$$

$$u^k_{rr't} \in \{0,1\} \qquad \forall k \in K, \forall r, r' \in R, r < r', r' = r+1, \forall t \in T \quad (22)$$

$$q^{kfp}_{irt} \geq 0 \qquad \forall k \in K, \forall f \in F_k, \forall p \in P, \forall i \in V, \forall r \in R, \forall t \in T \quad (23)$$

$$S^k_{irt} \geq 0 \qquad \forall k \in K, \forall i \in V, \forall r \in R, \forall t \in T \quad (24)$$

$$I^p_{it} \geq 0 \qquad \forall p \in P, \forall i \in N, \forall t \in T \quad (25)$$

The objective function (1) minimises the total number of kilometres driven by all vehicles during the entire time horizon. Constraints (2) and (3) ensure that inventory levels for fuel in underground tanks stay above the safety stock level and below the maximum capacity. Constraints (4) keep track of the daily inventory level, taking into account the demand and deliveries. Station restrictions are imposed by constraints (5), which means that some vehicles cannot access all stations. Constraints (6) ensure that all vehicles start and end at the depot. Constraints (7) represent the flow conservation constraints. Constraints (8) and (9) link x and q variables to z, such that a vehicle can only drive to a station and deliver fuel when it is visited by that vehicle on a certain day. Constraints (10) ensure that compartment capacities are respected and constraints (11) make sure that only a single product is loaded into a compartment, if any.

Constraints (12–13) ensure that operating hours of the vehicles are respected. Constraints (14) ensure the consistency of start times at different stations based on the driving and service times. Constraints (15–17) make sure that, in case a vehicle performs multiple trips during a time period, these trips are driven consecutively. Lastly, x, y, z, w and u are defined as binary variables by (18)–(22) and constraints (19) maintain nonnegativity.

5   Heuristic Solution Method

We investigated two solution methods: (i) using an exact solver, Gurobi Optimizer version 8.1.1 [14], for MILP that is implemented in Python, (ii) a decomposition heuristic. In this section we describe the decomposition heuristic.

5.1   Decomposition Heuristic

A decomposition heuristic, based on decomposing the decision process of the supplier, is considered to solve the rich variant of the PSRP for real-life size instances. To create the planning for a single day, the decision process is decomposed into five phases. Since the planning for a certain day affects the inventory levels of the next day, a dynamic programming approach is required to create the planning day by day. After each iteration, inventory levels are adjusted with the delivery quantities. An overview of the heuristic procedure is shown in Fig. 2.

To improve the initial solution created by the decomposition heuristic, an improvement procedure is proposed (discussed in Sect. 5.2). We now discuss the five phases considered for the decomposition, which are used to generate the planning for a single day. This process is repeated for each day in the time horizon, that is T_e days, and the day in the considered iteration is noted as t_c.

Phase 1 - Order Generation. An order is generated for each underground tank and the expected day of depletion is determined, by deducting the daily demand from the inventory level. The day of depletion is the time period the inventory level is expected to drop below the safety stock level. An order is identified by the station, product and depletion day, since a station is assumed to have maximum one tank per product. The resulting list contains all underground tanks that are expected to deplete during the remainder of the considered time horizon $[t_c, T_e]$.

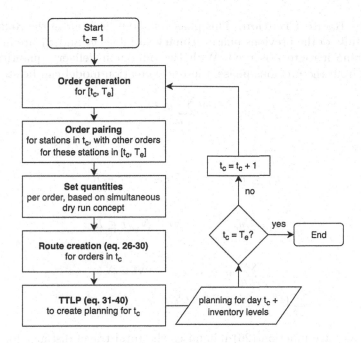

Fig. 2. Heuristic procedure, with T_e days in time horizon

Phase 2 - Order Pairing. The resulting list from phase 1 is filtered on underground tanks that deplete during the day for which the planning is generated t_c. Orders for the same stations as on this filtered list, with an expected depletion day in the future, are also added to the resulting list of phase 2. The output is a list of stations, with a set of tanks per station that are expected to deplete during t_c or a future time period.

Phase 3 - Set Quantities. Minimum and maximum delivery quantities are set according to the *simultaneous dry run* inventory policy, which we will now introduce. The maximum delivery quantity is set to the remaining tank's capacity. Minimum delivery quantities are set to a level that ensures the next delivery to a station to be postponed for as long as possible. When one of the tanks at a station depletes, the station needs to be visited. Postponing the next delivery is done by filling the tank with the highest consumption rate to the maximum, since this tank depletes the fastest. For the other tanks at the same station, the minimum delivery quantity is set to the expected sales during the same time that the tank with the highest consumption rate depletes again. This process, shown by Fig. 3, ensures that a station is visited as least as possible.

Phase 4 - Route Creation. This phase is about generating the routes based on the results of the previous phases. Binary variables y_r and z_{ir} are introduced to determine if route r is used. With the minimum delivery quantity $q^p_{ir,min}$ following from the previous phase, the route creation model can be stated as:

$$\min \sum_{r \in R} y_r\, c_r \tag{26}$$

Subject to

$$z_{ir} \leq x_{ir} \qquad \forall i \in N, \forall r \in R \tag{27}$$

$$z_{ir} \leq y_r \qquad \forall i \in N, \forall r \in R \tag{28}$$

$$\sum_{r \in R} z_{ir} = 1 \qquad \forall i \in N \tag{29}$$

$$\sum_{i \in N} (q^p_{ir,min} z_{ir}) \leq 0.9\, C_{k,min} \qquad \forall r \in R \tag{30}$$

The objective function (26) minimises the total travel distance for the considered time period. Constraints (27) make the choice to visit station i during route r only possible when the station is included in the predetermined route. Constraints (28) link variables y and z. Constraints (29) are used to ensure that each station is visited once. Constraints (30) limit the sum of the minimum delivery quantities to 90% of the total capacity of the largest vehicle. 90% of the capacity is used as maximum based on practical experience since different products need to be loaded into different compartments and a higher value may hinder feasibility, i.e., the next phase of the heuristic may not be able to find feasible solutions.

Phase 5 - Tank Truck Loading. In the final phase, routes are assigned to trucks while maximising vehicle utilisation for an efficient use of the vehicles. A variant of the Tank Truck Loading Problem (TTLP) by Cornillier et al. [10], is developed to execute this assignment procedure. Binary variable y^k_r is introduced to determine which vehicle k drives a route r and w^{kfp}_r is introduced to set in which compartment product p is loaded. The model is given as:

$$\max \sum_{r \in R} \sum_{i \in N} \sum_{k \in K} \sum_{f \in F} \sum_{p \in P} q^{kfp}_{ir} \tag{31}$$

Subject to

$$\sum_{k \in K} \sum_{f \in F} q_{ir}^{kfp} \geq q_{ir,min}^{p} \qquad \forall p \in P, \forall i \in N, \forall r \in R \qquad (32)$$

$$\sum_{k \in K} \sum_{f \in F} q_{ir}^{kfp} \leq q_{ir,max}^{p} \qquad \forall p \in P, \forall i \in N, \forall r \in R \qquad (33)$$

$$\sum_{p \in P} \sum_{f \in F} q_{ir}^{kfp} \leq M \, \delta_{i}^{k} \qquad \forall i \in N, \forall k \in K \forall r \in R \qquad (34)$$

$$\sum_{i \in N} q_{ir}^{kfp} \leq w_{r}^{kfp} Q^{kf} \qquad \forall k \in K, \forall f \in F, \forall p \in P, \forall r \in R \qquad (35)$$

$$\sum_{p \in P} w_{r}^{kfp} \leq 1 \qquad \forall k \in K, \forall f \in F, \forall r \in R \qquad (36)$$

$$\sum_{k \in K} y_{r}^{k} = 1 \qquad \forall r \in R \qquad (37)$$

$$\sum_{r \in R} (y_{r}^{k} \, t_{r}) \leq b^{k} - a^{k} \qquad \forall k \in K \qquad (38)$$

$$w_{r}^{kfp} \leq y_{r}^{k} \qquad \forall k \in K, \forall f \in F, \forall p \in P, \forall r \in R \qquad (39)$$

$$q_{ir}^{kfp} \geq 0 \qquad \forall k \in K, \forall f \in F, \forall p \in P, \forall r \in R \qquad (40)$$

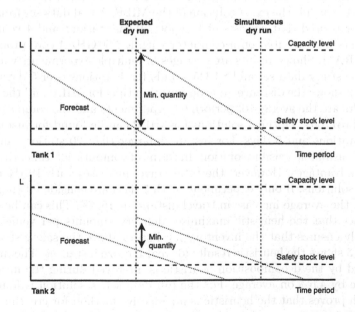

Fig. 3. Visualisation of the simultaneous dry run inventory policy. Shown graphs represent the inventory levels for two tanks at the same station. Minimum delivery quantities are set to ensure simultaneous dry run in the future.

The objective function (31) maximises the total delivered quantity, to ensure efficient vehicle utilisation. Constraints (32–33) set the delivery quantity to be within the range previously determined by the minimum and maximum delivery quantities. Constraints (34) implement station restrictions and constraints (35) limit the delivery quantity per compartment to its capacity. The fact that a compartment can only be filled with one type of product is implemented with constraints (36). Constraints (37) ensure that each route is driven by a vehicle exactly once and constraints (38) limit the duration of all routes driven by a vehicle by the driver schedule. Lastly, constraints (39) link variables w and y.

5.2   Improvement Procedure

For the initial solution, the decision to visit a station is based on the depletion day. This means that routing is not optimised over the entire time horizon and that the stations can not be visited later. To improve the initial solution, an improvement procedure is developed with solution candidates that are based on visiting stations one time period earlier. To evaluate if the solution improves, the planning is recreated for the remaining days. Since this is an extensive process, the number of candidates is limited to the number of station visits.

6   Computational Results

The performance of the decomposition heuristic is evaluated in reference to the benchmark which is the exact solution of the MILP. A real data set from a petrol distributor is used that consists of 1 depot, 59 gas stations and 4 vehicles. The experiments are executed on a computer with a 3.50 GHz 4-core processor and 32 GB of RAM. Shown results are averages of multiple experiments with subsets of the case study data set and S4-D5 stands for 4 stations over 5 days.

Table 2 shows the distance and computation time for MILP and the heuristic. The results are the average of performed experiments and the computation time is limited to 7200 s. Optimal solutions for MILP can be found for instances with up to 8 stations and 5 days. For instances larger than 20 stations and 7 days, there is no available feasible solution. In terms of computation time, the heuristic provides advantages. However, the total travel increases with 19.1% compared to MILP solutions. If only experiments with 7 days are considered (representing practice), the average increase in travel distance is 15.6%. This can be explained by the fact that the heuristic maximises delivery amounts per vehicle and the MILP only ensures that the inventory level stays above the safety stock level.

Table 3 shows the heuristic results for real-life size instances. The initial solution found by the decomposition heuristic is improved during the improvement procedure by 4.6% on average. For the full data set, a solution is found within 2 h, which proves that the heuristic is an effective method for creating solutions for real-life instances.

As a validation of the heuristic, we also compared the results for 59 stations across 14 days to the results from the actual planning at the petrol distributor.

Table 2. Benchmark comparison. CT: computation time, Δ: difference in distance relative to MILP, *: not optimal, **: no feasible solution

Experiment	MILP		Heuristic		
	Distance (km)	CT (s)	Distance (km)	Δ	CT (s)
S4-D5	267	2	304	13.8%	2
S4-D7	480	469	550	14.6%	4
S6-D5	321	544	413	28.8%	3
S6-D7	582*	7200	690	18.5%	6
S8-D5	399	1955	501	25.5%	5
S8-D7	753*	7200	849	12.7%	8
S10-D5	454*	7200	581	28.1%	6
S10-D7	873*	7200	984	12.7%	14
S12-D5	478*	7200	606	26.8%	8
S12-D7	972*	7200	1063	9.4%	18
S20-D7	1376*	7200	1642	19.3%	39
S30-D7	–**	–	2281	–	79
Average				**19.1%**	

Table 3. Computational results for larger instances. CT: computation time, InSol, FinSol: initial and final solution.

Experiment	InSol (km)	FinSol (km)	Δ	CT InSol (s)	CT FinSol (s)
S20-D14	3931	3670	−6.6%	2	162
S30-D14	5588	5365	−4.0%	4	589
S40-D14	6965	6735	−3.3%	12	727
S50-D14	10267	9813	−4.4%	29	3747
S59-D14	11426	10877	−4.8%	14	5103

As this was not straightforward to analyse in detail due to differences in the algorithmic approach we can only mention indications for the reduction in travel distance (around 12%) and average number of stops per trip (around 26%). This shows that the proposed approach has a potential to be used in practice.

7   Conclusions and Future Research

We presented planning methods for the MP-PSRP with real-life characteristics and increased complexity. In order to deal with the increased computational complexity, a heuristic is developed, which is a combination of a decomposition heuristic and an improvement procedure. The decomposition heuristic uses the newly introduced *simultaneous dry run* inventory policy to determine maximum and minimum delivery quantities. The models have been tested with a data set based on the real-life situation for a petrol distribution company. It is found that no feasible solution is available for MILP within the two hour time limit for instances larger than 20 stations and 7 days. The heuristic can create the planning for the full case study with 59 stations over 14 days and compared to the actual planning used at the company shows a potential of reducing the travel distance. Nevertheless, the performance of the heuristic algorithm needs improvements as small size instances show gaps compared to the MILP solution.

Future research in this area is encouraged especially in the efficient solution algorithm development. The value of the *simultaneous dry run* inventory policy could be further explored by considering the exact time of delivery instead of the day of delivery. This would allow to also replenish the quantity of fuel that has already been sold during the day till the moment of delivery. Furthermore, the decomposition of the problem into days might be hindering the potential of our heuristic for a multi-period setting. Therefore, further research into different decomposition approaches might be promising. Another direction for further research could be to simulate deliveries with unexpected events, to determine the effect of uncertainty on the distribution performance.

Acknowledgements. We are grateful for the support of AMCS B.V. by providing the case study data, especially Jelmer Brandt and Kristian Milo Hauge with valuable contributions.

References

1. Al-Hinai, N., Triki, C.: A two-level evolutionary algorithm for solving the petrol station replenishment problem with periodicity constraints and service choice. Ann. Oper. Res. **286**(1), 325–350 (2018)
2. Archetti, C., Speranza, M.G.: A survey on matheuristics for routing problems. EURO J. Comput. Optim. **2**(4), 223–246 (2014)
3. Azi, N., Gendreau, M., Potvin, J.Y.: An exact algorithm for a vehicle routing problem with time windows and multiple use of vehicles. Eur. J. Oper. Res. **202**(3), 756–763 (2010)
4. Benantar, A., Ouafi, R., Boukachour, J.: A petrol station replenishment problem: new variant and formulation. Logist. Res. **9**(1), 1–18 (2016)
5. Brown, G.G., Graves, G.W.: Real-time dispatch of petroleum tank trucks. Manag. Sci. **27**(1), 19–32 (1981)
6. Caceres-Cruz, J., Arias, P., Guimarans, D., Riera, D., Juan, A.: Rich vehicle routing problem: survey. ACM Comput. Surv. **47**(2), 1–28 (2014)
7. Coelho, L.C., Cordeau, J.F., Laporte, G.: Thirty years of inventory routing. Transp. Sci. **48**(1), 1–19 (2014)
8. Coelho, L.C., Laporte, G.: Classification, models and exact algorithms for multi-compartment delivery problems. Eur. J. Oper. Res. **242**(3), 854–864 (2015)
9. Cordeau, J.F., Laganà, D., Musmanno, R., Vocaturo, F.: A decomposition-based heuristic for the multiple-product inventory-routing problem. Comput. Oper. Res. **55**, 153–166 (2015)
10. Cornillier, F., Boctor, F.F., Laporte, G., Renaud, J.: An exact algorithm for the petrol station replenishment problem. J. Oper. Res. Soc. **59**(5), 607–615 (2007)

11. Cornillier, F., Boctor, F., Renaud, J.: Heuristics for the multi-depot petrol station replenishment problem with time windows. Eur. J. Oper. Res. **220**(2), 361–369 (2012)
12. Cornillier, F., Boctor, F.F., Laporte, G., Renaud, J.: A heuristic for the multi-period petrol station replenishment problem. Eur. J. Oper. Res. **191**(2), 295–305 (2008)
13. Derigs, U., Gottlieb, J., Kalkoff, J., Piesche, M., Rothlauf, F.: Vehicle routing with compartment: applications, modeling and heuristics. OR Spectr. **33**(4), 885–914 (2011)
14. LLC Gurobi Optimization: Gurobi Optimizer Reference Manual (2019). http://www.gurobi.com
15. Kazemi, Y., Szmerekovsky, J.: Modeling downstream petroleum supply chain: the importance of multi-mode transportation to strategic planning strategic planning. Transp. Res. Part E: Logist. Transp. Rev. **83**, 111–125 (2015)
16. Li, K., Chen, B., Sivakumar, A.I., Wu, Y.: An inventory-routing problem with the objective of travel time minimization. Eur. J. Oper. Res. **236**(3), 936–945 (2014)
17. Macedo, R., Alves, C., De Carvalho, J.M., Clautiaux, F., Hanafi, S.: Solving the vehicle routing problem with time windows and multiple routes exactly using a pseudo-polynomial model. Eur. J. Oper. Res. **214**(3), 536–545 (2011)
18. Ng, W.L., Leung, S.C., Lam, J.K., Pan, S.W.: Petrol delivery tanker assignment and routing: a case study in Hong Kong. J. Oper. Res. Soc. **59**(9), 1191–1200 (2008)
19. Popović, D., Bjelić, N., Radivojević, G.: Simulation approach to analyse deterministic IRP solution of the stochastic fuel delivery problem. Proc. Soc. Behav. Sci. **20**, 273–282 (2011)
20. Popović, D., Vidović, M., Radivojević, G.: Variable neighborhood search heuristic for the inventory routing problem in fuel delivery. Expert Syst. Appl. **39**(18), 13390–13398 (2012)
21. Triki, C., Al-hinai, N., Kaabachi, I., Krichen, S.: An optimization framework for combining the petroleum replenishment problem with the optimal bidding in combinatorial auctions. Int. J. Supply Oper. Manag. **3**(2), 1318–1331 (2016)
22. Triki, C.: Solution methods for the periodic petrol station. J. Eng. Res. **10**(2), 69–77 (2013)
23. Vidović, M., Popović, D., Ratković, B.: Mixed integer and heuristics model for the inventory routing problem in fuel delivery. Int. J. Prod. Econ. Part C **147**, 593–604 (2014)

Simulation Approach for Container Assignment Under Uncertainty

Wouter J. de Koning[1,2], Frank Phillipson[2](✉)(iD), and Irina Chiscop[2]

[1] Delft University of Technology, Delft, The Netherlands
[2] TNO, PO Box 96800, 2509 JE, The Hague, The Netherlands
frank.phillipson@tno.nl

Abstract. In this paper an online optimisation approach is proposed which can be used to find an appropriate combined schedule and container assignment in a Network Design Problem under uncertainty. For this, a simulation based approach on a multi-period time window is proposed, moving forward on the time window after each decision made, assuming that the status of the system is updated as soon as the stochastic and unknown elements become deterministic and known. This approach provides new insight and knowledge into synchromodal and multimodal planning problems. The results of the approach are compared to the results of three simpler online optimisation methods and to the solution of the offline approach where all information is known.

Keywords: Intermodal transport · Synchromodal transport · Online optimisation · Multiperiod time window · Simulation algorithm

1 Introduction

In recent years, a remarkable growth is noticeable in the number of containers that have to be transported from one place to another by different kinds of resources, e.g., trucks, trains and barges. A set of these resources linked together with the purpose of transporting freight (or people) from one place to another, is called a logistics network. A logistics network is usually run by a logistics service provider (LSP), who faces the problem of delivering the right amount of freight in the right place at the right time. Due to the ever-growing complexity of these networks, an LSP needs efficient tools to support his decisions in order to strive for the optimal network performance at minimal cost [10]. The decision making process could be classified into three levels: strategic, tactical and operational [4,19]. The operational level is concerned with short term decisions that need to be made by local management. The most important operational decisions relate to scheduling the transport and maintenance services, routing and dispatching of vehicles and allocating freight to transport modes.

In this work we look at the challenge faced by a Dutch LSP, responsible for the transportation of containers from the eastern part of the Netherlands to the port of Rotterdam and vice versa. Every day, multiple barges depart from the

E. Lalla-Ruiz et al. (Eds.): ICCL 2020, LNCS 12433, pp. 616–630, 2020.
https://doi.org/10.1007/978-3-030-59747-4_40

single inland terminal in the east to different deep-sea terminals within the port of Rotterdam. The orders arrive randomly in time at the planner, this being the first source of uncertainty. At each decision moment, a planner has to decide which containers to allocate to which barges and/or trucks. This decision has to be made in such a way that the network performance of the Dutch LSP is optimised over time. The planner needs to obtain a slot at each terminal the barge has to visit. The terminals within the Rotterdam region are controlled by other agents, who confirm the requested calls from the LSP with a delay of approximately half a day. Most of the time, these confirmed slots may deviate from the requested ones, giving the second source of uncertainty. This means that we have two elements of uncertainty in this problem: the requested appointment times that have to be confirmed and the orders (of containers to be shipped) that have not been announced yet. This online assignment problem under uncertainty falls under sychromodal transportation problems. The framework of [5] would summarise the problem as:

$$\overline{R}, [RD], [RDT] \mid \overline{D}, [D2R], \widehat{DRD}, \widehat{DDD} \mid \text{selfish}(1+) \mid \text{isolated}.$$

This problem has not been studied earlier. However, there exists work on related problems. The work of Rivera and Mes [17,18] also addresses future assignments. The authors formulate the container-to-mode assignment problem as a Markov Decision Process (MDP) and approximate the solution by means of Approximate Dynamic Programming (ADP). A future simulation approach in logistics can be found in [14], which is based on the general approach presented in [15,16]. To account for uncertain release times of the containers a simulation algorithm is used when making online decisions whether to assign a container to a barge or not. The general underlying problems are the Multi-Commodity Network Design Problem (MCNDP) [6,8,11] and Multi Commodity Minimum Cost Flow Problem (MCMCFP) [3,20], which disregard the stochastic nature of some of the problem's elements. The paper by Fragkos et al. [7] generalises the basic MCNDP to a multi-period setting, where demand for each commodity expands dynamically over a discrete time window. In the paper of Han et al. [9] a robust scenario approach is presented for the vehicle routing problem (VRP) with uncertain travel times. The work of Chiscop [2] also proposes a robust formulation, to be able to do simultaneous vehicle routing and container-to-mode assignment including uncertainty in the release times.

In this paper, in order to address the presence of uncertainty, a multi-period time window (MPTW) approach is introduced. This extends the traditional multi-commodity network design problems by introducing a multi-period time window setting. Although such multiperiod network design problems can provide useful input for strategic and tactical decisions, finding their optimal solution is computationally challenging. Our approach solves iteratively the planning problem, using a simulation approach, by moving forward on the MPTW after each decision made, assuming that the status of the system is updated as soon as the stochastic and unknown elements (i.e., orders) become deterministic and known, respectively, combining [7] and [14].

We attempt to obtain new insights and knowledge into synchromodal planning problems, including stochastic elements, by proposing a simulation based approach on a multi-period time window. To the best of our knowledge, this research is the first to address both vehicle routing (explicitly) and a container-to-mode assignment (implicitly), including uncertainty in the pick-up and delivery appointments, by generating potential future scenarios in order to obtain the best decision(s) that is resistant to change. The uncertainty element in our model is based on probability distributions, which has the benefits of incorporating distributional information and hence results in less moderate solutions than the classical robust optimisation approaches where probability distributions are ignored.

In Sect. 2 we present the problem and make some assumptions to create a computationally tractable mathematical model. Then in Sect. 3 we present our simulation approach for this problem. Sect. 4 presents some benchmark problems and the results for a case study. We end with some conclusions and ideas for further research.

2 Problem Description

We use a specific network structure in this paper. This network structure is relatively simple, however, it is close to the daily operations of a Dutch LSP. We assume three types of terminals in our problem, see Fig. 1: one inland terminal, T_{Origin} and one container terminal T_{Rot} in the Port of Rotterdam, both operated by the LSP and t deep-sea terminals $I = (T_1, T_2, ..., T_t)$, operated by other agents. Every day, multiple barges depart from T_{Origin} to different deep-sea terminals within the port of Rotterdam. We consider the transportation of freight from (i) T_{Origin} to multiple deep-sea terminals, denoted by outland orders, and from (ii) deep-sea terminals back to T_{Origin}, denoted by inland orders. Notice that no freight needs to be shipped between any two deep-sea terminals within the port of Rotterdam. The terminals within the port region are denoted by 'region D'. Besides the use of a limited number of barges, we assume that there is an unlimited number of trucks that can be used for urgent freight that cannot be transported by barge.

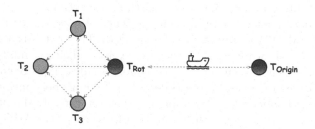

Fig. 1. The transportation network under consideration with $t = 3$.

We propose to use a MPTW approach combined with simulation. We need to simplify our mathematical model by making several assumptions. The MPTW is divided into a finite number of time steps (i.e., discrete approach), where each time step corresponds to three hours in real-life. The multi-period time window starts at time step 0 and covers nine days, until time step 72. At each decision moment, we have a Controlled Time Window (CTW), which is the next time step, and the Single Period Time Window (SPTW), which is the time window containing all the relevant information known, i.e., the planning horizon of 32 time steps. In Fig. 2 the MPTW approach is visualised. At the start of each decision moment a decision has to be made for the upcoming CTW, based on the information available in the concerned SPTW. This information could be both deterministic and stochastic.

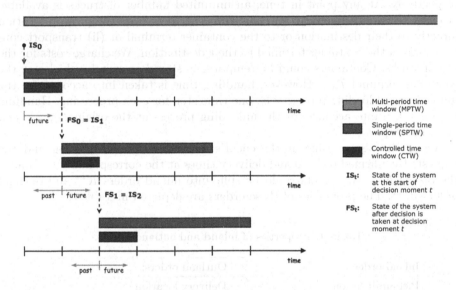

Fig. 2. Solving the planning problem using a multi-period time window approach.

When inland orders become known, the barge planners request an appointment, 12 time steps in advance relative to the requested appointment time. This requested appointment is confirmed 4 time steps later, i.e., 8 time steps in advance. Outland orders become known 12 time steps in advance relative to the release time. The corresponding requested appointment is confirmed in the same way. The confirmed appointment time could be scheduled at the requested appointment time (0), earlier (at most one time step) or later (one until five time steps), with probability distribution $p = (p_{-1}, p_0, p_{+1}, p_{+2}, p_{+3}, p_{+4}, p_{+5})$.

This means that the SPTW can be divided into three parts relative to the requested appointment times:

1. Orders having a requested appointment time in the interval $[0, 8]$ that is confirmed already.
2. Orders having a requested appointment time in the interval $(8, 12]$ that is not confirmed yet.
3. Outland orders having a pick-up time in the interval $[0, 12]$ and a requested appointment time strictly greater than 12.

The three deep-sea terminals in the Rotterdam region may only be visited in case of a confirmed appointment. The number of barges that may visit an appointment is restricted to one. Observe that this restriction does only apply to barges. The travel times of the barges are known and fixed, 1 time step in the Port area and 7 time steps between the origin and the container terminal. The travel times of the trucks are also known and fixed, 1 and 2 time steps respectively. At any point in time, an unlimited number of trucks is available at every terminal, which can (i) transport containers from the pick-up location directly to their destination or to the container terminal or (ii) transport containers from the container terminal to their destination. We charge costs for the use of trucks. Containers could be temporarily stored or switch vehicles at the container terminal T_{Rot}. However, handling time is taken into account for the unloading and loading process, i.e., one time step for each processing. Handling time is taken into account for the unloading process at the origin T_{Origin}, i.e., one time step.

Using the agreed time at the client's warehouse for (un)loading and the requested/confirmed pick-up and delivery times at the corresponding terminals, the orders K of the clients could be split into inland orders K^{in} and outland orders K^{out}. The properties of these orders are depicted in Table 1.

Table 1. Properties of inland and outland orders.

Inland orders:	Outland orders:
Pick-up location	Delivery location
Requested/confirmed pick-up time	Pick-up time
Delivery time	Requested/confirmed delivery time
Size of the order	Size of the order

As mentioned before, the travel time of the long-haul trip between the single inland terminal and the port of Rotterdam is around twenty to twenty-four hours. Since the other agents confirm the requested calls only 24 h in advance, a planning may become subject to changes when beneficial. For example, at some point in time, the LSP assigns outland order $k \in K^{out}$ to barge B, located at the origin, while the order is not confirmed yet. At that time, based on the requested pick-up and delivery times, the LSP benefits the most when the barge first picks up inland order $k' \in K^{in}$, then delivers the outland order and finally picks up inland order $k'' \in K^{in}$. However, when time passes by, the requested times are confirmed and might deviate. Based on the real-time data it might be more beneficial to unload the outland order at the container terminal T_{Rot} and deliver the order at the delivery appointment by truck, such that the barge is able to visit some other confirmed appointments. Since the LSP has the ability to change the plan when beneficial, using multiple modes of transport, the problem described coincides with a synchromodal planning problem.

3 Simulation Approach

We propose an algorithm in which future scenarios are simulated for the requested appointment times, given their probability vector p. A future scenario (or realisation) is not a specific forecast of the future, but a plausible description of what might happen. These scenarios are generated by sampling from the probability distribution of the uncertainty elements. By analysing various possible future scenarios, the planning and decision making process will be more efficient. For example, given two potential decisions for some barge (i.e., routing and container assignment), say decision I and II, decision I might perform better for certain scenarios, while decision II achieves better results for some other scenarios. Within the decision making process, the goal is to find the best decision(s) for each CTW that is resistant to change, i.e., feasible and (sub)optimal for every potential future scenario that has been simulated, such that a proper solution is obtained for the entire MPTW. The approach is visualised in Fig. 3.

3.1 Start of the Algorithm

The decision making process consists of both routing of the barges and container assignment to the barges (and trucks) such that the total cost is minimised over the entire multi-period time window. Since the problem is twofold, the decision space grows rapidly. To be able to manage this immense space, the container-to-mode assignment is not included in the decision space explicitly, but is taken into account afterwards, implicitly. By using a flowchart of the algorithm, shown in Fig. 3, the simulation based model is presented and explained. Due to complexity reasons, the length of a CTW is set to one, i.e., $d = 1$.

Although a MPTW consisting of 72 time steps is solved, it is sufficient to consider only 55 decision moments. At the 55th decision moment (i.e., at time step $t = 54$) no uncertainty is involved anymore. Just by the construction of the in- and outland orders, every requested appointment time is scheduled before or at time step 62, implying that every order is confirmed at time step 54. Therefore, the remaining interval [54, 72] can be solved offline. In the flowchart, the decision moment is denoted as period number (PeriodNr), but it is equivalent terminology. For each period number less than 54, the algorithm checks if a decision has to be made at all, which is almost always the case. Only if all barges are on their way from the origin to the container terminal or vice versa, the decision moment can be skipped until a barge arrives at one of the locations.

3.2   Decision Space

As an example, we use a set of three barges. At each decision moment t_a, each barge could be located at the origin (t_a, T_{Origin}), the container terminal (t_a, T_{Rot}) or one of the deep-sea terminals $(t_a, T_i)_{i \in I}$ in the region D.

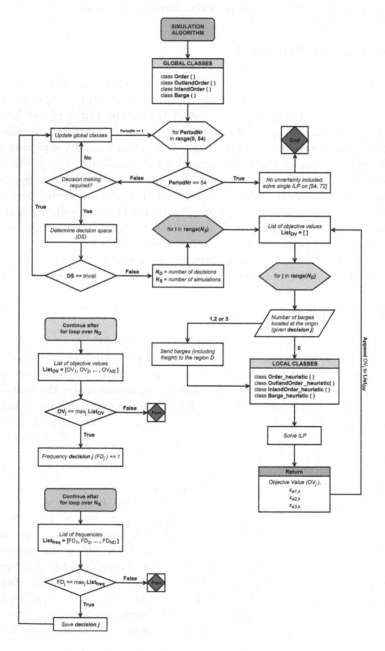

Fig. 3. Flow chart of the simulation algorithm.

Additionally, a barge could be on the move from the origin to the container terminal or vice versa, in case the initial node of the barge is (t, T_{Rot}) or (t, T_{Origin}), respectively, for some $t_a + 1 \leq t \leq t_a + 6$. In the latter case no decision has to be made for the barge under consideration. We distinguish between trivial and non-trivial decisions. Trivial decisions occur when there is only one direction for a barge, non-trivial decisions have several options to choose from.

If a barge is located at the origin, two possible decisions can be made. The barge could depart to the container terminal or stay another time step at the origin. If a barge is located at the container terminal, at most five possible decisions can be made. The barge could depart to the origin, it could stay at the container terminal or the barge could visit one of the three deep-sea terminals in case an appointment is scheduled at the upcoming time step. In case a barge is located at one of the deep-sea terminals, at most four possible decisions can be made. The barge could depart to the container terminal or it could visit one of the three deep-sea terminals in case an appointment is scheduled at the upcoming time step. From a theoretical point of view it could happen that 5^3 decisions could be made. However, in practice such a scenario would never happen. Moreover, due to symmetry, the number of decisions can be reduced drastically. During the performed experiments, on average 3.14 decisions could be made at each non-trivial decision moment, having a maximum of 20 decisions. In the model, a decision is denoted as a triple $(decision_{B1}, decision_{B2}, decision_{B3})$, where the i-th element corresponds to the (potential) upcoming location of barge i. Observe that the notation excludes the container-to-mode assignment.

Trivial Decisions. Quite often there is only one possible direction for a barge. Decisions could be trivial in different ways. In case no appointment is scheduled at the upcoming time step, a barge located at one of the deep-sea terminals can only return to the container terminal. Moreover, in case a pick-up appointment was scheduled at the current location, the order has to be (partially) assigned to the barge based on its remaining capacity. In case a barge, located at the region D, does have some containers on board corresponding to an outland order having its delivery appointment at the upcoming time step, the barge is obliged to visit the appointment. Observe that decisions belonging to delivery appointments must be taken at an earlier stage. Furthermore, the decision is trivial when a barge is located at the origin and its previous location was the container terminal, i.e., the barge just arrived. Since a barge must stay at least one time step at the origin to unload the containers on board (and possibly load some new containers), the decision is fixed.

Decision (t_a, T_{Rot}) to $(t_a + 1, T_{Rot})$. Although at first sight this might seem a trivial decision, it is not. At the container terminal a barge is allowed to unload or load some containers, implying that the decision includes the assignment of the containers located at the container terminal and on board of the barge itself. Even orders may be split into suborders, which causes some extra difficulties. Even if there is only one possible decision, the simulation process has to be done to reveal what containers to load and unload. For each potential decision, in which at least one barge decides to stay at the container terminal, we keep track of how frequently an order is transported by that barge. If so, the order could be transported fully or partially. Therefore, the number of containers per order is recorded as well. In the end, orders that occur in more than half of the simulations are taken into account in the final decision. The actual quantity equals the average number of containers transported by barge, rounded to the nearest integer.

Decision $(t_a, Origin)$ to $(t_a + 7, T_{Rot})$. At the origin, the only prerequisite is that a barge has to wait at least one time step after arrival (to unload the containers on board). After this, however, no loading time is taken into account, implying that the assignment is not based on the freight on board of the barge. Hence we need to determine what orders are, fully or partially, transported to the container terminal by the barge under consideration. As will be described in Sect. 3.3, the ILP used to find the (estimated) objective value for each possible decision is a heuristic excluding the container flow from the origin to the container terminal. The container-to-mode assignment has to be done manually. Just as for the previous decision, we keep track of the frequency an order is transported by that barge, including the number of containers per order. In the end, orders that occur in more than $\alpha\%$ of the simulations are taken into account in the final decision, where α is a predefined threshold value. This percentage has to be significantly higher than before, because we want to ensure that no conflicting appointments could occur, which might lead to infeasibility. During the experiments, α is set to 95, 90 and 85.

Remaining Decisions. The container assignment for the remaining decision space is straightforward. A concrete example is if a barge is located at the container terminal T_{Rot} and there is a single potential decision: departure to the origin. In that case, only the containers on board of that barge are forced to be transported to the origin. Just like for the delivery appointments mentioned above, the assignment of the containers to the barge has to be done at an earlier stage. In a similar way, the container-to-mode assignment for other decisions is based on the freight on board of the barge.

3.3 Solving the ILP

If the decision is non-trivial, a pre-specified number of simulations, denoted by N_S, is performed to seek the best decision(s) that is resistant to change. For every future scenario (or simulation) and every decision, an ILP, representing the SPTW problem, has to be solved. In case the number of simulations and decisions increases, the computational time significantly increases. Therefore a less time consuming heuristic is preferred. The output of each ILP does not have to be precise, because we are only interested in finding the best decision(s), given a possible future scenario. Therefore, an estimated objective value is sufficient. The time-space graph can be modified in various ways as can be found in [12,13].

4   Results

In order to benchmark the Simulation Approach, we conducted experiments for a set randomly generated instances. In this section the benchmarked results of Solution Approach are presented, interpreted and compared to the lower bounds computed for the benchmark solution methods. We will first shortly introduce how the instances are generated and which benchmark solution methods are used.

4.1   Design of Experiments

For the experiment we used $t = 3$, the network as depicted in Fig. 1. In the experiment we use a set of randomly generated instances, each containing a specific realisation of orders. For each instance a number of orders is generated, setting the pick-up location, the pick-up time, the delivery location, the delivery time and the size of the order. The pick-up location (for inland orders) and the delivery location (for the outland orders) is chosen from T_1, T_2 and T_3 with equal probability. For inland orders the requested pick-up time comes from a Uniform distribution $\{1, 59\}$ and the confirmed pick-up time follows from the probability vector as defined earlier. The due time is uniformly chosen among discrete values between 13 and 20 time steps after the requested pick-up time. For outland orders the pick-up time comes from a Uniform distribution $\{0, 62\}$. The due time is discrete uniformly chosen between 9 and 15 time steps after the pick-up time. For all orders the size of the order is also discrete uniformly chosen between 1 and 5.

4.2   Benchmark Solution Methods

In this section we present the benchmark methods. First we introduce the method for achieving a lower bound (the B_x-models), then we present three simple online optimisation methods.

In the normal setting, orders become known 12 time steps in advance. In practice those orders include uncertainty. However, in order to determine a lower bound for the problem, we may disregard this uncertainty element, implying that orders are confirmed immediately after they become known: we call this the B_{12} model. Even better approximations can be found if the orders are announced at an earlier stage. The ultimate version of this is when all orders are known for the whole period, the B_{72} model. For these models the ILP is solved, based on the certain input data. For the B_{12} model this means that 51 ILPs for an SPTW have to be solved. For The B_{72} model only one, very big, ILP for one SPTW has to be solved. These are offline methods, as all input is considered known and certain. The difference between the score of these methods and the online methods can be seen as the price of uncertainty.

We consider three simple online optimisation methods. The *RC method* (Requested as Confirmed) is the most obvious method to solve the problem, in which the uncertainty is not taken into account. In other words, at each decision moment in the model the requested appointment times are assumed to be the confirmed ones. Given that assumption, each single-period time window is solved by solving only one ILP, whereafter the solution on the interval $[t_a, t_a + \delta]$ is actually saved. For inland orders, the RC method works fine. For the outland orders, however, the method has some disadvantages. If the confirmed appointment time turns out to be earlier than the requested one, and the model had decided (based on the requested appointment time) to send the order last minute to its destination, possibly unnecessary costs are incurred because the order has to be trucked. Especially orders of large size may cause problems. To ensure such problems will not occur, the *EC method* (Earliest as Confirmed) is proposed. The method does assume that the confirmation of each requested appointment time is the 'worst case'. In other words, the confirmed appointment time is assumed to be the earliest possible appointment time. Observe that the problem faced in the RC method does not relate to the inland orders, so it would probably not benefit to assume the earliest possible appointment time for both type of orders. Therefore, the requested appointment time belonging to an inland order is assumed to be the average appointment time. Although the first possibility of infeasibility is avoided, the second possibility based on the container assignment at the origin could still occur. For both the RC and EC method, to deal with the uncertainty, the assumption is made to regard the appointment times of the requested ones in the beginning of the uncertainty interval to ensure that the transportation of outland orders by barge is possible (and no unnecessary costs are incurred). However, in most cases (to be precise five out of seven) the actual confirmed appointment time will be scheduled later than the requested one. Naturally, we do not charge any cost for being on time, but if an outland order does arrive at the container terminal way too early it is not beneficial. The containers corresponding to the order could stay on board of the barge the remaining time or the containers could be (partially) unloaded at the container terminal. The main drawback of the first option is the unnecessary use of the capacity, implying that some other orders cannot be loaded (fully) on the barge. Moreover, a pick-up appointment can only be visited if the delivery time does not collide with the delivery time of the outland order. The second option does avoid those drawbacks, but another disadvantage does appear. In the model, handling time is taken into account for both the unloading and loading processes at the container terminal, implying that the barge has to wait at least one time step after arrival at the container terminal. After the order has been unloaded, the order could be trucked to its destination, implying that cost has to be taken into account, or the order could be loaded on another (or the same) barge at a later moment, and transported to its destination without any cost, implying that this barge is forced to wait at least one time step at the container terminal as well. In other words, the model does not charge cost for being way too early, but the model does charge time, which could (again) lead to extra cost. Therefore, the *AC method* (Average as Confirmed) is added as a third model in order to investigate if shifting to the middle of the interval (i.e. the average) does benefit. Observe that the drawback of the RC method does emerge even more, and infeasibility could occur again in both ways.

4.3 Numerical Results

As can be seen in Table 2, the difference between the B_{12} model and the Simulation Approach is positive in terms of the average cost and the average number of trucks used, implying that the B_{12} model has overall better results. On the other hand, the Simulation Approach surpasses the performance of the simple methods. By surprise, the results of the AC method are much better than expected. It is even the solution method that used on average the least number of trucks for the long trips corresponding to outland orders, which is the part dealing the most with the uncertainty element. With the exception of one instance, the results for the Simulation Approach were at most within 20% of the B_{12} benchmark. As shown in Table 2, the gap was 12.5% on average, were some instances performed even better for the Simulation Approach than the B_{12} model (containing less uncertainty). The robustness is represented by the standard deviation of the average differences. Observe that the EC method is the most robust solution method, but also has the worst performance in terms of average cost. Disregarding the EC method, the Simulation Approach surpasses the simple methods both in terms of average cost and robustness. Besides that, no penalties occurred during the Simulation Approach, whilst during the other methods penalties did occur. We may conclude that the Simulation Approach is more reliable.

Table 2. Comparison of the results.

	Mean	SD	Gap	Time MPTW	Time SPTW
B_{72}	−1181.8	780.4	−8.9%	22.52 h	22.52 h
B_{12}	0.0	0.0	0.0%	1.00 h	48.41 s
SIM	1647.7	1665.1	12.5%	11.74 h	0.21 h
AC	2134.1	1744.2	16.2%	0.81 h	48.31 s
RC	3102.3	2000.2	23.5%	0.79 h	46.94 s
EC	3815.9	1334.6	28.9%	0.76 h	45.26 s

The results also give an overview of the computational time of the solution methods. The models have been implemented in Python and were solved with the commercial solver CPLEX 12.7 through the Python API. The experiments were conducted using 16 cores of 2.4 GHz each, working with 16 GB of RAM. To put the running time of the Simulation Approaches into perspective, we should realise that the running time per multi-period time window (MPTW) refers to the transportation of containers distributed over the entire network. In actual applications, we are only interested in the running time per single-period time window (SPTW), where a decision need to be made for the upcoming hours. Concerning the SIM model, almost all SPTWs can be solved within 10 min, except for some outliers. In each instance, it might occur once or twice that the decision space is quite large, implying that the number of ILPs that need to be solved increases significantly. For example, during the experiments, it occurred that the decision space consisted of 20 potential decisions. It took 58 min to find the best decision, what is too time consuming. Although 15 decisions were discarded after the first phase (i.e., after the check that is performed after 11 simulations), the computational time of the first phase was 44 min. In this specific example, the 5 contenders had nonzero frequency already after three simulations. If the check was done right then, the computational time of the decision moment had shrunk to 34 min, where the first phase took only 12 min. Therefore, it might be a good idea to improve the first phase if the decision space is large. This could be done by performing the check at an earlier stage, by discarding decisions after one or two simulations if the objective value deviates too much from the others or by taking into account the symmetry of some decisions even more.

In addition, because of the tree structure of the algorithm, the Simulation Approach can be parallelised easily. Around 85% of the computational time is spend on solving ILPs, implying that the computational time on a PRAM computer with infinite many processors and zero communication cost is less than a minute [1]. Although this is practically unrealistic, it shows that the average running time per SPTW can be reduced.

As it can be seen the simple methods are advantageous in terms of running time. Solving a SPTW takes only 48 s, because only one normal ILP has to be solved. Finally, the heuristic ILP turns out to be almost four times faster in terms of running time. Since the extra amount of ILPs that need to be solved is increased only by a factor 1.36, the algorithm does benefit considerably. Without using the heuristic, running the SIM model would take around 28.85 h, respectively, implying that the algorithm has been speed up by a factor of approximately 2.25.

5   Conclusions and Further Research

In this paper, an online optimisation approach is proposed, where the input data come in sequentially and decisions have to be taken while part of the relevant information is still uncertain or unknown. At each decision moment, the uncertainty element in the requested appointment times is converted to an offline optimisation problem by simulating various potential future scenarios. The approach is benchmarked against three simple online methods, in which the uncertainty is partially disregarded. The models assume that the requested appointment times will be confirmed at the requested, the earliest possible and the average appointment time, respectively. For this benchmark, experiments were carried out for 11 randomly generated instances. To say something about the quality and the practical relevance, the results were presented as the difference in results of the

B_{12} model and the solution methods. Although the B_{12} model does not guarantee optimality, the outcome can still be used as a benchmark for the problem. With the exception of one instance, the results of the cost function for the simulation model were within 20% of the B_{12} model. The gap was 12.5% on average, where some instances performed even better for the simulation model than the B_{12} model (containing less uncertainty). Although not optimal, the simulation model provides a reliable vehicle routing and a container-to-mode assignment. Within the decision making process, the model finds the best decisions that are resistant to change. The practical relevance of the simulation model is restricted in the sense that the model is build on several assumptions. Every order is announced exactly 36 h in advance, and confirmed exactly 12 h later. In practice, the announcement and confirmation times are more scattered. Furthermore, the assumption is made that the confirmed appointment can only be scheduled within an uncertainty interval of length seven, where the confirmation is based on the probability vector p that is uniformly distributed. Finally, due to the lack of real-world data, no adequate comparison can be made between the decisions made by the simulation algorithm and the decisions that barge planners would make in practice.

To conclude this research, we discuss some further research directions that may be developed and possibly lead to future success or usefulness. First of all, the network under consideration can be extended to a more practice oriented model. That extended network should take into account the farther away deep-sea terminals located in the Maasvlakte I and II and waiting nodes on water located in between the two terminal clusters. Besides that, the model can be generalised in terms of the number of barges and orders or the size of the orders. Even more general, the simulation based model can be applied to any multi-commodity network design problem including uncertainty (based on probability distributions) using the idea of solving explicitly a vehicle routing problem and implicitly a container-to-mode assignment. Furthermore, a better comparison can be made if the probability vector p is inferred from real-world data. The most ideal would be when the probability distribution can be extracted from the real-world data. If not, a sensitivity analysis could be carried out for different kinds of probability distributions. Finally, because of the tree structure of the algorithm, the simulation model can be parallelised easily. By doing so, the algorithm should benefit in terms of computational time.

Acknowledgement. This work has been carried out within the project 'Complexity Methods for Predictive Synchromodality' (Comet-PS), supported by NWO (the Netherlands Organisation for Scientific Research), TKI-Dinalog (Top Consortium Knowledge and Innovation) and the Early Research Program 'Grip on Complexity' of TNO (The Netherlands Organisation for Applied Scientific Research).

References

1. Chatterjee, S., Prins, J.: Parallel and distributed computing pram algorithms. COMP **203**, 13 (2002)

2. Chiscop, I.: A robust optimization approach to synchromodal container transportation. Master's thesis, Delft University of Technology (2018)
3. Crainic, T.G.: Service network design in freight transportation. Eur. J. Oper. Res. **122**(2), 272–288 (2000)
4. Crainic, T.G., Laporte, G.: Planning models for freight transportation. In: Design and Operation of Civil and Environmental Engineering Systems, p. 343 (1997)
5. De Juncker, M.A.M., Huizing, D., del Vecchyo, M.R.O., Phillipson, F., Sangers, A.: Framework of synchromodal transportation problems. ICCL 2017. LNCS, vol. 10572, pp. 383–403. Springer, Cham (2017). https://doi.org/10.1007/978-3-319-68496-3_26
6. Foulds, L.: A multi-commodity flow network design problem. Transp. Res. Part B: Methodol. **15**(4), 273–283 (1981)
7. Fragkos, I., Cordeau, J.F., Jans, R.: The multi-period multi-commodity network design problem. CIRRELT (2017)
8. Gendron, B., Crainic, T.G.: Relaxations for multicommodity capacitated network design problems. Technical report. Centre de recherche sur les transports, Université de Montréal (1994)
9. Han, J., Lee, C., Park, S.: A robust scenario approach for the vehicle routing problem with uncertain travel times. Transp. Sci. **48**(3), 373–390 (2014)
10. Hendriks, M.P.: Multi-step optimization of logistics networks: strategic, tactical, and operational decisions. Ph.D. thesis, Eindhoven University of Technology (2009)
11. Johnson, D.S., Lenstra, J.K., Rinnooy Kan, A.H.G.: The complexity of the network design problem. Networks **8**(4), 279–285 (1978)
12. Kalicharan, K., Phillipson, F., Sangers, A., Juncker, M.D.: Reduction of variables for solving logistic flow problems. In: 6th International Physical Internet Conference (IPIC) (2019)
13. de Koning, W.: A simulation based approach to synchromodal container transport. Master's thesis, Delft University of Technology (2019)
14. Kooiman, K., Phillipson, F., Sangers, A.: Planning inland container shipping: a stochastic assignment problem. In: Wittevrongel, S., Phung-Duc, T. (eds.) ASMTA 2016. LNCS, vol. 9845, pp. 179–192. Springer, Cham (2016). https://doi.org/10.1007/978-3-319-43904-4_13
15. Kooiman, K., Phillipson, F., Sangers, A.: A classification framework time stamp stochastic assignment problems. In: 9th International Conference on Operations Research and Enterprise Systems (ICORES), Valletta (Malta) (2020)
16. Phillipson, F.: Planning nurses in maternity care: a stochastic assignment problem. J. Phys.: Conf. Ser. **616**, 012006 (2015)
17. Rivera, A.E.P., Mes, M.R.: Anticipatory freight selection in intermodal long-haul round-trips. Transp. Res. Part E: Logist. Transp. Rev. **105**, 176–194 (2017)
18. Pérez Rivera, A., Mes, M.: Service and transfer selection for freights in a synchromodal network. In: Paias, A., Ruthmair, M., Voß, S. (eds.) ICCL 2016. LNCS, vol. 9855, pp. 227–242. Springer, Cham (2016). https://doi.org/10.1007/978-3-319-44896-1_15
19. Schmidt, G., Wilhelm, W.E.: Strategic, tactical and operational decisions in multinational logistics networks: a review and discussion of modelling issues. Int. J. Prod. Res. **38**(7), 1501–1523 (2000)
20. Ortega del Vecchyo, M., Phillipson, F., Sangers, A.: Decision making in a dynamic transportation network: a multi-objective approach. In: 6th International Physical Internet Conference (IPIC) (2019)

A Mathematical Model to Route Technicians for Inland Waterway Shipping

Melissa Buballa[1], Daniel Wetzel[1(✉)], Kay Lenkenhoff[2], and Kevin Tierney[1(✉)]

[1] Decision and Operation Technologies Group,
Bielefeld University, 33615 Bielefeld, Germany
{melissa.buballa,daniel.wetzel,kevin.tierney}@uni-bielefeld.de
[2] BIOM GmbH, 42349 Wuppertal, Germany
lenkenhoff@biom.info

Abstract. Inland shipping is a critical part of the global transport network that links population centers over rivers for both cargo and passenger transportation. Inland ships follow tight schedules, leaving little time for required maintenance or emergency repairs. Maintenance providers must therefore send their technicians out to ships during the ships' operation and quickly perform their work during regular calls on the ships' schedules. The resulting technician routing problem is challenging for maintenance providers to solve, not only due to time-dependent distance matrix, but also because of variable task durations, technician car pooling and the long planning horizon. We use an extended time space graph to formulate a binary linear model to provide routes for technicians and their vehicles. We evaluate the model on a benchmark of instances inspired from our industrial collaborator, showing that it can find optimal solutions to small and mid-sized instances.

Keywords: Time-dependent routing · Technician carpooling · Inland shipping

1 Introduction

There are over 40,000 km of navigable canals and lakes in Europe [11]. Inland waterways provide connections between seaports and inland industrial centers, and host a large tourism industry consisting of river cruise ships. The European inland fleet consists of over 15,000 cargo ships and over 350 cruise ships [3]. These ships require regular maintenance and repairs to remain operational, and service tight schedules to remain economically viable for their operators. A dedicated industry has thus emerged to provide fast and online services to inland ships.

There are two standard ways to maintain and repair inland ships. The first is to sail the ship to a drydock where the ship is removed from the water so servicing can commence over the period of several days. A clear drawback of doing this is that the ship cannot perform its normal duties while in drydock, meaning passengers must disembark or freight transfers must be delayed. Especially for

© Springer Nature Switzerland AG 2020
E. Lalla-Ruiz et al. (Eds.): ICCL 2020, LNCS 12433, pp. 631–647, 2020.
https://doi.org/10.1007/978-3-030-59747-4_41

cruise ships, which only have a short period in the summer in which they can be operated, this is not commercially viable. The second option is "on board" servicing, in which technicians travel to ships and service them in the course of their normal port calls. While this option allows vessels to continue their normal operations, it creates a daunting scheduling and routing task for the companies providing maintenance to inland ships.

Service providers have contracts to perform regular maintenance and repairs to multiple ships. The goal of these companies is to create a routing plan for their technicians over a multi-week time frame such that the driving and overnight stay costs are minimized, all maintenance and repair tasks are completed within specified time frames, and technicians' working time does not exceed contractually agreed upon limits. The routing of technicians for inland ships is especially interesting from a vehicle routing problem (VRP) perspective due several problem aspects. First, the ships are always moving, thus the distance matrix between tasks changes in each time step similar to time dependent vehicle routing problems (TDVRPs) (see [9]). Second, technicians can carpool together, leading not only to cost savings, but also savings in the total working time of the technicians.

The maintenance and repair tasks are diverse, posing challenges for service providers. Different tasks require different skills or qualifications as in the skill VRP (SVRP) [2], for example, a technician trained as a plumber may not carry out electrical work. Furthermore, tasks are assigned time windows over which they must be completed, as is often the case in technician VRPs (TVRP) [18]. These are often very flexible, as routine maintenance might have a multi-week window in which it can be carried out. Some tasks can be completed faster if multiple technicians work on them at the same time. Finally, some tasks involve multiple steps requiring waiting time in between in which a technician can complete a different task, for example while glue is drying.

In this paper, we introduce the inland shipping technician routing problem (ISTR) to address the problem described above. We base our model on an extended time-space graph in which graph nodes represent carrying out a particular task (repairs or regular maintenance) on a ship at a specific port at a certain time, which we call a time-space-task (TST) graph. The TST allows us to model multiple tasks per ship that can be performed over the entire planning horizon, as well as the time-dependent distance matrix that are not generally present in SVRP or TVRP problems. Ships usually have multiple tasks that must be completed during the planning horizon, corresponding to a technician visiting the same node in the TVRP several times. The ISTR contains elements of a number of VRP variants. Nonetheless, our model has a number of novel aspects, such as a time-dependent distance matrix, variable task durations, and technician car pooling. We conduct experiments using our model on a benchmark of instances inspired by data from our industrial partner. We show that the model is capable of finding solutions to small and mid-sized instances and analyze the benefits the model can provide maintenance providers in operative settings.

This paper is organized as follows. We first discuss related work in Sect. 2 before we introduce the graph structure and mathematical model in Sect. 3. We provide an experimental evaluation in Sect. 4 and conclude in Sect. 5.

2   Related Work

The vehicle routing literature has become extremely diverse, and contains a wide range of models touching numerous industries. Lahyani et al. (2015) [16] provide a taxonomy of *rich* vehicle routing problems, which we use to categorize and discuss our contribution. Under this taxonomy, the ISTR involves a deterministic, static routing and driver scheduling problem with a single depot over multiple periods with multiple trips, a fixed number of capacitated, heterogeneous vehicles with service times and specific constraints, in particular technician skill and task completion. Based on this categorization, we organize our discussion of related work to address several key aspects of the ISTR in VRP contexts: periodic task execution, time-dependent distances, and variable task durations.

Table 1 summarizes the most relevant literature and contrasts it with our work. We differentiate between approaches that using a time-space graph and those that do not, as these VRPs more closely resemble our work. We note that while a number of approaches have multi-day planning horizons, and include some kind of technician skill criteria, the ISTR's variable task durations and dynamic car pooling set it apart from the related work. Although the ISTR contains aspects of several existing VRP models, the combination of individual characteristics makes it necessary to present them in a new model. In particular, the time-dependent distances and variable task durations make it necessary to consider technician activities in detail. Furthermore, instead pre-assigning technicians to teams, dynamic carpooling allows the technicians to be employed flexibly.

Task Execution. We categorize task execution into three types: *(i)* tasks associated with a specific execution time, *(ii)* multi-period tasks that have time windows over several periods in which they can be executed [20,26], and *(iii)* recurring tasks, often with a fixed number of time periods between repeated executions [7,24]. The ISTR supports tasks with a fixed execution as well as multi-period tasks. The ISTR over a long time period involves recurring tasks, however these all recur at roughly the same time. Thus, we do not need to model minimum/maximum durations between repeating tasks as in some other problems.

Time-Dependent Distances. Time dependent distances in the VRP usually refer to varying travel times over the course of the day due to, e.g., rush hour traffic [10,19], and can also include multiple paths between nodes [14]. An important property of these distances in the literature is that they generally can be thought of as being drawn from an underlying distribution. In the ISTR this is not the case, as on the one hand we ignore the effects of traffic, resulting in constant

Table 1. Overview of the literature for the ISTR, where graphs are grouped into basis (B) graphs (i.e., no time-space graph), time-space (TS) and time-space-task (TST); the time horizon is either a single day (SD) or multi-day (MD); skill requirements for tasks can be single (S) or multiple (M); the task type (TT) is periodic (P) or not; the task duration (TD) is either constant (C) or variable (V); carpools (CP) can be formed dynamically (D) or given (G) as input.

Article	Graph	Horizon	Time dep.	Skills	TD	TT	CP
Schwarze and Voß (2013) [22]	B	x	x	M	x	x	x
Çimen and Soysal (2017) [6]	B	x	✓	S	C	x	x
Chen et al. (2016) [5]	B	MD	x	M	V	x	x
Meneghetti and de Zan (2016) [21]	B	MD	x	M	C	P	x
Zamorano and Stolletz (2017) [26]	B	MD	x	M	C	P	G
Budai et al. (2006) [1]	B	MD	x	x	C	P	x
Chen et al. (2006) [4]	B	MD	✓	x	x	x	x
López-Santana et al. (2016) [18]	B	MD	x	S	C	P	x
Huang et al. (2017) [14]	B	MD	✓	x	C	x	x
Yan and Shih (2007) [25]	TS	SD	x	S	C	x	G
Lawley et al. (2008) [17]	TS	MD	x	x	C	x	x
Jeenanunta et al. (2011) [15]	TS	MD	x	M	C	P	x
This work	TST	MD	✓	M	V	P	D

traveling time, but vessel movements result in a different set of places that can be traveled to in each time period.

Variable Task Durations. In reality, task durations depend on a number of factors, such as the number of technicians working on the task, experience, qualifications, and have random variations. Chen et al. [5] reduce task completion times based on the experience of a technician. Souyris et al. [23] include service time uncertainty to the problem, based on external influences and historical data about each technician's performance. In the ISTR, we reduce task times according to the number of technicians assigned to the task, which can be thought of as a type of job teaming [8], except that in the literature this has not been traditionally associated with variable task durations.

3   Mathematical Model

We introduce a binary linear programming model for the ISTR using a TST graph. We first examine model assumptions, then define the TST graph and finally provide our model.

3.1 Model Assumptions

The ISTR is a highly complex problem that we attempt to model as realistically as possible. However, we need to make a number of assumptions to model the problem mathematically in a reasonable way. Regarding vehicle movement, *(1)* the matrix of distance costs is symmetrical, and *(2)* only one vehicle can be used to go from one location to another. Technicians are subject to a number of working time constraints. We simplify them into the following assumptions. *(3)* Technicians are only allowed to travel and work between 06:00 and 24:00. Furthermore, they may only work a fixed total time per day. *(4)* The travel time of technicians is included in the total daily working time. If several technicians travel in the same vehicle the traveling time considered as working time is reduced linearly in terms of the number of technicians. *(5)* After returning to the depot a technician must take a break before leaving the depot again.

We consider two types of tasks in the ISTR: single-step and multistep tasks. The former are performed without interruption while the latter contains a break between two or more steps. To simplify our model *(6)* work at a single-step task cannot be interrupted, nor can the work in any pre-assigned portion of a multistep task. *(7)* Multi-step tasks have a break assigned to the task in advance and allow at most two subtasks in total. During the break between the subtasks, technicians can perform other tasks. Modeling more than two subtasks is too detailed for our research prototype. We ensure that a technician that starts a multistep task must finish it before leaving the ship. Furthermore, *(8)* all tasks must be carried out and *(9)* time windows in which a task can be performed are known in advance.

3.2 The ISTR Described Using a TST Graph

The ISTR is represented by a TST graph, including the information about the executed task. A node represents a specific task at a specific port to a specific time. The task durations are modeled on stationary arcs, i.e., those connecting two nodes of the same task at the same place. The same applies for travel times, which are assigned to arcs connecting different ports. The TST graph is easily constructed using the schedules of the ships requiring servicing.

The depot is represented as a single node that is not associated with any specific time, as technicians' tours do not have a fixed duration, so they can leave and return freely. In addition, the graph contains two overnight stay nodes at each port, representing the start and end of the stay. If a technician does not return to the depot at the end of the day, they must go to an arrival node of an overnight stay. The path continues on the next day at the departure node.

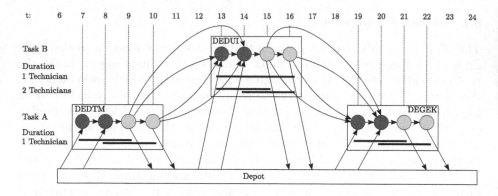

Fig. 1. TST graph of the ISTR with two tasks.

The ISTR contains two synchronized flows: one for technicians and one for vehicles. This allows carpools to be formed dynamically as needed to move technicians between ships. The time driving between tasks counts towards a technician's working time, but only if they are the one driving. Thus, several technicians can form car pool to reduce their working times. We reduce the working time linearly, assuming every technician takes an equal turn driving the vehicle, which is a necessary simplification of reality in which there are many different options for splitting the working time between technicians.

TST Graph Example. Figure 1 shows an example of the TST graph for two tasks (A and B), where task A can be performed at one of two ports, labeled with their UN/LOCODEs, an global identifier for ports; DEDTM or DEGEK, and task B can be performed at port DEDUI. Dark circles represent TST nodes in which a technician can start work on the task, and light nodes show where a technician may stop working if the task duration is completed. Note that task B is a variable length task, meaning if two technicians are assigned to it it only takes three time periods, as opposed to four with one technician. One example solution to the example instance is for a single technician to leave the depot for DEDTM at time 6, begin working on task A at time 7, then at time 9 travel to DEDUI, arriving at time 13. The technician then works alone until time 16 and leaves DEDUI for the depot, as both tasks are completed. There are a number of other feasible solutions, including performing task B before task A, or completing task B with multiple technicians.

TST Graph Formalism. Formally, the extended TST is defined by the following sets:

Ω	Set of all tasks
S	Set of all technicians (staff)
D	Set of all days
A	Set of all arcs with $i, j \in V$
A_d^D	Set of all arcs with $i, j \in V$ starting in day $d \in D$
A^P	Set of all arcs with $i, j \in V$ where node i and j are at different ports
A_d^{PD}	Set of all arcs with $i, j \in V$ starting in day $d \in D$ and where node i and j are at different ports
A_d^{WD}	Set of all arcs with $i, j \in V$ starting in day $d \in D$ and where node i and j are at the same port. $A_d^{WD} \cap A_d^{PD} = \emptyset$
D_s^S	Set of all days on which technician $s \in S$ is not available
D_ω^T	Set of all days in which task $\omega \in \Omega$ can be executed
K	Set of all vehicles
L	Set of all technician and task combinations (s, ω), where technician $s \in S$ has the qualification to work on task $\omega \in \Omega$
P	Set of all ports
P_ω^T	Set of all ports where task $\omega \in \Omega$ can be executed
T	Set of time
V	Set of all nodes
V'	Set of all nodes without the depot
V_d^D	Set of all nodes on day $d \in D$
V_ω^T	Set of all nodes that belong to task $\omega \in \Omega$
$V_\omega^{T'}$	Set of the earliest nodes at each port call where work on task $\omega \in \Omega$ can start
$V_{\omega p d}^{TPD}$	Set of all nodes that belong to task $\omega \in \Omega$ at port $p \in P$ on day $d \in D$
τ	Time discretization

Pseudo Technicians. To ensure work and health regulation a technician must return to the depot after a maximum tour duration and take a break. Since multiple tours of the same technician are required over the planning horizon, we introduce *pseudo technicians* all representing the same real technician. Each pseudo technician can undertake at most one tour. Pseudo technicians representing the same real technician are not allowed to work at the same time. We enforce a minimum break time between different pseudo technician tours.

3.3   Binary Linear Model

The following parameters are used in the mathematical model.

c_{ij}^T	Technician costs on arc $(i,j) \in A$
c_{ij}^V	Vehicle costs on arc $(i,j) \in A$
d_i	Day of node $i \in V'$
t_i	Time of node $i \in V'$
t^B	Break time a technician has between two tours
t_ω^T	Time required to complete task $\omega \in \Omega$
$t_{\omega q}^{TRS}$	Reduction of the required time to complete task $\omega \in \Omega$ if the q-th technician works on the task
$t_{\omega q}^{TR}$	Overall reduction of the required time to complete task $\omega \in \Omega$ if the q-th technician works on the task
t_{max}^S	Maximum time a technician can travel before returning to the depot
t_{max}^{SD}	Maximum time that a technician $s \in S$ can work in one day
t_{ij}^V	Travel duration on arc $(i,j) \in A^P$
t_{ijq}^{VR}	Reduction of the realized travel duration on arc $(i,j) \in A^P$ for the q-th technician
t_{ij}^W	Work duration on arc $(i,j) \in A_d^{WD}$
u_ω^T	Number of technicians that can work on task $\omega \in \Omega$
u_k^V	Number of technicians that can travel in vehicle $k \in K$
u_{max}^V	Maximum vehicle capacity, $\max_{k \in K} u_k^V$
δ_{ij}	Takes the value 1, iff for task $\omega \in \Omega$ on day $d \in D_\omega^T$ at port P_ω node $i,j \in V_{\omega pd}^{TPD}$ are sequential in the order of time
$\epsilon_{ss'}$	Takes the value 1, iff technicians $s, s' \in S$ are sequential in the order of pseudo technicians
ν_q	Parameter needed to connect the counting variables for the number of technicians working on a task, where q represents the q-th technician
M	Upper bound for the order restriction of an technician. $M := |T| + \max_{i \in V'}\{t_{i0}^V\}$

The following binary variables are used in the mathematical model.

x_{kij}	Set to value 1 iff vehicle $k \in K$ travels on arc $(i,j) \in A$
y_{sij}	Set to value 1 iff technician $s \in S$ travels on arc $(i,j) \in A$
$z_{s\omega i}$	Set to value 1 iff technician $s \in S$ works on task ω, $(s,\omega) \in L$ at node $i \in V_\omega^T$
β_{qij}	Set to value 1 iff at least q technicians travels on arc $(i,j) \in A^P$
λ_{sqij}	Set to value 1 iff technician $s \in S$ as the q-th technician travels on arc $(i,j) \in A^P$
$\sigma_{\omega i}$	Set to value 1 iff task $\omega \in \Omega$ starts in node $i \in V_\omega^T$
$\theta_{q\omega}$	Set to value 1 iff at least q technicians work on task $\omega \in \Omega$

We use the following binary model to solve the ISTR.

Minimize

$$\sum_{(i,j)\in A}\sum_{k\in K}c_{ij}^V x_{kij} + \sum_{(i,j)\in A}\sum_{s\in S}c_{ij}^T y_{sij} \tag{1}$$

subject to

$$\sum_{(i,j)\in A} y_{sij} \leq 1 \qquad\qquad\qquad \forall s \in S, i \in V \tag{2}$$

$$\sum_{(i,j)\in A} y_{sij} - \sum_{(j,l)\in A} y_{sjl} = 0 \qquad\qquad\qquad \forall s \in S, j \in V' \tag{3}$$

$$\sum_{(0j)\in A} y_{s0j} \leq \sum_{(s,\omega)\in L}\sum_{i\in V_\omega^T} z_{s\omega i} \qquad\qquad\qquad \forall s \in S \tag{4}$$

$$y_{sij} = 0 \qquad\qquad \forall s \in S, d \in D_s^S, j \in V_d^D, (i,j) \in A \tag{5}$$

$$\sum_{(i,j)\in A} y_{sij} \geq z_{s\omega j} \qquad\qquad\qquad \forall (s,\omega) \in L, j \in V_\omega^T \tag{6}$$

$$\lambda_{sqij} \leq y_{sij} \qquad\qquad \forall s \in S, (i,j) \in A^P, q \in \{1,...,u_{max}^V\} \tag{7}$$

$$\sum_{q\in\{1,...,u_{max}^V\}} \beta_{qij} = \sum_{s\in S} y_{sij} \qquad\qquad\qquad \forall (i,j) \in A^P \tag{8}$$

$$\sum_{s\in S}\sum_{q\in\{1,...,u_{max}^V\}} \lambda_{sqij} = \sum_{q\in\{1,...,u_{max}^V\}} \nu_q \beta_{qij} \qquad\qquad\qquad \forall (i,j) \in A^P \tag{9}$$

$$\sum_{q\in\{1,...,u_{max}^V\}} \lambda_{sqij} \leq \sum_{q\in\{1,...,u_{max}^V\}} \beta_{qij} \qquad\qquad\qquad \forall s \in S, (i,j) \in A^P \tag{10}$$

$$\beta_{(q+1)ij} \leq \beta_{qij} \qquad\qquad \forall (i,j) \in A^P, q \in \{1,...,u_{max}^V - 1\} \tag{11}$$

$$\lambda_{s(q+1)ij} \leq \lambda_{sqij} \qquad\qquad \forall s \in S, (i,j) \in A^P, q \in \{1,...,u_{max}^V - 1\} \tag{12}$$

$$\sum_{(i,j)\in A} x_{kij} \leq 1 \qquad\qquad\qquad \forall k \in K, i \in V \tag{13}$$

$$\sum_{(i,j)\in A} x_{kij} - \sum_{(j,l)\in A} x_{kjl} = 0 \qquad\qquad\qquad \forall k \in K, j \in V' \tag{14}$$

$$\sum_{k\in K} x_{kij} \leq 1 \qquad\qquad\qquad \forall (i,j) \in A^P \tag{15}$$

$$\sum_{k\in K} x_{kij} \leq \sum_{s\in S} y_{sij} \qquad\qquad\qquad \forall (i,j) \in A \tag{16}$$

$$\sum_{s\in S} y_{sij} \leq \sum_{k\in K} u_k^V x_{kij} \qquad\qquad\qquad \forall (i,j) \in A^P \tag{17}$$

$$\sum_{i\in V_\omega^T} \sigma_{\omega i} = 1 \qquad\qquad\qquad \forall \omega \in \Omega \tag{18}$$

$$z_{s\omega i} \leq \sigma_{\omega i} \qquad\qquad\qquad \forall (s,\omega) \in L, i \in V_\omega^{T'} \tag{19}$$

$$z_{swj} \leq z_{swi} + \sigma_{wj} \qquad \forall (s, \omega) \in L, p \in P_\omega^T, d \in D_\omega^T, i, j \in V_{\omega pd}^{TPD}, \delta_{ij} = 1 \quad (20)$$

$$\sum_{(s,\omega) \in L} z_{swi} \leq \sum_{q \in \{1,...,u_\omega^T\}} \theta_{qw} \qquad \forall \omega \in \Omega, i \in V_\omega^T \quad (21)$$

$$\theta_{(q+1)w} \leq \theta_{qw} \qquad \forall \omega \in \Omega, q \in \{1, ..., u_\omega^T - 1\} \quad (22)$$

$$\sum_{q \in \{1,...,u_\omega^T\}} \theta_{wq} \geq 1 \qquad \forall \omega \in \Omega \quad (23)$$

$$\sum_{i \in V_\omega^T} \tau z_{swi} \leq \tau + t_\omega^T - \sum_{q \in \{2,...,u_\omega^T\}} t_{wq}^{TRS} \theta_{qw} \qquad \forall (s, \omega) \in L \quad (24)$$

$$\sum_{(s,\omega) \in L} \sum_{i \in V_\omega^T} \tau z_{swi} = \sum_{q \in \{1,...,u_\omega^T\}} (\tau + t_\omega^T) \theta_{qw} - \sum_{q \in \{2,...,u_\omega^T\}} t_{wq}^{TR} \theta_{qw} \quad \forall \omega \in \Omega \quad (25)$$

$$\sum_{(i,j) \in A_d^{PD}} t_{ij}^V y_{sij} - \sum_{(i,j) \in A_d^{PD}} \sum_{q \in \{2,...,u_{max}^V\}} t_{ijq}^{VR} \lambda_{sqij} + \sum_{(i,j) \in A_d^{WD}} t_{ij}^W y_{sij} \leq t_{max}^{SD}$$
$$\forall s \in S, d \in D \quad (26)$$

$$\sum_{(i,0) \in A} (t_i + t_{i0}^V) y_{si0} - \sum_{(0,j) \in A} (t_j - t_{0j}^V) y_{s0j} \leq t_{max}^S \qquad \forall s \in S \quad (27)$$

$$\sum_{(i,0) \in A} (t_i + t_{i0}^V) y_{si0} + t^B \leq M(1 - \sum_{(0,j) \in A} y_{s'0j}) + \sum_{(0,j) \in A} (t_j - t_{0j}^V) y_{s'0j}$$
$$\forall s, s' \in S, \epsilon_{ss'} = 1 \quad (28)$$

$$\sum_{(0,j) \in A} y_{s'0j} \leq \sum_{(0,j) \in A} y_{s0j} \qquad \forall s, s' \in S, \epsilon_{ss'} = 1 \quad (29)$$

The objective function minimize the traveling costs of all vehicles and the hotel costs for technicians in Term (1). Constraints (2) to (11) represent the flow of the technicians through the graph and the associated connections. Technicians can only leave a node on a single arc (constraints (2)) and together with the flow constraints in (3), a technician always returns to the depot. To prevent solutions where technicians only leave the depot to reduce traveling times of other technicians, constraints (4) only allow a technician to leave the depot if they work on at least one task. For the time a technician is not available the variables are set to zero (constraints (5)).

A technician can only work at a node if the technician visits that node (constraints (6)). To calculate the correct reduction for the traveling time when more then one technician travels on the same arc, we count the number of technicians on a non-stationary arc. First, a technician can only be considered for the reduction if the technician travels on the arc (constraints (7)). Then, we count the number of technicians in general (constraints (8)) before we can link it to the technicians that are actually traveling on the arc in constraints (9). Constraints

(10) enforce the relation between the counting variables, i.e., a technician cannot exceed the number of all technicians. We make sure that the counting variables are ordered in constraints (11) and (12) for a correct time reduction.

Constraints (13) to (17) represent the flow of the vehicles trough the graph and technician synchronization. Constraints (13) ensure a vehicle can only leave a node on a single arc, and the flow constraints (14) guarantee that a vehicle will (eventually) return to the depot. Regarding our assumptions, we only allow one vehicle to take the same change in location (constraints (15)). The next group of constraints synchronize technicians and vehicles. In constraints (16), we only allow a vehicle to travel on an arc if there is at least one technician driving it. Then, the capacity of a vehicle must be sufficient to transport all the technicians traveling on the arc (constraints (17)).

Constraints (18) to (25) consider the tasks. Constraints (18) define that a task can only be started once. Furthermore, if a technician works at a node then the node must be the starting point of the task (constraints (19)) or the technician also works on the task at the previous node (constraints (20)). For variable length tasks, we need to keep track of the number of technicians working on the task. Constraints (21) count the amount of technicians working on a task while Constraints (22) guarantee that the counting variables are used in the correct order. In addition, at least one technician must work on each task (constraints (23)). Constraints (24) control the maximum duration a technician can work at one task where constraints (25) makes sure that the duration of all technicians working on a task equals the required task duration.

Constraints (26) and (27) consider the working time of the technicians. The maximum working time for a technician in a day is restricted by constraints (26). The first term represents the travel duration, minus the reduction of the travel duration for car pools and adds the work duration of a technician. Furthermore, the time a technician can be underway before going back to the depot is considered in constraints (27), which subtract the arrival time at the depot from the departure time.

Constraints (28) and (29) consider the representation of pseudo technicians. First, technicians that represent the same real technician cannot leave the depot at the same time (constraints (28)). Therefore, the departure of the following technician cannot be before the arrival of the previous technician, including the break time. The parameter M guarantees that the constraints are not infeasible if the following technician does not leave the depot. Second, technicians representing the same real technician will be used in ascending order due to constraints (29).

Table 2. The instances of the ISTR with the size and structure of the TST graph using the notation from the model description.

Instance (V-A-L-τ)	V	A	D	P	Ω	S	L	τ
070-0372-24-1.00	70	372	5	4	6	3	24	1.00
081-0469-32-1.00	81	469	3	4	8	5	32	1.00
100-0700-24-0.50	100	700	5	4	6	3	24	0.50
101-0724-30-1.00	101	724	5	7	5	2	30	1.00
103-0744-42-1.00	103	744	5	7	7	3	42	1.00
110-0887-24-0.50	110	887	5	5	6	3	24	0.50
120-1009-06-1.00	120	1,009	5	4	3	3	6	1.00
120-1050-38-1.00	120	1,050	7	5	10	5	38	1.00
120-1106-33-1.00	120	1,106	7	5	9	5	33	1.00
128-0903-26-0.25	128	903	8	5	7	5	26	0.25
148-1870-06-1.00	148	1,870	7	10	3	2	6	1.00
159-1223-48-1.00	159	1,223	6	8	12	5	48	1.00
169-1826-52-1.00	169	1,826	8	8	12	6	52	1.00
203-1807-46-1.00	203	1,807	7	11	12	5	46	1.00
238-2450-13-1.00	238	2,450	6	8	5	5	13	1.00
240-4373-53-1.00	240	4,373	11	9	9	7	53	1.00
250-3087-60-1.00	250	3,087	9	10	10	7	60	1.00
272-3198-19-1.00	272	3,198	6	9	5	5	19	1.00
297-4769-65-1.00	297	4,769	9	11	11	7	65	1.00
342-9346-46-1.00	342	9,346	16	9	8	7	46	1.00

4   Computational Results

We evaluate our mathematical model on a dataset of instances based on data from our industrial partner. We investigate the runtime and solution quality of our BP model to evaluate the integration of the model in a decision support system (DSS). Furthermore, we check whether a reformulation of constraints (28) changes the performance of the model.

4.1   Experimental Setting

Table 2 gives an overview of the instances for the ISTR. The number of nodes and arcs of the TST graph is determined by the planing horizon, the number of ports and tasks and the time discretization. Of course, smaller time discretizations lead to larger graphs, but this is not the only measurement of instance difficulty. The size of the overlap between technician's skillsets and the skills required to completing tasks is also an important driver of instance difficulty, as a high overlap makes the problem underconstrained (every technician can complete

Table 3. Runtime of Gurobi (wall clock time) and solution quality of the instances.

Instance (V-A-L-τ)	Runtime [s]	Gap [%]	Optimal solution found		Costs [EUR]
			At time [s]	with Gap [%]	
070-0372-24-1.00	17.7	0.0	7.0	19.2	548.80
081-0469-32-1.00	1,657.9	0.0	96.0	56.7	302.40
101-0724-30-1.00	1,732.1	0.0	61.0	69.8	441.70
103-0744-42-1.00	2,870.9	0.0	372.0	44.9	633.70
110-0887-24-0.50	10,800.0	23.4	–	–	1,059.80
100-0700-24-0.50	36.4	0.0	5.0	74.6	193.20
120-1009-06-1.00	5.3	0.0	3.0	82.5	35.40
120-1050-38-1.00	10,800.0	13.9	–	–	1,630.80
120-1106-33-1.00	1,088.9	0.0	191.0	23.8	1,114.00
128-0903-26-0.25	274.1	0.0	18.0	77.8	482.50
148-1870-06-1.00	135.0	0.0	21.0	66.3	607.30
159-1223-48-1.00	10,800.0	34.3	–	–	1,292.10
169-1826-52-1.00	10,800.0	30.0	–	–	1,304.70
203-1807-46-1.00	10,800.0	24.8	–	–	659.90
238-2450-13-1.00	10,800.0	66.1	–	–	896.30
240-4373-53-1.00	10,800.0	44.2	–	–	797.00
250-3087-60-1.00	10,800.0	48.6	–	–	475.10
272-3198-19-1.00	10,800.0	82.1	–	–	993.40
297-4769-65-1.00	10,800.0	66.4	–	–	535.90
342-9346-46-1.00	10,800.0	41.7	–	–	701.90

almost any task) and can lead to symmetries, whereas a low overlap starts to overconstrain the problem. We note that our instance set is meant to provide a variety of instance sizes that represent different scenarios from our industrial partner to test out our mathematical model. They are somewhat smaller than realistic instances but include structural aspects our industrial partner has to consider during operation.

4.2 Runtime Analysis

We use eight cores of an Intel Xeon E5-2670 CPU at 2.60 GHz with 32 GB of RAM and Gurobi 9.0.0 [13] for solving our model within a time limit of 3 h[1].

Table 3 contains an overview of the runtimes with the corresponding gap to Gurobi's lower bound and the solutions found. Within three hours, we are able to find optimal solutions to 9 out of our 20 instances. At first glance, this may seem disappointing, especially taken together with the relatively high gaps to Gurobi's lower bound on the unsolved instances. However, we note that most of the computation time is spent trying to prove that the solution found is optimal.

---

[1] We note that more time does not necessarily lead to much better results due to the difficulty of the instances.

The columns under "Optimal solution found" indicate when the optimal solution was found and what the gap to the lower bound was when it was found. On average, the optimal solution is found after just 86 s, and on average another 783 s is needed to prove its optimality. Considering the geometric mean to avoid the effect of a couple long runtimes, we find the optimal solution after 29 s and require another 172 s to prove its optimality.

Once an optimal solution is found, the gap to the lower bound tends to still be rather high. A large part of this is due to the consideration of the vehicles, which often still have free capacity. The relaxation allows the model to increase the utilization of a vehicle by "splitting" it and sending it on different routes. This is certainly an indicator that more work is needed to tighten the model. However, it could indicate that the high gaps in the unsolved instances are just an illusion, and that the solutions available for a DSS are of high quality.

The three key contributors to the difficulty of solving an instance are the length of the planning horizon, the number of nodes or arcs, and the number of tasks. This should not come as a big surprise, as these three quantities are the main contributors of the size of the graph. However, a fourth aspect of instance difficulty is the set L, which describes the possible combinations of technicians and jobs. For the instances 120-1009-6-1.00 and 148-1870-6-1.00 an optimal solution can be found within a few seconds despite the large size of the graph, since there are only a few tasks and technicians. The chosen time discretization also plays a role in instance difficulty, as well as in the level of abstraction of the instance. A low discretization allows for highly detailed planning of technician's working plans, of course at the cost of a larger model.

4.3   Symmetry Breaking Analysis

Constraints (29) are not required if constraints (28) are formulated with the parameter M on both sides. The resulting set of constraints is as follows:

$$
M\left(1 - \sum_{(i,0)\in A} y_{s'i0}\right) + \sum_{(i,0)\in A} (t_i + t_{i0}^V)y_{si0} + t^B \leq M\left(1 - \sum_{(0,j)\in A} y_{s'0j}\right)
$$
$$
+ \sum_{(0,j)\in A} (t_j - t_{0j}^V)y_{s'0j} \qquad \forall s, s' \in S, \epsilon_{ss'} = 1 \quad (30)
$$

Figure 2 provides the runtimes (left) for instances for which we were able to find the optimal solution, and the gaps (right) of all other instances. Both model approaches of the constraints perform equally well on average. The scatter plot is given with the line $y = x$. Points below the line indicate better performance for constraints (30), whereas points above the line mean the performance of constraints (28) and (29) is better. Constraints (28) and (29) offer slightly lower gaps than constraints (30), although there is one outlier that is able to be solved to optimality only with constraints (30). The higher gaps for constraints (30) are due to the additional parameter M, which allows more invalid solutions in the relaxation. Of course, these results are subject to erraticism [12] and should not be considered to necessarily favor either formulation.

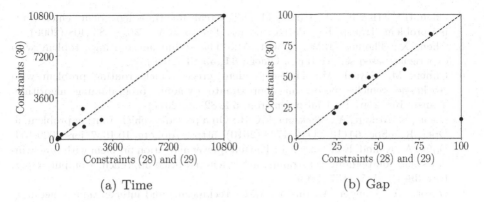

(a) Time   (b) Gap

Fig. 2. Comparison of the runtime and gap using the different model approaches for the order of technicians.

5   Conclusion

We presented a novel mathematical model for technician routing in the setting of inland shipping using a time-space-task graph. The model contains a number of components, such as time-dependent distances and variable task durations, that have not been solved together before in the VRP literature. The mathematical model provides solutions to all of the instances in our dataset, with the instances solved to optimality providing encouraging evidence that even the solutions not proven optimal are of high quality.

For future research, we intend to explore the following directions. As the instances in this paper are somewhat smaller than those solved by our industrial partner, we intend to make the model more effective for large-scale instances. This will include tightening the linear programming relaxation, as well as developing an effective primal heuristic. Another avenue of research is including stochastic components, as there are a number of uncertain input parameters to the ISTR, e.g. task completion times, travel times and ship arrival times.

Acknowledgments. We thank the Paderborn Center for Parallel Computation (PC²) for the use of the *OCuLUS* cluster.

References

1. Budai, G., Huisman, D., Dekker, R.: Scheduling preventive railway maintenance activities. J. Oper. Res. Soc. **57**(9), 1035–1044 (2006). https://doi.org/10.1057/palgrave.jors.2602085
2. Cappanera, P., Gouveia, L., Scutellà, M.G.: The skill vehicle routing problem. In: Pahl, J., Reiners, T., Voß, S. (eds.) INOC 2011. LNCS, vol. 6701, pp. 354–364. Springer, Heidelberg (2011). https://doi.org/10.1007/978-3-642-21527-8_40
3. Central Commission for the Navigation of the Rhine: CCNR Market Observation - Annual Report 2019. Central Commission for the Navigation of the Rhine (2019)

4. Chen, H.K., Hsueh, C.F., Chang, M.S.: The real-time time-dependent vehicle routing problem. Transp. Res. Part E: Logist. Transp. Rev. **42**(5), 383–408 (2006)
5. Chen, X., Thomas, B.W., Hewitt, M.: The technician routing problem with experience-based service times. Omega **61**, 49–61 (2016)
6. Çimen, M., Soysal, M.: Time-dependent green vehicle routing problem with stochastic vehicle speeds: an approximate dynamic programming algorithm. Transp. Res. Part D: Transp. Environ. **54**, 82–98 (2017)
7. Coene, S., Arnout, A., Spieksma, F.C.R.: On a periodic vehicle routing problem. J. Oper. Res. Soc. **61**(12), 1719–1728 (2010). https://doi.org/10.1057/jors.2009.154
8. Dohn, A., Kolind, E., Clausen, J.: The manpower allocation problem with time windows and job-teaming constraints: a branch-and-price approach. Comput. Oper. Res. **36**(4), 1145–1157 (2009)
9. Dutot, P.F., Laugier, A., Bustos, A.M.: Technicians and interventions scheduling for telecommunications. France Telecom R&D (2006)
10. Ehmke, J.F., Steinert, A., Mattfeld, D.C.: Advanced routing for city logistics service providers based on time-dependent travel times. J. Comput. Sci. **3**(4), 193–205 (2012)
11. Eurostat: Navigable inland waterways, by waterways type (2020). https://ec.europa.eu/eurostat/web/transport/data/database. Accessed 18 May 2020
12. Fischetti, M., Monaci, M.: Exploiting erraticism in search. Oper. Res. **62**(1), 114–122 (2014)
13. Gurobi Optimization: Gurobi Optimizer Reference Manual (2020). http://www.gurobi.com
14. Huang, Y., Zhao, L., van Woensel, T., Gross, J.P.: Time-dependent vehicle routing problem with path flexibility. Transp. Res. Part B: Methodol. **95**, 169–195 (2017)
15. Jeenanunta, C., Kasemsontitum, B., Noichawee, T.: A multi-commodity flow approach for aircraft routing and maintenance problem. In: 2011 IEEE International Conference on Quality and Reliability, pp. 150–155. IEEE (2011)
16. Lahyani, R., Khemakhem, M., Semet, F.: Rich vehicle routing problems: from a taxonomy to a definition. Eur. J. Oper. Res. **241**(1), 1–14 (2015)
17. Lawley, M., Parmeshwaran, V., Richard, J.P., Turkcan, A., Dalal, M., Ramcharan, D.: A time-space scheduling model for optimizing recurring bulk railcar deliveries. Transp. Res. Part B: Methodol. **42**(5), 438–454 (2008)
18. López-Santana, E., Akhavan-Tabatabaei, R., Dieulle, L., Labadie, N., Medaglia, A.L.: On the combined maintenance and routing optimization problem. Reliab. Eng. Syst. Saf. **145**, 199–214 (2016)
19. Malandraki, C., Daskin, M.S.: Time dependent vehicle routing problems: formulations, properties and heuristic algorithms. Transp. Sci. **26**(3), 185–200 (1992)
20. Mancini, S.: A real-life multi depot multi period vehicle routing problem with a heterogeneous fleet: formulation and adaptive large neighborhood search based matheuristic. Transp. Res. Part C: Emerg. Technol. **70**, 100–112 (2016)
21. Meneghetti, A., de Zan, E.: Technicians and interventions scheduling for the maintenance service of container ships. Proc. CIRP **47**, 216–221 (2016)
22. Schwarze, S., Voß, S.: Improved load balancing and resource utilization for the skill vehicle routing problem. Optimiz. Lett. **7**(8), 1805–1823 (2013). https://doi.org/10.1007/s11590-012-0524-2
23. Souyris, S., Cortés, C.E., Ordóñez, F., Weintraub, A.: A robust optimization approach to dispatching technicians under stochastic service times. Optimiz. Lett. **7**(7), 1549–1568 (2012). https://doi.org/10.1007/s11590-012-0557-6

24. Vidal, T., Crainic, T.G., Gendreau, M., Lahrichi, N., Rei, W.: A hybrid genetic algorithm for multidepot and periodic vehicle routing problems. Oper. Res. **60**(3), 611–624 (2012)
25. Yan, S., Shih, Y.L.: A time-space network model for work team scheduling after a major disaster. J. Chin. Inst. Eng. **30**(1), 63–75 (2007)
26. Zamorano, E., Stolletz, R.: Branch-and-price approaches for the multiperiod technician routing and scheduling problem. Eur. J. Oper. Res. **257**(1), 55–68 (2017)

Selected Topics in Logistics

Reactive GRASP-Based Algorithm
for Pallet Building Problem
with Visibility and Contiguity Constraints

Manuel Iori[1] [iD], Marco Locatelli[2] [iD], Mayron C. O. Moreira[3] [iD],
and Tiago Silveira[2($\boxtimes$)] [iD]

[1] Department of Sciences and Methods for Engineering,
University of Modena and Reggio Emilia, Reggio Emilia, Italy
manuel.iori@unimore.it
[2] Department of Engineering and Architecture, University of Parma, Parma, Italy
{marco.locatelli,tiago.silveira}@unipr.it
[3] Department of Computer Science, Federal University of Lavras, Lavras, Brazil
mayron.moreira@ufla.br

Abstract. In this paper, we study a pallet building problem that originates from a case study in a company that produces robotized systems
for freight transportation and logistics. The problem takes into account
well-known constraints, such as rotation and stackability, and other specific constraints such as visibility and contiguity among items belonging
to the same family. We formalize the problem and then solve it by means
of a GRASP metaheuristic. The algorithm is based on an Extreme Points
heuristic and a reactive mechanism. It uses a two-step strategy, in which
items are first grouped into horizontal layers, and then layers are stacked
one over the other to form pallets. The performance of the algorithm is
assessed through extensive computational tests on real-world instances.
The results show that the GRASP is able to create very compact packings for most of the instances with a limited computational effort.

Keywords: Pallet Building Problem · Practical constraints · Two-step
heuristic · Reactive GRASP · Real-world instances

1   Introduction

Cutting and Packing (C&P) is a field of the optimization area that involves
several interesting practical problems, being one of the most widely studied fields
of Operations Research [4,7,13,23]. In cutting problems, a set of stock units
has to be cut to produce smaller items, while in packing problems, a set of
items has to be packed into one or more containers. Some applications involve
the production of materials that come in panels (such as wood or glass), the

Supported by University of Parma, and by University of Modena and Reggio Emilia
under grant FAR 2018.

© Springer Nature Switzerland AG 2020
E. Lalla-Ruiz et al. (Eds.): ICCL 2020, LNCS 12433, pp. 651–665, 2020.
https://doi.org/10.1007/978-3-030-59747-4_42

optimization of layouts (as in industry or newspaper paging), and the loading and subsequent transportation of items employing containers, to mention a few.

A typology of C&P problems has been proposed in [28]. Later, Bortfeldt and Wäscher [4] extended the paper [28], considering the area of container loading and its main constraints. Specifically, Bortfeldt and Wäscher [4] made an important contribution by formalizing the main concepts of the container loading problems and the related constraints. Several interesting surveys and books have been published in recent years to try to review the fast-growing C&P literature [7, 21, 23, 25]. For a survey on C&P problems in freight transportation and vehicle routings, we refer to [15].

Most C&P problems are associated with mass-production operations in a company, as is the case for the problem we face in this work, a packing problem named Pallet Building Problem (PBP). Basically, through the solution of this problem we aim at loading a given set of items into one or more pallets meeting general and specific constraints so as to minimize the number of pallets used. That problem originates from a real-world robotized application and is thus subject to some non-trivial operational constraints. Typical items include, e.g., food packaging, soft drink bottles and cans. Items should be packed into layers, that must then be piled one over the other while respecting given stackability rules. In addition, items are grouped into families, and to facilitate loading/unloading operations, items from the same family packed into the same layer should be contiguous one with the other (as detailed in Sect. 2). That said, the loading of items and, therefore, the creation of pallets for this problem is a fundamental area for logistics, as it impacts not only the company's costs, but also the customer's final price (e.g., with the impact of freight logistics).

The PBP is NP-hard because it is a generalization of the Bin Packing Problem, which is known to be NP-hard [9]. In addition, it needs to be solved fast because it is frequently encountered at the operational level during the everyday working activity of a robotized packing system. For these reasons, we found it necessary to adopt heuristic solution algorithms. We derived these algorithms from the most successful and recent C&P studies, by embedding in them in a tailored way the additional operational constraints of the problem at hand. In a preliminary work, which was presented in [14], we developed a greedy heuristic and performed some preliminary computational tests.

The main contributions of this paper can be sketched as follows: (*i*) a real-world industrial application which addresses the concept of family, contiguity and visibility is presented, based on a concise literature review; (*ii*) a new heuristic to solve this problem is proposed, made up by a GRASP metaheuristic, using a reactive mechanism and efficient packing heuristics; and (*iii*) extensive computational tests on instances derived from the real-world case study are given.

The remainder of the paper is organized in five further sections. Section 2 provides a formal description of the problem. Section 3 briefly reviews the related literature. Section 4 presents the heuristic algorithms that we implemented. Section 5 gives the outcome of extensive computational tests. Conclusions and some future research directions are given in Section 6.

2   Problem Description

We are given a set R of identical pallets. Each pallet has a two-dimensional loading surface of width $W \in \mathbb{Z}_+^*$ and length $L \in \mathbb{Z}_+^*$, which can be used to load items up to a maximum height $H \in \mathbb{Z}_+^*$. We are also given a set $I = \{1, 2, \ldots, n\}$ of 3D rectangular item types, where each item type $i \in I$ contains b_i identical items, each having width $w_i \in \mathbb{Z}_+^*$, length $l_i \in \mathbb{Z}_+^*$, and height $h_i \in \mathbb{Z}_+^*$, such that $w_i \leq W$, $l_i \leq L$, and $h_i \leq H$.

In addition to item type, the concept of family is also essential to describe this problem. Type only refers to a specific characteristic, while family is a more general concept, covering at least one characteristic, e.g., geometric dimensions, material type, purpose of use and so on. As we are mainly interested in the packing problem, it is enough to take into account only geometric characteristics.

Considering the previous concepts, item types are partitioned into a set F of families as follows. Each item type i belongs to a given family $f \in F$, which, in the real instances we have addressed, is defined as a set of item types having similar height and weight. Note, however, that in other applications families could also be defined in different ways, e.g., each family could be made up by products of the same company. Items belonging to the same family can be used to form layers. Each layer is a 2D packing of items whose total width does not exceed W, and whose total length does not exceed L. In general, we consider three types of layers:

- *single-item type layers* are formed by a unique type of items;
- *single-family layers* are formed by different item types, but all belonging to the same family;
- *residual layers* are formed by a combination of items of different families or by items belonging to the same family but with occupation lower than a pre-defined threshold.

Let us call a *group* a set of items having the same item type and being loaded in the same layer. Packings of items in a layer should fulfill two operational constraints that concern groups and are aimed at easing unloading operations when the pallet is delivered. These constraints are named *contiguity* and *visibility* constraints, and are defined by the following contiguity and visibility concepts:

- *contiguity*: two items of the same type cannot be placed far apart in a layer because of the contiguity constraint. For this purpose, we establish the maximum Euclidean distance that can separate the two items without violating the constraint as follows. Let ℓ be the smallest edge length among all items in I. Let also $G \subseteq I$ be a generic subset of items of the same type packed into a layer. Then, two items $i, j \in G$ satisfy the contiguity constraint if the smallest Euclidean distance between the edges of i and the edges of j is lower than ℓ. Roughly speaking, in this way, we guarantee that no other item can fit between i and j. Therefore, the contiguity constraint for a generic layer r is met if, for each group, G packed in r, any item in G meets the minimum required Euclidean distance from at least another item in G, and there are no separated sub-groups of G (i.e., subgroups whose distance is ℓ or more).

– *visibility*: similarly to what we stated for the contiguity, we say that a group is visible from the outside if, for at least one item in the group, the Euclidean distance between its edges and the borders of the layer is lower than ℓ.

Single-item type layers and single-family layers can be used in a 3D packing to support other layers that are packed on top of them. For this purpose, we establish two additional conditions:

– a *stackability constraint* imposes that resistent items can not be on top of fragile ones. Formally, each family $f \in F$ is assigned with a level of resistance ρ_f, with small values indicating fragile items and large values indicating resistent ones. Items belonging to family f cannot be put below items belonging to family g if $\rho_f < \rho_g$;
– a layer can be used to support other layers only if its total area loaded with items reaches a minimum fraction α of the total loading surface WL. Parameter $0 < \alpha < 1$ is called *fill-factor*. A layer with loaded area lower than αWL can still be used to build a pallet, but can only be the topmost layer. We call this the *minimum supporting area constraint*.

We note that the stackability constraint above introduces a simplification of the real weight that an item has to bear in a load. The simplification is widely adopted in the literature as it works well in practice, see, e.g., [4]. For a more elaborated formulation of load bearing constraints, we refer to [8].

The aim of the PBP that we face is to load all items into the minimum number of pallets, by meeting the constraints: (i) all items should be packed in layers by satisfying contiguity and visibility constraints; (ii) at most one residual layer can be used per pallet, and, in such a case, it must be placed at the top of the pallet; (iii) single-item layers can be used to support any type of layers on top of them, as well as single-family layers can be used to support single-family and residual layers, as long as support and fill-factor constraints are satisfied; and (iv) the total height of the layers in any pallet should not exceed H.

3   Literature Review

The PBP emerges as a variant of the *Container Loading Problem* (CLP), which has received a good amount of attention in the last years. In [4] a comprehensive survey of the main constraints used in the literature is presented. In [25] the *Pallet Loading Problem* (PLP) is considered. In this problem a set of 2D rectangular items needs to be packed without overlapping and by allowing a 90° rotation into a 2D bin. In [7] a survey is presented about 2D and 3D Orthogonal Packing Problems, focusing on data structures for the packing representation and the item-positioning rules. Recently, Iori et al. [13] proposed a survey on variants of 2D packing problems, considering techniques to represent and handle items, relaxation methods, as well as exact and heuristic approaches. We also refer to [10] for a state-of-the-art computational analysis.

Considering the existing techniques in the literature to create solutions for the PBP, we separated them into two subsequent decisions: the first one consists in creating 2D layers, while the second one involves stacking layers to form pallets and thus considers the 3D characteristics.

For what concerns heuristics for 2D problems, Burke et al. [5] presented a new placement heuristic, called best-fit, for a 2D cutting problem, allowing non-guillotine packings and a 90° rotation. This technique uses a dynamic search based on the "niches", which are the available bottom-most gaps for an item in the partial packing. Imahori and Yagiura [12] improved the technique proposed in [5] by presenting a quicker implementation based on a balanced binary search tree and a priority heap. In [20] a complete set of techniques to deal with the 2D strip packing problem is presented. The authors use the so-called "skyline" approach in conjunction with greedy local search, a simulated annealing metaheuristic, and a multi-start diversification strategy.

Regarding 3D problems, Terno et al. [26] proposed the parallel generalized layer-wise loading approach (PGL-approach) for the CLP, using a complex branch-and-bound algorithm. Bortfeldt and Gehring [3] proposed a hybrid genetic algorithm to solve the CLP with a single container and a strongly heterogeneous set of boxes, considering orientation, stability, stacking, weight, and balance. Józefowska et al. [18] study the CLP considering rotation, stackability, and stability constraints. They considered a case study arising from a household equipment factory, proposing a best fit heuristic based on the idea of wall-building over available space. Kurpel et al. [19] presented techniques to obtain bounds and exact approaches to solving input minimization and output maximization versions of the multiple CLP with rectangular boxes, considering practical constraints such as rotation, vertical stability, and separation of the boxes. For what concerns the use of 3D packing problems arising in freight transportation, we refer to the surveys in [15, 24, 27].

The works that most resembles ours are the ones in [1, 22], however without addressing the concept of family, and contiguity and visibility constraints. Ranck Júnior et al. [22] addressed a real problem of a beverage company for packing boxes into a multi-compartment container and delivering over a predefined route, meeting the practical constraints of orientation, stability, load-bearing strength, and load balancing. Alonso et al. [1] considered practical constraints through a real example originating from a logistics company required to load of products into pallets (pallet building) and then load the created pallets into trucks (truck loading), by considering several practical constraints. For the pallet building, they incorporated orientation, support, priority, and stackability constraints. Regarding the truck loading, they adopted restrictions due to priority among pallets, stability, and stackability. They proposed a GRASP algorithm using a constructive phase, a randomized strategy to diversify the solutions, and an improvement phase.

4   Solution Algorithm

This section presents the full technique to solve the problem addressed, which we call *Reactive GRASP with Extreme Points Modified Heuristic* (GREP). GREP produces feasible solutions by using a two-step heuristic (Sect. 4.1) inside the GRASP framework tailored to a reactive method (Sect. 4.2).

4.1 Two-Step Heuristic

Creating Layers. The first step is related to the creation of the 2D layers. All of them are created considering only the dimensions l_i and w_i of item $i \in I$. This two-step heuristic is named *Extreme Points Modified Heuristic* (EPMH) and consists of the following parts.

Item Positioning . To find the position of an item in a layer, we use an adaptation of the Extreme Points Heuristic (EPH) proposed by Crainic et al. [6].

EPH works with the concept of extreme points. An extreme point e is a point in the 2D space, where an item $k \in I$ can be packed by taking into account a partial packing solution built so far. For the sake of clarity, packing an item k in an extreme point e means packing the bottom-left corner of k in e.

In EPH, the items are packed one at a time in the layer, by considering a set E of available extreme points. The set E is initialized with the origin point $(0,0)$. Then, each time a new item is packed, E is updated by removing the point used for the packing of the item, and possibly inserting new extreme points. These new extreme points are obtained by computing the projection of k over the partial packing solution under construction, considering both x and y axes. For the x-axis, EPH horizontally projects the top edge of item k to its left, until the projection touches a previously packed item or the left border of the layer (i.e., the y-axis). This is the first extreme point that is possibly created. For the y-axis, instead, EPH considers the right edge of item k and vertically projects it towards the bottom until the projection reaches a previously packed item or the bottom border of the layer. This is the second extreme point possibly created. The limitations of the original EPH and the way we overcome these ones when we deal with contiguity and visibility constraints are detailed in [14].

Item Grouping. This step is based on the extreme points set E. We divide it in two sets: *feasible extreme points*, E_f, and *infeasible extreme points*, E_i, representing, respectively, points that meet or do not meet the visibility and contiguity constraints for item k. Therefore, before adding k to the partial solution, we first update both sets, and later we check if k overlaps with previously packed items. An example of sets E_f and E_i is provided in Fig. 1.

That said, given the next item k, the point $e \in E_f$ that results in the best packing has to be chosen. For that purpose, the algorithm uses an evaluation function d to calculate the fitness for each e to aggregate k into a group. Therefore, the fitness of k is calculated in the following way: when k is the first item in a group, its fitness is calculated considering all items of the partial packing in the layer; when there is at least one item of the same type of k, the fitness is calculated by considering the items of this specific group.

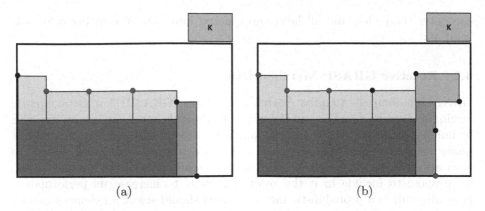

(a)   (b)

Fig. 1. Partial solutions and their feasible (black) and infeasible (red) extreme points for the next item k: representation of the extreme points that meet the boundary (1a), and contiguity (1b) constraints. (Color figure online)

Layer Creation. The main idea of EPMH is to create as many single-item and single-family layers as possible, since residual layers have to be inserted at the top of pallets, being at most one residual layer per pallet.

The layer generation that we adopted analyzes geometric characteristics of the items. EPMH sorts the family items by a specific criterion and, within each family, item types are also sorted by a specific criterion. Using this order, the heuristic tries to generate single-item layers by packing items one at a time according to the concepts previously described. If the packing obtained with a single item type meets the fill-factor constraint, but it is not enough to fill up the layer yet, EPMH tries adding more items of the same family to generate a single-family layer. Items are inserted in the residual list when: (a) the area of the remaining unpacked items of a specific family does not meet the fill factor constraint; or (b) the current layer found by the packing heuristic creates a packing that does not meet the fill factor constraint. After all families have been analyzed, the items of the residual list will be packed in other layers, thus forming residual layers.

Creating Pallets. EPMH uses a greedy heuristic to put layers together into pallets. This heuristic is described as follows: single-item, single-family and residual layers are sorted according to non increasing *stackability* (computed as the maximum stackability value among the items in the layer), breaking ties by non increasing *height* (calculated as the height of the highest item in the layer). Since residual layers need to be packed in separated pallets, the greedy heuristic starts by choosing the first residual layer, if any, in the order, and using it to initialize a pallet. Then, it fills the current pallet with as many single-item layers as possible, one at a time in the order, by fulfilling stackability and maximum height constraint. If the current pallet has still unused height, the heuristic attempts filling the pallet with single-family layers. The process is repeated until no more layer

can enter the pallet, and all layers are packed into pallets, creating a feasible
solution.

4.2 Reactive GRASP Metaheuristic

Greedy Randomized Adaptive Search Procedures (GRASP) is a metaheuristic
originally developed by Feo and Resende [11]. Roughly speaking, it is an iterative
technique that mixes greedy and randomized processes, divided in a *constructive
phase* to explore the solution space and in an *improvement phase* to try to
improve solutions. Although the efficiency of the original GRASP metaheuristic,
we propose to include in it the *reactive method* to increase its performance.
Basically, this is a probabilistic method which should select an element among
many options, where each option receives an independent probability, which is
adaptively modified according to the quality of the solution generated. We detail
all phases of the proposed reactive GRASP below.

Constructive Phase. This phase controls EPMH to create a feasible solution.

Choosing an Item. The GRASP idea is to mix greedy and random choices in
order to explore the search space more widely. In this way, this concept is easily
adapted to the layer creation heuristic (Sect. 4.1 – *Layer Creation*). First, the
algorithm creates the data structure S by classifying the item types $i \in I$ following a *random* order for families, and a non increasing order of *width* for items.
It is important to highlight that all solutions returned by the constructive phase
are generated from the initial order of S, while this order changes during the
local search phase.

Considering the selection process over S, we define the selectable range based
on the parameter ϵ, which stands for the percentage of elements analyzed on a
random choice. Let F_S be the sorted set of families which represents the order of
the families in S, and $G_f \subseteq S$ the sorted set of item types $s \in S$ which represents
the order of the item types of a family $f \in F_S$. In this case, a family f is selected
randomly among the first $\epsilon|F_S|$ families, and then, $s \in G_f$ is selected among the
first $\epsilon|G_f|$ item types.

Choosing a Fitness Evaluation Function . This method is based on the *reactive
method*, which is used to select a fitness evaluation function to evaluate the
extreme points chosen from E_f. Thus, considering the next item s, we use the
set D, that stands for the set of fitness evaluation functions, formed by the
functions *Lower X*, *Lower Y*, *Bounding Box*, *Bounding Square*, *Simple Contacts*,
Complex Contacts, *Distance Sum*, and *Center of Gravity*. Details on each of
these functions are described in [14].

The reactive method works as follows: given a fitness evaluation functions
set D and a probability function $P(d_s)$ to choose the function $d_s \in D$ related to
the item type $s \in S$, the method initializes $P(d_s)$ with the uniform distribution
over D and updates its values after a certain number of iterations (fixed by

parameter ψ), according to the quality of the respective generated solutions. The probabilities $P(d_s)$ are updated according to equations in the lines 27 and 28 on Algorithm 1. Note that the better the partial solution found by d_s, the greater the probability $P(d_s)$ to select d_s in the next iterations.

Choosing an Extreme Point . This step is an adaptation of the EPMH when positioning items (Sect. 4.1 – *Item Positioning*). To tailor the random GRASP methods to the deterministic EPMH ideas, the heuristic uses the parameter ϵ in the following way: let T be the sorted set composed by all extreme points of E_f referring to the item type s evaluated by d_s in a non decreasing order, and the parameter ϵ that stands for the percentage of extreme points analyzed on a random choice, the heuristic selects an extreme point among the first $\epsilon|T|$ extreme points of T, i.e., the parameter ϵ stands for the percentage of the best extreme points of E_f that can be chosen randomly.

Final Solution . After creating the layers, the pallets are generated by the greedy heuristic (Sect. 4.1 – *Creating Pallets*). In fact, the GRASP heuristic could be used also in this phase, so as to generate the pallets. We are actually investigating the use of an exact approach for this simpler phase.

Improvement Phase. This phase generates the solution from scratch, applying small modifications in S, since it is difficult to change the position of individual items without violating the contiguity and visibility constraints.

The improvement phase reconstructs the solution through a local search. Given S and the evaluation function d_s used in the constructive phase, the method repacks each $s \in S$ after applying the following modification in S: considering all families $f \in F$, select randomly f_a and f_b (if any) and switch the order of the respective group of items in S; later, for each family $f \in F$, select randomly the item types i_c and i_d (if any) in this group, and switch the order of the respective items in S. This local search uses the *First Improvement Strategy*, which considers the original data structure S and applies the previous local search up to either the quality of the solution is improved or a certain number of repetitions is reached (we set this value to be equal to 25).

Despite the improvement phase constitutes an essential part of the GRASP metaheuristic, this phase is not always carried out, since bad starting solutions tend to produce bad final solutions. Thus, we consider a threshold to perform this phase, using an upper bound UB, which is initialized with the value of the first solution created and updated whenever a new solution has a fitness better than the current UB. To avoid stagnation during this phase, GRASP controls UB in the following way: if the fitness of a new solution does not reach the value UB, the method increases the number of consecutive rejections κ. After a certain number of rejected solutions (constant MAX_REJECTED), the UB value is updated by the formula $UB = 0.98 * UB$ and κ is reset equal to 0. Thus, the algorithm forces the improvement phase for solutions which are not necessarily the best ones but are of "good enough" quality.

Evaluation of the Solution. The structure of the solution of the problem addressed contains several information that can help the algorithm to explore the search space. Thus, instead of using the basic bin packing objective function, we modify it in this way: let n_r be the number of residual layers, n_l be the total number of layers, n_p be the total number of pallets and f_l be the 2D fill factor of the layers, the algorithm calculates the value of the objective function as a maximization of $(v_{residual} + v_{pallets} + f_l)/3$, where $v_{residual}$ is the value of the logarithm function for the residual layers, that considers the proportion of n_r over n_l, being defined as $v_{residual} = -\log_{n_l+1}\frac{n_r+1}{n_l+1}$, and $v_{pallets}$ is the value of the logarithm function for the total number of pallets, that considers the proportion of n_p over n_l, being defined as $v_{pallets} = -\log_{n_l+1}\frac{n_p+1}{n_l+1}$. All individual values of the objective function are in the range between 0 and 1. About the logarithmic functions, the idea is to do the evaluation function more sensitive to small variations of residual layers and the number of pallets.

Algorithm. GREP is described in Algorithm 1. The algorithm can be divided into two distinct parts. First, related to the standard GRASP, the item type set is sorted (line 2) and, until the stopping condition (execution time) is not fulfilled (line 3), the algorithm selects a fitness evaluation function (line 4) to construct a feasible solution to the problem (line 7). The solution is evaluated (line 8) and compared to the current reference value UB (line 9): if the value of the solution is higher, the algorithm tries to improve the solution (line 11); otherwise, the reference value is decreased after a prefixed number of iterations without an improvement (lines 16–18). The second part is related to the reactive method. Here, the best (line 19) and worst (line 22) values of the fitness evaluation function are possibly updated. Next, the mean value of the current fitness evaluation function is updated (lines 24–25). In the end, after a prefixed number of iterations (line 26), all fitness evaluation functions are evaluated individually (line 27) and the probability function is updated (line 28).

5   Computational Results

All experiments have been conducted on a Virtual Machine VMware®, Intel® Xeon® CPU E5-2640 v2 2.00 GHz, 16 GB RAM, Ubuntu Server 18.04 OS. The algorithms have been implemented in Java and ran using Oracle® JDK 11.

We solved the proposed instances with GREP (Sect. 4). For each instance, we set the time limit to 5 min, running the algorithm 10 times. We carried out a simple test for parametric configuration of ϵ using a restrict set of values, and we have chosen $\epsilon = 0.15$. The remaining parameters are $\varrho = 10$, and MAX_REJECTED = 5, as suggested in [2].

We used the same 24 instances presented in [14], that are separated into 4 groups, each containing 6 instances. Table 1 summarizes the details of the instances, reporting an instance field and its respective value by row: ID number, number of item types, number of families, and total of items. For all instances, the fill factor was set to 75%, and the container dimensions were set equal to

---

Algorithm 1: REACTIVEGRASP

---
1 **begin**
2      $S \leftarrow$ SORTITEMS(I, $order\_family$, $order\_type$);
3   **while** NOTSTOPCONDITION$(numIter, maxIter, time)$ **do**
4          $d_s \leftarrow$ CHOOSECRITERION(d_s^*, $P_{d_s^*}$);
5          $n_{d_s^*} = n_{d_s^*} + 1$;
6          $numIter = numIter + 1$;
7          $Sol \leftarrow$ CONSTRUCTIVE(S,R,d_s,ϵ);
8          $V \leftarrow$ EVALUATESOLUTION(Sol);
9   **if** $V > UB$ **then**
10             $\kappa = 0$;
11             $Sol \leftarrow$ IMPROVEMENT(S,R,d_s,ϵ);
12             $V \leftarrow$ EVALUATESOLUTION(Sol);
13             $UB \leftarrow V$;
14   **else**
15             $\kappa \leftarrow \kappa + 1$;
16   **if** $\kappa >$ MAX_REJECTED **then**
17                 $UB \leftarrow 0.98 * UB$;
18                 $\kappa = 0$;
19   **if** $V > V_{best}$ **then**
20             $V_{best} \leftarrow V$;
21             $Sol_{best} \leftarrow Sol$;
22   **if** $V < V_{worst}$ **then**
23             $V_{worst} \leftarrow V$;
24         $Sum_{d_s^*} = Sum_{d_s^*} + V$;
25         $mean_{d_s^*} = \frac{Sum_{d_s^*}}{n_{d_s^*}}$;
26   **if** $mod(numIter, \psi) = 0$ **then**
27             $eval_{d_s^*} \leftarrow (\frac{mean_{d_s^*} - V_{worst}}{V_{best} - V_{worst}})^\varrho$, $\forall \, d_s^* \in D$;
28             $P(d_s^*) \leftarrow \frac{eval_{d_s^*}}{\sum_{d_s' \in D}(eval_{d_s'})}$, $\forall \, d_s^* \in D$;
29   **return** Sol_{best};

1500, 1250, and 1050 for height, width, and length, respectively. We tested it allowing rotation of 90° of the items.

5.1 Evaluation

We report the individual and average results for GREP to analyze its performance. Besides that, we show the best average results obtained by EPMH in [14] over the same instances, in order to compare the performance between both strategies in a consistent way. These results are summarized in Table 2.

Table 2 reports: algorithm; instance (average or individual ones), total number of pallets in the solution; total number of layers created; in the six successive

Table 1. Instances settings.

Field	Value																							
ID	01	02	03	04	05	06	07	08	09	10	11	12	13	14	15	16	17	18	19	20	21	22	23	24
n	20		23		29		34		37		48		59		64		61		75		79		66	
N. of families	4	12	4	13	6	15	7	17	6	17	9	18	10	19	11	19	10	19	16	20	17	21	13	19
Sum b_i	877	269	388	115	438	2103	698	1322	300	449	395	748	455	633	658	683	300	797	790	829	855	944	738	767

columns it reports the minimum, maximum and average pallet utilization and fill factor (2D space of all layers), respectively; average number of single-item, single-family and residual layers; maximum percentage of residual layers found among the instances (worst case result); minimum, maximum and average values of the objective function; total number of iterations; total number of local searches; ratio between the total number of local searches and the total number of iterations. Considering GREP, each row provides the average individual results after 10 iterations, except the last line which reports the average among all individual results, excluding the value for the column *Max percent. RL*, which stands for the largest value among all. Considering EPMH, the respective row reports the best average among all individual results when using the Bounding Box function, meeting all constraints used in this work, i.e., those ones meeting contiguity, rotation (R), and visibility (B) constraints. We highlight in bold the best average values for each column.

From Table 2, considering the average results, we notice that the number of layers in EPMH is slightly lower than in GREP, but the number of pallets is considerably larger. Thus, we highlight that the minimization of the number of layers is less relevant than the way in which these are created, since the overall number of pallets depends on the disposition of items within the layers. Considering layer type fields, we observe an increase in the number of single-item and single-family layers, while the number of residual layers is reduced, when using GREP. About the quality metric that analyze the worst case result (*Max percent. RL*), the reported value is significantly better when using GREP (at most 50%). Regarding to execution time, EPMH carried out in 104 ms (not reported in that table), in contrast to 5 min for GREP.

Considering the individual results of GREP from Table 2, let us focus first on the utilization of layers and pallets. Regarding the 2D fill factor, this value is quite stable (85% in average). In contrast, this behaviour is quite different when we analyze the pallet filling, in which the values fluctuate between 25% and 84% in average.

For what concerns the GRASP metaheuristic, we highlight the influence of the strategy to readapt the UB value. As the UB value is related to the local search process, it is interesting to adjust it according to the quality and time spent to find a new solution. In particular, the rate of change of the UB value is quite important: large and frequent variations of UB tend to favor a larger number of local searches, while small and not frequent variations tend to reduce the number of local searches. Thus, we balance this trade-off using a small (2%)

Table 2. Computational results (individual and average).

Alg.	Inst.	N. of pallets	N. of layers	Pallet filling Min	Max	Avg	2D fill factor Min	Max	Avg	Single-item layers	Single-family layers	Resid. layers (RL)	Max. perc. RL(%)	Objective funciton Min	Max	Avg	Total iterat. (TI)	Tot. l. search. (LS)	Ratio LS/TI (%)
GREP	01	11.00	46.00	0.44	0.84	0.73	0.55	0.94	0.83	32.10	12.90	1.00	2.17	0.668	0.668	0.668	6984.3	486.7	6.97
	02	6.40	16.00	0.14	0.76	0.40	0.76	0.89	0.82	9.80	2.10	4.10	25.63	0.500	0.522	0.513	29773.3	1636.9	5.50
	03	6.00	27.00	0.65	0.89	0.78	0.66	0.95	0.84	17.00	9.00	1.00	3.70	0.682	0.682	0.682	19551.4	1047.0	5.36
	04	3.00	6.00	0.12	0.59	0.28	0.64	0.92	0.79	1.00	2.00	3.00	50.00	0.456	0.456	0.456	45275.8	2560.9	5.66
	05	6.00	29.30	0.35	0.85	0.70	0.78	0.94	0.87	20.30	7.00	2.00	6.83	0.654	0.661	0.659	18060.2	1381.5	7.65
	06	29.00	108.00	0.13	0.89	0.77	0.69	0.98	0.87	100.00	4.00	4.00	3.70	0.600	0.600	0.600	3448.4	306.6	8.89
	07	12.20	52.00	0.43	0.88	0.75	0.71	0.93	0.86	36.30	13.70	2.00	3.85	0.639	0.645	0.644	10153.4	827.0	8.15
	08	22.40	91.10	0.20	0.85	0.66	0.68	0.95	0.86	61.70	15.50	13.90	15.26	0.521	0.526	0.523	4749.0	576.5	12.14
	09	4.90	16.00	0.23	0.86	0.63	0.74	0.96	0.86	8.60	5.40	2.00	12.50	0.613	0.634	0.615	13610.7	1315.5	9.67
	10	9.00	24.00	0.13	0.77	0.42	0.71	0.94	0.82	8.60	8.60	6.00	25.00	0.499	0.499	0.499	11022.2	778.8	7.07
	11	7.00	19.00	0.11	0.85	0.46	0.76	0.96	0.85	7.60	8.40	3.00	15.79	0.566	0.566	0.566	10075.0	795.1	7.89
	12	14.80	42.00	0.11	0.84	0.47	0.62	0.95	0.84	16.30	17.60	8.10	19.29	0.502	0.512	0.506	6744.8	652.7	9.68
	13	8.70	33.00	0.24	0.88	0.66	0.69	0.95	0.86	13.70	14.70	4.60	13.94	0.565	0.593	0.575	12603.4	819.7	6.50
	14	10.00	32.20	0.11	0.87	0.51	0.69	0.98	0.83	13.60	13.60	5.00	15.53	0.542	0.547	0.546	6946.1	525.7	7.57
	15	11.10	48.00	0.47	0.85	0.74	0.68	0.95	0.85	20.70	23.30	4.00	8.33	0.593	0.599	0.599	9303.9	709.1	7.62
	16	12.10	50.00	0.54	0.85	0.72	0.72	0.97	0.87	22.90	19.40	7.70	15.40	0.552	0.562	0.554	8637.0	711.3	8.24
	17	6.00	16.00	0.12	0.82	0.42	0.70	0.96	0.83	2.80	10.20	3.00	18.75	0.552	0.552	0.552	15302.9	1216.7	7.95
	18	12.60	38.10	0.11	0.89	0.50	0.71	0.98	0.85	13.40	16.80	7.90	20.73	0.511	0.518	0.515	5332.9	489.8	9.18
	19	12.00	50.10	0.32	0.86	0.69	0.75	0.96	0.86	19.70	24.60	5.80	11.58	0.568	0.591	0.574	6464.5	530.3	8.21
	20	13.60	55.20	0.16	0.87	0.69	0.58	0.95	0.86	25.60	23.30	6.30	11.41	0.564	0.575	0.568	5897.0	518.2	8.79
	21	12.10	53.00	0.44	0.85	0.70	0.68	0.95	0.85	20.60	26.50	5.90	11.13	0.572	0.579	0.573	5692.7	418.4	7.35
	22	15.20	59.60	0.15	0.84	0.63	0.63	0.95	0.84	28.80	22.80	8.00	13.42	0.537	0.552	0.543	4468.1	386.7	8.66
	23	10.70	44.90	0.27	0.86	0.69	0.67	0.95	0.85	13.20	26.40	5.30	11.80	0.564	0.585	0.576	6203.8	433.6	6.99
	24	12.50	46.30	0.12	0.84	0.61	0.58	0.95	0.84	16.60	22.80	6.90	14.90	0.541	0.559	0.544	6125.2	465.3	7.60
	AVG	**11.18**	**41.78**	0.25	0.84	0.61	0.68	0.95	**0.85**	**22.15**	**14.61**	**5.02**	**50.00**	0.5650	0.5742	0.5687	11351.1	816.25	7.89
EPMH	**AVG**	14.46	**41.00**	-	-	-	-	-	**0.86**	21.79	11.58	7.63	66.67	-	-	-	1	-	-

but fast (after 5 iterations without improvement) decrement in UB, which contributes to both exploitation and exploration of the search space. In the end, GREP carried out on average a percentage of local searches equal to 8%.

6   Conclusions

In this paper, we studied a pallet building problem with item rotations and practical constraints involving visibility and contiguity. We proposed an extension of the work proposed in [14] based on the GRASP metaheuristic with reactive method when applying the Extreme Points heuristic for creating 2D layers and the Greedy heuristic for creating 3D pallets. Regarding the reactive method, we tailored GRASP to Extreme Points heuristics to find a new place to pack the next item based on several fitness evaluation functions. Extensive computational experiments on real-world instances reported good final results, thus showing that GRASP is an efficient strategy for this type of problem.

As future work, we intend to develop other types of local searches to try to enhance the quality of the solutions generated so far, and to propose formal mathematical models to express the concept of contiguity and visibility of items. About the GRASP metaheuristic, it is possible to extend it using a learning mechanism through the recently developed fixed set search metaheuristic, as presented in [16,17]. We are also interested in extending the concept of family to address characteristics beyond the geometric ones. In that way, it will be possible to address more complex problems when using the contiguity and visibility constraints, as for example, the Vehicle Routing Problem (VRP). Bringing both problems together (PBP and VRP), the shared knowledge about well-defined families is useful for the whole process (packing and delivery), helping to solve both problems in a more efficient way.

References

1. Alonso, M., Alvarez-Valdes, R., Parreño, F., Tamarit, J.: Algorithms for pallet building and truck loading in an interdepot transportation problem. Math. Probl. Eng. **2016**, 1–11 (2016)
2. Alonso, M., Alvarez-Valdes, R., Tamarit, J., Parreño, F.: A reactive GRASP algorithm for the container loading problem with load-bearing constraints. Eur. J. Ind. Eng. **8**, 669–694 (2014)
3. Bortfeldt, A., Gehring, H.: A hybrid genetic algorithm for the container loading problem. Eur. J. Oper. Res. **131**, 143–161 (2001)
4. Bortfeldt, A., Wäscher, G.: Constraints in container loading - a state-of-the-art review. Eur. J. Oper. Res. **229**, 1–20 (2013)
5. Burke, E., Kendall, G., Whitwell, G.: A new placement heuristic for the orthogonal stock-cutting problem. Oper. Res. **52**, 655–671 (2004)
6. Crainic, T., Perboli, G., Tadei, R.: Extreme point-based heuristics for three-dimensional bin packing. INFORMS J. Comput. **20**, 368–384 (2008)
7. Crainic, T., Perboli, G., Tadei, R.: Recent advances in multi-dimensional packing problems. In: New Technologies, Chap. 5. IntechOpen (2012)

8. de Queiroz, T., Miyazawa, F.: Two-dimensional strip packing problem with load balancing, load bearing and multi-drop constraints. Int. J. Prod. Econ. **145**, 511–530 (2013)
9. Delorme, M., Iori, M., Martello, S.: Bin packing and cutting stock problems: mathematical models and exact algorithms. Eur. J. Oper. Res. **255**, 1–20 (2016)
10. Delorme, M., Iori, M., Martello, S.: Logic based benders decomposition for orthogonal stock cutting problems. Comput. Oper. Res. **78**, 290–298 (2017)
11. Feo, T., Resende, M.: Greedy randomized adaptive search procedures. J. Glob. Optim. **6**, 109–133 (1995)
12. Imahori, S., Yagiura, M.: The best-fit heuristic for the rectangular strip packing problem: an efficient implementation and the worst-case approximation ratio. Comput. Oper. Res. **37**, 325–333 (2010)
13. Iori, M., Lima, V., Martello, S., Miyazawa, F., Monaci, M.: Two-dimensional cutting and packing: problems and solution techniques. Technical report, University of Bologna (2019)
14. Iori, M., Locatelli, M., Moreira, M., Silveira, T.: Solution of a practical pallet building problem with visibility and contiguity constraints. In: International Conference on Enterprise Information Systems, vol. 1, pp. 327–338. SciTePress (2020)
15. Iori, M., Martello, S.: Routing problems with loading constraints. TOP **18**, 4–27 (2010)
16. Jovanovic, R., Voß, S.: Fixed set search applied to the minimum weighted vertex cover problem. In: Kotsireas, I., Pardalos, P., Parsopoulos, K.E., Souravlias, D., Tsokas, A. (eds.) SEA 2019. LNCS, vol. 11544, pp. 490–504. Springer, Cham (2019). https://doi.org/10.1007/978-3-030-34029-2_31
17. Jovanovic, R., Voß, S.: The fixed set search applied to the power dominating set problem. Expert Syst. e12559 (2020)
18. Józefowska, J., Pawlak, G., Pesch, E., Morze, M., Kowalski, D.: Fast truck-packing of 3D boxes. Eng. Manag. Prod. Serv. **10**, 29–40 (2018)
19. Kurpel, D., Scarpin, C., Pécora Junior, J., Schenekemberg, C., Coelho, L.: The exact solutions of several types of container loading problems. Eur. J. Oper. Res. **284**, 87–107 (2020)
20. Leung, S., Zhang, D., Sim, K.: A two-stage intelligent search algorithm for the two-dimensional strip packing problem. Eur. J. Oper. Res. **215**, 57–69 (2011)
21. Lodi, A., Martello, S., Monaci, M., Vigo, D.: Two-Dimensional Bin Packing Problems, pp. 107–129. Wiley, Hoboken (2014)
22. Ranck Júnior, R., Yanasse, H., Morabito, R., Junqueira, L.: A hybrid approach for a multi-compartment container loading problem. Expert Syst. Appl. **137**, 471–492 (2019)
23. Scheithauer, G.: Introduction to Cutting and Packing Optimization. Springer, Cham (2018)
24. Schmid, V., Doerner, K., Laporte, G.: Rich routing problems arising in supply chain management. Eur. J. Oper. Res. **224**, 435–448 (2013)
25. Silva, E., Oliveira, J., Wäscher, G.: The pallet loading problem: a review of solution methods and computational experiments. Int. Trans. Oper. Res. **23**, 147–172 (2016)
26. Terno, J., Scheithauer, G., Sommerweiß, U., Riehme, J.: An efficient approach for the multi-pallet loading problem. Eur. J. Oper. Res. **123**, 372–381 (2000)
27. Vidal, T., Crainic, T., Gendreau, M., Prins, C.: Heuristics for multi-attribute vehicle routing problems: a survey and synthesis. Eur. J. Oper. Res. **231**, 1–21 (2013)
28. Wäscher, G., Haußner, H., Schumann, H.: An improved typology of cutting and packing problems. Eur. J. Oper. Res. **183**, 1109–1130 (2007)

Game Theoretic Analysis of State Interventions to Reduce Customer Returns in E-Commerce

Maria Beranek[✉]

Chair of Business Management, esp. Industrial Management,
Faculty of Business and Economics, TU Dresden, 01062 Dresden, Germany
maria.beranek@tu-dresden.de

Abstract. The constantly growing online trade offers various opportunities for companies, but is also associated with the issue of an increasing number of customer returns. Since these are both economically and ecologically problematic, policymakers are currently discussing strategies to avoid these returns and the associated disposals. In a game theoretic model, different options of state intervention in the supply chain are investigated and compared with each other, i.e., the prohibition of disposal, the remission of value added tax on donations and a state-imposed return fee. For the resulting complex optimization problem, a solution approach is first presented to determine the Stackelberg equilibrium of the game. A comprehensive numerical analysis shows that above all the remission of the value added tax on donations as well as a state-imposed return fee for customers can lead to promising results. Nevertheless, the analysis also reveals that even without intervention in the market, members of the supply chain always have a personal interest in avoiding returns and disposal whenever possible.

Keywords: Reverse logistics · Customer returns · State interventions

1 Introduction

At a time in which online trade is constantly growing and displacing the stationary trade, returns management is also becoming increasingly important and is regarded as one of the main challenges of reverse logistics [5,20]. On the one hand, customer friendly return policies are a strategic instrument for companies. On the other hand, large amounts of returns are a problem for firms - in average, as at least 30% of all products ordered online are sent back to the retailer [18]. These not only generate costs, they also have a negative impact on the environment, for example, because additional transport is required or because resale is not always possible. For example, the online retailer Amazon was massively criticized in the German media for disposing of in large quantities products that were actually still functional but could not be resold [4]. According to studies, the impression of excessive disposal is deceptive, as the proportion of goods

© Springer Nature Switzerland AG 2020
E. Lalla-Ruiz et al. (Eds.): ICCL 2020, LNCS 12433, pp. 666–681, 2020.
https://doi.org/10.1007/978-3-030-59747-4_43

disposed of is about 4% [16]. Nevertheless, this scandal of the destruction of goods has provoked a debate within German politics. For example, the German Recycling Act has been updated, forcing manufacturers and retailers to report transparently on how they deal with surplus products. This step is partly seen as too weak and instead a complete prohibition of disposal is demanded by some parties, like it is also planned in France.

However, a prohibition of disposal is controversial and only one possible instrument to reduce return-based disposals. In this paper, methods of game theory are used to investigate various possibilities of state intervention in the supply chain to avoid returns and their disposal. In addition to the option of a prohibition of disposals, a tax remission on donations in kind as well as a state-imposed return fee to be borne by the customers are considered.

This analysis contributes to existing research in several ways. Currently, there is an increasing number of publications addressing customer returns in the supply chain. For a general overview on literature about customer returns, see [1]. Often, it is a common assumption that returned goods are as salable as new goods. For example, [19] and [12] consider newsboy problems including a return option for customers. Returns are assumed to have the same quality as new products so that they can be resold, if there is still enough demand. In [14] the original Wagner-Whitin problem is extended and includes product returns, which are all remanufactured and then sold as new. Also in [8], returns are resold at the same market price as the regular products.

In this paper instead, we assume that returns cannot be sold along with new items, as it is, e.g., generally handled by the MediaMarktSaturn Retail Group, the leading consumer electronics retailer in Europe [7], for instance due to warranty reasons. Returns can instead be sold on a secondary market at a reduced price. Due to the added complexity, only few papers in the context of return management include secondary markets into their analysis, see, e.g., [9,15]. These articles and others involving secondary markets (see, e.g., [6,11]), have in common that they typically assume that all items are salable to secondary customers or that the demand of those customers is fixed. We, however, explicitly consider different options, and allow the disposal or donation of goods that is unsaleable with the intention of being closer to reality. For this purpose we introduce deterministic demand functions for both the primary and secondary market.

Furthermore, a typical problem that is discussed in the field of customer returns is the optimal return policy. This is usually considered to be how much of the original purchase price is refunded to the customer. Typical options include full, partial or no refunds, see, e.g., [2,10,13]. In our paper we consider full refunds and analyze instead the certainly less considered impact of return fees on the customer behavior, i.e., their demand (see also [8]), and additionally on the proportion of items being returned.

To the best of our knowledge, all problems described so far have only been analyzed in settings of free markets. Therefore, we want to take up current political issues and investigate how returns and related disposals can be reduced through state interventions.

In Sect. 2, we will first introduce a general basic model for which no market interventions occur. For this model, a solution approach is presented in Sect. 3. In Sect. 4, a numerical analysis is performed for the basic model, i.e., from the perspective of a free market. The results are then compared with those obtained under the occurrence of state interventions in Sect. 5, which are special cases of the basic model. Section 6 concludes the paper. Supplementary material is provided in the electronic appendix at https://t1p.de/6yjs.

2   The Basic Model

In the following, the game theoretic basic model is presented. Its general formulation allows first to examine the decisions of the players without state interventions in the game. These interventions can then be examined later as special cases of the basic model.

2.1   Model Description

We consider a two-echelon supply chain, consisting of a manufacturer and a retailer. We assume that the retailer has the market power and acts as the Stackelberg leader. The manufacturer acts as the Stackelberg follower. All notations used in this paper are summarized in Table 5 in the electronic appendix. The structure of the supply chain and its material and cash flows are illustrated in Fig. 1 and explained as follows.

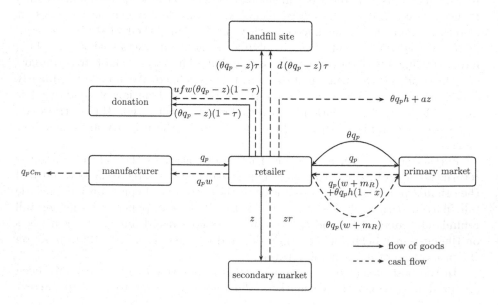

Fig. 1. Flow of goods and cash flow in the basic model

- The manufacturer produces the amount q_p of items demanded by the primary market p at costs c_m per item before selling them at the wholesale price $w \geq 0$ per unit to the retailer. The retailer adds its margin $m_R \geq 0$ before distributing the items to the primary market.
- The customers of the primary market return their purchased products to the retailer with a probability of θ, as some customers decide that the product does not match their expectations (see, e.g., [12,20]). We neglect the occurrence of products which are actually non-functional.

  Depending on the retailer's return policy, the costs h associated with the return must be borne by the retailer ($x = 1$) or by the customers themselves ($x = 0$). As in practice, the return rate is also influenced by this return policy:

$$\theta = \phi + \psi x \tag{1}$$

  where $\phi > 0$ is the basic return rate and $\psi > 0$ is the fraction of customers that is tempted to return if a free return policy is offered. See also [3,13] and [8], for example, where similar linear return functions are used. Note that $\phi + \psi \leq 1$ must hold.

  As it is common in many online retail stores, the complete purchase price will be refunded to the customers who return the product [12].
- The primary customer's demand q_p is described by a linear function

$$q_p = \alpha_p - \beta_p(w + m_R) - \lambda(1 - x) \cdot h \cdot y \tag{2}$$

  where $\alpha_p > 0$ is the primary market's basic demand. $\beta_p > 0$ is the customer's sensitivity to the retail price ($w + m_R$). It is further assumed that the customer's demand is also influenced by the return policy the retailer offers. If the retailer covers the cost of h and $x = 1$, this will prevent customers from migrating to other retailers. Otherwise, if $x = 0$, the customer's demand might decrease with sensitivity λ [8].

  For simplicity, it is assumed that the return fee h is the same for everyone in the market. If the government then dictates that customers pay the return costs themselves ($x = 0$), the same conditions apply to everyone in the market. This means that although the number of returns is still declining, it would not be advantageous for any customer to migrate to other retailers despite the return fee. Hence, the negative impact on demand would be offset by this state intervention. This effect is described by means of the binary variable y which in this case would take the value 0. Without state interventions, $y = 1$ holds.
- As in many industries, we assume that it is not possible to simply resell returned items due to warranty reasons and the customer's expectation to receive faultless, undamaged and unused goods. Typical types of products considered in this paper are therefore, e.g., those that consist of several parts and where it cannot be guaranteed that all these parts are still there after they have been returned. For example, it is not uncommon in the consumer electronics or home appliance industry to resell such products as open-box items with limited warranty at reduced prices.

Thus, after the end of the selling season on the primary market, the retailer is faced with various options for the processing of the returns: (i) selling them on a secondary market at a (reduced) price, (ii) disposal or (iii) donation.

(i) On the secondary market, returned items can be resold at a (reduced) selling price. The secondary market's demand is described by a linear function

$$q_s = \alpha_s - \beta_s r \tag{3}$$

where $\alpha_s > 0$ is the secondary customers' basic market demand and $\beta_s > 0$ is the sensitivity to the selling price r.

The domain of the retail price r and thus its relation to the primary price is specified as follows:

$$fw \leq r \leq fw + m_R \tag{4}$$

where $0 \leq f \leq 1$ is used to determine the residual value of returns. First, the equation above ensures that returns are not sold at a higher price than new goods. On the other hand, it prevents the items from being sold at symbolic prices in order to protect the brand image and prevent unfair competition.

Each product to be sold on the secondary market causes reconditioning costs a per unit. There is no return option for secondary customers.

Returned items, which are not salable at the secondary market can be either disposed of at a landfill site or donated.

(ii) Returned, unsaleable goods can be disposed of at unit costs d if the retailer chooses to do so ($\tau = 1$).

(iii) If the retailer decides against disposing of leftovers ($\tau = 0$), it can donate them instead. With regard to the current German tax law, value added tax u must be paid on the fictitious purchase price, i.e., the current residual value of the product, which leads to costs of ufw per item. In the case of material goods, 19% value added tax is usually charged. If the value of the product is practically zero at the time of the donation, i.e., $f = 0$, the donation would be free of charge.

– As mentioned above, the amount that is resold, disposed of or donated depends on the demand of the secondary market. If the quantity of returned items is smaller than the demand q_s of the secondary market at a certain price, only θq_p units can be sold. In the opposite case, only q_s can be sold and the difference quantity $\theta q_p - q_s$ must be disposed of or donated. In some cases it might not be possible or advantageous to serve the secondary market. For example, when the secondary market's basic demand is too small compared to the minimum price customers would have to pay, the secondary demand might become formally negative so that no products can be sold at that market. In other cases, reconditioning costs might be too high to economically serve the secondary market and disposal or donation would be the better option. To capture the actual sales volume on the secondary market, we introduce a variable z with

$$z \in \{0; \min\{q_s; \theta q_p\}\}. \tag{5}$$

2.2   Profit Functions

Taking all the considerations described above into account, the following profit functions result for the players.

Manufacturer:

$$\pi^M = \underbrace{q_p(w - c_m)}_{\text{sales to the retailer}} \tag{6}$$

Retailer:

$$\pi^R = \underbrace{q_p m_R}_{\text{profit on the primary market}} \underbrace{-\theta q_p(w + m_R)+}_{\text{refund}} \underbrace{zr}_{\text{sales to the secondary market}}$$
$$\underbrace{-d(\theta q_p - z)\tau}_{\text{disposal costs}} \underbrace{-ufw(\theta q_p - z)(1-\tau)-}_{\text{donation costs}} \underbrace{\theta q_p hx}_{\text{handling costs}} \underbrace{-\quad az}_{\substack{\text{reconditioning} \\ \text{costs}}} . \tag{7}$$

3   Solution Approach

In this section we present a general solution approach for the basic model. Here, the manufacturer decides its wholesale price; the retailer chooses its optimal margin, return policy, the quantity to be sold on the secondary market and the (reduced) selling price on that market. In addition, it can choose to either dispose of or donate leftovers.

To determine the optimal strategies of the players and the equilibrium of the game we apply backward induction. The manufacturer acts as the Stackelberg follower and determines its optimal wholesale price, given any decisions made by the retailer:

$$\max_w \pi^M = q_p(w - c_m). \tag{8}$$

The problem is solved by setting the first order derivative with respect to w equal to zero which yields:

$$w = \frac{\beta_p(c_m - m_R) + h\lambda(x - 1)y + \alpha_p}{2\beta_p}. \tag{9}$$

In addition, we have to check the second order condition, $\frac{\partial^2 \pi^M}{\partial w^2} = -2\beta_p \overset{!}{\leq} 0$, to make sure the profit function is concave in w. Since $\beta_p > 0$, the condition is always satisfied.

The optimization problem of the retailer is more complex and requires a special solution procedure. As stated before, $z \in \{0; \min\{q_s; \theta q_p\}\}$ holds. To provide analytical solvability, we split the problem into subproblems (see Table 1) which are first solved separately and then compared with each other. For example, it might be advantageous not to sell any products on the secondary market ($z = 0$), when the secondary customer's willingness to pay is too low compared to the primary market (case I). If, in contrast, the secondary market is served, either the returned quantity θq_p or the demand q_s is sold. When considering these cases as self-contained optimization problems, we must take into account, that, in contrast to case I, the retailer's profit function is not always jointly concave in m_R and r and that the selling price r might exceed or deceed its feasible range. Therefore, we can either obtain interior solutions (IS) or boundary solutions (BS) (cases II–V). After the optimal expressions for those cases are derived, they have to be checked for feasibility. For example, in cases II and III, the actual demand q_s on the secondary market has to be greater or equal to the amount of returns to be able to sell θq_p. If not, the decision variables must be adjusted in such a way that cases VI or VII would hold ($\theta q_p = q_s$) which are therefore included in the analysis to be compared with the other cases.

Table 1. Division of the problem into different subproblems

z	0	θq_p		q_s		$\theta q_p = q_s$	
Case	I	II	III	IV	V	VI	VII
IS vs. BS	IS	IS	BS	IS	BS	IS	BS

In the following, the derivation of the optimal expressions of the individual cases is illustrated by means of the first three cases. All other expression are provided in the electronic appendix. We derive the optimal expressions of the margin m_R and the price r on the secondary market. The optimal values of the binary variables τ and x can only be determined by numerical variation and therefore, are for now treated as parameters.

Case I: $z = 0$

In this scenario, the case is examined in which the secondary market is not served. Then, the value of r need not be determined. Inserting $z = 0$ into Eq. (7) and setting the first order derivative with respect to m_R equal to zero leads to

$$m_R = -\frac{\beta_p \left[c_m(x\psi + \phi - 1) + (x\psi + \phi)(d\tau + hx)\right] - \left[h\lambda(x-1)y + \alpha_p\right]\left[f(\tau - 1)u(x\psi + \phi) - 1\right]}{\beta_p \left[f(\tau - 1)u(x\psi + \phi) + x\psi + \phi - 2\right]}. \tag{10}$$

As the second order derivative of Eq. (7) with respect to m_R

$$\frac{\partial^2 \pi^R}{\partial m_R^2} = \frac{1}{2}\beta_p \left[f(\tau - 1)u(x\psi + \phi) + x\psi + \phi - 2\right] \overset{!}{\leq} 0 \tag{11}$$

is always smaller than zero, we are sure the profit function is always concave in m_R.

Case II: $z = \theta q_p$, interior solution

If $z = \theta q_p$, all returned items are resold and there is no need to dispose of or donate any items. Inserting $z = \theta q_p$ in Eq. (7) turns out that the profit function is linear in r. An interior solution can therefore be excluded.

Case III: $z = \theta q_p$, boundary solution

The retailer's profit function in Eq. (7) increases linear in r, so that it chooses its selling price as high as possible, meaning that we have to set $r = fw + m_R$. Inserting this equation into (7) and setting the first order derivative with respect to m_R equal to zero leads to

$$m_R = \frac{[(f-1)x\psi + (f-1)\phi - 1][h\lambda(x-1)y + \alpha_p] - \beta_p[(a + hx)(x\psi + \phi) - c_m]}{\beta_p[(f-1)x\psi + (f-1)\phi - 2]}. \tag{12}$$

Note, that the second order condition is always fulfilled as $\frac{\partial^2 \pi^R}{\partial m_R^2} = \frac{1}{2}\beta_p[(f-1)x\psi + (f-1)\phi - 2] \leq 0$.

Therefore, r results in

$$r = \frac{\begin{array}{l}\beta_p[(f-2)(a+hx)(x\psi + \phi) + c_m(f((f-1)x\psi + (f-1)\phi - 3) + 2)] \\ + (h\lambda(x-1)y + \alpha_p)[f(2x\psi + 2\phi - 1) - 2(x\psi + \phi + 1)]\end{array}}{2\beta_p[(f-1)x\psi + (f-1)\phi - 2]}. \tag{13}$$

It has to be checked if $\theta q_p \leq q_s$ holds to gain a feasible solution. If not, it can be excluded.

The derivations of the other cases are shown in the electronic appendix. For clarity, we summarize the complete solution procedure for the retailer as follows. Due to its complexity it is recommended to implement the solution algorithm with suitable software.

Solution Procedure:

Step 1: Exclude case II as a possible optimum, as it is never feasible.

Step 2: Calculate the value of m_R in case I.

Step 3: Calculate the values of m_R and r as suggested for each of the cases III, IV and VI. If needed, i.e., the concavity condition in IV is not fulfilled and/or r is outside of its domain in IV and VI, calculate the boundary solutions (cases V/VII)

Step 4: Determine the optimal value of x in cases I–VII and the optimal value of τ in cases I, IV and V by numerical variation and comparison.

Step 5: Exclude solutions that are not feasible, i.e., if $q_s < \theta q_p$ in case III or if $\theta q_p < q_s$ in cases IV and V.

Step 6: Among all feasible solutions, choose the solution which leads to the highest profit for the retailer as the optimum.

4 Numerical Analysis of the Basic Model

4.1 Basic Example

The following parameter values are used as the basis for the subsequent numerical analysis:

$$\alpha_p = 100, \quad \alpha_s = 70, \quad \beta_p = 0.5, \quad \beta_s = 1, \quad c_m = 2, \quad \phi = 0.1, \quad \psi = 0.2, \quad d = 0.5, \quad u = 0.19, \quad h = 1, \quad \lambda = 2, \quad a = 1, \quad f = 0.9, \quad y = 1.$$

Applying the solution procedure suggested in Sect. 3, we obtain the following results:

$$w = 49.585, \quad m_R = 98.829, \quad r = 67.621, \quad z = 2.379, \quad x = 0, \quad \pi^M = 1132.180, \quad \pi^R = 2156.804.$$

For this numerical example, the secondary demand $q_s = 2.379$ equals the amount returned to the retailer $\theta q_p = 0.1 \cdot 23.793$. This means that case VI applies. τ does not need to be determined because no quantities are disposed of or donated. In addition, the retailer decides here, despite the possible decline in demand, to charge customers for the return costs.

4.2 Analysis

To perform comprehensive numerical calculations, the solution algorithm proposed in Sect. 3 was implemented in a program in C# with Visual Studio 2019. The example above was then used as a basis for the numerical analysis in which the parameter values were varied successively as part of a sensitivity analysis. Thereby the equilibrium solutions were recalculated for each new parameter situation until no noticeable changes in the players' strategies were detected. Using this procedure, about 120 parameter combinations were tested.

The objective of the following analysis is to identify the cases in which unsaleable returns arise and when it is decided to dispose of or donate them when no state intervention occurs. Decisions on the retailer's return policy will also be discussed. To illustrate the results, we show extracts of the analysis in the form of selected figures and tables.

The Return Policy: It is observable that the decision whether to offer a free return policy depends mainly on the characteristics of the primary market. When the market potential is low, the retailer offers a free return policy, as it is shown in Fig. 2. Same applies if the customer's sensitivity to the return policy or the costs of return are high (see Figures 4 and 5 in the electronic appendix).

This behavior is logical and comprehensible, and yet the results are interesting. In practice, 74% of the smaller retailers and 53% of the larger retailers, who currently do not charge a fee, would like to pass on the return costs to the customers [17]. However, in many cases the strong competition would not allow

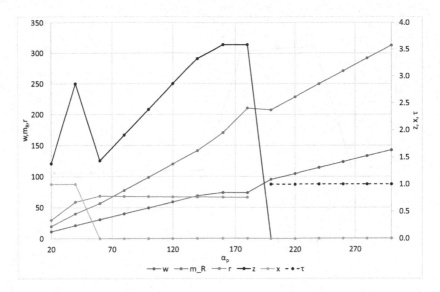

Fig. 2. Optimal values of the decision variables at variation of α_p

this to happen. Nevertheless, in practice it is mainly small and medium-sized companies operating in niches that charge return fees.

If customer demand did not respond to the return policy, i.e., $\lambda = 0$, we observed it would be possible for smaller companies to charge a return fee. This leads to the assumption, that small and medium-sized companies can only charge a return fee if they have a fixed customer base or are the only suppliers on the market. Otherwise they will have to deal with a too great loss of demand. Larger companies have more flexibility and freedom in the choice of the return policy and may use the return fee as a marketing instrument when suitable.

With regard to the price sensitivity, it is interesting to note that the retailer offers free returns only to customers in the medium sensitivity range (see Fig. 3). If the sensitivity to price is low, it is of course easier to demand additional fees from the customers. If the price sensitivity increases, the retailer then offers free returns. However, if the price sensitivity then increases even further, not only price sensitivity becomes a problem, but also the high return rate associated with free returns. This combination then again leads to the costs being passed on to the customer.

Decision on the Handling of Leftovers: In most of the cases analyzed, the retailer tries to avoid the occurrence of goods that cannot be resold. In other words, if possible, it tries to sell all returned goods on the secondary market, i.e., $\theta q_p \leq q_s$ holds in most cases. However, it is sometimes not possible or not advantageous to resell all returned products.

For example, if the market potential of the primary market is very large compared to the secondary market, it is not possible to sell new and returned

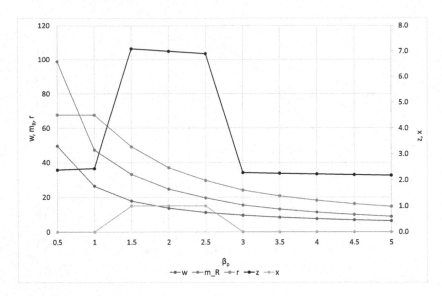

Fig. 3. Optimal values of the decision variables at variation of β_p

products at realistically related prices, since the retailer wants to fully exploit the willingness of the primary market to pay and charges high prices (see Fig. 2). Other reasons are, for example, a high price sensitivity β_s or high reconditioning costs a which would make serving the secondary market inefficient (see Figures 6 and 7 in the electronic appendix).

In most of the cases analyzed, the retailer decides to dispose of surplus goods, as this is simply cheaper than paying taxes on the donation. Only when the disposal costs exceed a certain threshold value it was observed that a donation is more economical despite the value added tax. In addition, if leftovers occur, in all cases we have investigated, the retailer charges the customer a return fee in order to reduce the amount of products returned and disposed of.

5   The Effects of State Interventions

Taking up current political discussions, the effects of various state interventions in the market aimed at avoiding returns and the associated disposal of functioning products are examined. We consider three scenarios as modifications of the basic model:

a) the prohibition of disposal, i.e., τ is fixed to $\tau = 0$
b) the remission of the value added tax on donations in kind, i.e., $u = 0$
c) the regulation that the return fee must be borne by the customers, i.e., x and y are fixed to $x = 0$ and $y = 0$.

The numerical analysis from the previous chapter was repeated for each of those three scenarios and under adjustment of the corresponding variables or parameters. The effectiveness of the political intervention can then be assessed by comparing the data with the basic scenario.

a) Prohibition of disposal:

The prohibition of disposal has been the subject of most debate in German politics to now and it has already been implemented in countries like France. The numerical analysis was carried out again from this point of view. Of course, it only has an influence on those cases where the retailer would previously have decided to dispose of the products.

There are reasons why this instrument is controversial. We have found that the prohibition leads to the retailer charging higher prices in order to reduce its additional donation costs, thereby reducing primary demand and thus the absolute quantity of returned, unsaleable goods. At the same time, however, it also reduces the economic welfare of all players. As an example, a sample of the numerical analyses is shown in Table 2. As it is observable, customers pay higher prices, manufacturers and retailers make fewer profits. Only in very rare cases could we observe that the prohibition led to more products being offered for resale, which was the case, for example, with very high reconditioning costs. However, as mentioned above, even without a prohibition, players would avoid disposal wherever possible due to intrinsic motivations.

Table 2. Comparison between the basic scenario and prohibition of disposal

	Basic scenario ($\tau = 1$)					$\tau = 0$				
α_p	w	m_R	q_p	π^M	π^R	w	m_R	q_p	π^M	π^R
200	95.25	207.50	46.63	4347.78	8260.78	94.42	209.16	46.21	4270.95	8187.83
220	104.72	228.55	51.36	5276.08	10024.55	103.81	230.38	50.91	5182.80	9935.94
240	114.20	249.61	56.10	6294.13	11958.84	113.20	251.60	55.60	6182.80	11853.05
260	123.67	270.66	60.84	7401.92	14063.65	122.59	272.82	60.30	7270.96	13939.16
280	133.15	291.71	65.57	8599.47	16339.00	131.98	294.04	64.99	8447.28	16194.28
300	142.62	312.76	70.31	9886.77	18784.86	141.37	315.26	69.68	9711.76	18618.41

b) Remission of the value added tax on donations:

Opponents of the strategy of a prohibition of disposal demanded a remission of the value added tax on donations. In our investigations, this intervention has almost solely impact on cases where the retailer would have previously opted for disposal. If it now had the choice, it would always opt for the free option ($\tau = 0$). See again a sample of the numerical analyses in Table 3 for a direct comparison. Interestingly, however, this instrument has almost no influence on the players' pricing policy. Depending on the parameter situation, the prices can rise or fall minimally, just like the demand of primary customers. No clear statement is possible here. The reason could be that the amount of leftovers is overall relatively small.

Table 3. Comparison between the basic scenario and remission of tax

	Basic scenario ($\tau = 1$)					$u = 0$				
α_p	w	m_R	q_p	π^M	π^R	w	m_R	q_p	π^M	π^R
200	95.25	207.50	46.63	4347.78	8260.78	95.26	207.47	46.63	4349.01	8263.12
220	104.72	228.55	51.36	5276.08	10024.55	104.74	228.53	51.37	5277.43	10027.12
240	114.20	249.61	56.10	6294.13	11958.84	114.21	249.58	56.11	6295.60	11961.64
260	123.67	270.66	60.84	7401.92	14063.65	123.68	270.63	60.84	7403.52	14066.70
280	133.15	291.71	65.57	8599.47	16339.00	133.16	291.68	65.58	8601.20	16342.27
300	142.62	312.76	70.31	9886.77	18784.86	142.63	312.74	70.32	9888.62	18788.38

Furthermore, in some cases, e.g., when reconditioning costs are relatively high, the retailer would be, compared to the basic scenario, more likely to decide not to resell returns and not to serve the secondary market. Instead, it decides now to donate which of course can be beneficial to society. In all cases considered, the remission of tax on donations led to higher profits for both players. However, it should be noted that the state's income then would naturally fall.

c) Return costs must be paid by the customer:

Of all the scenarios examined, the greatest effects can be observed here. Since this intervention eliminates the competitive advantage of free returns, it has an impact on each individual parameter combination. Thus, in cases where a return fee was charged in the basic scenario, the negative effect on customer demand is eliminated, so that the profits of all players increase. For the customer, in contrast, this intervention can be both positive and negative. In those cases where the retailer has so far paid the return fee, all customers have had to bear the cost collectively via an increased price, regardless of whether they decide later to return the goods or not. The directive of charging a return fee is fairer and allows lower prices in comparison. For companies that have already charged a return fee, however, it is interesting to note that in this scenario they have the possibility to increase their prices, as some customers who previously migrated to other retailers because of the return fee now return.

In those cases where no return fee has been charged so far, the intervention also leads to a significant decrease in returns. In the other cases, the increase in primary demand may lead to higher absolute number of returns, although the percentage of course remains constant. Furthermore, the intervention has no influence on the disposal behavior. In the case of surplus goods, the retailer would in most cases opt for disposal again as in the basic scenario. See a sample of the analysis in Table 4 for a direct comparison.

Table 4. Comparison between the basic scenario and mandatory return fee

	Basic scenario							$x = 0,\quad y = 0$					
α_p	w	m_R	q_p	x	τ	π^M	π^R	w	m_R	q_p	τ	π^M	π^R
20	11.20	19.61	4.60	1	-	42.29	85.85	11.42	19.15	4.71	-	44.40	89.24
40	21.05	39.90	9.53	1	-	181.44	368.32	21.37	39.25	9.69	-	187.66	377.20
200	95.25	207.50	46.63	0	1	4347.78	8260.78	96.20	209.61	47.10	1	4436.57	8429.49
220	104.72	228.55	51.36	0	1	5276.08	10024.55	105.67	230.66	51.84	1	5373.84	10210.30
240	114.20	249.61	56.10	0	1	6294.13	11958.84	115.15	251.71	56.57	1	6400.87	12161.65
260	123.67	270.66	60.84	0	1	7401.92	14063.65	124.62	272.76	61.31	1	7517.64	14283.51
280	133.15	291.71	65.57	0	1	8599.47	16339.00	134.09	293.82	66.05	1	8724.16	16575.91
300	142.62	312.76	70.31	0	1	9886.77	18784.86	143.57	314.87	70.78	1	10020.44	19038.83

6 Conclusion

In this article, we presented a game theoretic model that was used to examine and compare different options for state intervention to reduce customer returns and associated disposals. Which of the interventions is to be recommended depends on the respective perspective. The results show that a prohibition of disposal is usually not advisable. On the one hand, it only leads to a very limited change in customer and player behavior, and on the other hand it leads to customers, manufacturers and retailers being worse off economically. The reason for this is that the players have an intrinsically motivated interest in avoiding disposal whenever possible. Disposal is usually only an option if reselling is not possible or economically viable. Nevertheless, this prohibition is of course an option that is primarily aimed at environmental sustainability.

However, the option of reducing taxes on donations is just as environmentally friendly. Since donations are now always cheaper, the retailer would donate in situations where he had previously decided to dispose of the leftovers. However, this option would involve losses for the state.

The most far-reaching option in our analyzed cases was a state-imposed return fee. Since the return policy does not offer a competitive advantage here, this can in many cases reduce returns and thus also the amount of leftovers without having negative economic consequences for the players. However, it has no influence on the retailer's decision for or against a disposal. In practice, the actual impact of this intervention might not only depend on the customer's sensitivity to the return policy, but also on the type of product.

Interventions in the market should only ever take place when it is really necessary. From our and other studies it is clear that the concern of excessive disposal cannot necessarily be confirmed. However, the best result from our point of view would be a combination of free donations and a prescribed return fee. On the one hand it reduces the incentive for disposal, but on the other hand it also helps to reduce the occurrence of returns. First, less restrictive steps could be to reduce the tax rate on donations or to require a mandatory minimum return fee. Future research could examine the optimal height of these tax rates and fees. In order to gain a better insight into the market, it may then be useful to extend the model by, e.g., involving several retailers and their cannibalization effects.

References

1. Abdulla, H., Ketzenberg, M., Abbey, J.: Taking stock of consumer returns: a review and classification of the literature. J. Oper. Manag. **65**, 560–605 (2019)
2. Chen, J., Bell, P.C.: Implementing market segmentation using full-refund and no-refund customer returns policies in a dual-channel supply chain structure.Int. J. Prod. Economics **136**, 56–66 (2012)
3. Choi, T.-M.: Optimal return service charging policy for a fashion mass customization program. Serv. Sci. **5**(1), 56–68 (2013)
4. Fashionunited.   https://fashionunited.uk/news/business/amazon-criticised-for-disposal-of-returned-and-unsold-items-in-germany/2018062130340.   Accessed 16 Apr 2020
5. Gecker, R., Vigoroso, M.W.: Revisiting Reverse Logistics in the Customer-centric Service Chain: Benchmark Report. Aberdeen Group, Boston (2006)
6. Guo, H., Li, C., Zhang, Y., Zhang, C., Lu, M.: A location-inventory problem in a closed-loop supply chain with secondary market consideration. Sustainability **10**(6), 1–20 (2018)
7. Kessler, M.: Neu oder nicht? Online-Händler verkaufen Rückläufer als Neuware. https://www.teltarif.de/online-shop-shopping-neuware-retoure-ruecklaeufer-verbraucherzentrale/news/47455.html. Accessed 16 Apr 2020
8. Hua, Z., Hou, H., Bian, Y.: Optimal shipping strategy and return service charge under no-reason return policy in online retailing. IEEE Trans. Syst. Man Cybern.: Syst. **47**(12), 3189–3206 (2017)
9. Huang, X., Gu, J.W., Ching, W.K., Siu, T.K.: Impact of secondary market on consumer return policies and supply chain coordination. Omega **45**, 57–70 (2014)
10. Li, G., Li, L., Sethi, S.P., Guan, X.: Return strategy and pricing in a dual-channel supply chain. Int. J. Prod. Econ. **215**, 153–164 (2019)
11. Maiti, T., Giri, B.: Two-way product recovery in a closed-loop supply chain with variable markup under price and quality dependent demand. Int. J. Prod. Econ. **183**, 259–272 (2017)
12. Mostard, J., Teunter, R.: The newsboy problem with resalable returns: a single period model and case study. Eur. J. Oper. Res. **169**, 81–96 (2006)
13. Mukhopadhyay, S.K., Setaputra, R.: Optimal return policy for e-business. In: Proceedings of Technology Management for the Global Future PICMET, Istanbul, Turkey, 2006, vol. 3, pp. 1203–1209 (2006)
14. Parsopoulosa, K.E., Konstantaras, I., Skouri, K.: Metaheuristic optimization for the single-item dynamic lot sizing problem with returns and remanufacturing. Comput. Ind. Eng. **83**, 307–315 (2015)
15. Radhi, M., Zhang, G.: Pricing policies for a dual-channel retailer with cross-channel returns. Comput. Ind. Eng. **119**, 63–75 (2018)
16. Retourenforschung Uni Bamberg. www.retourenforschung.de/info-hintergruende-der-retourenentsorgung--studie-ausgewertet.html. Accessed 16 Apr 2020
17. Retourenforschung Uni Bamberg. www.retourenforschung.de/info-praeventives-retourenmanagement-und-ruecksendegebuehren--neue-studienergebnisse.html. Accessed 16 Apr 2020

18. Saleh, K.: E-commerce product return rate - statistics and trends [infographic]. https://www.invespcro.com/blog/ecommerce-product-return-rate-statistics/. Accessed 16 Apr 2020
19. Vlachos, D., Dekker, R.: Return handling options and order quantities for single period products. Eur. J. Oper. Res. **151**, 38–52 (2003)
20. Yang, F., Hu, P., Zhao, F.: Customer returns model in a dual-channel supply chain. J. Model. Manag. **10**, 360–379 (2015)

Fair User Equilibrium in a Transportation Space-Time Network

Lianne A. M. Bruijns[1,2], Frank Phillipson[2(✉)] [iD], and Alex Sangers[2]

[1] Delft University of Technology, Delft, The Netherlands
[2] TNO, PO Box 96800, 2509 JE The Hague, The Netherlands
frank.phillipson@tno.nl

Abstract. Central in this paper is a transportation network, in which containers are transported for multiple agents. This network is modelled by a Space Time Network, in which the travel time of modalities is fixed and independent of the occupancy of the network. To find the best allocation of containers to paths in this network, a flow problem can be solved. The System Optimal solution found then is the solution in which the total costs of the network are minimised. This paper introduces the idea of a fair User Equilibrium solution in such problem. The proposed approach changes the network, using a toll scheme, such that the fair User Equilibrium Solution in this changed network equals the System Optimal solution in the original network. This can be used to fairly redistribute the cost of the network among the users.

Keywords: User Equilibrium · System Optimal solution · Space Time Network · Intermodal and synchromodal transport

1 Introduction

Space-Time Networks (STN) are an often used representation in logistic network optimisation [4,12]. Solving a non-negative integral Minimum Cost Multi-Commodity Flow problem (MCMCF) on this STN [15] gives an overall optimal solution, the System Optimal (SO) solution, for the transportation flows in the logistic network. However, as in other kind of system optimisation problems, if there are multiple logistic agents in this network, not every agent will get its shortest or most economical path in this SO solution. This can, for example, be caused by capacity constraints. To reach a solution in which all agents are satisfied, and, therefor, do not want to change their paths, a User Equilibrium (UE) solution if preferred. The relationship between the UE and the SO solution can be examined by the Price of Anarchy [14] that measures how the efficiency of a system degrades due to the selfish behaviour of its customers. Bar-Gera et al. [1] consider the UE problem with the focus on spreading flow over the network and introduce the condition of proportionality: the same proportions apply to all travellers facing a choice between a pair of alternative paths, regardless of their origins and destinations.

© Springer Nature Switzerland AG 2020
E. Lalla-Ruiz et al. (Eds.): ICCL 2020, LNCS 12433, pp. 682–697, 2020.
https://doi.org/10.1007/978-3-030-59747-4_44

Most of the literature about User Equilibria is related to network congestion, where travel times on roads depend on occupancy of travelling arcs, as in traffic assignment and network design problems [6,7,11,16]. For application in logistic networks, Corman et al. [3] consider the application of multimodal transport to provide a UE solution, with the choice of modality based on the wishes of the agents. Yao et al. [19] use the User Equilibrium concept and game theory for transit line allocation. User Equilibria in (multi-) agent environments are also described as consensus seeking agents [13]. One commonly used approach for creating a UE solution is by using tolls. Hearn and Ramana [9] make use of a toll pricing system and describe the Robinhood formulation, in which the sum of all tolls must be zero. Other examples can be found in [5,18]. Yang [17] proved the existence of a Pareto refunding scheme that returns the congestion pricing revenues to all users to make everyone better off.

In [2] we showed how a UE solution can be created in an STN, where the UE solution is equal to the SO solution. The idea here is, that optimising the total network and then sharing the benefits from a overall optimal solution between all agents is beneficial for all. This sharing was done by defining tolls on paths in the STN network. This approach is partly based on the solution algorithms used by Hearn and Ramana [9] and Jiang and Mahmassani [10]. In general, tolls can be assigned to orders and paths in a STN. Assigning tolls to the orders occurs after obtaining the SO solution, to create a UE solution in which costs are divided over the orders. Assigning tolls to paths occurs after obtaining the SO solution and creates tolled path costs on the STN, in which the paths of the SO solution have cheapest (tolled) paths costs and thus a UE solution is obtained.

In a system where all agents make their own decisions, this approach might look very theoretical. However, in practice this approach can be helpful for a LSP in organising and pricing its system and services. The LSP has a system with bottlenecks and priorities certain orders and clients. How can he do that, without having clients complaining, if they would have total knowledge about the system, about their service and pricing in comparison with other clients. Creating a UE would partially solve this, the clients cannot find a better solution themselves, however, it would be even more interesting to have an approach to find a *fair* UE solution: their realised service level might be lower, but they get a fair compensation for that. In this paper the fairness of the UE solution in a logistic STN is defined for the first time and a method is presented to find a fair UE in an order-based STN and how to translate this to a fair UE solution in a path based STN.

In the next section, the general STN is defined and a definition for fairness is proposed, when creating a User Equilibrium in an STN. Fairness will be defined for a group of agents or flows over the STN that share a bottleneck link in their shortest or cheapest path. For this, in Sect. 3, an algorithm is presented to find connected components in an STN. With these connected components, the fair order-based toll scheme will be created in Sect. 4 and the existence of a toll set that realises the fair redistribution is proved. Next, in Sect. 5, the fair path-based

toll scheme is created and again the existence of a solution is proved. We end
with some conclusions and ideas for future research.

Table 1. Used notation.

$\mathcal{G} = (\mathcal{V}, \mathcal{A})$	STN Graph
$\mathcal{V}$	Set of nodes of the STN
$\mathcal{A}$	Set of directed arcs of the STN
x_a	The number of units of flow along arc a
$w = (w_O, w_D)$	Origin-Destination-pair (OD-pair) or order between origin location w_O and destination location w_D
$\mathcal{W}$	Set of all OD-pairs/orders
d_w	Demand of order w
p	Path, order of adjacent arcs, in the STN
$\mathcal{P}_w$	Set of all paths for OD-pair w
$\mathcal{P}$	Total path set
f_p	Path flow of path p
c_a	Cost of arc a/
C_w^p or C^p	Path cost (of order w)
m_a or m_p	Capacity of arc a or path p
δ_{ap}	Indicator whether arc a is in path p
k_w	Cost of sortest possible path of order w in the empty STN
r_w	Cost ratio of order w
$r_{\beta w}$	Tolled cost ratio of order w
$h_{in,w}$	Set of paths used in SO solution by order w
$h_{out,w}$	Set of paths not used in SO solution by order w
$NP - \beta$	Optimisation problem for finding the tolls
η_a and Γ_a	Bottleneck sets of paths and orders for arc a
$\mathcal{A}_\eta$	Bottleneck set
$\mathcal{Q}_w$	Set of cheapest paths for order w
$\mathcal{V}_s$	Connected components s, which is a list of visited nodes in connected component s

2   Fair User Equilibrium in STN

In this paper, a way to construct a fair User Equilibrium within an STN is
proposed. All used notation can be found in Table 1. The Space-Time Network
that represents the transportation network is a directed graph $\mathcal{G} = (\mathcal{V}, \mathcal{A})$. Each
arc $a \in \mathcal{A}$ is a link between two nodes, an origin node v_1 and an end node
v_2, both in $\mathcal{V}$: $a = (v_1, v_2)$, along which a transportation unit, for example a

container, can travel. The variable x_a is used to denote the number of units of flow along arc a. An Origin-Destination-pair (OD-pair) or order w is a pair of two nodes, origin location w_O and destination location w_D, so $w = (w_O, w_D)$, which is not necessarily an arc. The number of containers that an order wants to transport from w_O to w_D is denoted by d_w, the demand of order w. A path p consists of a sequence of (non horizontal) adjacent arcs between two nodes. Here only paths between origin and destination nodes are considered. f_p denotes the path flow of path p (always integer), with $p \in \mathcal{P}_w$, $w \in \mathcal{W}$, where $\mathcal{P}_w$ is the set of all paths for OD-pair w and $\mathcal{W}$ is the set of all OD-pairs/orders. The total path set is $\mathcal{P} := \bigcup_{w \in W} \mathcal{P}_w$. The costs of an arc a are denoted by c_a and the path costs of path p are denoted by C_w^p or C^p. The capacity of an arc is denoted by m_a and the capacity of a path is denoted by m_p. The available arcs in a path are denoted by

$$\delta_{ap} = \begin{cases} 1 \text{ if } a \text{ is contained in } p, \ \forall\, a \in \mathcal{A},\ p \in \mathcal{P}, \\ 0 \text{ otherwise.} \end{cases}$$

For each order w there may be multiple paths to travel by within the STN. The definition of [2] for a UE within an STN is used:

Definition. User Equilibrium in a transportation STN: A UE is reached when each agent can use their cheapest paths.

Next, the concept of fairness is added to this User Equilibrium. For this the cost ratio

$$r_w = \frac{C_w}{k_w}$$

is used to calculate how much the cost of the path in the solution for order w (C_w) is, compared to the cheapest costs he could have paid when he would be the only order on the network (k_w). Also the tolled cost ratio

$$r_{\beta w} = \frac{C_{\beta w}}{k_w} = \frac{C_w + \beta_w}{k_w}$$

is introduced, which denotes the ratio of a tolled solution, where β_w denotes the toll paid by order w.

Definition. Fair User Equilibrium in a transportation STN: A fair UE is reached when each agent can use their cheapest paths and all agents that would use some same bottleneck arc in the original STN, have the same tolled cost ratio.

The overall approach to find the tolls is equal to the approach in [2]. It starts with finding an SO solution, which results in the optimal flows $\underline{f_p}$. Now, define the set of paths used in the SO solution by $h_{in,w} := \left\{ p \mid \underline{f_p} > 0,\ p \in \mathcal{P}_w \right\}$, and the sets of all other paths (which are not in the SO solution) by $h_{out,w} := \left\{ p \mid \underline{f_p} = 0,\ p \in \mathcal{P}_w \right\}$. Then an new Problem NP-β can be solved that consists of an objective function that minimises the path tolls of a certain path set under a set of constraints.

3   Finding Connected Components in STN

For future use, it is important to know which agents use, in their shortest or cheapest path, the same (congested) connection or which orders share a bottleneck link in the original STN. This means that all connected components in the STN have to be found. The proposed method is presented in Algorithm 1. There, the connected components are found by constructing a graph G, consisting of orders $w \in \mathcal{W}$, where two orders in this graph can share an arc when those orders contain a joint bottleneck. To obtain these arcs, the cheapest paths per order are found (in Step 4). For each arc a, check if this arc is a bottleneck, that is when the amount of cheapest paths on that arc is higher than the capacity of that arc (this happens in Step 7), assuming every order travels via its cheapest path. If in this step bottlenecks are found and bottleneck sets are created, in which paths (bottleneck sets η_a) and orders (bottleneck sets Γ_a) are listed per bottleneck arc a. Also an arc in G is added between each pair of orders that are in the same bottleneck set. Then, for each cheapest path of an order that is in the SO solution, this path is fixed (so state that this path is taken by that order) and then recalculate the cheapest paths for all remaining orders (Step 19). If new bottlenecks arise, arcs are added between each pair of orders in this bottleneck set to the graph G. The fixing process is iterated until no new bottlenecks arise. Then in Step 49 the connected components are found in graph G. This set can be used to compare only the (tolled) cost ratio of orders that are in the same connected component, and to make sure that for each connected component the tolls sum up to zero such that orders only pay/receive for bottlenecks that influence the route choice for them.

4   Tolls on Orders

In this section, a method is presented to find tolls on orders to create a fair UE. Next, the existence of a (unique) solution will be proven.

4.1   Finding a User Equilibrium

Here, the goal is to find a fair order-tolled User Equilibrium. The same structure as presented in [2] for path tolled UE, is used here to obtain fair order tolls. First, the SO problem is solved in an STN. Second, the costs are adjusted by adding tolls. Note that here tolls are assigned to the total costs of orders, and thus the value of the tolls does not influence the path choices of customers. The tolls assigned to orders will make a fair redistribution of the costs of all orders using the network.

   The way of finding tolls that provide a UE solution in a initial SO problem is described in Algorithm 2. First, the SO is defined and solved in step 1 and 2 in

Algorithm 1. Finding connected components in STN

1: Let $\mathcal{Q}_w = \emptyset \; \forall \; w \in \mathcal{W}$ be the set of cheapest paths per order w, $\mathcal{A}_\eta = \emptyset$ the bottleneck set.
2: Create graph G with nodes $V = \mathcal{W}$ and arc set $E = \emptyset$.
3: **for** $w \in \mathcal{W}$ **do**
4:    Find cheapest paths $q_{w,n}$, $n \in \{1, \ldots, d_w\}$, $q_{w,n} \in \mathcal{P}_w$.
5:    Add paths $q_{w,n}$ to $\mathcal{Q}_w$.
6: **end for**
7: **for** $a \in \mathcal{A}$ **do**
8:    **if** $o_a > m_a$ (o_a the occupancy on arc a) **then**
9:        Create bottleneck set: $\eta_a = \Big\{ q_{w,n} \mid \delta_{a q_{w,n}} = 1, \; q_{w,n} \in \mathcal{Q}_w, \; \forall \; w \in \mathcal{W} \Big\}$.
10:        Create order set: $\Gamma_a = \{ w \mid q_{w,n} \in \eta_a, \; q_{w,n} \in \mathcal{Q}_w \}$.
11:        $\mathcal{A}_\eta := \mathcal{A}_\eta \bigcup a$.
12:        **for** $w_1, w_2 \in \Gamma_a$ **do**
13:            Add $e = (w_1, w_2)$ to E.
14:        **end for**
15:    **else**
16:        $\eta_a = \emptyset$.
17:    **end if**
18: **end for**
19: **for** $a_1 \in \mathcal{A}_\eta$ **do**
20:    **for** $q_{w,n} \in \eta_{a_1}$ and $q_{w,n} \in \bigcup_{w \in \mathcal{W}} h_{in,w}$ **do**
21:        Fix $q_{w,n}$: update $o_a = \delta_{a q_{w,n}} f_{q_{w,n}} \; \forall \; a \in \mathcal{A}$.
22:        Recalculate the cheapest paths for remaining orders and update $\mathcal{Q}_w$.
23:        Define $l = (q_{w,n})$ (a list of all previous fixed paths) and $\mathcal{A}_\eta^l = \emptyset$.
24:        **if** $o_{a_2} > m_{a_2}$ for $a_2 \notin \mathcal{A}_\eta$ **then**
25:            Create new bottleneck set η_{a_2}.
26:            Create order set: $\Gamma_{a_2} = \{ w \mid q_{w,n} \in \eta_{a_2}, \; q_{w,n} \in \mathcal{Q}_w \}$.
27:            Define $\mathcal{A}_\eta^l := \mathcal{A}_\eta^l \bigcup a_2$.
28:            **for** $w_1, w_2 \in \Gamma_{a_2}$ **do**
29:                Add $e = (w_1, w_2)$ to E.
30:            **end for**
31:        **end if**
32:        **for** $a_2 \in \mathcal{A}_\eta^l$ **do**
33:            **for** $r_{w,n} \in \eta_{a_2}$ and $r_{w,n} \in \bigcup_{w \in \mathcal{W}} h_{in,w}$ **do**
34:                Fix $r_{w,n}$: update $o_a = \sum_{q_{w,n} \in \text{fixed paths}} \delta_{a q_{w,n}} f_{q_{w,n}} \; \forall \; a \in \mathcal{A}$
35:                Recalculate the cheapest paths for remaining orders and update $\mathcal{Q}_w$.
36:                **if** $o_{a_2} > m_{a_2}$ for $a_2 \notin \mathcal{A}_\eta$ **then**
37:                    Create new bottleneck set η_{a_2}.
38:                    Create order set: $\Gamma_{a_2} = \{ w \mid q_{w,n} \in \eta_{a_2}, \; q_{w,n} \in \mathcal{Q}_w \}$.
39:                    $l := (l, q_{w,n})$.
40:                    Define $\mathcal{A}_\eta^l := \mathcal{A}_\eta^l \bigcup a_2$.
41:                    **for** $w_1, w_2 \in \Gamma_{a_2}$ **do**
42:                        Add $e = (w_1, w_2)$ to E.
43:                    **end for**
44:                **end if**
45:            **end for**
46:        **end for**
47:    **end for**
48: **end for**
49: $s = 1$.
50: $\mathcal{V}_s$ is the set of visited nodes in connected component s.
51: **for** $w_1 \in V \setminus \bigcup_{1 \leq j \leq s} \mathcal{V}_j$ **do**
52:    $\mathcal{V}_s := \{ w_1 \}$.
53:    **for** $w_2 \in \bigcup_{v \in \mathcal{V}_s} N_G(v) \setminus \bigcup_{1 \leq j \leq s} \mathcal{V}_j$ **do**
54:        $\mathcal{V}_s := \mathcal{V}_s \cup w_2$.
55:    **end for**
56:    $s := s + 1$.
57: **end for**
58: $k := s - 1$ are the number of connected components of G.
59: $\mathcal{V}_s$ are the connected components of graph G.

Algorithm 2. In step 3 and 4, the alternative problem is formulated, minimising the differences in cost ratio within connected components, and solved to get a fair payment regulation and a UE is reached. The sum of all tolls paid and received by all customers within a connected component has to be zero to ensure the total system has no profit or loss. The problem in step 3 can be linearised easily.

Algorithm 2. Calculating order tolls

1: Create SO problem:

$$\min \sum_{p \in \mathcal{P}} C_w^p f_p$$

$$\text{s.t.} \quad x_a = \sum_{p \in \mathcal{P}} \delta_{ap} f_p \ \forall \, a \in \mathcal{A}$$

$$\sum_{p \in \mathcal{P}_w} f_p = d_w \ \forall \, w \in \mathcal{W}$$

$$x_a \le m_a \ \forall \, a \in \mathcal{A}$$

$$f_p \in \mathbb{N}_0 \ \forall \, p \in \mathcal{P}$$

$$x_a \in \mathbb{N}_0 \ \forall \, a \in \mathcal{A}$$

2: Solve SO problem, output: $C_w = \sum_{p \in \mathcal{P}_w} C_w^p \underline{f_p} \ \forall \, w \in \mathcal{W}$.

3: Create the nonlinear programming problem NP-β (minimising over the absolute value of the difference of ratios for all pairs of orders in the same set of connected components):

$$\min \sum_{s=1}^{k} \sum_{w_1, w_2 \in \mathcal{V}_s} \left| \frac{C_{w_1} + \beta_{w_1}}{k_{w_1}} - \frac{C_{w_2} + \beta_{w_2}}{k_{w_2}} \right|$$

$$\text{s.t.} \quad \sum_{w \in \mathcal{W}} \beta_w = 0$$

$$\sum_{w \in \mathcal{V}_s} \beta_w = 0 \ \forall \, 1 \le s \le k$$

$$\beta_w \ge -C_w \ \forall \, w \in \mathcal{W}$$

where the objective function minimises the ratio differences for all pairs of orders. Note that we sum twice over the set of orders: when $w_1 = w_2$, that term of the objective becomes zero. The constraints ensures the total toll sum to be zero, and that no path can have a negative $C_{\beta w}$ cost.

4: Solve NP-β, output: β_w.
5: Add tolls β_w to the SO problem, SO-β:

$$\min \sum_{w \in \mathcal{W}} \left(\sum_{p \in \mathcal{P}_w} C_w^p f_p + \beta_w \right)$$

$$\text{s.t.} \quad x_a = \sum_{p \in \mathcal{P}} \delta_{ap} f_p \ \forall \, a \in \mathcal{A}$$

$$\sum_{p \in \mathcal{P}_w} f_p = d_w \ \forall \, w \in \mathcal{W}$$

$$x_a \le m_a \ \forall \, a \in \mathcal{A}$$

$$f_p \in \mathbb{N}_0 \ \forall \, p \in \mathcal{P}$$

$$x_a \in \mathbb{N}_0 \ \forall \, a \in \mathcal{A}$$

6: Solve SO-β problem, output path flow vector $\underline{f}$.

Adding the tolls to the SO problem (step 5 and 6) defines a new SO problem, which solution (in flows) should be the same as the original SO problem.

4.2   Existence of Solutions

Now the question arises whether every NP-β of Algorithm 2 has a (unique) solution. For each component $\mathcal{V}_s$, there are $\frac{1}{2}|\mathcal{V}_s|(|\mathcal{V}_s| - 1)$ terms in the objective, and we can state that the best solution possible has objective value 0, meaning that each term has to be equal to zero, leading to:

$$k_i\beta_j - k_j\beta_i = k_jC_i - k_iC_j. \tag{1}$$

A generalisation can be made of the optimal solution for tolls on orders: Given the problem with m orders, the linear system can be created $A\beta = b$ with A a block diagonal matrix:

$$A = \begin{bmatrix} A_1 & 0 & \cdots & 0 \\ 0 & A_2 & \ddots & 0 \\ \vdots & \ddots & \ddots & 0 \\ 0 & \cdots & 0 & A_m \end{bmatrix}$$

So, A consists of m block matrices, one for each component $\mathcal{V}_s = \{1,\ldots,n\} \,\forall\, 1 \leq s \leq m$, with $n = |\mathcal{V}_s|$ the number of orders in $\mathcal{V}_s$:

$$A_i = \begin{bmatrix} D_1 \\ D_2 \\ \vdots \\ D_{n-1} \\ \mathbf{1}_{1,n} \end{bmatrix} \quad \text{with } D_j = \begin{bmatrix} \mathbf{0}_{1,j-1} & k_{j+1} & -k_j & 0 & \cdots & 0 \\ \mathbf{0}_{1,j-1} & k_{j+2} & 0 & -k_j & \ddots & \vdots \\ \mathbf{0}_{1,j-1} & \vdots & \vdots & \ddots & \ddots & 0 \\ \mathbf{0}_{1,j-1} & k_n & 0 & \cdots & 0 & -k_j \end{bmatrix}, \; 1 \leq j \leq n-1, \tag{2}$$

and $\mathbf{1}_{1,n}$ is a row vector of n ones, $\mathbf{0}_{1,j-1}$ a row vector of $j-1$ zeros and $\mathbf{0}_{1,0} := \emptyset$. The vector b consists of vectors b_s for each component $\mathcal{V}_s = \{1,\ldots,n\} \,\forall\, 1 \leq s \leq m$ with $n = |\mathcal{V}_s|$:

$$b_i = \begin{bmatrix} z_1 \\ z_2 \\ \vdots \\ z_{n-1} \\ 0 \end{bmatrix} \quad \text{with } z_j = \begin{bmatrix} k_jC_{j+1} - k_{j+1}C_j \\ k_jC_{j+2} - k_{j+2}C_j \\ \vdots \\ k_jC_n - k_nC_j \end{bmatrix} \tag{3}$$

where A is a $\sum_{s=1}^{m}\left(\frac{1}{2}|\mathcal{V}_s| \cdot (|\mathcal{V}_s| - 1) + 1\right) \times |\mathcal{W}|$ matrix and b has length $\sum_{s=1}^{m}\left(\frac{1}{2}|\mathcal{V}_s| \cdot (|\mathcal{V}_s| - 1) + 1\right)$. To draw some conclusions from this equality $A\beta = b$, first some definitions from Linear Algebra are introduced:

Definition. Row-echelon form: A matrix is in row-echelon form if:

- All zero rows have been moved to the bottom.
- The leading nonzero element (also called a pivot) in any row is farther to the right than the leading nonzero element in the row just above it.
- In each column containing a leading nonzero element, the entries below that leading nonzero element are 0.

The elementary row operations can be applied to modify the matrix until a row-echelon form is obtained.

Theorem 1 [8, Theorem 1.7]. Let $A\boldsymbol{x} = \boldsymbol{b}$ be a linear system, and let $[A|\boldsymbol{b}] \sim [H|\boldsymbol{c}]$, where H is in row-echelon form.

1. The system $A\boldsymbol{x} = \boldsymbol{b}$ is inconsistent if and only if the augmented matrix $[H|\boldsymbol{c}]$ has a row with all entries 0 to the left of the partition and a nonzero entry to the right of the partition.
2. If $A\boldsymbol{x} = \boldsymbol{b}$ is consistent and every column of H contains a pivot, the system has a unique solution.
3. If $A\boldsymbol{x} = \boldsymbol{b}$ is consistent and some column of H has no pivot, the system has infinitely many solutions, with as many free variables as there are pivot-free columns in H.

The problem $A\boldsymbol{\beta} = \boldsymbol{b}$ can be reduced to $H\boldsymbol{\beta} = \boldsymbol{c}$, where H is in row-echelon form. When solving NP-β with two orders and one connected component $\mathcal{V}_1$, one can easily verify that there always exists a unique solution by reducing the initial system:

$$\begin{bmatrix} [cc|c]k_2 & -k_1 & k_1C_2 - k_2C_1 \\ 1 & 1 & 0 \end{bmatrix} \rightarrow \begin{bmatrix} [cc|c]k_2 & -k_1 & k_1C_2 - k_2C_1 \\ 0 & k_1 + k_2 & k_2C_1 - k_1C_2 \end{bmatrix}$$

This shows that Statement 2 of Theorem 1 holds, because $k_w > 0 \ \forall \ w \in \mathcal{W}$.

Then the solution is

$$\beta_2 = \frac{k_2C_1 - k_1C_2}{k_1 + k_2},$$

$$\beta_1 = \frac{k_1C_2 - k_2C_1}{k_2} + \frac{k_1}{k_2}\beta_2 = \frac{k_1C_2 - k_2C_1}{k_2} + \frac{k_1(k_2C_1 - k_1C_2)}{k_2(k_1 + k_2)} = \frac{k_1C_2 - k_2C_1}{k_1 + k_2}.$$

We only need to show that the constraints $\beta_w \geq -C_w$ are satisfied for all $w \in \mathcal{W}$:

$$-C_2 \leq \beta_2 = \frac{k_2C_1 - k_1C_2}{k_1 + k_2} \iff 0 \leq \frac{k_1(C_1 + C_2)}{k_1 + k_2}$$

$$-C_1 \leq \beta_1 = \frac{k_1C_2 - k_2C_1}{k_1 + k_2} \iff 0 \leq \frac{k_2(C_1 + C_2)}{k_1 + k_2}$$

These constraints are always satisfied, since $k_1, k_2, C_1, C_2 \geq 0$. This problem can be generalised to a problem with n orders with m components: Suppose there is an NP-β problem with n orders, and $\mathcal{V}_i = \{1, \ldots, n\}$, so $|\mathcal{V}_i| = n$ for all

$1 \leq i \leq m$. This gives the problem $A\beta = b$, with A being a block matrix. Now, the existence of a unique solution for each sub-problem $A_i\beta = b_i$ is proved, and so that a unique solution exist for the original problem.

The row-echelon form consists of the first row of each matrix D_j, meaning the rows $\begin{bmatrix} \mathbf{0}_{1,j-1} & k_{j+1} & -k_j & \mathbf{0}_{1,n-(j+1)} \end{bmatrix}$ $\forall\, 1 \leq j \leq n-1$. All other rows in the matrices D_j can be written as a linear combination of rows $\begin{bmatrix} \mathbf{0}_{1,j-1} & k_{j+1} & -k_j & \mathbf{0}_{1,n-(j+1)} \end{bmatrix}$, so those rows are equal to a zero row in the row-echelon form.

For block matrix A_i and corresponding vector b_i, the following row-echelon form $[H_i|c_i]$ can be obtained:

$$
H_i = \begin{bmatrix}
k_2 & -k_1 & 0 & \cdots & \cdots & \cdots & & 0 \\
0 & k_3 & -k_2 & 0 & \ddots & & \ddots & 0 \\
0 & 0 & k_4 & -k_3 & 0 & & \ddots & 0 \\
\vdots & \ddots & \ddots & \ddots & \ddots & & \ddots & \vdots \\
0 & \ddots & \ddots & 0 & k_{n-1} & -k_{n-2} & & 0 \\
0 & \ddots & \ddots & \ddots & 0 & k_n & & -k_{n-1} \\
0 & \ddots & \ddots & \ddots & \ddots & 0 & & -\sum_{i=1}^{n} k_i \\
0 & \ddots & \ddots & \ddots & \ddots & & \ddots & 0 \\
\vdots & \ddots & \ddots & \ddots & \ddots & & \ddots & \vdots \\
0 & \cdots & \cdots & \cdots & \cdots & \cdots & & 0
\end{bmatrix},
\quad
c_i = \begin{bmatrix}
k_1 C_2 - k_2 C_1 \\
k_2 C_3 - k_3 C_2 \\
k_3 C_4 - k_4 C_3 \\
\vdots \\
k_{n-2} C_{n-1} - k_{n-1} C_{n-2} \\
k_{n-1} C_n - k_n C_{n-1} \\
\sum_{j=1}^{n-1} k_j C_n - \sum_{j=1}^{n-1} k_n C_j \\
0 \\
\vdots \\
0
\end{bmatrix}
$$

Concluding, using Theorem 1 shows that for each toll problem with one connected component, there is a unique toll solution, because each column in H_i contains a pivot. Then, it follows that each row in block diagonal matrix H has a pivot in each column, and for the zero rows, c contain a zero in that row number, so together with the inequality constraints $\beta_w \geq -C_w \,\forall\, w \in \mathcal{W}$ are satisfied, Theorem 1 holds. It can be concluded that if a solution exists for a toll order problem given the inequality constraints, the equality constraints provide a unique solution.

5   Path Tolls Based on Order Fairness

In [2] is shown how path tolls can be found to create new tolled costs for the STN, in which the customers can choose their own travelling paths, and the path costs are constructed in such a way that they will choose paths that minimise the total cost of the network (SO) and are the cheapest paths for themselves (UE). In Sect. 4 is shown how the realised costs can be redivided fairly over all orders, such that the use of the network is paid by all customers, and no customer is more harmed regarding costs than others, when they are using the same part of the network. When adding tolls to paths, as in [2], it may feel like the customers are being misled, because the tolled path costs can differ a lot from the initial path costs, when taking the costs of the original networks into account. For this, the constraints of fairness, as used in the objective function of order tolls, can be coupled to make the path based solutions a more fair User Equilibrium, by dividing the costs over all orders in the network, instead of assign higher path costs to certain orders only. In this section the procedure is explained.

5.1   Finding a User Equilibrium

We start with the SO problem of [2]. To find path tolls, first the SO problem is solved, as presented step 1 if Algorithm 2. With the SO solution found, the next step is calculating the path tolls. Therefore the NP-β of [2] Equations 21–26 is used, but with the extra constraints ($\forall\ w_1, w_2 \in \mathcal{V}_s,\ \forall\ s \in \{1, \dots, k\}$):

$$r_{\beta w_1} = r_{\beta w_2} \iff \frac{C_{w_1} + \beta_{w_1}}{k_{w_1}} = \frac{C_{w_2} + \beta_{w_2}}{k_{w_2}}$$

$$\iff \frac{\sum_{p \in \mathcal{P}_{w_1}} \left(C^p_{w_1} + \beta^p_{w_1}\right) f_p}{k_{w_1}} = \frac{\sum_{p \in \mathcal{P}_{w_2}} \left(C^p_{w_2} + \beta^p_{w_2}\right) f_p}{k_{w_2}},$$

with order sets $\mathcal{V}_s$ as in Sect. 2. Again, the objective can be linearised easily.

5.2   Existence of Solutions

The question arises again whether a combined toll solution can be obtained. For the inequality constraints always a valid solution can be found:

$$\beta^i_w \geq -C^i_w \ \forall\ i \in \mathcal{P}_w$$

$$\beta^i_w - \beta^j_w \leq C^j_w - C^i_w \ \forall\ (i, j),\ i \in h_{in,w},\ j \in h_{out,w}$$

The first set of constraints provides a lower bound for all path tolls, and the last set of constraints gives an upper bound for all paths tolls for paths $p \in \bigcup_{w \in \mathcal{W}} h_{in,w}$, the path tolls for the other paths are unbounded. We can always find a toll vector $\boldsymbol{\beta}$ that satisfies those inequality constraints. If $C^j_w - C^i_w < 0$ for some (i, j), $i \in h_{in,w}$, $j \in h_{out,w}$, set $\beta^j_w := C^i_w - C^j_w$ for all those paths j and $\beta^p_w := 0$ for all other paths. This shows the solution space is non-empty.

Now, it has to be investigated if the equality constraints provide a valid solution in combination with the inequality constraints. The equality constraints are:

$$\sum_{w \in \mathcal{W}} \sum_{p \in h_{in,w}} \beta^p_w = 0 \tag{4}$$

$$\sum_{w \in \mathcal{V}_s} \sum_{p \in h_{in,w}} \beta^p_w = 0 \ \forall\ s \in \{1, \dots, k\} \tag{5}$$

$$\frac{\sum_{p \in \mathcal{P}_{w_1}} \left(C^p_{w_1} + \beta^p_{w_1}\right) \underline{f_p}}{k_{w_1}} = \frac{\sum_{p \in \mathcal{P}_{w_2}} \left(C^p_{w_2} + \beta^p_{w_2}\right) \underline{f_p}}{k_{w_2}} \ \forall\ w_1, w_2 \in \mathcal{V}_s,\ \forall\ s \in \{1, \dots, k\}. \tag{6}$$

Constraint (4) is superfluous, because it is equal to summing up Constraints (5):

$$\sum_{w \in \mathcal{W}} \sum_{p \in h_{in,w}} \beta_w^p = 0 \iff \sum_{s=1}^{k} \sum_{w \in \mathcal{V}_s} \sum_{p \in h_{in,w}} \beta_w^p = 0.$$

If $d_w = 1 \; \forall \; w \in \mathcal{W}$, this problem corresponds to finding solutions in Subsect. 4.2. If $d_w \geq 1 \; \forall \; w \in \mathcal{W}$, constraint (6) can be rewritten for a pair of two orders i and j, $i, j \in \mathcal{W}$ (we assume $h_{in,i} = \{p_1, \ldots, p_k\}$, $h_{in,j} = \{q_1, \ldots, q_l\}$):

$$\frac{C_i + \beta_i}{k_i} = \frac{C_j + \beta_j}{k_j} \iff k_j \beta_i - k_i \beta_j = k_i C_j - k_j C_i$$

$$\iff k_j \sum_{p \in \mathcal{P}_i} \beta_i^p \underline{f_p} - k_i \sum_{p \in \mathcal{P}_j} \beta_j^p \underline{f_p} = k_i \sum_{p \in \mathcal{P}_j} C_j^p \underline{f_p} - k_j \sum_{p \in \mathcal{P}_i} C_i^p \underline{f_p}.$$

The tolls can be calculated per connected component.

- If $\mathcal{V}_s = \{1\}$, then constraint (5) states: $\sum_{p \in h_{in,1}} \beta_1^p \underline{f_p} = 0$. So no tolls are added to the STN, because this order can take its cheapest paths, because it does not use any bottleneck arcs, which indicates there are no issues in travelling via its cheapest paths.
- If $\mathcal{V}_s = \{1, 2\}$, then constraint (5) states :

$$\beta_i + \beta_j = 0 \iff \beta_i = -\beta_j \iff \sum_{p \in \mathcal{P}_i} \beta_i^p \underline{f_p} = -\sum_{p \in \mathcal{P}_j} \beta_j^p \underline{f_p}.$$

We can use this to continue our rewriting of constraint (6):

$$(k_i + k_j) \sum_{p \in \mathcal{P}_i} \beta_i^p \underline{f_p} = k_i \sum_{p \in \mathcal{P}_j} C_j^p \underline{f_p} - k_j \sum_{p \in \mathcal{P}_i} C_i^p \underline{f_p}$$

$$\iff \sum_{p \in \mathcal{P}_i} \beta_i^p \underline{f_p} = \frac{k_i \sum_{p \in \mathcal{P}_j} C_j^p \underline{f_p} - k_j \sum_{p \in \mathcal{P}_i} C_i^p \underline{f_p}}{k_i + k_j}.$$

The equality always has a solution because $k_i + k_j \neq 0$.
- If $\mathcal{V}_s = \{1, 2, 3\}$, then based on (5):

$$\sum_{p \in \mathcal{P}_1} \beta_1^p \underline{f_p} + \sum_{p \in \mathcal{P}_2} \beta_1^p \underline{f_p} + \sum_{p \in \mathcal{P}_3} \beta_3^p \underline{f_p} = 0,$$

and (6):

$$k_2 \sum_{p \in \mathcal{P}_1} \beta_1^p \underline{f_p} - k_1 \sum_{p \in \mathcal{P}_2} \beta_2^p \underline{f_p} = k_1 \sum_{p \in \mathcal{P}_2} C_2^p \underline{f_p} - k_2 \sum_{p \in \mathcal{P}_1} C_1^p \underline{f_p}$$

$$k_3 \sum_{p \in \mathcal{P}_1} \beta_1^p \underline{f_p} - k_1 \sum_{p \in \mathcal{P}_3} \beta_3^p \underline{f_p} = k_1 \sum_{p \in \mathcal{P}_3} C_3^p \underline{f_p} - k_3 \sum_{p \in \mathcal{P}_1} C_1^p \underline{f_p}$$

$$k_3 \sum_{p \in \mathcal{P}_2} \beta_2^p \underline{f_p} - k_2 \sum_{p \in \mathcal{P}_3} \beta_3^p \underline{f_p} = k_2 \sum_{p \in \mathcal{P}_3} C_3^p \underline{f_p} - k_3 \sum_{p \in \mathcal{P}_2} C_2^p \underline{f_p}.$$

This problem corresponds to the order toll problem, where the constraints, as just observed, are contained in the objective function (see (1)), and so a solution exist for each problem (see Subsect. 4.2). In this case there are infinitely many solutions, because the row-echelon form of the problem satisfies Statement 3 of Theorem 1. We will show this, but first introduce some extra notation: with x_{j-1} we denote the number of paths for orders 1 up until $j-1$: $x_j = \left| \bigcup_{1 \leq i \leq j} \mathcal{P}_i \right|$, and we denote path flow found in the SO solution by f_w^p instead of $\underline{f_p}$. We assume $l = |\mathcal{P}_j| \; \forall \; j \in \mathcal{W}$.

We have $A\boldsymbol{\beta} = \boldsymbol{b}$ with $A = \begin{bmatrix} A_1 & 0 & \cdots & 0 \\ 0 & A_2 & \ddots & \vdots \\ \vdots & \ddots & \ddots & 0 \\ 0 & \cdots & 0 & A_m \end{bmatrix}$, with sub-matrix $A_i = \begin{bmatrix} D_1 \\ \vdots \\ D_{n-1} \\ \boldsymbol{g}_{1,x_n} \end{bmatrix}$

for each $i \in \{1, \ldots, m\}$ with $\mathcal{V}_i$ a connected component, $\mathcal{V}_i = \{1, \ldots, n\}$. The matrices D_j, $1 \leq j \leq n-1$ are defined as follows:

$$D_j = \begin{bmatrix} \boldsymbol{0}_{1,x_{j-1}} & k_{j+1}f_j^{p_1} & \cdots & k_{j+1}f_j^{p_l} & -k_jf_{j+1}^{p_1} & \cdots & -k_jf_{j+1}^{p_l} & 0 & \cdots & \cdots & \cdots & \cdots & 0 \\ \boldsymbol{0}_{1,x_{j-1}} & k_{j+2}f_j^{p_1} & \cdots & k_{j+2}f_j^{p_l} & 0 & \cdots & 0 & -k_jf_{j+2}^{p_1} & \cdots & -k_jf_{j+2}^{p_l} & 0 & \ddots & \vdots \\ \vdots & \vdots & \cdots & \vdots & \vdots & \ddots & \ddots & \ddots & \ddots & \ddots & \ddots & 0 \\ \boldsymbol{0}_{1,x_{j-1}} & k_nf_j^{p_1} & \cdots & k_nf_j^{p_l} & 0 & \cdots & \cdots & \cdots & \cdots & 0 & -k_jf_n^{p_1} & \cdots & -k_jf_n^{p_l} \end{bmatrix},$$

and vector $\boldsymbol{g}_{1,x_n}$ consists of all path flows for orders the connected component i:

$$\boldsymbol{g}_{1,x_n} = \begin{bmatrix} f_1^{p_1} \cdots f_1^{p_l} & f_2^{p_1} \cdots f_2^{p_l} & \cdots\cdots\cdots & f_n^{p_1} \cdots f_n^{p_l} \end{bmatrix}.$$

Vector $\boldsymbol{b}$ consists of $\boldsymbol{b}_i = \begin{bmatrix} \boldsymbol{z}_1 \\ \boldsymbol{z}_2 \\ \vdots \\ \boldsymbol{z}_{n-1} \\ 0 \end{bmatrix}$ $\forall \; 1 \leq i \leq m$ with $\boldsymbol{z}_j = \begin{bmatrix} k_jC_{j+1} - k_{j+1}C_j \\ k_jC_{j+2} - k_{j+2}C_j \\ \vdots \\ k_jC_n - k_nC_j \end{bmatrix}$.

Now it is shown that this system $A\boldsymbol{\beta} = \boldsymbol{b}$ has infinitely many solutions. We therefore need to show that in the row-echelon form $H\boldsymbol{\beta} = \boldsymbol{c}$, matrix H contains columns with no pivots. The row-echelon form of sub-matrix A_i is

$$H_i = \begin{bmatrix} k_2f_1^{p_1} & \cdots & k_2f_1^{p_l} & -k_1f_2^{p_1} & \cdots & -k_1f_2^{p_l} & 0 & \cdots & \cdots & \cdots & \cdots & \cdots & 0 \\ 0 & \cdots & 0 & k_3f_2^{p_1} & \cdots & k_3f_2^{p_l} & -k_2f_3^{p_1} & \cdots & -k_2f_3^{p_l} & 0 & \ddots & \ddots & \vdots \\ \vdots & \ddots & \ddots & \ddots & \ddots & \ddots & \ddots & \ddots & \ddots & \ddots & \ddots & \ddots & 0 \\ 0 & \ddots & \ddots & \ddots & \ddots & \ddots & 0 & k_nf_{n-1}^{p_1} & \cdots & k_nf_{n-1}^{p_l} & -k_{n-1}f_n^{p_1} & \cdots & -k_{n-1}f_n^{p_l} \\ 0 & \cdots & \cdots & \cdots & \cdots & \cdots & \cdots & \cdots & \cdots & 0 & -\sum_{j=1}^{n} k_jf_n^{p_1} & \cdots & -\sum_{j=1}^{n} k_jf_n^{p_l} \\ 0 & \cdots & \cdots & \cdots & \cdots & \cdots & \cdots & \cdots & \cdots & \cdots & \cdots & \cdots & 0 \\ \vdots & \ddots & \ddots & \ddots & \ddots & \ddots & \ddots & \ddots & \ddots & \ddots & \ddots & \ddots & \vdots \\ 0 & \cdots & \cdots & \cdots & \cdots & \cdots & \cdots & \cdots & \cdots & \cdots & \cdots & \cdots & 0 \end{bmatrix}$$

and the vector

$$
c_i = \begin{bmatrix}
k_1 C_2 - k_2 C_1 \\
k_2 C_3 - k_3 C_2 \\
\vdots \\
k_{n-1} C_n - k_n C_{n-1} \\
\sum_{j=1}^{n-1} k_j C_n - \sum_{j=1}^{n-1} k_n C_j \\
0 \\
\vdots \\
0
\end{bmatrix} .
$$

The number of pivots in H_i equals the number of orders, which is less than the number of path toll variables, so according to Statement 3 of Theorem 1: if a solution exists, there are infinitely many solutions for this toll problem.

6   Conclusions and Future Research

The goal of this work was to provide a method to obtain a fair User Equilibrium solution in a Space Time Network used for representation and optimisation of a logistic network. As extra constraint we wanted the solution to be both System Optimal as well as User Equilibrium.

In order to provide an SO solution in which a UE is reached as well, we applied tolls to the network costs. But in order to obtain a User Equilibrium, we need to define when a User Equilibrium is reached. For order tolls, we say a UE is reached when all extra costs (compared to the cheapest path costs) made in the network, are divided over the orders in a fair way, concerning the ratio of the paid costs compared to the cheapest path cost. For fair path tolls, we say a UE is reached when all orders can travel via their cheapest paths, and the extra costs in the network are divided in a fair way over the orders.

The first step in all toll algorithms is to calculate the SO solution based on the path costs of orders travelling from their origin to their destination. The next step is to calculate tolls that are added to the path or order costs, depending on what kind of tolls we considered. We succeeded in finding an approach to obtain both an SO and a UE solution on an STN. For order tolls we showed there always exists a unique toll solution and for fair path tolls there always exist infinitely many solutions.

For future research we recommend to look at the scalability and computational effectiveness of the proposed methodology. As indicated, the methodology can be used by a LSP to divide the capacity and to price the services in a fair way. We propose to bring this methodology in practice in such a case and perform a case study.

Declarations

This work has been carried out within the project 'Complexity Methods for Predictive Synchromodality' (Comet-PS), supported and funded by NWO (the Netherlands Organisation for Scientific Research), TKI-Dinalog (Top Consortium Knowledge and Innovation) and the Early Research Program 'Grip on Complexity' of TNO (The Netherlands Organisation for Applied Scientific Research).

References

1. Bar-Gera, H., Boyce, D., Nie, Y.M.: User-equilibrium route flows and the condition of proportionality. Transp. Res. Part B: Methodol. **46**(3), 440–462 (2012)
2. Bruijns, L., Phillipson, F., Sangers, A.: User equilibrium in a transportation space-time network. In: 6th International Physical Internet Conference (IPIC) (2019)
3. Corman, F., Viti, F., Negenborn, R.R.: Equilibrium models in multimodal container transport systems. Flex. Serv. Manuf. J. **29**(1), 125–153 (2015). https://doi.org/10.1007/s10696-015-9224-4
4. De Juncker, M.A.M., Huizing, D., del Vecchyo, M.R.O., Phillipson, F., Sangers, A.: Framework of synchromodal transportation problems. ICCL 2017. LNCS, vol. 10572, pp. 383–403. Springer, Cham (2017). https://doi.org/10.1007/978-3-319-68496-3_26
5. Didi-Biha, M., Marcotte, P., Savard, G.: Path-based formulations of a bilevel toll setting problem. In: Dempe, S., Kalashnikov, V. (eds.) Optimization with Multivalued Mappings. Springer Optimization and its Applications, vol. 2. Springer, Boston (2006). https://doi.org/10.1007/0-387-34221-4_2
6. Eikenbroek, O.A., Still, G.J., van Berkum, E.C., Kern, W.: The boundedly rational user equilibrium: a parametric analysis with application to the network design problem. Transp. Res. Part B: Methodol. **107**, 1–17 (2018)
7. van Essen, M., Thomas, T., van Berkum, E., Chorus, C.: From user equilibrium to system optimum: a literature review on the role of travel information, bounded rationality and non-selfish behaviour at the network and individual levels. Transp. Rev. **36**(4), 527–548 (2016)
8. Fraleigh, J., Beauregard, R., Katz, V.: Linear Algebra. No. v. 1 in Featured Titles for Linear Algebra. Addison-Wesley (1995)
9. Hearn, D., Ramana, M.: Solving congestion toll pricing models. In: Marcotte, P., Nguyen, S. (eds.) Equilibrium and Advanced Transportation Modelling. Centre for Research on Transportation (1998)
10. Jiang, L., Mahmassani, H.: Toll pricing: computational tests for capturing heterogeneity of user preferences. Transp. Res. Rec. **2343**, 105–115 (2013). Journal of the Transportation Research Board
11. Liu, H., Wang, D.Z.: Global optimization method for network design problem with stochastic user equilibrium. Transp. Res. Part B: Methodol. **72**, 20–39 (2015)
12. Liu, J., Zhou, X.: Observability quantification of public transportation systems with heterogeneous data sources: an information-space projection approach based on discretized space-time network flow models. Transp. Res. Part B: Methodol. **128**, 302–323 (2019)
13. Ren, W., Beard, R.W.: Consensus seeking in multiagent systems under dynamically changing interaction topologies. IEEE Trans. Autom. Control **50**(5), 655–661 (2005)

14. Roughgarden, T.: Selfish routing and the price of anarchy. OPTIMA-2007 (2006)
15. Ortega del Vecchyo, M.R., Phillipson, F., Sangers, A.: Alternative performance indicators for optimizing container assignment in a synchromodal transportation network. In: Cerulli, R., Raiconi, A., Voß, S. (eds.) ICCL 2018. LNCS, vol. 11184, pp. 222–235. Springer, Cham (2018). https://doi.org/10.1007/978-3-030-00898-7_14
16. Wada, K., Satsukawa, K., Smith, M., Akamatsu, T.: Network throughput under dynamic user equilibrium: queue spillback, paradox and traffic control. Transp. Res. Part B: Methodol. **126**, 391–413 (2019)
17. Yang, H., Huang, H.J.: Social and spatial equities and revenue redistribution. In: Mathematical and Economic Theory of Road Pricing, pp. 203–238. Elsevier Amsterdam (2005)
18. Yang, H., Zhang, X.: Existence of anonymous link tolls for system optimum on networks with mixed equilibrium behaviors. Transp. Res. Part B: Methodol. **42**(2), 99–112 (2008)
19. Yao, B., Chen, C., Zhang, L., Feng, T., Yu, B., Wang, Y.: Allocation method for transit lines considering the user equilibrium for operators. Transp. Res. Part C: Emerg. Technol. **105**, 666–682 (2019)

Comparison of Manual and Automated Decision-Making with a Logistics Serious Game

Martijn Mes[✉] and Wouter van Heeswijk

Department of Industrial Engineering and Business Information Systems,
University of Twente, Enschede, The Netherlands
m.r.k.mes@utwente.nl

Abstract. This paper presents a logistics serious game that describes an anticipatory planning problem for the dispatching of trucks, barges, and trains, considering uncertainty in future container arrivals. The problem setting is conceptually easy to grasp, yet difficult to solve optimally. For this problem, we deploy a variety of benchmark algorithms, including two heuristics and two reinforcement learning implementations. We use the serious game to compare the manual performance of human decision makers with those algorithms. Furthermore, the game allows humans to create their own automated planning rules, which can also be compared with the implemented algorithms and manual game play. To illustrate the potential use of the game, we report the results of three gaming sessions: with students, with job seekers, and with logistics professionals. The experimental results show that reinforcement learning typically outperforms the human decision makers, but that the top tier of humans come very close to this algorithmic performance.

Keywords: Intermodal transport · Serious gaming · Reinforcement learning · Approximate dynamic programming · Heuristics

1 Introduction

Despite the development of sophisticated logistics planning algorithms to automate decisions and the increasing availability of real-time data, planning in the logistics sector still heavily relies on human planners. There are several reasons why manual planning is often preferred. First, human planners require decisions to be sensible and explicable [18]. They tend to quickly lose faith in decision support algorithms when presented with counter-intuitive suggestions, even if consistently following the decision rules would work well in the long term. Second, humans are able to perform surprisingly well on certain planning tasks with vast numbers of potential solutions [8,25], therefore not always recognizing the benefits of automated planning. Third, the algorithmic expertise and experience of logistics companies with sophisticated decision support systems is

© Springer Nature Switzerland AG 2020
E. Lalla-Ruiz et al. (Eds.): ICCL 2020, LNCS 12433, pp. 698–714, 2020.
https://doi.org/10.1007/978-3-030-59747-4_45

often limited, yet experience is a key determinant for successfully introducing new technologies [23].

Serious games may overcome some of the aforementioned challenges. Such games can be used to educate and stimulate a "mental switch" towards decision support and automated planning within the logistics sector. They offer an opportunity for (future) planners to learn about the challenges involved in logistics planning, to gain experience with new technologies, and to become convinced about the advantages such technologies may bring. In addition, games may demonstrate the benefits of decision support, increasing faith in such systems by experimenting in an environment without real-life consequences. Finally, they illustrate the use of automated planning rules and the way such rules can be designed. Venkatesh [22] shows that game-based training is more effective than other forms of training with respect to user acceptance of new technologies. He also indicates that the effects of perceived usefulness and perceived ease of use of a new system – the main drivers behind technology acceptance – are stronger for people who have enjoyed game-based training.

This paper presents a logistics serious game that mimics an anticipatory planning problem in intermodal transport, considering uncertainty in future container arrivals. This anticipatory planning problem is based on Pérez Rivera and Mes [13] and can formally be defined as a Delivery Dispatching Problem (DDP) [12]. In its simplest form, this single-player game with group competition simulates a logistics service provider (LSP) that needs to assign containers to trucks, barges, and trains on a daily basis. The game consists of various predefined scenarios (varying in number of containers, container characteristics, and costs structures) that can be modified by a game master. For the planning algorithms, we make use of two heuristics and two implementations of reinforcement learning (RL). Implementation of these algorithms in practice is not always easy, especially for RL, due to the aforementioned lack of experience from the human planners and due to often being perceived as a 'black box' [18]. To address this phenomenon, we compare the performance of various algorithms with the human performance. Depending on the game mode, human players can either plan the containers manually, use decision support from our RL algorithms, or create their own automated planning rules.

The remainder of this paper is structured as follows. Section 2 positions our research in the body of existing literature and highlights its contributions. In Sect. 3, we describe the decision problem as represented in the game. Section 4 discusses the various solution methods deployed in this paper. The solution methods can all be evaluated using our serious game as introduced in Sect. 5. The experiments with this game are described in Sect. 6. We end with conclusions in Sect. 7.

2   Literature

This literature section is composed as follows. First, we present some related serious games. Second, we reflect on several aspects of human decision-making

that are relevant to logistics planners, and highlight various experiments that
have been conducted on human performance in this context, including the use
of serious games. Third, we briefly describe the reinforcement learning framework that we use as a benchmark as well as for providing decision support to
the human. Fourth, we discuss the anticipatory planning problem and several
reinforcement learning algorithms that have been developed for variants of this
problem.

In the transportation domain, serious games have mostly been developed for
raising awareness about the interaction among different actors in a transportation system [17]. For example, the rail cargo management game [11] simulates
the interaction among transporters, clients, and network managers. Games about
training a single-actor are scarce and focus mostly on passenger or public transport as seen in the review of Raghothama and Meijer [16]. For example, Ecodeal-
ers and Waze are two location-based games (using a mobile phone) described in
Rossetti et al. [17], where a single player is trained for the improvement of public
and passenger transport, respectively. Similarly, Drakoulis et al. [4] considered
an interactive game to motivate public transport users to participate and behave
correctly with the proposed demand-responsive transport service. Examples of
single player games that are closely related to ours are SynchroMania [3], the
follow-up game MasterShipper, and the Modal Manager game [10].

In human decision-making, bounded rationality has a major impact on everyday decisions. Due to time pressure and cognitive limitations, humans often set-
tle for an acceptable solution rather than the optimal one [19]. In this spirit,
so-called *fast-and-frugal* heuristics are often used to make decisions [5]. Such
decisions are constructed out of three building blocks, requiring limited information and processing: (i) search rules that specify how information is collected, (ii)
stopping rules that specify when the information search is halted, and (iii) decision rules that specify which decision should be selected. Heuristic algorithms,
as often used in logistics, reflect such intuitive human decision-making methods,
yet are faster (especially for large problem instances) and more consistent.

We may extract some insightful results from experiments with humans in
logistics planning problems. For example, experiments have been performed with
the MIT 'Beer Distribution Game', in which multiple participants manage part
of a simulated inventory distribution system [20]. Human performance is rather
poor, with identified causes being anchoring (initial stock levels strongly influence decisions later on), failure to take into account time lags in supply, and a ten-
dency to perceive controllable events as external influences. Other experiments
consider capacited VRPs with time windows, for which Anderson et al. [1] show
that humans – with visual aid – are able to find good solutions. For the Traveling Salesman Problem (TSP), Wiener et al. [25] conclude that humans tend to
quickly identify good general solution structures, which they subsequently refine.
In Kefalidou and Ormerod [7] it is shown that human participants came close
to optimal VRP solutions, especially those relying on visual solution methods.
Finally, Keller and Katsikopoulos [8] evaluate various human solution approaches
in operations management, claiming that such methods are particularly

effective when the model contains a single attribute that typifies good solutions (e.g., efficient capacity utilization). Furthermore, the authors state that humans perform well after relatively few trials, implying a steep learning curve. However, they also identify diminishing performance when dealing with larger problem instances. Summarizing, experimental studies show that humans perform well with visual cues and clear solution structures, but performance quickly declines when facing larger and more complex tasks.

Whereas logistics planners rely on manual planning for many decisions, sophisticated planning algorithms are widely spread in the industry as well. This paper considers an anticipatory planning problem, which may be formalized mathematically by a Markov Decision Process (MDP) that in theory may be solved to optimality. However, for realistic-sized problems in logistics planning this is typically not feasible [15]. To overcome computational limitations in solving the model, reinforcement learning (RL) techniques are often applied. For comprehensive and broad descriptions of RL, we refer to Powell [15] and Bertsekas [2]. RL exploits Monte Carlo simulation techniques to learn value functions by observation. Often Value Function Approximation (VFA) is used to computationally simplify the problem; for human designers the key challenge is to define a set of attributes (explanatory variables) that help estimating the downstream costs. In our serious game, we use this VFA to offer the player decision support.

The anticipatory planning problem that we study in this paper may formally be defined as a Delivery Dispatching Problem (DDP) [12]. The DDP involves one or more capacitated transport modalities that may be dispatched at certain decision moments. Containers with stochastic properties arrive dynamically over time and must be dispatched to their destination using the available transport modalities. Costs are minimized by utilizing the modalities' capacity as efficiently as possible, both considering the currently available containers and anticipating future arrivals. Many variants of the DDP exist; we build upon the variant presented by Pérez Rivera and Mes [13], involving a barge that can carry multiple containers and trucks that serve as alternative transport modality. For closely related DDP variants, Pérez Rivera and Mes [14] and Van Heeswijk et al. [21] present several baseline heuristics composed of simple decision rules that achieve consolidation, yet these heuristics ignore various considerations that humans would intuitively make. The aforementioned papers also develop VFA-based RL algorithms, testing a variety of attribute designs. In contrast, Voccia et al. [24] and Klapp et al. [9] present RL algorithms that utilize policy rollout, relying on scenario sampling to estimate downstream costs.

The main contribution of this paper is that we quantitatively compare between human performance and a variety of logistics planning algorithms, utilizing a serious game for this purpose. Such a comparison has not yet been made for the DDP. Furthermore, we provide insights into the drivers of human performance for the DDP and how well they are able to translate their own decision-making strategy into automated planning rules.

3   Problem Description

We formalize the DDP for intermodal transport, which forms the basis of our serious game, as a Markov Decision Process (MDP) model. The objective is to minimize the dispatching costs over a planning horizon of T days (representing decision moments), with dispatching decisions being made at day $t \in \mathcal{T} = \{0, \ldots, T\}$. New containers arrive daily; they are characterized by a destination $d \in \mathcal{D}$, a release day $r \in \mathcal{R} = \{0, 1, \ldots, R^{max}\}$ relative to t, and a time window length $k \in \mathcal{K} = \{0, 1, \ldots, K^{max}\}$ relative to r. Containers with $r > 0$ are deterministically known to arrive at $t + r$, but cannot be dispatched until $r = 0$. Each container characterized by $r = 0$ must be dispatched at or before $t + k$ to guarantee timely delivery; the window length only starts decreasing when $r = 0$.

Every day t, we decide which containers to transport by which transport modality $m \in \mathcal{M}$: trucks ($m = 0$), a barge ($m = 1$), and a train ($m = 2$). Capacities are restricted by Q^m. The costs for both barge and train transport are given by a fixed component depending on the subset of destinations visited and variable costs depending on the number of containers per destination visited. However, the train can visit only one destination per day. Economies of scale apply to both barge and train, as there is a fixed cost component, but the variable costs per container are lower than for the truck. Trucks have a capacity of one container ($Q^0 = 1$), and we assume the number of trucks is infinite. A container with $r = 0$ and $k = 0$ must always be transported; the infinite truck fleet guarantees that each container can be delivered on time. The container dock also has infinite capacity. Each unique combination of destination, release day, and time window length constitutes a *container type*. The problem state $S_t \in \mathcal{S}$ is a vector that describes the number of containers of each type:

$$S_t = [S_{t,d,r,k}]_{\forall [d,r,k] \in \mathcal{D} \times \mathcal{R} \times \mathcal{K}}.$$

At each day $t \in \mathcal{T}$, we decide how many containers of each type to dispatch, and whether we deliver them by trucks, barge or train. Recall that only containers with a release day $r = 0$ can be dispatched, that containers with time window $k > 0$ do not need to be dispatched, and that each dispatched container must be assigned to a transport modality $m \in \mathcal{M}$. Let $\mathcal{X}(S_t)$ be the set of feasible decisions while being in state S_t, and $x_t \in \mathcal{X}(S_t)$ the decision defined by:

$$x_t = [x_{t,m,d,k}]_{\forall [m,d,k] \in \mathcal{M} \times \mathcal{D} \times \mathcal{K}},$$

s.t.

$$x_{t,m,d,k} \leq S_{t,d,0,k} \qquad \forall [m, d, k] \in \mathcal{M} \times \mathcal{D} \times \mathcal{K},$$

$$\sum_{m \in \mathcal{M}} x_{t,m,d,0} = S_{t,d,0,0} \qquad \forall d \in \mathcal{D},$$

$$\sum_{[d,k] \in \mathcal{D} \times \mathcal{K}} x_{t,m,d,k} \leq Q^m \qquad \forall m \in \mathcal{M},$$

$$x_{t,m,d,k} \in \mathbb{N} \qquad \forall [m, d, k] \in \mathcal{M} \times \mathcal{D} \times \mathcal{K}.$$

Each decision x_t has an associated cost $C(S_t, x_t)$. We introduce some necessary notation. Let $c^f_{m,\mathcal{D}'}$ be the fixed costs for modality m for visiting the subset of destinations $\mathcal{D}' \subseteq \mathcal{D}$ (for the train $\mathcal{D}'$ consists of at most one destination, and for the truck the costs $c^f_{m,\mathcal{D}'}$ are always zero). Next, we define $c^v_{m,d}$ as the variable costs per container, i.e., the marginal costs of transporting a single container to destination d by modality m. Let $I_{m,\mathcal{D}'} \in \{0, 1\}$ be a binary variable indicating whether destination subset $\mathcal{D}' \subseteq \mathcal{D}$ is visited by modality m. To prevent postponing shipments until T and to consistently compare solution methods, we define so-called cleanup costs for the freight remaining at T, approximating the costs to dispatch the remaining containers at the end of the time horizon. We define cleanup costs with a function $C^T : (S_T, x_t) \mapsto \mathbb{R}^+$ that is added to the cost function, and $I_t \in \{0, 1\}$ the corresponding binary variable that only activates when $t = T$. The cost function at day t is defined as follows:

$$C(S_t, x_t) = \sum_{m \in \mathcal{M}} \left(\sum_{\mathcal{D}' \subseteq \mathcal{D}} I_{m,\mathcal{D}'} \cdot c^f_{m,\mathcal{D}'} \right) + \sum_{[m,d,k] \in \mathcal{M} \times \mathcal{D} \times \mathcal{K}} c^v_{m,d} \cdot x_{t,m,d,k} + I_t C^T(S_t, x_t),$$

s.t.

$$I_{m,\mathcal{D}'} = \begin{cases} 1 & \text{if } \left(\prod_{d \in \mathcal{D}'} \left(\sum_{k \in \mathcal{K}} x_{t,m,d,k} \right) > 0 \right) \wedge \left(\sum_{[d,k] \in \mathcal{D} \backslash \mathcal{D}' \times \mathcal{K}} x_{t,m,d,k} = 0 \right), \\ 0 & \text{otherwise} \end{cases}$$

$$I_t = \begin{cases} 1 & \text{if } t = T \\ 0 & \text{otherwise} \end{cases}.$$

We aim to find the policy that minimizes the costs over our planning horizon. A policy $\pi \in \Pi$ is a function $\pi : S_t \mapsto x_t$ that maps each state to a corresponding decision. The optimal policy π^* may be found by solving the well-known Bellman optimality equations for each state:

$$V^{\pi^*}_t(S_t) = \min_{x_t \in \mathcal{X}(S_t)} \left(C(S_t, x_t) + \sum_{S_{t+1} \in \mathcal{S}} \mathbb{P}(S_{t+1} \mid S_t, x_t) \cdot V^{\pi^*}_{t+1}(S_{t+1}) \right) \quad \forall S_t \in \mathcal{S}.$$

The problem definition supplied in this section enables us to outline our solution methods to tackle the anticipatory planning problem. A graphical illustration of the problem can be found in Fig. 1.

Container stack (r=0) Known arrivals (r>1)

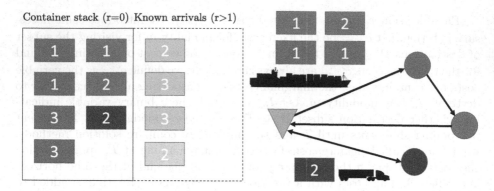

Fig. 1. Schematic representation of the problem. Left is the state, showing containers and their due dates. Right is a possible decision that allocates a subset of containers to barge and truck. Assuming a barge capacity of 8 containers, over 100 decisions exist for this example state, yet decision rules may be readily derived.

4   Solution Methods

This section discusses the following solution methods to the problem described in the previous section: (i) a heuristic policy, (ii) a myopic deterministic optimization policy, (iii) two reinforcement learning policies, (iv) human decision-making, (v) manually created planning rules, and (vi) human decision-making using decision support from one of the reinforcement learning policies. These methods are briefly described below. To ease the presentation, and because the train is not included as a modality in our experimental scenarios from Sect. 6, we only consider trucks and barges.

Heuristic. The heuristic follows three steps. In step 1 it calculates – for each possible destination for which we have an urgent container $(k = 0)$ – the costs for filling up the remaining barge capacity using containers with this destination. For those destinations for which the barge is cheaper than truck, all urgent containers are assigned to the barge. In step 2, for all destinations already visited by the barge, remaining containers of the same destinations are also assigned to the barge, starting with those with smaller time windows, as long as there is capacity left. In step 3, we check which destination has the most containers remaining. We fill up the remaining barge capacity with these containers, starting with the lower time windows, when it is cheaper to transport these containers by barge compared to truck, and when either (i) the total number of containers with this destination, both released and non-released, is above a specified threshold or (ii) we do not have any non-released containers with this destination. The first condition accounts for future capacity problems when postponing the transport of containers. The second condition accounts for the idea that it is less likely that these containers can be consolidated more efficiently the next day.

Direct Cost Minimization. A flawed yet deliberate approach to tackle the planning problem is to simply minimize the direct costs at day t, without considering downstream effects: $\sum_{t \in \mathcal{T}} \min_{x_t \in \mathcal{X}_t(S_t)} C(S_t, x_t)$. When multiple decisions yield the same costs, we select the one that loads the highest number of containers onto the barge, thereby stimulating capacity utilization. This method corresponds to a naive application of traditional OR techniques such as linear programming, optimizing only for the information deterministically known at the decision moment.

Reinforcement Learning. Even for the relatively small problem instances considered in our game scenarios, it is not possible to solve the MDP model exactly. Therefore, we resort to the reinforcement learning (RL) framework to approximately solve the optimality equations through Monte Carlo simulations. More specifically, the algorithm performs N learning iterations, and in each iteration, we loop over the planning horizon $\mathcal{T}$ and use the resulting observations to improve our estimates of the downstream costs, thereby facilitating better decisions. Instead of storing estimates for each possible state (the so-called lookup table approach), we apply value function approximation (VFA) using the basis function approach, where we estimate the state-decision costs $V_t^n(S_t, x_t)$ by $\bar{V}_t^n(S_t, x_t) = \sum_{a \in \mathcal{A}} \theta_{t,a}^n \phi_a(S_t, x_t)$. Here $\phi_a : (S_t, x_t) \mapsto \mathbb{R}$ returns a given attribute from the state-decision pair (e.g., the total number of containers) that explains – to some extent – the cost of the state-decision pair. The attribute value is multiplied with a weight $\theta_{t,a}^n \in \mathbb{R}$. The weights $\theta_{t,a}^n, \forall [t,a] \in \mathcal{T} \setminus \{T\} \times \mathcal{A}$ are updated after every iteration. So, the value of a state is using a weighted linear combination of the basis functions; for more information we refer to Powell [15]. Our RL implementation is exactly the same as the one described in Pérez and Mes [14], except that we consider the single trip version, i.e., we only consider deliveries and not pickups.

Reinforcement Learning with Extended VFA. The extended RL algorithm only differs in the features used in the basis function approach. To explain the features, we introduce the notion of MayGo and MustGo containers. MustGo containers are those that must be transported today, i.e., containers with $r = 0 \wedge k = 0$. MayGo containers are those that we might transport today, i.e., containers with $r = 0 \wedge k > 0$. The basis function approach considered in our standard RL implementation uses the following features: (i) the number of containers per type (resulting in $|\mathcal{D}| \times |\mathcal{R}| \times |\mathcal{K}|$ features), (ii) the number of destinations having MustGo containers, (iii) the number of MustGo containers, (iv) the number of destinations with MayGo containers, (v) the number of MayGo containers, (vi) the number of destinations of the non-released containers, (vii) the number of non-released containers, and (viii) a constant. For our extended RL algorithm, we introduce additional features that are based on the set of containers that remain after applying our decision x_t. For each possible destination subset $\mathcal{D}'$, we introduce two binary variables indicating whether the subset may or must be visited the next day.

Manual Planning. For the human planners, the notion of bounded rationality applies. The planner has access to all cost information as well as the probabilities of container arrivals. However, as the decision time to solve the decision problem for each day is limited, players might cognitively not able to evaluate all feasible decisions. In addition, the human planner cannot possibly anticipate the potential downstream effects of their decisions. It is therefore expected that players seek a satisfactory solution rather than an optimal one. Note that in practical business settings, the combination of time restrictions and cognitive limitations would typically also apply. Humans are known to be good at decisions that involve clustering, this is reflected in the observed decision-making processes during the game. Common decision rules are to combine containers with the same destination onto the barge, postpone visiting a certain destination when containers with similar destinations are known to arrive the next day, and utilize the capacity of the barge as well as possible.

Planning Rules. The game includes a graphical algorithm creator. With this tool, the players can define their own decision rules. These rules typically have a structure similar to the manual strategies used by the players. To create an algorithm, players first define filters. A filter is a collection of container types, e.g., all containers having a time window of 1. The filters are strongly connected to the features considered in our RL methods. There is no restriction on the number of filters that can be created. After defining filters, the decision rules can be created. Each rule consists of an action and a condition. The action is applied to a given filter, and consists of transport by a certain modality or withholding transport. The action will only be performed when the conditions are met. There are three types of conditions. First, the condition that the selected transport modality in the action can only be used for containers whose destination is already assigned to the transport modality. Second, conditions related to certain thresholds that compare ($\leq, <, =, >, \geq$) the number of containers in some filter with (i) some number, (ii) the capacity of a modality, or (iii) the number of containers in another filter. Third, conditions related to costs, where we compare the costs of the proposed action with the costs of another action (combination of a filter and transport mode). The player can use as many conditions as needed for each action, and all conditions can be combined with *and/or* operators. Also for the number of decision rules, there is no limit. Players may change the sequence of decision rules; each rule will act only on the containers that are not yet assigned by one of the previous rules. After creating the algorithm, the players can apply them in the game. Depending on the game settings, the player might be allowed to (i) overrule the decisions taken by their algorithm, i.e., manually change them or (ii) adjust their algorithm during the game.

Decision Support. For any decision and its corresponding features, the learned VFA weights can be used to compute the expected downstream costs. We use the VFA to provide decision support in the form of estimated marginal costs or savings. More specifically, we show the difference in estimated value $\bar{V}_t^n(S_t, x_t)$ of the decision x_t (certain assignment of containers to modalities) and the decision of doing nothing. These estimated marginal costs can be balanced against the direct costs of the decision x_t. As the calculation of $\bar{V}_t^n(S_t, x_t)$ only requires multiplying (fixed) weights and features for a single manual decision at a time, this form of decision support can easily be provided in real-time environments.

5   Serious Game: Trucks and Barges

This section introduces the serious game that is used to compare the human planning performance with those of the algorithms from Sect. 4. The game is called Trucks & Barges and is publicly available at www.trucksandbarges.nl.

The purpose of the game is to let players gain experience with transport planning under uncertainty, raise awareness about some of the trade-offs in anticipatory planning, and familiarize them with decision support and automated planning. The game is designed to provide the player with insight into (i) a typical intermodal planning problem, (ii) the benefits and challenges in anticipatory planning, (iii) the benefits of decision support and automated planning rules, (iv) the complexity of the planning problem, and (v) the formalization of automated planning rules. On the other hand, the game also provides the game master with insights related to the behavior of the participants, their awareness about the trade-offs in anticipatory planning, their learning process, and the way they respond to various forms of decision support, automated planning rules and optimization algorithms.

The game can be played individually as well as within a serious gaming session under the guidance of a game master (e.g., a classroom setting). When playing the game within a serious gaming session, the game master first selects a scenario that describes all problem settings, such as the modalities, costs, container arrival probabilities, destination probabilities, etc. Using these settings, the game master can represent different logistics challenges. As such, human performance can be evaluated from various perspectives. Next, the game master defines the rounds to be played. Each round consists of a pre-defined number of weeks where a player is in the same mode: practice, normal, support, planning, or automated. In the *practice* and *normal* round, the player only sees the direct costs of each selected decision. The normal round corresponds with "manual planning" in Sect. 4. The practice round has a build-in tutorial where players receive information on all elements within the game. Furthermore, the performance in the practice round does not affect the player's game score. The *support* round corresponds with "decision support" in Sect. 4. Here, the learned VFA weights are used to estimate the downstream costs of decisions. For each manual decision, the player sees both the direct costs and the estimated marginal downstream costs on top of the playing screen (see Fig. 2). The sum of these two costs supports the player in evaluating the marginal future impact of decisions with different immediate costs, i.e., to find the decision that is expected to be beneficial in the long run. The *planning* round corresponds with "planning rules" from Sect. 4. Here, the player uses the algorithm creator to make decisions according to his/her own fixed rules (but depending on the game settings, the player can either overrule these decisions or change the planning rules during the game). Finally, in the *automated* round, the player can see all the algorithms from Sect. 4 into action, without the option to manually intervene.

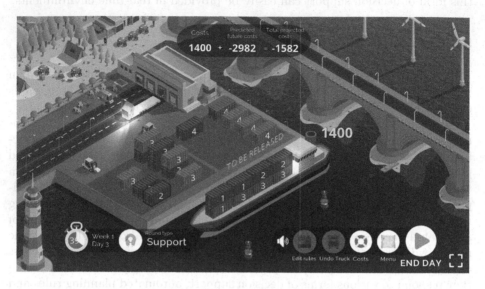

Fig. 2. Screenshot of Trucks & Barges serious game. Containers to be transported can be dragged to truck, barge, or train. Container colors indicate destination, container numbers reflect the remaining time window. (Color figure online)

The player takes the role of an LSP planner who schedules the transport of containers from the hinterland to a deep-sea port using trucks, barges, and trains. The underlying problem is as described in Sect. 3. The main playing screen is shown in Fig. 2. Containers are colored according to their destination (red, green, and blue for the three destinations considered in the game) and are located in one of two container yards. The container yard to the left holds containers that are released for transport ($r = 0$) and the yard on the right holds container that are to be released the next day ($r = 1$). Furthermore, containers are labeled with a white number in the middle according to their current time window, which decreases as days pass and containers are not transported. In the game, the possible time windows are $k \in \{0, 1, 2\}$ (incremented in-game by 1 to reflect travel times of 1 day) after the release day r. To schedule the transport of containers, the player can drag-and-drop containers from the left container yard onto a truck, barge, or train. The player can also undo such movements, dragging containers back from the modalities onto the container yard. The daily barge and train, as well as the trucks, take one day to bring a container to its destination, meaning that a container with a time window of 1 must be transported today. All containers must be transported within their time window; the unlimited number of trucks guarantees this is always feasible. The daily plan is finalized and executed when the end button is pressed or when the maximum time for a day's decision has elapsed, which is indicated by a clock in the bottom left corner.

Dispatch decisions result in "immediate costs", which are displayed next to the used modalities. At the end of each turn, containers that had a time window of 1 and were not transported will be automatically assigned to the trucks. Then, the barge, train, and trucks depart – visualized by an animation – and a daily report is presented to the player with the costs of his or her decisions. In the transition to the next turn, two things happen: (i) containers to be released the next day (i.e., containers in the right-hand yard) are moved to the left-hand yard, and (ii) new containers arrive to the two container yards. The turns continue until the end of the week, where the game "cleans" the containers that were left and assigns cleaning costs to the player. At the end of a week, the player gets a report on his or her costs for each day and the cleanup costs. At the end of a round, a round report is displayed providing insights into the player's performance (or algorithmic performance). The game also has a dynamic leaderboard, where players can see their ranking and the performance of other players in the game session in real-time.

The initial state at the beginning of each week, as well as the daily order arrivals are generated up front, such that all players face exactly the same game instance. However, even though this information is generated up front, none of the policies from the previous section will utilize information regarding future events, e.g., the RL policies only use the probabilities used to generate the container arrivals. All costs components and container arrival probabilities are accessible by the player through the info button.

6   Experimental Results

To illustrate the possible usage of the game, we now report on three gaming sessions with a different audience: students, job seekers, and logistics professionals. Depending on the audience, we consider different game scenarios and round types. For all game scenarios, we exclude the train as transport modality to not overly complicate the human decision-making process. We distinguish between two game scenarios: easy and difficult. In the easy scenario, the barge is always cheaper per container compared to truck, even though there are still setup costs for using the barge, depending on the combinations of destinations that need to be visited. In the difficult scenario, the barge is only cheaper compared to truck when sufficiently being utilized. Each rounds consist of 3 weeks, and each week consists of 5 days/turns. For each turn, we use a time limit of 60 s, which seems to be more than sufficient given that the average decision time of the players in all of the three gaming sessions was 17.8 s, and 85.4% of the decisions were made within 30 s. Note that the times for our heuristics and RL algorithms to make decisions are negligible ($\ll 1$ s). Here the RL algorithms benefit from the fact that the VFA is learned offline once per game scenario, which typically requires a couple of seconds.

The settings of the game scenarios can be found in the publicly available 'rooms' denoted by "low/high barge costs 4 rounds" at www.trucksandbarges.nl. Note that the rounds themselves are different in these publicly available games compared to the rounds of the serious gaming session as described in Sect. 4.

Two psychological effects are important with respect to the performance of the players: the anchoring effect and the reference effect [6]. Within our gaming sessions, there is a heavy reliance of players on the information initially offered. Also, if the player already played a round using decision support, this typically affects his/her behavior in subsequent rounds. Similarly, the costs made in the first round will serve as a reference for the performance in later rounds. To filter our these effects as much as possible, all players in all sessions first had to complete 3 weeks in the practice round.

For all groups, we studied various aspects, such as the relation between performance and decision time, and the relation between performance and the number of times the participants consulted the screens with cost information. However, given the limited number of participants and the huge fluctuations in performance, none of these relations were significant ($\alpha = 0.05$). Therefore, we only show the results of the performance of the players and algorithms in terms of costs. These results are all summarized in graphs showing the cumulative distribution function of the human players, scaled relative to the performance of our heuristics and RL policies. With respect to the cumulative distribution function, we first rank the players from good (low costs) to bad (high costs), and plot their scaled performance against the fraction of players that scored as least as well. With respect to the scaled performance, we compare the human performance against the four algorithms from Sect. 4: Heuristic, Myopic (direct cost minimization), RL (reinforcement learning), and RLext (reinforcement learning with extended VFA). We index the performance of the best performing algorithm to 0 and the performance of the worst performing algorithm to 1. In all experiments, RLext resulted in the best performance. The worst algorithmic performance was achieved by either Heuristic or Myopic. A player having a score higher than 1 means that all four algorithms performed better than this player.

6.1   Gaming Session 1: With Students

We first performed an extensive gaming session with 40 students from the master program Industrial Engineering and Management at the University of Twente. All students had to play 3 rounds: *normal*, *support*, and *planning*. We divided the group of students into two: one group first playing a normal round followed by a support round and the other group playing the rounds in reverse order. All groups ended with the planning round. Furthermore, all students had to play both the easy and difficult gaming scenario.

We first assess the difference in performance due to changing the sequence of the normal and support round. Players that first played support had on average 3.7% lower costs in the normal round. This suggests that lessons from the support round might be transferred to the normal round. However, given the huge fluctuations among the limited number of players, this difference is not significant. As only minor differences were observed between normal and support rounds, these results have been aggregated in Fig. 3 under the term *manual* (hence the graph corresponding with manual has twice as many observations as the graph corresponding with rules).

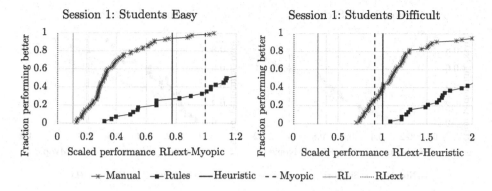

Fig. 3. Cumulative distribution in Session 1 of the scaled human performance relative to RLext (=0) and the worst-performing heuristic (=1). Both RLext and RL consistently outperform human players. In the difficult scenario, players' results considerably decrease.

Figure 3 visualizes the game results. When looking at the left-hand graph (representing the easy scenario), we observe that 98% and 94% of the students outperformed Myopic and Heuristic, respectively. With the algorithm creator, only 33% of the students outperformed the myopic solution method. For the difficult scenario (right-hand graph), we observe that 38% and 26% of the students outperformed the Heuristic and Myopic, respectively. In both scenarios, students had a hard time creating planning rules that improved their manual game play or one of the heuristics.

6.2 Gaming Session 2: With Job Seekers

The second gaming session was performed at a logistics fair organized in the Netherlands. This fair was organized for everyone looking for a job in the logistics sector, specifically aimed at students in pre-vocational secondary schools. At this fair, visitors could, e.g., drive trucks and forklifts, control drones, design a warehouse, stack pallets, but also play our game. As time is limited in such a situation, we let players first practice, then play only one round to measure their performance, and end up with an automated round in which they could see our algorithms in action. The results of 60 players are shown on the left-hand side of Fig. 4. Average performance is worse than for master students, possibly due to a lack of domain knowledge inherent to young job seekers. Best- and worst-case performance are comparable to that of students though.

712   M. Mes and W. van Heeswijk

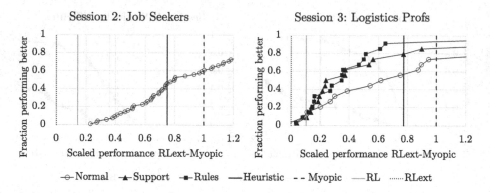

Fig. 4. Cumulative distribution in Sessions 2+3 of the scaled human performance relative to RLext (=0) and the myopic algorithm (=1). Note that some logistics professionals outperform the RL algorithms.

6.3 Gaming Session 3: With Logistics Professionals

Finally, we performed a gaming session at one of the larger logistics companies within The Netherlands. With 17 logistics professionals, we played the same rounds as with the students, but only considering the easy scenario and using the following sequence of rounds for all players: normal, support, and planning. The results are shown on the right-hand side of Fig. 4. In contrast with the results of the students, we now show the results of the two manual rounds (normal and support) separately, as there is a clear increase in performance when using support (but differences are still not significant given the limited number of players). Furthermore, a few players actually outperformed the RL algorithm. Finally, we observe that the logistics professionals were able to create planning rules, using the algorithm creator, that improved their manual game play.

6.4 Interpretation of Algorithmic Performance

We conclude the assessment of our results by briefly reflecting on algorithmic performance. For the easy scenario, the performance of the myopic policy is poor, being outperformed by most human players. This result highlights the challenges of anticipating the future impact of current dispatching decisions. For the difficult scenario, myopic performance drastically improves though. In this scenario, rules-of-thumb no longer work well; evaluating many solutions pays off here. The heuristic performs relatively well for the simple scenario, yet most humans are able to obtain better results. The heuristic embeds some rudimentary logic, but cannot handle exceptions and information about the future. These flaws are aggravated in the difficult scenario. Finally, RL outperforms virtually all players even in the easy scenario; only a handful of logistics professionals can beat its score. It is our only algorithm that explicitly considers downstream costs, which is crucial in anticipatory planning.

7   Conclusions and Further Research

This paper describes an anticipatory planning problem for the dispatching of trucks, barges, and trains, considering uncertainty in future container arrivals. We design several algorithms – a myopic policy, a heuristic and two reinforcement learning strategies – to solve the problem. Furthermore, we develop a serious game called Trucks & Barges to compare the performance of algorithms and human planners. Within the game, players can plan the containers manually both with and without decision support. In addition, the players may create their own planning rules using a graphical algorithm creator.

Test results are obtained through three serious gaming sessions: with students, with job seekers in the logistics sector, and with logistics professionals. The experimental results show that sophisticated heuristics and reinforcement learning on average outperform the human decision makers, but that the top tier of humans comes very close to the algorithmic performance. Both the creation of heuristic rules and of value function approximations in reinforcement learning require considerable domain knowledge. The results of the best logistics professionals in particular highlight the importance of domain knowledge in algorithmic design. Nevertheless, well-designed algorithms outperform most human decision makers. These insights imply that both human expertise and algorithmic developments remain necessary to advance the art of anticipatory planning in the logistics sector.

References

1. Anderson, D., et al.: Human-guided simple search. In: AAAI/IAAI, pp. 209–216 (2000)
2. Bertsekas, D.P.: Dynamic Programming and Optimal Control, vol. 1, 2nd edn. Athena Scientific, Belmont (2017)
3. Buiel, E., et al.: Synchro mania - design and evaluation of a serious game creating a mind shift in transport planning. In: 46th International Simulation and Gaming Association Conference, ISAGA, pp. 1–12 (2015)
4. Drakoulis, R., et al.: A gamified flexible transportation service for on-demand public transport. IEEE Trans. Intell. Transp. Syst. 19(3), 921–933 (2018)
5. Gigerenzer, G., Todd, P.M.: Fast and frugal heuristics: the adaptive toolbox. In: Simple Heuristics that make us Smart, pp. 3–34. Oxford University Press, Oxford (1999)
6. Kahneman, D.: Thinking, Fast and Slow. Macmillan, New York City (2011)
7. Kefalidou, G., Ormerod, T.C.: The fast and the not-so-frugal: human heuristics for optimization problem solving. In: Proceedings of the Annual Meeting of the Cognitive Science Society, vol. 36 (2014)
8. Keller, N., Katsikopoulos, K.V.: On the role of psychological heuristics in operational research; and a demonstration in military stability operations. Eur. J. Oper. Res. 249(3), 1063–1073 (2016)
9. Klapp, M.A., Erera, A.L., Toriello, A.: The dynamic dispatch waves problem for same-day delivery. Eur. J. Oper. Res. 271(2), 519–534 (2018)

10. Kurapati, S., Kourounioti, I., Lukosch, H., Tavasszy, L., Verbraeck, A.: Fostering sustainable transportation operations through corridor management: a simulation gaming approach. Sustainability **10**(2), 1–18 (2018)
11. Meijer, S.A., Mayer, I.S., van Luipen, J., Weitenberg, N.: Gaming rail cargo management: exploring and validating alternative modes of organization. Simul. Gaming **43**(1), 85–101 (2012)
12. Minkoff, A.S.: A Markov decision model and decomposition heuristic for dynamic vehicle dispatching. Oper. Res. **41**(1), 77–90 (1993)
13. Rivera, A.P., Mes, M.: Dynamic multi-period freight consolidation. In: Corman, F., Voß, S., Negenborn, R.R. (eds.) ICCL 2015. LNCS, vol. 9335, pp. 370–385. Springer, Cham (2015). https://doi.org/10.1007/978-3-319-24264-4_26
14. Pérez Rivera, A.E., Mes, M.R.K.: Anticipatory freight selection in intermodal long-haul round-trips. Transp. Res. Part E: Logist. Transp. Rev. **105**, 176–194 (2017)
15. Powell, W.B.: Approximate Dynamic Programming: Solving the Curses of Dimensionality. Wiley Series in Probability and Statistics, 2nd edn. Wiley, Hoboken (2011)
16. Raghothama, J., Meijer, S.A.: A review of gaming simulation in transportation. In: Meijer, S.A., Smeds, R. (eds.) ISAGA 2013. LNCS, vol. 8264, pp. 237–244. Springer, Cham (2014). https://doi.org/10.1007/978-3-319-04954-0_28
17. Rossetti, R.J.F., Almeida, J.A.E., Kokkinogenis, Z., Gonçalves, J.: Playing transportation seriously: applications of serious games to artificial transportation systems. IEEE Intell. Syst. **28**(4), 107–112 (2013). https://doi.org/10.1109/MIS.2013.113
18. Samek, W., Montavon, G., Vedaldi, A., Hansen, L.K., Müller, K.-R. (eds.): Explainable AI: Interpreting, Explaining and Visualizing Deep Learning. LNCS (LNAI), vol. 11700. Springer, Cham (2019). https://doi.org/10.1007/978-3-030-28954-6
19. Simon, H.A.: Bounded rationality. In: Eatwell, J., Milgate, M., Newman, P. (eds.) Utility and Probability. The New Palgrave, pp. 15–18. Palgrave Macmillan, London (1990). https://doi.org/10.1007/978-1-349-20568-4_5
20. Sterman, J.D.: Modeling managerial behavior: misperceptions of feedback in a dynamic decision making experiment. Manag. Sci. **35**(3), 321–339 (1989)
21. Van Heeswijk, W.J.A., Mes, M.R.K., Schutten, J.M.J.: The delivery dispatching problem with time windows for urban consolidation centers. Transp. Sci. **53**(1), 203–221 (2019)
22. Venkatesh, V.: Creation of favorable user perceptions: exploring the role of intrinsic motivation. MIS Q. **23**(2), 239–260 (1999)
23. Venkatesh, V., Bala, H.: Technology acceptance model 3 and a research agenda on interventions. Decis. Sci. **39**(2), 273–315 (2008)
24. Voccia, S.A., Campbell, A.M., Thomas, B.W.: The same-day delivery problem for online purchases. Transp. Sci. **53**(1), 167–184 (2017)
25. Wiener, J.M., Ehbauer, N.N., Mallot, H.A.: Path planning and optimization in the traveling salesman problem: nearest neighbor vs. region-based strategies. In: Dagstuhl Seminar Proceedings, pp. 1–21 (2007)

Pricing and Quality Investments
in a Mixed Brown-Green Product Market

Arka Mukherjee$^{(\boxtimes)}$ and Margarida Carvalho

CIRRELT and Département d'informatique et de recherche opérationnelle,
Université de Montréal, Montréal, Quebéc H3T 1J4, Canada
arka.mukherjee@umontreal.ca, carvalho@iro.umontreal.ca

Abstract. Sustainable Supply Chain Management (SSCM) has assumed
a position of prominence for academics and industry over the last two
decades. The sustainability literature shows that typically manufacturers
aim to optimize their pricing and greening level decisions in a mixed (green
and brown) consumer market. In this work, we capture a manufacturer's
classic dilemma on the pricing of green and brown products, and greening
investments, while subject to budget constraint. We compute and analyze
the variations of optimal decisions over time. Our findings underscore the
importance of investing in greening technologies and learning for the survival of green products. Furthermore, we show that a manufacturer's optimal pricing strategy is to enter the market with a lower price for the green
product and to increase it over time, eventually, surpassing the price for the
brown product. Our analysis reveals that the greening level attraction can
nullify the effect of a high price on the green product, resulting in higher
green demand than brown. Higher green product demand is a win-win situation for both the manufacturer and the environment.

Keywords: Green products · Pricing · Greening level · Learning ·
Sustainability · Optimal control

1 Introduction

The global emphasis on sustainable environmental practises in the last two
decades has encouraged many manufacturers and retailers to envisage future
consumer behaviour to be progressively green. Consequently, these manufacturers have invested in green practices and have been seeking to use green manufacturing, products, services or processes as means of competitive advantage.
Manufacturing is one of the salient activities influencing the cost and environmental impact on supply chains [14,15], yet there are many drivers and barriers
to green manufacturing practices. For example, [8] used a Delphi Survey method
to explore the various stimulus and obstacles. While it was found that elements

A. Mukherjee and M. Carvalho—This work was funded by the FRQ-IVADO Research
Chair in Data Science for Combinatorial Game Theory and the NSERC grant 2019-04557.

such as organizational commitment for Good Manufacturer Practice (GMP), eco-knowledge, society influences (green demand), financial incentives (government support), and innovation are drivers of green initiatives, few barriers also hinder them. Examples of such barriers are weak organizational structure to support GMP, lack of GMP knowledge, weak market positions for GMP-based products/processes, a society with low green attitudes, inadequate technology, the existence of sunk costs in GMP which can cause organizations to incur losses, inadequate supplier commitments towards GMP.

Greening of a product comes at a cost and, while greening the processes is more achievable, the subsequent deeper dive into green practises is costlier [18]. As a result, price of green products is usually much higher than the brown counterpart. Many consumers may be environmentally conscious. However, due to the price premium for green products, many consumers refrain from buying green despite their intentions to do so [1]. Thus, for most of the consumer goods, green products remain as a mere product line extension, while the brown counterparts far exceed the demand for green products. Deloitte conducted a direct study of more than 6,000 shopper experiences in 11 major retailers of varying formats to investigate the characteristics of the green shopper and to examine their shopping responses to sustainability issues. The survey revealed that while 95% of the respondents say they will buy green, only 22% have bought green, and 75% know what a green product is. The 2013 survey "*Consumer Trends in sustainability*", by Solarcity [17], shows that consumers are becoming more environmentally conscious and aware, and they wish to buy sustainable products and brands, but they are not always willing to pay more for the green products. Thus, there is a conflict between willingness to pay and willingness to act.

Motivated by the necessity of objectively understanding the conditions that potentiate the survival of green products, we propose an optimal control model that accounts for a manufacturer producing both green and brown substitutable products. The goal is to determine the optimal pricing and greening strategies over time under the following assumptions: *(i)* the manufacturer benefits from economies of scale; *(ii)* the manufacturer learning is increasing with green demand and this reduces greening costs; *(iii)* the manufacturer cannot exceed an investment budget. Through the determination of the model optimal outcomes, we provide theoretical results and numerical experiments allowing to identify the critical parameters for the success of the green product. The rest of the paper is arranged in the following manner. In Sect. 2, we provide a literature review of the related papers. Section 3 develops the model and Sect. 4 provides the analytical results. In Sect. 5, we present a comprehensive numerical study of different influential parameters of our model. Finally, in Sect. 6, we conclude with the implication of our findings and directions for future research.

2   Literature Review

A considerable part of the literature in Green Supply Chain management focus on the pricing and green quality of these products. In a comprehensive literature review, [11] shows that the recent articles on sustainability focus on different dimensions like economical, social, environmental, ethical and temporal. Many decision-support models are derived, leading to a myriad of solutions for sustainable societies. In the same line, our work also articulates a decision problem of pricing and quality, integrating the economic and environmental aspects. In particular, the literature can be broadly classified into two categories: *(i)* research on green products only (for example, [3,4,9,23]); *(ii)* research on both green and brown products (for example, [19–21]). In the first category (green products), these works investigate different directions such us the development and introduction of green products [4], the competition between green products [4,5,12,22] or chain to chain competition [13], green pricing and greening investment decisions under supply chain collaboration [9,10], government intervention for green product developments or promotions [5,5–7,24], eco-labelling [3] and diffusion of green products [16].

Our paper contributes in the second category - brown and green products. Therefore, we detail the literature in this direction. Various research problems have been explored in this area. In [21], it is investigated how a manufacturer's choice of green and brown products is determined in a market with environmentally conscious customers. The authors also shed light on fraudulent green attributes. Precisely, a manufacturer might have a strong inclination to behave fraudulently leading to the enforcement of strict supervision for such behaviour. Using a consumer utility based model, [19] shows that while extending a brown product line with green products, manufacturers can strategically avoid product cannibalization with a two-level pricing structure based on consumer segmentation. The static game theoretic model also incorporates learning and capacity constraints. The green quality appeal can also downsize and eliminate the brown demand under certain conditions. [20] considers the manufacturer strategies of *greening out* or *greening up*. Based on market segmentation of consumers into three different groups - the traditional segment, the fence sitter segment and the green segment - the authors find that better economic and environmental performance can persist together. Yenipazarli and Vakharia [20] consider a competition between a green and a brown manufacturer where there are two groups of consumers - brown consumers who are not willing to pay for green products and green consumers who are willing to pay for the green products. The authors highlight that the size of each consumer group can result in different findings. For example, the manufacturers are in a loss-loss situation when the size of the green customer group is larger. On the other hand, an increasing premium for the green product may lead to a win-win situation for both manufacturers.

In this paper, we propose a novel model where the demand for green and brown products is a dynamic function of both product prices and greening level. There is a vast literature focusing in this area of pricing and greening level investments, and some studies treat this classic dilemma of a manufacturer (*e.g.* [19,20,23]). However, to the best of our knowledge, our paper is one of the first to simultaneously incorporate a market with green and brown products, pricing and greening investments, budgets, learning of green practices and mutual interactions among these elements. We account for time when analyzing the optimal manufacturer decisions related to green and brown products. We emphasize the appropriateness of a dynamic model since greening level and learning evolve with time. Thus a dynamic model accurately enables an understanding and planing of long term optimal decisions (strategies). Moreover, since we derive feedback strategies, the manufacturer does not use static or pre-committed pricing and greening policies. Instead, given that its decisions are a function of greening level and learning, they enable the manufacturer to adjust them to improve its profit.

3   The Model

In this section, we present the manufacturer model within a monopolist context selling both green and brown products. Contrary to most of the previous literature, we consider a dynamic setup, i.e., the decisions to be taken by the manufacturer and hence, the consumers' demands and manufacturer's budget restrictions are all dynamic entities depending on time and on the evolving state of the economy. In this context, the manufacturer sells a green and a brown products which are substitutable (e.g., electric vehicles and conventional cars, organic food and GMO food, thermal or renewable power source). The manufacturer has as decision variables $p_g(t)$ and $p_b(t)$ which represent the price of the green and brown products, respectively, at time t, as well as, $I(t)$ corresponding to the investment efforts in green quality at time t. The state variables are $S(t)$, describing the greening level (or green quality), and $\lambda(t)$, modeling the learning of green practices. In the remainder of the paper, the subscript indices g and b will be used to designate association with green and brown products, respectively. Next, we devise and explain the manufacturer's optimization model.

Demand. The demand for the products depends on their prices. In particular, the demand functions for the green and brown products are:

$$
\begin{aligned}
D_g(t) &= \alpha_g - \beta_g p_g(t) + \gamma_g p_b(t) + \eta S(t) \\
D_b(t) &= \alpha_b - \beta_b p_b(t) + \gamma_b p_g(t) - \delta S(t).
\end{aligned}
\tag{1}
$$

The parameters α_g and α_b are the market potentials, β_g and β_b are the individual price sensitivities, γ_g and γ_b are the cross price sensitivities, and, η and δ are the green and brown consumer's attraction, respectively, towards green products. We assume that the following relations hold: $\beta_k > \gamma_k$, where $k \in \{g, b\}$, i.e., the green product demand $D_g(t)$ is more sensitive to its price $p_g(t)$ than to the brown product price $p_b(t)$; similarly, for $D_b(t)$. Thus, this is reasonable assumption in practice. As the demand functions (1) reflect, it is considered that green customers are not restricted to buying green products neither the reverse. Customers can indeed switch to brown products from green if they are not satisfied by the green level obtained at a premium price rises due to manufacturer's constraints. Similarly, brown customers can be attracted towards the green product due to green quality $S(t)$. However, following some of the existing literature (*e.g.* [19]), we assume that the influence of greening level on green customers is superior to the negative influence of greening level on brown customers, i.e., $\eta > \delta$. The total instantaneous demand for the manufacturer is $D(t) = D_g(t) + D_b(t)$.

Learning. We assume that the manufacturer can reduce the production cost of green products by economies of scale. In other words, as demand increases, learning from more production takes place. Consequently, learning is a state variable of this model. We define learning by the following equation:

$$\dot{\lambda}(t) = \phi D_g(t) - \omega\lambda(t) \text{ and } \lambda(0) = 0, \tag{2}$$

where ϕ and ω are non-negative numbers providing the rate of learning increase due to green demand and decrease due to decay in learning. Let us further discuss their interpretation. There are several factors influencing these parameters - (i) a firm failing to adopt a new technology, resulting in learning decay, (ii) improper development of business processes may result in learning loss, (iii) information asymmetry or lack of information in a supply chain can cause a higher decay (ω) or a lower ϕ, (iv) stringent budget constraints may result in learning decay and lastly, (v) efficiency of employees or technology being used can also be determinant for the values of ϕ and ω. While the above list is insightful it might not be exhaustive.

Learning will occur if $\lambda(t) > 0$. The complexity of our parametric space does not allow a straightforward derivation of a condition for positive learning. However, we have numerically verified that for a set of parameter values providing feasible equilibrium solutions, learning is always positive and increasing, as long as the initial value of learning is non-negative.

Green Quality. The greening level is given by the following equation:

$$\dot{S}(t) = k_1 I(t) + k_2\lambda(t) - \epsilon S(t) \text{ and } S(0) = 0, \tag{3}$$

where k_1, k_2 and ϵ are non-negative numbers reflecting the rate of greening level increase due to investments and learning, and decay in greening level. The above evolution of greening quality shows that marginal greening is positively influenced by the direct greening investments and by learning. One may argue that a higher price for the green product than for the brown one can lead consumers to perceive the green product as of superior quality. Nevertheless, [2] reveals that this is not significant and thus, we do not consider it in Eq. (3).

Green Product Budget. In the industry, manufacturers are always constrained by budgets that limit investments and thus, the greening level. Therefore, we assume that there is a budget constraint given by

$$0 \leq I(t) \leq M_g(t). \tag{4}$$

The above equation enforces a budget controlling the investment effort.

This captures the classic trade off between the economic and environmental dimensions of sustainability. Since managers of manufacturers are aware that learning reduces greening costs. Therefore, we assume that the budget $M_g(t)$ is not constant but reduces with learning increases with greening level. Therefore we assume the following structure for the budget:

$$M_g(t) = \xi_s S(t) - \xi \lambda(t). \tag{5}$$

The non-negative parameter ξ_s is the initial constant budget for green quality and green production. The rationale behind choosing such a function is that it allows us to capture two important aspects of the greening budget: *(i)* if learning is high management may decrease the budget, *(ii)* if greening quality is high, the management my increase the budget to avoid to limit it.

Cost Structure. The cost of greening is quadratic in the investment efforts and is given by:

$$\frac{\mu}{2}I^2(t) - \sigma\lambda(t), \tag{6}$$

where the non-negative parameters μ and σ are the proportionality constant for investment costs and cost reduction per unit learning. Given that the accumulated learning at time t, $\lambda(t)$, is increasing with the green demand, cost structure signifies that with an increasing green demand, we have a reducing greening cost due to learning. The higher the learning $\lambda(t)$, the lower the cost (6). Here σ can be interpreted as how efficiency of a manufacturer in leveraging the learning. If a manufacturer is efficient, it can employ proper resources to reduce more the cost (i.e., σ is high).

Model. Therefore, the manufacturer's infinite horizon decision problem is given by:

$$V(S(t), \lambda(t)) = \underset{p_g, p_b, I}{\text{Max}} \int_0^\infty e^{-rt}[D_g p_g + D_b p_b - \left(\frac{\mu}{2}I^2 - \sigma\lambda\right)]dt,$$
$$\text{Subject to } (2),(3),(4) \tag{7}$$
$$p_g \geq 0, p_b \geq 0.$$

For sake of simplicity, we have dropped the dependence on the time in the objective function of (7), and we will do it in the remaining of the paper, whenever this dependence is clear from the context. We stress that the consideration of an infinite time horizon is suitable for the questions addressed in this work as it enables a long-term analysis and thus, planning.

The above problem can be solved using the Hamilton-Jacobi-Bellman (HJB) equations, in order to obtain the optimal feedback strategies:

$$rV(S, \lambda) = \underset{p_g, p_b, I}{\text{Max}} \left(D_b p_b + D_g p_g + \frac{\partial V}{\partial \lambda}(\phi D_g - \omega\lambda) \right.$$
$$\left. + \frac{\partial V}{\partial S}(\lambda k_2 + k_1 I - \epsilon S) - \frac{\mu I^2}{2} + \sigma\lambda \right). \tag{8}$$

The HJB equation (8) does not incorporate the budget constraint. However, we consider the feasible solutions obtained by solving (8) which are characterised by Lemma 2 established in Sect. 4.

We conjecture that the value function is of the following form and later prove it in Proposition 1:

$$V(S, \lambda) = A_1 S^2 + A_2 \lambda^2 + A_3 \lambda S + A_4 S + A_5 \lambda + A_6. \tag{9}$$

4 Analytical Results

In this section, we present our analytical findings. First, we find the manufacturer's optimal pricing of the green and brown products and the optimal investment for the green product. We show how the prices and investments vary with time, the greening level and learning. Fundamental sensitivity analysis on the effect of our model parameters is performed, namely, learning sensitivity, price sensitivity and green level sensitivity on the pricing and investment strategies.

We have conjectured the structure of the value function in Eq. (9) and, in Proposition 1, we will show how to solve for this value function. Before presenting Proposition 1, we provide the following technical lemma which is essential for establishing the non-negativity of the optimal decision variables values.

Lemma 1. *The following condition holds:* $4\beta_g\beta_b - (\gamma_g + \gamma_b)^2 > 0$.

Proof. According to our model assumptions, we have the relations $\beta_g > \gamma_g, \gamma_b$ and $\beta_b > \gamma_b, \gamma_g$. Note that $4\beta_g\beta_b - (\gamma_g + \gamma_b)^2 = (2\beta_g\beta_b - 2\gamma_b\gamma_g) + (\beta_g\beta_b - \gamma_g^2) + (\beta_g\beta_b - \gamma_b^2)$, where each term in the brackets is positive.

Proposition 1. *In the Problem* (7), *the optimal prices of the green and brown products and the greening investment decisions of the manufacturer are given by:*

$$p_g(t) = \frac{1}{4\beta_b\beta_g - (\gamma_b + \gamma_g)^2} \Big(2\beta_b \left(-\phi\beta_g \left(2A_2\lambda + A_3 S + A_5\right) + \alpha_g + \eta S\right) $$

$$+ (\gamma_b + \gamma_g)(\phi\gamma_g (2A_2\lambda + A_3 S + A_5) + \alpha_b + \delta(-S)) \Big), \tag{10}$$

$$p_b(t) = \frac{\beta_g \left(\phi \left(2A_2\lambda + A_3 S + A_5\right) \left(\gamma_g - \gamma_b\right) + 2\alpha_b - 2\delta S\right) + (\gamma_b + \gamma_g)(\alpha_g + \eta S)}{4\beta_b\beta_g - (\gamma_b + \gamma_g)^2}, \tag{11}$$

$$I(t) = \frac{k_1 \left(A_3\lambda + 2A_1 S + A_4\right)}{\mu}. \tag{12}$$

The value function of the manufacturer is given by

$$V(S, \lambda) = A_1 S^2 + A_2 \lambda^2 + A_3 \lambda S + A_4 S + A_5 \lambda + A_6 \tag{13}$$

where $A_i s$, $i \in \{1, 2, 3, 4, 5, 6\}$ are constant coefficients of the state variable associated terms of the value function $V(S, \lambda)$ given in Eq. (9).

Proof. The right hand side of the HJB equations (8) is given by

$$HJB_{RHS} = D_b p_b + D_g p_g + \frac{\partial V}{\partial \lambda} \left(\phi D_g - \lambda\omega\right) + \lambda\sigma + \frac{\partial V}{\partial S} \left(\lambda k_2 + k_1 Z - S\epsilon\right) - \frac{\mu Z^2}{2}.$$

Next, as standard, we take the first order conditions:

$$\frac{\partial (HJB_{RHS})}{\partial p_g} = -\phi\beta_g \left(2A_2\lambda + A_3 S + A_5\right) + p_b\gamma_g + \gamma_b p_b + \alpha_g - 2\beta_g p_g + \eta S = 0 \tag{14}$$

$$\frac{\partial (HJB_{RHS})}{\partial p_b} = \phi\gamma_g \left(2A_2\lambda + A_3 S + A_5\right) + \alpha_b + \gamma_b p_g - 2\beta_b p_b + \gamma_g p_g + \delta(-S) = 0 \tag{15}$$

$$\frac{\partial (HJB_{RHS})}{\partial I} = k_1 \left(A_3\lambda + 2A_1 S + A_4\right) - \mu I = 0. \tag{16}$$

The system of equations given by (14) and (15), leads to the solutions in Eqs. (10) and (11) for p_g and p_b. Solving Eqs. (16) for I, gives the expression in Eq. (13).

Thereafter, these expressions of p_g, p_b and I are placed in the right-hand-side of the HJB equation. Finally, we compare the coefficients of the state variables or its associations from the two sides of the equation:

$$r \times (A_1 S^2 + A_2 \lambda^2 + A_3 \lambda S + A_4 S + A_5 \lambda + A_6)$$
$$= D_b p_b + D_g p_g + \frac{\partial V}{\partial \lambda} (\phi D_g - \lambda \omega) + \lambda \sigma + \frac{\partial V}{\partial S} (\lambda k_2 + k_1 Z - S\epsilon) - \frac{\mu Z^2}{2} \quad (17)$$

to obtain a set of six non-linear equations which are solved to get the coefficients A_i. We used Mathematica software (version 12) to solve the equations as these are not solvable manually[1].

Remark: For our model, the complexity of the parametric space is such that we are able to solve the value function only numerically. We have assumed suitable numerical values (given in the GitHub code) of the parameters which are well articulated to our model assumptions and the reality. Therefore, we confidently assert that our numerical results are quite robust. Moreover, the coefficients of the state variables (A_is) in our value function have multiple solutions and therefore, the value function is not unique. Hence, we have chosen the most suitable solution in which all A_is are positive. All other solutions result in a negative investment or pricing decision which is infeasible.

The above are the feedback pricing and green investment decisions of the manufacturer. One can note that the optimal prices and investment decisions are linear in the state variables, greening level S and learning λ. Therefore, an important question is: how do the optimal decisions vary with the state variables and other model parameters? Another, is on the comparison between the green and brown demands under the optimal policies. Nevertheless, before answering to these questions in the next sections, it remains to ensure that the optimal investment decision satisfies the budget constraint (4).

The parameters ξ_s and ξ in the budget constraint are known ex-ante by the manufacturer. In addition, the optimal decisions are also known to the manufacturer. Therefore, for a green product to exist in the market, the values of ξ_s and ξ must be suitable to design an admissible investment strategy. The following lemma shows the conditions feasible for producing green products.

Lemma 2. *The manufacturer will produce green products only if the following relationship between greening level and learning holds*

$$S(t) \geq \frac{\left(\xi_s + \frac{A_3}{\mu}\right)\lambda(t) + \frac{A_4 k_1}{\mu}}{\left(\xi - \frac{2A_1 k_1}{\mu}\right)}. \quad (18)$$

---

[1] The code used in this paper for solving the HJB equations and for the sensitivity analysis of Sect. 5 is publicly available on GitHub: https://github.com/arkamukherjee80/RagingSun.

Proof. We know that the green investment constraint is given by $0 \leq I(t) \leq M_g(t) = \xi_s S(t) - \xi \lambda(t)$. From Proposition 1 we note that $I(t) = \frac{k_1(A_3\lambda + 2A_1 S + A_4)}{\mu}$. Therefore, for the budget constraint to be satisfied, we must have $\frac{k_1(A_3\lambda + 2A_1 S + A_4)}{\mu} \leq M_g(t)$. Rearranging the terms, we get the inequality (18).

In inequality (18), ξ_s represents the manufacturer's (or management's) enthusiasm to invest in green quality and ξ represents the management's anticipation of how demand learning will decrease the budget for green investment. The above relation, therefore, signifies that given any values of ξ_s and ξ an admissible investment policy $I(t)$ might not exist at any given point of time.

4.1 Qualitative Analysis of Optimal Policies

In this section, we investigate how the decisions of the manufacturers vary with the state variables, greening level and learning, and the different model parameters. While we provide a comprehensive analysis of the optimal decisions, it is often more tractable to consider symmetry of the system parameters (e.g., $\beta_g = \beta_b = \beta$ and $\gamma_g = \gamma_b = \gamma$) without compromising the quality of the insights obtained. We carry out such simplifications in some cases.

Lemma 3. *The price of the green product is:*

(i) *increasing with the greening level $S(t)$ if and only if $\beta_g < \frac{1}{A_3}\left(\gamma_g + \frac{\eta - \delta A_3}{\phi}\right)$, and decreasing otherwise,*

(ii) *always decreasing in the learning $\lambda(t)$,*

(iii) *always increasing with η and decreasing with δ*

where A_3 is the coefficient of the term λS of the value function given in Eq. (9).

Proof. The lemma follows from the first order condition of the pricing decision p_g as given in Proposition 1.

$$\frac{\partial p_g}{\partial S} = \frac{2\beta_b(\eta - A_3\phi\beta_g) + (\gamma_b + \gamma_g)(A_3\phi\gamma_g - \delta)}{4\beta_b\beta_g - (\gamma_b + \gamma_g)^2} > 0, \quad \frac{\partial p_g}{\partial \lambda} = \frac{2A_2\phi\gamma_g(\gamma_b + \gamma_g) - 4A_2\phi\beta_b\beta_g}{4\beta_b\beta_g - (\gamma_b + \gamma_g)^2} < 0$$

$$\frac{\partial p_g}{\partial \eta} = \frac{2S\beta_b}{4\beta_b\beta_g - (\gamma_b + \gamma_g)^2} > 0, \quad \frac{\partial p_g}{\partial \delta} = -\frac{S(\gamma_b + \gamma_g)}{4\beta_b\beta_g - (\gamma_b + \gamma_g)^2} < 0.$$

Algebraic manipulations of the above inequalities together with the assumption $\beta_i > \gamma_i$ for $i \in \{g, b\}$ yield the inequalities above.

From the Lemma 3, we conclude that the price of the green product is not necessarily always increasing in the greening level. This is apparently a counterintuitive finding. The condition for a higher price premium for a higher greening level is a complex interrelationship among the price sensitivities, efficiency of demand learning ϕ, A_3 (the coefficient of λS in the profit (9)), η and δ. Learning helps in reducing the greening costs. The direct effect of this is a price reduction with a higher learning. Lastly, while the "green appeal", η, increases the green product price, the attraction of brown consumers, δ can reduce the same.

Lemma 4. *The price of the brown product is:*

(i) decreasing with the greening level $S(t)$ if and only if $\beta_g > \dfrac{\eta(\gamma_g + \gamma_b)}{2\delta - \phi A_3(\gamma_g - \gamma_b)}$

(ii) increasing in the learning $\lambda(t)$ if and only if $\gamma_g > \gamma_b$

(iii) increasing with η and decreasing with δ.

Proof. The proof of this lemma is similar to the proof of Lemma 3.

The price of a brown product decreases if the price sensitivity of the green productivity is greater than a certain threshold which depends on γ_g and γ_b. We can interpret γ_g as the increase in demand for the green product per unit increase in the brown product price and γ_b as the increase in demand for the brown product per unit increase in price of the green product. Surprisingly the equilibrium price of a brown product increases with the green preference level (η) of green consumers and decreases with a brown consumers' attraction (δ) towards green products.

The manufacturer's pricing strategies for brown and green products seems similar with respect to η and δ. In our model, though we consider a single manufacturer, there is a competitive environment between the green and brown products. Therefore, with an increase in greening level and subsequent green product price enhancement, the price of brown product rises because the manufacturer wants to reduce product differentiation by bridging the gap between the brown and green prices. Secondly, when brown consumers' attraction (δ) towards the green product is high, the approach for the manufacturer is more of retaining consumer loyalty by lowering brown product's price.

4.2   Comparative Analysis of Equilibrium Price and Demand

Typically, the green products are priced higher than the brown products [7,19]. However, under our model assumption of learning and budget constraints, we address the following questions:

(i) Is it possible to have a higher green demand?

(ii) Is there any situation in which a manufacturer may charge lower prices for the green product?

To answer the above questions we assume symmetry of the model parameters (i.e., $\beta_g = \beta_b = \beta; \gamma_g = \gamma_b = \gamma$). Examining and simplifying the condition $D_g > D_b$, we obtain:

$$\phi(\beta + \gamma)(2A_2\lambda + A_3S + A_5) - \alpha_b + \alpha_g + S(\delta + \eta) > 0$$
$$\implies \alpha_g > \alpha_b - \phi(\beta + \gamma)(2A_2\lambda + A_3S + A_5) - S(\delta + \eta). \tag{19}$$

All the terms in the RHS of Eq. (19) are positive. Therefore, if the market potential for the green product is high enough, the demand for green product can be higher than that of the brown product at any point of time. However, in most industries brown consumption far surpasses the green consumption. We may conclude here that if the green market potential is higher, the green demand is higher.

Similarly for $p_b > p_g$, we have:

$$\phi(\beta + \gamma)\,(2A_2\lambda + A_3 S + A_5) + \alpha_b - \alpha_g - S(\delta + \eta) > 0$$
$$\alpha_g < \alpha_b + \phi(\beta + \gamma)\,(2A_2\lambda + A_3 S + A_5) + \alpha_b - \alpha_g + S(\delta + \eta). \qquad (20)$$

From Eqs. (19) and (20), we note that the marketing potential α_g and α_b have an important role to play in determining green product price and demand. The finding implies that the manufacturer should strategically focus on increasing the marketing potential which in turn will enhance the green demand (*e.g.* by advertising, eco labelling, promotions, etc.).

Lemma 5. *The manufacturer's greening investments are increasing in the greening level and learning.*

Proof. Recall that $I(t) = \dfrac{k_1\,(A_3\lambda + 2A_1 S + A_4)}{\mu}$. Therefore, $\frac{\partial I}{\partial S} = \frac{k_1 2 A_1}{\mu} > 0$ and $\frac{\partial I}{\partial \lambda} = \frac{k_1 A_3}{\mu} > 0$. The positivity follows from $A_i > 0$. Numerically, it was found that a feasible solution for the HJB equation requires $A_i > 0$.

While high green investment will enhance green quality, one may comprehend that green investments should decrease with learning. However, learning λ indirectly affects the investments in two opposite ways: (i) by decreasing greening costs through the expression $\frac{\mu}{2}I^2 - \sigma\lambda$ in Eq. (7) and (ii) by enhancing greening level and, consequently, raising greening through the term $k_2\lambda(t)$ in the state evolution Eq. (3). At optimality, the "incremental force" of learning influences the investments more significantly.

Using the method of equating the coefficients of two equivalent polynomials, we found that each coefficient has four solutions. We want to reiterate that the only feasible solution is the one where all the coefficients are positive. Clearly, the state variables, learning and greening level, as well as their multiplicative association have a positive effect on the value function.

5   Sensitivity Analysis

Our model has many parameters each of which influences the behaviour of the decisions and the state variables. We identify ϕ, σ, β_g, β_b, γ_g, γ_b, k_1 and k_2, as the most important parameters of the model which enables us to answer our salient research questions.

In the numerical analysis, the parameter values were fixed or their variation was restricted as follows: $\alpha_g = \alpha_b = 10, k_1 = k_2 = 1, \mu = 10, r = 0.05, \epsilon = 0.1, \omega = 0.1, \phi \in \{0.001, 0.005\}, \delta \in \{0.03, 0.04\}, \sigma \in (0, 3), \beta = \beta_g = \beta_b \in \{1.8, 2.2, 2.6\}, \lambda = \lambda_g = \lambda_b \in \{1.8, 2.2, 2.6\}$.

Efficiency of Demand Learning. The demand learning efficiency ϕ can be interpreted as the manufacturer's ability to capitalize economies of scale. A manufacturer may be a highly efficient learner due to, e.g., technology innovation or the skills of its employees. On the other hand, a manufacturer can be a slow learner when it lacks such technology or skills. Succinctly, a higher ϕ represents a quick learner.

It is straightforward that learning and greening level will increase with ϕ. As per our model, learning has a positive impact on greening level. Therefore, the greening level also increases with the learning efficiency as shown in Fig. (1). Less direct, it is the impact of ϕ in the optimal decisions. Recall that the optimal greening investment is $\frac{k_1(A_3\lambda+2A_1S+A_4)}{\mu}$. Therefore, the investment increases with λ and S given that A_3 and A_1 are positive. Since learning λ and greening level S increase with ϕ, then, by a transitive relationship, the investment also increases with ϕ; see Fig. 3 for an illustration. A counter intuitive result is that the investment and the price of green product is increasing with the efficiency ϕ. One may apprehend that an efficient learning may decrease price while keeping the greening level high. This, in turn, increases the greening level, the learning and the corresponding green product price. A high greening level ensures more green demand. In this particular case, the attractiveness of a high greening level outplays the negative effect of the higher price on demand. On the other hand, the price of the brown counterpart decreases, although the effect of ϕ is much less marked for this decision variable. As the learning level increases, the firm makes more profit by enhancing the price difference rather than by bridging the gap. These intricate relations are illustrated in Figs. 2 and 4.

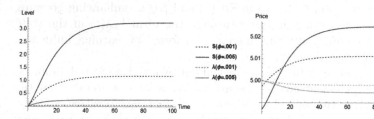

Fig. 1. Variation of green level and learning with ϕ

Fig. 2. Price variation with ϕ

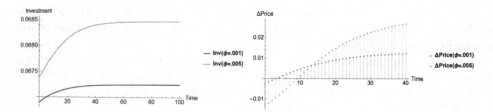

Fig. 3. Variation of investment with ϕ

Fig. 4. Price difference with ϕ

Green Level Appeal for Brown Consumers. The parameter δ in our model is the brown consumer's attraction towards green products. In Fig. 5, we observe that the greening level and learning both drop as this attraction increases[2]. If the brown consumers are considerably attracted by the green quality, the manufacturer looses motivation to increase the greening level. The greening investment therefore also decreases as δ becomes higher (Fig. 7). A higher value of δ also means more brown consumers are opting against brown products and increasing the demand for green products. This results in a price drop for the green product. The price of the brown product also decreases as a reaction to drop in green product price (Fig. 6). A higher efficiency of demand learning results in a higher price difference between green and brown products with $p_g(t) > p_b(t)$ for most of the life cycle of the product (Fig. 8).

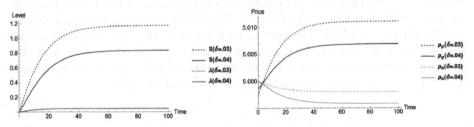

Fig. 5. Variation of green level and learning with δ

Fig. 6. Price variation with δ

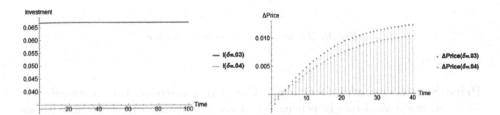

Fig. 7. Variation of investment with δ

Fig. 8. Price difference with δ

The Cost Efficiency of Learning. The parameter σ, the cost efficiency of learning, represents how responsive a company's cost savings are to the learning level λ. In Fig. 9, we observe that the greening level slowly increases with σ. This is not surprising, because at a given point of time, a manufacturer would achieve higher greening level if costs are lesser (the other parameters are fixed).

---

[2] Due to the scale difference of greening level and learning it is not obvious from the figure that the learning curve for $\delta = .04$ is below the learning curve for $\delta = .03$. However, this is true.

A high cost efficiency can lead to a lower cost of green product than the brown product and the investments in greening level increase with the cost efficiency (Fig. 11). Obviously, a higher σ implies a lower cost of greening. When the cost efficiency increases, the greening investments increase. We posit that a higher cost efficiency (higher σ) has an overall positive impact on the manufacturer's profit. Therefore, the manufacturer can afford and is motivated to make higher greening investments when σ is high. The importance of the parameter is strategic. A manufacturer may strategically save more costs given a certain learning level. Judicious resource allocation, optimization of operational techniques and so on are examples of such strategies.[3]

While in modern business in most industries we usually see that the prices of green products are higher, we show theoretically it is possible to reduce green product price below the brown price when cost efficiency of learning is high enough (Fig. 10). Therefore, price difference between green and brown products decreases with cost efficiency (Fig. 12). The significance of this result is that manufacturers can adopt strategies to increase cost efficiency of learning. This will help them in reducing the price of green products and, in the long term, the green and brown products can have similar prices resulting in increasing demand for green products and, consequently, environmental benefits.

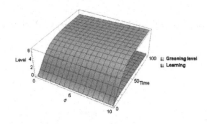

Fig. 9. Green level and learning with σ

Price Sensitivity and Decisions. The price sensitivity, here assumed $\beta = \beta_g = \beta_b$, has a vital role in pricing decisions. From Figs. 13, 14, 15 and 16, we observe that higher price sensitivities of green and brown products *(i)* reduce greening level and learning, *(ii)* reduce price of both green and brown products, *(iii)* reduce the price difference between green and brown products and *(iv)* reduce the optimal greening investments. From the Figs. 2, 6, 10 and 14, we can see a trend for all optimal decisions. For the manufacturers offering both green and brown products from the start of the planning horizon, it is the equilibrium policy to start with a lower price for the green product and then increase the

---

[3] In regards to the observations, Mathematica software was not able to solve the value function without exact parametric values like $\phi = .001$ and $\delta = .03$ However, for σ, we were able to obtain parametric solutions of the value function coefficients in terms of σ. Consequently, we are able to depict the variation of $S(t), \lambda(t), p_g(t), p_b(t), I(t)$ for the entire range ($[0, 10]$ in this case) of values of σ.

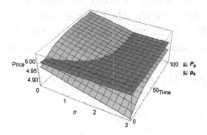

Fig. 10. Price variation with σ

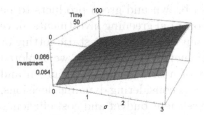

Fig. 11. Investments vs σ

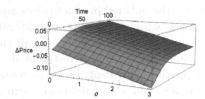

Fig. 12. Price difference with σ

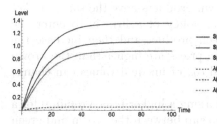

Fig. 13. Variation of green level and learning with β

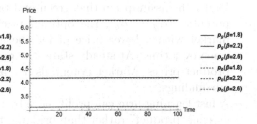

Fig. 14. Price variation with β

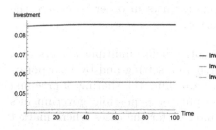

Fig. 15. Green investments with β

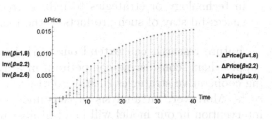

Fig. 16. Price difference with β

green product price, while simultaneously decreasing the brown product price. In general, the green investments should also increase with time. Finally, in what concerns the profits, from equation (13), we see that all the state variables positively influence the profit function since the coefficients of the states are positive. We also see from the above Figs. 1, 5, 9 and 13 that the state variables are increasing with time. Therefore, the profit function will also increase with time.

6   Conclusion

The urge to benefit the environment by enhancing green demand while operating under a strict budget often places a manufacturer in a strategic dilemma. A number of decisions encompassing quantity of brown and green products to be produced, the optimal product prices and the optimal greening investments, have been widely explored in the extant literature, but mostly under a static setting or not accounting simultaneously for all those elements. In our study, we explored the optimal pricing and investment decisions of a firm, selling both green and brown products. We contributed incrementally by considering dynamic decisions. We have also considered demand learning, investment budget and cost efficiency parameters to be some of the determinants of the optimal decisions. These give us several insights, both surprising and confirming empirical evidence.

Shortly, the most fundamental findings of our study are the following:

- Under the assumption that green and brown products have the same market potential ($\alpha_g = \alpha_b$), the optimal pricing policy of a firm is to enter the market with a lower price of for the green product and then increase the same over time. At steady state, the green prices are higher than the brown product prices. Market potentials, α_g and α_b, of unequal values can change our findings.
- A fast learning firm can profit more by charging a higher price premium for a greener "product" rather than bridging the gap between the brown and green product price.
- If the cost efficiency of learning σ is very high, theoretically, the firm can afford to have a lower green product price than the brown product's price. From a managerial perspective, this highlights the importance of firms investing in technology or strategies to reduce greening costs in order to ensure the successful stay of such products in the market.

Future research can extend our work by introducing multiple players of a supply chain, considering competition in a dynamic setting and by incorporating cooperative strategies such as contracts establishing the sharing of greening costs. Moreover, an analysis of consumer surplus or a possible government's intervention in our model will be of utmost interest for the cases where market potential α_g is not sufficiently high.

References

1. Benveniste, A.: Average Americans Can't Afford to Buy Green (2019). https://www.bloomberg.com/news/articles/2019-03-07/it-s-not-cheap-being-a-green-consumer
2. Berger, J.: Signaling can increase consumers' willingness to pay for green products. Theoretical model and experimental evidence. J. Consum. Behav. **18**(3), 233–246 (2019)
3. Brécard, D.: Consumer misperception of eco-labels, green market structure and welfare. J. Regul. Econ. **51**(3), 340–364 (2017). https://doi.org/10.1007/s11149-017-9328-8
4. Chen, C.: Design for the environment: a quality-based model for green product development. Manag. Sci. **47**(2), 250–263 (2001)
5. Chen, Y.J., Sheu, J.B.: Environmental-regulation pricing strategies for green supply chain management. Transp. Res. Part E: Logist. Transp. Rev. **45**(5), 667–677 (2009)
6. Cohen, M.A., Cui, S., Gao, F.: The effect of government support on green product design and environmental impact. Available at SSRN 3291017 (2019)
7. Ding, J., Wang, W.: Information sharing in a green supply chain with promotional effort. Kybernetes **ahead-of-print** (2020)
8. Ghazilla, R.A.R., Sakundarini, N., Abdul-Rashid, S.H., Ayub, N.S., Olugu, E.U., Musa, S.N.: Drivers and barriers analysis for green manufacturing practices in Malaysian SMEs: a preliminary findings. Proc. CIRP **26**(1), 658–663 (2015)
9. Ghosh, D., Shah, J.: Supply chain analysis under green sensitive consumer demand and cost sharing contract. Int. J. Prod. Econ. **164**, 319–329 (2015)
10. Ghosh, D., Shah, J., Swami, S.: Product greening and pricing strategies of firms under green sensitive consumer demand and environmental regulations. Ann. Oper. Res. **290**, 491–520 (2018). https://doi.org/10.1007/s10479-018-2903-2
11. Gonzalez, E.D., et al.: Making real progress toward more sustainable societies using decision support models and tools: introduction to the special volume. J. Cleaner Prod. **105**, 1–13 (2015)
12. Li, B., Zhu, M., Jiang, Y., Li, Z.: Pricing policies of a competitive dual-channel green supply chain. J. Clean. Prod. **112**, 2029–2042 (2016)
13. Li, X., Li, Y.: Chain-to-chain competition on product sustainability. J. Clean. Prod. **112**, 2058–2065 (2016)
14. Montoya-Torres, J.R., Gutierrez-Franco, E., Blanco, E.E.: Conceptual framework for measuring carbon footprint in supply chains. Prod. Plan. Control **26**(4), 265–279 (2015)
15. Neto, J.Q.F., Bloemhof-Ruwaard, J.M., van Nunen, J.A., van Heck, E.: Designing and evaluating sustainable logistics networks. Int. J. Prod. Econ. **111**(2), 195–208 (2008)
16. Peng, H.: Optimal subsidy policy for accelerating the diffusion of green products. J. Ind. Eng. Manag. (JIEM) **6**(2), 626–641 (2013)
17. Solarcity: Solar City Inside Energy. Consumer trends in sustainability: insights to grow your market share and defend your brand (2013). https://www.solarcity.com/sites/default/files/reports/reports-consumer-trends-in-sustainability.pdf
18. Walley, N., Whitehead, B.: It's not easy being green. Harvard Bus. Rev. **72**(3), 46–52 (1994)
19. Yenipazarli, A., Vakharia, A.: Pricing, market coverage and capacity: can green and brown products co-exist? Eur. J. Oper. Res. **242**(1), 304–315 (2015)

20. Yenipazarli, A., Vakharia, A.J.: Green, greener or brown: choosing the right color of the product. Ann. Oper. Res. **250**(2), 537–567 (2015). https://doi.org/10.1007/s10479-014-1781-5
21. Zhang, Q., Zhao, Q., Zhao, X.: Manufacturer's product choice in the presence of environment-conscious consumers: brown product or green product. Int. J. Prod. Res. **57**(23), 7423–7438 (2019)
22. Zhang, Q., Zhao, Q., Zhao, X., Tang, L.: On the introduction of green product to a market with environmentally conscious consumers. Comput. Ind. Eng. **139**, 106190 (2020)
23. Zhou, Y.: The role of green customers under competition: a mixed blessing? J. Clean. Prod. **170**, 857–866 (2018)
24. Zu, Y., Chen, L., Fan, Y.: Research on low-carbon strategies in supply chain with environmental regulations based on differential game. J. Clean. Prod. **177**, 527–546 (2018)

Increasing the Practical Applicability of Order Picking Operations by Integrating Classification, Labelling and Packaging Regulations

Sarah Vanheusden(✉)[iD], Teun van Gils[iD], Katrien Ramaekers[iD],
and An Caris[iD]

Hasselt University, Hasselt, Belgium
{sarah.vanheusden,teun.vangils,katrien.ramaekers,an.caris}@uhasselt.be,
https://www.uhasselt.be/Research-group-Logistics

Abstract. Warehouses play a vital role in every supply chain. The focus of warehouses is often on organising efficient and flexible order picking systems. However, warehouse managers indicate that planning order picking operations becomes extra complicated as they have to comply to many legislations. Warehouses in Europe are subject to the classification, labelling and packaging (CLP) regulation. Accounting for this regulation is vital in order to limit the risk of chemical reactions in the warehouse, therefore this regulation mainly affects storage decisions. The first objective of this study is to integrate the CLP regulation in storage assignment. An integer linear programming model is developed to formulate the CLP restricted problem. The second objective is to design an efficient order picking system by simulating different storage, batching and routing policies for a real-life warehouse subject to the CLP regulation.

Keywords: Order picking · Storage assignment · Simulation · Practical factors

1 Introduction

Managing order picking operations is a complex task. Trends such as e-commerce, globalisation, and increased customer expectations pose new challenges on warehouse management and increase the need for efficient order picking systems [10,17]. Scientific research focusses on the design and control of individual warehouse operations and more recently on the interaction or integration of multiple order picking planning problems and policies [15]. Despite the valuable contribution of these research papers, the application of the proposed solution algorithms is sometimes limited in practice due to insufficient attention for practical factors that characterise real-life order picking systems.

This study aims to increase the practical applicability of research in manual order picking by accounting for perspectives of practitioners. Manual systems are

© Springer Nature Switzerland AG 2020
E. Lalla-Ruiz et al. (Eds.): ICCL 2020, LNCS 12433, pp. 733–746, 2020.
https://doi.org/10.1007/978-3-030-59747-4_47

still the most popular in practice due to the flexibility of human pickers and high investment costs of automated systems [18]. Warehouse managers emphasize the increased difficulties in managing warehouse operations due to a changing classification, labelling and packaging (CLP) regulation. The CLP regulation is a European Union regulation from 2008, which aligns the European Union system of classification, labelling and packaging of chemical substances and mixtures to the Globally Harmonised System (GHS). The aim of the CLP regulation is to limit the risks on chemical reactions in a warehouse and therefore results in strong restrictions to store products in the warehouse. Not all type of products (i.e., regarding chemical composition) are allowed to be stored next to each other. For example, if products are damaged during handling and are stored next to a product that chemically interacts with the damaged product, severe damage and injury may be caused not only to the warehouse and its employees, but also to the surrounding environment. Varying product properties such as the size and weight of products further complicate the planning of order picking operations. By ignoring varying product properties, solution algorithms create unrealistic and often infeasible solutions in practice [3,5]. Product properties may restrict the allocation of products to storage locations and influence order picker routing as, for example, heavy products need to be retrieved before light products to prevent products from getting damaged (i.e., precedence constraints) [19].

The main contributions can be summarised as follows. First, a mathematical model is introduced to formulate the problem of a CLP restricted storage assignment, as existing storage assignment policies in literature do not meet the strict requirements of the CLP regulation. Second, this study contributes to the design of efficient order picking systems by introducing practically relevant decision support for planning order picking operations. The CLP restricted storage assignment policies are simulated in combination with batching and routing policies, accounting for the varying weight of products, to reduce order picking travel time in a real-life warehouse.

The remainder of the paper is organised as follows. Section 2 describes relevant literature. In Sect. 3, the case study, problem context and respective problem formulation are elaborated. Subsequently, the experimental design is presented in Sect. 4, followed by the results of the simulation study and managerial implications in Sect. 5. Section 6 is devoted to the concluding remarks and future research directions.

2   Literature Review

Customers order products and often demand next day delivery. Orders are composed of one or more order lines, each order line representing a single stock keeping unit (SKU) [16]. In order to ensure a fast and correct delivery of the ordered products, warehouse managers have to make several operational policy decisions: storage assignment, order batching and routing [15].

Storage assignment composes of a set of rules to allocate products to storage locations [16]. A random storage assignment (i.e., randomly assigning products to locations) may result in high storage utilisation, but that is at the expense of the distance travelled by order pickers. On the other hand, a dedicated storage policy assigns each product to a fixed location. Order pickers get familiar with the product locations, but space must be reserved for every product, resulting in low space utilisation. Dedicated storage may work well if products have different weights. For example, products are stored from heavy to lighter products and pickers are routed accordingly, preventing products getting damaged after being stacked on the pick vehicle [4]. However, to obtain a more efficient order picking process, fast moving items are often allocated to locations closely located to the depot. Therefore, class based storage, where products are assigned to classes based on a measure of demand frequency, is often used in literature [15, 16]. Product classes are assigned to a dedicated area of the warehouse. Products are assigned randomly to storage locations within each product class [4]. Various possibilities exist on how to assign product classes to areas in the warehouse. The most common policies are: within-aisle storage (i.e., each aisle contains a single product class), across-aisle storage (i.e., each product class is assigned to all pick aisles), diagonal storage (i.e., product classes are assigned in function of their distance to the depot) and perimeter storage (i.e., product classes are stored around the perimeter of the warehouse) [15]. Despite the relevance of above mentioned storage policies, these policies do not lend themselves for usage in a CLP restricted environment.

Order batching composes a set of rules on how to combine multiple orders in a single pick tour in order to minimise travel distance [9]. Batching is possible as long as capacity constraints (e.g., capacity of the pick truck) are respected [2]. First-in-first-out (FIFO) batching is very straightforward but does not take into account the storage location of the products that are batched [15]. Other batching policies try to assign orders to batches based on the proximity of their storage locations. The main question to be raised is how this proximity should be measured [4]. Two types of batching heuristics are often used in literature: seed and savings algorithms. Seed algorithms construct batches in two phases: seed selection and order congruency [9]. Savings based algorithms combine orders into batches to maximise travel time savings [16]. More sophisticated batching algorithms exist, but heavily impact computation times in simulation studies [15]. The reader is referred to [7–9] for more extensive overviews on algorithms for order batching. These batching methods do not explicitly account for the CLP restrictions and product properties, which might result in suboptimal order batching.

After products are allocated to storage locations and batches are formed, the shortest route to collect all items on the pick list needs to be determined. In literature, both optimal and heuristic routing policies exist. Research on routing disagrees whether heuristic or optimal routing policies should be used in practice [11]. Solving the routing problem to optimality for all warehouse layouts is not possible. Computation times heavily increase with a growing number of aisles and the size of pick lists [16]. Optimal routes are often approximated by the use of the Lin Kernighan Helsgaun (LKH) heuristic. On average, routes established by the LKH heuristic in a warehousing context, deviate only 0.1% from optimality [14]. As an alternative to the optimal routing policy, several other, intuitive and simple routing heuristics exist including S-shape, aisle-by-aisle, return, midpoint and largest gap. Precedence constraints (e.g., picking heavy items before light items) can severely restrict possible pick sequences. Precedence constraints in order picking routing received little attention although the integration of such constraints increases the practical applicability of routing policies. Precedence constraints make sure that some items can be picked before others due to variations in weight, fragility, shape, size, stackability, preferred unloading sequence or other specific customer requests that may limit the possible picking sequence [1,5,12,19]. The reader is referred to [11] for an extensive overview of routing policies in warehousing.

Previous research has focussed on several storage, batching and routing policies. However, existing storage and batching policies do not meet the strict CLP requirements and existing routing policies hardly account for weight restrictions. This paper differs from previous studies by integrating CLP restrictions when assigning products to locations, making sure no weight restrictions are violated during picking.

3 CLP Restricted Storage Problem

In order to analyse the impact of the CLP regulation in order picking planning, real-life data are used. Section 3.1 describes the problem context of the case study warehouse. Section 3.2 introduces and discusses the mathematical formulation of considering CLP restrictions in an optimal storage assignment. Section 3.3 discusses the results of an optimal storage assignment restricted by the CLP regulation.

3.1 Problem Description

The case study is based on a 3PL warehouse located in Belgium. The warehouse is responsible for the storage and distribution of dangerous chemical and cleaning products and is therefore obliged to meet the imposed CLP regulation of the European Union. The warehouse under consideration is shown in Fig. 1. The warehouse has a traditional multiple-block warehouse layout with nine parallel pick aisles and three cross-aisles perpendicular to the pick aisles. The pick aisles are two-sided and wide enough for two-way travel. Results of the study are easy transferable to other warehouses as this traditional layout is often used in practice [13].

The biggest challenge of the warehouse is to store products so that CLP distance barriers are satisfied. Each product is assigned to a single CLP product class. Within each CLP class, products have similar chemical compositions. Between storage locations of two CLP product classes, a pre-specified minimal distance should be met to prevent chemical reactions between those products. During picking, rules on minimal distance barriers do not apply, as products of different CLP classes are allowed to be transported together. Currently, the

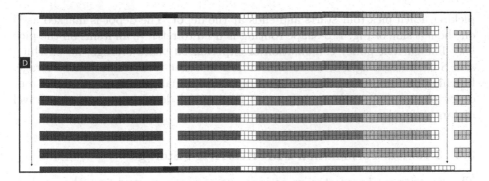

Fig. 1. Warehouse layout

storage assignment of the warehouse is based on the experience of warehouse managers and is shown in Fig. 1, with the different colours representing different CLP classes to which a product can belong. Definitions and distance barriers for these CLP classes are shown in Fig. 2. For example, between acid products of type 1 and other products, a minimal distance of 7 m needs to be met during storage, while normal products can be stored next to all other products. Not only the chemical composition of the products in the warehouse is important but also the measurements of these products. The warehouse stores products going from heavy barrels to small and light boxes which should be accounted for during picking. If product properties would be ignored during picking, products may get damaged.

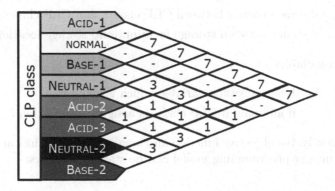

Fig. 2. CLP distance barriers

Order picking is performed manually using a pick vehicle. The capacity of the pick vehicle is restricted to two orders. Products for each order are collected on a single pallet. In the current situation a single order is collected each pick tour so that there is room to collect empty pallets on the pick vehicle during order picking. Each pick tour starts and ends at the depot. The depot is marked as D on the left side of Fig. 1. S-shape routing is used to retrieve all items on the pick list. The current policy combination of experienced based storage, no batching and S-shape routing is used as benchmark in order to evaluate other storage, batching and routing policies. Choosing the optimal combination of different order picking policies is an important managerial decision to minimise travel distance of order pickers.

3.2   Problem Formulation CLP Restricted Storage

The experienced based storage assignment of the case study warehouse does satisfy CLP distance barriers but does not guarantee an optimal assignment of products to storage locations. Furthermore, current storage policies in literature are not accounting for the CLP regulation. Therefore, an integer linear programming (ILP) model is developed to formulate the CLP restricted storage problem. To formulate the problem, following notations are used:

Sets

$$\lambda = \{1, 2, ..., L\} \text{ set of storage locations with index } l.$$
$$\gamma = \{1, 2, ..., C\} \text{ set of CLP classes with index } c.$$

Parameters

q_l cost of visiting storage location l.

p_c number of picks for CLP class c

s_c minimum number of storage locations for CLP class c

$d^*_{c_1 c_2}$ distance barrier between CLP class c_1 and CLP class c_2

$d_{l_1 l_2}$ distance between storage location l_1 and storage location l_2

Decision variables

X_{lc} binary decision variable which is equal to 1

if and only if CLP class c is assigned to location l

Subsequently, the objective function and associated constraints are discussed. The linear integer programming model can be stated as follows:

$$\min \sum_{l \in \lambda} \sum_{c \in \gamma} q_l p_c X_{lc} \tag{1}$$

Subject to

$$\sum_{l \in \lambda} X_{lc} \geq s_c \qquad\qquad \forall c \in \gamma \qquad\qquad (2)$$

$$\sum_{c \in \gamma} X_{lc} = 1 \qquad\qquad \forall l \in \lambda \qquad\qquad (3)$$

$$1 - X_{l_2 c_2} \geq X_{l_1 c_1} \qquad\qquad \forall c_1, c_2 \in \gamma : d^*_{c_1 c_2} > 0 \qquad (4)$$
$$\forall l_2 \in \lambda$$
$$\forall l_1 \in \lambda : d_{l_1 l_2} < d^*_{c_1 c_2}$$

The objective function of the ILP CLP storage assignment is defined by Eq. 1. The objective function minimises the mean monthly travel distance which is calculated based on the cost of a location and the mean pick frequency for a CLP class per location. The cost of visiting a location is calculated by the distance between the depot and the respective locations through their xy-coordinates. Constraints 2 reserve a minimal number of storage locations for each CLP class. Constraints 3 assign at least 1 CLP class to each storage location. Constraints 4 make sure that CLP distance barriers (e.g., Fig. 2) are respected. Constraints are only added between a CLP class and a location if the distance barrier could be violated in a solution. CLP barriers cannot be violated if $d^*_{c_1 c_2}$ is equal to zero or if the distance between two locations l_1 and l_2 exceeds the required minimal distance between CLP classes.

3.3   CLP Regulation in Storage Assignment

The ILP model is implemented in C++. To solve the ILP formulation, ILOG Cplex 12.7 is used with a runtime limit of 1 h. Cplex is not able to solve the storage assignment with CLP restrictions to optimality within the runtime limit, resulting in an optimality gap of 0.02%. The respective storage assignment is shown in Fig. 3. CLP classes have shifted significantly, except for base products of type 2 due to the high number of picks for this CLP class. The remaining CLP classes shifted from rectangular blocks to arches, with the top of the arch at the height of the depot.

From a practitioners point of view, the implementation of this near-optimal storage assignment may lead to some difficulties. Order pickers may get confused as CLP classes are no longer stored in rectangular blocks, requiring new and more extensive signalling as order pickers often need to replenish or return products manually to their respective storage locations. Therefore, the ILP model is solved once more with a run time limit of 1 h, but forcing the respective solution into rectangular blocks. Blocks are formed with the following operation: y-coordinate + (M × x-coordinate) with M being a very small number to prevent symmetry in solutions. The near-optimal storage assignment adapted to the needs of practitioners is shown in Fig. 4.

4   Simulation Experiments

In the simulation experiments of this study, multiple combinations of storage, batching and routing policies are simulated and evaluated in order to design a more efficient order picking system. By means of a factorial design, insights are provided about the impact of the different order picking decisions on the distance travelled by order pickers. Five storage location assignment policies, four order batching polices and two routing policies are analysed. The three factors and their associated factor levels are summarised in Table 1. The benchmark policy combination is indicated in italic.

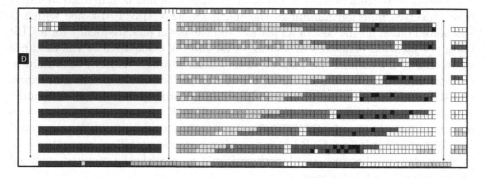

Fig. 3. Near-optimal storage assignment

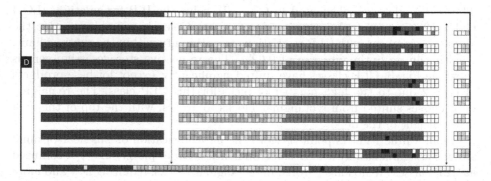

Fig. 4. Near-optimal storage assignment adapted to practitioners needs

Besides the assignment of products to storage locations based on the experience of the warehouse, four optimised CLP storage policies are tested by means of the ILP model (i.e., ILP CLP) outlined in Sect. 3.2. First, the CLP restricted storage policies assign CLP classes to locations, either in arches (i.e., ILP CLP) or in rectangular blocks (i.e., ILP CLP in blocks). Second, seven weight classes are assigned to each storage location. Finally, both ILP CLP policies are extended with an ABC classification (i.e., ILP CLP ABC and ILP CLP in blocks ABC). An ABC class is assigned to each location with fast moving classes assigned to the locations most closely located to the depot within each combination of CLP and weight class.

Despite the capacity of two orders on a pick truck, the warehouse collects a single order each pick tour. Logically, the warehouse could attain tremendous savings in travel time by batching orders. First, a simple but straightforward batching method is added to the experimental factor setting: FIFO batching. Furthermore, two seed algorithms are added to the experimental design. The first seed algorithm selects an order with the smallest number of CLP and weight class combinations as seed order. Next, the order that minimises the additional CLP and weight class combinations to visit in the route is added to the pick list. The second seed algorithm selects an order with the largest number of CLP and weight class combinations as seed order and adds an order to the pick list that minimises the additional CLP and weight class combinations to visit in a route.

Currently the warehouse uses S-shape routing to sort items on the pick list. The travel distance is also computed with the LKH heuristic. The LKH heuristic provides excellent results in the context of routing order pickers [14]. However, adaptations are made to the LKH heuristic as the current problem is asymmetric due to weight restrictions: a picker can be routed from the location of product A (e.g., heavy barrel) to the location of product B (e.g., light box), but routing the picker the other way around is impossible as product B would get damaged. Solving the routing problem to optimality for multiple-block warehouses would take too long for operational purposes and the LKH heuristic makes sure that routes can be evaluated quickly in the simulation experiments.

In summary, the simulation experiment consists of 40 policy combinations (five storage policies × four batching policies × two routing policies). To reduce the stochastic effect from order generation, 30 replications per policy combination are performed, resulting in 1200 observations. For each replication, combinations of storage assignment, batching and routing policies are tested for the same 1300 randomly generated orders in order to stress the effects of policy decisions. The 1300 generated orders represent the workload for a single working day with an average of 2,81 order lines per order (i.e., order size). Order generation is based on historical data of the real-life warehouse. An empirical distribution is fitted to the data of the warehouse to determine the number of order lines in each order, the CLP class of an order line, the weight class of an order line and the ABC class of an order line.

Table 1. Experimental design.

Factor	Factor levels
Storage	(5) *Experience based*; ILP CLP; ILP CLP ABC; ILP CLP in blocks; ILP CLP in blocks ABC
Batching	(4) *No batching*; FIFO; Seed 1; Seed 2
Routing	(2) *S-shape*; LKH heuristic

5   Results and Discussion

First, the results of the simulation experiments are discussed in Sect. 5.1. Section 5.2 discusses the practical implications of this research for warehouse managers.

5.1   Results Simulation Study

The results of the simulation experiments are graphically illustrated in Fig. 5. The graph shows the average travel time in hours (i.e., vertical axis) in function of different storage, batching and routing policies.

The benchmark policy combination (i.e., experience based storage, no batching and S-shape routing) is one of the worst performing policy combinations with an average travel time of 50.58 h over 30 replications. Changing the experience based storage policy to a more sophisticated policy has no effect or only a negligibly positive effect on average travel time, except for the ILP CLP with ABC, which slightly improves average travel time for all policy combinations. Changing the storage policy from experienced based to ILP CLP with ABC (i.e., keeping other policies from the benchmark fixed) results in an average travel time of 48,12 h and can be further reduced if batching is performed with a more sophisticated batching rule instead of no batching (i.e., average travel time of 46,26 h for seed 1 and 43.05 h for seed 2).

Batching orders, in this case study, means that two orders are picked during each pick tour (i.e., limited capacity on pick vehicle) instead of a single order. If orders are thoughtfully batched, large savings in travel time can be reached. Therefore, more sophisticated batching rules (e.g., seed 1 and seed 2) will perform better than FIFO batching, as FIFO batching may lead to the creation of inefficient batches. Figure 5 shows that the positive effect of batching orders is larger in case of LKH routing instead of S-shape routing. Routing order pickers by sorting items on the pick list using the LKH policy outperforms the S-shape routing for all combinations of storage assignment and batching policies.

It can be concluded that certain policy combinations yield excellent results (e.g., all storage policies in combination with one of the seed algorithms and LKH routing), while other combinations result in larger average travel times (e.g., all storage policies if no batching or FIFO batching is performed and S-shape routing is used). Moving from no batching or FIFO batching to a more sophisticated batching rule (i.e., seed 1 or seed 2) and moving to a more sophisticated routing policy positively impacts the efficiency of the warehouse, as opposed to the effect of more sophisticated storage policies. The very small effect of changing storage policies can be explained by the heavy restrictions the CLP regulation poses on allocating products to storage locations.

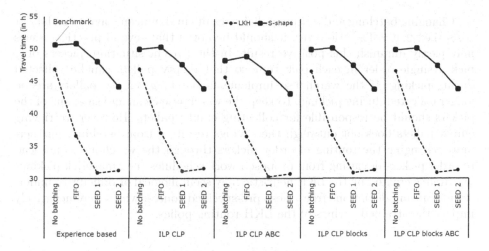

Fig. 5. Travel time in hours for each combination of storage, batching and routing policy

5.2 Managerial Implications

Results of the simulation study show the importance of and interaction among storage, batching and routing decisions when managing order picking operations. This section discusses the practical implications of this research.

Warehouse managers should be aware that complying with the CLP regulation in order picking strongly affects the allocation of products to storage locations. Further increasing order picking efficiency by changing the storage policy becomes difficult as solution possibilities are heavily restricted by CLP barriers. Compared to the benchmark policies with an average travel time of 50.58 h (i.e., experience based storage, no batching and S-shape routing), the warehouse could lower average travel time up to 30.24 h by adopting the best performing policy combination (i.e., ILP CLP ABC, seed 1 and LKH routing). However, as already stated in Sect. 3.3, changing to an optimal storage policy would require several adaptations in the warehouse (e.g., new and more extensive signalling). The small decrease in travel time caused by the new storage assignment may not make up for the effort that is needed to implement necessary changes in the warehouse. Therefore, managers can increase the performance of their warehouse by considering other batching and routing methods, keeping their experienced based storage policy in place.

Table 2 shows the savings in full time equivalent (FTE) (i.e., 1 FTE = 8 h = 1 shift) compared to the benchmark situation by changing the batching and routing policy. Warehouse managers can save 0.47 FTE by only changing the routing policy from S-shape to LKH routing and can even save up to 0.8 FTE by only changing the batching policy from no batching to seed algorithm 2. However, due to the strong relation between batching and routing, savings increase substantially if both batching and routing policies are changed. The warehouse can save up to 2.46 FTE each shift as shown in the last column of Table 2.

Changing batching and routing policies results in significant savings on labour costs (i.e., 2.46 FTE). However, it should be noted that several practical issues may partly diminish this positive result. In the current situation, pickers only pick a single order in each pick tour so that empty pallets can be collected during picking. If the warehouse implements batching, empty pallets are no longer collected during picking. To keep the warehouse clean and safe, one of the pickers should be responsible for collecting empty pallets. However, retrieving empty pallets does not outweigh the savings resulting from batching. Furthermore, changing the routing of order pickers through the warehouse, may lead to order pickers deviating from proposed work schedules (i.e., maverick picking) [6]. Routes created by the LKH heuristic may seem illogical or difficult to understand, causing deviations from these pre-specified routes, which may negatively impact the attained savings of the LKH routing policy.

Table 2. Changes in travel time and number of order pickers

	Experience No batching S-shape	Experience No batching LKH	Experience Seed 2 S-shape	Experience Seed 1 LKH
Travel time (in h)	50.58	46.82	44.12	30.86
Savings in FTE		0.47	0.8	2.46

6 Conclusions

Managing warehouse operations becomes increasingly difficult due to the extensive CLP regulation. Accounting for the CLP regulation in storage assignment is highly important as this regulation limits the risk on chemical reactions in the warehouse and makes sure that products can be handled safely without harming people or the environment. The new ILP CLP storage assignment policy shows very small savings in travel time as solution possibilities are heavily restricted by the CLP regulation. However, by simultaneously considering storage, batching and routing policies, efficiency of the warehouse can be increased. The simulations provide insights into excellent performing combinations (e.g., multiple storage assignment policies with seed batching and LKH routing), but also show that the current warehouse situation lacks efficiency. This paper is limited to three main order picking decisions (i.e., storage assignment, batching and routing) and deals with a limited number of policy options. In future research, the current simulation experiments could be extended with extra order picking policies, providing more insights into excellent performing policy combinations (e.g., extra routing policies), helping warehouse managers attain even better results. Furthermore, simulating other warehouse layouts, studying the effect different order sizes and batch capacities may allow us to further generalise results.

References

1. Bódis, T., Botzheim, J.: Bacterial memetic algorithms for order picking routing problem with loading constraints. Expert Syst. Appl. **105**, 196–220 (2018). https://doi.org/10.1016/j.eswa.2018.03.043
2. Briant, O., Cambazard, H., Cattaruzza, D., Catusse, N., Ladier, A.L., Ogier, M.: An efficient and general approach for the joint order batching and picker routing problem. Eur. J. Oper. Res. (2020). https://doi.org/10.1016/j.ejor.2020.01.059
3. Chabot, T., Lahyani, R., Coelho, L.C., Renaud, J.: Order picking problems under weight, fragility and category constraints. Int. J. Prod. Res. **55**(21), 6361–6379 (2017). https://doi.org/10.1080/00207543.2016.1251625
4. De Koster, R.B.M., Le-Duc, T., Roodbergen, K.J.: Design and control of warehouse order picking: a literature review. Eur. J. Oper. Res. **182**(2), 481–501 (2007). https://doi.org/10.1016/j.ejor.2006.07.009
5. Dekker, R., De Koster, R.B.M., Roodbergen, K.J., Van Kalleveen, H.: Improving order-picking response time at Ankor's warehouse. Interfaces **34**(4), 303–313 (2004). https://doi.org/10.1287/inte.1040.0083
6. Glock, C.H., Grosse, E.H., Elbert, R.M., Franzke, T.: Maverick picking: the impact of modifications in work schedules on manual order picking processes. Int. J. Prod. Res. **55**(21), 6344–6360 (2017). https://doi.org/10.1080/00207543.2016.1252862
7. Henn, S.: Algorithms for on-line order batching in an order picking warehouse. Comput. Oper. Res. **39**(11), 2549–2563 (2012). https://doi.org/10.1016/j.cor.2011.12.019
8. Henn, S., Wäscher, G.: Tabu search heuristics for the order batching problem in manual order picking systems. Eur. J. Oper. Res. **222**(3), 484–494 (2012). https://doi.org/10.1016/j.ejor.2012.05.049
9. Ho, Y.C., Su, T.S., Shi, Z.B.: Order-batching methods for an order-picking warehouse with two cross aisles. Comput. Ind. Eng. **55**(2), 321–347 (2008). https://doi.org/10.1016/j.cie.2007.12.018
10. Marchet, G., Melacini, M., Perotti, S.: Investigating order picking system adoption: a case-study-based approach. Int. J. Logist. Res. Appl. **18**(1), 82–98 (2015). https://doi.org/10.1080/13675567.2014.945400
11. Masae, M., Glock, C.H., Grosse, E.H.: Order picker routing in warehouses: a systematic literature review. Int. J. Prod. Econ. **224**, 107564 (2020). https://doi.org/10.1016/j.ijpe.2019.107564
12. Matusiak, M., De Koster, R.B.M., Kroon, L., Saarinen, J.: A fast simulated annealing method for batching precedence-constrained customer orders in a warehouse. Eur. J. Oper. Res. **236**(3), 968–977 (2014). https://doi.org/10.1016/j.ejor.2013.06.001
13. Roodbergen, K.J.: Storage assignment for order picking in multiple-block warehouses. In: Manzini, R. (ed.) Warehousing in the Global Supply Chain, pp. 139–155. Springer, London (2012). https://doi.org/10.1007/978-1-4471-2274-6_7
14. Theys, C., Bräysy, O., Dullaert, W., Raa, B.: Using a TSP heuristic for routing order pickers in warehouses. Eur. J. Oper. Res. **200**(3), 755–763 (2010). https://doi.org/10.1016/j.ejor.2009.01.036
15. Van Gils, T., Caris, A., Ramaekers, K., Braekers, K., de Koster, R.B.M.: Designing efficient order picking systems: the effect of real-life features on the relationship among planning problems. Transp. Res. Part E: Logist. Transp. Rev. **125**, 47–73 (2019). https://doi.org/10.1016/j.tre.2019.02.010

16. Van Gils, T., Ramaekers, K., Braekers, K., Depaire, B., Caris, A.: Increasing order picking efficiency by integrating storage, batching, zone picking, and routing policy decisions. Int. J. Prod. Econ. **197**(Part C), 243–261 (2018). https://doi.org/10.1016/j.ijpe.2017.11.021
17. Van Gils, T., Ramaekers, K., Caris, A., De Koster, R.B.M.: Designing efficient order picking systems by combining planning problems: state-of-the-art classification and review. Eur. J. Oper. Res. **267**(1), 1–15 (2018). https://doi.org/10.1016/j.ejor.2017.09.002
18. Vanheusden, S., van Gils, T., Caris, A., Ramaekers, K., Braekers, K.: Operational workload balancing in manual order picking. Comput. Ind. Eng. **141**, 106269 (2020). https://doi.org/10.1016/j.cie.2020.106269
19. Žulj, I., Glock, C.H., Grosse, E.H., Schneider, M.: Picker routing and storage-assignment strategies for precedence-constrained order picking. Comput. Ind. Eng. **123**, 338–347 (2018). https://doi.org/10.1016/j.cie.2018.06.015

A Solution Approach to The Problem of Nesting Rectangles with Arbitrary Rotations into Containers of Irregular Convex and Non-Convex Shapes

Alexandre Romanelli$^{(\boxtimes)}$ and André R. S. Amaral

Graduate School of Computer Science (PPGI), Federal University of Espírito Santo
(UFES), Vitória, ES 29075-910, Brazil
alexromanelli@gmail.com, amaral@inf.ufes.br

Abstract. This paper introduces the problem of nesting rectangles, without overlapping, into containers of irregular shapes, in order to maximize the number of items positioned. This problem occurs in tasks of loading steel sheets into empty spaces of partially occupied ship's cargo hold. This is a NP-hard problem. We present a solution approach to this problem based on the search over sequences, which are decoded by a bottom-left constructive method, and we use the Iterated Local Search metaheuristic to escape local minima. The neighborhood structure is defined by variations in the rotation of the rectangles. Non-regularized Boolean operations are used by the constructive method to compute collision-free regions. The results indicate the reliability of the proposed approach.

Keywords: Nesting problems · Combinatorial optimization · Heuristic search

1 Introduction

This work deals with the problem of nesting rectangles, without overlapping, into containers of irregular shapes, to maximize the number of items placed. As far as we know, there is no other published work on this specific problem. The problem occurs when loading stacks of rectangular steel sheets into spaces not yet occupied in a ship's cargo hold. The use of the available space to be occupied with the sheets can lead to the possibility of allocating a smaller number of ships and thereby simplifying the process of loading and unloading the products. Therefore, the solution to this problem can be useful for activities in ports used to transport products from the steel industries. The problem can be considered as a type of 2-dimensional knapsack problem.

Some considerations are made in this work, which are related to the abstraction of the problem's data. By simplicity, all stacks of sheets are assumed to have the same parallelepiped shape and the same size, and that the ship's cargo hold

© Springer Nature Switzerland AG 2020
E. Lalla-Ruiz et al. (Eds.): ICCL 2020, LNCS 12433, pp. 747–762, 2020.
https://doi.org/10.1007/978-3-030-59747-4_48

has an irregular shape as it is already partially occupied. It is also assumed that the height of the cargo hold's ceiling is sufficient to store the stacks of sheets, so a 2-dimensional representation based on the upper view of the hold can be used. Thus, each item to be positioned is viewed as a rectangle. We will assume that it is allowed the use of an arbitrary, predefined set of angles to rotate each rectangle, not necessarily multiples of 90°. When dealing with this problem, the objective is to determine a layout for positioning rectangular items so that the maximum number of items can be loaded. This resembles the Identical Item Packing Problem as defined in Wäscher, Haußner, and Schumann's typology in [27], which is NP-hard [15]. Consequently, practical solution approaches can focus on searching for sufficiently good solutions, rather than just optimal ones.

We propose an algorithm to solve the problem, based on the representation of a layout as a sequence of rotations that will be applied individually to each item to be positioned. A sequence is mapped to a layout by a constructive method that uses the collision-free region concept proposed in [25], and the bottom-left positioning heuristic, which consists of choosing for each item the available place with the shortest x-coordinates first, and solving ties by choosing that with the shortest y-coordinates – if we use a Cartesian coordinate system to represent the cargo hold area. The method of searching for better solutions consists of making changes in the sequence and checking the quality of the obtained layout. This process was inspired by the search methods proposed by [19] and [14]. To escape from local optima, the Iterated Local Search metaheuristic was adopted, with a proposed perturbation method that makes changes of sequence's elements in quantities randomly chosen within a predefined interval.

The contribution of this work is the introduction of a new problem in the context of two-dimensional nesting, which is presented together with a solution approach that can be used to compare results in future work. This paper is divided into six sections. In Sect. 2, the problem definition is presented. In Sect. 3, there is a brief overview of works that address similar problems or apply usable solution methods. In Sect. 4, intrinsic geometric subproblems of two-dimensional nesting problems are described. In Sect. 5, the proposed positioning algorithm is explained. In Sect. 6, the experiments that were carried out to evaluate the efficiency of the proposed method are presented. Finally, in Sect. 7, conclusions are drawn.

2   Problem Definition

The problem of nesting rectangular sheets in irregular cargo holds of a ship, or simply nesting rectangles in irregular containers (NRIC), can be defined as follows. Consider the following input data:

  i. $\mathcal{P} = \{P_i \mid i \in [1, N]\}$ is the set of N different types of sheets that need to be loaded. In this work, $N = 1$ will be assumed.
 ii. $P_i = (w_i, h_i, \Theta_i, d_i)$ defines the i-th type of sheet, which is a tuple formed by the following elements: w_i is the width of the rectangle; h_i is the height

of the rectangle; Θ_i is the set of angles that can be used to rotate a sheet of type i; and d_i is the demand of sheets of type i to be loaded.

iii. C represents the shape of the cargo hold that can be occupied with the sheets. In this work, this representation is a polygon that possibly has concavities and holes. Both the external contour and the possible holes are described by simple polygons, that is, without intersections between edges, except consecutive edges in their vertices in common.

Let $T_{ij} = (P_i^{\theta_k}, r_{ij})$ be the placement of an item of type i, rotated with an angle $\theta_k \in \Theta_i$ and translated by the vector $\overrightarrow{p_1 r_{ij}}$ (details are given in Sect. 4), where $i \in [1, N]$ and $j \in [1, d_i]$. T_{ij} is, therefore, a copy of P_i already positioned. A layout for nesting all items is defined as the set $\mathcal{T} = \{T_{ij}\}, \forall i \in [1, N], \forall j \in [1, d_i]$.

The NRIC problem is how to find a layout $\mathcal{T}$ that satisfies the Constraints (1) and (2), and maximizes the number of nested items. Constraint (1) requires that there should be no overlap between two positioned items. Constraint (2), on the other hand, ensures that all positioned items must be completely inside the cargo hold.

$$T_{ij} \cap T_{kl} = \emptyset, \quad \forall i, k \in [1, N], \forall j \in [1, d_i], \forall l \in [1, d_k], (i = k \rightarrow j \neq l) \quad (1)$$

$$T_{ij} \cap C = T_{ij}, \quad \forall i \in [1, N], \forall j \in [1, d_i] \quad (2)$$

3   Related Works

There are several studies in the literature related to the problem of nesting rectangles, as well as two-dimensional irregular shapes, which can be used as the foundation for developing an approach to solving the NRIC problem. The nesting of rectangles can be found with different characteristics, such as the orthogonal positioning of items in areas delimited by rectangles, or the planning of cutting materials, which can be guillotined or not, and the positioning of items in convex and non-rectangular areas. Some works that deal with these problems can be found in [4, 5, 10, 13, 17, 22].

The problem of nesting irregular shapes has been studied since the mid-1960s, and approaches to solve it can be found in [2, 6, 7, 18, 21]. In [3], constructive methods for generating layouts for cutting leather are presented. Analogously to the present work, the leather material is an irregularly shaped area on which the shapes (represented as polygons possibly with concavities) must be positioned to be cut. In that work, the authors used the concepts of the no-fit polygon and the inner fit polygon, which are discussed in Sects. 4.1 and 4.2 respectively, but they did not present the computational methods used to perform the calculations of these elements. However, in [8, 11] methods to calculate the no-fit polygon between two polygons, regular or not, with or without holes, are presented. Both the no-fit polygon and the inner fit polygon are also discussed in [24] and [25]. In these works, the concept of Collision-Free Region, which combines the previous concepts to determine all the points that can be used to make the valid placement of an item, was also presented. This concept is covered in Sect. 4.3.

All the problems studied in the works cited above differ from the NRIC in some aspect. Some of these problems deal with the packing of rectangles in rectangular containers, or with the nesting of rectangles or polygons in rectangular containers, while one of them deals with the packing of irregular polygons in irregular containers. The study in [3] can be seen as a generalization of NRIC, but its proposed methods are greedy and focused on exploring different geometric features of the items and of their NFPs to infer good placements. As in NRIC there are no differences between the items, and the objective of the present work is to explore the space of solutions to find better layouts, we consider that it would not be advantageous to use the methods of that work.

4   Computational Geometry Subproblems

In this work, the same subproblems of the nesting of irregular polygons will be addressed. This is justified by the irregular shape of the cargo hold making the positioning, in the problem of this work, a task similar to positioning a rectangular item in a partial layout of irregular shapes. Therefore, the No-Fit Polygon (NFP), the Inner Fit Polygon (IFP) and, through their combination, the Collision-Free Region (CFR) will be observed.

4.1   No-Fit Polygon

The NFP between two polygons P_i and P_j, NFP_{ij}, allows the identification of overlapping occurrence between these by checking for the inclusion of r_j within NFP_{ij}, where r_j is a candidate point for the nesting of P_j. This can simplify the overlap occurrence identification between two pieces, because the calculations involved in the polygon overlap test are computationally more expensive than verifying the inclusion of a point inside of a polygon. The following three situations are possible:

  i. If r_j is neither inside NFP_{ij} nor on any edge of its outline, then P_i and P_j are neither overlapping nor touching, i.e., there is no intersection between the sets of points of the contours of P_i and P_j;
 ii. If r_j is on some edge of the NFP_{ij} contour, then there is some touch between P_i and P_j, but these do not overlap;
iii. If r_j is inside NFP_{ij}, then there is some overlapping between P_i and P_j.

The NFP_{ij} is the result of the Minkowski sum $P_i \oplus \check{P}_j$, according to [9]. In this operation, P_i is the item whose positioning is considered fixed, while it is considered that P_j can be "moved" or relocated. The result of the subexpression $\check{P}_j$ is obtained by multiplication of the coordinates of each vertex of P_j by -1. An example of NFP between two polygons is shown in Fig. 1, which is divided into three parts. At 1a, items P_i and P_j, and the reference point r_j, are displayed.

In 1b, the NFP_{ij} is shown. In 1c, three possible translations of P_j are represented. If P_j were translated to tp_1, which is in the interior of NFP_{ij}, an overlap situation would occur. If the point tp_2, at the boundary of the NFP_{ij}, were used to translate P_j, it would touch P_i, without overlap. And if P_j were translated to a position tp_3, outside of the NFP_{ij}, P_j would not touch nor overlap P_i.

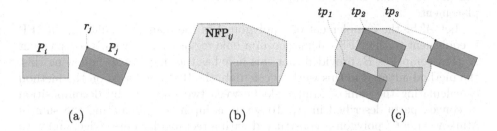

Fig. 1. NFP between two items.

NFP_{ij} is a polygon that can have holes and degenerations, such as isolated points, antennas, or line segments inside, if a point of these places is used to position P_j, there will be no overlap between it and P_i. However, as for this work, items to be positioned are rectangular, the NFP will always be a convex polygon without holes or degenerations. And for the same reason, the NFP calculation comes down to the process illustrated in Fig. 2, which makes $A \oplus \check{B}$ following the algorithm presented in [16]. In this figure, the two polygons, A and B, for which to calculate the NFP, and the transformation $\check{B}$, are presented in 2a. In 2b, the edges of A and $\check{B}$ are arranged in a slope diagram. In 2c, the sum of Minkowski is calculated using a path through the previous diagram, which is equivalent to ordering the edges by their inclinations.

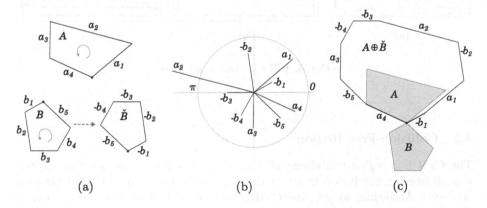

Fig. 2. Method to compute the NFP.

4.2   Inner Fit Polygon

The IFP for a type i of sheets to be positioned describes the region of the cargo hold in which the positioning point r_{ij} can be located. If an item is placed in any region of your IFP, this item will be completely inside the cargo hold. However, if a point outside the IFP is used to do the positioning, some part of the item will not be within that area and, consequently, this point does not offer a valid placement.

Let A' be the complement of a polygon A in the plane. Calculating the IFP is equivalent to the NFP calculation in a hole region of a polygon's complement A' that comprises B, provided that this hole has the shape of A. Following this, the method adopted in this work to calculate the IFP was based on the method of calculating the sum of Minkowski between two polygons by decomposition in convex parts described in [1]. To serve as input for calculating the sum of Minkowski, a C' polygon is constructed with a rectangular outer edge, and with a hole formed through the cargo hold. The outer edge of C' must be large enough so that there is no intersection at all between it and the hole.

Figure 3 presents an example of calculating the IFP of a rectangle P_i and a cargo hold C. In 3a, the objects are displayed, and point p_1 is indicated, which will be used to do P_i positioning. In 3b there is the polygon C', which has a rectangular shape with a hole shaped as C. Calculation of NFP is performed between C', fixed, and P_i, orbiting. The IFP between C and P_i, $IFP(C, P_i)$, which is the NFP part that is inside the hole of C', is displayed in 3c. Moreover, the rectangle P_i can be positioned anywhere on the contour or inside the IFP so that $C \cap P_i = P_i$.

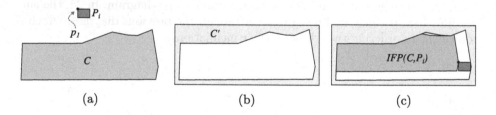

Fig. 3. IFP calculation strategy.

4.3   Collision-Free Region

The CFR is a region containing all the points possible to use so that an item is positioned in the layout in a way that the two constraints of the problem are observed. According to [24], the CFR is defined with three parameters. One is the cargo hold C, which is the container for the items. Another is the set $\mathcal{T}'$ that contains the nestings already performed. That is, $\mathcal{T}' \subset \mathcal{T}$ and represents the current state of the layout, still incomplete. The third parameter is the item for which one wishes to calculate the CFR, which is $P_i^{\theta_k}$. The definition of CFR is given by Eq. 3.

$$CFR(C, \mathcal{T}', P_i^{\theta_k}) = IFP(C, P_i^{\theta_k}) - \bigcup_{T_{ij} \in \mathcal{T}'} NFP(T_{ij}, P_i^{\theta_k}) \qquad (3)$$

It is important to emphasize that the edges of the NFPs' contours, as well as their degenerations, if any, are not a hindrance to positioning. Therefore, the Boolean operations between geometric shapes in Eq. 3 should not be regularized and should only consider the interior of each NFP. A resulting CFR can have degenerations, such as an NFP, but also be formed by unconnected polygons and by isolated vertices and line segments.

Figure 4 presents an example of CFR for a given item $P_i^{\theta_k}$, in a cargo hold C and with a partial layout $\mathcal{T}' = \{T_{1,1}, T_{1,2}, T_{1,3}, T_{1,4}, T_{1,5}\}$, as shown in part 4a of this figure, still indicating the point used as a reference for the item positioning, and the $CFR(C, \mathcal{T}', P_i^{\theta_k})$ is highlighted inside C. In 4b, examples of the item positioning at points of the CFR contour and inside it, which are valid locations, are presented, and two cases of invalid positioning, shown outside the CFR, which result in overlap between items and positioning partially outside the cargo hold, are displayed.

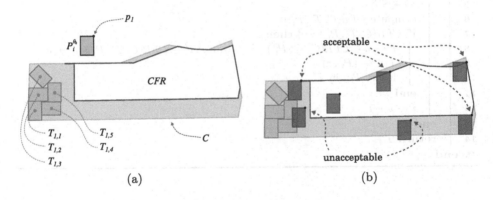

Fig. 4. CFR and its application.

5 The Proposed Positioning Approach

The proposed solution for the NRIC problem in this paper uses a "bottom-left" constructive method and a sequential search using the Iterated Local Search (ILS) metaheuristic [23,26]. The description of this approach is divided into four parts. The first deals with the constructive method used to transform sequences into layouts. In the second part, the explanation of the local search method is done, including the neighborhood structure used. The third part is dedicated to the description of the method for perturbing solutions, which is part of the ILS metaheuristic. Lastly, the main algorithm, which is the ILS implementation for the NRIC problem, is presented.

5.1   Constructive Method

The construction of a layout is done according to the method described in Algorithm 1. It receives three elements as input, which are: a sequence S of angles that must be applied to the items to be positioned; the type of these items; and the description of the cargo hold C. The output is the layout, partial or complete, T'.

Algorithm 1: Constructive-BL

---

input : $S, \mathcal{P} = \{P_1\}, C$
output: T'

1 **begin**
2 $\quad$ $T' \leftarrow \emptyset$
3 $\quad$ $i \leftarrow 1$
4 $\quad$ **while** $i \leq d_1$ **do**
5 $\quad\quad$ $\gamma \leftarrow S[i]$
6 $\quad\quad$ compute $CFR(C, T', P_1^\gamma)$
7 $\quad\quad$ **if** $CFR(C, T', P_1^\gamma) \neq \emptyset$ **then**
8 $\quad\quad\quad$ $r \leftarrow v \in CFR(C, T', P_1^\gamma) \mid v \leq_{(bl)} v', \forall v' \in CFR(C, T', P_1^\gamma), v' \neq v$
9 $\quad\quad\quad$ $T_{1,i} \leftarrow (P_1^\gamma, r)$
10 $\quad\quad\quad$ insert $T_{1,i}$ in T'
11 $\quad\quad$ **end**
12 $\quad\quad$ $i \leftarrow i + 1$
13 $\quad$ **end**
14 $\quad$ **return** T'
15 **end**

Algorithm 1 starts with $T' = \emptyset$. Then it moves through each position in the sequence S and, for each angle γ of this, calculates the CFR of P_1^γ, considering the items that have already been positioned, if any. If the CFR is not empty, then the positioning of an item rotated with an angle γ is possible.

The vertex for positioning, r, will be the vertex v of the CFR selected according to the bottom-left rule. This rule indicates that the point to be selected for positioning should be the one that is "below" and, in the event of a tie, the one that is more "to the left" prevails. The original meaning of this is that the point must be chosen because it has the smallest coordinate in the direction of the dimension to be minimized, usually the length, and the tiebreaker aims to keep the items together. In this work, the use of this rule is justified by the minimization of length during layout construction to preserve free area for items not yet positioned. The relation between two points according to the bottom-left rule, here represented by the operation $v \leq_{(bl)} v'$, is true if $v.x < v'.x$ or if $v.x = v'.x \wedge v.y \leq v'.y$, where ".$x$" and ".$y$" indicate the x and y coordinates of a point, respectively.

The vertex r is then used to position $T_{1,i}$, which is included in the layout T'. When all angles of S have been used to try to position an item, T' will contain the possible layout, with the bottom-left rule for the sequence S. This layout will be then returned as a result.

5.2   Local Search Method

The adopted local search algorithm receives as input data an sequence S' of angles to be used in the rotations of the items to be positioned, the type of these items, and the definition of the cargo hold C. This algorithm has two output elements: a layout T_l, which represents the local optimum found, and the sequence S of angles used to form this layout. This procedure uses a neighborhood structure that consists of changing one of the angles of the sequence S, followed by the reconstruction of the layout with the new sequence by calling Constructive-BL. Since S has d_1 elements and each item can be rotated by m different angles, $m = |\Theta_1|$, $m - 1$ angles remain to be tested on each item in the sequence. Therefore, each solution has a quantity of neighbors equal to $d_1 \times (m - 1)$. In the adopted method, when walking through the neighborhood of the current solution, represented by the sequence S, if a change of angle that leads to a layout with more items positioned is found, this neighboring solution is immediately adopted as the current one and a new iteration of search is started.

5.3   The Main Algorithm

Algorithm 2 describes the NRIC solver method that was developed. In addition to the item type, the algorithm receives the description of the cargo hold C and three parameters used as input to control the metaheuristic search that will be described below. The generated output is T_*, a set of nestings in C, which has number of elements $|T_*| \leq d_i$.

Algorithm 2 starts with the generation of an sequence S of items for positioning, in line 2. In this case, this sequence is formed by angles γ_i randomly selected in Θ_1. Each angle will be used to rotate an item to be positioned. The number of elements in S is therefore equal to d_1. In line 3, a local search procedure that finds a local optimal solution for the problem instance, as described in Sect. 5.2, is performed.

Afterwards in line 5, the algorithm enters a cycle of actions that are repeated while two conditions are met. One is that the number of positioned items, $|T_*|$, is smaller than the number of items to position, d_1. The other is that the number of iterations without improvement, i, is less than or equal to the maximum number of failed attempts to improve, $MaxFAI$, which is a parameter of the algorithm. Repeated actions start in line 6 with the choice of the perturbation size, which is a random value between the values of the parameters $MinPS$ and

---

Algorithm 2: NRIC-Solver

---

    input : $\mathcal{P} = \{P_1\}$, C, *MaxFAI*, *MinPS*, *MaxPS*
    output: $\mathcal{T}_*$

1 **begin**
2      $S \leftarrow (\gamma_1, \gamma_2, \ldots, \gamma_m)$, $m = d_1$, each $\gamma_i \in \Theta_1$ is randomly chosen
3      $\mathcal{T}_*, S_* \leftarrow$ Local-Search$(S, \mathcal{P}, C)$
4      $i \leftarrow 0$
5   **while** $|\mathcal{T}_*| < d_1 \wedge i \leq$ *MaxFAI* **do**
6   TP $\leftarrow$ random-between(*MinPS*, *MaxPS*)
7          $S \leftarrow$ Perturb(S_*, TP)
8          $\mathcal{T}_l, S_l \leftarrow$ Local-Search$(S, \mathcal{P}, C)$
9   **if** $|\mathcal{T}_l| > |\mathcal{T}_*|$ **then**
10             $\mathcal{T}_* \leftarrow \mathcal{T}_l$
11             $S_* \leftarrow S_l$
12             $i \leftarrow 0$
13   **else**
14             $i \leftarrow i + 1$
15   **end**
16   **end**
17   **return** $\mathcal{T}_*$
18 **end**

MaxPS, which represent, respectively, the minimum and maximum perturbation size. In line 7, the sequence perturbation method is performed. This procedure receives two elements as input, the original sequence of angles and the size of the perturbation, which indicates how many items in the sequence should be changed. The output of the algorithm is the modified sequence. The procedure just selects a subset of the sequence's elements and, for each value in it, changes the angle by randomly choosing a different one from Θ_1.

The sequence resulting from the perturbation is delivered, in line 8, for the execution of the local search method. This search, therefore, starts from a solution that is the random modification of the best solution found so far. This is intended to diversify the search, which means finding a local optimum solution different from the best solution previously known, and possibly better than this one. In line 9, a comparison between the quantities of items positioned in the local optimum found, $|\mathcal{T}_l|$, and in the best previously known solution, $|\mathcal{T}_*|$ is performed. If the newly found local optimum is better, then the best-known solution and the sequence that generated it are updated, in lines 10 and 11, and the iteration counter without improvement is reset by the command in line 12. If the result of the local search for the current cycle is no better than the $\mathcal{T}_*$, the iteration counter without improvement is incremented by one (line 14).

When the repetitive command in line 5 is finished, the algorithm will return $\mathcal{T}_*$. Due to the conditions of continuity of the "while", it is possible that the solution has reached the total number of positioned items, which is intended. But it is also possible that the execution algorithm has reached the limit of iterations without improving the solution. In this case, $\mathcal{T}_*$ is an incomplete solution, containing the layout with the maximum number of items positioned between the layouts that were evaluated in the search.

6   Results

The method described in Sect. 5 was implemented in the C++ language. The integrated development environment Qt Creator 4.7.2 on the Qt 5.11.2 development kit, and with the GCC compiler 5.3.1, was employed. The experiments were run on a computer with the AMD Ryzen™ 7 1700X processor with eight cores and clock of 3.4 GHz, with 16 GB of main memory, and Linux system with kernel's version 4.15.0-39. The geometric operations required to compute the IFP was implemented using packages of classes related to Nef polygons and Minkowski sum, which are part of the Computational Geometry Algorithms Library [12].

The proposed algorithm is evaluated on artificial instances of the problem, due to the unavailability of real data. Two test instances groups were created, with cargo holds described[1] by polygons C_1 and C_2, where C_1 has a randomly created shape and C_2 is equal to a item arbitrarily selected from the irregular nesting problem's benchmark instance named "Mao", gathered in [20]. Each of these groups were divided in two subgroups, according to the size and demand of the rectangular items to be packed. Finally, three different combinations of rotations allowed were applied to each subgroup to generate 12 instances, which are represented in Fig. 5, where "un" is an abbreviation for units, which references the item's demand.

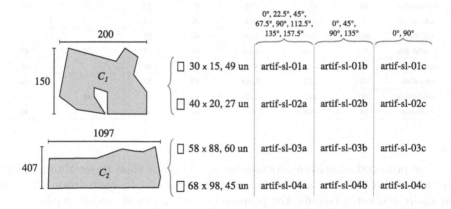

Fig. 5. Instances used in tests.

The proposed algorithm was run 10 times for each of the 12 test instances, with the *MaxFAI* set to 5, and the size of perturbation between 5% and 10% of

---

[1] The dimension's units used to describe the elements of the instances do not reflect any real metric unit, and they are used just to establish the proportion between the containers and rectangles' sizes.

the total demand. These arguments were defined after trying different values by running a limited number of experiments.

The quality of the produced layouts was evaluated by comparison with the best results obtained by manual improvement attempts and by using a greedy bottom-left method. For each instance in the last column in Fig. 5, a manually generated solution was obtained and its value was used as a lower bound for the solution values of the other instances in its respective subgroup. The greedy bottom-left method is a modification of the constructive method described in Sect. 5.1, including a step to select the piece orientation that leads to the best placement by the bottom-left rule.

Table 1 shows for the proposed algorithm average values of time, number of items in layout, and number of evaluated solutions followed by the minimum and maximum numbers of items nested. The table also presents the number of items nested in a manually generated layout; and the number of items nested with greedy bottom-left.

Table 1. Summary of the results with $MaxFAI = 5$.

Instance	Avg values of 10 executions			Max # of Items in layout	Min # of Items in layout	# of Items in a manually generated layout	# of Items with greedy bottom-left
	Time (s)	# of Items in layout	# of Evaluated sequences				
artif-sl-01a	963	38.9	3,242	39	38		37
artif-sl-01b	175	38.7	1,381	39	38	40	37
artif-sl-01c	21	38.9	446	40	38		37
artif-sl-02a	248	20.2	1,903	21	20		19
artif-sl-02b	53	20.4	839	21	20	21	19
artif-sl-02c	4	20.0	214	21	19		19
artif-sl-03a	967	59.1	3,280	60	59		57
artif-sl-03b	361	57.4	1,968	59	57	60	57
artif-sl-03c	51	57.3	684	58	56		57
artif-sl-04a	638	43.1	2,963	44	43		42
artif-sl-04b	151	43.1	1,167	44	43	45	42
artif-sl-04c	24	43.8	445	45	43		42

The proposed algorithm provides better solutions than those obtained with the greedy bottom-left method for all test instances. In comparison with the manually generated layouts, the proposed algorithm yields results equivalent to the best ones for 6 instances, and it falls short by one positioned item for 5 instances; for one instance it falls short by 2 items. However, the task of finding good layouts manually is difficult, requires an experient professional, and takes a long time to achieve acceptable quality. In this work, the manually generation of each layout took no less than one hour.

The number of solutions evaluated by the proposed algorithm and, consequently, the execution time are affected by the number of different rotations allowed. The greater this quantity, the larger the solution neighborhood to be verified. There was no significant difference between the results obtained with only orthogonal rotations and the variations with more permitted angles, which indicates that the search wasted effort with item rotations that did not lead to improvements. An exception is the instance "artif-sl-03a", for which better layouts were achieved when more rotation angles were allowed.

The detailed observation of the behavior of the algorithm revealed that the perturbation method adopted in the implementation of the ILS allowed 30% of the executions to escape the first local optimum found and achieve layouts with more items positioned. The local search method found better results than the start solutions in 89% of the times it was called in the tests, and the number of items added to the layout was 2.1, on average, with a standard deviation of 1.4. The best layouts found for each instance, over all sets of acceptable angles for rotations, are shown in Fig. 6.

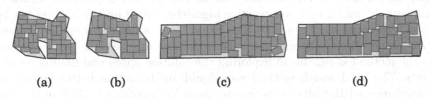

(a)   (b)   (c)   (d)

Fig. 6. Best layouts found: (a) 40 items in artif-01-c; (b) 21 in artif-02-c; (c) 60 in artif-03-a; and (d) 45 in artif-04-c.

Two groups of additional tests were carried out to check whether higher numbers of *MaxFAI*, and consequently more execution time, would lead the algorithm to obtain better results. In the first, called *Test A*, the program was run once for each instance with $MaxFAI = 15$. In the second, *Test B*, the program was also executed once for each instance[2], but this argument was calculated individually for each one as the maximum number different neighbors that a given solution could have. This was done with formula $MaxFAI = d_1 \times (|\Theta_1| - 1)$. The results of these tests are summarized in Table 2. There was no significant difference between these results and those obtained with $MaxFAI = 5$, which suggests that this initially defined value was sufficient to assess the behavior of the algorithm with the available instances.

---

[2] Except for instances with 8 different rotation angles, due to time constraints.

Table 2. Summary of the results of additional tests.

Instance	Test A		MaxFAI	Test B		Instance	Test A		MaxFAI	Test B	
	# of Items in layout	Time (s)		# of Items in layout	Time (s)		# of Items in layout	Time (s)		# of Items in layout	Time (s)
artif-sl-01a	39	2,717	n/d	n/d	n/d	artif-sl-03a	59	2,543	n/d	n/d	n/d
artif-sl-01b	39	445	196	39	5,813	artif-sl-03b	58	1,375	240	58	11,866
artif-sl-01c	40	50	98	40	308	artif-sl-03c	57	176	120	59	1,235
artif-sl-02a	20	616	n/d	n/d	n/d	artif-sl-04a	43	1,364	n/d	n/d	n/d
artif-sl-02b	21	159	108	21	843	artif-sl-04b	43	399	180	45	422
artif-sl-02c	21	16	54	20	42	artif-sl-04c	44	61	90	44	419

7   Conclusions

In this work, a solution method was proposed for the problem of nesting rect-angular items into irregular areas, which occurs in the loading of sheet metal on ships. The possibility of arbitrary rotation of items with a finite set of predefined angles was considered. This method combines search over sequences with the ILS metaheuristic, and uses a constructive algorithm based on the bottom-left rule and on techniques used in solvers for the problem of nesting irregular shapes.

In computational experiments with artificial instances, the results indicate that the method is capable of exploring the solution space and finding compact layouts. The local search method was significant to obtain better layouts and the implemented ILS allowed to escape from local optima in 30% of the tests. Comparison with other methods was not possible due to the lack of works in the literature that deal with this same problem.

As in other cutting and packing problems, the search over item sequences is limited by the ability that the constructive method has to represent layouts. Therefore, in future works other construction methods can be considered, or they can use techniques to search over the layout as alternatives to achieve better results. It would also be important to elaborate the mathematical optimization model and verify the applicability of exact methods to solve the problem.

References

1. Agarwal, P.K., Flato, E., Halperin, D.: Polygon decomposition for efficient con-struction of Minkowski sums. In: Computational Geometry, 16th European Work-shop on Computational Geometry - EUROCG-2000, vol. 21, no.1, pp. 39–61 (2002)
2. Albano, A., Sapuppo, G.: Optimal allocation of two-dimensional irregular shapes using heuristic search methods. IEEE Trans. Syst. Man Cybern. **10**(5), 242–248 (1980)
3. Alves, C., Brás, P., de Carvalho, J.V., Pinto, T.: New constructive algorithms for leather nesting in the automotive industry. Comput. Oper. Res. **39**(7), 1487–1505 (2012)
4. Amaral, A.R.S., Wright, M.: Efficient algorithm for the constrained two-dimensional cutting stock problem. Int. Trans. Oper. Res. **8**(1), 3–13 (2001)

5. Amaral, A.R.S., Wright, M.: Experiments with a strategic oscillation algorithm for the pallet loading problem. Int. J. Prod. Res. **39**(11), 2341–2351 (2001)
6. Art, R.: An approach to the two dimensional irregular cutting stock problem. Technical Report 320–2006, IBM Cambridge Scientific Center, Cambridge, MA (1966)
7. Bennell, J.A., Oliveira, J.F.: A tutorial in irregular shape packing problems. J. Oper. Res. Soc. **60**(1), S93–S105 (2009). https://doi.org/10.1057/jors.2008.169
8. Bennell, J.A., Song, X.: A comprehensive and robust procedure for obtaining the nofit polygon using Minkowski sums. Comput. Oper. Res. **35**(1), 267–281 (2008)
9. Bennell, J.A.: Incorporating problem specific knowledge into a local search framework for the irregular shape packing problem. Ph.D. thesis, University of Wales Swansea (1998)
10. Birgin, E.G., Lobato, R.D.: Orthogonal packing of identical rectangles within isotropic convex regions. Comput. Ind. Eng. **59**(4), 595–602 (2010)
11. Burke, E.K., Hellier, R.S., Kendall, G., Whitwell, G.: Complete and robust nofit polygon generation for the irregular stock cutting problem. Eur. J. Oper. Res. **179**(1), 27–49 (2007)
12. CGAL: Computational geometry algorithms library. http://www.cgal.org
13. Chazelle, B.: The bottom-left bin-packing heuristic: an efficient implementation. IEEE Trans. Comput. **C–32**(8), 697–707 (1983)
14. Dowsland, K., Dowsland, W., Bennell, J.: Jostling for position: local improvement for irregular cutting patterns. J. Oper. Res. Soc. **49**(6), 647–658 (1998)
15. Fowler, R.J., Paterson, M.S., Tanimoto, S.L.: Optimal packing and covering in the plane are NP-Complete. Inf. Process. Lett. **12**(3), 133–137 (1981)
16. Ghosh, P.K.: An algebra of polygons through the notion of negative shapes. CVGIP Image Underst. **54**(1), 119–144 (1991)
17. Gilmore, P.C., Gomory, R.E.: Multistage cutting stock problems of two and more dimensions. Oper. Res. **13**(1), 94–120 (1965)
18. Gomes, A.M., Oliveira, J.F.: Solving Irregular Strip Packing problems by hybridising simulated annealing and linear programming. Eur. J. Oper. Res. **171**(3), 811–829 (2006)
19. Gomes, A., Oliveira, J.: A GRASP approach to the nesting problem. In: Proceedings of MIC, pp. 47–52 (2001)
20. Hopper, E.: Two-dimensional packing utilising evolutionary algorithms and other meta-heuristic methods. Ph.D. thesis, University of Wales, Cardiff (2000)
21. Imamichi, T., Yagiura, M., Nagamochi, H.: An iterated local search algorithm based on nonlinear programming for the irregular strip packing problem. Discrete Optim. **6**(4), 345–361 (2009)
22. Letchford, A.N., Amaral, A.R.S.: Analysis of upper bounds for the pallet loading problem. Eur. J. Oper. Res. **132**(3), 582–593 (2001)
23. Lourenço, H.R., Martin, O.C., Stützle, T.: Iterated local search. In: Handbook of Metaheuristics, pp. 320–353. Springer (2003). https://doi.org/10.1007/0-306-48056-5_11
24. Sato, A.K., Martins, T.C., Tsuzuki, M.S.G.: An algorithm for the strip packing problem using collision free region and exact fitting placement. Comput. Aided Des. **44**(8), 766–777 (2012)
25. Sato, A.K., Martins, T.C., Tsuzuki, M.S.G.: Collision free region determination by modified polygonal Boolean operations. Comput. Aided Des. **45**(7), 1029–1041 (2013)

26. Stützle, T.: Applying iterated local search to the permutation flow shop problem. Technical Report, Technical Report AIDA-98-04, FG Intellektik, TU Darmstadt (1998)
27. Wäscher, G., Haußner, H., Schumann, H.: An improved typology of cutting and packing problems. Eur. J. Oper. Res. **183**(3), 1109–1130 (2007)

Cash Distribution Model with Safety Constraints

William J. Guerrero[1]([✉])[iD], Angélica Sarmiento-Lepesqueur[2][iD],
and Cristian Martínez-Agaton[2]

[1] Faculty of Engineering, Universidad de La Sabana,
Campus del Puente del Com ún, Km. 7, Autopista norte, Chía, Colombia
william.guerrero1@unisabana.edu.co
[2] Escuela Colombiana de Ingeniería Julio Garavito, AK.45 No.205-59,
Bogotá, Colombia

Abstract. This article studies the cash distribution problem for bank correspondents that are geographically dispersed, and the associated risk indicators, service times, and logistics costs. The proposed model is a variant of the Inventory Routing Problem (IRP) that considers risk-management strategies. The model considers a single cash center with unlimited capacity, from which cash deliveries are carried out by a single vehicle with limited capacity for cash distribution. The bank correspondents to which the cash deliveries are made handles a limited storage capacity. This paper considers the routing decisions of vehicles with hard time window, and risk constraints focused on inducing unpredictability of routes in a cash supply chain. The proposed model is denoted as a risk constrained inventory routing problem with time Windows (RcIRPTW). A mathematical formulation based on mixed-integer programming is proposed, studying the impact of incidents risks in the transport of cash, generating computational experiments on test instances where four types of variations of the IRP are evaluated with several random demand scenarios. The results show the importance of simultaneously optimizing inventory decisions considering routing and inventory costs along with the consideration of risk mitigation strategies. These risk constraints force changing the routes of the vehicle, reducing incidents rates, and reducing route predictability for secure transportation and logistics.

Keywords: Cash distribution · Inventory routing · Time windows · Branch banking · Risk management · Currency supply chain

1 Introduction

Globally, around 2.5 billion people do not use financial services and 75% of the poor do not have a bank account [14]. Financial inclusion is the key to reduce poverty and boost prosperity, enabling people to have access to useful and affordable financial products that meet their needs for transactions, payments, savings, credit, and insurance responsibly and sustainably [14]. Since 2010, more

© Springer Nature Switzerland AG 2020
E. Lalla-Ruiz et al. (Eds.): ICCL 2020, LNCS 12433, pp. 763–777, 2020.
https://doi.org/10.1007/978-3-030-59747-4_49

than 55 countries have committed to implementing financial inclusion, and more than 30 of them have prepared a national strategy on financial inclusion. The countries that have made the most progress towards financial inclusion are those that have created a regulatory environment and have fostered competition by allowing banking and non-banking institutions to innovate and expand access to financial services. Digital financial technology, and in particular the increased use of smartphones globally, has facilitated the expansion of access for small businesses and vulnerable populations in rural areas to financial services at a lower cost and lower risk.

Financial inclusion has a direct correlation with economic growth, social development, and poverty reduction [12]. Given this impact, public policies aimed at facilitating access to financial services. Colombia has not been oblivious to this trend. In recent years, significant efforts to increasing access to financial services exist. Since 2006, the national government has launched a strategy with the support of the Opportunities Bank policy, which has made it possible to implement several financial inclusion initiatives, such as expanding regional geographical coverage, combined with a strategy of public incentives aimed at the industry and the private sector, allowing considerable progress in financial inclusion in the country [12].

In 2006, 71% of the country's municipalities had a banking presence. However, the coverage of private banks is only 25% [12]. Thus, credit institutions are authorized to sign correspondent contracts with non-financial third parties, such as supermarkets and drugstores, to provide financial services through them. The strategy aims to reach areas where the operation of traditional channels becomes costly. This figure, known as Bank Correspondents, enables banks to reach a 100% municipality coverage in 2015. Further, through the use of technology and alternative networks, more transactions can be performed than those of the traditional financial system.

Thus, Bank correspondents are a low-cost channel that allows banks and finance companies to provide their services through commercial establishments such as neighborhood stores, drugstores, and supermarkets. It is called a branch banking scheme. This model allows financial institutions to achieve increased coverage in places where there are insufficient incentives or capacity to establish a branch, such as in exceedingly small municipalities, rural areas, or slums [11]. In that regard, they have become a key channel for expanding financial sector coverage. The implementation model and strategy differ between different countries and even between financial institutions: while some use bank correspondents with a "mini-branch" model to expand coverage and reach remote areas, others use them as a human cashier to decongest offices and expand the cashier network. Others use them as a satellite to serve new segments in areas close to their influence area. Despite the advances in the extension of bank correspondents, significant logistic challenges remain, such as the efficient management, distribution, and cash storage of banking correspondents [1].

Therefore, the optimal cash distribution and storage becomes the focus of financial institutions and distribution providers. With the expansion of covered areas with different socioeconomic conditions, transportation and storing cash may become a risky operation with a high probability of theft. Therefore, planning becomes an essential activity for such operations. In addition to traditional transport constraints and cost minimization criteria, safety constraints on a vehicle route and cash inventory management must be taken into consideration to ensure the proper satisfaction of demand for cash at bank correspondents.

One of the typical problems that cash management entails for financial institutions is the vehicle routing problem (VRP) and its variations applied to the valuables transport sector. The VRP emerges as a central problem in the fields of transportation, distribution, and logistics, being thus a classic problem of combinatorial optimization with multiple applications that seeks to determine the lowest cost routes that a fleet of vehicles must perform to meet the demand of customers that are geographically dispersed [8]. Recently, variations of the problem are proposed to include other criteria, besides costs, in the routing schemes. For example, profit maximization [5] or avoiding predictability [9].

Furthermore, [10] and [15] previously analyzed the dependency between cash inventory management decisions and transportation decisions. First, [15] and [7] propose to analyze an inventory-routing problem for cash distribution, neglecting risk-management elements. The problem with dynamic demands is analyzed by [6]. Then, [10] proposes a MIP model to optimize cash inventory levels and transportation decisions for a network of offices. They ignore routing decisions and risk management constraints. [16] studied the risk of transporting cash, where the robbery risk is a function of the amount of transported cash and the distance covered by the vehicle carrying the cash. A literature review on currency supply chains is presented by [4]. In a different setting, [3] presents a bi-objective model to optimize inventory-routing decisions considering risk measures of holding stock in the case of humanitarian logistics.

However, for the scope of this paper, we consider the application of risk management strategies that may constraint the solution space, allowing a safe and efficient cash replenishment to bank correspondents [9]. To the best of our knowledge, this is the first time that the currency inventory-routing problem is formally studied together with risk-mitigation strategies.

The cash inventory management problem is also a challenging logistic problem [10]. The presented situation considers an environment in which inventory replenishment policies are managed by the supplier, allowing the selection of time and amount of cash delivered to the correspondents, aiming to achieve an overall reduction in logistical costs and risks. Thus, the article proposes a model in which the problem of allocating cash inventories and the routing for a set of bank correspondents served by secure vehicles are optimized jointly, through a centralized decision setting.

The proposed study aims to generate a model that provides security strategies for current cash distribution based in Colombia's situation and social conditions in each of its municipalities where we detected evident insecurity rates. Besides, it seeks to simultaneously optimize routing and inventory decisions while considering risk mitigation strategies that allow the cash distribution for valuables transport companies in bank correspondents. The model takes into account different inventory levels, significantly contributing to the optimization of distribution costs, minimizing risks in cash delivery, reducing the planning times and helping to achieve the goals associated with financial inclusion.

The main contribution of the article is the study of new perspectives and research gaps in the financial sector in terms of currency supply chain and logistics. A literature review on this topic is presented by [4]. In the same way, we discuss future research directions to further knowledge development to improve planning processes in this sector.

The paper is structured in four sections as follows: The next section presents the mathematical formulation of the studied currency supply chain problem, together with different risk management strategies for cash distribution and management. The results of the proposed model and computational tests are presented in Sect. 3. Finally, Sect. 4 presents conclusions and future research.

2 Methodology

The cash distribution operation is intrinsically dangerous with high incident exposure. Therefore, operations planning requires to consider the physical safety conditions of the fleet. Thus, we propose a mathematical model to trade-off service-levels, operational costs, and risk mitigation strategies.

In cash distribution, the possible loss of valuables in the face of vulnerability to a known hazard is a risk. Given this situation, it is not only necessary to implement security measures, such as the use of armored vehicles, trained staff, and use of weapons, but it is also necessary to implement additional strategies in the planning of routes as the risk increases with the frequency of delivery to specific points [13]. For example, less predictable routes in order to avoid possible attacks on the system can be implemented.

2.1 Inventory-Routing Model

This proposal considers routing decisions of vehicles with inventories of cash, hard time windows, and risk constraints focused on inducing route unpredictability and risk mitigation strategies in a cash supply chain consisting of a depot (Cash Center) and multiple retailers (correspondent points and banking offices).

Given this context, we introduce risk management constraints when planning inventory policies and vehicle routes. These include the calculation of the cumulative risks on routes, time windows, and a limit on the frequency of chosen arcs over a certain number of consecutive periods. These constraints are necessary for the delivery of bank correspondents to optimize distribution and inventory management operations in terms of logistics costs and risks. This model will be henceforth denoted as the Risk constrained inventory routing problem with time windows (RcIRPTW) in bank correspondents.

The RcIRPTW is introduced for cash distribution. Therefore, consider a cash distribution network with $N = \{0, 1, 2, 3, \cdots, n\}$ nodes where cash is sent from a cash center (CC) $i = \{0\}$ with unlimited capacity, to a subset of bank correspondents (BC) $j = \{1, 2, 3, \cdots, n\}$ over a period of time $T = \{1, 2, 3, \cdots, t\}$ using a single vehicle with limited capacity Q.

The bank correspondent that receives cash deliveries has a limited storage capacity, a known demand for each period, and it has a defined time interval for deliveries (time windows). We assume a service time of zero time units, and losses of cash from incidents are zero. The parameters and decision variables of the model are the following:

Parameters:

- a_j Bank correspondent's j cash storage capacity [$]
- C_{ij} Travel cost from node i to node j [$]
- h_j Inventory holding cost at the bank correspondent j [$]
- $Initial_j$ Initial cash inventory of the bank correspondent j [$]
- $d_{i,j}$ Distance in kilometers from node i to node j [Km]
- $o_{i,j}$ Travel time between node i and node j [Min]
- $s_{j,t}$ Demand of cash at node j in a period of time t [$]
- $e_{j,t}$ Early window of BC j in the period of time t [Min]
- $l_{j,t}$ Late window of the BC j in a period of time t [Min]
- Q Vehicle's cash capacity [$]
- Tm Maximum Risk to be assumed in the cash distribution [$-Km]
- φ Risk penalty in cash distribution per kilometer. [% of transported cash]

Decision variables:

- $x_{i,j,t} = 1$ If the vehicle travels from node i to node j in time period t
- $In_{j,t}$ Bank correspondent j inventory level in time period t [$]
- $b_{j,t}$ Amount of cash to be delivered to BC j in the period of time t [$]
- $z_{n,t} = 1$ If node n is visited in the time period t
- $w_{j,t}$ Time of arrival at the bank correspondent j in the period of time t
- $q_{n,t}$ Amount of cash transported by the vehicle in time period t
- $R_{n,t}$ Risk at delivery in the time period t

the RcIRPTW can be expressed as follows:

$$Min \sum_i \sum_j \sum_t C_{i,j} \cdot x_{i,j,t} + \sum_j \sum_t h_j \cdot In_{j,t} \qquad (1)$$

Subject to:

$$In_{j,t} = In_{j,t-1} + b_{j,t} - s_{j,t} \forall j \in BC, \quad \forall t \in T | t > 1 \qquad (2)$$

$$In_{j,1} = Initial_j + b_{j,1} - s_{j,1}, \quad \forall j \in BC \qquad (3)$$

$$\sum_j b_{j,t} \leq Q, \quad \forall i \in T | t > 1 \qquad (4)$$

$$\sum_n x_{n,j,t} + \sum_n x_{j,n,t} = 2 \cdot z_{j,t}, \quad \forall j \in BC, \forall t \in T | t > 1 \qquad (5)$$

$$\sum_j x_{n,j,t} = z_{n,t}, \quad \forall t \in T | t > 1, \forall n \in BC \tag{6}$$

$$\sum_i x_{i,n,t} = z_{n,t}, \quad \forall t \in T | t > 1, \forall n \in BC \tag{7}$$

$$\sum_t x_{n,n,t} = 0, \quad \forall n \in BC \tag{8}$$

$$q_{j,t} \geq q_{n,t} - b_{j,t} - (1 - x_{n,j,t} \cdot 2 \cdot Q), \quad \forall n \in BC, \forall j \in BC, \forall t \in T \tag{9}$$

$$q_{0,t} = \sum_j b_{j,t}, \quad \forall t \in T \tag{10}$$

$$x_{i,j,t} \in \{0,1\}, \quad \forall (i,j) \in N, \forall t \in T \tag{11}$$

$$z_{n,t} \in \{0,1\}, \quad \forall n \in BC, \forall t \in T \tag{12}$$

$$In_{j,t} \geq 0, \quad \forall j \in BC, \forall t \in T \tag{13}$$

$$b_{j,t} \geq 0, \quad \forall j \in BC, \forall t \in T \tag{14}$$

$$w_{j,t} \geq 0, \quad \forall j \in BC, \forall t \in T \tag{15}$$

$$q_{n,t} \geq 0, \quad \forall j \in BC, \forall t \in T \tag{16}$$

$$R_{n,t} \geq 0, \quad \forall j \in BC, \forall t \in T \tag{17}$$

The objective of the model is to minimize the sum of the cash inventory holding costs at bank correspondents and the cost of transporting the cash over the planning horizon, as described in Eq. (1). The cost of going from one correspondent point to another takes into account the distance of travel. The inventory holding cost is a percentage of the total money kept in inventory by the bank correspondent.

The constraints (2) and (3) consider the cash flow of bank correspondents for any period t and period 1, respectively. Equation (4) establishes the capacity of the armored vehicle used for cash distribution. The constraints (5), (6), (7) and (8) guarantee the feasibility the routes from end to end (Cash center- Bank correspondent-Cash center), where (5) ensures that the vehicle visiting a bank correspondent goes out to visit the next correspondent in the time period t, where (6) and (7) ensure that correspondents have been visited and therefore, at the end of the journey (8) guarantees that the vehicle does not visit the same node in a time period t. Thereby seeking to prevent subtours at any period. The constraint set (9) measures the decrease in cash that the vehicle presents each time it executes deliveries to a bank correspondent. Equation (10) ensures that the amount of cash leaving the CC covers the distribution route to each bank correspondent. Finally, Eqs. (11) to (17) indicate the nature of the decision variables. This base version of the model is inspired by the model studied in the literature. See [2] for further reading.

2.2   Risk Management Strategies and Mathematical Modeling

The base model is enriched by some strategies to handle risks. This first strategy to mitigate the risk of the operation focuses on limiting the level of cash inventory at bank correspondents. That is, the maximum level of cash delivery is restricted, according to the maximum inventory policy allowed by the bank to the bank correspondent considering the available inventory in each period. The risk management policies evaluated by the bank impose a maximum inventory level assigned to correspondents, taking into account the incidents rate or loss of cash probabilities and the maximum coverage of the insurance policy according to the criticality and location of the bank correspondent. The following equations model this strategy:

$$b_{j,t} \leq a_j - In_{j,t-1}, \quad \forall j \in BC, \forall t \in T | t > 1 \tag{18}$$

$$b_{j,1} \leq a_j - Initial_j, \quad \forall j \in BC \tag{19}$$

$$b_{j,t} \leq a_j \cdot z_{j,t}, \quad \forall j \in BC, \forall t \in T \tag{20}$$

Equation (18) controls the quantity to be delivered, taking into account the bank correspondent's maximum inventory capacity. Equation (19) controls the first delivery to the correspondent according to the available initial cash and the maximum cash capacity of the bank correspondent. Finally, Eq. (20) satisfies the maximum inventory quantity if the correspondent bank is visited or not.

The second strategy to mitigate risk is to limit the amount and distance that the cash travels per period. A similar constraint is proposed by [16] for a vehicle routing problem. We set a threshold on the amount of cash at risk multiplied by the traveled distance, taking into account an assumed risk factor on the route. Thus, we propose that the cumulative risk of cash delivery on a scheduled route should not exceed the maximum risk limit imposed by the bank for each scheduled period. Taking these assumptions into account, the maximum value of loss within the operating model is limited.

$$R_{j,t} \geq R_{i,t} + q_{i,t} \cdot \varphi \cdot d_{i,j} - (1 - x_{i,j,t}) \cdot 2 \cdot Tm, \quad \forall i,j \in BC, \forall t \in T \tag{21}$$

$$R_{0,t} = 0, \quad \forall t \in T \tag{22}$$

$$R_{n,t} \leq Tm, \quad \forall n \in BC, \forall t \in T \tag{23}$$

In Eq. (21), the amount of cumulative risk of the route is computed considering a factor φ that represents the risk percentage penalty on the distribution value. That is, the risk function is the amount of cash transported multiplied by the distance traveled by a vehicle.

It comes from the fact that the longer distances imply higher risks for the cash. Equation (22) ensures that the cumulative risk level at the cash center or starting point is zero. Equation (23) ensures that the cumulative risk of cash delivery on a scheduled route does not exceed the maximum risk limit Tm per period. The parameter φ is set considering the coverage of the insurance in the cash distribution process.

Time windows in vehicle routing refer to the existence of a time interval within which a correspondent must be served. The third strategy is to create random time windows per period, which allows us to generate a diversity of correspondents' attention intervals, reducing the routine movements that the armored vehicle makes when delivering cash to the bank correspondents. Thus, routing can become highly unpredictable. Within the mathematical model random hard time windows are proposed as a risk mitigation strategy.

$$w_{j,t} \geq e_{j,t} \cdot z_{j,t}, \quad \forall j \in BC, \forall t \in T \tag{24}$$

$$w_{j,t} \leq l_{j,t} \cdot z_{j,t}, \quad \forall j \in BC, \forall t \in T \tag{25}$$

$$w_{j,t} \geq w_{i,t} + o_{i,j} - ((1 - x_{i,j,t}) \cdot (l_{it} + o_{i,j})), \quad \forall j \in BC, \forall t \in T \tag{26}$$

Equations (24) and (25) present traditional hard time windows constraints. These equations guarantee that the vehicle visits the correspondent within the corresponding time windows. Equation (26) seeks that the arrival time to the correspondent takes into account the travel time from one correspondent to another. The parameters $e_{j,t}$ and $l_{j,t}$ must be random to induce route unpredictability without losing the feasibility of the solution.

The fourth strategy to manage risk is associated with the number of periods that an arc is used by a vehicle on consecutive days. This constraint reduces the predictability of routes.

$$x_{i,j,t} + x_{i,j,t+1} + x_{i,j,t+2} \leq 1, \quad \forall i, j \in BC, \forall t \in T \tag{27}$$

The constraint (27) limits the use of an arc in three consecutive days to be up to one. That is, for every three consecutive days, each arc is used once at the most.

Finally, these strategies are not mutually exclusive. That is, combining strategies can increase the security levels in transportation and inventory. Nevertheless, we expect increased logistic costs, when including all of them. Thus, we need to trade-off logistic costs and security. In the remainder, we expose the strategies and the associated IRP mathematical models using prefix and suffix, as presented in Table 1.

Table 1. Notation for risk management strategies and IRP prefix and suffix.

Strategy	Prefix/suffix
limiting the level of cash inventory	–
limit the amount and distance that the cash travels per period	Prefix Rc
Random time windows	Suffix TW
Limit the consecutive use of arcs	Suffix AFC

The first strategy is implemented in every model since it is common to limit the cash inventory levels in the network. We denote the AFC Rc IRPTW, for the model implementing all the strategies.

3   Computational Results

The risk-constrained cash distribution model is developed using the mathematical programming solver CPLEX version 12.8 under the GAMS language to find an optimal solution to the problems with a different combination of constraints as exposed in the previous section. The workstation for these experiments is an Intel processor Core ^{TM} i7-3537U CPU @2.50 Ghz and 8 GB RAM.

Computer experiments are performed on 4 test instances with different demand patterns for each period. We randomly generated the demand per period between 0 and 120 million COP. Also, random time windows with a uniform discrete distribution in a range of 0–2 h are assumed. The distance matrix in the test instances, using real data of bank correspondents, is given in kilometers, and the travel times and windows are in minutes. The test instances have 50 periods.

3.1   Analysis of Risk Management Strategies

The following is an analysis of the Key Performance Indicators evaluated for the IRP model and the different variations. We compare the indicators against the classic version of the IRP. When analyzing the average cost function of the different IRP models, shown in Fig. 1, we conclude that the IRPTW and AFC Risk IRPTW models are the ones that produce the highest costs. The main reason is that the number of visits to the correspondents and the inventory levels increase. In these versions, the cash inventory is significantly higher to compensate for the constraints in the routing.

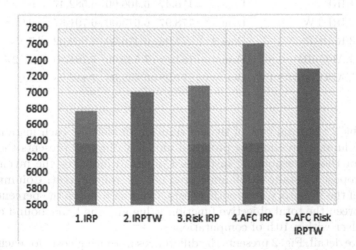

Fig. 1. Average total cost for each IRP strategy. Blue bar shows the lower bound. Orange bar shows the upper bound after 10 h of computation. (Color figure online)

The scenario with the highest GAP versus the lower bound is the one with arc frequency constraints since limiting the number of consecutive uses of arcs implies that the search for an optimal solution harder. The IRPTW and the RcIRP (Risk IRP) seem to have similar objective function values.

Table 2. Summary for total costs of IRP solutions.

Model	Instance	IC	RC	Total cost	GAP
1.IRP	Dem 1	169,72	6.684,00	6.853,72	5,9%
2.IRPTW	Dem 1	170,15	6.903,00	7.073,15	0,0%
3.Rc IRP	Dem 1	169,96	6.851,00	7.020,96	8,5%
4.AFC IRP	Dem 1	174,47	7.086,00	7.260,47	12,1%
5.AFC Rc IRPTW	Dem 1	185,64	7.120,00	7.305,64	0,0%
1.IRP	Dem 2	169,72	6.355,00	6.524,72	7,1%
2.IRPTW	Dem 2	161,94	6.461,00	6.622,94	0,0%
3.Rc IRP	Dem 2	188,40	6.432,00	6.620,40	8,7%
4.AFC IRP	Dem 2	148,32	7.711,00	7.859,32	24,8%
5.AFC Rc IRPTW	Dem 2	189,99	6.674,00	6.863,99	0,0%
1.IRP	Dem 3	165,84	6.968,00	7.133,84	4,6%
2.IRPTW	Dem 3	160,44	7.389,00	7.549,44	0,0%
3.Rc IRP	Dem 3	153,75	7.917,00	8.070,75	16,7%
4.AFC IRP	Dem 3	178,07	7.441,00	7.619,07	9,8%
5.AFC Rc IRPTW	Dem 3	167,54	7.699,00	7.866,54	0,0%
1.IRP	Dem 4	176,47	6.406,00	6.582,47	6,7%
2.IRPTW	Dem 4	178,97	6.613,00	6.791,97	0,0%
3.Rc IRP	Dem 4	174,02	6.476,00	6.650,02	7,3%
4.AFC IRP	Dem 4	161,39	7.540,00	7.701,39	21,2%
5.AFC Rc IRPTW	Dem 4	177,28	6.935,00	7.112,28	0,0%

In Table 2 the total cost of the distribution models for each instance is presented. Column 1 presents the proposed model. Column 2 presents the demand pattern for the corresponding instance. Column 3 indicates the inventory cost for the proposed instance. Column 4 presents the routing cost. Column 5 shows the sum of the inventory and routing costs. Column 6 shows the percentage variation between the total objective function value and the lower bound computed by the solver within 10 h of computation.

In more detail, Fig. 2 presents the differences in routing costs for each strategy as a percentage increase over the base model (IRP). We observe that, when applying a variation, the largest routing cost increase appears when considering the arc frequency constraint for delivery in each node (AFC IRP). Similarly, there is considerable variation when applying combined constraints between arc frequency constraint and maximum risk constraint (AFC Risk IRPTW).

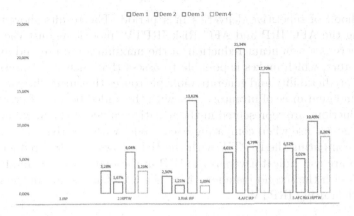

Fig. 2. Average routing cost for each IRP strategy

Figure 3 depicts the inventory costs for each strategy. As constraints are placed on the model to mitigate the risk of cash losses, the average inventory increases as risk is concentrated on the correspondent. On the other hand, the level of inventory tends to increase because it is less expensive to maintain cash inventory at the correspondent than the risk taken while distributing the cash. Thus, the AFC IRP and RcIRPTW models tend to have larger inventory levels in the system.

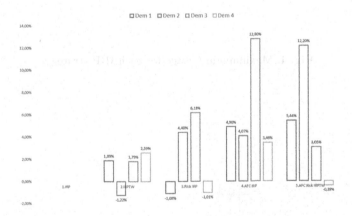

Fig. 3. Average inventory holding cost for each IRP strategy

3.2   Risk Performance Indicators

The maximum and average arc use indicators, presented in Figs. 4 and 5, show how the AFC IRP and AFC Rc IRPTW models mitigate the unpredictability of distribution routes and thus mitigate the risk of incidents by decreasing the likelihood of repetitive deliveries in a period. The results show that when comparing the AFC IRP and AFC Risk IRPTW models against the base IRP model, there is a significant reduction in the maximum arc use and average arc use indicators, which makes it possible to assess that such constraints mitigate the route predictability and generate multiple routes that meet the conditions for delivery and guarantee of inventory, but with the added benefit of greater safety. These reductions are represented in the negative values of the maximum arc use and average arc use when comparing each model with the IRP base model. For example, comparing the IRPTW with the IRP shows a 15.38% reduction in the maximum arc use indicator versus the IRP in the first instance. Similarly, when evaluated with the second instance, there is a 38.1% reduction in the maximum arc use when using IRPTW.

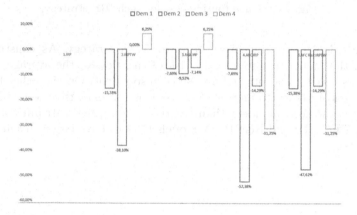

Fig. 4. Maximum arc usage for each IRP strategy

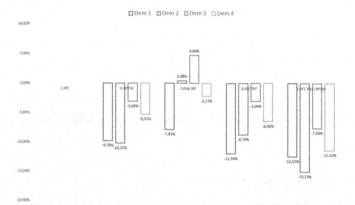

Fig. 5. Average arc usage for each IRP strategy

Finally, when evaluating the risk indicator in Fig. 6, it is shown that the models that reduce and mitigate the cash in transit risk in a route are the models of Rc IRP and AFC Rc IRP that contain within their models the constraint to limit the risk in transit indicator that the bank assumes during the process of cash distribution to the different nodes. The value for Tm takes into account the coverage policy that the insurance company offers the bank.

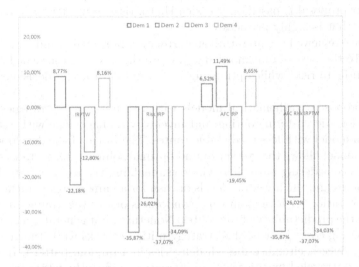

Fig. 6. Maximum risk indicator for each IRP strategy

Thus, we observe under the four evaluated instances that the different strategies trade-off costs and safety concerns. In general, the IRPTW and AFC Risk IRPTW are optimization models that can be solved to optimality, while less constrained models such as the IRP, Rc IRP, and AFC IRP, makes the optimization problem to be difficult to solve within short computational times. Further, we have noted that including random time windows does not provide a significant decrease in risk indicators. On the other hand, limiting the risk in transit seems to be the best strategy to mitigate risks without increasing logistic costs significantly.

4 Conclusions and Future Research

This research presents the formulation of a mathematical model with the implementation of different strategies that allow enhancement of risk levels, distribution costs, and cash holding costs associated with the process of cash distribution in a network of bank correspondents.

Currently, Colombia uses cash distribution models based on the establishment of security conditions and the strengthening of the fleet with armament. However, these conditions may become vulnerable when distribution routes become predictable. This research proposes the use of alternative strategies such as random visit times to distribution points, as well as a limited frequency on the delivery conditions between points, in order to reduce predictability and risk of theft of the fleet designated for cash distribution.

Managing the cash distribution planning with this type of model allows us to compute routing schemes with dynamic conditions that allow the system to make efficient use of resources and to significantly reduce their risks associated with theft. Our proposal is based on the idea that a risky route for cash distribution is a route that is highly predictable.

We have reviewed the literature en currency supply chains and cash-in-transit models. To the best of our knowledge, we are the first to propose safety strategies to mitigate risks while optimizing inventory and routing decisions simultaneously.

The proposed mathematical models with risk mitigation strategies allow to trade-off logistic costs in routing and inventory management with risks. That includes a model with less predictable routes. The usage of the developed mathematical model allows the system to find optimal solutions for instances of up to 50 periods considering hard time windows, enabling the user to plan the distribution routes and the inventory levels of cash for a bank correspondent network.

The operation with random time windows is one of the evaluated strategies to reduce the predictability of the routes. Nonetheless, it generates a significantly higher routing cost. That is, this strategy mitigates risks while the vehicle is on the route, since it circumscribes all deliveries in a random pattern. In contrast, the distance traveled by the cash can increase significantly, which increases the risks in transit in the system.

Based on these results, we can conclude that the best strategy to manage risk in this setting is to set a limit on the amount of cash at risk multiplied by the traveled distance. Previously this has been studied by [16] for a single-period routing problem. With our model, we acknowledge the dependencies between decisions in consecutive periods, and thus, we can plan cash inventory levels and routing decisions for several periods in the future.

For future research, we propose to analyze the model as a bi-objective problem, minimizing logistic costs and risk indicators. Further, since delivery times and travel times might be stochastic parameters, the measurement of risk levels to decrease the probability of theft of securities vehicles by using stochastic programming or simulation models is suggested as a topic for further research.

We propose to work on heuristic and meta-heuristic methods for this problem and to address cash centers location issues to optimize distribution costs and the expansion of more delivery routes, modeling cash delivery problems with heterogeneous fleet or multiple vehicles and implementing heuristic models considering the risk factor within the objective function.

References

1. Banca de Oportunidades: Reportes de inclusión financiera. http://bancadelas oportunidades.gov.co/es/reportes/312 (2020). Accessed 25 May 2020

2. Coelho, L.C., Laporte, G.: The exact solution of several classes of inventory-routing problems. Comput. Oper. Res. **40**(2), 558–565 (2013)
3. Espejo-Díaz, J.A., Guerrero, W.J.: A bi-objective model for the humanitarian aid distribution problem: analyzing the trade-off between shortage and inventory at risk. In: Figueroa-García, J.C., Duarte-González, M., Jaramillo-Isaza, S., Orjuela-Cañon, A.D., Díaz-Gutierrez, Y. (eds.) WEA 2019. CCIS, vol. 1052, pp. 752–763. Springer, Cham (2019). https://doi.org/10.1007/978-3-030-31019-6_63
4. Geismar, H.N., Sriskandarajah, C., Zhu, Y.: A review of operational issues in managing physical currency supply chains. Prod. Oper. Manage. **26**(6), 976–996 (2017)
5. Guerrero, W.J., Velasco, N., Prodhon, C., Amaya, C.A.: On the generalized elementary shortest path problem: a heuristic approach. Electron. Notes Discrete Math. **41**, 503–510 (2013)
6. van der Heide, L.M., Coelho, L.C., Vis, I.F., van Anholt, R.G.: Replenishment and denomination mix of automated teller machines with dynamic forecast demands. Comput. Oper. Res. **114**, 104828 (2020)
7. Larrain, H., Coelho, L.C., Cataldo, A.: A variable MIP neighborhood descent algorithm for managing inventory and distribution of cash in automated teller machines. Comput. Oper. Res. **85**, 22–31 (2017)
8. Lüer, A., Benavente, M., Bustos, J., Venegas, B.: El problema de rutas de vehículos: Extensiones y métodos de resolución, estado del arte. In: EIG (2009)
9. Michallet, J., Prins, C., Amodeo, L., Yalaoui, F., Vitry, G.: Multi-start iterated local search for the periodic vehicle routing problem with time windows and time spread constraints on services. Comput. Oper. Res. **41**, 196–207 (2014)
10. Osorio, A.F., Toro, H.: An MIP model to optimize a Colombian cash supply chain. Int. Trans. Oper. Res. **19**(5), 659–673 (2012)
11. Peña, P., Vázquez, A.: El impacto de los corresponsales bancarios en la inclusión financiera: una primera evaluación. Estudios Económicos CNBV **1** (2012)
12. Superintendencia Financiera de Colombia: Estrategia nacional de inclusión financiera en colombia. https://www.superfinanciera.gov.co/inicio/informes-y-cifras/informes/inclusion-financiera-10084716 (2020). Accessed 25 May 2020
13. Talarico, L., Sörensen, K., Springael, J.: Metaheuristics for the risk-constrained cash-in-transit vehicle routing problem. Eur. J. Oper. Res. **244**(2), 457–470 (2015)
14. The World Bank Group: financial inclusion. https://www.bancomundial.org/es/topic/financialinclusion/overview (2020). Accessed 25 May 2020
15. Wagner, M.: Analyzing cost structures of inventory-routing: application to cash supply chains. Lect. Notes Manage. Sci. **2**, 110–122 (2010)
16. Xu, G., Li, Y., Szeto, W.Y., Li, J.: A cash transportation vehicle routing problem with combinations of different cash denominations. Int. Trans. Oper. Res. **26**(6), 2179–2198 (2019)

Correction to: Stowage Planning with Optimal Ballast Water

Beizhen Jia, Kjetil Fagerholt, Line Blander Reinhardt,
and Niels Gorm Malý Rytter

Correction to:
Chapter "Stowage Planning with Optimal Ballast Water"
in: E. Lalla-Ruiz et al. (Eds.): *Computational Logistics*,
LNCS 12433, https://doi.org/10.1007/978-3-030-59747-4_6

In the original version of this chapter Figure 1 was published incorrectly. Figure 1 has now been corrected.

The updated version of this chapter can be found at
https://doi.org/10.1007/978-3-030-59747-4_6

Author Index

Ahuja, Nitin 507
Akkerman, Fabian 356
Alarcon-Gerbier, Eduardo 396
Alves, Júlio César 584
Amaral, André R. S. 747
Ambrosino, Daniela 119
Anand, Sajini 342
Andersson, Henrik 261
Aslaksen, Ingvild Eide 36
Assbrock, Gerrit 101
Atasoy, Bilge 18, 476, 553, 600

Beelaerts van Blokland, Wouter 553
Beirigo, Breno 492
Beranek, Maria 666
Bergman, Mark 183
Boers, Luke 600
Bruijns, Lianne A. M. 682
Buballa, Melissa 631
Buscher, Udo 396

Caris, An 733
Carvalho, Margarida 715
Castro, Carlos 277
Celius, Ebba 326
Chiscop, Irina 616
Christiansen, Marielle 261
Correia, Gonçalo 600

Daduna, Joachim R. 457
Dafnomilis, Ioannis 101
Dahle, Lars 261
de Koning, Wouter J. 616
Dreyer, Heidi 326
Duinkerken, Mark B. 101

Erikstad, Stein Ove 3

Fagerholt, Kjetil 3, 36, 68, 84
Fernández Gil, Alejandro 277

Gansterer, Margaretha 215
Gómez Sánchez, Mariam 277
Guericke, Stefan 342

Guerrero, William J. 763
Gunawan, Aldy 167
Guo, Wenjing 553

Hadj-Hamou, Khaled 151
Hartl, Richard F. 215
Heijnen, Wouter 356
Huang, He 412
Hvattum, Lars Magnus 261

Iori, Manuel 651

Jia, Beizhen 84
Jin, Jiangang 522
Johnsen, Lennart Christian 36

Kalicharan, Kishan 569

Ladier, Anne-Laure 151
Lalla-Ruiz, Eduardo 277
Larsen, Rie B. 476
Lau, Hoong Chuin 200
Lenkenhoff, Kay 631
Lewis, Rhyd 384, 539
Ley, Jens 101
Li, Mingyu 68
Locatelli, Marco 651
Los, Johan 215
Los, Kim J. 135

Manguino, João L. V. 231
Martínez-Agaton, Cristian 763
Mateus, Geraldo Robson 584
Meisel, Frank 36
Mes, Martijn 183, 356, 698
Meyer, Anne 412, 507
Moreira, Mayron C. O. 651
Moura, Ana 311
Mukherjee, Arka 715

Negenborn, Rudy R. 18, 215, 428, 443, 476,
    492, 553, 600
Neijmeijer, Nout 443

Neufeld, Janis Sebastian 371
Nunes, Pedro 311

Ormevik, Andreas Breivik 3

Pantuso, Giovanni 295
Pauly, Markus 412
Phillipson, Frank 135, 569, 616, 682
Polinder, Henk 443
Pouls, Martin 412, 507
Pourmohammad-Zia, Nadia 428

Quak, Hans J. 135
Queck, Bertran 200

Ramaekers, Katrien 733
Reehorst, Madeleine 326
Reinhardt, Line Blander 84
Romanelli, Alexandre 747
Römer, Michael 246
Ronconi, Débora P. 231
Rytter, Niels Gorm Malý 84

Sangers, Alex 569, 682
Santos, José 311
Sarmiento-Lepesqueur, Angélica 763
Scheffler, Martin 371
Schott, Dingena L. 101
Schulte, Frederik 215, 428, 443, 492
Schulte, Jakob 246

Schütz, Peter 68, 326
Shi, Xiaoning 522
Silveira, Tiago 651
Skålnes, Jørgen 261
Souravlias, Dimitris 18, 428
Spaan, Matthijs T. J. 215
Stelwagen, Uilke 135
Sun, Wenchen 522
Svanberg, Elisabeth 36

Tierney, Kevin 246, 443, 631
Touzout, Faycal A. 151

van Benthem, Tim 183
van Gils, Teun 733
van Heeswijk, Wouter 52, 698
van Kempen, Elisah A. 135
Vanheusden, Sarah 733
Vansteenwegen, Pieter 167
Voß, Stefan 522

Wetzel, Daniel 631
Widjaja, Audrey Tedja 167

Xie, Haoqi 119

Yu, Vincent F. 167

Zhang, Yimeng 18

Printed in the United States
By Bookmasters

Printed in the United States
By Bookmasters